CRIME
in Modern Society

By **MABEL A. ELLIOTT, Ph.D.**

PROFESSOR OF SOCIOLOGY AND
CHAIRMAN OF THE DEPARTMENT OF SOCIOLOGY
PENNSYLVANIA COLLEGE FOR WOMEN

Harper & Brothers – PUBLISHERS – *New York*

Library of Congress catalog card number: 52-10829

Crime in Modern Society

To the Devoted Memory
of My Brother
LEE ELLIOTT
and
His Creative Intelligence

CONTENTS

Editor's Introduction   xi

Preface   xiii

SECTION I. THE NATURE AND EXTENT OF CRIME

1. Introduction   3
2. Crime and Criminology   11
3. The Extent and Distribution of Crime   32

SECTION II. CRIMINALS

4. Who Are the Criminals?   77
5. The Major Types of Offenders   102
6. The Professional Criminal and Organized Crime   133
7. Special Types of Offenders   171
8. The Woman Offender   199
9. Types of Women Who Break the Law   226

SECTION III. FACTORS IN CRIMINALITY

10. Crime and American Culture   259
11. Nativity, Race, and Crime   284
12. Biological, Mental, and Emotional Factors in Crime   313
13. Social Relationships and Economic Factors in Crime   347
14. Theories of Criminality   383

SECTION IV. THE TREATMENT OF CRIMINALS

15. Penal Methods Past and Present   409
16. The Conflict in Penal Theories   435

Contents

17. Police   455
18. Jails, Workhouses, and Houses of Correction   495
19. Criminal Procedure   513
20. Criminal Procedure: The Trial   531
21. Probation and the Suspended Sentence   553
22. The American Prison System: State and Federal   579
23. Prison Administration and Services   612
24. Prison Discipline   648
25. Prison Labor   677
26. Women's Prisons and Reformatories   702
27. Parole and the Indeterminate Sentence   726

SECTION V. CRIME PREVENTION

28. Crime Prevention on the Juvenile Level   773
29. Crime Prevention on the Adult Level   805

Index of Names   841

Index of Subjects   848

ILLUSTRATIONS

These pictures follow page 432.

Plate

I. Housing in a Delinquency Area in Pittsburgh.

II. Once Such Indignities as the Pillory Were Society's Answer to the Crime Problem.

III. The Caged Man.

IV. The United States Federal Penitentiary at Leavenworth.

V. Air View of the United States Penitentiary at Alcatraz.

VI. Solid Block—Outside Cells as Developed at the Federal Reformatory at Terre Haute.

VII. A Single Cell in a Modern Prison.

VIII. Close-Up View of Inside Cell for Single Occupant.

IX. Maximum-Security Inside-Cell Block at Federal Reformatory, Chillicothe.

X. Athletic Field at the Federal Reformatory at Terre Haute.

XI. At Seagoville Men Eat at Small Tables.

XII. Superior Library Facilities as Developed at the Federal Reformatory at Terre Haute.

XIII. The Chapel at Western Penitentiary, Pittsburgh, Pennsylvania.

XIV. Corridor Disciplinary Unit.

XV. The Administration Building, Federal Reformatory for Women, Alderson, West Virginia.

XVI.   A Cottage at the Federal Reformatory for Women at Alderson, West Virginia.

XVII.   A Typical Single Room in a Women's Prison.

XVIII.   Women Prisoners at Work in the Federal Reformatory for
Women at Alderson, West Virginia.

XIX.   Spinning Mill Manned by Inmates.

XX.   Beaming Cloth Is Part of a Successful Prison Industry.

XXI.   Cub Scouts, Fricot Ranch School for Boys, Planting Cedar
Tree at Annual Fricot Day Ceremonies.

XXII.   Forestry Camp Fire Suppression Detail.

EDITOR'S INTRODUCTION

Throughout her professional career Dr. Elliott has been a research student of the forms of delinquent behavior. As a social researcher she has had direct contact with delinquents. Added to these rich experiences she has shared in the planning efforts of official state boards charged with the responsibility of crime prevention and prison administration. Further than this, she is a distinguished sociologist whose breadth of scholarship and social insight into complex problems of human relations lend perspective and imaginative approach to any task she undertakes. When these capabilities are brought to bear upon the writing of a new text on criminology, the result is an integrated treatment of the main facets of the problem of adult crime.

As the author states in Chapter 1, the juvenile offender is not dealt with in the present book, except incidentally. It is usual in college and university courses of instruction to treat separately the problems of juvenile delinquency and adult crime. For this reason the present book concentrates attention on the adult offender. As a consequence of this division of subject matter, it is possible to provide a thorough treatment of the varied and interesting aspects of the problem of criminal behavior and the efforts of society to deal with it.

F. Stuart Chapin

PREFACE

This textbook, dealing primarily with adult offenders and their treatment, aims to provide all the material, new and old, vital to a well-rounded course in criminology. It should be suitable not only for upper-class college students, but for graduate students and students of social work. It also should provide an up-to-date reference work for probation and parole officers, for police and for the administrative personnel of penal institutions.

It was thus organized with the idea of giving an adequate orientation to the student on the extent and nature of crime and the various factors which research has indicated to be related to criminal behavior. Recent research as every criminologist knows has greatly altered earlier conceptions of crime. The chapters on penal treatment not only give factual data on the treatment of problems. They were developed with the idea of providing both students and persons engaged in working with offenders the conclusions of outstanding authorities with reference to improved methods of penal treatment so that prisoners will be more likely to succeed on release. For despite all the reformer's demands that prisons be abolished, there is no likelihood that prisons will be abolished unless the whole structure of criminal law is changed. It seems likely that major alterations in treatment within prisons may do far more to facilitate a program of intelligent reform than demands for the abolition of prisons, per se. Once a program proves workable, lawmakers will be much more willing to conform to existing practices and write them into law. For criminal procedures and penal procedures and penal treatment alike are deeply rooted in thinking, in tradition and reinforced by the prejudices of the average man and woman. The material on crime prevention likewise should be useful to civic committees and crime prevention commissions as well as college students.

The book in a sense is a culmination of my training, research, and professional career up to now. Many years ago I wrote my master's thesis under the general direction of Dr. Herman M. Adler, who was then Director of the Institute of Juvenile Research in Chicago. Shortly thereafter (while I was a graduate student at Bryn Mawr College) I made a special study of the post-institutional careers of girls who had been released from the Sleighton Farm Reformatory in Pennsylvania. Following this I returned to Northwestern University where I completed the requirements for my Ph.D. with my dissertation, *Conflicting Penal Theories in Statutory Criminal Law*. Immediately after this I went to the University of Kansas where I taught the courses in criminology and delinquency for a period of seventeen years. While at the latter institution I conducted many research projects in the field and directed numerous graduate theses in criminology. During part of this time I also served as Research Director of the Kansas Public Welfare Commission, and in discharging my duties in this connection, I personally supervised or conducted many studies of inmates in the state correctional and penal institutions. I also conducted a number of studies on my own. Since coming to Pennsylvania College for Women in 1947, I have conducted a number of further studies. Most of these materials are incorporated in the text and thus make available a large amount of original data and help in giving the book whatever originality of approach it may possess.

This, however, is in no sense to diminish the great debt which I (and all authors of criminology texts) owe to the whole list of scholars in the field of criminological research, and in particular to those who have explored new areas and given new perspectives to criminological theory.

This book has been ten years in preparation, chiefly because I have interrupted my writing at various junctures to do further research. When I began to outline the various chapters, I found numerous gaps in the available information on material I wished to include despite the enormous range of available materials. There was, for example, little organized data on the cultural roots of lawlessness. I therefore took time out to delve into lawlessness in our frontier mores. There was likewise little definitive material on the woman offender based on any intensive study of criminal women as persons. I therefore paused again on my book to conduct a series of studies at the Federal Women's Reformatory, at the House of Detention in New York City, and the Kansas State Women's Industrial Farm. These women represent cross sections of the women incarcerated at these three institutions. Following this I undertook a special project for the Quakers, namely,

Coercion in Penal Treatment: Past and Present, which incorporated a survey I made of penal practices within the prisons in 1945. This was done with the understanding that any or all material might be incorporated in this text. During this same period, Mary Goshorn Williams, a graduate student, also assisted me in making a survey of the basis of determining insanity in criminal trials throughout the United States, and the methods of treating those adjudged criminally insane. These materials have likewise been incorporated in the book.

Although historical materials are covered, the major emphasis of the text is in current aspects of crime and its treatment, and many persons have aided me by preparing special data or tables, by permitting me access to case records, or by supplying newly gathered information. All these have been of immeasurable help in presenting what is a very complex matter, *Crime in Modern Society*.

It would be impossible to recount here all the persons to whom I am indebted, but I should like to acknowledge special appreciation to the following: Dean John H. Nelson, Chairman of the Graduate Research Fund at the University of Kansas for a special research grant which covered my expenses in studying the woman offender; the Honorable Estes Kefauver, Chairman of the Special Senate Committee to Investigate Crime in Interstate Commerce, of the 81st Congress, and the secretary to this committee, Miss Joyce Mack, who made all nineteen volumes of the Senate hearings available as well as other material; the Honorable James V. Bennett, Director of the Federal Bureau of Prisons, who gave time to make many thoughtful suggestions with reference to materials this book should include as well as supplying me with much recent statistical data, a large number of photographs, and several important studies on classification and orientation in prison work; Mr. Victor Evjen, the Managing Editor of *Federal Probation* for other valuable suggestions; Mr. Sol Rubin who drew up recent data on probation and parole; the Honorable J. Edgar Hoover who provided numerous statistical studies as well as information on the F.B.I.; the Census Bureau of the U.S. Department of Commerce which supplied me with data on prisoners up to 1946; Mr. Virgil W. Peterson, Operating Director of the Chicago Crime Commission, who gave me fresh material on organized crime as well as other data; Dr. Robert H. Gault, Editor of the *Journal of Criminal Law, Criminology and Police Science*, who permitted me to quote tables and other material from various articles and also allowed me to reproduce material from my own articles in this journal; the editors of the *American Sociological Review* for permission to reproduce portions of my article "Crime and the Frontier Mores"; and to the University of Chicago Press for permission to reproduce part of my book, *Conflicting Penal Theories in Statutory Criminal Law*; Mrs. R. Templeton Smith, President of the Allegheny County League of Women Voters, for permission to reproduce the chart summarizing data on the League's survey of the police situation in cities of over 100,000 in the United States; and to Mr. Ray Sprigle, reporter on the Pittsburgh *Post Gazette* for special information on local police corruption.

The librarians at Carnegie Library, Pittsburgh, the University of Pittsburgh Library, the University of Kansas Library, the Library of Congress, the University of Colorado Library, especially those of its Law School and its Pioneer Library, and of the Laughlin Library at Pennsylvania College for Women, have all given me special service.

I am also grateful to Miss Helen Hironimus, former warden of the Federal Women's Reformatory, for arranging interviews with prisoners there and for supplying me with statistics. Miss Hironimus was also of major assistance in providing insight from her experience to the analysis of women offenders. (I am also indebted to her successor, Miss Nina Kinsella, for supplying recent data and photographs.) Miss Ruth E. Collins, Superintendent of the House of Detention, New York City, was equally co-operative in permitting me to interview women serving sentence there and permitting me to attend staff conferences. She has also supplied recent statistical data. Mrs. Etta Beavers, former Superintendent of the Women's Industrial Farm at Lansing, Kansas, was also very helpful in my study of women in that institution. I wish also to thank the women prisoners themselves for being so co-operative in submitting to interrogation. Many of these women expressed the hope that their experience might save other women from similar difficulties.

In addition, I wish to thank Dr. Paul R. Anderson, President of Pennsylvania College for Women, for permitting me to teach on a reduced schedule for one semester so that I could complete this textbook; my students in criminology who through the years have contributed to my understanding and insight as to what should be incorporated in a "teaching text"; George L. Murphy, Lecturer in Sociology at the University of Pittsburgh, who typed the manuscript with such critical intelligence and who has assisted in making the indexes; and Dr. F. Stuart Chapin, Editor of Harper's Social Science Series, for his constructive suggestions.

MABEL A. ELLIOTT

Pennsylvania College for Women
July 22, 1952

SECTION I

The Nature and Extent of Crime

CHAPTER 1

Introduction

Criminology as a Field of Study

As a field of study, criminology is basic preparation (or should be) for persons entering various types of social work as well as for the probation and parole officer who is actively engaged in helping the offender become readjusted (or stay adjusted) to his community life. The student who expects to work with offenders will see the relationship between criminology and his chosen vocation at once. But the family case worker and the child welfare worker will also find the study of criminology profitable because they also will have many cases in which the client is an offender. In the case of the child welfare worker, many instances of delinquent or criminal parents may arise. For persons who contemplate a career in case work some understanding of these problems is essential. Psychology students are also basically concerned with problems of human behavior and many students in the field will find employment as clinical psychologists or as resident psychologists in institutions dealing with delinquents and criminals. Psychology students who expect to do graduate work will find many research topics in criminology. But whether they pursue this or some other area in psychology, criminology offers an essential part of the psychologist's training in human behavior. Administrators of penal and correctional institutions obviously need some training in criminology, although many are still woefully lacking in this respect. Likewise lawyers, in their roles both as practicing attorneys and as judges on the bench, will also find it important to have training in criminology. For by the very nature of their professional activities they will need to understand the criminal and the treatment provided him whether they are defending him, prosecuting him, or sentencing him to prison. Many clergymen in their work as counselors will deal with persons who have broken the law and will find a knowledge of criminology to their advantage. So too will newspapermen who write so positively about crime for the press.

For the student who aspires to a career in teaching and research in sociology, the study of criminology is important. Criminology is concerned in a basic sense with the problems of social organization and social disorganization and with problems of social structure. Crime is one of the major threats to social organization, because it is an attack on basic social values incorporated in accepted concepts of government, in notions of ethical conduct which are widely accepted by the group, and in the law itself. All sociology students are likewise concerned with the extent and variety of social problems as such, and of these crime is certainly one of the important local, state, and national problems. In general the college student is presumed to have some background in both sociology and psychology before he enrolls in a criminology course.

Popular Interest in Criminology

Since so many persons are interested in crime (whether from a professional or a human-interest angle), the criminology course often has the largest enrollment of all the subjects offered by sociology departments. (In a few colleges and universities criminology is offered by the psychology department, but the number of students interested remains relatively constant.) Some people are attracted to the subject because they consider criminals pathological and they regard criminology as fascinating because of its morbid ramifications. Others hold themselves aloof from the subject on the same grounds. Such notions have arisen from the popular belief that criminals are a type of person markedly different from the law-abiding population. This belief is not scientifically tenable, but its effect is everywhere observable. For criminals have almost universally been socially "marked" men and women who have been ostracized and punished for the injuries they have done to individuals and society as a whole. Throughout the course of civilized history many persons, learned and unlearned, have pondered upon the nature and characteristics of criminals. For generations they have been concerned with the reasons which led criminals to break the laws and suffer the humiliation and shame that trial and punishment entail. In consequence theologians, philosophers, jurists, and legislators (as well as interested laymen) have developed many theories as to the mainsprings of criminal behavior.

Truly scientific research into the motivating factors of criminal conduct is relatively recent, however, and the best-informed scholars in the field are still reluctant either to pose any final answers to the "causes" of crime or to frame any simple statements as to the most effective means of treating the criminal. "Crime" itself is a broad subsuming term used to designate many varieties of human conduct which range from violating parking regulations and selling on the black market to holdups and sex murders. Modern criminologists are therefore dubious about finding any meaningful over-all explanation of crime that can apply to such varied activities.

Earlier criminologists had no such inhibitions; they were quite willing to say that criminal behavior was the function of some such factor as differentiated bodily or cranial structure, low-grade intelligence, bad housing, lack of religion, or some other factor that seemed at the time to be characteristic of the persons arrested, tried, and convicted. We know today that certain individuals (chiefly members of the lower economic classes) are punished more frequently (and often more severely) than others. We are not so positive, however, that this fact offers a complete explanation of crime. This the student will come to recognize as he pursues his study of the subject.

Prejudice and Criminal Theory

Much criminal theory, as this book hopes to make clear, is the result of the prejudices of the theorists who have oriented their thinking from a particular point of view. Thus religionists may regard criminals as sinners, psychologists regard them as persons who have been motivated to antisocial conduct by inner frustrations and conflict, and sociologists tend to explain conduct in terms of response to a social situation. The uninformed man in the street (who may be an artist, a businessman, or a mathematician) may hold that the real explanation of crime is that the criminal is "mean," a person who has no regard for the property and lives of others. There is a certain amount of truth in these explanations, but none of them tells the whole story. There are many facets to human behavior and we need to obtain a picture of the whole criminal.

Statistics on Crime

Statistics on crime give us a superficial understanding of the extent and distribution of crime. This understanding is incomplete because many crimes are not reported. Many criminals are not arrested and many of those who are arrested are never prosecuted or convicted, even though guilty. Many factors contribute to this, but all of them necessarily affect the validity of any conclusions we may reach. Thus if crimes occur widely in the upper middle class, but are not reported, the theory of economic need as a factor in crime must of necessity be discounted. Similarly if urban people are arrested for behavior that goes unnoticed among rural people, it is the situation rather than the activity that should be held responsible for the crime. These are only two of many questions that concern us in interpreting statistics, which will be discussed in a later chapter.

Case Studies and Crime

In order to supplement the over-all (if faulty) picture of crime which we may derive from statistics, this text presents a variety of case studies (and detailed summaries of cases) of persons who have been convicted of different types of crime. Some of these studies are more detailed than others, because of the extent of materials available. These studies, particularly those involving women offenders, should make it clear that *criminal behavior is human behavior*. For in the background of all these individuals there are circumstances and situations which have prompted them to break the law. We need, however, to keep in mind that there is usually a subjective factor involved in assigning motivations to human conduct and that scientific conclusions are difficult to establish on any verifiable basis.

Treatment of Crime

A large part of this book is devoted to the problems entailed in apprehending offenders and in their detention, trial, and conviction. Following conviction the criminal is usually either put on probation or committed to prison. Later he is either released without formality or placed on parole. Most of our practices in treating criminals are rooted in antiquity and have little reference as to whether or not the treatment restores the offender to society as a rehabilitated or reformed individual. The treatment of the offender, like that of the mentally ill, has often been a matter of sequestering him from public view. The court in passing sentence gets the criminal out of the public's way, and the public has paid little attention to whether the treatment was productive of any effective results. In general, however, society has been more interested in punishing criminals than in their reformation. Since most criminals are released within two years and the majority of them become recidivists, the treatment of crime has become a pressing social problem. Fortunately there have been a few constructive developments in recent years, but prison treatment is still a significant example of cultural lag, of the failure of prison authorities to envision their problem as one of re-education. In consequence few prisons have any real program for helping the prisoner become a better-adjusted member of society. Criminal behavior, like all problems of human conduct, is (in a peculiar sense) a problem of its own generation and one which each generation must face for itself. Through sanitary precautions, through "miracle" drugs, and through surgical techniques medicine may be able to reduce many of the illnesses which plague the human body. In consequence mortality rates from diseases like malaria, pneumonia, and appendicitis have declined markedly. Behavior is a different matter. From the social viewpoint, as we shall see later, new situations create new crimes and impose new restrictions on human behavior. From the individual viewpoint every person has to learn to accept the social controls of the particular society in which he lives. To conform willingly to the taboos and restrictions of the group the individual must believe in the essential validity of such rules, but their validity is not always apparent to him.

Crime Prevention

It seems likely therefore that there is no final solution to the crime problem. Even if one generation were able to produce a very high degree of social conformity and thus "put down crime," the social changes that are more or less bound to occur in a subsequent generation would result in a new "crime wave." In any event each generation has to learn anew and for itself the importance of social orderliness and of respect for the rights and welfare of other members of society. Preventing crime is in one respect part of the whole problem of good government, and as the political scientists continually remind us, this requires eternal vigilance.

Crime prevention is more than "good government," however; it is just as much a matter of "good education," of sound family life, of suitable leisure-time activities, and of a socially oriented philosophy of life. It is also a matter of helping the person who has made a misstep so that he can become a useful member of society. Religious organizations, social case workers, educators, families, and communities as a whole are all involved in setting standards of human conduct. They are also involved in "helping people out of trouble." The pooling of knowledge and skills, as we shall see, is essential in preventing crime in the first place and in preventing the recurrence of criminal behavior.

Criminology from a Sociological Frame of Reference

Since this text is written by a sociologist, it will unquestionably bear the earmarks of a sociological frame of reference. Criminology, however, is a borderline subject to which psychologists (and psychiatrists) as well as sociologists have made a significant contribution. Because there have been so many researches in recent years on crime and criminology, no textbook can hope to cover all the contributions in the field. The comprehensive list discussed in this book aims to give the student a perspective from which to view modern understanding of criminal behavior. All ideas, including those of our generation, have roots in the past, and in this author's opinion it is very important for the student to see how criminal theories arose and how they have been superseded by other conclusions as the result of further research.

With reference to prisons and prison treatment it is likewise important for sociology students and others to understand how penal institutions arose and how they have developed and endured to the present time, despite their relative ineffectiveness in reducing criminality. Prisons are an excellent example of the difficulties involved in altering the structure and function of institutions. Like other institutions, they have remained relatively static in the midst of dynamic social change.

These, then, are a few of the topics which this text will present in detail in the chapters which follow.

Limitations of the Study of Criminology

Much of our understanding of the criminal is limited by our present inability to measure scientifically the subtle and unseen aspects of human personality. Much psychological and psychiatric theory may seem to explain human conduct, but thus far at least such explanations cannot be verified. Hence there are many frontiers in criminology. This book is offered in the profound hope that it may stimulate some of the critical and creative intelligence of the students who use it to extend their interest to criminological research. For it is the students of this generation who must explore the new horizons to which present developments in the field may point.

The Scope of the Book

This text is limited to the study of the adult offender for two reasons. One is that modern departments of sociology rather generally offer courses in both juvenile delinquency and criminology, the latter dealing chiefly with adult criminals. The second reason is that there is such an extensive literature in both fields that neither one course nor one book can cover both satisfactorily. The student of criminology should recognize, however, that adult criminality is often the sequel to juvenile delinquency and that many criminals began their careers in lawbreaking as juvenile offenders. Any student who is planning to become a specialist in criminology should take as extensive courses in delinquent and criminal behavior as possible; this book can cover only a segment of the material on the subject. Graduate students in particular should take additional courses in probation and in criminological research.

All that textbooks should do, at best, is to provide an adequate skeleton for courses. Many new researches that will appear in the various sociological journals, in *Mental Hygiene*, in the *Journal of Criminal Law and Criminology and Police Science*, in the *American Journal of Ortho-Psychiatry*, and in other publications, will give new insights to the study of criminology.

Many technical terms are employed in this book, because criminology itself is a technical subject. Some of the students, probation officers, prison officials, and other persons using this book as a text or as a reference may find it profitable to consult the *Dictionary of Sociology* and the *Encyclopedia of Criminology* where special terms are unfamiliar or seem confusing. The latest unabridged edition of Webster's dictionary also gives special definitions for most legal, psychiatric, and criminological terms. Ordinarily, advanced students in psychology and sociology will have little difficulty with the special vocabularies employed. All fields of knowledge have developed scientific terms in order to discuss various matters precisely, and this is true of criminology.

Since many students are inclined to ignore footnotes, they are urged to pay particular attention to those in this text. Many contain valuable information.

CHAPTER 2

Crime and Criminology

WHAT IS CRIME?

There are many perspectives from which we may view the crime problem, just as there are many opinions as to why men commit crimes. There are many pseudoscientists and self-appointed experts on the nature of crime because the subject is fascinating to such a great variety of people. Every corner grocer and every filling-station operator and nearly everybody's Aunt Lizzie can tell you just what should be done to curb the present crime rate. Serious students of criminology can assume no such optimistic role. They are instead confronted with a large body of facts and relationships which scholars in the field have built up from a variety of approaches. The approaches to the study of crime in themselves tend to color the interpretations and conclusions drawn. The approaches that are particularly important for the student to consider view crime as a social problem, as a psychological problem, as a combination of both these problems, as a psychosocial problem, and as a legal-social problem. Crime in fact may be regarded as a moral or religious problem; laws restraining crimes are rooted in religious and ethical concepts. As part of the background for a course in criminology, we may profitably review these approaches.

Crime as a Social Problem

Modern sociology has placed much emphasis on the study of the structure and functioning of present-day society. This entails an examination of how both society and its institutions are organized, of

11

what factors contribute to effective social functioning and what factors produce social disruption and social disorganization. From a sociological perspective crime is therefore one of the most serious problems of social disorganization, because criminals are engaged in activities which threaten the basis of government, law, order and social welfare. Some crimes represent the purely hedonistic interests of the individual who seeks to satisfy his desires without concern for the welfare, safety, or property of others, as the case may be. More powerful criminals are apparently united in a lawless combination with corrupt forces within our government so as to subvert the very purpose of government to their own mercenary ends. There are many varieties of social disorganization in a society so vast and complicated as ours, but the far-flung network of activities sponsored by professional criminals has created a virtual struggle for power within the fabric of government itself.

Technically such crimes are against the law. In a very real sense they are offenses against society and against the values of honesty, decency, and general welfare which the average citizen regards as basic to our way of life. Crime is therefore one of the important areas of social disorganization for the sociology student to consider.

Crime as a Psychological Problem

Crime is committed by criminals, the psychologists remind us, and criminals are human beings who for whatever reasons are motivated to act in ways which law condemns. Viewed from a psychological perspective, crime is thus not only criminal behavior, it is behavior of persons who are much the same as the rest of us. Psychologists have consequently been interested in the personality traits which characterize criminals in the belief that certain traits must differentiate criminals from the noncriminal group.

Psychologists have done much patient research in their attempts to determine the nature of the delinquent's and criminal's personality. Personality itself is not easy to describe exactly. Robert H. Gault, distinguished psychologist, says, "Personality is overt behavior and implicit taken as a whole."[1] Sociologists generally define personality as *the interrelated traits which determine an individual's role in the group.* But neither psychologists nor sociologists can say just how these various traits are related to each other and to the impression they make

[1] Robert H. Gault, *Criminology,* Heath, Boston, 1932, p. 38. This is one of the few textbooks written from a psychological perspective.

on the group. Mental ability, for example, is a personality trait. Measurements of mental ability made by psychologists indicate, however, that neither lack of mental ability (feeble-mindedness) nor high mental ability is of itself conducive to criminal conduct, as some had previously supposed. Other psychologists and psychiatrists have held that marked emotionality or emotional conflicts are basic factors in delinquent behavior. Studies they have made seem to indicate that many delinquents and criminals are frustrated, have a deep sense of guilt, or are emotionally disturbed. Nobody knows, unfortunately, how many nondelinquents have such disturbances. Nevertheless, crime is human behavior and we need all the insights that psychology has to offer criminology.

Crime as a Psychosocial Problem

Criminal behavior is deviant behavior from the point of view of society. We have reason to believe that persistent criminal activity is based upon antisocial attitudes. The psychologist tends to think of attitudes as internally organized tendencies to react in a certain way. The sociologist often holds the community responsible for the development of such attitudes.

To the objective student of criminology—if there is such a person—this may seem like arguing whether the chicken came from the egg or the egg from the chicken. Both psychology and sociology have made important contributions to criminal theory. Most of the important textbooks in criminology have been written by sociologists, however. The present book aims to cover relevant psychological data on crime and its treatment, but like most treatises by sociologists it will undoubtedly emphasize the sociological point of view. Criminals as individuals may be a psychological problem. But they are also a social problem, and their problems have arisen because of their failure to conform to the laws which represent the will of the larger social group. Criminals may be in harmony, however, within the disorganized community in which they live and the disorganized group within which they function.

Crime as a Legal-Social Problem

CRIME: A DEFINITION

In one sense crime is a legal problem, for, so far as modern Western culture is concerned, crime may be defined as any act, or failure to act, which is forbidden or prescribed by law, the failure to abide by such law being punishable by fine, imprisonment, banishment, death, or other punitive treatment, as the particular state may prescribe. Crimes may be classified with reference to (1) degree of reprehensibility, (2) party injured, (3) and whether they are traditional or recent concepts.

FELONIES AND MISDEMEANORS. When crimes are classified on the basis of degree of reprehensibility they are usually designated as *felonies* and *misdemeanors*. Major crimes are generally classified as felonies, and minor offenses as misdemeanors. Felonies are usually punishable by imprisonment in a state prison or penitentiary or by death. They are occasionally punishable by fine or by both fine and imprisonment. What is designated as a misdemeanor or a felony varies somewhat from state to state; but murder, burglary, rape, grand larceny, arson, treason, and perjury are usually classified as felonies, while drunkenness, petit larceny, "disturbing the peace," traffic violations which do not involve serious injury, and so-called minor offenses are usually designated misdemeanors. The latter are usually punished by a moderate or small fine or a short jail sentence. However, some states consider as felonies certain offenses that are classified as misdemeanors in other states. This disparity in definition of felonies and misdemeanors is one of the confusing aspects of the crime problem in the United States. We have 49 criminal codes governing the United States and the District of Columbia, and a federal code covers offenses against the federal government.

Crimes classified according to the party injured include personal offenses, crimes against the state, and crimes against the social welfare.

PERSONAL OFFENSES. The crimes of murder and rape always injure individuals, and in most cases theft, burglary, and arson incur loss for the individual whose property is destroyed. These are in a sense "personal" crimes, but not necessarily crimes against the person. The latter involve physical or moral injury to the person.

CRIMES AGAINST THE DIGNITY AND SECURITY OF THE STATE. Certain crimes may be considered as crimes against the government itself. With the rise of feudal kingdoms and the various national states in western Europe, certain activities came to be condemned as disturbing the peace and dignity of the king. In fact, under the old English law any crime committed by one citizen against another was considered an affront to the king's peace if it took place within the grounds around his castle. Later, as the kingdom extended to all England, Scotland, and Ireland, the king's peace covered all territory ruled by the Crown. To this day the indictments for crime in England charge the accused with an offense "against the peace and dignity of the King."

Many of our own states have retained a modification of this concept, except that it is the *people* rather than the king who are considered offended. In Illinois, for example, a criminal indictment alleges that the accused has committed an offense "against the peace and dignity of the people of the State of Illinois."

CRIMES AGAINST THE SOCIAL WELFARE. With increases in the complexity of our society and the numerous maladjustments which have appeared because of the need for sanitation and public health regulations, and for care and protection for the indigent, sick, widows, children, aged, foot passengers, and others, many new laws providing greater security for all persons have been enacted. Many acts are now forbidden, such as "spitting on sidewalks," speeding within city limits, making undue noise in a city, adulterating foods, fraudulently using the mails, etc. Various tax laws provide means for taking care of people who are without funds. Thus evasion of income taxes becomes a serious offense against the public welfare because it means that the individual is not accepting his pro rata share of the expense involved in maintaining social benefits. Regulation of the sale and manufacture of intoxicating beverages is regarded as essential to the social well-being; hence bootlegging is a serious crime. Application for relief by a person who has an adequate income is likewise considered a crime, and contrary to acceptable concepts of social welfare. Parents are required to bring up their children suitably, but their restraint over their children is limited. The state now protects the child from cruelty on the part of his parents. The list of modern crimes includes so many varieties of forbidden conduct that almost everyone is unwittingly a lawbreaker.

Traditional as Compared to Newer Conceptions of Crime

The crimes we have called personal offenses constitute most of the crimes that may also be considered traditional. They are offenses which have been condemned since time immemorial, and they are recognized as offenses in present-day primitive societies as well as civilized societies. These offenses carry the weight of historical and prehistorical disapproval and are abhorrent to virtually all peoples. In early primitive society, however, such offenses apparently were not considered offenses against the group; they were punished not by group action but by retaliation on the part of the person injured or his family. In turn the culprit's family, as well as the culprit, might be subject to reprisals. When personal injuries or damage was avenged by individuals it was usually in kind, and eventually group reprisals were of the same nature. These ideas were later codified in law. Thus the ancient Hebrew codes, derived from the Code of Hammurabi, provided for "an eye for an eye, a tooth for a tooth and a life for a life."[2]

Primitive Crimes

Primitive crimes in the sense of offenses punished by the whole tribe were acts which were regarded as endangering the entire group, rather than an individual or family. They included such behavior as sacrilege (which angered the gods), endangering the food supply (and hence the life of the group), and offenses like black magic, sorcery, the breaking of sex taboos, etc. There have been many studies of primitive crimes and practically all of them agree that the offenses punished by primitive societies included the following socially feared categories of behavior:

Witchcraft.
Treason.
Sacrilege and offenses against religion.
Incest and other breaches of sexual morality.
Poisoning and allied offenses.
Breaches of hunting rules.

These primitive crimes obviously entailed special dangers for the group. A witch was a fearful person who might wreak vengeance on whomsoever she chose. Treason, then as now, involved placing the safety of the group in the hands of the enemy. Sacrilege was a crime because it might occasion the wrath of the gods. Incest and sex offenses were closely allied to black magic, because both were held to tamper with the ill-understood biological processes of reproduction. Such offenses also violated whatever notions of personal decency the group had evolved. Poisoning was long vested with fear and mystery because death might ensue from tiny amounts of deadly drugs which could be administered in the victim's food or drink without his knowledge. Few people knew enough about the natural properties of drugs and chemicals to understand either their nature or their dangerous properties. A poisoner was thus regarded as a potential and mysterious

[2] Early punishments are discussed in detail in chap. 15.

danger to everyone; none could predict who might be his next victim. Breaches of the hunting rules might bring death. Destruction of young animals and female animals was forbidden because such wanton killing endangered the future food supply. The rules themselves were reinforced by superstitions, but offending rules was tantamount to starvation; this gave such practices the status of evil (or black) magic.

Among many present-day primitive societies, as among the Trobrianders, the basic punishment for such crimes is humiliation which induces the guilty person to commit suicide and thus punish himself.[3] In primitive as in civilized society rules and regulations do not operate rigidly; hence many primitives avoid punishment through stealth, family prestige, or purely practical consideration of the problems the punishment itself entails. There is great discrepancy between practice and theory in the operation of criminal law among primitives just as there is in civilized society. Today the Trobrianders rather generally punish murder and theft as offenses against the group, in contrast to the earlier primitives who regarded them as a purely personal matter. Murderers now receive a sentence and a thief is subjected to ostracism.[4]

Transitional Stages from Primitive to Civilized Society

There was of course no abrupt break between punishment based on personal vengeance and the development of a penal system which imposed punishment by the group. The evolution of concepts of law and justice involved transitional stages in which offenses against the individual came to be recognized as offenses against the tribe or group. Men who live in groups are bound to develop opinions regarding persons who harm members of their group. Most primitives have developed some form of court or tribunal, even though it may be merely a conclave of the elders to take action against an act disapproved by the group. Criminal law and criminal justice grew out of the consideration of ways and means of treating or disposing of persons who injured members of the group.[5] Thus notions of atonement for wrongdoing and of composition (a term meaning affixing penalty in other

[3] Cf. Bronislaw Malinowski, *Crime and Custom in Savage Society*, Kegan Paul, Trench, Trubner, London, 1932, Part II. Cf. also Herbert I. Hogben, *Law and Order in Polynesia*, Harcourt, Brace, New York, 1934, chaps. 7, 9.

[4] Bronislaw Malinowski, *op. cit.*, chaps. 3, 4.

[5] Cf. L. T. Hobhouse, *Morals in Evolution*, Chapman & Hall, London, rev. ed., 1951, chap. 3, "Law and Justice."

than kind) developed. As Hobhouse says, "Condemnation of the act takes the form of a fear for the commonweal. . . ."[6] In other words, all concepts of crimes as offenses against the group involve consideration of the social welfare, and of the safety and security of members of the group. Thus the thief is condemned by the whole group by extending the concept of injury to the individual to injury of a member of the group. He who steals my purse may steal trash, but no one's purse is safe so long as the thief is able to steal mine.

We cannot trace in detail the steps in the evolution of criminal law. Some tribes exhibit more vengeance in treating offenders than others. Ethnological studies indicate many developments in the transition from primitive to modern concepts of crime. At the same time much modern criminal law is deeply rooted in primitive custom.

Briefly, social condemnation of wrong came to possess a certain economy; that is, it became a prudent means to an end. Through its institutions of its police and courts society thus punishes the offender on an impartial basis (theoretically at least), with a minimum of bother to the individual but while assuring of the same degree of protection for all.

Newer Conceptions of Crime

Modern extensions of the concepts of crime have developed out of the complications in modern life which make it increasingly difficult for an individual to solve his problems of health, safety, and economic security without assistance from fellow members of society. In consequence crimes today are not merely *different from* and *more extensive than* those in primitive society. They also include many forms of conduct not condemned as late as 150 years ago. This may be accounted for by the vast changes involved in the transition from a rural to an urban economy and from an agricultural to an industrial civilization with all the attendant mechanical and chemical inventions. Moreover, many hazards are entailed in living in great urban centers, hazards ranging from the danger of epidemics to dislocations in industry and widespread unemployment. Modern warfare endangers the civilian population to a degree unimagined in earlier times. The possibility of a breakdown in our transportation system and in the distribution of the food supply in wartime involves basic problems of survival. Hence black markets, sabotage of railroads, etc., become serious crimes. The hazard of unemployment is so serious a problem of modern times that

[6] *Ibid.*, p. 99.

a new tax structure became imperative. Evasion of the tax laws today is thus a new crime created by new concepts of the social welfare. These are but a few examples.

Many persons who offend the new laws do not consider themselves criminals, however, because the new laws have arbitrarily made what was previously considered lawful behavior a crime. In fact, penalties for most of the new crimes are met with opposition, with many people insisting that their personal liberties are being infringed. There is no such defense, for traditional crimes since custom has long since established that no man shall be free to steal, to murder, to rape, etc. Defense for these crimes can be based only on pleas of unsound mind, nonage, duress, etc.[7]

Sociology, Crime, and the Law

To the sociologist all present-day definitions of crime are negative aspects of the public welfare. Crimes are acts or omissions of acts which endanger members of society in some way. The traditional crimes are in general more condemned than the recently defined crimes, because there is almost complete consensus with reference to the harm the former entail. Hence, the newer laws that restrain conduct which was formerly either accepted or "winked at" are harder to enforce and, as we have said, persons who disobey them do not ordinarily consider themselves criminal. In consequence offenses against such laws are both extensive and difficult to punish. Offenses against the liquor laws during prohibition and against the rationing laws in wartime are good examples. Yet changing social conditions may mean that these new crimes involve serious danger for the group.

Only when the group as a whole holds that a certain type of behavior is dangerous and to be condemned is it regarded as a serious offense. Public opinion often lags behind the social consciousness of those who write the laws in time of emergency. Even in normal times the lawmakers tend to write laws only after the need for them has long been evident and has created a social demand.

Religious Ethics, Moral Concepts, and Criminal Law

Modern criminal law thus not only has many roots in primitive practices and early civilizations but also includes recent addenda to our concepts of forbidden conduct. Criminal law incorporates many

[7] Cf. chap. 15, pp. 396–399.

moral and religious concepts; but even so, moral and religious principles today often go much further in defining acceptable conduct than the law requires, as for example in the Christian precepts "Love the Lord thy God with all thy soul" and "Love thy neighbor as thyself." No modern state can claim in any true sense to be a Christian state, although the Western world has often called itself "Christendom." Nevertheless, the concepts of fair trade, fair labor practices, civil rights, racial equality, social security, and aid to dependents all incorporate principles rooted in Christian teaching, for all these principles manifest significant concern for the welfare of persons who are unable to secure such benefits unaided.

Lawmakers are themselves inevitably affected by whatever religious ideals they hold as individuals, and this is true both of our own legislators and of those of earlier generations. Historically the present-day traditional crimes of the Western world were initially condemned by the religious tenets of the Ten Commandments and the Mosaic Code, which are part of our Judaic-Christian heritage. Apparently (according to modern scholars) the Mosaic Code was largely derived from the Code of Hammurabi.[8] The Hebrews reinforced these rules by what they considered divine authority. These rules represented their basic moral concepts of right and wrong and of good and evil. The ideas of both good and God, we have reason to believe, have grown out of social experience. Religious belief may transcend experience, but it is nevertheless an interpretation of experience. All the great religions of civilization are ethical religions which postulate a universe based upon moral law. Today, however, both moral and religious law tend to be less rigid than civil or criminal law. The latter two always try—none too successfully—to apply their principles universally and impartially.

Criminal law is likewise far more rigid than the Christian concept of salvation and forgiveness for the sinner. But both the church and the law place responsibility upon the offender. The church insists that the sinner must "repent and accept salvation"; the law holds that the offender is responsible for his own conduct and that he must take punishment in consequence. Religious teaching similarly recognizes that it is often difficult to lead a good life, whereas the law holds that anyone who knows the difference between right and wrong can be expected to do right.[9]

[8] Cf. chap. 15 for a detailed discussion of this point.
[9] Cf. James Ten Broeke, *The Moral Life and Religion*, Macmillan, New York, 1922, for a discussion of morality and religion.

Democratic government is undoubtedly rooted in the Christian concept "Love thy neighbor as thyself," although it cannot be said to be in exact harmony with this teaching.[10] So far as the concept has been adopted, it applies much more significantly to civil than to criminal law. Most civilian government services evidence concern for the welfare of those for whom the services are provided. The institutions for punishing criminals, however, have incorporated little concern for the prisoners' welfare within their functions until relatively recently.

In outlining the position of the Christian church on civilian matters, St. Thomas Aquinas maintained that civil law cannot apply as universally as divine (or religious) law and that civil (or human) law is concerned only with maintaining civil order. Furthermore, civil or human laws may be unjust and acts of tyranny, in which case the laws themselves "do not oblige anyone's conscience." Change in law, like all change, St. Thomas regarded as disruptive because it upsets custom and "custom is a great help to the observance of the law."[11]

Man's Conscience and the Law

When Christian teachings are in conflict with law, St. Thomas held that "we should obey God rather than men."[12] In modern society the state theoretically permits no such interference with law enforcement; but religious teaching as crystallized by St. Thomas, as well as that of the Puritans, the Quakers, and others, places man's conscience above the law. Roman Catholics accept the teachings of St. Thomas with reference to conscience and the law, but Protestants in general have revolted from what they considered tyrannical authority even more frequently than have the Roman Catholics.

The American people have been basically Protestant in tradition, and in line with their Protestantism they have been noted for reserving the right to reject laws which they do not approve. Part of this tendency to rejection undoubtedly stems from an unwillingness to promote the general welfare at the expense of individual liberty. The Constitution of the United States is committed to protecting men from unjust laws, but there has been an obvious tendency on our part to regard new laws as restrictions on our liberty. Thus many of our "test case" lawsuits are aimed primarily at setting aside new laws as

[10] Cf. Eleanor Roosevelt, The Moral Basis of Democracy, Howell, Soskin, New York, 1940, pp. 12–13.
[11] Cf. Etienne Gilson, Moral Values and the Moral Life (The System of St. Thomas Aquinas), transl. by Leo R. Ward, Herder, St. Louis, 1931, Part I, chap. 5, "Law on the Human Level."
[12] Ibid., p. 206.

unconstitutional because they are allegedly unwarranted interferences with civil liberty.

Law, Morality, and the Ruling Class

Part of the failure in law enforcement in America stems from our theory of government, which *identifies the government with the people*. According to this theory, the state is none other than its collective members, whom it aims both to protect and to restrain. This identification of the ruler with the ruled creates certain difficulties of both a philosophical and a practical sort. In a modern democracy it is true that ideally "we the people" are presumed to be both the state and the ruling class. But unfortunately this ideal is a pious delusion which few students of political science or law can be persuaded to accept in its practical application. A much truer statement of fact is to say that, *in the final analysis, the state is the ruling class.* It seems to be true in both Western democracies and dictatorships that the ruling class is the group that is in political control. This conception of the state does not ignore the powerful political aspects of public opinion, but it recognizes the practical facts of politics.

As the years have passed, different groups have been enfranchised so that the number who vote and make their vote heard has become increasingly more representative of the total adult population. Even so, our political party system permits a very small group to determine the list of candidates for office. With few exceptions, those who run for office represent those who pull the political strings; and those who are elected owe their first allegiance to those who selected them for candidates. The successful candidates become the executives and lawmakers of our nation, but as a ruling class they also represent the social and economic ideologies of their economic and social group, the middle class; for the most part this means the upper middle class. Occasionally a representative of labor or a person with lower-class interests or affiliations is elected to office or to a legislative body; but in general the only persons who can afford to assume office or become lawmakers are those who have achieved comfortable economic status or else they must receive salaries, gifts, or bribes on the side. Examples of the latter are lawyers elected to a state legislature who are employed on "retainers" by holding companies or railroads and hence tend to represent the interests of their employers in the legislative assembly. Insurance agents run for election as state representatives and keep the interests of the insurance corporations in mind in opposing social security legislation. Part of the moral tone underlying our law is thus derived from an acceptance of the *status quo* and the economic practices on which our industrial civilization is based.

Law and the enforceability of law rest upon the accepted values of the society which enacts the law, despite the fact that those values may seem nebulous when we attempt to define them. The criminal code of the United States may be assailed, but in general our lawmakers have adhered persistently to belief in God and religious values, in the sanctity of life, in the sacredness of private property, and in the desirability of personal liberty. When this country declared its independence from Great Britain, Jefferson summed up our beliefs—somewhat prematurely, perhaps—when he said that all men are created equal and that all have the right to life, liberty, and the pursuit of happiness. He was a Virginian, and he believed in enjoying life. Many of our forefathers did not take much stock in the right to happiness. If a man worked and behaved himself, all concurred in holding that he had a right to life and a right to liberty. Our bill of rights granted him the right of freedom of enterprise which enabled him to acquire property. But thus far man's constitutional right to be happy has not been enforceable nor can we do much to punish people who make us unhappy unless they commit specifically condemned offenses.

The Arbitrary Character of the Law

The arbitrary and specific character of our criminal codes which define and limit the number and types of punishable offenses has often been attacked by criminologists as well as by other social critics. It is obviously absurd to attempt to protect society by opposing certain petty or relatively unimportant types of antisocial conduct while ignoring equally important and much more serious evidences of such conduct. Thus it may be alleged that the lack of social conscience on the part of businessmen, lawyers, and even many physicians probably results in far greater suffering and more deaths than are involved in the few thousand persons murdered each year.

So far as morality is concerned, it may likewise be maintained that many antisocial acts are far more opposed to social welfare than crimes which are defined as such. In the final analysis, however, generalized social opinion as expressed by the laws and the lawmakers and as interpreted by the law enforcers must always lag behind the seers and the social prophets. Meanwhile, if the social definitions of crime were not rigorously limited to the specific offenses for which common and statutory law have provided penalties, no person would be safe from the capricious judgment of the police and the judges. Whenever statutory and common law are pushed aside for law by decree, there is no gain for social ethics. The brutal tactics of the Nazis which ignored the protection of the individual by labeling as criminal every attempt to evade the outrages of the Nazi dictatorship is an example par excellence of the dangers law by decree presents. Law by decree might on occasion be an advantage. If, for example, our President could alter laws without reference to Congressional action he might enact provisions which would be socially desirable. But in the long run it is safer to go through the slow processes of legislation than it is to provide for services without legislative enactment. For the legislature protects individual liberty, without which life itself has little value. In enacting laws, however, there are many ways in which society "strains at gnats and swallows camels." In viewing crime and the criminal from any idealistic perspective man's petty attempts to deal with those who subvert the social order may seem a bit pathetic. Yet, as von Hentig has wisely pointed out, the law must of necessity be highly formalized. That much behavior which is injurious to the welfare of the community, the state, and society as a whole is not subsumed under our criminal law cannot be denied. Some extension of social controls over areas of conduct heretofore ignored would unquestionably be desirable. Yet only as such controls are evolved through democratic processes can we anticipate any true gain in social perspective. Arbitrary law, despite its dangers, is infinitely preferable to the capricious justice of law by decree.[13]

CRIMINOLOGY: WHAT IT IS

Criminology: A Definition

Criminology may be defined as the scientific study of crime and its treatment. To date this study has produced a large body of facts which relate to (1) the nature of crime, (2) factors which are associated with criminal behavior, (3) case studies of offenders, and (4) the treatment or punishment of criminals.

Because the term "crime" covers the wide variety of behavior which is forbidden and punished by the state, there are many reasons why criminology has not become a science in the sense of developing precise laws with reference to the genesis of criminal behavior and its con-

[13] For an exposition of this idea, see the important book by Hans von Hentig, Crime: Causes and Conditions, McGraw-Hill, New York, 1947, pp. 5–7.

trol. That is, we cannot state with mathematical precision the exact relationship between factors which appear to be associated with criminality or criminal activity. There are too many imponderables to permit us to establish and verify such laws.

The development of criminological research is in a sense a record of correlative developments in psychology, psychiatry, and sociology. Most of what we may call scientific research in criminology has been done in the fields of psychology and sociology, although psychiatry has made many stimulating contributions to criminological literature with reference to motivation in criminal conduct. Some research has tried to incorporate or "integrate" the techniques of both psychology and sociology; but on the whole psychologists have worked on the problem of differentiating personality traits of criminals, and sociologists have studied social relationships and environmental factors in the backgrounds of criminals. Research which integrates the findings from both fields will probably go much further in getting at basic explanations for criminal conduct.

Virtually all the important research in criminology in America has been done since 1910. As a matter of fact, most of the important psychological and sociological research in the various areas of human behavior and social relationships has been carried on since that date. Criminological research may therefore be regarded as dependent upon scientific developments in these two fields.

The National Conference of Criminal Law and Criminology in 1909

One event, however, appears to have precipitated much of the immediate interest in criminology in the United States. This event was the National Conference of Criminal Law and Criminology held at Northwestern University School of Law in Chicago in 1909. This conference was called in recognition of a need on the part of the legal profession for revising criminal law and procedure, but was also part of the celebration of the Fiftieth Anniversary of Northwestern University Law School. One hundred and fifty leaders in the academic fields of medicine, psychology, sociology, and penology, as well as representatives from the juvenile courts and legal aid societies, judges of criminal courts, prosecuting attorneys, and practicing lawyers, were brought together to pool their ideas on how to develop a more intelligent approach to problems of criminal justice.[14]

[14] Robert H. Gault, "Criminology in Northwestern University," *Journal of Criminal Law, Criminology and Police Science*, 42:2–17 (May–June, 1951).

From this conference emerged the American Institute of Criminal Law and Criminology as an organization. This institute in turn established a number of committees whose activities gave major impetus to scientific study and research in the field of crime. The Committee on Translation of European Treatises was of special importance, for it was responsible for publishing, in translation, nine important works by leading European scholars. These translations made a vast area of criminological material available in English to American students and scholars.[15] These volumes, published by Little, Brown & Company of Boston in the Modern Criminal Science Series, are listed below with dates of publication:

Modern Theories of Criminality, by C. Bernaldo de Quiros of
    Madrid (1911).
Criminal Psychology, by Hans Gross, Professor of Criminal Law
    at the University of Gratz (1911).
Crime, Its Causes and Remedies, by Cesare Lombroso, Professor
    of Legal Medicine at the University of Turin (1911).
The Individualization of Punishment, by Raymond Saleilles, Pro-
    fessor of Comparative Law at the University of Paris (1913).
Criminal Sociology, by Enrico Ferri, Professor of Criminal Law
    at the University of Rome (1917).
Penal Philosophy, by Gabriel Tarde, Professor of Modern Phi-
    losophy at the College of France (1912).
Criminality and Economic Conditions, by William A. Bonger,
    Dutch publicist (1916).
Criminology, by Raffaele Garofalo, Jurist of the Court of Appeals
    of Naples (1914).
Crime and Its Repression, by Gustav Aschaffenburg, Professor of
    Psychiatry at the Academy of Practical Medicine in Cologne
    (1913).

The publication of these books had a salutary effect. In both theory and practice, criminal law in the United States had been based almost exclusively on British common law and case decisions. Hence a tremendous intellectual stimulus was given to American scholars and lawyers when these major contributions of Continental criminologists and jurists were made available. Although Henderson had touched briefly on the personal, social, and environmental factors in his text, The Dependent, Defective and Delinquent Classes, published in 1893 and subsequently revised, there was no satisfactory textbook in crim-

[15] Ibid.

inology for college courses. Maurice Parmalee, who attended the conference in 1909, produced the first comprehensive standard text in 1918.[16] This book drew largely from European sources. In the meantime many research projects in this and other countries were published. Two of the more important of these were Goring's study, *The English Convict*, published in 1913,[17] and Healy's intensive case studies of 1000 delinquents from which he compiled statistical data with reference to factors causing delinquency in 1915.[18] William I. Thomas and Florian Znaniecki's great contribution to sociological literature, *The Polish Peasant in Europe and America* (in 1918–1920), also made sociologists conscious of how the crime problem among immigrants was related to problems of cultural conflict and assimilation.[19]

By 1924 so many research projects had been completed that Edwin H. Sutherland was able to publish his closely reasoned text, *Criminology*,[20] based largely on new research. In 1926 John L. Gillin brought out his text, *Criminology and Penology*,[21] which provided extensive historical material on the development of prisons, probation, parole, and other aspects of penal treatment. In the meantime many graduate research projects in criminology were launched. The University of Chicago initiated its systematic studies of various urban communities, out of which emerged both Clifford R. Shaw's and Henry D. McKay's studies of "delinquency areas" and the Chicago Area Project in delinquency prevention. The present author made an ecological and cultural study of juvenile court cases in Chicago in 1923 under the direction of Dr. Herman M. Adler, State Criminologist of Illinois,[22] and later made a follow-up study of delinquent girls who had been released from Sleighton Farm Reformatory in Pennsylvania in 1924–1926.[23] In 1928, Healy and Bronner published their more extensive study covering 4000 cases of delinquents from Chicago and Boston.[24] The Gluecks began their monumental studies of Massa-

[16] *Criminology*, Macmillan, New York.
[17] Published by His Majesty's Stationery Office, London.
[18] *The Individual Delinquent*, Little, Brown, Boston.
[19] Initially published by University of Chicago Press, Chicago, in five volumes. A two-volume edition published in 1927 by Knopf, New York.
[20] Published by Lippincott, Philadelphia.
[21] Published by Appleton-Century-Crofts, New York.
[22] Mabel A. Elliott, *A Correlation Between Rate of Juvenile Delinquency and Racial Heterogeneity*, Department of Welfare, Springfield, 1926.
[23] Mabel A. Elliott, *Correctional Education and the Delinquent Girl*, Commonwealth of Pennsylvania, Harrisburg, 1929.
[24] William Healy and Augusta F. Bronner, *Delinquents and Criminals, Their Making and Unmaking*, Macmillan, New York, 1928.

chusetts delinquents and criminals in the late 1920's,[25] and literally hundreds of small research projects concerned with psychological measurements of delinquents and criminals or environmental factors in criminal behavior were completed in the period 1920–1930.[26] Meanwhile Cyril L. Burt published his statistical study comparing delinquents and nondelinquents in London in 1925.[27]

Nearly all these studies showed that delinquents and criminals came from a background of poverty, bad neighborhoods, broken homes, incompetent or shiftless or immoral parents, faulty home training, or inadequate education; or they were living in a community in which established patterns of delinquency and crime were operating—if not in the family. In general, delinquent girls had much worse home situations than delinquent boys, but boys were subjected to many undesirable contacts with patterns of delinquent behavior in their neighborhood associates. During the decade 1920–1930 sociologists concluded that delinquents had more handicaps than nondelinquents. Furthermore virtually all delinquents brought before courts were shown to live in the slums—those deteriorating interstitial areas between the business zones and better residential sections.

In the meantime psychiatrists (as we shall discuss later) have developed their theory that crime is rooted in emotional frustration. This idea has thus far convinced few but the psychiatrists, for it defies any objective scientific measurement. Psychologists, on the other hand, have devised many scales for measuring intelligence and attitudes and have tried to correlate them with delinquent behavior. It is possible that psychiatry may develop more exact methods of criminal research in the future.

In the period since 1930 many refinements in research techniques have taken place. The Gluecks' research into the behavior patterns of delinquents whom they had previously studied showed that many who had at first failed to adjust had subsequently reformed. Austin L. Porterfield has studied the admitted delinquencies of college students and found them to be similar to those of juvenile court cases, and Edwin H. Sutherland startled the American public by declaring that the executives of the leading business and industrial corporations in America had wittingly broken the criminal codes or laws where infractions carried heavy penalties. These studies indicated that delinquency

[25] Sheldon and Eleanor T. Glueck, *500 Criminal Careers*, Knopf, New York, 1930. This was the first in an impressive series of follow-up studies.
[26] Cf. Marshall B. Clinard, "Sociologists and American Criminology," *Journal of Criminal Law and Criminology*, 41:549–577 (January–February, 1951).
[27] Cyril L. Burt, *The Young Delinquent*, University of London, London, 1925.

is not necessarily the product of all the unfavorable social and economic factors which previous research seemed to indicate. On the other hand persons who are brought before the court tend to be members of the lower economic and social class.

Roscoe Pound and Jerome Hall, among others, have traced the social origins of the concepts of crime and the relation of criminal laws to the social order in which we live.[28] Many laws are actually in conflict and contribute to the confusion in the fields of criminology and criminal law. All these new insights into crime require a new orientation to the whole problem. Religious teachers have long taught that *all men are sinners*. Modern criminal research likewise indicates that the tendency to commit crime is not limited to the handicapped and underprivileged groups. There is, however, a tendency to punish those of the lower class more severely.

The Contribution of Sociologists to Criminology

Sociologists have made major contributions to the treatment of crime by their research which in turn has led to various community reorganization projects. In these projects the people themselves have made strenuous effort to improve the patterns of behavior in the community and turn the delinquency areas into areas in which it is safe for children to grow up. Sociologists have also made numerous studies of prisons, probation, and parole as institutions for penal treatment. Psychology and sociology have both made important contributions to the case-work techniques employed in working with men on probation and ex-prisoners on parole. Sociologists, along with lawyers and other interested persons, have assisted in many of the crime surveys which modern interest in crime has evoked.

Thus many sources of information are available to the student interested in learning why men persist in behaving in ways which are defined as criminal and which are harmful both to themselves and to society. There are still gaps in our information that need to be filled in before we can be sure we know what factors produce either criminality or effective readjustment. In studying criminal behavior we are not permitted by ethical and other considerations to put the criminal in a test tube and control all the variables which affect him. But we can control our research projects much more effectively today than was possible in an earlier period because of the work which has gone

[28] Cf. Roscoe Pound, *Criminal Justice in America*, Holt, New York, 1930, and Jerome Hall, *Theft, Law and Society*, Little, Brown, Boston, 1935.

before. We might also conduct the treatment of crime on much more scientific bases.

Undoubtedly many new directions will appear in criminal research. The extent of crime in modern society (as discussed in the succeeding chapter) is startling evidence of the great need for developing and applying social science if we are to achieve a more effective social organization. The students of this text are the heirs of previous research, but they can go further because they can stand on the data thus far accumulated.

Every newspaper presents new material on the extent of crime. Scare headlines and first-page publicity provide an index to the current interest in crime. Modern society may be crime ridden, but it is also crime conscious. Articles dealing with criminal research appear regularly in the *American Sociological Review*, the *American Journal of Sociology*, the *Journal of Criminal Law, Criminology and Police Science*, and *Federal Probation*. These are usually oriented from the sociological frame of reference. Other articles of equal importance will be found in *Mental Hygiene*, the *American Journal of Ortho-Psychiatry*, the *Prison Journal*, and the *Journal of Abnormal and Social Psychology*. The serious student will wish to become acquainted with current materials in the field.

SELECTED BIBLIOGRAPHY

Allen, Carleton Kemp, *Law in the Making*, Oxford University Press, New York, 3rd ed., 1939. This book, although basically devoted to law of equity, gives an excellent history of the development of law out of custom and moral ideas with a summary of various viewpoints. It may be considered a classic reference.

Clinard, Marshall B., "Sociologists and American Criminology," *Journal of Criminal Law and Criminology*, 41:549–577 (January–February, 1951). This article gives a brief history of the contribution of American sociologists to criminology.

Gault, Robert H., "Criminology in Northwestern University," *Journal of Criminal Law, Criminology and Police Science* (new title), 42:2–17 (May–June, 1951). This article gives an excellent survey of the development of criminology after the 1909 Conference on Criminal Law and Criminology at Northwestern University.

Gilson, Etienne, *Moral Values and the Moral Life* (The System of St. Thomas Aquinas), transl. by Leo R. Ward, Harder, St. Louis, 1931. This book summarizes Christian teaching as developed by St. Thomas Aquinas in reference to moral conduct and the law.

Hobhouse, L. T., *Morals in Evolution*, Chapman & Hall, London, rev. ed., 1951. A comprehensive treatise on the common origins of morality and justice is given in chapter 3, "Law and Justice."

Quiros, C. Bernaldo de, *Theories of Criminality*, transl. by Alfonso de Salvio, Little, Brown, Boston, 1911. This book summarizes the earlier contributions of European criminologists and pseudocriminologists.

Roosevelt, Eleanor, *The Moral Basis of Democracy*, Howell, Soskin, New York, 1940. This is a brief statement by America's leading woman citizen on the relation between Christian religion and democratic government.

CHAPTER 3

The Extent and Distribution of Crime

From a social point of view the failure of our citizens to abide by the restraints imposed by our criminal codes constitutes a major problem of social disorganization; and the degree to which such failure exists indicates the degree of failure inherent in our social controls. The crime rate is thus a matter of perennial interest, not only to the sociologist, the government official, and the civic-minded layman, but to the *public*, as the headlines and the detailed reports in our newspapers testify.

Both modern research and general observation must convince us, however, that lawbreaking is a rather common characteristic of human behavior and that most persons have at some time or other committed offenses for which they might have been punished by either state or federal laws. Many laws apparently run counter to the general propensities of human beings to act selfishly, passionately, deceptively, and aggressively without concern for the values or the welfare of the group.

When serious-minded people have lived long enough to know something about human behavior (their own and that of their neighbors), they are often frank enough to admit that they have sometimes broken the law. The present author once had occasion to interview a district judge with reference to the case of a young boy charged with grand larceny. His was a peculiarly emotional case. His father (a prominent lawyer) and mother (a cultivated, educated woman) had been divorced following a rather serious scandal involving bootleg liquor. His mother was attempting to meet the bills for herself and her three children on the small wages she drew as secretary to a state official. She had moved into a cheap three-room flat in a lower-middle-class neighborhood. The two boys resented their change in status, their lack of weekly allowances, the broken family. The younger one responded by joining forces with another boy who already had a series of delinquencies. Together this boy and he broke into a jewelry store and escaped with $10,000 worth of watches, bracelets, and rings. In attempting to dispose of these items they were apprehended.

Anyone with any psychological insight could see reasons for the younger boy's motivation. He was a bright lad of 15 years, who because of the value of the things he had stolen faced a sentence to the state penitentiary. Because of his youth it seemed reasonable to ask the judge for leniency. There was some question as to what attitude he might take toward the youngster. The judge, however, recognized the boy's behavior for what it was; a youthful protest against the outrages of his experience. He arranged to have the boy committed to an institution for psychiatric treatment and said in passing, "I remember the first time I stole something. The amount was smaller but my psychological reactions were a bit similar. My father had done something I seriously deplored and I went out and stole the refreshments for a church social."

Sometimes older persons recall their youthful delinquencies with glee, recounting how they stole a pig for a fraternity banquet or "walked" a fraternity brother to keep him from being arrested for being drunk. To date there has been no general census or survey of the past criminal activities of the population as a whole. But we do have enough partial surveys of the unpunished delinquent and of the criminal behavior of young persons and adults to give us some new perspectives on the crime problem.

SURVEYS OF OFFENSES AMONG THE GENERAL POPULATION

Four noteworthy studies of delinquent and criminal behavior among persons not punished for lawbreaking are (1) the Cambridge-Somerville study in Massachusetts, (2) the Porterfield study in Fort Worth, Texas, (3) the Wallerstein-Wyle study of crimes among "law-abiding" citizens, and (4) Sutherland's famous study of the crimes committed by our great industrial and public utility corporations.

The Cambridge-Somerville Study

In 1946 Fred J. Murphy, Mary M. Shirley, and Helen L. Witmer published their research on the hidden delinquencies of 61 boys who never had been brought to court and 40 who had been court cases. These boys, from the communities of Cambridge and Somerville, admitted that they had committed a total of 6416 offenses. Of these only 95, or 1.5 per cent, had ever been brought to court for a hearing. Approximately 1400 of the 6416 offenses were infractions of city ordinances, none of which even so much as resulted in a complaint. There were 4400 minor offenses of which only 27, or $6/10$ of 1 per cent, were prosecuted. Moreover, of 616 serious offenses only 11 per cent (68) were punished. These youngsters admitted the delinquencies to social workers who knew them well enough to gain their confidence. Many of the offenses had occurred years before and were known to neither the court nor the social agency at the time they were committed.[1]

The Porterfield Study in Fort Worth, Texas

Another study published the same year by Professor Austin L. Porterfield of Texas Christian University compared the frequency of criminal and delinquent offenses of 337 college students (200 men and 137 women) with the number of offenses committed by 2049 boys whose cases were brought into the Fort Worth juvenile court. The court cases were charged with 55 specific offenses ranging from "shooting spit wads at a wrestling match" to murder. What is more striking is that 100 per cent of both men and women students admitted they had committed offenses, as Table 3.1 indicates. In fact one theological

TABLE 3.1.　Percentage of Texas Christian University Students Reporting the Commission of 1 or More of the 55 Offenses

	Number in Group	Percentage Reporting One or More of the Offenses	Average Number of Offenses Reported
Precollege men	200	100.0	17.6
College men	100	100.0	11.2
Precollege women	137	100.0	4.7

SOURCE: Austin L. Porterfield, *Youth in Trouble*, Leo Potishman Foundation, Fort Worth, 1946, Table 1, p. 38. Quoted by permission.

student said he had committed 27 of the 55 listed offenses! Moreover, the offenses were just as serious as those committed by the delinquents brought before the court. There was even one case of murder

[1] Fred J. Murphy, Mary M. Shirley, and Helen L. Witmer, "The Incidence of Hidden Delinquency," *American Journal of Ortho-Psychiatry*, 16:686–696 (October, 1946). Cf. Edwin Powers and Helen L. Witmer, *An Experiment in Prevention of Delinquency— The Cambridge-Somerville Youth Study*, Columbia University Press, New York, 1951, for a detailed report on this study.

and one case of negligent homicide, for which no charges were ever pressed. A comparison of the frequency with which the same offenses were committed on the average by 100 college men and the boys in court shows that the college men committed far more offenses than the juvenile court boys were charged with, yet only in cases of traffic violations were any significant charges brought against the college boys, as Table 3.2 shows.[2] Traffic violations, however, as every one

TABLE 3.2. Frequency with Which Offenses of Various Types Were Reported by and Charged Against the Average 100 Texas Christian University Men Students Compared with the Frequency with Which the Same Offenses Were Charged Against the Average 100 Boys in Court at Fort Worth

Type of Offense	Frequency with Which Reported by the Average 100 Men Students		Frequency with Which Charged Against the Average 100 Men or Boys			Number of Times Reported by 100 Students for Each Time Charged Against 100 Boys in Court	
	Pre-college	College	Pre-college	College	Boys	Pre-college	College
Acts of public annoyance	366.0	131.0	0.0	0.0	2.8	130.7	46.8
Traffic violations	255.0	189.0	31.0	28.0	0.9	283.3	210.0
Malicious mischief	235.5	145.0	0.0	0.0	5.0	47.0	29.0
Encroaching	170.5	79.0	0.0	0.0	2.6	65.6	30.4
Personal affronts	143.0	105.0	0.0	0.0	1.7	84.1	61.8
Vagabondage	134.5	100.0	0.0	0.0	53.3	2.5	1.9
Liquor violations	120.5	143.0	0.5	0.0	1.2	100.4	119.4
Theft	116.0	36.0	0.0	0.0	27.2	4.3	1.3
Dishonesty, except theft	113.0	99.0	0.0	0.0	2.6	43.4	38.1
Sex offenses	36.5	85.0	0.0	0.0	0.7	123.7	121.4
Other cases	15.0	4.0	2.5	4.0	2.0	7.5	2.0
All types of offenses	1705.5	1116.0	34.0	32.0	100.0	17.6	11.2

SOURCE: Austin L. Porterfield, *Youth in Trouble*, Leo Potishman Foundation, Fort Worth, 1946, Table 4, p. 44. Quoted by permission.

who has ever filled in a civil service examination data sheet knows, are not regarded by public officials as serious offenses. Sex offenses ran high among the college men with 5.5 per cent of the men admitting attempted rape in precollege days, 24.5 per cent indecent exposure, and 58.5 per cent extramarital coitus. In contrast only 0.7 per cent of the boys in court were charged with sex offenses, although this figure probably represents only a small percentage of this type of offense among the juvenile court cases.[3] (At least we are fairly safe in thinking that rates for sex offenses were higher if we may believe the ratios established in the Kinsey report. In this latter study more illicit sex

[2] Austin L. Porterfield, *Youth in Trouble*, Leo Potishman Foundation, Fort Worth, 1946, Table 3, pp. 40–41.
[3] *Ibid.*, Cf. chap. 5 for an analysis of the sex offenses by males as revealed by the Kinsey report.

relations were found to occur in the less well-educated classes than in the college-trained group.)

In any event the major distinction between the delinquent behavior of college students and the cases brought into court seemed to lie in the relative impunity accorded the students because they belonged to a more favored group. College students represented a higher economic and social level, their family backgrounds were more stable, and their post-delinquent behavior was not followed by social ostracism which seems to incline the institutionalized offender to further delinquencies and misconduct.[4]

Data from these studies, partial and limited though they may be, give us rather significant evidence that many lawbreakers in favored economic and social groups (probably the majority) receive no penalty at all for their offenses but instead escape punishment completely. Most of these nonconvicted offenders seemed to be leading pretty decent lives as respected citizens in their communities. We are therefore forced to speculate as to what might have happened to those persons who were prosecuted and given penal sentences if they had likewise escaped detection and conviction. Might they too have profited from the opportunity to maintain their self-respect and have become decent law-abiding citizens? This question has no satisfactory answer, but it seems likely that many might have become well-adjusted citizens. Certainly it is well for us to keep in mind that the so-called law-abiding have many offenses to their discredit. Furthermore the man who escapes penal sentence escapes far more than the sentence. He escapes condemnation and stigma in the community as well. For, as Porterfield has well pointed out, the college man who has committed offenses moves in respectable society. He has status in the community and enjoys the respect of his fellow men. On the other hand the young person who is condemned and rejected by the community sinks both in his own and in others' estimation by reason of the progressive segregation imposed upon him by an outraged public opinion.[5]

The Wallerstein-Wyle Study

Impressed with the findings of these two studies, James S. Wallerstein and Clement J. Wyle of the Randen Foundation in New York City devised a questionnaire which they submitted to a cross section

[4] *Ibid.*, pp. 46–51.
[5] *Ibid.*, p. 48.

of the population (in which there was an effort to balance racial and religious groups).[6] The questionnaire listed 49 offenses and covered the following general groups of offenses. (Apparently no one was asked if he had committed murder, as in the Texas study.)

Malicious mischief.
Disorderly conduct.
Assault.
Auto misdemeanors.
Health law violations.
Indecency.
Gambling.
Larceny.
Burglary and possession of burglar's tools.
Robbery and illegal possession of firearms.
Bribery.
Perjury.
Falsification and fraud.
Election frauds.
Tax evasion.
Coercion and extortion.
Conspiracy and compounding a crime.
Criminal libel.

There were 1698 persons who replied to the questionnaire, including 1020 men and 678 women. Of these, 91 per cent admitted they had committed one or more offenses after the age of 16, for which they might have received penal sentences. (Under the age of 16 all offenses in New York are considered juvenile delinquencies.)

A partial list given in a summary of the study showed the percentages of men and women committing certain offenses to be as follows:[7]

Offense	Per Cent Men	Per Cent Women
Malicious mischief	84	81
Disorderly conduct	85	76
Assault	49	5
Auto misdemeanors	61	39
Indecency	77	74
Gambling	74	54
Larceny	89	83
Grand larceny (except auto)	13	11

[6] James S. Wallerstein and Clement J. Wyle, Our Law Abiding Law Breakers. Reprint from Probation, April, 1947, p. 2.

[7] Ibid., p. 4.

	Per Cent Men	Per Cent Women
Auto theft	26	8
Burglary	17	4
Robbery	11	1
Concealed weapons	35	3
Perjury	23	17
Falsification and fraud	46	34
Election frauds	7	4
Tax exasion	57	40
Coercion	16	6
Conspiracy	23	7
Criminal libel	36	29

More detailed analysis also disclosed that the number of instances of lawbreaking ran high among this so-called noncriminal group. In fact, the mean number of offenses committed by all the men included in the returns was 18, with an average of 8.2 for the clergymen and 20.2 for laborers. Perhaps one might conclude that theological training had a somewhat lessening effect on the crime rate! Women laborers, on the other hand, admitted only 9.8 offenses after reaching 16 years of age, while women in government and military jobs committed 14.4 offenses. The mean average for the women was 11 offenses.

Perhaps more important, both groups admitted they had committed more offenses after reaching 16 years than earlier; the men reported a mean average of only 3.2 juvenile offenses, and the women only 1.6. Moreover, both men and women reported that their offenses increased progressively from the age of 21 to 40 and then declined. The authors were a bit skeptical of these statements with reference to declining criminality, but other researches, notably that of the Gluecks, confirm the idea that maturity brings social conformity among court-convicted delinquents.[8] It would be reasonable to suppose that the nonconvicted offenders tend eventually to conform to the social dictates just as do those who are arrested and convicted.

Sutherland's Study of the White Collar Criminal

Under the classification of "white collar criminals" the late Edwin H. Sutherland has recently ventilated the extensive lawbreaking which occurs among businessmen, particularly among the executives of our

[8] Sheldon and Eleanor T. Glueck, *Later Criminal Careers*, Commonwealth Fund, New York, 1937, p. 109.

great corporations. Dr. Sutherland made his initial indictment of the American businessman's illegal and criminal conduct in his presidential address delivered at the thirty-fourth annual meeting of the American Sociological Society held in Philadelphia on December 27, 1939. He declared that all our statistics on crime were misleading and incorrect because they almost completely ignored the high rate of lawbreaking among the leading business and professional groups. Instead, he charged, arrests, convictions, and punishment were reserved chiefly for the lower economic and social classes.[9] While certain glaring instances of crime in the upper brackets have been exposed in the notorious exploits of Kreuger, Stavisky, Whitney, Mitchell, Foshay, Insull, the van Sweringens, Musica, Coster, Fall, Sinclair, and others, the great majority of fraudulent manipulators of big business go on relatively unnoticed by both the law enforcement agencies and the community in general. Similarly fee-splitting on the part of physicians, though forbidden by law and professional ethics, has hiked up the medical fees of the average surgical patient.[10]

Following this body blow Sutherland carried his research into the far reaches of criminal activity among 70 of the 200 largest manufacturing, mining, and mercantile corporations in America. He also made a special analysis of 15 power and light corporations. The findings from this research (published in 1949) provide us with a shocking picture of lawlessness on the part of big business in the United States.[11] Since case histories of individual criminals are ordinarily withheld in published materials, Sutherland decided to give the "criminal" corporations the benefit of anonymity in his report and referred to each one by number instead of name. The records of these corporations were carefully checked, however, and in certain highly publicized instances of lawbreaking the corporations are referred to by name. In brief, Sutherland made a digest of the number of recorded instances in which the respective corporations violated federal and state laws governing the following categories:

1. Restraint of trade.
2. Misrepresentation in advertising.
3. Infringement of patents, trade-marks, and copyrights.
4. Unfair labor practices (as defined by the National Labor Relations Act and other laws).
5. Financial fraud and violation of trust.

[9] Edwin H. Sutherland, "White Collar Criminality," *American Sociological Review*, 5:1–2 (February, 1940).
[10] *Ibid.*
[11] Edwin H. Sutherland, *White Collar Crime*, Dryden, New York, 1949.

6. Violations of war regulations and other offenses.[12]

From his research Sutherland discovered that these 70 corporations had received 980 decisions against them indicating their illegal activities, with the number of counts against the various corporations ranging from 1 to 50.[13] More than half of these decisions that the corporations were guilty were concentrated in the period 1935–1949, and 60 per cent were between 1935 and 1944. Only one corporation had but a single decision against it. Two corporations were guilty of 50 violations, and the average for all the corporations was 14. Of the decisions against 41 of the 70 corporations, only 158 or 16 per cent were rendered by criminal courts; 298 decisions against 59 corporations were made by civil courts; 129 decisions against 43 corporations were rendered by equity courts. All told, 583 of the decisions were made initially by the courts. In 361 instances the decisions were rendered by commissions and of these one-fourth were later referred to courts for settlement and were sustained. In 25 additional cases against corporations their illegal goods were confiscated at the order of commissions. Eleven cases were settled out of court but in accordance with court orders.[14] In addition to the court and commission decisions, there must have been hundreds of violations of law by corporations which were not brought before the courts. These untried and unpunished violations were obviously not included in the tabulations.

As we have mentioned, only 158 of these decisions were rendered by criminal courts, but Sutherland maintains that *all* of the cases tried by other agencies were *truly criminal*. He concludes that in each instance there was socially harmful action, the laws forbade such conduct, and penalties were provided in the laws which were violated. These considerations are ordinarily enough to classify *any* behavior as crime. Sutherland further made a detailed analysis of the laws violated in each type of offense and the penalties attached to such violations. This convinced him that the corporations were tried in each instance for conduct that was essentially criminal in character even though some cases were tried in the civil courts or before commissions. Nevertheless in these instances the stigma of crime was essentially eliminated by the exacting of civil fines or penalties imposed by commissions.

Some of the actual violations of these corporations should be mentioned to give us a notion of the types of illegal conduct in which they engaged. Offenses classified as "restraint of trade" included violations of the Sherman Antitrust Law, which forbids monopolistic con-

---

[12] *Ibid.*, chap. 2.   [13] *Ibid.*, p. 25.   [14] *Ibid.*

trol of industries. A great packing firm was indicted and penalized for securing preferential railway rates and controlling virtually all the equipment necessary to operate such an industry, including the stockyards, refrigerator cars, cold-storage plants, fertilizer plants, trade journals, etc. A great dairy was declared guilty of purchasing hundreds of dairies, pasteurization plants, bottle exchanges, and butter, cheese, and ice cream factories in order to control the dairy business. An aluminum company was penalized and reprimanded when a commission declared that virtually all aluminum was under the control of that company, a condition accomplished through a series of expansions which gave it a strangle hold on the industry. Many of the corporations were indicted for price fixing, the latter usually accomplished through "gentlemen's agreements," or through the price leadership of an important firm which more or less forced other firms to conform. Often price agreements were made verbally so that there was no written record, but these were discovered by commissions. International cartels by which trade associations restricted output were also disclosed.[15]

Decisions were rendered against 44 of the 62 manufacturing and mining corporations for infringements on patents. These involved 81 explicit decisions, 21 stipulations as to necessary amendments in present practices, and 31 consent decrees, or a total of 133 in all. Eight mercantile corporations were included in the 70 corporations and Sutherland found these firms had 72 decisions against them for patent violations. Often it was disclosed that a great corporation manufactured an item in full knowledge that it was patented by another person or firm, with the idea of paying damages if prosecuted. Sometimes the firm settled the case out of court for a very high fee, when the rightful owner of the patent brought suit.[16]

One of the most flagrant instances of patent violations occurred in a mercantile corporation which sold commodities ranging from electric fans to cream separators. This corporation violated 19 patent rights. Another large mercantile establishment (in this case a mail-order house) owned many small manufacturing plants secretly and produced such commodities illegally; thus it was liable for patent infringement violation.[17]

In addition to these bona fide cases of patent infringement certain firms engaged in patent manipulation, securing patents for minor alterations in existing patents in order to obtain the right to initiate damage suits in case of infringements. This practice has become a virtual racket in the major mechanical and electrical industries. Cer-

---

[15] *Ibid.*, chap. 4.   [16] *Ibid.*, chap. 6.   [17] *Ibid.*

tain clever engineers take out patents which make minor improvements on existing patents. Principles involved in these alterations are more or less bound to occur to other inventors and the holder of the patent initiates a suit as soon as slight changes are introduced by the other manufacturer. Such infringement suits may literally have the law on their side and yet be a form of coercion which amounts to a definite restraint of trade.[18] Many inventors make fortunes out of such suits. Some such abuses have been restrained by recent court decision.

Misrepresentation in advertising is a special variety of fraud that went quite unrestricted until the Pure Food and Drug Act of 1906 made false statements in labels (as well as adulteration) a punishable crime. The Federal Trade Commission Law of 1914 further prohibited misrepresentation in advertising in the press. Many corporations producing home-consumed commodities ranging from breakfast foods to shirts and from laxatives to automobiles have since had decisions rendered against them. Pharmaceutical houses manufacturing patented medicines and in recent years those manufacturing vitamins and patented forms of the miracle drugs have been major violators of laws governing such misrepresentation. A cigarette company, for example, whose cigarettes were reported by *Reader's Digest* to contain a smaller amount of nicotine than other brands publicized this article in its advertising and, failing to state that the difference was so small as to be negligible, was penalized for it. All manner of extravagant advertising claims have been condemned as misrepresentation, including alleged half-price sales when few, if any, actual reductions occurred.[19]

Decisions against 43 of the 70 corporations were rendered for unfair labor practices. The following labor practices on the part of the corporation are forbidden by law:

Refusal to bargain collectively.
Interference with activities of labor.
Restraint.
Coercion.
Company union.
Intimidation.
Espionage.
Violence.
Other interference.

Most of these unfair labor practices are self-explanatory as classified, but a few deserve further explanation. Espionage, in connection with

[18] *Ibid.*   [19] *Ibid.*, chap. 7.

a corporation, means spying on the activities of labor unions. One corporation whose activities were condemned had spent nearly a million dollars for the 200 labor spies it hired for its plant; these men even shadowed the representatives of the United States Department of Labor. Another company so distrusted its spies that it actually hired other spies to spy on them! Some companies used machine guns and tear gas against their workmen during the 1930's.[20] We should point out, however, that the relations between corporation administrators and unions have improved since then and that many corporations are no longer guilty of such offenses. Nevertheless, Sutherland contends that the greatest violators of the Unfair Labor Practices Act have been among the heaviest contributors to the National Association of Manufacturers. This group has consistently sponsored a variety of federal laws which authorize practices and legal controls aimed at thwarting the unions.[21]

Financial manipulations by corporations (or their executives) constitute a special variety of fraud or violation of trust in handling corporation funds and in particular the funds of stockholders. Forty-one of the 70 corporations covered by Sutherland's study were involved in 64 decisions of this nature. Some of the offenses were virtual embezzlement. Sometimes the executives of a corporation had formed other companies (among themselves) to supply their corporation with goods or services. In general the high salaries paid to executives, the bonuses given to the board of directors, et al., eat up a large share of the corporation's income. The average stockholder knows little about how the corporation whose stock he owns is run and the executives take advantage of his ignorance. The financial reports are drawn up so as to give little notion of the actual financial transactions of the corporations involved.[22]

Violations of War Regulations

The war crimes of industrial and manufacturing corporations would fill many volumes. The vast majority of violations of price regulation were never taken to court. Only the most serious and long-continued violations were prosecuted. Violations of priority regulations were the reasons for decisions against only 3 of the corporations. Defective war materials were allegedly far more extensive and characteristic of wartime production than the official decisions might indicate since only 1 of the 70 corporations was convicted of fraud on this count.[23]

[20] *Ibid.*, chap. 8.   [21] *Ibid.*, p. 147.   [22] *Ibid.*, chap. 9.
[23] *Ibid.*, chap. 10. (This subject is also discussed in chap. 6 under "The Black Market.")

Tax evasion by corporations was a special aspect of offenses against the excess-profits tax and according to Sutherland corporation profits were often manipulated in order to reduce taxes. Identical bids were the source of other alleged illegal activities on the part of companies supplying war materials—steel and chemicals, for example. Violations of war embargoes which were investigated by the Nye Commission and other agencies have shown pretty conclusively that certain munitions manufacturers engaged in illegal activities in times past. Three of the 70 corporations covered were literally accused of treason, but up to the time Sutherland's book was published no decision had been made.[24] Despite their excessive illegal machinations these corporations apparently are not subject to much vilification or "ordeal through slander" as are individuals who are merely suspected of such crimes.

The 15 Power and Light Corporations

The public utility corporations are all theoretically regulated by state and federal law, but the records of many of them show numerous instances of illegal activities. There were 38 decisions (including 18 settlements) rendered by courts against 10 of the 15 such corporations studied by Sutherland. Besides these court decisions the light and power companies received 386 orders from commissions with reference to their violations of regulations.[25] The reports of the Federal Trade Commission and other investigation commissions listed 293 further violations of the law. In general these public utility violations defrauded either the consumer or the investor. Frauds against the consumer arise for the most part out of figuring rate costs on the basis of fraudulent estimates of cost of power-plant construction, etc. Sutherland cites one corporation that sold a completed power plant to a sub-holding company for 4 million dollars (the stated actual cost) whereas the plant had really cost only $2,500,000. Sometimes a holding company charged a service fee to a subsidiary for what were virtually no services at all, but the public paid utility rates based on these alleged costs.

A wide variety of fictitious costs have characterized the illegal operations of many utility companies. They may, for example, "milk" the subsidiaries. This practice leaves little left over for paying dividends to stockholders and at the same time results in high rates to consumers. Such frauds were alleged in 47 instances against 12 of the 15 public utility corporations Sutherland studied.[26]

From these and many unrecounted instances, Sutherland contends

[24] *Ibid.*, pp. 173–174.   [25] *Ibid.*, chap. 12.   [26] *Ibid.*

that the white-collar crime of our great corporations is organized and deliberate. Some white-collar crime obviously may be unintentional because of the detailed character of certain laws governing corporations. But these corporations and power and light companies employ excellent legal staffs and for the most part were repeatedly guilty of illegal practices—and practices they knew to be illegal.[27] Apparently they were willing to risk suits, court orders, and adverse verdicts, chiefly because the profits from their illegal activities were sufficient to offset the fines. Moreover these white-collar criminals do not consider themselves to be criminal even though they know they are breaking the law. Instead they regard the laws covering such activities as an infringement of their rights, hence believe the corporations justified in violating them. Even so, corporations tend to be selective in their illicit activities and usually commit violations they think unlikely to be detected or punished. For such activities tend to be punished only as the investigations of governmental agencies or Congressional committees bring them to light.[28]

Consumers do not usually object to illegal charges on their monthly gas or light bill unless the bill is considerably larger than usual or "out of proportion." When the amount seems unreasonable the consumer may occasionally demand an adjustment but virtually no consumer carries a case to court because the cost would be prohibitive. A former employee of a city light and power corporation once reported to the author that one out of every twelve bills of the company for which he had worked was padded; when customers complained, the "errors" were adjusted, but relatively few protests were received.

Unwitting Lawlessness

Many citizens commit crimes without knowing it. L. M. Hussey holds that this unintentional lawlessness of the average citizen stems both from the complexity of the law and from the fact that it is virtually impossible for the average person to keep informed of the law.[29] Nevertheless our courts adhere to the notion that "ignorance of the law excuses no one." Even so, the average respected citizen who commits an individual offense is seldom caught in the toils of the law. If caught, the influential citizen can usually persuade the judge or the police that he had no intention of breaking the law. The ignorant

[27] *Ibid.*, chap. 13.   [28] *Ibid.*, especially pp. 222–229.
[29] L. M. Hussey, "Twenty Four Hours as a Lawbreaker," *Harper's Magazine*, 160: 436–439 (March, 1930).

and friendless person has no such advantage. Since no one will swear to his character and reputation the hapless victim of the law is routed to prison, often without any opportunity for adequate legal advice. Once incarcerated he frequently becomes convinced that society is against him and strikes back by further and willful lawlessness on release. If anyone would verify these statements let him attend a few sessions in the police courts and the district courts. Unemployed Negroes, down-and-out immigrants, petty thieves are seldom given a real chance to defend themselves or explain their conduct in terms the court is willing to excuse.

Part of the crimes in high places, especially so-called unpunished and neglected crimes among businessmen, on the other hand, grow out of the fact that our criminal laws were written to apply to individuals. As President Wilson said in his book The New Freedom, "Our laws . . . have not been satisfactorily adjusted to business done by great combinations and we have got to adjust them."[30] Through legal fiction the corporation assumes the status of a person. This makes it difficult to attach blame to the individual members of the corporation. Efforts to fix criminal responsibility on officers or agents of a company usually entail a "slow and defective" process.[31] Needless to say, the powerful corporation lawyers constitute a formidable lobby against more effective criminal legislation and procedure covering the activities of "big business."

The lobbyists for our great industrialists also exert every conceivable pressure upon Congress to support the economic structure of the country, that is, to support the current practices which will enable modern industry to flourish with as much aid and as little restriction as possible.

At the same time, the complicated nature of various restrictive laws leads inevitably to lawbreaking: first by the connivance of corporation lawyers who seek every loophole by which they may evade the law; second through willful violation with the implicit idea of forcing a test case if the law-enforcing agents raise an issue of illegality; third because of the old argument that true criminal malice depends upon intent and any intent on the part of individual executives of the corporation (which is usually sued on an impersonal basis) becomes very difficult to establish.

On the other hand the acts of persons which were punished through

[30] Quoted by Albert Lieck in his article, "The Administration of Criminal Justice," in Penal Reform in England, ed. by L. Radzinowicz and J. W. C. Turner, Macmillan, London, 1946, p. 52.
[31] Ibid.

retaliation and revenge in primitive society are still those most roundly denounced and punished at the present time. They are the "ordinary crimes," and curiously enough the lawmakers and the ruling class condemn these offenses almost as much for their own group as for others. A millionaire who murders his wife or his wife's lover is as apt to be convicted as is the lower-class murderer. Nor would the businessman who engages in sharp practices, manipulates reports, or employs illegal and fictitious costs in estimating rates think of robbing his neighbor or of burglarizing his neighbor's home. His crimes (which he does not regard as crimes) are impersonal and are distributed so that the illegal gains are derived through the voluntary payments of a wide number of people. He may even justify such behavior as being "good business."

Professional or Organized Crime

Although Sutherland shocked and disturbed many businessmen in ventilating the organized, illegal activities of the upper ranks of industry, society has long recognized the powerful underworld variety of organized crime which flourishes under the protection of corrupt political officials. One of the darkest chapters of American politics is the widespread corruption of public officials. Police often refrain from arresting persons known to be involved in serious crimes because it is financially advantageous for them to co-operate with big-time criminals.

These persons, usually known as professional or organized criminals, are not engaged (as are big businessmen) in creating necessary goods and services for the consumer. Their chief occupation is crime and their illicit activities constitute their only source of livelihood. White-collar criminals commit their crimes in connection with the operation of legitimate businesses and preserve an aura of respectability. Those who direct criminal empires, crime syndicates, do not purport to engage in legitimate business. They exploit the weaknesses of men for their illicit gains, knowing well that the services they provide are a source of community and personal disorganization. Thus the gangsters, the racketeers, the gamblers, whether they operate gambling machines, slot machines, or number policies, or are engaged in the illicit liquor and narcotic trade, are part of this unsavory chapter in social disorganization.

The losses due to these crimes cannot be estimated accurately, but they must total far more than those from the unorganized crimes. Yet criminologists have not given such crimes as much consideration as the exploits of the simple thief and robber because the majority of professional big-time criminals have so successfully evaded the law. These plunderers of society, be they politicians who raid the city treasury through fraudulent contracts (or "dishonest" graft[32]) or the gamblers and swindlers who take their toll from the citizens' pocket-books, roll up an unbelievable amount of money, probably as much as some of the major industries. Systematic stealing from the public through fraudulent and padded pay rolls, and contracts let at enormous profit for public buildings or for paving streets involves the corruption of the politicians who take their slice of the illicit profits. In an earlier period, prohibition gave an impetus to organized crime with its accompanying corruption of both the police and the citizenry. Because of its extensive ramifications we shall devote a whole chapter to organized crime. We should point out here, however, that corruption of the police is an important aspect of organized crime. The more corruption the more crimes (and the fewer arrests), for the police do not usually include these crimes in their reports to the Federal Bureau of Investigation.

THE STATISTICS OF CRIME

As we have seen, criminal behavior is relatively characteristic of all "sorts and conditions of men." The statistics of crime (or the crimes recorded by the law-enforcing agencies) are unfortunately fragmentary, since so many crimes go undetected and unpunished. The student may well inquire what advantage is to be derived from studying an inaccurate array of numbers. However, the statistics of crime are accurate in one sense at least: they represent the crimes that we as members of the community have considered important enough to report and the arrests police were alert enough (or willing) to make, and the statistics on prisoners give us a picture of the persons whose offenses were adjudged serious and for which penal sentences were exacted. They represent, if you will, the persons whose lawbreaking is regarded by the citizens as antisocial and injurious to the welfare of the group.

These offenders, as later analysis will make clear, come chiefly from

[32] Politicians also engage in so-called "honest" graft which involves an unfair or unethical manipulation of their office. Such conduct is, strictly speaking, often illegal and cannot be punished by the courts. The recent demand that federal employees engage in no unethical use of their position or special knowledge may induce improved ethics in local and state politics.

the lower economic and social classes. It seems obvious that the officials and the community as a whole believe their behavior to be more offensive than either the organized crime of the underworld or the unreported crimes of the middle or upper classes. The average middle-class or upper-class lawbreaker retains a certain position in the group despite his illegal activities. The underworld racketeer retains his freedom through his financial acumen and his connections with corrupt officials who find it profitable to co-operate in his illicit activities.

The upper middle class, however, are the lawmakers and *they believe in the law even when they break it*. Religious traditions and democratic concepts lay back of the middle-class notions of honesty, decency, and respect for other persons' property. This hypocrisy of the norm-defining and ruling groups has been discussed in vivid language by many of our severest social critics.[33] Our moral hypocrisy has been condemned by cynical journalists, criminal lawyers, leading jurists, and social philosophers. Jean Paul Sartre contends that our taboos and our behavior (sexual and otherwise) represent the discrepancy between our behavior and our myths. Puritan in our ideals, Sartre maintains, we are literally afraid to live up to the ideals because we are afraid of not being as American as our neighbors.[34] Part of our hypocrisy, as some contend, seems also to lie in not being willing to admit that we believe in our ideals. Moreover, hypocrisy has been described as the homage vice pays to virtue. Even when breaking the law, the respected middle-class and upper-class members still believe in the law. Those who are arrested, tried, and convicted may well be the scapegoats for their respected fellow citizens. Psychiatrists have long been telling us that we condemn that for which we ourselves feel guilty. It may be that we as a group condemn the petty offenses because we as a group feel so guilty for our extensive illegal activities.

In any event the statistics that we gather on crime and criminals refer to the condemned group of offenses and offenders and for that reason deserve our serious attention.

General Character of Crime Statistics in the United States

The statistics for crime in the United States thus refer not to those persons guilty of extensive lawbreaking among the rank and file of the population but to the number of (1) crimes reported, (2) arrests made, (3) persons charged with or indicted for crimes, (4) persons

[33] Cf. Harry Elmer Barnes and Negley K. Teeters, *New Horizons in Criminology*, Prentice-Hall, New York, 1943, pp. 29–31.

[34] Cf. Jean Paul Sartre, "Americans and Their Myths," *The Nation*, 165:402–403 (October 18, 1947).

convicted, (5) those convicted and placed on probation, (6) those sentenced to prison, and (7) those released upon either (a) parole or (b) expiration of sentence. Many variables affect these statistics so far as their reliability as an index to the number of crimes and criminals is concerned. For this reason minor variations in the number of crimes reported from year to year do not necessarily indicate any true picture of the variation in crime trends over the particular period. Such variations may equally well indicate (1) differences in the degree of effective and extensive policing, (2) a more (or less) rigid enforcement of laws during one year than another, or (3) changes in the criminal and penal laws themselves, (4) accuracy of local officials in keeping reports and in computing rates also varies from time to time. Some police stations, for example, record every reported violation. Others record relatively few, and the seriousness of the offense is no necessary criterion for reporting.

Limitations of United States Crime Statistics

As Thorsten Sellin has pointed out, certain limitations of the crime statistics in America are also inherent in the nature of our government. That is, they exist because ours is a federated government of the separate 48 states, and each of the states has its own system of criminal codes, police, courts, penal institutions, and treatment agencies. Our state criminal codes and methods of gathering statistics vary markedly, frequently as much as separate nations of Europe.[35]

Federal crime statistics consequently relate only to offenses against the federal government, but even these are not all available in a single report because the police activities of the federal government are scattered through many of the federal bureaus and departments.[36] There are, for example, federal police in the Coast Guard, in the Treasury Department, in the Post Office Department, and in the customs service, not to mention others. The federal civilian courts and federal military courts also issue separate reports. Even so, national crime statistics were gathered from 1926 to 1946 by the Census Bureau. Since 1946 they have been compiled by the United States Department of Justice. These statistics are not complete, however, because the federal government has no legal authority to compel returns from the several states. Nor has there been an adequate Congressional

[35] Thorsten Sellin, *Status and Prospects of Criminal Statistics in the United States, Sartryck ur Svensk Juristtidning Fest Krift fir Karl Schlyter*, Stockholm, 1949, pp. 295–302.

[36] Cf. chap. 17, "Police," pp. 475–480.

appropriation to publish these data since they have been gathered by the Department of Justice.

Judicial statistics for various states were also published from 1932 through 1946. For these statistics only 16 states initially co-operated, but by 1935, 36 states supplied figures on the number and types of offenders convicted by the courts. Police statistics have been gathered by the Federal Bureau of Investigation since 1930 with a gradually increased coverage. By 1948 nearly half of the population of the country was covered by these reports and from them relatively accurate estimates for the nation as a whole could be drawn.[37]

Censuses of prisoners were taken every ten years from 1850 through 1890. In 1900 there was a decision to make a detailed statistical study of prisoners, which was published in 1904. After that detailed censuses were made in 1910, 1923, and 1933, the report of 1923 being the most comprehensive.[38] From 1926 to 1947 detailed annual reports on prisoners admitted and those discharged were made.

Several states have kept criminal statistics over a long period. In New York, a law requiring the state to keep records concerning the name, nationality, occupation, sex, and age of each offender was adopted in 1839.[39] For our purposes, however, it will be sufficient to consider only the more recent statistics for the United States as a whole. Our concern is primarily with understanding the current crime problem.

The Number of Crimes Reported by Police

The estimated number of major crimes for the United States as a whole for the year 1950 was 1,790,030, which was 26,740 or 1.5 per cent more than for the year 1949. In 1949 an estimated 1,763,290 major crimes were committed, as Table 3.3 shows. These estimations were based upon the filed reports of 4200 police agencies.[40] The major crimes according to these data, include:

> Murder and nonnegligent manslaughter.
> Manslaughter by negligence.
> Rape.
> Robbery.
> Aggravated assault.

[37] Sellin, op. cit.   [38] Ibid.   [39] Ibid.
[40] Uniform Crime Reports, Annual Bulletin, 1949, Federal Bureau of Investigation, U.S. Department of Justice, Washington, 1950, p. 78, and ibid., Annual Bulletin, 1950, Washington, 1951, p. 74.

Burglary—breaking or entering.

Larceny—theft.

Auto theft.

These categories refer only to certain serious crimes. They are obviously selective, omitting a sizable share of offenses for which criminals are arrested and convicted, for they do not cover the extensive crimes committed under the aegis of organized crime syndicates or big-time racketeers. Drug act violations, drunkenness, prostitution, arson, and other important crimes are also omitted. Except for murder these data virtually exclude the crimes for which the majority of criminal women are arrested and convicted. They make no mention at all

TABLE 3.3. Crime Trends, Urban and Rural
(Estimated number of major crimes in the United States, 1949–1950)

Offense	Number of Offenses		Change	
	1949	1950	Number	Per Cent
Total	1,763,290	1,790,030	+26,740	+1.5
Murder and nonnegligent manslaughter	6,990	7,020	+30	+.4
Manslaughter by negligence	4,880	5,330	+450	+9.2
Rape	16,380	16,580	+200	+1.2
Robbery	59,120	53,230	−5,890	−10.0
Aggravated assault	78,860	80,950	+2,090	+2.7
Burglary—breaking or entering	409,400	411,980	+2,580	+.6
Larceny—theft	1,024,520	1,044,160	+19,640	+1.9
Auto theft	163,140	170,780	+7,640	+4.7

SOURCE: Table 26, *Uniform Crime Reports*, Annual Bulletin, 1950, Federal Bureau of Investigation, U.S. Department of Justice, Washington, 1951, p. 74.

of the political crimes of espionage or treason which have received so much publicity and have created so much internal and international furor in connection with the prosecution of Communists following World War II. Nevertheless these are the types of crimes which bulk largest in the daily grist of police activities even though they may not constitute the major social hazards in lawbreaking. In any event these crimes (as reported to the police) indicate *the significant hazards facing individuals* who are the victims of crimes in the United States; they represent the main threats to the bodily safety and the property security of the average citizen. For this reason they are condemned by virtually all societies. Life is man's most precious possession so long as he is motivated by the will to live. In consequence we reserve our highest condemnation for the person who willfully kills or attempts to kill another person. Rape, regarded as the most serious of condemned sex offenses, has its roots in the social values which are ascribed to chastity, and the attempt to restrict sex relations to married persons. As rape is both a violation of the body of the person and a violation of marriage mores, it is condemned for social reasons as well as by psychological factors such as jealousy and revulsion. A man must also have ways and means of providing himself with food, clothing, and shelter. Survival itself has been dependent in times past upon the ability to provide these essentials. The "provident" man accumulated enough for the "rainy day" and the future. But unless the group protected his property he could not be certain of its preservation for future needs. In the course of his cultural development, man has built up an elaborate and complex system of property law and a body of criminal law dealing with those who appropriate or damage other people's property.

There are thus universal and basic reasons why the number of cases of rape and murder (because they are psychological and biological phenomena) are not affected greatly by urban or rural residence. If anything, the reported rates for rape are somewhat higher in rural areas. Perhaps this is because the urban rapist takes advantage of the anonymity and the sophistication of the city. He may also be better versed in protecting himself from the law. Property crimes are disproportionately higher in cities, as a comparison between Tables 3.4 and 3.5 indicates. There are many explanations for this. The competitive aspect of urban life is greater than that of the rural areas and therefore stimulates more economic crimes in cities. The observable disparities in wealth in cities create greater dissatisfactions with economic status which the majority of workers are not able to overcome by increasing their earnings through honest effort. There is also much more stimulation through advertising for the individual to consume expensive goods, to dress well, and to spend money on entertainment in the city than in the country. Consumer goods themselves are usually displayed in such a fashion that it is relatively easy for shoplifters to steal merchandise. Large sums of money are often within easy reach in stores and banks. The anonymity of city life makes it possible for a man to commit crimes without great fear of detection since few people in cities pay much attention to what other people are doing. In consequence the criminal who plans and stages a robbery or burglary or steals merchandise from a store counts on executing his plot without being caught. The pickpocket on the city street plans to lose himself in the crowd. The thief who picks up a purse at a post-office window, for example, relies on the temporary absorption of the customer who is buying stamps. The bystanders are strangers. Each intent on getting his own stamps pays little attention to others.

The complexity of city life itself also increases the number of controls (and definitions of illegal conduct) imposed upon human behavior. Many acts are forbidden under penalty in the city which might be accepted or at least permitted without penalty in the open country. The farmer may call his hogs in sonorous voice with impunity. The city dweller may not raise a great racket without disturbing the peace. The farmer's wife may throw the dishwater out the pantry window if she chooses. The city housewife obviously must refrain from any such threat to the passers-by.

Comparative Crime Rates in Cities in 1949 and 1950

For the 2069 cities which reported offenses there were 1,036,334 crimes in 1949 and 1,040,249 in 1950, which may be broken down as follows:[41]

Classification of Crimes in 1949		Classification of Crimes in 1950	
Total	1,036,334	Total	1,040,249
Murder and nonnegligent manslaughter	3,390		3,467
Manslaughter by negligence	1,966		2,268
Rape	7,420		7,365
Robbery	38,646		34,308
Aggravated assault	49,391		50,014
Burglary—breaking or entering	244,179		241,100
Larceny—theft	592,975		597,086
Auto theft	98,367		104,641

It is generally accepted that most crime occurs in urban communities, as can be easily deduced from the ratio of reported rural and urban crimes. In 1949 only 176,561 major crimes were reported from rural areas and in 1950 only 184,415.[42] Proportionately, however, the reported cases of murder and nonnegligent manslaughter occurred at virtually the same rate so far as ratio to population is concerned, and the negligent manslaughter was somewhat higher in rural areas. Since

[41] From *Uniform Crime Reports*, Annual Bulletin, 1950, p. 77.
[42] *Ibid.*, p. 84.

this category includes deaths from reckless driving it is not necessarily true that the members of the rural population are involved in all these crimes. Highway deaths from negligent manslaughter are reported by

TABLE 3.4.   Rural Crime Trends, 1949–1950
(Offenses known as reported by 1566 sheriffs, 97 rural village officers, and 11 state police. Total rural population 34,617,887, based on 1940 decennial census)

| | Number of Offenses | | |
Offense	1949	1950	Per Cent Change
Total	176,561	184,415	+4.4
Murder and nonnegligent manslaughter	1,823	1,776	−2.6
Manslaughter by negligence	1,847	1,903	+3.0
Rape	4,076	4,231	+3.8
Robbery	6,595	6,299	−4.5
Aggravated assault	11,140	11,959	+7.4
Burglary—breaking or entering	58,028	61,992	+6.8
Larceny—theft	76,451	79,760	+4.3
Auto theft	16,601	16,495	−.6

SOURCE: Table 29 in *Uniform Crime Reports*, Annual Bulletin, 1950, Federal Bureau of Investigation; U.S. Department of Justice, Washington, 1951, p. 84.

sheriffs of the counties in which the deaths occur, but the persons charged with the offense may be city residents. The rural population thus may or may not be responsible for the particular crime. As a matter of fact the *Uniform Crime Reports* have published statistics indicating a significant increase in rural crimes for the whole post-World War II period. From the published data, however, it is impossible to determine whether these crimes were committed by rural residents or not. It seems likely that many of the property offenses were committed by persons operating out of near-by small towns or even the larger cities. In recent years farmers have reported that grain has been stolen from both open and sealed bins, and that cattle, hogs, chickens, or horses are stolen at night or when families have gone to town or to county fairs, etc. It is relatively easy for trucks to drive up to grain bins on large farms or ranches and fill up with grain, or for other trucks to drive into the farm lots or pastures and steal livestock when farmers are away from home. The thieves may even haul the stolen goods to an adjoining state and sell them to unsuspecting grain or livestock merchants. Or they may operate in illicit conjunction with merchants who know they are receiving stolen goods. The comparatively high prices for farm products in recent years and the fact that few rural areas have adequate means of protection against such lawlessness have been conducive to increases in rural crimes.

It is also true that more farmers have valuable household equipment in the shape of electric refrigerators, radios, and furniture than formerly. A large percentage of farmers never lock their houses while they are away from home, whether for an afternoon or evening in town or even on a vacation trip. The considerable distances between farmhouses make it easy for thieves and burglars to raid farmhouses, granaries, or herds of livestock without detection if the farmer is not on the premises. In a few instances, of course, farmers may steal from their neighbors, but most thieving on farms is now believed to be an organized variety of stealing and the long-distance hauling makes the identification of farm thefts difficult. The lack of adequate rural police that has always been a problem has now become a serious threat to the safety of rural property.

Regional Variations in Crime Rates

One of the striking aspects of crime in the United States is the regional variation in rates. This is especially true with reference to specific offenses, as Table 3.5 shows. These rates, although based upon the 1950 preliminary census figures because computation on the basis of the 1950 census had not been completed, may be regarded as indicating certain differences:

In New England, as the table shows, all crime rates were markedly less than the national average; and the murder, robbery, and aggravated assault rates were lower than the rates for these offenses in any other region. Vermont had the lowest rates of any state for these offenses. The East South Central states region, including Alabama, Kentucky, Mississippi, and Tennessee, on the other hand, had the highest murder, and the South Atlantic states, including all states on the east coast below Pennsylvania, had the highest aggravated assault rates. Considering the states separately, however, Georgia had the second highest murder rate of any state and North Carolina's rate was higher than that of Mississippi or Kentucky. Illinois had the highest robbery rate and North Carolina the highest aggravated assault rate.

According to these same estimations the Pacific states had the highest burglary, larceny, and auto theft rates. The Mountain states ranked next for these particular crimes, although Arizona had higher rates for almost all crimes than the Pacific region as a whole and Nevada had the highest rates for murder and burglary and second highest for auto theft. The Middle Atlantic states region (New Jersey, New York, and Pennsylvania) ranked lowest for burglary, larceny, and auto theft. New Hampshire ranked lowest of the states in auto theft. It

TABLE 3.5. Urban Crime Rates, 1950, by Geographic Divisions and States

(Offenses known per 100,000 inhabitants. Population figures based on 1950 decennial census preliminary counts)

Division and State	Murder, Nonnegligent Manslaughter	Robbery	Aggravated Assault	Burglary—Breaking or Entering	Larceny—Theft	Auto Theft
Total	5.11	50.0	73.4	356.4[a]	894.9[a]	153.4
New England	1.07	16.5	11.7	251.5	600.3	109.6
Connecticut	1.35	14.5	20.8	272.7	577.5	97.1
Maine	1.42	10.0	8.0	232.2	724.8	97.4
Massachusetts	1.00	19.9	9.8	238.3	594.7	123.8
New Hampshire	.74	5.6	3.3	192.8	496.7	52.4
Rhode Island	1.09	12.9	14.7	345.5	649.1	91.4
Vermont	—	.9	.9	169.8	586.0	85.8
Middle Atlantic	2.60	27.6	35.4	224.9[b]	447.4[b]	96.6
New Jersey	2.27	25.8	46.3	277.4	465.7	104.5
New York	1.56	9.9	19.6	204.8	516.2	89.0
Pennsylvania	3.46	40.4	40.4	204.2[c]	360.0[c]	97.7
East North Central	4.21	66.0	67.5	325.8	861.4	128.0
Illinois	5.26	104.9	86.0	314.4	560.0	128.3
Indiana	4.65	33.5	40.0	375.7	921.2	153.4
Michigan	4.11	74.7	116.4	422.4	1,306.1	159.7
Ohio	4.08	45.8	38.2	303.1	874.1	102.6
Wisconsin	.84	9.7	10.7	161.5	801.4	100.4
West North Central	3.70	40.1	53.4	292.2	824.7	134.5
Iowa	1.30	11.4	6.5	220.4	770.8	126.6
Kansas	3.73	37.3	28.1	364.6	932.8	132.2
Minnesota	1.64	27.7	6.2	216.9	747.7	106.2
Missouri	7.23	76.6	141.0	370.8	830.6	154.5
Nebraska	3.32	24.6	29.4	265.4	976.0	187.6
North Dakota	—	4.5	3.2	272.9	927.1	101.2
South Dakota	1.11	9.4	5.5	250.0	663.3	74.7
South Atlantic[d]	10.97	50.1	218.7	430.9	929.6	192.0
Delaware	6.18	36.3	13.9	357.5	1,013.9	213.9
Florida	11.86	55.0	106.6	665.6	1,148.7	177.8
Georgia	17.79	40.0	156.8	318.5	773.3	174.1
Maryland	7.59	49.0	104.8	240.7	566.7	284.9
North Carolina	13.23	30.8	451.1	431.4	768.2	159.4
South Carolina	9.41	25.0	107.5	395.9	1,012.2	157.1
Virginia	11.81	64.6	212.4	509.9	1,257.5	217.6
West Virginia	2.69	32.5	51.8	326.4	584.0	137.1
East South Central	14.44	53.7	119.7	394.0	662.5	193.1
Alabama	18.96	40.3	146.3	372.9	617.3	154.1
Kentucky	10.26	82.2	114.6	509.6	852.6	258.6
Mississippi	12.14	23.9	104.7	286.0	529.6	102.8
Tennessee	14.68	56.6	106.6	370.9	614.2	216.8
West South Central	9.59	42.2	74.7	457.3	1,001.8	207.1
Arkansas	6.98	27.9	84.2	329.7	581.3	102.9
Louisiana	9.87	42.9	79.5	283.9	580.8	165.2
Oklahoma	3.76	41.1	36.2	499.3	1,186.7	205.5
Texas	11.11	43.9	80.8	517.4	1,141.6	232.6
Mountain	3.10	52.9	37.2	492.8	1,549.5	224.2
Arizona	5.42	78.2	92.7	622.4	2,138.0	347.6
Colorado	2.73	71.1	29.1	614.6	1,670.8	199.5
Idaho	4.07	34.6	19.3	437.2	1,423.4	166.7
Montana	2.12	51.4	41.9	350.9	1,319.8	258.7
Nevada	7.20	72.0	62.0	710.3	2,117.9	335.7
New Mexico	3.11	26.8	40.1	306.1	948.6	271.5
Utah	1.64	26.5	18.9	428.7	1,467.3	166.1
Wyoming	2.78	65.8	36.1	354.8	1,578.4	178.8
Pacific	3.07	79.3	59.6	512.4	1,568.1	229.0
California	3.21	84.5	69.7	522.4	1,590.5	233.0
Oregon	1.81	49.8	29.6	467.5	1,446.4	208.2
Washington	2.98	66.8	20.3	481.5	1,510.5	218.3

a The rates for burglary and larceny are based on the reports of 2296 cities with a total population of 67,578,820.
b The rates for burglary and larceny are based on the reports of 504 cities with a total population of 10,221,704.
c The rates for burglary and larceny are based on the reports of 210 cities.
d Includes the report of the District of Columbia.

SOURCE: Table 32 in *Uniform Crime Reports*, Annual Bulletin, 1950, Federal Bureau of Investigation, U.S. Department of Justice, Washington, 1951, p. 90.

seems likely that the great increases in population in the Pacific states may account for some of the difference between the Pacific states' rates and those of other areas. However, some regions had nearly the same ranks for these offenses in 1940, as Table 3.6 shows.

TABLE 3.6.   Number of Offenses Known to the Police per 100,000 Inhabitants, January to December, Inclusive, 1940, by States

Division and State	Murder, Nonnegligent Manslaughter	Robbery	Aggravated Assault	Burglary —Breaking or Entering	Larceny —Theft	Auto Theft
New England	1.2	15.5	10.5	269.3	571.5	172.3
Middle Atlantic	3.1	26.3	31.1	259.0	471.0	145.7
East North Central	4.1	81.6	32.1	326.5	891.7	144.0
West North Central	3.1	37.7	14.1	267.0	912.2	140.2
South Atlantic	15.2	72.0	135.6	430.3	1,175.7	222.6
East South Central	21.6	85.6	210.7	519.2	1,009.4	182.4
West South Central	11.4	50.9	83.5	405.3	1,316.9	155.4
Mountain	3.7	46.8	19.3	372.5	1,429.3	197.6
Pacific	3.7	78.1	29.5	522.8	1,499.1	344.2

SOURCE: Table 81, *Uniform Crime Reports*, Fourth Quarterly Bulletin, 1940, Federal Bureau of Investigation, U.S. Department of Justice, Washington, 1941, p. 175.

Unpublished Figures on Crime

Figures for the extent of such crimes as fraud and embezzlement, although very important, are not published, for reasons we shall discuss more fully in our chapter on organized crime. Figures on the number of persons received in state and federal prisons for these offenses may seem to indicate that the rate has gone down. Sutherland insisted, however, that the rate has actually gone up. He held that there is much fraud, for example, in collecting insurance and that "murders are committed, houses burned, automobiles destroyed and sickness or injury feigned in order to collect insurance."[43]

It seems equally certain that insurance companies sometimes bribe coroners to declare persons found dead to be suicides in order to avoid paying insurance. Certainly much of the public sentiment against "ambulance chasers" has been aroused partly by zealous insurance agents who rush to the scene of accidents to get dazed and seriously injured persons to sign waivers of the insurance company's further responsibility. At the same time these agents object strenuously to any attempt by lawyers to represent interests of the injured persons, as we shall mention later.

[43] Edwin H. Sutherland, *Principles of Criminology*, Lippincott, Philadelphia, 4th ed., 1947, p. 39.

Fraudulent medical testimony on the part of physicians who represent insurance companies is virtually never punished. An unethical physician can cloak himself under his right to offer his medical opinion. Since physicians are often honestly mistaken it is difficult to fasten a charge of fraud, even in notorious cases.

Likewise misappropriation of funds of private character is seldom punished unless there is a glaring embezzlement. Mere using of funds bequeathed for one purpose for another is seldom either reported or punished, since boards of trustees or other controlling agencies often decide to use the funds as they see fit. Strictly speaking, many widows mismanage or willfully appropriate funds which belong technically to their children. In such cases there is usually no malice of intent. Frequently, in fact, the widow uses funds which are legally those of her children for the latter's support, hence few courts would be willing to render a penal verdict against her.

The Relative Accuracy of Reported Crimes

Of all crime statistics those reported by police are probably more accurate than others, but they too must be accepted with reservations. For example, according to the annual bulletin issued by the Federal Bureau of Investigation for crimes reported in 1948, there was little change over 1947 (0.3 per cent increase) although moderate increases occurred in the following categories: aggravated assault, 4.7 per cent; burglary, 0.8 per cent; and larceny, 2.3 per cent.[44] Anyone familiar with statistical theory will recognize that these differences are negligible and are likely to be due to variations in reporting.

On the other hand the crime reports issued during the war and the newspaper publicity attached to these reports emphasized the great increase in crimes among women and especially among girls under 21, particularly for prostitution, vagrancy, and sex crimes in general.[45] These reports do not make clear, however, that a concerted drive was made against prostitution and commercialized vice at the behest of military authorities and the United States Public Health Service during this period. Because police were alerted in a co-operative program to put down the spread of venereal disease, many more arrests were made proportionately than in preceding years. The increase in arrests

[44] *Uniform Crime Reports, for the United States and Its Possessions*, Annual Bulletin, 1948, Federal Bureau of Investigation, U.S. Department of Justice, Washington, 1949, p. 73.

[45] *Ibid.*, Semi-Annual Bulletin, 1943, Washington, 1943, p. 46.

is thus no accurate index as to whether or not prostitution actually increased.

We should also keep in mind that the number of crimes reported in the *Uniform Crime Reports*, which are issued (at present semiannually) by the Federal Bureau of Investigation, are computed from reports *voluntarily* made by the police departments of our various cities, and by the rural police agencies (usually county sheriffs) throughout the country. *Some communities, both in rural and in urban areas, do not make reports at all.* The crime rates themselves are computed on the basis of the decennial census population, which means that computed rates in areas in which there have been tremendous population shifts are apt to be grossly at variance with actual rates during the period immediately preceding a new census count. For example, crime rates in Los Angeles for 1949, computed on the basis of the 1940 census, must be regarded as decidedly inaccurate since Los Angeles grew by leaps and bounds during the period of wartime and postwar expansion. Similarly the alleged increases in crime rates following World War II, 1946–1950, were not corrected for the notable increases in the population as a whole, or for the number of soldiers who were "separated" from military service and returned to the civilian population at that time.

There are additional reasons why one must maintain a certain amount of healthy skepticism as to whether alleged increases in crime rates are actual increases. There is no certainty at all, for example, that the *number of crimes reported* corresponds in any constant ratio, from year to year, to the *number of crimes committed*. It is in fact well known that many crimes similar to those recorded are never reported. Many household employees, for example, commit petty thefts of food and clothing and sometimes steal significant items of jewelry, art objects, etc. But because of difficulty in proving that such thefts have been committed by employees, and because any person accusing another of a crime which cannot be proved may be liable for damages, householders often believe they would be in danger of suit if they reported the offenses. Furthermore some employers are reluctant to bring servants to trial and thus "ruin their lives," though other employers have no such inhibitions. Many thefts, also, are never discovered until much later. Few householders make regular inventories of their possessions and most persons cannot tell when an article they have just missed disappeared. All merchants and particularly grocers and "ten-cent" and variety stores lose a sizable amount of merchandise yearly which they do not ordinarily report as stolen. They merely count such losses as a part of operating costs.

When important items like rugs, valuable paintings, clothing, money, or jewelry are stolen from a private residence, the householder ordinarily reports the fact to the police, and the same is true of important and observed losses on the part of merchants. On the other hand, a significant proportion of losses reported to insurance companies (which must be reported to police) are known to be fraudulent. In addition, many people report jewelry and other valuables stolen when such items have merely been misplaced, yet frequently fail to report that their "lost" articles are "found" when they turn up. Travelers often have luggage and other possessions stolen and having little or no extra time do not report their loss unless their insurance company requires it. It seems likely therefore, that the number of petty crimes is much greater than the number of such offenses reported.

Unreported Sex Crimes

No one knows how many sex offenses are committed; the number reported appears to have little or no relation to the actual number. The Kinsey report has shown this fact pretty conclusively in indicating the high ratio of unpunished sex offenses among the group of 12,214 men surveyed, outside of prostitution (which is itself illegal).[46] Even with rape, which is often considered as serious as murder or "a fate worse than death," we may believe many cases to be concealed because the victim might suffer more from the publicity attending the punishment of the rapist than from "hushing up" the affair. Families, in fact, may try to cover up such crimes to protect their daughters from serious gossip. In cases of seduction in rural areas and in immigrant sections of cities the father of the injured girl may demand payment from the father of the young man who has violated his daughter if he knows who the culprit is. This extralegal penal practice is a survival of an ancient custom, but its private character detracts from the publicity and scandal which might otherwise occur. When the parties involved in sexual crimes are older there is still a tendency to forgo punishment in order "to protect the name" of the woman unless the sex attack is accompanied by murder, or other brutal treatment.

[46] Alfred C. Kinsey, Wardell B. Pomeroy, and Clyde E. Martin, *Sexual Behavior in the Human Male*, Saunders, Philadelphia, 1948, pp. 30 and 546.

Other Unreported Crimes

There are many other varieties of unreported crimes. (1) Some crimes are too negligible to be reported.[47] (2) Others are not reported because they occur when the victims are out of town, or are traveling and have little time for reporting the incident, as we have mentioned. (3) The major reason serious crimes are not reported, however, seems to be that the prestige or character of the victim would itself be adversely affected by reporting the crime. Men of good reputation, for example, may be the victims of blackmail and pay off the blackmailer rather than bring the culprit to trial because of the attendant publicity. Often men believe they will suffer suspicion from the publicity, hence keep the whole matter quiet. Cardsharpers and confidence men also swindle many persons who would hesitate to have it known that they were so gullible. Receivers of stolen goods, who are a part of the criminal racket themselves, may be sorely exploited themselves on occasion and be required to turn over their goods to other criminals (who may perchance be dressed in police uniforms). The latter may literally fleece the "fences" (as receivers of stolen goods are called) before the "fences" realize they are being victimized. Since they themselves are lawbreakers they obviously prefer not to report the crimes against them.[48]

In addition to the limitations on the accuracy of crime statistics as recounted above, we should bear in mind that legal definitions of crime vary in the different states; the sale of liquor, for example, is a crime in a state where it is prohibited but not a crime in other states. Similarly what is defined as murder in one state may be classified as manslaughter in another. Any comparison of crime rates between states is difficult unless laws governing offenses are identical. There are thus many factors which affect the matter of reporting crimes to police. And even where crimes are reported we cannot always be sure that police make a record in every instance. In a recent inquiry into the police department in Pittsburgh, for example, it was alleged that the police made no record at all in the case of a brutal murder.

Presumably, however, murder rates are fairly reliable, since most murders are reported and few persons would report a case of nonexistent murder. Likewise most reports of auto theft and burglary are pretty certain to occur only when the crimes have been committed.

[47] Cf. Hans von Hentig, *Crime: Causes and Conditions*, McGraw-Hill, New York, 1947, pp. 57–61.

[48] Cf. Charles L. Clark and Earle E. Eubank, *Lockstep and Corridor*, University of Cincinnati Press, Cincinnati, 1927, p. 105.

Instances of robbery and petty thieving may be more difficult to establish unless the person witnessed his robbery or saw a thief departing with his property; when a person "loses" a wallet he may literally be unable to state whether it was stolen while he was not looking or whether he dropped it in a store or on the street.

Jealousy and Revenge as Factors in Crime Reporting

Since so many crimes go unreported, the question arises as to why any crimes are reported and who reports them. Evidence indicates that virtually all people apparently report certain crimes: (1) those which outrage their sense of moral values and (2) those which entail serious losses to themselves or others (but at the same time no serious loss of prestige or status for themselves). Thus a group of college girls who heard a policeman using profane and abusive language in speaking to a young woman (he later forced the girl to enter an automobile) reported the case to police headquarters and the policeman was tried and fined for the offense. A woman who saw a man hit a woman over the head with a club, mortally wounding her, and drag her body into an alley rushed to report the crime. A man whose place of business was broken into and robbed during the night reported the offense. A clergyman whose automobile was stolen from his garage notified the police as soon as he discovered the theft. Offenses such as these are almost certain to be reported.

Many crimes of the underworld, however, are reported by enemies or persons motivated more by a desire for revenge or a desire to divert attention from their own criminal activities than by any abstract sense of justice. For example, a jealous jilted lover may report his former paramour for another illicit sex affair. A woman madly in love with a man who marries another woman may contrive in her bitterness to have her rival arrested by framing a plot against her. A woman wise in the ways of the narcotic trade may secure drugs from an unethical physician catering to such a market, mail them to her rival, and report the fact anonymously to the F.B.I. If an innocent woman falls in love with an underworld criminal (as sometimes happens) she is very likely to be the prey to some such device. Many cases reported to police detectives thus come through jealous or revenge motives rather than from any true acceptance of the social principles involved in the law.

Detectives on the alert to discover clues to crimes know this and often try to find out what enemies the person under suspicion may have. Sometimes businessmen report their rivals for suspected illegal activities. Disgruntled employees likewise report the delinquencies of their employers on occasion.

The Criminal's Loyalty to His Kind

Nevertheless the majority of criminals maintain a conspiracy of silence about the criminal activities of rival racketeers, gangsters, and gamblers. They know that their own empires are built on shaky foundations and that retaliation in kind and with vengeance will swiftly follow any information or testimony which they give against rivals in their vocation. The underworld criminal does not withhold information about his rivals from any sense of loyalty to his profession but chiefly because his own safety is at stake. Similarly, corrupt public officials tend to protect each other and usually contrive to keep under cover facts which if known would result in conviction for dishonesty or misuse of funds, as well as discharge for inefficient service.

ARRESTS

The number of arrests made in a community depends not only on the number of offenses but upon the efficiency and number of police and their sleuthing skills, whether or not they ride about in automobiles (and fail to observe many crimes committed on their beats), and whether they arrest on the basis of evidence or on suspicion. The number of arrests also depends significantly upon the integrity or lack of corruption among police. If the police are involved in the numbers racket they obviously will not arrest the persons with whom they are in league. In such instances they may make token arrests to satisfy certain public criticisms but they do little more.

False Arrests

Police often make false arrests in the vicinity where a serious crime has taken place simply because almost anyone may be under suspicion. Sometimes every person known to have a record (as well as all persons who might conceivably have committed the crime) is arrested and held for questioning in case of a serious offense such as kidnaping or a brutal and mysterious murder. In the summer of 1928, for example, a young woman who was a graduate student at Northwestern University was attacked and slain on the lawn of a prominent Evanstonian. It eventually turned out that the crime was committed by a feeble-minded Negro bootblack. But before the murderer was apprehended virtually every old man, every other male person who was regarded as "queer" in the neighborhood, and a few men known to be strangers or newcomers who had been seen in the general area after the murder were arrested and subjected to intensive grilling. These persons virtually had to prove they did not commit the murder despite their innocence.[49]

The Number of Arrests

The number of arrests is more or less meaningless as an index to crime because many innocent people are arrested and many guilty people are not. Furthermore a large proportion of the guilty who are arrested are either not brought to trial or not convicted. Even so, there are many more crimes reported than there are arrests. In 1950, for example, there were 793,671 arrests, as Table 3.7 shows, 46,194 of which were on suspicion without specific entry of the charge. Forty-one per cent (330,794) of the arrests were for major offenses, 26.9 per cent (213,713) being for murder, robbery, assault, burglary, larceny, and auto theft.[50]

PRISON STATISTICS

Prison statistics, whether for state or federal prisoners, give us no complete picture of persons tried and convicted, since convicts placed on probation or fined are not included in the enumeration. The federal government's probation service probably has higher professional standards than those of the majority of states, and many federal judges are inclined to give a man or woman a chance, particularly for a first offense. The decision as to whether or not a federal offender shall be placed upon probation rests with the federal judge (and not with any legal stipulation), however. In consequence there is great disparity in the matter of placing convicts on probation. A federal judge who feels personally outraged by an offense may exact a severe sentence, whereas another judge may be inclined to consider such items as motives, youth, or other mitigating factors and place the convicted person on probation. Similarly the different judges in the several states vary markedly in whether or not they sentence first offenders (or others) under probation instead of committing them to prison.

[49] The third degree is discussed in chap. 17, "Police."
[50] *Uniform Crime Reports*, Annual Bulletin, 1950, p. 106.

Prisoners in State and Federal Prisons and Reformatories

TABLE 3.7.   Distribution of Arrests by Sex, 1950

Offense Charged	Total	Number Male	Female	Per Cent Total	Male	Female
Total	793,671	717,088	76,583	100.0	100.0	100.0
Criminal homicide	6,336	5,482	854	.8	.8	1.1
Robbery	19,779	18,930	849	2.5	2.6	1.1
Assault	59,496	53,168	6,328	7.5	7.4	8.3
Burglary—breaking or entering	43,673	42,564	1,109	5.5	5.9	1.4
Larceny—theft	66,031	58,409	7,622	8.3	8.2	10.0
Auto theft	18,398	17,905	493	2.3	2.5	.6
Embezzlement and fraud	21,439	19,505	1,934	2.7	2.7	2.5
Stolen property; buying, receiving, etc.	3,289	3,014	275	.4	.4	.4
Arson	1,054	932	122	.1	.1	.2
Forgery and counterfeiting	11,743	10,395	1,348	1.5	1.4	1.8
Rape	9,323	9,323	—	1.2	1.3	—
Prostitution and commercialized vice	8,579	3,338	5,241	1.1	.5	6.8
Other sex offenses	19,725	16,851	2,874	2.5	2.3	3.8
Narcotic drug laws	8,539	7,495	1,044	1.1	1.0	1.4
Weapons; carrying, possessing, etc.	10,376	9,887	489	1.3	1.4	.6
Offenses against family and children	15,238	14,419	819	1.9	2.0	1.1
Liquor laws	11,260	9,466	1,794	1.4	1.3	2.3
Driving while intoxicated	51,318	49,190	2,129	6.5	6.9	2.8
Road and driving laws	14,571	14,255	316	1.8	2.0	.4
Parking violations	309	293	16	a	a	a
Other traffic and motor vehicle laws	13,052	12,649	403	1.6	1.8	.5
Disorderly conduct	45,438	39,078	6,360	5.7	5.4	8.3
Drunkenness	178,165	162,202	15,963	22.6	22.8	20.9
Vagrancy	48,604	41,598	7,006	6.1	5.8	9.1
Gambling	15,490	13,965	1,525	2.0	1.9	2.0
Suspicion	46,194	41,291	4,903	5.8	5.8	6.4
Not stated	7,930	7,083	847	1.0	1.0	1.1
All other offenses	38,322	34,401	3,921	4.8	4.8	5.1

a Less than $\frac{1}{10}$ of 1 per cent.

SOURCE: Table 40, in *Uniform Crime Reports*, Annual Bulletin, 1950, Federal Bureau of Investigation, U.S Department of Justice, Washington, 1951, p. 107.

The latest statistics on prisoners available for the United States as a whole as this book is being written are the estimated data for 1949. For that year there were 165,127 on December 31. The year previous there had been 157,154. The increase in the number of prisoners at the end of 1949 was thus nearly 8000, or approximately 5 per cent more than the year before. Nearly all of this increase was in state prisons.[51]

[51] *National Prisoner Statistics, Movement of Prisoners in State and Federal Prisons and Reformatories: 1949*, U.S. Department of Justice, Washington, June 25, 1951, p. 1 (preliminary data subject to revision).

Compared to the number of prisoners during the period 1939–1948, this number represents a sizable decline from the peak prison population of 182,330 in 1939 but is significantly more than the 134,069 and 134,669 at the end of the years 1944 and 1945 respectively. The latter were war years, however, and the decline then may be attributed to the war. Certain of the variations are at least partially due to irregularity in reports. Mississippi, for example, did not report in 1939 or 1945. Georgia made a report for the first time in 1945, and in 1947 the number of prisoners in Georgia was an estimate based on a partial report and on the trends in the neighboring state of Alabama. The data in Table 3.8 include only prisons in which felonious prisoners are incarcerated, although not all the prisoners were felons.[52]

Students must keep in mind that the significant drop in the total number of prisoners since 1939 does not of itself indicate that the number of convicted prisoners has declined, or that the rate of crime has necessarily fallen. It merely shows that the rate of imprisonment for the general population is declining, presumably because of wider use of probation. Unfortunately, since there are no adequate statistics on the extent of probation, it is difficult to give any exact figures for the number of convicted criminals on an annual basis. Nor are there satisfactory detailed statistics for parole.

As Table 3.9 shows, there are certain admissions during the year at prisons which are not on court order. These supposedly include transfers from other institutions, just as discharges include persons transferred to other institutions.

The Statistics Covering Commitments to Federal Prisons

In Chapter 23 we discuss the organization and services of federal prisons and in that connection refer again to the statistics covering prisoners in these institutions. Since most of the jurisdiction with reference to criminal conduct is vested in the states where the crimes are committed, only those crimes relating to the national security, or involving commerce in articles forbidden by federal statute, or some such matter, or ordinary offenses committed on government reservations, in the District of Columbia, in federally controlled territory, or on the high seas are subject to federal punishment. Certain events in recent years have resulted in additions to the federal criminal code. The wave of kidnapings during the thirties, climaxed by the extortion-kidnaping of the Lindberghs' infant son, caused kidnaping across state

[52] *Ibid.*, p. 2.

lines to be made a federal offense. (Although kidnaping is always a dramatic type of crime, the number of kidnapings has never been great in comparison to the number of other offenses.) The ease with which stolen automobiles may be transported across state lines made a federal law more or less essential.

TABLE 3.8.   Prisoners Present at End of Year and Prisoners Received from Court, by Type of Institution, for the United States, 1939 to 1949

(Includes estimates for certain state institutions. The difference between the state figures for 1939 to 1948 presented in this table and figures for the same years previously published is caused by the elimination of one institution from the group of included institutions.)

Year	Prisoners Present at End of Year			Prisoners Received from Court		
	All Institutions	Federal Institutions	State Institutions	All Institutions	Federal Institutions	State Institutions
	Number					
1949	165,127	16,808	148,319	71,703	13,130	58,573
1948	157,154	16,307	140,847	65,931	12,430	53,501
1947	152,295	17,146	135,149	66,230	12,948	53,282
1946	141,242	17,622	123,620	62,874	14,950	47,924
1945	134,669	18,638	116,031	54,954	14,171	40,783
1944	134,069	18,139	115,930	51,648	14,047	37,601
1943	138,498	16,113	122,385	51,491	12,203	39,288
1942	152,703	16,623	136,080	62,187	13,725	48,462
1941	166,655	18,465	148,190	73,288	15,350	57,938
1940	175,231	19,260	155,971	77,424	15,109	62,315
1939	182,330	19,730	162,600	a	a	a
	Rate per 100,000 of the estimated civilian population					
1949	111.9	11.4	100.5	48.6	8.9	39.7
1948	108.3	11.2	97.0	45.4	8.6	36.9
1947	106.8	12.0	94.8	46.4	9.1	37.4
1946	102.1	12.7	89.3	45.4	10.8	34.6
1945	105.6	14.6	91.0	43.1	11.1	32.0
1944	105.9	14.3	91.6	40.8	11.1	29.7
1943	108.7	12.6	96.1	40.4	9.6	30.8
1942	116.7	12.7	104.0	47.5	10.5	37.0
1941	126.7	14.0	112.6	55.7	11.7	44.0
1940	133.1	14.6	118.5	58.8	11.5	47.3
1939	139.6	15.1	124.5	a	a	a

a Comparable data not available.
SOURCE: Table 1, *National Prisoner Statistics, Movement of Prisoners in State and Federal Prisons and Reformatories: 1949*, U.S. Department of Justice, Washington, June 25, 1951, p. 2.

The number of certain federal offenses has been much the same over the years, as Table 3.10 shows, whereas other offenses have evidenced marked variation. Counterfeiting and forgery reached an all-time high in 1939, declined abruptly in 1942, dropped even further during 1943 and 1944, but rose again in 1946, and both have increased consistently

TABLE 3.9. Movement of Prison Population, by Type of Institution and Sex, for the United States, 1949
(Includes estimates for state institutions in Georgia and Mississippi)

Movement of Population	All Institutions			Federal Institutions			State Institutions		
	Total	Male	Female	Total	Male	Female	Total	Male	Female
Prisoners present January 1[a]	157,459	150,986	6,473	16,307	15,865	442	141,152	135,121	6,031
Admissions, total	110,710	105,408	5,302	18,043	17,544	499	92,667	87,864	4,803
Admitted, except transfers	87,169	82,082	5,087	15,412	14,942	470	71,757	67,140	4,617
Received from court	71,703	67,726	3,977	13,130	12,696	434	58,573	55,030	3,543
Returned as a conditional-release violator	9,079	8,481	598	1,529	1,505	24	7,550	6,976	574
Returned from escape	2,494	2,404	90	113	109	4	2,381	2,295	86
Other	3,893	3,471	422	640	632	8	3,253	2,839	414
Transferred from other institutions	23,541	23,326	215	2,631	2,602	29	20,910	20,724	186
Discharges, total	103,042	97,583	5,459	17,542	17,059	483	85,500	80,524	4,976
Discharged, except transfers	79,298	74,319	4,979	14,900	14,452	448	64,398	59,867	4,531
Unconditional and conditional releases	69,051	64,718	4,333	13,999	13,569	430	55,052	51,149	3,903
Unconditional	29,547	27,839	1,708	5,352	5,288	64	24,195	22,551	1,644
Expiration of sentence	27,685	26,171	1,514	5,317	5,253	64	22,368	20,918	1,450
Pardon	35	33	2	—	—	—	35	33	2
Commutation	1,827	1,635	192	35	35	—	1,792	1,600	192
Conditional	39,504	36,879	2,625	8,647	8,281	366	30,857	28,598	2,259
Parole	31,318	29,181	2,137	3,051	2,935	116	28,267	26,246	2,021
Conditional pardon	1,502	1,435	67	—	—	—	1,502	1,435	67
Other conditional release	6,684	6,263	421	5,596	5,346	250	1,088	917	171
Death, except execution	734	716	18	38	36	2	696	680	16
Execution	77	77	—	—	—	—	77	77	—
Escape	2,677	2,574	103	117	113	4	2,560	2,461	99
Other	6,759	6,234	525	746	734	12	6,013	5,500	513
Transferred to other institutions	23,744	23,264	480	2,642	2,607	35	21,102	20,657	445
Prisoners present December 31	165,127	158,811	6,316	16,808	16,350	458	148,319	142,461	5,858

[a] The difference between the January 1, 1949, totals shown in this table and the totals for the end of 1948 shown in the preceding table is caused by the reclassification, as of January 1, 1949, of a state receiving unit whose prisoner population was not formerly included to the status of an institution whose population is hereafter to be included.

Source: Table 2, National Prisoner Statistics, Movement of Prisoners in State and Federal Prisons and Reformatories: 1949, U.S. Department of Justice, Washington, June 25, 1951.

since that time. However, virtually all federal offenses declined during the war except those involving espionage, national defense, court-martial, and the selective service. While World War II was in progress, all espionage offenses naturally increased, since there were more enemy agents then. The far-flung activities of selective service involved many instances of violation because so large a number of persons with personal objections to military service were called "in the draft." As a matter of fact, national security offenses were not classified as such during this time.

In 1949, as the table shows, violations of our immigration laws, including illegal entry, formed the largest category of federal offenses. These have bulked consistently high since the end of World War II, but were also relatively high in 1939. The disturbed conditions under Nazi- and Fascist-dominated sections of Europe made many desperate persons seek illegal refuge here after the close of World War II. Displaced persons in considerable numbers have allegedly crossed into this country from Canada or Mexico without visas. The stimulus to find a haven in the "land of the free" has made them willing to risk detection. Crossing boundaries illegally has been a common practice in war-torn Europe. There the crime involved is often in leaving one's homeland, and many refugees are unable to comprehend the rigidity of American immigration laws.

Because the "narcotic ring" is international in character, the only way the sale of narcotic drugs can be controlled is through federal legislation. The number of narcotic offenses dropped off markedly during World War II (with the obvious restraints on nonmilitary travel) but has been rising more recently. The number of auto thefts for the country as a whole dropped precipitately after 1945 but has since risen sharply,[53] and the number of offenses under the Dyer Act, which makes transporting stolen automobiles across a state line a federal offense, has increased, as the accompanying chart shows. A large percentage of cars stolen are apparently being transported into other states and perhaps for longer distances than earlier.

The number of juvenile cases has declined, with the general decline in juvenile delinquency in the postwar period. Part of the drop in juvenile cases, however, is due to the practice of handling federal juvenile cases through the local welfare agencies and courts so far as possible. This seems preferable to bringing juveniles before federal courts (unless the children are residents of federal territory or the District of Columbia, when no other recourse is possible).

[53] Cf. *Uniform Crime Reports,* Annual Bulletin, 1950, Federal Bureau of Investigation, U.S. Department of Justice, 1951, p. 1.

TABLE 3.10.   All Sentenced Federal Prisoners Received from the Courts, by Offense, Fiscal Years Ended June 30, 1937 to 1949

Offense	1937	1938	1939	1940	1941	1942	1943	1944	1945	1946	1947	1948	1949
Total	24,202	23,597	24,750	23,003	21,706	20,027	16,630	19,216	21,200	20,112	19,626	16,787	16,733
Counterfeiting and forgery	1,486	1,710	1,965	1,589	1,289	824	522	536	673	891	1,083	1,018	1,204
Embezzlement and fraud	510	704	809	750	796	733	473	452	340	350	396	531	582
Immigration	2,802	2,844	2,541	2,270	1,695	1,428	1,466	2,674	3,996	3,629	3,989	3,200	3,526
Juvenile Delinquency Act	—	—	—	216	428	478	488	834	911	1,221	870	677	607
Kidnaping	44	41	32	37	31	25	42	31	20	21	32	36	23
Liquor laws	12,238	10,520	11,362	10,735	10,123	8,155	3,502	2,635	2,988	2,425	1,996	1,838	2,035
National Bank and Federal Reserve Act	120	155	167	157	161	110	74	67	51	69	50	141	90
Narcotic drug laws	1,866	2,332	2,610	2,250	1,596	1,522	1,241	1,306	1,134	1,261	1,447	1,443	1,503
National Motor Vehicle Theft Act	1,312	1,563	1,588	1,512	1,498	1,623	1,150	1,079	1,072	1,997	2,740	2,612	2,471
Theft from interstate commerce	308	358	354	313	342	178	216	362	475	448	524	430	378
White Slave Traffic Act	370	447	396	378	357	359	376	255	209	157	183	221	160
Government reservation, D.C., high seas, territorial cases	1,033	994	999	1,021	1,139	1,112	933	991	986	873	974	1,069	1,054
Other	2,083	1,859	1,895	1,719	1,772	1,419	1,370	1,392	1,757	1,965	1,867	1,898	2,012
National security offenses													
Selective Service Act of 1940	30	70	32	56	479	2,061	4,777	6,602	6,588	4,805	3,475	1,673	1,088
Selective Service Act of 1948	—	—	—	—	228	1,049	3,145	3,930	2,613	1,446	833	236	152
Other national defense and security laws[a]	—	—	—	11	151	751	1,121	1,710	2,150	1,143	578	319	182
Military court-martial cases:													
Army	30	70	32	45	100	261	511	954	1,793	2,176	2,014	851	592
Navy	—	—	—	—	—	—	—	8	32	40	50	267	88

[a] Commitments under national defense and security laws in effect prior to 1940 not classified separately.

SOURCE: Table 2 in Federal Prisons, 1949, U.S. Department of Justice, Washington, D.C., 1950, p. 9.

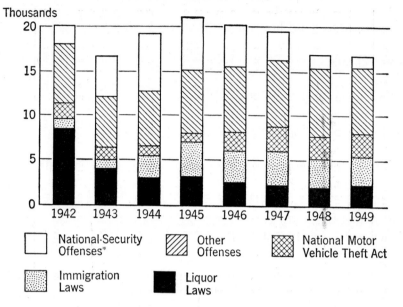

National-Security Offenses*   Other Offenses   National Motor Vehicle Theft Act

Immigration Laws   Liquor Laws

* Court-martial cases; violations of the Selective Service Act and of other war-related or national-security laws

Federal Prisoners Received from Courts: Fiscal Years 1942–1949 (Beginning July 1), According to Major Offenses. (From *Federal Prisons, 1949*, Bureau of Prisons, U.S. Department of Justice, Washington, 1950.)

The shift in the relative importance of federal offenses during the fiscal years from June 30, 1942, to June 30, 1949, is shown in the chart. Obviously offenses vary with the times, the type of legislation in force, the problems of security in war and postwar periods, as these graphs indicate.

Prisoners as Criminals

Most of our detailed information and most of the research with reference to criminals, aside from the important recent data on unreported crimes, professional criminals, and the white-collar criminal, refer to prisoners. These are, in a very real sense, the one group of criminals we know something about, for they have been studied intensively. Even so, our so-called scientific material about this group is not extensive. We have no large body of detailed case studies from which to derive conclusions for prisoners. We do know certain details with reference to superficial characteristics of age, sex, occupation, residence, type of offense, whether the prisoners are recidivists, etc. These facts give us certain insights into criminals, but they supply little information as to why the crimes were committed. Nor do they help us understand how these people differ from more altruistic men except that we know they are chiefly from the lower economic and social classes.

In comparison with the enormous illicit gains of organized crime or with the illegal activities of modern industrial corporations, many of the offenses for which prisoners have been arrested and convicted seem very petty indeed. At the same time it seems likely that modern industry has been subjected to far more extensive investigation and has paid far heavier penalties for breaking the laws than has the fabulous network of underworld criminals. There are many reasons for this disparity in law enforcement but the major explanation must lie in the fact that most corporations are controlled by federal laws. The plunderous activities of organized criminals have successfully evaded the law because of the inefficiencies and corruption of the local officials who have the duty of apprehending the big-time criminals and bringing them to justice. The problem of organized crime is one of the most serious aspects of social disorganization within the local, state, and national community. Because of its extensive ramifications we shall discuss it in detail in another chapter.

SELECTED BIBLIOGRAPHY

Federal Prisons, 1949, U.S. Department of Justice, Washington, D.C., 1950. This report gives statistical data on federal prisoners in the United States. Later reports should also be consulted.

Hentig, Hans von, *Crime: Causes and Conditions,* McGraw-Hill, New York, 1947, chaps. 3, 4, 5, 6, and 7. These chapters give an excellent statistical analysis of the various aspects of crime.

Murphy, Fred J., Shirley, Mary M., and Witmer, Helen L., "The Incidence of Hidden Delinquency," *American Journal of Ortho-Psychiatry,* 16:686–696 (October, 1946). This study shows that a significant percentage of delinquencies of boys, both court cases and non-court cases, had never been brought to court for hearing.

Porterfield, Austin L., *Youth in Trouble,* Leo Potishman Foundation, Fort Worth, 1946. This is an important comparative study of the delinquencies of juvenile court cases and the admitted and unreported cases of delinquency among college students.

Powers, Edwin, and Witmer, Helen L., *An Experiment in Prevention of Delinquency—The Cambridge-Somerville Youth Study,* Columbia University Press, New York, 1951. This gives a detailed report on the study cited above, with data on the preventive aspects of the project.

Prisoners in State and Federal Prisons and Reformatories, 1945, Bureau of the Census, U.S. Department of Commerce, Washington, 1947. This is a detailed statistical analysis of the prison population.

Sellin, Thorsten, *Status and Prospects of Criminal Statistics in the United States*, Sartryck ur Svensk Juristtidning fir Karl Shlyrter, Stockholm, 1949. This gives an excellent analysis of the limitations of criminal statistics because of our peculiar division of powers between state and federal government.

Sutherland, Edwin H., *White Collar Crime*, Dryden, New York, 1949. Dr. Sutherland gives an account of the extensive lawbreaking on the part of the great industrial corporations of America.

Uniform Crime Reports for the United States and Its Possessions, Annual Bulletins, 1949 and 1950, Federal Bureau of Investigation, U.S. Department of Justice, Washington, 1950 and 1951. A summary of the crimes "known to police" and estimations of crimes for the population as a whole are given in these bulletins. Consult later bulletins.

Wallerstein, James S., and Wyle, Clement J., *Our Law Abiding Law Breakers*. Reprint from *Probation*, April, 1947. This is an impressive study of the admitted crimes of a cross section of persons living in New York.

SECTION II

Criminals

CHAPTER 4

Who Are the Criminals?

The only criminals we know much about are convicts in our prisons and reformatories. This group is probably overweighted with the less skillful type of criminals—those not clever enough to escape detection. Even so, prisoners represent a fair cross section of human society. A certain percentage are vicious, hard-boiled creatures who shoot straight and kill whenever their fancied need arises. Many more are chronic weaklings, obviously unable to adjust in a competitive society according to whatever legal rules are entailed. A small group are neither weaklings nor avowed enemies of society and are sometimes as surprised and chagrined as their friends to find themselves lawbreakers. In a crisis, such men have failed to live up to the statutory and common-law provisions which they themselves respect. Prisoners have thought long and hard on why they are set apart from the group. One noteworthy attempt at self-analysis comes from the somewhat literary pen of a federal offender at the United States Penitentiary at Leavenworth, Kansas. It is reprinted in full here.

What Is a Criminal?[1]

Tonight we pace the narrow confines of our cell and ask ourselves for the hundredth time: What is a criminal? Is he, as Lombroso claimed, a moral degenerate? Is he the mental imbecile that metaphysicians, in flowing, learned verbiage, assert he is? Is he the hardened, desperate malefactor, the slinking, murderous beast that penologists would have us believe? Is he the victim of adverse circumstances, unsavory environment, and changing social conditions? Or does he wage war on organized society merely for the sake of adventure? Why is he a criminal?

[1] Anonymous, reprint from *The New Era*. Published by inmates of the United States Penitentiary at Leavenworth.

Garbed in the unholy vestments of dishonor and disgrace, we ourselves are what the world terms a criminal. Should we not know the meaning of the appellation far better than the casual observer? For some years our life has been the life of a prisoner—a criminal, if you please. Criminals, so called, have been our associates, and our friends. We have known them in the moments of their success, and we have known them in the long bitter hours of their failure. Failure that spells oblivion, the oblivion of high, bleak walls, iron bars, monotonous, heartbreaking, and man-killing routine. We have seen how recklessly they can live, and we have also seen how gamely they can die. We have known them intimately, lived with them, but never have we been able to discover any difference between them and their brethren upon whom Fortune chose to smile. They entertain in their heart of hearts the same ideals, the same hopes, and the same ambitions as does the man who never saw a towering prison wall.

Those who commit crime as a matter of choice are few indeed. Many follow it as a means of livelihood because it is the only vocation open to them; and they must be men of stamina, courage, and brains, if they would survive. Those who match their wits against the vast resources of the Powers That Be must be clever rogues, indeed. They are, in truth, just such men as those who attain success in other walks of life—there is no iota of difference. The same ability to think and plan, the same nerve, the same determination, the same unswerving loyalty, and the same persistent application which, if diverted into legitimate channels, would have won recognition for them in any sphere of endeavor. These are the men who have chosen crime as a vocation, because their talents and training, in the majority of instances, equipped them for that career, just as you have chosen the law, or the field of high finance, for similar reasons. And these men, in a limited degree, succeed as law breakers, but they, the same as anyone else, must pay for their success. The toll is heavier by far than that of success in any other field of endeavor.

There are others who follow crime as a profession—men who were born a hundred years too late. Men who live as their kind have always lived— by the strength of their own right arms. To them might is right, they know no other code. Still, they, too, are criminals. These are the men who have never learned to turn the other cheek. These are the men who strike back. Society tramples them under its feet, and they arise from the dust with grim murder in their hearts. They cannot forget; they cannot forgive, and so they fight to the bitter end with the blind courage of their breed.

Some there are whom the very machinery of the courts has converted into criminals. We see them every day in the chrysalis stage. They commit some minor infraction of the law, some petty offense, for which they are sent to jail. In jail they receive scant consideration and little or no courtesy from either their fellow prisoners or from the police. They are neither fish nor fowl. They note the fact that the "good thief" is respected and feared by one, and extended the hand of good fellowship by the other. Straightway they determine to become real criminals, and some few of them succeed, but most of them are cast into prison—scrap iron in Society's junk yard.

Others are criminals by accident. Under the influence of liquor, drugs, sudden passion, and sometimes actual hunger, they commit a crime. They cannot truthfully be termed criminals—they are "accidents." Sometimes serious accidents, no doubt, but still accidents. Surely you would not call them criminals.

What is a criminal? In the final analysis the question is unanswerable. One might as readily ask: What is a man? and the definition would be as vague as this. What is a criminal? Out of the depths of our experience, we would say that a criminal is a thousand changing moods, a thousand inherited tendencies, a thousand mistakes, a thousand injustices, welded into a thousand ever-changing personalities; and from the furnace of the melting pot, you could, perhaps, find the answer . . . What is a criminal?

The Average Person Is a Lawbreaker

Just as "All men are liars," according to Socrates, all men are, in a sense, criminals. "Fellow citizens and criminals," a prominent criminologist once addressed a popular-lecture audience. And in America we must admit the truth of the implication. As we discussed in the previous chapter, almost everyone who has reached adulthood has probably at some time or other committed an offense for which he might have received penal sentence. Although there are no official statistics to prove this statement, the studies of Porterfield, and Wallerstein and Wyle do much to confirm it. We can think of other examples. During prohibition many persons were guilty of transporting liquor which they secured from bootleggers. In states which have been technically "dry" since repeal there has been a widespread tendency among otherwise law-abiding citizens to purchase liquor in adjoining states. This inclination of Americans to pick and choose the laws to which they conform is unquestionably an important factor in American lawlessness. The majority of persons break speed laws, drive through traffc lights, and do many petty things which are technically offenses. But they also do more serious things. Men commit rape and are not reported because the scandal would involve the victim. A child steals from his parents and the offense is overlooked. Vicious women forge checks on male acquaintances and are not arrested because they would undoubtedly resort to blackmailing the men who are their prey. Frauds are perpetrated with such cunning that an extremely clever lawyer would find difficulty in prosecuting the case.

On the other hand, thousands of persons steal small articles without getting caught. Maids "take home" quantities of food from the kitchens of employers. Thousands of library books are taken annually. Rural young people plunder watermelon patches for a jovial lark. College students steal and roast the traditional pig for their fraternity dinner. The treasurer of a women's church organization turns over books which do not balance when her successor is elected. A well-known city manager in a western city admits his "country bookkeeping." All of these persons are guilty of offenses which carry sentence to a state prison. In the case of rape, at least, a few states provide for the death penalty. Yet these offenders have not been punished. Social position, the fear that exposure would be worse than punishment, and lenient public attitudes all result in minimizing their offenses. Are these persons criminal? Unquestionably their motivations varied little from those of the rather drab-looking men who face life behind prison bars. With the eloquent young man from Leavenworth, we also can ask, "What is a criminal?"

Criminals Have Broken Laws

Many attempts have been made by scientific and pseudoscientific students to determine the peculiar characteristics of criminals. Theologians have said such men have "sinned in their hearts against God." Lombroso, from his series of physical measurements of prisoners, concluded they were a special anthropological type—atavistic creatures, born as it were to be criminals. Goring and others who have come after him have sought to establish the low-grade intelligence of the criminals. They broke laws, it is said, because they lacked the intelligence necessary to comply with social demands. As a corollary, they could not foresee the consequences of their evil deeds.[2] Later, however, tests showed that American criminals rated higher in intelligence than the rank and file of men in the United States Army during the First World War.[3] This cannot be taken as absolute proof of the superiority of prisoners, since men serving in the army say that many soldiers had such a hilarious time while taking the tests that they refused to concentrate, hence showed up worse than they would have if they had

[2] Charles B. Goring, The English Convict, His Majesty's Stationery Office, London, 1913, p. 262.
[3] Herman M. Adler and Myrtle R. Worthington, "The Scope of the Problem of Delinquency and Crime as Related to Mental Deficiency," Journal of Psycho-Asthenics, 30:47–57 (1925). Cf. also Carl Murchison, "American Criminal White Intelligence," Journal of Criminal Law and Criminology, 15:239–316, 434–494 (1924).

given the test serious thought. Be that as it may, there seems to be good ground for believing that intelligence *per se* is no key to behavior.

Education and Crime

Lack of education also had had its protagonists as an explanation for criminal behavior. At least several studies seem to show that criminals are set off from the civilian population by their lower educational achievements. According to the federal study of prisoners' antecedents covering the prison population for the year 1923, however, there are no sensational differences between prisoners and non-prisoners. The number of prisoners with little or no schooling is not markedly greater than in the general population. That is, 10.7 per cent of the prison population was illiterate in that year in contrast to 7.1 per cent of the general population. True, the number of prisoners who attended high school and college was markedly lower than in the general population and we may well believe that a differential still exists. But the increases in educational training now more or less compulsory throughout the country will undoubtedly produce higher educational achievement among prisoners.

These characteristics of criminals apply only to prisoners—the criminals who have been not only caught but convicted. Criminals who do not get caught are not arrested; those who are arrested but not punished must have the education and intelligence necessary for an adequate defense. Not many studies have been made of these untamed criminals, but the few in existence are enough to convince us that men who commit crimes need not be stupid or untutored men, as we shall discuss later.

Criminals are thus most safely described as those who have broken laws. But since all or most of us have broken laws, some further characterization for the group punished is necessary. The major factor · differentiating the persons considered criminal seems to be their rejection of social values. Many men outside of prison are basically selfish and egoistic in their pursuit of life, liberty, and happiness. Motivated by a "what's in it for me?" philosophy, such men may be basically antisocial, yet stay within the law or bend the law to meet their own egotistic purposes. Or, because of power and influence in community affairs, they may be criminal in every sense except the purely technical matter of having been arrested and condemned for their behavior.

These unpunished criminals and the recidivists behind the bars are the real criminals for they have organized their lives without reference to social values. They have justified their lifework, whether it be safe-blowing, racketeering, promoting bonanza schemes, or unfair merchandising, on a basis of the material rewards. It is in their primary rejection of the ethical values demanded by that articulate section of society which makes the laws that the main difference between the criminal and the noncriminal lies. And, as we shall point out later, whatever hope we may have for rehabilitating the offender must lie in some conversion of his values. His readjustment must be effected through his sincere rejection of his purely egotistic motivations in favor of some fundamental concern for the welfare of his fellows and especially for the victims of his antisocial drives.

Criminals Obey Most Laws

Lest any smug sense of self-righteousness overcome the civilian noncriminal or uncaught white-collar criminal, he would do well to remember the relative lawlessness of all men. He should recognize, moreover, that the condemned criminal has obeyed most laws. Criminals have usually broken only one or two of the serious legal taboos. Fundamentally, the man in prison is law abiding and has lived according to the majority of social rules. This is not so much because of any matter of "honor among thieves" as because of the simple fact that no man can live at all without some general adherence to the socially acceptable rules of conduct. Thus criminals tend to observe laws of decency with reference to dress, do not jeopardize their neighbor's life, pay their rent, and seldom run off with their neighbor's wife.

There are thousands of laws on our statute books and in most respects the criminal conforms to them quite as well as does the average citizen. He is set apart chiefly because he has broken one or two rules that society considers especially important. Naturally, society usually has a good reason for thinking these rules important.

But the universal tendency to lump all lawbreakers, at least those who are convicts, into a despised and rejected group is absurd. The criminal may have exploded emotionally and killed his wife, his neighbor, or one of his own accomplices who double-crossed him. He may have cold-bloodedly shot his man for a price. Probably, however, he stole from a commercial concern, robbed a bank, or was caught in housebreaking. For many and various reasons the criminal has accepted certain values antithetical to the welfare of the group. Whether because of faulty training or defective personality traits, he has behaved contrary to what our collective social conscience considers inimical to social well-being.

The Prisoner

All prisoners, with the rare exception of those falsely convicted, are criminals and these include a wide variety of men. *In toto*, prisoners should give a fair picture of criminal men. There is little that is subtle in prisoner statistics, but they furnish rough information as to age, sex, type of offense, and the place where the crime was committed. The varied life experiences which lie back of the offender's lawbreaking and explain his particular behavior are seldom indicated in raw numbers. For these one must look to the case history, and we may point out here that only when detailed studies are made of each offender can we hope to have any satisfactory understanding of crime or will statistics have much meaning.

Data with reference to prisoners give no accurate indication of the extent and nature of crime in the United States. It is a notorious fact that only a small percentage of criminals are arrested; a much smaller number are tried, and a far lesser number convicted. In consequence, prison statistics pertain to only a selected group of criminals.

To remedy this situation, the Federal Bureau of Investigation has requested the co-operation of the various state and municipal police in filling out reports on crimes committed. Larger cities and towns have been uniformly co-operative in making returns, as have most smaller towns and rural townships. Altogether, 102,083,360 out of the 150-odd million comprising our total population were accounted for in computing the crime rate for the year 1950.[4] The figures may be considered to represent a fairly adequate picture of crimes committed in America as reported by local police.

We shall have occasion to refer to these statistical reports in other chapters. Here our major concern is data bearing on the prisoners themselves.

Most Criminals Are Men

Most criminals are men—young and inexperienced men. More criminals fall in the group 20 to 24 years of age (inclusive) than in any other 5-year age group. Usually these men have committed a theft in

[4] *Uniform Crime Reports*, Annual Bulletin, 1950, Federal Bureau of Investigation, U.S. Department of Justice, Washington, 1951, pp. 77, 84.

a city and often they are away from home at the time. Thus briefly we may sum up the age, sex, offense, and residence data with reference to convicted prisoners.

We need further explanation, however, to make the picture clearer. There are, of course, some women prisoners. But women numbered only 5302 of the 110,710 prisoners admitted to state and federal institutions in 1949, and of the total 165,127 prisoners incarcerated in institutions on December 31, 1949, 158,811 were men and 6316 were women. Stated differently, women constituted approximately 3.9 per cent of prisoners committed during 1949 and approximately 3.9 per cent of the number of prisoners present on December 31 of that year.[5]

May we assume that women are so much more law abiding than men? On the surface the answer appears to be in the affirmative. Despite the large numbers of women and girls in industry, the family still exerts a greater restraint over women. Most women are married fairly young and their contacts with industry and the competitive wage-earning group tend to be temporary. Personal rather than impersonal relationships thus bulk most extensively in their associations. A woman's happiness is consequently based essentially upon the integrity of human relationships. She must "trust" her husband and her father because her whole life scheme is built up on acceptance of honesty. So far as the chicanery of modern industry is concerned, she is more often its victim than its accomplice. For, in a life whose whole meaning rests essentially on honesty, dishonesty has little appeal.

Men and boys, on the other hand, are schooled from early childhood in the rougher ethics of the street and of the market place. David Harum's succinct advice to "Do it unto others as they'd like to do unto you, but do it first" has been the first law of life for many persons in our competitive economic society. Parents in the lower economic class seldom take the trouble to instruct their sons in the niceties of ethical considerations. When parents of the upper middle class do impose standards of polite conduct upon their well-dressed children their sons may get trounced by those who reject such sissified ethics, as Booth Tarkington attests in his autobiography. Tarkington tells how the well-brought-up boys in his neighborhood were rolled in the dust by the small "gangsters" (none over eleven).[6]

[5] *National Prisoner Statistics, Movement of Prisoners in State and Federal Prisons and Reformatories: 1949*, U.S. Department of Justice, Washington, June 25, 1951, p. 2 (preliminary data).

[6] Cf. Booth Tarkington, "As I Seem to Me," *Saturday Evening Post*, 214:22–23 ff. (July 12, 1941).

A woman's life tends to be spent in a domestic realm where personal relations and personal morality are emphasized. Men, so far as their business and most of their working-day pursuits are concerned, live on a different plane of our culture. This is a public culture, where the values of private integrity are overshadowed by all the encroachments that an impersonal public will stand for. All too often its philosophy is expressed by "What's in it for me?"

Of course, there are a few notorious women in the criminal world and there are many undetected crimes among women as well as men, but the average woman, because of her relative isolation, is naïvely honest, despite the relatively selfish character of her motivations.[7]

The Youth of Criminals

A few criminals grow old in their ill-favored profession. A few begin their criminal activities in their declining years. Most of the latter offenders commit offenses which are observably related to senility. Old men, for example, commit a disproportionately high number of sex offenses and are frequently guilty of ravishing preadolescent girls. A mentally deteriorated old man may commit a stealthy theft or an explosive murder. Strictly speaking, these men should not be regarded as criminal, because their behavior may be attributed to their disturbed mental functioning. Nevertheless, such offenders often receive sentences in our courts.

By and large, lawbreakers are young men. The 20- to 24-year-olds have consistently committed more offenses than any other age groups, as Table 4.1 shows. In a sense, their criminality represents in part the rebellion of youth. For 1946 the median age for federal prisoners was 27.6 years, and that for state prisoners was 26.3 years. The mean age varied somewhat in the various states from 23.5 years in Colorado to 32.1 years in Nevada. The Bureau of the Census concluded that states which have a high median age for prisoners tend to be those states where young men 16 to 21 years of age are sent to juvenile rather than adult reformatories. The median age is also affected by the degree to which young persons are put on probation.[8]

There is, of course, nothing peculiarly American about youth's coming to grips with the law. In European prisons we find virtually the same situation. Laws are made for all generations, but it is the young men in particular who rebel against social authority. Because

[7] Criminal women are discussed in detail in chaps. 8 and 9.

[8] *Prisoners in State and Federal Prisons and Reformatories, 1946*, Bureau of the Census, U.S. Department of Commerce, Washington, 1948, p. 24.

TABLE 4.1. Felony Prisoners Received from Court in State Institutions, by Age and Sex, by Regions, 1946

Age and Sex	Number					Per Cent Distribution				
	United States	The North-eastern States	The North Central States	The South	The West	United States	The North-eastern States	The North Central States	The South	The West
Total	43,679	6,999	11,937	18,697	6,046	100.0	100.0	100.0	100.0	100.0
Male	41,240	6,401	11,311	17,684	5,844	100.0	100.0	100.0	100.0	100.0
Under 15 years	31	2	2	22	5	0.1	—	—	0.1	0.1
15 to 19 years	7,632	1,526	2,092	3,256	758	18.5	23.8	18.5	18.4	13.0
20 to 24 years	11,061	1,802	3,051	4,682	1,526	26.8	28.2	27.0	26.5	26.1
25 to 29 years	7,299	997	1,982	3,295	1,025	17.7	15.6	17.5	18.6	17.5
30 to 34 years	5,076	696	1,421	2,177	782	12.3	10.9	12.6	12.3	13.4
35 to 39 years	3,727	469	922	1,702	634	9.0	7.3	8.2	9.6	10.8
40 to 44 years	2,544	378	712	1,031	423	6.2	5.9	6.3	5.8	7.2
45 to 49 years	1,719	212	493	704	310	4.2	3.3	4.4	4.0	5.3
50 to 54 years	973	142	282	383	166	2.4	2.2	2.5	2.2	2.8
55 to 59 years	573	99	167	216	91	1.4	1.5	1.5	1.2	1.6
60 to 64 years	306	39	93	115	59	0.7	0.6	0.8	0.7	1.0
65 to 69 years	181	25	62	57	37	0.4	0.4	0.5	0.3	0.6
70 years and over	118	14	32	44	28	0.3	0.2	0.3	0.2	0.5
Detail, 15 to 24 years										
15 to 17 years	2,835	593	764	1,248	230	6.9	9.3	6.8	7.1	3.9
18 years	2,445	473	686	1,018	268	5.9	7.4	6.1	5.8	4.6
19 years	2,352	460	642	990	260	5.7	7.2	5.7	5.6	4.4

	(1) No.	(1) %	(2) No.	(2) %	(3) No.	(3) %	(4) No.	(4) %	Total No.	Total %
20 years	320	5.5	928	5.2	646	5.7	428	6.7	2,322	5.6
21 to 24 years	1,206	20.6	3,754	21.2	2,405	21.3	1,374	21.5	8,739	21.2
Median age	28.1	—	26.3	—	26.3	—	24.6	—	26.3	—
Female	202	100.0	1,013	100.0	626	100.0	598	100.0	2,439	100.0
Under 15 years	—	—	2	0.2	—	—	—	—	2	0.1
15 to 19 years	22	10.9	183	18.1	76	12.1	94	15.7	375	15.4
20 to 24 years	63	31.2	290	28.6	200	31.9	166	27.8	719	29.5
25 to 29 years	27	13.4	196	19.3	113	18.1	119	19.9	455	18.7
30 to 34 years	27	13.4	110	10.9	76	12.1	82	13.7	295	12.1
35 to 39 years	24	11.9	120	11.8	62	9.9	63	10.5	269	11.0
40 to 44 years	15	7.4	50	4.9	49	7.8	31	5.2	145	5.9
45 to 49 years	11	5.4	39	3.8	23	3.7	20	3.3	93	3.8
50 to 54 years	8	4.0	11	1.1	13	2.1	9	1.5	41	1.7
55 to 59 years	4	2.0	3	0.3	7	1.1	8	1.3	22	0.9
60 to 64 years	1	0.5	3	0.3	3	0.5	2	0.3	9	0.4
65 to 69 years	—	—	6	0.6	4	0.6	4	0.7	14	0.6
70 years and over	—	—	—	—	—	—	—	—	—	—
Detail, 15 to 24 years										
15 to 17 years	1	0.5	51	5.0	26	4.2	36	6.0	114	4.7
18 years	7	3.5	55	5.4	19	3.0	30	5.0	111	4.6
19 years	14	6.9	77	7.6	31	5.0	28	4.7	150	6.2
20 years	7	3.5	61	6.0	43	6.9	36	6.0	147	6.0
21 to 24 years	56	27.7	229	22.6	157	25.1	130	21.7	572	23.5
Median age	28.0	—	25.8	—	26.6	—	26.6	—	26.4	—

SOURCE: Table 11 in *Prisoners in State and Federal Prisons and Reformatories, 1946*, Bureau of the Census, U.S. Department of Commerce, Washington, 1948, pp. 23–24.

of their lack of experience, they fail to see any folly in their disavowal of personal and social responsibility. They are lured by present advantage and for them there has been no testing of the validity of the common conscience underlying our criminal law.

Detailed statistics are not available for prisoners since 1946 because of lack of Congressional appropriation. We have little reason to believe that age groupings have altered markedly since that time, however. A glance at Table 4.1 shows that it is the 18- and 19-year-olds who were most frequently convicted that year. Physically developed but socially immature, these young people are most likely to find themselves in conflict with the law so far as serious offenses are concerned. The rate of felonies for the age grouping 25 to 29 is lower than that for the 20-to-24-year group, and at age 30, the rate drops again. At 35 it declines still further and after a man reaches 50 to 54 he soon fades out of the criminal group.[9] Figures for previous years show these groupings applied rather consistently during the five years 1942 to 1946, inclusive.

Of course there are a few convicts for the upper age group—men who suddenly go "haywire" after a lifetime of unquestioned integrity —but they represent the exceptions rather than the rule. "But," someone may protest, "I have seen many old men in prison." True, for prisoners include men who are serving long sentences. Men in prison also look older than their age. A man in his upper thirties when convicted does not keep his youth well when imprisoned for 10 or 12 years. The deadly routine, the monotonous, gloomy surroundings are destructive to the interest which keeps a man in the world outside alert. There are also many men serving life sentences, either as murderers or as habitual offenders. These men grow old in prison, but they too, it must be remembered, look older than they are, for they are often men without hope.

But let us return to our subject. Prisoners are young when committed; the median age for all male felons received in state institutions in 1946 was 26.3 years. For women prisoners it was 26.4.[10] A few years earlier (in 1940) women prisoners tended to be older, their median age being 29.5 years in contrast to 27.9 years for men.[11] Federal offenders tend to be older than state prisoners when they commit their crimes. The median age for federal male felony offenders for 1946 was

[9] Ibid., pp. 21–23.   [10] Ibid., pp. 25–26.

[11] Prisoners in State and Federal Prisons and Reformatories, 1940, Bureau of the Census, U.S. Department of Commerce, Washington, 1942, p. 17.

27.6.[12] In 1940 the federal prisoners' median was 32.1, in contrast to the state prisoners' median of 26.7.[13] Federal offenders are thus becoming younger. However, the largest number of federal offenders in 1940 were engaged in bootlegging and liquor law violations. These were largely older men. The number of liquor law violators declined markedly with repeal of prohibition laws. Many other federal offenses are by nature less likely to involve young men. The latter seldom have income enough to attempt any serious evasion of our income tax laws, for example, nor do they ordinarily have sufficient business experience to get involved in illegal business enterprises. The largest 5-year classification for federal offenders in 1950, as Table 4.2 shows, was for the age group 25–29.

TABLE 4.2. Ages of All Federal Sentenced Prisoners Received from Courts for Fiscal Year Ending June 30, 1950

Age	Total	All Offenses Male	Female
Median	28.1	28.1	27.9
All ages	18,063	17,351	712
21 and under	3,911	3,758	153
Under 15	44	44	—
15	119	118	1
16	225	220	5
17	374	363	11
18	533	510	23
19	778	747	31
20	895	853	41
21	943	902	41
22 and over	14,152	13,593	559
22	992	949	43
23	906	870	36
24	885	849	36
25 to 29	3,797	3,646	151
30 to 34	2,352	2,266	86
35 to 39	1,855	1,786	69
40 to 44	1,342	1,289	53
45 to 49	972	927	45
50 to 54	497	466	31
55 to 59	289	282	7
60 to 64	158	157	1
65 to 69	83	83	—
70 and over	24	23	1

SOURCE: Table 15, *Federal Prisons, 1950*, Federal Bureau of Prisons, U.S. Department of Justice, Washington, 1951, p. 63.

[12] Cf. *Federal Offenders, 1946*, Bureau of Prisons, U.S. Department of Justice, Washington, 1941, p. 292.

[13] *Prisoners in State and Federal Prisons and Reformatories, 1940*, pp. 30–36.

Most Criminals Are Unmarried

According to the statistics for 1946, 50.4 per cent of the male felony prisoners were single. Of the female prisoners 54.6 per cent were married. As we discuss more in detail in Chapter 8, an unsatisfactory marriage is probably a factor in many a woman's criminal activities. Since a large number of prisoners are very young, age alone explains why many of the men are unmarried. The percentages of prisoners under 30 in 1946 were as follows: 56.7 per cent of all prisoners; the same percentage of male prisoners; and 55.6 per cent of women prisoners.

Since more adult men are married than are single, we can probably attach some importance to marriage as a factor in stabilizing male conduct. Age itself should account for a degree of social maturity, but when a man has a family to support, a life of crime involves many risks. Even men who have been first offenders can probably see valid reasons for a steady job when there are children to be fed and clothed. Nor can we ignore the influence of the wife. All women do not have a stabilizing effect, but a virtuous wife unquestionably exerts a strong influence toward desirable conduct on the part of her husband. Women seem to be, by nature, relatively conservative—their status as mothers probably makes them so. A desire for the security of their children makes them place a high value on stable home relationships. Obviously the pursuit of an honest trade or profession offers fewer hazards than a life spent in criminal activities and mature men recognize this fact.

The woman who has abandoned herself to crime, on the other hand, has, more often than not, been married, although in a high percentage of cases she is divorced, widowed, or separated from her husband. In 1940, for example, only 29.2 per cent of women prisoners were single, 49.9 per cent were married, the rest were either divorced, widowed, or separated. In 1946 only 28.5 per cent were single, 54.6 per cent were married, and 16.8 per cent were widowed and divorced, as Table 4.3 shows. Why women who are or have been married commit more crimes than unmarried women may seem to be a perplexing question. There are several explanations which bear on the matter. Most women who are convicted are involved either in crimes with their husbands or sweethearts or in sex or liquor offenses. Women who are unhappy in marriage and in consequence engage in extramarital sex offenses are more likely to be punished than married men in a similar situation. Married women also have more freedom than unmarried women in

TABLE 4-3. Female Felony Prisoners Received from Court in Federal and State Institutions, by Offense and Marital Status, for the United States, 1946

(Includes statistics covering year ending May 31 for state institutions in Pennsylvania, and for those in Georgia, statistics for year ending March 31; excludes statistics for state institutions in Mississippi. Per cent not shown where base is less than 100)

Offense	Total Prisoners Received	Marital Status Reported					Per Cent of Total Reported		
		Total	Single	Married	Widowed and Divorced	Marital Status Not Reported	Single	Married	Widowed and Divorced
All offenses	2,889	2,737	781	1,495	461	152	28.5	54.6	16.8
Murder	142	133	38	53	42	9	28.6	39.8	31.6
Manslaughter	232	216	66	94	56	16	30.6	43.5	25.9
Robbery	98	98	27	55	16	—	—	—	—
Aggravated assault	180	157	54	89	14	23	34.4	56.7	8.9
Burglary	133	123	51	61	11	10	41.5	49.6	8.9
Larceny, etc.[a]	831	772	274	394	104	59	35.5	51.0	13.5
Forgery	326	320	88	158	74	6	27.5	49.4	23.1
Commercialized vice	26	26	4	16	6	—	—	—	—
Other sex offenses	143	129	16	93	20	14	12.4	72.1	15.5
Violating drug laws	145	145	29	93	23	—	20.0	64.1	15.9
Violating liquor laws	51	43	2	35	6	8	—	—	—
Other offenses	582	575	132	354	89	7	23.0	61.6	15.5

[a] Includes auto theft, embezzlement, fraud, and stolen property.

SOURCE: Table 36, Prisoners in State and Federal Prisons and Reformatories, 1946, Bureau of the Census, U.S. Department of Commerce, Washington, 1948, p. 52.

their social relationships. This may be a factor in their lawbreaking. We shall discuss this problem in greater detail in Chapter 8. In any event women, married or unmarried, constitute but a very small share of the total criminal group. The criminal world, in a special sense, is a man's world.

Most Prisoners Are Recidivists

All studies show that a large proportion of offenders are recidivists. A detailed study of prisoners committed to reformatories, jails, and workhouses in 1923 showed that 50 per cent of those for whom there was information had prior commitments to penal institutions. Over half of these were second offenders. The rest were serving time for their third, fourth, or more offense.[14] In 1950 the Federal Bureau of Investigation found that 60.2 per cent of the 793,671 persons arrested in that year had been previously arrested and their fingerprints were on file in Washington.[15]

Figures for felony prisoners released from prisons in 1946 showed that 51.1 per cent of those for whom there was information had previous commitments, as Table 4.4 shows. The Census Bureau regards this as a rough indication of the extent of recidivism, but states that it is probably an understatement since many states do not have facilities for gathering accurate information.[16] If these statistics were completely reliable we might infer that approximately 49 per cent of the men go straight when released from prison. Actually we can take no such optimistic outlook, for many released convicts commit further offenses for which they are not apprehended. Follow-up studies of released prisoners have indicated that almost 80 per cent commit serious offenses following parole, as we shall discuss in detail later.[17] Studies in Great Britain indicate that confirmed recidivists usually commit several types of crime, as we shall mention in Chapter 5.

Recidivism is apparently greater today among the men who serve sentences in prison than among the women. At least 67.6 per cent of the women released in 1946 had no previous commitment, as Table 4.4 indicates. For women sent to jails and workhouses the prior commitment rate is higher. In 1923 the rate was 50.7 and we have reason

[14] The Prisoner's Antecedents, 1923, Bureau of the Census, U.S. Department of Commerce, Washington, 1929, p. 41.
[15] Uniform Crime Reports, Annual Bulletin, 1950, p. 111.
[16] Prisoners in State and Federal Prisons and Reformatories, 1946, p. 94.
[17] Cf. Sheldon and Eleanor T. Glueck, 500 Criminal Careers, Knopf, New York, 1930, pp. 184–185.

TABLE 4.4. Felony Prisoners Released, by Type of Institution, Prior Commitment, and Sex, for the United States, 1946

Prior Commitment	All Institutions			Federal Institutions			State Institutions[a]		
	Total	Male	Female	Total	Male	Female	Total	Male	Female
Total	50,059	47,312	2,747	13,133	12,668	465	36,926	34,644	2,282
Prior commitment reported	46,680	44,106	2,574	13,133	12,668	465	33,547	31,438	2,109
No prior commitment	22,819	21,079	1,740	7,343	7,122	221	15,476	13,957	1,519
Jail or juvenile institution	9,442	8,949	493	2,418	2,262	156	7,024	6,687	337
1 prison commitment	8,418	8,199	219	1,912	1,849	63	6,506	6,350	156
2 prison commitments	3,338	3,266	72	805	789	16	2,533	2,477	56
3 or more prison commitments	2,663	2,613	50	655	646	9	2,008	1,967	41
Prior commitment not reported	3,379	3,206	173	—	—	—	3,379	3,206	173
Per Cent Distribution									
Prior commitment reported	100.0	100.0	100.0	100.0	100.0	100.0	100.0	100.0	100.0
No prior commitment	48.9	47.8	67.6	55.9	56.2	47.5	46.1	44.4	72.0
Jail or juvenile institution	20.2	20.3	19.2	18.4	17.9	33.5	20.9	21.3	16.0
1 prison commitment	18.0	18.6	8.5	14.6	14.6	13.5	19.4	20.2	7.4
2 prison commitments	7.2	7.4	2.8	6.1	6.2	3.4	7.6	7.9	2.7
3 or more prison commitments	5.7	5.9	1.9	5.0	5.1	1.9	6.0	6.3	1.9

[a] Includes statistics covering year ending May 31 for Pennsylvania, and for Georgia, statistics for year ending March 31, 1947, adjusted to a calendar year basis; excludes statistics for Michigan and Mississippi.

Source: Table 59 in *Prisoners in State and Federal Prisons and Reformatories, 1946*, Bureau of the Census, U.S. Department of Commerce, Washington, 1948, p. 94.

to believe it is as high or higher today. The majority of women sentenced to local penal institutions are arrested for prostitution and other sex offenses and the uncounted repetition of offenses among prostitutes is notorious. For non-sex offense categories of crime women apparently do not tend to become repeaters so frequently.

Residence

Many criminals are nonresidents of the places where their crimes are committed. According to the survey in 1923, men serving sentences in prison were nonresidents of the community in which the crime was committed in 28.3 per cent of the cases (although only 10.4 per cent of the women were convicted of offenses committed while away from home). Furthermore, the larger the city, the larger the proportion of nonresident offenders. Many of the crimes were committed by rural residents, although the rural offender usually confined his criminal activities to the smaller cities.[18] Women criminals are chiefly urban in residence, for the reason that the largest group of women offenders are arrested for prostitution, and prostitution is definitely an urban phenomenon. The ratio of urban women prisoners to rural female offenders was approximately 6:1 in 1930.[19] Unfortunately we have little data on prisoners' residence since that date.

Despite the fact that urban residents are convicted more frequently than rural dwellers it seems likely that the continual migration of rural young people to the city has swelled the ranks of American criminals. Unaccustomed to the complexities and stimulations of city life these displaced country people are easy prey to the temptations to crime. Sociologists are well aware that some country boys and girls become demoralized by the new patterns and pressures of urban life. We have no way of knowing, however, whether or not the urban crime rate is appreciably swelled by the continuous trek of rural youth to the city.

Presumably the persistent draining off of rural populations to the city accounts in a minor degree for the low rural crime rate. Migrants to the city are certainly more adventurous young persons than those who stay on the farms, and are no longer under the watchful eye of family and neighbors. It is thus probably safe to say these young people swell the city crime rates slightly. But we must also remember

[18] The Prisoner's Antecedents, 1923, p. 12.
[19] Prisoners in State and Federal Prisons and Reformatories, 1929–1930, Bureau of the Census, U.S. Department of Commerce, Washington, 1932, p. 10.

that it is mostly the better educated and brightest rural young people who seek the opportunities of city life. These groups in turn rank low in crime, hence cannot bear any major responsibility for the urban rate.

TABLE 4.5. Commitments to Prisons and Reformatories During the First Six Months of 1923—Proportion Resident and Nonresident of Place Where Crime Occurred, by Sex and Offense

Sex and Offense	Total	Total with Report as to Both Residence and Place of Crime	Residing at Place of Crime		Residing Elsewhere		No Report as to Residence or Place of Crime
			Number	Per Cent of Total (¹)	Number	Per Cent of Total (¹)	
Both sexes	19,080	15,991	11,654	72.9	4,337	27.1	3,089
Male	17,882	14,926	10,700	71.7	4,226	28.3	2,956
Female	1,198	1,065	954	89.6	111	10.4	133

SOURCE: Table 5 in *The Prisoner's Antecedents, 1923*, Bureau of the Census, U.S. Department of Commerce, Washington, 1929, p. 12.

Rural Versus Urban Crimes

Crimes committed in the open country differ significantly from urban crimes in their lack of cunning, strategy, and complex planning, comparatively speaking. Urban crimes are predominantly offenses against property (including theft, fraud, forgery, and embezzlement). They also include abortion, vice, political corruption, and the like. Most rural crimes involve property but they tend to be direct and naïve.[20] Often the individual is in revolt against laws which are contrary to his beliefs rather than "doing what he knows to be wrong." Thus Iowa farmers revolted several years ago against the compulsory tuberculin tests for their dairy herds as an invasion of their "private rights."

A study of crime in Hutchinson County, South Dakota, made by John Useem and Marie Waldner, gives an illuminating picture of the rural crime problem. In this county two-thirds of the people live in the open country and the rest in small towns, none exceeding 1300 population.[21] When the court convictions for the period 1890 to 1940 were analyzed, certain definite differences existed between the crimes committed during 1890–1915 and those committed during 1915–1940. Misdemeanors increased markedly in the latter period. Crimes of vio-

[20] Cf. John Useem and Marie Waldner, "Patterns of Rural Crime," *Rural Sociology*, 7:175–185 (June, 1942).
[21] *Ibid.*

lence dropped from 52 to 7 per cent while "crimes against the public," which included for the most part offenses against school laws and liquor law violations, increased.

This South Dakota county was settled by several foreign-born immigrant groups, the German Hutterites, German-Russian Mennonites, and German Catholics. Each of these groups settled in somewhat isolated sections and perpetuated their own customs and practices. The American "Yankee" population, being regarded as a shiftless lot, was not emulated in these communities. Even so, the "Yankees" were elected to the legislature and wrote the laws for the state as a whole. Conflict between the mores of the foreign-born groups and the laws of the Yankees inevitably ensued. The foreign groups saw no reason for educating their children unless they were to be teachers or ministers. The foreigners had always been moderate drinkers. Thus the liquor laws and compulsory education laws were in violation of their own cultural patterns; they experienced no stigma within their group for offending them. On the other hand, deviations from their own cultural traits were severely frowned on.

Property crimes were committed most often by persons 20 to 25, conforming to the general tendency of this age group to be the modal group. Offenses against the public or violations of school and liquor laws were committed by those 45 to 55. The latter naturally include the men with families and because of their age the majority of those with the largest number of children. Since they were also those whose Old World habits of liquor consumption were most deeply ingrained, the explanation for the difference in the types of lawbreaking among this age group is obvious.

As might be expected there were few professional criminals in this rural area. Part of the crimes of younger people were to be explained in the lack of wholesome rural recreation, of "something to do" in their leisure time. The dearth of amusement led many young people to seek out the taverns and poolrooms which seem always to have been the "dens of rural iniquity."[22]

The Criminal According to Offense

If we classify criminals by type of offense it is obvious that the majority of rank-and-file criminals are property offenders. Although the statistics do not indicate this, it is petty thievery that bulks largest

[22] *Ibid.* Cf. also Mabel A. Elliott and Francis E. Merrill, *Social Disorganization*, Harper, New York, rev. ed., 1950, chap. 23, "The Small Town."

among economic crimes. Petty offenders are usually not sentenced to prison, however. Instead they receive sentences from 30 days up to a year, hence do not figure in the "felony" classification. Even so, in 1946 nearly one-fifth of all male felons committed to prisons and reformatories were burglars, more than a sixth had committed larceny, nearly one-tenth were involved in auto thefts, and another tenth were convicted of robbery, as Table 4.6 shows. These, with sex offenders and murderers, constitute the important categories of the traditional types of offenders. Problems of social welfare, of increased taxation, of warfare, etc., meanwhile have introduced a variety of new taboos with reference to individual conduct in modern society. Modern technology has permitted the development of new varieties of professional criminals who make lawbreaking their basic occupation. In order to give the student some insight into the types of persons who commit crimes the various types of offenders will be discussed in detail in several succeeding chapters. The activities of the woman offender will be given special consideration, and case histories of different types of women offenders will be presented. Throughout, the author hopes to make clear that criminals are human beings, often misguided and misdirected, but just as often enmeshed in a series of situations which have evoked the behavior society condemns and punishes.

SELECTED BIBLIOGRAPHY

Cavan, Ruth Shonle, *Criminology*, Crowell, New York, 1948, chap. 11, "Characteristics of Criminals." This chapter reviews the major characteristics of prisoners.

Federal Prisons (1946–1950). Annual reports of the Federal Bureau of Prisons are published containing much valuable material on prisoners in federal prisons.

Glueck, Sheldon and Eleanor T., *500 Criminal Careers*, Knopf, New York, 1930. This book contains excellent pre-institutional and post-institutional information on 510 criminals.

Prisoners, 1923, Bureau of the Census, U.S. Department of Commerce, Washington, 1926. This is an excellent detailed study of the various characteristics of prisoners. No subsequent census report has supplied so much information.

Prisoners in State and Federal Prisons and Reformatories (1926 to 1946), Bureau of the Census, U.S. Department of Commerce, Washington, published from 1929 to 1948. This series of statistical compilations constitutes the only significant data we have on the characteristics of prisoners for the period covered. Since 1948 summary data have been pub-

TABLE 4.6. Male Felony Prisoners Received from Court, by Type of Institution, Offense, and Age, for the United States, 1946
(Median not shown where base is less than 100)

Type of Institution and Offense	All Ages	Under 15 Years	15 to 19 Years	20 to 24 Years	25 to 29 Years	30 to 34 Years	35 to 39 Years	40 to 44 Years	45 to 54 Years	55 to 64 Years	65 and Over	Median Age
All institutions	53,543	34	8,748	14,767	9,830	6,768	4,962	3,342	3,584	1,140	368	26.6
Murder	1,837	1	154	386	353	267	240	139	181	88	28	30.5
Manslaughter	1,501	—	109	307	302	221	180	112	163	83	24	30.7
Robbery	5,109	4	1,013	1,944	1,032	549	295	140	113	15	4	24.0
Aggravated assault	3,358	1	331	846	674	482	388	262	241	91	42	28.7
Burglary	10,017	14	2,670	2,988	1,651	1,078	687	441	379	84	25	23.9
Larceny, except auto theft	9,044	2	1,731	2,639	1,649	1,047	763	526	523	129	35	25.5
Auto theft	5,151	3	1,485	2,037	895	383	194	96	52	5	1	22.7
Embezzlement and fraud	1,436	—	65	215	253	242	189	152	209	83	28	33.8
Stolen property	482	—	40	107	92	73	61	36	63	8	2	30.1
Forgery	3,682	2	274	870	802	556	408	302	347	99	22	29.3
Rape	2,327	2	256	749	480	293	203	124	144	53	23	26.6
Commercialized vice	189	—	4	30	34	44	25	30	14	6	2	33.0
Other sex offenses	1,249	1	69	155	174	161	154	150	226	102	57	37.1
Violating drug laws	1,246	—	40	157	213	237	186	151	200	53	9	34.5
Carrying and possessing weapons	397	—	69	110	68	50	38	23	31	5	3	26.4
Nonsupport or neglect	726	—	7	60	155	184	134	100	76	10	—	33.8
Violating liquor laws	1,840	1	35	216	276	309	297	238	309	117	42	36.4
Violating traffic laws	187	—	5	41	49	24	29	15	16	8	—	29.8
Violating national defense laws	1,130	—	170	291	207	194	148	55	52	12	1	27.5
Other offenses	2,635	3	221	619	471	374	343	250	245	89	20	30.0

Federal institutions	12,303	3	1,116	3,706	2,531	1,692	1,235	798	892	261	69	27.6
Murder	220	—	4	70	89	33	18	3	2	—	—	27.0
Manslaughter	167	—	1	69	57	26	9	4	1	—	—	26.2
Robbery	345	—	16	181	79	40	22	6	1	—	—	24.3
Aggravated assault	429	—	7	181	136	67	20	10	5	1	2	26.0
Burglary	225	—	27	92	44	30	14	7	8	2	1	24.6
Larceny, except auto theft	1,600	—	111	545	388	207	148	89	85	20	7	26.9
Auto theft	2,459	1	574	1,078	457	177	90	59	19	4	—	23.0
Embezzlement and fraud	529	—	17	85	77	81	69	52	105	33	10	35.3
Stolen property	157	—	3	17	23	30	26	19	36	3	—	36.1
Forgery	722	1	48	231	167	103	64	44	50	11	3	27.4
Rape	488	—	8	242	148	57	27	5	1	—	—	24.9
Commercialized vice	125	—	3	24	26	29	17	14	9	2	1	31.6
Other sex offenses	64	—	4	28	20	5	3	2	—	1	1	—
Violating drug laws	1,063	—	29	128	177	200	165	132	177	47	8	34.9
Carrying and possessing weapons	25	—	1	8	8	2	4	1	1	—	—	—
Nonsupport or neglect	—	—	—	—	—	—	—	—	—	—	—	—
Violating liquor laws	1,530	1	29	178	233	262	251	192	252	100	32	36.2
Violating traffic laws	—	—	—	—	—	—	—	—	—	—	—	—
Violating national defense laws	1,125	—	170	288	206	194	147	55	52	12	1	27.5
Other offenses	1,030	—	64	261	196	149	141	104	88	25	2	29.8
State institutions[a]	41,240	31	7,632	11,061	7,299	5,076	3,727	2,544	2,692	879	299	26.3
Murder	1,617	1	150	316	264	234	222	136	179	88	27	31.7
Manslaughter	1,334	—	108	238	245	195	171	108	162	83	24	31.9
Robbery	4,764	4	997	1,763	953	509	273	134	112	15	4	23.9
Aggravated assault	2,929	1	324	665	538	415	368	252	236	90	40	29.4
Burglary	9,792	14	2,643	2,896	1,607	1,048	673	434	371	82	24	23.9

[a] Includes statistics covering year ending May 31 for Pennsylvania, and for Georgia, statistics for year ending March 31, 1947, adjusted to a calendar year basis; excludes statistics for Mississippi.

TABLE 4.6. Male Felony Prisoners Received from Court, by Type of Institution, Offense, and Age, for the United States, 1946 (*Continued*)
(Median not shown where base is less than 100)

Type of Institution and Offense	All Ages	Under 15 Years	15 to 19 Years	20 to 24 Years	25 to 29 Years	30 to 34 Years	35 to 39 Years	40 to 44 Years	45 to 54 Years	55 to 64 Years	65 and Over	Median Age
Larceny, except auto theft	7,444	2	1,620	2,094	1,261	840	615	437	438	109	28	25.0
Auto theft	2,692	2	911	959	438	206	104	37	33	1	1	22.3
Embezzlement and fraud	907	—	48	130	176	161	120	100	104	50	18	33.1
Stolen property	325	—	37	90	69	43	35	17	27	5	2	27.6
Forgery	2,960	1	226	639	635	453	344	258	297	88	19	29.8
Rape	1,839	2	248	507	332	236	176	119	143	53	23	27.4
Commercialized vice	64	—	1	6	8	15	8	16	5	4	1	—
Other sex offenses	1,185	1	65	127	154	156	151	148	226	101	56	38.0
Violating drug laws	183	—	11	29	36	37	21	19	23	6	1	32.1
Carrying and possessing weapons	372	—	68	102	60	48	34	22	30	5	3	26.3
Nonsupport or neglect	726	—	7	60	155	184	134	100	76	10	3	33.8
Violating liquor laws	310	—	6	38	43	47	46	46	57	17	10	37.3
Violating traffic laws	187	—	5	41	49	24	29	15	16	8	—	29.8
Violating national defense laws	5	—	—	3	1	—	1	—	—	—	—	—
Other offenses	1,605	3	157	358	275	225	202	146	157	64	18	30.2

SOURCE: Table 33, *Prisoners in State and Federal Prisons and Reformatories, 1946*, Bureau of the Census, U.S. Department of Commerce, Washington, 1948, pp. 46–47.

lished by the Federal Bureau of Prisons, which will publish more detailed data in the future.

The Prisoner's Antecedents, 1923, Bureau of the Census, U.S. Department of Commerce, Washington, 1929. This is the only extensive study made by the federal government with reference to the background of prisoners prior to their commitment to prison.

Uniform Crime Reports, Federal Bureau of Investigation, U.S. Department of Justice, Washington. These annual and semiannual bulletins have been published since 1929 and contain data compiled from cities, towns, and counties throughout the country with reference to persons arrested and their offenses.

CHAPTER 5

The Major Types of Offenders

All the mass data about prisoners obscure the picture of the criminal himself. We need to keep in mind that criminals are men—men with families and friends, men out of work and ill advised, men who staged a holdup under the influence of liquor, men driven by sexual impulses, greedy men, men in the depths of economic despair, men with false ambitions, all adjudged guilty in the courts of men, their misdeeds written down in the permanent records. Their good deeds —and there were probably many—are ignored. If the courts had been impressed with their good record, they probably would not have gone to prison.

Classification of Offenders

All scientific study tends to result in the classification and description of phenomena and criminology is no exception. When scientists in the fields of anthropology and psychiatry turned to a study of the criminal the merit of adjusting punishment to fit the offender seemed obvious. They soon emerged with definite classifications of offenders. The most notable series of classification were made by Italian scientists who, because they made their conclusions from actual observation of criminals, were called positivists. Of this group Lombroso, Garofalo, and Ferri have been the most significant.

LOMBROSO (1836–1909)

Slightly more than a century after Beccaria published his famous essay on *Crimes and Punishments*, which led to the classical school of penology,[1] Lombroso (in 1878) published the results of his first re-

[1] Cf. chap. 16, pp. 437–440.

search in criminal anthropology.[2] Lombroso was a prison physician and from his study he concluded that the criminal was a distinct anthropological type, possessing definite physical stigmata. Such a man was a "born criminal," an atavistic being, inferior in development to normal man; in fact the criminal reproduced in his person the ferocious instincts of primitive humanity and the lower animals. Subsequent research has resulted in the rejection of Lombroso's conclusions, but he must be credited with first directing the penologist's primary concern from the crime to the offender, an epoch-making fact in the annals of penology. [3]

Later Lombroso revised his point of view and recognized other types of criminals in addition to the "born" or "atavistic," namely, (1) the insane criminal, (2) the criminal by passion, and (3) the occasional criminal, with three subclassifications: (a) the pseudocriminal, (b) the habitual criminal, and (c) the criminaloid.

GAROFALO (1852–1934)

Garofalo, Italian jurist, differed from Lombroso, physician and anthropologist, in his classification of criminals. Garofalo maintained that in the main criminals are characterized by psychological rather than physical anomalies; that is, they are deficient in pity or in probity. These defectives, he believed, fall into four categories: (1) typical criminals, or murderers, (2) violent criminals, (3) criminals deficient in pity and probity, and (4) lascivious criminals.[4]

The grosser offenders, that is, the murderers who kill for egotistic motives (for brutal enjoyment or rape), he believed to be destitute of all moral sense and incapable of reformation; hence death was the only effective punishment for them. The violent offenders, whose acts are due to false notions of honor, necessity for vengeance, or traditional prejudices, he would have eliminated by "marooning" on an island or in a penal colony. Habitual criminals should be interred for life in an overseas penal colony. Sentences for youthful offenders and lascivious criminals should be indeterminate. For offenders deficient only in moral training or restraint, who commit only the less serious

[2] This was made available in German in 1881 in Lombroso's article, "Über den Ursprung das Wesen und die Bestrebungen der neuen anthropologish Kriminalistischen Schule in Italien," in *Zeitschrift für die gesamte Strafrechtwissenschaft*, vol. I (1881), no. I.

[3] Goring's study, *The English Convict*, published in 1913, showed by actual anthropological measurements that criminals vary little from the rank and file of the population.

[4] Raffaele Garofalo, *Criminology*, transl. by Robert W. Millar, Little, Brown, Boston, 1914, Part II, chap. 1.

violations of the sentiment, reparation rather than elimination should be the method of treatment.

Ferri (1856–1929)

According to Ferri there were five classes of criminals: the insane, the born, the habitual, the occasional, and the passionate.[5] Accepting the contributions of psychology and psychiatry, as well as those of sociology and anthropology, Ferri concluded that punishment should rest on the psychological motive prompting the criminal action.

Since all attempts to classify criminals according to their personal characteristics have proved relatively futile, the only significant way to classify them today is by the type of offense committed. Thus we may designate the criminals as murderers, sex offenders, thieves, bank robbers, habitual criminals, criminally insane, etc. What sort of men are these? Case studies cannot supply complete information but they will increase our understanding of the criminal. For crime is primarily a human problem—in particular, the problem of human beings in conflict with the law.

The Wisconsin Survey

The recent researches of Professor John L. Gillin and his graduate students at the University of Wisconsin have done much to fill in a great gap in our information about prisoners. Limiting their inquiry to three types of offenders, they studied 486 men in the Wisconsin prison population of approximately 1700. These included (1) all of the 128 sex offenders convicted of sodomy and rape. There were a few convicted of adultery who were excluded because the number was so small. (2) Of 108 men serving a life sentence, 92 were included, the 16 others being omitted only because of death during the period of study, serious illness, or their inability to speak and understand English. (3) An additional 266 of the 933 property offenders completed the group studied.[6]

These men were interviewed for the most part by graduate students at the university, although Dr. Gillin personally conducted some of the interviews, as well as supervising the whole project. From the prison records basic information with reference to the prisoner's offense, his trial and sentence, his physical, psychological, and psychiatric ratings upon admission, names of friends and relatives, and

[5] Enrico Ferri, *Criminal Sociology*, transl. by Kelley and Lisle, Little, Brown, Boston, 1917, pp. 138–139.
[6] John L. Gillin, *The Wisconsin Prisoner*, University of Wisconsin Press, Madison, 1946, pp. 4–5.

previous criminal records including the Federal Bureau of Investigation reports were available. This material was augmented by reports from social agencies, police, and parole officers from the communities in which the prisoner previously lived.[7]

As anyone who has done criminal research knows, all this information still seemed too sketchy to give any satisfactory picture of the prisoners' personalities. Hence the data were supplemented by life histories which were written by the prisoners who were willing to do so, and in every instance additional material was secured through a personal interview.

Because it has been generally believed that criminals seldom tell the truth, their stories were further checked by trained investigators who visited the communities where the prisoners lived. The field investigations provided little additional data, however, and in Professor Gillin's opinion they were not worth the effort and cost entailed. Surprisingly or not, the Wisconsin prisoners apparently were truthful about everything except the circumstances under which they committed their crimes. Here they seemed to rationalize. But with the exception of "a few pathological liars" they told the truth about facts unrelated to the crime. [8]

In order to obtain analogous data with reference to a comparable group of non-prisoners, the law-abiding brothers (all that were available) of 172 prisoners were interviewed and compared with their brothers in prison.

Dr. Gillin is probably unduly cautious when he warns us of the possible faults in the conclusions of the study. It is true of course that interpretations made by the interviewers may be faulty, and Gillin warns that the sample may not be representative.[9] From a statistical point of view, however, the group studied is a fair sample of the men in the Wisconsin prison. In many instances the data are more likely to be lacking than to be basically wrong or distorted. We shall summarize the major findings in our analysis of types of prisoners. But certain generalizations with reference to differentiations between prisoners and their non-prisoner brothers are important for us to keep in mind here.

The Wisconsin researchers concluded that there were 14 significant differences between the two groups. Some applied only to certain types of offenders. These we may summarize briefly:[10]

1. A significantly larger proportion of murderers left school at an earlier age than their brothers.

[7] *Ibid.*   [8] *Ibid.*, p. 6.   [9] *Ibid.*, pp. 7–8.   [10] *Ibid.*, pp. 21–25.

2. Twenty-five per cent of all prisoners went to work earlier than their non-prison brothers, and of murderers 40.7 per cent went to work earlier.

3. A significant proportion (33.3 per cent) of the prisoners thought they were their mothers' favorites whereas only 9.9 per cent of the brothers so considered themselves. This was not true in the case of the sex offenders however.[11]

4. Prisoners also had a considerably higher appreciation for their mothers than did their brothers, and this was markedly true of murderers, of whom 87.5 per cent (in contrast to 44 per cent of their brothers) had great appreciation for their mothers.[12]

5. Significantly less of all the prisoners (56 per cent) held a job for more than a year, in contrast to 75.1 per cent of their brothers, who held jobs for this length of time, although this difference did not apply to sex offenders.[13]

6. A somewhat smaller percentage (15.8) of the prisoners than of their brothers (26.4 per cent) were farmers. However, in the case of murderers the percentage of farmers for both the prisoner and his brother was higher. Property offenders, on the other hand, came from skilled trades more frequently than did their brothers.[14]

7. The property offenders indicated less stability on their jobs than did their brothers, as indicated by the number of job turnovers.[15]

8. A significantly larger percentage (46.3) of all prisoners had never married (27.3 per cent of their brothers had).[16]

9. But 27.5 per cent of the prisoners had been divorced or separated, in contrast to 4 per cent of the non-prisoner brothers. Domestic relations were thought to be a possible factor in their criminal conduct.[17]

10. Fifty-four per cent of the prisoners had disharmonious relationships with their wives in contrast to only 8.9 per cent among their non-prisoner brothers. Eighteen of the 92 murderers had killed their wives.[18]

11. There was greater disparity between the education of the prisoner and his wife than was true of the non-prisoner and his wife; i.e., 50.6 per cent of the wives of prisoners had more education than their husbands, whereas the brothers' wives were better educated than their

---

[11] *Ibid.*, and also Table 49.
[12] *Ibid.*, and also Table 50.
[13] *Ibid.*, and also Table 51.
[14] *Ibid.*, and also Table 52.
[15] *Ibid.*, and also Tables 53 and 54.
[16] *Ibid.*, and also Table 55.
[17] *Ibid.*, and also Table 56.
[18] *Ibid.*, and also Table 57.

husbands in only 31.8 per cent of the cases. This fact was considered a partial explanation for disharmony.[19]

12. A larger proportion (40.9 per cent) of prisoners than their brothers (24.0 per cent) had married women of different nationalities. Cultural differences were regarded as possible sources of serious friction.[20]

13. Differences in religious affiliation existed much more frequently in the case of prisoners and their wives (40.5 per cent) than was true of the brothers and their wives (11.9 per cent)—another likely source of disharmony in marital relationships.[21]

14. The property offenders had married women from a higher economic status in a significantly higher proportion (23.2 per cent) of cases than had their brothers (4.9 per cent). For others there was no great difference but among property offenders this factor may have contributed to marital disharmony.[22]

From their data Gillin and his assistants conclude that the brothers of the prisoners seldom had their economic security, their emotional satisfactions, or their personal safety thwarted or threatened to the same extent as had the prisoners. The conduct of both groups they believe to have been "born of the interaction of the innate constitution with life experiences." While in some instances the innate constitution played the greater role, they believe the life experiences of the prisoners were generally significant in precipitating their criminal behavior.[23]

The mainsprings of human conduct are not easy to measure. After these detailed individual case studies were concluded the authors modestly admitted that they could not weight the factors.[24] The Gillin study may, however, contain clues. Certainly the data from this research is important in pointing out the need for further case studies of prisoners with greater refinements in technique. At the same time they may be regarded as a contribution to the science of criminology. There have been so many brash statements with reference to criminals based on insufficient and scanty data that it is salutary to be reminded that behavior is a very complicated thing and that no simple formula can be applied in establishing causes of criminal conduct.

[19] *Ibid.*, and also Table 58.
[20] *Ibid.*, and also Table 59.
[21] *Ibid.*, and also Table 60.
[22] *Ibid.*, and also Table 61. In this author's opinion this circumstance may also have been an impetus to seeking illegal gains.
[23] *Ibid.*, p. 196.   [24] *Ibid.*, p. 197.

The research of Gillin and his assistants yields the definite conclusion that frustrating experiences have been factors producing the criminal, that situations which undermine the ego and destroy the self-esteem can cause disintegration of the personality and produce delinquent and criminal conduct. They assert that prison officials and persons dealing with offenders should recognize these conclusions, and that teachers and others responsible for developing youthful personalities should realize their important role in helping individuals find themselves.[25] We shall give specific conclusions from the Wisconsin survey along with other conclusions in the discussion of different types of offenders.

As we have already indicated and as everyone who deals in any capacity with crime or criminals knows, most offenders are property offenders. The vast majority of those whose offenses are reported, as well as those who get caught in the toils of the law, are thieves, robbers, burglars, forgers, and embezzlers. If Gillin is right these men are more likely to be skilled workers than their non-prisoner brothers but are characterized by high job mobility. They were married to women of a higher economic status in a significant number of cases. Thus the attempt to maintain a fairly high standard of living may be a factor in many economic crimes.

There have been many efforts to explain why men steal, rob, forge, and embezzle, which Barnes and Teeters have summarized succinctly by stating that need and greed cause most offenses against the property rights of others.[26] Like all simple explanations this cliché fails to get at the basic motivations of individuals who steal. One man may steal chiefly because he has easy access to money or materials placed in his charge. Another may work out an extensive plot to extort money, or carry out a perfect burglary in order to live in luxury otherwise impossible. Another may steal to pay for the medical expenses of a sick child, unaware of the social resources in the community which are available to meet such needs. Yet Gillin's study of Wisconsin prisoners showed that property offenders tend to come from better economic and social backgrounds than either sex offenders or murderers.[27] We must remember, however, that Gillin bases his conclusions on cases of men who were imprisoned at a time when welfare funds were

---

[25] Ibid., pp. 198–199.

[26] Harry E. Barnes and Negley K. Teeters, New Horizons in Criminology, Prentice-Hall, New York, rev. ed., 1949, p. 6. Cf. Thorsten Sellin, Research Memorandum on Crime in the Depression, Social Science Research Council, New York, 1937, for a summary of literature in the field.

[27] John L. Gillin, op. cit., p. 142.

generally available to meet the relief problems of all persons genuinely in need. It would be interesting to compare these men with a group of prisoners committed prior to 1930, when public opinion generally condemned the acceptance of relief on the part of able-bodied men.

Even though Gillin's study indicates that greed as well as need plays an important role in economic offenses, he maintains that the social importance placed upon achieving economic success in our culture rather than grave poverty has been an important factor in the criminality of the Wisconsin prisoner. It is true that most of the Wisconsin property offenders came from the lower economic classes, but it is also true that the majority of Wisconsin people living under similar economic conditions "did not steal, rob, break and enter, forge, or burn buildings."[28] This of course is not the whole story, as our survey of unpunished crimes indicates. For those who have failed to respect the property rights of others our educational and religious institutions must assume part of the blame. We have not impressed upon our young people the importance which property rights have in our whole culture, nor have we emphasized the major spiritual values in the development of our required educational curricula.

Case analyses of the Wisconsin prisoners show that factors other than need are important. Economic adversity, according to Gillin and his assistants, explained the personality disintegration of only a few of the men. Most of them had been demoralized by mental attitudes of defeatism, negativism, and inferiority. The economic situation provided a precipitating crisis which they were unable to meet.[29]

Embezzlers

The men who embezzle yield to what is a very easy temptation, that of taking for their own purposes money already legally in their possession and control. Embezzlers have always been previously trusted persons; in fact they are often so-called "solid citizens" with good reputations. Otherwise they would not have been entrusted with access to the funds in the first place.

As a matter of fact, most embezzlers do not really intend to steal. They usually "intend to return" the money they take but once started they find it hard to stop, and ordinarily the inspectors, auditors, or bank examiners catch up with them before they can replace the funds or after they have taken so much that replacement is impossible.[30]

[28] Ibid., p. 191. [29] Ibid., p. 195.
[30] Myron Stearns, "Embezzlement, the Easiest Crime," Reader's Digest, 48:73–75 (January, 1946). Condensed from Banking.

The bank clerk or cashier who handles thousands or hundreds of thousands of dollars every day is unquestionably seriously tempted. Enormous amounts of money are continually in his hands while he ordinarily draws but a very modest salary. At the same time his contact with large sums may easily influence him "to lead a banker's life." The first step of the embezzler is usually to "shingle" accounts a few dollars at a time. Embezzlers often shingle from nonindustrial corporations, where there are fewer audits on accounts from day to day.[31] Others may take larger amounts, with the expectation of returning the money before anyone notices the loss.

A post-office employee in Utah, for example, took $400 from the safe to play the stock market, in order to pay off some debts. He had some "inside information" and hoped to retrieve his finances by "taking a flier." He sincerely expected to return all that he "borrowed" within a couple of weeks. During those two weeks the federal post-office inspector arrived in town and immediately, detected what he had done. The offense was serious and the man could easily have been sent to prison. Because of his own and his family's reputation, however, he was not sentenced but placed on probation. Actually, this man justified the opportunity extended him and has never since had any difficulties with the law.[32]

While most embezzlers cannot live within their incomes, some embezzlers are in the upper income groups. Myron Stearns reports on a president of a gas company who received $75,000 a year but even so could not pay his debts and took $200,000 of his company's funds.[33] Greed rather than need was thus the basic motivation.[34]

An educator who was the head of a western state teachers' organization similarly yielded to the desire to improve his finances, taking sizable amounts, several hundred dollars each month appropriated from the teachers' annual dues, which he charged to "postage." He did not squander the money, but bought farms and other property. The organization's auditor had never checked up on the validity of the expenditures and these illegal extractions went on for years. Eventually the man became seriously ill and his successor began checking into the accounts. There was much more outgoing mail, he found, than there had been under his predecessor, whereas the bills for postage amounted to less than one-third of the previously alleged postage

[31] Based on data obtained by the author from interviews with embezzlers.
[32] Case interviewed by the author; identification changed to preserve anonymity of offender.
[33] Myron Stearns, op. cit.
[34] Harry E. Barnes and Negley K. Teeters, op. cit.

bills. By that time the "defaulter" was on his deathbed and no charges were brought against him. It was generally agreed by the officials of the organization that exposure at that time would not punish the culprit, would bring shame to his family, and would bring dishonor to the organization. There was not even any attempt to get the heirs to repay the organization.[35]

A much better evidence of embezzlement by well-to-do persons occurred during the thirties when a western state was rocked by a "bond scandal." The state auditor had turned over to one of the leading bankers and his son several million dollars in bonds and in return had received a set of bogus bonds. Both of the bankers, father and son, were highly respected citizens and their behavior nonplused the good people of the state. Nevertheless public sentiment was outraged and father and son received two of the highest sentences ever imposed—the son's for 600 years, the father's for 900 years.[36] Crushed by his loss of status the father committed suicide before his sentence began. The son, a graduate of a well-known eastern university, entered prison. The class aspect of justice was soon to manifest itself, however, for 11 years later he was released on parole.

Offenders Against Banking Laws

During the depression, legislation affecting banking greatly increased in rigidity and banking regulations were much more strictly enforced. In consequence, many bankers languished in prisons for offenses which either would have been overlooked or would not have been considered illegal a few years previously. Obviously it was sound social policy to alter the banking laws for the protection of the depositors' funds. Laxities in regulating banks had undermined an important segment of our national economy.[37] However, this precipitate alteration in the enforcement of laws created serious offenses overnight out of conduct previously either accepted or winked at. Some bankers were indeed behaving in ways which had to be curbed but many bankers were not aware of all the technicalities involved in the new law enforcement and some relatively innocent men went to prison.

A banker in a midwestern state, for example, had always looked

[35] The data in this case were obtained confidentially. It seems quite likely that many such cases exist.

[36] These absurd sentences were based on conviction on several counts.

[37] Cf. Paul F. Gemmill and Ralph H. Blodgett, *Current Economic Problems*, Harper, New York, 1947, pp. 195–197.

after his wife's financial investments. She had been ill for several years and had been unable to attend to her business affairs personally. During her final illness this man was so upset that he forgot some essentials pertaining to his wife's affairs. The day following her death he went to the bank and performed certain routine tasks which should have been looked after some days earlier. Obviously this was against the law for he was now handling an estate without any proper authority to act. A bank examiner who came in a few days later reported the banker for illicit use of his dead wife's funds. Because banks were being rigidly checked on during the depression, both the examiners and the court were also rigid in their interpretation of the law and the man went to prison for ten years. His wife's brother was nationally famous but could not save him from this disgrace. Here a man was caught in the technicalities of the law with no malice of intent whatsoever. He was heir to half the money he was handling. Public sentiment, however, was strongly in favor of the strict bank laws because so many persons had lost heavily in the era in which banks had so generally ignored the safety of their depositors.[38]

There are of course bankers who intentionally juggle figures to their own advantage. Before the enactment of federal insurance for depositors' accounts the depositors took serious losses in such cases. Today insurance regulations protect deposits up to $10,000.

A recent rash of bank embezzlements in western Pennsylvania and adjoining West Virginia would seem to indicate that better enforcement of banking audits might disclose a much higher proportion of embezzling bankers. During a period of 13 months $3,364,087 was embezzled from seven banks.[39] The first shortage was noticed in September, 1950, when $1,300,000 was revealed to be missing after the cashier of the bank shot and killed himself. Two of the embezzlers were bank presidents in the same Pittsburgh suburb (New Kensington). One was indicted for embezzling $600,000 and the other is reported to have embezzled $550,000.[40] While a bank teller in Parkersburg, West Virginia, took $363,000 another in Indiana, Pennsylvania, took $148,479.[41] One cashier literally stole bank funds to "buy" the bank through a dummy outside investor allegedly from Cleveland. This investor was found to be nonexistent.[42]

In each of the above cases the men involved were respected mem-

[38] Case data in author's files.
[39] Pittsburgh *Post-Gazette*, October 1, 1951, p. 1, and October 27, 1951, p. 2.
[40] *Ibid.*, September 14, 1951, p. 1.
[41] *Ibid.*, September 25, 1951, p. 1.
[42] *Ibid.*, August 16, 1951, p. 1.

bers of the community and were taking an active part in local civic and social affairs.

The Habitual Offender

Occasionally a man with a serious record makes a notable readjustment. Criminologists have reason to believe that readjustment takes place much more readily when the ex-convict is given an opportunity to regain the respect of his neighbors and his own self-respect. The novelist Karin Michaelis tells a remarkable story about a cultivated burglar, Hans Petersen, who specialized in looting wealthy homes of their rare antiques. He had spent 20 of his 40 years in prison and when he was released started again to acquire antiques in his old fashion. His defense was that people had promised to help him to go straight but no one had helped him beyond giving him an old pair of trousers. Miss Michaelis became interested in him and applied for a pardon, which was granted him. He arrived looking "like a college professor" and was given a small bungalow in her garden. Eventually he opened a rare book shop with capital supplied him by friends he made under Miss Michaelis' sponsorship. He later married an attractive woman and set up his own establishment.[43]

When the Germans came to Denmark, they sought out Hans Petersen for his previous skills. All of his new friends were distressed to think he turned Nazi. Petersen wore a fine German uniform, but it eventually developed that he was plotting against the Nazis. The time came when the underground planned to seize a Nazi airplane parts factory. Then Hans Petersen cleared with the underground, met them at the factory, unlocked the doors, and helped set the fuses himself. He alone did not escape but in this act of patriotism against the common enemy cleared his name. He achieved real respect from his community and was willing to sacrifice not only his temporary reputation but his life for its advantage.

That some unfortunate people may be the victims of circumstances is apparent to almost everyone. When a man becomes a repeater, a recidivist, or a habitual criminal, there is generally no such kindly solicitude as was extended to Hans Petersen. Usually it is held that the habitual offender has not profited from his mistakes but is instead an avowed enemy of the state, a *real* criminal. The general reaction against the man who commits several offenses has been written into our "habitual criminal" laws.

[43] Karin Michaelis, "The Reformation of H. P., Burglar Extraordinary," *Reader's Digest*, 48:107–110 (May, 1946).

In 1926 New York enacted what were popularly known as Baumes Laws. These made life sentences compulsory for persons who were known to have committed four felonies. Provisions of this kind had been incorporated in the laws of a much earlier time, both in this country and in Europe.[44] Many states actually had such laws, but they had fallen into disuse. The Baumes Laws promoted their revival and stimulated new legislation. In fact, within two years other states adopted similar provisions or so revised old laws that their stringency was increased.[45] In some states life sentences were imposed for fourth offenses; in Kansas, for the third felony.[46] In all cases progressive penalties were enacted for second and third convictions.

The criminologist immediately raises two questions: "Who are these habitual offenders?" "Are they different from other offenders?" Hence the decision to study a representative group of habitual criminals sentenced to life imprisonment under the Kansas habitual criminal act. The Kansas law, adopted in 1927, provides that a person convicted of a second offense be given double the sentence for his first conviction and if convicted a third time, a life sentence.[47] During the year beginning June 30, 1930, and ending June 30, 1931, the 15 men sentenced under this act were interviewed by Sam R. Carter in a study of the history and operation of the Kansas habitual offender law.[48]

Since these men constituted the total number sentenced during one year under the provisions of the act relating to those who had committed three or more offenses, they presumably give a fair picture of habitual criminals in Kansas. In connection with the study all of the judges in the 36 active judicial districts in the state were asked to comment on the effectiveness of the law's operation, however, and it seemed obvious from their replies that the majority of the courts did not enforce the mandatory clause of the law.[49] These prisoners thus represented only the cases in which the law was enforced. In any event they were habitual criminals.

With these limitations in view we may examine the 15 cases. Thir-

[44] Cf. Mabel A. Elliott, *Conflicting Penal Theories in Statutory Criminal Law*, University of Chicago Press, Chicago, 1931, chap. 10. Cf. also Boris Brasol, *The Elements of Crime*, Oxford University Press, New York, 1927. This topic is discussed in greater detail in a latter section. Cf. chap. 15, pp. 423–424.

[45] These were Florida, New Jersey, North Dakota, Oregon, South Dakota, Vermont, and Louisiana. Cf. Sam R. Carter, "The History and Operation of the Habitual Offender Law in Kansas," unpublished Master's thesis, University of Kansas library, 1935. (This study was made under the direction of the author.)

[46] *Laws of Kansas*, 1927, chap. 1, ser. 1, 2, 3, p. 247.

[47] *Ibid.*   [48] Sam R. Carter, op. cit.   [49] *Ibid.*

teen of the men were guilty of offenses against property; one was convicted for "intent to do great bodily harm" and one for persistent liquor law violation.

Those committing offenses against property included 6 convicted on charges of robbery, 3 on charges of larceny, 3 on charges of burglary, and 1 on charges of forgery. All of the men except 1 had been convicted more than twice before; 5 had been convicted of 3 previous offenses, 4 had been convicted 4 times, and 1 had been convicted 8 times. Prior arrests, on the other hand, ranged from 2 to 11. These habitual offenders thus showed a propensity to commit a variety of crimes.[50]

Although this group is statistically too small to warrant any sweeping conclusions, there is no doubt that the men were pretty well habituated to a life of crime, for each had an average of over four felonies to his credit. Two of the men were especially dangerous; they were actually caught cooking a quantity of dynamite (which had been smuggled in) on the prison stove while working in the kitchen. This "nitro-soup," as it is known in prison parlance, was to be used to blow up the prison but the plot was foiled. These men were caught while the interviews were in process and since they were put into solitary confinement could not be interviewed.[51] Earlier one of the two men had insisted he was not guilty of the offense for which he was indicted but had been convicted on his past record.

Seven of the men pleaded "guilty" at the time of their trial, but four of the eight who pleaded "not guilty" admitted their guilt later to Mr. Carter. These admissions reinforce Gillin's conclusion that prisoners are unexpectedly truthful![52] However, the men knew when they talked to Mr. Carter that the truth would not hurt them. Three of them stated they committed the crimes because they were in need of funds —because they were out of work. Four of them insisted they were not guilty but were convicted by circumstances; 1 claimed he was convicted by false testimony, 1 insisted he was "framed," and the other 2 insisted they were convicted on circumstantial evidence. All had criminal records, however. At the same time it is probably true that a man with a record has less chance of proving his innocence than a man indicted for the first time. One prisoner, a Negro, insisted that he was guilty of only two offenses and a check made of state prison and F.B.I.

[50] *Ibid.*, pp. 40–41. Norval Morris' study of 270 confirmed offenders in Great Britain showed that 60 per cent committed more than one type of crime and that many recidivists committed both sex and property offenses. Cf. Norval Morris, *The Habitual Criminal*, Harvard University Press, Cambridge, 1951, pp. 360–366.

[51] *Ibid.*   [52] John L. Gillin, *op. cit.*, p. 6.

records gave no evidence that he had ever served more than one sentence previous to his conviction under the habitual criminal act.

Only one of the men said the offense was his own fault in admitting his guilt. Practically all blamed other people or their home circumstances for their criminal careers. And to a large extent they were right. Most of them either had unfortunate home circumstances, were maladjusted at school, or were vocationally maladjusted. As habitual criminals they had served several sentences in either industrial schools and reformatories or penitentiaries.[53] From the various studies made by Glueck and others only a few of the men would seem to be markedly dangerous or markedly different from the general run of recidivists who make up the majority of our convicted criminals. A blanket habitual criminal law based on a number of offenses does not necessarily apply to the most dangerous offenders.

The Sex Offender[54]

Two recent studies of male sex behavior raise the question of whether the prisoners who are sex offenders are much more guilty of illicit behavior than unselected civilian groups. These are (1) the famous Kinsey report and (2) the research of Hohman and Schaffner on army draftees. The much-discussed Kinsey report indicates that premarital and extramarital sex relations are common among men in all walks of life. This study, based upon a survey of 12,214 cases, showed that educational and social level were correlated with both the extent and the frequency of such experience. Thus 98 per cent of the boys who had not gone beyond the eighth grade had had premarital sex experience, 84 per cent of those who went into high school but not beyond had had such experience, and 67 per cent of those who went to college had had some premarital sex experience.[55] The highest frequency of such sex experience was among the lowest educational level, where the average was 3 times a week during the late teens; frequencies for the high school group were 1.5 per week and for the college group once in 3 weeks. There were some in the college group who had had only 1 premarital sex experience.[56] According to this research, except for the 15 per cent which goes to college, most males actually accept premarital sex intercourse as suitable and expected behavior.[57]

[53] Sam R. Carter, op. cit.   [54] Women sex offenders are treated in chap. 9.
[55] Alfred C. Kinsey, Wardell B. Pomeroy, and Clyde E. Martin, Sexual Behavior in the Human Male, Saunders, Philadelphia, 1948, pp. 552–553, 557.
[56] Ibid., p. 10.   [57] Ibid., p. 559.

Information as to the extramarital sex relations of men was more difficult to obtain than the premarital data, apparently because of fear of social consequences. About 40 per cent of men with a high school and college education admitted such infidelities; moreover for those in the upper age groups the high school and college-educated groups indulged in more extramarital excursions than did those from the lower educational levels. Kinsey and his associates are inclined to think the men they interviewed tended to cover up their extramarital experience and that approximately 50 per cent have had some sex contacts outside of marriage, even though there is little social acceptance for such behavior.[58]

Homosexual activity, which is so universally condemned, Kinsey and his associates found to be much more common than is ordinarily believed. According to their figures, 27.3 per cent of young unmarried males and 38.7 per cent of the single men between 36 and 40 years of age had such relations.[59] Kinsey rightly contends that if one-fourth to one-third of the male population actually engages occasionally in such experiences, the young boy who is ostracized or severely punished for discovery in a lone experience is unreasonably condemned. They point out that 20 to 30 per cent of the unmarried males might be so arrested, but that these men are not necessarily social menaces. There are in fact many gradations of homosexuality. Some persons are predominantly homosexual whereas some who are relatively heterosexual have had homosexual experience. In any case homosexual tendencies are markedly increased by institutional segregation and by the very prisons where homosexuals may be sentenced.[60]

Sodomy, though much less prevalent than homosexuality, is estimated to occur (according to the Kinsey report) among approximately 6 per cent of the total population. It is much higher in rural areas than elsewhere and is highest among the college-level rural group, chiefly because such contacts are available in rural areas.[61] Incest, on the other hand, despite the Freudian's insistence on its general prevalence, was found to exist scarcely at all, except during early boyhood.[62]

Dr. Hohman and Dr. Schaffner in 1947 published an earlier account of the sex experiences of 4664 unmarried draftees. During the psy-

[58] Ibid., chap. 19.   [59] Ibid., p. 261.
[60] Ibid., p. 664. Cf. also chap. 24, "Prison Discipline," section on "Sex Offenses in Prison."
[61] Ibid., p. 262.
[62] Kinsey in fact condemns the psychoanalysts who interpret all mankind on the basis of their patients. Ibid., p. 558.

chiatric examinations given when they were inducted into the United States Army these men were questioned with reference to their previous sex life, if any. Of the total, 500 were Negroes, all of whom with the exception of 7 had had sex relations by the time they were 21. Three of the 7 virgins were homosexuals.[63]

Of the 4164 white men in the sample, 20.6 per cent were virgins, with the ratio of urban men virginal 20.8 per cent, of rural men 19.5 per cent. Most of the 79.4 per cent of white inductees who had had sex relations ranged from 21 to 29 years of age; 0.57 per cent were under 21, 4.6 per cent were past 29, and approximately 84 per cent ranged in age from 21 to 26.[64]

Classified according to the time of first sex experience, 57.3 per cent had had their first sexual intercourse by the time they were 16 and 63 per cent by the time they were 18. Before they reached 21, 92.8 per cent had indulged in illicit sex relations. Moreover, 80 per cent of this group had had sex relations with "nice" girls, that is, girls whom they would have been willing to marry.[65]

Despite all this evidence of the existence of widespread illicit sex relations they are nevertheless condemned both by mores and by law. Yet notwithstanding the relative hypocrisy indicated in the difference between the sex standards and practice of Americans, few people regard promiscuity with any favor, and, as we all know, women who offend the mores are condemned and punished more severely than men. In spite of the frequency of extramarital sexual lapses, men as lawmakers have expressed their revulsion against certain types of sex offenders—rapists, homosexuals, and persons guilty of incest—with severe punishments. In some states rape is considered as heinous an offense as murder, and prisoners themselves tend to ostracize those serving sentences for rape as depraved and despicable creatures.

The social opprobrium attached to incest cases is even greater than that inherent in the law. For this reason, in Wisconsin, at least, there is a tendency to convict the men who have committed incest of rape in order to assess a heavier penalty.[66] Of the 178 sex offenders who were studied in Wisconsin there were 26 cases of sodomy, 25 cases of statutory rape, and 127 cases of rape.

SODOMY AND HOMOSEXUALITY

By statute in Wisconsin sodomy consists in bestiality (sex relations with animals), homosexuality, and unnatural forms of sex relations

[63] Leslie B. Hohman and Bertram Schaffner, "The Sex Lives of Unmarried Men," *American Journal of Sociology*, 52:289–294 (May, 1947).
[64] *Ibid.*   [65] *Ibid.*   [66] John L. Gillin, *op. cit.*, p. 116.

generally known as perversions. There were 20 cases of such perverts among the Wisconsin prisoners surveyed.

The Freudian psychoanalysts and sexologists have held that homosexuals have their root in the sexual feelings a boy has for his mother which he does not shed with maturity.[67] Freud contends in fact that the organic heredity does not of itself establish any sexual barriers between mother and child. A child learns to condition his sex impulses according to the cultural pattern.[68]

Confidential testimony in a famous case in which a small boy was murdered by two wealthy young men is said to have revealed that the boy was killed during sexual abuse, but this testimony was never released to the press.[69] Here the pattern of homosexuality seems to have been accompanied by sadism of an obviously brutal variety. There has been much aroused public sentiment on sex criminals because of the publicity attending certain sex murders. Actually, though the few cases have produced reactions of horror and fear, the danger is not great.[70]

To detect and detain brutal sex offenders before they commit their distressing offenses is not easy. Certain types of criminals, those suffering from mental deficiency or paresis, are easy to diagnose, but the "obsessive-compulsive" type may commit a savage sex offense or sex murder without evidencing a certifiable mental disorder. Legal and medical definitions are still too much at variance to allow for a workable medico-legal definition of "insanity" and the institutionalization of the potentially dangerous sex offender.[71] On the other hand, the relatively normal character of many sex offenders points to the need for better sex education and more wholesome recreational facilities, and better training in controlling sex impulses.

The Wisconsin sodomists, as mentioned above, represented a wide range of types and included cases of bestiality and homosexuality. The I.Q.'s of the sodomists ranged from a low of 40 to 49 to an upper limit of 110 to 119.[72] Those convicted of bestiality were for the most part

[67] See Edward E. Mayer, "The Sex Deviate," *Pennsylvania Medical Journal*, 53:32–37 (January, 1950), for a summary of psychiatric and psychoanalytical theory concerning homosexuality.

[68] Cf. Sigmund Freud, *New Introductory Lectures on Psychoanalysis*, Norton, New York, 1933. Cf. also William H. Perloff, "Roles of Hormones in Human Sexuality," *Psychosomatic Medicine*, 12:00 (May–June, 1949).

[69] This is confidential information obtained from a medical witness.

[70] Cf. Howard Whitman, *Terror in the Streets*, Dial, New York, 1951, for an account of the public (and Mr. Whitman's) reaction to current sex murders.

[71] Ira S. Wile, "Society and Sex Offenders," *Survey Graphic*, 26:569–572 (November, 1937).

[72] John L. Gillin, *op. cit.*, Table 22, p. 218.

low grade in intelligence whereas the homosexuals tended to be of average or superior intelligence. In most cases of overt homosexuality, Gillin concludes, men who were homosexual possessed physical and mental traits which repelled women, or had been seduced early in life, or could not afford either to marry or to pay for illicit heterosexual relationships. The majority were already more or less demoralized and had at the same time a history of emotional frustration, along with stimulations to perversion in their environment.[73]

Men who lead a restricted social life and have most of their contacts with members of their own sex are more likely to become homosexuals than those who have greater association with the opposite sex. Homosexuality is a problem in prisons, as is discussed in Chapter 24. But it is also a problem in theological seminaries, in boys' schools, and in other isolated sex groups. In general there is less overt homosexuality in isolated women's groups because the sex drives of most women are less imperious. But homosexuality is a problem among women criminals even though it is less extensive.

INCEST CASES

Those who committed incest among the survey group of Wisconsin prisoners tended to be men of low I.Q. and were more likely than the sodomists to be farmers or skilled laborers. The incest cases were said to be more apathetic emotionally. Fifty-one per cent had an I.Q. of less than 70. In 53.3 per cent of the cases there was marital disharmony but to a lesser degree than among the other types of sex offenders. It has been generally known that incest cases usually involve young and inexperienced girls who are the victims of their parents, stepparents, or older male relatives. To what extent incest exists undiscovered we do not know but because of the social disapproval probably a far greater number of offenders go unpunished than are ever convicted. As we have previously mentioned, one striking fact from the study of incest cases showed that not all of those guilty of this offense were charged with incest, but many were charged with rape.

STATUTORY RAPE CASES

In fact, 46 of the 89 Wisconsin statutory rape cases were really incest cases. This discrepancy seems to be accounted for largely because a severer punishment was possible if the sex offender was indicted under such a charge.[74] According to Gillin it is easier to secure a conviction in Wisconsin on a rape charge than on an incest charge,

[73] Ibid., pp. 97–107.   [74] Ibid.

despite the fact that the penalty for rape may be greater. The sentence for incest is 2 to 10 years, whereas the sentence for statutory rape is from 1 to 35 years or a fine of $200.[75] Incest is apparently so tabooed by the average jury that there is reluctance to exact any but the severest penalty.

Statutory rape does not involve force; it consists in sex relations with young women under age and includes all cases under 18 years of age in Wisconsin. Of the 89 rapists, information on the social and economic background was available for only 44. For 34 legitimate sex relations were not possible at the time; 15 were single, 2 were widowers, 4 were divorced or separated, and 13 although married were denied sex relations because of incompatibility, health, disharmony, or pregnancy of the wife. Most of the men convicted of rape came from bad home situations which provided them no acquaintance with acceptable moral standards. Although these facts do not excuse the seduction of young women they were nevertheless apparently operative in inducing the men to seek illicit sex outlets. Twelve of the 44 men were under the influence of drink at the time the offense occurred—further evidence that alcoholism is a factor in other crimes.[76] Most of the men were mature (86 per cent were over 30), but only 2 corresponded to the popular notion of the "senile rapists" who lure young children into sex relations.[77]

The *Report of the Mayor's Committee for the Study of Sex Offenders in New York City*[78] shows a striking rise in rape cases with a rise in the business index. Von Hentig points out that there is also an increase in the marriage rate at such times and that it may be true that sexual urges are greater in times of prosperity.[79] He is not the first to urge this interpretation; Parmalee held in his book published in 1918 that the intemperate use of alcohol and riotous amusements are both more common in prosperity and these give rise to an increase in sexual crimes as well as other crimes against persons.[80]

FORCIBLE RAPE

Forcible rape is a very serious charge and only 14 of the 128 Wisconsin sex offenders were convicted of it. After interviewing the men

[75] It is difficult to consider a fine of $200 as commensurate with a possible 35-year sentence, obviously.

[76] Cf. chap. 7.

[77] Ibid., pp. 119–120.

[78] New York, 1942, p. 39, quoted by Hans von Hentig, *Crime: Causes and Conditions*, McGraw-Hill, New York, 1947, p. 223.

[79] Ibid.

[80] Maurice Parmalee, *Criminology*, Macmillan, New York, 1918, pp. 77–79.

those conducting the research concluded that only 4 of the cases were in fact forced, but that the girls' testimony had been accepted without much investigation by the court. (This conclusion was not verified.) In several instances the men were young foreigners who had accepted the sex standards of groups with which they were associated and did not know they were under the influence of the "lower elements of the American community." Several of these rapists had very low I.Q.'s, but the intelligence ratings of 2 of them were thought to have been low because of their inability to speak English.

In one case a young farm boy of Polish extraction with an I.Q. of 61 (whose formal education stopped at 9 years of age) became involved with a girl he met at dance halls and skating rinks. The girl, whom he insisted he jilted, filed a complaint against him because she was furious at his "letting her down."[81]

On the whole the male sex offenders in the Wisconsin prison came from the most sordid economic and social backgrounds. Frequently the researchers found that the prisoners' physical disabilities were apparently factors in their failure to make normal and socially sanctioned sex adjustment. For those who had married there was usually a problem of marital disharmony. A few of the rapists were actually so ignorant they did not realize their behavior was illegal, since it was characteristic of the cultural groups with which they associated. In fact, some of the young men apparently had achieved status in their groups by reason of their illicit sex experience, which had established their claims to manliness and virility!

The whole problem of sex offenses presents many difficult angles. The double standard condones the patron of prostitution and condemns the prostitute. Illicit sex behavior while obviously not commended exacts little penalty for the man if he is "discreet" and confines his attention to prostitutes or to those adult women who are willing to yield to his embraces. At the same time society is horrified by rape and sex crimes committed against children or young persons under the age of consent.

Brutal sex crimes, especially forcible rape as a prelude to murder, are especially condemned, as we have mentioned. Most sex murderers, however, are psychopathic, and the murder itself may be incidental or accidentally involved in the sexual offense where the motive of the individual has been to ravish the victim. Sometimes violent sex murders stem from social and racial barriers to marriage. Sometimes they are the result of such extremely psychopathic personalities as that of

[81] John L. Gillin, op. cit., p. 130.

William Heirens, who perpetrated three brutal sex murders while pursuing the relatively calm life of a student at the University of Chicago. This young man was diagnosed as a hysterical personality. He had no psychosis but he was almost completely insensitive emotionally with a deep sexual perversion.[82]

Murderers

In no phase of crime is there so much popular interest as in murder. We have already discussed sex murderers, who are among the most perverted types of persons who kill. Much more space is allotted proportionally in the press to murders than to other crimes whatever the variey of murder. In fact, people in general seem to derive a certain horrified fascination from probing into the motives and mysteries of murder, as is amply evidenced in the best-selling detective novels. Since many other crimes involve as much cunning and planning as murder, we are forced to believe that the nature of crime accounts for part of the interest.[83]

Psychologists and criminologists also seem to have developed more theories and conducted more case studies with reference to murders than for other types of adult offenses. Perhaps it is easier to understand why men steal. Many people unquestionably are made jealous or are thwarted and frustrated by their associates, for whom they entertain intense dislike. They may even retaliate in all sorts of "knife-in-the-back" tactics. But they seldom reach the extreme of taking the life of the disliked person, however much they may contribute to his economic and social ruin. What is it that drives certain men to murder?

Unlike other offenders, murderers come from all walks of life, at least so far as prisoners are concerned. The murder rate is not significantly less among farmers and in rural areas than in the city. Jealousy and bitter hatred are not restricted to certain occupations or residence groups.[84]

In Gillin's survey of Wisconsin prisoners murderers were more

[82] Cf. Foster Kennedy, Harry R. Hoffman, and William H. Haines, "Psychiatric Study of William Heirens," *Journal of Criminal Law and Criminology*, 38:311–341 (November–December, 1947).

[83] Cf., for example, Ted Collins, ed., *New York Murders* (by Angelica Gibbs and others), Duell, Sloan and Pearce, New York, 1944, and Stewart H. Holbrook, *Murder Out Yonder*, Macmillan, New York, 1945. For detective stories consult weekly reviews of the *Saturday Review of Literature* and local newsstands. For murder stories consult files of any newspaper.

[84] Cf. *Uniform Crime Reports*, Annual Bulletin, 1950, pp. 74, 84.

frequently found to be foreign born than were robbers, burglars, and larcenists, however.[85] In their marginal status as immigrants the foreign-born unquestionably experience many frustrations. This fact may account for their high rate.[86] The Wisconsin murderers, also, had been pushed into the competitive economic arena to add to the family income at an early age. They were more frequently the first or the only child than was true of those committing other types of offenses. They had to leave school early to go to work, a large number were unskilled laborers (more or less inevitably), and they had a less steady employment history than the sex offenders.[87]

On the other hand the Wisconsin murderers had fewer previous arrests than other offenders. We have long known rather generally that the murderer frequently has had no previous criminal record when he commits a capital offense. In fact, prison authorities have often agreed that murderers represent the best type of prisoner, since their offense is often their sole conflict with law. Many of these men are deeply penitent for their act of fury and cause little or no trouble in the prison.[88] In Wisconsin, however, the most emotionally unstable murderers are committed to insane hospitals, hence are out of the picture, as may be true in other states.

From their analysis of the case histories of murderers, Gillin and his assistants conclude that murderers are basically frustrated persons who lack capacity to make a normal adjustment. Most of them have a history of early emotional maladjustment and have met crises too severe for them to meet sanely.[89] These conclusions are not new, but Gillin's findings reinforce them.

Gillin also draws some further conclusions:

1. Murderers tend to be organically defective persons, by heredity, disease, or accident, and hence are lacking in the physical vigor, nervous ability, or mental capacity required to make a satisfactory life adjustment.

2. The environment of murderers has limited their ability for self-support and economic adjustment.

3. Early emotional experiences have established deep-seated grudges, irritability, and tendencies to compensate for frustrations.

[85] John L. Gillin, op. cit., p. 9.
[86] Cf. Mabel A. Elliott and Francis E. Merrill, Social Disorganization, Harper, New York, 3rd ed., 1950, chap. 28.
[87] John L. Gillin, op. cit., pp. 9–10.
[88] Former Warden M. F. Amrine of the Kansas State Penitentiary has often spoken of these characteristics of murderers.
[89] John L. Gillin, op. cit., p. 7.

4. The educational background of murderers is insufficient to insure well-developed personalities.

5. Many murderers were addicted to behavior condemned by the community such as excessive drinking, sexual promiscuity, or violent behavior.

6. The murderer's frustrations have fostered antisocial methods of satisfying his ego.

7. Disrupted relationships with spouse or lover have frequently resulted in the murderer's emotional upheaval.

8. A crisis has precipitated the explosive conduct of the individual.

9. In more than 30 per cent of the cases the murderers were drunk or had been drinking at the time of the murder. An additional 26 per cent either were insane when the murder was committed or became so after they were imprisoned. A further 6 per cent were psychopathic. Four murderers were both insane and drunk, and in 1 case the murderer was drunk and psychopathic. Most of the others were temporarily upset or committed murder in connection with a robbery or sex crime.[90] The Wisconsin survey, in fact, lends a great deal of support to the popular notion that murderers are insane at the time they commit their offenses.

KANSAS MURDERERS

In connection with his study of habitual offenders in Kansas, Sam R. Carter made a brief comparative study of 20 murderers; these men constituted the total number committed to the Kansas State Penitentiary for this charge during the period June 30, 1930, to June 30, 1931. Of this group of murderers 14 were first offenders, 4 were second offenders, 1 was a fourth-time offender, and 1 had a fifth offense to his debit.[91] Nine of these men had never been arrested, much less convicted, before they committed the murder for which they were serving sentence. Five had been arrested once before; 2 had been arrested 3 times; 3, 3 times; and 1, 6 times.

Since the professional criminal usually has several aliases this item was checked and 15 of the group had no aliases; 1 man had 1 alias, 3 had 2 aliases, and 1 had 5 aliases. So far as these data furnish any information, we may conclude that 14 of the men were not habitual criminals as indicated by either past offenses or aliases and that 6 had some previous serious record, with 5 of them having aliases.[92]

So far as social data are concerned, 17 of the men were white, 3 were Negroes. Twelve were legal citizens of Kansas, 5 of them natives

90 *Ibid.*, pp. 86–87.   91 Sam R. Carter, *op. cit.*, pp. 70–73.   92 *Ibid.*

to the state; 8 were transients. The average educational achievement was 8 years' schooling although 5 men had not completed the sixth grade. There were a high school graduate and a medical school graduate in the group. The occupations of the murderers ranged as follows:[93]

Occupation	Number
Common laborer	4
Farmer	4
Mechanic	4
Butcher	2
Schoolboy	3
Cook	1
Shoemaker	1
Physician	1

Eleven were not employed, however, at the time of the murder. This circumstance may or may not have been a factor in their crime. We have no data on the family interactions of these murderers; only 8 of the 20 were married. So far as religious affiliation goes, 8 professed no belief in religion and 3 classified themselves "Protestant" without affiliation—seeming to indicate that there was no serious religious influence in their lives. On the other hand 4 were Methodists, 2 were Catholics, and 1 each belonged to the Baptist, Christian, and Presbyterian denominations.[94]

The murderers were less willing to admit their guilt than were the habitual offenders; only 9 pleaded guilty whereas 11 pleaded self-defense.[95]

A number of other studies give us further data on killers. In his book *Homicide in the United States* H. C. Brearley has summarized most of the material on "slayers."[96] The study made by the U.S. Bureau of the Census, *The Prisoner's Antecedents,*[97] also makes a special analysis of murders from data compiled for 1923. For the first six months of that year there were 19,080 persons committed to state and federal institutions for homicide. This group included, of course, all those who committed first- and second-degree murder as well as manslaughter. Since more Negroes than white persons were convicted of murder the conclusions with reference to the social and economic backgrounds of the total groups are skewed by the fact that racial discrimination against Negroes has resulted in low educational opportunities and low economic and social opportunities. Negroes have

[93] *Ibid.*　　　　[94] *Ibid.*　　　　[95] *Ibid.*
[96] University of North Carolina Press, Chapel Hill, 1932.
[97] Department of Commerce, Washington, 1926, p. 21.

a greater propensity to commit murder. Those who do commit it often have little education because Negroes in southern states generally have little education. Hence when we read that the median school achievement for the 19,080 was only the *fifth* grade we must remember that many of the Negroes had much less schooling. Even so, murderers had less education than any group of offenders except those convicted of felonious assault.[98]

ADDITIONAL THEORIES WITH REFERENCE TO MURDERERS

Many psychologists, criminologists, and psychiatrists have advanced explanations as to why men kill. Lombroso believed that murderers were true criminals because they were biologically degenerate.[99] The biological theories of criminality have now been pretty thoroughly discredited, as we shall discuss later, but analysis of intelligence tests administered to different types of offenders indicates that murderers rank lower than any save those convicted of "felonious assault." This does not mean that all murderers are low grade in intelligence, however. It is rather more likely that the imbeciles and borderline slayers skewed the median average.[100] It is also true that up to now no intelligence test devised has been completely satisfactory in separating the factors of intelligence and education and we have already spoken of the Negroes' educational handicap. Moreover, the murderers, by the fact of their particular crime, are usually in a greater state of emotional upset when taking intelligence tests than are persons who have committed offenses against property. Unquestionably the average murderer tends to feel greater remorse and guilt than other offenders do. In consequence he would be less likely to show up to advantage when an intelligence test was administered.

Various psychiatrists have attempted to analyze and classify murderers. Schlapp and Smith have developed a biological-personality classification into four types: (1) the insane, (2) the feeble-minded, (3) the epileptic, and (4) the emotionally defective, including those who have become emotionally disordered through the effect of drugs of various sorts.[101]

In Russia as well as in other European countries the murderer has often been classified as to his personality type—as one who is a "weak-

[98] *Ibid.*
[99] Cesare Lombroso, *Crime, Its Causes and Remedies*, Little, Brown, Boston, 1911, p. 416.
[100] H. C. Brearley, *op. cit.*, pp. 84–85.
[101] Max G. Schlapp and Edward H. Smith, *The New Criminology*, Boni & Liveright, New York, 1928.

ling in conflict." The All-Ukrainian Cabinet for Research in Criminality and the Criminal made a detailed biosociological analysis of 216 murderers and concluded that 153 or 70 per cent fell within this category. That is, such persons had resolved a mental conflict by annihilating their adversary. These murderers were diagnosed as being in a state of highly emotionalized fear which led to their explosive behavior.[102]

Andreas Bjerre, the Swedish criminal psychologist, has also held that weakness is the determining factor in all crime but that it is especially true in the case of the murderers, "who seek to escape from the realities of life."[103] Murderers succeed in escaping, he maintains, in several different ways: (1) The largest category are those who escape self-condemnation by means of self-deception. (2) The second largest group escapes reality by renunciation and maintains a complete passivity to everything except animal-like existence. These murderers "brood" and try to explain their crimes while living in what Bjerre calls "anguished fear." (3) The third category escape reality through "shamming."[104]

If one reads Dr. Bjerre's case studies, however, it is obvious that he is studying the reactions of murderers to their crimes, for what he describes is how men who have killed react to their own behavior. Men in and out of prison make mistakes and blunders in the course of their lives and tend to excuse themselves. The rank and file of people, in fact, rationalize some of their behavior with "Well, *I did the best I could.*" Some people, more sensitive souls than most, experience a greater sense of guilt for their conduct and continually worry about past events. Others are great shams. In modern parlance we should probably call them "stuffed shirts," pompous persons, well impressed with themselves, but in the final analysis all their self-importance is based on fraud. The fact that prisoners must live with themselves, hence are more or less driven to extremes in order to build up pictures of themselves worthy of self-respect seems to this author an obvious fact of human psychology and not especially truer of prisoners than of civilians.

Certain important facts emerge from Dr. Bjerre's patient study of murderers, however. One is that in the background of murderers there tends to be a great sense of insecurity and a constant sense of failure.[105] (This classification corresponds roughly at least with Gillin's conclusion that frustration is an important factor in crime.) Bjerre also be-

[102] *Social Science Abstracts*, 2:947.
[103] Andreas Bjerre, *The Psychology of Murder*, transl. by E. Classen, Longmans, Green, London, 1927, p. 5.
[104] *Ibid.*, p. 6.   [105] *Ibid.*, p. 96.

lieves that the hatred on the part of the weak, suffering, and incompetent for the strong, happy, and self-assured grows out of their sense of inferiority. At the same time he holds that childhood impressions exert a decisive effect upon the human personality and are a factor in the background of criminal conduct. Hence persons with a "predisposition to criminal characteristics" might be saved under proper guidance. Hatred of one's fellows, unexpressed, may be translated years later into violence and murder.[106]

Bjerre's classification of certain murderers as belonging to the "shamming" type may lend some insight as to why some murderers attempt to conceal their crime by planting evidence which will attach blame to someone else, or try to make it seem that their victims were suicides. He cites an interesting case of one Olaf Malmstrom, who killed his wife. Malmstrom sought by a series of letters, presumably written by his wife but which he wrote himself, to convince investigators he was not guilty. First he pretended that his wife wrote a suicide note and disappeared. Later he received further letters purportedly from the wife stating she was mentally ill but could not tell where she was. Finally the woman's body was found in the Malmstrom potato patch. Then her husband invented the story that she was slain by a vagrant, an itinerant Mormon missionary, who wrote a full confession in a letter. Eventually the full facts disclosed that Malmstrom was guilty of incest with his three daughters and that he previously had set fire to his valuable house. His dead wife must have known of his misconduct; evidently he killed her lest she disclose what she knew. His daughters' testimony against him convicted him, but throughout his sentence he continued to assert his innocence. In Bjerre's estimation Malmstrom's belief in his innocence was genuine. Malmstrom constructed his belief in his lack of guilt skillfully, maintaining that it had never been really *proved* that he had committed the crimes for which he was convicted. He maintained that unless an act was committed in the presence of two witnesses it could not be proved and since he had never confessed he could never have transgressed the law. He had, it is true, confessed to the charge of incest only to escape the charge of murder subsequently imposed.

Malmstrom's lies obviously rivaled those of Munchausen, but in themselves they are indications of his mental and emotional distortions. They do not necessarily show innate moral defectiveness as Bjerre contends.[107] Malmstrom's relations with his wife—indeed, his whole marriage—were based on purely practical considerations and

[106] *Ibid.*, p. 110.   [107] *Ibid.*, chap. 3.

were without affection. His peculiar experiences had warped his personality until he became completely abnormal in his emotional reactions. At least modern criminologists would so conclude.

On the other extreme stands the man who killed but had committed no previous crimes. Such was the case of Bailey Smith. Bailey Smith had lived most of his 70 years on the farm near ———, Michigan, where he was born. Industrious and hard working, he had paid for his 360 acres of good land by the time he was 50 and had then been content to slacken his efforts and spend more of his income. He had built a new house, owned a fine car, belonged to the Kiwanis Club "in town," and was an influential member of the Baptist Church. Always his neighbors had regarded him as "reasonable and square." Then his line-fence neighbors to the south moved to town because they were getting on in years and leased their farm to a hopeful young man of Dutch descent. This young farmer, Peter Van Huyten, was striving anxiously to get ahead and bought cattle to put on the fodder in a field adjoining Mr. Smith's. There never had been anything but a hedge of willows on the line. Van Huyten insisted that there be a fence and finally got the landlord to agree. There was some question about where to put the fence. Since Smith objected to uprooting the hedge, Van Huyten insisted the fence would have to go on Mr. Smith's land and started digging the holes for it. Smith was furious. He grabbed his gun and rushed down to the line. Although he was outraged, he probably never intended to shoot his neighbor. A few sharp words were exchanged and the old farmer yielded to his impulse, reached for the trigger, and shot Peter Van Huyten through the heart. At his trial the old man sobbed as he confessed his guilt. He was convicted of first-degree murder.[108]

WILLIAM HEIRENS

Sex murderers are practically all psychopathic. We have already referred to the case of William Heirens in the section on sex offenders. He is a good example of a psychopathic murderer. Chicagoans were terrified by this young man, a college sophomore of good parentage, who confessed to attacking sexually and then murdering two women and a child in Chicago after the three murders had gone unsolved for months. His was unquestionably a dual personality since he carried on his college work very satisfactorily with no indication of serious emotional disturbances. As the detectives delved into the

---

[108] Names, etc., are changed but the case is a true case of a respectable farmer serving a sentence in a midwestern prison.

case, it seems obvious that he committed many additional offenses, and 29 robbery and assault charges were held against him. Under drugs he confessed to the three murders for which he was convicted and sentenced for three life sentences despite attempts to clear him on insanity charges. After the sentence was pronounced, young Heirens tried unsuccessfully to commit suicide. After his incarceration his mental unbalance became increasingly apparent and a month later he was transferred to the Minors Penitentiary for the Criminally Insane.[109]

FIREARMS AND MURDER

While premeditated murders may often be the result of the peculiar emotional distortions described by Bjerre and others, we must remember that a large number of homicides are not sudden explosions resulting from long-time hatreds. Many manslaughter cases would never have occurred if firearms had not been available. Most murders occur where people are accustomed to carry weapons.[110] In the United States more people carry firearms than anywhere else in the world, and a large share of them do so illegally. The mores supporting the male practice of carrying a gun are strong, especially in the South and West, and the law is often disregarded where law and mores are at variance.[111] Of course there are many other ways of committing murder—cutting, bludgeoning, poisoning, etc.—but firearms are the weapons most frequently used.[112]

In the South and West guns are carried too generally for it to be presumed that all who "wear a pistol" are special personality types. Moreover, firearms are too easily purchased in most areas. In any event, we cannot expect murder rates to go down while concealed weapons are so commonly carried and "whipped out" with little provocation. Only when laws forbidding the carrying of such weapons are effectively enforced can we count on a lower homicide rate.[113]

SELECTED BIBLIOGRAPHY

Barnes, Harry E., and Teeters, Negley K., New Horizons in Criminology, Prentice-Hall, New York, rev. ed., 1951. Consult this book for extensive information on various types of offenders.

Bjerre, Andreas, The Psychology of Murder, transl. by E. Classen, Long-

[109] Cf. New York Times, January 8, 1946, p. 1, col. 2; July 2, 1946, p. 26, col. 3; July 15, 1946, p. 26, col. 2; July 27, 1946, p. 32, col. 1; July 28, 1946, p. 13, col. 3; August 3, 1946, p. 28, col. 6; August 7, 1946, p. 46, col. 5; September 6, 1946, p. 38, col. 3; and October 12, 1946, p. 21, col. 4.

[110] H. C. Brearley, op. cit., p. 71.

[111] Ibid., p. 74.　　[112] Ibid., p. 70.　　[113] Ibid., pp. 76–77.

mans, Green, London, 1927. An analysis of the psychological characteristics of murderers is made by a distinguished Swedish criminal psychologist.

Brearley, Howard C., *Homicide in the United States*, University of North Carolina Press, Chapel Hill, 1932. This excellent analysis of the background of murderers gives information on the area differences in homicides, methods, etc.

Ferri, Enrico, *Criminal Sociology*, transl. by Kelley and Lisle, Little, Brown, Boston, 1917. Ferri, with Garofalo, tried to classify offenders on the basis of motivating factors.

Garofalo, Raffaele, *Criminology*, transl. by Robert W. Millar, Little, Brown, Boston, 1914. This book gives Garofalo's juridical classification of offenders. This distinguished Italian jurist did much to promote a scientific study of factors in crime.

Gillin, John L., *The Wisconsin Prisoner*, University of Wisconsin Press, Madison, 1946. This is an important analysis of factors in the backgrounds of various types of offenders classified on the basis of offense.

Hentig, Hans von, *Crime: Causes and Conditions*, McGraw-Hill, New York, 1947. Dr. von Hentig gives an excellent analysis of factors in crime.

Hohman, Leslie B., and Schaffner, Bertram, "The Sex Lives of Unmarried Men," *American Journal of Sociology*, 52:289–294 (May, 1947). This article reviews extensive information concerning the sex behavior of 4664 unmarried draftees.

Morris, Norval, *The Habitual Criminal*, Harvard University Press, Cambridge, 1951. This is a comprehensive study of habitual criminality, with a summary of comparative legislation on habitual criminals and case studies on 270 confirmed recidivists.

CHAPTER 6

The Professional Criminal and Organized Crime

Anyone who makes his living by carrying on illegal activities may be called a professional criminal. There are of course many types and varieties of professional criminals. Some are the "overlords" or "big shots" in illicit undertakings whereas a large number of lesser men and women participate in the various underworld activities such as gambling, bootlegging, prostitution, the narcotics trade, organized thieving and swindling, kidnaping, counterfeiting, and other activities in which the promoters of illegal enterprises reap high monetary gains. Making "big money quick" is the major aim of the professional criminal and he often reaches the goal. Such criminals have developed skills and techniques both for deluding honest people and for playing upon the weaknesses which are common to men in general. Professional criminals may be skilled technicians, as in the case of counterfeiters, or crude gunmen, as in the case of gangsters. Occasionally they carry on as marginal men in the half-world between assumed respectability and avowed criminality. A reformed professional thief, speaking before a group of sociologists in Chicago, told of how a "colleague" of his lived a Dr. Jekyll and Mr. Hyde existence. As a burglar he was a super upper-story man. But his family was unaware of his source of income and his daughter (whose family credentials presumably were examined) was a student at Vassar.

Antecedents of the Professional Criminal

Many people believe that the Camorra and the Mafia (outlaw "black hand societies") in Naples and Sicily are the cultural ancestors of professional and organized crime in the United States. To a large extent this idea is aprocryphal; furthermore, much professional crime existed in the United States before the Italian and Sicilian immigration. It is likely, however, that certain patterns of crime were introduced through various national sources, and many professional criminals seem to have immigrant backgrounds, as we discuss in Chapter 11.

The degrading poverty of the slums has unquestionably stimulated their children to seek a life which permitted some of the luxuries of life they could so easily observe in near-by neighborhoods. Few who lived in the tenements could aspire to win high rewards honestly, hence were easy prey to those who lured them into the "easy life" of bootlegging, gambling, etc. Meanwhile the fabulous rise of many relatively poor businessmen to positions of wealth and dominance and the emphasis placed upon a high material standard of living are all a part of the stimulus to criminal activity. It is of course equally true that America has been founded upon hard work, upon reward for honest effort and the general acceptance of the common decencies and the Ten Commandments. The people who have followed these precepts generally consider themselves the true Americans. But the children of underprivileged peoples of Europe who sought our shores in the last fifty years are also Americans. Our cities and our nation as a whole have failed signally to provide many of them with the basic values of the American people and at the same time we have displayed a standard of living which no poor person could achieve honestly.

The Extent of Organized Crime

In recent years the American public has been shocked by the extent of organized crime and the degree of corruption among government officials. During 1950 and 1951 the investigations of crime conducted by the Special Committee of the Senate of the Eighty-First Congress (popularly known as the Kefauver Committee) were front-page news throughout the United States. Many persons had known of the extensive underworld connections of the great vice lords and gangsters during the prohibition era, but there was general presumption that the end of prohibition had removed the major impetus to a network of interrelated illicit industries. The Kefauver Committee hearings made it abundantly clear that widespread organized crime is a major internal problem in our city government and a threat to our democratic way of life.

The published reports of the committee give us some notion of the extensive illegal operations, but they furnish us with few accurate statistics. They show merely what informed people are willing to tell. Most organized crime is unreported crime, and it is unreported chiefly because its victims have collaborated in it. The professional criminals in turn have operated under cover and with the protection of law enforcement officials. But we have enough information to believe that the monetary returns of these unreported crimes are fabulously large, even far in excess of the reported crimes for which men are arrested, convicted, and serve sentence.

These organized, big-money crimes are the special province of the professional criminals who operate for high stakes, who steal not from sudden impulse, or to secure a minimum of food, clothing, or shelter, but for fabulous goals, and in order to live on a luxury standard.

Organized crime is one of the amazing aspects of social disorganization when we think of how little concern there is on the part of individual citizens and local officials for this sort of crime. For in ordinary crimes the victim usually reports his loss. Moreover the local community is likely to be up in arms about a local murder, a daring holdup, or a rape case. Although organized crime exacts a far greater toll, the community usually does nothing. Instead the officials and a fair segment of the population permit it to exist chiefly because they themselves hope to profit from such corruption. The organized criminals achieve their ends only as they are able to corrupt both their victims and their accomplices in the process.

Most professional criminals and all those engaged in so-called criminal syndicates are able to operate only because they possess rare insight into human weaknesses and exploit them. Thus the swindlers are able to part fools from their money because the men they swindle have the same urges for dishonest gain. Gamblers make enormous profits because their "clients" would like to make enormous profits from gambling. The professional criminals are in a sense the evil priests of our generation. They possess a peculiar black magic, the power to corrupt other men and women and to subvert the institutions of government while amassing enormous fortunes for themselves. Skilled in applied human psychology, they use their skills to engage other men in criminal activities and in particular to make it lucrative for government officials to protect their crimes. These circumstances obviously account for the fact that machine politicians seldom arrest the large-scale criminals, much less bring them to trial. The petty criminal or the criminal operating on an individual basis has no such protective devices, nor does he ordinarily involve his victim in his crime. Thus, as has often been said, "crime does not pay" (in the long run) for the petty or individually operating criminal for he has no power over the forces which bring about his downfall. Organized crime, on the other hand, is plotted social disorganization in which the group vested with the power of enforcing the law co-operates in breaking the law. Hence for organized criminals and their political accomplices crime pays very well. Criminals often have huge incomes—far higher incomes than they could ever expect to receive from any legitimate source. In fact the incomes of racketeers and gangsters often exceed those of the heads of our largest industrial corporations, although it is the latter's standard of living which has sparked the professional criminal's desire for his illicit gains. The professional criminals want luxury, conspicuous wealth, beautiful homes, fine automobiles, expensive food, and impressive clothes. It is a sad commentary on our culture that the material values of a wealthy segment of our population often have outweighed the spiritual, ethical, and moral values of our society.

The Professional Criminal—A Definition

Any person who makes his living at lawless pursuits may be defined as a professional criminal. His time, his effort, and often his capital are invested in activities which the state has forbidden, whether he is a small-time operator or a criminal gangster with far-flung connections with other criminals in widely separated parts of the country.

Most professional criminals are organized criminals. When we use the term "organized criminals" we do not mean they are members of formally set up state or national associations. Criminals do not belong to any such formal groups. There is no nation-wide syndicate which solicits dues or maintains an extensive membership. Nevertheless there formerly was organized bootlegging and there now is organized gambling and prostitution in the sense that a syndicate may control several "spots" in one city or in adjoining cities or even in separated states.[1]

We are using organized crime at this point as a term to subsume the interlocking collusion between professional criminals to aid themselves in various ways. In particular we are referring to the silent covenants which professional criminals secure with law-enforcing and administrative government officials so as to protect themselves from arrest and punishment.

Obviously these illegal activities are not carried on in accordance

[1] Edwin H. Sutherland, *The Professional Thief*, written by "Chic" Conwell, University of Chicago Press, Chicago, 1937, p. 26.

with formally executed contracts. They operate through verbal contracts, through bribes, through a slice in the returns. These bribes or "percentages" are not listed in any corporation tax returns or in any accounting to the Department of Commerce. No one can say how extensive such connections are but we have reason to believe that the economic losses from organized crime and political corruption far exceed the losses from other forms of crime.

The Changing Aspects of Organized Crime

Modern society has produced its peculiar variety of professional criminals (as we shall discuss), but there have been professional criminals since time immemorial who have engaged in a wide variety of illicit trades and practices. For professional crimes change with the times and the development of civilization. They vary with the opportunities which are presented to greedy, dishonest, and unscrupulous men. Professional crime is a business, a means of making money while engaged in activities specifically forbidden by law. This is true whether the professional criminal robs a bank, cheats a schoolteacher out of her hard-earned savings by offering her stocks in a nonexistent gold mine, or shoots a rival gangster for a specified price. All these crimes are perpetrated for material gain and are merely means to that end.

With changing situations certain types of professional crime which once perplexed the law enforcement agencies have virtually disappeared. Piracy, a major hazard in international and coastwise shipping during our colonial and early federal period, is no longer a problem with the acceptance of "freedom of the seas." Rumrunning and bootlegging were major crimes during prohibition days, but the availability of legal liquor has reduced the lure of illicit liquor for both buyer and seller, although high liquor taxes have increased bootlegging recently.

Following the repeal of prohibition, criminals turned to other activities. Some went into the legal liquor business but a majority of those once engaged in bootlegging have apparently gone into the gambling racket.

The Extent of Organized Crime in Modern America During the Prohibition Era

During the bootlegging era, from 1919 (the date of the enactment of the Volstead Act) until 1934, one of the most fabulous structures of organized crime that ever existed came into being. Huge organizations were engaged in rumrunning, the secret importation of liquor on small boats which evaded our coast guard. Enormous fleets of trucks, under guard of gangsters, carried liquor produced in illegally operating breweries and distilleries in our own country. These boot-leggers delivered their stock to countless speak-easies which operated under cover of police protection and by civil connivance in virtually every city in America. Some bootleggers delivered their liquor to pri- vate clubs and residences. During the "roaring twenties" such lawless-ness threatened to break down the very structure of our government and prohibition, as such, became a major political issue.

During 1929–1930 the cost of the various police activities of the federal government in attempting to enforce the prohibition law was estimated by the National Commission on Law Observance and En-forcement to be $25,644,069.57 or 74.1 per cent of the total police costs.[2] For the same period the costs of prosecution chargeable to enforcing the Volstead Act were $996,720.33 out of a total of $1,996,-976.86 expended for all federal prosecutions.[3] The criminal business of the federal courts for the same period amounted to $6,331,015.21, of which 68.1 per cent was assignable to prosecuting bootleggers.[4] Additional costs of federal probation and parole brought the final cost even higher.

There simply is no way of estimating the staggering amounts which the bootleggers themselves made. Al Capone, for example, became the head of a multi-million-dollar business. Not all of his profits were in bootlegging, for he was also a major promoter of prostitution and gambling. We might add that this tie-up between vice, gambling, and illicit liquor interests was a perennial problem during prohibition. Hundreds of murders were committed by Al Capone's henchmen at his behest. Through his armed agents he literally enforced a reign of terror on Chicago. Occasionally innocent people were killed by chance bullets in the gunplay between Capone's gang and rival gangsters. Country girls were lured into prostitution by advertisements (in small-town newspapers not far from Chicago) purporting to offer legitimate employment. For all of these offenses Capone escaped punishment. He maintained a high-powered detective service to keep watch on all efforts of police to obtain evidence. This made it both dangerous and difficult for undercover agents to operate. One federal official, for example, laid his hands on a ledger for one of Capone's gambling

---

[2] Cf. Report on the Cost of Crime, Report No. 12 of the National Commission on Law Observance and Enforcement, Washington, 1931, p. 106.
[3] Ibid., p. 114.   [4] Ibid., p. 129.

establishments—the Hawthorne Smoke Shop in Cicero, a west-side Chicago suburb—but never made any use of it. It was located later among a great number of other old records stored at the Chicago Post Office and contained an exact account of the Smoke Shop's business. From this ledger government officials discovered that Capone's profits for a 3-year period were approximately $600,000, none of which had been reported to the Bureau of Internal Revenue. Obviously this was but a fraction of Capone's illegal income, but it was upon the basis of this evidence that he was sentenced to 11 years' imprisonment in a federal penitentiary for evasion of his income tax. In the words of Alan Hynd, Capone, was a member of the "get-it-while-you-can epoch" following World War I.[5]

Many other criminals in New York, Miami, New Orleans, Los Angeles, Kansas City, and elsewhere were involved in similar rackets. The "Pretty Boy Floyds," the "Legs" Diamonds, the John Dillingers, the Frank Nittis, the Verne Sankeys all made the headlines during the early thirties while supplying willing customers who sought their special services.

During the depth of depression and World War II organized crime was on the decline but since World War II it is apparently increasing again. The new wage scales have meant more money in circulation and thus a greater potential number of persons for professional criminals to exploit. For organized crime must depend upon victims who have money with which they can afford to take chances. Such lawlessness relies upon the co-operation not only of the victims but of the law enforcement agents who are sitting in the political saddle and betraying public trust for the bribes which the professional criminals pay in order to operate.[6] But let us consider the organized types of crime in greater detail.

Current Types and Varieties of Organized Crime

The major types of crime in vogue among professional criminals today are: (1) thieving, i.e., stealing personal property or money, usually subclassified as burglary, larceny, and robbery; (2) receiving stolen goods, a crime committed by persons who do business in stolen goods

[5] Cf. Alan Hynd, The Giant Killers, McBride, New York, 1945, for a detailed account of the difficulties involved in securing information on Capone's vast empire of organized crime.

[6] Cf. Mabel A. Elliott and Francis E. Merrill, Social Disorganization, Harper, New York, 3rd ed., 1950, chap. 25, "Political Corruption," for a detailed survey of the collusion between crime and politics.

either by buying outright or receiving them as agents; (3) swindling in all its manifold forms; (4) racketeering; (5) gambling in its several varieties. We shall discuss each of these types of crime briefly.

THIEVING

Burglary, larceny, and robbery all involve stealing property belonging to others, but the terms refer technically and legally to specific varieties of stealing. Burglary is technically the offense of breaking and entering a house, store, factory, or other establishment for the purpose of stealing property of whatever nature. Larceny is the term usually applied to stealing from or looting of stores or other places where goods are relatively accessible. He who steals articles from a store counter or who steals an automobile parked in the street is called a thief. A robber, on the other hand, takes property from the person or in the presence of the person. A bank is thus robbed if the thieves stage and execute the stealing of bank funds in daylight while those who operate the bank witness the procedure. A holdup is likewise a robbery whether a person or a bank is robbed. If thieves break into a bank at night and escape with the funds the bank is said to have been burglarized rather than robbed.

The loss from burglaries in the United States constitutes a sizable annual sum. In 1950 it was $23,635,685.[7] Obviously not all such thieving is professional. There are many individual thieves, some of whom steal large amounts. But the successful thief is ordinarily the professional thief.

The professional thief usually works with a group which is variously designated "mob," "troupe," or "outfit." Some individual thieves shift from mob to mob. Since there is "honor among thieves" a thief must co-operate to remain a member of a mob. He may in fact be fired for lack of co-operation. Usually one person steals while another steers the stolen goods to a fence or pawnbroker. All expenses are paid from the sale of goods, and what remains is divided equally. If someone is caught a "fixer" tries to pay the policeman a sufficient amount to keep him from following through with the case.

In large cities there are always certain persons who are engaged in stealing in department stores, apartment houses, hotels, and jewelry stores, etc. When stealing from banks thieves often try to get a bank employee to co-operate in return for a share in the stolen bonds or currency. Other thieves may be "confidence" men who purport to be

[7] *Uniform Crime Reports*, Annual Bulletin, 1950, Federal Bureau of Investigation, U.S. Department of Justice, Washington, 1951, p. 105.

operating gambling houses or broker houses. Professional thieves develop great skill in all forms of thieving. They must depend upon others for tips as to people carrying sizable sums or going away from home where articles of value may be taken. Frequently they work in collaboration with ostensible employees of a bank or hotel. Bellboys themselves often act as thieves as well as informers.[8] Thieves may watch a luggage counter for luggage highly insured. Signs in railway trains reading "Beware of pickpockets" give much information to the pickpockets for passengers in reacting to such notice invariably place their hands over pockets carrying their wallets.

The Fix

One of the major facets of organized professional thieving is the "fix." We discuss this in Chapter 19,[9] but it should be pointed out here that if the professional thief is to succeed he must keep out of jail. To be convicted he has to be identified by the victim or by witnesses, and the police, bailiff, clerk, prosecuting attorneys, jury, judge, and others must see the case through the tedious processes of arrest, hearing (or indictment), trial, conviction, and sentence. These steps involve many loopholes and the clever thief (as well as other lawbreakers) takes full advantage of them. Sometimes he hires a bondsman; sometimes he fixes the case himself by paying off the policeman. Friends of the thief who is arrested may lure the victim to the wrong court building and in the guise of police officers offer him full restitution. The victim may also be advised that he will be notified about the time of trial, but since he is led to believe this is the actual court of jurisdiction he never appears at the trial. Sometimes judges are bribed to refuse to hear the case, or to direct a verdict of not guilty. Sometimes when victims are not bought off they are caught in compromising circumstances and in consequence yield to demands for a settlement on the promise that their private lives will be kept secret. Sometimes the testimony of a policeman fails to corroborate the victim's (and this is usually because the policeman is bribed). In general there is little fixing by thieves in federal courts except in narcotic drug charges. Formerly many cases involved in prohibition charges were alleged to have been fixed. Since all members of the underworld tend to have contacts, thieves and narcotic drug peddlers may aid each other. Thieves may in fact steal narcotics for peddlers.[10]

[8] Edwin H. Sutherland, op. cit., pp. 43–55.
[9] Cf. the section "Bail or Jail," pp. 522–524.
[10] Cf. Edwin H. Sutherland, op. cit., chap. 4.

FENCES

Persons who knowingly receive stolen goods are as guilty of theft as the thieves or burglars who supply them with goods, but the majority of these particular operators of illicit business are seldom punished. Some fences operate dress or fur shops where customers secure wearing apparel at cut-rate prices. In Kansas City it is well known that a certain auto and radio supply shop was a receiver of stolen goods. Here everything from radiator caps to handsome radios could be purchased at prices much lower than regular market prices.

Other fences have been known to sell their stolen wares on the street and in office buildings. During the depression many sidewalk merchants were selling furs or hose on the streets, near subway stations, etc. In not a few instances pawnshop dealers have served as outlets for stolen goods. For this reason many states now require pawnshop operators to register all pawned merchandise with local police departments.

SWINDLING

A major form of professional crime is swindling or "bunco." In this type of crime the professional criminal usually has one or more confederates, but there is no organized community collusion. Swindlers simply must have assistants who co-operate on such a casual basis that the victim of the swindling presumes them to be would-be clients like himself or innocent bystanders. Generally known as confidence men or "con" men, swindlers carry on their illicit operations with all the techniques of high-pressure salesmen; in fact they usually pose as salesmen. Their victims are often so-called "respectable" people who are influenced to participate in a get-rich scheme. Indeed, the victims recognize that some illicit or unfair advantage must be involved in the scheme or the returns for the investment offered could not be so great. They imagine, as it were, that some fabulous transaction is to take place in which they are to make a killing. All too late (after the confidence men have departed with the cash) they realize that it is they—the victims—who are the "suckers."

There are a wide variety of con men abroad, each with his particular specialty. The number and variety of swindling or bunco operations are as extensive as the imagination of the swindlers. All swindlers are adept at the use of suggestion and in exploiting the gullibility of their victims. They take advantage of a common human frailty, as we mentioned earlier: the desire to get something for nothing. The victim is always led to believe that he is to share in the opportunity for gain, whether it be in purchasing stolen goods, in participating in a bonanza scheme, or in dividing the contents of a lost wallet. He is eventually persuaded to part with his own money (usually a sizable sum) only to find that he has been mercilessly cheated. The fraud may be perpetrated by some quick-change operation or the victim may be given worthless securities or goods of little value in exchange. For example, when he thinks he is to receive diamonds he receives glass baubles, or a cardsharp "wipes him out" by playing with a marked deck.

In general the procedure which the swindler employs is as follows: First he flatters the victim. Then he engages him in conversation in order to discover his financial status. If it seems likely that the proposed victim has sufficient cash a third person (well known to the operator) is "accidentally" made a part of the situation. The two may discuss a sure-fire tip on a stockmarket, an investment in Texas oil, or a California gold mine, all with the idea of inducing the victim to participate. Once the swindler has obtained the confidence of his victim (who has to be a relatively gullible person) he may proceed to take the latter's savings for his bogus scheme. Or he may rob the victim of all his valuables while the latter is not watching, then disappear. Generally speaking, two men operate in getting a third into a bunco game. One is the "steerer," who directs the victim to the operator by some such device as "finding" a wallet or through a prearranged "accidental" meeting.[11] John C. R. MacDonald gives an example of a "sick old man" who arouses the victim's sympathy. The sick man loses a wallet. He allegedly has not long to live and has "spells." During one of these spells the swindler tells his victim he needs help in distributing his money before he dies and the victim is roped into helping him. The victim may be asked to establish his own integrity by bringing money from his bank to verify his financial reliability. Later the old man may be seized with another spell while they are en route to a drug store for medicine. The old man's assistant leaves his money with the old man while he goes for the medicine. When the former returns he is told the medicine is wrong. Then the victim is asked to go for the medicine and to leave his money as proof that he can be trusted to return. When the victim comes back the old man has disappeared with his (the victim's) money.[12]

[11] John C. R. MacDonald, *Crime Is a Business*, Stanford University Press, Stanford University, California, 1939.
[12] *Ibid.*, pp. 12–16.

Use of Mails to Defraud

In an earlier period many get-rich schemes were circulated through the mails. Today federal laws make it a very serious offense to use the mails to defraud. Nevertheless people are still being defrauded through buying stocks in nonexistent corporations or investing in non-producing oil wells which are advertised through the mail.

Confidence Men

Prior to 1900 most "con" men played for small stakes and were content to fleece their victims of the money they had on their persons. The amounts taken usually ranged from $25 to $200. Later the "big con" games or swindling procedures developed into complicated practices in which large stakes were often involved. The major varieties of these games are, in the vernacular, the "wire," the "rag," and the "pay-off." The "wire" is simply an abbreviated term for wiretapping. The victim is a race fan, who is persuaded that the con man can tap telegraph wires, secure advance information on results of races and make it possible for the victim to place a bet with a bookmaker in time to win on the basis of the advance information. In such instances a man with sizable savings is located by one of several means. He may have decided to retire and has advertised that his store, business, or practice is for sale. Or he may be one of the persons who responds to a neat advertisement reading something like this:

> WANTED: Reliable business man with $20,000 to invest in a successful business. References exchanged.[13]

From the replies to such an advertisement the con man can pick a victim, or a series of victims. The only real essential is that the victim has money. Tourists provide excellent prospects; well-to-do-farmers at a World's Fair, ranchers in the big city on a business trip, wealthy widows at resort hotels all are likely marks for the con men. Even officials of important religious organizations sometimes yield to such temptations. According to David W. Mawrer, professional men are notoriously gullible, but anyone who has money is fair game.[14] Very wealthy men are often taken in.

When such a person is given a "hot tip" the trick is to have him win on a relatively low bet. This convinces him that he is playing a sure game. He is then willing to place a huge sum. He may even wire

[13] Cf. David W. Mawrer, *The Big Con*, Bobbs-Merrill, Indianapolis, 1940, p. 121.
[14] *Ibid.*, pp. 111–115.

his banker for a large amount of money. Meanwhile he watches others place large bets and sees enormous winnings paid by the bookmakers' cashier to other players. These players of course are "shills"—that is, accomplices of the con men. Their winnings make the victim anxious to place his money on such certain rewards. The mark, or victim, may get nervous while waiting for his money, but he is given no time to himself. As soon as his money comes a winner is announced, and he bets an enormous sum—usually through some prompting to the effect that small bets are not usually made there. There is then great excitement. There is in fact something wrong. The "winner" comes out second. The mark has lost. The con men talk about the possibility that the police heard about the wire tapping. They extend their sympathy; they may even lend the victim carfare, talking all the while of the importance of keeping the whole thing quiet and "clear of the police." They see their victim to his train, after which they divide their loot.[15]

The "pay-off" is simply a more complicated series of bet-placings in which the victim is led to bet $25,000 or more, after he has seen others win. He then wins ten times the amount. By this time he is hypersuggestible and is asked to place everything on the winning horse. He does this and the horse comes in second. The con man explains he said "place," not "win," while the victim is literally wiped out. Often a fake murder of one of the accomplices is staged so as to scare the victim. The other con men agree to meet the victim in another city. He goes there but never sees the con men again. He fears the police. He goes on to another city and eventually home, still fearful the police will follow him. But they never do.[16] He has already "paid off" well.

When the "roper" or con man is conducting a bogus deal in stocks the game is called the "rag." In this type of swindling operation the con man, through his ally, purports to be working on inside tips on stock prices. He gives a $50 bill to be invested while in company with his victim. The investment immediately yields $150. This in turn is multiplied ten times the next day. The victim is later taken to a fake brokerage office with all the normal paraphernalia. All the customers are "shills" (accomplices) but the victim never suspects but what they are buying genuine stock. Prices fluctuate; then the stock they have been told to watch goes down. They buy. The stock goes further down. Then it starts to rise. In the meantime the victim has written a large check because he has been told that the winnings are a sure

---

[15] *Ibid.*, pp. 62–63.   [16] *Ibid.*, pp. 63–88.

thing and that he can cover the check with them. Complications always arise and the victim always loses. He seldom recognizes, until too late, that he never purchased any stock at all and that the stock quotations themselves are false, for his time has been completely absorbed by the con men. Eventually the victim is himself so involved that the con men plant so-called detectives to make it look as though he is to be arrested for his illicit activities. Then the con men plead his cause with detectives and help him escape—but his money is gone. When and if he calls the police the con men are gone too.[17]

Other Swindling Games

The Spanish prisoner letter is another old ruse against which the federal postal officials are continually warning the American public. In this game the victim is offered one-third of a large sum (or some such portion) if he will only help the Spaniard (now in a Spanish prison for bankruptcy) recover funds from a portmanteau held in America and pay the expenses of the prisoner's trial. Several Americans have literally lost all their money by handing it over to the so-called agent of this prisoner. Many Americans have even gone to Europe on this amazing adventure.

College professors are sometimes gullible and one of the favorite frauds perpetrated on them is the election to some especially distinguished body of scholars. There are a number of honorary biographical listings such as *Who's Who in America*, *American Scholars*, and special directories of important persons in particular fields. There are also several listings which are of dubious merit, and in recent years several money-making rackets have developed in which professors are asked to send $10 immediately for listing in an order which is to be the greatest distinction in the world! Or large sums may be requested for listings in a volume of prominent families, but no volume ever appears.

Street solicitations by unknown "charity" organizations are another means of extracting hundreds of dollars, usually in small contributions, from street crowds, especially during the holiday season, when sympathy for a cheerless Christmas is easily aroused.

RACKETEERING

The major unreported crimes are unquestionably the organized crimes of racketeering and gambling and the relatively "respectable"

[17] *Ibid.*, pp. 88–109.

crimes of those whom Sutherland has dubbed "the white collar criminals." Gambling is discussed more extensively in a later section and white-collar crime in a previous chapter, so we shall mention them only briefly here. We may point out again the bulk of crime committed under the aegis of the so-called criminal syndicates with the protection of hoodlums, gangsters, and those businessmen willing to sell out for a price is so enormous both in the extensiveness of its interlocking underworld communication and in its organization that criminal activities amount to petty offenses in comparison.

Racketeering may be defined as a form of criminal conspiracy in which underworld characters co-operate in exploiting either legal or illegal businesses for excessive profit. The exploitation may be accomplished (1) under threat of violence, or (2) by preferred shares in illicit gains. Such methods and activities are not new. We have had holdup men, pirates, highwaymen ever since people have acquired valuable property or carried money which others have sought to wrest from them. Swindlers likewise have long engaged in their corrupt practices. Many of the great family fortunes in this and other countries have been products of the manipulative devices of men in key positions—financiers, railroad magnates, oil speculators, and the like. In fact the whole structure of our capitalistic system has a considerable underpinning of the "let-the-buyer beware" philosophy. Honesty (within limits) has, however, been more or less imposed upon business by virtue of general standards of religion and personal decency as well as by federal legislation, "Better Business Bureaus," and the commonly accepted beliefs that "honesty is the best policy" and "a satisfied customer is the best advertisement." Nevertheless many crimes still persist in high places and not all have been those of underworld characters, as we have discussed in Chapter 3. The point here is that the cutthroat character of much competitive business has built up great financial enterprises both through shameless exploitation of our natural resources and through ruthless lack of concern for the financial welfare of the individuals or corporations that were annihilated. Much of the stimulus to illegal racketeering stems from the successful achievements of respected men who drove their competitors out of business by hiring legislators as retainers (who in turn sponsored legislation favoring their companies), by employing detectives for the purpose of discovering their competitors' secrets, and by bribing legislators. That is, while criminal syndicates have literally become big business they have patterned much of their organization along the lines of industrial corporations. They have aimed at (1) securing special protection and

(2) paying off persons in authority so that their activities either are not reported by authorities or if reported tend never to come up for trial, much less conviction.

During the 1920's and early 1930's much of the racketeering was, as stated earlier, concentrated in bootlegging. This eventuated in the gang warfare in Chicago and other cities—in an effort to control this illicit industry and its profits. There were, however, many other rackets.[18]

In 1935 Martin Mooney maintained that there were 16 major rackets including:

Pinball games	Hot ice (diamonds)
Policy or numbers	Gambling (dice, cards)
Race tracks	Garages and automobiles
Commercialized vice	Abortions
Loan sharks	Gunrunning and counterfeit-
Night clubs	ing
Union and industrial shake-	Stocks and bonds
downs	Narcotics
Real estate	

Most of these rackets and numerous others are still flourishing. Slot machines, for example, have long been controlled by the underworld element and the juke-box racket is one of the more lucrative businesses of the criminal syndicate in recent years.[19] Frank Costello's far-flung underworld interests, which have recently been investigated, first consisted of crap games. Then he went into a variety of businesses involving Kewpie dolls, razor blades, punchboards, and slot machines. During prohibition he went into bootlegging. From the moneys accruing from his rackets Costello, in the vernacular of his associates, "went legit." He bought controlling interests in real estate where he can maintain a modicum of respectability. Now many other gangsters have brought their underworld tactics into the "real-estate game." Here they have manipulated rents, entered into fraudulent construction contracts, and otherwise operated on the fringe of the law. Flimsy materials and shoddy construction have gone into many postwar building projects, despite the high construction charges. Under the cover of government contracts, gangsters have allegedly misled honest government clerks into approving contracts in which frauds were involved.

[18] Martin Mooney, Crime Incorporated, McGraw-Hill, New York, 1935, chap. 3.
[19] Virgil W. Peterson, "Vitalizing Liquor Control," Journal of Criminal Law and Criminology, 40:119–134 (July–August, 1949).

Legal liquor industries, because of their identification with the unsavory saloon, have always had a tie-up with the underworld. There are, of course, certain inherent dangers in this latter situation.[20] We shall discuss this topic more fully in a later section of this chapter.

The Gangster

The gangster exists because of the service he renders to racketeers and other professional criminals. The latter often find it necessary to resort to violence, blood, and plunder in order to pursue their illegal activities and those who kill for a price constitute the group we ordinarily refer to as gangsters. They are the hireling criminals who work for criminals. There have always been outlaws who "shot it out," but during the prohibition era gangsters instituted a virtual reign of lawlessness in many cities. During the heyday of Al Capone's dictatorship of his $60,000,000-a-year illicit liquor trade in Chicago he terrorized the city. His competitors engaged him in gang warfare.[21] In Chicago on a fateful Valentine's Day seven gangsters disguised as policemen were mowed down by machine guns of Capone's gangsters. In Kansas City gangsters shot five persons in Union Station and injured the sheriff of Jackson County. A group of notorious gangsters in New York City was actually known as Murder, Incorporated. Innocent bystanders, federal agents, and policemen were occasionally killed by gangsters, but the toll was greatest among racketeers themselves.

Gangsters' activities included taking criminals or other persons for a "ride," i.e., kidnaping a victim and leaving his body bullet ridden by the side of the road or at some bizarre destination. Gangsters also blew up buildings or businesses to order when the owners failed to pay tribute to their particular racket. Between October 1, 1928, and January 15, 1929, at least 157 businesses were bombed for refusing to have dealings with racketeers.[22]

The pattern of gangsters slugging it out has declined since the lawless twenties and thirties, but mysterious murders still happen. Sometimes a racketeer talks too much; then he is considered a liability. John Lazia, gambling king of Kansas City, was found slain in 1934. Charles Binaggio, who was in the bootlegging business during prohibition in

---

[20] Cf. *Time*, 54:15–17 (November 28, 1949), for a summary of Costello's racketeering enterprises. Cf. also Mabel A. Elliott and Francis E. Merrill, *op. cit.*, pp. 548–550.

[21] Fred D. Pasley, *Al Capone, The Biography of a Self-Made Man*, Garden City Publishing Co., Garden City, 1930, pp. 1–9.

[22] Cf. Gordon L. Hostetter and Thomas Q. Beesley, *It's a Racket*, Les Quins Books, Chicago, 1929, pp. 25–27.

that city and later an operator of a gambling club, and Charles Gargotta, another notorious Kansas City gambler and bootlegger, were allegedly killed by St. Louis gangsters in 1950 for not "co-operating" in their gambling activities.

The problem of securing information or evidence in gangsters' trials makes it difficult for the police and the courts either to arrest or to convict gangsters guilty of murder, bombings, or participating in gambling or other illegal activities. Despite the enmity between rival gangsters and their lack of any normal inhibitions about undertaking a cold-blooded murder, gangsters maintain a conspiracy of silence and never testify against one another in court unless they are caught in the act. At a Kansas City investigation (conducted by the Special Committee on Organized Crime in Interstate Commerce) gangsters who were brought in to testify repeatedly maintained they knew nothing about the very offenses for which they had been arrested and convicted until they discovered the investigating committee had full records of their cases.[23]

Racketeering in Legitimate Industry

Frank Costello, in his testimony before the Senate investigating committee, has maintained that he is no longer interested in gambling and other illicit activities and is now basically concerned with legitimate business.[24] Actually of course, gangsters' methods of getting something for nothing are also involved in the operation of their so-called legitimate business. Virgil W. Peterson of the Chicago Crime Commission and others with wide information concerning gangster activities say that gangsters have invested heavily in real estate, the liquor industry, and the manufacture of juke boxes, as well as in the hotel and restaurant business.[25] We shall discuss these in more detail.

REAL ESTATE

The housing shortage following World War II offered special temptations for men anxious to make a dishonest dollar. Government loans on a cost basis gave them a chance to pad building costs and to divide the difference between actual and alleged costs both with

[23] Cf. Investigation of Organized Crime in Interstate Commerce, Hearings Before the Special Committee to Investigate Organized Crime in Interstate Commerce, U.S. Senate, 81st Congress, Washington, 1950, Part 4, "Missouri," pp. 313–340.

[24] Ibid., Part 2, pp. 125–213.

[25] Cf. Interim Report of the Special Committee to Investigate Organized Crime in Interstate Commerce, U.S. Senate, Washington, August 18, 1950.

persons supplying materials and with those furnishing labor. Thousands of apartment buildings erected under government subsidy have been constructed by reputable and honest concerns. A great many buildings of flimsy construction have also been erected. The costs were based upon estimates calling for sturdy materials, heavy walls, soundproof floors, and high-grade plumbing. Rents were then established in ratio to the alleged costs. The racketeers in real estate were thus able to secure handsome returns through their deals with contractors and merchants selling building materials. They were also able to establish high rents based upon their alleged costs of construction.

Liquor Manufacture and Distribution

Most of the existing gangster organizations started during prohibition, when organized lawlessness literally prevented any semblance of enforcement of the Volstead Act. Gangsters owned and controlled the manufacture and distribution of liquor during that period. It was almost inevitable that the illicit tie-up between liquor and racketeers continue when prohibition was repealed. Certainly gangsters hold large shares of stock in many breweries and distilleries. They also control the wholesale and retail distribution of liquor in many areas where liquor is not sold in state-supervised stores, as was brought out in the testimony before the Senate's Committee to Investigate Organized Crime in Interstate Commerce at the hearings at Kansas City, Missouri.[26] The attempt to build up a prestige aspect to liquor consumption by advertisements indicating that consumers of liquor are persons of good taste and social influence stems at least partially from the long-time association of liquor with crime and racketeering.

Hotels and Restaurants as Bases for Gambling Operations

The earnings of gambling racketeers, whom we shall discuss shortly, have also been enormous, probably as high as any bootlegger's in prohibition times. In order to conduct their enterprises with as little interference as possible these racketeers have not only bribed public officials but invaded legitimate businesses.[27] Since they must first have a base of operation, they have invested heavily in hotels, night clubs, restaurants. These places must be supplied with food and liquor, so they have bought large holdings in meat and provision companies, in breweries and distilleries. They have also bought automobile agencies,

[26] Cf. *Investigation of Organized Crime in Interstate Commerce*, Part 4, "Missouri," pp. 313–324. Cf. also Virgil W. Peterson, *op. cit.*
[27] Cf. *Interim Report of the Special Committee to Investigate Organized Crime in Interstate Commerce.*

transportation companies, and banks. They are even said to dominate some of the smaller steel companies.[28]

Because these gangsters can supply so much ready cash certain unscrupulous businessmen have been willing to compromise any business ethics they might otherwise possess both in order to finance their operations and in order to secure an enormous income through the monopolies maintained by the gangsters. In a certain city, for example, it has been alleged that a prominent banking family was greatly indebted to "well-heeled" gangsters for financial support.[29] The investigation conducted by the Kefauver Committee in Kansas City recently disclosed that the late gangster Binaggio met with city officials in the business office of the head of a large lithographing company.[30]

Ambulance Chasing

Certain rackets operate almost wholly within the law. "Ambulance chasing" is one of the most widely publicized. Unfortunately all the angles of this racket have never been disclosed. The term itself has been applied to the group of lawyers who rush to the scene of an accident and prevail upon accident victims to push suits for serious damages against the parties allegedly responsible. Such lawyers try to convince injured persons that they have a good case for securing judgments against the drivers of automobiles, railroad companies, building owners in case of accidents in buildings, etc. They often urge persons with relatively minor injuries to sue for a large amount, particularly if those who are either technically or actually responsible for the accident are financially able to pay a sizable sum if a judgment is rendered. Unquestionably ambulance chasers are responsible for a significant number of suits in which damages are awarded.

The unethical ambulance chasing on the part of the insurance agents representing those responsible for accidents has seldom been effectively aired. The number of insurance adjusters who call on victims of accidents while the latter are (1) at the scene of the accident or (2) still in a dazed condition at the hospital or elsewhere must total many times the number of lawyers who are anxious to help the victims bring suit. In fact it is a common practice for an insurance adjuster to take advantage of the weakened or dazed condition of the

[28] *Ibid.*

[29] A special investigation conducted by a criminology student of the author's (at the University of Kansas) revealed this allegation.

[30] *Investigation of Organized Crime in Interstate Commerce*, Part 4, "Missouri," p. 194.

victim and induce him to sign a release absolving the insurance agency from any further responsibility. Often the agent in such cases agrees to make a token payment, or he may agree to pay the ambulance and hospital bill, if these are involved.

It is a well known medical fact that persons suffering from shock, from brain injury, or even from nervous tension following an accident are in a highly suggestible state and under duress of insurance agents may sign releases when the true extent of injuries is still by no means obvious. This pressure on the part of insurance agencies is a nefarious and unethical exploitation of the injured person. In fact some lawyers who have investigated such activities insist that insurance agencies have been responsible for most of the propaganda against lawyers who represent accident victims in court. Certain accident insurance companies have even sponsored legislation in some states which forbids lawyers to appear at the scenes of accidents, thus making it much more likely that a victim will sign a release. In view of the number of persons who sign releases following serious injuries at the behest of unethical insurance companies and consequently receive no suitable compensation for hospital bills, or for long weeks of invalidism during periods of enforced unemployment, it seems obvious that a more ethical plan for protecting victims of accidents is in order. Such a plan might require that no injured person be allowed to sign a release until he had consulted a reputable member of the legal profession.

Unquestionably certain ambulance chasers have been in league with persons involved in fraudulent accidents, and with persons who claim to be seriously injured when at worst they have suffered minor injuries. But it seems equally patent that the powerful influence of insurance companies has created a one-sided picture of the ambulance chaser with an idea of reducing the number of legitimate claims. By vilifying thus the members of the legal profession who defend victims of accidents, the companies cause laws, juries, and public opinion to tend to put legitimate and illegal (or unethical) claims in the same category.[31]

The Black Market

During World War II racketeering reared its ugly head in the excessive profits engineered by clever crooks within the framework of the legitimate businesses which were covered by O.P.A. regulations.

[31] The author is indebted to a well-known Chicago attorney for this insight into the way insurance companies have built up the mythology of ambulance chasing.

Leon Henderson, who served as Chief of the Office of Price Administration, has maintained in fact that most of the black-market operations during this time were carried on by persons in legitimate business and that criminal racketeers played an insignificant role in the evasion of wartime rationing restrictions, price restrictions on commodities, or rent control.[32]

Certainly the black market in meat introduced a relatively new lawbreaker, the American farmer, to the scene. Since many farmers resented the restrictions on their presumed right to butcher livestock for their own consumption, there was undoubtedly widespread violation of the rules in rural areas. Some of these farmers unquestionably supplied black-market meat to both small-town and city butchers. Butchers also often violated the regulations with reference to saving fats. There simply was no effective way to enforce these restrictions where merchants were not basically honest.

Dr. Marshall B. Clinard, who was Chief of the Analysis and Reports Branch of the Enforcement Department of the Office of Price Administration during World War II, claims that the public was overwhelmingly in favor of such regulations, although he admits there were extensive violations. For the year 1944 alone there were 338,029 violations but only 11 per cent of the total number of retail and pre-retail concerns in the United States were involved. The major violators were engaged in the manufacture or processing of foods or commodities used in the production of foods. However, since all concerns were not investigated the actual rate must have been considerably higher.[33]

Even so, prosecutions of violations constituted approximately one-half of the civil court actions and one-sixth of the criminal cases for 1945.[34] Many of the offenses which might have been prosecuted in the criminal court were treated as civil cases, obviously because of the reluctance of officials to bring businessmen to criminal trial. That most of these operations were willful violations seems evident. But some grocers and food dealers accused of violations were only guilty of faulty bookkeeping in the matter of ration stamps. These tiny stamps were easily lost and preserving them for accurate records became a serious problem.

On the other hand there were certain definite instances of racketeering, both in printing fraudulent ration stamps and in securing enor-

[32] Leon Henderson, "How Black Is Our Market?" *Atlantic Monthly*, 178:46–53 (July, 1946).

[33] Marshall B. Clinard, "Criminological Theories of Violations of Wartime Regulations," *American Sociological Review*, 11:258–270 (June, 1946).

[34] *Ibid.*

mous supplies of rationed goods. Recent hearings of the Special Committee to Investigate Organized Crime in Interstate Commerce make it plain that numerous persons with long criminal records entered into extensive black-market operations. A number of large-scale food and candy manufacturers have admitted that they paid over-ceiling prices to obtain sugar and syrup. One enterprising company (according to testimony before the committee) secured sugar and syrup in the black market which it made into jelly that was sold later to the large baking companies for sweetening breads, doughnuts, cakes, and cookies. The government had sanctioned increased manufacture of jellies because the O.P.A. thought they could be used as a spread in place of butter and margarine (because of shortages in civilian supplies of fat).

The Office of Price Administration must have been subject to many pressures. Testimony before the Senate investigating committee disclosed, for example, that a certain person responsible for enforcing the O.P.A. restrictions in New York actually resigned to become an employee of a firm for which he had previously "worked out a settlement" for a violation.[35] The clever manipulation of the laws to the advantage of the racketeers was undoubtedly an important factor in the enormous profits of some food manufacturers and processors. Probably the most significant fact revealed thus far, however, is that money of criminal racketeers was invested in these quasi-legitimate industries. Frank Costello, for example, whose network of illegal and quasi-legal operations we have already discussed, was alleged to have been engaged in the glucose business, supplying glucose to one of the large candy corporations which was investigated by the Senate committee.[36]

Whether or not the economic controls put in force in 1951 will lead to illegal activities and to operations within the law but outside its intended purpose remains to be seen.

GAMBLING

Gambling is probably the most widespread of all illicit activities, largely because it presents persisting lure for its victims. They long for the chance to get something for nothing, despite the fact that the gambler seldom wins. Gambling is at the same time closely allied with the liquor interests, prostitution, and the illicit traffic in narcotic drugs.

[35] Cf. *Investigation of Organized Crime in Interstate Commerce*, Part 3, "Black Market Operations."
[36] *Ibid.*, p. 136.

At least these activities always seem to be closely interlocked in the underworld in our various cities.

The far-flung criminal connections of those engaged in organized gambling have been generally recognized but never effectively verified by any official bodies until rather recently. The hearings conducted in 1950 by the Special Committee of the United States Senate for Investigating Organized Crime in Interstate Commerce indicated the national network of relationships which is maintained by gambling organizations. In the Miami, Florida, area, for example, gangsters formerly operating with the Costello organization in New York, the Capone gang of Chicago, the Blumenfield syndicate in Minneapolis, the Purple gang in Detroit, the Cleveland syndicate, and Phil Kastel's associates from New York have all converged, according to the testimony of Virgil W. Peterson. Earlier (during prohibition) these groups operated as bootleggers but today the gangsters have transferred their interest largely from liquor to gambling, maintaining at the same time wide operations in hotels, restaurants, and other legitimate businesses, as we mentioned earlier in this chapter.[37]

Furthermore, as the Senate investigating committee has brought out, the gamblers who operate in fashionable resort communities often contribute handsome sums to local charities, to the Red Cross, and to other worthy welfare projects. In so doing they contribute to their own "public relations" and create a certain toleration on the part of people interested in community well-being.[38]

Gambling an Age-Old Problem

Like many other aspects of antisocial or criminal behavior the whole problem of gambling is shot through with hypocrisy and has been so for generations. Statutes prohibiting gambling are not new; laws have been enacted throughout history. And always there has been difficulty in enforcing the laws.[39] In England, for example, a law was passed during Henry VIII's reign which prohibited the operation of a gambling establishment. By common-law practice, however, there was no prohibition against gambling contracts. Not until Victoria's reign were all gambling contracts declared null and void.[40] Even so, gambling debts have been generally collected in accordance with the

[37] Cf. *ibid.*, Part 1, "Florida," pp. 135–170.
[38] *Ibid.*
[39] Cf. John Philip Quinn, *Fools of Fortune*, Howe, Chicago, 1890, pp. 100–101.
[40] Cf. Morris Ploscowe, "The Law of Gambling," *Annals of the American Academy of Political and Social Science*, 269:1–8 (May, 1950).

unwritten code of gamblers. And "gentlemen pay their gambling debts."

In the United States during the 1830's most states which were organized by that time had enacted statutes forbidding gambling. New York, Massachusetts, and Pennsylvania were the first states to adopt such legislation. The laws could not guarantee that gambling would cease to exist, however. They merely made it illegal, and gave gamblers a powerful impetus to seek the frontier. Following the disruptions of the Civil War, Governor Warmoth ("carpet-bag" governor of Louisiana from Illinois) sponsored a legalized lottery in Louisiana. Here the abuses eventually became so notorious that the people of the state forced the enactment of laws prohibiting gambling.[41]

In the majority of states today gambling is illegal. But in Nevada it has been wide open since 1931. As a matter of fact gambling was wide open, with very few restrictions, in Nevada prior to 1910. In that year it was forbidden by law, although it seems never to have been prevented thereby. Consequently Nevada decided in 1931 to regulate and license gambling and thus achieve a revenue for the state. Today virtually every type of gambling game (including the roulette wheel, tumbling cages, etc.) flourishes in the casinos there. A few other states have legalized games of chance, lotteries, and in a few instances slot machines when the proceeds are to go to charity. A number of states allow pari-mutuel betting at horse races. Idaho allows slot machines to be licensed on a local-option basis. Washington State formerly permitted them to operate in clubs.[42]

All laws which regulate or forbid certain types of activity as crime do so because there is general agreement that such behavior is harmful to the group. The harm in gambling lies in the fact that the professional gamblers exploit those who are lured by the games of chance and deprive them of money for which they receive nothing in return. Usually the people who can least afford to lose their money are the ones most exploited. From a social viewpoint most gambling operations could be designated as a form of fraud.

The widespread existence of so-called gambling syndicates is due to the corruption of local politics. Easy money accrues to the corrupt politician, who in turn finds such corruption possible chiefly because of the extensive collaboration in lawbreaking which exists among the general population.

The extent to which corrupt officials protect gambling is illustrated

[41] Virgil W. Peterson, "Obstacles to the Enforcement of Gambling Laws," *Annals of the American Academy of Political and Social Science*, 269:9–20 (May, 1950).

[42] Morris Ploscowe, *op. cit.*

by the testimony given the Senate Committee on Organized Crime at a hearing on February 7, 1951, when Sheriff Frank J. Clancy of the Jefferson Parish (where New Orleans is located) admitted that he himself participated in the gambling games and that he had made $78,000 in betting on races during the 4 years preceding. He acknowledged that most people lose betting on horse races but that tips from stableboys and jockeys had enabled him to "play the last race and win." Clancy admitted he did all this despite his sworn oath to abolish gambling and said he was moved to permit gambling in his parish in order to give the old and unemployed jobs in the casinos![43]

The Major Forms of Gambling

We cannot consider all types of gambling here, but we may say briefly that the major forms of gambling in the United States are the unorganized type connected with cards and poker and the organized variety including bookmaking, the numbers racket, and slot machines and pinball machines. In addition there are the gambling casinos which depend upon the roulette wheel and other mechanical devices (such as the bird cage), which are set with mathematical precision to pay a certain percentage to the players and to return the major proportion to those who operate or own them. Despite the fact that all states except Nevada make the operation of mechanical devices illegal, they are to be found in many gambling establishments in other states. The only widely distributed mechanical contrivance has been the slot machine. We shall confine our major discussion to bookmaking, the numbers game, and slot machines.

BOOKMAKING

Bookmaking is the term applied to what may be called organized illegal betting, usually on the outcome of horse races, athletic contests, and other sports events in which the results theoretically are uncertain, but on which odds are placed. Actually bookmaking relies seriously on tips relayed, in the case of horse races, through jockeys or others who in certain instances are able to have a hand in fixing the race. In athletic events the outcome is occasionally fixed by gamblers who pay certain athletes to fumble the ball and lose the game to their opponents. Horse racing constitutes the major business of bookmakers, however. In the United States the only legal betting on races is at those race tracks where pari-mutuel betting is permitted. Here race

43 Pittsburgh Post-Gazette, February 8, 1951, p. 2, cols. 5–6.

fans may place bets on the winner, on the horse which is to come in second or to place, etc.

It should be stated that friendly wagers between friends are not bookmaking. Bookmaking is making a business of betting; the person taking the bets keeps the money unless the better wins and it is usually arranged so that relatively few of those who place bets win. The business of booking depends upon information sent out by news or press services over leased wires or by telephones to distributors, who in turn relay it to sub-distributors, who again relay it to their sub-sub-distributors or bookmakers. Actually the distributors (called "drops") and sub-distributors are usually bookmakers too. The amounts charged for their service depend generally upon the number of customers to whom the information is relayed. Department of Justice officials estimate that there are approximately 150,000 "bookies" (persons engaged in bookmaking) operating on such a basis.

The gambling wire services are virtually all controlled by men who are identified with so-called criminal syndicates. Thus the Continental Press of Chicago (the major racing information service) is allegedly controlled by the Capone interests. The Harmony Publishing Company in Kansas City has been controlled by gambling interests in that city including those of the recently slain Charles Gargotta. According to sworn testimony before the Senate investigating committee, this company secured its information from the General News Service of Chicago and had bought its right to do business from the Trans-American News and Publishing Company. The Pioneer News Company operates in St. Louis. These are only a few important middle-western "drops." The Armstrong Racing Publications and the Daily Racing Form in New York City (the latter a service of Triangle Publications) are distributed on even more extensive circuits throughout the country. There are literally thousands of channels of distribution through the elaborate system which has been developed by the Continental Press Service and many other such services exist. Until some federal legislation is enacted which prohibits the interstate transmission of this information or hot tips on the way races are to go such transmission of information is for the most part legal, even though the betting is not.

At the same time practically all such information (with the exception of the racing services of regular newspapers) is backed by criminal and gambling interests. The information is necessary for the numerous gambling establishments to operate, and their operation is for the most part illegal. That is, the practice of bookmaking or the accepting of wagers on horse.races is illegal in the District of Columbia and every state in the Union except Nevada. There are also a few states which make the dissemination of racing news illegal. In Michigan, for example, it is illegal to publish betting odds before the event takes place but not afterwards. Nevada prohibits transmitting betting information from within the state to outside the state by telephone, telegraph, teletype, radio, or signaling devices. In Pennsylvania it is illegal for any public utility to provide private wires for gambling information. In Oklahoma penalties are attached to transmitting or delivering information for horse-racing bets, and in Texas knowingly furnishing telephone, telegraph, teletype, teleprint, or radio service or equipment or placing such service on property used for bookmaking is a crime.

Obviously there would be many difficulties involved in requiring telephone and telegraph companies to enforce gambling laws although in numerous instances these companies have denied service to parties they know to be operating gambling establishments. Administrative officers of such business enterprises seldom investigate the character of their customers; and telephone and telegraph installation men can hardly be expected to check on the legality of business establishments. But bookmaking is one of the most serious of the various gambling activities. Federal legislation prohibiting the dissemination of race news seems to be one way in which it might be outlawed.[44]

An even lower (swindling) form of bookmaking is fake bookmaking. Here the bookmaking establishment leads victims known to have money to place enormous bets on "sure" things, only to discover they have written checks for all their available cash and that there never was the slightest chance they would ever secure any return. This we discussed earlier. As in all gambling, the aim is to make great gain on the advance information or "fixed" race, but actually there is no fixing and only complete certainty of losing. This form of bogus bookmaking is usually called the "pay-off," for that, in slang parlance, is what it is.[45]

There are other varieties of bookmaking, most of them in connection with athletic events, some within the field of collegiate athletics. In January, 1951, for example, the center on the Manhattan College basketball team, a high scorer, was offered $1000 to lose the game to

[44] Cf. Transmission of Gambling Information, Hearings Before a Subcommittee of the Committee on Interstate and Foreign Commerce, U.S. Senate, 81st Congress, Washington, 1950, pp. 888–962. This volume covers extensive information and sworn testimony on the problem of bookmaking and the sources of information.

[45] David W. Mawrer, op. cit., pp. 63–88.

De Paul University. Instead he talked to the coach, who called him out of the game, and another player was put in. Police later found that the co-captains had thrown three games the year before in return for a $40 weekly salary and $5000. In the meantime the bookmakers had been able to tip off certain gamblers on a sure outcome of the game. Two previous scandals had occurred in games played at Madison Square Garden, one in 1945 and one in 1949,[46] and there have been many others in other parts of the country. Similar gangster corruption of football scores has long been rumored in collegiate circles.

THE NUMBERS GAME

The numbers or policy game is a special type of lottery in which the individual pays to guess the lucky number with the hope that he will receive a large sum for guessing correctly. The numbers may be football scores, pari-mutuel figures at a race track, stock market quotations, or some other easily verified number. When the number is associated with racing the horse race is often allegedly fixed in order to pay off well to gamblers.[47]

It has been estimated that billions of dollars are lost every year in the policy racket and the ignorant classes are the most exploited. Ray Sprigle, for example, estimated that the numbers racket took 50 million dollars annually from Pittsburghers and that an additional 50 million is derived by the same racket from the surrounding county. The numbers racket in adjoining counties in this industrial area took another large amount. Sprigle, an ace reporter of the Pittsburgh *Post-Gazette*, claimed that these figures are a reasonably reliable estimate.[48] During the summer of 1950 he published a series of articles, naming names and giving addresses of operators of stationery stores, newsstands, novelty stores, etc., all of whom he accused of dealing extensively in the numbers racket with the co-operation (and profit sharing) of the police. The far-flung network of the policy racket in Pittsburgh extends to surrounding suburbs in Allegheny, Westmoreland, and other counties. One of the most serious aspects of the racket is its widespread patronage among the lower-income and working classes and especially in the Negro residential area in the "hill" district. Many of those who play the numbers regularly can ill afford to lose the amounts they so regularly do, but all are motivated by the high returns, often of 600 or 800 to 1, due the lucky person. Some people

[46] *Time*, 57:85 (January 29, 1951).
[47] Courtney Ryley Cooper, *Here's to Crime*, Little, Brown, Boston, 1937, chap. 3.
[48] Ray Sprigle, "Inside the Rackets," Pittsburgh *Post-Gazette*, July 10, 1950, p. 1, cols. 1–2.

condone such betting on the ground that only small amounts are involved. Actually the amounts are not small, but total an enormous sum.

As Herbert Asbury has recounted, people often play numbers on the authority of their dream books or consult fortunetellers on their lucky numbers. Pennsylvania was the first state to attempt to control the policy racket and passed a law forbidding it in 1805, but, as the recent investigations indicate, it is still going strong. Technically the numbers racket is illegal in most states. Louisiana, in fact, is the only state that ever made it legal.[49] The Kansas City grand jury estimated that 3½ million dollars are contributed by the poor in that city in the numbers game.[50] In view of the estimates for Pittsburgh it seems likely that the figures for Kansas City are an understatement.

SLOT MACHINES

Slot machines have been called "one-armed bandits" because they take their money from such willing victims. These victims play the machines in the vain hope that they will "hit the jackpot," even though they all must realize that the machines are set against them. At least they are usually adjusted so as to return only 20 per cent of the money taken in.[51] The majority of slot machines are in private clubs, resort hotels, suburban night clubs. Except for the few states which license them they are illegal, yet operate with the full knowledge of the police in most cases. They are often in fact located in fraternal organizations to which the police belong. Some clubs receive their major revenue from slot machines. Many otherwise law-abiding citizens take a chance on a pocketful of quarters or lesser amounts. Because so many people who play the slot machines are relatively well-to-do, public officials often say there is no great harm in such gambling. It again contributes to the illicit income of our worst (and least penalized) criminal element.

With the recently enacted federal legislation slot machines may cease to exist in any large numbers. For on January 2, 1951, President Truman signed the bill forbidding the shipment of slot machines in interstate commerce. At about the same time slot machines were ordered confiscated in the various army and navy clubs. Slot machines

[49] Herbert Asbury, Sucker's Progress (An Informal History of Gambling in America from the Colonies to Canfield), Dodd, Mead, New York, 1938, chap. 6.

[50] Cf. Report of the Kansas City Grand Jury, quoted in Transmission of Gambling Information, Hearings Before a Subcommittee of the Committee on Interstate and Foreign Commerce, on Senate 3358, pp. 687–688.

[51] Ernest Blanche, You Can't Win, Public Affairs Press, Washington, 1949, p. 89.

had previously been outlawed in all states but Nevada, Montana, and Maryland (and were legal in only three of the counties of Maryland) but continued to operate in virtually all states. Since all slot machines are produced by a series of companies in Chicago there is some chance the business may be wiped out by the restrictions on shipping.[52] The same companies have also made juke boxes and vending machines and can easily shift to their legitimate business. At least it should be easier to prevent the shipment of slot machines than to control their operation.

Whether gambling can ever be eliminated by law or not is hard to say. Some people hold that state-regulated gambling—in which the state, rather than private concerns, secures the percentage—would be a more effective means of controlling the obvious human desire to take a chance. The enormous toll involved in the current operation of the various gambling rackets and the enormous "take" of the racketeers indicate the extent to which political corruption exists, as the author hopes to have made plain.

Many problems complicate the enforcement of the various laws against gambling, bookmaking, and slot machines. So far as those who supply news to bookmaking gamblers and numbers for the numbers racket are concerned, there seems to be an organized conspiracy to operate within the law in giving out information and to pretend complete innocence as to how their "news" is distributed to the numerous persons acting as "drops" for the news and in turn taking bets and receiving the money played in the numbers game. It thus becomes very difficult if not completely impossible to invoke federal laws with reference to the transmission of gambling information. Meanwhile gambling itself usually takes place in a local establishment, whether it be an elaborate gambling casino, a night club, or a dingy tavern. Chances on numbers similarly are sold locally, frequently at small newsstands, on the street close to a newsstand, in saloons, or elsewhere. Sometimes they are sold in hotel lobbies, or by waiters in bars or dining rooms, and occasionally in the best hotels.

Because most states outlaw slot machines, the manufacturers usually loan them as concessions in private clubs where the police cannot enter without a warrant. Highly respectable resort hotels and country clubs "patronized by the best people" (even army and navy clubs, as we have seen) have often co-operated with these one-armed bandits.

[52] *Facts on Files*, 11:5 (January 5–January 11, 1951). Cf. *Time*, 57:72 (January 15, 1951).

The Hazards of Gambling

The hazards of gambling are primarily for the "suckers"—those who invest with so little chance of return. The professional gambler seldom really gambles. Through chicanery, dishonesty, stacking the cards, loaded dice, etc., he eliminates the chances from games of chance for himself. Similarly in the numbers racket the "pay-off" is fixed so as to make enormous profits. In fact the person picking a number has about one chance in a thousand of choosing the lucky number.[53] In the case of pinball machines any skill which the players may acquire is offset either by transferring the machine to another location or by "gimmicking" the plungers with extra springs (which may be removed later). Pinball machines are usually fixed to pay off when first installed in order to lure customers, but later "the machine gets the nickels."[54]

The Relation Between Big Business and Gambling

In a sense every business enterprise is a risk and for that reason even the most honest of businesses bears a certain resemblance to gambling. Merchants cannot be certain that their merchandise will sell at the prices asked or that new types of goods will sell at all. It is the operations of great holding companies, however, that have borne the greatest resemblance to gambling. Some holding companies have been in a sense looting companies in which the stockholders have staked their earnings in the shares of the subsidiary companies. Certain business activities have been condemned by law, as we have said in our discussion of white-collar crime.[55] Before the present regulations of the Securities and Exchange Commission were established investment banks often overcapitalized a company and then manipulated its watered stock so as to reduce their prices with all the numerical accuracy of an actuary table. The companies became "unable to pay dividends," which in fact they never intended to pay, while the moneys invested by the stockholders were absorbed by investment banks or boards of directors. Such business methods fleeced the stockholders as surely and effectively as any "con" man ever swindled his victim. Some such promoters, as for example Samuel Insull, achieved the status of civic leaders until their empires crashed like a stack of cards. So long as their clients anticipated high dividends they offered no complaints at shady methods. Only when they saw their invest-

[53] Ernest Blanche, op. cit., p. 71.   [54] Ibid., p. 95.   [55] Chap. 3, pp. 38–45.

ments vanishing were the stockholders willing to give information to the Federal Trade Commission.[56]

The various overcapitalized real-estate "booms," the Wall Street manipulations preceding the crash in 1929, the extensive unregulated banking practices which existed prior to the New Deal—all in their respective fashions resemble to gambling. For gambling feeds upon the same lure, the same desire to secure something, if not for nothing, at least for very little expenditure. The novice who gambles fails to consider the fact that his chances of winning are small. He is merely impressed with the fact that someone will win a large amount and conceivably he could be the winner.

ORGANIZED CRIME AND CORRUPT POLITICS

Since organized crime and political corruption exist in reciprocal relationship they go hand in hand in disorganizing the community. Organized crime strikes deeply into the basic disturbances which threaten the community, as the author has stated elsewhere.[57]

The very officials who are supposed to enforce the law are thus often interested in the profits in local criminal activities. Glaring instances of such corruption could undoubtedly be established in every community where crime is rife, as in Pittsburgh, where Ray Sprigle, as we have said, has fearlessly exposed corruption in the police department in connection with the numbers racket.

During the heyday of the Pendergast regime in Kansas City police extracted protection money from houses of prostitution and gambling; even the city manager, McElroy, was a tool of machine politics while election frauds made it impossible for the honest people "to turn the rascals out." Under the Pendergast regime when a criminal who "had connections" was brought to justice he was almost certain to be tried in a court where the jury was "fixed." Not until a federal investigation of the vote fraud resulted in prosecution by the federal courts was there any opportunity to put men with a social conscience in office.[58]

Finally through the effective co-operation of the United States District Attorney, the governor of Missouri, and the United States Department of Justice, the machine government in Kansas City was driven out and in 1940 a reform government was installed. Hundreds

[56] Cf. in this connection Edwin H. Sutherland, "Crime and Business," *Annals of the American Academy of Political and Social Science*, 217:112–118 (September, 1941).

[57] Mabel A. Elliott and Francis E. Merrill, *op. cit.*, p. 542.

[58] Cf. Mabel A. Elliott and Francis E. Merrill, *Social Disorganization*, Harper, New York, 2nd ed., 1941, pp. 934–935. This material is not available in the 1950 edition.

of houses of prostitution and gambling dens were closed, a well-trained and conscientious city manager was installed, and Thomas Pendergast went to prison for income tax evasion. Kansas City was allegedly quiet.[59]

But not for long. Too many members of the old political machine had tasted of the fruits of corruption. Thomas Pendergast died, but his organization lived on to regain a considerable degree of political power within a few short years. Certain men in legitimate business had always profited from the lucrative contracts they secured from city officials. These men often urged the police to relax their enforcement of the law. Some of the gangster elements moved to the periphery of the city. Others moved to that imaginary boundary which separates Missouri and Kansas so as to make the problem of law enforcement extremely difficult.[60] Even federal officials who try to enforce federal laws in local communities are often stymied. Certainly they have a much better record for high standards of official conduct than state and local politicians. Even so it has been alleged that the crooks themselves have often secured access to federal files through "leaks." Leaks are often difficult to trace since they may occur through janitors, plumbers, etc., as well as through those who are "entrusted" with secret documents. The vast army of protection which the professional criminals have thrown up has become a virtual counterspy organization.

In recent years many earnest citizens have been up in arms about racketeering, but in few cities has there been any truly satisfactory effort to put an end to it. Even where a relatively successful attack has been made on the intermeshed activities of corrupt politicians and the underworld the changed conditions seldom endure over any extended period unless there is continuous vigilance on the part of the local citizens. As it is, most citizens are unwilling to devote themselves permanently to keeping corruption out of politics. The zeal of a reform movement may result in "turning the rascals out" temporarily, but once this is accomplished the aroused citizens settle back into their accustomed routine. They become absorbed in their own problems of making a living and in concerns related to their families and themselves. Not so with the corrupt politicians. Scarcely are they unseated by so-called honest citizens than they plot ways and means of making a comeback and of controlling the next election. Houses of

---

[59] *Ibid.*, pp. 935–936.
[60] *Investigation of Organized Crime in Interstate Commerce*, Part 4, "Missouri," pp. 232–233.

prostitution which were locked and padlocked reappear in other parts of town; or, if the surveillance is strong, prostitutes may operate as call girls under cover of legitimate jobs as waitresses, manicurists, etc. Slot machines driven out of public restaurants, drugstores, etc., find a refuge in private clubs. Gangsters driven out of town move outside the city limits or to a rural area where there are no police. Only by constant effort can organized crime be kept down. So long as we fail in developing an adequate system of social values—that is, one to which the citizens adhere almost universally—organized crime will continue to be a problem.

As a result of the Congressional committee hearings on organized crime, Congress passed a law in October, 1951, requiring all gamblers to register with the Bureau of Internal Revenue before December 1, 1951; all who signed were required to pay an "occupational" tax of 50 dollars. Failure to comply with this law may be punished with a fine up to $10,000 and 5 years in prison. Gamblers who run a gambling agency are also required to pay a tax of 10 per cent on all bets, whether the gamblers win or lose. All lists of gamblers are to be open to the public and to law enforcement agencies.[61]

The purpose of this registration obviously is not to raise revenue, but to bring the local gambling establishments to the attention of the government officials. Since bookmaking is legal in no state except Nevada, the law is tantamount to requiring lawbreakers to give public notice of their intent to break the law. *The law does not license lawbreaking.*

On December 4, 1951, the Bureau of Internal Revenue announced that 7706 gamblers throughout the country had applied for occupational tax stamps.[62] We may presume many gamblers did not register. Meanwhile the federal government has also initiated a movement to confiscate all slot machines. How successful these attempts to curtail gambling may be none can foresee. The legality of a law requiring gamblers to register may be questioned, but since the purpose of the law is to prevent gambling it seems likely that few judges will oppose the bill; nor is it likely that gamblers will have the temerity to fight the law in the courts. One of the most obvious effects of the gambling tax law has been the decision of the Continental Press Service to discontinue its national race wire news after March 12, 1952. This news service alleged that the demand for its racing information had declined as much as 80 per cent.[63]

[61] *Pittsburgh Post Gazette*, October 29, 1951, p. 23.
[62] *Pittsburgh Post Gazette*, December 5, 1951, p. 1.
[63] *Pittsburgh Post Gazette*, March 10, 1952, p. 2.

One of the striking revelations of the Kefauver Committee was the tie-up between gangsters and politicians in New York City. During the hearings held there William O'Dwyer, former mayor and currently ambassador to Mexico, admitted that he had given jobs to persons with underworld connections. Other testimony was to the effect that certain groups had attempted to secure political favors by "good will" payments. Although most of the exposures were with reference to the collusion between Tammany Hall (the major Democratic machine in New York) and organized crime, there were also sensational charges that the state police had knowingly permitted gambling at the state-operated resort Saratoga Springs.[64] Earlier in his career the governor of New York had been elevated to national prominence as a "gang-busting" district attorney in New York.

The Senate investigation thus has served an important function in disclosing the links between the criminal world and the professional politician. It has also made plain the interstate character of organized gambling and bookmaking and may (or may not) eventuate in attempts at control through federal legislation aimed at preventing the transmission of gambling information unless the gambling tax law virtually forces all the race news services to shut down because of decline in demand. The federal government cannot legislate against local tie-ups between crime and politics, but it has been suggested that a National Crime Commission serve as a national watchdog. Certainly the incomes of gangsters under suspicion can be investigated by the Treasury Department.[65]

SELECTED BIBLIOGRAPHY

Annals of the American Academy of Political and Social Science, 269:1–149 (May, 1950). With the exception of the book review section, the entire volume of this journal is devoted to the subject of gambling.

Barnes, Harry E., and Teeters, Negley K., New Horizons in Criminology, Prentice-Hall, New York, rev. ed., 1951, chaps. 1 and 2. These chapters contain excellent material on organized crime and the tie-up with corrupt politics.

Cooper, Courtney Ryley, Designs in Scarlet, Little, Brown, Boston, 1939. This is a fearless exposé of the tie-up between prostitution, crime, the liquor interests, and politics.

Elliott, Mabel A., and Merrill, Francis E., Social Disorganization, Harper, New York, 3rd ed., 1950, chaps. 25 and 26. These chapters, entitled "Po-

[64] New York Times, Sunday, March 25, 1951, Section 4, E1 and 2.
[65] Ibid.

litical Corruption" and "Crime and the Community," discuss many facets of organized crime.

Hoover, J. Edgar, *Persons in Hiding*, Little, Brown, 1938. This book gives a colorful account of famous professional criminals, chiefly gangsters, who have been "hunted" by the Federal Bureau of Investigation.

Hynd, Alan, *The Giant Killers*, McBride, New York, 1945. This book presents vivid, factual reporting on gangsters, professional racketeers, gamblers, and corrupt politicans in various cities in the United States. Data are given on Al Capone, the Pendergast regime, Moses Annenberg, operator of the race-track tipster sheet, James Monroe Smith, and many others.

Interim Report of the Special Committee to Investigate Organized Crime in Interstate Commerce, U.S. Senate, Washington, August 18, 1950. This describes an initial investigation of the far-reaching underworld connections in American cities.

Investigation of Organized Crime in Interstate Commerce, Hearings Before the Special Committee to Investigate Organized Crime in Interstate Commerce, U.S. Senate, 81st Congress, May 26 and 27, July 13, 14, and 15, August 9 and 10, and September 19, 22, and 26, 1950, Washington, 1950, Part 1, "Florida." These hearings present significant materials with reference to organized crime in Florida and give revealing testimony with reference to the gangsters who have invaded Florida from other parts of the country. Evidence of the real-estate holdings of the criminal element is also presented.

Investigation of Organized Crime in Interstate Commerce, Hearings Before the Special Committee to Investigate Organized Crime in Interstate Commerce, U.S. Senate, 81st Congress, July 6 and September 28, 29, and 30, 1950, Washington, 1950, Part 4, "Missouri." This presents hearings in Kansas City, Missouri, with reference to the extent of gambling and its relation to other criminal activities within Missouri and other states.

Kinsey, Alfred C., Pomeroy, Wardell B., and Martin, Clyde E., *Sexual Behavior in the Human Male*, Saunders, Philadelphia, 1948. This book reveals widespread sexual activity outside the bonds of marriage.

MacDonald, John C. R., *Crime Is a Business*, Stanford University Press, Stanford University, California, 1939. An excellent treatise on organized swindling and racketeering has been written by a competent and intelligent police inspector. Aimed primarily at policemen, it provides valuable information to the student of crime.

Mawrer, David W., *The Big Con*, Bobbs-Merrill, Indianapolis, 1940. This book gives significant information about swindlers and their operations.

Transmission of Gambling Information, Hearings Before a Subcommittee of the Committee on Interstate and Foreign Commerce, U.S. Senate, 81st Congress, April 17, 20, 21, 24, 26, 27, and 28 and May 1, 2, 3, and

4, 1950, Washington, 1950. This volume gives detailed information on the methods employed in transmitting gambling information and discloses the network of relationships among gamblers in various cities.

Whitman, Howard, *Terror in the Streets*, Dial, New York, 1951. This gives a vivid popular account of violent offenses and offenders in recent years. The "dangers" are probably exaggerated, however.

CHAPTER 7

Special Types of Offenders

We have discussed the rank-and-file offender who is imprisoned for his criminal conduct in Chapter 5. Other types of present-day offenders have attracted wide attention in the press, however, because of either the special nature of their offense or the special dangers their criminal activity imposes. We refer first to those offenders who are primarily behavior problems—whose personal maladjustment involves personal rejection by the group, as in case of the drug addict and the alcoholic. A second type of offender, the national political offender, has aroused particular interest because his offenses are so closely related to security and the machinery of war. This category includes the traitor, the spy, and the selective service violator, who may be a draft evader with no ethical scruples or a conscientious objector to war.

THE SUMPTUARY OFFENDERS

The drug addict is a criminal because of his illegal consumption; the alcoholic because of his excessive consumption. Both are apparently adjudged offensive because their conduct not only involves serious danger or deterioration to themselves but is also morally repulsive to the majority of persons. The drug addict and the alcoholic are generally regarded as disorganized individuals who are escaping the difficulties in their life situations by the dubious euphoria derived from drugs or alcohol.

The Origins of Drug Control

By the terms of the opium law, popularly known as the Harrison Anti-Narcotic Act (enacted in 1914), all persons in possession of narcotics or engaged in their sale, except upon a physician's prescription, are subject to severe penalties and imprisonment in our federal penitentiaries. The Harrison Act was a direct outgrowth of the work of the International Opium Convention, which began to negotiate restrictive measures in the international opium trade in 1911–1912. In 1915 three nations, China, the United States, and the Netherlands, agreed to restrict all traffic in drugs save for medical purposes. Previous agitation over the drug situation had begun in earnest in the United States when the spread of the opium habit in the Philippines reached such serious proportions that an International Opium Commission met in Shanghai to discuss the problem in February, 1909. This meeting ended in a recommendation for a conference to be held at the Hague with representatives of the various governments empowered to devise means of restricting traffic in opium, morphine, and cocaine. In consequence the United States was committed to an early enactment of legislation covering the use of opiates at home. The provisions for the restrictions as drawn up by the several nations are most severe.[1]

Our opium control law (the Harrison Anti-Narcotic Act), which went into effect on March 1, 1915, restricts the sale, manufacture, or importation of opiates except for medicinal purposes and requires all physicians to prescribe such drugs under rigid regulations.[2] Various states also have laws governing narcotics, but the majority of persons imprisoned for violating drug acts are sentenced under the Harrison Act. The Marihuana Tax Act which went into effect in 1937 has been responsible for a sizable increase in the number of convictions.

Initially these various drug acts augmented our prison populations. In 1938 there were, for example, 2369 cases, whereas in 1937, 2557 persons were convicted for violating the federal narcotics revenue laws, with 61 additional cases for violating the Marihuana Tax Act, which was in effect only November and December of that year. For the same year, 2829 more persons were convicted of violating state narcotic acts.[3] The rigid enforcement of the narcotic laws has resulted in a tremendous decline in drug consumption. By 1940 the number convicted of violating drug acts and sentenced to institutions was only

---

[1] Hamilton Wright, "The End of the Opium Question," *Review of Reviews*, 51:464–466 (April, 1915).

[2] *United States Statutes at Large*, 63rd Congress, 1913, 1915, Vol. 38, Part I, "Public Laws," pp. 275–279, 785–790.

[3] Cf. *Prisoners in State and Federal Reformatories*, 1938, Bureau of the Census, U.S. Department of Commerce, Washington, 1941, p. 13.

2225. In 1946 the number stood at 1391, but the majority of these (1172) were convicted under the federal law.[4]

Heated controversy has arisen over whether drug addiction is a medical or a criminal problem. Most medical authorities contend that drug addicts are in need of medical attention and supervision and that the Harrison Act really creates criminals instead of reducing crime. This is doubtful since before the laws which have restricted drugs were enacted there was widespread association of the addict with the underworld and especially with prostitution.[5]

The Extent of Drug Addiction

Meanwhile critics of the Harrison Act maintain it has never been effectively enforced. At least relatively few persons are arrested and convicted as narcotic offenders. In 1950, for example, only 8539 persons were arrested for narcotic offenses.[6] Yet authorities maintain that less than 1 per cent of the users is ever apprehended. The actual number of persons addicted to narcotics is of course unknown, but estimates range from 100,000 to 4,000,000.[7] The latter estimate is probably too high. There are, however, many types of narcotics involved in drug addiction, including morphine, heroin, opium, cocaine, hashish, and marihuana. The widespread use of barbiturates is also becoming a drug problem, but it is not a violation of criminal law, although many states restrict their sale to persons presenting a physician's prescription.

The drug problem, like many other problems which involve value judgments with reference to behavior, presents a dilemma. Rigid restriction of the sale of narcotics has unquestionably decreased the number who use them in certain areas. But it has made possible the profitable "drug racket." The truly salutary aspect of the law probably lies in the reduction of the medical use of narcotics. Physicians have recognized more keenly the dangers of drugs and have been more careful in prescribing them, and self-medication by many potential users has been definitely curtailed.

In general the medical profession regards narcotic addiction as an

---

[4] *Prisoners in State and Federal Prisons and Reformatories*, 1946, Bureau of the Census, U.S. Department of Commerce, Washington, 1948, p. 53.

[5] Lawrence Kolb, "Drug Addiction in Relation to Crime," *Mental Hygiene*, 9:74–89 (January, 1925).

[6] *Uniform Crime Reports*, Annual Bulletin, 1950, Federal Bureau of Investigation, U.S. Department of Justice, Washington, 1951, p. 111.

[7] Cf. Donald P. Wilson, *My Six Convicts*, Rinehart, New York, 1951, p. 330.

illness and the layman regards it as a vice or crime. In any case addiction stems from the use of drugs, and the narcotic is often a criminal on other counts. As an illness most narcotic addiction is difficult to cure, with the exception of addiction to cocaine and marihuana. Users of the latter do not have serious physical withdrawal symptoms when the drug is discontinued. However, some of them have an "emotional" dependency on it and may shift to another drug if they give up one of these.[8] Meanwhile morphine, heroin, and opium addiction will probably always be problems until some non-addictive substitute with the sedative and analgesic character of opium and its derivatives is found.[9]

Unfortunately addiction is often the sequel to taking opiates for medical purposes, as we have implied. There are several types of addicts who may be considered criminals. A distinction should be made, as Dr. Wolff suggests,[10] between the *criminal addict*, who commits offenses in order to secure the drug, or as a result of using the drug, the *addicted criminal*, who as a member of the underworld becomes addicted to the drug, and the addict who uses the drug to annul any inhibitions he might have when he wishes to commit a crime. Some get into the drug racket, which is itself a crime, in order to secure drugs for their own consumption.

In any case, the addict's problem, though essentially a medical one, has been complicated seriously by the penal nature of the law. At the same time the addict's craving may become so intense that he will steal to obtain the drug. Moreover, the prices demanded by the narcotic racketeers are so high that the addict is frequently unable to obtain sufficient money by honorable means to purchase the drug. Because addicts must associate with the underworld and be continually on the alert to evade law enforcement officers, they may occasionally commit other crimes because of this involvement.[11] The press has further complicated all this by sensational news stories about the numerous crimes committed by dope fiends.[12] Such stories are for the most part unfounded. Opiates, instead of inducing belligerent activity,

[8] Cf. *Investigation of Organized Crime in Interstate Commerce*, Hearings Before the Special Committee to Investigate Organized Crime in Interstate Commerce, U.S. Senate, 82nd Congress, May 29 and June 7, 12, 26, and 27, 1951, Washington, 1951, Part 14, "Narcotics," especially pp. 138–150.

[9] Pablo O. Wolff, "Narcotic Addiction and Criminality," *Journal of Criminal Psycho-Pathology*, 5:35–58 (July, 1942).

[10] *Ibid.*

[11] Lawrence Kolb, *op. cit.* Cf. also Alfred R. Lindesmith, "Dope Fiend Mythology," *Journal of Criminal Law and Criminology*, 31:199–208 (July–August, 1940).

[12] Alfred R. Lindesmith, *op. cit.* Cf. also Alfred R. Lindesmith, *Opiate Addiction*, Principia Press, Bloomington, Indiana, 1947, for a detailed discussion.

as Dr. Kolb points out, promote a sense of peace and calm.[13] Extreme nervous irritability and restlessness, the sense of being ready to "jump out of one's skin" disappear with the administration of the drug. The psychopathic or neurotic addict loses his sense of inferiority, fear, and discontent and feels confident and self-possessed. If he has sufficient food, he in no way belies by conduct or appearance that he is an addict. Only when addicts sacrifice food for the drug are they likely to manifest evidences of addiction. Persons under the influence of marihuana are another question; like the alcoholic, they may become so intoxicated by the drug as to be a menace to others.[14]

Cure of the patient is what the public should demand and what our legal provisions should promote. Compulsory hospitalization of addicts until cured might be a much better solution to the problem than committing them to prison. As a matter of fact the addicts who are imprisoned are often hospitalized. Many authorities, however, especially medical men, think it should be possible to hospitalize them without the stigma of a prison sentence. Ordinarily a drug addict may be cured in a year. If he has a relapse he is not hopeless but can usually be cured eventually. He is a sick individual, and the penologist of tomorrow will undoubtedly point to the present-day treatment as one evidence of the ignorance of our generation.

Among adult drug addicts who are apprehended and sentenced those addicted to morphine constitute the largest group. The great majority of these offenders, as is true of most prisoners, come from the lower economic and social stratum. These, however, are the addicts who get caught, and are only a small fraction of the total number of addicts. Physicians are found among drug addicts far out of proportion to their numbers. In fact, drug addiction may be regarded as an occupational hazard of the medical profession. The physician is tempted because of his special knowledge to use the drug for its relief and he has it available without resort to racketeers.[15] So far as types of crimes are concerned there is some disparity of opinion as to whether opiate smokers and heroin and morphine addicts commit crimes while under their influence.[16] Those addicted to opiates may, however, commit crimes in order to secure money to buy the drugs. Heroin, which is 5 times stronger than morphine, creates a greater craving, hence is more likely to lead to criminal behavior.[17]

[13] Lawrence Kolb, op. cit.   [14] Ibid.
[15] M. J. Pescor, Physician Drug Addicts. Reprint from Diseases of the Nervous System, 3:2 (June, 1942).
[16] Lawrence Kolb, op. cit.   [17] Ibid.

The use of marihuana is probably even more serious than the use of other drugs so far as its effect upon behavior is concerned. Marihuana seems to produce greater mental and moral degeneration than the others. Inhibitions of all sorts disappear with its use and reason is apparently impaired. On the other hand, courage seems to be greatly increased and if a person is mentally deteriorated he may be impelled to aggressive criminal conduct. Marihuana makes the average person act as though intoxicated because it interferes with his perception of space. It is known to have been widely used in India by persons who commit premeditated crimes.[18]

Marihuana and the "hashish" drug widely used in India and Egypt are one and the same. The association of this drug with criminal conduct is directly evidenced in our own word "assassin," which is derived from the word *hashshashin* meaning one who kills under the influence of the drug.[19] Science has not thus far established the degree of addiction which marihuana may produce, but it is generally believed that the habit may be broken more easily than opiate addiction. There are apparently considerable variations in the effects upon individual users.[20]

TEEN-AGERS AND DRUG ADDICTION

One of the appalling aspects of narcotic addiction has been its marked increase among teen-agers growing out of the drug peddlers' heartless solicitation of customers among young persons. It has been a matter of common knowledge among law-enforcing agents that narcotic peddlers have been enticing children of high school age into the illegal drug market for many years. Recent disclosures indicate that a shocking number of school boys and girls have become victims of heroin and other narcotics. In New York City William Jansen, superintendent of the city's schools, testified that he believed one out of every 200 school children was using habit-forming drugs. Sensational revelations of narcotic addiction among New York City high school students were made by press and radio in June, 1951. Tragic instances were recounted of young people who were led to commit crimes or become prostitutes to secure money for narcotics. These disclosures have aroused many persons, both to the actual and to the potential menace of the drugs.[21] Eight other cities—Philadelphia, Detroit, Chicago, St. Louis, New Orleans, San Francisco, Washington, and Balti-

[18] R. N. and G. S. Chopra, "The Present Position of Hemp Drug Addiction in India," *Indian Journal of Med. Res.* Memoirs, No. 31, 1939, quoted by Pablo O. Wolff, *op. cit.*
[19] Pablo O. Wolff, *op. cit.*   [20] *Ibid.*
[21] Cf. New York *Times*, June 18, 1951, p. 1, col. 3 and p. 24, col. 4.

more—were also reported to have alarming increases in the consumption of narcotics by young people.[22]

On November 2, 1951, President Truman signed a bill tightening penalties for the violation of narcotic and marihuana laws and set up a commission to study ways of improving the control of narcotics.[23] Since that time F.B.I. agents throughout the country have assisted in "narcotic raids" and have disclosed that many youthful persons are engaged in the narcotic trade.[24]

Most young addicts apparently begin the habit for the thrill of adventure and with little or no comprehension of the dangers involved. In one tragic case brought out in the investigations of the narcotic traffic in New York a talented young woman musician who made an income of $245 a week at her profession turned to prostitution for additional money because she was so enslaved by the heroin habit. The "dope" peddlers allegedly have invaded every section of New York City and have recruited scores of drugstores, restaurants, bars, night clubs, and cheap hotels as adjuncts to their illicit business. Certain movie theaters and subway stations have yielded to the high returns of the narcotic trade.

The Alcoholic

The alcoholic—the man or woman given to excessive consumption of alcoholic beverages—presents a variety of facets. From a psychological and sociological viewpoint, alcoholics constitute a major category among disorganized persons. Alcoholism at the same time is an important public health, psychiatric, and personality problem.

The criminologist's concern with alcoholism is less extensive and may be confined to two counts: (1) alcoholic intoxication, which is itself a misdemeanor; and (2) crimes which are committed while under the influence of alcohol. Although alcoholism is often regarded essentially as a medical and personality problem, drunkenness or alcoholic intoxication has long been a crime. Apparently it was not a social problem of serious proportions until the invention of spirituous or "hard" liquors, however. The first English law concerning drunkenness was enacted in 1606, during the reign of James I. It recognized that drunkenness was not merely a "loathsome sin" but "the Root and Foundation of many other Sins as Bloodshed, Stabbing, Murder, Swearing, Fornication, Adultry and such like, to the great Dishonour

[22] *Time*, 57:23 (June 25, 1951).
[23] *Pittsburgh Post Gazette*, November 3, 1951, p. 1.
[24] Cf. New York *Times*, January 12, 1952, p. 1, and p. 26.

of God of our Nation, the overthrow of Many good Arts, and Manual Trades, the Disability of Workmen, and the general Impoverishing of Many good Subjects, abusively wasting the good Creatures of God."[25]

Then as now, drunkenness was offensive not merely because the person's condition was disagreeable but also because intoxicated persons often committed serious offenses while under the influence of alcohol. Today, drunkenness is the largest single category of offenses for which arrests are made in the United States. In 1950 there were 178,165 arrests for drunkenness; 162,202 were men and 15,963 were women, as Table 3.7 (p. 66) shows.[26] No one supposes this represents the total number of alcoholics. Nobody knows how many alcoholics there are in the United States, since intoxicated persons of sufficiently high social standing are seldom arrested. Estimates of the number of chronic alcoholics range from 700,000 to 900,000,[27] and about 3,000,000 are believed to drink to excess.[28]

Members of the family or friends usually try to protect alcoholics who belong to the middle and upper classes and police themselves are not disposed to arrest intoxicated persons who are guests at a fashionable night club, a country club, or a first-class hotel unless some serious complication arises. Despite the number of women who drink, most of those who drink to excess are men.

DRIVING WHILE INTOXICATED

Driving while intoxicated presents a public hazard. Most states impose serious penalties for endangering the lives and limbs of others while driving in an unsober state. Many drunken drivers escape arrest, but 51,318 persons were arrested for drunken driving in 1950, of whom 49,190 were men and 2128 were women.[29]

ALCOHOL AS A FACTOR IN OTHER CRIMES

Today it is widely believed that increased drinking has been a major "cause" of increases in the crime rate. This belief is held not only by active "drys" and prohibitionists but by the general public. Most

[25] Law cited by W. M. Maltbie, "Penal Handling of Inebriates," in Alcohol, Science and Society, published by Quarterly Journal of Studies on Alcohol, Yale University Press, New Haven, 1945, p. 373.
[26] Cf. also Uniform Crime Reports, Annual Bulletin, 1950, p. 107.
[27] E. M. Jellinek, "The Problems of Alcohol," Alcohol, Science and Society, pp. 23–24.
[28] Cf. Mabel A. Elliott and Francis E. Merrill, Social Disorganization, Harper, New York, 3rd ed., 1950, chap. 9, "The Alcoholic," p. 181.
[29] Uniform Crime Reports, Annual Bulletin, 1950, p. 107.

data on this subject are inconclusive but are supported by common knowledge. We have no reliable statistics with reference to the number of other misdemeanors and felonies committed while under the influence of drink. "Drunken sex offenses, drunken murders, drunken assault," etc., are not recorded as such. And where alcoholism is acute it is usually not recorded. In 1946, for example, only 3 out of 37,281 deaths in Chicago were attributed to alcohol; thus family considerations and insurance motives must have been responsible for classifying deaths from alcohol as due to other causes.[30] Many divorces are granted to wives who allege their husbands are drunkards when they have never been arrested for drunkenness. Wives actually have been "beaten up" by their spouses and these erring husbands are literally guilty of assault and battery even though not reported. A sizable number of murders are committed in the "bellicose" state of intoxication. The fact that sex inhibitions are weaker under the vinous haze undoubtedly contributes to certain cases of fornication and rape, as well as to "disorderly conduct" in general. Many husbands and wives neglect their children because of the drink habit but if arrested in such cases are usually charged with neglect.

At the same time alcoholism is often advanced as a defense for the person who allegedly committed an offense when he was intoxicated and hence was not in full possession of his mental powers.[31] We are thus in the absurd position of making drink both a crime and an excuse for a crime.

Why the person drinks is another question. Many who drink to excess do so because they have lost their self-respect or are discouraged and frustrated in their daily lives. The Alcoholics Anonymous group with their religious approach to the problem and their emphasis upon the alcoholic's need for support in withstanding the temptation to drink has demonstrated the essential need of the alcoholic for spiritual help instead of punishment. Nevertheless drunkenness continues to be the major classification of the minor offenses.

THE POLITICAL OFFENDER

In one sense all crimes are offenses against the state, but most crimes have been designated as such because individual members of the group have been injured. Political offenses, on the other hand,

---

[30] David B. Rotnam, "Alcoholism and Crime," *Federal Probation*, 11:31–33 (July–September, 1947).
[31] *Ibid.*

are those which threaten or endanger the existence of the established government itself.

General Characteristics of Political Offenders

Although some political offenders are persons without integrity who have yielded to the extensive bribes paid either by foreign powers or by local groups, the vast majority are conscientious adherents to a political philosophy which threatens the existence of the government they are opposing. This was true of attempts to wrest power from a tyrannical monarch and is equally true of those who aim to overthrow our own government or that of any foreign power today. Political offenders thus represent a paradox for they are criminals who carry on their illegal activities in pursuit of their ideals. They are not imbued with sordid schemes for extracting vast sums of money from unsuspecting victims, nor are they motivated by basic desires to destroy or kill, although these crimes may be necessary in the pursuit of their ends. They are generally idealists devoted to a cause (however mistaken it may be) which they place higher than patriotism or personal safety. In most cases of treason the traitors place their cause higher than the existence of their own government. In cases of espionage the spies may be loyal agents of their own country and place its survival above that of the country whose national interests they would destroy—or whose secret papers they would secure. Or they may be hired agents of a foreign power and thus are guilty of treason. All spies are heroes, then, to their native land or the country whose cause they are espousing, while they are archenemies to those governments whose secrets they secure.

Political Offenders Under the Totalitarian State

With the rise of totalitarianism, the term "political offender" took on new meaning and the offenders themselves multiplied by geometric proportions. For the very existence of the dictator state has depended upon complete acquiescence of the citizens to all policies of state. Thus in Nazi Germany those who opposed the totalitarian power of the Nazis were either exiled, routed to a concentration camp or prison, or condemned to death for "political unreliability." Millions of Jews were by pronouncement declared the archenemies of the German people and faced either the concentration camp or the gas chamber. Most of these were denied any semblance of trial.

In Soviet Russia the process of "liquidating" the enemies of the state has involved the death or "disappearance" of untold numbers, many of whom likewise have been denied a fair trial. Dallin estimates that 10 to 25 million have been sent to the slave labor camps. He says the former may be too low, the latter too great a number.[32]

In a totalitarian government little importance is attached to the sanctity and dignity of human personality. In its ruthless quest for power, the state conceives of itself as the end-all and be-all of existence before which all other values must bow and yield.

Political Offenders in the United States

The United States of America is a democracy established on the premises of human liberty and equality, both extended by our justly famous Bill of Rights. In consequence our federal government has operated in behalf of the people in the several states (rather than in behalf of the states per se) and has had little interest in coercing its citizens or involking laws that entailed any limitation of their right of protest or of opposition to the party in power. Above all rights Americans have cherished their freedom to do what they want to do and protest vociferously when they are prevented from doing so. Nevertheless all freedom, including that of Americans, is relative, hedged in by considerations of suitable conduct, public safety, and general well-being. Moreover such freedom is more or less unconsciously limited by the taboos and mores of the group. We have freedom of speech, but it is subjected to laws governing libelous or slanderous statements. We have freedom of worship but limit the rights of citizens to promote polygamy, sexual lewdness, or promiscuity as a religious doctrine. We likewise prohibit such antireligious practices as swearing and in many states limit the Sunday activities of everybody as a concession to the religious beliefs of the majority of citizens (or at least of the majority of lawmakers).

Freedom of speech, press, and assembly is similarly relative and in times of national danger tend to be greatly restricted in the interest of national security. Civil rights are thus always in danger in times of international tension. We have in no sense approximated the ruthless control which totalitarian states have imposed upon the expression of political opinion. We permit scurrilous attacks upon the party in power within the operation of our two-party system. A Democrat may

[32] David J. Dallin and Boris J. Nicolaevsky, *Forced Labor in Soviet Russia*, Yale University Press, New Haven, 1947, pp. 84–87.

safely denounce the theory and practices of Republicans and vice versa. With the growing threat of Soviet communism and the increased recognition of the control which the Politburo in Moscow exercises over the activities and tactics of Communists all over the world, the political freedom formerly accorded American Communists has been very generally restricted. This has been justified on the grounds that the basic tenets of Marxian communism support the overthrow of the existing political structure of our country and the economic system of capitalism under which it has operated. Communism has thus been conceived as a basic threat to our national existence. In the minds of most loyal American citizens, as well as of our legislators and our judiciary, the extension of full freedom to the Communists would eventually sound the death knell to our form of government. A certain hedging of our political principles has thus been inevitable, but it has been born of a necessity and of a danger which did not threaten us seriously at any earlier period. Never before in our history has a political party fought for an accepted legal status when that party was engaged in an effort to overthrow the government.

Complete freedom is always a pure chimera, but certainly governmental acquiescence to subversive activities was not guaranteed by the Bill of Rights. The times and conditions have changed and the legislative, executive, and judicial branches of our government have been thrown into confusion and have adopted contradictory policies because of the fears (both real and potential) that the present exigency arouses. In a situation taut with these fears for our national safety, the number of persons charged with committing political offenses has naturally increased. Some of these persons are guilty, but in the emotionally charged atmosphere of world wars and ideological conflicts many innocent people are likely to be victims of suspicion. Correlatively, many guilty of collaborating with foreign agents may avoid detection. A few renegades who have betrayed their trust may thus imperil the security of the innocent. Accusations which are made without established evidence have created complicated problems within our federal government.

Although the relative number of political offenders brought to trial and punished is small, the importance of these criminals far outweighs their numerical significance. If international tensions between the Soviet Union and the United States continue we can expect a mounting list of political offenders.

Types of Political Offenders

The major types of political offenders may be subsumed under the categories of (1) traitors, (2) spies, (3) draft evaders, and (4) conscientious objectors. We have referred incidentally to the first two, but shall discuss all in further detail here.

THE TRAITOR

Traitors must have existed as long as established governments have engaged in a struggle for power with other governments. All nations in time of peace, as well as war, are guilty of trying to secure secret information which it is advantageous for them to possess. Thus they must engage in espionage, and each government's agents can operate effectively only as they are able to secure the co-operation of certain citizens in the countries where they wish to secure information. In short, the several nations all engage in espionage, operating partly at least through inducing other nationals to become traitors. Traitors and spies act in collusion and occasionally a man may be a foreign agent or spy for another country. Most spies are nationals of the country they serve. Political offenders are thus the natural sequence of international peacetime rivalries as well as the inevitable corollary of war.

The traitor is one guilty of treason, and treason consists in (1) making war against one's own state, (2) adhering to enemies of the state, or (3) giving aid and succor to an enemy power.[33] Because treason involves the possible downfall of the state it is universally regarded as the worst of all offenses from a legal point of view although in peacetime the betrayal of secrets to a foreign agent has seldom resulted in any extreme punishment. In the spring of 1951 Morton Sobell and Mr. and Mrs. Julius Rosenberg, along with David Greenglass, who had previously confessed spying, were convicted of espionage as spies for a foreign country. Their treason was considered particularly serious because of their part in passing atomic bomb secrets to Soviet Russia and was marked by the first death sentence ever invoked by a civilian court for treason in the United States.[34] That their treasonous conduct entailed giving information which threatened the safety and security of the United States there can be no doubt. The enormity of their act dwarfed any humanitarian considerations which

[33] Cf. Vernon C. Branham and Samuel B. Kutash, *Encyclopedia of Criminology*, Philosophical Library, New York, 1949, pp. 499–500.
[34] Cf. *Time*, 57:23 (April 9, 1951).

the judge might otherwise have permitted to influence the sentence imposed.

Certain other cases in recent times have involved concepts of treason even though treason was not the alleged offense. This was true in the now famous trial of Alger Hiss, which involved the controversial issue as to whether or not Hiss had ever been a member of the Communist party. Hiss was convicted, on the basis of the oral testimony of Whittaker Chambers, not of being a Communist, or of treason, but of perjury. That is, he was convicted of lying under oath, saying he was not a Communist and never had been a member of the Communist party when evidence to the contrary indicated that he was. Indirectly, however, Hiss' conviction was a conviction for treason since it was Chambers' confession and testimony that he had secured confidential State Department papers from Hiss that led to the latter's conviction of perjury.

This case aroused widespread controversy because Hiss maintained his innocence throughout two trials and through appeal to a higher court. The evidence was circumstantial but substantial enough to convince two juries and the appealing courts of its admissibility. If he is guilty, as convicted, he has been one of the greatest traitors this country has ever produced.[35] If not, he has suffered outrageous wrong.

Following the conviction of Alger Hiss and those passing on atomic bomb secrets, numerous leaders of the Communist party in America were convicted or indicted for their subversive or treasonous activities. In October, 1949, 11 top Communist leaders were convicted of conspiring to advocate and teach the violent overthrow of the government. Their convictions were subsequently upheld by the United States Supreme Court on June 4, 1951.[36] Shortly after this decision, 21 other Communists were indicted and 17 arrested on similar charges.[37]

THE SPY

THE NATURE OF ESPIONAGE.   Espionage, as we have already intimated, is the term applied to the activities involved in seeking, obtaining, and transmitting secret information, usually of valuable military nature, to a foreign country by the secret agents of that country. All important countries and some of the lesser ones operate an

[35] Cf. Alistair Cooke, Generation on Trial, Knopf, New York, 1950, and Ralph De Toledano, Seeds of Treason, Funk and Wagnalls, New York, 1950, for two divergent viewpoints.
[36] Cf. Facts on File, June 1–June 7, 1951, p. 181.
[37] Cf. New York Times, June 21, 1951, p. 1.

"intelligence" or secret service system. Each one is actively engaged in running down military secrets and in keeping abreast of all military developments in other countries, particularly in those considered hostile or potentially hostile. All important nations are thus equally guilty of espionage yet the practice is recognized by international law as a legitimate means of protecting national security. At the same time the several nations punish the foreign agents of other countries severely, and in time of war spying becomes a dangerous and difficult vocation. All spying involves grave personal dangers; in wartime the penalty is usually death. When spies receive such a penalty they may become national heroes like Nathan Hale. Other spies like Hede Massing or Whittaker Chambers may betray a country's secrets but confess their guilt and be absolved from punishment because of the aid they give in the prosecution of others who are equally guilty.[38]

The wartime spy, therefore, must be clever and daring in order to secure and transmit valuable information to his country—or from his country if he is a traitor—and he is always subject to severe penalties, usually death, if apprehended. In the United States the wartime penalty for spying is death or imprisonment up to 30 years. In peacetime the highest penalty is imprisonment for 20 years.[39]

Sometimes nationals of one country can be led to act as spies for a hostile country, as seems to have been true of Whittaker Chambers, Alger Hiss, et al. Those who do this are guilty both of treason and of espionage. In the post-World War II period the most widely publicized espionage has been in connection with the Russian secret-service agents who secured information from Canadian and American scientists concerning the process of manufacturing atomic bombs. It has been estimated that there have been 10,000 to 12,000 secret Soviet agents in the United States in addition to the embassy employees of the Soviet Union and the various Soviet-dominated countries. Their major goal has been to secure the secret processes used in producing atomic bombs. Networks of spies have infiltrated the various research laboratories and information with reference to most (if not all) of the materials and processes employed in nuclear fission have probably been passed on by scientists working in league with "couriers" who transmitted the information to the Soviets. Obtaining this information obviously required the co-operation of American scientists. Thus Elizabeth Bentley admitted that she gathered secret information from

[38] Cf. Hede Massing, *This Deception*, Duell, Sloan and Pearce, New York, 1951, for her story of the Soviet spy net.
[39] Cf. *United States Code*, Title 50, chap. 4.

32 employees in various departments or agencies of the federal government. Whittaker Chambers testified at Alger Hiss' trial that he obtained vital information from Henry Julian Wadleigh and Alger Hiss.[40] Harry Gold, American chemist, admitted that he acted as a Russian agent,[41] as did Dr. Klaus E. J. Fuchs, the German-born British scientist. Fuchs betrayed highly confidential American and Canadian material to Russian agents over a period of seven years, by his own testimony.[42]

The processes by which respectable men become spies may be illustrated by the case of Alfred Dean Slack, a man who became friends with an American who was a Russian agent. This man, Buggs by name, bought industrial chemical information from Slack. Later, during World War II, Slack worked at an ordinance plant and Harry Gold tried to induce him to sell "war secrets." That, Slack maintained, was different and he refused to give further information. Then Gold threatened to expose his previous sale of chemical formulas to Russia. In desperation Slack yielded, fearing that his job and future were at stake. In 1950 the F.B.I. arrested Slack and in a few months he was sentenced to 15 years in prison. Government officials recognized that he had been intimidated and asked for only a 10-year sentence but the Judge held that 15 years was not too much for such conspiring with a foreign power.[43]

In the Russian spy network in the United States several "spy rings" allegedly operate, each apparently without knowledge of the others. This method provides several sources of clues or actual information. It also permits a double check on the activities of each ring, and reveals any possible counterspying (spying upon the spies).[44]

COUNTERSPYING. Because of the dangers of espionage modern nations have built networks of counterespionage in order to prevent secrets from leaking to foreign agents. In the United States the major counterespionage agency functions as a part of the Federal Bureau of Investigation. In the Soviet Union there are four different espionage agencies: the M.V.D. or State Security Police, the diplomatic information service secured by the Foreign Office espionage, the military and naval attachés (who are often called "legal spies" in diplo-

[40] "How Russia Got U.S. Secrets: 10,000 Spies in Key Places," United States News and World Report, 27:11–13 (February 17, 1950).
[41] "Gold Pleads Guilty," Newsweek, 35:22 (June 12, 1950).
[42] Cf. "The Super-Spy," New Republic, 122:10 (February 20, 1950).
[43] "Inside Story of a Native American Who Turned a Spy," United States News and World Report, 29:15–17 (November 24, 1950).
[44] "How Russia Got U.S. Secrets: 10,000 Spies in Key Places," United States News and World Report, 27:11–13 (February 17, 1950).

matic parlance), and the Foreign Section of the Central Committee of the Communist Party. These spying agencies not only secure important information for their government but operate as veritable spies on each other in order to reduce the "political unreliability" of which totalitarian states are so afraid.[45]

The operation of an intelligence agency requires expert ability. All the social sciences, including economics, geography, history, political science, and sociology, have something important to contribute to understanding what is happening in other countries. How to coordinate the various departments and assist in making an intelligent foreign policy is an extremely complicated problem. In a country such as ours it is not surprising that both congressmen and the general public should be confused. National security does not admit publishing intelligence data and in consequence no one seems to know what is going on. Spying has become a profession, although it carries with it the possibility of severest condemnation under the penal law of the state spied upon.[46]

Selective Service Violators

Selective Service Act violators are classified in this text as political offenders because they are not ordinary criminals; that is, they have not committed what are normally considered crimes. They are offenders because they have opposed the military effort of the country; many have protested on moral, philosophical, or religious grounds against war as an instrument of national policy. James V. Bennett, Director of the Bureau of Prisons, has held that such persons are not to be considered political offenders.[47] Their offenses are, however, truly political in that they have refused to support the government's call to the armed services. They have not betrayed military secrets to the enemy, it is true. But persons who refuse to serve their country in time of war are in a sense lending aid and comfort to the enemy, irrespective of their motives in refusing military service. During World War II all such selective service violators were tried under provisions of the Selective Service Act of 1940. This act expired in 1947 and a new Selective Service Act was adopted in 1948. During the period 1941–1950 a total of 12,311 persons served sentences as selective service violators

[45] George Fielding Eliot, "Espionage and Counterespionage," *Collier's Encyclopedia*, 7:416–418 (1950).

[46] For a short but comprehensive discussion of American secret intelligence consult George S. Pettee, *The Future of American Secret Intelligence*, Infantry Journal Press, Washington, 1946.

[47] Cf. James V. Bennett in *Federal Prisons, 1946*, Bureau of Prisons, U.S. Department of Justice, Washington, 1947, p. 10.

of the act of 1940 as Table 7.1 shows. An additional 102 served sentences in 1949–1950 for violating the act of 1948.

TYPES OF SELECTIVE SERVICE VIOLATORS.   Beginning in 1944 the Federal Bureau of Prisons classified all Selective Service Act violators under three categories: (1) conscientious objectors, (2) Jehovah's Witnesses, and (3) others. Jehovah's Witnesses were held distinct from conscientious objectors chiefly because they claimed all their members were ministers of religion and thus entitled to exemption from military duty.[48] However, the Jehovah's Witnesses have considered themselves as religious conscientious objectors and they have been generally so considered by the Quakers and other religious groups which have opposed war. They therefore will be included as conscientious objectors in this discussion.

THE "OTHER" SELECTIVE SERVICE ACT VIOLATORS.   The largest number of selective service violators were those who had no religious or philosophical objections to war as such (so far as could be determined). They were those who were negligent about registering for the draft or were out-and-out "draft evaders." During the period 1941 to 1950, 6958 such persons served sentences under the act of 1940, as Table 7.1 shows. Approximately 40 per cent of this third category had criminal records. Many were socially and mentally inadequate and, in Mr. Bennett's opinion, would have been rejected by the draft if they had registered. Or if accepted, he believes they would have been discharged for medical or dishonorable reasons.[49] Of the 5777 granted parole, many were members of this group, but they were not classified separately, as the table indicates.

It seems reasonable to suppose that some of the religious or conscientious objectors to military service might have been rejected by the draft boards or might have been discharged for being "psychoneurotic." Some may have claimed religious reasons for objection to military service when they had none, but we cannot establish these facts.

THE CONSCIENTIOUS OBJECTOR

Conscientious objector is the term generally applied to persons who refuse to bear arms or enter active military duty in time of war because of religious or moral convictions.

The constitutional right of the conscientious objector to refuse to perform military services stems from the extension of the right of religious freedom guaranteed by Article I of the Bill of Rights: "Con-

[48] *Ibid.*, pp. 12–13.   [49] *Ibid.*

TABLE 7.1   Violators of the Selective Training and Service Act of 1940: Commitments, Median Ages, Average Lengths of Sentence, End-of-Year Populations, and Paroles, Fiscal Years Ended June 30, 1941 to 1950

	Total	1941	1942	1943	1944	1945	1946	1947	1948	1949	1950	Selective Service Act of 1948 (fiscal years)		
												Total	1949	1950
Received from the courts into federal institutions	12,311	196	806	2,764	3,585	2,477	1,312	739	210	141	81	102	65	37
Conscientious objectors	1,217[a]	139[a]	—	495[a]	251	214	106	11	—	1	—	70	48	22
Jehovah's Witnesses	4,136[a]	106[a]	—	901[a]	1,735	899	409	70	11	2	3	—	—	—
Others	6,958[a]	757[a]	—	1,368[a]	1,599	1,364	797	658	199	138	78	32	17	15
Median age (years)	b	b	28.5	29.9	27.4	27.0	26.5	26.9	29.9	31.0	33.0	b	b	b
Average length of sentence (months)	b	12.0[a]	21.0	32.4	35.2	32.7	22.5	16.3	15.0	15.1	16.0	15.1	15.1	10.1
Conscientious objectors	b	b	b	b	34.0	30.9	20.7	15.9	—	18.0	—	b	b	b
Jehovah's Witnesses	b	b	b	b	42.0	40.1	25.9	24.0	19.6	21.0	12.0	b	b	b
Others	b	b	b	b	28.1	28.0	23.0	19.0	14.8	15.0	16.1	b	b	b
Serving sentence in federal institutions—June 30	—	161	706	2,650	4,679	4,703	2,797	829	328	172	87	70	55	15
Conscientious objectors	—	b	b	588	694	475	204	13	—	—	—	46	39	7
Jehovah's Witnesses	—	b	b	981	2,530	2,724	1,339	63	11	3	5	—	—	—
Others	—	b	b	1,081	1,455	1,504	1,254	753	317	169	82	24	16	8
Parole granted	5,777	12	79	405	928	1,112	1,450	1,539	140	85	27	55	—	—
U.S. Board of Parole	3,952	—	9	140	428	400	1,338	1,385	140	85	27	55	—	—
Under Executive Order No. 8641[c]	1,825	12	70	265[d]	500[d]	712	112	154	—	—	—	—	—	—

[a] Estimated.
b Data not available.
[c] By the Attorney General upon the recommendation of the Selective Service System.
[d] The proportion for each year of the 765 paroles granted in 1943 and 1944 is estimated.

SOURCE: Table specially compiled for this book by Henry Coe Lanpher, Research and Statistical Assistant to the Director of the Bureau of Prisons, U.S. Department of Justice.

gress shall make no law respecting an establishment of religions, or prohibiting the free exercise thereof. . . ." This was undoubtedly a concession to the Quakers, who are opposed on religious grounds to resorting to violence as a means of settling international disputes. Since joining the army was rather generally a voluntary matter in our earlier history the conscientious objectors to war posed no serious problem. Compulsory military duty was long in effect on Continental Europe and many immigrants came to this country to escape it. With the implementation of the draft as the major means of recruiting an army for World War I approximately 600 conscientious objectors served sentences in civil and military prisons in the United States. Following World War I the futility of war seemed apparent both to many ex-soldiers and to many serious students of international relations. In consequence peace movements gained numerous adherents from these groups. The Jehovah's Witnesses sect also greatly expanded in membership during this period. The number of persons who conscientiously opposed war as an instrument for adjudicating international conflicts thus markedly increased, and commanded sufficient respect to receive consideration in the Selective Training and Service Act of 1940.

In fact Article I of the Bill of Rights was accepted as providing sufficient basis for the exemption of persons who "by reason of religious training and belief [were] conscientiously opposed to participation in war in any form," provided their claims to such exemption were sustained by draft authorities according to Section 5(g) of the Selective Service Act. Such persons were not exempt from national service, however; they were to be assigned to noncombatant military service or "to work of national importance under civilian direction." Persons whose claims were not granted were permitted to appeal their cases to appeal boards set up under provisions of the law. The appellant in such instances was entitled to a hearing conducted by the United States Department of Justice. The Justice Department then would make a recommendation to the appeal board, which on consideration might or might not follow the recommendation.[50]

Many conscientious objectors, of both the religious and the philosophical varieties, maintained that the Selective Service Act of 1940 (when we were still not at war) obliterated other safeguards of the Bill of Rights including freedom of speech, freedom of the press, freedom of petition and assembly, the right to trial by jury, and the right

[50] Mulford Q. Sibley and Ada Wardlaw, *Conscientious Objectors in Prison*, Pacifist Research Bureau, Ithaca, New York, 1940–1945, p. 1.

of habeas corpus.[51] All these were declared involved because so many conscientious objectors were denied proper judicial review, and were often summarily arrested and otherwise mistreated.[52]

Previous to the attack on Pearl Harbor, the conscientious objectors also denied the constitutionality of the Selective Service Act on grounds that the only power Congress had to call forth a militia was "to execute the laws of the Union, suppress insurrection and repel invasion."[53] After that date this argument obviously had no weight.[54] The conscientious objectors still raised the further question, however, of whether miltary conscription was not involuntary servitude imposed by the state although the courts ruled that no such servitude was imposed by the draft law.[55]

We cannot go into all the differential factors which determined the decisions of local draft boards or appeal boards, but it is safe to say that there was great disparity in the interpretation of what constituted a conscientious objector and whether a claim of such objection to military service was allowed.

The important clause in the Selective Service Law of 1940 so far as conscientious objectors were concerned was that limiting such persons to those whose beliefs were "by reason of religious training and belief." Initially religious training was defined by the Director of Selective Service, Clarence A. Dykstra, as a matter of the individual's religious belief and did not require specific membership in any religious group. Later, by ruling of General Hershey all conscientious objectors were required to specify a belief in a Divine Creator. This ruling was in effect after March, 1942.[56]

Any conscientious objector who could convince his draft board of the religious basis for his disavowal of war and was willing to enter noncombatant military service or to accept an assignment to civilian public service had no further problem if he co-operated in his particular assignment.

THE NUMBER OF CONSCIENTIOUS OBJECTORS. From October 16, 1940, to June 30, 1945, 5516 conscientious objectors (the vast majority of whom were religious objectors to war) were convicted on various charges, according to figures compiled by the National Service

[51] All these rights are guaranteed in the first article of the Bill of Rights.
[52] Cf. Julien Cornell, The Conscientious Objector and the Law, John Day, New York, 1943, pp. 78–79.
[53] Ibid., p. 82.   [54] Ibid., p. 83.
[55] United States vs. Mroz, 136 Federal Reports, 2nd series, cited by Julien Cornell, op. cit., pp. 89–91.
[56] Julien Cornell, op. cit., pp. 2–3.

Board for Religious Objectors. Four of this group were dismissed with a fine, and 218 were placed on probation, as Table 7.2 shows. The rest served prison sentences ranging from a month or less to over 5 years.

TABLE 7.2.   Sentences Received by Conscientious Objectors in 4 Successive Periods, 1940–1945, by Type and Length of Sentence[a]

Type and Length of Sentence	Oct. 16, 1940, to June 30, 1942	July 1, 1942, to June 30, 1943	July 1, 1943, to June 30, 1944	July 1, 1944, to June 30, 1945	Total
Fine only	2	—	—	2	4
Probation	30	56	77	55	218
1 month or less	5	5	7	3	20
1 to 6 months	18	18	12	6	54
6 months to 1 year and 1 day	83	87	130	106	406
1 year and 1 day to 2 years	112	246	391	268	1,017
2 to 3 years	68	675	713	265	1,721
3 to 4 years	39	191	224	127	581
4 to 5 years	29	405	738	321	1,493
More than 5 years	—	2	—	—	2
Total	386	1,685	2,292	1,153	5,516

[a] Adapted from Department of Justice figures as arranged by the National Service Board for Religious Objectors. A number of men received fines in addition to prison terms.
    SOURCE: Table 3 in Mulford Q. Sibley and Ada Wardlaw, *Conscientious Objectors in Prison*, Pacifist Research Bureau, Ithaca, New York, 1940–1945, p. 9. These figures do not agree with those in Table 7.1.

Figures published by the Federal Bureau of Prisons show that only 5353 persons have been classified as either conscientious objectors or Jehovah's Witnesses for the whole period 1941 to 1950, as Table 7.1 shows. This table also shows the violators of the Selective Service Act of 1948 for the fiscal years 1949 and 1950. The number of violators declined markedly after 1944, presumably because the number of persons drafted declined. The number of violators of the Selective Service Act of 1948 has also declined, however, in the two years covered by Table 7.1. Whether this seeming decline is due to the relatively small number of persons called to active service cannot be accurately stated. Some religious groups oppose communism more avowedly than they have opposed war. The Korean conflict has thus posed additional problems to certain conscientious objectors, particularly to those of the Roman Catholic faith. But, in any event, all classes of offenses against national security have declined considerably, including those against the Selective Service Acts of 1940 and 1948.[57]

[57] Cf. Table 22.3 in chap. 22 on federal offenders.

RELIGIOUS AFFILIATION OF CONVICTED CONSCIENTIOUS OBJECTORS. The majority of conscientious objectors convicted during World War II were Jehovah's Witnesses, as we have said. Table 7.3 shows that 72.4 per cent of those convicted belonged to this sect. Members of the "historic peace churches" also bulked large in the convictions. This group includes the Society of Friends (Quakers), the Mennonites, and the Church of the Brethren, all of whom are committed to the opposition to war by their fundamental doctrines. Jehovah's Witnesses constitute a relative newcomer among religious sects. (They were not organized until 1878, although they claim that Abel was the first Witness.)[58] Jehovah's Witnesses oppose allegiance to nationalism in all its forms as idolatrous and their pacifism stems from this doctrine.

TABLE 7.3.   Religious Affiliations of Conscientious Objectors Convicted During 4 Periods of Selective Service Act Administration, to June 30, 1945[a]

Religious Affiliation	Oct. 16, 1940, to June 30, 1942	July 1, 1942, to June 30, 1943	July 1, 1943, to June 30, 1944	July 1, 1944, to June 30, 1945	Total	Per Cent of Total C.O.'s
Jehovah's Witnesses	167	1,086	1,826	913	3,992	72.4
Negro Moslems and "Hebrews"	10	128	17	11	166	3.0
Large religious groups	65	173	143	81	462	8.4
Small religious groups	29	60	97	81	267	4.8
Nonaffiliated religious objectors	53	113	93	32	291	5.3
Philosophical or political objectors	55	112	70	13	250	4.5
Not classified	7	13	46	22	88	1.6
Total	386	1,685	2,292	1,153	5,516	100.0

[a] Figures prepared by the National Service Board for Religious Objectors, based upon reports of the Department of Justice.
SOURCE: Table 2 in Mulford Q. Sibley and Ada Wardlaw, *Conscientious Objectors in Prison, 1940–1945*, Pacifist Research Bureau, Ithaca, New York, 1945, p. 12.

There were also many conscientious objectors in other religious groups. In fact the majority of other Christian religious bodies (although they have not condemned all participation in war) have for the most part affirmed the *right* of all their members to oppose war on religious and conscientious grounds.[59] Methodists, in fact, although not classified in Table 7.3, ranked next to Jehovah's Witnesses in

[58] Mulford Q. Sibley and Ada Wardlaw, op. cit., p. 2.
[59] *Congress Looks at the Conscientious Objector*, National Service Board for Religious Objectors, Washington, 1943, pp. 86–89.

number of conscientious objectors convicted. There were also many Roman Catholics among those conscientious objectors who served sentences. Catholics frequently had difficulty gaining exemption on religious grounds, however, although the doctrines laid down by both St. Augustine and St. Thomas Aquinas permitted conscientious objection. In any event Catholics, along with Presbyterians, Baptists, and Episcopalians made up the bulk of objectors outside of the so-called "peace" churches.[60] In addition a small number of Jews and Moslems and some nonaffiliated religious objectors claimed exemption.

PHILOSOPHICAL OBJECTORS. The philosophical objectors were usually the most articulate and attracted attention far out of proportion to their numbers, since they constituted only 4.5 per cent of the total group. So far as comparisons between religious and philosophical objectors are concerned there was no great difference in their viewpoints on war except that religious objectors claimed their religious faith to be the reason for taking their particular stand. The philosophical objectors were often united with religious objectors in working organizations such as the Pacifist Research Bureau, the War Resisters League, the National Council Against Conscription, etc. All these groups were alike in their idealism and, as is true in many other idealist movements, a lunatic fringe among their members was inevitable.

As it worked out many conscientious objectors voluntarily presented their cases to the draft boards and were assigned to civilian wartime duty. Others volunteered for agricultural work, as "guinea pigs" for medical research, etc.

Although the position of the "philosophical" objector was akin to that of the religious objector his objection to war was not a matter of his religious ideology. Obviously the philosophical objector derives part of his disavowal of war from the social, economic, and cultural milieu in which he lives.

The conscientious objector of the philosophical type was likely to be a highly educated person (a few in fact have been college professors) who could see little hope of solving human or international problems effectively through violence. A young university instructor who failed to register for the draft would have been exempted from military service by his draft board had he been willing to claim exemption on religious grounds. He insisted he had no religious basis for claiming exemption, that his only grounds were ethical and philosophical. These arguments did not please the draft board and the

[60] Mulford Q. Sibley and Ada Wardlaw, op. cit., pp. 12–13.

young man was subsequently sentenced to a federal prison. This objector purposely took a stand to force the issue, to see what the draft board would do. James V. Bennett has characterized this type of objector as an activist.[61] Such an objector is a fighter, albeit an intellectual one, against the *status quo*, rather than a thoroughgoing pacifist. Men of this type were frequently sentenced to prison for evasion of military duty.

Many religious objectors got into trouble, along with the philosophical objectors, because of their obstructive opposition. That is, (1) some were arrested and prosecuted because they objected not merely to military service but to *registering* for military service. (2) Others accepted an assignment to a nonmilitary or civilian service but later became convinced that they could not conscientiously continue in such service. (3) Others had religious grounds for objecting to military service, but these grounds were so liberally constructed that they were not acceptable to the selective service boards. Certain members of the Unitarian Church, for example, were unwilling to assent to belief in a Divine Creator (although other members of this church made such assent).

Some of the religious objectors, like the philosophical objectors, were also activists. If sentenced to prison, they usually continued their protests within the prison. They objected to the discipline, to the classification system, to alleged discrimination on the basis of race, and to the whole authoritarian nature of prison administration. Some of these objections to prison regime were well taken. But since, as we have mentioned, a large number of the conscientious objectors were highly educated and refined persons, they were ill fitted by training and experience for prison. Nor did they realize that prison regime (with all its defects, and they are legion) was organized primarily to take care of the recidivist offenders who come under the regular criminal code—the crooks, the thieves, the rapists, the embezzlers, and the murderers. Conscientious objectors, therefore, evaluated the prison regime from the perspective of the person who is not normally a prisoner. At the same time they were idealists rather than enemies of society and the prison life was not geared for such persons. Some were *objectors to prison*, in fact, as well as to war, and thus complicated every phase of the prison regime. Others sought to reform prisons through their protests both while in prison and after release. Though many of the objections which the "conchies" raised were

[61] *Federal Prisons, 1943*, Bureau of Prisons, U.S. Department of Justice, Washington, 1944, pp. 10–13.

legitimate some grew out of the general ignorance of the objectors concerning problems of dealing with hardened offenders.

Some of the conscientious objectors in prison were extremely neurotic and a few were genuinely psychotic. These—the "lunatic fringe" —made the problem of dealing with the conscientious objector in prison extremely difficult. In at least 4 prisons, in Danbury, Lewisburg, Petersburg, and Ashland, the conscientious objectors staged strikes against racial segregation. These men unquestionably believed that there should be some semblance of democracy in prison. Actually racial segregation in prison involves many other considerations including the omnipresent problem in prisons of homosexual attraction between the races.

TYPES OF NONCOMPLIANCE. The types of noncompliance on the part of conscientious objectors during World War II were thus varied. As Table 7.4 shows, 3331 of the 5516 conscientious objectors convicted during the years 1940 to 1945 were charged with failure to report for induction to the army. Members of this group obviously either had not been accepted as valid religious conscientious objectors or had not presented their claims. Some failed either to register, to return questionnaires, or to report for physical examination. Those assigned to nonmilitary duty constituted nearly a third of those who were eventually convicted.

TABLE 7.4. Number of Conscientious Objectors Convicted on Various Charges in Three Different Periods, to June 30, 1945[a]

Charges on Which Convicted	Convictions to June 30, 1943	July 1, 1943, to June 30, 1944	July 1, 1944, to June 30, 1945	Total	Per Cent Convicted on Each Charge
Failure to register	245	13	8	266	4.8
Failure to return question- naire	39	9	1	49	.9
Failure to report for physical examination	50	19	1	70	1.3
Failure to report for induc- tion into army	1,045	1,551	735	3,331	60.4
Failure to report to CPS camp	618	618	303	1,539	27.9
Non-co-operation in CPS (including walkouts)	50	79	104	233	4.2
Counseling or aiding evasion	24	3	1	28	.5
Total	2,071	2,292	1,153	5,516	100.0

[a] Arranged from Department of Justice figures. Those for 1944–1945 are preliminary figures supplied by the National Service Board for Religious Objectors.
SOURCE: Table 1 in Mulford Q. Sibley and Ada Wardlaw, *Conscientious Objectors in Prison, 1940–1945*, Pacifist Research Bureau, Ithaca, New York, 1945, p. 5.

The conscientious objectors are thus a phenomenon of wartime and in peacetime tend to disappear. In 1950 there were only 97 persons committed for offenses under the Selective Service Act of 1940 and 39 under the Selective Service Act of 1948.[62] None of those convicted under the 1940 act was a "conscientious objector" and only 12 of those convicted under the 1948 act were objectors on religious grounds, while one was a "philosophical" objector.[63]

SPECIAL TYPES OF OFFENDERS AS RELATED TO THE TIMES

The special types of offenders considered in this chapter represent special problems of conduct which the state has defined in modern society. The alcoholic and the narcotic addict are condemned by the modern state because they are irresponsible. Moral ideas thus affect the judgment of the state. The conscientious objector, on the other hand, is pitting his moral concepts against the political strength of the state. To him moral law transcends the authority of the state. Although the modern state theoretically adheres to freedom of religion and freedom of thought (so far as the latter is implied in freedom of press and freedom of speech), it does not admit any action which threatens its power. In this fact lies both the strength and the weakness of the state as an instrument for social well-being.

SELECTED BIBLIOGRAPHY

Alcohol, Science and Society, published by the Quarterly Journal of Studies on Alcohol, Yale University Press, New Haven, 1945. The various aspects of the alcohol problem are presented in 29 lectures.

Congress Looks at the Conscientious Objector, National Service Board for Religious Objectors, Washington, 1943. A summary of 13 hearings before Congress on the subject of the conscientious objector.

Investigation of Organized Crime in Interstate Commerce, Hearings Before the Special Committee to Investigate Organized Crime in Interstate Commerce, U.S. Senate, 82nd Congress, May 29 and June 7, 12, 26, and 27, 1951, Washington, 1951, Part 14, "Narcotics." This report gives extensive testimony on the narcotic problem in the United States.

Lindesmith, Alfred R., "Dope Fiend Mythology," *Journal of Criminal Law and Criminology,* 31:199–208 (July–August, 1940). Dr. Lindesmith maintains the press has greatly complicated the picture of drug addiction by sensational news stories.

---

[62] *Federal Prisons, 1950,* Bureau of Prisons, U.S. Department of Justice, Washington, 1951, Table 19, p. 66.

[63] *Ibid.,* p. 47.

Lindesmith, Alfred R., *Opiate Addiction*, Principia Press, Bloomington, Indiana, 1947. This is one of the sanest discussions of opiate addiction from a sociological viewpoint.

Massing, Hede, *This Deception*, Duell, Sloan and Pearce, New York, 1951. A report on the Communist network is given by one of the Communists' former most active agents.

Pettee, George S., *The Future of American Secret Intelligence*, Infantry Journal Press, Washington, 1946. This is a dicussion of the extent and nature of our intelligence service. Much of our intelligence service is naturally secret.

Rotnam, David B., "Alcoholism and Crime," *Federal Probation*, 11:31–33 (July–September, 1947). The relation between alcoholism and crime is ably presented.

Sibley, Mulford Q., and Wardlaw, Ada, *Conscientious Objectors in Prison, 1940–1945*, Pacifist Research Bureau, Ithaca, New York, 1945. This is a well-documented and for the most part objective appraisal of the conscientious objectors who served prison sentences in World War II.

West, Rebecca, *The Meaning of Treason*, Viking, New York, 1947. A well-known British writer attempts to probe the antecedents to treasonous conduct.

CHAPTER 8

The Woman Offender

There is real need for definitive research on the subject of criminal women, and a recent book by Dr. Otto Pollak purports to give reliable data on the extent of women's crime.[1] Dr. Pollak has undoubtedly combed literature on crime and criminals in order to write his book, but he provides very little truly scientific material on the criminal activities of women. His data, which are chiefly secondary, are given a liberal subjective interpretation by which he purports to shatter the notion that women are less criminal than men. Instead, he concludes, women (because they are *deceitful*) merely conceal their crimes more frequently than do men.

Women are deceitful, in turn (Pollak avers), because of their sexual passivity, a matter which makes it easy for the wife to deceive her husband, and this biological fact conditions a woman's ability to mask her offenses. This interesting theory of woman's nature is derived from the psychiatric theory of Eric Fromm, but Dr. Pollak educes little scientific evidence to prove his contention. He gives a number of instances in which women criminals have deceived their victims, it is true, including the sham prostitutes who demand pay in advance and walk out on their patrons. But such shyster methods are not peculiar to women. Getting something for nothing is a primary characteristic of all mercenary crimes, irrespective of the sex of the offender. We have ample evidence of male spouses who delude their wives. We also have ample evidence that gangsters, racketeers, and corrupt politicians, all of whom are chiefly male, are not altogether lacking in deceit in dealing with their victims, members of rival

[1] Cf. Otto Pollak, *The Criminality of Women*, University of Pennsylvania Press, Philadelphia, 1950.

groups, officials of the law, or the public interest (where the latter is involved).

Pollak also believes women commit a much larger number of secret (presumably undiscovered) murders, since they could poison people without being suspected. It is doubtful, however, if as many women murderers escape detection as men, since their guilt reactions are generally observable and women murderers usually kill either their husbands or their children. Furthermore, members of the family are the first persons suspected and modern criminal science can easily detect most poisoning. The majority of the undetected murderers are male gangsters, as every criminologist knows. Nevertheless, Dr. Pollak is right in attributing responsibility for abortion to women (although he ignores the many instances in which their husbands or lovers collaborate in providing funds for the abortion).

One of the crimes for which women are more frequently arrested and convicted than men is child abandonment (or neglect). This fact convinces Dr. Pollak of women's essential criminality. It is well known, however, that men desert their children and wives far oftener than women desert their children or husbands, yet deserting husbands and fathers are often neither arrested nor punished. As far as child abandonment is concerned, society is much more aroused when a woman is the offender than in the case of a deserting father. Women social workers will usually testify in court against such a mother. Yet they are often unwilling to take action against a deserting father who leaves his family without support because, they argue, it is useless to antagonize a father and he certainly will not support his family if sent to prison!

Despite Pollak's contentions, all statistical analyses of crime show that women as compared to men are relatively law abiding. At least women are much less frequently involved in offenses which bring them into direct conflict with the law. At the same time women constitute the bulk of sex offenders brought into court, but this fact can be explained largely by the double standard and is not because women are essentially less chaste than men. Men buy sex favors illicitly but are seldom punished whereas women are often punished and are always condemned for selling such favors. Somewhat paradoxically, women actually break laws pertaining to sex less frequently than men, but the laws with reference to sex are invoked more often against women. For other than sex offenses women are seldom arrested and convicted.

Private Culture and Its Effect upon the Conduct Pattern of Women

There must be some reason for these apparent differences in criminality. We have no reason for believing that women are inherently
"better" and therefore less criminal. The chief explanation for the
disparity in crime rates of men and women seems rather to lie in the
special characteristics of their respective cultures. Men and women
live in different worlds. Some of the crimes women commit grow out
of this fact. For the average woman is more gullible and naïve than
the average man, perhaps because she lives in a private world in which
the virtues of honesty, faith, and trust form the web, woof, and pattern of responsible family life. Marriage is the lot of most women and
if the marriage is to be satisfactory it must be a co-operative relationship based upon love and confidence. Crime, Sutherland continually
insisted, is the result of a person and a situation. The situations in
which women find themselves apparently are not so conducive to
crimes as are the situations men face. Despite the so-called emancipa-
tion of women, the average woman spends her life and fulfills her
purposes in the home.

A further reason for there being fewer criminals among women is
that the average woman experiences less conflict between her ethical
values (and mode of life) and the achievement of her goals than does
the average man. If a woman's husband is faithless, her marriage is a
failure. If her children are dishonest or delinquent she has failed at
her personal and racial task of bringing up the next generation. The
driving motivations in the average woman's life tend, therefore, to
be emotional.

Since a woman spends most of her life in devotion and service to
her family, this concentration of interest in her family's welfare results in a peculiar type of emotional selfishness. She is primarily concerned about *her* family, *her* husband, *her* children, *her* home. So long
as she receives the expressed love of her family, other concerns do not
seem to matter much. Emotional security tends to be her major aim
and highest goal.

The major satisfactions of women are thus measured by the nonma-
terial values of love, affection, and service to her family. A woman's
success as a wife and as a mother has no monetary measure, hence
money and financial status have relatively less importance in her scale
of values. Of course, some women are very mercenary, but the average woman achieves her goal if her children grow up to be attractive

and competent and if she retains her husband's love and devotion. "Marriage," as Elizabeth Browning wisely wrote in "Aurora Leigh," "is a woman's whole existence."

TABLE 8.1.   Distribution of Arrests by Sex, 1950

Offense Charged	Number			Per Cent		
	Total	Male	Female	Total	Male	Female
Total	793,671	717,088	76,583	100.0	100.0	100.0
Criminal homicide	6,336	5,482	854	.8	.8	1.1
Robbery	19,779	18,930	849	2.5	2.6	1.1
Assault	59,496	53,168	6,328	7.5	7.4	8.3
Burglary—breaking or entering	43,673	42,564	1,109	5.5	5.9	1.4
Larceny—theft	66,031	58,409	7,622	8.3	8.2	10.0
Auto theft	18,398	17,905	493	2.3	2.5	.6
Embezzlement and fraud	21,439	19,505	1,934	2.7	2.7	2.5
Stolen property; buying, receiving, etc.	3,289	3,014	275	.4	.4	.4
Arson	1,054	932	122	.1	.1	.2
Forgery and counterfeiting	11,743	10,395	1,348	1.5	1.4	1.8
Rape	9,323	9,323	—	1.2	1.3	—
Prostitution and commercialized vice	8,579	3,338	5,241	1.1	.5	6.8
Other sex offenses	19,725	16,851	2,874	2.5	2.3	3.8
Narcotic drug laws	8,539	7,495	1,044	1.1	1.0	1.4
Weapons; carrying, possessing, etc.	10,376	9,887	489	1.3	1.4	.6
Offenses against family and children	15,238	14,419	819	1.9	2.0	1.1
Liquor laws	11,260	9,466	1,794	1.4	1.3	2.3
Driving while intoxicated	51,318	49,190	2,128	6.5	6.9	2.8
Road and driving laws	14,571	14,255	316	1.8	2.0	.4
Parking violations	309	293	16	*a*	*a*	*a*
Other traffic and motor vehicle laws	13,052	12,649	403	1.6	1.8	.5
Disorderly conduct	45,438	39,078	6,360	5.7	5.4	8.3
Drunkenness	178,165	162,202	15,963	22.6	22.8	20.9
Vagrancy	48,604	41,598	7,006	6.1	5.8	9.1
Gambling	15,490	13,965	1,525	2.0	1.9	2.0
Suspicion	46,194	41,291	4,903	5.8	5.8	6.4
Not stated	7,930	7,083	847	1.0	1.0	1.1
All other offenses	38,322	34,401	3,921	4.8	4.8	5.1

a Less than $\frac{1}{10}$ of 1 per cent.

SOURCE: Table 40 in *Uniform Crime Reports*, Annual Bulletin, 1950, Federal Bureau of Investigation, U.S. Department of Justice, Washington, 1951, p. 107.

On the other hand, a family and marriage represent only a segment of a man's interest. When the average man leaves the house in the morning, he leaves a private culture, dominated by personal ethics, for a public culture, dominated by struggle for economic success and financial reward. Competition in the market place, in the office, or at his profession is frequently a battle of wits, a matter of outwitting one's contemporaries, without any desire for the welfare of all. "Success" for men in western urban society depends all too frequently on how effectively one man eliminates his competitors, while he secures more orders, more customers, more patients, or more clients, as the case may be.

Offenses Women Commit

Despite their lower rate of crime, women commit a wide variety of crimes. In fact, with the exception of rape, women are arrested for and convicted of all the crimes listed in the *Uniform Crime Reports* issued by the Federal Bureau of Investigation for 1950, as Table 8.1 shows. But prostitution is the only category in which women are arrested more frequently than men. However, the women arrested for vagrancy are usually prostitutes too, "vagrancy" being a mere euphemistic term for prostitution in most cases.

Actually the largest single category of women arrested in 1950 was drunkenness, which accounted for 20.9 per cent of female offenders. If we total those arrested for "prostitution and commercialized vice," "other sex offenses," "disorderly conduct," "vagrancy," and "suspicion," all terms frequently employed to designate women sex offenders, they add up to 28 per cent of the women arrested.[2] As stated, the men constitute a far greater proportion of those arrested for all sex offenses except prostitution. The listing below shows that men commit 45 times as many road and driving offenses, 42 times as many auto thefts, 38 times as many burglaries, 21 times as many robberies, and 6 times as many murders, as well as exceeding women in all of-

Proportion of Men to Women Offenders[3]

Rape (exclusively masculine offense)	
Road and driving laws	45 to 1
Auto theft	42 to 1
Burglary	38 to 1
Other traffic and motor vehicle laws	31 to 1
Driving while intoxicated	23 to 1
Robbery	21 to 1
Carrying and possessing weapons	20 to 1
Offenses against family and children	17 to 1
Drunkenness	10 to 1
Gambling	9 to 1
Criminal homicide	6 to 1
Prostitution	.6 to 1

[2] Cf. chap. 9 for a treatment of female sex offenders, and pp. 116–123 for a discussion of male sex behavior.

[3] Ratios computed by writer from data in *Uniform Crime Reports*, Annual Bulletin, 1950, Federal Bureau of Investigation, U.S. Department of Justice, Washington, 1951, p. 109. The author acknowledges her debt to Walter C. Reckless for this idea.

fenses except prostitution. Even prostitution is an offense for which men are arrested in their role as pimps and panderers.

Comparative Crime Rates Among Men and Women

If we make any comparative analysis of arrests and convictions of men and women offenders, the latest data giving figures for both (as this is written) are for the year 1946. In that year there were 68,742 women among the 645,431 arrests. On January 1 women constituted 16.8 per cent of the 134,852 prisoners who were inmates of state and federal prisons. During the year 60,241 prisoners were released, 4552 of them female, while 64,044 prisoners were received through court commitment, 4168 of whom were women.[4] In other words, during 1946, 16.8 per cent of the arrests in the United States and its possessions, 7.5 per cent of the prisoners received in state and federal institutions, and 6.5 per cent of the prisoners released from such institutions were women.[5] Men constituted 83.2 per cent of the arrests.

We have no data to show what percentage of those arrested were convicted and admitted to state and federal prisons, since many of them were released without trial and many who were tried and convicted did not receive sentence during the year of their arrest. There is presumptive evidence, however, that a smaller percentage of women who are arrested serve sentences in state and federal prisons; many women are arrested for misdemeanors and as such are either released or if convicted are sentenced to a local jail or house of detention.

The Number of Convictions in Relation to Arrests

The number of women convicted in proportion to those arrested is unquestionably much lower than is true in the case of men. In 1946, for example, 68,742 women were arrested in the United States, according to the F.B.I. records, but only 4198 women prisoners were received in state and federal institutions, whereas for the same period 576,689 men were arrested and 59,876 were received by all institutions.[6] That is, 10.3 per cent of men received serious sentences in contrast to 5.7 per cent of women.[7]

[4] Ibid.

[5] Prisoners in State and Federal Prisons and Reformatories, 1946, Bureau of the Census, U.S. Department of Commerce, Washington, 1948, p. 6.

[6] Uniform Crime Reports for the United States and Its Possessions, Annual Bulletin, 1946, Washington, 1947; Prisoners in State and Federal Prisons and Reformatories, 1946, p. 37. (These are the latest available data on both arrests and convictions as this book goes to press.)

[7] Obviously, not all of the men and women arrested in 1946 came up for trial that

In some respects, however, women receive more severe treatment at the hands of law-enforcing agencies than men. Women with a police record, for example, are much more frequently arrested on suspicion than are men. Women who have been previously arrested for prostitution are often picked up by police simply for being on the streets after dark. Because jail facilities for women are often poor, a much larger percentage of those sentenced for misdemeanors are committed to the state and federal prisons. In 1946 over one-fourth (1101 out of 4168) of the women committed to state and federal institutions were misdemeanants.[8] Relatively few male misdemeanants are committed to prison.

Sensational Literature on Women Offenders

The average person is horrified by the mere thought of a woman criminal, and much literature concerning female offenders capitalizes on this fact. Hargrave L. Adam, in a sensational British study published in 1914, classified criminal women into seven groups:[9]

The prostitutes.
The poisoners.
The murderers.
The baby farmers.
The vitriol throwers.
The financial defrauders.
The aiders and abettors.

Obviously, as Mr. Adam must have known, a large number of women criminals are not subsumed under these categories. Instead his categories represent the types of women offenders most likely to attract the reader's interest. Such a classification takes no account of the less dramatic and less sensational offenses. Except for sex offenses, to which exaggerated importance is attached, the range of antisocial conduct for which women are punished is about as extensive as that of men, as Table 8.1 indicates. Mr. Adam points out, however, that fewer women commit crimes in spite of their being exposed to untoward home and neighborhood influences in very nearly the same numbers

---

year, hence the statistical picture is not quite accurate. There are no figures to indicate the exact number of persons arrested who were later convicted since data are not collected so as to follow the cases through.

[8] *Prisoners in State and Federal Prisons and Reformatories, 1946*, p. 18.

[9] Hargrave L. Adam, *Women and Crime*, T. Werner Laurie, Cliffords Inn, London, 1914.

as men.[10] He, like many present-day criminologists, ignores the differences between the private milieu in which the average woman lives and the public existence which characterizes the lot of men.

The statistics for crimes committed, arrests made, and convictions, because of their inaccuracy, give us no complete picture of crime, whether the statistics are for men or women, as we have discussed in Chapter 3. Although there are relatively few women offenders, it is probably true that a somewhat larger proportion of women who break the law are not prosecuted than is true in the case of men. We have no exact data to prove this statement and there is no reason to believe Dr. Pollak's contention that women commit as many crimes as men. It is well known, however, that a large number of petty thefts are committed by servants. Most servants are women and nearly everyone who ever hired servants has had some trouble with their petty pilfering. For such minor thefts or "petty larceny," however, there is a general disinclination to institute proceedings. Often the maid, cleaning woman, laundress, or other suspected servant is given opportunity to return whatever she has taken. Sometimes she is dismissed summarily, but unless the amount is large the average employer usually prefers not to press charges. Often, of course, it is difficult to establish guilt in such instances since the articles missing are taken surreptitiously. Intelligent servants (who are at the same time dishonest) may take advantage of employers since it is a serious offense to accuse a person of stealing unless the charge can be proved. To make a false accusation is to make oneself liable for damages.

Judges are generally more likely to be lenient in dealing with women on trial than in dealing with men, although usually neither the number of acquittals nor the statistics of cases on probation are classified on the basis of sex. At least it is commonly taken for granted that the woman offender does not receive as severe a penalty for criminal conduct as does the male offender, unless she is a sex offender or is guilty of neglecting her children. In both of these latter instances women are more severely punished than men.

War and Its Effect on Women's Crime Rates

Wartime conditions are often said to increase criminality among women.[11] The number of women arrested for violation of state laws

---

[10] *Ibid.*, p. 8.
[11] Francis E. Merrill, *Social Problems on the Home Front*, Harper, New York, 1948, p. 199.

and municipal ordinances increased from 79,122 in 1943 to 83,600 in 1944, or 5.7 per cent. This rise was widely publicized in the press as an index to women's increasing criminality, but the percentage of increase is too small to be significant from a statistical point of view.[12]

What is more important to keep in mind is that during the war police were alerted to be on the watch for women sex offenders in the special united effort of military officials, public health officials, and police to reduce prostitution. Much of whatever increase took place in women's crime rates may be attributed to this fact.

During World War II the crime rate and the number of arrests for women thus increased for three reasons: (1) There was an actual increase in arrests. (2) There was greater vigilance with reference to prostitution. (3) The proportion of women in the total crime rate went up because of the decline in the number of men arrested. A large number of men in the younger age categories most likely to be arrested were in the army.

We may be reasonably certain that a large number of women arrested for prostitution were arrested more than once. Indeed prostitutes are commonly arrested and released several times a year. An unknown but unquestionably large number of prostitutes also are arrested without having a fingerprint card sent to Washington.[13]

The effect of war upon the women's crime rate, however, is rather complicated. The percentage, as well as the actual number, of arrests among women rose in several categories, e.g., drunkenness, disorderly conduct, vagrancy, and commercialized vice. At the same time the percentage of women arrested for prostitution actually went down, despite the fact that the number of arrests for this category increased.[14]

One of the greatest internal migrations in history occurred during 1940–1947 in the United States.[15] Many of the migrants were women who swelled the number of factory workers, and many of these shifted from plant to plant. Previously sheltered young women were exposed to many temptations. Drunkenness increased among women as well as sex offenses and disorderly conduct, but the arrest rates for larceny, homicide, and assault declined in percentage. Women had

[12] Taken from *Uniform Crime Reports,* Annual Bulletin, 1944, Federal Bureau of Investigation, U.S. Department of Justice, Washington, 1945.

[13] Cf. *Uniform Crime Reports,* Annual Bulletin, 1945, Federal Bureau of Investigation, U.S. Department of Justice, Washington, 1946, p. 113.

[14] Cf. Hans von Hentig's analysis of statistical data with reference to sex and crime in his book, *Crime: Causes and Conditions,* McGraw-Hill, New York, 1947, pp. 117–120.

[15] According to the Census Bureau 71 million persons changed their residences in the internal migration between 1940 and 1947.

more money and could pay for their hearts' desires. They could walk out on their husbands; they could even pay for a divorce. But in this new freedom there were social dangers.

The disorganization accompanying war always seems to yield its toll of disorganized personalities. It is always reflected in changing behavior patterns, in disrupted families, in the increase in sexual laxity, and in the twisted moral values of bewildered and disturbed individuals. The increase in illicit sex behavior and drunkenness among women should not be surprising.

What may seem surprising is the decline in the percentage of homicides and assault among women. Dr. von Hentig attributes this decline to the improvement in women's economic condition.[16] It is a well-known if unverified fact, however, that most women murderers kill either their husbands (because their love has turned to hate) or their lovers (who have double-crossed them). There is probably no serious economic motive involved. In wartime husbands and wives are often separated and the same is true of sweethearts. The separation may lead to unfaithfulness and divorce but it automatically precludes murdering the absent party. The wartime decline in murder among women may be partially explained thus.

In 1946 the number of arrests for prostitution and vice remained close to what it was for the year previous, but the total number of women arrested decreased almost one-fifth, as the accompanying table shows. However, the number of women arrested increased somewhat during the years 1947–1949. There is no way of telling whether this is merely an increase in reported arrests, an increase in line with the greater number of women reaching adult status, or an increase in police activity. In 1947 there was an upturn of arrests of nearly 10 per cent, as Table 8.2 shows, followed by small increases in 1948 and 1949. There was, however, a slight decrease in 1950. The number of male arrests for 1950 increased only 0.5 per cent—that is, it remained almost stationary.

WOMEN IN STATE AND CITY PENAL INSTITUTIONS

Since Euro-American culture places high social value upon the Christian ideal of a "chaste and sober life" for women, the woman who either flouts the conventional sex code openly or merely fails to abide by it is generally regarded as both a law-breaker and a sinner.

[16] Hans von Hentig, op. cit., p. 119.

In fact, the sex offender (despite changing sex mores), still tends to be the most condemned of all women, and we may presume it is largely in consequence of this social attitude that sex offenders constitute so large a part of the women offenders serving sentence in penal institutions.

TABLE 8.2. Number of Women Arrested, 1937 to 1950
(Including those under 18 years of age)

Years	Total	Percentage Change from Preceding Year
1937	35,976	—
1938	37,780	+5.0
1939	43,818	+16.0
1940	51,950	+18.6
1941	57,799	+11.3
1942	70,353	+21.7
1943	79,122	+12.5
1944	83,600	+5.7
1945	84,144	+0.7
1946	68,742	−18.3
1947	75,391	+9.7
1948	76,977	+2.1
1949	78,585	+2.1
1950	76,583	−2.5

SOURCE: Table 47 in *Uniform Crime Reports*, Annual Bulletin, 1945, Federal Bureau of Investigation, U.S. Department of Justice, Washington, 1946, p. 123; and subsequent *Uniform Crime Reports*, 1947 to 1950, inclusive.

Statistics for local and state institutions indicate that prostitution and other sex offenses bulk large among the offenses women commit, as Tables 8.3 and 8.4 show. In New York City, for example, for the period January 1, 1950, to December 31, 1950, there were 6377 cases admitted to the House of Detention—of whom 1299 were sentenced and 5078 were for detention. Of these, 3235 were brought in for prostitution under the law known as Vagrancy Act No. 887. This was slightly more than 50 per cent of the cases. An additional 536, or 8.4 per cent, were sentenced for disorderly conduct. Most of this group was actually arrested for prostitution, whereas 4 were arrested for compulsory prostitution.

The same situation applies in the less densely populated areas. In Kansas, for example, prostitution or illicit sex conduct was formerly the foremost reason for committing women to the State Industrial Farm. The majority of those committed to the Kansas institution were sent, in fact, under the quarantine law for venereal diseases rather than for sex misconduct, *per se*. In that state any woman suffering from ve-

TABLE 8.3. Classification by Offense for Sentenced and Detention Cases Committed to the House of Detention, New York City, January to December, 1950

Offense	Sentenced	Detention	Total
Abandonment	0	13	13
Abortion	2	21	23
Act 887 (Vagrancy Act)	496	2739	3235
Alcoholic Beverage Code violation	20	23	43
Arson	1	13	14
Assault	39	314	353
Bail surrender	0	0	0
Bigamy	0	2	2
Bookmaking	1	3	4
Burglary	4	35	39
Burglary tools	1	1	2
Compulsory prostitution	1	0	1
Conspiracy	1	10	11
Conspiracy to assassinate	0	2	2
Counterfeit money	0	4	4
Criminally receiving stolen goods	2	7	9
Dangerous weapon	3	28	31
Disorderly conduct	256	280	536
Disorderly House	1	0	1
Drugs	84	192	276
Ending life of child	0	14	14
Escape, aid to	1	1	2
Extortion	0	1	1
False alarm	3	9	12
Federal stop-over	0	7	7
Forgery	8	69	77
Forgery prescription	0	2	2
Fortune Telling	1	5	6
Fraud	3	1	4
Fraud re check	1	10	11
Fraud re hotel	0	3	3
Fraud re property	0	1	1
Fraud re relief	26	7	33
Fugitive	0	23	23
Gambling	1	0	1
Gambling house	0	13	13
General business law	0	2	2
Grand larceny	10	131	141
Homicide	0	43	43
House of good shepherd	0	1	1
Impairing morals of a minor	0	1	1
Indecent exposure	2	3	5
Injury to property	0	1	1
Interrupting quiet enjoyment	0	1	1
Jostling	0	7	7
Jumped bail	0	1	1
Kidnaping	0	3	3
Leaving scene of crime	0	1	1
Lottery tickets	0	3	3
Mail theft	12	57	69
Maiming	0	1	1
Malicious mischief	4	17	21
Manslaughter	1	4	5
Material witness	0	16	16

TABLE 8.3. Classification by Offense for Sentenced and Detention Cases Committed to the House of Detention, New York City, January to December, 1950 (*Continued*)

Offense	Sentenced	Detention	Total
Murder	0	3	3
Neglect of child	3	6	9
No heat	0	2	2
No hot water	0	1	1
Non-Support	1	2	3
Park rules and regulations	11	0	11
Perjury	0	2	2
Petit larceny	121	403	524
Policy (numbers racket)	81	60	141
Railroad property	6	4	10
Rape	0	1	1
Receiving stolen property	0	1	1
Resisting arrest	0	1	1
Robbery	3	56	59
Sanitary code, violation of	5	7	12
Self-Committers	0	16	16
Shop theft	0	2	2
Sodomy	0	2	2
Stealing automobiles	0	1	1
Stop-Overs	0	6	6
United States documents theft	0	1	1
Unlawful entry	3	1	4
Unlawful practice of medicine	2	0	2
Unlawful use of mail	0	1	1
Vagrancy	22	27	49
Viol. admin. code	11	6	17
Viol. Albion parole	0	6	6
Viol. building code	0	1	1
Viol. education law	0	1	1
Viol. federal probation	0	1	1
Viol. housing law	1	0	1
Viol. labor law	2	1	3
Viol. liquor law	2	1	3
Viol. multiple dwell. law	9	7	16
Viol. N.Y. State Warrant	0	3	3
Viol. parole and probation	25	52	77
Viol. property law	0	4	4
Viol. state parole	0	14	14
Viol. term lease	0	6	6
Viol. traffic law	6	4	10
Viol. welfare law	0	13	13
Warrants	0	2	2
Albion Warrant	0	6	6
Bedford Warrant	0	1	1
Hudson Warrant	0	30	30
Westfield Warrant	0	19	19
Wayward minor	0	103	103
Westfield parole	0	36	36
Youthful offender	0	9	9
Totals	1299	5078	6377

SOURCE: Data furnished by Ruth E. Collins, Superintendent.

nereal disease may be sent to the prison for treatment, but in actual practice only women with a record of immorality are actually sent. Women of good reputation who contract such a disease from their husbands, for example, would not be likely to be sent to the prison.

During the period from July 1, 1944, to July 1, 1945, 132 out of the 209 women received at the Kansas State Industrial Farm were sent under the quarantine law, while 20 additional were sentenced for sex offenses, or for "vagrancy," a term which is also used to cover the charge of prostitution in Kansas. During the war period, 156 of 209 cases were thus sex offenses.

Since penicillin and other "miracle" drugs have provided swift treatment for venereal disease, few prostitutes are now committed to the Kansas State Industrial Farm. The number of women offenders in Kansas has, however, gone down precipitately on all counts. As Table 8.4 shows, only 38 women were serving sentence in the Kansas State

TABLE 8.4. Offenses for Women Committed to Kansas State Industrial Farm, on October 13, 1951

Murder 1st degree	3
Murder 2nd degree	2
Manslaughter 1st degree	2
Robbery 1st degree	2
Felonious assault	2
Forgery 2nd degree	7
Worthless check	2
No fund check	2
False pretense	1
Grand larceny	2
Abetting statutory rape	1
Pocket picking	1
Conceal mortgaged property	1
Adultery	1
Bigamy	1
Petty larceny	1
Aid and abetting escape	1
Venereal disease (health cases)	6
Total	38

SOURCE: Data supplied by C. W. Wilson, Record Clerk, Kansas State Industrial Farm for Women, Lansing, Kansas.

Industrial Farm in October, 1951. Of these, 6 were sentenced for venereal disease and 3 others for violating sex codes (1 for adultery, 1 for abetting statutory rape, and 1 for bigamy).

In New York City the convictions for offenses against property included 121 cases of petit larceny, 10 of grand larceny, 4 of burglary,

3 of fraud, and 8 of forgery. All told these constituted but 146 or 11.2 per cent of the total convictions among the women convicted to the House of Detention. In Kansas 18 of the total 38 cases, or almost one-half, were convicted on economic charges. Only one woman was convicted of impairing the morals of a minor and no other offense involving the mistreatment or contribution to the delinquency of a child was represented in the charges. The impersonality of city life and lack of concern on the part of neighbors for whatever Mrs. Doe may do is probably a reason for so few women being charged with such an offense in New York City.

Women convicted of murder in New York State are not sentenced to prison, since the death penalty is mandatory for capital offenses. There are therefore no murderers among those sentenced to the House of Detention, but 43 who were accused of homicide were detained there awaiting trial. Many of the so-called worst offenders in New York City are sentenced to the Westfield Prison or Bedford Hills Reformatory for Women, but equally serious offenders are also sentenced to the House of Detention. (This is dependent upon the decision of the judge.) The population of the House of Detention thus represents a fair cross section of metropolitan women offenders. Malicious mischief accounted for 4 incarcerations, abortion for 2, gambling for 1, the numbers policy for 81. A modern trend in women's crimes is evidenced in the 26 cases sentenced to the House of Detention for obtaining relief fraudulently. One of the major offenses, other than prostitution, was using drugs. As material presented in an earlier chapter indicates, prostitutes are often narcotic addicts.

In Kansas, 3 women were convicted of first degree murder; 2 of second degree murder; and 2 of manslaughter of the first degree. These offenses do not vary markedly from those covered in the Glueck's study some 20 years ago. Of the 500 women committed to the Massachusetts Reformatory for Women, 54 per cent were sentenced for sex offenses which included cases of adultery, fornication, keeping houses of ill fame, night walking, being "lewd and lascivious," and other sex offenses. An additional 23.8 per cent were sentenced for offenses against public health, safety, and morals which were also chiefly for sex immorality. Another 6.6 per cent were imprisoned for drunkenness, 2 per cent were convicted under narcotics laws, and 0.8 per cent were serving for offenses against person. Only 11.2 per cent were serving for offenses against property.[17]

[17] Cf. Sheldon and Eleanor T. Glueck, *Five Hundred Delinquent Women*, Knopf, New York, 1934, Tables 1–9 in Appendix D, p. 423.

Federal Women Offenders

Women sentenced to the Federal Reformatory for Women at Alderson are not representative of the rank-and-file women offenders since they are convicted under federal laws. Federal criminal laws cover offenses against the federal government, offenses involving interstate activities which have been declared illegal, offenses committed on federal territory, or offenses endangering the national interest which are covered by some specific federal law. Thus sex offenders do not ordinarily bulk large in the group of women convicted by federal courts.

During World War II, however, women were prosecuted under federal law for prostitution carried on in or near an army camp under Public Law 193, popularly known as the May Act.[18] For a time approximately one-half of the women serving sentence at Alderson were committed under this act and as late as September, 1945, 18.2 per cent of the inmates at Alderson were committed under charge of prostitution.[19] Most of those arrested under this act were not true or hardened prostitutes but were young girls. Hence it is questionable if the act accomplished any measurable reduction in venereal disease (which was its avowed purpose).

Certainly the problem of controlling prostitution around army camps and training centers demanded immediate attention. Women "in the racket" flocked to all the Fort Rileys, Fort Roberts, and Fort Sumters in America. Sometimes neither local authorities nor the War Department clamped down hard enough. In other instances the May Act[20] was so vigorously enforced that a young girl who was on a legitimate errand and found in a bus station near an army camp was fair game for arrest by zealous federal officials.

A survey of the first 100 cases received under the May Act at the Federal Reformatory for Women showed all but 10 to be under 35 years of age; 68 per cent were under 25 and 37 per cent under 20. Twelve per cent were juveniles under 18.[21] Often these younger girls could have been much more suitably treated under juvenile codes and it is a large question whether or not the F.B.I. officials did wisely in

[18] Helen Hironimus, Warden, correspondence dated September 3, 1945.

[19] United States Code, Title 18, sec. 518a, enacted July 1, 1941.

[20] Some women, in the opinion of social workers investigating the cases, have been so arrested simply because they were out late at night. Obviously most of the convictions were for bona fide cases.

[21] Helen Hironimus, "Survey of 100 May Act Violators Committed to the Federal Reformatory for Women," Federal Probation, 7:31–34 (April–June, 1943).

more or less "railroading" them into the prison at Alderson. Certainly there are few soldiers who could not protect themselves from the advances of such young girls. Most men who have sex relationships with girls 15 or 16 years old are willing victims, and Congress might very suitably have protected the young girls from the advances of the soldiers. The May Act was an "emergency measure" and remained in effect only until May 15, 1945.

Although prostitution is normally punished under state legislation and local ordinances, women engaged in "white slavery" are subject to federal law. According to the Mann Act this involves transporting women across state lines for immoral purposes. Only 2.2 per cent of the women committed to federal prisons in 1951 came in this category —a somewhat lower percentage than in preceding years.

The largest category of federal women offenders are convicted of violation of the narcotics laws. In July, 1951, they constituted 32.8 per cent of the total group, as Table 8.5 shows. These women were prosecuted under federal legislation for possessing narcotics, but many of them also have a checkered record of prostitution. It is well known that prostitutes are frequently involved in the drug racket, chiefly because many of them become addicts themselves. Federal agents on the lookout for drug law violators are often given tips about prostitutes in local communities. The federal government through its Public Health Service is also interested in stamping out venereal disease and it seems likely that many drug law violators are arrested chiefly because they are prostitutes, even though prostitution is not charged.

Any federal prisoner must obviously be convicted of violation of a federal law. Postal law violations are chiefly a matter of robbing mails. Forging as a federal offense usually involves either forging government checks or taking checks from the mail in apartment house mailboxes. These two categories constitute the reasons for committing 21.5 per cent of the women at the Federal Reformatory in 1951. Motor vehicle theft under federal law entails taking a vehicle across state lines, and many of the women arrested for such an offense have been convicted by reason of their presence in a stolen automobile, whether or not they aided in stealing the car. More women were convicted for such offenses earlier than at the present time. In 1945 slightly over 15 per cent were so arrested; in 1951 the percentage was 8.6.

During World War II a larger number of women than usual were convicted for securing servicemen's allowances illegally. In certain instances the woman would marry several men in order to secure their allowances and a considerable number of women were convicted of this offense during the war. In 1951 only 1.7 per cent of the federal women offenders were committed under this charge. Liquor law violations are chiefly a matter of evasion of liquor tax laws by restaurant owners, etc. Few women were convicted of immigration law violations, espionage, or treason.

TABLE 8.5.   Women Prisoners at the Federal Reformatory for Women at Alderson, West Virginia, on July 19, 1951

Type of Offense	Number	Percentage
Narcotic violators	148	32.8
Postal violations	97	21.5
Forgery	56	12.1
Motor Vehicle Theft Act	39	8.6
National Stolen Property Act	16	3.5
Liquor laws	12	2.6
White Slave Traffic Act (Mann Act)	10	2.2
Immigration laws	8	1.7
Servicemen's Dependents Allowance Act violation	8	1.7
Counterfeiting: altering money	7	1.6
Robbery—grand larceny and petty larceny	7	1.6
Manslaughter and murder	6	1.3
Interstate commerce violations	6	1.3
Embezzling	5	1.1
Assault	4	Less than 1
Bank robbery	4	"
Kidnaping	3	"
Espionage	2	"
Treason	2	"
Custom laws	2	"
Perjury	2	"
Veterans' Administration offenses	1	"
False pretenses	1	"
Harboring	1	"
Prostitution—army camp	1	"
Bankruptcy	1	"
Income tax evasion	1	"
Impersonation	1	"
	451	

SOURCE: Data supplied by Nina Kinsella, Warden.

These women, along with those convicted under the National Stolen Property Act and the federal Kidnapping Act and a few embezzlers, constituted most of the offenders, although there was a sprinkling of other types.[22]

During World War II and for several years following, certain female offenders sentenced under the Federal Juvenile Delinquency Act, Title 18, Section 921, were also incarcerated at Alderson. This act provided that a juvenile who violates a federal law may be tried and

[22] Cf. chap. 9 for discussion in greater detail.

sentenced, have his (or her) case heard informally, and be committed to the custody of the United States Attorney General. Such juvenile offenders were eligible for parole at any time. In some instances young girls are brought before federal courts who were not truthful about their ages and are sentenced as adult, or who refuse to be sentenced as juveniles.[23] At present juvenile offenders are not sentenced to Alderson.

Marital Status of Women Offenders

Because marriage itself provides women with protection from the economic competition in the market place, they can more easily maintain their relatively law-abiding role. We might suppose, then, that most female offenders would be unmarried, but the reverse is true. The average female felon is or has been married, whereas the average male felon has never taken vows of matrimony although the differences in proportion are less for men than for women.

Statistics for female prisoners in 1946, for example, showed that only 28.5 per cent of those whose marital status was reported were single, 54.6 per cent were married, 7.3 per cent were widowed, and 9.6 per cent were divorced. The percentages for these categories have remained fairly constant for a good many years. So far as the women prisoners are concerned, marriage has not been a stabilizing influence. Instead, it has often seemed to contribute to women's delinquency.[24] Actually what this means is that criminal and delinquent women tend to be those who have made an unhappy or unsavory marriage.

In preparing the manuscript for this book the author interviewed a large number of women offenders in order to give fresh insight into their problems. Over and over again the prisoners related stories of unhappy marriages. Sometimes there was a love triangle; the woman's felonious conduct was the result of her infatuation with some other man. In other cases the love for her own husband prompted her to act as her husband's accomplice. Sex attraction seems to have no bounds and occasionally a relatively decent woman may become infatuated with a man who has a long criminal record. A woman offender has sometimes been unwittingly the abettor of her lawbreaking husband while uninformed of his criminal activities. In still other instances an emotionally disturbing divorce has led the woman to re-

[23] Helen Hironimus, former warden, Federal Reformatory for Women, correspondence dated October 20, 1948.
[24] Cf. table on marital status of prisoners in chap. 4, p. 91.

solve her frustrations through reckless antisocial conduct. Just as the delinquent child so often "gets even" with his parents by stealing, the adult woman may "get even" by forging checks or getting drunk— and sometimes by a combination of both methods.

When marriage is unsatisfactory or unhappy for a man, the double standard allows him to satisfy his sex desires outside of marriage and still conduct other areas of his life on a socially approved plane. For women illicit sex conduct is much more frequently condemned and adjudged criminal.

Of the unmarried women prisoners, a sizable number have a record of prostitution, whether or not they are serving sentence for such a charge. Some of these women who were reared in good homes have basic personality conflicts over thus offending the moral standards of the group. Others among them become more or less adjusted to their way of life and feel little or no remorse over their behavior. While these attitudes are largely a matter of rationalization, many prostitutes have built up a system of values which accepts illicit sex experience. As one of them said: "I have learned a great deal. I have met many interesting men, and I am convinced that marriage is not a very satisfactory arrangement or so many married men would not seek relationships with other women."[25]

Age of Women Offenders

Previous to World War II the median age of women convicted of felonies was slightly higher than for men. In 1938, for example, the median age for male felons was 27.7, whereas that for female felons was 28.9.[26] In 1939 the median age for men was 27.6 and for women 29.2.[27] During and after World War II both the female and the male median age declined, but the female median declined the most for the years 1944, 1945, and 1946. The male and female median ages for felonious offenders are as follows:[28]

Year	Male	Female
1944	27.1	26.0
1945	26.9	25.8
1946	26.3	26.4

[25] Interview with the author.

[26] Prisoners in State and Federal Prisons and Reformatories, 1938, Bureau of the Census, U.S. Department of Commerce, Washington, 1940, p. 11.

[27] Prisoners in State and Federal Prisons and Reformatories, 1939, Bureau of the Census, U.S. Department of Commerce, Washington, 1941, p. 11.

[28] Material taken from Prisoners in State and Federal Prisons and Reformatories, 1944, 1945, 1946 (reports published in 1946, 1947, 1948), pp. 18, 18, and 24 respectively.

As is obvious from these figures, the median ages for both sexes have been approximately the same in recent years. The decrease in the median age of women prisoners may have been the result of war conditions; whether or not it will continue remains to be seen. In any event the median age for women committing serious offenses has been consistently higher than for women committing misdemeanors while the reverse has been true of men. In 1938, for example, the median age of women misdemeanants was 24.5 years, for men 36.7 years.[29] For more recent years age data for misdemeanants have not been published because Congress has not appropriated funds.

In 1946 felonious offenses among women had their highest incidence during the years 20 to 24 inclusive and there was a decline for every 5-year grouping after that time, as Table 8.6 shows.

In England the proportion of female offenders to male offenders apparently increases with age. For example, during the period 1932 to

TABLE 8.6. Percentage of Felonies Committed by Females Received in All State and Federal Prisons and Reformatories in 1946

Age	Percentage
All ages	100.0
Under 15 years	0.1
15 to 19 years	15.3
20 to 24 years	29.4
25 to 29 years	18.5
30 to 34 years	11.9
35 to 39 years	10.7
40 to 44 years	6.3
45 to 49 years	4.2
50 to 54 years	1.9
55 to 59 years	0.9
60 to 64 years	0.3
65 to 69 years	0.5
70 years and over	—

Detail, 15 to 24 years

15 to 17 years	4.3
18 years	4.6
19 years	6.3
20 years	6.5
21 to 24 years	22.8

SOURCE: *Prisoners in State and Federal Prisons and Reformatories, 1946*, Bureau of the Census, U.S. Department of Commerce, Washington, 1948, p. 22.

[29] *Prisoners in State and Federal Prisons and Reformatories, 1938*, p. 11.

1936 there was only 1 female offender under 14 years of age for every 18.1 males; for those 14 to 16 there was 1 female for every 13 males; for those 30 to 40 there was 1 woman for every 6 males; for those 40 to 50 there was 1 for every 4.2 males; and for the age group 50 to 60 there were 3.8 males for each female offender.[30]

This analysis might seem to indicate that English women become increasingly criminal with age. This is not true, however. Rather, English men seem to become increasingly improved in social behavior with age and the marked differences between the crime rates of men and women thus diminish. English young men 14 to 16 committed 897 offenses per 100,000 population for the 5 years 1932–1936, the highest rate for any age group—the rate was 55 per 100,000 for men over 60. In other words the delinquency rate of boys 14 to 16 was 18 times as high as the crime rate for men over 60. The highest rate for women was 88 offenses per 100,000, which was slightly less than 9 times the 10.2 rate per 100,000 for women past 60. At present we have no comparable analysis of comparative age ratios of men and women convicts in America.

Figures for other countries show substantial sex differences. It is obvious of course that crime rates depend as much upon the social definition of antisocial behavior as anything else. Mere comparative ratios between the sexes for particular offenses may easily be falsely interpreted. Mannheim points this fact out, for example, in cases of larceny committed by servants. English statistics for all courts show that women servants committed 2.9 offenses to every 1 committed by men servants, which ratio seems on the surface to indicate a propensity for thievery among female servants. Actually there were at that time more than 17 times as many women servants as men servants; hence despite the larger number of women arrested their rate was actually much less than that of the men.[31]

The Occupation of Women Offenders

Since the various types of sex offenses constitute the largest category for which women are generally arrested and convicted many people might suppose that prostitution was a major occupation of women offenders. We have already noted that most women offenders are married, and if those in Omaha, Nebraska, are typical of women criminals in general, it is the housewife more frequently than the members

[30] Hermann Mannheim, *Social Aspects of Crime in England Between Wars*, George Allen and Unwin, London, 1940, p. 336.

[31] Cf. *ibid.*, pp. 340–341.

of any other occupational group who comes into conflict with the law. As Table 8.7 indicates, 38.2 per cent of the women arrested in Omaha during the years 1930–1934 were housewives and 30.1 per cent were domestics. Prostitution ranked third as an occupation, with waitresses, students, and teachers accounting for negligible percentages.[32]

TABLE 8.7.   Distribution of Occupations of Women Arrested in Omaha 1930–1934 by Percentages

Occupation	No. of Women	Per Cent
Housewives	3,551	38.2
Domestics	2,795	30.1
Prostitutes	1,815	19.5
Waitresses	327	3.5
Students	41	.4
Teachers	15	.1

SOURCE: T. Earl Sullenger, "Female Criminality in Omaha," *Journal of Criminal Law and Criminology*, 27:706–711 (January–February, 1937).

Sullenger's data contrast markedly with the occupational data revealed in the Gluecks' study of 500 criminal women in Massachusetts. The Gluecks found that 71.6 per cent of the women in their study were idle at the time of arrest and 4.8 per cent were spending their time in keeping house; only 23.6 per cent were employed. This information, however, was collected during a period of peak unemployment. When these women had been last employed approximately one-fifth (19.4 per cent) had been in domestic service, 44.4 per cent had been working in factories, 14.2 per cent had been in restaurant or hotel work, 10.3 per cent had worked as scrub and cleaning women, 3.4 per cent had been salesgirls, 2.1 per cent had been clerical workers, and 4.6 per cent had fallen into a miscellaneous list of occupations.[33]

Early Home and Environmental Backgrounds

If our population continues to be limited by immigration restrictions eventually most American women criminals will inevitably come from native stock. Heretofore, however, most studies of women offenders in America show a significant percentage to be from immigrant parentage.[34] The Gluecks found that the parents of 60 per cent of the women they studied had been born in Canada or Europe. The

[32] T. Earl Sullenger, "Female Criminality in Omaha," *Journal of Criminal Law and Criminology*, 27:706–711 (January–February, 1937).

[33] Sheldon and Eleanor T. Glueck, *op. cit.*, p. 107.

[34] *Ibid.*, chap. 3.

Sleighton Farm survey, however, showed that only 29.1 per cent of the girls who were committed to that institution were from immigrant stock[35] whereas 7.8 per cent were foreign born, as Table 8.8 shows.

TABLE 8.8.   Nativity of Sleighton Farm Girls Committed During Years 1913–1915

Nativity	Number	Per Cent
Total	203	100.0
Native Born	128	63.1
Native Parentage		
Native born	59	29.1
Foreign Parentage		
Russian	16	—
German	12	—
Irish	6	—
Polish	5	—
Italian	4	—
Austrian	3	—
English	3	—
Swedish	3	—
Scotch	2	—
Welsh	2	—
Hungarian	1	—
Australian	1	—
French	1	—
Foreign Born	16	7.8
Russian	7	—
German	2	—
Scotch	2	—
Austrian	2	—
Polish	1	—
Swedish	1	—
French	1	—

SOURCE: Mabel A. Elliott, *Correctional Education and the Delinquent Girl*, Commonwealth of Pennsylvania, Harrisburg, 1929, p. 24.

It seems to be true that the proportion of immigrant extraction among delinquent girls and criminal women varies with the size of the community in which they resided. Seventy-five per cent of the women in the Massachusetts study had lived in urban districts.[36] And a much earlier study in Chicago made by Breckenridge and Abbott pointed out that only 21.6 per cent of the white girls brought before the court were native born of native parents.[37]

The problems which children of the foreign born encounter involve more than cultural conflict. A sizable part of their adjustment prob-

[35] Mabel A. Elliott, *Correctional Education and the Delinquent Girl*, Commonwealth of Pennsylvania, Harrisburg, 1929, pp. 23–24.
[36] Sheldon and Eleanor T. Glueck, op. cit., p. 105.
[37] Sophonisba P. Breckenridge and Edith Abbott, *The Delinquent Girl*, Russell Sage Foundation, New York, 1912, p. 57.

lem lies in the poverty and economic struggles which have been so frequently the lot of the foreign laborer's family. For both the Sleighton Farm and the Massachusetts Reformatory women, parents ranked low in occupational status, the majority were living on a very low income, and families were so large as to make the poverty appreciably greater than if there had been fewer children. At Sleighton Farm the average girl came from a family with 5 or more children. The average number of children in the family of the inmate at the Massachusetts Reformatory was 6.43. In both groups there was considerable parental infelicity. Only 30 per cent of the parents of the Sleighton Farm girls were listed as moral and more than half of the girls' homes were broken.[38] The Massachusetts survey showed that 58.4 per cent of the homes were broken[39] and 31.8 per cent of the parents were considered unfit because of either quarrelsome relationship, lax discipline, or unwholesome surroundings. Only 9.8 per cent of the women offenders in the Massachusetts group were reared in homes adjudged adequate. Moral standards were low; there were records of criminality in 45.5 per cent of the families; and in 31 per cent the conduct of members of the family was notorious despite the lack of any arrest for their behavior.[40]

These Massachusetts women and the Sleighton Farm girls were committed to state institutions. Because of the technical nature of certain federal charges it seems likely that a larger number of women in federal institutions have no record previous to their commitment although this assumption has not been established by any published research. That is, illegal entry and espionage, for example, are types of behavior which are not necessarily associated with long histories of delinquency and crime.

Recidivism Among Women Prisoners

Once in trouble, the woman offender, like her male counterpart, tends to become a recidivist, irrespective of the charge on which she was convicted. In the study made in New York State in 1920, 51.3 per cent of the women serving sentences for sex offenses had been previously convicted, and 26.9 per cent had been convicted two or more times. Even more of the women whose offenses were against property had been previously convicted. Sixty-four per cent had served one or more sentences and 36.8 per cent had served two or more. Those

[38] Mabel A. Elliott, op. cit., p. 27.
[39] Sheldon and Eleanor T. Glueck, op. cit., pp. 71–73.
[40] Ibid.

sentenced for intoxication were not included in this computation or (it is stated) the rate would have been even higher.[41]

The proportion of women prisoners to women arrested is somewhat less than that of male prisoners to males arrested. For example, the number of women arrested for violation of state and municipal ordinances in 1946 was 68,742, or approximately 10.6 per cent of the total number of 645,431 arrests. The number of women prisoners received from the court in 1946 was 4168, or approximately 6 per cent of the number arrested, whereas there were 59,876 men received, or approximately 9.6 per cent of the number arrested that year.[42] The difference between the proportionate numbers of men and women arrested and those serving sentence is popularly regarded as an evidence of the general tendency of judges to be more lenient with women than men. However, the majority of women commit misdemeanors, hence are more likely to be dealt with lightly for that reason, as we mentioned earlier. On the other hand, many women, especially streetwalkers, were arrested many times. Sometimes such a woman is arrested as often as once a month, and each arrest appears as a separate offense, whereas if she were sentenced the woman would ordinarily be counted only once in the annual statistics. Since many women are released to be rearrested and fewer men are so released, the proportionate difference in number arrested and number serving sentence is probably accounted for by this fact.

In any event, only 1 per cent of the 500 women surveyed by Glueck and Glueck either had never been arrested or had not committed offenses for which they might have been arrested and 66.4 per cent either had been arrested or had had warrants issued for their arrest.[43]

Similarly, in the author's study of Sleighton Farm girls, there was virtually the same background of delinquency, except that an even larger percentage (76 per cent) had had previous formal charges brought against them and either had been placed on probation or had been inmates of quasi-penal institutions. The remaining 24 per cent were well-known behavior problems in their home communities and many of them were practicing prostitution.[44]

[41] Mabel R. Fernald, Mary H. S. Hayes, and Almena Dawley, A Study of Women Delinquents in New York State, Appleton-Century-Crofts, New York, 1920, p. 119.

[42] These figures were compiled by the author from data for arrests and imprisonment. They are not an exact indication of the proportion of commitments to arrests since not all cases are tried the same year they are arrested. We have no means of securing accurate information for this from existing statistics.

[43] Cf. Sheldon and Eleanor T. Glueck, op. cit., p. 101. In view of the delinquent and criminal behavior among the rank-and-file population, this situation may not be so serious as the Gluecks thought. Cf. pp. 33–47 in this text.

[44] Mabel A. Elliott, op. cit., p. 34.

The statistical data give us a composite picture of the type of women who commit offenses. The majority of women offenders who come before the courts are unquestionably products of the unsavory aspects of modern urban civilization. In order to present a clearer view of the individuals who furnish the raw material for these statistics a series of case histories are presented in the following chapter.

SELECTED BIBLIOGRAPHY

Adam, Hargrave L., *Women and Crime*, T. Werner Laurie, Cliffords Inn, London, 1912. This study points up spectacular women criminals, who are not typical of the rank-and-file women offenders.

Elliott, Mabel A., *Correctional Education and the Delinquent Girl*, Commonwealth of Pennsylvania, Harrisburg, 1929. This monograph contains considerable material about young women who were released from Sleighton Farm, Darlington, Pennsylvania, after attaining 21 years of age. The follow-up study took place from 5 to 9 years after the expiration of their parole.

Elliott, Mabel A., and Merrill, Francis E., *Social Disorganization*, Harper, New York, 3rd ed., 1950, chap. 6, "The Sex Offender," and chap. 7, "The Prostitute." These chapters survey in some detail female sex offenders and prostitutes.

Fernald, Mabel R., Hayes, Mary H. S., and Dawley, Almena, *A study of Women Delinquents in New York State*, Appleton-Century-Crofts, New York, 1920. This is one of the first extensive surveys of women offenders.

Glueck, Sheldon and Eleanor T., *Five Hundred Delinquent Women*, Knopf, New York, 1934. A comprehensive survey is made of criminal women who served sentences in the Massachusetts Reformatory.

Hironimus, Helen, "Survey of One Hundred May Act Violators Committed to the Federal Reformatory for Women," *Federal Probation*, 7:31–34 (April–June, 1943). This is an analysis of the types committed under the May Act by the former warden of the Federal Reformatory for Women.

Merrill, Francis E., *Social Problems on the Home Front*, Harper, New York, 1948, chaps. 5 and 6. These chapters are concerned with the impact of war on sex and offenses and prostitution (two major categories of female offenses).

CHAPTER 9

Types of Women Who Break the Law

Despite the drab and unhappy lives of most women criminals, the spectacular news stories concerning the activities of a few notorious women bandits have grossly distorted the picture of the average woman criminal for the general reader. The lay public believes the woman criminal to be a quasi-glamorous, stylishly dressed, semi-Holly-wood personality who has mastered all the arts of deception and all the lures of sex appeal. Flaming-haired Kathryne Thorne Kelley, who aided and abetted her husband, "Machine Gun" George Kelley, in his extortion kidnaping of Charles Urschel, is a case in point. Her love of luxury, her attractive "good looks," and her obvious intelligence as described in the press convinced many people that the criminal woman is the "brains of the gang." The clever, refined-looking wife of John Dillinger is another example of a woman who made a quiet respectable "front" for her gangster husband. Actually these women are the exceptions which prove the rule. Even when indicted as a member of a gang, the average criminal woman is more often a victim of the gang than the one who does the plotting and scheming to carry through a spectacular exploit. She is much more likely to have misplaced her faith in some crook who gets her into trouble than to be the one who instigates a crime or influences some man to undertake a bank robbery, a holdup, or an extortion kidnaping in order to satisfy her own greedy desires for a luxurious existence. Sometimes a woman's love for an undeserving man exceeds whatever scruples she might otherwise have. Many a woman who gets into trouble with the law is so infatuated by a man that she forsakes whatever principles she may have to his predatory ambitions. Sex attraction follows no rules of logic and exists between both the social and the antisocial. Some of

226

the case studies cited below should make this plain. When a woman reared in an atmosphere of social respectability "on the right side of the tracks" has become a criminal, we must look for some special explanation. Crisis situations, sudden impulses, and extreme temptations in times of real or fancied need may account for such social and moral lapses. Sudden enticements may throw the well-brought-up young woman off her guard.

The Background of Criminal Women

The average criminal woman is not a clever, well-educated girl gone wrong. She is usually the product of an unsavory environment. Frequently she is a child of a broken home; one or both of her parents may be immoral. Usually her family is in the throes of poverty—poverty made worse by the fact that a large number of children must share the scanty income. The housing and neighborhood standards are usually low, and frequently the only recreational facilities available are themselves conducive to personal disorganization.

Few criminal women in conflict with the law have had a good education. Most of them had to quit school to go to work at an early age. Indeed, many of them are handicapped mentally, hence would not have profited from extensive education. Most of their homes have offered little emotional security. Most criminal girls and women are driven by frustration and conflicting desires and by the low standards under which they have been reared. Hence their behavior is deeply rooted in the situations in which chance has placed them.[1]

Even so, not all criminal women come from a background of social depravity and economic insecurity. Some are the daughters of respectable parents and have always lived in a good neighborhood.

Because women have been generally idealized in Western civilization, the very thought of a woman criminal brings a thrill of horror to many men. In consequence women criminals are regarded as being somehow untrue to their sex, and much of the literature with reference to women and crime has intensified this opinion. Even persons who know better have often exploited their information in order to appeal to the human penchant for demanding horrible examples of women in conflict with the law. Such treatises ignore the simple fact that the average woman offender is actually a rather pathetic creature, a victim of circumstances, exploitation, and her own poor judgment.

[1] Cf. Mabel A. Elliott, *Correctional Education and the Delinquent Girl*, Commonwealth of Pennsylvania, Harrisburg, 1929, pp. 23–35.

To most wardens of women's prisons the run-of-the-institution inmate is unquestionably a mundane offender, yet wardens have sometimes presented the bizarre or unusual woman inmate or a striking
prison incident as though these were typical of prisoners and prison
life. Thus Mary B. Harris in *I Knew Them in Prison* relates the high
spots in her career as a penologist and the spectacular cases under her
custody.[2] Similarly, Florence Monahan in her book, *Women in Crime*,
picks out cases of special interest rather than "typical cases."[3]

In order to acquaint the serious student of criminology with a more
accurate picture of the woman who breaks the law, the author of this
text conducted a series of interviews with women inmates of three
different types of penal institutions: the Federal Reformatory for
Women at Alderson, West Virginia, the House of Detention in New
York City, and the Kansas State Industrial Farm for Women at Lansing, Kansas.[4] Space limitations make it impossible to present all the
cases interviewed, but study of all the cases has been of immeasurable
value in interpreting women's role in crime.

Certain facts have been altered in each instance in order to protect
the woman's identity, but the essential characteristics of these female
offenders have been retained and are given below as illustrations of the
type of women who come in conflict with the law.

Sex Offenders

The paradox and hypocrisy of sex morals makes it difficult to deal
with illicit sex behavior and prostitution objectively. To condemn a
woman for yielding to the man who is excused for making his imperious demands is to ignore the fundamental legal principle of "accessory to the act." Although male sex aberrations are generally more
leniently treated than women's, most adult males object strenuously
to the sexual exploitation of young girls by men. Men as fathers and
as responsible adults shudder at the thought of 12- to 15-year-olds
yielding to unscrupulous men. In consequence, all males who seduce
young girls are condemned as rapists and as being only slightly, if at all,
above murderers in heinousness of their offense. Laws vary widely but
all states recognize an age of consent, below which any sex relation-

[2] Viking, New York, 1936.   [3] Ives Washburn, New York, 1941.
[4] The author wishes to pay special thanks to Miss Helen Hironimus, former Warden
at the Federal Reformatory for Women, to Miss Ruth E. Collins, Superintendent of
the House of Detention, and to Mrs. Etta Beavers, former Superintendent of the Kansas
State Industrial Farm, for their co-operation in securing these case histories.

ship is technically defined as rape. Any man who forces sex relations upon any woman above the age of consent is also condemned as a rapist. On the other hand, a woman who yields to the successive entreaties of a man is often condemned not merely as his accomplice but as his temptress. Legal definitions of sex conduct thus ignore the psychological aspects of sex attraction and any purposeful arousing of sex desires so as to induce subsequent yielding, etc. To sum up what might well be an extended discussion of the subject, illicit sex behavior is chiefly a matter of biology outwitting sociology. The mores condemn illicit sex relationships, the laws punish them, the social institutions are disrupted by them, and health is often wrecked by the venereal disease which is their toll. Rationality, however, has not thus far conquered the deeply rooted impulse to continue the race. How to spiritualize and curb human sex desires remains one of our unsolved and recurring behavior problems.

We have already pointed out that sex offenses are the only important category of offenses for which more women than men suffer penalties. Yet men and women are both involved in all illicit sex behavior and men more often than women seek sex experience outside the bonds of matrimony. It is only the double standard of morals which causes a greater number of women to receive punishment.

The law actually condemns 3 different categories of offenses against chastity. These are:[5]

1. Voluntary nonmercenary sex misconduct.
2. Aggressive sex conduct.
3. Mercenary sex offenses.

Under the first category come offenses usually classified as delinquency on the part of young girls, fornication on the part of unmarried persons, and adultery on the part of married people. These offenses are variously punished. A young girl from an underprivileged or immoral home who becomes a sex delinquent is more likely to become a court case than is the child of parents of a higher economic and social level. Middle- and upper-class parents (able to cope with a problem daughter) usually try to meet the situation personally. Furthermore, social workers seldom have an opportunity to investigate homes in the middle and upper social circles. As a matter of fact they would probably be quickly ejected if they ever tried to investigate. The upper-class

[5] Cf. the Herrick Committee Report, *Women and Girl Offenders in Massachusetts.* Massachusetts Child Council, Boston, 1938, pp. 17–18.

girl's behavior in such a case is often carefully covered up. If she is pregnant she may either have her baby in another city or have an abortion—without too much danger of disclosure. The latter in turn is technically a serious offense, but actually very few cases of abortion are punished.[6]

The voluntary nonmonetary sex offenses are for the most part confined to younger girls of the lower economic class, especially insofar as they come into contact with the law, and such offenses properly fall under the category of juvenile delinquency. On the other hand, everyone knows that a considerable number of women are mistresses of men to whom they are not married. Some of these women are in the upper economic and social group. Modern prodigal women are not all in the lower social strata, but few except those in the lower classes or those with a notorious public record are ever caught in the net of the law. Of course the mistress of a wealthy businessman suffers a certain social stigma, but in the anonymity of a great city she also may enjoy many of the luxuries of modern urban life—the theater, café society, good food, beautiful clothes, and pleasant living quarters. Most of the penalty which she experiences is psychological but if her conscience has become sufficiently calloused she may rationalize well enough to be fairly well adjusted to her way of life. Naturally hers is a precarious existence and the mental conflict she suffers in trying to live in two worlds may well exact a serious toll.

Obviously it is socially important to protect the institution of marriage and the sanctity of family life. It is a large question, however, whether the criminal court is the best agency for dealing with persons who are involved in illicit sex relations. In any event, to condemn the woman for entering into such relationships and to excuse the man is clearly contrary to the legal principle of "accessory to the act." This a "man's world" tacitly permits.

Aggressive sexual conduct or rape, on the other hand, has always been condemned by both sexes, as we have indicated previously, especially so far as the sexual exploitation of young girls is concerned. Fathers as lawmakers have written rigid laws for punishing the unscrupulous men who seduce young girls. Whatever the difficulties involved in establishing a suitable criterion for rape, men rather than women constitute the bulk of rapists, and have been discussed in Chapter 7.

[6] It has been estimated that 800,000 to 2,000,000 abortions take place in the United States each year, most of which are never punished.

The Prostitute

Most women sex criminals fall into the category of mercenary sex offenders or prostitutes. These women as a group reap the greatest social stigma of all women sex offenders since they have debased sex not by thoughtless or impulsive love but for a price. The prostitute has no romantic excuse for her "unwise" love.

All extramarital sex excursions threaten the stability of the family and marriage, hence receive social disapproval, but the prostitute is the greatest threat and the most condemned. The case histories of such women show, however, that most of them are, like delinquent girls, the products of underprivilege and neglect.

Because of the cultural differences which mark the backgrounds of men and women, few women from good family backgrounds go about enticing men into illicit behavior. Yet men of education and otherwise impeccable manners often see nothing essentially wrong in "making passes" at so-called good women. That they are sometimes successful in getting women to yield to their entreaties is no valid evidence that the women are thereby worse sinners or offenders than the men.

Social controls derived from religious and moral values seek to regulate sex conduct largely because uncontrolled sex behavior disrupts the family, produces disease, and wrecks personalities. What lawyers, legislators, judges, and social workers often forget is that nonpromiscuous illicit sex relations are very little different from legal sex relations, except that they are outside of matrimony.

The prostitute, however, represents a very special variety of sex offender.[7] The prostitute, who nearly always is a woman (although there are a few unprosecuted male prostitutes), has entered into sex relations for gain and outside the bonds of matrimony.[8] Her (or his) accomplice pays for the favors of sex. Both parties are guilty of fornication, but as the laws in this country function, the seller is the one usually punished and the buyer ordinarily goes free. Whatever the leniency that may be granted women who have committed other types of offenses, the woman who is a prostitute with a record tends "to pay and pay." The judge looks at the record and notices that she has been arrested several times. Some of these arrests may have been on "suspicion" only, but even so the record "looks bad." Hence the judge,

---

[7] Cf. Mabel A. Elliott and Francis E. Merrill, *Social Disorganization*, Harper, 3rd ed., New York, 1950, chap. 7, p. 155.

[8] Some marriages are obviously mercenary, but mercenary marriages have never been condemned to the same degree as illicit mercenary relationships.

in moral revulsion, exacts a severe penalty. In fact, a woman with a record cannot even wait on a corner for a streetcar. The police know her and assume she is "soliciting." A woman who has been booked on charges of prostitution often cannot meet a friend or relative on legitimate business without danger of being picked up by the police.

Such a pickup is obviously a false arrest, but a false arrest nevertheless adds to the woman's criminal record. Police frequently profit from such pickups since their arrests show them to be on the alert and doing their job well.[9]

On the other hand many promiscuous offenders have also been committed to the Federal Reformatory and other institutions (through the vigilance of the F.B.I.) on other charges. The Bureau of Public Health of the Federal Security Agency has launched a well-deserved attack on prostitution and venereal disease. Prostitution, except around army camps, is not a federal charge, however. If the federal government is to co-operate, the prostitutes arrested by the F.B.I. must be charged with other offenses.

We have already mentioned the arrests for prostitution under the May Act during the war.[10] Many promiscuous sex offenders were also arrested by federal officials on other charges through the vigilance of the Federal Bureau of Investigation. Prostitutes are so frequently narcotic addicts that a prostitute can often be presumed to have secured narcotics illegally. The detective's problem is to get the evidence and in certain instances prostitutes have complained bitterly that the evidence was planted against them. Since there is ample indication that the prostitute is a social menace her conviction on other grounds is held to be socially justified by some detectives and police.

Dorothea Hart

Dorothea Hart was such a prostitute. Known throughout the underworld of the Pacific coast city in which she lived as the "Queen of Hearts," Dorothea Hart was the luxury-loving "Madam" of a "fashionable" house of prostitution. Among her patrons were those who had carved fortunes out of the opening of the West—captains of finance, shipping, and industry. Many patrons held important political positions and in general were representatives of a class which could afford to spend lavishly and pay well for their illicit pleasures. The "Queen of Hearts" conducted her "house" on "refined" lines. There was a beautiful ballroom where the "girls" (attired in modish evening

[9] Social workers in a large city women's prison insist that this is characteristic police practice with reference to prostitutes.

[10] Cf. pp. 214–215.

dresses) danced with the men. An excellent restaurant and bar provided expensive food and drink for the customer and his partner. Admission was by "introduction" by other customers. Many of these customers were members of exclusive clubs in the city. Each customer was "protected" by the "Madam" and in return he paid handsomely for the favor.

For fifty-odd years Dorothea Hart catered to such "broadcloth indiscretions." Often there was some attempt to thwart her activities, but her unsolicited contributions to the political coffers of local city officials gave her such political protection as to make her well-nigh invulnerable. A notable clergyman denounced her publicly, a dynamic woman lawyer attempted to have her place of business padlocked, the Salvation Army held prayer meetings outside the mansion where she reigned. (She had bought the house from one of the wealthiest families in the city.) But despite all attacks the "Queen of Hearts" sat entrenched through the political corruption of the local government, the licentious desires of a powerful clientele, and her own conniving skill in catering to them.

Coupled with all this there was a curious sentimentalism and maternal concern for the men who were her patrons and for the girls who were hostesses. For her patrons, in her own words, she "gave every protection," that is, she protected their identity and their health. No one outside could learn who her clients were and no man who entered ever needed to fear venereal disease. A highly trained medical service assured both the men and the girls of safety in that respect.

As for the "Queen of Hearts," she herself had long since given up any illicit sex relations. She was simply the hostess. But for thirty years or more she had used narcotics—not, she insisted, as a sedative, but as a stimulant. Periodically she had tried to break the habit, but there had been no real desire to give it up, and 10 different times she had been pronounced cured only to return to the drug habit. Meanwhile her business flourished and Dorothea Hart actually believed that her "racket" was good for life. Nothing could touch her. She had laid her plans well. Then the impossible happened. She was arrested for the sale, possession, and use of narcotics.

According to Dorothea, this all came about through the disloyalty of one of her newly appointed hostesses, Eloise Artwig. Eloise was a beautiful girl who applied for a job with "Madam" Hart. She agreed eagerly to the terms which the "Queen of Hearts" offered her. Shortly after she came into the house, however, she developed a case of nerves and asked her "hostess" to help her out. Dorothea claims she was sorry for Eloise because she thought her afraid. She let her have a few pills and gave her a "prescription" to be filled through a leading gangster. In exchange for the prescription, Eloise turned state's evidence for the federal officers. The gangsters suspected something, however, and shot Eloise through a window as she stood in the federal district attorney's office.

But Eloise's signed deposition had been made, and this was sufficient to convict Dorothea Hart. At 72 the latter was sentenced to 10 years in the Federal Reformatory for Women. Thus the career of a colorful underworld character came to an abrupt end.

When the author interviewed "Madam" Hart, she frequently complained of her decline in social and financial status. She missed the finery, good food, wines, and extravagant surroundings in which she had taken such pride. She had hobnobbed with the celebrities who frequented her establishment; she knew all the important politicians through her contributions to campaign funds and her active participation in the various political battles. Her presence had graced many a political gathering and political festivity. She also knew the clergy and made generous contributions to the various charities. She had accounts at the best stores. On the other hand, the gangsters and the "mobs" who made up the underworld were her particular friends. And Dorothea Hart took especial pleasure both in the dual role from which she surveyed her world and in her secret knowledge of the frailties of the men who played such an important part in the civic and industrial life of her community. Of course, Dorothea Hart never posed as a good woman. She merely knew the so-called civic leaders and knew too that their virtue was often tarnished.

Dorothea Hart is now an old and garrulous woman, who loves to recount the splendor of her former establishment. Once in a while there has been a slight hint of remorse for a life spent in promoting the evils of the flesh and for wrecking the life of many a foolish girl who sold herself for the finery that Madam Hart provided. Despite these momentary flashes of penitence, however, there is little hope for any favorable prognosis. A lifetime spent in rationalizing the "high" character of her establishment gives little reason to expect any sense of guilt or desire to readjust. In her own way Dorothea has been honored among sinners for she has been a veritable dowager among underworld madams.

Angelina Russo

Angelina Russo is a less romantic offender. When interviewed by the author, she was serving a year's sentence in a large city "House of Detention" for compulsory prostitution. In the parlance of the underworld, she was a "bookie" for girls. That is, she made contacts with girls in a beauty parlor and was convicted of having induced them to work in the various houses of prostitution from which she secured a commission.

Angelina has many opinions as to her own life history and likewise many rationalizations for her conduct. She came from a good home in the Middle West where there was constant surveillance and she says this made her wild. Because her mother was ill she was placed in a Catholic convent as a boarding student where she remained until she finished the eighth grade. She then went home to help her mother with the housework. She stayed at home for several years but finally decided she could not stand all her mother's supervision and ran away when she was 19 years old. She joined a vaudeville troupe where she sang and danced in a Hawaiian act.

While on the road, she fell in love with a man she did not know was married. She soon found out he had a wife, but she decided to live with him despite the fact. His wife was a Catholic and apparently never discovered the affair. Since this first illicit adventure, Angelina has been married twice but insists she was never in love with either husband.

Angelina thinks her whole career started with her affair with the married man. She loved him, but it was obvious that the relationship could not continue and, as she said, she "didn't care what she did afterwards." Her early upbringing made her feel very guilty. As she expressed it: "When you have lost your virginity you have lost everything. Nothing else matters." Hence her decision to become a prostitute. She subsequently worked on call, in hotels, on the street, and in houses. In one of these houses she met a man who took a fancy to her and whom she married. He said he did not hold her past against her but she was always sure he did. At least he was very jealous and a miser. She left him and he got a divorce.

Then Angelina went to New York, where she has been ever since. Her present marriage is a "common-law" arrangement, which she thinks is best. She justifies this by saying: "If a man is not sure of you, he treats you possessively and tries to run you." Angelina says her present "husband" made her give up prostitution. Since this common-law marriage Angelina maintains that she has never been in prostitution. Before her "marriage" she ran a house in which two or three girls worked and lived. She herself never lived there at any time. "After all" she said, "I have a family. My sister and her children know nothing of this part of my past. I have had to keep this from them."

Questioned as to how she could be charged with compulsory prostitution if she was not in the business, she admitted she has "told girls where they could get a job." Girls came to the beauty parlor to inquire about such opportunities. Some of them, she holds, turned in evidence against her. Angelina is very bitter about her conviction and sentence. She argues rather logically that it was obviously impossible to compel anyone to enter prostitution. She says one of the girls who alleged such compulsion was 32 years of age. The girl claimed she was required to give 10 per cent of her earnings to Angelina. Actually, Angelina maintains, the girl had been in the sporting business for years and was smarter than that!

Angelina says, and she is probably right, that there is a great deal of political corruption in securing convictions for prostitution. Her lawyer told her that if she could plead guilty she could then get bail. She says she was ill with asthma at the time or she would have reasoned more intelligently.

It is difficult to verify the truth of any of Angelina's allegations, of course. There seems to be a common complaint among women serving for sex offenses, however, that the police and lawyers promise to get them off if they admit their guilt and then proceed to exact the full penalty of the law. The woman "with a past" has little chance for leniency from the court. In fact some judges seem to think that subterfuge is allowable in obtaining a conviction of such women. Social workers at one prison say that a judge always tends to be severe with a woman with a record, even when the evidence against her is not well established. Her past record is often considered evidence enough of her general culpability in the present situation, irrespective of any proof.

MANN ACT VIOLATORS

Thelma Anderson

Thelma Anderson came from a very strict and highly respected family. Her father was especially stern and a member of a narrow religious group which frowned on most present-day leisure-time activities. In fact the sect to which he belonged believed dancing was a prelude to sin, if not a sin itself. Thelma lived at home in a small town in Illinois where she was a junior in college. She was an accomplished musician and a student of superior intelligence. But here is her story: Thelma left home after a violent quarrel with her father over a "date." She had accepted an invitation to the junior-senior prom and her father had told her point-blank that she could not go to the party. This seemed to be the last straw, and Thelma decided life was hopeless at home and left. She went to the capital of an adjoining state where she got a job as a maid. A few days later she saw her picture in the paper with the caption "Prairie City Girl Missing." Realizing the alarm she had caused her family, she telephoned home and told her parents she was all right. In great excitement they drove to see her the same day

but she refused to go home with them. After she had worked at a number of places in this same city her father came to see her again. This time he insisted that she return home. She refused again, stating that she was going to be married. As a matter of fact she had not even met anyone who wanted to marry her, but she decided she could surely pick up someone. Thelma was in fact attractive enough to make that relatively easy. She walked down the main thoroughfare several times on the Sunday evening following. Then a young man who had passed her by came back and started talking to her. She felt she must carry out her statement to her father and walked down the street with him. She saw him again the next evening.

Thelma realized from the first that the young man, Jimmy, was attracted to her. He was handsome, a good dancer, and a good conversationalist. Thelma felt her prayers answered when he proposed within a week. Her protected background had given her no understanding at all of the sordid underworld, but she was soon to be fully initiated. The night she was married her husband took her to a house of prostitution. She could scarcely believe she could be involved in such a mess but she was terribly frightened and somehow felt that if she got out of the jam the publicity would be worse than any ignominy she might suffer by staying in it. Like many women who are thus exploited, she had a false sense of loyalty, chiefly because Jimmy was so attractive despite his immorality. Things began to happen fast. The first house she was in was padlocked but she and Jimmy escaped. Later they met a girl who had been at the same house. She had been arrested previously and released by the police. They picked her up and drove to Chicago. The girl later turned state's evidence against Thelma and her husband and both were convicted and sentenced for violating the Mann Act. Thelma was only 19 years old. If Thelma's story is correct, the girl who turned in the evidence had a much more checkered career than she did. Prison officials, it should be stated, believe her story. But it has been a practice to release the prisoner who turns in the evidence which convicts another. Where one criminal is equally guilty if not more guilty than the other, there is a large question as to the judicial or police ethics involved in such a release. Thelma, who had been a college girl a few short months earlier, was sentenced under the Mann Act for procuring women for white slavery.

Since her commitment to prison Thelma has done some quiet thinking. She has resolved to make every effort to deserve the love and respect of her parents when she is paroled. She is wise enough to see that they erred in being so strict, but her career in prostitution was so completely repulsive to her that the prognosis for an acceptable adjustment for her is highly favorable.

Illegal Entry

Many of the cases of women prosecuted under our immigration laws for illegal entry into the United States have been punished as much because they were prostitutes as because of their entry. Otherwise they would have been merely deported.

Helen Roskoff

Helen was the daughter of a Czech peasant who had settled in the wheat lands of Saskatchewan and later decided to take up residence in South Dakota where he believed he could make more money. He bought a farm which was heavily mortgaged and his family of four sons and two daughters were all required to work hard to pay off the debt. Helen never had any pretty dresses or silk hose like the neighboring farm girls. How she hated the ugly black cotton hose and the coarse dark ginghams she had to wear because they would not show the dirt. She had little social life and was never allowed to go to parties or to have dates with young men like other 16-year-old girls. One Sunday she begged to stay home from church and the farm boy who lived across the road came over to see her. They were sitting in the barren "parlor" when the family came home from church.

Helen's father was very angry at the deception and ordered the young man to leave. Greatly embarrassed by her father's behavior, Helen decided to run away. She took some $12 from her mother's purse and got on a bus for Minneapolis. There she secured a job working in a lunchroom and presently met a girl who told her she could make much better money in a club she knew. Helen says she was so naïve she didn't realize it was a house of prostitution the girl had in mind. She literally had never heard of such a place. Two days later the house was raided and she was placed under arrest. Questioned as to her birthplace, she replied truthfully that she had been born in Canada and was promptly turned over to the Federal Bureau of Investigation. It had not occurred to her that she was not a citizen of the United States, but within three weeks she, a poor ignorant country girl, was deported to Canada. Homeless and penniless she entered prostitution in Winnipeg. Several years later Helen drifted to Windsor and crossed over to Detroit. From there she went to Chicago, where she met a man with whom she lived for nearly a month. He really wanted her to marry him but Helen refused. In a fit of jealous rage he said: "Well, you are a Canadian. I will turn you over to the immigration authorities." The incident occurred during World War II and this time she was not deported but sentenced for illegal entry.

Helen is very bitter. She contends it was wrong for government officials to send a young girl out of the country when her family was allowed to remain. She insists that she got into trouble innocently and that the government virtually forced her into her illegal profession by its rigid interpretation of the law. The plight of an inexperienced girl without legal or friendly aid certainly indicates the need for greater intelligence in interpreting federal laws.

Women Gangsters

Because most people are not familiar with the type of women who get embroiled with gangsters or who become members of gangs, they tend to regard such women as the ultimate in evil human beings, as the quintessence of female moral turpitude. Actually "women gangsters" are often simple and misled young girls who become involved with unprincipled men through a series of circumstances. There are exceptions of course, but women gangsters have seldom been intellectually and emotionally conditioned to an acceptance of criminal activities. Frequently they get into a criminal activity "without meaning to" and once involved see no way to escape a situation in which they seem to be enmeshed. Such was the case of Manya Vanek.

Manya Vanek

Manya Vanek was enrolled as a junior in a midwestern university when she came to the author in apparent distress. It was obvious that she had something on her mind, yet she was reluctant to talk. She would say, "I want to talk to you," and then her throat would tighten. She did this several times. Finally she gulped, "No one likes me," and asked nervously, "Could you tell me how to make people like me?"

Several suggestions were offered as to the importance of being friendly and of developing interest in other people if one expected to be interesting and have friends. A few days later the girl returned, this time in hysterics. "I am a criminal," she blurted out. I smiled, wondering what she wanted to tell me. "Yes, I am," she continued threateningly. "I am one of those people you talk about in the criminology class." "What do you mean?" I inquired and then her story came out.

As a child of 2 Manya had been brought to America by her uncle and his wife. Her parents remained in Czechoslovakia where the father's poor health required the mother's constant attention. Manya grew up without much affection on the South Side of Chicago. Her uncle worked in the steel mills, her aunt did hand embroidery at home for a dress factory. The aunt continually chided Manya with the importance of being a good child. She kept telling her what a great care she was, and that some day she must repay her aunt and uncle for her board and keep.

Manya began to slip off with a group of boys who "played robbers" in the neighborhood. Before long they became more venturesome and started holding up people on dark streets near alley entrances. Manya went along to help hide the loot. At first she protested she was afraid but after she had helped them once they threatened to tell all they knew about her if she did not keep on helping them. About this time her parents came to America. The father was in good health and able to provide for his family and Manya went to make her home with her parents in northern Michigan. She was now 16 and the young gangsters had found her such an asset to their group that they followed her to her new home in the Iron Range country. She had just finished high school when she and the young men were caught red-handed robbing a filling station. The father, who was a professional musician, was deeply pained and puzzled. Because he was highly regarded in the community, the judge put the girl on probation and required her to go to junior college and make a "B" average. This she did and when she finished at the junior college she enrolled at a neighboring state university. Here the young men trailed her. They began branching out in a book-stealing racket. Again they threatened the young woman. She must steal books from the university library or they would tell the university officials all about her. In desperation she had stolen some 300 books. And her despair and guilt brought her to the author.

This case was officially investigated and all the girl's story was found to be substantially true. Here obviously was a young woman of good mentality who had become a criminal because of the emotional factors in her background. Once involved she was frightened and felt that she would be found out unless she complied with what the leaders of the gang told her to do. Eventually she saw she could not continue and disclosed the whole situation.

Quite a different person was Lenore Bowe, and yet she too was not the vicious, calculating, scheming, selfish woman that many might believe her to be. She was sentenced to the Federal Reformatory for Women for 20 years on the charge of possessing and transporting a stolen motorcar across state lines, with an accompanying charge of armed robbery. Technically she would be eligible for parole after 17 years.

One might expect Lenore to be a hardened, underworld character. Instead she is an alert, attractive, somewhat wistful young woman. Her story is given here as she wrote it because it shows the progressive nature of antisocial conduct as well as a surprising degree of insight on the part of the offender herself. The names, offenses, and places are of course fictitious.

Lenore Bowe

I was born in Pennsylvania, the youngest of 10 children. I was born 5 years after the next older child, and my oldest brothers and sisters were married when my parents died. By that time we were living in Indiana. Our family was broken up early because my mother died with tuberculosis when I was 5. Daddy tried very hard to look after me and the 3 other children still at home but he contracted pneumonia and died when I was 7. He was a tenant farmer and spent lots of time outside in bad weather.

After his funeral the family had a council and decided that the next older sister and I should take turns living with the 4 eldest brothers and sisters. That left a brother 15 and a sister 17 to look after themselves but my brother got a job in Pittsburgh and lived with an aunt, paying her for room and board, and my sister Clara worked as a waitress in a hotel and lived with my grandmother in southern Illinois.

Because nobody wanted to pay for all of my keep, I had to live for 3 months with each of the brothers and sisters who had agreed to share the expense of looking after me and my brother. I missed Daddy very much as he had been very kind. He brought me pretty clothes, let me go to the movies, and I could always have an ice-cream cone whenever we went into town. He helped me with my reading when I went to school. I really worshiped Daddy.

My brothers and sisters actually did not want to have me live with them. My sister used to complain about how hard I was on shoes and how I kept silent all the time. She did not know how lonesome I was for Daddy. My brothers thought I did not need any money for candy or gum. I never knew what was going to happen to me for I always had to go to live with someone else just when I was getting settled in school. I never had a room of my own or any place to put my clothes. My sister had a cot in her dining room for me to sleep on when I stayed there. My elder brother's wife did not like me and used to say: "You cost us more money than we can afford, Lenore." I used to cry because my clothes were so ugly. I always wanted a pale blue dress and white shoes.

Sometimes my brother would say he could not keep me any longer and would take me over to my sister's house after I had stayed there only 1 month. The last time I was at my brother's was when I was 13. I was growing rapidly then and was tall for my age and I felt awkward at times. I had trouble with schoolwork because I had to move so often. We would be in the middle of fractions in arithmetic and I would have to move. Maybe they were through with fractions at the next school. Then I would move again and they would just be starting them. I can see now why it was so hard for me to learn.

At any rate my brother decided I was no good in school and might just as well be earning my living. He got a job for me working in a family where I had to help with the housework and take care of 4 children. I liked the children and the woman was pretty nice to me at first.

But when I was 15 a fellow I knew asked me to go to the carnival. He was 19. We went with another boy and girl and we stayed out terribly late. Mrs. Wolfe, the lady where I worked, didn't like that. She told my brother I was "running around nights." My brother was very angry. He told me he'd put me in the reform school. He said I was "running wild." Maybe I was, but I hadn't done anything really bad. I think he did not want to support me and Mrs. Wolfe didn't want me to work for her any more for fear I'd get into more serious trouble. Then my brother went to see the judge and told him how "bad" I was. All I ever did was to go riding until 1:30 in the morning with this boy and the other couple. But even so I was sent to the girls' reformatory. I was just a green country girl and didn't know much about life. But I learned a great deal at the reform school. I knew scarcely anything about sex and had never heard of girls getting paid for having relations with men. It all sounded very mysterious to me.

I really got to know some of the girls at the reformatory and felt that they were my friends. Because I was young and there was no serious charge against me I was released from the reform school in 9 months. I then went to live with my sister again. She felt pretty upset about my brother's sending me there. But she kept nagging me. She kept saying that I'd have to be very careful about how I behaved or they'd send me back. "When you are once in a reform school, they can always send you back," she told me. I decided to leave her home when she told me that so they couldn't send me back. I went to Louisville, Kentucky, and I got into the "racket." I did what every girl does who hasn't got a job. I met some girls I knew at the reform school. They told me how to get in touch with men at a hotel. It was easy enough. I met them in a drugstore or sometimes at a railway station. I'd ask them if I could have a match. Then we'd go to a hotel and the man would register me as his wife. To keep from being arrested, I followed a friend's advice. She said "never stay in one place too long."

Anyway, I liked to travel. I went on to Nashville and Memphis and then to New Orleans. I tried to be "choosy" but I contracted syphilis when I was only 18. I went to a doctor who gave me shots in the hip and he said he cured me, but I guess he really didn't. When he said I was O.K., I decided to go back to Indiana for a visit. It's strange how you think you do not like your family, and then get homesick to see them. I took a bus to Indianapolis and visited one of my sisters there. Then I went on to Fort Wayne and other towns. I told all the folks I had worked in a restaurant and made big tips. I had some nice-looking clothes.

While I was home I met a boy who lived in Fort Wayne. His name was Thomas M——. Tom liked me right away. My sister said he was a fine young man. I am sure he was and still is. All his family have a good reputation. I was tired of traveling and the racket. What I really wanted was for someone to care about me. This boy never knew I had been a prostitute or he would never have looked at me. He was very religious, a Catholic, and his sister is a nun.

We were married by a justice of the peace because I wasn't a Catholic. We were happy, I thought, but I suppose I just liked being looked after. Sometimes I used to worry for fear Tom would find out about me. I lived with him about a year and I always intended to be decent. I don't know why I left him except my old trouble with syphilis seemed to be coming back. I knew I had to have treatment for I went to a doctor in Indianapolis who told me that the syphilis had broken out again. I couldn't tell my husband. Rather than tell Tom, I left. I didn't tell any of my folks where I went. I had about $25 in my purse so I took a bus to Kansas City and answered an ad in the newspaper for a nursemaid. The woman hired me and I stayed there for about 8 months. I used most of my wages for treatment, but I saved a little money. The family I worked for was rich and paid good wages. They lived in the country club section.

One day I decided to go to Denver and see the West on a little vacation trip. I was still going straight. I went to a hotel and when I had been there about a week I met Max Ertle, who really got me in trouble. He was just a kid, poor boy. Well, he was 26. I was 23. He was out of a job. It was during the depression. He didn't have any money and he fell in love with me. I had nice clothes and I suppose he thought I was used to having plenty. He seemed to figure that the only way he could get me was to get money first. So he stole a car in Denver. I didn't know it was a stolen car and he asked me to go with him to Santa Fe. I don't know why I decided to go, but I went. I suppose I wanted an adventure. He told me that he was going to sell the car so we'd have some money and that he was in love with me. When we got to Santa Fe, we got married. We went to a Presbyterian minister. I kept thinking: "You are already married, Lenore. You cannot do this." But I felt sort of dazed and numb and decided to go through with it. Naturally Max did not know I was already married and I did not know he was a thief. I guess he never had been a thief before. We were arrested in Santa Fe and Max was sent to El Reno and I was sent to Alderson on a federal charge of transporting a motor vehicle across a state line. They said he tried to rob a filling station but that is not true.

I received a conditional release in 10 months and I decided to go back to Max's folks in Santa Fe and the institution released me to them. Nobody at Alderson had ever heard of my own family, or of my husband in Indiana. I was afraid to tell my family I was in prison—or to tell the institution about my folks. No one else in the family has ever been in trouble. And I didn't want the prison authorities to know about my husband in Indiana either for he is a good man. I was also afraid that I would be arrested for bigamy. I guess I was just plain scared. I was certainly worried. That explains why I went back to Santa Fe.

My in-laws in Indiana seemed poor to me but they don't know what being poor is. Max's father lives in a shack in the Mexican section of Santa Fe. He is on relief and has only broken-down, worn-out furniture. But since the institution thought I had no relatives of my own, I went back there. I had forgotten what awful squalor my father-in-law lived in. It was terrible and I simply couldn't stand it. I went downtown to a bar and bought some liquor and drank so much I got drunk. I am not an experienced drinker. Within an hour I was arrested for being drunk and sent to a federal jail for breaking my conditional release. I hadn't supposed they could do things that fast.

In jail I worked in the kitchen and cooked for the men prisoners. One of the men was the handsomest man I have ever met, George Watson. It was a case of love at sight. I would do anything for him. One day he whispered to me: "Baby, would you like to get out of here?" "I surely would," I replied.

"Will you help us?" he inquired. "Of course, if I can," I replied. "Well all we need is some sharp knives. Then we can cut through these bars. Bring us some from the kitchen," he told me.

The rest was easy. The three boys sawed through the bars with the knives. They then seized the jailer and took his revolver and a machine gun away from him. They searched his pockets and took his keys. They then tied his arms and locked him up.

I walked out with the three boys. They unlocked the garage. George backed out the car, we all got in, and drove away. Two of the boys sat in front. I was in love with George then. I still am.

I sat in the back seat with one of the boys and we held the machine gun. Neither of us knew how to use one, but when we drove into a filling station we pointed it at the men while George and the other boy robbed the cash drawer. Then we did the same thing while George filled up the gasoline tank. Actually I have never fired a gun in my life and I doubt if the boys ever have. Certainly I have never been a robber and I know none of the boys would ever kill anybody.

You may think it is queer, but I could have got off easy if I had testified against the 3 men. The F.B.I. men told me this. But I could not do that for I was in love with George. I was really madly in love with him. We could not get a good lawyer to give proper advice. No one would defend a "machine gunner." But that is no reason they should give me so much time because I would not talk. They sentenced me for 20 years on 4 counts. I will have to serve 17 years for helping steal a car, for possessing and transporting a machine gun, and escaping federal officers. George is in Alcatraz as a dangerous offender and he has a 25-year sentence, but he would never kill anyone. He got an extra 5 years for white slavery, for taking me across a state border, and he never touched me.

Since I came back to Alderson, I have worried a good deal about my marriage to Max. Recently I told the officers. The warden here tells me I can get a divorce and that I won't have to serve another sentence for bigamy. I was just a foolish kid who was too scared to be honest before. I was sure they'd arrest me for that too. If I get a divorce from Max that will square me with the law. But I still don't know what to do about my legal husband, Tom. Because he is a Catholic he does not want a divorce. When we were married he told me it must be "forever." He is a decent man and has never wanted to live with any other woman. Since I came back to Alderson, the warden told me to write to him and I did. He says he wants me to come back to him. I think he should divorce me for I have caused him a lot of trouble.

They tell me I can never have a parole because I broke parole once, and even with good time I shall be here for 17 years. That is too long to plan for. I love George and I know he loves me. It might be better if I loved Tom. But I don't.

I could take training for some sort of work so I could get a job when I get out. But the world will be changed before that time comes. I am not going to plan now for what I shall do then. Maybe when my time is almost up I can make some plans. George and I would like to be together.

Personally I don't think I am such a terrible person. I was shoved from one person to another when I was a child. I ran away from home because I was scared. Nobody cared much what happened to me. No one taught me what a young girl should know. I got in the racket without realizing what the end might be. I married a decent man, but was afraid of my past coming to light and ran away.

People say I am dangerous. But I know I am not dangerous. Probably most folks think I was a fool for refusing to testify against George. But I wasn't that mean. I loved him. I knew he would do as much for me. When we get out we will no longer be young, but if we can be together we may be able to plan something decent and legal. We both got a wrong start but we still have something to hope for.

Economic Offenders

Women who commit economic crimes are of 2 general types: (1) those who receive very low legitimate wages (maids, scrub women) and (2) those who are commercially employed but whose pay is also low. Both are constantly entrusted with other people's personal possessions or with merchandise or money. Thus the maid who steals hose or takes small sums of money from her employer or carries home a little bag full of food each night often quite literally adds to her income for a period of years before being detected. The basic reason for her thieving obviously lies in her economic status. Such thefts frequently escape attention until the servant takes a really valuable possession which is bound to be missed. A missing diamond ring, valuable bracelet, or string of pearls will inevitably be noticed and the thief will usually confess. Smaller thefts when discovered are often not reported to the police since a decent employer usually hesitates to ruin a servant's future. Countless instances of petty pilfering are unrecorded in the annals of crime and account for a part of the differential in the reported crime rates of men and women.

When women invade the commercial world the low-paid clerk faces much the same temptation as the domestic employee, but the facilities for discovery and the tendency to prosecute are much greater in the business world. Often women who hold positions of trust in the mercantile establishments, banks, and other firms are expected somehow to pay board and room and to dress well on very low wages. The desire to achieve a standard of living beyond the reach of the meager pay envelope accounts for certain economic crimes. Frequently a refined, well-dressed woman may appear so honest and trustworthy that her dishonest activities are never suspected by her immediate associates.

Such is true of women who embezzle. Women embezzlers are, of course, much like men embezzlers. That is, they are usually persons in positions of responsibility and trust whose work entails direct contact with large sums of money. Women embezzlers take small sums over a series of years so as to avoid detection for a long time. In Kansas City a number of years ago the treasurer of the Women's City Club was found to have taken many thousands of dollars from the club over a period of years. None of the other officers could believe that this woman they so admired and respected could be guilty of so serious an offense. There had been no official auditing and, as in the case of many civic organizations, the funds were carelessly handled.

Even when a woman embezzles in a bank she tends to take no spectacular sum, but rather to shingle small amounts from large accounts. Often accounts of philanthropic organizations are depleted of small amounts because less rigid attention is likely to be paid to the amounts deposited. Yet always the day of reckoning comes as in the case of Imogene Carter.

Imogene Carter

Imogene was born on a farm in western Indiana and moved to a near-by small city when she was about 5. Her father went into the nursery business and made a comfortable living before the depression came. Then no one wanted a new hedge or a few trees for the lawn or garden. Business became so bad that finally he was forced to sell out.

These financial troubles came just at the time Imogene finished high school. She had planned to attend a well-known eastern women's college but obviously could not because of lack of funds. Instead her uncle loaned her money to go to a business college where she completed a course in six months. She then worked as a stenographer in an office for a time. Later she accepted an opening in a bank for $50 a month and subsequently was promoted, receiving $85 a month. Later she received a $5-a-month raise every year until her salary was $135 a month. All this time she lived at home, where she contributed to the family expenses. Her father's income from a job he obtained in a hardware store barely kept the house going.

Imogene then began to shingle the larger accounts in order to have decent clothes and to replace the shabby home furnishings. In the course of 10 years she actually embezzled almost $18,000. During none of this time had she ever lived extravagantly, but she bought an occasional new coat or dress for her mother, new living-room and dining-room furniture, new curtains, and other household items.

In order to avoid detection she very carefully kept two sets of books, one with the shingled accounts, one with the actual amounts that had been deposited. She knew she would eventually get caught but had always been able to present the books with the shingled accounts to bank examiners so that her books were in agreement with the money in the bank.

In the meantime her mother became seriously ill and it was necessary to take her to another city for medical attention. While she was gone the bank examiners arrived. Imogene's time was up. The officers of the bank were nonplused. They insisted that Imogene was honest and that the discrepancies must surely be a mistake. They assured the examiners this was the case, but telephoned to Imogene to ask her if she could come home to straighten out the whole affair. She told them in a quavering voice that her mother had died and they were taking the body to Michigan but that she would return two days later.

After the funeral, while she was still in Michigan, Imogene went to her hotel and wrote a letter to the bank confessing everything. Her associates at the bank were deeply shocked, as were her friends in the community. The bank was reluctant to prosecute but there was nothing else to be done. Banking authorities turned in the evidence. Imogene pleaded guilty and was sentenced to the Federal Reformatory for 10 years.

FORGERS

Forgers also tend to be a relatively high type of criminal. Like embezzlers they usually take money to meet some pressing financial problem, but woman forgers seem to be extraordinarily upset persons as well as in need of money.

Eugenia Harwood

Eugenia Harwood was an attractive young woman who married a conscientious objector, Henry Wilson. Eugenia was so troubled about her husband's insisting that he would not fight for his country that she got her pastor to talk to him. This minister tried to influence him to accept his military duties co-operatively. Finally, Henry decided to enlist in a noncombat branch of the service. This he did. Eugenia and Henry had had many previous arguments over his going into the army and he had slapped her several times when she tried to convince him he was wrong. Eugenia thought he was a coward but he insisted that he was a "C.O." for religious reasons. Eventually, however, he yielded to pressure and went into the Army Air Corps.

While Henry was in training Eugenia went back to Michigan to live with her parents. Henry in the meantime was operated on for appendicitis and later was given an emergency furlough and recuperated at the home of his in-laws. Eugenia went back with him when he returned to his camp in Florida and they secured an apartment there. Here their really serious trouble began. Henry did not dance, but he thought it all right for Eugenia to serve as hostess at the U.S.O. dances. He stipulated, however, that she was not to dance. She decided to take part in some amateur dramatics and because she wore a negligee on the stage her husband became insanely jealous and kicked and slapped her. Eugenia was pregnant at the time and as a consequence of this mistreatment she had a miscarriage. Henry returned to the post without realizing his wife was ill for she was too emotionally upset to tell him. She had no money and in desperation telephoned her family in Michigan. They sent her money to come home but after she reached home they persuaded her to return to her husband, who had transferred to another post. He, however, refused to speak to her when she arrived. At first she was desperate.

She then decided to go to St. Louis to see her uncle and told him she thought she could get a job in Wichita if he would lend her carfare, which he did. She never tried to get a job there, however. Instead she walked into a department store, bought a coat and dress, and gave a check for $100, receiving $25 in cash. She had no money at all in the bank on which she wrote the check. Then she took a bus to New Mexico. She says she does not know why. She merely decided to go to Santa Fe. There she passed further worthless checks, but within a couple of weeks she was arrested for giving the Wichita check and extradition papers were served for her return for trial in Wichita. There she was sentenced to the Kansas State Industrial Farm for Women for 1 to 10 years.

At the prison her conduct was exemplary and her family secured a parole within 9 months. She decided she could not stay in Michigan, however, and went to Chicago. Having very little money with her, she wrote some more checks and was soon returned to the Industrial Farm. A forger such as Eugenia is obviously an emotionally upset person. She is intelligent enough to "know better," and the forgeries themselves are symptomatic of her distressed condition. All facts in this case were verified.

Paula Manson

Another interesting forgery case is that of Paula Manson. A divorcee, she was trying to adjust herself to post-divorce trauma by getting a position in a New York department store. She and her husband had been divorced in California in February, 1946. He had been very brutal to her, refused to have children, and insisted on her having three abortions. Paula came to New York in early March and had a serious abdominal operation which involved so much expense that her finances were practically exhausted.

Paula was a tall, dark, rather handsome woman, alert and obviously intelligent. She had no trouble in securing a position as saleswoman with a fashionable store and she was anxious to succeed. The head of the ready-to-wear department was much impressed with her ability and said she would undoubtedly have been promoted had she not become involved in the forgeries. Paula had discussed her financial straits with a fellow saleswoman, Mrs. McBeth, and the latter suggested that she might buy necessary clothing easily at another department store simply by charging it to a regular customer's name. This woman supplied a name for her and she tried. Because her appearance was so respectable, she had no difficulty whatever in walking out of the store with the garments she had purchased and charged to the unsuspecting customer.

Later she went to a near-by cocktail room with another woman friend for a drink. After two highballs she asked the cashier if she could cash a check. She signed a fictitious name and cashed the check without difficulty. Because Paula seemed to think there would be no way of tracing her identity, she cashed several such checks, all for amounts of $15 or less, each time signing a different name. It somehow never occurred to her that eventually all the checks would be compared for handwriting and that she would inevitably face a charge of forgery.

Meanwhile her ability as a saleswoman became recognized and she was considered for the position of buyer in the dress department. She seemed to be "on the way up." Then without warning a store detective asked her to come to the office, where police were waiting to arrest her. She confessed to all the charges and was sentenced to 2 years.

Paula's case involves a woman who came from a good family background. Her difficulties have emotional roots and her maladjustment indicates a need for psychiatric treatment, although she has a good deal of insight into her own problem. She would like to make a new start in a business career, but no reputable department store would consider her for an opening in merchandising—at least not in New York. The rector of her church was trying to help her and because of her superior background it seems likely that she will make a satisfactory adjustment if she is willing to live within a salary she can earn.

TAX EVASION

Many crimes are a matter of evasion of new laws—sometimes willful evasion, sometimes unwitting evasion. Every new law which redefines conduct requires an adjustment of old habits, whether it be a question of ration points, of paying new taxes, or of observing new regulations. Sometimes one is simply caught in the intricacies of the law—as in the case of Rhoda Roberts.

Rhoda Roberts

Rhoda Roberts, with her husband James, ran a night club in Ocean City. They served dinners, but a large share of their business consisted in serving drinks to the people who came out to their attractive place overlooking the ocean. The Robertses knew that the liquor floor tax was going into effect on October 1, 1942, and decided to avoid paying the tax by buying a lot of liquor in September and storing it in Pennsylvania in Rhoda's mother's cellar.

Rhoda claims they did not realize that the law required a floor tax on all liquor owned on October 1 irrespective of when it was purchased. She said they simply misunderstood the law. Obviously she and her husband did not want to pay the tax, but she holds that they certainly would never have risked the stigma and prison penalty for the $400-tax, and that would seem to be a logical conclusion. However, there is some reason to assume they willfully evaded the law and thought they could escape detection.

Rhoda maintains that a man who helped her husband store the liquor at her mother's told a woman whom she regards as her enemy about what they had done. This woman kept a rival establishment across the street and it was she who informed the F.B.I. If the woman had not been her enemy, Rhoda thinks she never would have been reported and arrested. However, since a record of all sales is kept at the warehouse, the existence of the liquor would have come to light eventually because it was unreasonable to suppose the Robertses could have disposed of it all before October 1.

In the end Rhoda's mother was indicted along with Rhoda and her husband on 2 counts: for evading interstate commerce laws and for tax evasion. Rhoda says she had never heard of the interstate commerce law. The mother was released upon payment of a fine, which Rhoda and her husband paid because they felt morally responsible. They themselves each received a sentence of a year and a day. Rhoda is very bitter about her conviction. She says that she was never in conflict with the law before, that it was all due to misunderstanding, and that she can see no reason why she and her husband should be treated like common criminals. Their business has been ruined and she fears they will never be able to get back on their feet financially. And all, in her estimation, because they did not read the "fine print part of the law."

Rhoda's case illustrates an important fact in crime detection, namely, that personal enmity and jealousy are frequently involved in the testimony which convicts the offender. Certain convictions apparently could not be made without such testimony.

The Alcoholic Woman

The alcoholic, whether man or woman, is usually a maladjusted person on other counts. The alcoholism is merely symptomatic of personality disorganization, as we have mentioned. Although certain persons are undoubtedly more or less allergic to alcohol, hence become intoxicated by the consumption of relatively small quantities, the majority of true alcoholics are persons who seek release from their frustrations, grief, or tensions through the sedative effects of alcohol.[11]

Agnes Brennan

Agnes Brennan was serving a term for alcoholism in the House of Detention in New York City. She grew up in a small town in New Hampshire and came to New York to take up nursing in one of the large hospitals. Agnes came from a respectable Catholic family. Her real purpose in coming to the city was to be near John McNary, a man from her home town, whom she hoped to marry. McNary had been on the police force in New York for 3 years. He and Agnes had never been formally engaged but had an "understanding," as she expressed it.

Since Agnes was 28 when she came to New York she was anxious to lose no time in marrying. McNary seemed to be fond of her, but instead of coming nearer to marriage they began to quarrel. On several occasions after a serious quarrel Agnes would go on a drinking bout, for when she started drinking she could not leave liquor alone. In fact she would drink continuously for several days at a time. She says she does not know why she keeps on drinking thus, but undoubtedly hers is a psychiatric problem. Periodically, every 8 or 10 months, she goes on such a "binge" and while under the influence of alcohol does something foolish for which she is arrested.

Agnes has served 5 sentences at the House of Detention. Twice she has gone out and pulled a fire alarm when highly intoxicated. The first time she did this she was sentenced for only 10 days. The judge had given her an alternative sentence of $50 or 10 days in the House of Detention but since she had only $19 she went to jail. John McNary was out of town at the time and she was not willing to ask anyone else to help her out. She was considerably upset about the front-page news story which was carried the first time she was sentenced. After her release, she got drunk 5 times in 1941 and for 3 of these sprees she served a short sentence. She says she kept worrying because everyone knew what she did and that drove her to drinking again!

After the last sentence her mother was notified and came to New York. She secured a parole for her daughter and Agnes went home with her. While she was home she felt that everybody there "knew" about her and was "talking about her." Her family and her home-town physician were convinced she was ill, however, and did everything to make things pleasant for her. Then her father was taken ill and had to have an operation. Agnes rose to the occasion and took care of him. Because he was not able to work for some time, Agnes

[11] Cf. Mabel A. Elliott and Francis E. Merrill, *Social Disorganization*, Harper, New York, 3rd ed., 1950, chap. 9, "The Alcoholic."

believed it important for her to contribute to the family income and she went back to New York and obtained a position with Dr. Jones, a physician in New York. She told Dr. Jones quite frankly about her problem and he treated her for acute alcoholism several times during the next year and kept her from getting into any difficulty with the law.

The next spring she had pneumonia but as soon as she was out of the hospital Dr. Jones asked her to take over a difficult case. She was still weak and became very tired and she began to take one drink, then another and another. Again she went out and rang the fire alarm and because she was a recidivist she was sentenced to 1 to 2 years in the House of Detention.

Agnes seems to have acquired some insight into her own case and says when she is released she is going to join Alcoholics Anonymous. She believes that if she could have proper help at the right time she would not go off on these "binges." Whether such moral assistance will do as much for her as deep psychiatric therapy is a question, but her courage in facing her problem is a favorable factor in an otherwise none-too-favorable prognosis.

Abandoning Children

As we have already mentioned, men are seldom punished for walking out on their families. Social workers seem to be generally agreed that sending a man to prison does not make him take better care of his children, but rather prevents him from making any financial contribution whatsoever to their support. Furthermore, antagonizing the father may only add to his already hostile family attitudes.

If a mother leaves her children to get along as best they may, however, both legal authorities and social workers act to see that she is taken in hand. Of course the mother usually assumes greater personal responsibility for seeing that the child's food is prepared and that he is kept clean and properly clothed than does the father. When the mother fails in these responsibilities there is obviously need for some immediate attention to the child on the part of local authorities. If a father takes a few days' vacation from family duties, he does not seem so reprehensible because the mother sees that the children are not neglected. This is probably the social explanation for punishing the women and letting the men go unpunished in neglect of their families. In either instance the parents are behaving immaturely and both probably are in need of psychiatric attention and case work. But since there must be some plan for providing adequate supervision for the children in case the mother fails in her task she is more likely to be treated as a criminal than as a personality problem. This was true in the case of Mrs. House.

Mary House

For several years Mrs. Mary House had been in difficulties with the truant officer because her children attended school so irregularly. Often they came only 2 or 3 days a week, spending the rest of the time at home, in the park, or on the street. Neighbors were known to have complained to the juvenile court several times because she neglected her children. As a matter of fact for 2 months before she was arrested Mrs. House took practically no care at all of them. Actually she had been away a month some time earlier when she went to California with a John Browder and married him there. After a brief honeymoon they returned to Moundsville. Shortly thereafter Mr. Browder decided that he wanted to go to Alaska to get a job driving a truck. They separated and Mrs. House applied for a divorce, obtained it, and took back her former name. All this time she spent many nights away from home talking her situation over with friends. What to do about John overshadowed any concern she might have had for the children. This incident occurred during World War II and she was working daytimes in an egg-dehydrating plant. She claims that she had too far to walk in the rain when caught without an umbrella and stayed with fellow workers who lived close to the plant.

Sometimes she would not come home for 48 hours and the neighbors objected to having to feed the 3 small children, who were hungry. Mrs. House insists that her 18-year-old daughter was perfectly capable of cooking their supper, which sounds reasonable. But in any event there seems to be no question but that Mrs. House neglected her children. They were without suitable clothing and were apparently half-starved for lack of regular meals. On investigation it was found that Mrs. House had never applied for any ration books with which to obtain sugar and meat for the children!

Whenever the neighbors or social workers tried to locate Mrs. House she was always found in a beer joint with a man. She was therefore suspected of staying with him on the nights she did not return home. In court Mrs. House admitted all of the testimony offered against her so far as leaving the children alone was concerned and she was sentenced to 2 years in the state prison. Further investigation of the case indicated that Mrs. House was in very poor health mentally, emotionally, and physically. She had suffered a recent attack of bronchopneumonia and was also suffering from a badly infected ovary. There is a large question whether suitable medical and psychiatric attention might not have been more satisfactory than a prison sentence.

Obviously her conduct is not defensible but it is doubtful if imprisonment will improve it.

From these case histories, typical of thousands of women who are in the clutches of the law, a fairly consistent picture of their moral and physical weakness, emotional imbalance, or bad home training emerges. Life has not been easy for these women, even for those who acquired temporary financial assets. The way of the transgressor is still hard; sometimes it has been a hard way that led to the transgression, itself.

SELECTED BIBLIOGRAPHY

Adam, Hargrave, *Women and Crime*, T. Werner Laurie, Cliffords Inn, London, 1914. This volume is concerned with sensational types of women offenders.

Asbury, Herbert, *Gem of the Prairie* (*An Informal History of the Chicago Underworld*), Knopf, New York, 1940. This book contains sketches of famous "madams" of the Chicago underworld.

Elliott, Mabel A., and Merrill, Francis E., *Social Disorganization*, Harper, New York, rev. ed., 1950, chap. 6, "The Sex Offender," and chap. 7, "The Prostitute." These chapters are devoted chiefly to these special types of women offenders.

Fernald, Mabel R., Hayes, Mary H. S., and Dawley, Almena, *A Study of Women Delinquents in New York State*, Appleton-Century-Crofts, New York, 1920. This is one of the earliest studies of criminal women and their backgrounds.

Glueck, Sheldon and Eleanor T., *Five Hundred Delinquent Women*, Knopf, New York, 1934. This book contains a number of case studies of women criminals.

Harris, Mary B., *I Knew Them in Prison*, Viking, New York, 1936. A vivid picture is given of outstanding prison personalities among the women offenders who were supervised by the author of this book while she was warden of various institutions.

The Herrick Committee Report, *Women and Girl Offenders in Massachusetts*, Massachusetts Child Council, Boston, 1938. This study contains some excellent material on sex offenders.

Hironimus, Helen, "Survey of 100 May Act Violators Committed to the Federal Reformatory for Women," *Federal Probation*, 7:31–34 (April–June, 1943). This analysis describes the type of young woman convicted under the May Act.

Monahan, Florence, *Women in Crime*, Ives Washburn, New York, 1941. Another autobiographical account of a woman warden, this book contains more information about the warden than her charges.

SECTION III

Factors in Criminality

CHAPTER 10

Crime and American Culture

Crime on the Colonial Frontier[1]

All sociologists and criminologists accept the idea that culture in its wider ramifications and culture conflict in particular provide the matrix out of which much of the modern crime problem emerges. Thus, for example, we recognize that race, class, national origins, and the varying cultural patterns of social behavior provide important sources of cultural conflict and resultant antisocial behavior.

We sometimes forget, however, that antisocial conduct is as much rooted in the past as it is a function of the present and that in America, as everywhere, crime bears an important relationship to our culture. In our country the frontier mores are related in a significant sense to lawlessness because our frontier was pushed ahead by "backwoodsmen" who formed a vanguard to organized society. That is, the first settlers usually preceded the establishment of governmental institutions, and lawlessness was therefore a part of the pattern of pioneer existence.

CRIME IN PURITAN NEW ENGLAND

In tracing the course of crime in America from the time of our Puritan forebears we find the primitiveness of the first early settlements in Massachusetts soon supplanted by a life which had lost any resemblance to a frontier existence. With the rapid development of ocean shipping life in the colonial New England city or countryside possessed few essential differences from life in Mother England except

[1] Part of this chapter is taken from the author's article, "Crime and the Frontier Mores," *American Sociological Review*, 9:185–192 (April, 1944), and is reproduced with permission.

in those areas of behavior where religious belief made for rigid definition and control.

The Puritan revolt was a twofold reaction against excessive ritualism in religious worship—and against the laxity in morals which characterized life in sixteenth- and seventeenth-century England. Somehow the Puritan mind concluded that there was some vital connection between the ceremonial worship of the Established Church and immoral conduct. That the latter was the product of the many disintegrating aspects of society (agricultural economy was giving way to the development of mercantile economy based upon foreign trade) never occurred to the average dissenter. As with many present-day persons who have sought for a simple explanation of human behavior, the kindly and honest folk who tried to live decently and to worship their Maker according to the dictates of long and careful thinking believed the church was at fault. It seemed obvious that the church was suffering from a goodly measure of corruption among both its laity and its clergy. That many of the clergy rushed through the prayers without much attention to their thought and meaning was undoubtedly true. That many parishioners then as now gave little heed to the creeds and prayers in which they joined must have been equally apparent. Yet the beautiful old prayers (as the distillation of religious thought of the ages) can scarcely be regarded as the basic reason for moral dissolution. Any modern sociologist would be more correct in ascribing the decline in morals to the general impact of social change —the factors which were disrupting the old manner of living—and to the fact that the culture had thus far developed no new stabilizing characteristics of its own.

There has probably never been a more significant event in human history than the discovery of the New World. No achievement of modern science has so startled the minds of men as the knowledge that beyond the Atlantic lay a vast land with unimaginable resources. The discovery, through the voyage of Sir Francis Drake, that the earth was round upset all the generally accepted ideas of the nature of the universe. That the extension of the world's boundaries, the inventing of the printing press, the distribution of the Bible, the development of mechanical invention all occurred in the same era makes understandable the great social and political upheavals of the time. When all that man had generally believed to be true about the earth was thus proved false it is small wonder that religious faith of the period should have suffered a profound shock. After all, the clergy were the best-educated men of the time. If all their teaching with reference to geography was wrong it was only reasonable to think they might be wrong with reference to spiritual teachings.

It seems likely that man has never been excessively devout or devoted to religious principles. But we can be certain that the stimulus of New World settlements, of the impact of the discovery on the imagination of man, was as disruptive as it was exciting. The effect on modern man of a successful round trip to the moon or to Mars might be somewhat comparable. Old ideas had been proved wrong; old truths were now susceptible of skepticism and complete rejection. Many clergymen also must have been affected by the cynicism occasioned by the impact of science on sixteenth-century religion.

The Puritan movement thus had much in common with the Fundamentalist movement which has emerged from the clash between twentieth-century science and religious ideology of our day. Failure to comprehend the complicated relation between religious dogma and the culture in which it flourishes is an understandable error on the part of the Puritans. Something was unquestionably wrong with the social order in which they lived. The social disorganization they saw all about them was a startling index to the need for some return to restraint and order in the lives of ordinary men. The eternal voice of experience has made obvious through the ages the fact that sex license and riotous living exact a serious toll in lives disorganized. Although man has failed miserably in his attempt to live by moral law, moral law as conceived by the wise men of all ages carries greater evidence of being near to what we have called universal law or the heart of the universe than any other achievement of man. In final analysis what we call science and what we accept as religion must converge on the basis of truth. But it was with no such penetrating insight that the Puritan looked at his world. He did recognize one fundamental fact in which all successive religionists are forced to concur, however, namely, that religion must be what a man truly believes and not what he recites in unthinking unison.

In his recognition of the importance of sexual restraint as a factor in effective personality development, the Puritan knew as well as we do that no phase of human behavior is so fraught with possibilities for social condemnation as illicit sex conduct. In addition to a diseased body, disillusioned emotional reactions, and social condemnation the sex offender faced eternal damnation at the hands of an angry God. Moreover, penal restrictions in early New England made no distinction between sins, vice, and crime.[2] All were deemed offenses against God's holy ordinances and therefore serious crimes against the colonial laws. Every law in the Massachusetts Bay colony appended a proper Biblical reference to indicate its essential authority.[3]

Thus the scriptural sins of slander, adultery, bestiality, irreverence, witchcraft, Sabbathbreaking, etc., were crimes in early Massachusetts, and records of those punished indicate that the majority of sins were for religious nonconformity and for sex aberrations. When it came to punishments the Puritans derived their scriptural authority for punishment chiefly from the old Testament.[4]

Baptism for all children conceived out of wedlock and born less than 7 months after marriage was prohibited, unless the parents made public confession of their sin. Since it was generally believed that the unbaptized child was doomed to eternal damnation, many guilty parents voluntarily exposed themselves to merciless publicity in order to achieve certainty of heavenly existence for their offspring.[5]

The Puritan treatment of the sex offender was a far cry from the forbearance of Christ, who so gently bade Magdalene, "Go and sin no more." By stern law and severe practice they hoped to keep their daughters pure and undefiled and worthy of full acceptance into the Kingdom of God. That the severity of their repressive measures led to serious mental illness we are well aware; but the Puritans attributed such illness to their own waywardness. Women driven to states of hysteria by their rigid laws were feared as accomplices of evil and punished far more severely than mere sex offenders. Not a few fragile, sensitive women met their fate high on the hangmen's hills of colonial New England. Truly the Puritans forgave not, neither the sins of the flesh nor the deterioration of the mind.

In keeping with Puritan notions of propriety elaborate dress was forbidden. Women were prohibited from wearing "silver, gold, silk laces, girdles or hatbands."[6] Women whose husbands were not "worth £200" could not wear silk in any form.[7]

Leaving their homeland in order to worship God according to the dictates of their conscience, they permitted no such liberty to other nonconforming groups. Baptists and Quakers were mercilessly condemned for their teaching and interpretations of what truths they believed God had revealed to them. With smug complacency the Puritans assumed that all who were not for them were against them.

---

[2] James G. Leyburn, *Frontier Folkways*, Yale University Press, New Haven, 1935, chap. 2, "The Massachusetts Bay Frontier," p. 22.
[3] *Ibid.*, p. 23.   [4] *Ibid.*   [5] *Ibid.*, p. 24.
[6] *Ibid.*, p. 27.   [7] *Ibid.*, p. 21.

Their belief that theirs was the only acceptable truth made them treat fellow dissenters as virtual criminals. Yet, despite any untoward aspects New England Puritanism may have had, it lent a stern quality to colonial life which was on the whole salutary. Life was hard, but the strong character of the settlers hewed cities out of the forest and produced crops from New England's rocky soil. Basically the Puritan was a Briton whose goals and ideals in the face of adversity have left their dent on American life. While not altogether lovely, and often lacking in forbearance and human understanding, the unyielding discipline of the New Englanders produced far more sturdy souls than it disorganized by its rigidity. Like many others, New Englanders found their strength in what were also their essential weaknesses.

The Puritan tradition, so inherent a part of the frontier mores of New England, has been written large in the matrix of American statutory criminal law, in the "thou shalt nots" which have been enacted by each successive generation, as the descendants of Puritans made their trek over the Alleghenies, across the plains and prairies of the Mississippi Valley, to push beyond to the mountains and eventually take the trail to the Pacific.

CRIME IN THE COLONIAL SOUTH

Although many have believed that Virginia and New England represented the two poles of colonial America, stringent rules concerning personal conduct were also in effect in early Virginia. In fact the first legislative assembly in America, the Virginia House of Burgesses which was organized in 1619, passed many detailed regulations of human conduct. One concerned drunkenness. For the first offense the minister was to reprove the offender privately; for the second, publicly. The third offense called for his being "put in the irons for twelve hours and a fine." For any further offenses more severe punishments might be given.[8]

In contrast to our present notable propensity for castigating our presidents and Congress, criticism of those in political authority was strictly forbidden in colonial Virginia. Any person "speaking against" the governor or council might be punished with the pillory.[9] Swearing was subject to fine.[10] Selling arms to an Indian carried imprisonment for life.[11] Even the milder blandishments of flirting were vigorously condemned, and either "man or maiden" was subject to fine or whip-

[8] John Fiske, *Old Virginia and Her Neighbors*, Houghton Mifflin, Boston, 1897, Vol. I, pp. 245–246.
[9] *Ibid.*, p. 247.   [10] *Ibid.*, p. 248.   [11] *Ibid.*

ping for seeking the affections of two persons at the same time.[12] Sexual crimes were especially serious in colonial Maryland and Virginia, possibly because of the sex ratios which made marriage impossible for so many.[13]

The earliest clergy in Virginia may have been men of estimable character, but by the time of the eighteenth century the Virginia parson set a very "low" religious tone. As John Fiske says, "He belonged to the class of wine-bibbing, card-playing, fox hunting parsons," of which there were so many examples in the mother country after the reaction against Puritanism set in.[14] In 1711 a bequest was made to the vestry of Christ Church, Middlesex, Virginia, providing that the rector preach 4 sermons a year against the 4 reigning vices: (1) atheism and irreligion, (2) swearing and cursing, (3) fornication and adultery, and (4) drunkenness. And it is related authentically that at least one rector who preached such sermons was guilty in all four categories.[15] Naturally not all clergy were as debauched as this one, but there was unquestionably a period in which the Anglican Church in Virginia was exceedingly corrupt. As a reaction against this corruption, more than half of the Virginians turned dissenter by the time of the American Revolution. Virginia, it must be remembered, was dominated by the Cavaliers who had reinstated Charles II. Shortly after Charles II's restoration to the throne great numbers of the Royalist party came to Virginia, many of whom were given large grants of land by their grateful king. Under these advantageous economic circumstances the Cavaliers became the founders of Virginian aristocracy and the graceful life which came to be so characteristic of the James River area. Not all the British who later migrated to the southern colonies were the competent, able men who were the progenitors of the "First Families of Virginia." Here too came the transported prisoners[16] who became the indentured servants of aristocracy. Many free but impecunious men also became indentured servants. However, we have no reason to believe that the early crimes in Virginia were due primarily to the transported convicts. As a matter of fact many petty offenses were severely punished in England at that time. Death sentences, in fact, were imposed in England for stealing anything worth

    [12] Ibid., p. 247.
    [13] Cf. Richard B. Morris's article on "Crime" in Dictionary of American History, Scribner, New York, 1940, Vol. II, pp. 87–88.
    [14] John Fiske, op. cit., Vol. II, p. 261.
    [15] Ibid., p. 262.
    [16] Cf. chap. 27, "Parole and the Indeterminate Sentence," for a discussion of the penal system of transportation in some detail.

more than a shilling. Transportation of petty offenders was partially a matter of mitigating the severe penalty otherwise imposed.[17]

Public fears as to the dangers accompanying the influx of so many criminals arose, however. Both Virginia and Maryland soon protested against this policy of sending criminals to the colonies. Feeling was so strong by 1700 that there were relatively few indentured white persons in the colonies. Meantime Negro slavery had become an accepted institution in the South. It is estimated that there were 6000 Negroes and 60,000 Englishmen in Virginia at the beginning of the eighteenth century. By 1750 there were approximately 250,000 of each group.[18]

The caste system imposed both in the slave status of the Negro and in the lowly position of the indentured convict gave rise to the discriminatory criminal law in the South. Many plantation owners had reason to fear the occasional Negro uprisings and many of the discriminatory laws arose in an attempt to put down racial conspiracies. Thus the law provided that any runaway slave might be killed if he resisted attempts to seize him. The male slave who worked in the house was also liable to emasculation for no white woman was considered safe in his presence. A master's control over his slave was regarded as absolute, and a master who murdered a slave could not be punished. Nor was testimony of a slave admissible as either evidence or information in court, save in case one of his own race was on trial for his life.[19] Slaves, in fact, could not even be freed by their masters except for meritorious service and only then by special license of the governor and his council.[20] By these early provisions Virginia set the standard for not extending basic civil rights to the Negro, a discrimination which has persisted to this day.[21]

Despite its vexing population problems, Virginia was, even so, relatively law abiding. Distinguished by the generally high social and economic status of the settlers and especially of its governing class, early Virginia experienced little of the lawlessness which later characterized North Carolina. For North Carolina was in a sense Virginia's frontier. Here migrated the poor whites who could not succeed in Virginia. Here too were small landowners. But North Carolina was also the Mecca for the escaped outlaws of Virginia to the North and of South Carolina to the South. There was little in early North Carolina which gave evidence of the aristocracy so characteristic of its border colonies. Life was simple and rough. Crimes ran high in the wilder-

[17] John Fiske, *op. cit.*, Vol. II, pp. 181–182.
[18] *Ibid.*, p. 191.   [19] *Ibid.*, pp. 197–198.   [20] *Ibid.*, p. 199.
[21] For a detailed treatment of the Negro and crime, consult chap. 11.

ness and pirates ransacked the coast. It was this frontier character of the colony of North Carolina that produced the first widespread lynch law in America. The substantial citizens arose in popular protest against threats to their property and to common decency. Almost completely agricultural in its economy, North Carolina had virtually no cities and few organized governmental agencies for social control. There was not even the refining influence of the church until the first clergyman arrived in 1703. There were no schools until much later, shortly before the Revolutionary War, although the Scotch-Irish migrations which began in 1719 made their dent in the colony by their insistence on sobriety and orderliness.[22] It was then that the less tractable elements of the population again sought the frontier. This time the poor whites and the more adventurous of the better stock made their way westward across the wilderness of Tennessee and Kentucky to the plains of Missouri and Illinois. Some pushed on into Kansas; according to American folklore the lineal descendants of these "degraded" Carolinians figured in Quantrill's raid in Lawrence, Kansas, while others were numbered among the desperadoes of Memphis. Such allegations undoubtedly are grossly exaggerated.

Today we have no reason to suppose that biological degeneracy was the primary source either of lawlessness or of the trek westward by the restive pioneer. Out of the wilderness have come some of the finest types of American manhood. But here too originated much of the American pattern of liberty and rejection of the restraining influence of urban life. In the wilderness a man was free of tax collectors, of lawmakers, even of his neighbors' opinion.[23]

PIRACY

One of the major crimes of the colonial period was piracy—plundering vessels on the high seas. Crimes which are not purely emotional in character tend always to be associated with economic conditions and situations. Piracy which was obviously a crime of this type was a problem from the beginning of the first colonial settlements. The first shipments from England to the Massachusetts Colony are said to have suffered from attacks of pirates and such attacks did not die out until well into the nineteenth century. In fact the whole period from 1632 to 1827 was marked by the excessive plundering of American ships by the desperadoes of the sea.[24]

[22] John Fiske, op. cit., Vol. II, p. 315.
[23] Ibid., chap. 15, "The Carolina Frontier."
[24] Cf. George Wycherley's article, "Pirates and Piracy on American Coasts," in Dictionary of American History, Vol. IV, pp. 277–278.

The robbing of ships is an ancient variety of crime which was given new impetus by shipments to the New World. Old English law condemned the pirate as the enemy of the human race and a deliberate outlaw. Pirates either committed their crimes on the high seas or sacked towns by invasion from the seas.[25] The early English settlements in the Carolinas provided an especially fine market for pirates, who sometimes went so far as to make fair exchange of their stolen wares for goods brought in British ships. By the despised Navigation Laws of 1661 and 1663 and others which were subsequently enacted, England tried to restrict all American trade to the mother country. These laws actually did much to promote piracy. Many wealthy men in the colonies were bitterly opposed to confining all their commerce to England when such a plan made it possible for the British merchants to exact exorbitant prices for their goods.[26] At least two governors of Carolina were in active collusion with the pirate trade.[27]

The ill-gotten gains of piracy were not to last long, for soon the colonies began to lose their own cargoes. The colonies were permitted to send whatever products England could not use to other countries and the Carolinas developed an extensive rice trade which was shortly imperiled by the pirates.[28] Similarly their shipments to New England never reached port. Eventually the English fleet came to the assistance of the southern colonies and stopped the pirates for the time being.[29]

The Navigation Acts seemed oppressive enough, but the Stamp Act on tea and the Molasses Act both entailed such prohibitive duties that they were virtually nonenforced. The organized smuggling and carrying of contraband which consequently developed was accorded a status very nearly comparable to legal trade.[30]

Following the Seven Years' War with the French the British decided to enforce the restrictions of the Molasses Act as modified by the Sugar Act of 1764.[31] Apparently Great Britain did not foresee that by enforcing the laws she was sowing the seeds of the American Revolution. But in the colonists' "lawless" revolt against those laws can be discerned that passion for freedom which has become an American tradition.

In the meantime the matter of piracy became complicated with

[25] Cf. John Franklin Jameson, *Privateering and Piracy*, Macmillan, New York, 1923, p. ix.
[26] John Fiske, *op. cit.*, Vol. II, p. 363.
[27] Ibid.   [28] Ibid.   [29] Ibid., p. 367.
[30] William Smith McClellan, *Smuggling in the American Colonies*, Moffat Yard, New York, 1912, chap. 5.
[31] Ibid., p. 64 n.

privateering. Lacking adequate naval facilities our Continental Congress authorized the commissioning of privateers, which, we may explain briefly, are armed private vessels commissioned by governmental authority to seize shipping or war vessels of an enemy country.

During the American Revolution 1151 American privateers are said to have captured 600 British vessels. Privateers also participated in the War of 1812, after which, unfortunately, many of them failed to serve the interests of state, but instead turned pirates themselves.[32] The spoils of war thus became an impelling inducement to plunder in peacetime. We cannot treat this subject exhaustively here, but piracy became an important step in the trail of the gangster on the American scene.

The Western Frontier and Crime

Life on the frontier plains and prairies was relatively peaceful. When the midwestern pioneers co-operated with nature in wresting a livelihood from the soil there was little occasion for sharp disputes and these early settlers evidenced little disposition to violence. Hence the farming sections of Ohio, Indiana, Illinois, Iowa, Minnesota, and Wisconsin took on the general orderliness of the northeastern states.

Further west, on America's last frontier, life assumed a different character. Many courageous and sturdy men of honor were tempted by economic opportunity and advantageous climate to take part in the development of Colorado, Wyoming, Montana, and points further to the west and southwest. But here also came the flotsam—outlaws from the eastern states, ex-convicts fleeing hostility and embittered by real or fancied injustice. Some paroled convicts came from as far away as Australia and Mexico.[33] Thus the Far West became the haven of refuge for the horse and cattle thief, for the escaped robber from an eastern penitentiary, for the counterfeiter, as well as the matrix which produced some first offenders.

So shady was the background of many of our pioneers that a special code of etiquette arose for conversing with strangers. As one Westerner put it:

"Never ask a stranger where he came from or he may draw a trigger. He may very well have come from jail."

[32] Cf. William M. Robinson, Jr., "Privateers and Privateering," in *Dictionary of American History*, Vol. IV, pp. 349–350.

[33] Cf. Thomas J. Dimsdale, *The Vigilantes of Montana*, McKee, Butte, Montana, 1929, chap. 1. Cf. also Stewart Edward White, *The Last Frontier*, in "Chronicles of America Series," Allen Johnson, ed., Yale University Press, New Haven, Vol. XVI, chap. 11, and James G. Leyburn, *op. cit.*, p. 215.

Indeed too much inquisitiveness, as Everett Dick expresses it, was "an invitation to gunplay."[34]

In California the signs of the times were well expressed in a song of the day:

> "Oh what was your name in the States?
> Was it Thompson or Johnson or Bates?
> Did you murder your wife
> And fly for your life?
> Say, what was your name in the States?"[35]

Legal, religious, and educational institutions and controls were virtually nonexistent in the mining camps and mountain frontiers. Here, too, there were few women, and thus little of the conserving influence of good women or the stabilizing values of family life. The distorted sex ratio in the almost exclusively male population was undoubtedly a factor in the frontier crime rates. It brought the inevitable influx of scarlet women who became the hostesses of the gambling dens and night clubs and the dancing partners at the "Hurdy-gurdy" houses, which offered the combined facilities of a bar, gambling house, and dance hall.

Shooting scrapes and jealous quarrels over the attentions of these willing ladies were a frequent accompaniment of strong liquor, frustrated impulses, and the code of the times. According to the latter, no red-blooded man was expected to take silently the curses and insults of his rivals. Personal insults, however much deserved, demanded immediate action. If a mountaineer was denounced as a liar, a thief, or worse he did not hesitate to annihilate his slanderer. He was quick on the trigger, aimed well and without remorse. Thus we may account for the emotional origins of many a mountaineer murder. Life was cheap but honor was long on the western frontier.

A large share of frontier crimes were economic in motivation. The vast sums of money afloat in the West stimulated an invasion of outlaws and hoodlums. It was common practice in the cattle country to drive thousands of cattle up the long trail from the Southwest to the markets. First these markets were in Illinois, Missouri, and Arkansas, but as the railroads pushed west, they were in Abilene, Great Bend, and Fort Dodge, Kansas, and finally in Utah, Nevada, Colorado, and

[34] Everett Dick, Vanguards of the Frontier, Appleton-Century-Crofts, New York, 1941, p. 389.
[35] Cf. Joseph Henry Jackson, Anybody's Gold, Appleton-Century-Crofts, New York, 1941, for an account of the flotsam in California.

Wyoming.[36] When the cattle were delivered, payment was made in cash, and thousands of dollars were turned over to the rangers because of the lack of banking facilities. Often the rangers were forced to protect the gold and silver in their saddlebags with their lives, and many a life was lost. Sometimes the life was that of a cattleman, sometimes it was the quick-shooting outlaw's. Even the United States marshals appointed to preserve law and order often had no other recourse than to shoot it out.

Many folk tales have grown up in the western plains country about the quick justice and lynch law of the men who subdued the wilderness quite as often with a six-shooter as with the plow and ax. Old-timers in Kansas can still recount the exciting adventures "West of Salina," at Dodge City and Abilene. In the parlance of the day "there was no law west of Leavenworth," although common law was theoretically enforceable by territorial governments. Boot Hill Cemetery outside of Dodge City is silent testimonial to the days when gambling, hard liquor, and holdups were outstanding accompaniments of the pay-off at the end of the cattle trail. Men either went about their own business peaceably or met with prompt and decisive lynch law.

In the silver and gold mining camps, riches were more fabulous than in the cattle country. In a Montana mountain valley 10,000 miners extracted more than $10,000,000 worth of gold in a year. Between Virginia City, Montana, and Salt Lake City lay a wilderness of 475 miles. Organized crime grew apace. Clever scoundrels posed as honest men. One of the most active outlaws was Henry Plummer, who got himself elected sheriff for two communities, Virginia City and Bannock, Montana. As a law enforcement officer he was naturally able to obtain information about shipments of gold by express. He also purported to be an expert mining engineer. In consequence he and his road agents were able to perpetrate some of the most astounding crimes in American history. While pretending to be in the pursuit of robbers fleeing from justice, he and his "road agents" are known to have killed 102 men in their plunderous activities.[37] Finally the outraged citizens organized a Vigilantes, a committee for the purpose of eliminating this road agent band. In short order they executed 24 of these early racketeers along with other marauders.[38] These two Montana communities are representative of the general lawlessness which

[36] Cf. Emerson Hough, "The Cattle Trails," chap. 2 in *The Passing Frontier*, Vol. XVI of "Chronicles of America Series," Allen Johnson, ed., Yale University Press, New Haven, 1918.

[37] *Ibid.* Cf. also Thomas J. Dimsdale, *op. cit.*

[38] Thomas J. Dimsdale, *op. cit.*, p. 15. Cf. also Emerson Hough, *op. cit.*, p. 77.

flourished all over the West. On the Pacific coast there were mining camps of similar varieties. Here too crimes were settled for the most part by lynch law, which afforded the "popular tribunals" of the period.

In Texas a more highly organized group, the Texas Rangers, fulfilled something of the functions of the popular tribunals of Colorado, Wyoming, and California. In Texas the frontier problem was both political and geographic. At first the Rangers were a privately financed organization which aimed to overcome the stealing and the interracial conflicts in an area in which Mexicans, Anglo-Americans, and Indians were all striving for supremacy. In 1834 Austin called a meeting of American militiamen to put down Indian uprisings, and a force of 20 to 30 full-time Rangers was created. These men were soldiers in the saddle, but they were also illegal agents of the United States government, since Texas was at that time under Mexican rule. The Rangers incidentally became known as the "horse marines" because of their capture of some Mexican vessels.[39]

Following Texas' admission to the Union, the Rangers made continuous war on the Indian tribes.[40] Later, during the Civil War, the Texas Rangers were subordinated to the demands of the Confederacy and virtually passed out of existence. With the carpetbag government organized in 1870, Governor Davis sponsored their rebirth in the creation of a state police. Murderers and other felons were rounded up with a notorious amount of lawlessness on the part of the police entrusted with the task.[41] Close upon this upheaval the Texas legislature created two military forces for protection of the frontier. One was the Frontier Battalion to control the Indians to the west, the other the Special Force of Rangers charged with suppressing bandits on the Mexican border.[42] As time passed their duties changed. The great cattle country became a Mecca for cattle thieves, who were dealt with summarily by the pistol. On the Mexican border bandits were continually stealing sheep, cattle, and saddle horses. Because Mexico was at the time in the throes of a revolution this presented other problems as well.

With our entry into World War I, the danger that German spies would cross the border from Mexico created new difficulties, and it also must be admitted that the Texas Rangers themselves were guilty of many irregular activities. They virtually took the law into their own hands. Following the war a legislative investigation of the Rangers

[39] Walter P. Webb, The Texas Rangers, Houghton Mifflin, Boston, 1935, chaps. 1, 2.
[40] Ibid., chap. 8.   [41] Ibid., chap. 11.   [42] Ibid., chap. 12.

took place. Frontier problems had come to be of little importance as relations with our neighbors to the south grew more friendly. In consequence the Rangers were reduced in 1935 to two mounted companies and a headquarters company. Border troubles were placed wholly in the hands of the United States Army, and a highway patrol was assigned to take the Rangers' place in regulating public safety.[43]

Disregard for the law was a major characteristic of antisocial behavior on the frontier. With the exhaustion of free lands, marked alterations in our social and economic structure appeared, and freedom in its more absolute form was, so to speak, dethroned. So long as there were new wildernesses to conquer any man with sufficient energy and initiative could make a living. No one bothered much about the general laxities in business honesty and financial integrity and in consequence there was little restriction. If a man felt hampered by competitive forces he could always "go west." Today we are only a few short generations removed from the last frontier and the cultural heritage of that era inevitably affects our administration of criminal justice today. Ours is no longer a simple culture, even though certain frontier residuals have become a part of the American way of life.

Culture Conflict and Crime

Today American culture is one of seething complexity, one into which the varied culture groups of Europe, Africa, and Asia have poured their heritages in a veritable mosaic. Thus the Scandinavian, German, Slavic, and Latin peoples have brought their respective cultural traits to be assimilated and amalgamated in our melting pot. The Japanese and Chinese—Orientals at variance with themselves—have increased our cultural complexity. The Negro still retains important vestiges of his African habits and customs. Each of these—and all others who have come to make up America—has added to the richness of American life. But each has also added confusion to our social values and to the difficulties which create maladjustments for individual citizens. Despite the heterogeneous origin of our people, our social ideas and ideals, our customs, folkways, and mores have been shaped basically by the transplanted English common law, English Protestant religious concepts, and the English language. With the American Revolution, we made no effort to free ourselves from what was our dominantly English culture.

[43] *Ibid.*, p. 567.

Ours was a vast, unpopulated continent and with the advent of industrial development we opened our gates to the foreigner who was anxious to share in the freedom we offered him, although this freedom was always limited to what would fit into the American pattern. Thus the Italian's love of wine came into conflict with our attempt to enforce prohibition. Meanwhile the Italian's subversive institutions of the Mafia and the Camorra found new forms in their development of a sinister variety of gangster-hoodlums in America; the transplanted Slovakian or Polish peasant found himself, in the words of William Bolitho, separated only by a plate-glass window from the unbelievable riches displayed by a great Chicago department store.[44] Unhappily the spectacular rise from "rags to riches" which has been so dramatically recorded in the history of a large number of American capitalists created the myth and folklore of equal and unlimited opportunity. After the last stake was driven into the last homestead the only way many men of brains and enterprise could reach great fortunes was by despoiling the gains of others. While some of the antecedents of gangsterdom, racketeering, and illicit profits stem from outlawed European groups, others have more than probably grown out of the frustrated hopes of the children of the economically depressed immigrants.[45]

The complexity of our culture has been due in part to the swift impact of mechanical invention upon the habits of our people. Mobility has become a major characteristic of the modern American.[46] The dynamic urban industrialism of America nevertheless has its roots in the relative simplicity of the Elizabethan colonial period. Our cultural heritage was in fact so simple that it has not provided a firm foundation for the economic, political, and social structures which have been reared above it. Correlatively our social organization has been unstable and liable to disruption and disorganization. That it has endured so well is a tribute to the genius of the American people. For ours is a society in which competition and conflict are inherent.[47] These in turn have produced the social disorganization which is at base responsible for much criminal behavior. Part of the competition has been in our economic system. Some of the conflict has been between immigrant parents and their children who wished to take on

[44] William Bolitho, "Gangster Traumatism," *Survey*, 63:661–665 (March 1, 1930).
[45] Cf. Arthur W. Train, *Courts, Criminals and the Camorra*, Scribner, New York, 1912, for a discussion of the Camorra.
[46] Mabel A. Elliott and Francis E. Merrill, *Social Disorganization*, Harper, New York, 3rd ed., 1950, chap. 27, "Mobility."
[47] *Ibid.*, chaps. 1, 2.

the traits of Americans. Much of it has been between the belligerent descendants of the foreign born and the established descendants of persons with several generations of American ancestry.

The majority of people are fairly law abiding, at least so far as the majority of rules are concerned. Of course many who consider themselves responsible citizens break some of the laws, but we should live in chaos and on the verge of constant revolution if it were not for our relative conformity to law. Conflicts between those who observe the rules and those who reject them must naturally occur. Certain groups, as Sutherland points out, become associated on a differential basis.[48] Organized and systematic crime becomes possible only because individuals associate with others who accept their lawbreaking. Thus we have the underworld, the "mobs," the gangsters who build up a veritable code for regulating their own group. This is in a sense an educational process by which criminals come to accept criminal patterns of conduct by their differential association. They even tend to justify their behavior. Thus a gambling racketeer may say, "I am only conducting a Wall Street for the little guy." Certainly many gangsters and racketeers consider themselves quite as worthy in their motives as business and professional men.[49] Al Capone gave his *apologia pro sua vita* when he said: "All I ever did was to sell beer and whisky to our best people. All I ever did was to supply a demand which is pretty popular. Why, the very guys that make my trade good are the ones that yell the loudest about me. Some of the leading judges use the stuff."[50]

Crime and National Patterns

The cultural differences of national groups are evidenced in many ways, but none is more striking than the patterns of criminal behavior in the various countries. Everyone who has traveled in the Orient or the Soviet Union, for example, can testify to the peculiar character of stealing there. The average American railroad passenger gives little thought to the safety of his luggage and virtually none at all if he travels by Pullman. Luggage in Russia, on the other hand, is never considered safe unless one more or less literally sits on it. While waiting for a train in a Russian railway station a foreigner will be

[48] Edwin H. Sutherland, *Principles of Criminology*, Lippincott, Philadelphia, rev. ed., 1947, pp. 6–7.
[49] *Ibid.*
[50] Fred D. Pasley, *Al Capone, The Biography of a Self-Made Man*, Ives Washburn, New York, 1939, p. 349.

continually reminded by authorities never to let his eyes stray from his baggage. Even in a sleeping car at night he is warned to keep his windows down. Otherwise thieves are apt to remove his baggage when the train stops at stations to receive passengers. Russian railway thieves, in fact, have been a special variety of organized criminals and have developed special tools—long-handled steel devices—by which they can hook the luggage from the overhead racks and pull it out the windows which are 4 or 5 feet away.

Household thieving is also an important variety of Russian crime. Of course we have household robberies in America, but the average home is relatively free from such depredations. Mr. and Mrs. America can lock up their house or apartment and depart on a month's vacation with the reasonable expectancy of finding things exactly as they left them on their return. Not so in Russia. Everyone who leaves for a holiday in Russia is more or less forced to retain a caretaker during his absence. Otherwise the chances are that his house will be ransacked and most of his valuables stolen. Even the method of thievery takes on a cultural character. In America every good burglar possesses expertly made burglary or "jimmy" tools. By the skillful connivance of the unethical manufacturers who cater to his illegal needs he can force virtually any lock. Russian thieves require no such elaborate equipment. They simply cut out around the lock with a jig saw and open the door.

In England, on the other hand, the low rate of thievery is amazing to the most law-abiding American traveler. Though our luggage is comparatively safe on trains in the United States we should never think of putting trunks in a baggage car without some definite receipt or claim check. In England one simply claims his luggage at journey's end. The writer in checking a trunk from London to Edinburgh once protested when no claim check was given her. It seemed so obvious that some dishonest person could easily claim the trunk as his own. No such dilemma resulted, however. Another Britisher commented (when questioned about this practice), "We expect a man to be a gentleman until he proves himself to be a rogue."

In America our culture complex is equally evident in our peculiar crime patterns. An automobile has become the veritable index to the American standard of living. Riding swiftly through the green countryside or city boulevards has become a virtual folkway. That one has no special reason for a journey does not reduce the desire to ride. Yet even so there remain many untutored, uneducated, unskilled persons for whom the right to a "joy ride" is forever denied—because of lack

of the initial "down payment." The urge to own a car and other
evidences of a high standard of living have unquestionably been a
spur to economic crimes of serious nature. It takes money to buy a
car, to dress well and live pleasantly in a good neighborhood. In consequence only thefts which yield high returns are considered to be of
any advantage. Thus the era of the automobile ushered in the era of
bank robberies and big-stake holdups. Illicit business throve on the
gambling activities, the numbers rackets, and the relentless threats
of the extortionists.

Petty thieving, with its smaller returns, has thus had no appeal for
the professional criminal in America. The professional thief exerts
his wits to make a living and he sets his standards high. He wants
what the industrialist and successful professional man accepts as his
due, and he often knows literally no other means of getting it. If the
big-time criminal is successful he soon becomes convinced that only
fools sweat for a few paltry dollars a day.

Crime and Social Disorganization

Despite our high standard of living and the enormous productivity
of the American economic system, our society has been sorely torn by
the social disorganization which has hounded us through the years
following World War I, on through the Great Depression, during
World War II, and in the subsequent struggle between Russian communism and the democratic countries. Much that is designated crime
today has been a function of these various disruptions which have
affected every aspect of American life.

Spurred by the desire to prolong wartime prosperity, speculation
and booms were a part of the madness which eventuated in the stock
market crash in the fall of 1929. Agriculture prices had taken a tremendous drop earlier with the decline in demand for our major crops
—wheat, corn, and cotton—through the destruction of European
markets. A minor employment crisis occurred in 1921 and 1922. Intellectually the period of the twenties was one of unbelievable ex-
cesses accompanied by cynical disillusionment. No one "believed in
God" and a goodly share of the emancipated students and artists also
rejected any belief in the sanctity of marriage. The jazz age was also
an age of lawbreaking. Thousands of would-be artists and modern
young radicals sought consolation on Montparnasse, exchanging the
deadly monotony of life in Dubuque or Toledo for a newer standard-
ization in the sidewalk cafés of Paris.

The prohibition amendment, which sought to end the liquor problem in America, created an unprecedented opportunity for racketeering, and introduced gin and "café society" into the upper ranks of the American social structure. Part of the crime rate of the era was an index to the extent to which customary behavior of certain groups was in direct antithesis to codes of restraint. The Volstead Act, for example, forbade the sale or manufacture of intoxicating beverages, and during the "prohibition" the violators of this act formed the largest group of federal offenders. These people were not willing to change their habits to suit the new definition. There was literally no "consensus," and unquestionably great numbers of American citizens who were the patrons of the illicit industry were not punished. The confusion in the enforcement of our laws has been in part at least a reason for our high crime rate, and for the belief that one has a fighting chance to escape the law.

American Lack of Respect for Law

The American lack of respect for law obviously was not born of the prohibition era, as we hope our discussion of frontier mores has made clear. Nevertheless the peculiar ethics of officials and the enforcement of the prohibition law were shot through with amazing hypocrisy. The mere possession of liquor was an offense for which the possessor might be sentenced to prison in some states. In others the Volstead Act alone was implemented and only the manufacture and sale of liquor were punished. Many more persons defied the law openly and brazenly and "got away with it" than were ever arrested and convicted. Even those who were imprisoned thought they were unlucky rather than criminals.

Similarly, many states have rigid laws against the selling of contraceptives although they are sold openly over the counters of newsstands and drug and department stores. Untold thousands of persons report on less than their total taxable income, and do not report all their taxable assets to the assessor. Few Americans who drive an automobile always conform to the speed limits in the various jurisdictions. Most Americans seem to believe that legislators are no better judges than they are of how a man should behave and insist upon the right to a little judicious lawbreaking, irrespective of the social dangers involved.

Lawlessness has many facets. Parents who are their children's guardians may spend their children's inheritance with no special qualms because the money is needed for the children's support. Investors lose much more money through the sharp practices of stock companies (which take the income for directors' salaries, etc.) than through actual stealing.

As a matter of practical expediency we must recognize that there are many pitfalls in attempting to control behavior through legal taboos. In the first place the highly formal classifications of behavior make it difficult to differentiate between the greater and lesser good. Frequently articulate middle-class opinion is not in line with desirable social ends even though the middle class writes the laws. For example, in recent years there has been a widespread middle-class opinion (and upper-middle-class in particular) that the tactics of organized labor should be limited. For the very fact that labor unions exist makes possible collective bargaining and the forcing of issues through strikes. Strikes may lead to shutdowns of industry, which in themselves may be deplorable. Yet the evils resulting from strikes may be slight in comparison to the conditions which might exist if labor unions were abolished and all workmen were forced to accept the wages offered by employers or starve. The loss of all right to have a voice in the conditions of work and rates of pay would penalize the great mass of workers inestimably.

Moral Concepts and Crime

Whatever the given culture, moral concepts of honesty, decency, suitable relationships between the sexes, and being a "good neighbor" (far more than laws on the statute books) are factors which determine the limits of human conduct. Out of his background of training and experience man builds up his pattern of living, his life organization, *the things he will and will not do.*[51] Yet even here we have no certainty that moral concepts will see a person safely through a crisis situation. Frequently the individual has no experience with which to meet the circumstances into which he is plunged. In a relatively homogeneous and unified society he might hope to meet his problems safely and acceptably by following the established patterns of the group. In the degree to which we can bring about social organization through effective social planning we can hope to avert the social disorganization of which crime is the function. Apparently we have made a start in the right direction. But who can say? The disruptive influences of World War II and the struggle between Russia and the United Na-

[51] Cf. Mabel A. Elliott and Francis E. Merrill, op. cit., chap. 3.

tions may offset the gains thus far made. Social disorganization is a function of the lack of stability and cohesion of the social group.

Crimes which seem to be essentially social and economic in their origin, on the other hand, find much of their impetus in cultural patterns, in the complicated stresses and strains of modern civilization which places such importance upon monetary rewards and social prestige. Yet envy, hatred, and all the untoward passions of men also break out in crimes, some against person, some against property. Cultural history, complexities of our modern urban civilization, and the peculiar characteristics of the offender's personality all play important roles in determining the nature of crimes. Recently Walter C. Reckless has called upon American sociologists to leave history out of textbooks on criminology. If sociologists and criminologists fail to see crime in the light of its cultural origins and historical background, however, they will be treading on dangerous ground. For they will inevitably ignore facts which explain many of the present-day social attitudes and cultural patterns implicit in the antisocial behavior classified as modern crime.

Business and Crime

In 1939 Edwin H. Sutherland threw a bombshell into the complacent theorizings of criminologists, sociologists, and social workers who have maintained that the major explanation for criminal behavior lies in poverty and the underprivileged environment. In his presidential address to the American Sociological Society in December of that year, Dr. Sutherland laid open to the bone much of the hypocrisy and cant which have characterized the analysis of the American crime problem. His thesis was that criminal behavior was as characteristic of business (especially big-business) and professional groups as it was of the members of the lower class. He maintained that criminal statistics gave a distorted picture of criminals as poverty-stricken, feeble-minded, and psychopathic persons who were members of deteriorated families and lived in the slums. To substantiate his views, Dr. Sutherland cited figures showing that the embezzling crimes in high places among highly "respectable," socially accepted persons were a hazard to innocent investors; that the crimes of political graft and bribery in upper governmental circles seldom result in official action; that if brought to trial a great many corporations, officials, and professional persons might receive convictions and heavy sentences.[52] Since the

[52] Cf. Edwin H. Sutherland, "White Collar Criminality," *American Sociological Review,* 5:1–12 (February, 1940).

majority of juvenile delinquents and criminals who become the inmates of industrial schools, reformatories, and prisons come from the economically and socially depressed groups, the men who head the industrial corporations, the banks, the retail businesses, and the chambers of commerce were both shocked and nonplused by the accusation.

Since his initial pronouncement Dr. Sutherland conducted extensive researches and concluded that virtually all the great corporations have committed criminal offenses or offenses which are criminal in nature even though they were frequently tried in civil courts. These studies are so important that we have summarized them in detail in another section. These upper-class criminals, or white-collar criminals as Sutherland designated them, are, however, not ordinarily thought of as criminals at all. Instead they are the respected, influential, powerful members of our social organization although their crimes involve enormous sums of money and affect the pocketbooks and economic well-being of thousands of persons.

The victims of white-collar criminality, as Sutherland pointed out, cannot protect themselves[53] because of their ignorance and their lack of financial ability to fight for their rights. In a sense they are in a position comparable to the lower-class criminals who have no advantage before the law. Protagonists for the Negro have held that a caste system dominates the administration of justice in the South. Truly the caste system operates in the administration of justice for all lower-class offenders. In fact despite our increase in social consciousness we have been content to think of crime as basically a function of the lower economic classes. If Sutherland has done nothing else he has made it necessary for us to reconsider the whole problem of the etiology of crime. If the most respected businessmen in our local communities and in our national life are lawbreakers we must raise many questions with reference to class justice as well as the nature of crime which cannot be answered here. There are innumerable unfinished tasks for the criminologist in the years ahead.[54]

Crime and Our High Standard of Living

Part of stimulation to crime among lower-class criminals stems from our standard of living—a standard which made possible a Ford in the workman's backyard and a television set in the living room with

[53] *Ibid.*
[54] We have discussed this aspect of the causes of crime in chap. 3.

a daily newspaper (unread) beside it. Man must work hard and compete with his skills or his brain power to achieve sufficient means to purchase these things. If he achieves all these gadgets he believes he is sharing in the good life. While many professional and learned Europeans never hope to own an automobile, virtually every skilled industrial worker in America can realize his desire to have one. Many unskilled persons lack the earning power to acquire automobiles, television sets, etc., however, and are constantly tempted to steal such items.

Restrictive Legislation and Crime

Restrictive legislation, meanwhile, has also added to our crime rate. With no more free lands available, our population began to seem excessive. Industrial centers could no longer absorb all the foreigners who pressed at our gate. It was then that Americans turned from the economic opportunity offered on the frontier and voiced insistent demands for restrictive laws. On the Pacific coast protest against Oriental immigration arose. In the eastern states the southern European loomed as a menace to the economic security of industrial workers. Increasingly the defenses of pioneer democracy shifted from free land to legislation. Instead of moving on when he was annoyed by the sound of his neighbor's ax, the son of the frontiersman demanded a muffling of the ax, as Turner has well pointed out.[55] The new faith in social action through legislative enactment was not always justified, as we pointed out in our discussion of lawlessness. It has been no easy step from freedom from law in the wilderness to freedom through law under an industrial civilization. When the social historian of the future writes of the epic period 1896 to 1950 he will probably find something naïvely tragic in the attempts of the American people to solve the problems of crime and personal maladjustment by writing restrictive laws. Even those of us too close to the scene to be truly objective must see that laws themselves may be conducive to disorder. As often as not they are the results of the agitation of special groups who have succeeded in convincing the legislators but not the populace. When social controls are precipitately imposed they thus often produce as much crime and disorganization as they seek to avert, especially if there has been no effective education of the general public in the need for such legislation.

[55] Frederick L. Turner, *The Frontier in American History*, Holt, New York, 1920, p. 32.

Social Legislation and Lawbreaking

Under the leadership of Franklin Delano Roosevelt the American people initiated a new type of legally implemented security. Widespread attacks were made on unemployment, dependency, and the hardships of old age under the Social Security Act, adopted in 1935. This act, with its successive revisions, has extended the protective arm of the law over groups previously subjected to the vagaries of the fluctuating business cycle. This and other protective legislation, along with its important functions in preserving social well-being, has also created certain opportunities for lawbreaking, e.g., graft and dishonesty in accepting relief or unemployment stipends. Such legislation has unquestionably diminished any importance we may attach to stealing as an alternative to starvation. Whatever stimulus the new legislation may give to dishonest practices is, however, slight in comparison with the social values to be derived from freeing great masses of people from the haunting specters of eviction, starvation, or freezing cold. The altered situation offers a temptation to the unscrupulous which is quite different from the temptation to steal for food, shelter, and clothing.

By and large (despite our lawbreaking) the American people are relatively law abiding, and the far-reaching extensions of big business are in final analysis dependent upon honest dealings, fair play, and good will. Honesty, decency, and humanitarianism are written large in the conscience of the people. Our hearts are touched by the annual roll call of the Community Chest; we dig down in our pockets for the relief of disaster victims; we believe in the brotherhood of man even though we have not achieved it in an ultimate sense. Crime is one of our notorious excrescences because we have found no answer to the need for universal moral education, and thus far at least we have not achieved any unity of definition of conduct except that diversity which finds its expression both in adhering to and in breaking the law. Our cultural heterogeneity and our lack of consensus have many facets, which must be viewed in proper perspective to understand them. Our much vaunted freedom, which we aim so hard to preserve, carries with it certain hazards and one of them is our crime rate.

Obviously it is far from this author's belief that either our culture or our frontier mores explain all or most of our crime rate. Nevertheless, the frontier culture constitutes an important part of our social heritage and explains much of the American's rejection of and disrespect for formal legislative controls. Unlike our European cousins, we have had our most serious frontier problems within our own borders. Perhaps, one might add facetiously, this is one reason crime looms large in the American mores—just as the mores were written in the lack of social consciousness of our forebears. In Europe, on the other hand, there has been much respect for laws within national boundaries, whereas cultural conflicts between nations have led to war. As Turner has pointed out, ours is a democracy born of free land, and such a democracy, "strong in selfishness and individualism, intolerant of administrative experience and education and pressing individual liberty beyond its proper bounds, has its dangers as well as its benefits."[56]

SELECTED BIBLIOGRAPHY

Arnold, Thurman, The Folklore of Capitalism, Yale University Press, New Haven, 1937. This book shows how the "myths" of capitalism have become a part of the thinking of the average man.

Dick, Everett, Vanguards of the Frontier, Appleton-Century-Crofts, New York, 1941. This is a popular account of the western frontier mores.

Dimsdale, Thomas J., The Vigilantes of Montana, McKee, Butte, Montana, 1929. Lynch law in the fabulous silver country is described in a factual account.

Fiske, John, Old Virginia and Her Neighbors, Houghton Mifflin, Boston, 1897. This is a classic account of early Virginia problems of law enforcement.

Hough, Emerson, "The Cattle Trails," chap. 2 in The Passing Frontier, Vol. XVI of "Chronicles of America Series," Allen Johnson, ed., Yale University Press, New Haven, 1918. An excellent picture is given of cattle "rustling" in an early day.

Leyburn, James, Frontier Folkways, Yale University Press, New Haven, 1935. This is one of the most important sociological interpretations of early America.

Sutherland, Edwin H., "White Collar Criminality," American Sociological Review, 5:1–12 (February, 1940). This is the first pronouncement concerning Professor Sutherland's excursions into crime in high places.

Webb, Walter P., The Texas Rangers, Houghton Mifflin, Boston, 1935. This volume gives a scholarly account of law enforcement on the western plains of Texas.

Wycherly, George, "Pirates and Piracy on American Coasts," in Dictionary of American History, Scribner, New York, 1940, Vol. IV. Piracy during the colonial period and the early years of our republic is well described.

[56] Ibid.

CHAPTER 11

Nativity, Race, and Crime

Most Americans, except for the 400,000-odd native Indians, are the descendants of immigrants. The rest are immigrants. Even so, Americans rather generally entertain the belief that our criminal element is derived largely from the immigrant group. Strangely enough, this is no recent notion. It existed in colonial days. The belief that "foreigners" were corrupting manners and morals was actually held by many eminent men in early America. Even Benjamin Franklin is known to have voiced the opinion that the Germans in Pennsylvania were a disrupting influence on the American way of life.

As Edith Abbott makes clear in her analysis of public opinion and crime in the *Report on Crime and the Foreign Born* of the National Commission on Law Observance and Enforcement, this notion has arisen from two rather different sources: First, the influx of peoples with unfamiliar cultures created a hostile attitude on the part of the established population groups. As a matter of fact strange costumes or slightly deviant behavior always creates suspicion. A number of years ago a Bavarian student was arrested in California, on grounds that he was a suspicious character, because he was wearing his native Alpine leather walking outfit. Differences in culture also lead to conflict between culture groups and this often is expressed in higher crime rates as well as in increases in arrests. Second, the English system of transporting convicts to America lent a different substance to the belief, for a sizable share of the British criminal population was more or less forced to migrate to America. Once in the new country, these criminals might earn their freedom, but many people regarded them as the source of our subsequent "born" criminals.[1]

[1] Cf. Edith Abbott, "Public Opinion at Different Periods of American History," Part I, *Report on Crime and the Foreign Born*, National Commission on Law Observance and Enforcement, Washington, 1931, Report No. 10, pp. 23–24.

Remittance Men

The sons of prominent and respectable British and Continental families who committed serious offenses or became involved in disgrace of sufficiently shameful variety were frequently sent to the colonies to start a new life. Their wealthy parents, thus chagrined, usually financed their wayward sons by buying land and building houses for them. Such black sheep came to be known as "remittance men," as they are still called today. Often famous families would send their delinquent members to America and the practice continued long after the colonies had declared their independence.[2] Many such men straightened up and became prominent members of the community.

The British Transportation System

Men of the lower economic status who came into conflict with the law could not be saved from disgrace by family pride. During the economic depressions of the seventeenth and eighteenth centuries many poor fellows whose sole offense was unemployment were arrested for vagrancy. The question of what to do with the great number of unhappy prisoners was solved by transporting them to the colonies where they earned their freedom after serving a period of indentured labor.[3] Most of these men would be on relief rolls rather than in prison today. Some, however, were unquestionably felons and "desperate villains."[4]

Many of these transported convicts were sent to the West Indies, and during Cromwell's regime political prisoners constituted a sizable share of them. In fact, during the rebellion he *barbadoed* so many to one island that it is known as *Barbados* to this day.[5]

While the colonial labor problem was met in part by the transportation system, stern objections to the practice soon arose. The House of Burgesses of Virginia in 1670 and Maryland in 1676 passed acts forbidding such malefactors to land. Mother England completely disregarded these affronts to the imperial government. Instead, in 1717, the British Parliament systematized the transportation procedure and provided that persons who had committed "robbery, lar-

[2] Cf. Roy L. Garis, *Immigration Restriction*, Macmillan, New York, 1928, p. 10.
[3] Cf. chap. 27 for a detailed discussion on transportation.
[4] Cf. *Journal of Prison Discipline and Philanthropy*, October, 1859, p. 15, cited by Harry E. Barnes and Negley K. Teeters, *New Horizons in Criminology*, Prentice-Hall, New York, rev. ed., 1949, pp. 438–439.
[5] Margaret Wilson gives some interesting data in this connection in her book, *The Crime of Punishment*, Harcourt, Brace, New York, 1936, p. 96.

ceny and other felonious acts," who might otherwise be whipped, burnt on the hand, or imprisoned, be transported for indentured labor for 7 years. Thus their labor might help in building the colony and be useful to the mother country. Even persons sentenced to death, and "idle persons" lurking in divers parts of London and elsewhere, might be transported. Idleness was apparently considered more serious than overt criminality, for idle persons might be indentured for 8 years.[6]

The colonies attempted to rebuff the overt act by placing a head tax on convicts thus summarily deposited in America. Pennsylvania imposed such a duty in 1722 and Delaware in 1740. Benjamin Franklin took an official part in these protests and charged that the transported persons continued in their evil ways and corrupted the morals of the servant class and poor people with whom they associated.[7]

What effects these indentured convicts had upon American lawlessness we shall never be able to state accurately. It may well be that they increased the temporary crime rate, but we must also remember that many of those guilty of theft had stolen food because their children were starving or they themselves were hungry. We do know that some of the colonists were convinced that these men became "new men" and honest citizens in their new surroundings.[8]

There was, however, no consensus as to the reorganizing impact of life in the colonies upon the former convicts. Most people believed that criminality was inherited because in so many instances the same family contributed a number of criminals. As a matter of fact Dr. Charles B. Davenport, in his introduction to Estabrook's revised edition of Richard L. Dugdale's book *The Jukes*, holds that the progenitors of this notoriously criminal and ne'er-do-well family might be traced to these transported convicts.[9]

After the Revolution, the Continental Congress recommended that all states pass statutes to prevent the admission of convicts, and to penalize them for entry in some way. Most of the states adopted some such statutory provisions, but none was very effective in eliminating all traffic in convicts. By virtue of the independence of the colonies,

[6] Edith Abbott, *op. cit.*, pp. 24–25. Cf. also J. D. Butler, "British Convicts Shipped to the American Colonies," *American Historical Review*, 2:12–33 (October, 1936), cited by Abbott.

[7] Edith Abbott, *op. cit.*, pp. 26–27.

[8] Miss Abbott quotes such an opinion from J. Hector St. John de Crèvecœur, *Letters from an American Farmer*, London, 1782, in *ibid.*, p. 29. Cf. also Roy L. Garis, *op. cit.*, pp. 18–19.

[9] Cf. Charles B. Davenport, Introduction to Arthur Howard Estabrook, *The Jukes in 1915*, Carnegie Institution, Washington, 1916.

most such transportation to America ceased and convicts were sent instead to Australia and other outlying colonies. There was, however, no satisfactory organization to carry out the prohibitory laws. Actually many convicts, both from England and from the Continent, slipped unnoticed into this country throughout the nineteenth century.

In the meantime, continuous charges were made to the effect that immigrants were swelling our crime rates. In 1855 the mayor of New York protested the "penal colony" which European nations had established at the port of New York. The Thirty-Fourth Congress made a report on *Foreign Criminals and Paupers*, declaring them to be the source of the great increase in juvenile delinquency. After the Civil War the New York Association for Improving the Condition of the Poor declared that the chief demoralizing element in the city lay in the 400,000 immigrants who, in 20 years, had brought so many paupers, felons, and convicts to their midst.[10]

Following the panic of 1873 and subsequent economic disruptions, the immigration to the United States shifted. Instead of people from the northern and western European countries, those from southern and eastern Europe began to arrive. By this time the Germans and Irish were becoming well assimilated by our national melting pot and a definite part of the American culture. The cultural differences between the Latin and Slavic and the Nordic populations were conducive to much greater adjustment problems.[11]

Morals and Immigration

Public sentiment soon expressed itself in law. In 1875 the first federal immigration law was passed, prohibiting the admission of felons or women "imported for purposes of prostitution." Congress failed, however, to pass any enabling act or to provide machinery for enforcing the law. Consequently, in 1882, another act of Congress provided that a foreigner convicted for any save a political offense was to be sent back to his native country at the expense of the steamship company by which he had traveled. There was no diminution in the charge that immigrants were increasing our crime rate. Hence, the Ford Committee for Investigating Crime Among Immigrants was created. In 1891 the immigration act was revised to the effect that no person convicted of a felony, other infamous crime, or misdemeanor involving

[10] Cf. *Twenty-Fourth Annual Report of the New York Association for Improving the Conditions of the Poor*, New York, 1867, pp. 36–37, quoted by Edith Abbott, *op. cit.*, p. 41.
[11] Edith Abbott, *op. cit.*, pp. 42–43.

moral turpitude might be admitted.[12] Political offenses were not to bar the immigrant, even though the political offense might have been designated as a felony, or a crime, or an offense involving moral turpitude.

In 1901 there was another investigation of crime and pauperism among criminals, by the Federal Industrial Commission. This commission found, after a careful study of statistics, that whites of foreign birth "were a trifle less criminal" than native whites. Prisoners with foreign-born parents, however, ranked out of all proportion to their numbers in committing crime. A further "inquest" was held by the Federal Immigration Commission of 1908–1911, as to the operation of the immigrant laws. Their report admitted that immigrants did not appear to increase crime in proportion to their numbers. Even so, the commission held that the admission of criminals and those of criminal tendencies was a serious social aspect of the immigration movement.[13]

The Immigration Act of 1917

In 1917 Congress passed a comprehensive immigration act which incorporated a rigid policy of deportation without any time limit and provided that all persons who had ever been convicted of a crime involving moral turpitude, all anarchists, and all aliens convicted in this country for a term of 1 year or more for a crime involving moral turpitude might be deported. Thus, a person who becomes a criminal or prostitute in this country may be deported even though it is social disorganization in our midst which has been basically responsible for his or her moral deterioration. The 1917 law, although modified, still remains basic to our immigration policy.

Quota Restriction as a Means of Reducing Lawlessness

In 1921 the act of 1917 was modified by limiting the nationals who were to be admitted from each country to 3 per cent of the number of the same foreign stock, as enumerated by the 1910 census. In 1924 the rate of admission was further restricted. The quota admissions were changed from 3 to 2 per cent and the quota basis was changed

[12] It must be admitted that the failure to define moral turpitude has led to many different types of court decision.

[13] Cf. *Abstracts of Reports of the Immigration Commission*, 61st Congress, 3rd Session, Senate Doc. No. 747, Vol. I, p. 27. Cf. also Edith Abbott, "The Modern Period of Federal Control," Section II, *Report on Crime and the Foreign Born*, pp. 51–52.

from the nationals present in 1910 to those present in the 1890 census. Although this act purported to be a means of restricting the number of Europeans who were flocking to our shores, actually it became a legalized method of supporting American prejudices against immigrants from southern and eastern Europe, since comparatively few had come to this country until after 1890. Just as objections had arisen to the German and Irish in the early immigration, so the entry of Italians, Hungarians, and Slavs was later opposed on grounds of their lawlessness. Our American institutions were considered to be in danger. These new people were held to have had no background in self-government, hence were unequal to the demands of democratic life.[14]

This viewpoint was reinforced by the figures compiled and analyzed by Alida C. Bowler in the *Report on Crime and the Foreign Born.*[15] In this report the immigrants from Scotland, England and Wales, Germany, Ireland, and France were shown to have notably low crime rates in comparison with the rates among Czechoslovakians, Lithuanians, Italians, and Greeks. In the smaller American cities the crime rates for foreign born, especially the southern and eastern Europeans, were markedly higher than in the larger cities, as the variations in Tables 11.1, 11.2, and 11.3 show. The adjustment difficulties of the new immigrants were probably enhanced by small-town suspiciousness, whereas greater tolerance of foreigners prevailed in metropolitan centers. At least the rates for the foreign born were lower in 7 of the 10 cities with populations over 500,000 than the native white rate. The cultural conflict thus represented takes on a regional aspect as well. As the tables show, the Chinese rate is exceedingly high in San Francisco. But the Scandinavian rate in San Francisco is the highest among foreign-born white groups.[16] In general, we may assume that the factor of social distance has a marked effect upon the crime rates of different national and racial groups. It seems evident that the Negro rate is partially a matter of prejudicial interpretation of behavior, as our discussion later indicates. The Turk, it has been suggested, "raises unpleasant historical memories." The Slovak's language is incomprehensible. So, too, are many of his customs. Teutonic or Nordic culture, on the other hand, has become a part of the background of American culture; the Schwartzes are as well accepted as the Worthingtons and the Wilsons. But a name like Svarc sounds queer to the American

[14] Cf. Roy L. Garis, *op. cit.,* p. 170.
[15] Alida C. Bowler, "Recent Statistics on Crime and the Foreign Born," *Report on Crime and the Foreign Born,* pp. 100–102.
[16] Cf. *ibid.,* pp. 103–108. The "small town suspiciousness" is the present authors interpretation.

TABLE 11.1. Number of Persons Arrested by Police, or Arraigned in City Magistrates' Courts, per 10,000 of Same Population Class, by Nativity and Color, and by Country of Birth, for 10 Cities Having More Than 500,000 Inhabitants in 1930[a]

Nativity and Country of Birth	Arraigned in Magistrates' Courts New York (1929)	Number of Persons per 10,000 of Same Population Class Arrested by Police									
		Chicago (1929)	Philadelphia (1930)	Detroit (1930)	Los Angeles (1929–30)	St. Louis (1930)	Baltimore (1930)	Boston (1930)	San Francisco (1929–30)	Milwaukee (1930)
Total[e]	559	642	826	130	410	1,315	687	1,198	992	725
Native white	{ 616	{ 555	{ 952	{ 96	{ 388	{ 973	{ 734	{ 1,322	{ 945	776
Negro		3,975		923		5,259				565
Foreign born										
Austria	454	385	377	97	488	631	330	937	1,098	899
Canada	474	166	280	129	674	1,045	324	847	737	630
Czechoslovakia	195	42	108	64	216	895	137	778	755	114
England, Scotland, and Wales	N.D.	141	N.D.	9	N.D.	114	108	N.D.	N.D.	410
France	188	67	158	81	210	359	204	503	616	183
Germany	185	232	106	98	210	206	241	768	498	327
Greece	203	152	212	41	198	253	101	447	380	1,456[b]
Hungary	3,152	1,532	1,512[b]	358	664	1,235	1,359	1,660	1,239	
Ireland	N.D.	129	360	66	N.D.	282	20	N.D.	N.D.	1,382
Italy	194	200	425	196	620	722	259	1,129	848	704
Yugoslavia	542	801	102	93	338	1,452	626	893	728	544
Lithuania	N.D.	467	842	55	N.D.	792	148	N.D.	N.D.	1,225
Poland	N.D.	1,157	962	115	N.D.	N.D.	248	1,164	N.D.	431
Russia	309	513	309	112	237	1,172	512	1,247	226	992
Scandinavian countries	590	174	678	72	368	678	216	775	953	1,170
China	307	305	1,143	131	431	739	1,517	1,170	1,280	625[c]
Japan	2,036	983	584[c]	29[c]	555	1,101[c]	2,618[c]	5,013	6,306	c
Mexico[d]	552	N.D.		191[c]	210	612[c]	1,250[c]	769[c]	191	
All others	464	940	402	154	635	683	1,346	1,233	1,113	1,247

a Rates computed from figures appearing in annual reports or special tabulations for year designated, and population estimates based on 1930 census, or on 1920–1930 increase for interim years, applying 1920 percentages to total to estimate nativity and nationality groups. N.D. is used to indicate that no data were available.
b Included with Austria in police reports.
c Estimated number in population so small as to make rate calculation of doubtful value.
d All estimates of Mexican population, based on 1920 census percentages, are open to such serious question that Mexican rates were not inserted, although the figures are included in total foreign-born rate.
e Total refers to number of persons arrested per 10,000 total population.

Source: Table 3, Based on Crime and the Foreign Born, National Commission on Law Observance and Enforcement, Washington, 1931, Report No. 10, p. 199.

TABLE 11.2. Number of Persons Arrested by Police, per 10,000 of Same Population Class, by Nativity and Color, and by Country of Birth, for 10 Cities Having 200,000 to 500,000 Inhabitants in 1930[a]

Nativity and Country of Birth	Number of Persons Arrested by Police, per 10,000 of Same Population Class Arrested by Police									
	Cincinnati, Ohio (1930)	Newark, N.J. (1930)	Kansas City, Mo. (1930)	Seattle, Wash. (1929)	Rochester, N.Y. (1929)[b]	Jersey City, N.J. (1930)	Denver, Colo. (1929)	St. Paul, Minn. (1929)	Akron, Ohio (1930)	Providence, R.I. (1930)
Total[c]	580	429	480	502	324	439	720	479	602	610
Native white	637	335	451	548	295	483	636	590	631	753
Negro	110	2,877	911	1,465	237	313	2,305	462	468	982
Foreign born	99	294	268	342	350	287	567	96	32	244
Austria	11	174	N.D.	310	123	118	1,218	108	29	39
Canada	N.D.	223	N.D.	69	—	71	38	56	3,057	78
Czechoslovakia	4	61	N.D.	520	143	102	210	15	49	—
England, Scotland, and Wales	7	117	N.D.	64	144	156	30	43	188	48
France	29	86	N.D.	354	115	126	—	240	305	—
Germany	1,278	146	N.D.	129	199	1,579	—	58	974	1,542
Greece	74	667	N.D.	618	184	187	—	198	343	94
Hungary	53	149	N.D.	—	403	145	—	—	218	674
Ireland	334	322	N.D.	215	363	489	109	49	1,366	—
Italy	N.D.	303	702	308	—	137	920	166	988	43
Yugoslavia	N.D.	208	N.D.	134	202	173	491	166	1,210	272
Lithuania	189	200	N.D.	N.D.	315	388	N.D.	—	812	N.D.
Poland	174	387	184	159	151	488	332	117	104	342
Russia	N.D.	222	N.D.	196	354	190	95	91	214	899
Scandinavian countries	N.D.	318	N.D.	608	c	c	141	117	c	127
China	N.D.	c	N.D.	486	—		1,695	c		332
Japan				183						c
Mexico[d]		—		—			311			—
All others[e]	268	765	156	1,079	248	551	1,394	140	766	831

[a] See note a, Table 11.1.
[b] A large number of "nativity-unknown" cases included in this figure.
[c] See note c, Table 11.1.
[d] See note d, Table 11.1.
[e] See note e, Table 11.1.

SOURCE: Table 2-A, Report on Crime and the Foreign Born, National Commission on Law Observance and Enforcement, Washington, 1931, Report No. 10, p. 101.

TABLE 11.3. Number of Persons Arrested by Police, per 10,000 of Same Population Class, by Nativity and Color, and by Country of Birth, for 11 Cities Having 100,000 to 200,000 Inhabitants in 1930[a]

Nativity and Country of Birth	Youngstown, Ohio (1930)	New Haven, Conn. (1929)	Bridgeport, Conn. (1930)	Scranton, Pa. (1930)	Salt Lake City, Utah (1929)	Paterson, N.J. (1930)[d]	Trenton, N.J. (1930)	Elizabeth, N.J. (1929)	New Bedford, Mass. (1930)	Wilmington, Del. (1929–30)	Lowell, Mass. (1929)
Total[f]	595	860	293	454	931	d	664[e]	473[e]	248	1,497	437
Native white	659	819	306	445	1,024	N.D.	643	476	229	1,124	424
Negro	—	2,143	1,238	—	1,871	2,772	—	—	276	5,507	463
Foreign born	409	830	223	485	447	400	432	474	1,047	754	N.D.
Austria	89	919	94	396	847	559	861	984	293	—	N.D.
Canada	N.D.	543	255	181	34	422	335	418	293	—	381
Czechoslovakia	899	198	9	738	N.D.	—	—	—	—	—	N.D.
England, Scotland, and Wales	5	468	91	140	59	161	192	335	151	8	258
France	119	619	87	259	641	285	389	359	172	74	N.D.
Germany	175	361	79	158	223	291	223	176	70	54	N.D.
Greece	492	1,592	244	1,726	3,089	1,250	2,214	1,053	183	814	354
Hungary	171	499	168	238	N.D.	303	428	219	—	—	N.D.
Ireland	25	889	193	268	760	356	284	344	244	102	522
Italy	765	772	269	680	1,362	403	545	608	238	1,300	N.D.
Yugoslavia	525	N.D.	3,807	—	923	213	232	—	—	—	N.D.
Lithuania	811	1,620	266	1,376	—	989	—	567	—	—	664
Poland	560	1,471	419	961	194	451	523	297	408	1,477	1,015
Russia	327	785	185	239	1,491	430	624	895	348	735	825
Scandinavian countries	162	854	257	N.D.	97	913	491	620	111	230	N.D.
China	b	b	b	b	1,500[b]	b	b	b	b	b	N.D.
Japan	N.D.	N.D.		b	807[b]	b	b	b	b	b	N.D.
Mexico[c]	N.D.	N.D.							b		N.D.
All others	781	1,770	547	1,494	358	532	604	1,340	319	222	529

[a] See note a, Table 11.1.
[b] See note c, Table 11.1.
[c] See note d, Table 11.1.
[d] Paterson sent list for known foreign born and "colored" only.
[e] Group of "unknown nativity" included in total.
[f] Total refers to rate per 10,000 total population.

Source: Table 11.B, Report on Crime and the Foreign Born, National Commission on Law Observance and Enforcement, Washington, 1931, Report No. 10, p. 102.

schoolboy. Even more so does Metropolous. Prejudice against the Roman Catholic likewise persists as a result of our Puritanical traditions. The Greek Orthodox is even less well understood, and Mohammedanism is almost completely antithetical to our religious culture.[17]

A detailed analysis of the figures for arrests in 5 cities—Detroit, Los Angeles, Cleveland, Buffalo, and Cincinnati—showed, however, that the rate for foreigners as a whole approximated the native white rate only in the more violent crimes of murder and aggravated assault.[18] Foreigners committed rape only half as often as native whites. Native whites committed 3 times as many robberies, 4 times as many burglaries. Mexicans, on the other hand, were listed as heavy offenders in all groups. But second-generation "Mexicans" are so generally listed as Mexicans that the statistics for this group are recognized to be of little value.[19]

A summary of convictions by nationality groups showed that the foreign-born rate most nearly equaled the native-white rate for murder, but that convictions for aggravated assaults were almost twice as high among the native whites.[20] In robbery and burglary, the convictions for the foreign born were approximately one-fourth those for the native born; in larceny they were but one-half.[21] On the other hand, the foreign born had a higher rate than natives in offenses against liquor laws, gambling, and assaults. Gambling and sale and consumption of liquor were not considered offenses in their own countries, and "protecting one's honor" by combat was an established cultural pattern. Despite these differences in defining criminal conduct, when the various rates were corrected for age and sex it became obvious that the criminality of these groups was grossly exaggerated. Most foreign groups in America contain a high proportion of adult males. When the conviction rates for the foreign male population in Chicago 17 years old and over as a whole were analyzed by Miss Bowler, they were shown to be actually less than the rates for the native-born group of the same age and sex. This was also true of arrests of males over 15 years of age in 9 American cities over a period of years, as Tables 11.4 and 11.5 indicate. (They were markedly less, too, than the Negro arrests.)

[17] Cf. Clara A. Hardin and Herbert A. Miller in Francis J. Brown and Joseph S. Roucek (eds.), *Our Racial and National Minorities*, Prentice-Hall, New York, 1937, chap. 23, "The Second Generation," p. 714.
[18] Alida C. Bowler, *op. cit.*, p. 116.
[19] *Ibid.*, p. 119.
[20] *Ibid.*, p. 131.
[21] *Ibid.*, pp. 119 and 117.

TABLE 11.4. Number of Persons, per 100,000 of Population of Same Class 15 Years and Over, Charged with Certain Important Offenses by the Police Departments of 9 Cities During a 1-Year Period, by Offense, by Nativity and Color, and by Country of Birth

	Total Number Charged, per 100,000 of Same Population Class, 9 Cities[a]					
Nativity and Country of Birth	Homi-cide	Rape	Rob-bery	Aggra-vated Assault	Bur-glary	Weap-ons
Native white	19.4	17.8	108.1	47.5	92.2	28.7
Negro[b]	120.5	64.0	481.2	543.5	421.0	222.0
Foreign-born white	12.3	11.2	28.1	44.5	34.2	19.1
Austria	16.0	4.9	19.7	31.9	9.8	18.4
Canada	4.4	3.3	14.8	4.9	38.4	2.7
Czechoslovakia	2.1	2.1	6.4	18.0	8.5	2.1
England, Scotland, and Wales	5.6	8.1	11.8	4.3	22.9	1.2
France	7.5	7.5	18.8	18.8	11.3	7.5
Germany	3.6	2.6	2.6	14.0	10.1	4.2
Greece	9.7	29.0	22.6	164.5	32.3	58.1
Hungary	2.2	2.2	24.7	15.7	4.5	3.4
Ireland	6.0	1.3	7.3	11.3	16.0	2.0
Italy	53.6	34.8	67.0	102.3	38.7	64.7
Yugoslavia	0.0	4.9	9.9	22.3	2.5	4.9
Lithuania	21.3	18.3	36.5	161.4	39.6	24.4
Poland	8.9	12.1	37.4	52.5	25.6	9.5
Russia	7.9	3.2	13.4	29.6	14.8	5.5
Scandinavian countries	4.2	1.2	4.8	17.5	22.9	3.0
Mexico[c]	77.2	132.7	267.8	417.4	579.1	349.9
All other (white)	22.5	23.3	85.1	105.1	77.0	36.1

[a] Rates computed from figures taken from annual reports, or from special tabulations provided by the police departments, and population estimates based on census data. Cities supplying these figures were: Chicago; Detroit; Los Angeles; Cleveland; Cincinnati; Kansas City, Mo.; Rochester, N.Y.; San Francisco; and Cambridge, Mass.

[b] Separate figures for native white and Negro were not supplied by San Francisco, but inasmuch as San Francisco's percentage of Negro population is only 0.5 of 1 per cent it was considered safe to disregard the deficiency.

[c] All Mexican rates are of very doubtful value because of the question as to validity of population estimates.

SOURCE: Table 6, *Report on Crime and the Foreign Born*, National Commission on Law Observance and Enforcement, Washington, 1931, Report No. 10, p. 119.

TABLE 11.5. Number of Men and Boys, per 10,000 of Male Population of the Same Class, 17 Years and Over, Convicted of Felonies, by Nativity and Color, for Three 5-Year Periods, as Reported by the Chicago Police Department[a]

	Average Number per Year per 10,000 of Male Population of Same Class, 17 Years and Over, Convicted of Felonies		
Nativity and Color	1915–1919	1920–1924	1925–1929
Total	43.2	36.7	28.0
Native white	47.5	42.5	32.4
Negro	116.9	163.5	144.2
Foreign born	30.1	16.1	10.1

[a] Rates computed from figures contained in the annual reports of the Chicago police department, 1915–1929, and population estimates based on United States census figures.

SOURCE: Table 7, *Report on Crime and the Foreign Born*, National Commission on Law Observance and Enforcement, Washington, 1931, Report No. 10, p. 126.

However, when the figures are broken down into various nationality groups, it is patent that the new immigration, whether east or southern European or Mexican, produces more criminals than the immigration of Anglo-Saxon and Nordic stock as Table 11.4 shows.[22]

The conclusions, as set forth by Miss Bowler, are confirmed by a later analysis. Sutherland's analysis of arrest rates for 1937 showed the rate per 100,000 adult population to be 514.2 for native whites, and 212.1 for foreign-born whites.[23] Courtlandt C. Van Vechten's analysis of commitment rates to prisons in 1940 for all age groups showed that the native-born rate per 10,000 was 11, the foreign-born rate 5.

However, when the commitment rates are broken down into age groups important differences appear, as one can see in Table 11.6.

TABLE 11.6.   Commitment Rates per 10,000 Male Persons in the United States by Nativity and Age in 1940

Nativity	All Ages	16–19	20–34	25–29	30–34	35–39	40–44	45–49	50–59	60–69	70 and Over
Native white	11	11.8	21.5	16.7	13.2	11.7	8.6	6.0	3.9	1.8	0.7
Foreign-born white	5	16.7	29.5	22.9	13.2	8.6	6.7	4.3	2.8	1.4	0.4

SOURCE: Courtlandt C. Van Vechten, "The Criminality of the Foreign Born," *Journal of Criminal Law and Criminology*, 32:139–148 (July–August, 1941). Reproduced by permission of the *Journal*.

The criminality of the foreign-born white male under 30 was considerably greater than that of the native-born white, but the rate decreased rapidly for the foreign born after the age of 30. The final statistics for prisoners admitted in 1940 further confirmed the conclusion that the foreigner tends to be more law abiding than the native born. In that year, native-born white persons constituted 66.3 per cent of the prisoners admitted, foreign-born white 4.3 per cent. Population

[22] Parenthetically we might say that the fact that rejection of the Mediterranean peoples and eastern Europeans and the Orientals, by our immigration acts, might produce international tensions with far-reaching repercussions did not dawn upon those earnest and misguided congressmen of the postwar twenties. But the Italians and Japanese resented the discriminations imposed upon their peoples. The complicated economic disruptions in Italy following World War I were augmented by the drastic restrictions against Italian immigration. They were regarded as insulting to the great Roman people. Highly organized collective methods for improving the economic peril resulting from the inability of their surplus population to migrate resulted in the Fascist movement. But we did not see that far ahead. Facts and figures, the latter both real and imagined, had made us believe that unrestricted immigration would destroy our law, our biological stock, our very national integrity. Statistics seemed to bear this out. Dr. H. H. Laughlin so testified at a Congressional hearing. Cf. Roy L. Garis, op. cit., pp. 247–248.

[23] Edwin H. Sutherland, *Principles of Criminology*, Lippincott, Philadelphia, rev. ed., 1939, p. 123.

figures for 1940, however, showed that there were 29,099,464 native-white males, 15 years of age or over, and 11,335,482 foreign-born males, 15 years of age and over. Of these groups, 41,258 native whites were admitted to prison and only 2717 foreign born.[24] In other words, the rate for native white, per 100,000 population, was 141.8 in contrast to the foreign-born rate of 23.9 per 100,000 males of the same age and sex group. The median age of the foreign-born group for 1940 may account for this marked contrast—it was 51.0 years; the median age for whites was 26.7 years. The fact that the foreigners are so much older than the native born must be considered a significant factor in the stability of the immigrant group's behavior.

The European immigrant tends also to come from a relatively unified cultural background where there has been great respect for law and order and a fundamental acceptance of governmental authority. The ways of the new country may seem strange, but in general the immigrant wishes to conform, both because it is in line with his mores and because he may be deported if he commits any serious offense.[25] He thus recognizes the importance of not breaking the law.

In his analysis made in 1941 Van Vechten concluded that foreigners are much less likely to be involved in crimes for personal gain than are the native born. Native-born rates are higher than foreign-born rates in the following ratios:

11 to 3 for robbery.

22 to 5 for burglary.

20 to 5 for larceny.

On the other hand, rates for personal violence are about the same for each group.[26] Van Vechten does not take into consideration the fact that Italian immigrants and persons of Italian descent have figured largely in organized crime in America.

The foregoing data confirm an earlier study made by the author, with reference to cultural conflict and juvenile delinquency. Juvenile delinquency rates in Chicago were examined with reference to the nationality groups represented and a much higher delinquency rate was found in the nationality groups differing most from the American cultural norm. That is, British and north European groups produced the lowest delinquency rates. South and eastern Europeans produced

---

[24] These data were derived from material presented in a release from the Bureau of the Census, Population Series, p. 10, No. 6, p. 1; and *Prisoners in State and Federal Prisons and Reformatories, 1940*, Bureau of the Census, U.S. Department of Commerce, Washington, 1942, Table 8, p. 8.

[25] Cf. also Edwin H. Sutherland, *op. cit.*, p. 113.

[26] Courtlandt C. Van Vechten, "The Criminality of the Foreign Born," *Journal of Criminal Law and Criminology*, 32:139–148 (July–August, 1941).

the highest. On the other hand, a relatively homogeneous nationality group produced a higher rate than a group which came from highly diverse cultures. The conclusion at that time was that the degree of delinquency was apparently in part a measure of the conflict between the mores of the American norm (or law-enforcing group) and those of the foreign culture. Since there was less disparity between German and English cultures and American habit patterns it seemed obvious that the conflict was naturally less than in case of the Mediterranean peoples and east Europeans.[27]

Alien Status and Arrest

Part of the foreigner's problem lies in his alien status. *Because he is a foreigner he is more likely to be arrested when innocent than is the native born.* Similarly, when he runs afoul of the law, he has much greater difficulty in securing justice. The Mexican, for example, seems to have been the victim of much lawlessness on the part of police. He is frequently subjected to "third degree" tactics. Often the ignorant foreigner does not know his legal rights. Cases are on record of Mexicans who literally did not know why they were arrested. Research has disclosed many gross miscarriages of justice against such helpless and impecunious aliens.

NEGROES AND CRIME

The preliminary estimation for the population of the United States in 1950 as released by the Census Bureau was 150,697,000, with the numbers of white persons estimated to be 135,215,000, Negroes 14,-894,000, and other races 588,000.[28] As earlier figures in Table 11.5 indicated, Negroes unquestionably are convicted for more crime in proportion to their numbers than white people. Figures for arrests for 1950 as given in Table 11.7 indicate that approximately 1 out of every 24 Negroes was arrested. However, the same Negro is often arrested several times. Even so the rate is very high. Many factors enter into this apparent propensity to disobey the law, as we shall discuss.[29] Analysis of the male prisoners received by courts during the years 1932 to 1936 shows Negroes exceed white men in proportion to the popula-

[27] Mabel A. Elliott, *A Correlation Between Racial Heterogeneity and Juvenile Delinquency in Chicago*, Department of Welfare, Springfield, Illinois, 1926, p. 41.

[28] *1950 Census of Population, Preliminary Reports*, Series P6–7, No. 1, Bureau of the Census, U.S. Department of Commerce, Washington, February 25, 1951, p. 6.

[29] Cf. W. A. Bonger, *Race and Crime*, transl. by Margaret M. Horduk, Columbia University Press, New York, 1943, chap. 3 for a detailed treatise on race and crime.

tion represented for every offense except embezzlement and fraud, as Table 11.7 indicates. Since embezzlement and fraud are possible only to those who have some economic opportunity to commit them, Negroes are more or less automatically excluded from these two types of crime.

TABLE 11.7. The Average Number of Male White and Negro Prisoners Received from Courts, per 1,000,000 Population for the Years 1932–1936

Crime	White	Negro
Homicide	3.6	25.3
Robbery	9.7	25.1
Aggravated assault	1.9	17.0
Burglary	17.1	64.7
Rape	2.0	4.5
Larceny	13.6	43.9
Auto theft	5.2	6.2
Embezzlement and fraud	3.1	2.0
Forgery	5.9	6.1

SOURCE: Hans von Hentig, "The Criminality of the Negro," *Journal of Criminal Law and Criminology*, 30:662–680 (January–February, 1940).

Negroes also are accused more frequently of crimes they do not commit and are more often punished for those they do commit than are whites. It is probably true, of course, that the white man commits more crimes for which he suffers no arrest than does the Negro.

Since the Negro suffers many handicaps growing out of the economic, social, and political discriminations against him, many social scientists have insisted that he is not necessarily a greater offender; he is more likely to live in situations which are conducive to criminal activity, and he is more likely to suffer punishment for any such activity. Certainly the Negro, more often than the white person, is a member of the economically depressed group.

We need not review the extensive literature on the American Negro to establish his economic and social disabilities. The economic discriminations against him affect not only opportunity for employment and rate of pay. There are also many occupations which are not open to him. Educational facilities for vocational and academic training are woefully inadequate in the South and Southwest where the majority of Negroes live. Even when Negroes can afford college and professional training, the doors of learning are often closed to them. Most state universities south of the Mason and Dixon line have consistently refused to admit Negroes, although they are partially supported by tax-paying Negroes. Lawsuits have been waged and courts have ruled in favor of the Negroes but public sentiment has never succeeded in opening the doors on any general basis. Graduate students and professional students in recent years have been more widely admitted to universities.

A study made in 1930 showed that white persons were arrested in Virginia more frequently than Negroes for only 2 offenses, forgery and drunken driving. Both of these offenses seldom occur in the lowest income groups for obvious reasons.[30] In all other offenses, Negroes committed twice as many crimes as white offenders, 10 to 20 per cent more frequently than white persons.[31]

Another special study, covering the years 1930–1936, showed the proportion of male prisoners received from courts in the United States to be racially divided as follows:[32]

Year	White Race	Negro
1930	120.4	353.5
1931	132.7	371.2
1932	124.6	351.3
1933	113.3	345.3
1934	109.8	356.2
1935	118.5	391.5
1936	109.0	370.0

The Report on Crime and the Foreign Born, referred to earlier, showed that Negroes committed 10 times as many murders, 6 times as many rape cases, 16 times as many robberies, 11 times as many burglaries, and 11 times as many offenses with armed weapons in proportion to their number as did foreign-born whites in 9 cities of over 100,000 population, as may be computed from Table 11.4. The proportion convicted in Chicago was likewise high although not as high as in the 9 cities taken together, as shown in Table 11.5.

Current Crime Rates Among Negroes

As we mentioned earlier, Negroes bulk even larger in the number of arrests. During the year 1950 there were 205,576 Negroes among the total of 793,671 persons arrested (or 26 per cent of the arrests), ac-

[30] Both offenses are possible only to persons within certain economic brackets. Ordinarily the impecunious person would not be able to cash a bad check, nor is he so likely to have a car.

[31] Workers Writers Program, The Negro in Virginia, Hastings House, New York, 1940, p. 341.

[32] Data from John H. Kliner and Thomas A. Hulton, Indiana and the Adult Offender, 1939, p. 98, quoted by Hans von Hentig, "The Criminality of the Negro," Journal of Criminal Law and Criminology, 30:662–680 (January–February, 1940).

cording to the records tabulated by the Federal Bureau of Investigation.[33] In proportion to their numbers Negroes apparently committed
far more crimes than Italians—the highest ranking of the foreign-born
group—as shown in the study on the foreign born in Table 11.4.
Mexican rates appear to be higher in all categories, but the Mexican
data are not reliable.

Negro Crime Rates as Related to Social and Economic Factors

These statistics on Negro crime rates have led many uncritical people to believe the Negroes' earlier status as an African primitive race
has made them less receptive to the rules and regulations of civilized
society. Unprejudiced consideration of facts, however, indicates that
the Negro is more likely to be placed under suspicion than the white
man and is often falsely arrested. Likewise, the Negro is more frequently arrested for petty offenses than the white man. Because he is
seldom financially able to pay fines when imposed, he must, in a far
greater number of instances, serve the alternative sentence. If guilty,
he is more likely to be convicted, and we are probably safe in assuming
that even if he is not guilty, the preponderance of prejudice is always
against him. All these items must be considered in accounting for the
relative crime rates. Certainly, as Guy B. Johnson insists, the simple
fact of race is not sufficient to explain the Negro crime rate. The
really important fact in accounting for it is the Negro's subordinate
social status; his economic and social disabilities are the antecedents
to criminal behavior in all groups.[34] But the caste system imposed
upon the Negro makes it well-nigh impossible for him to conquer
his disabilities. Race prejudice prevents him from living where he
chooses, even when he is financially able to have decent surroundings.
The Negro undoubtedly commits more crimes in proportion to numbers than white persons, but it is partly because he is the victim of
prejudice and is hampered in his opportunities.

In the northern and western sections of the United States the Negro crime rate is an essentially urban phenomenon and the urban
factors, which are important in all crime rates, intensify the Negro's
conflict with the law. During the depression, when white men found

[33] Cf. chap. 3, "The Extent and Distribution of Crime." Cf. also *Uniform Crime
Reports, Annual Bulletin,* 1950, Federal Bureau of Investigation, U.S. Department of
Justice, Washington, 1951, p. 112.

[34] See Guy B. Johnson, "The Negro and Crime," *Annals of the American Academy
of Political and Social Science,* 217:93–104 (September, 1941). Cf. also Mabel A.
Elliott and Francis E. Merrill, *Social Disorganization,* Harper, New York, 3rd ed., 1950,
p. 647.

it hard to secure employment, Negroes were the first to be laid off, if white men could do their work. Young colored men employed as ushers in theaters or as bellhops, for example, were soon superseded by white men when employment opportunities were scarce. In consequence, Negroes, during the depressed thirties, knew the full impact of the disorganizing aspects of relief.

The wages of colored persons in the past, especially colored women, were always lower than for white people.[35] The Federal Wage and Hour Law has paved the way for more equitable wages, but Negroes are so largely employed in service industries that local prejudices will have to undergo important changes before any generally effective adjustment in wages is made. The bitter demand on the part of articulate Negroes and their champions for some fair acceptance of their services in defense industries and for recognition of ability in the armed services during the war has resulted in a more satisfactory status for the Negro in the American social hierarchy, but there is still far to go. In view of all the barriers to his full participation in American culture it is not surprising that the Negro feels less constrained to abide by the laws than does the white person.

Murder Among Negroes

Although it is true that Negroes are punished for many petty offenses, their crimes are often of a serious nature, as Table 11.8 shows. The Negro homicide rate is especially high. In 1950, 2889 of the 6336 persons arrested for criminal homicide were Negroes. Psychologically, murder is associated with frustration and the Negro experiences frustration on every hand. Murder is also associated with sexual jealousy. Dr. von Hentig insists that the disturbed sex ratio which characterizes our colored population augments the problem of sex jealousy and consequent murder rates.[36]

Sex and Age Ratios in Relation to Negro Murders

Probably because of the greater incidence of disease (as well as from other causes) the Negro population evidences certain disturbances in sex and age ratios. These disturbances also may well account for at least part of the disparity between native-white and Negro crime

[35] Cf. *The Negro Woman Worker*, Bulletin of the Women's Bureau No. 165, U.S. Department of Labor, Washington, 1935, p. 3. Cf. also Mabel A. Elliott and Francis E. Merrill, *op. cit.*, pp. 230–231.

[36] Hans von Hentig, *op. cit.*

TABLE 11.8. Arrests by Race, 1950

Offense Charged	Total All Races	Race				
		White	Negro	In-dian	Chi-nese	Japa-nese	All Others
Total	793,671	576,422	205,576	7,334	842	285	3,212
Criminal homicide	6,336	3,372	2,889	36	2	2	35
Robbery	19,779	12,517	7,060	93	14	2	93
Assault	59,496	31,277	27,619	281	41	13	265
Burglary—breaking or entering	43,673	31,776	11,534	196	21	13	133
Larceny—theft	66,031	44,776	20,672	307	49	25	202
Auto theft	18,398	14,695	3,500	144	6	4	49
Embezzlement and fraud	21,439	18,346	2,962	65	10	14	42
Stolen property; buying, receiving, etc.	3,289	2,209	1,050	12	6	3	9
Arson	1,054	806	241	6	—	—	1
Forgery and counterfeiting	11,743	9,927	1,689	89	7	3	28
Rape	9,323	6,473	2,717	46	3	2	82
Prostitution and commercialized vice	8,579	5,190	3,260	38	32	21	38
Other sex offenses	19,725	16,057	3,473	75	14	7	99
Narcotic drug laws	8,539	3,939	4,262	18	175	3	142
Weapons; carrying, possessing, etc.	10,376	5,082	5,198	24	12	2	58
Offenses against the family and children	15,238	11,708	3,415	69	4	2	40
Liquor laws	11,260	5,841	5,306	80	11	3	19
Driving while intoxicated	51,318	44,911	5,706	508	9	16	168
Road and driving laws	14,571	10,746	3,662	118	3	7	35
Parking violations	309	210	98	1	—	—	—
Other traffic and motor vehicle laws	13,052	9,463	3,431	83	8	4	63
Disorderly conduct	45,438	31,217	13,610	405	20	11	175
Drunkenness	178,165	143,867	30,040	3,513	33	50	662
Vagrancy	48,604	37,157	10,657	504	57	18	211
Gambling	15,490	7,584	7,462	10	172	41	221
Suspicion	46,194	32,751	13,054	251	26	2	110
Not stated	7,930	6,179	1,555	133	11	5	47
All other offenses	38,322	28,346	9,454	229	96	12	185

SOURCE: Table 44, *Uniform Crime Reports*, Annual Bulletin, 1950, Federal Bureau of Investigation, U.S. Department of Justice, Washington, 1951, p. 112.

rates because they promote the factor of jealousy. For the United States as a whole, the number of young colored males, 15 to 39, was 42.7 per cent of the total male colored population in 1940. In contrast, only 40.3 per cent of white males are 15 to 39 of age. The difference here may seem slight, but it swells the ranks of the potential criminal group. Youth and male sex are, as Dr. von Hentig points out, the dynamic factors in crime.[37]

Not only do more male Negroes belong to the group most likely to get into conduct difficulties. The disparity between Negro males and

[37] *Ibid.*

Negro females is more marked than is the difference in sex ratios for white persons. According to figures for the 1950 census there were slightly less than 98 nonwhite males for every 100 nonwhite females in the United States, but for the age group 15 to 39 there were only 92.6 nonwhite males for every 100 nonwhite females.[38]

For the urban communities however, where the majority of crimes are committed, the number of male Negroes is markedly lower than the number of females. The disproportion is, at the same time, greatest in the young adult groups in the ages most commonly given to mating. Where two women are seeking the attention of one man, and where there are fewer men than women, or where the reverse is true, it has been held that Negroes are prone to emotional explosions. This disparity in Negro sex ratios is more pronounced in some cities than others. In Columbus, Ohio, which has a large colored population, there were 109.4 males per 100 females in 1940. In Natchez, Mississippi, on the other hand, there were only 70.7 males per 100 females. Such a disparity inevitably makes monogamic matings impossible for some and may well account for certain sex crimes and jealous murders.[39] In any case, *Negroes commit more murders proportionately than white people.* Whether they are naturally more explosive than white persons is a question difficult to answer. Certainly violent murders or stabbings occur with greater frequency among Negroes than white persons. A survey of the death rate in Chicago shows that 27 per cent of the Negro males and 25 per cent of the Negro females met death from stabbing, in contrast to 7 per cent of white males and 8 per cent of white females.[40]

Mortality and Desertion Rates Among Negroes

In 1940 the male Negro death rate from all causes in the United States was 1523.6 per 1,000,000 population, in contrast to 1162.2 per 1,000,000 for white males. For Negro men 35 to 39 years of age the rate was 1145.2, in contrast to 413.2 for white men of the same age. For the years 40 to 44 the death rate for Negro males was 1578.5 per 1,000,000, whereas the white rate was 607.3. For Negro males 45 to 49 years old the rate was 2093.0, the white rate 714.4. Only Negroes

[38] Cf. *1950 Census of Population, Preliminary Reports*, p. 7. These figures are computed from the preliminary data. Since most nonwhites are Negroes, they give an approximate picture of Negro sex ratios.

[39] Cf. Hans von Hentig, *op. cit.* Data on race, broken down for cities, are not thus far available for the 1950 census.

[40] *Ibid.*

who have attained the age of 70 have a death rate comparable to that of the white man.[41]

Figures for 1948 (which, however, do not separate Negroes from other nonwhites) give a relatively accurate picture of the Negro death rate. (For Negroes constitute approximately 96.5 per cent of the nonwhite group.) As Table 11.9 shows, the death rate for nonwhite males is far more than twice as high as for white males of the same age group —25 to 44. It is also considerably higher than the female nonwhite rate and accounts for the many widows among the younger married Negro group. The higher death rate of males in itself greatly augments the economic problems of Negro families. For the loss of the breadwinner lowers an already stringent standard of living. It is also true that many more Negro husbands than white husbands desert their wives. Both facts swell the proportion of Negro women who are heads of families. Many Negro women thus go out to work and leave their children unsupervised as they play in the cities' worst slums. The cycle of criminal conduct is not hard to complete. The higher mortality and desertion rates among Negroes are thus apparently significant factors in the Negro's economic problems, which in turn tend to be conducive to crime.

Morbidity Rates

Disease is, of course, a factor in disturbing the population age and sex groups. Tuberculosis and syphilis exact a particularly high toll among Negroes.[42] The high rate of tuberculosis must be attributed largely to the extreme economic handicaps of the Negro, whose small wages are often insufficient for decent shelter and an adequate diet. The syphilis rate seems to be related to promiscuous sex habits among Negroes as well as their low economic status.

Negroes and Sex Crimes

Although sex crimes run especially high among Negroes, there is no need to presume that the propensity to such crimes is a matter of innate social depravity. The Negro's sex mores have evolved from his cultural history. Before the Civil War, many Negroes lived in a virtual

[41] *Deaths and Death Rates for Selected Causes by Age, Race and Sex, United States,* 1940, Special Report, Vital Statistics, Bureau of the Census, U.S. Department of Commerce, Washington, April 15, 1942, pp. 230–232.

[42] Cf. E. Franklin Frazier, *The Negro Family in Chicago,* University of Chicago Press, Chicago, 1932, chaps. 7, 8, for a discussion of these problems.

TABLE 11.9. Death Rates by Age, Race, and Sex, United States, 1948
(Exclusive of stillbirths and of deaths among armed forces overseas. Rates per 1000 estimated midyear population excluding armed forces overseas)

Age	All Races			White			Nonwhite		
	Both Sexes	Male	Female	Both Sexes	Male	Female	Both Sexes	Male	Female
All Ages[a]	9.9	11.3	8.5	9.7	11.2	8.3	11.3	12.6	10.0
Under 1 year	35.0	39.4	30.4	32.2	36.4	27.8	56.5	63.1	49.9
1–4 years	1.6	1.7	1.4	1.5	1.6	1.3	2.4	2.6	2.3
5–9 years	0.7	0.8	0.6	0.6	0.8	0.5	0.8	0.9	0.8
10–14 years	0.7	0.8	0.5	0.6	0.8	0.5	0.9	1.0	0.9
15–19 years	1.2	1.5	0.9	1.1	1.4	0.7	2.2	2.3	2.1
20–24 years	1.6	2.1	1.2	1.4	1.9	0.9	3.6	3.9	3.3
25–29 years	1.8	2.1	1.4	1.5	1.8	1.1	4.4	4.9	3.9
30–34 years	2.2	2.6	1.8	1.8	2.3	1.4	5.3	5.9	4.7
35–39 years	3.2	3.8	2.7	2.7	3.3	2.2	7.8	8.6	7.1
40–44 years	4.8	5.8	3.8	4.1	5.1	3.1	11.0	12.3	9.9
45–49 years	7.2	8.9	5.5	6.3	8.0	4.6	15.0	16.8	13.2
50–54 years	11.1	14.1	8.2	10.0	13.0	7.1	23.0	26.3	19.7
55–59 years	15.9	20.1	11.7	14.8	19.0	10.6	28.5	32.8	24.3
60–64 years	23.7	29.3	17.9	22.6	28.5	16.8	37.6	40.5	34.6
65–69 years	36.7	44.3	29.4	35.6	43.4	28.1	52.3	55.2	49.2
70–74 years	54.2	63.4	45.9	53.7	63.1	45.3	61.2	68.3	53.9
75–79 years	81.6	92.8	71.9	82.3	93.6	72.7	70.7	81.5	60.3
80–84 years	126.3	136.5	117.5	130.1	140.3	121.6	77.0	89.2	66.6
85 years and over	247.1	254.9	241.3	267.0	271.8	263.3	105.7	124.9	93.0

[a] Includes deaths for which age was not stated.

SOURCE: Table A, in *Deaths and Death Rates for Selected Causes by Age, Race and Sex, United States, 1948*, Special Report, Vital Statistics, U.S. Bureau of Public Health, Federal Security Agency, Washington, November 27, 1950, p. 317.

TABLE 11.10. Death Rates from Certain Diseases per 100,000 Estimated Population in 1948 for Male and Female According to White and Nonwhite Races

Causes of Death	Total Rate
Tuberculosis (all forms)	30.0
White male	33.3
female	15.4
Nonwhite male	92.1
female	65.4
Syphilis	8.0
White male	8.6
female	2.9
Nonwhite male	38.2
female	16.0

SOURCE: Table 2, *Deaths and Death Rates for Selected Causes by Age, Race and Sex, United States, 1948*, Special Report, Vital Statistics, U.S. Bureau of Public Health, Federal Security Agency, Washington, November 27, 1950, pp. 334 and 336.

state of imposed promiscuity. Nor did the masters and slaveholders set any exemplary standards, for their conduct was equally promiscuous. We are apparently safe in presuming that not many southern gentlemen lived in accordance with the rigid monogamic ideals which they required their womenfolk to follow. In fact, high-ranking men in the old South often admitted that some of their slaves were their own flesh and blood.[43] The present hybrid character of our colored population attests to this fact; Herskovits maintains that approximately 80 per cent of the American Negroes have some white blood.[44]

Under slavery, the Negro woman had no protection whatsoever from the sexual advances of her master. As a matter of fact, she was often pleased to bear a child by him, for it frequently helped to improve her lot on the plantation and meant she could work in the "big house" instead of the fields. If it was a matter of mutual attraction, she was given definite advantages by the relationship. Usually, however, it was the prestige of the white race rather than any personal effection which induced the slave girl to accept the white man's embraces. The mulatto, who resented her hybrid status, had the added reason of resentment to make her develop seductive wiles for the slaveowner. At least Frazier so argues.[45] She could then boast that her children had "the best blood in the South" in their veins. Despite the widespread existing social prejudice to racial amalgamation, a powerful sex attraction between the races was probably a more important factor in the problem of miscegenation during slave days than the mere desire to increase the slave stock for purely mercenary reasons.

We must not think all the illicit unions of slave days were between Negro women and white men. Frazier furnishes numerous instances of the bastard-hybrid progeny of white women. Usually these were a matter of casual relations between indentured white women and Negro men during our early colonial and federal period.[46]

Nor was monogamy established for the Negroes by their freed state. The period immediately following the Civil War completely disrupted the old social structure. The great social economic revolution which accompanied the end of slavery uprooted whatever stability the Negro of the old South had previously known. Small wonder that sex irregularities should increase with all the other forms of social disorgani-

[43] Arthur W. Calhoun, *Social History of the American Family*, Clark, Cleveland, 1917–1918, Vol. II, chap. 9.

[44] Melville J. Herskovits, *The American Negro*, Knopf, New York, 1930, chap. 1.

[45] Cf. E. Franklin Frazier, *The Negro Family in the United States*, University of Chicago Press, Chicago, 1939, chap. 4.

[46] *Ibid.*

zation which were rife during the "carpetbag" era. Ignorant, untutored, and impecunious, the Negro faced many baffling problems. Biological satisfactions, temporary though they might be, were immediately available. In fact, every social upheaval seems to be marked by extreme social disorganization and disorganized sex mores in particular. And in the Negro's case, it must be said that the white man failed to set any commendable example.

Although there has been a gradual acceptance of traditional Anglo-Saxon notions of permanent monogamy, some illiterate Negroes in rural sections of the South and in the poverty-stricken slums of the cities have retained many of the loose habits of their slave mores. This is well brought out in the pathetic comedy, *Porgy*, the story of poor blacks in Catfish Row, Charleston. A shyster colored lawyer persuades Porgy to pay him a dollar to get Bess, with whom he is in love, a divorce from "Crown." When the lawyer asks when they were married, her friends maintain she "ain't neber been marry." That, according to the lawyer, presents "complications" and he demands two dollars! Finally he compromises for a dollar and a half, for, as he says, "It take expert fuh divorce 'oman whut ain't marry."[47]

Cultural Explanation for Negro Crime

Besides the many cultural explanations for the Negroes' seeming propensity for crime, we must keep in mind that the caste system which makes them liable for every petty offense also restricts their chance for justice in the law courts. In the South in particular there is an essentially caste definition of crime. Such relatively simple acts as "failure to keep one's place," "talking back" to a white person, even "looking at a white woman" may be conceived as dangerous conduct. If a Negro is insolent, homicide may result, and as often as not go unpunished.[48] On the other hand, if a Negro commits an offense against one of his own race, even a serious crime, he frequently is not arrested. There seems to be a general notion that Negroes should not clutter up the white man's courts.[49]

In not a few instances the Negro has been the victim of a frame-up —of being accused of committing a white man's crime with the evidence planted against him. Because of the caste system, the Negro has practically no protection against the testimony of white persons, es-

[47] Cf. Dorothy and DuBose Heyward, *Porgy*, Act II, Doubleday, New York, 1927, pp. 62–67.
[48] Guy B. Johnson, *op. cit.*
[49] Cf. J. D. Bowles, Master's thesis, University of Kansas Library.

pecially if he is used as a scapegoat for a woman's sex delinquency.[50] A woman who has become pregnant through illicit sex relationships can thus get an innocent Negro indicted for rape and have a legal abortion—with only sympathy instead of blame for her condition.[51]

Emotional Basis for Negro Crimes

Small wonder then that the emotional basis for crime should also be significantly represented among Negroes. Life presents many frustrations to the Negro, which are not the lot of white men. Discriminated against, kept in his place, condemned to low income and poor living quarters, it is only natural that he should feel impelled by hate and revenge.[52] White men have more money than Negroes. Why not steal? White men make it impossible for the Negro to enjoy many of the fruits of the good life—if only the "foamy beauties of a chocolate soda at the corner drug store," as one Negro student has said. We cannot very well expect anything but a rebellious attitude from the Negro.

Housing and Negro Crime

At least 90 per cent of our Negro population in the North lives in cities. Here living quarters available to them are everywhere restricted to the slum areas and areas immediately adjacent. Slums are in no sense responsible for crime as such, but crime always breeds in them. Here, too, lack of sanitation is a serious factor in promoting disease. In Kansas City, Kansas, for example, a large number of the houses in the Negro district have no modern plumbing, and at least 1 school building in the area has been furnished with nothing but outdoor toilets. And this in modern America. Grim, ramshackle, unsanitary housing is prevalent in Negro neighborhoods throughout the United States.[53]

We cannot attribute the high morbidity rate among Negroes entirely to crowded housing and appalling sanitation, but it is inevitably affected by both.

Drink, Recreation, and Crime

Although drunkenness is a misdemeanor, it is an especially serious problem among Negroes and accounts for a major part of their arrests

[50] Cf. Monroe N. Work (ed.), Negro Year Book (1931–1932), pp. 289–292 (1938).
[51] Lillian Smith's novel, Strange Fruit, exploits this theme.
[52] Guy B. Johnson, op. cit.
[53] Cf. Mabel A. Elliott and Francis E. Merrill, op. cit., chap. 31, "Racial Minorities," especially pp. 648–649.

and jail sentences. Drink, moreover, is also a factor in other crimes, especially in murder and sex crimes.

The lack of decent recreational facilities is a matter of concern for all underprivileged groups but is especially serious for Negroes. The low-grade cabaret dance hall probably reaches its lowest depths in the Negro "joints," known as "Free and Easys." Every stimulus exists to promote immorality. Here in turn sex jealousies are aroused which result in murder. The commercialization of sex in such places is recreation at its worst, yet in many communities no decent places exist where young Negroes may dine and dance. Though disreputable dives also cater to white people in most American cities, there are usually wholesome places where they may spend their leisure time. Negro young people should not be condemned too severely for patronizing the only places open to them.[54]

THE AMERICAN INDIAN AND CRIME

Indians do not constitute any significant proportion of our criminals, but the Indian crime rate in proportion to their total number is relatively high. In 1950 there were 7334 Indians arrested for reported crimes, as Table 11.8 shows. One out of every 54 Indians thus appears to be arrested. However, as with the Negroes, the same person tends to be arrested many times, while the average Indian is comparatively law abiding. The American Indian's crime rate, like that of the Negro, is undoubtedly seriously affected by his minority status, particularly in the Southwest. In general the Indian may be said to have been glamorized in the folklore while he has been pushed aside and ignored by our lawmaking bodies so far as his welfare is concerned. The economic plight of the Indians of Arizona and New Mexico is one of the darkest blots on the American escutcheon. And because there are so few Indians they have not been able to raise a compelling voice of protest, as have the Negroes. There is, admittedly, an Indian Rights Association, but its members are few and the majority of Indians are more or less segregated in the West and Southwest. The Indians have posed no significant threat to white Americans nor have they been able to make as effective demands as the Negroes.

Types of Offenses Indians Commit

Of the 7334 Indians arrested in 1950, 3513, or approximately 48 per cent, were charged with drunkenness, as Table 11.8 shows. Drunken-

[54] T. L. Woofter, *Negro Problems in Cities*, Doubleday, New York, 1928, chap. 17, "Commercial Recreation."

ness is a far commoner cause for arrest among Indians than for any other racial group. The problem of drunkenness is one of the most serious problems in the administration of Indian Affairs.[55] Alcoholism itself is often an index to personal disorganization, in addition to being a misdemeanor. The next highest Indian offense was driving while intoxicated (508 cases), which accounted for 6.9 per cent of the arrests, and vagrancy cases ranked next with 504 cases. There were 405 cases of disorderly conduct. We are probably safe in assuming that both vagrancy and disorderly conduct cases were conditioned by consumption of alcohol.

According to a special study of 100 typical families among the Navajo Indians in 5 communities, 34 arrests were made among members of the families in 1943–1944. These arrests were as follows:[56]

Disorderly conduct (drunkenness)	22
Liquor violation	4
Trespassing	2
Assault and battery	3
Transmitting venereal disease	1
Adultery	1
Illicit cohabitation	1

Thus, the major crime of the Navajos, like other Indians, is drunkenness or obnoxious or disorderly conduct while drunk. Half of the arrests were in a community situated near the police service. The report alleged that had there been more police there would have been more arrests since it was well known that drunkenness was proportionately greater in the other four communities. These Navajo families were characterized by many of the social and economic factors which seem to exist in the backgrounds of many lawbreakers. They were unbelievably poor. (Their annual average per capita income was $63.75.) Many were victims of tuberculosis; many were physically defective; none of their homes was sanitary. The Indian has not been well treated in New Mexico and Arizona. Both states have failed in the past to give social security benefits to Indians on the same basis as other citizens.[57] "The People" as the Navajos call themselves, have been more or less demoralized by the impact of the Western civilization in which they are permitted only a marginal status.[58]

[55] Cf. G. E. E. Lindquist, The Indian in American Life, Friendship Press, New York, 1944, pp. 84–87.

[56] J. A. Krug, The Navajo, U.S. Department of Interior, Washington, 1948, p. 9.

[57] Ibid., pp. 8–9.

[58] Cf. Edwin Corle, People on the Earth, Wallace Hebberd, Santa Barbara, California, 1950, for an excellent fictionalized account of the Navajos.

Certain Indian crimes stem from the conflict between their culture and Euro-American culture. Bigamy thus may be acceptable to the tribal mores while it is outlawed by American law. Hence illegitimacy and fornication may exist only from the white man's point of view.[59]

This is not the place to discuss the various ramifications of the Indian problem. However, it is a fact that the United States military men who controlled the government's policy with reference to the Indians failed notoriously to carry out treaty obligations with the Indians and subjected them to a pitiable dependent status. The cruel ruthlessness of federal officials was often expressed in the words, "The only good Indian is a dead Indian." Despite all this the Indian has somehow preserved much of the essential integrity of his culture and has remained relatively unabsorbed by the white man's way of life. But it is not surprising that where he has been partially absorbed he has often been demoralized by his marginal status.

Other Racial Groups

Other racial groups are too small in number to be considered here. The Orientals have had their problems of maladjustment but their crime rate is too small to constitute any serious problem except for the offenders themselves. In some of our large cities the Chinese have their own courts in "Chinatown" and try their own members for offenses virtually without the knowledge or notice of our law-enforcing agencies.

SELECTED BIBLIOGRAPHY

Abbott, Edith, "Public Opinion at Different Periods in American History," Part I, Report on Crime and the Foreign Born, National Commission on Law Observance and Enforcement, Washington, 1931, Report No. 10, pp. 23–78. This gives an excellent historical review of attitudes toward foreigners with reference to their relation to our crime rate.

Bonger, William A., Race and Crime, transl. by Margaret M. Horduk, Columbia University Press, New York, 1943. This is one of the best studies on race and crime, written by the distinguished Dutch criminologist.

Bowler, Alida C., "Recent Statistics on Crime and the Foreign Born," Part II, Report on Crime and the Foreign Born, supra, pp. 79–196. This

[59] Cf. Hans von Hentig, "The Delinquency of the American Indian," Journal of Criminal Law and Criminology, 36:75–86 (July–August, 1945).

is a survey of important crime statistics pertaining to both foreigners and Negroes in the decade 1920 to 1930.

Brown, Francis J., and Roucek, Joseph S., *Our Racial and National Minorities*, Prentice-Hall, New York, 1937. This book contains some excellent material on racial and cultural antagonisms which are factors in crime rates among Negroes, Indians, and the foreign born.

Hentig, Hans von, "The Criminality of the Negro," *Journal of Criminal Law and Criminology*, 30:662–680 (January–February, 1940). Dr. von Hentig gives a penetrating analysis of factors which contribute to the Negro's high crime rate.

Hentig, Hans von, "The Delinquency of the American Indian," *Journal of Criminal Law and Criminology*, 36:75–86 (July–August, 1945). Here von Hentig analyzes the factors responsible for the high rate of delinquency among American Indians.

Johnson, Guy B., "The Negro and Crime," *Annals of the American Academy of Political and Social Science*, 217:93–104 (September, 1941). This gives a summary of the various social factors which account for much of the Negro crime rate.

Krug, J. A., *The Navajo*, U.S. Department of Interior, Washington, 1948. The Secretary of the Interior gives a brief but important analysis of factors in this tribe's crime rate.

Uniform Crime Reports, published annually by the Federal Bureau of Investigation, U.S. Department of Justice, Washington. These reports give semiannual and annual data on arrests for Negroes and other races and for the foreign born.

CHAPTER 12

Biological, Mental, and Emotional Factors in Crime

Literally hundreds, perhaps thousands, of studies have been made with reference to the special characteristics of criminals. The underlying presumption back of such research obviously has been that criminals are different from noncriminals and that the differences may be observed and measured. Recent studies on the extensive lawbreaking among respectable persons (as we have discussed in Chapter 3) make it clear that the majority of people commit crimes at some time or other. This conclusion gives us little reason, therefore, to take too seriously any belief in the existence of basic physical, mental, or emotional differences between criminals and noncriminals.

Perhaps it would be better to look for the differences (if any) between amateur and confirmed criminals. But this too would involve practical problems since many amateurs are caught, convicted, and sentenced while confirmed or professional criminals often elude conviction (even when detected). Almost all of the research material on offenders refers to a special group of offenders: those who are serving prison sentences. In any event a summary of the various researches should be a part of the information of every student of criminology. All such information is significant in reviewing historical developments in the field and some of the data are important for the insight they give us into the characteristics of prisoners.

Pronouncements on the relation between defective physique, low mentality, or emotional disorders and criminal behavior should be taken *cum grano salis*, however. As has often been said, any person with a theory of human behavior probably should be psychoanalyzed. At least it is possible that the theorist may be expressing a deep-seated sense of guilt or a similarly deep-seated grudge or hostile attitude

313

buried in *his* unconscious. On the other hand part of the tendency to assign importance to the special or peculiar characteristics of criminals may stem from the particular background of him who makes such pronouncements. An examination of the research literature, both recent and of an earlier date, shows that medical men and others trained in biology tend to emphasize biological factors while psychiatrists and psychologists emphasize motivation and attitudes which drive criminals to their antisocial behavior. Sociologists usually tend to find ample explanation for crime and delinquency in social factors surrounding the criminal—in his low-grade economic status, the bad neighborhood in which he grew up, and his immoral home environment—while the clergyman finds the criminal to be the man who has sinned against the laws of God. Each according to his training can thus account for the criminal.

Actually there is a certain amount of truth in each of these various conclusions, but each such explanation usually ignores other equally important factors. In final analysis the truly objective approach is to consider all the factors in a given situation which may have been significant in inducing behavior. At the same time everyone must be on guard to avoid emphasizing data which substantiate his hunches, prejudices, or unconscious attitudes while ignoring equally pertinent material which does not confirm his theories of human behavior.

PHYSICAL CHARACTERISTICS OF PRISONERS

It is easy to understand why certain early "scientific" criminologists emphasized the biological characteristics of criminals as factors conditioning their activities. Many of the early scientists in the field of criminology were physicians. Since their training was rooted in physiology and anatomy, they looked rather naturally for physical differences between prisoners and the non-prison population. Actually the earliest researchers confined their studies to prison and jail populations and did not examine the non-prison population. For the latter they depended upon general impressions from persons they chanced to meet in their everyday associations outside of institutions. Various conclusions with reference to the physical characteristics of criminals have been summarized in two important treatises, that of Arthur E. Fink, *Causes of Crime (Biological Theories in the United States 1800–1915)*,[1] that of Hans von Hentig, *The Criminal and His Victim.*[2] Dr. Fink's book is devoted exclusively to biological theories of crime

[1] University of Pennsylvania Press, Philadelphia, 1938.
[2] Yale University Press, New Haven, 1948.

in the United States, and Dr. von Hentig's volume, which is concerned with the sociobiology of crime, employs many European as well as American sources. Dr. Fink's is an exhaustive survey of biological research and theories; Dr. von Hentig's equally scholarly book summarizes psychological and social factors also. Von Hentig gives credence, however, to the possible relationship between certain physical traits and criminal behavior, as we shall see. Our discussion of physical factors is largely derived from these two sources.

The Phrenologists' Theory of Crime

Franz Joseph Gall (1758–1828), the Viennese physician, developed phrenology as a result of his physiological and anatomical studies. From his study of the brain and the contour of the skull Gall became convinced that behavior was related to the size and shape of the head. He concluded that the brain was divided into some 26 organs (increased by his disciple John Gaspar Spurzheim to 35). These "organs" were classified into "propensities," "sentiments," and "perceptive" and "reflective faculties." The "propensities" were divided into higher and lower and it was the lower propensities which eventuated in criminal behavior unless they were made subservient to the perceptive and reflective faculties.[3] (Here, perhaps, Gall and his followers grasped a little of what modern psychoanalysts call "sublimation.") Later an American, Dr. Charles Caldwell (1772–1853), while identified with the Medical Department at Transylvania University in Lexington, Kentucky, introduced phrenology into this country. He had attended Spurzheim's lectures in Paris in 1821 and returned to give lectures in this field and to become a stanch exponent of phrenology. Caldwell reduced the psychological "organs" to 34 but kept the essential framework of Gall and Spurzheim. Three phrenological characteristics—philoprogenitiveness, destructiveness, and "covetiveness"—were held to be closely associated with criminal behavior. Philoprogenitiveness Caldwell associated with infanticide in 27 out of 29 females guilty of this crime. Destructiveness led, he believed, to murder unless regulated and held in balance by superior faculties. Covetiveness (which other phrenologists called "acquisitiveness") led to both selfishness and economic crimes. Caldwell recognized individual differences in propensities and maintained that a strong propensity did not mean a crime necessarily would be committed.[4]

[3] Arthur E. Fink, op. cit., p. 3.

[4] Charles Caldwell, Elements of Phrenology, Lexington, Kentucky, 1874, cited by Arthur E. Fink, op. cit., pp. 5–7.

Many respectable scholars and physicians as well as prison and insane-hospital superintendents supported phrenology as scientifically accurate. Because there was a certain coincidence between the phrenologists' findings and behavior it was not long before phrenology was widely exploited by quacks and sidewalk fakirs. Meanwhile scientific physiological and psychological research soon established the fact that behavior could not be resolved into functions of small sections of the brain. However, phrenology served as the impetus both to later research in the causes of crime and to the whole science of psychology.[5]

Anatomical Characteristics

Lombroso may be credited with making the first extensive anthropometric study of criminal man.[6] He was not, as some have believed, however, the first to make a scientific study of the criminal. Serious study of the criminal was apparent in the work of early prison reformers of the eighteenth century and must also have been of some concern to the clergy, who controlled prisons during the Middle Ages. Certainly the application of scientific statistical techniques to the study of crime preceded Lombroso by a half-century, as Lindesmith and Levin have pointed out.[7] A. M. Guerry (1802–1866) was particularly interested in the ecological distribution of crime, and A. Quetlet (1796–1874) emphasized the effects of sex, age, climate, and other factors upon the incidence of crime. Many others were of similar opinion. Lombroso's research merely directed the interest temporarily to the biological characteristics of the criminals, but the extensive scientific social data on crime prevented Lombroso from gaining any complete acceptance.[8]

Lombroso (1836–1909), who was a prison physician, conducted his series of anthropometric studies on Italian prisoners. At the time of his first publications on the subject he concluded that the criminal was atavistic, i.e., a throwback to more primitive ancestors and in general characterized by physical stigmata. These stigmata were commonly low forehead, cauliflower ears, projecting ears, receding chin, too many digits, etc. Other men had believed criminals had special physical deviations, but Lombroso was the first to try to measure them

[5] Cf. Edwin G. Boring, A History of Experimental Psychology, Appleton-Century, New York, 1929, p. 55, cited by Arthur E. Fink, op. cit., p. 19.
[6] Cf. chap. 5.
[7] Alfred Lindesmith and Yale Levin, "The Lombrosian Myth," American Journal of Sociology, 42:653–671 (March, 1937).
[8] Ibid.

exactly.[9] From the data Lombroso collected he educed his belief in the born criminal. That is, he maintained the true criminal was born with certain defects which more or less conditioned him to "moral depravity" and to violent and criminal behavior. Later he revised his viewpoint and added the epileptic criminal, the criminaloid, and the habitual criminal to his original classification. For the criminaloid the peculiar physical anomalies differed in degree but not in kind.[10] Criminaloids, he held, might become so habitually criminal through long confinement in prison as to be indistinguishable from born criminals aside from their slighter stigmata.[11] The epileptics were classified along with hysterical offenders and those who commit crimes under influence of liquor.

Lombroso even went so far as to relate physical characteristics of criminals to the type of offense they committed. He described the mobility of hands and face of the thief, and mentioned his scanty beard, projecting ears, abundant hair, thick lips, hoarse voice, etc. Murderers he found to have bloodshot eyes, aquiline noses, curly black hair, strong jaws, long ears, thin lips, and a menacing grin. Forgers and swindlers were described as wearing amiable smiles, having pale faces, small eyes, and large twisted noses, and being bald and gray at an early year, and of a feminine facial cast. Most criminologists have come to regard all this as so much nonsense. But the first effective disproof of any distinctive physical traits among criminals was that of Charles B. Goring, whose monumental study, *The English Convict*, we discuss later on in this chapter.

Meanwhile some of the leading penologists and sociologists of this period were unable to accept the notion that criminals were a special biological type because of evidence to the contrary. Frederick H. Wines, writing in 1895, for example, was unable to disprove "atavism" but he insisted that it was not a satisfactory explanation; that the tendency to commit crimes was not due to heredity but to environmental causes.[12] Similarly Charles R. Henderson, in his book on *Dependents, Defectives and Delinquents* in 1901, insisted that there was no true criminal type.[13]

[9] Cf. C. Bernaldo de Quiros, *Modern Theories of Criminality*, Little, Brown, Boston, 1911, pp. 4–5.

[10] Cesare Lombroso, *Crime, Its Causes and Remedies*, transl. by Henry P. Horton, Little, Brown, Boston, 1911, pp. 369–374.

[11] *Ibid.*, p. 374.

[12] Frederick H. Wines, *Punishment and Reformation*, Crowell, New York, 1895, pp. 247–249.

[13] Charles R. Henderson, *Introduction to the Study of the Dependent, Defective and Delinquent Classes*, Heath, Boston, 1901, chap. 2, "Causes of Crime," especially pp. 238–244.

There were a number of studies on the criminal brain during this period, but the research which was most important in leading to the abandonment of the general notion of a distinct criminal type was that of August Drähms and Frances Kellor. Drähms' book, an anthropometric study published in 1900, compared the cranial measurements of European criminals, Elmira Reformatory inmates, and Amherst students. From his data Drähms could find no evidence of a distinct criminal type. A year later Miss Kellor published her study of the cephalic indexes of 55 students, 60 white female criminals, and 90 Negro women criminals. These measurements showed relatively little difference between these three groups so far as their average cephalic index was concerned. Moreover, Kellor also pointed out that they all were not far different from the prostitutes and felons in Lombroso's study of female offenders.[14]

Specific Physical Traits and Criminality

Earnest A. Hooton revived the early interest in the physical traits of criminals a few years ago when he undertook an extensive study of the bodily characteristics of 10,953 male prisoners in prisons and reformatories, 2004 prisoners in county jails, 743 criminally insane persons, and 173 defective delinquents. These were divided into "Old American" native-white criminals and "New American" criminals, the latter including native white of foreign-born parentage and foreign born. These prisoners were compared with 1227 insane civilians and 1976 normal civilians (909 of the latter were white and 1067 were Negro or Negroid).

From his measurements Hooton summarized his findings as to the differences between Old American criminals and the civilian sample in Table 12.1. Analyzing these measurements according to offense, he came to certain other conclusions: Tall thin men were most likely to murder or to rob. Assaults were associated with short slender types. Burglary and larceny (in contrast to robbery) were associated with short slender or short medium build. The majority of forgers were tall. Sex offenders tended to be short and heavy. Recidivism, however, was most frequent among short slender groups; the minimum recidivism was with the tall heavy groups.[15]

[14] Frances Kellor, *Experimental Sociology*, Macmillan, New York, 1901, pp. 37–38, cited by Arthur E. Fink, *op. cit.*, pp. 120–121.

[15] Earnest A. Hooton, *Crime and the Man*, Harvard University Press, Cambridge, 1939, pp. 87–88. (This book is a popular account of the larger volume.)

TABLE 12.1.   Crude Metric Differences of Old
American Stock Criminals in Contrast with
Civilian Sample

Age	−3.80 years
Weight	−11.70 lbs.
Height	−1.02 cm.
Bicromial diameter	−0.45
Chest depth	−0.66
Chest breadth	−0.69
Head breadth	−0.81 mm.
Head height	−0.84 mm.
Circumference	−6.60
Face height	−0.70
Nose height	−1.84
Ear length	−2.40
Relative sitting height	+0.22
Facial index	−0.76
Nasal index	+1.96
Ear index	+1.88
Zygo-frontal	+0.48
Frontal-parietal	+0.69

SOURCE: Earnest A. Hooton, *The American Criminal*, Harvard
University Press, Cambridge, 1939, Vol. I. Table derived from
Table XI-32, Appendix.

Hooton also attached importance to the following morphological characteristics of criminals, as differentiated from civilians:

1. Tattooing is commoner among criminals.
2. Thinner beards and body hair and thicker head hair are commoner among criminals.
3. Criminals have straighter hair than civilians.
4. Red-brown hair is more characteristic of criminals, with less gray and white.
5. Criminals have blue-gray and mixed eyes to an excessive degree while civilians have more blue eyes and dark eyes. Eye-folds are commoner in criminals as are thin eyebrows.
6. Low and sloping foreheads are excessively common among criminals.
7. High, narrow nasal roots, high nasal bridges, undulating nasal profiles, nasal septa inclined upward and deflected laterally, with extreme variations in the thickness of the nasal tip are more frequent in criminals than in civilians.
8. Thin lips and compressed jaw angles are more frequent among criminals than civilians.
9. Criminals seldom have a marked over-bite.
10. The criminal's ear is more likely to have a roll helix, to protrude farther, and to be small than is a civilian's.

11. Long thin necks and sloping shoulders apply more frequently among criminals.[16]

Hooton made a special point of isolating the physical characteristics of persons committing first-degree murder and those committing second-degree murder. Such a refinement lacks scientific validity, as von Hentig points out. Whether or not a murder is classified as "first degree" or "second degree" depends on many items. Laws are often a bit hazy about the exact difference between the two, although first-degree murder is usually defined as premeditated killing. Many persons committing murder are permitted to plead guilty to the lesser offense of second-degree murder so that a conviction can be secured. Resisting a policeman and killing him in a gunfire duel is usually punished as first-degree murder, even though the murderer regards it as "shooting in self-defense." Killing a victim in the course of committing burglary or robbery often involves a first-degree conviction despite the lack of premeditation.[17]

Even so, von Hentig believes certain physical traits may be linked with crime and delinquency. In this connection he summarizes the views of a number of authorities pointing to the relation between "excessive vigor" and criminal behavior. The exceptional strength evidenced in wrestlers, prize fighters, "strong-arm" men is often displayed by criminals. It may also be displayed by policemen. The deformed noses so common among criminals he attributes to blows from police or other strong "opponents."[18] Dr. von Hentig was trained in medicine as well as in law and criminology, hence he probably gives greater credence to certain physiological traits than do most criminologists. One of these is red hair. He also believes physical defects may be related to delinquent behavior.

HEREDITY

The idea that criminality is a hereditary factor has been completely discredited by present-day criminologists. Surprising as it may seem to contemporary students, the belief that man inherited proclivities to steal, murder, lie, plunder, and commit rape has been widely held throughout history and actually has been discarded only recently. The notion that criminality was inherited stems, it would seem, from two different concepts: (1) the idea that criminality is associated with specific criminal traits and (2) the theological view that the sins of the fathers are visited upon their children unto the third and fourth

16 *Ibid.*, p. 301.   17 Hans von Hentig, *op. cit.*, pp. 13–15.   18 *Ibid.*, p. 48.

generation. Obviously the Lombrosian doctrine of the relation between defective physical structure and criminal behavior inevitably
promoted belief in the hereditary character of criminality since physical traits are inherited according to fairly definite laws.

Most of the criminologists and penologists of the latter part of the
nineteenth century gave credence to such a theory. In fact this idea
was thought to be established because studies of criminals showed
them to have criminal ancestry. The reports of the inspectors of the
Pennsylvania Eastern State Penitentiary during the last quarter of the
nineteenth century are replete with findings of this sort. A study of
37 criminals convicted in 1878 showed every one had relatives in
prison. Reports beginning with 1880 listed the causes of crime, and
heredity, inherent depravity, and physical disease far outweighed all
the other 22 factors listed. (It is significant, however, that even then
environmental and family factors were recognized as important.[19]) Dr.
R. E. McVey of Kansas Medical College even attributed criminality
to "poverty of the blood," with which instability of brain and nervous
structure was associated, while the latter led to unstable habits and
vacillations in morality. McVey further stated that criminals were frequently offspring of alcoholics, epileptics, and those of unsound
mind.[20]

Henry M. Boies went so far as to regard all crime as a disease and
employed the technical jargon of causes of disease, then in vogue
among physicians, viz., the procatarctic, the proegumenal, and the
synectic. Moral depravity was thus regarded as the synectic cause of
depravity, which was due to abnormal condition of the organic structure. The proegumenal cause of criminality lay in the unbalanced relations between organs. These organs (witness to belief in phrenology)
included organs of selfish gratification and evil propensity! The
procatarctic causes of moral depravity (which produces the crime)
lay in inherited peculiarities, arrested nutrition, infection, etc. Boies
admitted, however, that there were social as well as physical causes of
crime.[21]

There were of course others who supported the idea that criminal
traits were inherited. Many medically trained men writing as late as
1914 adhered to such a view.[22] Many sociologists and psychologists of

[19] Cf. Arthur E. Fink, op. cit., pp. 151–164.
[20] R. E. McVey ,"Crime, Its Physiology and Pathogenesis, How Can Medical Men Aid
in Its Prevention," Kansas Medical Journal, 1–2:500 (June, 1890), cited by Arthur E.
Fink, op. cit., p. 163.
[21] Cf. Henry M. Boies, The Science of Penology, Putnam, New York, 1901, pp. 39–43.
[22] Cf. Winfield Scott Hall, "The Relation of Crime to Adolescence," Bulletin of the
Academy of Medicine, 15:86–96 (April, 1914).

the period also accepted it. Philip A. Parsons in his treatise *Responsibility for Crime* agreed with Dugdale that the tendency to criminality was inherited,[23] and Paul E. Bowers in his study of 100 recidivists claimed that 56 bore a neuropathic taint, while 17 were psychopaths.[24] Naturally many professors of criminology trained in this period held to a belief in inherited criminality until it was adequately disproved.

PHYSICAL HANDICAPS AND CRIMINALITY
The Crippled

The lame, the deformed, and the maimed all unquestionably suffer from social ostracism and are handicapped in marriage opportunities, in securing employment, and in numerous other ways. Effective education and exceptional personality qualities are required to face life serenely with the knowledge that one is physically handicapped, particularly if one is physically repulsive. The pent-up resentment of the man with a club foot or the woman with a twisted cheek may find expression in thieving or in crimes of a violent, emotional sort, and on occasion against a person more favored in physical attributes. Even an abnormally ugly nose can cause a man to writhe when taunted, as the play *Cyrano de Bergerac* well demonstrates.

Nevertheless cripples and defectives constitute only a small proportion of criminals and delinquents. A study of German prisoners in 93 penal institutions showed that there were approximately 5.5 cripples per 1000 prisoners.[25] Many of those crippled are so because of injuries received accidentally or in warfare, but some prisoners are congenital cripples and others have undoubtedly been wounded in the course of their illegal activities.

In general we must believe that it is the mental and emotional reaction to the crippled condition that results in abnormal behavior rather than the defect itself. This is of course conditioned by the shrinking attitudes and pity of the physically normal. Were there no rejection of the crippled the latter would hold no resentment. A sizable share of the defectives have been wards of the state in times past because of economic and other disadvantages, but modern methods of vocational rehabilitation of the handicapped should reduce the

[23] Philip A. Parsons, *Responsibility for Crime*, Columbia University Studies in History, Economics and Public Law, 34:70–83 (1909), cited by Arthur E. Fink, op. cit., p. 173.

[24] Paul E. Bowers, "The Recidivist," *Journal of Criminal Law and Criminology*, 5:404–415 (September, 1914).

[25] Max Hagemann, "Gebrechen," *Handworterbuch der Kriminologie*, Vol. I, p. 498, cited by von Hentig, op. cit., p. 70.

hazard of violent or antisocial conduct, as well as need for relief, among this group.

Blindness and Other Ailments of the Eye and Criminality

BLINDNESS

Because of the widespread public and private facilities for aiding the blind, most blind persons have some sort of assistance in overcoming their handicap. Many of the blind unquestionably resent living in darkness and the need for securing their impressions of the world chiefly through tactile and auditory impressions. Nervous and emotional disturbances are far more frequent among the blind than are any real delinquencies.

STRABISMUS

Strabismus is an eye disorder occasioned by inability to co-ordinate the muscles of both eyes. There are two forms, "wall-eyed" strabismus and "cross-eyed" strabismus. According to Salsetto, strabismus affected 10 per cent of the women prisoners and 7.5 per cent of those convicted of homicide.[26] Lombroso also held that 16 per cent of thieves were cross-eyed.[27] We must remember that these conclusions were for a much earlier period and if the data are reliable they still give no certainty of any causal relation between defect and delinquency. Undoubtedly many other factors—poverty, neglect, associations, etc.— were relevant in the specific crimes.

Left-Handedness

According to Havelock Ellis left-handedness is common among criminals.[28] Ellis, Lombroso, and others have assumed that greater strength or squeezing power in the left hand gave the criminal special advantage over his victim, even where there was no true left-handedness.[29] Hans von Hentig surveyed a wide number of researches in the field but came to the conclusion that the existing data were inconclusive with reference to this factor. Even so he is unwilling to dismiss altogether the disdain for left-handedness as expressed in literature,

[26] Cited by Cesare Lombroso in *The Female Offender*, p. 79.
[27] *Ibid.*, p. 80.
[28] Havelock Ellis, *The Criminal*, London, p. 76, cited by Hans von Hentig, *op. cit.*, p. 51.
[29] Cf. Gina Lombroso Ferrero, *Criminal Man According to the Classification of Cesare Lombroso*, Putnam, New York, 1911, p. 21.

folklore, proverbs, and mores. Where ambidexterity, or left-handedness, enters the picture von Hentig believes it may have some relation to crime, particularly in the case of left-handed murderers, whose victims could not parry their thrusts.[30]

Red Hair

Red hair, according to von Hentig, is probably associated with criminal behavior, as we mentioned earlier. Dr. von Hentig is a brilliant scholar and obviously does not think all redheads are criminal. He believes that social attitudes toward red hair and the aversion many persons have for it may affect the behavior of persons with such coloring. He also suggests that "red heads suffer for their non-conformity." From this he concludes that the redhead's irritation may result in antisocial behavior.[31]

In an article on "Redhead and Outlaw" von Hentig further contends that there was a surprising number of redheads among the outlaws on the advancing American frontier. He is of the opinion that the quick, nervous, and irritable reactions of red-haired persons have been a factor in their outlawry. Indeed he cites numerous books dealing with bandits and outlaws which indicate that Jesse James, Sam Brown, and Sam Bass had red beards, and James Casey had sandy hair. Quantrill's hair is said to have had a reddish luster, and Charlie Harper and Wild Bill Hickock had auburn hair, to mention a few others. Von Hentig includes many more.[32] Since most red-haired persons appear to be relatively well-adjusted members of society any serious acceptance of hair color as a factor in crime seems dubious, however.

Endocrine Imbalance and Crime

Physicians have long associated certain types of disease with emotional and behavior disturbances. In fact, disturbed behavior is often a symptom of disease. Persons who are ill (or fatigued, for that matter) often are irritable, unreasonable, and less controlled in their behavior than usual. They likewise may be temporarily irrational while running a high temperature. Endocrine imbalance has been definitely correlated with peculiar personality characteristics which latter have been definitely altered in turn by proper medication. In consequence

[30] Hans von Hentig, op. cit., pp. 57–64.

[31] Ibid., p. 55.

[32] Hans von Hentig, "Redhead and Outlaw," Journal of Criminal Law and Criminology, 38:1–6 (May–June, 1947).

certain specialists in biochemistry became enthusiastic supporters of the theory that crime is a function of glandular disturbances. Walter B. Cannon and George W. Crile were among the first to relate bodily ailments and emotional disturbances to defective functioning of the endocrine glands.[33] This view was carried a step further by Kretschmer and S. J. Smith[34] and was popularized by Max G. Schlapp and Edward H. Smith in their book *The New Criminology*. The latter maintained that crime itself is rooted in the emotional disturbances occasioned by undersecretion or oversecretion from the endocrine glands.[35]

Louis Berman's researches gave further impetus to the idea. In fact, he believed he had established a conclusive relationship between crime and glandular malfunctioning in his study of prisoners at Sing Sing in 1931.[36] Here he maintained the prisoners were found to have defective glandular activity 2 or 3 times as frequently as was true of the general population.[37] The idea that criminal behavior is rooted in glandular defects has had wide popular appeal, but there has been little scientific evidence supporting Berman's point of view. For one thing, criminality is much more widespread than might be supposed from the number of the persons arrested and convicted, as we have already made clear. Nevertheless it has been comforting to many persons to be able to differentiate criminals thus.

The dangers inherent in accepting such conclusions before they are confirmed by much more extensive research are legion. For example, the author knows a medical officer of a boys' industrial school in the Middle West who ordered all the boys to be given mild doses of thyroid, without checking the metabolism of a single boy, with the idea that their antisocial tendencies would automatically decrease.

Goring's Study of the English Convict

Although many intelligent persons did not accept the conclusions of Lombroso nor for that matter those of the neo-Lombrosianists, they had no data to offset them. It was not until Charles B. Goring made a comparative anthropometric study of 3000 English convicts and an

[33] Cf. Walter B. Cannon, *Bodily Changes in Pain, Hunger, Fear and Rage*, Appleton-Century-Crofts, New York, 1915, and George W. Crile, *The Origins and Nature of the Emotions*, Saunders, Philadelphia, 1915.

[34] Cf. E. Kretschmer, *Physique and Character*, Harcourt, Brace, New York, 1925, and S. J. Smith, "The Relation Between Persistent Thymus Gland to Criminology," *Medical Record*, 99:438 (March, 1931).

[35] Published by Boni and Liveright, New York, 1928.

[36] Cf. Louis Berman, *Glands Regulating Personality*, Macmillan, New York, 1921, and Louis Berman, *New Creations in Human Beings*, Doubleday, New York, 1938.

[37] Louis Berman, *New Creations in Human Beings*, pp. 242–250.

equal number of Cambridge University students that any proof that criminals did not carry distinctive physical characteristics could be offered. Goring's research was published in 1913. Goring not only took the skull measurements of the two groups. He also recorded the height, weight, and arm span as well as general physical characteristics of strength and muscular condition of each group.

From these measurements Goring found no differences between prisoners and non-prisoners except that the prisoners were slightly shorter, weighed less, and had slightly smaller skulls. These differences he considered too small to be significant. He then made comparative studies of students from Oxford, Cambridge, London, and Aberdeen universities, officers and men from the Royal Engineers, and faculty members of the University of London. From these data he concluded that prisoners differed less from the total group than the Oxford and Cambridge students differed from each other. So far as peculiarities of physique or stigmata were concerned, they thus were no more characteristic of criminals than of students. Goring believed, however, that the slighter weight and height might be partially responsible for their conviction in that they were related to poor economic status. In the light of today's understanding it would seem to be their economic condition, rather than their undersize, that led to conviction.

On the other hand, Goring was reluctant to ignore the factor of heredity altogether and with somewhat dubious reasoning decided that because there was a correlation of +.60 for imprisonment of father and son and a correlation for brothers of +.45 the tendency to criminality was inherited.[38] Sutherland has made a very adequate disposal of Goring's conclusions on this point by showing that Goring virtually ignored family influence and other environmental factors which would account for the son's following in his father's footsteps.[39]

INTELLIGENCE AND CRIME

Looking for some differentiation between criminals and university students and officers, Goring concluded that criminals were essentially less intelligent than the others.[40] Since the students and officers were a selected group, he was probably right. Any fair study of the mental differences between criminal and noncriminal groups should be made

[38] Cf. Charles B. Goring, The English Convict: A Statistical Study, His Majesty's Stationery Office, London, 1913, pp. 200, 263, 365.

[39] Edwin H. Sutherland, Principles of Criminology, Lippincott, Philadelphia, rev. ed., 1947, pp. 85–86.

[40] Charles B. Goring, op. cit., p. 262.

by comparing persons from similar economic and social backgrounds. The lower mental ability of prisoners seemed plausible at the time Goring made his study on other counts. Psychological testing was a new device and many psychologists and sociologists of the period were convinced that criminals (along with other social deviates) were behavior problems chiefly because they were lacking in intelligence. It was held that such persons could not make satisfactory decisions and govern their conduct accordingly.

Henry H. Goddard, a prominent psychologist of the time, was particularly enthusiastic about the theory that feeble-mindedness was *the clue to delinquency*. In 1914 he stated in his book, *Juvenile Delinquent*,[41] that feeble-mindedness was the single most proximate cause of delinquency, and again in 1920 he stated that the greatest single cause of delinquency and crime was low-grade mentality.[42] Goddard subsequently revised his viewpoint and has more lately admitted that everyone is a potential delinquent.

Virtually all the studies made during this time, however, indicated that a high percentage of juvenile delinquents were subnormal mentally. Healy and Bronner found 14 per cent of the Chicago children in their study were feeble-minded, 14 per cent were psychopathic, 5 per cent were psychotic, and 2 per cent were neurotic.[43]

The present author's study of Sleighton Farm girls published in 1929 covered cases which had been given mental tests by various psychologists during the period from 1916 through 1920. According to these tests, the Sleighton Farm girls were of normal mentality in only 27 per cent of the cases, dull normal in 10 per cent, borderline in 21.5 per cent, and moron in 41.5 per cent. Three cases in the group were imbeciles.[44] These girls were chiefly sex delinquents, and sex delinquency is more generally associated with low mentality than are other types of delinquency and crime. However, the commonly accepted notion that criminals and delinquents are low grade in mentality may well have influenced the psychologists unwittingly in giving the scores, although this is impossible to prove.

What constitutes feeble-mindedness had not been accurately defined at that time. Even so, it must be admitted that the feeble-minded are probably more easily led into crime and delinquency than

[41] Published by Macmillan, New York, 1914, p. 22.

[42] Cf. Henry H. Goddard, *Human Efficiency and Levels of Intelligence*, Princeton University Press, Princeton, 1920, pp. 73–74.

[43] William Healy and Augusta F. Bronner, *Delinquents and Criminals, Their Making and Unmaking*, Macmillan, New York, 1926, Table 49, p. 274.

[44] Mabel A. Elliott, *Correctional Education and the Delinquent Girl*, Commonwealth of Pennsylvania, Harrisburg, 1929, p. 30.

more intelligent persons, if only because the former have less ability to think critically. Subsequent studies seem to indicate, however, that criminals are not very different in intelligence from the rank-and-file population. For Dr. Herman M. Adler and Myrtle R. Worthington concluded from their study of the prisoners at Joliet State Prison, in Illinois, that the Illinois prisoners ranked higher mentally than the men in the United States Army in World War I.[45] Later, after making a comparison of a number of studies, Leslie D. Zeleny concluded that the ratio of mental deficiency among delinquents and criminals and that of the general population was 1.2 to 1—not any enormous difference.[46] Because some persons alleged that the Adler and Worthington study should have compared Illinois prisoners with Illinois soldiers, Simon H. Tulchin carried the research a step further by comparing the men in the Illinois State Penitentiary and at the Illinois State Reformatory at Pontiac with men from the Illinois army draft for World War I. Tulchin found that the Illinois prisoners and the Illinois draftees ranked much the same in intelligence.[47] (There meanwhile is some presumption that Illinois soldiers ranked higher than the average draftees in World War I because of the illiteracy among Negroes in the southern states.)

Today it is thus generally recognized that whatever the relationship of intelligence to crime it is not ordinarily a precipitating factor. Certain types of crime require a high type of intelligence, as in case of the embezzler, who otherwise would not have a position in which it was possible to embezzle. On the other hand, a stupid man of low mentality is more likely to be led into a plot in which he takes excessive risks for relatively little reward. By and large, mental ability varies among criminals just as it does among the general population. There are clever crooks, but even these occasionally get caught, as the indictments following the Kefauver Crime Commission hearings have so well witnessed.

EMOTIONAL DISORDERS AND CRIMINALITY

The fact that low-grade mental ability was shown not to be the key to criminal behavior did not detract from the belief that criminal be-

[45] Herman M. Adler and Myrtle R. Worthington, "The Scope of the Problem of Delinquency and Crime as Related to Mental Deficiency," *Journal of Psycho-Asthenics,* 30:47–57 (1925).

[46] Leslie D. Zeleny, "Feeblemindedness and Criminal Conduct," *American Journal of Sociology,* 38:564–578 (January, 1933).

[47] Simon H. Tulchin, *Intelligence and Crime,* University of Chicago Press, Chicago, 1939, p. 12.

havior was closely related to the personality of the offender. Research into the personality characteristics of the criminal still persisted. To persons dealing with criminals it seemed obvious that something in the criminals' make-up made them rebel against the socially accepted rules of conduct. All ideas are said to be related to the intellectual climate in which they develop and this theory appears to be well illustrated in the emotional theories which developed with reference to human conduct.

Ours is the age of Freud, or the psychiatric age, just as truly as it is the age of chemistry and the age of the atomic bomb. Psychiatrists are physicians who are specialists in mental and emotional disorders. They deal with patients who are unhappy, frustrated persons, beset by fears and inhibitions, as well as with those who are psychotic and the victims of delusions and hallucinations. From their study and analysis of these persons the psychiatrists have become convinced that human behavior can be explained effectively only by its drives or motivations.

The Psychiatrist's Conception of Emotional Disturbances

Since criminals are sometimes mentally disturbed, the psychiatrist soon extended his interest to the field of criminal behavior. Although psychiatrists do not all agree in all the details of human motivation they more or less concur in their acceptance of certain basic concepts. Chief among the concepts which refer to human personality are the *id*, the *libido*, the *ego*, and the *super-ego*.

The *id* is the term employed to indicate the great reservoir of human drives, which seldom come to the surface of awareness. In other words the *id* is the *unconscious*. The *libido* is the sexual energy of the individual and (according to Freud in particular) is the basic aspect of all life energy, or the "will to live."[48] The *ego* is the conscious personality whereas the *id* is submerged. The *id* is the source of all the primitive animal drives or what were formerly called instincts. The *super-ego* is the evaluative and standard enforcing aspect of personality and is more or less synonymous with what we call "conscience" in popular parlance. The *super-ego* is the force which restrains us when we reply politely to someone who annoys us, makes us offer food to others first when we are ravenous ourselves, or leads us to treat a person kindly when he has intentionally injured us. The *super-ego* thus incorporates the individual's "social training" which he has received

[48] Cf. Sigmund Freud, *Civilization and Its Discontents*, transl. by Jean Riviere, Hogarth, London, 1930.

at the hands of his parents, the church, the school, and the community in general.

Sometimes, according to the psychiatrists, the restraints imposed on the ego by the super-ego result in serious tensions which manifest themselves in fears, resentments, or overt criminal behavior. In consequence many persons fail to measure up to their standard of conduct as reflected in the super-ego and develop a strong sense of guilt. This may lead to neuroses or psychoses, or to overt criminal conduct which occurs (according to many psychiatrists) literally because of a desire for punishment in order to offset the deep sense of guilt.

Personality, as we now understand it (sociologically), is the related traits of the individual which determine his role in the group. These in turn are largely the result of the individual's training and experiences within the group. They stem from the generally accepted standards of the group and the admonitions and prohibitions which are enforced with varying degrees of rigidity by the society in which the individual is born, is reared, and grows to adulthood.

The emotionally mature individual, according to psychiatric thinking, is he who has learned to control his emotions effectively and who lives at peace with himself and in harmony with the standards of conduct which are acceptable to the group. The concept of emotional maturity is difficult to define effectively yet everyone recognizes what for want of better words is called "immature" or "childish" behavior. According to Bromberg, immature persons (1) rebel against rules and regulations, (2) tend to engage in hyperactivity, (3) wear bizarre or unusual clothing or indulge in tattooing, or (4) have feelings of inferiority or guilt with reference to sex.[49]

The psychiatrist does not ignore environmental or other factors completely, but he believes criminal behavior is the result (in part at least) of unconscious motives. Thus the thief who steals some article for which he has no use may be striking back at the victim or may be getting even with a despised parent. Some crimes are not motivated basically by either of these desires but by a sense of guilt which yearns for punishment. Thus many criminals (murderers, for example) leave clues for detection. A piece of string, a fingerprint, or a weapon may be a means of locating the criminal. Similarly one whose crime involves a neurotic element—such as a sex murder, arson, or kleptomania—usually revisits the scene of his crime. Psychiatrists are pretty well agreed that a criminal of this type wants to be arrested and convicted. In other words he seeks punishment, usually wishes to remain de-

[49] Walter Bromberg, *Crime and the Mind*, Lippincott, Philadelphia, 1948, p. 117.

pendent, and at the same time has great resentment toward society. These attitudes result in a mixed feeling, the desire for revenge and guilt reactions which demand punishment. Committing a crime is thus a variety of chronic suicide. Alexander and Staub say that punishment provides the motive for the neurotic criminal's crimes.[50]

The Psychoses and Criminality

The conflict between the *super-ego* and the *ego* may occur without affecting the individual's intellectual orientation. Even if the conflict becomes serious it may result in neuroses or physical illnesses of a psychosomatic nature without any emotional disturbance. Or the emotional strain may be so great that the individual escapes reality into the world of delusions and hallucinations and develops a true psychosis.

Psychoses are generally classified as (1) those due to organic disease and brain injury and (2) those which are functional disturbances of emotional origin. Obviously any brain injury or diseased condition of the brain which alters the individual's judgment or capacity for self-restraint will affect his behavior. If the organic condition is such that he is mentally disoriented his behavior may take absurd, dangerous, or antisocial directions. When the deranged individual suffers delusions he may attack his alleged "enemies" or commit very serious crimes.[51]

The most common types of psychoses, the manic-depressive psychoses, schizophrenia, paranoia, and involutional melancholia, bulk large among the group of offenders known as the "criminal insane."

Manic-Depressive Psychoses and Crime

If the psychosis is pronounced and violent (as it often is in well-developed manic-depressive cases), the patient is usually placed under supervision in an institution where he is unable to commit any very serious offense, but he may still commit minor offenses. If his mania is less advanced it may go undetected until he commits some grave offense. Such persons sometimes play rather serious "practical jokes," disregard decencies in dress, or commit sex offenses. In the

[50] Karl A. Menninger, *Man Against Himself*, Harcourt, Brace, New York, 1938, Part II, chap. 4, "Anti-Social Behavior." Cf. also Franz Alexander and Hugo Staub, *The Criminal, the Judge and the Public*, transl. by Gregory Zilborg, Macmillan, New York, 1931.

[51] J. R. Rees, "Mental Variations and Criminal Behavior," chap. 1 in L. Radzinowicz and J. W. C. Turner (eds.), *Mental Abnormality and Crime*, English Studies in Criminal Science, Vol. II, Macmillan, London, 1944, pp. 1–7.

depressive phase of the manic-depressive syndrome or in pure melancholia cases the patient may attempt suicide or murder. Usually the depressed patient believes he is saving the victim or victims of murder from torture.[52] The author of this text once gave mental tests to manic-depressive cases in a state hospital. One such case cut up her baby and fried it on top of a stove in order "to keep it from suffering." Obviously these "altruistic" motives are the unconscious motives of destruction, hate, and fear which need to be uncovered before the patient can be cured (if the psychoanalytic theory is correct).

Involutional Melancholia

Involutional melancholia is a depressive mental disease of late middle life and apparently occurs more frequently among women than men. It involves no retardation in intellectual function but is characterized by great anxiety, a sense of guilt, feelings of inferiority. Often there is also an imaginary physical illness. The patient is irritable and aggressive and may occasionally assault another person violently with a mallet, skillet, etc.[53]

Schizophrenia

Schizophrenia is the term now generally applied to what was formerly called dementia praecox. The disease is characterized by progressive mental deterioration (along with deterioration of the whole personality). There are numerous forms of schizophrenia which we shall not attempt to discuss in detail. All forms are serious; relatively few schizophrenics recover. Likewise relatively few commit serious offenses, and for 2 reasons: The patients are so emotionally disorganized that they are usually institutionalized hence have little opportunity to commit crimes. And most such persons are quiet, timid, and withdrawn into the realm of their hallucinations. Some are paranoiac and believe they are God—or acting as His emissary. At other times the paranoiac is Napoleon, or some other notable historic figure.

Paranoia

Paranoia is also classified as a distinct type of chronic mental illness. In this disease there are systematic delusions but the memory

[52] Angus Macniven, "Psychoses and Criminal Responsibility," in L. Radzinowicz and J. W. C. Turner (eds.), op. cit., pp. 8–16.
[53] Ibid., p. 18.

is unimpaired. The individual is full of suspicion and believes he is the victim of hostility on every hand. Paranoia is, according to Freud, closely associated with homosexual interests which have been denied and projected. Paranoid types of personalities seldom are hospitalized because they are usually able to take care of themselves and are in general harmless.

Nevertheless paranoiacs sometimes commit murder and other violent crimes and *they are potentially dangerous*. Sometimes they assault or try to kill persons whom they have never known. Sometimes they try to assassinate public officials. Sometimes they commit libel or assassinate the character of innocent persons orally.[54] Such paranoiacs frequently write obscene letters—in fact the majority of obscene letter writers are paranoiacs. They also commit embezzlement. Other types of offenses include drunkenness and neglect of family.[55]

Paranoia is a difficult disease to diagnose for the patient usually protests against any diagnosis or detention. If the case comes to court he may be clever enough to make the diagnosing physician the one who "looks queer." Nevertheless even though "relatively harmless," such persons may commit many petty offenses, and in case of libelous conduct or in the writing of obscene or threatening letters they may be a menace to other persons' peace of mind.

The Extent of Mental Disease Among Prisoners

Reports on the extent of psychopathic or mentally ill offenders in prison have varied remarkably. For example, statistics gathered with reference to mental disorders among New York City and Massachusetts offenders showed that approximately 16 per cent of the New York prisoners were mentally disturbed or genuinely psychotic. Three-fourths of the 82.3 per cent considered normal were classified as having personality defects.[56] In contrast, from 90 to 96.7 per cent of the murderers, burglars, embezzlers, and those convicted of fraud, rape, and other sex offenses who were committed to Illinois State Penitentiary in 1939–1940 were considered to have some gross defect from a psychiatric point of view.[57] The utility and reliability of psychiatric judgment behind these opinions have been questioned by many per-

[54] Cf. Lawson G. Lowrey, *Psychiatry for Social Workers*, Columbia University Press, New, York, 1950, pp. 213–220.

[55] *Ibid.*

[56] Walter Bromberg and Charles B. Thompson, "The Relation of Psychoses, Mental Defect and Personality Type to Types of Crime," *Journal of Criminal Law and Criminology*, 28:70–89 (May–June, 1937).

[57] Data cited by Hans von Hentig, *The Criminal and His Victim*, p. 171.

sons. Among the various critics, Michael Hakeem has made a devastating attack upon what he calls the naïve, unscientific pronunciamentos which he found in reading 825 psychiatric reports chosen at random from 3500 cases of prisoners in the Illinois State Penitentiary. Hakeem declared, in fact, that the prison psychiatrists made trivial, obvious, and unscientific statements concerning prisoners and frequently summarized their whole reaction to their interviewees in a moralistic evaluation of the offender. Dr. Hakeem further maintained that few psychiatrists conducted any sort of tests from which they derived their conclusions, but that they recorded the reactions of the prisoner during the interview and presumed this to be characteristic of the convict's total behavior.[58]

In addition to the mental diseases resulting from organic lesions and functional psychoses many authorities give considerable space to the disturbing effects of alcohol and narcotic addiction in precipitating criminal offenses. These are discussed in Chapter 7. "Special Types of Offenders," hence will not be considered here.

From our knowledge of the nature of emotional conflicts and the relation between emotional disturbances (or mental illnesses) and crimes it should be clear that some offenses are unquestionably committed by persons who are seriously disturbed. We have no reason to believe, however, that crime is essentially a result of mental illness, unless we subscribe to the notion that all criminality is *ipso facto* an evidence of mental illness. Psychiatrists who are familiar with sociological literature on crime seldom make such an assumption.

The evidence as to the extent of mental disease among criminals is itself confusing. Since the most serious cases of mental illness are usually exempt from criminal prosecution, they are not a part of the statistics of crime. Where psychiatrists have examined the rank and file of criminals under consideration they have usually reported a rather high incidence of mental disorders, psychopathic conditions, or emotional instability, as we have stated.

Neuroses and Criminality

A neurosis is a mild nervous disorder in which there is neither intellectual disorientation nor systematic delusions. The neurotic who becomes a criminal is in Bromberg's opinion acting in a symbolic way

[58] Michael Hakeem, "An Evaluation of Case Reports Prepared by Psychiatrists in Penal and Correctional Institutions and Set Ups of Various Types," unpublished paper delivered at the American Sociological Society in Chicago, December 28, 1946.

to gratify an unconscious impulse. Theft may be an expression of a neurosis, particularly burglary since it is a furtive, stealthy crime and thus in itself is (according to Bromberg) an indication of inferiority feelings. Similarly the "low-value" type of burglaries in which lead pipe, scrap metal, etc., are stolen from an abandoned house may be regarded as an expression of self-depreciation. There are many varieties of stealing which involve taking objects for which the offender has no use. Most of these crimes psychiatrists would explain as the result of early hostility to parents, or sibling rivalry. Even the professional burglar may have a deep sense of early deprivation which he is unconsciously trying to offset. Robbers are a different matter, for their offenses require aggression for items they consciously desire, but they too may have hidden feelings of inferiority (which are to be offset by the value of the robbery). Larceny and swindling similarly may involve desire for self-esteem through acquiring valuable goods. Arson or pyromania may be related to other neurotic ambitions but are usually associated with sex impulses.[59]

The Psychopathic Personality and Crime

The psychopaths (popularly known as cranks, eccentrics, or just plain "queer") are borderline mental cases. They are not psychotic, but they are ill balanced, are often very depressed or very exalted, and include the group frequently described as hysterical.[60] Since the term includes such a variety of deviations from the norm, most psychiatrists do not consider this classification a specific type of mental deviate, although Karpman so regards it.[61] According to Abrahamsen, psychopaths fall into three general groups: (1) the predominantly aggressive, (2) the predominantly passive or inadequate, and (3) the predominantly creative.[62]

The psychopaths who are predominantly aggressive are the ones who commit crimes, especially murder, suicide, and sex offenses. The nonaggressive and creative psychopaths obviously do not fall into the criminal group. Many sexual deviates, particularly the homosexual, also fall under the psychopathic classification. Drug addicts and alcoholics are likewise sometimes called psychopathic. In any event alco-

[59] Walter Bromberg, op. cit., chap. 6, "The Neurotic Offender."
[60] David Abrahamsen, Crime and the Human Mind, Columbia University Press, New York, 1945, p. 113.
[61] Benjamin Karpman, "The Problem of the Psychopathist," Psychiatric Quarterly, 4:495–526 (1929), cited by David Abrahamsen, op. cit., p. 114.
[62] David Abrahamsen, op. cit., p. 113.

holism may be considered a symptom of defective personality. Gray and Moore's research on the type of offenses committed under influence of alcohol showed a much higher percentage of assault and violence among alcoholics than among nonalcoholic offenders.[63]

Offenders with Distorted Super-Egos

According to Abrahamsen the habitual or professional criminals and gangsters are persons whose *ego* and *super-ego* approve of their criminal conduct. These persons show no remorse and fear no punishment. They are in no sense insane, but they have no consideration for social well-being or the welfare of the group.[64]

Psychiatry and Scientific Criminology

Despite the widespread general interest in psychiatry and the public attention and lip service paid to psychiatrists, we are forced to recognize that many aspects of human personality and its motivations are still *terra incognita*. For with all of our psychological and psychiatric devices for probing the inner recesses of the mind the isolated character of mental processes still remains. Everyone must live within himself and there are limits beyond which the most skilled psychoanalyst cannot penetrate. Much of what psychiatrists advance as scientific cannot be tested; whatever the validity of psychiatric theories at present they have not been scientifically proved. Many psychiatrists make nebulous and hazy statements about prisoners or other patients that defy substantiation, as Hakeem has pointed out. Much of psychiatry is thus still a matter of faith. Psychiatrists repeat a jargon and apply a schematized pattern of analysis to virtually all their cases. Even so, they have opened up a whole new field for personality research in their explorations of the forgotten and deeply buried experiences and the unconscious motivations of men.

Since all offenders have rebelled against social codes and many have continuously flouted them, they have obviously acted unwisely or "immaturely" from the point of view of the group. Their particular behavior has got them in trouble. Sociologists are interested in discovering whether the persons arrested and convicted of crimes are more emotionally unstable than the general population. At present

---

[63] M. A. Gray and Merrill Moore, "Incidence and Significance of Alcoholism in the History of Criminals," *Journal of Criminal Psychopathology*, 111:316 (October, 1941).

[64] David Abrahamsen, *op. cit.*, pp. 125–126.

that question cannot be answered. We have not thus far devised satisfactory emotional tests, much less applied them to the general population. In an age when there are so many international tensions and
such understandable fears of atomic warfare, many people are anxious
and worried. Their fears and anxieties explain why books entitled
Peace of Mind and *Confident Living* have been best sellers. Other
persons beset by fears have sought out the psychoanalyst's couch—
when they could afford it. But we have no reason to assume that emotional instability or fears or tensions always result in criminal offenses, even though these emotional disturbances may make living
difficult both for those affected and for their associates. People who are
motivated by selfish tendencies, who are aggressive and even hostile,
may achieve success as corporation heads or members of Congress, or
they may rule their families with an iron hand. The psychiatrist is a
trifle like the Quaker in finding everyone queer "but thee and me."
The sociologist sometimes thinks the psychiatrist is a little queer,
whereas the sociologist probably appears to be a bit emotionally immature in the eyes of the psychiatrist.

In conclusion, we may agree with the psychiatrist in recognizing
that any type of mental illness or emotional disturbance, even though
slight, affects the individual's behavior. It is important, however, for
us to recognize that the irritability and tensions characteristic of such
disturbance need not result in criminal behavior.

Personality Differences Between Delinquents and Nondelinquents

THE MONACHESI STUDY

In a recent study conducted by Dr. Elio D. Monachesi and a group
of graduate students at the University of Minnesota there was an attempt to differentiate the personality characteristics of delinquents
and nondelinquents by giving them the Minnesota Multiphasic Personality Inventory. This inventory was made up of 12 personality
scales which aimed to measure any similarity in response between
the individuals tested and a sample of persons tested who had been
diagnosed as emotionally disturbed.[65]

When the inventory was given to a group of 101 delinquent girls
and 85 nondelinquent girls who came from approximately the same
school grades and were equated for rural-urban residence, the delin-

[65] Elio D. Monachesi, "Some Personality Characteristics of Delinquents and Non-
Delinquents," *Journal of Criminal Law and Criminology*, 38:487–500 (January–February,
1948).

quent girls were found to differ markedly from the nondelinquents. Furthermore, the delinquent girls were much more like the emotionally disturbed group in their responses than were the nondelinquent.[66] In order to test the inventory further, it was given to 55 other delinquent girls and 90 nondelinquent girls and to 75 delinquent boys and 85 nondelinquents. In each case the individuals were selected because of their availablity and their comparable social and economic status. Thirty-three of the 55 delinquent girls were on probation from the juvenile court in St. Paul, 22 were confined in the Hennepin County (Minnesota) Home School (for delinquents). Of the 75 delinquent boys 29 were in the Hennepin County Home School and 22 were from the adjoining Ramsey County Home School. Nine were on probation from the Minneapolis juvenile court. The nondelinquent girls and boys were members of organized groups or high school classes. Forty-eight girls belonged to the Girl Reserves, 12 to the Girl Scouts, 30 attended 2 high school classes. The Boy Scouts claimed membership of 33 of the boys, 15 belonged to recreational groups in a settlement house, 15 belonged to a Hi-Y group, 22 were attending two high school classes.[67] The nondelinquents all belonged to groups in neighborhoods in which the delinquents lived then or at some previous time. The neighborhoods belonged chiefly to the lower-income group.

The second instance again showed a marked difference in the mean standard scores as achieved by the delinquent and nondelinquent girls. The results for the boys, however, were upsetting. Even more frequently than the delinquents, the nondelinquents exhibited the same personality traits as those clinically diagnosed as suffering with psycho-asthenia, schizophrenia, hypomania! Pressed to explain these findings, Monachesi suggested that it is possible that a large share of the boys in the "character building" groups may be boys "with personality difficulties just as serious as those found among delinquents."[68] The findings would seem to indicate to this author, however, that the nondelinquent boys were more abnormal in their personality make-up than the delinquents! In any event there is some reason to suppose that all persons have behavior problems and have to learn to adjust to social demands. Dr. Karl A. Menninger has said that all children are born criminals in the sense that they have no innate sense of proper behavior and no inborn tendency to respect the rights, interests, and property of others. We are probably going too far in assuming either that delinquents are much worse than non-

[66] *Ibid.*   [67] *Ibid.*   [68] *Ibid.*

delinquents or that differences in personality make-up between delinquents and nondelinquents are great enough to measure objectively. As Monachesi himself points out, many youngsters grow up in neighborhoods where status is achieved by delinquent behavior. Shaw also points out this fact.[69]

On the other hand, well-behaved girls live in a different cultural milieu from that of delinquent girls in what we have defined earlier as an essentially private culture.[70]

Social Immaturity as a Factor in Behavior

The Sleighton Farm Study

Several studies including the present author's follow-up survey of the young women who had once been inmates of Sleighton Farm[71] show the delinquents (or criminals) who may be recidivists on parole often later straighten up and become law-abiding citizens. The latter was made at a period 5 to 10 years after the girls were released from custody of Sleighton Farm and the girls ranged in age from 25 to 29 when the study was made.[72]

So far as the Sleighton Farm girls were concerned only 26, or 23.6 per cent, of the 110 cases for whom detailed information was obtained in a follow-up study made a completely successful adjustment. Fifteen girls, or 13.6 per cent, had serious personality disturbances although they were not offenders against the law; 43, or 39.2 per cent, had serious sexual delinquencies *but eventually made a seemingly stable adjustment*; 26, or 23.6 per cent, failed completely in making an adjustment.[73]

Actually only 11 of the girls, or 10 per cent, were arrested after release from the farm and all but 1 of those were arrested on a morals charge.[74] Nevertheless the admitted or discovered delinquencies of these young women were just as serious (and as illegal) as those for which they had been committed. They had merely become more skillful in evading detection.

[69] Clifford R. Shaw and Henry D. McKay, *Juvenile Delinquency and Urban Areas,* University of Chicago Press, Chicago, 1942, pp. 435–437.
[70] Cf. chap. 8.
[71] Mabel A. Elliott, op. cit.
[72] *Ibid.*, p. 13. (It was considered important that the girls be at least 25 at the time of the study so as to permit a certain maturity.)
[73] *Ibid.*, pp. 37–38. The same percentage thus was wholly successful and failed completely.
[74] *Ibid.*, p. 39.

The important fact remains, however, that eventually, and within a period of 4 to 8 years after they were released, 76.4 per cent had been able to make a seemingly satisfactory adjustment. And even when the type of home, intelligence, occupation, educational training, or marriage was related to the girls' adjustments, none of these accounted for the earlier stability of the completely successful group.[75] Fortunately, most of those who adjusted, late or early, married reliable men. But we have large reason to believe that the physical and emotional maturity of the girls (plus whatever standards of conduct they may have come to see value in) was in a significant degree responsible for their adjustment.[76]

The Gluecks' Follow-Up Studies

The Gluecks' monumental follow-up studies of juveniles and adult criminals through a series of checkups at regular intervals give us more important information on the question of maturity in relation to behavior. Initially the Gluecks conducted a survey of 1000 delinquent boys who had been referred by the Boston juvenile court between the years 1917 and 1922 to the Judge Baker Foundation Clinic devoted to study of delinquents and operating in connection with the court. The behavior of 923 of these boys was analyzed over a 5-year period, after the treatment at the clinic was closed.[77] The follow-up study revealed that 88.2 per cent of the boys were recidivists, that only 11.8 per cent were non-delinquent during this 5-year period. That is, 798 boys were delinquent, 107 were not delinquent, and of the 18 remaining 12 had died, 1 was in a mental hospital, 2 were in other nonpenal institutions, and 3 were in the army.[78]

Of the 798 recidivists, 568 or 71.2 per cent were convicted for serious offenses, 167 or 20 per cent were convicted for minor offenses, and the rest either committed offenses for which they were arrested but not convicted, committed offenses for which they were not arrested, or were guilty of desertion or received dishonorable discharge from the army or navy. All told, 97 per cent of the recidivists committed offenses which came to the attention of officials.[79]

Some 5 years after the study just described was completed the Gluecks again interviewed the boys, who by this time were grown men. By then 39 of the 1000 were dead, but one of those who died lived long enough to be included in the study. All told, 962 young

[75] Ibid., pp. 38–39.   [76] Ibid.
[77] Sheldon and Eleanor T. Glueck, One Thousand Juvenile Delinquents, Harvard University Press, Cambridge, 1934, p. 5. Reliable information was available for only 923.
[78] Ibid., p. 151.   [79] Ibid., pp. 151–152.

men were included in the second follow-up. Their ages then averaged 24 years, with 9.2 per cent under 21, 61.7 per cent from 21 to 25, 28.9 per cent from 26 to 30, and 2 cases (less than 1 per cent) between 31 and 35.[80] Of the 962, information with reference to subsequent arrests was obtained for 877; it could not be checked for the remaining 85. For the 877, approximately one-third (33.9 per cent) had no arrests, while the remaining two-thirds (66.1 per cent) had 1 or more. Only 19.2 per cent of these had but 1 arrest. The average young man was arrested 3.76 times, but more than half had 4 arrests, 16.9 per cent had 5 or 6 arrests, and 18.0 per cent had 7 or more.[81] However, 46 of the group not arrested were known to have behaved in a delinquent or criminal manner. Hence only 26.8 per cent had become wholly law-abiding.[82]

Frequency of conviction was about the same for those brought up for offenses as in the preceding study, but the number of young men brought to trial who were convicted dropped markedly, from 78.0 per cent to 61.5 per cent. Perhaps even more significant, 65.6 per cent of the youths spent no time at all in penal or correctional institutions for the second 5-year period because more of them paid fines. There were 307 who served sentences, however, and of this group 55.7 per cent served 1 term, 23.5 per cent served 2 terms, 12 per cent served 3, and 8.8 per cent 4 or more. One-eighth (14 per cent) of these boys spent time in correctional schools, approximately one-third (31.3 per cent) spent time in reformatories, and one-fifth (19.9 per cent) were sentenced to prisons. More than half (52.4 per cent) were sentenced to jails, houses of correction, or state farms, and a small number (3.2 per cent) were committed to institutions for defective delinquents.[83] The small number sentenced to correctional institutions is explained by the fact that most of the boys were past 21 and too old to be sent there again. So far as increasing stability of behavior is concerned, the fact that 26.8 per cent had become non-offenders was the most important finding.[84]

The Gluecks therefore resolved to carry their analysis further by following the young men through a third 5-year span. By this time an additional 21 had died and 2 were in nonpenal institutions so that only only 938 cases remained for study. Now relatively mature, these young men had reached an average age of 29. The percentage in each age group is as follows:[85]

[80] Sheldon and Eleanor T. Glueck, *Juvenile Delinquents Grown Up*, Commonwealth Fund, New York, 1940, p. 43.
[81] *Ibid*.   [82] *Ibid*., p. 51.   [83] *Ibid*., p. 49.   [84] *Ibid*., p. 58.
[85] *Ibid*., p. 59. (Both follow-up studies are published in the same volume.)

Per Cent	Age Group
9	21–25
62	26–30
28.7	31–35
less than 1	36–40

Information could not be obtained for 92 (nearly one-tenth) of the 938 young men for the third follow-up study but of the remaining 846, 42.1 per cent had not been arrested. Of the 490 arrested, 23.7 per cent had been arrested once, 17.3 per cent twice, 12.7 per cent 3 times, the rest 4 or more times, with 21.1 per cent arrested 7 or more times. The average boy arrested had almost the same number of arrests as in the previous 5-year span, or 3.78.[86]

When the records of those arrested in the second 5-year period were checked with their records in the third 5-year period it was found that 79.4 per cent of those arrested in the second period were arrested once or oftener in the third. On the other hand 86.3 per cent of the 285 not arrested in the second 5-year period had no arrests in the third period.[87] A few were arrested more than once and 2.6 per cent were arrested 4 or more times.[88] In addition to the crimes for which these young men were arrested an additional 50 men either committed civilian crimes for which they were not arrested or were offenders in the army or navy.[89]

The Gluecks' most significant conclusion from these follow-up surveys was that there was a decline in criminality among the group and a decrease in the seriousness of crimes of those who continued to behave in a criminal fashion.[90] From these findings the Gluecks developed their theory that the maturation of the offender is a basic factor in his adjustment. Age they found to be less important than the number of years which elapsed after the onset of the delinquent behavior. That is, with increased maturity the tendency to commit delinquent acts decreases. Some persons, however, never reach such maturity. According to the Gluecks the time of abandoning the delinquent behavior depends thus not so much upon biological maturity as upon time itself. For the boys studied the most significant chances of reformation were held to be between the ages of 15 and 21.[91]

These findings with reference to the later careers of delinquent boys were later confirmed in another follow-up study on adult crimi-

---

[86] *Ibid.*   [87] *Ibid.*   [88] *Ibid.*, pp. 60–61.
[89] *Ibid.*, p. 62.   [90] *Ibid.*, p. 89.   [91] *Ibid.*, pp. 143–145.

nals published in 1937. It covered the later careers of 510 criminal men whose parole and post-parole behavior had been previously studied in 1930.[92] Information on 422 of the men in the initial study was obtained for their post-parole period; 21.1 per cent were successes, 16.8 per cent were partial failures, and 62.1 per cent were total failures.[93]

A second 5-year follow-up study was made of the 454 of the 510 men who were still living at the beginning of the period. Of this group information concerning their behavior could not be obtained for 57, and 34 were confined in penal institutions practically the whole period.[94] For the remaining 363 men, 200 had been arrested and 63 had not been arrested, although 2 had been dishonorably discharged from the army. Of the 363 men for whom there was information a total of 118 were nondelinquents during the entire second 5-year period, in contrast to 89 of 414 men in the first 5-year period.[95] Moreover by the fifth year of the second period 42.1 per cent of 321 men for whom information was available were judged to have become nondelinquent. This increase in law-abiding behavior, as in the case of the boys, was attributed to the maturation process, but among the men the Gluecks found the rate of improvement in conduct increased up to the age of 36, after which it declined. The Gluecks therefore concluded in their second follow-up study of adult offenders that persons with a record who had not become stable by their thirty-sixth year were not likely to become so later.[96]

In 1943 the Gluecks' third follow-up survey of the 510 adult criminals was published covering another 5-year period.[97] At the beginning of the third period 439 of the original 510 were living. By the end of the period 49 (or 11.2 per cent) were in jails or prisons, 16 were in mental hospitals or chronically ill, 27 more (or 6.2 per cent) had died, and the whereabouts of 40 were unknown.[98]

Since the group had apparently improved in conduct during the second 5-year period the major question was whether or not such improvement continued. Actually the number of arrests remained ap-

[92] Cf. Sheldon and Eleanor T. Glueck, Five Hundred Criminal Careers, Knopf, New York, 1930.
[93] Ibid.
[94] Sheldon and Eleanor T. Glueck, Later Criminal Careers, Commonwealth Fund, New York, 1937, pp. 63–64.
[95] Ibid., pp. 75–76.
[96] Ibid., pp. 111–112.
[97] Sheldon and Eleanor T. Glueck, Criminal Careers in Retrospect, Commonwealth Fund, New York, 1943.
[98] Ibid., p. 73.

proximately the same since 208 men (or approximately 57 per cent) of the group were known to have been arrested. This percentage is close to the 55.1 per cent arrested during the second period, but was markedly less than the 70.7 per cent arrested in period 1. The average number of arrests of those arrested remained more or less the same, however: 3.30 for the first period, 3.71 for the second, and 3.56 for the third. Moreover the actual (in contrast to average) frequency of arrest did not vary greatly.[99] Arrests for crimes against property decreased; arrests for drunkenness remained approximately the same. The amount of actual drunkenness was known to have increased, however. The predominant offense was, in fact, drunkenness, with offenses against public health, safety, and welfare second, property offenses third, and a variety of offenses, including chiefly drug offenses, family offenses, and those against person fourth.[100]

When the men were classified as serious offenders, minor offenders, and nonoffenders during the third period the number of serious offenders dropped significantly from 51 per cent (to 38 per cent in the second period) to 30.4 per cent.[101] Meanwhile the number of minor offenders was upped slightly (from 29.1 per cent) in the second period to 39.9 per cent and still remained at 38.8 per cent in the third period. The percentage of nonoffenders remained at 30.8 per cent for the whole period. However, the Gluecks believe that 21 of the men who had reformed for 5 years previous to the third period and who had had only a brief relapse at the beginning of the third period should be counted as nondelinquent. This shift in classification obviously yields weight to their argument that the improvement of offenders is progressive, and raised the total of nondelinquents to 41.8 per cent.[102]

In the meantime the Gluecks accepted as further evidence of declining criminality the fact that many of the serious offenders had become minor (or at least nonproperty) offenders.[103] That a man actually improves when he turns from stealing to family desertion is a value judgment in which not everyone would concur with the Gluecks! But maturity, as their impressive studies indicate, is an important factor in inducing willingness to abide by the rules and regulations of the group. It may be that many offenders become increasingly aware of the need for conformity with the passing years.

[99] *Ibid.*, pp. 109–110. [100] *Ibid.*, pp. 110–112.
[101] *Ibid.*, pp. 118–119. [102] *Ibid.*, pp. 118–119.
[103] *Ibid.*, pp. 121–122.

The Importance of Personality Studies

This survey of literature with reference to the special physical, mental, and emotional characteristics of criminals and the question of the effect of the offenders' maturity or lack of maturity has its chief value for the student in the insight it gives to man's extensive effort to find what is wrong with the offender. The underlying assumption of all such researches is that something is definitely and distinctively amiss with a criminal which differentiates him from the rank and file of men.

Our earlier discussion on the hidden crimes of respected members of the community (as well as the extensive operations of organized crime) and the widespread tendency of businessmen to break the law gives us little reason to suppose criminals are much different from other persons, since the majority of us are at least occasional offenders. Criminals may be less socially oriented than noncriminals. Indeed, crimes are often merely the illegal expression of perfectly normal tendencies. Crime itself may also be an artificial fact created by law rather than anything which has been long tabooed by the group. The strength of social acceptance of the new definition must depend upon the degree to which it disrupts old customs and folkways. Black markets are thus always a problem in times of price control, because the government is attempting to control sumptuary habits and buying habits of individuals who are unaccustomed to such restraints.

There are doubtless personality factors in every crime situation in which an individual knowingly disobeys a law. But there are also social, economic, and community factors which sociologists believe are important in stimulating criminal activity. These we shall discuss in the next chapter.

SELECTED BIBLIOGRAPHY

Abrahamsen, David, *Crime and the Human Mind*, Columbia University Press, New York, 1945. A leading psychiatrist makes a comprehensive statement on the emotional factors in crime.

Bromberg, Walter, *Crime and the Mind*, Lippincott, Philadelphia, 1948. A fair appraisal of emotional factors in crime is made by a psychiatrist who recognizes the importance of social factors as well.

Ferrero, Gina Lombroso, *Criminal Man According to the Classification of Cesare Lombroso*, Putnam, New York, 1911. Lombroso's talented daughter gives a pithy summary of his conclusions.

Fink, Arthur E., *Causes of Crime, Biological Theories in the United States, 1810–1915*, University of Pennsylvania Press, Philadelphia, 1938. This is an exhaustive survey of research on the biological characteristics of criminals.

Goring, Charles B., *The English Convict*, His Majesty's Stationery Office, London, 1913. The original data in Goring's famous comparative anthropometric study of convicts and university students are recorded in this massive tome.

Hentig, Hans von, *The Criminal and His Victim*, Yale University Press, New Haven, 1948, Part I. This section is devoted to physical traits and mental disorders as they allegedly occur among criminals. The book also considers social factors and the victim in relation to crime.

Hooton, Earnest A., *Crime and the Man*, Harvard University Press, Cambridge, 1939. A neo-Lombrosian reports on his extensive physical measurements of criminals and civilians. His conclusions have been widely rejected by sociologists.

Lombroso, Cesare, *Crime, Its Causes and Remedies*, transl. by Henry P. Horton, Little, Brown, Boston, 1911. Here are the basic conclusions of the outstanding exponent of the notion of the "born" criminal.

Radzinowicz, L., and Turner, J. W. C. (eds.), *Mental Abnormality and Crime*, English Studies in Criminal Science, Vol. II, Macmillan, London, 1944. A symposium of leading psychiatrists discusses the relation of mental abnormality to crime.

Schlapp, Max G., and Smith, Edward, *The New Criminology*, Boni and Liveright, New York, 1928. Crime, according to these authors, is a matter of glandular activity and biochemistry.

Tulchin, Simon, *Intelligence and Crime*, University of Chicago Press, Chicago, 1939. The intelligence of Illinois prisoners is compared with the intelligence of Illinois draftees in World War I.

Zeleny, Leslie D., "Feeblemindedness and Criminal Conduct," *American Journal of Sociology*, 38:564–578 (January, 1933). This study showed that the mental ratings of criminals and the general population were not very different.

CHAPTER 13

Social Relationships and Economic Factors in Crime

Although certain explanations for the delinquent's or criminal's immediate reaction (or behavior) appear to lie in the personal characteristics of offenders, the person who engages in criminal activity must always do so in reference to a social situation. Crime is always a personal-situation complex, as Sutherland has maintained.[1] Criminal activity is behavior which occurs because of the stimulus to the individual which his relationships to other persons and groups involve. Emotional reactions and motivations of individuals which lead to various types of criminal conduct are thus stimulated by group situations. Sutherland maintains that criminal behavior is learned in interaction with other persons, that in final analysis it is as the result of differential association with groups that a person becomes delinquent. Thus the individual learns by association in his particular family, gang, or other group the special ways of counterfeiting, bank robbing, picking pockets, breaking locks, etc. He comes to regard such behavior as suitable, and in conformity to the patterns of the group in which he lives.

Thus the child in the slums, born in an area where the boys in the neighborhood have acquired a variety of skills in picking pockets, stealing small articles from the five-and-ten-cent stores, swiping junk from junk yards, etc., will soon be indoctrinated in such techniques.

This theory may explain the confirmed criminal, the person who persists in antisocial or criminal behavior and becomes the recidivist or habitual offender. It does not offer the basic explanation for the

[1] Edwin H. Sutherland, *Principles of Criminology*, Lippincott, Philadelphia, rev. ed., 1947, p. 5.

criminal activity of the person under emotional stress who commits a theft, murders his wife, or commits rape without any special social education for his antisocial behavior. In a sense differential association may account for a person's becoming a chronic sex offender if he lives in a group which tolerates or approves such offenses. To the present author the effect of the differential association of the criminal is best explained not by the *education* of the person in criminal activities but by the *stimulation* to antisocial activities. Some of the differential associations may provide patterns for criminal conduct. Other associations provide the stimulus to crimes of personal violence or economic offenses without supplying any techniques in how to murder, steal, or embezzle. Most bank clerks or post-office employees, for example, are not taught to embezzle. Rather they are *stimulated* to embezzle by the desire for more material goods and pleasures than their modest salaries permit, while the money is as close as their fingertips. The man or woman who kills his or her spouse ordinarily has not been taught to kill. He may have learned to use a firearm or knife, or he may know of the killing properties of poison, sleeping tablets, etc., but the motivation comes from the feelings of hatred and frustration which the murderer has toward his victim. Stimulus to particular criminal activity which the criminal may or may not regard as offensive conduct thus appears to be derived from the particular relationships of the individual.

Certain factors in producing crimes thus appear to be inherent in the community. Others are related to the ineffectiveness of institutions in meeting human needs. Still others are inherent in the economic structure of modern society and defects in social relationships.

GROUP RELATIONSHIPS AND CRIME

All persons have to make adjustments in terms of their relationships to other persons, groups, and institutions. When these relationships frustrate the individual he may commit antisocial acts—sometimes emotional offenses, sometimes offenses which are in a sense symbolic. When the relationships stimulate him to group participation he may indulge in antisocial behavior more because he has learned to accept the practices of the group and wishes to identify himself with the group than because any deep-seated emotional tension is driving him.

The groups which stimulate individuals to antisocial behavior are much the same as those of law-abiding persons. It is the peculiar or differential character of the relationships which stimulates antisocial conduct. Such relationships include:

1. Those within his immediate family and his larger kith and kin groups.
2. His age group.
3. His sex group.
4. Friendship and rival groups.
5. The nationality or cultural groups with which he comes in contact.
6. Occupational associations.
7. The community and neighborhood in which he lives and their cultural homogeneity or heterogeneity, as the case may be.
8. Institutional associations in school, church, club, lodge.[2]

The Family

The educational and value-setting functions of the family are basic influences in the lives of all children reared in family settings. The juvenile delinquent who is brought into court is very often the product of either a broken home or one in which the parents are incompetent, immoral, or otherwise unable to help their children make a satisfactory adjustment to the rules and regulations which society imposes.

Virtually all studies relating to the family backgrounds of delinquents and criminals show a larger than normal percentage (to the civilian population) of broken homes, of immoral parents and siblings, of homes of low educational and economic status and high mobility. Earlier studies showed a high percentage of parents of immigrant stock.

The Glueck Study of Adult Criminals

In the Gluecks' study of 510 criminals committed to the Massachusetts Reformatory, 60 per cent of the young men came from homes in which there was either a long or a complete absence of 1 parent. Two and one-half times as many of these prisoners were of foreign-born or mixed parentage as the general population. (These prisoners may have been affected by cultural conflicts similar to those mentioned in Chapter 10.) Seventy-five per cent of the families were

[2] This list is altered somewhat but was suggested by Mary van Kleeck's list in *Work and Law Observance*, Report No. 13 of the *Report on the Causes of Crime*, Vol. I, National Commission on Law Observance and Enforcement, Washington, 1931, pp. 186–187.

handicapped economically and although only 15 per cent were completely dependent on relief at the time, 60 per cent had been aided by some welfare organization. Only 13 per cent of 1 or both parents had attended the common school. More than half of the families had official criminal records and an additional 30 per cent had committed crimes but had not been arrested. The picture of training in crime and frustrations involved in the family life of these young men is not hard to reconstruct.[3]

THE ELLIOTT SLEIGHTON FARM STUDY

Analysis of the family factors in the background of 203 Sleighton Farm girls showed a lesser number (29.1 per cent) to be of foreign or mixed parentage. Three of the girls were illegitimate and of the remaining 200 the home was broken in 103 cases, or 51.5 per cent. (Shideler's study in Cincinnati indicated only 25 per cent of the school children in that city came from broken homes.[4] Hazel Ormsbee's study of the young employed girl, presumably from somewhat similar economic status, showed only 12 per cent were from broken homes.[5]) These comparisons indicate that broken homes are apparently more characteristic of delinquent girls than non-delinquents. In 37.8 per cent of the broken homes of the Sleighton Farm girls the mother was head, in which case these girls generally had no supervision. Probably more important than the broken home was the fact that 56.3 per cent of one or both parents were immoral. In addition many were regarded as shiftless and incompetent—an influence probably nearly as deterimental for the growing girl.

Economically 63.6 per cent of the parents belonged to the lower skilled and unskilled laboring group, and there were 5 or more children in 60.4 per cent of the families. Nearly 20 per cent had 8 or more children and 6 families had either 13 or 14. The economic problems in these homes should be obvious.[6]

THE HEALY-BRONNER STUDY

In the Healy-Bronner study of 4000 cases of delinquents (2000 each in Chicago and Boston) 1000 cases in Chicago and Boston were

[3] Sheldon and Eleanor T. Glueck, *Five Hundred Criminal Careers*, Knopf, New York, 1930, pp. 306–307.

[4] Ernest H. Shideler, "Family Disintegration and the Delinquent Boy," *Journal of Criminal Law and Criminology*, 8:715 (January–February, 1918).

[5] Hazel Grant Ormsbee, *The Young Employed Girl*, The Woman's Press, New York, 1927, pp. 58–60.

[6] Mabel A. Elliott, *Correctional Education and the Delinquent Girl—A Follow-Up Study of One Hundred and Ten Sleighton Farm Girls*, Commonwealth of Pennsylvania, Harrisburg, 1929, pp. 26–30.

selected for determining how many came from "really good" homes. This famous pair ruled out families where there were unfortunate conditions such as poverty, neglect, poor discipline, overcrowding, lack of sanitation, excessive quarreling, drunkenness, criminality, obscenity, immorality, mother working, mentally ill parent at home. They found that only 7.6 per cent of the delinquents had reasonably good homes. As it happened, 10.3 per cent of the Boston homes were rated good and only 5 per cent of the Chicago homes.[7]

THE GLUECKS' STUDY OF 500 MATCHED PAIRS OF DELINQUENTS AND NONDELINQUENTS

The Gluecks' recent study of 500 matched pairs of delinquents and nondelinquents (mostly from the Boston area) gives further evidence of the importance of family influences in developing delinquency patterns. The two groups of delinquents came from approximately the same economic background. But the delinquents came from homes in which there were far more emotional disturbances. A much larger proportion came from homes broken by desertion, separation, divorce, or death. The delinquents' parents (or substitute parents) were more often harsh or lax in their discipline, or else neglectful of the children. Relationships within the delinquents' families were often disorganized; there was lack of respect and affection and, in general, the delinquent's parents gave him no adequate conception of the cultural pattern to which society expected him to conform. Instead the delinquent families had a tendency to select an "antisocial culture." In consequence, the Gluecks conclude that the delinquents developed consistent antisocial tendencies because they were never adequately socialized.[8] Their families in other words failed the delinquents in a major family function—that of socializing the child through introducing him to acceptable patterns of conduct.

"Age" Groups

Part of delinquency and crime must be recognized as the tribute which members of a gang or play group or other associates of similar age exact in return for "belonging." For boys and young men in particular many delinquencies and crimes are group activities, entered

---

[7] William Healy and Augusta F. Bronner, *Delinquents and Criminals, Their Making and Unmaking*, Macmillan, New York, 1928, pp. 128–129.
[8] Sheldon and Eleanor Glueck, *Unraveling Juvenile Delinquency*, The Commonwealth Fund, Harvard University Press, Cambridge, 1951, pp. 278–280.

into as much for the thrill and excitement as for any mercenary value to be derived from stealing.

In rural areas robbing watermelon patches has been a variety of rural recreation even though the outraged farmer may take his shotgun to frighten off the unwelcome revelers. So far as boys' gangs are concerned they apparently arise spontaneously in the boys' efforts to create a society for themselves, as Frederick H. Thrasher has said. Before there were widespread efforts to provide suitable recreational facilities for boys in Chicago, Thrasher found 1313 gangs in Chicago and the surrounding area, to which at least 25,000 (perhaps more) boys and young men belonged.[9]

Spontaneous play groups always arise among children living in the same neighborhood, and the gangs themselves develop rather naturally out of the struggles of rival groups for possession of play space in vacant lots or street corners, for hideouts, or even for the loot in rubbish heaps.[10] The areas in which these youngsters live afford few opportunities for wholesome play. Hence lawlessness is almost certain to develop out of the struggles between these youthful groups. Gangs vary markedly, but they all tend to possess leadership, loyalty, and *esprit de corps*, which they exercise in opposition to other gangs as well as in opposition to law and the "cops."

The boys' gangs are generally early adolescent, but their group activities in crime may extend into their twenties, if not beyond. Many boy gangsters are, in the words of Thrasher, "reincorporated into family and community life."[11] Those who are sentenced to correctional institutions are more likely to become adult criminal gangsters—the combined effect of their continuous social relationships with persons (chiefly of their own age group) who have defined their values in terms of "fellowship, excitement and security."[12] The adult criminal gangs are mostly made up of young persons, but their major motivation tends to be economic rather than excitement *per se*. The young adult criminal gangs tend to be of three varieties: (1) The temporary associations are composed of the permanent, relatively powerless gangsters who aid each other in committing crimes but have little political influence or wealth for their efforts.[13] (2) The powerful gangs (also young men) usually have become specialists in crime, with highly developed techniques in stealing, safeblowing, robbing freight trains, blackmailing, dope peddling, gambling, vice rings, etc.[14]

[9] Frederick H. Thrasher, *The Gang*, University of Chicago Press, Chicago, 1927, p. 5.
[10] *Ibid.*, pp. 26–27.   [11] *Ibid.*, p. 418.   [12] *Ibid.*, p. 420.   [13] *Ibid.*, p. 431.
[14] *Ibid.*, chap. 20, "The Gang and Organized Crime."

(3) The super gangsters, rings, or syndicates may be older master technicians who operate through the offices of younger men in the various communities.

All gangs from the point of view of their members thus represent "in-groups" and both their rival gangs and society as a whole are "out-groups." Much crime is unorganized and many adult criminals have never belonged to gangs, but, as the statistics in Chapter 4 indicate, most criminals are fairly young. Part of the reason young persons are in conflict with society must lie in the fact that the older and socially minded members of society have failed to educate them with reference to the need and desirability of social conformity. Some crimes represent conflicts between rival lawbreaking groups, as has been indicated, in which both define the social situation in terms of their own selfish and hedonistic interests rather than on any basis of the general welfare of the group.

Dr. von Hentig maintains that criminality may be closely connected with the organic aggressiveness of puberty. Life processes themselves demand that young persons divest themselves of family protection in order to achieve the biological perpetuation of the race.[15] Unhappily most juvenile delinquents who come into contact with the courts have no great family protection. In any event youth has always been willing to take great risks.

Sex Groups

Most criminal gangs are male. The gangster thus represents a very definite adjustment to the leadership and stimulus of members of his own sex in participating in lawless activities. Much of our culture is obviously sex linked and the conservative attitudes toward women's behavior undoubtedly stem at least partially from women's function in conserving the race by the bearing of children. The fact that the male sex is biologically endowed with greater muscular strength and stronger tendencies to aggressive activity probably accounts for the much greater tendency of boys to engage in wrestling, fisticuffs, and gang activities. Dr. von Hentig holds that these facts explain the high crime rate among males.

Some crimes are perpetrated by members of one sex within their own sex group (as in gang warfare, etc.). But many crimes are committed by men against women, and vice versa. Men snatch women's

[15] Hans von Hentig, *Crime: Causes and Conditions*, McGraw-Hill, New York, 1947, "The Biological Aspect of Youth," pp. 140–145.

purses, cheat women of their inheritances, rape women, murder women, etc. The element of sex attraction enters into the various facets of all such crimes, although the economic motive is probably paramount in most economic crimes. Similarly women commit offenses against men. How much such conduct is due to distorted or frustrated sexual desires cannot be answered scientifically, but there is reason to believe that emotional disorders may have a bearing on nonsexual as well as sexual crimes, as mentioned earlier.[16] As the instigators of masculine crimes, women allegedly are often accomplices. Men, on the other hand, often steal for women, just as other men work to support women.

Occupational Maladjustments and Crime

We are just beginning to recognize the full importance of deriving satisfactions from one's job and with this the fact that much industrial strife is derived from failure to consider the worker's social interests as well as his need for decent pay and suitable working conditions. Some dissatisfactions arise from shifting workers from job to job without their consent.[17] Other tensions grow out of inability to live decently on wage scales, inhuman working conditions or unsanitary working conditions, etc. Sometimes these tensions and frustrations on the job lead to violent hostility such as characterized the mining industry a few decades ago. The struggles between miners and mine owners led to brutal killings on both sides of the labor-management conflict. Even within the relative calm of the university setting there have been rare instances in which a member of the faculty in an embittered and frustrated struggle for promotion or status took arms against a department head or college president as the object of his envy or the believed source of his frustration. Most academic struggle or rivalry does not end in violence. But it may result in "ordeals by slander," or in the undermining of the status of the resented person in more subtle but equally disastrous ways.

Thus comparatively few crimes of violence take place in educated circles, whereas they have been rather common in the field of heavy industry. We may presume that part of the difference in violence is due to differences in the satisfactions derived from the occupational

[16] Cf. Dr. von Hentig's extended discussion of "Sex and Crime," chap. 5 in *ibid.*
[17] F. J. Roethlisberger, *Management and Morale*, Harvard University Press, Cambridge, 1941, pp. 46–66.

associations. The average college professor enjoys his work, whereas many engaged in heavy industry resent the unpleasant aspects of their labor.

As all students of sociology are aware, every person's existence is not merely one of simple relationships to groups but a complex network of interrelationships which are affected by attitudes and values. Increased understanding of the mutual problems of labor and management (as well as opportunity to present and air grievances) has gone a long way in reducing industrial violence. Since many of the factors in occupational tensions are closely related to the economic organization and structure of society, they will be discussed under "The Economic Structure and Crime" later on in this chapter.

WORK HISTORY

In connection with the *Report on the Causes of Crime*, published by the National Commission on Law Observance and Enforcement, Mary van Kleeck analyzed, for 300 of the 1051 prisoners committed to Sing Sing in the year ending February 28, 1930, the last type of work in which they were employed prior to commitment.[18] Her analysis showed these men to represent a cross section of occupations in industry, business, and the professions. More than one-third were employed in "the various processes of industry," and about one-sixth were employed as laborers, cleaners, and porters (it was these occupations in which the Negroes chiefly worked). Of the 300 prisoners, 233 were white men and of this group 31 were owners or partners in business or officers or executives of businesses. None of the 67 Negroes were in this classification. Miss van Kleeck's study thus showed that so far as the prisoners at Sing Sing were concerned they were for the most part skilled workmen or men with businesses of their own, rather than unskilled, incompetent workmen.[19]

UNEMPLOYMENT

Miss van Kleeck found unemployment to be a much more significant characteristic than lack of earning capacity. For the year ending June 30, 1929, 37.9 per cent of the 1098 prisoners were out of work, and for the 10-year period 1920–1929 inclusive, from 26 to 38.1 per cent were out of work when they committed their crimes.[20] Thus the

[18] Mary van Kleeck, *op. cit.*, "Work and Law Observance in the Histories of Men in Sing Sing Prison," pp. 193–218.
[19] *Ibid.*, pp. 197–199.
[20] *Ibid.*, p. 200.

prisoners represented a larger proportion of unemployed than would have been found in the general population for the period covered.

While extreme need is not the only factor accounting for economic crimes Miss van Kleeck found that, when she related the type of crime to whether or not the prisoner was employed, 45 per cent of the economic crimes were committed by the unemployed and only 25 per cent of the crimes against person were committed by the unemployed. However, the fact that 55 per cent of those who committed economic crimes were employed indicates that economic standards beyond individual income were probably more important factors in this group's crimes than extreme need itself.

Of the 300 men set apart for special study, only 56 had had favorable occupational opportunities by reason of possessing the following characteristics: (1) 1 type of employment, (2) 5 years or more of employment in one position, or (3) evidence of satisfactory service as reported by probation officer with verified report of employment record. The first classification was regarded as evidence of favorable opportunity with or without classification 2 or 3. Or the last 2 were regarded also as favorable. Ordinarily each person rated favorable received at least 2 counts.[21]

The 300 prisoners selected for special study were also analyzed with reference to the following categories:

1. Experience in work which requires time to learn.
2. Training in a vocational or industrial school.
3. Training in a professional school.
4. Schooling beyond elementary grades.
5. High rating in stability as measured in individual's having stable employment record.
6. Physical strength.
7. Managerial or executive experience.
8. Other assets.[22]

Of the 300 men, 194 had one or more assets, 106 had none.[23]

From the above data Miss van Kleeck concluded that unemployment ranked as a factor in the prisoners' crimes (although it was not necessarily the direct factor) and that a greater number of unemployed men were committed in bad times than in good times. Most of the men had not made their livelihood through lawbreaking.[24]

---

[21] *Ibid.*, pp. 206–207.
[22] *Ibid.*, p. 208.
[23] *Ibid.*, p. 209.
[24] *Ibid.*, pp. 217–218.

The Victim as a Factor in Crime

In the relationships which are part and parcel of crimes, the victim is always important. This fact has led Hans von Hentig to study the victim as a determining factor in crime. This interesting orientation to the problem of crime deserves further exploration than the brief mention possible here. But von Hentig is right in maintaining that the victim provides the precipitating stimulus to the crime which is the offender's response to the situation. So far as murder is concerned, most murdered persons have inspired great hate and desire for vengeance in their murderers. Women who are victims of murder are usually killed by their husbands or paramours. Men who are victims of murder are more likely to be murdered by former friends or acquaintances,[25] but when a woman commits murder her husband is usually the victim.

The victims of swindlers are usually trying to make dishonest gain themselves, as we discussed in Chapter 6. Sex offenses are unquestionably affected by the sex attraction of the victim for the offender, but must also be affected by mutual attraction in many instances.[26] Some victims are stimuli to crime because they are physically defenseless, e.g., children, women, and old persons. Inexperienced persons, whether country girls in the great city or foreigners in a strange land, may be duped by criminals. Lonesome and heartbroken persons are especially luring victims. Bereaved persons in particular are often taken in by memorial biography rackets. Many "moochers" cut the obituary columns for possible easy sources of clothing, etc., if not for outright cash.

Even the state, as the theoretical victim of crime, may allow conditions to exist which call forth rebellious and aggressive criminal conduct. Moreover the type of treatment in prisons and on parole which is fostered by the state tends to reinforce the criminal tendencies of many offenders.[27] It is impossible to summarize all of von Hentig's examples here. The relationship between the victim and the criminal offers many fascinating opportunities for further study and verification.

The Community and Crime

The Kefauver Crime Committee hearings during 1950-1951 made the American public aware of how intrenched organized crime was in

[25] Hans von Hentig, *The Criminal and His Victim*, Yale University Press, New Haven, 1948, chap. 12, "The Victim's Contribution to the Genesis of Crime."
[26] *Ibid.*   [27] *Ibid.*

the various urban communities throughout the country. The law-abiding public was shocked to realize how extensive the gambling, narcotic, prostitution, labor, and business rackets were and how boldly the black-market operators carried on their activities during World War II when rationing was so essential to our general well-being.[28] Many people were aroused from their usual apathy and believed that the federal government should take some action. Actually most of the responsibility for permitting crime to exist must be attached to the local community.

Because of its customs, ideas, and practices, the community may be said to generate crime, tolerate crime, and in turn be disorganized by crime.[29] Crime may be defined as antisocial behavior which the group rejects and to which it attaches penalties. Practically all members of society accept the validity of defining crime by law. In our society penalties are also established by law. Hence it is not always easy for members of the community to believe that they collectively are responsible for the existence of crime or that their culture determines to a major degree the character of crime. The lack of community responsibility stems from public apathy, from the failure of the group to do anything about conditions which are known to exist. Part of the responsibility must be attached to the peculiar features of our culture.

Culture and crime have so many interrelated facets that we can consider only the more important ways in which culture affects the definitions and treatment of antisocial conduct. Modern criminologists are fairly well agreed on certain relations between crime and culture. We may summarize these here: (1) The cultural norms of group behavior are conducive to the peculiar aspects of crime in a particular community. (2) Crime is related to the particular type of social organization in a given society. (3) A differential patterning of crime tends to exist within the various cultural groups in a community. (4) American lawlessness is deeply rooted in the frontier mores. (5) Social disorganization and confusion with reference to basic social values are accompanied by a high crime rate. (6) Crime is more constant in all classes within a community than the crime rates seem to indicate because of the differential treatment which is accorded persons in different social

---

[28] Cf. General Conclusions, Third Interim Report of the Special Committee to Investigate Organized Crime in Interstate Commerce, Washington, 1951, p. 1.

[29] Nathaniel Cantor, Crime, Criminals and Criminal Justice, Holt, New York, 1932, pp. 37–40, 63–65. Cf. also Ruth Shonle Cavan, Criminology, Crowell, New York, 1948, pp. 3–20.

strata. This in turn creates much of the confusion and lack of consensus as to whose conduct should be punished and whose should not.[30]

1. NORMS OF BEHAVIOR IN RELATION TO CRIME

Norms of behavior which define our conduct give rise to the stability of our social order. Hence it is often difficult for us to understand that the norms which are expressed in laws contribute to lawbreaking. The fact is that these norms may correspond to the ethical concepts of legislators and be at the same time wholly unrepresentative of the behavior norms of the lower economic and social classes which bulk so large in the group arrested and convicted for crimes. Laws tend to be class-conscious regulations laid down by successful and respectable members of the upper middle class because it is from this group that the majority of our legislators come. Hence the values of sexual morality, honesty, and property which are considered so pertinent and so obvious to the well-to-do and to lawmakers may be neither obvious nor especially important to the illiterate, the unsuccessful, the frustrated, and the impecunious members of the lower class. People on the whole obey laws which they regard as reasonable standards of behavior and in which they have been more or less indoctrinated by their associates. Laws which incorporate upper-middle-class thinking often seem to be mere interferences with accepted patterns of behavior among the lower economic and social groups. Stealing from a wealthy employer who has more food, linen, silverware, etc., than he can possibly use, for example, may be regarded as a justifiable procedure. Any law which defines as illegal the common practices within a particular group is bound to be disobeyed by many of those who do not accept its initial premises.

Persons reared in squalor and poverty and denied the benefits of education and refinement often see little advantage or meaning in "high-minded ideals." Their exposure to the morals of what Whyte calls "Street Corner Society" gives them little motive to develop concepts consonant with those of people who have never felt the urge to steal, who have never been initiated into promiscuous sex habits in their early youth, or who have never experienced the bitter frustrations imposed by extreme poverty. It is not difficult to understand why

[30] Cf. Mabel A. Elliott, "Delinquent Behavior of People," *Phylon* (Atlanta University Review of Race and Culture), 5:242–251 (Third Quarter, 1949). Much of the material discussed under these categories is derived from this article. Cf. also Mabel A. Elliott and Francis E. Merrill, *Social Disorganization*, Harper, New York, 3rd ed., 1950, chap. 26, "Crime and the Community."

the majority of our racketeers, wealthy gamblers, and "underworld" leaders are recruited from the poverty-stricken and slum-dwelling immigrant groups.[31] This is evidenced in the gangs which Thrasher studied (to which we referred earlier) which were products of the slums of Chicago. All came from dismal and deteriorating areas. Some were from the West Side; some from the near North Side (north of the Loop and west of the "Gold Coast"); others from the Negro districts and the South Side "badlands." All were poverty-stricken areas located between the encroaching industrial and business section and the better residential areas.[32]

Our much vaunted high standard of living and the stimulus which great wealth affords to those who wish to acquire a fortune but who cannot hope to achieve it legally have unquestionably been factors in producing our notorious gangsters. Gangsters are in a very real sense frustrated personalities hell-bent on becoming millionaires.[33] In the bitter struggle for survival in the slums, primitive urges characterize social relationships far more than polite considerations for the welfare of others.

2. Crime and Modern Social Organization

The complexity of our urban type of civilization, with its anonymity, its dependence upon secondary rather than primary group controls, its mobile population, and its high degree of economic insecurity, is closely linked with the crime rate. The emphasis placed upon material well-being, the amazing production of complicated gadgets, and the yearning to possess them which advertisers have stimulated are all factors in creating desire to achieve material comforts by illegal means. Crimes are also definitely related to urbanization, as we noted in Chapter 3. They occur much more frequently in large cities than in smaller cities or rural areas. Moreover, the disparity in rates decreases as the proximity of the rural areas to a large city increases. Cultural norms of city behavior are spilling over into the countryside, and the rural areas are becoming more and more urbanized with good roads and the automobile. Rural crime rates have also risen as a result of the new and extended relationships with near-by cities.[34]

[31] William F. Whyte, *Street Corner Society*, University of Chicago Press, Chicago, 1943.
[32] Frederick H. Thrasher, *op. cit.*
[33] Mabel A. Elliott, "Delinquent Behavior of People," *Phylon*, 5:242–251 (Third Quarter, 1949). Cf. also Ruth Shonle Cavan, *op. cit.*, pp. 54–90.
[34] Edwin H. Sutherland, *op. cit.*, pp. 44–45, 135–138.

3. The Differential Patterning of Crime

Where sufficient inhibiting forces operate and control the conduct of individuals crime rates tend to be low. The subtler aspects of social control appear to be even more important than the law-enforcing agencies. The essential honesty of the Englishman as a cultural trait is more important in maintaining a low crime rate than the English "bobbies" or the detectives from Scotland Yard. Stealing is a serious offense in the criminal code of Soviet Russia, but the stern impact of the law has not prevented widespread thieving, as most travelers in that country can testify. We too have our characteristic crimes. Bank robberies, for example, are common occurrences in America, but such crimes seldom take place in European countries. Personal property thefts seem to be more characteristic offenses in eastern Europe and Russia. American lawbreaking possesses a lusty distinctiveness insofar as it is exemplified in bank robberies and other bold exploits of criminals. Much of this differential patterning of American crime is a product of the lawless heritage of pioneer days.

4. Crime and the Frontier Mores

Although crimes change with the times, much of our current lawlessness is undoubtedly rooted in the frontier mores, as discussed in Chapter 10. Revolt from authority has been a part of the cultural heritage, for our nation was born out of a revolt against oppressive restraining laws, and out of this demand for liberty has sprung much of our unwillingness to accept the restraint of law.

5. Social Disorganization (and Confusion in Social Values) and Crime

American cities afford an excellent example of how the impact of heterogeneous cultural groups makes any consensus on basic values difficult. As we shall discuss more fully, war exemplifies even better how social disorganization affects the crime rate by upsetting the normal concept of the sanctity of life. Murder rates appear in particular to be affected. A revolutionary period so calls into question the basic values of the group that theft is often rampant and normally enforced sex controls decline.

6. Crime and the Class Structure

As our discussion in Chapter 3 made clear, there is a good deal of crime among all classes, but lower-class criminals are more likely to suffer penalty for their offenses. This circumstance probably creates rebellious attitudes among the lower-class criminals and makes them less willing to abide by rules and regulations. "Class" justice is an important facet of modern crime control which needs more exploration than it has thus far received. But Sutherland's research on the white-collar criminal gives us evidence that upper- and upper-middle-class lawbreakers feel free to pick and choose as to which laws they will obey, whereas low-status lawbreakers are not permitted to decide for themselves about the validity of a law.

Cultural Tensions Within the Community

The tendency to regard one's own nation and culture as best and to ridicule and condemn practices of another people is universal. Considerable education is required to recognize that other persons may be equally sensible and intelligent or even superior when they act in such peculiar ways.

It is not surprising therefore that children who differ both from the major group and from the policemen in cultural background should figure prominently among those arrested and brought into court. We have discussed nativity in an earlier chapter. Of course there is always some criminality and so far as we ourselves are concerned the number of foreign born and those of foreign-born extraction is rapidly decreasing among our delinquent and criminal groups because of the reduction in immigration. Even so, we should point out here that cultural homogeneity reduces conflict because there is a tendency to define social situations similarly. Children of the foreign born are often struggling between the desires for their parents' approval at home and the approval of the children (and the teacher) at school. American children are in general treated much more democratically than is customary in European families. The child of foreign parentage may rebel against parental authority and his rebellious behavior may result in conflict with the law.

In the author's study of cultural heterogeneity as a factor in delinquency in Chicago, the proportion of nonnative-white population in each ward to the native-white population was considered the proportion of heterogeneity. The coefficient of correlation between the rate of delinquency in each ward and the proportion of heterogeneity was then determined according to the Pearsonian formula. The correlation (r) corrected according to percentage of error was then estimated to be from $+.57$ to $+.707$.[35] The 3 wards with the highest rate of

[35] Mabel A. Elliott, A Correlation Between Rate of Juvenile Delinquency and Racial Heterogeneity. Reprint from Welfare Magazine (July and August, 1926), pp. 14–20.

delinquency and the 3 with the lowest rate were then studied with reference to the racial and nationality groups in their respective populations. In the 3 wards with the highest delinquency rates the proportion of the foreign born and Negroes was found to be much greater than in those with the lowest delinquency rates. Furthermore the foreign-born white population in the wards with highest delinquency had a much higher proportion of south Europeans and Slavs than was true in the wards with low rates, in which the foreign born were predominantly north European.

It is well known that the problems of assimilation vary with the degrees of difference of the alien group from the native or *absorbing* group. American cultural norms are rooted in those of England and northern Europe, hence the southern and eastern Europeans face many more adjustment problems than do those from northern Europe.[36]

Heterogeneity of population in large political subdivisions such as states shows no such correlation with crime. However, in this case heterogeneity may not involve significant mixing of populations within close proximity. Austin L. Porterfield and Robert H. Talbert maintain that heterogeneity of population in the several states is accompanied by a negative correlation so far as crimes are concerned. Mississippi, which has the highest percentage of Negro population (and heterogeneity on basis of proportion of nonnative white population), has a crime rate less than half that of North Carolina.[37] In Mississippi, however, as Porterfield and Talbert show, there is no significant cultural conflict. Moreover, as these authors should have pointed out, many communities in the deep South do not "clutter up their courts" with Negro crimes.[38]

INSTITUTIONAL RELATIONSHIPS AND CRIME

Institutions, as every student in the social sciences knows, are organized methods of meeting human needs. Some are only partially successful in meeting those needs in present-day society, as research on the family, the church, the school, political institutions, and correctional institutions has made clear. All of these institutions are intimately and specifically concerned with the conduct of the indi-

[36] *Ibid.*, pp. 21–25.

[37] Austin L. Porterfield and Robert H. Talbert, *Crime, Suicide and Social Well-being*, Leo Potishman Foundation, Fort Worth, 1948, p. 38.

[38] Cf. Charles S. Johnson, *The Negro in American Civilization*, Holt, New York, p. 316.

viduals whose needs or problems they serve, hence deserve special consideration in a textbook on crime. Other institutions including the economic might also be analyzed, but for the purposes of presentation in this chapter we shall consider economic factors from the point of view of economic status and economic conditions. The wide variety of economic organizations engaged in production and distribution makes it difficult to analyze crime in relation to a specific factory, industry, or economic service. The family we have discussed under "Group Relationships and Crime." It should be pointed out here that training for family life is an institutional problem and one which has community and educational and religious ramifications.

Religious Affiliation and Criminal Behavior

The major functions of the church from a sociological point of view are to help the individual live and die in consonance with the highest values which the church has developed in interpreting the nature of the universe, God, and moral conduct. The effectiveness of the church is at least partially determined by the degree to which its members conform with its moral laws. These religious-moral laws are largely incorporated in the legal restraints which are imposed upon the common crimes of murder, rape, stealing, burglary, perjury, etc., hence the church may be rightly expected to produce law-abiding citizens, except insofar as political controls (as in the case of Communist countries, for example) are in opposition to the expressed beliefs or creeds of religious groups.

From one point of view, crime thus represents a failure upon the part of organized religion to train members of society to behave morally and "in love and charity with their neighbors." Criminals, insofar as they have behaved in ways contrary to the church's precepts, are certainly out of harmony with the church. The question therefore arises as to what degree of relationship has existed between the offender and the church.

Certain persons have insisted that church membership is conducive to crime. Others have conducted investigations which appear to indicate that a large share of both delinquents and criminals have a religious affiliation and that many delinquent children have attended religious services or Sunday school more or less regularly. Kvaraceus' study, for example, shows that 92 per cent of the delinquent children brought before the Passaic Children's Bureau were affiliated with some church and that 58 per cent attended services regularly.[39] For adult criminals, Franklin Steiner claimed that 80 per cent of 85,000 convicts considered themselves Christians, and C. V. Dunn found that 71.8 per cent of 25,726 prisoners claimed church affiliation.[40]

Those who have assumed there was any positive relationship between the church and criminality have ignored two important facts, however. First, such persons have not shown what percentage of church members and regular attendants commit crimes and delinquencies for which they are arrested. The percentage conceivably may be very small and in any event would give the only fair picture of the relation between religious affiliation and behavior. Second, the influence of the church is profoundly affected by both the social milieu and class attitudes of the community in which it functions. According to information cited by Philip M. Smith, a survey conducted by the Federal Council of Churches showed that two-thirds of the membership in the Roman Catholic and Baptist churches comes from the lower class.[41] These two denominations have the highest number of affiliations among prisoners, as Sutherland has pointed out. It is absurd, as the latter makes clear, to assume that they are criminal because of these affiliations. Their low social and economic status is unquestionably more important in determining their delinquent and criminal behavior.[42]

Many prisoners of south or eastern European extraction are nominal members of the Roman Catholic Church, and often the Catholic Church in the immigrant community is Polish Catholic or Italian Catholic or is designated by some other national group name. The young people tend to break away from these "foreign" churches because of their wish to be identified with Americans. Sometimes such young persons identify themselves with American churches. But in any event it is the decay both in social solidarity and in the general acceptance of rules and regulations in the community which produces disorganized behavior of the church member. The churches may not

[39] William C. Kvaraceus, "Delinquent Behavior and Church Attendance," *Sociology and Social Research*, 28:284–289 (March–April, 1944).

[40] Cf. Harry E. Barnes and Negley K. Teeters, *New Horizons in Criminology*, Prentice-Hall, New York, rev. ed., 1951, p. 184. Cf. also C. V. Dunn, "The Church and Crime in the United States," *The Annals of the American Academy of Political Science*, 125:200–228 (May, 1926).

[41] *Information Service*, Department of Research and Education of the Federal Council of Churches in America, May 15, 1948, p. 3. Cf. also Philip M. Smith, "Organized Religion and Criminal Behavior," *Sociology and Social Research*, 33:362–367 (May–June, 1949).

[42] Edwin H. Sutherland, *op. cit.*, pp. 193–194.

be doing an effective piece of work in preventing crime, but they are not engaged in promoting delinquency any more than the school is. The need for promoting good behavior is, however, a major challenge to all religious organizations.

It is also important to recognize that, though a large number of prisoners may have indicated some religious background or affiliation, actually very few of them have had any serious religious convictions; nor have they pursued Christian goals, save for the few religious conscientious objectors who have faced prison sentence rather than abandon their ideals. These latter, good or misguided as they may be, are persons who have dared to challenge the methods and ideals of the state. The crimes of most criminals, however, are tacit evidence that they have had little concern or love for either their neighbor or God and are in direct contradiction to both the first and the second great commandments as stated by Christ, as well as the ten commandments which are the common heritage of Judaic-Christian ethics. It is therefore nonsense to attach much importance to the fact that many criminals profess religious affiliations. As a matter of fact people not connected with any church often designate themselves as "Protestant" chiefly because they are not Catholic. Many whose families were nominally Roman Catholic, Jewish, or affiliated with some Protestant sect have long since quit attending the church or observing its precepts but may say they are Catholic or Jewish. No thoroughgoing acceptance of the ethical precepts of the Jewish or Christian religion is or can be consonant with avowed criminality. The church, on the other hand, takes the stand that all men are sinners and admits forgiveness to all who "offend God's holy ordinances" but are "heartily sorry for their misdoings," irrespective of the offense. In this view church and state have never agreed.

The blame we may attach to the church must be for its failing to offer parishioners (particularly young persons) vital help in meeting and adjusting to life problems. This Dr. Miriam van Waters holds to be a major dysfunction of the church.[43] Many churches are in a state of disorganization because of shifting population in the area in which they are located. Old members have moved away and newcomers may be unchurched or members of churches in other neighborhoods.[44] Most pastors do some counseling and a few churches employ social workers to help meet the various problems for which parishioners seek help. Such problems are often related to marital crises, extreme need,

[43] Miriam van Waters, *Youth in Conflict*, Republic, New York, 1925, p. 141.

[44] Robert E. Lee Faris, *Social Disorganization*, Ronald, New York, 1948, chap. 11, "Disorganization of Religious Institutions."

and bereavement.[45] But many mothers and fathers seek help in dealing with their behavior children. Here the clergyman and his assistants are called upon to do real social work, which after all is only "the art of helping people out of trouble." The church may be credited with doing the first social work and establishing the first agencies for meeting problems of the ill, the homeless, the friendless, and the down and out, as well as the several varieties of "sinners." The early church also gave refuge to many criminals and attempted to help them reorganize their lives.

Techniques for helping people have become so refined that most of the burden has been shifted (and wisely) to the social welfare agencies. Few social agencies, however, can offer people an opportunity to change their ways and an uplift of spirit which the "poor in spirit" so sorely need, as can the church. If the church is to accept Christ's mission it must keep in mind that He came not to call the righteous but sinners to repentance. It must also extend its help and counsel in time to reach the man or woman in need of help.[46]

Part of the reason the churches have failed to help the delinquents and criminals is that most of them have not reached beyond their own portals. The various evangelical missions, the Salvation Army, the Volunteers of America have been among the few who have recognized this challenge to religion.

What does work with pre-delinquents, delinquents, and criminals entail on the part of the church? Georgia E. Harkness has outlined the tasks in preventing crime among immigrants as follows: (1) removing the corrupting influences from the community, (2) helping the individual to develop a character which will resist temptation, (3) teaching the law and language, and (4) making sure that the accused secures justice in the courts.[47] These suggestions could be applied equally well by any church serving an underprivileged group. Unfortunately, few churches have assumed this form of stewardship toward their members.

The School, Delinquency, and Crime

TRUANCY

The failure of the school to interest and stimulate students is evidenced in the number who fail for other than intellectual reasons, and

[45] Cf. William H. Leach, *Toward a More Efficient Church*, Revell, New York, 1947, pp. 62–64.
[46] Wisser 'T Hooft and J. A. Oldham, *The Church and Its Foundation in Society*, Willett, Clark, Chicago, 1937, pp. 137–138.
[47] Georgia E. Harkness, *The Church and the Immigrant*, Doubleday, New York. 1921, p. 52.

in the number who leave school when there is no economic necessity for so doing. But it is most significantly evidenced in the children who are truants or attendance problems.

Truancy has long been considered a first step in delinquency and one that frequently leads to more serious difficulties because the child who skips school usually has some plan for spending his time. Of course he may be interested in nothing more than seeing what is beyond the bridge or exploring the business section. Some boys play truant in groups, as was true in the case of 54 out of 251 truants studied in New York City. Of these 251 adolescents who were released from the Truant School in 1922 and followed for at least 2 years thereafter 124 had no subsequent delinquency and 127 or 51 per cent had juvenile court or criminal records as follows:[48]

Number with Criminal or Delinquency Record	Classification of Offense	Per Cent
54	Juvenile delinquency	21
38	Misdemeanor	16
35	Felony	14

Number Without Criminal or Delinquency Record	Per Cent
124	49
251	100

Thirty per cent of the truants had records as adult offenders, which is a significant fact. However, felons were arraigned on an average of 5 times, misdemeanants 4.3 times, juvenile delinquents 3 times, whereas truants were arraigned only 1.4 times.[49]

EDUCATIONAL ACHIEVEMENT AND CRIMINALITY

There is at least limited evidence to the effect that crime rates decrease with educational achievement. An analysis of comparative crime rates in 1923 showed crime rates of 42.8 per 100,000 of the adult population and of only 14.3 per 100,000 of those who had pursued some study of college rank. In that year only 6.7 per cent of the population had attended college, as the following classification indicates. Unfortunately recent data on prisoners' educational status for the country as a whole are not available. For the first 6 months of 1923 the educational achievements of prisoners in federal and state prisons and re-

[48] Crime Commission of New York State, Subcommission on the Causes and Effects of Crime, *From Truancy to Crime*, Albany, 1928, p. 10.
[49] *Ibid.*, p. 11.

formatories in comparison to the adult population over 21 years old were as follows:[50]

Educational Classification	General Population	Prisoners
Illiterate	7.1%	10.7%
Able to read and write	92.9	89.3
Last school attended:		
Elementary	61.1	67.5
High school	25.1	15.4
College	6.7	3.4
Not reported	—	3.0

The percentage of college graduates in the general population has increased notably in recent years but we have no comparable figures with reference to college-trained civilians and prisoners. In 1923 no offense appears to have required a college degree except that of illegal abortion. Prisoners who had had some college training fell into certain groups, however, constituting 22.5 per cent of the embezzlers, 16.6 per cent of those convicted for fraud, and 8.5 per cent of the forgery group.[51] The highest grade attained by at least 50 per cent of the prisoners is as follows:[52]

Grade Attained	Offense for Which Committed
4	Assault
5	Homicide and violating liquor laws
6	Rape, violating drug laws, burglary
7	Rape, violating drug laws, burglary
8	Forgery, fraud
High school	Embezzlement

EDUCATIONAL DIFFERENTIALS BETWEEN LOWER-CLASS ITALIANS AND JEWS AND THEIR CRIME RATES

Jackson Toby has recently made an interesting study on the disparity in crime rates between lower-class Italian and Jewish groups in the United States. His general hypothesis is that those who pursue crime as a career are recruited from lower-class males "who fail to introject the goal of social mobility." Toby believes that boys from this group do not think they can make a success at a legitimate career. For one thing they do not have enough education to succeed in a legitimate occupation, failing either because of lack of native ability or from

---

[50] These data are derived from Table 12, *The Prisoner's Antecedents*, 1923, Bureau of the Census, U.S. Department of Commerce, Washington, 1929, p. 21.
[51] *Ibid.*, p. 21.   [52] *Ibid.*

lack of motivation. Yet because of our high standard of living they crave financial success.

The reason for the differential in crime rate between lower-class Jewish and Italian groups, Toby concludes, is that Jewish boys are motivated to secure an education because of Jewish cultural tradition, whereas southern Italy (where most of our Italian immigrants originated) is hostile toward education.[53]

EMOTIONAL TRAINING

In general we have been far more effective in framing definitions of delinquency than in educating young persons in the meaning and importance of the social values which are incorporated in our laws and customs. Parents and teachers both could do much to help children understand the values of chastity, truthfulness, holding one's temper, and respecting the personal property of others. Children have to learn that these things are important and often they receive no education in such matters.[54] Children also need help in the emotional adjustments entailed in growing up. Frankwood Williams has accused teachers and parents of behaving as though becoming acquainted with literature and history and mastering algebra were the most important educational achievements of young persons. Actually it is probably more important to help them emancipate themselves from controls and learn to make suitable heterosexual adjustments, upon which secure and happy family life depends.[55]

MORAL EDUCATION

Moral or character education within the schools has never been very effectively implemented. The schools all too often turn their moral problems over to the juvenile court instead of recognizing them for what they are, educational problems. If schools envisioned their task as one of preparing for life instead of a matter of teaching children to read, do sums, and acquire a series of facts in a series of subjects, they could assume a major role in helping children to adjust adequately to life situations. Ways in which this might be done are discussed in Chapter 28.

[53] Cf. Jackson Toby, "Educational Maladjustment as a Predisposing Factor in Criminal Careers," Doctoral dissertation, Harvard University Library, 1950. A summary of the thesis was furnished for this discussion by Jackson Toby, in correspondence, dated July 24, 1951.

[54] Much of the material in this section is based on an article by the author. Cf. Mabel A. Elliott, "Can Your Community Control Delinquency?" *National Parent Teacher*, 38:4–6 (December, 1943).

[55] Cf. Frankwood Williams, *Adolescence*, Farrar & Rinehart, New York, 1930, pp. 101–120.

In connection with this discussion we must keep in mind that differences in educational attainment have been marked in the past by differences in economic and social background. Within recent years a high school education has become rather common and there has been a great increase in the number of college graduates. It is therefore probable that the number of prisoners with high school and college training will increase—unless, that is, we greatly revamp the emphasis of our educational program so that with each successive year of training the individual becomes better trained to meet the obligations of a law-abiding citizen.

Political Institutions and Crime

Because crime involves breaking the law, the political or governmental structure of the community may be regarded as responsible in a major degree for keeping down crime. The political structure of the community, however, is a function of the collective will of the people; the degree to which citizens expend effective effort will determine the type and quality of government they enjoy or endure. Good government requires eternal vigilance on the part of the good citizens. Where dishonesty, corruption, and incompetence become intrenched in local government, crime always flourishes. For political corruption not only promotes crime, political corruption *is* crime.[56]

There are many ways in which the political organization is responsible for crime, but the four most important are through (1) weak government, (2) political corruption of the government's administrative officers, (3) ineffective or corrupt police, (4) the difficulties inherent in the operation of our system of criminal justice.

POLITICAL CORRUPTION

There probably will always be a residue of petty thieves and a certain number of violent crimes such as murder, as well as other violations, under the best of municipal governments. Many crimes do not require malfeasance on the part of those who are responsible for the administration of local politics. Organized crime could not exist, however, if local government officials were wholeheartedly engaged in enforcing the law and in bringing to justice those who are making a business of crime, as we have discussed in Chapter 6.

[56] Cf. Mabel A. Elliott and Francis E. Merrill, *op. cit.*, chaps. 25 and 26, for a more extended discussion of the interlocking relationships between corrupt politics, crime, and community disorganization.

The corrupt politicians may commit crimes themselves when they pad pay rolls, hire people to perform nonexistent jobs, take slices out of the payments made to contractors for paving and for erecting municipal buildings and bridges, or pay political cohorts high salaries to look for nonexistent leaks in the water system, to hang up towels once a day in a washroom in a park, or to appear at a desk in the city hall once a month. Such graft has been a part of the cost of government in many cities.[57]

Dishonest men in office frequently take bribes from the big-time gamblers and houses of prostitution and racketeers in return for allowing them to carry on their illicit enterprises unmolested by local police. Often the police, too, exact a toll for ignoring the operation of lotteries and for not investigating the activities of racketeers. When the public becomes aroused over some notorious offense a corrupt police system may make a few token arrests and raids. The public is temporarily satisfied and never notices that many of the cases never come to trial, for the political corruption extends to fixing the cases in court.

That desire for political office and the power that goes with it corrupts many men is a truism long since established. And politicians who ordinarily stand for decency in government sometimes compromise themselves in order to get elected. The recent disclosures on the close relationship between the former mayor of New York City and the notorious and fabulously wealthy Frank Costello ("kingpin racketeer") and other gangsters are a case in point.[58] Many other city officials in other communities have had just as unholy alliances. The underworld henchmen of Big Bill Thompson of Chicago, the Thomas Pendergast machine in Kansas City, the notorious gas ring in Philadelphia afford further illustration.

CORRECTIONAL INSTITUTIONS AND CRIME

Since so great a proportion of criminals are recidivists there seems to be large reason for believing that penal experience in our correctional institutions is a stimulus to further crimes. The offender's criminal habits are reinforced by the hardening process of imprisonment. He is also introduced to new methods of committing crimes.

So far as jails are concerned there is little that can be said in their favor, as the discussion in Chapter 18 will make clear. Yet the vast majority of offenders are misdemeanants who are exposed not only to one another but to the old hardened felons, drug addicts, liquor

[57] Ibid., chap. 25.　　[58] Newsweek, 37:30 (May 14, 1951).

law violators, murderers, and gangsters in detention awaiting trial. In 1923 it was estimated that 58.1 per cent of all commitments were to county jails and that county and municipal workhouses, chain gangs, and county penal farms received an additional 28.7 per cent. That is, 86.8 per cent of offenders were committed to institutions whose whole effect was regarded as unsavory; the surroundings for the most part were dirty and unsanitary. In general such institutions were training schools for further crimes.[59] This situation is still true.

Meanwhile, we have no general agreement as to what should determine the basis of treatment or punishment of the offender, as we discuss in a later section. On the one hand, there is loud-spoken and insistent belief on part of the classical school of penology that any "responsible" person guilty of an offense should receive a penalty commensurate with the seriousness of the crime. The "positive" school, on the other hand, believes that treatment should be the major consideration and should be based on a careful study of the personality and social dangerousness of the individual offender. In the main, this theory is the one held by the majority of criminologists and psychiatrists today. The latter maintain that society can profit in the long run only through the readjustment of the offender. Modern criminologists believe, too, that the severity and vengeance involved in the classical point of view defeat its purposes, for prisoners are for the most part returned to society. Follow-up studies appear to indicate that prisoners have often been damaged by long sentences and institutional experience, rather than improved. The prison's part in promoting crime will be treated in detail in Section IV.

THE ECONOMIC STRUCTURE AND CRIME
Economic Status and Crime

It is not necessary to be a radical to believe that there is a significant relationship between economic status and the crime rate. Disparities in economic status result in disparities in social status, in the ability to achieve a desirable standard of living, and in the opportunity for privilege and leadership within the group.

Not all crimes are due to misery or poverty, as our previous discussion of organized crime should have made clear. Nevertheless, the relationship between low economic and social status and delinquency

[59] National Crime Commission, Subcommittee on Pardons, Parole, Probation, Penal Laws and Institutional Correction, *Propagating Crime Through the Jail and Other Institutions for Short Term Offenders*. New York, 1929, pp. 6–7 and 17.

and crime is everywhere observable. This fact has given rise to the Marxian doctrine that crime is a normal residue of the capitalistic system, just as poverty and wealth are assumed to be the necessary extremes of such a system. Capitalistic society protects private property, which is sacrosanct to capitalists, according to the Communist viewpoint. But to the proletariat there is nothing sacrosanct about what he does not possess. Hence, Engels asks, "What adequate reason has the proletarian for refraining from theft?"[60] Today we know that antisocial behavior is not confined to the lowest economic and social classes and that many big-time professional criminals become wealthy. It is nevertheless true that those arrested and convicted for conventional crimes come largely from the lowest economic groups.

When the majority of any nation or community is poor it is not necessary to assume that poverty itself is a causal factor in crime. The majority of lawbreakers are bound to come from the largest group. In the United States, however, we have much evidence that the lowest economic and social groups are contributing a disproportionate number of the delinquents and criminals who are brought into court.

This fact has been established by many studies; those cited in the section dealing with disturbed occupational relationships should suffice for example. Another effective demonstration of the relation between economics and delinquency is evidenced in Clifford R. Shaw and Henry D. McKay's research on delinquency areas. Shaw and McKay studied the distribution of boys who were juvenile delinquents in Chicago, Philadelphia, Greater Boston, Cincinnati, Greater Cleveland, Richmond (Virginia), Columbus, Birmingham (Alabama), Little Rock (Arkansas), and Denver. Briefly stated, their conclusion was that persons of low economic status were segregated into areas which were deteriorating physically and therefore losing population.[61] Here a much higher percentage of the families was on relief than in other areas, the median rental for the areas was much lower than for the city as a whole, and a disproportionate number of the breadwinners were industrial workers. (Shaw's figures were for 1934 when wages in industry were notably low.) The foreign born and the Negroes, who are at the bottom of the economic ladder, were concentrated in these deteriorated areas, and far more families of these groups than of native-born whites were on relief. Tuberculosis, which is a disease

[60] Cf. Karl Marx and Friedrich Engels, The Communist Manifesto, transl. by Eden and Cedar Paul, International, New York, 1930, pp. 128–131.
[61] Clifford R. Shaw and Henry D. McKay, Juvenile Delinquency and Urban Areas, University of Chicago Press, Chicago, 1942, pp. 43–85.

much more common among the poor than among the comfortable or well-to-do, was also concentrated in these areas.[62]

Economic Conditions and Crime

In times past economic need has generally become more acute with rising prices, since wage rates have usually lagged behind increases in prices. Since World War II we have had the phenomenon of a rise in wages for industrial workers before price adjustments; hence economic need has not been a serious reason for crimes or increases in crimes among this group. White-collar workers have had less increase in wages (so far as buying power is concerned) but no study has been made of the increases (or decreases) in crime among this group. The crimes of the white-collar worker—as well as those of the executives of industry—should be studied more exhaustively.

In the meantime there have been significant analyses made of the cost of certain commodities in relation to crime. In 1918 Parmalee wrote an important textbook on criminology covering many studies on the relation between economic conditions and crime.[63] Parmalee believed that it was not only poverty but the desire for a higher standard of living which led to crime. One of the earlier studies was that of William A. Bonger, the Dutch criminologist, who made an extensive analysis of the relation between the cost of cereals and the crime rate. In England, France, and Wales he correlated the price of wheat with the crimes against property and in Germany he studied the price of rye in relation to the number of thefts; in each instance he found an inverse ratio between the cost of each and the crime rate. Thus poverty was in his estimation a major reason for crime. Bonger recognized, however, that many economic crimes are motivated by a desire for luxuries rather than for absolute necessities.[64]

Dorothy Swaine Thomas made an important study of the effect of general economic conditions on crime in her analysis of the relation between the business cycle and crimes in England for the period 1857–1913. Here she found a slightly inverse ratio between increase in prosperity and the crime rate.[65] Because all indictable offenses included crimes of violence, murder, malicious injury, she established a separate

[62] *Ibid.*, pp. 32–42.
[63] Maurice Parmalee, *Criminology*, Macmillan, New York, 1918, chap. 6, "The Economic Basis of Crime."
[64] William A. Bonger, *Criminality and Economic Conditions*, Little, Brown, Boston, 1916, pp. 564–571.
[65] Dorothy S. Thomas, *Social Aspects of the Business Cycle*, Routledge, London, 1925, p. 138. Cf. also Mabel A. Elliott and Francis E. Merrill, *op. cit.*, pp. 125–126.

category for crimes. She then found that the correlation between property crimes with violence and the business cycle for the same period was +.44 when correlated synchronously. A somewhat smaller coefficient of correlation of +.37 occurred when a two-year lag was allowed. That is, she found a marked tendency for crimes of burglary, house- and shop-breaking, and robbery to occur in times of economic depression and to decrease with better times. There was little correlation between malicious crimes and injuries and the business cycle, but sex crimes seemed to decrease with hard times.[66]

The frequency of crimes against person in fact tends to be higher in good times than in poor times. Sex crimes appear to increase in good times, as Dorothy Thomas points out.[67] Luxurious living and the consumption of large amounts of spirituous liquor require money. These are often associated with sexual offenses. Since the number of rapes in New York during the period 1930–1939 went up and down with the business index[68] von Hentig concludes that there is a relation between prosperity and rape. He recognizes that part of this may be due to the fact that fewer parents or victims are paid off (outside the court) in boom times. Wealth may be a factor in the seduction in the first place. Von Hentig holds there is also an additional factor. Prosperity seems to stimulate sexual activity, as is expressed both in higher marriage rates during business booms and in illegal sexual behavior.[69]

We have mentioned the unemployment rate among prisoners. The extent of unemployment in the general population likewise has been studied, with the conclusion that unemployment is conducive to crimes against property. This was true following the stock market break in 1929 up to and through 1932, but between that date and 1934 there was no widespread increase in crimes despite the great increase in the ranks of the unemployed. However, by that time the nation-wide federal relief program had been initiated and this must have done much to maintain a relatively high level of morale among those out of work by offsetting the fears of hunger and starvation as well as of eviction for lack of rent.[70] On the other hand we know from previously cited studies that many prisoners had been unemployed prior to committing their crimes.

[66] Dorothy S. Thomas, op. cit., pp. 139 and 141–142.
[67] Ibid.
[68] Cf. Report of the Mayor's Committee for Study of Sex Offenses, New York, 1942, p. 39.
[69] Hans von Hentig, Crime: Causes and Conditions, pp. 222–223.
[70] George B. Vold, "The Amount and Nature of Crime," American Journal of Sociology, 40:796–803 (May, 1935).

There is no basis for assuming that poverty is the sole factor in crime. As Cyril Burt pointed out in his study of *The Young Delinquent*, it is not so much poverty as "relative poverty" which has promoted irresistible desires that are conducive to crime.[71] If they cannot share in the fancied advantages of consuming highly desired and advertised goods otherwise, many persons are willing to steal.

The author's study of Sleighton Farm girls showed that it was not poverty alone or broken homes alone that caused a girl to be delinquent. It was rather the poverty-stricken broken home (where the father or mother was dead or had deserted) of low moral status which seemed to produce the delinquent girl. Even so, the girl seldom was convicted for stealing but was usually brought to court for a sex offense. Morality, as we have pointed out before, seems to be a middle-class virtue and it is probably easier for middle-class persons to be "moral" than for either the extremely wealthy or the very poor.[72]

Sutherland's study on the white-collar criminal and other studies of criminality among unpunished groups indicate that lawbreaking is a rather common human trait. If society respects one type of criminal while it subjects another to stern disapproval, it is difficult to reorganize our approach to the treatment of crime. For we can reconcile differences in social definitions of crime only by shifting the basic requirement for achieving respect from the possession of wealth to an acceptance of individual responsibility for abiding by legal restrictions which promote the general welfare.

The Economic Aspects of Seasonal and Geographic Differences in Crime

It is well known that crime rates vary both with the seasons and with climate. Economic crimes, for example, are greater in winter, apparently because it costs more to live. Fuel costs increase and warm winter clothing is much more expensive than summer apparel. Economic need is also greater in the winter months because unemployment increases with the decline in agricultural work, building trades, and other employment. Not all robberies and burglaries can be accounted for by economic need but it is significant that the highest number take place in winter when economic need is greatest. In 1950, for example, the greatest number of both robberies and burglaries was

[71] Cyril Burt, *The Young Delinquent*, University of London, London, 1938, pp. 68–69.

[72] Cf. Mabel A. Elliott, *Correctional Education and the Delinquent Girl*, especially pp. 26–28.

in January and December, while the low month for these offenses was June.[73]

Crimes against persons also vary with season. More crimes of violence and more sex crimes are committed in summer than winter, as discussed in Chapter 3. We can presume that the high rate of crimes against person in summer is partially a matter of increased social relationships. More people spend more time out of doors in summer and thus come into contact with a greater variety of persons than is true in winter. More people are also on vacation in summer away from the restraining and inhibiting influences of family and community. Young women are more likely to be sexually assaulted away from home than in their own homes. In 1950 murder, rape, and assaults were all at their peaks during the summer months. The greatest number of murders was in late August, the highest number of rapes in late July, and the highest number of assaults in mid-June.[74]

CRIME AND THE LARGER COMMUNITY

Our discussion of crime in its relation to community disorganization has emphasized the local community. We must also recognize that modern crime is not a local problem but national and even international in character. Modern means of communication and rapid transportation have so mobilized criminals that the agencies which deal with their apprehension, conviction, and treatment should not be those of the isolated community. Effective organization against crime will entail a centralization of effort and co-operation within and between states, as well as between states and the federal government. Ultimately, the only solution to crime lies in prevention, and in building up a more generally accepted code of behavior among all ranks and conditions of men. The local, state, and national communities are all responsible for permitting crime to exist without greater effort to combat it.

SOCIAL DISORGANIZATION AND CRIME

Thus whether we are discussing disturbed relationships within the family, age and sex groups, or occupational groups, or within the larger community, social disorganization is definitely related to crime. These relationships produce the frustrations leading to violence and the stimuli to economic crimes. Institutions which no longer meet the

[73] Uniform Crime Reports, Annual Bulletin, 1950, Federal Bureau of Investigation, U.S. Department of Justice, Washington, 1951, p. 87.
[74] Ibid., pp. 84–85.

needs of human beings on a satisfactory basis contribute to the failure of individuals to define situations on a socially acceptable basis. Part of the social disorganization which is responsible for crime grows out of lack of standards, as in case of persons growing up in the slum areas, or out of the organized attempts on the part of gangsters, racketeers, corrupt politicians, and other antisocial groups to subvert social institutions to their own selfish ends.

War, as the most violent form of social disorganization, accomplishes its ends by disrupting the stability of family life, by destroying the economic foundations of society, and by channeling the normal functions of the church, educational institutions, welfare agencies, and even government itself into the war effort. We cannot recount the extensive disruptions of war here in any detail. But it is in the transvaluation of the moral values of peoples—so that they come to accept illicit sex experience, violence, death, and destruction almost callously—that much of the most serious social disorganization of the soldier takes place.

War and Crime

As our discussion on the extent of crime indicates in Chapter 3, crime rates went down sharply during the war chiefly, we may presume, because the young men (who constitute the largest number of offenders) were inducted into the armed services. So far as children are concerned, war appears to make an immediate impact. Sex delinquency among young girls tends to increase for a number of reasons. (1) They are exposed to many additional temptations because they are often left to shift for themselves while their mothers are employed in war plants or because the families have moved to new and crowded areas. (Stealing rates for boys also go up in crowded areas.) (2) They are exploited by soldiers in military camps and training centers.

The statistics gathered by the Children's Bureau in Washington for the war years showed that there was a 56 per cent increase in all juvenile delinquency for the years 1939 to 1944 over 1938. The delinquency rate for girls, though still far lower than that for boys, increased more proportionately than the boys' rate—that is, 82 per cent in contrast to 51 per cent among the boys.[75] However, these statistics cover only the courts in the larger urban communities throughout the

[75] Preliminary Statement—Juvenile Court Statistics, 1944, Division of Statistical Research, Children's Bureau, Federal Security Agency, Washington (February 24, 1945), p. 1.

country and these are the communities in which many abnormal conditions resulted from the war, including an enormous increase in mobile population, overcrowding, lack of sufficient recreational facilities for war workers' children, etc.[76]

So far as sex offenses were concerned, they went up for both sexes, and for adults as well as children. But because of the double standard, boys and men, including soldiers, seldom figured in the statistics except where rape was alleged. Rape cases went up during the war. The average annual number for the years 1939–1941 was 4286. By 1944 the annual number was 5443, as the following figures show:[77]

Rape Cases Annual Number	Year or Years
4,286	1939–1941
4,754	1942
5,224	1943
5,443	1944

The number of rape cases reported is unquestionably inaccurate; the notoriety to which the victim is exposed is a powerful deterrent to reporting the incident, as is mentioned in the chapter on the woman offender. It is also true that some cases of rape are alleged when the victim was a willing participant in the sex relationship.[78] The major rape cases during wartime, however, are undoubtedly in the fighting zones and areas of occupation, where soldiers take abnormal license with women of the enemy country. For these we have no reliable statistics. The stories of almost unbelievable sexual license by German and Russian soldiers in enemy or occupied territory have some basis in fact. The United States Army has enforced rigid punishment for rape where reported and verified, but it has never been able to curb illicit sex relationships.

When the soldier returns to civilian life many problems complicate his readjustments. Moreover he belongs to the age group which commits the most crimes. But we cannot ignore the fact that war has taught men to lie, to steal, to destroy, to kill, even to rape, and that it must be hard for many soldiers to adjust to the moral values which are so important for effective community life.[79]

[76] Cf. Francis E. Merrill, *Social Problems on the Home Front*, Harper, New York, 1948, pp. 151–159.

[77] *Ibid.*, p. 109.

[78] Cf. chap. 6, pp. 121–122.

[79] Cf. Mabel A. Elliott and Francis E. Merrill, *op. cit.*, pp. 87–88, 107–108, and chap. 34, "War."

SELECTED BIBLIOGRAPHY

Bonger, William, *Criminality and Economic Conditions*, Little, Brown, Boston, 1916. A thoroughgoing economic determinist presents his case for the economic basis of crime.

Elliott, Mabel A., *Conflicting Penal Theories in Statutory Criminal Law*, University of Chicago Press, Chicago, 1931, chap. 13, "The Conflicting Trends in Statutory Penal Law." This chapter summarizes the confusion in our penal thinking which complicates the whole problem of crime in the United States. The author contends this has an effect on the incidence of crime itself.

Elliott, Mabel A., *Correctional Education and the Delinquent Girl*, Commonwealth of Pennsylvania, Harrisburg, 1929. Important details are given with reference to the low economic and social status of delinquent girls committed to Sleighton Farm, Darlington, Pennsylvania.

Elliott, Mabel A., and Merrill, Francis E., *Social Disorganization*, Harper, New York, 1950, chaps. 5, 6, 25, 26, and 34. These chapters cover material on social and economic factors in delinquency and crime, as well as the impact of war on behavior.

Glueck, Sheldon and Eleanor T., *Five Hundred Criminal Careers*, Knopf, New York, 1930, chaps. 6 and 7. These chapters give an excellent picture of the family, nativity, associates, industrial history, etc., of the 510 men whom the authors followed through several successive studies to determine their later adjustments.

Glueck, Sheldon and Eleanor, *Unraveling Juvenile Delinquency*, The Commonwealth Fund, Harvard University Press, 1951. This book, although devoted to juvenile delinquency, gives important comparative data on the genesis of antisocial attitudes, particularly with reference to the delinquents' families.

Healy, William, and Bronner, Augusta F., *Delinquents and Criminals, Their Making and Unmaking*, Macmillan, New York, 1928. A classic among studies shows both the factors producing delinquency and those which condition subsequent adjustment.

Hentig, Hans von, *Crime: Causes and Conditions*, McGraw-Hill, New York, 1947. In a scholarly and exhaustive book Dr. von Hentig covers various causes including the social and economic.

Hentig, Hans von, *The Criminal and His Victim*, Yale University Press, New Haven, 1948. This book deals with the social factors in the criminal's background as well as biological and psychological data. The victim's role in crime is especially emphasized.

Merrill, Francis E., *Social Problems on the Home Front*, Harper, New York, 1948. This book gives some excellent statistical data covering the period 1939–1944 on the immediate impact of war on juvenile delinquency and sex offenses. The material is too close to the war to show the long-run impact of war on adult antisocial behavior since most crime rates increase following a war, not during a war, however.

Parmelee, Maurice, *Criminology*, Macmillan, New York, 1918, chap. 6, "The Economic Basis of Crime." This chapter gives an excellent summary, especially of the nineteenth century, of early statistical analyses of economic conditions in relation to crime.

Shaw, Clifford R., and McKay, Henry D., *Juvenile Delinquency in Urban Areas*, University of Chicago Press, Chicago, 1942. Representing the summation of 20 years' study, this book shows that juvenile delinquents as brought before courts come almost entirely from the depressed, deteriorating slum and interstitial areas in every city where the problem has been studied.

The Prisoner's Antecedents, 1923, Bureau of the Census, U.S. Department of Commerce, Washington, 1929. This publication gives a statistical analysis of social data for all prisoners in reformatories and prisons in the United States. Although conditions have changed in certain respects much of the data are still applicable.

Thomas, Dorothy S., *Social Aspects of the Business Cycle*, Routledge, London, 1925. This book examines the relationship between trends in the business cycle and various social phenomena including different types of crime.

Thrasher, Frederick H., *The Gang*, University of Chicago Press, Chicago, 1927. This is the classic study of 1313 young and adolescent boys' gangs in Chicago.

Van Kleeck, Mary, Winslow, Emma A., and Reid, Ira de A., *Work and Law Observance*, in *Report on the Causes of Crime*, Vol. I, Report No. 13 of the National Commission on Law Observance and Enforcement, Washington, 1931. Unemployment and work relationships in the background of prisoners at Sing Sing are examined.

CHAPTER 14

Theories of Criminality

(A Summary of the Reasoned Conceptions as to the Causes of Crime)

From our survey of the various researches on the personal, group, and environmental factors in crime in the preceding chapters it should be obvious that criminality is a complicated problem. The question "What causes crime?" admits no easy answer. Many of the theories of criminality have been built upon prejudiced thinking which has militated against any truly scientific approach. No present theory of criminality can be considered final; most sociologists regard the group associations and social environment of the individual as setting the pattern for criminal behavior, and psychologists and psychiatrists emphasize the internal motivations which prompt the offender to behave as he does. It seems likely that both approaches are correct but that each represents a different perspective from which the crime problem is viewed. These and other theories will be discussed in detail later in the chapter. Interest in the cause or causes of crime is in itself a sociological phenomenon and arose in connection with the development of the psychological and social sciences.

Penology Antedates Criminal Research

As material in Section IV will make clear, scientific study in the field of criminology was preceded by earnest considerations with reference to penology. Since established theological and philosophical opinion both regarded man as a free creature able to decide for himself the course of his own behavior, there was little interest in any research into causes of criminal activity. The criminal was regarded as one who willfully chose to do wrong. The major social interest in criminals lay in what action society should take against them. Hence theories of punishment, or more properly theories justifying punishment, developed in connection with the types of penalties attached. These theories of deterrence, retribution, reformation, reparation, and social utility are discussed in Chapter 16.[1]

Eventually thoughtful men became distressed with the types of punishments exacted. The savage exercise of the death penalty was reduced and what was then believed to be more rational and humane treatment of prisoners was developed. It is noteworthy that these reforms did not begin in western Europe and in the British colonies until the seventeenth and eighteenth centuries. Such reforms were led by both religious leaders (especially the Quakers and notably Elizabeth Fry and John Howard) and learned philosophers of the period including Jeremy Bentham, Romilly, Beccaria, and Feuerbach, but even they were more concerned with treating criminals than with exploring the causes and nature of criminal conduct.[2]

Early Research into Causes of Crime

No significant research into the causes of crime developed until scholars became interested in the general subjects of psychology, psychiatry, biology, and sociology. For it is these branches of learning that have attempted on a scientific basis to find out what causes crime. The occult "sciences" of physiognomy and phrenology preceded true scientific research by trying to relate the appearance and structure of the face and the cranial structure of criminals to their delinquent behavior, as we have discussed in Chapter 12. These pseudosciences were widely accepted as late as the middle of the nineteenth century as providing adequate bases for determining the criminality of offenders. In fact these ideas probably stimulated Lombroso to make his anthropometric study of criminals which in turn led him to believe that he had discovered the anomalies which distinguish "criminal man." Preceding Lombroso early psychiatrists also made studious inquiries into the nature of criminals. The French psychiatrist Phillipe Pinel (1745–1826) developed his conception of mental illness as a degeneration in the mental faculties, which theory was carried further through Bene-

[1] Cf. Mabel A. Elliott, *Conflicting Theories in Statutory Criminal Law*, University of Chicago Press, Chicago, 1931, chap. 2, especially pp. 20–22.

[2] C. Bernaldo de Quiros, *Modern Theories of Criminality*, transl. by Alfonso de Salvio, Little, Brown, Boston, 1911, pp. xiii–xiv.

dict A. Morel (1809–1872) to a conception of moral insanity. Morel believed from his researches that mental degeneration was hereditary and he and later psychiatrists of the nineteenth century did much to perpetuate a belief in heredity as a major factor in criminality. Henry Maudsley (1835–1918), the British psychiatrist, diagnosed the criminal as morally insane and wrote an important article on "The Heredity Nature of Crime" in 1870.[3] Maudsley published many books relating to mind and body, the matter of responsibility and disease, and the relation between physical pathology and mental disease.

Meanwhile A. M. Guerry (1802–1866) had advanced the opinion that there was an ecological factor in crime and A. Quetelet (1796–1874) held that age, sex, and climate all affected crime rates.

By the middle of the nineteenth century Marx and Engels developed their theory of socialism and maintained that all crime was the effect of the capitalist system. The idea of the economic roots of crime gained many adherents, of whom William A. Bonger, the Dutch sociologist, was the leading exponent. His book, published in 1905 in Amsterdam, discussed the various preceding biological and psychological approaches to crime, which he more or less thought to demolish by extensive statistics showing crime to be closely related to the economic status of the individual offender and to economic conditions in general.[4]

Most early sociology consisted in armchair inspection of man's activities and was chiefly introspective analysis. Charles R. Henderson apparently wrote the first significant sociological treatise on the causes of crime in America in 1893 when he published *An Introduction to the Defective, Dependent and Delinquent Classes*.[5] This book went through numerous editions, and in 1914 Henderson published a small brochure on *The Causes and Cure of Crime*.[6] In brief, Henderson held that the causes of crime are factors of "*personality and environment* and of the reaction of personality upon environment in the formation of habits and new nature!" The environmental influences he mentioned included the external physical world of climate, seasons, and meteorological changes. Under social conditions he listed conjugal relations, social position, density of population, customs, economic conditions, food, famine, beliefs, industrial education, political factors, association and suggestion, lynching, and immigration. Under "the physical and

[3] *Ibid.*, pp. 5–9.
[4] Cf. William A. Bonger, *Criminality and Economic Conditions*, transl. by Henry P. Horton, Little, Brown, Boston, 1916.
[5] Published by Heath, Boston, 1893.
[6] Published by McClurg, Chicago.

psychical nature of the individual" he regarded sex, education, occupation, alcoholism, heredity, and individual degeneration as important. Of these various factors Henderson believed the social factors were the most significant causes of crime and he also held that these were the causes which society could most hopefully expect to eliminate.[7] Henderson was obviously an eclectic who recognized that behavior was affected by many stimuli. Most of the criminal research since he made this compilation of causes has explored some facet of his suggested list.

Following extensive developments in the fields of psychology and the social sciences, a National Conference on Criminal Law and Criminology was called at Northwestern University in 1909 in celebration of the fiftieth anniversary of the founding of the university's School of Law. The 150 delegates were outstanding leaders in medicine, psychology, sociology, and penology, as well as persons actively engaged in juvenile court work and legal aid societies, judges of the criminal court, leaders of the bar, and representatives from state attorneys' offices.[8] The conference itself gave impetus to the study of criminology on a university level in the United States. Since that time many important and trivial researches into the causes of crime have been completed. We now know a great many facts about crime and criminals, but it is difficult to establish any precise relation between criminality and factors associated with crime. Out of the numerous reasons which could probably be invoked in explanation for this lack of precise scientific conclusions, two in particular appear to be of importance: (1) Criminal behavior is human behavior. (2) There is great disparity in definitions of crime itself.

Crime Is Human Behavior

The causes of criminal behavior are hard to measure because criminal behavior is human behavior. Human behavior is hard to measure because behavior involves the attitudes, habits, and thinking processes of men as well as their overt conduct. An act involves internal as well as external stimuli just as surely as this book is as much the product of the author's mind as it is of the hand which wrote it. No student

---

[7] Cf. Charles R. Henderson, *Dependent, Defective and Delinquent Classes*, Heath, Boston, 2nd ed., 1901, pp. 237–253.

[8] Cf. Robert H. Gault, "Criminology in Northwestern University," *Journal of Criminal Law and Criminology and Police Science*, 42:2–17 (May–June, 1951). (This conference is discussed in chap. 1.)

can see what goes on within the author's mind. He can only see what is put down on paper in black and white. Nor can anyone see what goes on in the mind of the offender preceding his overt criminal act or while he is committing it. Why a criminal commits an offense is a matter involving many imponderables. Mathematical precision has exploded the atom. It is conceivable that it may eventually lay bare the mysteries locked together in human personality, but human personality is much more complicated than the atom. It is not surprising, therefore, that there are so many interpretations of antisocial behavior.

Variations in Definition of Crime and Criminal Theory

What is defined as a crime varies somewhat from state to state, as we have mentioned. This fact likewise complicates any valid theory of crime. For what indeed may be held to induce criminal behavior if an act is a crime in one state and not in another? Does something sinister motivate the gambler in California when he may legally enter into a variety of gambling activities in Nevada and commit no crime? What, for example, is drunken driving? Is a driver with liquor on his breath culpable? Must his blood show a certain percentage of alcohol, or must he be involved in a traffic accident? The purely legal interpretation of crime and consequent criminality becomes very confusing. It may thus be a logical question as to whether the crime is culturally precipitated or is a matter of willful misbehavior.

Michael and Adler's Rejection of Criminal Research

After reviewing the various researches in (1) crime, (2) its treatment, and (3) its prevention, Jerome Michael and Mortimer J. Adler dismissed all such studies as useless in a polemical treatise on the subject. Their contention was that these researches were based on faulty analyses, used bad statistical techniques, and led to no precise theory of crime. Such an extreme conclusion is, in the present author's viewpoint, unwarranted, but we may profitably consider Michael and Adler's viewpoint.[9]

These two gentlemen maintained that criminality must be a function of other factors, that criminality must be in fact a *dependent variable*. All psychological and sociological research up to that date

[9] Jerome Michael and Mortimer J. Adler, *Crime, Law and Social Science*, Bureau of Social Hygiene, New York, 1932. This book was subsequently published by Harcourt, Brace, New York, in 1933.

they declared invalid because of the lack of control groups. There had been a failure to establish the significance of percentages in statistical computations, to compute percentages of error, or to consider that factors in association need not be causal. Such criticism was in effect a devastating attack on existing sociological and psychological techniques in all research, not merely that in the field of criminology.

Michael and Adler's sweeping rejection of all criminological research has been virtually ignored by criminologists, perhaps partly because these two men made such an incisive criticism of the latter's allegedly futile efforts. Because Michael and Adler believed sociologists and psychologists had produced so many useless studies, they proposed that an institute of criminology and criminal justice be created within a great university, autonomous in operation but closely related to the law school of such an institution. The institute they proposed should have two divisions, one in criminology, and one in criminal justice, both under a single director. The criminological division was to have a logician, a statistician, a mathematician, a theoretical and experimental physicist, a mathematical economist. Michael and Adler held the mathematical economist to be the only social scientist who is really a scientist and the psychometrician to be the only psychologist whose work meets the criterion of possessing a scientific method.[10]

One may question whether the theories of mathematical economics can stand the test of complete exactness. Michael and Adler hold, for example, that the law of demand can be tested without reference to human nature, whereas criminal theories cannot. The law of demand which they so admire is to this effect: "Demand for any article in a given interval of time is a function not only of its price but of the prices of all other articles at that time."[11] This they say can be tested without any knowledge whatsoever of human nature. It is empirically established like a law in physics. To the advertising manager and sales promoter this conclusion must amount to so much nonsense. It is a well-known fact, for example, that the ball point pen was sold for as much as $19.98 when it initially cost approximately 80¢ to make (and later only 8¢) and that the pen's sale was stimulated by the rather ridiculous slogan, "It writes under water." After all, most people do not write under water nor is there any reason for their so doing. The novelty of a pen which would write for weeks without filling also appealed to human nature. The demand so far as observable had little to do with all other prices, whether we consider ink, sugar, soup, furniture, or mink coats. Eventually the novelty wore off and the disad-

[10] *Ibid.* (1933 ed.), pp. 401–409.   [11] *Ibid.*, p. 84.

vantages of writing with a crayon-like ink which rubs off on the fingers reduced the price and the demand as well.[12]

This proposal of Michael and Adler deserves extensive mention here, not only because it is representative of the legal-logical approach to a social problem, but also because there is much truth in their denunciation of the previous researches. Their allegation ignores three important considerations, however. First, *criminologists have made a large body of data available from which relationships can be and have been established*, notwithstanding the arguments to the contrary. Second, many of the researches Michael and Adler condemned as futile actually have been provocative enough to be carried further into more productive study. Finally, no research in crime can reasonably expect to measure criminality as an entity by means of a precise mathematical formula. Any such attempt is doomed at the outset, because human behavior (whether criminal or law abiding) cannot be resolved into a measurable entity or a mathematical formula by any known psychological or sociological device. Behavior, we have reason to believe, is always a function of many variables within the personality of the individual, his group relationships, and the stimuli within the community and the general cultural milieu.

Complications Involved in Developing a Theory of Crime

Crimes range from petty thievery to premeditated murder and it should be obvious that the lure of an apple to a hungry child is something different from the murderer's impulse to kill a rival gangster or a wife's lover. Yet many serious students have tried to reduce the causes of antisocial behavior to some unitary factor which would account for such completely different types of forbidden behavior.

Behavior—like history—defies simple description, and any simple explanation of crime is virtually bound to be no explanation at all. Some crimes are committed unwittingly, we say. Others are committed with the avowed intention of breaking the law. But unwitting behavior may be the result of ignorance, of absent-mindedness, of mental defect or mental illness. Ignorance may exist because of lack of education, isolation, unfamiliarity with foreign customs, or immaturity. Or the criminal may be a repressed individual and as such he rebels against or "flouts" the law. The biologist, anthropologist, psychologist, psychiatrist, clergyman, and the sociologist all want to

[12] Cf. Thomas Whiteside, "Where Are They Now: The Amphibious Pen," *New Yorker*, 27:40–41 ff. (February 17, 1951).

know what it is about the individual which makes him break the law. All these persons recognize that some men may commit crimes because they are ignorant, and if the criminals are feeble-minded there would appear to be a basis for such ignorance. That idea once satisfied many psychologists. Biologists held meanwhile that a large number of criminals are biologically defective. Some undoubtedly are, but research has shown that criminals are not especially differentiated biologically from the civilian population. The psychiatrist has been concerned with the emotional frustrations and hatreds which have led men into open opposition.

Psychiatric explanations that frustrations are a cause of crime have been widely accepted despite the fact that no control studies have been made as to the degree to which frustrations affect the rank-and-file civilian population. Most people are probably confronted by a variety of rebuffs and frustrations in the course of their life experiences yet most people work out a fairly satisfactory adjustment without getting into conflict with the law.

Clifford R. Shaw, for example, does not believe that the majority of delinquent children are delinquent because of basic emotional disturbances. In fact his famous studies of delinquency areas made it rather clear that boys and girls from good homes in bad areas often got in trouble and that the community's negative influences were a major menace to the children. Others have held that it is poverty per se which is back of all these problems since poverty is the basic reason for people's living in deteriorated areas. Still others maintain that the poverty of the industrial classes who live in these areas is the inevitable result of the class conflict inherent in the capitalistic economic system which grinds down workers in order to secure more profits for the controllers of industry.

Emotional insecurity may account for certain crimes, but the sociologist insists that most crimes are *learned* forms of behavior and have their roots in the deteriorated, depressed, and poverty-stricken areas where antisocial behavior patterns are established and passed on from generation to generation. These "delinquency areas," as Clifford R. Shaw and others have called them, are in another sense "disorganized" communities. They are communities in which patterns of conduct which are opposed to social well-being have developed and been allowed to remain, chiefly because the members of the community have not taken constructive measures to build law-abiding attitudes. Nor have they provided wholesome patterns of recreation in which the children could be directed toward any appreciation of the desirability of law-abiding behavior. Moreover the small groups with which the child or the adult criminal associates often promote the type of conduct called delinquency and crime.

At the same time we have built up a complex structure of laws regulating conduct in an attempt to retain existing social, economic, and political institutions. The tremendous number and variety of acts which are classified as crime cannot help but increase the likelihood of lawbreaking among the general population. Many of the newer laws such as those prohibiting black markets are in direct opposition to established patterns of behavior, hence the widespread willingness to take a chance in breaking the law.

The psychiatrists meanwhile became interested in the fact that some of the siblings of delinquents who were theoretically exposed to the same neighborhood and family influences did not become delinquent. Healy and Bronner came to the conclusion that the children who become delinquent in families where other children are not delinquent are characterized by emotional conflicts and frustration and contend that their delinquent behavior is an expression of emotional insecurity.[13]

The types of offensive behavior may be presumed to be as varied as the diseases which plague the human organism and it is possible that crimes are produced by as varied a number of situations and circumstances, internal and external to the individual offender. Avowed and repeated criminal activities unquestionably distort the offender's attitudes toward the rules and regulations (or values) implicit in a law-abiding society. Nevertheless many prisoners do reform. As they grow older an increasing number become nonoffenders, as the Gluecks' follow-up studies attest. The one-time (or x times) offender can and often does adjust himself to the demands of the society in which he lives, even though he may protest and rebel against such social constraints as a young person.

The notion that youth is a factor in delinquency and crime and that maturity brings more responsible behavior did not originate with the Gluecks. Their research merely adds weight to the argument. It has long been a popular adage that a man who marries "settles down." William Bolitho, the British journalist, advanced the idea that crime was an anachronism or a primitive immature sort of behavior which the criminal usually discarded when he grew older and married.[14]

[13] William Healy and Augusta F. Bronner, *New Light on Delinquency*, Yale University Press, New Haven, 1936, especially pp. 128–129 and 491–492.
[14] Cf. William Bolitho, "The Psychosis of the Gang," *Survey*, 63:500–506 (February 1, 1930), and "Gangster Traumatism," *Survey*, 63:661–665 (March 1, 1930).

Bolitho's idea is purely an impression from observations and is not based on careful and exact study.

The variety and types of crime militate against accepting any single precipitating entity which will function as a variable. Murder, bigamy, rape, thieving, stuffing the ballot box, perjury, embezzlement, treason, failing to report income, driving through a red light—all are crimes, but we have no reason to suppose that the motivations involved in committing them all spring from the same source or are stimulated by the same sorts of environmental factors. Few scientific medical men would accept the theory of the chiropractor that all disease is a matter of spinal maladjustment, even though it can be established that much pain (which is "dis"-ease) is referred through that part of the nervous system.

Medical science has made great headway since the discovery of bacteria as the source of infectious disease. But medicine has never been able to discard Galen's theory that it is as important to know the patient as the disease. Furthermore the psychogenic origin of certain physical ailments and the present-day developments in the field of psychosomatic medicine cannot be ignored in considering factors which produce disease. An equally important fact which all medical men further recognize is that the body has capacity to cure itself through the recuperative processes which disease or injury sets to work in the human organism by disease or injury (when it is not so sorely diseased or injured that recovery is impossible). Similarly it may be true that the human personality carries within itself facility to overcome habits and patterns of behavior which are adjudged criminal by the society in which it exists.

Meanwhile the sociologists and psychologists who are best qualified to judge the validity of criminological research will agree with Michael and Adler when they declare that the investigators who have done the most trivial and glaringly defective research have made the most sweeping conclusions with reference to the etiology of crime.[15] Every competent criminologist recognizes the fact that most criminal theory is defective, and that the less the researcher knows about the subject the more dogmatic he tends to be. Moreover, there are many gaps in criminological science, as there are in every area of information. We may profitably classify the approaches to criminal theory as they have developed up to now, however. These theories will give the student some notion of the amount of progress being made in criminological research.

[15] Jerome Michael and Mortimer J. Adler, op. cit., p. 169.

Current Theories of Criminality

The various theories of criminality derived from criminal research range from those which we may quite properly reject as worthless (as have Michael and Adler) to those which may be regarded as tenable working hypotheses. Any such conclusions, if scientific, must admit the possibility of being superseded by later and more adequate research. The theories of criminality derived from the various studies may be classified roughly on several bases. The classifications as developed in this text represent the perspectives from which the crime problem is analyzed, i.e., (1) as to whether a unitary or a multiple-factor approach is emphasized; (2) as to whether a legal-philosophical concept of the criminal's responsibility for his own conduct is accepted or there is a belief that all behavior is "conditioned" or "determined" by factors external to the offender; (3) as to whether the factors in crime are explained by factors in the individual's mental, physical, and emotional make-up (or personality), or by group and environmental relationships, or by a combination of both; (4) as to whether crime is thought to be a matter of social organization or group definition or a matter of social disorganization and lack of consensus.

These theories will be discussed briefly in the order given.

UNITARY AND MULTIPLE-FACTOR THEORIES OF CRIME

The Unitary or Single-Explanation Theories

Modern sociologists generally regard as untenable the unitary theories of criminal behavior which attach extreme importance to 1 specific factor. This is true whether the factor is a personality trait or an aspect of the physical or social environment, if all other factors are disregarded. Simple unitary explanations for crime include all the attempts to explain criminality by single personality characteristics, whether "heredity," physical handicaps or defective physical structure, low mentality or emotional frustration. They also include all theories which would attach the mainsprings of criminal conduct to a single environmental factor, whether it be broken family, immoral parents, bad neighborhood, poor housing, lack of recreational facilities, lack of adequate schooling, the police, correctional institutions, poverty, the capitalistic system, lack of religion, etc.

The discussion in the two preceding chapters should make it abundantly clear that no one factor can be safely considered to be the sole or a basic cause for crime. There are too many noncriminals or non-delinquents to whom these same characteristics apply. The conduct of some individuals may perchance be explained by a single precipitating factor, but it is also true that there are *several* untoward or handicapping factors in the background of most delinquents. When a straw breaks a camel's back there are other preceding weights and strains to be considered.

That no specific factor can be regarded as the cause of crime should be further evident in the fact that the term "crime" covers so many varieties of forbidden conduct. It is ridiculous to suppose that the same factor induces a woman to murder her husband, a banker to embezzle funds of a bank, a child to steal a toy pistol, the conscientious objector to refuse to register for military service, or the Communist to commit perjury.

Multiple-Factor Theories

In recent years many criminologists have accepted the multiple-factor theory of delinquency or crime, because the various researches have shown that most persons brought before the courts for crimes have had a series of handicaps. That is, usually there has been not 1 or 2 factors but a series of 4, 5, 6, or more untoward conditions which appear to have made it difficult for the offender to grow up into a socially adjusted person or to live a law-abiding life. The typical juvenile delinquent is thus not only from a broken home and a poverty-striken home. One or both parents also may be immoral. There is likely to be retarded schooling, a poor neighborhood, and a neighborhood tradition of delinquency in the child's history.[16] As many court workers are well aware, an immoral mother, a drunken father, a low income, a poor neighborhood, school retardation, and early employment in industry are all common factors in the background of a large share of delinquent girls. Any one of these handicaps might be satisfactorily surmounted if other, desirable influences contributed sufficiently to produce acceptable social conduct. But few girls could be expected to live "a moral and righteous life" when everything in their home background and environment militated so seriously against it. Most boys brought before the juvenile court come from poverty-striken homes, in poor or deteriorated neighborhoods, where they have played with other youngsters and have committed their

---

[16] Cf. Cyril Burt, The Young Delinquent, University of London, London, rev. ed., 1938, for a development of this point of view.

delinquencies with the help of their companions. Often there is a tradition of delinquency in the community.[17]

Similarly in the studies of adult criminals (for example, those carried on by the Gluecks) unfavorable home conditions, mobility, poor work history, unemployment, low educational attainment, poor church attendance, lack of suitable leisure-time activities all appear in a significantly high percentage of the cases.[18] Such multiple handicaps may accompany criminal activities but do not necessarily explain crime, since some criminals have no such variety of handicaps. They do not explain, for example, why a wealthy man shoots his wife or why a banker embezzles huge sums of money.

We need, then, to study the community background of the criminal with its over-all situational influences, as William I. Thomas and Dorothy S. Thomas suggest, before we can be sure that it is the factors which have been isolated for study that are truly basic in any multiple-factor theory of delinquency or crime.[19]

LEGAL-PHILOSOPHICAL THEORIES OF CRIME

The legal-philosophical theories of crime are concerned with the degree to which man may be considered responsible for his own behavior, and accordingly with what degree of culpability may be attached to his behaving in ways condemned by the group. These concepts may be roughly classified into three groups: (1) the theory of complete responsibility, (2) the theory of limited or partial responsibility, (3) the theory of determinism. All are based more or less on a priori reasoning with reference to the nature of man's capacity for self-direction and are closely related to theories of punishment, as discussed in Chapter 16. They are, however, also basically concerned with causes of criminal conduct.

The Theory of Moral Responsibility

The theory of moral responsibility represents a fusion of Christian theology and moral philosophy, and the latter is in a general way de-

[17] Cf. Clifford R. Shaw and Henry D. McKay, *Juvenile Delinquency in Urban Areas,* University of Chicago Press, Chicago, 1942, pp. 141 ff.; Sheldon and Eleanor T. Glueck, *One Thousand Juvenile Delinquents,* Harvard University Press, Cambridge, 1934, pp. 89–90; and Cyril Burt, op. cit.

[18] Sheldon and Eleanor T. Glueck, *Five Hundred Criminal Careers,* Knopf, New York, 1930, chaps. 6 and 7.

[19] Cf. William I. Thomas and Dorothy S. Thomas, *The Child in America,* Knopf, New York, 1928, pp. 574–575.

rived from theological concepts as to the nature of man and his struggles against evil-doing or sin. Man is to be condemned for his transgressions because he knowingly commits an act which he himself realizes is wrong. Actually it appears that what is considered right and wrong is always interpreted according to the social insights of the group. That is, ideas of right and wrong are based upon the ethical concepts of the group. These ethical concepts, in turn, are largely drawn from the religious tenets of the group involved.

Most Christian leaders recognize that some people have greater temptations than others but insist at the same time that all behavior involves choice or freedom of will. Otherwise no blame could be attached to "sinful" conduct. Accepting the Christian premise that men are free moral agents, Rousseau developed the theory of social contract as the basis for all law. That is, laws (and thus punishment) arose only because men were collectively willing to be governed by law. Punishment was justified only because men knowingly chose to do wrong, not because of any right of tyrants to impose their wills upon the group. This in essence is part of the underlying philosophy of democratic government.

Theories of Limited Responsibility

The democratic basis for the acceptance of law or legal restrictions obviously lies in the conception that all persons prefer such rules and regulations to the chaos or hardships which would exist without them. But it soon became apparent to lawmakers and jurists alike that there were limits to the responsibility which could be attached to any persons incapacitated because of (1) mental defect and derangement (or insanity), (2) "nonage," (3) alcoholism, and (4) coercion or duress.

The Mentally Defective and Mentally Deranged

Persons "not in their right minds" or "insane persons" have thus been recognized as individuals who, though they might commit nominal crimes, could not be held responsible because of their lack of mental ability (or feeble-mindedness) or because they were unable to comprehend what they were doing because of mental illness or emotional disturbance. Psychiatrists (who are specialists in mental disorders) and lawyers (who have a legal conception of mental ability) have had many battles over what constitutes responsibility. In general the law has traditionally considered a man sane and in his

right mind if he "knows the difference between right and wrong."
This legal dictum was laid down by the British courts in the famous
McNaghten case of 1843 when it was held that *a criminal is sane
and therefore responsible if he knows the difference between right and
wrong and he is not to be adjudged either sane or criminal if he does
not comprehend that his behavior is wrong*.[20] Since law is based much
more upon logic than upon research into the dynamics of human behavior, such a viewpoint has seemed sensible to many lawyers, but
psychiatrists and persons familiar with abnormal psychology maintain (with good reason) that a mentally ill or emotionally disturbed
person may be intellectually aware that he is doing something the
group condemns as wrong *but may still be under strong compulsion
to commit such an act*. Psychiatrists in consequence often argue that
to say a person knows the difference between right and wrong is
meaningless in trying to establish the responsibility of the offender.
The psychiatrist also frequently insists that it is difficult to say what
is right and wrong, whereas the lawyer often thinks the issues are
clear cut.[21]

The question of exemption from responsibility in case of feeble-
mindedness is likewise a complicated problem so far as the court procedures are concerned. Most psychologists would hold with good
reason that low-grade mentality should give presumptive evidence of
irresponsibility. But technically the offender may still be held "to
know he is doing wrong," when he lacks the capacity to inhibit his conduct.

NONAGE

Nonage, or irresponsibility for conduct because the individual is
too young to understand the import of what he is doing, has long
been accepted as a reason for not punishing or for dealing lightly with
offenses committed by children and young persons. Under English
common law a child under 7 was considered incapable of committing
a crime (*doli incapax*).[22] In 1908 the Children's Act raised the presumptive age for knowing the difference between right and wrong
to 14 in Great Britain. This act stated that a child under 14 could not
be convicted for a crime unless the jury was satisfied that such a child

[20] F. H. Bradley, "Anglo-American Philosophies of Penal Law," *Journal of Criminal
Law and Criminology*, 2:186–98 (July, 1911).
[21] William Alanson White, "Need for Cooperation Between Lawyers and Psychiatrists Dealing with Crime," *American Bar Association Journal*, 13:551–555 (October,
1927).
[22] O. C. M. Davis and F. A. Wilshire, *Mentality and the Criminal Law*, Wright,
Bristol (England), 1935, pp. 143–144.

knew he or she was doing wrong.[23] The act of 1932 retained the presumptive age of 14, and the absolute age was raised to 8. This act also abolished the death penalty for persons under 16. In 1933 the minimum age for the death penalty was raised to 18 years.[24]

In the United States much the same provisions now apply with reference to children and young persons except that in a few states the juvenile court extends its jurisdiction until 21. In case of capital offenses, however, many states provide for regular criminal court hearings and trial for young persons. We are in the rather ambiguous position of saying that a person knows he is doing wrong when he murders but may be considered less responsible when he steals or commits other noncapital offenses!

ALCOHOLISM AND CRIMINAL INTENT

Courts in Great Britain and the United States have often mitigated penalties in offenses on grounds that the person was intoxicated when he committed the crime. Drunkenness is, however, a penal offense, even though it may be alleged as a defense in other crimes. (It is not an offense if not committed in public, and upper-class persons who become intoxicated in public places are seldom arrested. The person who disturbs the peace or becomes noisy and uncontrolled in public is subject to arrest.) But when a person commits another crime while under the influence of alcohol the question of whether or not he is responsible has been variously interpreted. In consonance with the acceptance of insanity as a limiting factor in criminal responsibility, proof of drunkenness has been a factor in reducing punishment, because any criminal intent was regarded as either less or nonexistent.[25]

Thus, a murder committed while the murderer was intoxicated is usually labeled manslaughter and the penalty is markedly less than in the case of first- or second-degree murder. Similarly, in sex offenses drunkenness is often brought up as a defense. But if a person is intoxicated when driving an automobile this usually increases the severity of the punishment in case there is a serious accident. It is usually argued that the driver voluntarily consumed the alcoholic beverage which (he knew) would make his driving hazardous. There is thus no consistent acceptance of alcoholism as evidence of irresponsibility. If it can be said that the person knowingly made himself more likely

---

[23] *Ibid.*, p. 134.   [24] *Ibid.*, pp. 143–144.
[25] G. M. Scott, "Alcoholism and Criminal Behavior," in L. Radzinowicz and J. W. C. Turner, *Mental Abnormality and Crime*, Macmillan, London, 1944, chap. 8.

to commit a crime by drinking he can reasonably be accused of adding to the gravity of his offense.[26]

COERCION OR DURESS

Coercion or duress may also reduce the responsibility of a person committing a criminal act when some other person threatens his life, safety, or reputation unless he commits or helps commit a crime. Thus a woman may be coerced by her husband or lover into the role of an accomplice in murder because of threats. If such coercion can be legally established the penalty is usually reduced.

Determinism

The extreme behavioristic school of psychology holds to the theory that all behavior is a more or less mechanical response to stimuli. This school of thought unquestionably did much to promote the belief that environmental factors are largely responsible for the individual's behavior, whether social or antisocial. Extreme determinists, in fact, go so far as to maintain that man is absolved from any moral responsibility for his behavior because it is the result of the various influences to which he has been exposed.

The psychiatrist goes even further in holding that the question of who is "responsible" is a metaphysical problem, and one for which there is no satisfactory answer. Instead the psychiatrist insists that there are a series of antecedents back of each individual act. Furthermore acts which appear to be the same on the surface are not the same at all but the result of a unique series of antecedents.[27] There is basic error, from the psychiatric view, in assuming that men are free to choose how they act and are therefore equal before the law. To the behaviorist and the psychiatrist and others who accept such views the factors which result in man's behavior give him very little freedom and, since each person's experiences are different, men cannot be said to be equal.

The sociologist, in recognizing that group influences, patterns of behavior, and unsavory surroundings of various sorts condition the criminal to act as he does, may also be said to adhere to a determinist viewpoint. The sociologist does not necessarily hold that delinquent or criminal behavior is inevitable or a mechanical result of these factors; he says rather that such behavior is likely to occur when many untoward conditioning factors are a part of the individual's back-

[26] *Ibid.*   [27] William Alanson White, *op. cit.*

ground and experience. Where delinquent or criminal activity does not take place, the presumption is that certain stabilizing influences may have offset the disorganizing influences. In some cases stable conduct may be due to chance or to nonobservable influences.

THEORIES WHICH CONSIDER CRIME A MATTER OF PERSONAL MALADJUSTMENT OR OF GROUP STIMULI OR OF A COMBINATION OF BOTH

Current theories of criminal behavior lean heavily at present toward those which stress personality factors, those which stress factors in group association, or those which stress the interrelation of these two approaches. These theories may be described briefly as: (1) theories which maintain that antisocial behavior or crime is a function of a maladjusted personality or defective personality; (2) theories which hold that crime is a result of environmental circumstances including social, economic, and geographical (and ecological) factors or a combination of these in what may be termed social disorganization; (3) theories which recognize that characteristics of the individual and the environment interact in all behavior situations including those defined as criminal.

As an example of the first classification the psychologist in an earlier period maintained that low-grade mental ability led the criminal to make the decision to steal (presumably an unwise choice befitting feeble intellect).[28] Similarly some psychiatrists have held that emotional conflict and frustration have led the criminal to rebel against society. The biologists have assumed that biological defects in physical structure, glandular malfunctioning, or physical disease has in some way induced the abnormal or criminal conduct.

The seeming conflict between the theories has developed out of the perspective from which criminal behavior is viewed. The biologist, psychologist, and psychiatrist have been concerned with the characteristics or motivations of the offender who rebels against the rules and regulations of the group. The psychiatrist with a psychoanalytic slant has long interpreted crime as the resolution of inner conflict between the individual's *id* and *ego* which is occasioned by the individual's *super-ego*. (Briefly, the *id* is the person's natural instinctive and selfish tendencies which he tries to suppress; the *ego* represents the individual's conscious adjustment to the world about

[28] H. H. Goddard, *Feeblemindedness, Its Causes and Consequences*, Macmillan, New York, 1914, p. 514.

him; the *super-ego*, which is more or less synonymous with conscience, forces the conflict into the unconscious because the individual experiences guilt at the thought of his selfish or ill-intentioned motives.) His criminal behavior thus may be explained as symbolic; the man or woman who steals may be seeking sexual satisfactions. The psychiatrist, then, holds little brief for the sociologist's contention that deteriorated neighborhoods, housing congestion, unemployment, lack of education, etc., explain criminality. He asks, rather, "Why did the person live in such a bad neighborhood, lose his job, fail to get an education, or fall in with criminal companions?" He tends to think that the mental inclinations of the individual are responsible for his crime. Thus the peculiar or particular aggressiveness of the individual which is manifest in criminal activities is occasioned by "inner weakness" or insufficient psychic activity. The criminal (from this viewpoint) has no tendencies that other persons do not have. He merely fails to keep his criminal tendencies in balance by mental resistance.[29]

The social scientist (whether sociologist, political scientist, or economist, socialist or social philosopher) is generally concerned with the factors which have stimulated the individual to behave in an antisocial fashion. The theories emphasizing group or environmental association maintain in general that crime is due to stimuli which exist external to the offender and cause him to react in antisocial ways. Here again the explanations range from consideration of a single factor to consideration of the whole social milieu. To the social geographer or ecologist crime may result from the physical environment or climate. To some sociologists crime stems from the individual's relationships to the family and other groups and the effects of these relationships upon the offender (who is interacting with other members of the group). To the economist crime often appears to grow out of economic need or comparative economic status. To the political scientist and social philosopher criminal behavior may be the result of the impact of the economic (or capitalist) system upon the underpriviledged, or the result of the impact of cultural values upon individual conduct.

Modern sociologists generally agree that criminal behavior is learned —and learned, in the opinion of Edwin H. Sutherland, in the differen-

---

[29] Cf. David Abrahamsen, *Crime and the Human Mind*, Columbia University Press, New York, 1944, chap. 2, especially pp. 25–31. Cf. also Franz Alexander and William Healy, *Roots of Crime*, Knopf, 1935, for detailed presentation of the psychoanalytic viewpoint.

tial group association with criminals.[30] Thus Sutherland holds that the criminal's conduct is usually approved (or at least is not rejected) by the immediate group to which he belongs, but this behavior is nevertheless considered antisocial by the lawmaking and crime-defining members of the larger group in which this differentiated group functions. The criminal becomes such by contact with criminal patterns of behavior, which he assimilates, and conversely by lack of contact with the law-abiding or anti-criminal world.[31]

This theory as developed by Sutherland has much to commend it insofar as both lower-class and upper-class or "white-collar" criminals are concerned. For both the traditional criminals and the respected white-collar criminals tend to behave as their associates do. The theory of differential association does not explain the incidental, the highly emotional, or the accidental crimes, but applies only to the confirmed types of criminality in which the offender accepts antisocial behavior as a suitable way of life. He is identified with the group whose behavior he copies. We must recognize, however, that the incidental and occasional criminals constitute a significant percentage of the criminal group. Differential group association seems, therefore, as faulty an over-all explanation for all crime as is emotional insecurity.

These "momentary" offenders Dr. Abrahamsen concludes are "not in reality offenders."[32] In this classification he includes the "situational," the accidental, and the associational criminal. However, the associational offender is so affected by his immediate surroundings that he falls into company with persons "of a criminal pattern."[33] Such association may obviously lead to chronic criminal behavior. From a sociological viewpoint associational offenders appear to be the largest group of criminals.

SOCIAL ORGANIZATION AND DISORGANIZATION AND CRIME

Social Organization

From one perspective we may well argue that crime is a matter of definition. Whatever the defining group, which in modern society is the state, declares crime to be, is crime. In this sense crime is a function of the social organization and is occasioned by the strictures

---

[30] Cf. Edwin H. Sutherland, *Principles of Criminology*, Lippincott, Philadelphia, rev. ed., 1947, chap. 1, "A Theory of Criminality," especially pp. 6–9.
[31] *Ibid.*　　　[32] David Abrahamsen, *op. cit.*, p. 94.　　　[33] *Ibid.*, p. 95.

imposed upon human conduct. Changes in the social organization create new problems in social well-being. New definitions arise in the shape of new laws which are contrary to old patterns of behavior, hence meet with resistance and this resistance constitutes new crimes. Thus new laws may be accused of creating new crimes. As social change and the enactment of laws accelerate the needs for social control, crimes increase. Directly they are a product of law. Indirectly they are inherent in the fact of social organization itself.

Social Disorganization

Actually of course it is not the agreement of the group to enforce controls that creates crime. Rather, crime is the result of disunity in the group: some members of the group define situations differently from the way the rules laid down by the lawmakers (another section of the group) have specified. Since there is no pre-existing harmony between the interests of the individual and the social values which are inherent in laws there probably will always be some crime. We have no reason to suppose that all persons will ever accede completely to the interests of the group. Furthermore we can always expect a certain amount of social disorganization so long as there is growth, invention, change, and decay. Likewise there will be crimes and changing definitions of crimes. This situation is manifest in Soviet Russia. The Soviets, it will be recalled, predicted a decline of crime with the decline of capitalist society. The Soviet Union must be credited with taking a constructive interest in remotivating the older and "conventional" types of criminals, but the political offenders in the U.S.S.R. meanwhile have apparently increased in manifold measure.

All crimes, whether the conventional "moral" crimes or the offenses against the state which have been defined in accordance with new functions and theories of government, require the restraint of individual tendencies to behave selfishly and without concern for the welfare of others. Every definition of a new crime, therefore, requires a reorganization in the individual's scheme of values. Social change thus induces a special variety of crime which is contingent upon the degree of social organization or social disorganization, depending upon the perspective from which the problem is viewed.[34] Some of the

[34] Cf. Mabel A. Elliott and Francis E. Merrill, *Social Disorganization*, Harper, New York, rev. ed., 1950, chaps. 1, 2, 4, 5, 25, and 26, for developments of the relation between social change and social disorganization.

crime rate is thus a matter of the degree to which the average citizen accepts his responsibility for making democratic government work. As Virgil W. Peterson has said, "Part of the crime problem in the United States stems from public apathy, indifference and lack of understanding, which has permitted a deterioration in the official agencies for combatting crime."[35]

FURTHER TESTING OF HYPOTHESES IS NEEDED

Any objective consideration of theories of criminality indicates that the various hypotheses need further testing. For example, there must be more study of the offenders' characteristics in contrast to those of nonoffenders (if any), and the precipitating effects of environmental influences must be studied for whatever insights they offer into why the criminal behaves in an antisocial fashion. Both the situation which stimulates the conduct and the internal reactions of the individual to the situation in which he functions are essential to any explanation of conduct. Meanwhile the fact of position and status of offenders in relation to number of arrests and types of punishment should also be studied. There has always been great reluctance to develop and execute social experiments for the purpose of ascertaining effects upon behavior, but studies in which the variable of social status is controlled while all behavior maladjustments are analyzed might bring out the deviations of conduct which are condemned within each group. Controlled experiments in which delinquents are transplanted in different types of neighborhoods might yield further insights. That is, certain delinquent children might be transplanted into low-delinquency areas (with no contact between former delinquents). Others might be transplanted together so that contacts could be maintained. Others could be kept in the same neighborhood which produced them without changing the influences. Others could be placed in areas where definite projects aimed at prevention of delinquency (such as the Chicago Area Project described in Chapter 28) are under way. Rates of progress might then be compared and factors most conducive both to improvement and to continued delinquency might thus be isolated.

If, as the Gluecks maintain, maturation is a major factor in conformity, educational experiments to accelerate the acceptance of a mature viewpoint should be developed to test this hypothesis. Since

[35] Virgil W. Peterson, *Crime Commissions in the United States,* Chicago Crime Commission, Chicago, 1945, p. 1.

learning seems so obviously related to acquiring both the motivations and the techniques for crime, controlled experiments in education for good citizenship in existing "delinquency areas" should be made to see how much delinquency rates may be offset by education.

All of these proposals have drawbacks, and all are likely to meet with social disapproval since tinkering with human lives is not generally condoned. It should be pointed out, however, that prisons, reformatories, and all the other instruments of correction are tinkering with human lives—and with none too favorable results. Controlled experiments in isolating factors in delinquency will present difficulties. One problem will be to eliminate the influence which observation of behavior may entail. There are also ethical objections to watching delinquents behaving delinquently. And there may be grave problems of scientific validity and reliability in recording what takes place. But watching and recording delinquent behavior in action offers some hope for the scientific understanding of such behavior.

SELECTED BIBLIOGRAPHY

Abrahamsen, David, *Crime and the Human Mind*, Columbia University Press, New York, 1944. This book advances the basic psychoanalytical concept of crime in relation to the mental make-up of the individual. The book has a valuable chapter on "Treatment and Research."

Alexander, Franz, and Healy, William, *The Roots of Crime*, Knopf, New York, 1935. This book gives an excellent statement of the roots of criminality in psychoanalytical concepts of the struggle in terms of the *id*, *ego*, and *super-ego*.

Barnes, Harry E., and Teeters, Negley K., *New Horizons in Criminology*, Prentice-Hall, New York, rev. ed., 1951, chaps. 4–11. Various explanations of crime are critically reviewed.

Bonger, William A., *Criminality and Economic Conditions*, transl. by Henry P. Horton, Little, Brown, Boston, 1916. Extensive European data on the relationship between crime and economic conditions are presented in this book. It also reviews previous economic theories.

Cavan, Ruth Shonle, *Criminology*, Crowell, New York, 1948, chap. 12. This chapter presents a simple systematic analysis of various criminal theories from the point of view of sociologists, biologists, psychologists, psychiatrists, and psychoanalysts. There is an especially good condensation of psychoanalytic theory in respect to crime.

Ferrero, Gina Lombroso, *Criminal Man According to the Classification of Cesare Lombroso*, Putnam, New York, 1911. The daughter of the famous Lombroso summarizes his research and his early and revised theories as to the nature of "criminal man."

Fink, Arthur E., *Causes of Crime: Biological Theories in the United States,*
1810–1915, University of Pennsylvania Press, Philadelphia, 1938. This
presents a comprehensive summary of attempts to relate criminality to
biological characteristics of offenders.

Michael, Jerome, and Adler, Mortimer J., *Crime, Law and Social Science,*
Harcourt, Brace, New York, 1933. One of the most provocative attacks
on existing criminal theory ever published, this book includes a proposed plan for developing scientific research.

Quiros, C. Bernaldo de, *Modern Theories of Criminality,* transl. by Alfonso
de Salvio, Little Brown, Boston, 1911. This classic analysis of European
criminal theories by a distinguished Spanish scholar also gives a historical
analysis of their development.

Reiwald, Paul, *Society and Its Criminals,* transl. by T. E. James, International Universities Press, New York, 1950. Reiwald's thesis is that society
is guilty of producing the criminal which it in turn condemns because of
guilt. The author applies psychoanalysis to the whole problem of crime.

Sutherland, Edwin H., *Principles of Criminology,* Lippincott, Philadelphia,
rev. ed., 1947, chap. 1, "A Theory of Criminality." This chapter presents
the closely reasoned theory of one of the most distinguished criminologists this country has produced.

SECTION IV

The Treatment of Criminals

CHAPTER 15

Penal Methods: Past and Present

Because man has made spectacular advances in the fields of physics, chemistry, biochemistry, and mechanical engineering he often believes that his achievements have been equally significant in all fields. Modern penologists have often assumed, for example, that there has been great progress in criminal law and an evolutionary development from the barbaric punishments of primitive man to the humane rehabilitation of the twentieth century.

Frederick H. Wines was one who held such a belief. In his book, *Punishment and Reformation*, Wines advanced the proposition that the treatment of the offender had gone through four stages: "first the era of vengeance or retribution; the second, that of repression; the third, that of attempted reformation or rehabilitation; the fourth, of which we see as yet but the early dawn, is that of prevention."[1] He then went on to show how these stages developed in precise order until treatment reached the definitely more advanced stage which is in vogue today.

Unfortunately, criminologists can no longer take such happy view of the progress in penal methods. For despite the zeal with which earnest reformers have brought their strong wills to bear upon public conscience and have labored for the achievement of much-needed legislative reforms, such reforms have seldom transformed the prevailing basic social attitudes toward the malefactor or changed the petty details of penal treatment. It is true that widespread use of capital punishment and painful physical torture characteristic of the colonial period has been replaced by the prison sentence. Although imprisonment may seem to be an advance over physical punishment,

[1] Frederick H. Wines, *Punishment and Reformation*, Crowell, New York, rev. ed., 1919, pp. 6-7.

inmates have very seldom been treated intelligently or humanely by wardens or guards. Prisons are still roundly denounced for their failure as a penal method. So-called reformatories emphasizing educational training and indeterminate sentences have supplanted prisons in the treatment of young offenders, but they can supply no evidence to show they are reforming their charges. Sporadic attempts to apply preventive measures have been made in various states, but few communities have any well-organized program for developing social consciousness or shouldering the responsibility for helping young persons (or older ones) become successfully adjusted citizens. We need not delude ourselves. The way of the transgressor is still hard, and vengeance still motivates our basic penal law. Public opinion still vacillates between the desire to restore the offender to the ranks of well-adjusted law-abiding citizens and the desire to make him pay the last full measure for his offense.[2] Society has long tried to force conformity through fear of punishment and the penal methods of modern society show little improvement.

Primitive Methods of Treating Crime

The actual measures early man used in punishing offenses which were condemned by primitive law and custom are lost in obscurity. We do know something of present-day primitive tribes, some of whom show marked compassion in dealing with criminals. In certain American Indian tribes, for example, there was a general procedure in the trial of murderers which resulted in breaking down any desire for revenge. Hickey, a missionary to the Indians in Michigan, gave a moving account of an Indian murder trial. The Indian court consisted of (1) the murdered man's immediate family, (2) the murdered man's relatives and those of his wife, (3) Indian chiefs of tribes concerned, (4) the murderer, and (5) the medicine man, who acted as mediator in 3 capacities—(a) as friend of the murderer, (b) as friend of both parties, and (c) as agent presenting gifts to the murdered man's family—and as the one who revealed the will of the Great Spirit.

When the court first convened gifts were brought, to be presented to the family of the murdered man. Then feasts were prepared—one for relatives of the murdered man, one for the murderer's relatives. Following this the court was held in solemn assembly. The criminal

[2] Cf. Mabel A. Elliott, *Conflicting Penal Theories in Statutory Criminal Law*, University of Chicago Press, Chicago, 1931.

himself presented a forlorn appearance with his face blackened, his blanket and leggings in holes. A speaker (one of the murderer's relatives) stressed the sorrow that one of their own had caused. It was then explained that the gifts for the murderer's family in no sense made up for the one who was gone. Another speaker from the criminal's side then asked for clemency in an eloquent speech comparing the murderer with a hunted animal. Still another made a plea for forgiveness. The medicine man then presented the gifts and pleaded for the young man's life. He lighted the pipe of peace. After several rejections of the pipe the widow of the murdered man finally prompted her son to accept it. The widow then also took a puff on the pipe— and by so doing was regarded as saying, "I forgive this murderer."[3]

Hickey described another instance in which an Indian mother adopted the young man who killed her son in a drunken brawl. In primitive society serious offenses within the tribe were generally considered shameful affairs, and the sooner hushed up the better. Often the culprit felt disgraced but he was not ordinarily treated very severely. In case there was a murder of one of equal rank the murderer often went free. If a man of low rank murdered a high-ranking person he might become a slave but in time he regains his free status.[4]

Compounding (translating the offense into monetary damage or fine) is frequent among primitive tribes, but the payment is made to the injured party and not to the state. Among the Bavenda (one of the Bantu tribes in Africa) assault, adultery, arson, damage to property, and theft are all compoundable because they are offenses against individuals. Certain crimes, considered more serious, including witchcraft, murder, homicide, incest or other abnormal sex relations, and plotting for the death of the chief, are not compoundable. Witches or wizards at an earlier time were always killed by being pushed from a high cliff. Now they are usually driven from the country (or banished) although their women and children may be appropriated by the king. Sometimes the wizard is able to pay a ransom for his wife (or wives) and children. Among the Bavenda murder is punished by death or banishment. Sometimes in fact the family of the murderer kill him. Homicide is generally treated as murder except where influential persons are involved in a murder plot, in which case they may be released on payment of fine. Incest is considered a horrible offense among the Bavenda and is punished by death or banishment.

[3] M. Hickey, "A Missionary Among the Indians," Michigan Pioneer Collections, 4:550–556 (1847), cited by William I. Thomas in Primitive Behavior, McGraw-Hill, New York, 1937, pp. 533–538.

[4] W. I. Thomas, op. cit., pp. 538–540.

There are obviously many variations as to how primitive societies treat crime, but these illustrations are fairly typical.[5]

As man's social consciousness grew, private wrongs came to be considered injuries to the group, as threats to the strength of the group through impairing individual members, as we discussed in Chapter 1. Also, as man's worldly goods increased and concepts of private property developed greater emphasis was placed on social protection of property. Similarly, with increases in power and authority rulers developed laws which specifically protected those in power against treason, disturbances, etc. In many ways our own earliest ancestors (if we can assume their practices were at all like those of present-day primitives—which of course we cannot establish) probably were not as cruel and barbarous in their treatment of criminals as the ancient Babylonians, Romans, and Hebrews, or our medieval forebears, because they had less to protect. Primitive man's severest penalties were directed against those offenses which he feared most.[6]

Ancient Penal Law

Code of Hammurabi

The Code of Hammurabi, sixth king of the first Babylonian dynasty, is apparently the oldest of codified laws respecting both civil and criminal law. Complete records of Babylonian history are not available but the latest research and study of archaeological data indicate that Hammurabi, who conquered all of Mesopotamia, reigned around 1950 B.C.[7]

The Code of Hammurabi has long been known to have existed but was not discovered until December, 1901, when archaeologists unearthed it on the site of Susa, an ancient Persian city. The text of the code is inscribed upon broken pillars of black diorite in cuneiform. (These stones had apparently been stolen by the Elamites around 1100 B.C. and taken to this particular location.) All told, 282 laws were inscribed on the broken pillars but five rows of the cuneiform inscriptions had been erased (in order to inscribe the names of the trophy-bearing conquerors). Fortunately three sections of the missing part of the code were replaced from fragments of clay tablets which the British Museum had previously received.

[5] Ibid., pp. 547–551.
[6] Cf. also Bronislaw Malinowski, Crime and Custom in Savage Society, Routledge, London, 1949, Part II, for a discussion of primitive crime and primitive law.
[7] William L. Langer, An Encyclopedia of World History, Houghton Mifflin, Boston, 1940, p. 26. Some authorities place Hammurabi as far back as 2150 B.C.

The text of this code has been one of the most important archae-ological discoveries, for study has revealed that it was the historical antecedent of both the Jewish and the Roman legal codes. Many of our laws governing family inheritance and property, contract and criminal law have their roots in this code, but it is the criminal code with which we are concerned here.

Retaliation, either in kind or by composition, is the characteristic penalty provided for in the Code of Hammurabi, with variations in the penalty based upon status. Filial ingratitude was one of the most important offenses and false witness in a capital case was a capital offense. Stealing from the gods or from the palace was also punished by death. Certain ethical concepts governed some of the provisions. For example, a man who paid a substitute to serve for him in the army might be slain. Anyone stealing from a house which was on fire might be thrown into the same fire. Certain of the specific provisions of the code which are given below indicate the rigidity of standards of con-duct.[8]

A person who made a false accusation was to be branded on the brow. Adulterers were bound together and thrown into the river to drown, except the husband might spare his wife and the king might spare his servant.

Men guilty of incest with their daughters were banished from the city.

If a son struck his father his hand was cut off.

If a man destroyed the eye of a free man, his own eyes were de-stroyed.

If the son of a foster father or a foster mother should say "Thou art not my mother" or "Thou art not my father" his tongue was to be cut out.

The status aspect of the law, on the other hand, is illustrated in the following provisions:

If a man had broken the bones of a free man his bones were broken.

If he had destroyed the eyes of a plebeian or broken a bone of a plebeian, he paid 1 mina of silver.

If he had destroyed the eyes of a man's slave or broken a bone of a man's slave, he had to pay one-half his value.

If he had knocked out the teeth of a man of the same rank his own teeth were to be knocked out.

[8] These regulations affecting crime are selected from Chilperic Edwards, *The Ham-murabi Code*, Watts, London, 1904, chap. 4, "The Text of the Inscriptions."

If he had knocked out the teeth of a plebeian he had to pay one-third of a mina of silver.

If a plebeian struck the body of a man greatly above him, he received 60 lashes with a cowhide whip in public.

If he struck the body of the son of a free man of like condition, he paid 1 mina of silver.

If a man struck the daughter of a free man and caused her fetus to fall he paid ten shekels of silver for her fetus.

If that woman died, his own daughter might be slain.

We cannot recount all the stipulations with reference to criminal offenses covered by the Hammurabi Code, because of lack of space, but these quotations should be sufficient to indicate that retaliation, graduated according to the status of the offender and that of the victim as well, characterized the nature of penalties under the ancient regime.[9]

THE MOSAIC CODE

Scholars agree rather generally that the Mosaic Code (as found in Exodus, Chapters 20–23, the Book of Deuteronomy, Leviticus, Chapters 17 and 26, all part of the Pentateuch of the Old Testament) was drawn up after the Jewish people fled from Egypt into the land of Canaan—roughly between 1400 and 1250 B.C. or some 600 to 700 years after the reign of Hammurabi. Many of the narrative accounts in Genesis correspond to those found in Babylonian literature, and a surprising number of the Mosaic laws correspond almost exactly to the earlier Babylonian code. There is thus little doubt that the Mosaic Code was drawn largely from that of Hammurabi.

In general, however, the Mosaic Code was more severe than the Babylonian code. This was true of the civil code as well as the criminal code, although the latter is all that we are concerned with here. Disobeying Jewish rituals was, for example, severely punished whereas there were no persecutions for religious offenses in the Babylonian code.[10]

A few comparisons between the codes should be of interest to sociology students because it may be seen that in ancient times (as well as later) laws once enacted often were copied by other groups, be they states or countries, but that some were altered in the process of adapting them to local needs. Thus both the Hebrew code and the Code of Hammurabi provided that a foster child might lose his tongue for denying his foster parents. The Hebrews did not diminish the pen-

[9] Cf. *ibid.*, chap. 4.   [10] *Ibid.*, chap. 6.

alty in case a slave (rather than a freeman) lost a tooth or an eye, as did the Babylonians. Neither the Hebrews nor the Babylonians condemned the owner of a goring ox, but the Hebrews provided punishment for the ox—namely, that it be stoned to death—and forbade that its flesh be eaten. Both the Code of Hammurabi and the Mosaic Code provided that a thief caught in the act might be slain, although the Hebrews limited this penalty to nighttime robbery. The treatment of adulterers was essentially the same in both codes. All told there were some 32 ordinances with reference to crime in the Hebrew code and 21 of these are almost identical to those of the Code of Hammurabi.[11] The Mosaic Code was based upon a philosophy of vengeance—"an eye for an eye" and "a tooth for a tooth."

Christianity introduced a new approach to the malefactor—that of loving one's enemy and doing good to those who despitefully treated one. So far as the impact of Christianity upon criminal law has been concerned its major effect has been in the substitution of imprisonment for torture and capital punishment, as we discussed in Chapter 22.

Roman Treatment of Crime

With the rise of the Roman Republic the famous Twelve Tables were adopted about 451–450 B.C. These were actually an enacted Code of Laws. Unfortunately only fragments of these tables remain, but scholars have pieced together the allusions and quotations by various Roman authors, particularly those quotations from Cicero, until we now have a fair idea of what the original Twelve Tables contained. Everything indicates that they mark a definite transition from a system of private vengeance for wrongs committed to a state system of fines which were paid as compensation to the person wronged, with the state fixing the amount. So far as is known, private vengeance was permitted only in the case of an assault ending in a broken bone. If a man received a broken bone he could retaliate in kind and break the bone of the one who had injured him. In all other cases monetary penalties were exacted. Thus a man who assaulted another might pay 25 asses for a blow. A theft was punished by having the thief pay the victim twice as much as the stolen article was worth.[12]

Later, in the Roman "classical period" crimes were classified into four groups: (1) theft, (2) robbery, (3) damages to property, and

[11] *Ibid.*, p. 132.
[12] Cf. *Encyclopaedia Britannica* (1947 ed.), Vol. XIX, p. 453.

(4) outrage to persons. A thief was required to restore the stolen articles. If he was seized or detected in the process of committing the act he paid fourfold. A robber could be required to pay fourfold but was not required to return the stolen goods. In case of damage to property the owner of the property was allowed compensation equal to the highest amount that the property would have brought in the preceding 30 days. If either a slave or a horse was injured or killed the owner was allowed an amount equal to the highest price that he could have obtained within the year preceding. If a man was injured by violence or his character was defamed by slander, libel, lampooning, or even by an offensive ditty, he might sue for damages. If these were awarded the amount was assessed by the court.[13]

Medieval Criminal Law

Georg Rusche and Otto Kirchheimer maintain that punishment is related primarily to the economic aspects of the social structure. They imply that criminal law is a function of the ruling class and involves an attempt to maintain the status of the ruling class against threats to their property and status. They contend with validity that private systems of meeting crime were generally in effect in Europe through the early Middle Ages. These systems were of two sorts, viz., feud and penance. So far as the serfs were concerned the lords maintained their authority because the serfs were socially dependent upon them, and this traditional relationship was reinforced by religious acceptance "of the established order of things." The major import of criminal law lay in controlling the offenses between persons of equal status, by private vengeance, wergeld or money paid in penance.[14]

Wergeld was the "man price" or value set on a person's life and varied markedly with his status. If a man injured or killed a nobleman, he paid an enormous price. If he injured or killed a serf, the wergeld was low.

The primary reason for punishment was to maintain order or peace on the feudal estates and this governing principle was later extended to the property of the kings. The traditional indictment in England, for example, is still in effect and accuses the criminal of an offense "against the peace and dignity" of the king. Technically "peace and

[13] James Hadley, *Introduction to Roman Law*, Appleton, New York, 1874, pp. 237–244.

[14] Georg Rusche and Otto Kirchheimer, *Punishment and the Social Structure*, International Institute of Social Research, Columbia University Press, New York, 1939, pp. 8–9.

dignity" first applied only to the land surrounding the king's castle but eventually it was extended to the whole country as the kingdom.[15] This extension of authority and discipline over persons on their lands, or kingdoms, was fostered by the royal houses in France and England and the petty potentates or princes in Germany.[16] The transition from private vengeance to an administration of justice on the part of rulers was accompanied by a decline in the blood feud or retaliation in kind with the substitution of the wergeld, or fine paid in penance. If an offender could not pay the prescribed fine he was punished corporally by being thrown into prison where he was forced to live on bread and water until others interceded or he was pardoned by the bishop. Even the king was subordinate to the rulings of the church in such matters.[17]

The process of compounding crimes—or translating them into monetary fines—has often been regarded as a humanitarian advance over the primitive retaliative justice. Also, it must be admitted, fines have served as a means of deriving revenue. In fact, many believe that fiscal considerations were basic in developing this form of justice. It was obviously much cleverer to make a man pay for his misbehavior than it was to subject him to torture and the practice seems to have spread throughout the European continent as well as in England.[18]

With the development of mercantilism and the rise of capitalism major conflicts between the masses and the wealthy landed gentry, merchants, and capitalists appeared. As early as the sixteenth century sharp cleavages between the wage earners and their employers arose and the discontent frequently led to strikes and boycotts at this early date (a fact not generally known). Crimes increased among the poverty-stricken workers which the ruling class sought to control through harsh penalties. Offenses against property were in fact more severely punished if the offender was a member of the lower (or villein) class than if he was an equal. The criminal Code of Charles V (Articles 128 and 129) thus provided immunity for offenders among the upper classes for offenses treated severely when committed by the lower class.[19] Medieval criminal law thus attempted to protect the status of

[15] This terminology is still retained in many indictment forms in various parts of the United States where the person under indictment is accused of "an offense against the peace and dignity of the citizens of the state of ————."

[16] Georg Rusche and Otto Kirchheimer, op. cit., p. 10.

[17] Ibid.

[18] Cf. J. C. Fox, The History of Contempt of Court, the Form of Trial and Mode of Punishment, Oxford University Press, Oxford, 1928, p. 138, and R. Garraud, Traité Théorique et Pratique du Droit Pénal Français, Paris, 2nd ed., 1898, Vol. 1, p. 111, cited by Rusche and Kirchheimer, op. cit., p. 212.

[19] A. Steinhausen, Geschichte der Deutschen Kultur, Leipzig, 3rd ed., 1929, p. 312, cited by Rusche and Kirchheimer, op. cit., p. 212.

the ruling class as well as to punish persons who were dishonest (and threatening the status of the ruling class). During this period the professional criminals were almost wholly persons from the lowest class.[20]

The Development of Severe Penal Measures

Since the development of the town economy entailed many serious economic maladjustments the number of offenders unable to pay their fines inevitably increased. Suppression of crime became a major problem, for "vagabonds, beggars and robbers were becoming a plague on the land." Punishments became harsher and harsher. If a man could not pay his fine he was punished severely. Floggings, brandings, mutilation, and capital punishment were common. The death penalty, which had not been widely used in early times, came to be generally accepted as the only means of getting rid of the professional criminals by the sixteenth century.[21] An estimated 72,000 thieves were hanged during the reign of Henry VIII. Even innocent people were frequently put to death and methods of execution became increasingly brutal.[22] Von Hentig recounts numerous examples of disemboweling and of having bodies torn asunder by horses.[23]

Punishment in the American Colonies

During our colonial period the colonists rather naturally operated under the system of laws which was in effect in England. Although it was true that many New Englanders initially came to the New World to escape religious persecution they imposed cruel treatment on other nonconformists and used numerous devices of torture and corporal punishment for the so-called minor offenses. For felonious offenses death was the chief penalty.

The varieties of corporal punishment in force during this period seem almost unbelievable today—for although it must be admitted that cruelty has not been eliminated from our penalties today, we can safely say that in general torture is no longer used as a form of punishment. Torture survives chiefly as a means of disciplining prisoners, as we shall see in Chapter 24. Since present-day practices grew out of dis-

[20] B. Schmidt, *Die Strafrechtsreform in ihren staaterechtlicher und politischen Bedenlung*, Leipzig, 1912, pp. 185–186, cited by Rusche and Kirchheimer, *op. cit.*, p. 214.

[21] Georg Rusche and Otto Kirchheimer, *op. cit.*, pp. 18–19.

[22] *Ibid.*, p. 19.

[23] Hans von Hentig, *Punishment, Its Origin, Purpose and Psychology*, Hodge, London, 1937, pp. 98–100.

content with colonial penal practices it will be valuable for us to consider these methods briefly.

BILBOES

Bilboes were iron bars with two sliding shackles into which the legs of the person punished were thrust and padlocked. Occasionally the offender in bilboes was also chained to the floor, but this was a needless precaution since he was already so shackled he could not move. It has been said that this type of punishment was of Spanish origin and that the Spanish Armada employed it for restraining captured enemy forces. In any event it was also widely used by the British and was likewise a common form of restraint imposed upon vicious or lawless colonists both in New England and in Virginia.[24]

THE PILLORY

The pillory was a device which held the head in a fast position and stretched the neck as well. Its use has been traced as far back as the twelfth century in England and it may well have been much older. The pillory was in fact a variety of scaffold, but instead of being nailed to the cross to die, the offender was merely held in place for ridicule. Sometimes he suffered lasting physical injury by having his ears nailed to the pillory.[25]

In England many were pilloried for such minor offenses as fortune-telling, drunkenness, and impudence. But treason, perjury, blasphemy, quarreling, slandering, etc., might subject the miscreant to the pillory. Many conscientious citizens including Puritans, Quakers, and other dissenters also suffered on the pillory. In general it was considered a disgrace to be pilloried even though the offense punished might not be so regarded.[26]

STOCKS

Because iron was often hard to secure, stocks made of planks were employed instead of bilboes during colonial days.[27] When stocks were the means of punishment, the offenders were displayed in public places on a wooden bench with their hands and often their heads thrust through holes in boards from which they could not escape until

[24] Alice Morse Earle, *Curious Punishments of Bygone Days*, Macmillan, New York, 1896, chap. 1.

[25] *Ibid.*, chap. 4. Cf. also "Pillory," *Encyclopaedia Brittanica*, Vol. XVII, p. 929.

[26] Alice Morse Earle, *op. cit.*, p. 48.

[27] *Ibid.*, p. 9 and chap. 3.

released. Usually such punishments were for several hours, sometimes longer. While such a position was decidedly uncomfortable, the chief punishment lay in the exposure to the taunts and ridicule of passers-by. Colonial history is replete with examples of such degradation.

THE BRANK

The brank was a cagelike device to cover the head and was fitted with a bar which pressed down over the offender's tongue. This was widely employed to punish gossiping and scolding women. Men who were "paupers, blasphemers and railers" also frequently were subjected to its torture in seventeenth-century England. In fact there were known instances of its use as late as the middle of the nineteenth century "to silence scolds."[28] In the colonies a device known as the cleft stick which pinched the tongue was also employed to keep idle gossips quiet—while exposed to public gaze. The cleft stick was also used as a punishment for "gross premeditated lying."[29]

MUTILATION

Mutilation has been employed since Biblical times and seems to possess scriptural authority. Even Jesus seems to favor the idea in his pronouncement, "If thine eye offend thee, cast it from thee." Castration has been widely inflicted for rape, thieves have had their hands cut off, gossips and blasphemers have had their tongues cut or injured. Mrs. Earle recounts many instances of mutilation in the early colonies. Dishonesty and cheating were frequently punished by lopping off the culprit's ears. Quaker religious leaders, who were unpopular in the Puritan circles, sometimes had their tongues bored through with a red-hot iron.[30]

BRANDING

Branding, which was among the earliest of punishments, combined disgrace with pain. Branding was employed by Athenians to mark their slaves, soldiers, and prisoners of war. Romans branded criminals on the forehead. In England vagabonds were branded with a V. Similarly the letter T stood for thief, M for murderer.[31] The adulteress in New England was forced to wear a scarlet letter, as every schoolboy familiar with Nathaniel Hawthorne's famous tale knows. It seems likely that our phrase "a marked person" may stem from this prac-

[28] Ibid., pp. 98–105.
[29] Ibid.
[30] Ibid., pp. 138–141.
[31] Frederick H. Wines, op. cit., pp. 75–76.

tice. At least it served to call attention to the misbehavior of the offender in a humiliating fashion.[32]

THE WHIPPING POST

Lashing at the whipping post and flogging have been used from earliest times and were common in our own country in colonial times. Servants were lashed frequently and until slavery was abolished Negro slaves were often severely flogged for recalcitrant behavior.[33] Ordinarily, men of higher birth did not receive such treatment.[34] Despite recent attempts to abolish the whipping post, Delaware still retains this relic of barbarism. In other states flogging as an authorized form of punishment has been abolished. Unhappily, flogging is still inflicted in a few of our prisons for infraction of prison rules and was a relatively common practice until widespread public opinion was aroused against it.

THE DUNKING STOOL

The dunking stool was a mechanically operated chair into which the offender was fastened and periodically dumped into a tank of water. This device was widely used for ridiculing persons guilty of gossip. Dunking was considered a relatively mild punishment. It apparently was a source of great amusement to passers-by.

THE DEATH PENALTY

The death penalty was the major form of punishment in the mother country and naturally was widely employed here since most of the colonies operated under transplanted British law. The Quakers in fact raised the first significant voice of protest against capital punishment in early America.

When William Penn received as a royal grant the land that was to become Pennsylvania he set himself to founding a Quaker model of the Christian state. Penn and 100 fellow members of the Society of Friends drew up the famous Great Law of 1682 which was to govern Pennsylvania. This law substituted hard labor as a method of punishment for all offenses except murder, for which the death penalty was retained.

The death penalty was meanwhile in force in England during Queen Anne's reign. Non-Quakers were instrumental in influencing the queen to abolish Penn's "lenient" provisions and to institute death penalty

[32] *Ibid.*
[33] See in this connection Raphael Semmes, *Crime and Punishment in Early Maryland*, Johns Hopkins Press, Baltimore, 1938, pp. 38–39.
[34] *Ibid.*

for virtually all offenses for which Penn had exacted imprisonment, as we discuss in a later chapter.[35] Penn was soon able to secure the re-enactment of his Great Law, however, but following his death in 1718 the death penalty was restored for virtually all felonies, ranging from treason to witchcraft and including all sex offenses.[36]

Present-Day Penal Methods

With the growth of the prison movement in our late colonial and early federal period corporal punishment very largely disappeared. In fact our Constitution is interpreted more or less to guarantee that the body of the culprit be exempt from maiming or torture, although we have reserved the right to deprive what are commonly called heinous offenders of their life.

Present-day methods of dealing with the offender vary markedly, however, once he has been tried and convicted (or caught in the act for minor offenses, such as traffic violations). Methods of treatment range in degree of severity, from (1) warning, (2) monetary fines, (3) probation, (4) imprisonment, (5) parole (as a means of lessening imprisonment), to (6) the death penalty, while (7) pardon absolves the accused from further punishment.

WARNING

Warning is in a sense no penalty at all, for the offender is admonished more or less severely and dismissed. Sometimes the police who catch the guilty party let him go, if it is a first offense, with a warning. Sometimes the police refer the offender to a magistrate who administers a warning and dismisses the case. For citizens who intend to obey the law, a single lapse may be treated as well by a warning as by any more severe method. The offender takes care not to repeat his offense.

THE EXACTION OF FINES

A fine is an assessment of a monetary payment to the state as a penalty for violating the law. The bulk of present-day punishments are unquestionably taken care of by fines, although we have no exact statistics. Laws provide in fact that fines may be exacted in the majority of offenses, with the exception of those crimes for which the

[35] Cf. chap. 22, pp. 581–582.
[36] Orlando F. Lewis, *The Development of Prisons and Prison Customs, 1776–1845,* Prison Association of New York, New York, 1922, pp. 12–13. Cf. p. 582 for a list of capital offenses in colonial times.

death penalty may be exacted. When a fine is assessed against an offender the sentence may or may not entail imprisonment as well. In general the guilty person may settle for his offense in case of a misdemeanor by a fine if he can furnish the money. In certain rather serious crimes, particularly those in which corporations are involved, large fines may be assessed as civil fines (rather than criminal fines), as we have discussed in our treatment of white-collar crime.[37]

Fines involve a significant aspect of justice since the person unable to pay may have to go to jail or prison in consequence. In general fines do not carry nearly as much stigma as a sentence to a penal institution. A system whereby the offender could pay a fine in installments might be a more democratic way of administering justice. If a defendant is committed to prison until the fine is paid it may be that he has merely refused to pay it. In other cases he may be completely unable to pay it. When the person is sent to prison in default of payment of fine the cost of crime is obviously enhanced since the state must pay for the offender's living while he is imprisoned.

Fines may also be exacted for contempt of court or for refusal to carry out previous court orders. The whole problem of fines deserves a thorough review by competent persons. As it is, there is little possibility of evaluating an offense effectively in monetary terms. Judges, too, are allowed considerable discretion in whether to exact a fine, imprisonment or both and as to what the fine, if any, is to be.[38] Sutherland estimates that approximately 75 per cent of all crimes are punished by fines.[39] Certainly it is obvious that the bulk of prisoners who are convicted are not sent to prison but some are placed on probation.

PROBATION

Probation is the conditional release from imprisonment and is contingent upon the co-operation and good behavior of the offender. This type of treatment ordinarily involves supervision on the part of the court but carries relatively little stigma so long as the offender behaves himself.

IMPRISONMENT

Depriving an offender of his liberty for a certain period because of his conviction for a crime is widely enforced both in case of offenses

---

[37] Chap. 3, pp. 38–45.

[38] Cf. Article on "Fines" in *Encyclopaedia of the Social Sciences*, Vol. VI, Section 249, for a detailed discussion on fines.

[39] Edwin H. Sutherland, *Principles of Criminology*, Lippincott, Philadelphia, rev. ed., 1947, p. 572.

which are considered serious and against persons who are unable to pay fines. Imprisonment involves not only the unpleasant and coercive deprivation of what freedom the normal civilian may possess. It also carries a definite stigma which in turn may be regarded as its most serious aspect. The offender becomes a person "who has served a term," a "jailbird," a "convict." In contrast the offender who pays a fine escapes a major share of the stigma which is attached to a sentence to prison. The length of sentence depends (1) on the nature of the offense and (2) the offender's previous record.

Parole

Parole is the conditional release from prison pending the completion of the offender's sentence. Ordinarily parole is extended only to those who have made a satisfactory record within the prison and who (after study by the parole board) are considered "good risks." That is, the paroling authority has occasion to believe that the paroled person will make a successful adjustment. The parolee is ordinarily supervised by a parole officer during this period. Parole is widely granted by the prison boards of our several states. Many criminologists believe all prisoners should be released under supervision before the expiration of their term.

Pardon

Certain persons who are serving prison sentences may be pardoned by the governor of the state or, in case of federal offenders, by the President of the United States. The pardon power is justified by the fact that occasionally an innocent person is convicted by circumstantial evidence, by high public feeling (as in case of war), or by other circumstances. Executive clemency also may be extended when the prisoner's offense has been redefined by state or federal law and any previous reason for the exaction of the penalty therefore no longer exists. Pardons unfortunately are frequently granted for political rather than for humanitarian or sound criminological reasons.[40]

The Death Penalty

In times past a great deal of emotion has been expended in newspaper editorials, in criminological journals, in textbooks, in high school debates, and on the floors of legislative assemblies on the question of whether or not the death penalty should be abolished. Inflamed ora-

---

[40] The general subjects of probation, imprisonment, and parole are dealt with at length in subsequent chapters.

tory has pointed out the wickedness of committing murder in the name of the law, the disutility of the death penalty as a reformative device, and its brutalizing impact on society in general. Equally aroused and impassioned speeches have been made in support of capital punishment, which has been alleged to protect womanhood, to prevent vicious crimes, and to give the heinous offender his due. The reasons pro and con for either permitting or requiring the death penalty have in fact been much more extensive.

The most important arguments against the death penalty are as follows: (1) There is no evidence whatsoever that the death penalty decreases the number of murders or other so-called capital offenses. (2) The punishment is irremediable in case of error and numerous cases of "third degree" convictions have resulted in the death of the innocent. Borchard cites 29 convictions of innocent men for murder.[41] (3) Where the death penalty is mandatory, the effect is to diminish certainty of punishment. In every instance in which an extremely severe, arbitrary, and rigid penalty is exacted by the commission of a particular offense it is more difficult to secure convictions than when there are alternative penalties. Juries are often reluctant to require a severe penalty.

Today there is relatively little interest in the subject of capital punishment. Few articles on the subject have been written in recent years and as a matter of fact very few civilian criminals have paid for their crimes with their lives, as we shall discuss presently. Nevertheless all states but Maine, Michigan, Minnesota, North Dakota, Rhode Island, and Wisconsin permit capital punishment. Arizona, Colorado, Kansas, Iowa, Missouri, Oregon, South Dakota, and Washington have at some time abolished the death penalty but have later restored it. There is widespread opinion that retaining the death penalty keeps down crime, but there is little scientific evidence to justify this belief. Numerous studies have shown clearly that the death penalty is in force in some states where the murder rate is high and in other states where it is low. England has had a *low* murder rate for years while the death penalty has been in force. But murder rates are *high* in the southern United States where there is also a death penalty. Meanwhile 42 states and our federal government still authorize the death penalty for murder. The federal government also authorizes it for treason, espionage, and kidnaping. Eighteen states authorize it for rape and in 16 states it is also a penalty for treason. Eight states permit capital punishment for armed robbery and for arson, 6 for burglary, and 5 for train wreck-

[41] Cf. Edwin M. Borchard, *Convicting the Innocent*, Yale University Press, New Haven, 1932.

ing. Murder is, however, the major civilian crime for which the death penalty is exacted. It is also the major crime for which military prisoners are executed.[42]

THE RATE OF EXECUTION

Relatively few murderers are executed, even though the death penalty exists on the statute books of most of the states. In the years 1947 and 1948, for example, there were 7760 and 7620 estimated cases of murder and negligent manslaughter, yet only 152 prisoners were executed in 1947 and only 118 in 1948. Moreover rape cases were estimated at 17,180 in 1947 and 16,180 in 1948 and only 23 rapists were executed in 1947 and 22 in 1948, as Table 15.1 indicates.[43]

TABLE 15.1.   Prisoners Executed in the United States by Race and Offense, 1930 to 1948[a]

Year	Total	White	Race Negro	Other	Murder	Offense Rape	Other
Total	2,831	1,268	1,528	35	2,470	316	45[b]
Per cent	100.0	44.8	54.0	1.2	87.2	11.2	1.6
1930	155	89	65	1	147	6	2
1931	153	77	72	4	137	15	1
1932	140	62	75	3	128	10	2
1933	159	77	80	2	151	6	2
1934	168	65	102	1	154	14	—
1935	199	119	77	3	184	13	2
1936	194	92	100	2	180	10	4
1937	147	69	74	4	133	13	1
1938	190	96	92	2	156	25	9
1939	159	80	77	2	144	12	3
1940	124	49	75	—	105	15	4
1941	123	59	63	1	102	20	1
1942	147	67	80	—	116	24	7
1943	135	56	76	3	118	17	—
1944	120	47	70	3	96	24	—
1945	117	41	75	1	90	26	1
1946	131	46	84	1	107	21	3
1947	152	42	110	—	128	23	1
1948	118	35	81	2	94	22	2

[a] Does not include executions in military installations. The army, including the air force, carried out 146 executions, all during the period 1942 to 1948; 93 were for murder (including 18 which also involved rape), 52 were for rape, and 1 was for desertion. The navy carried out no executions during the period.
[b] Includes 14 armed robbery, 12 kidnaping, 8 burglary, 6 espionage (all in 1942), 3 assault with deadly weapon, 2 offense not reported.
SOURCE: Table 1, *Prisoners Executed: 1948, Prisoners in State and Federal Prisons and Reformatories, 1948*, Federal Bureau of Prisons, U.S. Department of Justice, Washington, 1950, p. 1.

[42] *Prisoners Executed: 1948, Prisoners in State and Federal Prisons and Reformatories, 1948*, Federal Bureau of Prisons, U.S. Department of Justice, Washington, 1950, p. 1.
[43] Cf. *Uniform Crime Reports for the United States and Its Possessions*, Annual Bulletin, 1948, Federal Bureau of Investigation, U.S. Department of Justice, Washington, 1949, p. 111, for estimates of major crimes in 1947 and 1948.

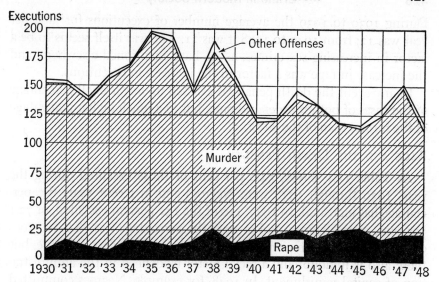

Executions

Other Offenses

Murder

Rape

1930 '31 '32 '33 '34 '35 '36 '37 '38 '39 '40 '41 '42 '43 '44 '45 '46 '47 '48

Prisoners Executed in the United States: 1930–1948, According to Offense. (From *Prisoners Executed: 1948, Prisoners in State and Federal Prisons and Reformatories, 1948*, Bureau of Prisons, U.S. Department of Justice, Washington, 1950.)

As a matter of fact the exaction of the death penalty for murder has declined markedly in the United States during the years 1930 to 1948 although there was a slight upsurge from 1930 to 1935, as indicated by the accompanying chart. The average number of executions from 1930 to 1939 was 166, and from 1940 to 1948 the average was 130. As Table 15.1 shows, the number of civilian executions in the 19-year period from 1930 through 1948 totaled 2831, of which 2470 were for murder, 316 were for rape, and 45 were for miscellaneous offenses, including 14 for armed robbery, 12 for kidnaping, 8 for burglary, 6 for espionage (all in one year, 1942), 3 for assault with deadly weapon, and 2 for offenses which were not recorded.[44]

In addition to these civilian executions, 146 military executions were carried out by the army (including the air force), all of which took place during the period 1942 through 1948. Even in the army the major capital crime was murder, although the death penalty was permitted for other military offenses. Ninety-three of the army executions were for murder (18 of which also entailed rape), 52 were for rape, and 1 was for desertion. The navy did not enforce a single execution.[45] Of course the period covered the war years, and civilian crimes also declined then. On the other hand executions for rape have increased.

[44] *Ibid.*   [45] *Ibid.*

During 1930 to 1939 the average number of executions for rape per year was 12; from 1940 to 1948 it was 21. The war itself seems to be a factor in increasing sex crimes, as we have mentioned elsewhere, and the increase in rape was a factor in the increase in executions.

In any event the death penalty is exacted in only a small percentage of the cases of both murder and rape, but in a much higher percentage of the former than of the latter.

RACE AND THE DEATH PENALTY

As Table 15.1 shows, 54.0 per cent of those executed during the years 1930 through 1948 were Negroes and in recent years the percentage has increased. In 1947, 110 of the 152 persons executed, or 72.1 per cent, were Negroes, and in 1948 the percentage was 68.6. Negroes commit a higher than proportionate number of murders, it is true, but there also is undoubtedly a racial factor evidenced in the administration of capital punishment. In 1948, for example, Negroes committed less than half of the murders but received more than two-thirds of the executions. That is, Negroes, who constitute less than 10 per cent of our population, committed 3072 of the 6703 murders; white persons committed 3579; Indians committed 26; Chinese 2; and "all others" 24. Obviously the death penalty is more frequently exacted today in case of Negroes than in case of white persons.[46]

In the early 1930's, on the other hand, more white persons than Negroes were executed. The basic reason for the shift in the position of the races is apparently the decline in the use of the death penalty in the northern states. As Table 15.2 shows, Ohio and New York are the only northern states which executed 6 or more prisoners in 1948 whereas 6 southern states, North Carolina, Georgia, Florida, Mississippi, Louisiana, and Texas, had 6 or more executions—as did California. In North Carolina, South Carolina, Louisiana, Virginia, and the District of Columbia all persons executed were Negro prisoners.

As is indicated in Table 15.3, there has been a gradual decline in the employment of the death penalty in all sections of the country except in the southern states. Furthermore, all of the states which have abolished the death penalty lie north of the Mason and Dixon line. The death penalty is apparently to be associated with regional practice.

METHODS OF EXECUTION

Hanging was the general method of enforcing capital punishment until relatively recently. Today at least 23 states authorize the electric

[46] *Ibid.*, p. 120.

TABLE 15.2. Prisoners Executed by Offense and Race, 1948

State	All Offenses				Murder				Rape			
	Total	White	Negro	American Indian	Total	White	Negro	American Indian	Total	White	Negro	American Indian
Total	118	35	81	2	94	32	60	2	22	1	21	—
Federal	4	3	1	—	4	3	1	—	—	—	—	—
Connecticut	1	—	1	—	1	—	1	—	—	—	—	—
New York	6	3	3	—	6	3	3	—	—	—	—	—
New Jersey	3	—	3	—	3	—	3	—	—	—	—	—
Pennsylvania	3	2	1	—	3	2	1	—	—	—	—	—
Ohio	7	3	4	—	7	3	4	—	—	—	—	—
Nebraska	1	—	—	1	1	—	—	1	—	—	—	—
Maryland	3	1	2	—	1	—	1	—	2	1	1	—
District of Columbia	2	—	2	—	2	—	2	—	—	—	—	—
Virginia	3	—	3	—	2	—	2	—	1	—	1	—
West Virginia	4	2	2	—	4	2	2	—	—	—	—	—
North Carolina	8	—	8	—	7	—	7	—	1	—	1	—
South Carolina	5	—	5	—	2	—	2	—	3	—	3	—
Georgia	13	2	11	—	12	2	10	—	1	—	1	—
Florida	7	1	6	—	4	1	3	—	3	—	3	—
Kentucky	3[a]	2[a]	1	—	1	—	1	—	—	—	—	—
Tennessee	5	2	3	—	2	2	—	—	3	—	3	—
Alabama	2	1	1	—	2	1	1	—	—	—	—	—
Mississippi	8	1	7	—	7	1	6	—	1	—	1	—
Arkansas	2	1	1	—	1	1	—	—	1	—	1	—
Louisiana	6	—	6	—	5	—	5	—	1	—	1	—
Oklahoma	2	—	2	—	1	—	1	—	1	—	1	—
Texas	11	5	6	—	7	5	2	—	4	—	4	—
Oregon	1	—	1	—	1	—	1	—	—	—	—	—
California	8	6	1	1	8	6	1	1	—	—	—	—

[a] Includes 2 prisoners executed for robbery.

SOURCE: Table 3, Prisoners Executed: 1948, Prisoners in State and Federal Prisons and Reformatories, 1948, Federal Bureau of Prisons, U.S. Department of Justice, Washington, 1950, p. 3.

TABLE 15.3.   Prisoners Executed in the United States Under Civil Authority, 1930 to 1948

Region and State	Total	1930	1931	1932	1933	1934	1935	1936	1937	1938	1939	1940	1941	1942	1943	1944	1945	1946	1947	1948
United States	2,831	155	153	140	159	168	199	194	147	190	159	124	123	147	135	120	117	131	152	118
Federal[a]	15	1	—	—	—	—	—	3	—	5	—	—	—	—	—	1	1	—	—	4
Northeastern States	466	36	36	31	24	28	36	28	23	30	28	20	22	23	19	26	4	13	26	13
New England:																				
Maine[b]	—	—	—	—	—	—	—	—	—	—	—	—	—	—	—	—	—	—	—	—
New Hampshire	1	—	—	—	—	—	—	—	—	—	1	—	—	—	—	—	—	—	—	—
Vermont	2	—	—	1	1	—	—	—	—	—	—	—	—	—	—	—	—	—	—	—
Massachusetts	27	2	2	—	—	4	4	2	—	3	2	—	1	—	3	—	1	1	2	—
Rhode Island[b]	—	—	—	—	—	—	—	—	—	—	—	—	—	—	—	—	—	—	—	—
Connecticut	15	2	—	—	—	—	—	1	1	—	—	—	—	2	2	1	1	3	—	1
Middle Atlantic:																				
New York	253	15	12	20	18	15	16	21	14	7	15	13	15	18	12	20	7	4	12	6
New Jersey	52	10	6	4	3	1	2	3	5	7	3	1	1	2	—	2	3	5	11	3
Pennsylvania	116	9	16	17	5	8	10	1	8	12	10	4	5	8	7	3	13	7	12	8
North Central States	301	20	22	17	25	21	30	11	17	36	19	9	9	8	7	10	13	7	12	8
East North Central:																				
Ohio	118	8	10	11	11	7	10	6	1	12	10	2	4	2	5	2	7	2	5	7
Indiana	35	1	1	—	3	4	2	2	5	8	3	—	1	1	—	2	7	1	—	—
Illinois	76	6	10	5	5	8	10	2	7	4	4	4	2	4	1	8	1	—	1	—
Michigan[b]	—	—	—	—	—	—	—	—	—	—	—	—	—	4	—	—	1	—	—	—
Wisconsin	—	—	—	—	—	—	—	—	—	—	—	—	—	—	—	—	—	—	—	—
West North Central:																				
Minnesota[b]	—	—	—	—	—	—	—	—	—	—	—	—	—	—	—	—	—	—	—	—
Iowa	14	—	1	—	—	—	3	1	4	4	2	1	1	1	—	1	1	2	—	—
Missouri	49	5	—	3	6	2	5	1	4	8	2	2	1	1	—	2	2	2	3	—
North Dakota[b]	—	—	—	—	—	—	—	—	—	—	—	—	—	—	—	—	—	—	1	—
South Dakota[e]	1	—	—	—	—	—	—	—	—	—	—	—	—	—	—	—	—	—	—	—
Nebraska	2	—	—	—	—	—	—	—	—	—	—	—	—	—	1	—	—	—	2	1
Kansas	6	—	—	—	—	—	—	—	—	—	—	—	—	—	—	3	—	—	—	—
The South	1,721	67	78	81	92	100	110	127	92	101	93	83	76	102	90	69	75	99	102	84
South Atlantic:																				
Delaware	12	2	—	—	—	—	—	1	2	—	1	—	1	1	—	—	1	1	1	—
Maryland	58	1	1	2	1	1	4	2	1	2	1	6	5	5	6	4	4	5	4	3

	Total																			
District of Columbia	37	1	1	4	3	—	6	—	1	8	—	—	1	1	2	1	—	1	4	1	2
Virginia	63	3	3	2	1	—	3	5	2	3		1	5	5	3	3	5	9	1	5	3
West Virginia	30	2	2		3		2			3			2	5	4	2	2	1	1	1	4
North Carolina	233	10	8	8	3	20	11	23	10	7	14	9	10	15	19	12	9	10	13	22	8
South Carolina	124	5	9	6	5	13	8	5	5	7	5	9	5	10	4	16	4	4	16	13	5
Georgia	259	7	18	12	14	23	11	11	2	17	8	9	14	8	15	16	19	5	16	16	13
Florida	105	1	7	1	5	1	6	11	16	7	4	10	3	4	2	6	5	5	6	6	7
East South Central:																					
Kentucky	83	2	—	4	9	6	6	11	5	8	2	3	2	8	4	5	4	—	4	4	3
Tennessee	81	2	1		3		9	9	10	5	4	5	4	10	2	2	2	5	5	2	5
Alabama	105	5	2	4	9	5	5	17	4	5	9	4	9	9	9	3	3	2	9	2	2
Mississippi	108	1	4	8	5	8	2	7	6	4	6	5	6	2	5	4	4	13	5	5	8
West South Central:																					
Arkansas	87	10	7	2	4	3	9	5	5	4	2	5	5	4	7	7	4	2	2	6	2
Louisiana	103	5	13	13	7	7	6	3	4	6	6	6	4	4	2	4	3	4	4	8	6
Oklahoma	47	2	2	4	4	2	5	4	2	1	2	1	2	—	2	2	2	2	2	2	2
Texas	186	8	10	14	9	12	20	14	2	11	4	6	8	12	18	8	9	4	5	8	11
The West	328	31	17	11	18	19	23	25	15	18	14	16	12	19	18	16	24	12	9
Mountain:																					
Montana	6	—	—	—	1	—	1	2	—	1	1	—	1	1	1	—	—	—	—
Idaho	6	—	—	—	—		—		—					—					
Wyoming	6	2	—	—	2	1	3	—	—	2	—	—	1	—	1	1	1	2	1
Colorado	36	7	4	2	2	—	3	3	1	2	2	2	4	1	3	—	3	2	—
New Mexico	4	—	—	2	—		—		—		—		1		—				
Arizona	28	2	1	1	4	—	4	3	3	7	1	1	2	2	4	—	1	3	1
Utah	6	—	—	—	1	—	1	1	—	1	1	—	1	—	3	—	3	—	—
Nevada	15	1	1	1	1	—	1	1	1	1	1	2	2	—	2	2	—	1	—
Pacific:																					
Washington	36	4	1	2	1	2	3	3	—	4	2	3	2	5	4	—	1	2	2	1	2
Oregon	14	—	1	—	—	—	—	—	—	1	1	—	1	1	—	—	—	—	3	1	1
California	177	15	9	6	10	11	17	17	8	11	9	3	10	6	4	9	7	13	24	6	7	8

a The 15 federal executions took place in the following states: 1930: Kansas; 1936: Indiana, Oklahoma, Arizona; 1938: Indiana, Illinois, Michigan, Kansas (2); 1943: Tennessee; 1945: Wyoming; 1948: Florida, California (3). The 3 in Kansas and the 1 in Michigan were carried out in federal prisons; the others, in state or local facilities. In statistics previously published by the Census Bureau, federal executions carried out in state and local facilities were charged to the states in which they occurred.

b Death penalty illegal during entire period.

c Death penalty illegal during the years 1930-1938.

SOURCE: Table 2, *Prisoners Executed: 1948*, Prisoners in State and Federal Prisons and Reformatories, 1948, Federal Bureau of Prisons, U.S. Department of Justice, Washington, 1950, p. 2.

chair and 8 provide lethal gas chambers.[47] Lethal gas is apparently pain-less, but there is some question as to whether electrocution is not a cruel method of inflicting death. Some authorities maintain that there is terrific pain involved in an electric shock strong enough to kill. Such pain is at least short and Sutherland is undoubtedly correct in saying that the greatest distress in capital punishment lies in awaiting the ad-ministration of the penalty rather than in the manner in which death is induced.[48]

The Administration of Criminal Justice

Although most offenses are punished by fines, monetary appease-ment of the state carries with it much less punishment than imprison-ment. Pardons occur occasionally but are unsystematic and often de-pend upon the whim of the governor or upon threats from his political enemies. The death penalty is a relatively insignificant method of pun-ishing offenders in the United States, as we have indicated. The major facets of our treatment of offenders lie thus in the institutionalized systems of police, the jails, the courts, the probation system, the pris-ons, and the parole system. Most of these systems are ineffective and cumbersome because of the accumulated weight of the outworn cul-ture patterns which have been in force these many years. Scientifically, as we shall come to see, there is not much to be commended in our penal system. But the complicated machinery which has been de-veloped to meet the problems of (1) dealing with the offender and (2) inducing conformity to the law is not easy to change. Cultural lag may be obvious on every hand, but social institutions which have en-dured over any long period tend to be revered. They also tend to per-sist because of the public's inertia and because of general public dis-trust of the innovator, as every student in sociology knows.

This section on penal treatment is devoted to an extensive analysis of the major aspects of our system of treating the offender. But before institutions can develop we know as sociologists that certain basic be-liefs and attitudes must have developed. As Sumner has said, an insti-tution is a concept plus a structure.[49] F. Stuart Chapin has carried the analysis of an institution further and indicated that all institutions in-volve (1) attitudes, (2) behavior patterns, (3) symbols, and (4) oral

[47] *Release Series P.N.*, Bureau of the Census, U.S. Department of Commerce, Wash-ington, June 30, 1945.
[48] Edwin H. Sutherland, *op. cit.*, p. 562.
[49] William Graham Sumner, *Folkways*, Ginn, Boston, 1906, pp. 2–30.

PLATE I. Housing in a Delinquency Area in Pittsburgh. (Photo, Richard Saunders, Pittsburgh Photographic Library.)

PLATE II. Once Such Indignities as the Pillory Were Society's Answer to the Crime Problem. (From *Federal Prisons, 1950,* Federal Bureau of Prisons, U.S. Department of Justice, Washington, 1951.)

PLATE III. The Caged Man. (From *Handbook of Correctional Institution Design and Construction*, Federal Bureau of Prisons, U.S. Department of Justice, Washington, 1949, p. 3.)

PLATE IV.   The United States Federal Penitentiary at Leavenworth. (Photo,
Courtesy Federal Bureau of Prisons.)

PLATE V.   Air View of the United States Penitentiary at Alcatraz. (Photo,
Courtesy Federal Bureau of Prisons.)

PLATE VI. Solid Block—Outside Cells as Developed at the Federal Reformatory at Terre Haute. (Photo, Courtesy Federal Bureau of Prisons.)

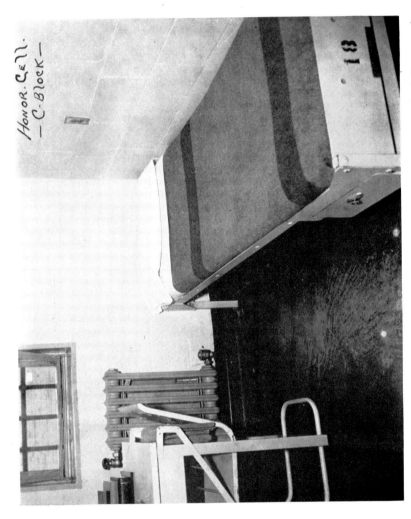

PLATE VII. A Single Cell in a Modern Prison. (Photo, Courtesy Federal Bureau of Prisons.)

PLATE VIII.   Close-Up View of Inside Cell for Single Occupant. (From *Handbook of Correctional Institution Design and Construction*, Federal Bureau of Prisons, U.S. Department of Justice, Washington, 1949, p. 209.)

PLATE IX. Maximum-Security Inside-Cell Block at Federal Reformatory, Chillicothe. (From *Handbook of Correctional Institution Design and Construction*, Federal Bureau of Prisons, U.S. Department of Justice, Washington, 1949, p. 209.)

PLATE X. Athletic Field at the Federal Reformatory at Terre Haute. (From *Handbook of Correctional Institution Design and Construction*, Federal Bureau of Prisons, U.S. Department of Justice, Washington, 1949, p. 217.)

PLATE XI. At Seagoville Men Eat at Small Tables (This Is Unique Among Prisons). (Photo, Courtesy Federal Bureau of Prisons.)

PLATE XII. Superior Library Facilities as Developed at the Federal Reformatory at Terre Haute. (Photo, Courtesy Federal Bureau of Prisons.)

PLATE XIII. The Chapel at Western Penitentiary, Pittsburgh, Pennsylvania.

PLATE XIV. Corridor Disciplinary Unit, with Doors Closed but with Hinged Shutter Open. (From *Handbook of Correctional Institution Design and Construction*, Federal Bureau of Prisons, U.S. Department of Justice, Washington, 1949, p. 212.)

PLATE XV.   The Administration Building, Federal Reformatory for Women, Alderson, West Virginia. (Photo, Courtesy Nina Kinsella, Warden.)

PLATE XVI.   A Cottage at the Federal Reformatory for Women at Alderson, West Virginia. (Photo, Courtesy Nina Kinsella, Warden.)

PLATE XVII. A Typical Single Room in a Women's Prison. (Photo, Courtesy Nina Kinsella, Warden.)

PLATE XVIII. Women Prisoners at Work in the Federal Reformatory for Women at Alderson, West Virginia. (Photo, Courtesy Nina Kinsella, Warden.)

PLATE XIX. Spinning Mill Manned by Inmates. (From *Handbook of Correctional Institution Design and Construction*, Federal Bureau of Prisons, U.S. Department of Justice, Washington, 1949, p. 290.)

PLATE XX. Beaming Cloth Is Part of a Successful Prison Industry. (From *Handbook of Correctional Institution Design and Construction*, Federal Bureau of Prisons, U.S. Department of Justice, Washington, 1949, p. 290.)

PLATE XXI. Cub Scouts, Fricot Ranch School for Boys, Planting Cedar Tree at Annual Fricot Day Ceremonies. (Photo, Courtesy California Youth Authority.)

PLATE XXII.   Forestry Camp Fire Suppression Detail (Showing Work with Older Boys). (Photo, Courtesy California Youth Authority.)

or written codes.[50] Thus the court has attitudes with reference to the sanctity of the law, the dignity of law enforcement (as exemplified in legal procedures), the symbols of the court, and the laws themselves under which the court functions. The prisons operate under notions as to the reprehensible character of the lawbreakers which are their charges; they have developed patterns of behavior which have endured for generations; they dress their charges in symbolic (uniform) fashion; and they operate under both written and unwritten law. One might extend the illustrations at great length.

Underlying all of our penal treatment, however, are the basic considerations by which we (rightly or wrongly) justify the institutional measures employed. These may be *apologia pro nostris institutis*,[51] or rationalizations, if you will, but they constitute the social reasons our society has been able to advance for treating the offenders thus.

It seems probable that groups as well as individuals often act first (as William James has said) and think afterwards. Some of the explanations that have been made for treating offenders as we do may be a matter of *ex post facto* reasoning. Some penal theory may be merely an attempt to persuade ourselves that society could act no differently under the circumstances. Thus some penal theory justifies brutal and coercive treatment. Other theories attempt to deal logically and mathematically with criminals on the basis of the degrees of seriousness of their offenses. Still others are concerned with helping the offender through redirecting his attitudes into a will to conform. Before attempting to understand our penal institutions we shall consider in some detail the present conflicts in penal theory.

SELECTED BIBLIOGRAPHY

Bar, Karl L. von, A *History of Continental Criminal Law*, Little, Brown, Boston, 1916. This is an authoritative history of European penal law.

Deets, Lee E., "Changes in Capital Punishment Since 1939," *Journal of Criminal Law and Criminology*, 38:584–594 (March–April, 1948). Recent trends in capital punishment are surveyed.

Earle, Alice Morse, *Curious Punishments of Bygone Days*, Stone, Chicago, 1896. Fascinating, if somewhat gruesome, this is an account of the penal methods of our relatively recent ancestors.

Edwards, Chilperic, *The Hammurabi Code*, Watts, London, 1904. This book contains the text of the ancient Hammurabi Code and compares its penal provisions with those of the Mosaic Code.

[50] F. Stuart Chapin, *Contemporary American Institutions*, Harper, New York, 1935, chap. 2.

[51] Apologies for our institutions.

Elliott, Mabel A., *Coercion in Penal Treatment: Past and Present*, Series II, No. 5, Pacifist Research Bureau, Ithaca, New York, 1947. This is a short concise survey of coercive penal methods.

Hadley, James, *Introduction to Roman Law*, Appleton, New York, 1874. An old but authoritative outline of Roman penal law is given in this book.

Hentig, Hans von, *Punishment, Its Origin, Purpose and Psychology*, Hodge, London, 1937. This is an especially important summary of varieties and purposes of punishment.

Lewis, Orlando F., *The Development of Prisons and Prison Customs, 1776–1845*, Prison Association of New York, New York, 1922. This monograph contains an excellent account of capital punishment as it applied in colonial times.

Rusche, Georg, and Kirchheimer, Otto, *Punishment and the Social Structure*, Columbia University Press, New York, 1939. In this scholarly volume the relationship between the desire of rulers to protect both property and power and the type of penalties exacted by law is shown.

Wines, Frederick H., *Punishment and Reformation*, Crowell, New York, rev. ed., 1919. This is a standard reference on the topic.

CHAPTER 16

The Conflict in Penal Theories

Penal theories, or the logical assumptions by which men have justified punishment, range from the average layman's opinion on the subject to the viewpoints held by research criminologists. Criminological
science is probably hampered more than most science relating to human behavior by the ignorance and prejudices of the average man.
Even the treatment of the insane, bad as it is, is for the most part
under the direction of persons who have had special medical and psychological training in mental disorders. Criminals, we are forced to admit, are usually subjected to laws, procedures, and treatment administered by persons who possess little if any specialized knowledge of
criminology or scientific understanding of criminal behavior. Penal
theory is thus often propounded by persons who know scarcely anything about why criminals commit crimes but who nevertheless purpose "to put down crime" and "to give the criminal his due."
Research criminologists, sociologists, psychologists, and psychiatrists
interested in dealing effectively with the offender insist that the major
emphasis should be focused on relating the treatment to the offender.

The theory of making the punishment fit the crime is age old. It
apparently found its earliest expression in the *lex talionis*, the "eye for
an eye" and "tooth for a tooth" type of justice, and this survives in
many facets of present-day criminal codes. The theory is well exemplified in every outraged citizen's demand for more severe penalties for
specific offenses, and particularly for the death penalty. When this
viewpoint is augmented by a logical refinement of a philosophical sort
we generally designate it as *classical*, not because it has persisted since

classical times (which of course it has) but because it is based upon a *priori* reasoning, and on the fairly logical notion that if penalties are severe people will fear the law, hence conform to the rules laid down.

The *positive* penal theory, on the other hand, is based less on rationalization and takes the offender into consideration. It insists that treatment be related to the offender's personality. This theory is rather generally held by the psychiatrist, the psychologist, the sociologist, and the research criminologist. Because these persons have worked directly with maladjusted individuals, the term "positive" in the sense of scientific (based on direct knowledge) i.e., employed to designate their viewpoint. Actually what the positive group is proposing is not punishment as such but treatment for one who has failed to meet the requirements of group life. Where reformation is considered possible this theory supports treatment which will result in the offender's rehabilitation. Where prognosis is unfavorable, isolation of the offender is usually recommended.

Between the extremes of these views many variations in penal theory have appeared, but they are broadly covered by the classical and positive theories. The classical and positive conceptions are obviously irreconcilable, yet both are incorporated in our present-day criminal codes. Consequently there is much confusion in present attempts at criminal treatment. We try to make the punishment fit the crime while we also try to reform or rehabilitate the offender. Unfortunately the character of the criminal is not reformed by treating him according to the type of offense. The motivations of the criminal are not automatically dependent upon or related to the type of offense committed, hence readjustment of the offender cannot proceed on such an assumption. Because psychiatrists (who so often are called to assist in dealing with difficult offenders) see this fact so clearly they frequently negate the whole purpose of criminal law. The lawyer, on the other hand, regards the offender as a willful misdoer who is trying to subvert the purposes of the group by disobeying the laws. Understanding something of the conflict between psychiatry and the law is thus extremely important to understanding the conflict in penal theory itself.[1] But let us consider in further detail the nature of the classical and positive penal theories.

[1] Cf. Mabel A. Elliott, *Conflicting Penal Theories in Statutory Criminal Law*, University of Chicago Press, Chicago, 1931, for a detailed discussion of this point, especially chaps. 1, 2, and 13. The author is indebted to the University of Chicago Press for permitting her to draw heavily on this book for the material in this chapter.

THE CLASSICAL SCHOOL

The classical school of penology originated in a revolt against the gross injustices of the penal system during the eighteenth century, and in particular against the exercise of discretionary power by the judges at that time. Such authority had been vested in the ecclesiastical courts which developed during the decline of the Roman Empire and was carried over later into the secular courts. In principle the purpose of discretionary power seems valid. Judges were permitted to make "due allowances" in administering justice, in order to take all the circumstances into consideration. In general an economic crime was judged partly with reference to the amount of property held by the person from whom the property was stolen. Thus a judge might consider it more heinous to harm the helpless or to rob the widow than to steal vast sums from the wealthy, or even to murder a man. On the other hand certain offenses might be considered so serious that penalties in addition to those prescribed by law could be attached by the judge.

In practice such discretionary power was inevitably subject to abuse. Many judges became veritable tyrants, using their so-called professional discretion to advance their personal interests. Others became grossly corrupt, and condemned their enemies in an arbitrary, highhanded fashion. Serious-thinking men of the time could not have failed to recognize how unjustly and unfairly the offender was often treated.[2]

The reaction against such arbitrary decisions on the part of judges was naturally closely related to the whole intellectual trend of the times. Rousseau's philosophy of "social contract" was widely accepted and a factor in facilitating the spread of the classical idea. According to Rousseau all punishment, like all law, could legitimately arise only because men collectively were willing to accept it as just.[3]

Rousseau's philosophy of law, which incorporated an acceptance of the belief in "freedom of the will" and of the individual's moral responsibility for his own conduct, thus gave further sanction to the classical movement. Punishment was consequently held to exist on the one hand because the group so willed and on the other hand because individuals had knowingly chosen to do the wrong act. Such a system of philosophy left no room for discretionary judgments upon the part of magistrates. At the same time it ruled out extremely cruel and severe punishment.[4]

[2] See Raymond Saleilles, The Individualization of Punishment, transl. by Rachel S. Jastrow, Little, Brown, Boston, 1911, pp. 45–51.
[3] Ibid., pp. 51–58.   [4] Ibid.

Although concerned primarily with the mitigation of extreme penalties, the classical group employed purely abstract, theoretical, and a priori methods of studying the crime because they believed consideration of circumstances had led to abuses of justice. Crime was therefore regarded as an abstract juridical entity, quite without any basic concern as to why criminals are criminals. The crime, as it were, was a "Ding an Sich." In fact the name "classical" has been applied to the group because their reasoning was based upon abstraction.[5]

It is to Beccaria, the Italian scholar, that credit has usually been given for inaugurating the classical movement. What his book, Crimes and Punishments, actually did, however, was to make articulate the generally prevailing sentiments of philosophers and reformers of the day. Among other outstanding representatives of the school, two of special note were Bentham of England and Feuerbach of Germany.

Beccaria (1738–1794)

In accepting Rousseau's position that "laws are conditions under which men, naturally independent, united themselves in society," Beccaria held that, likewise, crime can be determined by law alone and that the authority for making the laws resides only with the legislators. Hence, he reasoned, judges have no right whatsoever to interpret penal laws, since such interpretation is tantamount to making laws, and judges are not legislators. Laws rather were to prescribe a fixed, specific, and definite penalty in such a way as to insure a fixed proportion between crime and punishment. That is, the more serious the crime, the more severe the punishment to be attached. The seriousness of the particular offense was to be determined according to the injury which society had suffered because of the crime. Hence Beccaria maintained there was to be a gradation of crimes and punishments, for only by such a plan could there be any justice in punishment. This scheme also provided the only means for deterring criminals from committing further offenses and preventing nonoffenders from breaking the law, he avowed. Nevertheless there was no room in his theory for the unduly severe penalty. Beccaria summarized his point of view in the following theorem: "That a punishment may not be an act of violence of one, or many against a private member of society it should be public, immediate and necessary: the least possible in the case given, proportioned to the crime and determined by law."[6]

[5] Enrico Ferri, Criminal Sociology, transl. by Joseph F. Kelley and John Lisle, Little, Brown, Boston, 1917, pp. 2–4.

[6] Cesare B. Beccaria, An Essay on Crimes and Punishments, transl. from the Italian with a commentary attributed to Voltaire, London, 1767, p. 5.

Jeremy Bentham (1748–1832)

One of the outstanding social philosophers and statesmen of his time, Jeremy Bentham was also a leading exponent of the classical theory. Intellectually Bentham was a utilitarian hedonist who propounded the theory that all law should be based on the premise that it would insure the greatest good to the greatest number. Believing that the general object of all laws was to augment happiness, he concluded that punishment was an evil which was to be permitted only when it promised to preclude a greater evil.[7] Whatever the punishment meted out, it should be in proportion to the offense committed, but with the further provision that it should outweigh the offense if it was to have any deterrent effect.

According to Bentham there were four objects of punishment, three of which were definitely deterrent. These objects were: (1) to prevent all offenses, (2) to prevent the worst offenses, (3) to keep down mischief, and (4) to act at the least expense.[8] He therefore maintained that the greater the offense, the greater the punishment to be inflicted; at the same time uniform sentences should be given for similar crimes. Bentham recognized, however, that circumstances influencing the criminal should always be taken into account.[9] Severity was to be condoned because of "its reforming effect." But to be effective, he shrewdly recognized, any punishment must be "acceptable to the majority of the people."[10]

Feuerbach (1804–1872)

Feuerbach, the German classicist, also adhered to a belief in the *a priori* method of establishing punishment on the basis of the abstract crime. For him there was "no punishment without law, no crime without law." Perhaps the following quotation will sum up his point of view:

"Every just punishment in the state is a logical consequence [of breaking a law] based on the necessity of preserving order. Every violation of the law must be a perceptible offense menacing to the order."[11]

[7] Jeremy Bentham, *An Introduction to the Principles of Morals and Legislation*, Vol. II, London, 1823, p. 1.

[8] *Ibid.*, p. 17.

[9] *Ibid.*, p. 22. To this extent his idea involved a slightly positivistic aspect.

[10] *Ibid.*, pp. 41–43.

[11] Paul J. A. Feuerbach, *Lehrbuch des Gemeinen in Deutschland Gültigen Peinlichen Rechts*, transl. the author's, Heyer, Giessen, 1847, p. 41.

Because of the political ferment during this period, particularly because of the French Revolution, the ideas promoted by the classical school bore almost immediate fruit. The French code of 1791 incorporated Beccaria's principle of "equal punishment for the same crime," fixing definite penalties for specific offenses, with gradations in penalty according to the gravity of the offense.[12]

Since, as we have stated, it was generally accepted that man was a "free moral agent," free to make his own decision, the criminal was held to have made a wrong choice voluntarily. Nothing remained for the court to do except ascertain the guilt of the accused and attach the proper penalty. In practice this precept frequently became both awkward and difficult since it made necessary many minute differentiations in the law in order to cover all types of offenses. Finally, because so many obvious injustices resulted from trying to ignore the criminal and place all the emphasis upon his crime, the French code of 1810 established the principle of minimum and maximum limits within which the judge might fix the penalty.[13]

In this early French code penalties were proportioned according to the grade of the offenses—(1) corporal and infamous, (2) correctional, and (3) municipal—and were levied against (1) crimes, (2) correctional offenses, and (3) municipal offenses. Fixed penalties were established in each category.

On the other hand brutal punishments, with the exception of the death penalty, were abolished—and the latter was limited to decapitation by the guillotine (which was presumably a quick and neat form of death). Pardons and life imprisonment were both abolished. All punishments save for capital offenses thus were intended to rehabilitate the offender.[14]

The classical system, then, initially permitted no consideration of the nature of the criminal, his background, handicaps, or extenuating circumstances under which the crime occurred. Later, as psychological science advanced it became impossible to regard all men as wholly "free" or "responsible." For the classical theory made no allowance for the numerous cases of insanity, immaturity, passion, or "irresistible impulse" that all reasonable persons, even those who have held in the main to the traditional tenets of the classical school, came to recognize as mitigating circumstances. These latter-day classicists thus came to

[12] John L. Gillin, *Criminology and Penology*, Appleton-Century-Crofts, New York, rev. ed., 1945, p. 230.

[13] *Ibid.*, pp. 230–231.

[14] Cf. Jean Brissand, *A History of French Public Law*, transl. by James W. Garner, Murray, London, 1915, p. 565.

be designated as "neoclassicists" because of their deviation from the rigid classical philosophy.[15]

THE POSITIVE SCHOOL

Despite the apparent philosophical logic underlying the classical theory, the findings of the positive (or scientific) criminologists, sociologists, and psychologists have almost completely discredited it. For when scientific interest in these fields and anthropology was turned to a study of the criminal the merit of adjusting punishment to fit the nature of the offender seemed obvious. If the behavior of the criminal is to be changed one must certainly deal with the peculiar characteristics of the criminal. Because their theories were based upon the study and observation of actual criminals this group has been called positivists. Among the many criminologists recruited from the various groups Italians made the most significant initial contributions, hence the terms "positive school" and "Italian school" were originally used almost interchangeably. Of the Italians, Lombroso, Garofalo, and Ferri probably made the most important early contributions.[16]

Cesare Lombroso (1836–1909)

In 1878, slightly more than a century after Beccaria published his essay on Crimes and Punishments, Cesare Lombroso published the results of his first research in criminal anthropology.[17] Lombroso was a physician who was at one time attached to military service. He had occasion to observe troublemakers in the army and later he continued his research among regular civilian prisoners. From his study he concluded that the criminal was a distinct anthropological type, possessing definite physical stigmata. These included low forehead, receding chin or excessively long chin, "cauliflower" ears, too many digits on the hand, and in addition marked resemblances to the opposite sex. But above all Lombroso contended that the criminal was marked by abnormalities in brain structure.[18] Such a man, he contended, was a "born criminal," an atavistic being, inferior in development to normal man, who reproduced in his person the ferocious instincts of primitive

[15] John L. Gillin, op. cit., pp. 230–231.
[16] Ibid., pp. 332–345.
[17] This was published in German in 1881 in Lombroso's article, "Uber den Ursprung das Wesen und die Bestrebungen der neuen anthropologish Kriminalistischen Schule in Italien," in Zeitschrift für die gesamte Strafrechtwissenschaft, Vol. I (1881), p. 1.
[18] Cf. Gina Lombroso, Ferrero, Criminal Man According to the Classification of Cesare Lombroso, Putnam, New York, 1911, pp. 10–24.

humanity and the lower animals. Subsequent research has resulted in the rejection of Lombroso's conclusions, but to him must go the credit for first directing the penologist's primary concern from the crime to the offender.

Later Lombroso revised his point of view somewhat and concluded that there were other types of criminals in addition to (1) the "born" or "atavistic," namely, (2) the insane criminal, (3) the criminal by passion, and (4) the occasional criminal, with 3 subclassifications: (a) the pseudocriminal, (b) the habitual criminal, and (c) the criminaloid.

As to theories of punishment Lombroso held that social welfare should be considered before the criminal, but that the criminal and his victim should both be considered before the crime. To this end he maintained that punishments should vary with the type of criminal. For the man guilty of repeated murders the death penalty might be applied (but only in a few instances). For criminals of passion, remorse itself constituted the greatest punishment. Generally speaking, fines, reprimands, or removal of the criminal from the environs of the person injured would, he thought, constitute adequate means of protecting society.[19] Punishment of insane criminals Lombroso believed unjust. Instead he insisted that such persons should be retained in asylums until admittedly cured.[20] Insofar as possible prison sentences should be abolished and corporal punishment, fines, or indemnity (or reparations) should be imposed. For minors he urged that preventative methods be employed so as to eliminate delinquency at the outset.

Raffaele Garofalo (1852–1934)

Garofalo, the Italian jurist, differed from Lombroso in his classification of criminals, holding that in the main criminals were characterized by psychological rather than physical anomalies. That is, criminals were deficient "in pity or in probity." These defectives he believed to fall into four categories: (1) typical criminals, or murderers, (2) violent criminals, (3) criminals deficient in probity, and (4) lascivious criminals.[21] Holding that the purpose of punishment was to "bring about the disappearance or at least, the progressive diminution of criminal phenomenon,"[22] he agreed with Lombroso that punishment

[19] Cesare Lombroso, *Crime, Its Causes and Remedies*, transl. by H. P. Horton, Little, Brown, Boston, 1911, p. 416. Lombroso was also discussed briefly in chap. 12.
[20] *Ibid.*, p. 402.
[21] Raffaele Garofalo, *Criminology*, transl. by Robert W. Millar, Little, Brown, Boston, 1914, Part II, chap. 1.
[22] *Ibid.*, p. 406.

itself had to be adapted to the wrongdoer, and that "the aim of pun-ishment was not to punish the criminal fact, but to strike the crim-inality of the agent as revealed by the fact."[23]

For Garofalo two methods of punishment were considered tenable: (1) elimination and (2) reparation. The grosser offenders, that is, the murderers who kill for egotistic motives (for brutal enjoyment or rape), he held to be lacking in all moral sense, hence incapable of reformation. For this group death was the only effective punishment. The violent offenders whose acts were frequently due to false notions of honor did not require vengeance; such might better be eliminated by "marooning" on an island or in a penal colony. For habitual crim-inals he proposed internment for life in an oversea penal colony. Sen-tences for youthful offenders and lascivious criminals, on the other hand, he believed should be indeterminate. For offenders deficient only in moral training or restraint, who committed only the less serious violations of the sentiment, reparation rather than elimination should be the method. In such cases Garofalo believed two fines should be levied, one as recompense to the state for creating a disturbance, and the other for the benefit of the injured party.[24]

Enrico Ferri (1856–1929)

Enrico Ferri was distinguished both as a jurist and for his interest in sociological theory. He also served as chairman of a committee for the revision of the Italian penal code, but his proposals were never implemented because of the development of Fascism. According to Ferri there were five criminal types: the insane, the born, the habitual, the occasional, and the passionate.[25] Ferri accepted the contributions of psychology and psychiatry, as well as those of sociology and an-thropology, and concluded that punishment should be based on the psychological motive prompting the criminal, rather than on other considerations. Social protection, however, must always be the funda-mental reason for punishment by the state, in his estimation.[26]

Ferri laid down three fundamental bases for establishing a positive system of social defense: (1) segregation of criminals for an indefinite period, (2) reparation in damages, and (3) the choice of defensive means according to the various types of criminals.[27] In line with the first principle, an absolute indeterminate sentence should be imposed.

---

[23] *Ibid.*, p. 408.
[24] *Ibid.*, pp. 372–401.
[25] Enrico Ferri, *op. cit.*, pp. 138–139.
[26] *Ibid.*, p. 442.
[27] *Ibid.*, p. 502.

In establishing the limits of the sentence both the conditions under which the offense took place and the personality of the criminal must be considered, with the dangerousness of the criminal to be the deciding factor. Reparations, according to the second criterion, should be made in order that the injured party might be indemnified. At the same time penalties should not be too severe. By the third principle Ferri sought to abolish uniformity of punishment, substituting punishment based upon the type of criminal.[28]

Although Ferri found individualization of punishment acceptable in theory, he held that complete individualization was not practicable under modern conditions because the number of prisoners is too large and prison staffs have no adequate notions of criminal biology and psychology. As long as these limitations exist there is little possibility of achieving wholly individual treatment.[29]

Ferri condemned all unnecessary severity of punishment and was unalterably opposed to the infliction of the death penalty. He reasoned that because of its brevity the death penalty is useless for social defense, and because of its intensity it is useless for individual reform.[30]

Among Ferri's most significant ideas of punishment was his emphasis upon the social factors producing crime, and what he calls "penal substitutes." By the latter he would aim to prevent crimes by removing the social factors precipitating them. That is, by such devices as the adoption of free trade, unrestricted emigration, lowering the tax rate on necessities, raising taxes on alcoholic drinks, substitution of metal money for paper currency, spread of birth control, legalizing of divorce, etc., he would prevent the situations which produce crime in the first place.[31] Of all the Italian positivists, Ferri's scheme seems to have been the most forward looking and most scientific, for it aimed to attack the crime problem at its source, instead of being concerned merely with dealing with "finished" criminals.

In points of emphasis these "positivists" obviously differed, but all agreed in the validity of adjusting punishments to the individual offenders. Contrary to a rather generally accepted notion, this consensus does not mean that they stood uniformly for lenient treatment. Instead what they all urged was an "efficient type of treatment" which should at the same time be compatible with social welfare.

On the other hand the classicists, although emphasizing the principles of abstract justice, also were aiming at the promotion of the welfare of the group. That punishment should incorporate social utility

[28] *Ibid.*, pp. 502–520.   [29] *Ibid.*, pp. 76–142.
[30] *Ibid.*, p. 534.   [31] *Ibid.*, pp. 226–227.

both groups agreed. They were far apart, however, in the means they sought to employ to achieve such ends.

In the main, the classicists subscribed to the dominant idea in eighteenth-century philosophy, namely, the belief that man is a free moral agent who exercises the capacity of choice in matters "right" or "wrong." This idea still survives and underlies much of our present-day penal theory.[32] If a criminal is held responsible for his actions, he must possess such a capacity. The positivist in general rejected this point of view. Most positivists subscribed to the determinist's position that neither the criminal nor the normal citizen has much freedom of choice in his conduct. If conduct is considered to be a resultant of biological inheritance, social environment, and past experience, it is obviously foolish to punish a man for something for which he was nowise responsible.[33]

In the period since the Italian positivists brought forth their opinions concerning the nature of criminal man, most of the important research in the field of criminology has appeared. In general criminologists have come to recognize that many factors are involved in the backgrounds of criminals and delinquents. Nevertheless the position or status of offenders in the social structure seems to be the determining factor in condemning them and bringing them to trial and conviction. We are just beginning to recognize that our much vaunted democracy has scarcely characterized the administration of criminal justice.

AN ANALYSIS OF THE MOTIVES OF PUNISHMENT

Briefly we have surveyed the general philosophy underlying the disparity in viewpoints of the classical and positive theorists. A more detailed analysis of the motives or aims of punishment shows that they ordinarily fall into some five categories. These McConnell has called (1) expiation, (2) retribution, (3) deterrence, (4) reformation, and (5) social utility.[34] To this list Kirchwey would add reparation,

---

[32] Cf. F. H. Bradley, "Anglo-American Philosophies of Penal Law," *Journal of Criminal Law and Criminology*, 2:186–198 (July, 1911).

[33] For further development of this point of view cf. Harry Elmer Barnes, *The Repression of Crime*, Doubleday, New York, 1926, p. 24; Clarence Darrow, *Crime: Its Causes and Treatment*, Crowell, New York, 1922, pp. 6 and 7; William A. White, *Insanity and the Criminal Law*, Macmillan, New York, 1923; also Karl A. Menninger, "The Psychiatrist in Relation to Crime," *American Bar Association Reports*, 51:751–757 (1926).

[34] Cf. Ray M. McConnell, *Criminal Responsibility and Social Constraint*, Scribner, New York, 1912, pp. 6–113.

and would subdivide deterrence into (1) deterrence of the criminal against future offenses and (2) deterrence of society by example.[35] Willoughby classifies the theories of punishment as (1) retribution, (2) deterrence, (3) prevention, and (4) reformation,[36] making retribution synonymous with vindication or expiation. With the retributory motive, the basis of punishment becomes the infliction of pain, by which the individual may expiate his offense or suffer retribution for the evil done. Such a motive was upheld by Kant.[37] To Thomas Hill Green punishment by its very nature involves three aspects, the retributive, the preventive, and the reformatory. On the other hand he holds that *legal* punishment can never involve vengeance, for "no equivalent of wrong done to society *can* be paid back to the doer of it."[38]

At the same time Green maintains that the idea of punishment implies a capacity for understanding that the nature of the individual rights accorded a man must be founded upon consideration of the public good. Likewise, judges, as the authority punishing misconduct, must possess a similar understanding which is made apparent in their behavior. "A punishment is unjust in which either element is absent."[39] Moreover, he who administers punishment and the person punished must both agree as to what constitutes public good, if punishment is to be efficacious.

Consideration of these various classifications would seem to indicate that five categories—(1) retribution (or vengeance), (2) deterrence, (3) reformation, (4) reparation, and (5) social utility—are comprehensive enough to embody the significant motives of penal law. The social utility motive is obviously a broad classification and may well include all save retribution. The expiation motive is not considered here since it is primarily a theological concept—that of atoning for offenses through suffering, the suffering meted out in proportion to the gravity of the crime. In a very real sense this concept is nothing but vengeance or retribution in the name of "moral law."[40]

We may consider briefly each of the motives. The vengeance or retributory theory,[41] disregarding theological implications, would ac-

[35] George W. Kirchwey, "Crime and Punishment," *Journal of Criminal Law and Criminology*, 1:718–734 (January, 1911).
[36] W. W. Willoughby, *Social Justice*, Macmillan, New York, 1900, chap. 10, "Punitive Justice."
[37] Immanuel Kant, *Rechtslehre*, pp. 201–202, cited by Willoughby, *op. cit.*
[38] Thomas Hill Green, "Anglo-American Philosophies in Penal Law," *Journal of Criminal Law and Criminology*, 1:19–43 (May, 1910). Reprint from *Principles of Political Obligation*, London, 1858–1888, chap. 1. (Italics mine.)
[39] *Ibid.*   [40] Ray M. McConnell, *op. cit.*, p. 7.   [41] *Ibid.*, chap. 2.

cord punishment in proportion to the wrong committed. Such an idea is held in the retaliative "eye for an eye" and "tooth for a tooth" principle of the Mosaic Code. It still operates in the provisions of death penalty for murder, and in the exactment of severe penalties for grave offenses. This motive affords opportunity for the expression of "righteous indignation" by society but is, after all, a vengeance principle, since it involves retaliation or expression of resentment.[42] As we have said, the vengeance principle involves certain notions of equality. Notions of equality before the law, however, have been greatly altered by modern psychology, physiology, and psychiatry, which have made us aware of individual differences and the importance of environment in molding personality.

The deterrence motive aims to instill fear of the law in the mind of the offender and to intimidate potential miscreants by the horrible example of what happens to those who break the law. According to this theory, punishment is inflicted not because of the past wrongs, but to prevent future wrong. It thus becomes theoretically a means of protecting the group.[43] Actually modern criminologists can find little objective evidence to support the deterrence motive. Criminals commit crimes in spite of the possibility of severe punishment.

The reformatory motive is concerned primarily with the rehabilitation of the offender in order to bring about his satisfactory adjustment within the group. Behind this motive the church has been the most important, if somewhat unrecognized, influence. Many of the eighteenth-century reformers did not realize their debt to the medieval church, which first emphasized the necessity for expiation, penitence, and reform.[44] The particular method by which the reformation is to be accomplished varies with the interpretation made of the delinquent's conduct. Solitary confinement as instituted by Pennsylvania Quakers was assumed to be a means of reforming the convict just as it was when used by the church fathers preceding them. With a technique diametrically opposed to such a practice the psychiatrists would also aim to cure the diseased personality of the criminal whenever they consider the prognosis favorable.

Those supporting the reparation motive aim to force the offender to pay damages to the person or persons injured. The requirement of

[42] Courtney S. Kenny, *Outlines of Criminal Law*, Macmillan, New York, 1907, pp. 33–34.

[43] For an elaboration of this point of view, cf. John H. Wigmore, "Introduction" to "Psychiatry in Relation to the Administration of Criminal Justice," chap. 14 of *Illinois Survey of Criminal Justice*, Illinois Association for Criminal Justice, Chicago, 1929.

[44] Prosanto Kumar Sen, *From Punishment to Prevention*, Oxford University Press, London, 1932, pp. 27–29.

an indemnity compels the criminal to make good the damage he has caused. Since the state, as well as the injured person, has suffered, the payment of a fine in a sense may be considered "reparation." The underlying principle of reparation, however, is the indemnification of the injured person.[45] According to the social utility theory, the basis for meting out punishment should be the consideration for the welfare of the group.[46] Whatever the punishment exacted, it may be justified if it results in promoting social well-being. Retribution, for example, may serve such an end. If men are deterred from criminal activity by stringency of the law and certainty of punishment, all is in favor of such procedure. The reformatory motive likewise is acceptable because there can be no social welfare which fails to consider the well-being of the individual. The group is strong only in the strength of its individual members. Rehabilitation is thus socially desirable.

The retribution or vengeance motive in meting punishment according to the gravity of the offense, and the deterrence theory which inflicts penalty as a means of preventing offenses by making an example of the lawbreaker, and which is concerned primarily with maintaining order, take little concern for the personality of the offender and in the long run subvert the social interests. The social utility motive, however, may permit treatment on the basis of the individual offender insofar as it is not incompatible with the interests of the group. The reparation motive involves more consideration for the injured party than for the offender but is nevertheless in a sense a part of the social utility theory. The reformatory idea, on the other hand, places the emphasis on the offender himself and aims to restore him to social health, although it is often expressed by methods much more nearly akin to the deterrence or vengeance type. During the past 70 years reformation has come to the fore as the major purpose of punishment. Prisons, as we shall see, are generally regarded as failures largely because they do not reform their inmates, not because they do not punish them.

Early English and Germanic law emphasized the vengeance motive although they both gave some thought to the deterrence, reformation, reparation, and social utility motives. Even the classical school, which thought to deter by vengeance, was also concerned with the deterrence, reformation, and reparation motives because of their obvious social utility aspects, since anything which prevents crime, restores the property of the person harmed or pays him for the life of a loved one, or

[45] Garofalo, op. cit., pp. 226–227.
[46] Ray M. McConnell, op. cit., chap. 5.

converts the criminal into a law-abiding citizen is admittedly socially desirable. There is no argument there.

The particular methods of punishment employed may be much alike despite allegedly different motivations, however. Thus the jurist may maintain he is merely interested in deterrence when he espouses the death penalty,[47] whereas what Lord Haldane aptly terms the "serves him right" school would employ the same form of treatment. Theoretically the vengeance or retaliation school is based upon a concept of justice, of equalizing the offense by inflicting the same suffering upon the offender. In fact the Hindu scholar and statesman, Prosanto Kumar Sen, maintains that the concept of justice entails both the idea of equality of punishment and the idea of punishment which equals the crime from the point of view of the suffering inflicted.[48]

There is thus much rationalization in any analysis of the social motives for punishment, whether we are speaking of the classical or the positive viewpoint. Both groups tend to apply their concepts of penal justice more generally to offenders in the lower classes apparently because they threaten the stability of the middle and upper classes. Similarly offenses in the upper-middle- and upper-class groups are more frequently overlooked or nol-prossed. Even if brought to trial offenders in these classes are less likely to be convicted than are lower-class offenders, as we have previously mentioned.

Existing cultural norms provide the justification for the rationalization and the acceptance of our confused and antiquated penal methods. As mentioned earlier, present-day criminal law and penal practices have retained much of the classical or vengeance motive. At the same time both have been definitely affected by the findings of scientific research. In consequence ideas which are in essential conflict exist side by side in our statute books and penal practices are antithetical both to themselves and to the rehabilitation of the prisoners subjected to their provisions. Some jurists, including Prosanto Kumar Sen, have praised present-day methods as a compromise which represents progress and will "lead the way to a final goal."[49] Unfortunately penal practices which place the major emphasis upon punishing the crime cannot be effectively concerned with rehabilitating the offender. The two viewpoints are irreconcilable and contradictory, and any penal system incorporating both must inevitably fail to achieve significant ends in penal treatment. To the sociologist retention of the classical idea is an

[47] John H. Wigmore, "Review of the Loeb-Leopold Case," *Journal of Criminal Law and Criminology*, 15:400–405 (November, 1924).

[48] Prosanto Kumar Sen, *op. cit.*, chap. 2.

[49] *Ibid.*, p. 35.

excellent example of cultural lag. Sociologists and sociology students must also recognize that penal practices are well entrenched, built upon deep-seated human emotions and patterns of thinking. Man has far to go before he will be willing to reclaim offenders, if they are persons of a lower social status who threaten the stability of the social structure. The conduct of a member of the upper or upper-middle class often is not considered so offensive nor is it generally penalized so severely as is that of members of the lower class.[50]

The Conflict Between Psychiatry and the Law

In Chapter 12 we discussed the relations between both mental deficiency and mental derangement and crime. In view of the significant advances in mental testing and psychiatry it may seem strange that legislators should be so slow to adopt penal practices incorporating these advances. This topic will be further discussed under "Criminal Procedure."

Our concern here is with the motivation of punishment. Psychiatrists in general agree with the position of Dr. William Alanson White, who said:

"Criminal law needs to change its point of view from that directed to the individual offender as a morally perverse person, who ought to be punished, to the welfare of society. Lawyers think this is the aim and object of the penal system it is true, but the efforts made to attain this aim and object is not by dealing with the real individual, but by dealing with a hypothetical individual. . . . Criminal law is based on an underlying implication that all men are born free and equal, at least before the law."[51] Speaking futher, Dr. White maintained: "Now we know, if we know anything at all, that men are not born equal, that no two men are alike, and that an act which appears to be the same on the surface when performed by many different men, has back of it in each instance a series of antecedents which stamp it as unique. To think of it otherwise would be the same as if we thought all fevers should be treated alike."[52]

The legalist, on the other hand, holds that justice must be specific, definite, and impartial. Lawyers fear that the psychiatric viewpoint, which allows for complete individualization of treatment, would de-

[50] Cf. chap. 3.
[51] William Alanson White, "Need for Cooperation Between Lawyers and Psychiatrists," *American Bar Association Journal*, 13:551–555 (October, 1927).
[52] *Ibid.*

stroy the whole basis of criminal law,[53] which of course is exactly what psychiatrists would like to do.

The whole conflict is complicated by three factors: (1) Psychiatrists and lawyers have such specialized training that their professional terminologies are more or less unintelligible to each other. The lawyer thinks of mental disorders in terms of insanity and of whether the accused "knows the difference between right and wrong." To the psychiatrist both concepts are meaningless because they are in no sense measures of mental abnormalities. Yet the lawyer regards them as definite and specific indications of whether the offender is responsible for his conduct. The psychiatrist contends no one is wholly responsible and both lawyer and psychiatrist regard the other's viewpoint as inaccurate and distorted. (2) The established legal basis for court procedure gives the psychiatrist little opportunity to present a clear-cut description of the offender's personality characteristics. This fact we shall discuss in detail later.[54] The lawyer thus has an *a priori* advantage because his profession made the rules for treatment of the offender and can stifle the implementation of psychiatric treatment. (3) Psychiatrists disagree markedly among themselves as to the nature of criminal conduct. Of course lawyers do not agree as to the nature of laws; otherwise litigation would disappear. But the disparity in psychiatric opinion creates much confusion in the minds of lawyers, lawmakers, and the public in general. Certain enthusiastic psychiatrists, like Dr. Benjamin Karpman, maintain that *all* criminals are victims of unconscious compulsions. Karpman holds that the mental abnormalities of criminals run the gamut of mental derangement and mental defect, that criminals may be psychotic, mentally deficient, neurotic, or psychopathic, but underlying all antisocial behavior is an unconsciously conditioned psychic reaction over which the individual has no conscious control.[55]

Since recent researches have established the high degree of criminal conduct that goes unpunished among respectable and relatively well adjusted persons, the psychiatrists who maintain that all criminals are abnormal are confronted with another intellectual dilemma, namely, that practically all persons are abnormal. If "everyone is queer but thee and me, and sometimes I think thee is a little queer," abnormality becomes so commonplace as to indicate little differentiation between persons. The psychiatrist who makes all lawbreaking an indication of

[53] Cf. John M. Zane, *The Story of Law*, Ives Washburn, New York, 1927, p. 459.
[54] Cf. chap. 20.
[55] Benjamin Karpman, "Criminality, Insanity and the Law," *Journal of Criminal Law and Criminology*, 39:584–605 (January–February, 1949).

abnormality must either ignore the high rate of lawbreaking or re-define motivations of antisocial conduct by some other term than ab-normality.

Fortunately most psychiatrists are not such extremists as Dr. Karp-man. But even less extreme psychiatrists must separate scientific data from speculative theory before they can expect an extension of psy-chiatric theory within the law. Lawyers and psychiatrists must co-operate if they would develop a common understanding of criminal behavior. Meanwhile it is the pious hope of sociologists that the large body of sociological research in crime may also shape the treatment of crime. Cultural forces in our community life cannot be safely ig-nored if we are to have a total picture of human behavior. Surely our culture shapes much of the patterning of human behavior even though individual emotions and drives may precipitate the particular indi-vidual reaction.

Planning Criminal Justice in the Light of New Insights in Penal Philosophy

Any resolution of the existing drawn-out dilemmas of criminal justice must obviously alter both the function of criminal law and the methods by which the law is implemented. Dr. Herman Mannheim of the University of London has made an incisive analysis of the variety of problems involved in reconstructing criminal justice. He contends with a measurable degree of validity that modern society is confronted with a long-continued crisis in values so far as criminal law is concerned. Concepts with reference to crimes and the laws regarding the treatment of criminals have remained virtually intact for centuries. Dr. Mannheim insists that each generation should work out its own views on crime and develop appropriate legislation to cover the recog-nized social needs. To that end he surveyed the whole problem of crimes and criminal justice with the idea of redefining both the social values which are inherent in any conception of crime and the laws which aim to safeguard those values. He divides crimes into three cate-gories: (1) crimes against human life, (2) crimes against the protec-tion of sexual and family life, and (3) economic crimes.

We cannot recount all the specific changes which Dr. Mannheim suggests for altering and improving British criminal law as related to these topics. In essence, a large share of what he proposes is equally applicable to our own crime problem. He maintains that an extension of administrative law would prevent much of the crime problem at the outset. He insists that criminal laws should be observed in operation and revised in the light of their operation; that the contribution of experts should be integrated within the court procedure; that treatment tribunals should serve in an advisory capacity in determining the type of treatment; that justice should become truly democratic.[56] These and many other suggestions are presented in his proposals. That the judges and lawyers will object to them is inevitable, for judges and lawyers have a vested interest in the *status quo*. Nevertheless scientific understanding of antisocial behavior demands some such alteration. Likewise new definitions of antisocial conduct are needed if our criminal law is to be related to modern social organization. Antiquated and obsolete legal concepts and cultural traditions must be succeeded by laws and procedures consonant with modern science and modern needs.[57] But to bring about these changes it seems obvious that we must decide once and for all to adopt intelligent and scientific objectives rather than muddle along with the vengeance motive.

SELECTED BIBLIOGRAPHY

Beccaria, Cesare B., *An Essay on Crimes and Punishments*, translation with commentary attributed to Voltaire, London, 1767. One of the notable eighteenth-century scholars attempts to reduce capricious administration of criminal law.

Bentham, Jeremy, *An Introduction to the Principles of Morals and Legislation*, II, London, 1823. The leading English exponent of the classical theory that punishment be administered in proportion to the offense committed gives his point of view.

Bradley, F. H., "Anglo-American Philosophies of Penal Law," *Journal of Criminal Law and Criminology*, 2:186–189 (July, 1911). An excellent summary of British-American penal philosophy is presented.

Elliott, Mabel A., *Conflicting Penal Theories in Statutory Criminal Law*, University of Chicago Press, Chicago, 1931. This book surveys statutory law during the period 1900–1925 with reference to the conflict between positive and classical penal theory. Much of the viewpoint of the present chapter is derived from this earlier study.

Ferrero, Gina Lombroso, *Criminal Man According to the Classification of Cesare Lombroso*, Putnam, New York, 1911. Lombroso's views on crime as summarized by his daughter.

Ferri, Enrico, *Criminal Sociology*, transl. by Joseph F. Kelley and John Lisle, Little, Brown, Boston, 1917. This book by the Italian jurist is one

---

[56] Cf. Hermann Mannheim, *Criminal Justice and Social Reconstruction*, Oxford University Press, New York, 1946, Part II.

[57] *Ibid.*, especially pp. 270–271.

of the most important of the positivists' contributions to the study of crime in relation to social conditions and to law.

Gillin, John L., *Criminology and Penology*, Appleton-Century-Crofts, New York, rev. ed., 1945, chaps. 13 and 14. These chapters give one of the best treatments of the classical and positive schools of penal theories.

Green, Thomas Hill, "Anglo-American Philosophies in Penal Law," *Journal of Criminal Law and Criminology*, 1:19–43 (May, 1910). This is a reprint of the famous jurist's discussion of penal law.

Karpman, Benjamin, "Criminality, Insanity and the Law," *Journal of Criminal Law and Criminology*, 39:584–605 (January–February, 1949). Karpman maintains that all criminals are victims of unconscious compulsions; thus "responsibility" for criminal conduct is impossible.

Saleilles, Raymond, *The Individualization of Punishment*, transl. by Rachel S. Jastrow, Little, Brown, Boston, 1911. This book is a notable discussion on modern attempts to relate punishment to the individual offender.

Sen, Prosanto Kumar, *From Punishment to Prevention*, Oxford University Press, London, 1932. This is an examination of the concepts of justice and of prevention of crime by a distinguished Hindu scholar.

Wigmore, John H., "Introduction" to "Psychiatry in Relation to the Administration of Criminal Justice," chap. 14 of *Illinois Survey of Criminal Justice*, Illinois Association for Criminal Justice, Chicago, 1929. A famous American jurist takes issue with the psychiatric view of how criminals should be treated.

Zane, John M., *The Story of Law*, Ives Washburn, New York, 1927. This book presents a plea for the classical viewpoint and conservatism in criminal justice.

CHAPTER 17

Police

The problems of enforcing law and maintaining order in our complicated urban society are in a sense a measure of the defects in our democratic form of government. The police, who are specially vested with the authority for keeping citizens within the law and for protecting life, liberty, and property of individuals, and who must at the same time see that life is kept relatively peaceable and tranquil, have a variety of difficult tasks. To accomplish them acceptably they need both unusual intelligence and the highest integrity. Unfortunately patterns of recruiting police and the public attitude toward police have handicapped any achievement of such ideals. Nowhere in the world are the police subjected to greater criticism than in the United States. No group is more subjected to periodical surveys and investigations. There are many facets to the police problem which we shall develop in this chapter, but personnel standards are the critical issue.

The Origins of Police

The American police system had its humble beginnings in two types of police service. (1) The night watchmen of early New England provided the first protection against thieves, robbers, and other offenders. Sometimes such watchmen were paid members of the community, but the general practice was for citizens to share the responsibility for "maintaining the watch."[1] (2) As soon as township and county governments were organized the offices of constable and sheriff were established as a matter of course. As long as the communities

[1] Raymond B. Fosdick, *American Police Systems*, Appleton-Century-Crofts, New York, 1915, p. 58.

were small these officials constituted the daytime police. Sometimes the constables were the night watchmen. As our cities grew following the Revolution, daytime police forces were organized, but for many years the number of night watchmen far exceeded those on day duty.[2] Night watchmen were more important than day police during the long period in which street lighting was either inadequate or nonexistent; darkness has always been the special accomplice of crime. But when electric lighting became general, the thief and burglar could no longer disappear into the night with little fear of apprehension as formerly.

The practice of vesting authority for maintaining order and security in a specially designated group of civilians is age old. It was common in the ancient Egyptian, Roman, and Grecian civilizations. Law enforcement, in fact, seems always to have depended upon police, and at times, as under Augustus in ancient Rome, police have been the instruments of terror and repression.[3] Under both Nazism and communism we have had a revival of this type of police as an instrument in the totalitarian state. Under such governments the police are concerned primarily with carrying out the instructions of the dictatorship. Under our government the police are basically concerned with protecting the rights of individuals to life, liberty, and property in the name of the law and the common welfare of all the citizens.

The Need for Police

The police needs in any community can be established by the particular hazards which exist. These are situations or incidents requiring the protection and other services which the police force is prepared to give. If there are numerous crimes committed in a community there is obviously need for police, both to prevent further crimes and to apprehend criminals. If there are numerous traffic accidents, more traffic regulation is necessary. If there is merely heavy traffic, considerable regulation is necessary. In areas where there are numerous taverns, dance halls, playgrounds, parking lots, etc., police are important. Police also protect the property of businessmen and keep a watchful eye on homes in residential areas, particularly when they know the owners to be absent from the city.

Briefly, the police service covers (1) answering calls for assistance when a murder, robbery, or auto accident, etc., is reported to the police, (2) the inspection of places which are known to be danger spots,

[2] Cf. Elmer D. Graper, *American Police Administration*, Macmillan, New York, 1921, pp. 3–4.
[3] Cf. "Police" in *Encyclopaedia Britannica* (1947 ed.), Vol. XVIII, pp. 158–159.

such as taverns, beer joints, lobbies of movie houses, waiting rooms of railway stations, etc., and (3) routine patrolling either on foot or in automobiles with the idea of reducing the incidence of crime through presence in the area at intervals throughout day and night.[4]

Types of Police

There are many varieties of police engaged in keeping order, arresting offenders, detective work, and protecting life and property. Police may be classified as public and private police and each variety may be divided into numerous subcategories.

PUBLIC POLICE

Public police are public officials paid by governmental agencies to protect the social interests of the citizens in their particular political unit. The conception of police as servants of the people rather than as coercive agents of the state represents a significant advance socially speaking in the development of the concept of government itself. Public police may be classified as local police, county police, state police, and federal police, each with definitely circumscribed jurisdictions. (1) The largest group of law enforcement officers are the local urban police. They constitute the most important group concerned with the detection and apprehension of the offender. Local police include urban police and rural police, chiefly township constables. (2) Sheriffs and their deputies are county police. (3) State police include state detectives or members of state bureaus of investigation, highway patrolmen, and bodyguards for state officials. (4) Federal police include a wide variety of officials, those with authority to investigate violations of federal law and those who arrest violators. (5) Private police are those hired by industrial corporations, stores, and other establishments, as well as by individuals, to protect individual owners (or persons in case of bodyguards).

Urban Police

Urban police constitute the most important police group, both numerically and insofar as their relation to crime and criminals is concerned. Theirs is a highly complicated task, and they are usually subdivided according to the specific functions they perform.

[4] Cf. J. A. Greening, "Beat Survey" (conducted by the Police Department), Berkeley, California, January, 1944, p. 3. (Mimeographed report.)

THE ORGANIZATION OF URBAN POLICE

The organization of urban police depends both upon the size of the community and upon the size of the police force. In larger cities there is a tendency to subdivide police by level of activity.

Police activities may be divided into patrol duties (these constitute the largest group), traffic regulation, records control, property maintenance (that is, guard duty at public buildings), criminal investigation, personnel management, crime prevention, and morals regulation.[5]

In some cities, Chicago, for example, there has been an extreme degree of fragmentation of the police services, as the accompanying illustration shows. In New York the city police authority is divided geographically, with one chief inspector having over-all supervision of four deputies who in turn supervise division inspectors in the boroughs under their direction. This type of supervision allocates authority and is generally considered a more effective basis for control than one in which a single police commissioner attempts to supervise all the divisions of police in the city.[6] In general most cities have three levels of police authority: (1) the chief of police, (2) the captains in charge of major activities or functions of police, and (3) the lieutenants in charge of platoons or shifts of police force.[7]

In cities where police are deeply enmeshed in corrupt politics the police may be directly responsible to the mayor instead of operating under a police board, which has authority to appoint the commissioner. Experience has shown the importance of divorcing politics from police control as much as possible.[8]

THE DISTRIBUTION OF POLICE

The efficient distribution of the available personnel is of major importance in preventing crime and in apprehending offenders as well as in the direction of traffic.[9] The need for police protection in urban areas varies with different communities since conditions in the communities are constantly changing. A shift in civic developments, population shifts, deterioration of neighborhoods with expansion of the business area, development of new business and industrial areas

[5] Bruce Smith, Police Systems in the United States, Harper, New York, 1949, pp. 245–246.
[6] Ibid., chap. 8, especially pp. 238–243.
[7] Ibid., p. 238.
[8] John C. Polcyn, Chief of Police of Milwaukee, correspondence dated May 5, 1950.
[9] J. D. Holstrom, Chief of Police, Berkeley, California, correspondence dated April 24, 1950.

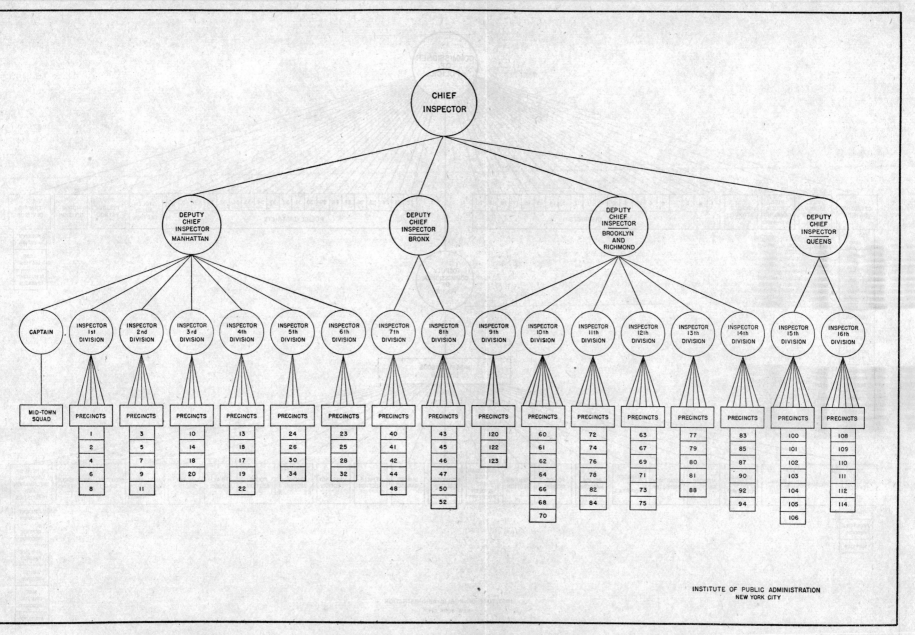

Generalized Organization Chart of the Patrol Force of the New York City Police Department, Showing Extensive Subdivision by Areas and Levels of Activity. (From Bruce Smith, *Police Systems in the United States*, rev. ed., Harper & Brothers, New York, 1949.)

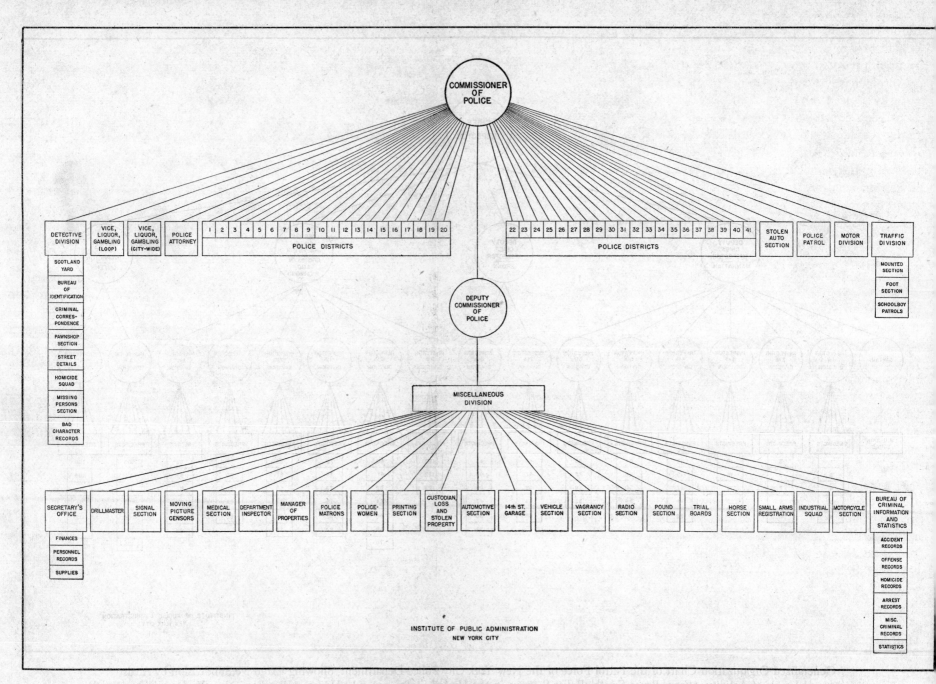

Organization of the Chicago Police Department in 1930–1931. An extreme example of administrative fragmentation, with 48 units directly responsible to the commissioner of police, and 23 to the deputy commissioner. In each case, the span of control was grossly exceeded. (From Bruce Smith, *Police Systems in the United States*, rev. ed., Harper & Brothers, New York, 1949.)

in outlying districts of a growing city—all affect the problem of policing.[10] The advent of a circus in town with all its followers is often an occasion when more policing than usual is necessary.

An efficiently organized police force keeps a constant record of the crimes reported, plotting them or pin-pointing them on city maps so as to keep continually alerted to danger zones in the community. If traffic accidents occur most frequently at certain intersections, those intersections are places where police should be stationed or traffic control lights installed. If holdups and attacks on women are occurring in certain neighborhoods at certain hours the platoons in those areas should be increased.

Effective distribution of police means putting the best-trained police on duty during the hours when police protection is most seriously needed. Most burglaries occur between 2 and 4 in the morning. Most purse snatching occurs between dark and midnight. Most sex attacks on women and sex murders occur during this time. It seems obvious that the ablest patrolmen should be on the night shifts. In many cities, however, there are fewer police on night duty than on the day shifts. Even where the same number of police are on duty the policy may be to give the least desirable night shift to the newest recruits.

In Pittsburgh, for example, police platoons are on shifts of 8 hours each: (1) from 7 A.M. to 3 P.M., (2) from 3 P.M. to 11 P.M., and (3) from 11 P.M. to 7 A.M. Because the hours from 7 A.M. to 3 P.M. are the pleasantest hours to work, the police with seniority status work then; those next in seniority work from 3 P.M. to 11 P.M., and the newest recruits are on the shift from 11 P.M. to 7 A.M. We have already mentioned that the most need for personal protection is at night before midnight and that property crimes occur most frequently in the early morning hours. Obviously the shifts should be altered and the platoons be assigned to different hours. In Berkeley, California, well-trained men are on the night shifts in recognition of the police needs.

Law Enforcement by the Police

Traffic laws probably occasion the greatest amount of lawbreaking and inequality in law enforcement. No traffic patrolmen or highway police can possibly arrest all offenders. Most patrolmen merely try to catch a small percentage of traffic violators, those who are the most flagrant offenders.[11]

In the United States the average citizens resents "highhanded" au-

[10] Cf. J. A. Greening, op. cit., p. 2. [11] Bruce Smith, op. cit., pp. 10–12.

thority and tends to resist laws which affect his personal liberty. Law-suits frequently involve contesting the constitutionality of the law, and police themselves tend to be tolerant of persons who break a law when there is general resentment against it. Where a rigid law is ruthlessly enforced, public reactions often lead to the general viola-tion of the law and it is either repealed or simply unenforced. Thou-sands of dead laws exist in our various statute books, laws which quite literally died under the weight of public disapproval. Others are in-termittently enforced and fines exacted while the violations continue. Almost every city where parking is a problem presents a major ex-ample of such trends in law enforcement.

Furthermore, traffic police have to direct traffic. They cannot keep traffic moving and also appear as witnesses against every traffic violator. If they appeared in court so frequently, traffic conditions would be-come worse while violators were being tried. Hence the more flagrant violations are arrested regularly while irregular and occasional spot checks on minor violators keep the average individual aware of the importance of safety regulations.[12]

Direction and regulation of traffic so as to prevent congestion has been taken over by the police largely because no other body seems to be vested with sufficient authority to deal with it. Maintaining an orderly flow of traffic is imperative to the life of a city. For the metro-politan city of the twentieth century this presents many problems. Cities have become too large for comfortable coming and going. Old cities like London, Paris, Berlin, and even New York, Boston, and Pittsburgh, contain many narrow streets. These were adequate for horse travel when the cities were small, but with rapid automobile transportation and enormous increases in population traffic is a major problem of city government. Keeping traffic moving has become therefore one of the most important functions of the police. Traffic police constitute the greatest number of police in most cities. Their job is essentially to maintain order, not to keep down crime.

HEADQUARTERS CONTROL AND RECORDS DEPARTMENT

Two important aspects of effective policing are (1) headquarters control and (2) the records department. Headquarters control should be well organized so that an emergency call can be quickly dispatched to police officials in the precinct where the offense occurred and ad-ditional police shifted to that area if necessary. Where inadequate standards exist, over-all supervision may be lacking. Pittsburgh, thus

[12] Ibid.

formerly had no headquarters control over complaints and requests. If an offense was reported to the police department, the call was transferred to the appropriate precinct. The precinct officer called the radio dispatcher by telephone if he thought the matter of sufficient importance to send a car. The radio dispatcher then requests a radio car to report to the scene of the offense. All told, three telephone conversations transpired before any action was possible. Sometimes this meant that the delay averted any possible or immediate apprehension in case of a holdup, murder, etc.[13] The cruising car and radio have altered the police structure in most cities from what it was when station houses were neighborhood institutions.

Nor have Pittsburgh police always kept records. Serious crimes have been reported when no record was made. Detectives were not trained and their equipment has been miserably inadequate until very recently. Yet Pittsburgh is the wealthiest city per capita in the United States. It could well afford adequate police protection. Pittsburgh politicians simply found it more profitable to play ball with certain lawless elements and to appoint policemen whose major qualification was political loyalty. Public protest against these outrages have brought certain improvements in recent years.

Keeping adequate records is obviously important to plotting crime trends in various areas and to developing programs and policies which will deal effectively with crimes. If no records of crimes are kept, police can hardly be assigned to duty on the basis of the need in a particular district.

PERSONNEL STANDARDS FOR POLICE

A good policeman should possess an adequate knowledge of criminal law so as to know what constitutes criminal conduct and what action he as a police officer should take in arresting or releasing a suspected person. He should have intelligence verging on the wisdom of Solomon, for he must decide whether the offender warrants arrest or whether a warning will suffice to keep the lawbreaker within the law in the future. The police must be informed enough to recognize clues in case the criminal has escaped before his offense is discovered. He must be strong physically in order to overcome the person resisting arrest as well as to protect himself and innocent persons from an armed criminal. He must know the places where crimes are likely to be committed and keep his eye on all the hazards we have already

---

[13] Confidential report of the Federal Bureau of Investigation, May 12, 1948.

mentioned. He should be schooled in police techniques and in the field of criminology.

Obviously few policemen can meet any of these standards except that of possessing good physical health and basic intelligence.

Educational training of police has improved in recent years and now approximately half of the cities require police to be high school graduates.[14] In Wichita, Kansas, a large number of the officers are college graduates. In Berkeley, California, 68 of the 128 policemen, including police officials, had training beyond high school in 1948. Of these, 12 had attended business college, 41 had some university training, and 15 were college graduates.[15]

A few police systems, it is true, have been able to develop very high standards for recruiting personnel. Milwaukee (Wisconsin), Toledo (Ohio), Berkeley (California), and Wichita (Kansas), are among the cities which have developed unusually satisfactory personnel requirements for their police.

THE MILWAUKEE POLICE PERSONNEL REQUIREMENTS. The Milwaukee Police Department has developed definite and specific job requirements for the various types of police work and has rigidly defined the duties and responsibilities of each member of the force, whether chief of police, captain of detectives, desk sergeant, superintendent of the bureau of identification, or patrolman on his beat. A 437-page book covering rules and regulations has been issued.[16]

All police are required to be at least high school graduates. All detectives, including the captain of detectives, are required to have a thorough knowledge of the criminal code of law and what constitutes a violation of the various sections. They must also be well acquainted with the rules of evidence and able to present cases in court effectively and intelligently.[17]

The Milwaukee police captain (or "district commander") is held responsible for the preservation of public peace, the protection of life and property, and the general good order of his district. He is particularly responsible for the suppression of crimes against person and property, prostitution, gambling, and vice. He is required to visit the scene of every major crime, is in charge of all prisoners at his station house, is responsible for investigation of all city licenses and for enforcement of liquor laws, supervises the patrolmen in detail,

---

[14] Bruce Smith, *op. cit.*, pp. 150–151.

[15] Cf. *Annual Report, Berkeley Police Department*, Berkeley, California, 1948, p. 54.

[16] *Rules and Regulations of the Department of the City of Milwaukee* (issued May 1, 1932).

[17] *Ibid.*, p. 66.

giving them proper instructions, etc., etc. He obviously must have an adequate understanding of all that is required of the patrolmen. The patrolmen on the beat are as much concerned with protecting property and maintaining order as they are with making arrests.[18]

MILWAUKEE POLICE TRAINING SCHOOL. All new men are required to take a 50-day intensive training program. During this time they attend classes 8 hours a day for 35 days. The last 15 days are spent with experienced police officers on foot patrol, in squad cars or ambulances, at desk duty, and on other assignments.[19] The training program consists in physical training in drill, first aid, use of police baton, self-defense, target and combat shooting. The academic training includes a study of types of crime, arrest, investigation, psychology, juvenile delinquency, public relations, report writing, and local, state, and federal law. A major part of this training consists in mastery of the rules and regulations of the Police Department of Milwaukee, as set forth in the rule book.[20]

It seems obvious that no policeman can absorb in 50 days all the training this course presumes to cover. For this reason all officers are required to attend further classes one hour a week on their own time, irrespective of the length of time they have served.[21] Much of the instruction is given through discussion so that the police recruits and those who already are in service can participate. Movies, problems of crime detection, and lectures by experts are employed to point up the training, in addition to discussion on preventing crimes, arresting offenders, and preserving order. Since police are frequently asked to render first aid, instructions in making tourniquets, artificial respiration, and the treatment of fractures are given.[22]

The Milwaukee Police Training School also does its bit of civic education by conducting a Law and Order School for citizens, as well as providing lecturers to various church, civic, and fraternal groups on problems of policing a city, public safety, etc.[23]

THE ALLEGHENY COUNTY LEAGUE OF WOMEN VOTERS POLICE SURVEY

In an effort to get a realistic picture of police in various sections of the country, the Allegheny County League of Women Voters submitted a questionnaire in 1950 to the chiefs of police of all cities of over 250,000 population in the United States with the exception of

[18] Ibid., pp. 37–51.
[19] Police Department mimeographed instructions, June 16, 1947, p. 1.
[20] Ibid.   [21] Ibid., p. 2.   [22] Ibid., p. 3.   [23] Ibid., p. 4.

TABLE 17. 1. Summarizing Data on Police in 31 Cities over 250[

City	Police per 1000	Pct. Beat Men	Education and Physical Req.	Character Investigation	Order of App.	Advantages for Vets.	Exams Given Applicants	Pct. of Failure
Atlanta, Ga.	1.5	25 pct.	High school Reg. physical	Police inv.	Highest	5 and 10 pct. after passing	Police aptitude High school equivalence test	75 pct.
Birmingham, Ala.	1.1	15 pct.	High school No disability	Police emp. credit	1 of 1st 3	None	Written	40 to 6 pct.
Boston, Mass.	3.2	30 pct.	Civil service standards Physical same	Police inv.	Eligible list of C.S.C.	Determined by C.S.	Civil service exams.	N.R.
Buffalo, N.Y.	1 per 724	1 per 3000 pop.	Elementary Good physical condition	Capt. of precinct where appl. resides makes inv.	Highest	Vets, 1st pref.	Police aptitude Genl. IQ	80 pct.
Chicago, Ill.	1 per 603	24 pct.	Elementary Be in good health	Civil serv. inv.	Highest	5 pct. for 30 mos. military service	Police aptitude High school equivalence test	42 pct.
Cincinnati, Ohio	1.7	61 pct.	High school pref. Perfect physical	FBI and Det. Bur. Inv.	Highest	20 pct. after passing	Police aptitude High school equivalence test	70 pct.
Cleveland, Ohio	1.9	12.5 pct.	No education req. Physical same	Complete inv.	1 of 1st 3	10 pct. on entrance exams.	C.S. exams.	N.R.
Columbus, Ohio	1.6	16 pct.	No education req. Rigid physical	Employment, credit, and police records	1 of 1st 3	20 pct. after passing	Police aptitude Written, mental	69 pct. physic 37 pct. mental
Denver, Colo.	1.5	9 pct.	High school Ext. med. exam.	Police, credit records	Highest	5 and 10 pct. after passing	IQ aptitude C.S. exam.	40 pct.
Detroit, Mich.	2.4	27 pct.	High school Perfect physical	Employment, social, credit, criminal record	Highest	Max. of ISPTS after passing	Standard IQ Police aptitude	80 pct.
Houston, Tex.	1.3	25 pct.	High school Physical req.	Thorough inv.	Highest	5 pts. on promotion exam.	Genl. knowledge exam.	N.R.
Indianapolis, Ind.	1.3	N.R.	Elementary Average physical req.	Character, credit, employment, etc.	Highest grades only	None	Written, oral Exam by merit comm.	70 pct.
Kansas City, Mo.	1 per 666	12 pct.	High school Rigid physical	Criminal and references	Class selected from highest	Credit for yrs. of milit. serv. in lieu of H.S. credits	Written 60 pct. Oral (before board) 40 pct.	60 pct.
Los Angeles, Calif.	2.1	10 pct.	High school Physical standards of West Point	Personnel div. check	Appl. from C.S. lists	10 pct. added to passing grade	Police aptitude Written, oral exams.	96.5 p
Louisville, Ky.	1	50 pct.	2 yrs. high school Rigid physical	Employers, neighbors, etc.	C.S. selects Highest	None	Written, oral	75 pct.
Milwaukee, Wis.	2.2	86 pct. Sq. & ptl.	High school Rigid physical	Background, credit, employers, etc.	Highest (el. list added to)	5 pts. added	Written, oral	(See te
Minneapolis, Minn.	8.8	50 pct.	High school No physical disab.	Local and FBI checks	Highest	Vets. have pref.	Written, oral	27 pct.
New Orleans, La.	N.R.	Maj. assgn. motor patrol. Rest Beat men	Civil service standards	Police, credit, and neighbors	Highest	Extra credit on exams.	C.S. exams.	N.R.
New York, N.Y.	.433	70 pct.	No spec. educ. req. Mental and physical by C.S.	Police, milit. serv., employers, etc.	Highest	Vets. given pref.	Genl. IQ exam.	40 pct
Oakland, Calif.	1.5	40 pct.	High school Excellent physical condition	Personal interview with appl. usual sources	Highest	5 pct. on passing grade	Written exam. Police interview appl.	65 pct.
Philadelphia, Penna.	2.51	N.R.	Elementary Complete physical	C.S. character inv.	Highest	10 pct. on passing grade	Genl. information and IQ	39 pct.
Portland, Ore.	1.35	16 pct.	High school C.S. physical	Employment and personal references checked	Highest	5 pts. 10 pts. on 10 pct. disability	Police aptitude Genl. mental	60 pct
Providence, R.I.	2.04	50 pct.	2 yrs. high school Police physical	FBI check and usual sources	Men selected from top 20	5 pct. and maybe 10 pct. depending on milit. record	Genl. mental exam.	N.R.
Rochester, N.Y.	3	16 pct.	High school Good physical condition	Police, credit records, etc.	Highest	Absolute pref. for vets.	Police aptitude Genl. IQ	75 pct.
San Antonio, Tex.	.6	55 pct.	No educ. req. Must pass written exam. Standard physical	FBI and personal inv.	Highest	5 pts. on entrance exam.	Written C.S. exam.	70 pct.

kly and Max. an Salary	Basis for Promotion	Cause for Suspensions and Firings	Police Responsibilities to Politicians	Any Overtime or Pay for Court Appearances	Pensions and Retirement
- $75	Police chief recom.	Conduct unbecoming officer	None	Officer testifying in court on own time receives $2 a day	Compulsory ret. at 65 Opt. plan after 25 yrs. not to exceed $100 mo. (See text)
- $60	Comp. prom. exams.	Chief decides firings, Appeal to Personnel Board permitted	None	None	Compulsory ret. after 30 yrs. Ret. at 60 after 15 yrs.
- $70	C.S. comp. exams.	Violations of dept. rules and reg.	None	Receives overtime pay	One-half to two-thirds annual pay depending on length of service
- $69	Comp. C.S. exams.	Violations of dept. rules	None	Time off at future date	Compulsory ret. at 70; two 25-yr. optional plans
- $70	C.C. comp. exams.	Violations of dept. rules and reg.	None	Time off at later date	Compulsory ret. at 63 at half pay. Ret. at 57 at half pay
- $77	Comp. exams.	Violations of rules Firings for assn. with pd. char., gambler, etc.	None	Time off for court time	Not recorded
- $80	C.S. exam.	Violations of dept. rules and reg.	None	Time off for court time	2 pct. of salary for a 5-year period, or $1200, whichever is greater but must not exceed 65 pct. of annual pay
- $72	C.S. exam. 1st man on list appointed	Violations of state law, city ord.	He votes as he sees fit	Receives 2 hrs. time for court appearances	Half of last 5 yrs. basic pay
- $72	C.S. exam. Seniority Eff. report	Violations of rules Firings for 2nd off. and severe violations	None	Receives 2 hrs. time for court appearances	Half basic pay after 25 yrs.
- $82	Written exam. Seniority Oral int. Serv. rate	Major infrac. dept. rules	None	Time off	Half of a patrolman salary after 25 yrs.
min.	Seniority Exams. on pt. basis	Infrac. against dept. rules	None	None	After 25 yrs. of service or at age 65
- $62	Ability to produce eff. results in dept.	Violations of rules Firings appeal Bd. of Safety	Vote only	None	After 20 yrs. $85 After 25 yrs. $100
- $65	Exam. and com. officer valuation	Infrac. of police manual	None	Overtime pay	Contributory Fund pension. Police contribute 4 pct. monthly wage up to $10. City contributes up to 6 pct.
- $80	C.S. exams. every 2 yrs.	Violations of police rules	None whatsoever	Time off	40 to 66-2/3 pct. of salary depending on length of service
- $60	Comp. exams.	Violations affecting deficiency of dept.	None	None	After 30 yrs. when age 55 $100
- $78	Seniority, ability, etc.	Violations of rules	None	Time off	1/2 average salary last 5 yrs. All entering since 1947 must serve 25 yrs. for this pension
- $75	Seniority C.S. exams.	Firings for 4 or more minor offenses	None	Overtime pay (See text)	Compulsory ret. at 65. After 20 yrs. at 55 $115. After 25 yrs. $125
- $55	C.S. exams.	Violations of rules and reg. police manual	None	None	50 pct. of basic salary after 20 yrs.
- $110	After 1 yr. serv. eligible for C.S. prom. exam.	Violations of rules Police comm. makes decision	None	Officers on night duty who must appear in court are excused at 5 A.M.	20 yr. plan - 5 pct. 25 yr. plan - 6 pct.
- $80	C.S. exam.	Violations of dept. rules	Police are specifically prohibited from participating in political activity of any sort	Two hrs. time off	Joint Contributory System. May retire at 55 after serving 20 yrs., after 25 yrs. irrespective of age
- $70	After 3 yrs. experience applicants given police exam.	Depends on seriousness of infraction	None	None	1/2 of average pay for last 5 yrs. for police serving 20 yrs.
- $70	Promotional exam.	Violations of rules of dept. Chief makes decision	None, except to cast his ballot	None	Contributory Fund Type Pension. Exact amount not indicated
- $62	Up to Lt.(inc.) comp. exam.	Chief can susp. Bureau of Police and Fire can fire	None	None	May retire at age 58 with pension based on yrs. service and pct. of last 10 yrs. annual salary
- $65	C.S. exam.	Violations of rules	None	If officer has to remain in court for most part of day he gets night off	5 pct. Contributory Fund pension for persons serving 20 yrs. 6 pct. Contributory for persons serving 25 yrs.
- $65	Prom. C.S. exams.	Violations of reg. of C.S. Commission	None	None	Pay 5 pct. into pension fund; retire at half pay

TABLE 17. 1. Summarizing Data on Police in 31 Cities over

City	Police per 1000	Pct. Beat Men	Education and Physical Req.	Character Investigation	Order of App.	Advantages for Vets.	Exams Given Applicants	Pct Fai
San Francisco, Calif.	1	60 pct.	High school Army physical standards	Complete inv.	Highest	5 pct. of passing grade	Police aptitude Genl. IQ	25
St. Louis, Mo.	2,3	58 pct.	2 yrs. high school Thorough physical	Police, credit, etc.	All who pass are equally available	Vets. 1st pref.	(See text)	48
St. Paul, Minn.	1,2	7 pct.	Elementary Reg. physical	C.S. inv.	Highest	Vets. 1st pref.	Genl. and police aptitude	N.
Seattle, Wash.	1.28	12 pct.	High school College pref.	FBI, local, crime record, etc.	Highest	10 pct. added to passing	Oral interview by Bd. of Ex.	80
Toledo, Ohio	1.1	5 pct.	High school Must be good physical	Thorough inv. (See text)	Highest	None	C.S. exam.	50
Washington, D.C.	2.18	42 pct.	No min. educ. req. Pass C.S. physical	Intensive inv.	Highest	5 pct. on entrance exams.	C.S. exams.	50

Pittsburgh. This group included 31 cities. Although the study does not probe deeply into local police problems it shows up certain very important facts. These are summarized in Table 17.1.

PERCENTAGE OF POLICE ON FOOT PATROL.   One of the significant disclosures of this survey is the small percentage of police who were designated as beat men (and in most instances this term was interpreted to mean those on foot patrol). As will be noted from Table 17.1, only 5 per cent of the police in Toledo, 7 per cent in St. Paul, 9 per cent in Denver, 10 per cent in Los Angeles, 12 per cent in Seattle, and 15 per cent in Birmingham, Alabama, were on beat patrol. On the other hand 61 per cent of the police force in Cincinnati, 50 per cent in Louisville (also Minneapolis and Providence), 58 per cent in St. Louis, 55 per cent in San Antonio, 70 per cent in New York City were on beat patrol. In Milwaukee, which we have already indicated has one of the best police departments in the country, 86 per cent of the men are either in squad cars or on beat patrol. Foot patrol is obviously the best means of detecting danger to property and discovering crimes, since police riding by in a motorcar can seldom notice the activities of criminals. The fact that so many cities have so few policemen on foot must weigh heavily in the large number of unsolved theft crimes and the fact that so little stolen property, other than automobiles, is ever recovered. A goodly number of police on patrol duty is one factor in keeping down crime. An adequate detective bureau is likewise important for apprehending the criminal who escapes before police arrive at the scene.

EDUCATIONAL REQUIREMENTS.   Although a high school education

◄ by Allegheny County League of Women Voters (Pittsburgh), 1950 (Continued)

Max. Salary	Basis for Promotion	Cause for Suspensions and Firings	Police Responsibilities to Politicians	Any Overtime or Pay for Court Appearances	Pensions and Retirement
0	C.S. exams to capt. (incl.)	Violations of dept. rules	None, whatever. The C.S. Comm. does not condone polit. activities while employed with city	2 hrs. time off for all appearances	Compulsory ret. at age 65 (See text)
5	(See text)	Violations of dept. rules	None	None. Commander can make time up to men	Contributory Fund pension. Rate of pay increases with age of retirement
2	Must be ptlman 5 yrs. to take Sgt. exam.	Violations of rules	None. City charter forbids any city employee from acting politically	Overtime paid	$100 per mo. for 20 yrs. at age 50 $2.50 per yr. per mo. over 20 yrs. and up to 30 max. $125 per mo.
)	C.S. exams. to rank of capt.	Violations of dept rules	City residency	Time off - hr. for hr.	1/2 pay at 25 yrs. or disability. Max. $125 a mo. 2 pct. cont. by members
3	After 5 yrs. ptlman duty C.S. exams.	Violations of rules police manual	Absolutely none. Divorced entirely from politics	None. All 8-hr. shifts change monthly	25 yrs. at age 52 1/2 pay. 2 pct. per yr. service after 25 yrs. up to 33 yrs.
)	C.S. exam. to capt. (incl.) rest by selection	Violations of dept. rules	Subject to same provisions as all District employees	At discretion of commanding officer	Retire on half pay after 25 yrs. service provided person is 55 years of age

would seem to be essential to present-day metropolitan police, there is no educational requirement beyond elementary schooling in Chicago, Cleveland, Columbus, Indianapolis, New York City, Philadelphia, St. Paul, San Antonio, Washington, and Buffalo. There would appear to be no reason to question the validity of the survey with reference to education. On the other hand, the majority of cities require some sort of examination and allegedly make selection from those highest on the list.

POLITICS. Since Pittsburgh personnel requirements have been notoriously low and many police hold their jobs chiefly because they have been good workers in their political party, the League of Women Voters survey raised the question to what extent "political responsibilities" were exacted of police in the 31 cities studied. As Table 17.1 indicates, virtually all chiefs of police claimed there was no such requirement of their police. This question obviously would not be answered in the affirmative. No police chief could be expected to write down the extent to which politics had aided appointments. In cities with high personnel standards a political basis for appointment could not exist. In an eastern city the chief of police was fired for appearing in court while intoxicated but was soon thereafter restored to office by the mayor. In general, cities may fire or suspend policemen for violation of rules or conduct unbecoming in a police official but they are often reinstated.

SALARIES. As Table 17.1 indicates, the weekly wage rate for patrolmen varies markedly in the cities covered. In Kansas City the minimum salary indicated was $42 a week, and in a number of cities the lowest salary was $50 or $55 weekly. The low salary scale is recognized to be a major reason for police corruption. Police can make huge sums by co-operating with the numbers racket, by taking fees from houses of prostitution and bootlegging establishments. When they have so little pay, the temptation is great.

In-Service Training

Because of salary scales and lack of opportunities for promotions it seems unlikely that the majority of police, particularly those in our larger cities, will ever be recruited from a highly trained group. Nevertheless, special training in the social sciences, criminology, and the law, and in the strong-arm methods and technical procedures which are entailed in the detection, apprehension, formal arrest, and fingerprinting of offenders is almost imperative for effective policing. For this reason on-the-job training of police offers a practical solution to the problem. New appointees should be given some comprehensive notion of the tasks they will encounter as well as definite information necessary to perform their responsibilities legally and effectively.

Most untrained and newly appointed policemen would welcome an organized presentation of basic information and techniques. The Los Angeles Police Department has instituted a "roll call" training program built upon suggestions submitted by the men themselves. Confronted with a police force 59 per cent of whom had less than 2 years' experience, the department believed the need for helping the men comprehend their responsibilities was obvious. It was finally decided to lengthen the working hours 15 minutes and attempt to train the men on certain principles in thumbnail lessons during a 15-minute roll-call training program in each patrol division. The results obtained varied markedly as did standards of presentation of materials.[24]

Then a concerted research program was developed as to what such a course should encompass. One hundred and fifty superior officers were interviewed and asked to indicate what information and skills police officers should have which they did not possess. These men interviewed 350 subordinate policemen and received a total of 1219 responses representing specific gaps in policemen's knowledge and techniques which they themselves recognized. The questions were later reduced to 156 work operations and these in turn were classified under 30 general subjects ranging from "field deployment" to fingerprinting. Many of the questions related to problems for which there

[24] Richard Simon, "Roll Call Training Program of Los Angeles Police Department," *Journal of Criminal Law and Criminology*, 40:507–518 (November–December, 1949).

was no easily available information. Police texts were found generally inadequate because they were written by persons with no experience in police work.

What to do when there's a call that "a burglar is there now" or that a murder has been committed is very important. Police muff the solution to many crimes by sounding sirens when approaching the scene of a burglary, by handling the victim's body before observing techniques for securing fingerprints, etc., etc.

The Los Angeles experiment has not only helped measurably to improve standards of police service. It has also made police aware that clear-cut policies do not exist in certain police problems, and that there is often disparity in policies within the same department. It also brought to light the deviations from policies presumed to be in force as well as special problems in which so-called policies were not workable.[25]

Roll-call training is obviously not as satisfactory as more extensive training programs, but it meets an important need.

The city of Wichita, Kansas, has developed a 'police science curriculum" in connection with the Municipal University of Wichita. This curriculum was instituted in connection with the recognition of the need for trained police. University students who meet the other requirements of the Police Department (including physical examination, intelligence tests, character investigation, etc.) may be appointed on active duty on a half-time basis while continuing their studies. They are required to take the following courses in police science:

1. Police organization and procedures—a course covering regulations, policies, tactics, distribution, general duties of police, record systems, report writing, etc.
2. Traffic control—covering important aspects of traffic direction, traffic hazards, and safety devices.
3. Criminal law and evidence—including all the important information on laws governing procedure, evidence, offenses, arrest, search and seizure, etc.
4. Specialized investigation—covering special techniques for collecting and preserving evidence, where to look for evidence, how to identify criminals, etc.
5. Scientific crime detection—a course in physical, chemical, and biological tests for crime, and evidence of deception, etc.

In addition to these courses the student officers are required to take 4 hours of military science, 5 hours of psychology, 8 hours of

[25] *Ibid.*

sociology, 4 hours of speech, 13 hours of political science, and 3 hours of cultural anthropology (a course designated as "customs and cultures"). They are required to carry at least 12-hour loads each semester. If they are elected regular officers they must carry 8 hours until they have completed the course. Police science certificates are awarded to students who complete all prescribed courses, satisfy all the requirements for a Bachelor of Arts degree, and at the same time have performed their duties as student officers with merit.[26]

Toledo, Ohio, has developed a Police Academy which offers detailed instruction in 12 different subjects with 65 subdivisions. These courses cover a variety of topics from the general aspects of police work—military courtesy, combat techniques, criminal law, police practice in criminal investigation, detection, and the like, medical aid, relation to the F.B.I., knowledge of counterfeiting, crime prevention, function of moral squads, history of government, juvenile court procedure, special aspects of felonies such as arson, burglary, auto theft, homicide, public relations, probation, and parole, etc.[27] These courses are given in a period of from 105 to 120 days. They are taught by 40 different persons, some specialists in the particular subject matter, others members of the police force who are well acquainted with the subject.

TEACHING MATERIALS. Because so many policemen have had so little formal education, the problem of textual material has been a complicated one. Rollin M. Perkins developed a text entitled *Elements of Police Science* in connection with a short course at the State University of Iowa, however, which covers adequately, although simply, the various aspects of crime detection, first aid, law of arrest, criminal law, and special date on crimes. This text supplies a vital need in the training of policemen.[28] Most textbooks for policemen have been of the question-and-answer variety and are presumably to be used in preparing for examinations.[29] They give correct information but no background or insight to the answers, and lead to "learning by rote" without any basic comprehension of materials. Of course, certain information will be of value but courses given by persons with broad training in law and criminology and with professional experience in

[26] R. L. Anderson, Lieutenant, Wichita Police Department, correspondence dated April 21, 1950.
[27] Mimeographed "Report of Toledo Police Academy," January, 1950.
[28] Rollin M. Perkins, *Elements of Police Science*, Foundation Press, Chicago, 1941.
[29] W. H. N. Stevens and Otto C. Kaffits, *The Policeman's Text Book*, College Book, Columbia, Ohio, 1941, and George Fletcher Downing, *The Policeman's Manual*, Funk and Wagnalls, New York, 1930, are examples of such books.

dealing with offenders will give the policeman perspective which no "cram book" can ever hope to give. Nevertheless published rules with which the police are expected to familiarlize themselves do help the policeman understand his job and keep him from making serious errors.[30] Obviously, he needs to understand more than rule-of-thumb procedures.

The State Police

Today there is some type of state police and criminal investigation bureau in each of the 48 states.[31] The first authorized state police were established in Texas in 1835 when Texas was a republic. The Texas Rangers, as these police were called, were created initially as a border patrol but later took over the general types of policing, including crime detection.[32] In 1865 Massachusetts established "state constables" vested with general police duties, but they were primarily concerned with the restriction of vice. In 1903 Connecticut created a small police force to keep down vice, to enforce liquor and gambling laws, and in particular to investigate fires of suspicious origin. Arizona in 1901 and New Mexico in 1905 established mounted police similar to the Texas Rangers.[33]

The Pennsylvania "State Constabulary" organized in 1905 grew out of Governor Pennypacker's demand for some agency which could carry out his executive orders.[34] About this time there was much industrial unrest in the coal and iron districts, many of which were relatively rural. Since the sheriffs and constables were generally unable to preserve order the need for better rural police was obvious. The Pennsylvania state police is under the direction of a state superintendent who is responsible to the governor alone. This state police patrols rural areas, a service which marks an important departure from the idea that local police are to look after the special needs of the local community.[35]

Other states followed in creating state police departments, many of them patterned after the Pennsylvania department. With the great increase in automobile ownership and travel, state regulation of motor traffic and state highway control have been established, and these ordinarily function under a commissioner of highways.

[30] The Police Department in Chicago, for example, gets out a small book of rules entitled "Instructions for Patrolmen" which defines general duties of all police and specific responsibilities of the different divisions.

[31] Bruce Smith, *op. cit.*, p. 22.   [32] Cf. chap. 10.

[33] Bruce Smith, *op. cit.*, p. 167.   [34] *Ibid.*, pp. 168–169.

[35] *Ibid.*

Most state police have limited authority. Some have emergency authority to arrest lawbreakers. Others do not. In several states, including Iowa, Nebraska, South Dakota, and California, the bureaus of criminal investigation are not a part of the state police. In general the American people are unwilling to vest complete police authority in the state police; only nine states confer such broad powers. Colorado has seen fit to emphasize the civilian service rendered by its highway police, who are designated as "State Highway Courtesy Patrol."[36]

Usually state police are vested with the same police powers as municipal police, constables and sheriffs, or other duly constituted police officers. Police in New Jersey, New York, Pennsylvania, and West Virginia, are also the fire, fish, and game wardens.[37] They do not have executive authority over local police ordinarily although they may assume such command in West Virginia on the request of the sheriff or the governor.[38]

Rural Police

Modern metropolitan communities require a variety of police services which the separate municipalities are meeting with varying degrees of effectiveness. Rural police remain essentially what they were in England in Anglo-Saxon times—the county sheriff and the village, town, or township constable. During early days both offices possessed considerably more power and prestige than they do today for they were truly administrative arms of the state. Sheriffs, in fact, were virtually viceroys who carried out orders of the king. They combined the functions of county judge, taxing agent, and war lord as well as pursuing and apprehending criminals. Since sheriffs derived their power from the king they were usually appointed by the king. During medieval times the constable was a local township marshal. He was responsible for apprehension of felons and acted as tax collector, highway supervisor, and minor magistrate as well. When local justices of the peace were established these petty judges diminished the importance and stature of both sheriff and constable.[39]

The Sheriff in the United States

Most of the civil authority formerly vested in the sheriff has been transferred to the county commissioners, and the sheriff's role has

---

[36] *Ibid.*, p. 174.   [37] *Ibid.*, p. 176.
[38] *Ibid.*   [39] *Ibid.*, pp. 74–80.

been restricted to his position as chief police officer in the county. In some southern and southwestern states the sheriff is also tax collector; in a few southern states he is administrator for estates where there are no known heirs and in certain other states he serves writs, subpoenas, and orders from the court.[40]

Sheriffs actually arrest very few persons today, although they occasionally take rural offenders into custody. They also accompany prisoners to state penal institutions after they have been tried and sentenced. They sometimes make journeys into other counties or states to take escaped prisoners into custody when they are held by other officials.

The major task of most sheriffs is supervising the county jail and feeding and caring for the county prisoners. This function of the sheriff will be discussed in some detail in the next chapter. Unfortunately the fee system prevails in many states and the sheriff's income often depends upon the difference between the fee he receives for feeding prisoners and the amount he expends. If he keeps the food expenses low enough, charitable persons and relatives may take a hand in supplying food to those in jail while the sheriff makes a profit on the deal.

The sheriff also receives a fee for rendering civil process and in urban counties this medieval practice sometimes runs into as much as $100,000 a year.[41] The fee basis for supporting the sheriff grew out of the idea that he who causes the trouble should pay for it, and such fees were originally paid by the offender. Because many arrested persons who are detained in jail have little income the fees finally came to be paid by the county. It seems obvious that such fees should be abolished and that sheriffs should be paid a straight salary.

There are no personnel requirements for sheriffs other than the simple requirements of age, residence, citizenship, and electoral status.[42] In case of gross misbehavior, such as flagrant immorality or misuse of official funds, the sheriff may be removed from office. Most sheriffs, other than those in the larger cities, are untrained men. Few have any education beyond high school and many have an eighth-grade education or less. In rural counties sheriffs are usually retired farmers. Occasionally an automobile dealer or some other businessman runs for sheriff. Blacksmiths frequently hold the office, presumably because of their strong right arms. In a case known to the author a blacksmith who advertised that he was a taxpayer and a church member was elected to office.

[40] *Ibid.*, p. 86.   [41] *Ibid.*, p. 83.   [42] *Ibid.*, p. 81.

Seldom does the sheriff have any knowledge of criminology or modern police methods antecedent to holding the position. Nor does he usually stay in office long enough to learn much about the suitable requirements for his particular tasks. The need for county police who have knowledge of the law and training for their administrative functions is patent.

THE CONSTABLE

Virtually all subdivisions of counties, whether designated as towns (in New England), townships, or magisterial or county districts, are provided with local constables who are the police officers in the local administrative units. In most states constables are elected by their neighbors, but in a few states—New York, Rhode Island, and South Carolina—they are appointed by county officials. In Delaware the governor appoints the constable in two of the three counties, and the county board appoints them in the third.

In New York State, although theoretically vested with power to arrest criminals, only a small percentage of constables exercise such power. In fact the rural constable's job seldom takes much of his time. He usually has other full-time employment and is literally unable to respond to any sudden demand for his services. The constable receives no regular income and obviously could not live on the small number of fees which he receives. At best his official tasks constitute a part-time job. Consequently most rural constables assume no responsibility for tracking down criminals, and any protection they lend in the community is relatively slight. Bruce Smith regards constables as outmoded in modern times.[43] On the other hand the constable still constitutes a local authority when pressing need arises, and acts as a legal representative for the local community on occasion.

Village constables or marshals do not differ much from the regular township constable except that they have more duties because of traffic, protection of small businesses, protection of school children, etc. Generally speaking villages now need full-time police service, at least for the business area and wherever there is a traffic problem.

COUNTY AND SUBURBAN POLICE

In every metropolitan area the problems of city and county police tend to coincide. In the suburban areas of some of our larger cities county police function as an extension of the sheriff's office. Sometimes special highway police operate from the sheriff's office, as in

43 *Ibid.*, p. 101.

Cook County, Illinois. In Nassau County, New York, adjacent to Queens County (which is a part of Greater New York City), a county police was organized in 1925 which operates independently from the sheriff's office and on a highly efficient basis. Many of the villages in Nassau County are under protection of the county police, but some of the villages with established police departments have been unwilling to give up their local police forces.

In addition to these rural police various states have local park and parkway police, e.g., Long Island, and Westchester County, New York. County prosecuting attorneys also exercise a certain police function in their investigation of local crimes and in bringing the offenders to justice.

Federal Police

With the extensive growth in the functions of our government and in particular with the increase in federal regulative laws affecting the individual, the need for federal police has increased. In consequence nine different systems of un-co-ordinated federal police have grown up to protect property, to protect citizens, to enforce federal laws, and to apprehend those breaking them. The lack of uniformity in police standards, the lack of supervisory control over federal police as a group, and the inevitable overlapping of jurisdictions all contribute to confusion in defining and assuming authority. The various federal police include:

1. The Coast Guard, which operates as a part of the Treasury Department, chiefly, we may presume, because there was no other really suitable department of the government to which it could be attached.
2. The Secret Service in the Treasury Department, which provides the official intelligence service of our government as well as investigating all cases of counterfeiting of money and stamps and cases of forgery of government pay checks. This division also lends official protection to the President and his family.
3. The intelligence unit of the Bureau of Internal Revenue, which is primarily concerned with investigations of frauds and income-tax evasions.
4. The intelligence unit of the Bureau of Internal Revenue, which investigates evasions of the Alcoholic Tax Act.
5. The customs officials of the Bureau of the Customs, who inspect luggage of returning American travelers and incoming immigrants and levy custom duties.

6. The post office inspectors, who inspect post offices at irregular intervals and check upon postal law violations.

7. The Bureau of Narcotics of the Treasury Department, which has police jurisdiction over violation of federal narcotic laws.

8. The federal military police, who serve an important role in wartime in apprehending dangerous offenders as well as arresting military personnel for violations of rules and regulations while traveling, on leave, etc.

9. The Federal Bureau of Investigation, popularly known as the F.B.I., which investigates infractions of the federal criminal laws and arrests guilty persons, checks on persons who allegedly break parole, and carries out "loyalty" checks on federal employees and in particular instances of espionage and attempts to overthrow the government. This group is generally considered the most important federal police agency. At least, it is the best known.

In addition there are other intelligence divisions vested with special confidential tasks, as well as federal police in charge of watching federal property, the investigators of the Veterans Bureau who protect the government against false claims, the police in our national parks, in our territories and island possessions, etc. There are a multitude of police functions which might well be simplified if we had a thoroughgoing reorganization of our federal police. On the other hand the various federal police and federal inspectors have such a variety of highly specialized duties that a degree of separation is more or less warranted.[44]

The Federal Bureau of Investigation

All of the various federal police perform services vital to the functioning of the various departments of government, but the Federal Bureau of Investigation probably performs more services which affect the welfare and safety of the nation as a whole than all the other federal police combined. It also receives the most publicity and has been on occasion the most roundly criticized. The Bureau was first organized in 1908 and remained relatively obscure until the thirties. The great increase in federal criminal legislation was a major reason for the expansion of its services.[45]

THE INVESTIGATIVE FUNCTIONS OF THE F.B.I.   Although the F.B.I.

[44] Cf. Arthur C. Millspaugh, *Crime Control in the Federal Government*, Institute for Government Research of the Brookings Institution, Washington, 1937, for a detailed account of federal police.

[45] *The Story of the Federal Bureau of Investigation*, U.S. Department of Justice, Washington, 1945, pp. 3–4.

has power to investigate all persons or situations in which the United States is or may be a party in interest, it ordinarily does not enter into the activities of the specially assigned federal police mentioned above. The F.B.I. has primary investigative jurisdiction over the following matters: administrative (or governmental) investigations; admiralty law violations; antitrust laws; applicants for positions; bankruptcy frauds; bondsmen and sureties; bribery; claims against the United States; claims by the United States; copyright violations; crimes on the high seas; crimes in Alaska; crimes on Indian reservations; crimes on government reservations; crime statistics; espionage; Federal Kidnapping (Lindbergh) Act; Federal Reserve Bank Act; frauds against the government; identification usages; illegal wearing of service uniforms; impersonation of federal officials; interstate commerce violations; interstate transportation of stolen property; irregularities in federal penal institutions; killing or assaulting a federal officer; larceny from interstate shipments; location of escaped federal prisoners; mail fraud; National Bank Act; national defense investigations; National Motor Vehicle Theft Act; neutrality violations; obstruction of justice; peonage statutes; passports and visas; patent violations; parole and probation violations; personnel investigations; Red Cross violations; robbery of national and Federal Reserve System banks; theft or embezzlement of government property; unlawful flight to avoid prosecution; Veterans Bureau violations; White Slave Traffic Act; and investigations of a confidential character covering a wide range of subjects requiring the exercise of tact, judgment, resourcefulness, initiative, an understanding of law, and the ability to develop evidence and to prepare it for orderly presentation to the prosecuting officers of the government.[46] These latter often concern the international relationships of the United States, espionage and counterespionage.

The need for a Federal Bureau of Investigation has grown out of the difficulties encountered by the local, county, and state authorities in dealing effectively with the growing complexity of certain types of crime in which the federal government has special interest and obligations.

PERSONNEL REQUIREMENTS FOR THE F.B.I. Personnel requirements are rather high. All applicants for service with the Bureau must be citizens of the United States and must be college graduates. Formerly they had to have a degree in law or accounting or a high proficiency of

---

[46] "Crime Report Bulletin," Federal Bureau of Investigation, U.S. Department of Justice, Washington, April 10, 1946, p. 4.

rating in a foreign language. They are not specialists in criminology and often know very little about the subject. The F.B.I. agents are men who know the law, who can detect errors or manipulations in bookkeeping easily, or whose linguistic ability is of special importance in the detection of foreign espionage, etc. The tactics of the F.B.I. do not involve any concern for the factors which have produced the criminal aside from the leads these offer in detecting him.

The applicants must be from 25 to 41 years of age and in good physical condition. They must pass certain tests for sight, hearing, and strength and must be at least 5 feet 7 inches tall.[47] Other qualifications such as character, employment record, habits, etc., are also investigated.

After their applications are accepted the recruits in the F.B.I. service must take special training of a concentrated sort for a period of 4 months. This training covers fingerprinting, accounting, photography, federal law, how to search at a scene of crime, how to interview different types of persons, how to operate firearms, and special training in jujitsu. In addition to the technical training they are briefed in the matter of criminal statistics and learn how to keep records and how to write reports. They are also taught how to organize and administer a regional office.

Simulated crime situations in which there has been a robbery, a kidnaping, or other offense committed are realistically presented. Every available device in the way of films, sound pictures, etc., is used to facilitate the instruction. Some of the training sessions are devoted to forums and discussions so as to teach the importance of sharing ideas in attacking difficult problems.

Some of the problems which the F.B.I. has met have included the capture of gangsters during the lawless thirties, the tracking down of the espionage rings within the secret Atomic Energy Commission (and the industries operating under the Commission's jurisdiction), ferreting out the black marketeers during World War II, and the general survey of the Communist threat in the United States. The capture of gangsters has involved grave dangers and a high loss of life among the F.B.I. men themselves. The majority of federal offenders are not violent, however, as is witnessed by the rather mild personalities of persons engaged in espionage or federal bank embezzlements, or even of soldiers who go "A.W.O.L."

Because the F.B.I. agents are on the whole intelligent and well

---

[47] *Qualifications of Special Agents* (pamphlet), Federal Bureau of Investigation, U.S. Department of Justice, Washington, April 10, 1946, p. 2.

trained in the art of crime detection they have established new records for the successful pursuit and arrest of criminals at relatively low cost. At least it has been claimed that the savings in peacetime years for the government and for private citizens have amounted to around 7 dollars for every dollar spent in maintaining the organization.[48]

THE F.B.I. NATIONAL ACADEMY. The F.B.I. National Academy was organized in 1935 for the purpose of training local police officers in crime detection, firearms practice, police records, laboratory methods of detecting crimes, and various materials from criminal law, government, mathematics, applied psychology, and sociology. Instruction is also given in typing, visual education, etc., to selected local police.

Police officers are chosen (by reason of their outstanding intelligence, education, and experience) to represent their local police departments. Often they learn for the first time about the importance of family disorganization to delinquency, or the emotional factors which contribute to the "sullen insolence" of a teen-aged delinquent. The police officer will be instructed in the importance of maintaining good public relations and taught how to speak to various clubs and civic organizations on law enforcement and public safety. He will also learn how to use chemical analysis in determining whether bloodstains are human blood, and how to tell what bullet shattered a glass window or windshield. Equally important, he will be trained in how to carry back what he has learned to other men on his staff. The F.B.I. National Academy has done much to improve police standards throughout the country. This service under the direction of J. Edgar Hoover is of immeasurable importance.

THE F.B.I. LABORATORY. An F.B.I. crime laboratory was developed in 1932 which experiments with the latest techniques in crime detection. Documents are examined for handwriting analysis. (Often papers are forged, and handwriting is erased with chemicals.) Plaster of Paris or other casts of footprints, tire tracks, etc., are often made. Hair, soil, fibers, etc., are microscopically examined; serological tests for blood are made.

The laboratory has developed a collection of more than a thousand types of bullets.[49]

THE CRIMINAL IDENTIFICATION DIVISION. Another important service of the Federal Bureau of Investigation is the fingerprint file which it maintains in Washington on a co-operative basis with police depart-

---

[48] Jolin Nash, "Efficiency of the FBI," *Atlantic Monthly*, 162:87–89 (June, 1944).
[49] Cf. J. Edgar Hoover, "Adventure in Crime Control," *Vital Speeches*, 3:559–562 (July 1, 1937). Cf. also *The Story of the Federal Bureau of Investigation*, p. 4.

ments throughout the country. The Bureau registers all cards sent to its files by the various police as well as all fingerprints of federal offenders. In addition it maintains a file of all employees whose fingerprints are referred for registry and check. Many employers request this service for their employees and war industries required such investigation in order to decrease liability to sabotage.

THE UNIFORM CRIME REPORTS. Another major service rendered by the F.B.I. is the annual and semiannual publication of the *Uniform Crime Reports*. These contain statistics for the number of arrests throughout the country and relevant data with respect to the value of property stolen, sex, age, and marital status of persons arrested, and analyses of the crime rates in various sections of the country, of crime trends, etc. The statistics, while admittedly inaccurate, give a rough picture of crime in America. The Bureau thus has been responsible for developing greater uniformity in crime reporting throughout the country. Unfortunately there is at present no way local police can be compelled to send in reports, hence all yearly crime rates are at best approximations and subject to many errors, as was discussed in Chapter 3.

PRIVATE POLICE

Private police assume a larger role in maintaining order than most of us realize. Private police consist chiefly in (1) industrial police, (2) private watchmen employed at factories, office buildings, and private estates, (3) private detectives, and (4) "voluntary" police.

Industrial Police

All types of police have been criticized, denounced, and investigated, but none has been in a more anomalous position than police who protect industrial interests. But it was the failure or inability of public police to protect the financial interests and property of certain corporations that led to the establishment of such police. Two of the most important examples of industrial police are railroad police and the coal and iron police of Pennsylvania.

Railroad police were authorized by state law in Pennsylvania in 1865. Today *all* railroads hire some form of police or "special agents," although Pennsylvania seems to be the only state making specific provision for such police. The early provision in Pennsylvania grew out of the raids made on state railroad property and freight following the

Civil War. In earlier days in the western states railroad holdups were a common form of banditry. Theft of valuable freight in fact has always been a serious problem in railroading. Disposability is a major factor in the theft of materials and, according to Shalloo, dry goods are the most frequently stolen. Tobacco, boots and shoes, and automobiles rank next, in the order given. The losses on railroads include all types of goods transported by railroads, as well as baggage and money and other personal possessions of passengers.[50] Passengers also indulge in pilferage of bedding, linens, etc., from railroads and of course there are always some thieves who rob other passengers traveling on the same trains.

Often dishonest employees are involved in these losses, for only through some such collusion can thieves know in which cars particular goods are located. In 1922, for example, several police on the New York Central Railroad were involved in the larceny of $6,000,000 worth of freight.[51] Indeed, losses on all railroads were so serious prior to 1920 that in that year the Protective Section of the American Railway Association was organized. The co-operative efforts of railroads reduced railway losses 92.7 per cent in 9 years.

Railroad police are armed; they often arrest persons upon suspicion without adequate evidence, and their pursuit of offenders often necessitates their operating off of railroad property. In such instances their authority is open to question. Occasionally police shoot innocent people merely for "trespassing" and with nothing to indicate that they are committing any offense. The secret service divisions of police are particularly difficult to regulate. Many authorities believe it would be far better for the state to provide public police protection for railroads than for them to assume the responsibility of such protection.[52]

Coal and iron police. In 1866 the Pennsylvania law covering railroad police was extended to provide special protection to coal and iron companies. These police were virtually armed spokesmen of the coal and iron companies who attempted to keep men at work through terrorism. In the company towns where miners lived in company houses and made their purchases in company stores, where their children went to company-owned schools, the coal barons maintained feudal-like control. The miners had no more rights than domestic servants. In case of protests against reductions in wages, inadequate safety

[50] Jeremiah P. Shalloo, *Private Police* (special monograph), Academy of Political and Social Science, Philadelphia, 1933, pp. 4–11.

[51] New York *Times*, March 17, 1922, p. 19, cited by Jeremiah P. Shalloo, *op. cit.*, p. 4.

[52] Jeremiah P. Shalloo, *op. cit.*

devices, and other practices, the police often engaged in a virtual civil war with the protesting strikers. Both sides were guilty of violence, but the power, ammunition, and legal authorization of violence put the balance in favor of the police. Class-conscious judges virtually always rendered verdicts in favor of the coal companies. The bituminous areas near Pittsburgh were scenes of bitter strikes during the years 1925–1929. Organized labor rose in protest against the ruthless conduct of the police. Coal companies complained of the enforced idleness of their mines and the destruction of their property. Finally in 1929 the coal and iron police senselessly beat a miner to death.[53] Organizations all over the state were aroused by such barbaric tactics. In 1935 the coal and iron police were abolished and maintenance of law and order was placed where it had always belonged—with the public police. Unfortunately public police had not always protected the miners' lawful interests in the past. As a matter of fact mine owners had previously bargained with sheriffs to appoint deputy sheriffs who in turn were commanded and controlled by the coal companies in the anthracite strike of 1922. These so-called deputies often employed the most brutal tactics in the name of the law.[54]

During the first quarter of the twentieth century thousands of miners were illiterate eastern Europeans. Many could not speak English. Today their children have had the advantage of a compulsory education and their children's children have gone to high school and some have gone to college. The standard of living has risen in the mining town. Miners often own their own homes—albeit heavily mortgaged under a federal loan. They have radios, electric refrigerators, and automobiles. More than this, they can protest against working conditions without fear of or display of violence. "Time marches on"—even in the coal industry.

Private Watchmen

Private watchmen are so widely employed by factories and other industrial organizations, as well as by private institutions such as colleges and hospitals and private residences and estates, that they need special treatment here. Millions of dollars are spent by various concerns and individuals for such protection. In Pennsylvania private watchmen are permitted police authority by reason of several diverse statutes, and their authority is derived from the agency under which they are commissioned. Their powers are essentially those of con-

---

[53] *Ibid.*, chaps. 6 and 7.   [54] *Ibid.*, p. 95.

stables but may be executed only on the property of their employer. In general such watchmen are required to possess the same qualifications as municipal police.[55]

Private Detectives

Private detectives often work for individuals interested in securing civil as well as criminal evidence. Occasionally they spend long periods tracking down some offender against whom the victim seeks revenge. The major private detective agencies are the William J. Burns International Detective Association, which handles the protective service of the American Bankers Association, and the Pinkerton National Detective Agency, which handles special protection and detection work for the Jewelers Security Alliance. Most bank detectives work after the offense is committed. Many of the losses suffered by banks are through forgeries and embezzlement despite the occasional spectacular bank robbery. Where extremely valuable jewelry is on exhibit, detectives are usually on guard. Otherwise detectives are simply on call at the nearest branch of the agency, where they are notified in case of robbery or burglary.[56]

The Willmark Service System offers a specialized private detective service for stores, theaters, and hotels, and much of their effort is directed toward detecting dishonesty and undesirable service standards on the part of employees. Store detectives also watch for evidences of dishonesty among patrons. Ordinarily customers are not arrested unless they are seen carrying goods out of the store, since they can easily claim they are looking at the goods, comparing or matching fabrics, etc., etc.

Voluntary Police or "Vigilantes"

During pioneer times farmers had vigilance organizations to prevent cattle and chicken thieving, etc. Such voluntary police were revived during the 1920's as a laymen's co-operative effort to aid in preventing bank robberies and were especially common in Illinois, Indiana, Iowa, Kansas, Wisconsin, and Michigan, particularly the first four states. Numerous rural bank holdups and thefts of livestock seem to have been responsible for these voluntary policemen.

The American Bankers Association sought help in protecting their depositors' funds in smaller towns and villages. Sheriffs appointed vol-

[55] *Ibid.*, chap. 14.   [56] *Ibid.*, chap. 11.

untary guards as deputies and the Bankers Association furnished the armed weapons and the insurance for any liability the sheriff might incur through any act of these deputies. With the development of state police the need for vigilantes has declined. These voluntary bank guards were in themselves testimony to the poor policing on the part of sheriffs and constables.[57]

POLICE CORRUPTION

One of the most serious problems in police administration is the problem of corrupt politics. Police often cater to corrupt party interests, lining their pockets through collusion with local racketeers who are making enormous sums of money by conducting illicit activities. Most police corruption is found among urban police because they constitute the major police group. Among the many factors contributing to the corruption of police the following are most important: (1) Corruption may be so prevalent among the upper echelons of the city administration as virtually to require co-operation in corruption among the police. (2) Bribes may be offered which make it very profitable for the police to protect illicit interests quite aside from corruption in higher places. (3) The low salary and personnel standards both contribute to the vulnerability of the individual police in situations where the corrupt policy is not enforced from above.

In any city in which there is extensive political corruption the police are in a particularly vulnerable position. In order to keep their jobs they must co-operate with the city administration. The city fathers in turn often secure an important part of their revenue from the unholy interests of gambling, liquor, and prostitution. Even where the liquor business is legal and regulated there are many illicit interests which try to evade the heavy taxes and the license fees. Laws against illicit activities are seldom impartially or universally enforced. The contributions of gamblers, liquor racketeers, and heads of vice syndicates to the coffers of the political party in power are notorious in the government of most large cities.[58]

Police may be instructed to make token arrests of prostitutes and gamblers but to let the powerfully organized vice groups alone. Gambling establishments may thus flourish under the name of night clubs while the party officials in power and the police share in the "take."

[57] Bruce Smith, op. cit., pp. 110–112.
[58] Cf. Mabel A. Elliott and Francis E. Merrill, Social Disorganization, Harper, New York, 3rd ed., 1950, chap. 25, "Political Corruption," pp. 539–540.

Houses of prostitution may contribute thousands of dollars to county or city political clubs and to the police. Bootleggers may line the pockets of corrupt politicians. All of these illicit activities invariably entail the collusion of the police.

On the other hand individual police may accept bribes to protect certain gamblers or houses of prostitution. They may accept "fees," as it were, from the "fences" which received stolen goods in a local community. Where such corruption flourishes the police naturally have to show some activity and they tend to hound the ex-convicts on parole in the community for the slightest offense. Or they may arrest the "lower class" prostitute or streetwalker who has no powerful "mob" or syndicate back of her. Again, they may arrest respectable people on false charges and fine them, but keep their names out of the paper so long as they make no protest. During the heyday of the Pendergast regime in Kansas City a professor from the University of Kansas was running to catch a streetcar to the Union Station after teaching an extension class. A police patrol wagon drew up, the police seized him, and he was kept incommunicado for 24 hours. A theft had been reported in the neighborhood and the police seized the first passer-by who seemed to be in a hurry.

In this same city police have hounded the ex-convicts released from the near-by federal prison at Leavenworth and the two state prisons at Lansing, Kansas, and Jefferson, Missouri. These men may have committed a crime but often it was pitiably small in comparison with the long list of continuously criminal activities of gangsters and corrupt politicians unmolested by the police.

The tremendous power of the vice interests over police makes it difficult for the honest police officer to maintain his personal integrity. The police commissioner is subject to approval of and removal by the mayor. The police officer must learn therefore to be discreet in his arrests if the mayor is involved in local graft. Activities of powerful persons and important individuals must be ignored or the police officer may quietly lose his job.[59] In small towns the same sort of corruption may exist on a lesser scale. In a western university town, for example, there were seven known bootlegging establishments in one block in a downtown section. They were never disturbed in the distribution of liquor, and the taxi drivers held what was tantamount to a franchise for delivering the illegal wares to consumers. An enterprising university student decided to compete with these bootleggers and

[59] V. O. Key, Jr., "Police Graft," *American Journal of Sociology*, 40:624–636 (March, 1935).

in a very short time was arrested and committed to the county jail. Obviously he knew he was breaking the law and "deserved" the punishment. The point is that other bootleggers known to the police operated unmolested for years, in fact until the prohibition law within the state was repealed.

Politicians often allege that the extensive and national organization of the underworld makes local law enforcement impossible. This is nonsense. The "National Crime Syndicate" is, in the estimation of persons extensively acquainted with rackets and racketeers, a smoke screen behind which local politicians and police hide. If police tried, they could enforce the law against racketeers and force them out of business. Racketeers stay in business because they make big money and are able to pay off the local corrupt politicians. It is true that certain syndicate organizations supply gambling paraphernalia, roulette wheels, slot machines, etc., but it is absurd to think that local politicians are defenseless against them. Any police force composed of honest and intelligent men can keep a city free from organized rackets. St. Louis, with an administrative force of 15 men, has demonstrated this. Columbus, Ohio, with 5 administrative officers, has virtually wiped out vice in that city by enforcing effective policing.

In the spring of 1950 Ray Sprigle, feature writer for the Pittsburgh *Post-Gazette*, relentlessly exposed what he characterized as the incompetence and corruption of the Pittsburgh police. According to Sprigle's articles, the Pittsburgh police made little or no effort to put down crime, police were not effectively distributed, and the whole police force was controlled by politics. Furthermore, the numbers racket was flourishing wide open because of the rake-off which the police and the party in power received. Sprigle's articles were stimulated by a series of unsolved murders in Pittsburgh. Public indignation meetings had reached a white heat over the case of a young woman from a well-known family who was the victim of a rape-murder. The young woman was knocked on the head by her assailant under a corner street light in a quiet residential area about 11 o'clock one evening. A neighbor who happened to be looking out the window saw the woman fall to the street. She rushed to a telephone and called the police. When she returned the man had disappeared with the woman. The damaging fact was that the police did not respond to the call for over an hour! Furthermore their methods of detection were outrageously ineffective. The woman's body was not found until the next morning although it lay at the rear of a house near the alley, only a short distance away.

Investigation of the police department disclosed that the detective bureau had virtually no suitable equipment and no personnel at all with any special skills in homicide detection. In response to enraged citizens and indignant members of the Allegheny County League of Women Voters, 100 policemen were added to the force. These new men were placed on the 11 P.M. to 7 A.M. shift, whereas it would have been more sensible to have put the best-trained police on duty then. Following the newspaper publicity attached to this murder, several other women were brutally attacked.

In the meantime the League of Women Voters accused the mayor of using the police as a political machine. The situation in this city is unfortunately duplicated in many cities throughout the country.

Other Lawlessness on the Part of the Police

In addition to co-operating with racketeers police often are extremely "lawless in the name of the law." That is, they frequently arrest persons by using methods which are specifically forbidden by law. Volumes have been written on this subject, but all such types of lawlessness characteristic of policemen may be described briefly as "direct action." That is, police employ violence, intimidation, brutality, and the "third degree," all of which practices are unconstitutional. They arrest many persons falsely and deprive many suspects of liberty, often to the extent of keeping them incommunicado until satisfied they are not guilty or until they have confessed.[60]

The widespread use of firearms, clubs, and blackjacks by police in making arrests has undoubtedly contributed to the increased use of arms among criminals. Police often justify such methods by maintaining that capturing the gangsters and hoodlums is more important than preserving the constitutional rights of criminals. Some police forget that criminals are human beings and entitled to decency in the name of the law, if merely to create a respect for the law and law-enforcing agencies.

Police often fire upon a suspected criminal when the offender is in no sense dangerous. For example, Kansas City police shot and killed a high school boy a few years ago when he was seen driving a car he had "swiped" to take a high school girl friend to a class party. The boy obviously was not armed and was a first offender. The state does not deprive a man of his life as punishment following a conviction for

[60] Cf. Ernest J. Hopkins, *Our Lawless Police*, Viking, New York, 1931, for a detailed discussion of lawlessness on the part of police.

stealing a car. There is no valid or legal justification for having the police exact such punishment. Sometimes police break up political or labor meetings by clubbing certain attendants. This practice has been particularly common in times of hysteria over communism or over industrial strikes in certain areas. Policemen obviously have no right to inflict punishment, and such activities are basic denials of the constitutional rights of freedom of assembly and of jury trial.

Trial-and-error arrest is another notorious custom of police. They may decide someone "looks suspicious" and take him into custody. Actually a false arrest is specifically prohibited by the Constitution of the United States. But few police are ever punished for arresting an innocent person. If a person has a record he may be arrested with almost complete impunity. Arresting without warrant is particularly common. An arrest, moreover, is often made to assure that the accused person will be on hand to answer charges, when police are reasonably sure that he has committed an offense.[61]

The problem of false arrest is part and parcel of the whole matter of graft and political corruption. Police may arrest persons falsely because they split the fees which shyster lawyers receive for representing these persons in court, or which the bonding company gets for going bail for the falsely arrested person. Incidentally, false arrests explain a portion, but not all, of the cases in which "nolle prosequis" are entered, as we describe in Chapter 19.

Occasionally a falsely arrested person sues the policeman, as happened in a police scandal in New York City during the thirties. In this instance policemen engaged in the nefarious practice of picking up innocent young women en route home from the theater or elsewhere on charges of streetwalking. They would then agree to release the girls on payment of 50 dollars. Otherwise the girls were held and their names published in the police court records in the daily papers. Obviously most young employed women could not afford the notoriety of publicity or the expenses of bringing suit and they meekly raised the money for the fines. Happily, a few respectable and relatively well-to-do married women were among the group arrested. These women brought suit for false arrest, there was a cleanup in the police department, and this racket was stopped.

The problem of false arrest in case of the person with a record still persists in New York, however. Social workers at the House of Detention in New York City have told the author that certain policemen hound women who have been previously arrested for prostitution and

[61] *Ibid.*, chap. 5, "Trial and Error Arrest."

accuse them of streetwalking if they are on the streets after dark, even if they are on legitimate business. The woman with a record has no status in court and the policeman keeps up his quota of arrests by picking up such characters.

The "third degree" is a slang phrase for the pressure methods by which police induce a suspected person under arrest to confess. The term covers a wide variety of oppressive techniques employed to compel the person to tell what he knows and to be a witness against himself. Such procedure involves a forcible "trial without jury" which is in itself illegal. Trial by police has no legal validity; it is contrary to the Fifth Amendment of the Constitution to compel a person in a criminal case to be a witness against himself.[62]

The compulsive techniques employed by police are as extensive as the imagination of the police. The most frequent device is "grilling." Under ceaseless, relentless questioning the hapless victim may confess to crimes he never committed. Or he may be put in a sweatbox where physical torture makes him beg to confess to escape the terrific heat. He may be strapped or beaten with a rubber tube until he admits nonexistent guilt. He may also confess to actual crimes he has committed.

This "pre-trial inquisition," as Hopkins styles it, convicts more men than our courts. As a secret, illegal instrument it has no valid place in the apprehension of offenders.[63] Yet many law-abiding persons and many police officials justify its use because in their estimation the criminal deserves no consideration. Unfortunately the third degree is about as effective in securing confessions from the innocent as it is from the guilty. Furthermore the police possess neither training nor authority for conducting trials. This relic of inquisition days should be abolished. Such lawlessness in the name of law only contributes to further lawlessness and to contempt for the machinery of justice.

Part of the crime problem itself might be reduced if policemen were not so heavily armed. Naturally the criminal who has become a desperado is dangerous, and a desperado confronted by a gunman from the F.B.I. or any other armed police group is very likely "to shoot it out." So long as the strategy of gun against gun applies, the need for arming policemen is a practical one.[64] If the manufacture, sale, and possession of firearms were under more rigid restriction and supervision, however, much of the gunplay in modern struggles between

[62] *Ibid.*, chap. 14, "The Third Degree."
[63] *Ibid.*
[64] J. Edgar Hoover, "Police Problems Today," mimeographed report of the speech of the Director of the Federal Bureau of Investigation to the International Association of Chiefs of Police at Kansas City, Missouri, September 22, 1936.

criminals and police might be averted. Thus far at least we have not made any notable campaign to reduce civilian possession of arms or to ferret out those illegally sold.

In Great Britain the "bobbies" are not armed. Armed bandits in America have been an especially serious problem since World War I, and another alleged reason for arming police. War itself has probably been a factor in the increase in criminals who kill. But the arming of police has probably taken as great a toll of police as it has of criminals. Furthermore it probably has increased the number of needless deaths of minor offenders who have been shot by police. Many F.B.I. men have lost their lives in struggles with armed criminals and there is some question as to whether this "dead end justice" achieves any desirable ends.

The Informer

The informer or "stool pigeon" plays an important role in the arrest of many criminals. A stool pigeon is usually either a shady character or an actual criminal who has a grudge against fellow criminals on whom he "snitches" and reports for criminal activities.[65] A tavern keeper, for example, dismissed an employee for dishonesty. A tavern near by hired the man, who told his new employer that he had quit his previous job because his former employer was evading the floor tax on liquor by storing quantities in his father-in-law's cellar. This tavern keeper saw a quick way to put his rival out of business. He reported the case to the federal authorities and both the tavern keeper and his wife were committed to federal penitentiaries.[66] In this case the informer was just about as unreliable a person as the one whom he reported. When an informer is engaged in just as serious lawbreaking as the one concerning whom he gives information, he is usually protected by the state or federal government by "turning state (or federal) witness." Sometimes informers literally sell information to the police. The stool pigeon's financial gain through the role of informer seems especially reprehensible. Actually many such informers are jealous, vicious characters whose reliability and veracity are questionable.

People in the vice racket and the narcotic trade are particularly likely to try to shift blame to innocent people. Narcotic dealers thus may send narcotics through the mail to unsuspecting recipients in order to clear themselves. They then notify the police that they have

[65] Ernest J. Hopkins, *op. cit.*, pp. 104–109.   [66] This is an actual federal case.

secret information that a certain woman is receiving drugs by mail and to watch the local post office. Detectives then may intercept the mail and arrest the person on whom the blame has been laid.

Probably no one has less ethics or less worthy motivations than the jealous, grudge-bearing criminal who turns stool pigeon. Police officers should certainly be wary about accepting tips from such a person. Protecting informers who have been equally guilty is scarcely a suitable practice for the state to countenance. Many police officers and detectives maintain, however, that this is one of the few methods by which they can secure information.[67]

Citizens' Responsibility for Police Corruption

In final analysis citizens themselves are responsible for police corruption. Many persons who consider themselves honest and reputable citizens have their parking tickets "fixed." They are contributing to political corruption. So, too, are those who play the numbers or bet on horse races. These latter are filling the coffers of racketeers. But everyone who loses gets something for his money, namely, a racket-ridden community. Smashing the racket or eliminating corruption requires vigilance; it requires honest police and an alert citizenry.[68]

POLICE AND CRIME PREVENTION

In recent years police departments have recognized the importance of preventing crime instead of watching offenders develop criminal tendencies and commit crimes, and then arresting them. Many young persons who become confirmed delinquents are frequently known to the police. The fact that they are known to police is one of the reasons they are ever arrested. In times past, police have usually operated on the theory that they could not interfere until a serious overt act had occurred. Today the social futility of waiting until something serious happens is obvious. The police certainly cannot arrest and punish the potential offender. But they can legitimately counsel him and aid in directing his activities into wholesome and law-abiding activities.

This idea is merely an extension of the protective function of the police into a broader conception of its welfare activities. The work of

[67] Cf. Don L. Kooken, "Ethics in Police Service," *Journal of Criminal Law and Criminology,* 38:172–186 (July–August, 1947).

[68] Edward J. Allen, address to Allegheny County League of Women Voters, March 23, 1950.

women police is largely concerned with protection of women and girls—to keep them from getting into delinquency, whether by seduction or by their own initiative. The idea underlying women's police work has inevitably spread to the prevention of delinquency among boys. New York City as early as 1914 started a Junior Police Department to "admonish and warn" young persons instead of arresting them. In 1918 a Welfare Bureau dealing with problems of young people was established in the Police Department. In 1929 New York created a Bureau of Crime Prevention in the Police Department which was succeeded in 1930 by the Juvenile Aid Bureau.

In the minds of many people the abolition of the Crime Prevention Bureau, which was staffed by social workers, was a serious mistake. But in any event the New York City police have developed within their own group a serious desire to help children keep out of trouble. Where serious involvements indicate the need for case work, the case is referred to a social work agency. The Police Department now arrests no children under 16 except on felonious charges. As many as 30,000 children a year are given advisory help.[69]

The men and police working in this division are college graduates who are trained in recognizing the home, school, and community factors which are conducive to delinquency. The police themselves have sponsored the Police Athletic League, which functions under paid recreational directors. Ball teams and other athletic groups as well as a summer camp are maintained by the aid of outside contributions. More recently co-ordinating councils in each of the 81 patrol districts in New York have been established to co-ordinate and develop existing facilities within the community.[70]

Many other cities have developed similar projects within their police departments. In fact, by 1930 at least 13 cities claimed to have crime prevention bureaus. In most cases these were staffed by women police. Nevertheless, the police departments of Philadelphia, Rochester, New York, Wichita, Kansas, Berkeley, California, and other places have been outstanding in their early acceptance of the crime prevention program. There is no question but that this function will develop in the years ahead.[71]

Some authorities, and among them Bruce Smith, question whether crime prevention is a legitimate function of the police, since they are

[69] James B. Nolan, "The Crime Prevention Work of New York City's Police," *Federal Probation*, 11:18–21 (April–June, 1947).
[70] *Ibid.*
[71] This subject is discussed further in chap. 28, "Crime Prevention on the Juvenile Level."

dealing with matters which may be outside their competence.[72] Certainly police should not attempt case work unless they are trained. But because police by their particular decisions often affect the whole future of young persons it seems obvious that a juvenile division of the police department whose members are trained in case work represents the best solution to this problem.

SELECTED BIBLIOGRAPHY

Fosdick, Raymond B., *American Police Systems*, Appleton-Century-Crofts, New York, 1915. This is the classic study of American police systems.

Hoover, J. Edgar, "Police Problems Today," mimeographed report of a speech by the Director of the Federal Bureau of Investigation to the International Association of Chiefs of Police at Kansas City, Missouri, September 22, 1936. The Director of the F.B.I. presents his justification for strong-arm methods on the part of the police.

Hopkins, Ernest J., *Our Lawless Police*, Viking, New York, 1931. This amazing document exposes the lawlessness of our law-enforcing agents.

Key, V. O., Jr., "Police Graft," *American Journal of Sociology*, 40:624–636 (March, 1935). The unholy alliance between graft and "the law" is made clear.

Kooken, Don L., "Ethics in the Police Service," *Journal of Criminal Law and Criminology*, 38:172–186 (July–August, 1947). This is an inquiry into certain unethical police practices.

Millspaugh, Arthur C., *Crime Control by the National Government*, Institute of Government Research of the Brookings Institution, Washington, 1937. This book is an excellent account of the various law-enforcing bodies of the federal government.

Perkins, Rollin M., *Elements of Police Science*, Foundation Press, Chicago, 1941. Here is an excellent summary of the gist of criminal law and police science necessary for the average policeman to know if he performs his task satisfactorily.

Shalloo, Jeremiah P., *Private Police*, American Academy of Political and Social Sciences, Philadelphia, 1933. In a revelatory study, private police, particularly the railroad and "coal and iron" police, are presented with disturbing details.

Simon, Richard, "Roll Call Training Program of the Los Angeles Police Department," *Journal of Criminal Law and Criminology*, 40:507–518 (November–December, 1948). A detailed account is given of the short-period training program in the Los Angeles Police Department.

Smith, Bruce, *Police Systems in the United States*, Harper, New York, 1949. This is the best single volume on contemporary police problems.

[72] Bruce Smith, *op. cit.*, pp. 262–265.

Sprigle, Ray, series of articles on Pittsburgh police in the Pittsburgh *Post-Gazette*, spring, 1950. These articles are a fearless attack on police corruption.

The Story of the F.B.I., Federal Bureau of Investigation, U.S. Department of Justice, Washington, 1945. This is a brief history of the organization and development of the F.B.I.

CHAPTER 18

Jails, Workhouses, and Houses of Correction

Historically, the jail, or "gaol" according to the British spelling, was the antecedent of the modern prison, but its function was to insure the detention of either (1) the accused who was awaiting trial or (2) the convicted who was awaiting punishment. Initially there was little notion that deprivation of liberty through confinement in itself constituted punishment. It was only with the decline of capital punishment, physical torture, and public ridicule as methods of punishment that deprivation of liberty became a general means of punishment. The imprisonment method of punishment developed at much the same time as the classical penal theory. This theory, it will be recalled, stressed (1) making the punishment fit the crime, (2) increasing the severity of punishment with the degree of heinousness of the offense, and (3) making the punishment as mild as possible under the circumstances. In other words the classical movement was purportedly a reform movement. Most of its proponents supported the abolishment of capital punishment and the substitution of incarceration save for the most serious offenses.[1] We shall discuss the prison movement in a later chapter.[2]

Suffice it to say here that when imprisonment became a basic form of punishment with long sentences exacted for serious crimes, new types of prisons, often designated as penitentiaries, were erected. The jails simply were not suited to long sentences. One may also question whether they are suited to short-time offenders, but at any rate the general practice developed of committing minor offenders or misdemeanants to jails and felons or persons punished by sentences of over

[1] Cf. chap. 17, pp. 437–441.   [2] Chap. 22.

a year to prisons or to reformatories, when this type of institution had developed.

Functions of Present-Day Jails

The present-day jail thus not only serves its original function of detention, but also serves as a place for committing the short-term offender. Virtually all minor offenders, save traffic violators and a few other misdemeanants, are released on bond, often for only $10 or $20 pending hearing. Minor offenders known to be reliable, those arrested on traffic violations, etc., are not usually required to give bond but are given a summons to appear in court. Most of these are released, either without fine or with small fines, at the hearing. Persons arrested on more serious charges are released on higher "bail," as we discuss in the next chapter. The dual function of the jail as both a place of detention and a place for imprisonment inevitably complicates its administration because of the variety of problems imposed.

The Number of Jails and Other Houses of Detention

Jails which are designated as such include the 3000-odd county jails and an undetermined number of municipal and village jails. Professor Sutherland estimated that there are 11,000 municipal jails, including regional and city jails and village lockups. All told, there must be approximately 14,000 institutions or buildings used for detaining persons after arrest, pending release or bail or sometimes for the whole period before trial.[3]

The county jails are in a sense state institutions since they are places where persons who have been arrested for breaking state laws are held pending trial and/or after sentence to the local jail for such lawbreaking. Local and county government is a dark and none-too-well-ventilated chapter of American politics and one which we cannot treat in detail here. It should be said, however, that counties are administrative but relatively unsupervised units of the state government. The jurisdiction of county officials has traditionally ended at the county boundaries and in the early days many criminals made a safe getaway simply by crossing county lines. Today the practice is for county officials to co-operate and much of the jurisdictional buffoonery involved in apprehending offenders has disappeared.

[3] Edwin H. Sutherland, *Principles of Criminology*, Lippincott, Philadelphia, rev. ed., 1947, p. 264.

Conditions in Jails an Old Problem

Conditions in jails have been notorious for centuries. Reformers have been continually distressed about jails, but the public apathy is hard to dispel. John Howard's famous inquiry first published in 1777 and later in 1784 on the *State of the Prisons* was as much an indictment of English jails as it was a protest about conditions in "prisons" in general. He was so shocked and appalled by the filth, the immorality, the poor food, the overcrowding and physical and mental disease that he found that he decided to make the whole matter of prison reform his lifework,[4] as we discuss in a later chapter.

In Howard's tour of the "principal lazarettos" of Europe he came to the conclusion that jail fever, which raged in most of these institutions, was the result of contagion. He anticipated far ahead of physicians that infectious and contagious diseases were due to germs—and spread through the air surrounding the person was ill. Howard contended that often disease was spread by riotous sailors who were arrested on shore leave for as he visited prisons throughout Europe he traced the spread of plagues from port to port. He consulted with prison keepers and physicians and found contagion seemed to spread much more rapidly when prisoners were closely confined and windows were kept shut. In fact, Howard took stern issue with the physicians who denied the contagious character of jail fevers.[5]

Later Howard made an extensive survey of British county jails. For each he prepared a short, succinct report. At Tower Hamlet's Gaol in London he reported briefly, "No alteration. The rooms dirty and the prison for some years going to ruin. 1787, April 14, two prisoners. 1788, August 20, one prisoner."[6]

Reading County Bridewell in Berkshire drew this comment: "A new prison, containing six close (called *refractory*) cells, nine feet and one half by seven and a half; eight solitary cells, ten feet by seven feet 9 inches with courts the same. . . . The rooms are furnished with bedsteads and straw mattresses, but no coverlets. The sewers make most of the rooms and courts offensive. . . . Terms of confinement are written on the doors of their cells. I observed some were for one year: a severe confinement, to be so long in solitude, unemployed, in nau-

[4] Cf. John Howard, *The State of the Prisons*, Eayres, Warrington (England), 1784, Section I, pp. 4–12.
[5] Cf. John Howard, *An Account of the Principal Lazarettos in Europe*, Eayres, Warrington (England), 1789, especially Sections I to IV, inclusive.
[6] John Howard, *The State of the Prisons*, Section II, "English Prisons and Hospitals," p. 122.

seous cells, and without fire in winter. 1788, July 12, Prisoners 17."[7]

The jail was obviously an outmoded and antiquated institution when it was transplanted to America. In fact, probably no institution has made so little improvement in the course of history as the jail. Throughout its existence it has been condemned and reviled. The only reason which can be found for its existence is that we have to have some place to keep certain offenders to be sure they do not escape before trial.

Despite the fact that county jails are state institutions and therefore should be accountable to some executive department of the state government, this is true in only four states—New York, Minnesota, New Jersey, and Oklahoma. Occasionally earnest citizens in the other states demand an investigation, and a survey of jails is made. Missouri, for example, made such a survey in 1940.[8] The author of this text directed a survey of Kansas jails in the early 1930's for the Kansas Public Welfare Commission.[9] Maryland made a survey, published in 1935.[10] Connecticut conducted a similar survey in 1948.[11] Dr. Edith Abbott published a survey of the jails in Illinois in 1916.[12] All these reports indicated that jails were in a generally appalling condition. The Missouri Jail Survey conducted by a member of the Federal Bureau of Prisons showed that only 10 per cent of the jails were regarded as fit to detain federal prisoners temporarily, while awaiting trial. Food was scanty, clothing and jails unsanitary, prisoners idle.

The Federal Jail Survey

The most comprehensive report on county jails was the survey made in 1938 by the Federal Bureau of Prisons. On a rating scale based on 100 points, 69 per cent of the jails rated under 50 and 96.7 per cent under 60. In fact the Federal Bureau of Prisons rated 1944 of the jails as *wholly unfit for the custody of a federal prisoner, even for one*

[7] *Ibid.*, p. 169.

[8] Roy Casey, "Missouri Jail Survey," *Proceedings of the Seventieth Annual Congress of the American Prison Association, Cincinnati, Ohio,* 1940, pp. 402–410.

[9] Foline Eppstein, "The County Jails in Kansas," in *Handbook of Kansas Social Resources,* ed. by Mabel A. Elliott, Carroll D. Clark, and Ruth D. Kolling, Kansas Conference of Social Work, Topeka, 1932, pp. 286–296.

[10] *Eleventh Annual Report of Inspection of the County Jails of Maryland by Director of Department of Welfare,* Baltimore, 1935, p. 12, cited by Louis N. Robinson, *Jails; Care and Treatment of Misdemeanant Prisoners in the United States,* Winston, Philadelphia, 1944, p. 18.

[11] *Report of the Legislative Commission on Jails,* Hartford, 1938, p. 10.

[12] Edith Abbott, *One Hundred and One Jails and Why They Ought to Be Abolished,* Juvenile Protective Association of Chicago, Chicago, 1916.

brief hour.[13] Furthermore the Bureau restricted 480 additional prisons to emergency use only. These jails were condemned for their filth, lack of sanitation, overcrowding, lack of privacy, lack of segregation for female offenders, and vicious practices, including the "kangaroo court."[14]

To any objective observer it is patently absurd to think that men and women who transgress the criminal laws of the United States deserve greater consideration and better treatment than John Doe who robs a grocery store or commits some other offense under the jurisdiction of the laws within a particular state. But the fact remains that personnel standards are so much higher in our federal government than they are in the administration of local government that federal officials have seen the importance of providing suitable and decent surroundings for men and women who come under their surveillance and jurisdiction.

The Missouri Jail Survey

The Missouri Jail Survey, conducted in 1939, covered 114 county jails in Missouri in addition to the Municipal Jail in St. Louis, which has a combined "city-county" status. Data and information with reference to 11 items were gathered. These included (1) administration and discipline, (2) building and equipment, (3) personnel, (4) food, (5) medical service, (6) hospital facilities, (7) cleanliness and sanitation, (8) personal hygiene, (9) rehabilitation, (10) employment, (11) religious instruction. The Federal Bureau of Prisons devised a scale based upon weighting these items, with a total possible score of 100 per cent. Because jails are so uniformly poor the Bureau set the minimum standard for jails in which federal prisoners are detained at 50 per cent, but less than 10 of Missouri's 115 jails rated that high! Only 3 jails rated "fairly good" in cleanliness and sanitation; the majority scored "very bad." Only 2 jails maintained a jail hospital; no jail had any rehabilitation program; food in only 3 was rated "good," in 34 it was rated "poor," and food expenditures in the majority of jails ranged from 10 to 15 cents a day! No jail had any employment program, although some prisoners performed routine maintenance duties. Only 19 had any religious instruction and this was "irregular and haphazard."

The degree of crowding varied; 38 jails were definitely overcrowded,

[13] Italics mine.
[14] Cf. Nina Kinsella, "The Untried Prisoner," *Prison Journal*, 18:416 (January, 1938).

but some jails had very few inmates and could have been economically combined with an institution in an adjoining county.[15]

The Kansas Jail Survey

The data for a survey of Kansas jails conducted under the general supervision of the present author in 1931 were analyzed by Foline Eppstein, who served as a research assistant with the Kansas Public Welfare Commission. Questionnaires were sent to every district judge in the state requesting detailed information for the 105 county jails. Information for 72 of these jails was secured, which gave a fairly representative picture of the jails throughout the state, since jails in all the counties with large populations responded as well as more than half of the remaining county jails located in the smaller cities and small towns which are county seats. Unfortunately, the data received were not complete for the 72 jails. Only 71 jails reported population.

All together, 12,685 prisoners were held in the 71 jails which reported their populations during the year, with the total yearly number in each jail ranging from 18 to 1246. The daily population varied from less than 1 to 94. Types of offenses were classified by reports from 68 jails with "alcoholism" (presumably drunkenness) constituting 31.7 per cent of the offenses, larceny 9.4, thieving 8.3, disturbing the peace 4.7, vagrancy 2.3, prostitution 1.0, and a wide number of miscellaneous charges accounting for 42.2 per cent of the cases—these ranged from bad checks to forgery, assault, bank robbery, "laying out fine," etc., etc.[16]

Only 7.5 per cent of the total prisoners were reported as recidivists but this small percentage should not be interpreted to mean that most of the jail inmates were first offenders. It may indicate rather that the local sheriffs did not clear their records with the F.B.I. in Washington. One county reported that 38.9 per cent were repeaters, and it seems likely that the percentage for the total group reporting could not have been as low as indicated.[17] This discrepancy affords another indictment of the average county jail, whose chief officer has little or no professional training for his job.

So far as the prisoners were concerned, the average Kansas jail prisoner spent 30 days awaiting trial, but many prisoners were held several months. Only 2.5 per cent of those held in jail were under 16, but in some jails the number was 10 per cent of the inmate population.

Fifty of the 72 jails had some type of labor provision. In 21 all

[15] Roy Casey, op. cit.   [16] Foline Eppstein, op. cit.   [17] Ibid.

prisoners were idle. Only one jail made any provision for employing women prisoners. In 41 of the 50 counties with work programs the men worked on building or maintaining the roads; in the other 9 the men were kept at odd jobs mostly around the courthouse or courthouse grounds. Where employed, the men received $2 a day which was applied toward their fines and costs.[18] (Incidentally, Kansas pays its prisoners in the state penitentiary only 4 cents a day unless they work in the mines. The reason for this disparity in pay for jail prisoners and for those in the penitentiary is not clear.) Sixty-nine of the 72 questionnaires replied to the question on kangaroo courts; in 32 cases such "courts" were openly permitted by the sheriff, and in one case the men held such courts on the sly.

Conditions in the jails varied markedly. In 32 instances there was only one cell in the jail. In 22 cases young boys were admittedly kept in the same cells as older prisoners. Ventilation was poor. One jail had no windows at all, and 12 had no outside ventilation in every cell.[19]

Some of the jails must have been very unsanitary. Only 69 answers were given to this question, and 10 of these reported the jail was cleaned less than once a month; 1 once a year. Blankets were the only form of bedding in all but 7 of the 57 reporting on this question. In 29 of the 57 the blankets were laundered every week, in 15 twice a month, in 9 once a month, in 2 every 2 months, in one 2 times a year, and "as necessary" was the laconic answer for 11 jails. Plumbing was inadequate in fully half of the jails.[20]

Only 31 of the jails submitted sample menus and in these cases the food seemed fairly adequate as to amount but decidedly lacking in vitamins and minerals. Most of the menus were of the meat, bread, and potatoes variety.[21]

Although it is illegal to detain women in a Kansas jail, virtually all county jails receive women. Men jailers look after their needs in all but 21 of the 60 jails reporting on this item.

Add to this generalized picture the fact that most jails are smelly and horribly dirty and one may have some conception of the average Kansas jail.

Why Are Jails What They Are?

Several reasons seem to account for the deplorable conditions in the majority of our jails. These are chiefly (1) the policy of having the jails run by the sheriff and the disgraceful fee system, (2) the lack of

[18] *Ibid.* [19] *Ibid.* [20] *Ibid.* [21] *Ibid.*

supervision mentioned above, (3) the fact that many sparsely settled counties cannot afford to keep up a well-organized jail, (4) local politics, and (5) public lethargy. These reasons may be subdivided, but they subsume the most important factors and we may profitably consider them further.

People in the mass do not care what happens in jails and the inarticulate and politically unimportant people who are committed to jail cannot talk back to the local government about the vermin, the poor food, and the indignities to which they are exposed. Few citizens, or for that matter few governmental officials, have ever visited a county jail.[22]

All judges should probably be required to make inspection visits to jails at unannounced but frequent intervals. This might do much both to clean up the jails and to keep judges from sentencing offenders to jails. Far more offenders could suitably be placed on probation or under some other form of supervision.

The Sheriff's Role as Jail Keeper

The sheriff technically is the chief police officer, as we have discussed in a previous chapter. But by common-law tradition he is also keeper of the jail, and a considerable part of his income is frequently derived from the fee system, by which he is reimbursed for feeding the prisoners. If the sheriff can keep the cost of the food much lower than the fee he is allotted for providing meals to the prisoners, he can add appreciably to his income. In a jail with a fair number of prisoners the sheriff thus has a chance to make money by cutting down on the quality and quantity of food. Roy Casey reports a sheriff in Missouri who made $13,000 a year from the item of feeding prisoners alone.[23] In other jails honest sheriffs "set a good table." In smaller jails the sheriff's wife may do the cooking and the prisoners may eat the family fare.

Sanitation in the smaller jails—and this is where the most serious sanitary problems tend to exist—is often closely related to the interest of the sheriff's wife. If the sheriff's wife is an excellent housekeeper and also takes an interest in the condition of the jail, the jail may be kept clean, the floors scrubbed, the linen and blankets laundered, and the mattresses aired and vacuumed. This author has visited many small

[22] William A. Tuck, "The Jail and the People," *Proceedings of the Seventieth Annual Congress of the American Prison Association, Cincinnati, Ohio,* 1940, pp. 411–423.
[23] Roy Casey, *op. cit.*

county jails in different parts of the country and in every instance where they were neat and clean it was because the wife of the sheriff insisted that the jail be kept clean. Where they were dirty, she "never set foot" in the jail.

Most of the smaller county jails consist of cells constructed at the back of the official residence provided for the sheriff. Hence keeping the jail clean is actually important to the jailer's household. The sheriff has to come into contact with prisoners, and disease and vermin should be kept down if only in self-defense and as a protection to his family.

We have discussed the sheriff's lack of professional training and insight in the chapter on police. This lack of training is further evidenced when he permits the kangaroo court to exist. Some sheriffs are so ignorant as to relish the prankish aspects of such deplorable practices. The kangaroo court, briefly, is the pseudo court at which prisoners preside when a newcomer is admitted to jail. Many of the prisoners are sentenced convicts, it must be remembered, whereas newcomers are frequently awaiting trial. The latter are often first offenders; some are innocent; but in any case older, experienced, and hardened offenders may be able to compel the newcomer to turn over all moneys in his possession and buy a variety of "treats for the crowd." If he objects he may be subjected to the crudest of horseplay; he may even be forced to perform the most menial of services for his fellow prisoners.

Some sheriffs get their chief enjoyment of office out of recounting the plight of prisoners in kangaroo court. This baleful habit is obviously closely related to the public ridicule type of punishment of another era. To permit prisoners to exercise such authority over fellow prisoners demeans both the whole process of punishment and human dignity which democratic government seeks to preserve. There is no democracy in ignominious activities like this and kangaroo courts should be outlawed—by legislation if necessary.

Installment Basis for Paying Fines Instead of Jail Sentence

Many prisoners go to jail because they are unable to pay a fine (a situation tantamount to imprisonment for debt). Any democratic system of justice should eliminate the practice of jailing people because they are too poor to pay a fine. If some plan for permitting fines to be paid on an installment basis were in effect many poor offenders could be kept out of jail. The fines seemingly should also be reduced somewhat in case of extreme poverty. Such a policy would do much to eliminate the inequalities of justice which now exist, yet requiring the offender to pay a fine might be a rehabilitative procedure. No good influence can be derived from sentence in any jail.

The Fee System

As mentioned, the sheriff's income is often dependent upon the number of arrests he makes and the amounts paid for feeding the prisoners. This practice is subject to many abuses. Some sheriffs allegedly round up people with a record and arrest them without evidence to augment their income. Other sheriffs serve poor food to their charges in order to make a greater amount, as has been explained. No county can afford to wreck the health of the men and women whom it returns to the community. Abolition of the fee system is imperative in any plan for improving the jails.

Children in Our Jails

One of the most lamentable aspects of the administration of criminal law is that of confining children to jails. This practice should make American citizens blush with guilt and shame. To expose young children to the physical and mental filth which confinement in jail usually involves may do them lasting damage. Actually 28 states and the District of Columbia have passed laws prohibiting the detention of children in the common jail. But despite these prohibitory laws the practice persists to an alarming degree in states where it is illegal as well as in states where no such law exists. Connecticut and New Hampshire were the only states where such a law existed which claimed never to use jails for juvenile offenders in 1949.[24]

According to the report submitted to the National Conference on Prevention and Control of Juvenile Delinquency held in Washington in 1946, some 40,000 children in the United States between the ages of 10 to 17 are sent to jails every year! This is considered an understatement, however, and the number probably is over 50,000.[25]

Ever since the prison reform movements began, the practice of keeping children in jails has been deplored. Jails are obviously seldom fit places in which to lock up adults. The only excuse that sheriffs and police can give is, "What else can I do? The county (or city or state)

[24] Austin H. MacCormick and James H. Dooling, "Keeping Children Out of Jails: It Can Be Done," Federal Probation, 13:40–45 (September, 1949).
[25] Ibid.

provides no other place." But sheriffs and police seldom call public attention to the need for providing suitable detention quarters. Since few in either group have any professional training they see little value in exposing such vital needs. Their major interest unfortunately is in a job with a salary.[26]

When juveniles are segregated in jails they are kept in an adjoining wing, which is merely a part of what MacCormick and Dooling call "cold storage . . . in a filthy, vermin-ridden vault."[27] No community can afford to treat its children as insensitive objects, whose physical custody is the only consideration. In communities of sufficient population a juvenile detention home should be a part of the local government's administrative equipment. In smaller communities a little ingenuity will generally locate respectable and intelligent couples who will undertake the supervision of one or more children at a reasonable fee. Often women who were social workers before marriage are happy to make some professional contribution to the communities in which they live. Today regional receiving homes could be made available for the cases in several adjoining counties or in given sections of the state. In many communities local orphanages could provide suitable temporary supervision and care. A special room could be set aside in the courthouse if need be to take care of children's cases. Certainly no county is forced to fall back on the jail. Probably most county commissioners have never had the problem raised in any official session. If county commissioners were required to visit the quarters occupied by children in jail the situation would probably be cleared up in 24 hours.

In Illinois, which proudly claims to have the first juvenile court law in the United States, the practice of putting children in jail either for "safekeeping" or to await court action is common. This has been true even in Chicago, where there are many suitable places where children might be detained. During the years 1938–1942, for example, 300 children were sent to the Cook County jail. The periods of jail detention ranged from 1 day to almost 3 years and, according to a study made at the time, most of these instances could have been avoided. Allegedly some children are "too tough" to be dealt with under the juvenile code, but in none of these cases was this the basic reason for their being assigned to jail.[28]

[26] Ibid.   [27] Ibid.
[28] Fred Gross, "Jail Detention and Criminal Prosecution of Children of Juvenile Court Age in Cook County," Master's thesis, University of Chicago, School of Social Service Administration, 1943, cited in "Notes and Comment," Social Service Review, 19:255–258 (June, 1945).

A satisfactory method of enforcing a state-wide prohibition against keeping children in jail would probably require a state agency authorized to inspect jails and see that children are not so confined. Merely to make the practice illegal and to provide no other facilities makes most of the laws virtually inoperative in all but large communities except in a few states. New Jersey and North Carolina have made concerted efforts to keep children out of jails. New Jersey has a state agency which supervises jails. North Carolina requires jails to report their inmate population monthly to the State Department of Public Welfare, and when children are found to be on the jail lists, local welfare agencies make arrangements to provide suitable places of detention for present and future cases. This method emphasizes a helpful solution rather than a "cracking-down" technique and has much to commend it.[29]

Education in Jails

Educational programs, either academic or vocational, are practically nonexistent in jails. There has been a general assumption that jails and all short-term institutions can do little or nothing effective in the way of education. Under present conditions this is more or less true. As long as all the unfortunate conditions of overcrowding, filth, immorality, and official incompetence apply, certainly no effective educational facilities can be expected to develop in jails or workhouses.[30]

Nevertheless a few institutions, including the Cincinnati workhouse, the Detroit House of Correction, and the Holmesburg Prison (local) in Philadelphia, have made a favorable start. Needless to say, any suitable educational program should be under professional supervision and preferably under the local department of education.[31]

Obviously nothing educational can be attempted when a person is held overnight or only a few days, but even this person can be supplied with suitable and wholesome reading material. For the person who remains from a month to a year a great deal can be accomplished. A man can learn how to be a janitor, how to take care of small boilers, how to make minor plumbing and electrical repairs, what the best cleansing agents are, etc., etc. Suitable instruction in health and hygiene can be given also.[2]

[29] Austin H. MacCormick and James H. Dooling, op. cit.
[30] Austin H. MacCormick, The Education of the Adult Prisoner, National Society for Penal Information, New York, 1931, chap. 20, "Education in Jails."
[31] Ibid., p. 312.   [32] Ibid., p. 313.

Those who remain from 60 to 90 days or more can profit from academic instruction. Classes cannot be organized but prisoners can be individually instructed and make measurable progress. Illiterates can learn to read simple materials and also to write in such a time. Longer-term prisoners can be encouraged to take correspondence courses of the short-unit variety. A well-rounded prison library should be developed; some larger jails have a really good selection. Sometimes fraternal or service organizations can be induced to supply suitable books.[33]

How to secure teachers for a jail educational venture is a difficult matter unless they can be recruited through the public schools. If sufficient effort and interest could be developed, many retired teachers or men who were teachers before undertaking a different career might be recruited for such worth-while work. Older women who were teachers before marriage might also be volunteer teachers. Teachers volunteering should be expected to carry through a project for two or three months at least. A volunteer school has to keep the spark of enthusiasm alive lest the volunteers drop out. Other aspects of prison education are discussed in Chapter 23.

Houses of Correction and Workhouses

Houses of correction, as they developed in England, originated essentially as an early effort to improve the common jails and to make them institutions for instilling honest work habits. The first house of correction, located on the site of St. Bridget's Well, which was later corrupted to Bridewell, was founded in London in 1557. Apparently this venture was favorably regarded for in 1576 the British Parliament ordered each county to set up such an institution. Houses of correction were public institutions, often designated "city hospitals." They were quasi-penal and quasi-relief in character and aimed to provide employment for the rowdy vagrants and paupers for whom no other social provision for food, clothing, and housing had been made, as well as to take care of "lewd and idle" people, including young persons, children, and prostitutes.

In general these institutions provided industrial training or at least work for dependents, whether or not delinquent. During the early part of the seventeenth century two such institutions developed. Persons who were merely poverty stricken were consigned to workhouses; the definitely delinquent or criminal in character were sent to houses

[33] *Ibid.*, pp. 315–316.

of correction. Both institutions carried a certain amount of stigma for it was an offense to be a vagrant and something of an offense to be unemployed. The Amsterdam House of Correction, established in 1589, was one of the most enlightened of such rehabilitative penal ventures. It provided vocational training, wages for inmates, academic education, and medical care, and in general subscribed to all of the accepted principles of modern penitentiaries.[34] This Amsterdam institution affected the development of the British house of correction, but later, under the system of transportation and other developments, the houses of correction were abolished. Meanwhile the workhouses became almshouses with their punitive character eliminated.[35]

In Scotland the workhouses were designated as "poor-houses" and it is from these that the poorhouses of the United States derive their name. In America county farms or poorhouses have always been regarded as the last resort of those without funds, and are chiefly refuges for indigent aged persons. Although they are not punitive in character, there has always been a stigma attached to commitment. As a matter of fact, until the depression of the 1930's in America many city police arrested the poor who had nowhere to go for lack of funds on the charge of vagrancy. And the local magistrate often smugly sentenced the vagrant to the county jail for a month's hard labor. This sentencing of the unemployed to jail in the United States grew out of the early confusion in the functions of the house of correction, the workhouse, and the jail. In fact in Pennsylvania the "Great Law of 1682" provided that a jail was to be erected in Philadelphia "for the restraint, correction, labor and punishment of all persons there committed."[36] The prison system of the United States is in a sense a development of this conception of the workhouse or house of correction.[37] New Jersey and Massachusetts soon followed Pennsylvania with similar provisions and many other states adopted such plans later. Today there are about 90 institutions designated as houses of correction or workhouses.[38]

From the beginning houses of correction were a part of the shift from corporal and capital punishment to incarceration for punish-

[34] Cf. Thorsten Sellin, *Pioneering in Penology: The Amsterdam House of Correction in the Sixteenth and Seventeenth Centuries*, University of Pennsylvania Press, Philadelphia, 1944.

[35] Louis N. Robinson, op. cit., p. 93.

[36] Orlando F. Lewis, *The Development of Prisons and Prison Customs, 1776–1845*, Prison Association of New York, New York, 1922, p. 11.

[37] Cf. chap. 22.

[38] There is no exact information on this point. Louis N. Robinson, op. cit., pp. 97–98, lists 69 institutions by name, says there are "a few" in Oregon and that allegedly there are 19 additional in Tennessee.

ment. The offenders so punished were chiefly misdemeanants. With the Quaker laws of Pennsylvania an important step was taken in providing incarceration under a work program for all offenses save murder.[39] With this transition came the inception of modern prisons for felonious offenders.[40] Some houses of correction have distinctive features and may be discussed briefly. The Detroit House of Correction has borne the stamp of the genius of its first superintendent, Zebulon R. Brockway, who later became the head of the first reformatory for men in America and carried with him many of the industrial practices he had earlier developed in Detroit.

The Detroit institution now sponsors an educational program. Extension courses at the University of Michigan are open to the men, and the police department conducts a special educational project for traffic violators, dealing with traffic rules and regulations. The Detroit House of Correction functions both as a local and as a state institution for prisoners sent from other counties.[41]

Any county may establish a house of correction in Wisconsin, but Milwaukee seems to have the only such institution and it also receives prisoners from other parts of the state. Sixty per cent of its prisoners are for 10 days or less, but it receives both misdemeanants and felons. At the House of Correction in Chicago sentences run from a few days to a year and may be accompanied by fine. This institution is now a farm colony and devoted to "the better class of prisoners." The St. Louis House of Correction, located within that city, is for local prisoners only. It is housed in buildings erected in 1841, with a few more recent additions. Here a stone quarry furnishes most of the work.[42]

New Hampshire boasts 10 houses of correction located on the same grounds as county farms, as well as 2 others. In 8 of these the county jail is combined with the house of correction. In one at Grafton, New Hampshire, women prisoners are kept in the almshouse. Massachusetts has 15 houses of correction. One of these, at Billerica, is located on a farm. The District of Columbia has a workhouse at Occoquan, Virginia, with a program of farming, a cannery, and a brick plant; the men also work on federal construction projects. These institutions all are far superior to most jails; they provide employment and some vocational training; but, like the jails, they do very little truly rehabilitative work.[43]

[39] Orlando F. Lewis, op. cit., p. 12.
[40] Mabel A. Elliott, Coercion in Penal Treatment: Past and Present, Pacifist Research Bureau, Ithaca, New York, 1947, p. 16.
[41] Louis N. Robinson, op. cit., pp. 107–110.
[42] Ibid., pp. 110–117.   [43] Ibid., pp. 119–124.

There are 2 states, New York and New Jersey, which have county penitentiaries as well as county jails. Technically, all the prisoners in New York County penitentiaries are misdemeanants. Actually many have been indicted on felony charges but convicted on a lesser charge, usually as part of the bargaining process described in Chapter 20. In New Jersey all first-class counties are required to provide penitentiaries for all persons serving less than 18 months. The remaining 19 counties are required to provide only for those prisoners sentenced less than a year. Both in New York and New Jersey the county penitentiaries have ranked high among penal institutions, and striving to be penitentiaries in fact, and not merely *prisons*.[44]

Should Jails Be Abolished?

Many outstanding American welfare leaders, including Stuart A. Queen, Edith Abbott, and Frank Bane, have contended that county jails should be abolished, that the average local rural counties are not in a financial position to maintain effective institutions for detaining persons awaiting trial or misdemeanants after conviction.[45] Instead, Bane recommends state prison farms where such offenders might profit from the physical exercise and healthful labor on farms, where sanitary conditions could be insured, and where the prisoners by their own labor could pay for the major costs of their maintenance.[46]

Many states have developed prison farms in connection with either their prison or their jail program. Los Angeles County, California, for example, has "honor road camps" and honor farms where prisoners are employed in useful outdoor labor. Los Angeles County has more county prisoners than the average state prison. In 1947 the high count was 2760, with an anticipated increase in the offing,[47] hence the short-sentenced convict constitutes a serious problem.

Any talk about abolishing jails altogether is so much nonsense. So long as there is crime we shall probably always have to have some place to detain vicious and dangerous offenders, or offenders who

[44] *Ibid.*, chap. 7, pp. 125-135.

[45] Cf. Stuart A. Queen, *The Passing of the County Jail*, Banta, Menasha, Wisconsin, 1920; Edith Abbott, *op. cit.*; Frank Bane, "How Virginia Is Solving the Jail Problem," in *The County Jail*, National Committee on Prisons and Prison Labor, New York, 1929, pp. 13-14.

[46] Frank Bane, *op. cit.*

[47] Eugene Biscailuz, "Los Angeles County Jail Units," *Proceedings of the Seventy-Seventh Annual Congress of Correction, Long Beach, California*, American Prison Association, 1947, pp. 58-60. Earlier these annual meetings were called Congresses of the American Prison Association, and the reader will find many such references in the chapters dealing with prisons.

would otherwise escape before coming up for trial. What we should decide on now is an improvement of our system of jails so that they are not of themselves a place for breeding crime and perversion and for the spreading of disease.[48]

For persons held a few hours or a few days, there obviously can be no detailed program of treatment or education. Even so, humane consideration for young persons and first offenders requires that they be given clean and wholesome surroundings. For the sentenced prisoner some really constructive rehabilitation program should be provided. Suitable food and decent surroundings should be available for all prisoners. So far as possible, misdemeanants should never be sentenced to jail. Instead all suitable men should be put on probation, and where corrective influences are desirable or mass treatment is necessary something in line with the best procedures in houses of correction should be developed. Since jail populations are composed largely of chronic misdemeanants, the desirability of educating the petty offender to law-abiding conduct and suitable work habits seems obvious. The fact that the average jail has such a small population makes it difficult to implement any program. The development of state institutions for sentenced misdemeanants might prove a more satisfactory plan than is possible under the county jail system.

SELECTED BIBLIOGRAPHY

Abbott, Edith, *One Hundred and One County Jails and Why They Ought to Be Abolished*, Juvenile Protective Association of Chicago, Chicago, 1916. This is a devastating denunciation of Illinois jails (which were not abolished).

Casey, Roy, "The Missouri Jail Survey," *Proceedings of the Seventieth Annual Congress of the American Prison Association, Cincinnati, Ohio,* 1940, pp. 402–410. This is a detailed survey of conditions in Missouri jails.

Eppstein, Foline, "The County Jails in Kansas," in *Handbook of Kansas Social Resources,* ed. by Mabel A. Elliott, Carroll D. Clark, and Ruth D. Kolling, Kansas Conference of Social Work, Topeka, 1932. An analysis is made of jail conditions in Kansas in a survey directed by the author of this text.

Gross, Fred, "Jail Detention and Criminal Prosecution of Children of Juvenile Court Age in Cook County," Master's thesis, University of Chicago, Chicago, 1943. A picture of the children held in the Cook County jail is carefully drawn.

[48] Roy Casey, "Children in Jail," *Delinquency and the Community in Wartime, National Probation Association Yearbook,* 1943, New York, 1944, pp. 175–182.

Howard, John, An Account of the Principal Lazarettos in Europe, Eayres, Warrington (England), 1789, especially Sections I to IV. This is a fascinating account of the disease-laden and disgraceful prisons or jails of the eighteenth century. Copies are available in some of our older libraries.

Howard, John, The State of the Prisons, Eayres, Warrington (England), 1784, Section IV. This gives a running description of the appalling conditions in the English county jails.

Kinsella, Nina, "The County Jails," Proceedings of the Sixty-Fifth Annual Congress of the American Prison Association, 1935, New York, 1935, pp. 283–289. A survey of county jails is made in behalf of federal prisoners who are sometimes kept in detention in local jails.

MacCormick, Austin H., The Education of the Adult Prisoner, National Society for Penal Information, New York, 1941, chap. 20, "Education in Jails." The author surveys the lack of suitable educational facilities in jails.

MacCormick, Austin H., and Dooling, James H., "Keeping Children Out of Jails: It Can Be Done," Federal Probation, 13:40–45 (September, 1949). This is a compelling statement of the need for keeping children out of jails.

Queen, Stuart A., The Passing of the County Jail, Banta, Menasha, Wisconsin, 1920. The prediction of this title has not been fulfilled but the reasons for suggesting it remain.

Robinson, Louis N., Jails; Care and Treatment of Misdemeanant Prisoners in the United States, Winston, Philadelphia, 1944. This is the best and most comprehensive study of jails in recent years.

CHAPTER 19

Criminal Procedure

During the depression an underpaid laborer sold his mortgaged car to pay for his baby's hospital bill. He was a stupid fellow and unaware of the serious offense involved. His sentence was two years in the state penitentiary. A wealthy investment banker manipulated thousands of dollars belonging to unsuspecting investors, but his lawyers found a loophole by which he escaped criminal conviction during a heated trial. A shabbily dressed woman stood in front of a drugstore waiting for a bus and was picked up by the vice squad. She "had a record" and the judge paid little attention to the fact that there was no evidence of criminal conduct in this instance. The wheels of criminal courts roll on—but every honest critic of the courts knows that public opinion and social attitudes play their part in dealing out "justice."

The occasional dramatic murder case, a horrifying rape case, or an accusation of mishandling of funds involving a wealthy insurance company or a public official gains widespread attention in the press. The public seldom hears nor little cares about the run-of-the-mine cases which clog our criminal courts. The daily or weekly docket of human miscreants, the drunks, the petty thieves, the traffic violators, the prostitutes and street brawlers are outside—and in general held to be beneath the dignity—of any social interest on the part of decent law-abiding citizens.

Lawyers likewise have held themselves rather generally aloof from the practice of criminal law. Occasionally there have been men like Clarence Darrow who have seen the need for protecting the interests of a man despite his shortcomings. Such lawyers have recognized that men may be crippled by adverse social circumstances, twisted by antisocial ambitions, or framed by the grossly motivated machinations of other men. Guilty though they may be, they are largely products of a competitive social order in which it is not given to every man to succeed. In any event, a guilty man has the right to whatever protection the law affords him.

There have been so many complaints about the administration of criminal justice that the socially minded group of lawyers and scholars who are members of the American Law Institute have made it their concern to do something about it. After careful study of the defects and merits of American criminal procedure a special committee of this group has proposed a code for American criminal procedure.

But first let us survey existent practices. Criminal procedure is of two sorts: first, that covering the cases coming under the jurisdiction of the federal courts; second, that covering prosecution of offenses against the several states.

American Federal Criminal Procedure

The origins of both our federal procedure and that of the several states lie in the practices and traditions of English common law, although even in colonial times new precedents were soon established in America. According to English common law criminal prosecutions were initiated and conducted by a private prosecutor in the name of the king. Obviously such procedure was subject to abuse and where abuse was apparent the Attorney General might refuse to permit the prosecution to proceed.

In the colonies the advantage of providing a public prosecutor as a servant of the people was by some happy chance recognized. In 1704 the first law providing for a public prosecutor was enacted in Connecticut. By the time of the Revolution the practice was well established and has been characteristic of American procedure ever since the separation from the mother country.

Private prosecution on the other hand was a typical medieval institution and undoubtedly had its roots in private vengeance. In primitive times, as may be recalled, civil and criminal offenses were not easily differentiated. Most wrongs were of a private sort and it was left to the sufferer to secure redress as best he might.[1] With the rise of democratic thought in France public prosecution was established there during the seventeenth century. Jefferson and other revo-

---

[1] Cf. chap. 15 for a discussion of primitive crimes.

lutionaries in America became protagonists for the public prosecutor and under their influence the French pattern of public initiation of trial proceedings was widely copied. Today the American official prosecutor for both federal and state courts combines the features of the British Attorney General and the French *avocat général et procureur du roi*.[2]

After the Constitution of the United States of America was adopted in 1789 provision was made for the appointment of United States district attorneys. These men were vested with the authority to look after the legal interests of the federal government and to initiate proceedings in both civil and criminal cases. Apparently the early district attorneys were left much to their own devices in deciding what cases were to be prosecuted. In 1861 an attorney general for the various United States was appointed to supervise the district attorneys, presumably because of the serious character of the decisions imposed by the War Between the States. It was not until 1870, however, that a Department of Justice was established and not until 1909 that any truly over-all control of federal prosecutions was placed with the Department of Justice. Today, fortunately, there is a well-organized central control over practice and policy.[3]

Even so, much responsibility and authority for decision is inevitably vested in the district attorneys. They decide whether there is sufficient evidence to prosecute and whether or not to dismiss proceedings once started. In occasional instances they have been known to yield to political considerations. Sometimes they have been downright dishonest. On the whole, however, the district attorneys have been men of integrity and of fealty to duty.

Political support for the office through the patronage of the Senate has been a problem in certain cases. Usually this has not been serious except when the Senators have been opposing the administration and have recommended men for office whose policies were certain to conflict with executive policies and the enforcement of current legislation. Any political office is subject to corruption and the most serious temptation to corruption lies in the financial *quid pro quo* by which a crafty businessman may seek escape from federal indictment. There is reason to believe that many attorneys have had offers to make it worth their while to quash an indictment or see that nolle prosequi is entered, or, as popularly expressed, that the case is "nol-prossed."

[2] National Commission on Law Observance and Enforcement, *Report on Prosecution*, No. 4, Washington, 1931, pp. 6–7.
[3] *Ibid.*, pp. 8–9.

The State Prosecuting Attorney

Each state has sovereign power with reference to the enactment and administration of all laws covering offenses within its boundaries which are not distinctly allocated to the province of the federal government. Naturally there is considerable variance in the penal laws and criminal procedure since local needs and traditions and the character of the population vary. However, modern science, transportation, and communication have had a unifying effect upon the states, not to mention the rest of the world. In consequence innovations in one state are frequently copied by another state and a considerable degree of uniformity marks both civil and criminal justice. Unfortunately the uniformity of the state prosecution systems is partly a matter of their being uniformly inefficient and badly organized. In most states the county is the unit of prosecution and a locally elected lawyer institutes criminal proceedings. This local attorney is variously designated as state's attorney, county attorney, district attorney, or prosecuting attorney. Whatever the particular title, his duties require him to prosecute infractions of the law, whether civil or criminal, and we shall refer to him as prosecuting attorney. One of his duties is to give legal advice to local officials and to citizens when the advice is of a public character.

Unlike the federal district attorneys the county or state prosecuting attorney has little central supervision. It is true that all states have an attorney general, but ordinarily his duties involve the protection of the interests of the state as a whole, particularly with reference to the various state departments, offices, and institutions. He may even interpret the law, making rulings in cases in which advice is sought where there is no litigation. Seldom, if at all, does he enter into the administration of criminal justice. In consequence the local prosecuting attorney is usually responsible only to his electorate. More than likely he is deeply interested in politics and has some other office as his goal. In general the lawyers with the greatest ability and the best training are unwilling to go through the stresses and strains of public service. The voters, therefore, may have little choice. Even where they have considerable choice few persons are competent to judge the candidates' qualifications.[4]

Because local prosecutors often use their office to promote future political advancement there are many temptations to play up popular opinion rather than to protect vital public interests. Powerful political

4 *Ibid.,* pp. 10–14.

figures may literally buy off the ambitious young attorney. Any man who wishes to be elected to public office knows he has to have sufficient votes and he cannot always afford to be too particular about the personal habits of his political supporters. Hence virtually all office seekers are forced to sully their record with a few unsavory contacts with the political underworld. They are then under continual threat of blackmail, undeserved though it may be, and are often forced to "play ball" with unscrupulous citizens.

At the same time the prosecuting attorney wields more authority in the administration of justice than does the presiding judge of the district court. For it is he who institutes proceedings against the person accused. He may dispose of the case without giving any reason for so doing. He may quash an indictment if he chooses. All in all he assumes the triple role of investigator, prosecutor, and veritable magistrate. He judges what is to be prosecuted, what is to be investigated. In addition he is a law enforcement officer with special aides to suppress lawbreaking. He may even become a virtual triumvirate of police, sheriff, and coroner. There is much more actual limitation on the authority of the judge than on the judicial function of the prosecutor, who so often becomes the arbiter in determining which law shall be enforced and which shall not.[5]

If a prosecuting attorney carries a case to court he tends to hound the accused unmercifully. Seldom, if ever, does it occur to him that it is his duty to protect the legal interests of the prisoner he is bringing to justice. He is concerned much more seriously with "making a good record." "A good record" means that he must at all odds secure convictions. Frequently the prosecutor's zest for law-abiding activities is not evidenced in his own virtually illegal representations against hapless criminals. This relentless pursuit of the accused by a public servant so as to bring about an emotionalized judgment on the part of a jury should have no place in criminal justice. Some method of procedure should be devised wherein the state's legal representative presents facts simply and unemotionally if we are to avoid patent miscarriages of justice. The high rate of reversals by courts of appeal is itself testimony to the excess fervor of prosecutors bent on a high conviction record.

That a high conviction record pays political dividends is well known. Many an aspirant to higher office points with pride to his law enforcement proclivities in the district attorney's office. If a prosecutor

[5] *Ibid.*, pp. 16–18. Cf. also *The Missouri Crime Survey*, Macmillan, New York, 1926, p. 156.

can secure a 95 per cent record of convictions for cases tried his reputation is established. Naturally many such zealous prosecutors labor in the public interest. No one doubts, for example, that Thomas E. Dewey as district attorney rendered a great service to the city of New York. And certainly he gained political stature in the process. But even Mr. Dewey is known to have been seriously mistaken about one victim of his war on crime, and he allegedly used wire tapping and other highhanded devices. Convicting the innocent is a serious hazard in our complicated criminal procedure.[6]

Despite the tremendous authority vested in the prosecuting attorney for bringing the guilty to justice, his power is by no means absolute. The *Report on Prosecution* of the National Commission on Law Observance and Enforcement cites ten checks which curb the prosecutor's authority:

1. The police exert wide discretion in making arrests (as we have elsewhere noted).

2. The magistrate has power to dismiss the case.

3. The grand jury may ignore charges.

4. A nolle prosequi may be entered or the case may be dismissed.

5. The prosecutor may accept a plea of lesser offense. Strong political pressure may be exerted on the prosecuting attorney to do this, but seldom if ever is the reason mentioned.

6. The trial jury may render a verdict which seems to ignore the guilt or innocence of the offender.

7. The judge exercises discretion in passing sentence.

8. A motion may be made by the jury to mitigate the sentence.

9. The offender may be paroled before expiration of the sentence.

10. When convicted the offender may receive executive pardon.

Six of these ten "mitigating devices" are outside the control of the prosecuting attorney and afford a certain amount of check on any extremity exercised on his part.[7]

The State Attorney General

Part of the attorney general's ineffectiveness in any state unquestionably is the result of the tremendous variety of duties which are imposed upon him. As a matter of fact nearly all his time is consumed by his civil duties and functions. A follow-up survey made of the law

[6] Oswald G. Villard, "The Facts About Mr. Dewey," *The Nation*, 150:282 (February 24, 1940); Cf. also Edwin M. Borchard, *Convicting the Innocent*, Yale University Press, New Haven, 1932.

[7] Cf. National Commission on Law Observance and Enforcement, *op. cit.*, pp. 23–24.

enforcement in Missouri from 1931 to 1941 showed that the attorney general's heaviest duty is rendering legal opinions to the General Assembly, to the various state and county officials and heads of state departments, to prosecuting attorneys, and finally to interested private citizens. These run into the hundreds. In all civil suits or proceedings of law in which the rights and interests of the state are involved the attorney general or a representative from his office must appear in court. In addition he must approve countless matters, appoint appraisers, collect taxes due the state, etc., etc. He must participate in criminal law enforcement in case of extradition proceedings and in criminal cases which are brought before the Supreme Court; occasionally he must take over or assist the local prosecuting attorney; and finally he must prepare and prosecute ouster cases against sheriffs and prosecutors.

Yet, because of the high number of civil duties, criminal functions amount to only 10 per cent of his total duties.[8] The fact that many cases which should be followed through are lost in the grist is not exactly surprising, but it remains one of the practical obstacles to effective administration of criminal law in most states.

THE STEPS IN CRIMINAL PROCESS

Form, ceremony, and dignity mark the convening of many courts, especially higher courts, where judges wear robes of office and an air of solemnity and formality prevails. British courts have been particularly given to ceremony, but even most of the informal midwestern American courts possess a certain degree of order. Witnesses are solemnly sworn in, the judge overrules the lawyers' objections gravely, noisy onlookers are quieted, and the jury is instructed by the judge according to custom.

The steps in the criminal process constitute a highly formalized plan.

The Arrest

First the person suspected and accused must be arrested. If anyone wishes to charge a particular person with an offense he must swear out a warrant to the effect that this individual has committed a specific offense. The police may then proceed to make the arrest provided the one so charged has not escaped.

[8] Cf. John G. Heinberg and A. C. Breckenridge, *Law Enforcement in Missouri*, University of Missouri Studies, Columbia, Vol. XVII, No. 1.

More precautions are taken to prevent false arrest in case of misdemeanors than is true in case of felonious charges. Whenever the police suspect an individual of committing a felonious offense he or she may be arrested without warrant. It seems ironical that the law protects one accused of a misdemeanor from false arrest more carefully than it does one accused of a felony. In case of a mysterious murder, for example, many innocent people are hounded by police and arrested, because it is important to apprehend the felon, even though the innocent may suffer.

A number of years ago, for example, a sensational murder was committed in Evanston, Illinois. A young woman graduate student at Northwestern University was brutally attacked and killed on her way home from the library one evening. Her body was discovered behind the hedge on the lawn of a prominent Evanstonian. The respectable community was outraged. Every man within a few miles' radius was a likely suspect. Nearly every man known to have been in the vicinity was held for questioning. Newspaper reporters blamed janitors, delivery men, students. Neighbors looked suspiciously at each other. Eventually the culprit was found. He happened to be a feeble-minded Negro, but many reputable servants, deliverymen, students, and businessmen were arrested and held for questioning. One elderly man was held on suspicion for days, but because a shocking felony had been committed the police felt no compunctions about arresting on virtually no grounds except that of *locus vivendi*.

The Accusation

All persons tried in criminal courts must be carefully and accurately informed of the offense they have allegedly committed. In order to protect the innocent against erroneous accusations legal usage has become unbelievably complicated and technical. Several paragraphs are often required to present a somewhat confusing accusation of breaking a criminal law, save in those states which have adopted simplified procedure. New York, for example, has eliminated archaic verbiage from such accusations.

According to common-law practice a person is usually accused by an indictment originating with a grand jury. The accusation is made upon the basis of available evidence which gives sufficient presumption of an individual's guilt to require a trial.[9]

[9] Clarence N. Callender, American Courts, Their Organization and Procedure, McGraw-Hill, New York, 1927, p. 179.

The Grand Jury

According to common law the grand jury consists of 24 persons, but in many states today the number usually authorized is 12 or 16. Some states allow a lesser number. In any case a majority vote is necessary for the indictment.

When the grand jury convenes the prosecuting attorney usually meets with them and produces witnesses against the persons under suspicion. If it seems obvious that there is presumable reason to prosecute, the examination is stopped at once, a vote is taken, and a "true bill of indictment" is rendered. If during the course of investigations evidence appears which incriminates other persons further accusations are made. The accusations which originate with the grand jury instead of the prosecuting attorney are termed "presentments." A presentment is an authorization for the presiding officer to prepare a bill of indictment, which the foreman marks as a "true bill."[10]

Information

In many of the western states a person may be accused through the filing of information, either by a private attorney or by the prosecuting attorney. If the former method is employed the accused person must be arrested, a preliminary hearing held, and the case returned to the court for trial. When the prosecuting attorney files the information with the court, if the court approves the accused may then be arrested, arraigned, and tried. This type of procedure is used in a few states for all offenders. For serious offenses such as murder or highly complicated property crimes the indictment seems to possess certain merits and is employed in the majority of states.

Not all indictments result in trial. Often the defendant can pick flaws in the indictment and even though the accused is guilty the indictment may be disqualified by demurrer or motion "to quash." The defendant may prepare a petition giving his reasons why the indictment should be set aside. The matter is argued before the court and if the charge appears to be unreasonable or unfounded and the alleged facts do not constitute the offense charged the demurrer may be sustained.[11]

Arraignment

If the indictment is not dropped the defendant is brought to court, where he is arraigned or charged with the offense.

[10] *Ibid.*, pp. 176–177.   [11] *Ibid.*, p. 181.

Hearing

In case of minor offenses—misdemeanors—trials may be held in short order without indictment. The procedure varies. Sometimes persons are arrested and held in jail for weeks or months pending trial, because of inability to give bail. Usually such delay occurs because the docket is crowded or the court not in session.

Preliminary Examination

For more serious offenders—those arrested for felonies—an immediate trial is not usually possible, but in any event a preliminary hearing must be held in the lower court. At this inferior court, whether a justice of the peace, magistrate's, or alderman's court, the prosecuting attorney presents the charge made against the prisoner at the bar and the judge decides whether or not there is just cause for "binding over" the accused to the grand jury for indictment (or to the prosecuting attorney in case an indictment is not called for in that state).[12]

Bail or Jail?

In a chapter entitled "Bail or Gaol?" Raymond Moley gives a vivid picture of how great an advantage accrues to the accused when he is able to secure bail in case of his indictment or the transfer of the case to the trial court. A man who is recognized as a responsible person may not even be required to give bail or a bond for his appearance at a later trial. Some offenders—chiefly persons charged with murder—are not allowed bail in most jurisdictions.

The practice of giving bail, as Moley makes clear, did not originate in order to preserve man's freedom and presumption of innocence. It developed as a means of preventing costly imprisonment pending trial and was generally considered a more satisfactory means of keeping the offender on hand than the earthen walls of many of the dungeon prisons in England. Moreover, sheriffs in particular were glad to get rid of the responsibility of providing food and shelter for those awaiting trial.[13]

Unhappily bail is no longer a successful means of guaranteeing that those charged will appear in court, at least in the United States.

[12] Nathaniel Cantor, *Crime, Criminals and Criminal Justice*, Holt, New York, 1932, pp. 176–178.
[13] Raymond Moley, *Our Criminal Courts*, Minton, Balch, New York, 1930, p. 45.

Nor is it a guarantee that the state will receive the amount of the surety in case the prisoner "jumps his bail." Nevertheless, the right to secure bail is a constitutionally guaranteed right in most states and our federal Constitution further guarantees that the amount shall not be excessive.

The seeming importance of the right of bail unfortunately has led to its widespread abuse. In fact, many persons arrested on serious charges give bail and are never heard of again. According to *The Missouri Crime Survey* there were 186 bail forfeitures in 1 year and in 73 cases the defendant never appeared. A large number of bail forfeitures are either uncollectible or else not collected. In 39 Missouri counties the sum of $292,400 was forfeited in 1 year. Actually only $25,900 was called for in judgment and only $1572.80 was subsequently collected. In St. Louis and Kansas City not a cent was collected.[14] Courts seem to be completely credulous about accepting the credit of personal or professional bondsmen. At the time the Missouri survey was made at least 85 persons charged with serious crimes were at large in the state.[15]

Nor is the responsibility for accepting a surety sufficiently guarded. Sometimes it is the policeman who accepts bail! Sometimes bail is accepted from completely unreliable persons with a record for bail jumping. Professional bondsmen have contributed an especially unsavory chapter to the bail problem. Often they are closely identified both in sympathy and in a business way with the underworld. Some of them are men with criminal records who are literally co-operating in the rackets of those for whom they act as bondsmen. Many have no financial integrity; not a few have no financial security and offer bonds far in excess of their ability to pay.[16] Surety companies have also been involved in bail scandals, although reputable insurance agencies are seldom participants in any dishonorable bail deals.

As matters stand, the impecunious and ignorant lawbreakers have no opportunity to secure bail. The professional criminal has a special advantage; the bondsmen have intimate contact with the underworld and are always on hand when he needs them. Often they are both playing for the same stakes and the bond is part of the game. The privilege of bail has thus become a privilege of scandal.

Bail has actually done more to aid the most unscrupulous variety of lawbreaker than it has done to help the innocent. Poor and igno-

[14] Raymond Moley, "Bail Bonds," Part V of *The Missouri Crime Survey*, pp. 197–199.
[15] *Ibid*. Cf. also Raymond Moley, *Our Criminal Courts*, p. 46.
[16] Raymond Moley, *Our Criminal Courts*, pp. 45–46.

rant persons accused of crimes can practically never secure bail. Indicted persons who are unable to secure release have far greater difficulty in securing adequate witnesses than does the man who can plot
his course of action with all the varieties of help that may be obtained
from friends, relatives, and legal advisers. Moreover, the poor man is
much more likely to suffer for his guilt since there is little likelihood
that he can escape. The marked disadvantage of poverty is obvious
even among thieves.

Frequently a temporary defaulting on bail is a device employed by
the bailee to delay trial. When a defendant fails to show up at his trial
the judges may order the surety to appear and give evidence as to
why the accused has not appeared or give reason why the judgment
shall not be rendered. The surety then presents the accused at the
next term of court while the defendant profits from all the advantages
of having his case delayed. This is in a sense a reward for not fulfilling
one's obligation to appear at the proper time.[17]

THE CRIMINAL COURTS

The criminal courts in the different states consist, generally speaking, of three types. (1) First, are the lower courts or courts of inferior jurisdiction in which misdemeanants under certain categories
are tried and in which persons charged with felonious offenses undergo
preliminary examination. In rural areas these are generally "justice of
the peace" courts. In larger communities they are variously designated
as magistrate's courts, municipal courts, or occasionally, alderman's
courts. No special legal training is required of the magistrates although
they are vested with definite judicial powers, both in determining
guilt and assessing punishments for minor offenders and in ascertaining probability of an offense's having been committed by the person
accused on a felonious charge. Actually these courts handle the great
mass of petty offenders, hence are vitally important in the administration of justice. (2) Second, there are the district or county courts,
which have original jurisdiction in the trial of felonious offenses as
well as in case of certain more serious misdemeanant charges. (3)
Third, there are the "supreme," "superior," or "appellate" courts,
which have the final voice in confirming or setting aside the verdict
by a district or county court when it is appealed.

In the larger cities there are in addition numerous special courts

[17] Raymond Moley, "Bail Bonds," Part V, *The Missouri Crime Survey*, pp. 197–199.

with jurisdiction over particular types of cases. In New York City, for example, the Women's Court deals with women sex offenders.[18]

Rural Courts

In rural areas and villages the justice of the peace or a local official conducts preliminary examinations and passes on misdemeanants. Usually this country squire possesses no legal training and the prosecuting attorney's word is taken at face value.

The average rural justice of the peace or village magistrate is, however, subject to a great deal of local social control. Although there are miscarriages of justice in all courts, actually the average small town brooks less deviation from what it considers the special duty of its elected officials than does the city. The methods of conducting the court tend to be simple and informal and the procedure is lacking in ceremony.

The fee basis for compensating judges arose because rural communities rather generally hold that the courts should put no financial burden on the taxpayers. "Those who cause the trouble should pay for it" is the philosophical justification for fee-supported justices of the peace. But with a township system of courts the fees are distributed among too large a number of justices to make the pay worth while to all.[19]

If the number of justices were reduced and their jurisdiction extended over a wider area, justices could be given more adequate remuneration. As matters stand, justices are under the serious temptation to solicit business. This situation contributes to a buyers' market. Plaintiffs, it is maintained, seek out a court which will render favorable verdicts. A survey made in Michigan substantiates this accusation.[20] Where criminal cases are concerned the justice tends to render verdicts favorable to the sheriff rather than to the defendant. Statistics for 63 counties in Michigan covering 35,800 traffic cases during 1931–1936, for example, showed that there were convictions in 91.5 per cent of the cases.[21]

Some plan for providing competently trained (and this means legally trained) justices for the minor courts should be developed for rural court work. Virginia has already provided for a system of part-

[18] Cf. Nathaniel Cantor, op. cit., chap. 12, "The Courts."
[19] Edson R. Sunderland, "Qualifications and Compensation of Minor Court Judges," *Journal of the American Judicature Society*, 29:111–116 (December, 1945).
[20] *Ibid.*   [21] *Ibid.*

time judges for what previously amounted to one-third-time work.[22]

College and legal training for rural judges would seem to be essential if it is their business to interpret the law. Many of our city magistrate's courts are manned by equally incompetent judges, as we shall presently discuss. It is a fact, however, that rural judges have a better record for personal integrity than can be said of city magistrates. In effect the rural judge is in the position of trying his neighbor. He also knows that every verdict he renders is mercilessly ventilated through small-town or rural gossip. Therein lies a strong constraint to maintain his standing among members of his community along with his responsibility for maintaining law and order.

Municipal Courts

In the larger cities the inferior criminal courts are usually divided into two categories: (1) the justice of the peace courts and (2) a second variety, variously designated as aldermen's, magistrates', or municipal courts. In some cities there are also special courts such as women's courts, morals courts, etc., as mentioned.

We shall discuss later the rural origins of American urban and district courts. The inferior city courts are blood cousins of the early rural courts and often unsuited to their function in metropolitan areas. Yet because they handle the bulk of all criminal cases (both rural and urban) their functioning is a matter of major concern to the whole administration of criminal justice.

Frequently the alderman's or magistrates' courts have been called the "poor man's" courts, because they have jurisdiction over all civil litigation involving amounts under $100. But they also conduct the preliminary examinations for more serious offenses and have the right to discharge or hold over cases for grand jury action. They issue warrants for arrest, detain witnesses, and fix bail. On nonjury cases they have extensive trial jurisdiction. In the area of criminal justice such courts thus exercise enormous power. In dismissing cases they may even give encouragement to the petty offender, who may have another and bigger try at making crime pay. Records are almost uniformly badly kept. Cases are "fixed" to an appalling degree and the alarming number of favors extended to the friends of ward heelers gives many a young criminal a false notion of security in his ill-chosen profession. He thinks it easy to "get by." The magistrates' courts (by whatever term they may be designated) must bear a large share of the onus for

[22] *Ibid.*

the youthful lawbreaker's credo that "*only saps work.*" Police, we concede, make many false arrests. But even so, the high percentage of dismissals are a frank commentary on corruption in our city courts.[23] And that so many offenders receive no penalty for their dishonest dealings gives an impetus to all the rackets and other illegal activities which so complicate our economic order. The dismissals literally make crime pay, at least for the time being.

District Courts

There are many explanations for the ineffective functioning of our criminal courts, but basic to them all is the retention of a pioneer system of justice within an urban court structure. All the increases in complex urban living have fostered personal and social disorganization. Modern crimes are in fact essentially urban in character. Crime and crime patterns have changed markedly but we still muddle along with the rural justice which sufficed fairly well in colonial New England as well as in frontier days.[24] Part of this retention of pioneer criminal procedure stems from the control of country lawyers over the administration of criminal justice. Everyone knows that the members of state legislatures are predominantly country lawyers and that these men make the laws which govern the criminal justice in cities. As Roscoe Pound points out, there is an apparent inability and disinclination of country lawyers to comprehend the legal problems of large cities. The pattern of decentralization, the diffusion of responsibility, and the variety of tasks make the prosecuting attorney's combination of duties far too great. It may be comparatively easy for a rural county attorney to carry on his functions as investigator, attorney, solicitor, and judge. In a large city these multiple duties quite properly should be divided among a well-co-ordinated and highly trained personnel.[25]

Another factor complicating criminal justice is the judicial hierarchy with the long-drawn-out proceedings entailed in appealing cases to a higher court. Such proceedings involve enormous waste of time and needless expense. Unhappily the item of cost in appealing is often so great as to make our courts wholly undemocratic. No poverty-stricken defendant can ever hope to appeal a case, whereas the gangster has the financial resources of his group to provide legal defense. And this in democratic America! Unification and simplification of our

[23] Cf. in this connection Spencer Ervin, *The Magistrates' Courts of Philadelphia,* Thomas Skelton Harrison Foundation, Philadelphia, 1931, especially chaps. 2, 3, and 4.
[24] Roscoe Pound, *Criminal Justice in America,* Holt, New York, 1930, chap. 4.
[25] *Ibid.*

courts is an imperative step in providing justice on a democratic basis. The American Bar Association could do much to foster uniform and simpler laws, if it chose.

The conflicting jurisdictions which occur because of the division of judicial powers between federal and state governments and between state and state likewise often result in gross miscarriage of justice.[26] Eventually, perhaps, laws may become uniform, but so long as state boundaries remain the jealous guardians of local law this problem will remain. Greater co-operation between states might be facilitated by appropriate federal legislation, however.

The Judge

The popular election of district judges is in itself a questionable exercise of democratic choice on the part of the average voter. Most citizens know little or nothing about what constitutes suitable professional qualifications for the lawyers who are competing for the bench. Since the only way the average judge can be known to his electorate is through the newspaper, he, like the prosecuting attorney, has to "keep in the public eye." In consequence he is tempted to be spectacular or to identify himself with so many petty civic groups and community organizations that he has little time for reflective and "judicial" thinking.

The popular election of the judge also subjects him to the whims and prejudices of the voters, and often a good man loses out. In any case there is always the problem of what Raymond Fosdick calls "transient administration," which makes any continuity of policy impossible. Of course, changes on the bench are not always bad and the appointed judge who is incompetent or who becomes so with increasing age also complicates the effective administration of our courts. However, our federal judges are, generally speaking, men of high integrity and ability. Usually we are safe in assuming that the appointed judge has had his credentials properly considered.

The Judge's Role in Interpreting the Law

The judge's role in interpreting the law is seldom recognized. Everyone knows that the judge presides over the hearing whether he is conducting a jury trial or is trying the offender himself. What few realize is the extent to which the judge's personal prejudices, philosophy

[26] Ibid.

of life, and personality enter into his legal decisions. These are especially likely to affect decisions in civil suits, but the implications are almost equally serious in the administration of criminal justice.

When conducting the trial the judge must rule quickly upon objections raised to testimony during the examination and cross-examination of the witnesses. Lawyers for both sides, as well as the defendant, must accept his decisions during the trial. Schooled in precedent and in case law, the judge can usually cite some generality to support his decision if he is ever required to do so. Ordinarily, however, he is not asked to give any justification for his rulings.

The personality of the judge, his temperament, and his economic and social philosophy inevitably influence his decisions. The judge with conservative economic views is thus generally opposed to the trade-union representative. The judge who can see no extenuating circumstances which may account for the crime will ordinarily exact a harsh penalty. The judge who has studied in a law office without benefit of liberal arts training usually has less understanding of the origins of criminal behavior than does the attorney with a background in psychology and sociology. These differences unquestionably have some effect upon the instructions he gives to the jury. Frequently the judge has less understanding than the student reading this text as to the personal motivations and social factors in criminal conduct.

Yet the only guarantee of justice rests in the personality of the judge, in his ability to differentiate between the spirit and the letter of the law, as Cardozo has pointed out. For law must always be applied to dynamic life situations and since it is interpreted by the judge it can never be said that the truly dead hand of the law is operating. And in all the numerous instances in which no law or precedent seems to fit, the judge quite literally makes the law through his own weighing of the situation.[27]

SALARIES FOR THE JUDICIARY

Since judges represent the legal-social interests of the state they should be adequately remunerated so that men of high caliber may be attracted. State and federal district judges are generally presumed to represent the upper 10 per cent of the legal profession, but their salaries seldom approximate anything resembling the income of leading corporation lawyers. This discrepancy poses many serious problems for the legal profession since the ablest men should be judges.

[27] Cf. Benjamin Cardozo, *The Nature of the Judicial Process*, Yale University Press, New Haven, 1921, Lecture III, "The Judge as Legislator," pp. 98–141.

Naturally there have been many demands to improve the judges' salary.

The Hobbs-Wagner bill proposed an annual increase of $5000 for federal judges of all rank.[28] Since judges' salaries are far superior to those in the academic profession and exceed the majority of those in the legal profession there may be some question as to whether salaries are in themselves a measure of a man's worth, but returns are generally high among the outstanding members of the bar. These same men have been marked more by ability to win cases by setting aside the basic purposes of lawmakers through detection of flaws in the laws' application than by concern about the protection of the social interests of government. Only as lawyers are imbued with a social conscience rather than mere desire to win cases can we expect to find a large group of legally trained men from which suitable judges may be selected. On the other hand, some opportunity for greater financial return should improve the caliber of men seeking the judicial office.

Lawlessness and Criminal Justice

Of course many of the problems of criminal justice cannot be attached to the personnel of the courts, or their lack of unification. Much of our crime problem lies in the lawless attitudes so characteristic of the American people, who do not wish their government to impose any restraints which affect them personally. Many of these lawless persons are in the comfortable and upper-income groups, as witness the black market during World War II and the patrons of the bootlegger during prohibition. This topic has been discussed in chapter 3.

A selected bibliography on criminal procedure is given at the end of chap. 20.

[28] Cf. "How to Get and Keep Competent and Independent Judges," *American Bar Association Journal*, 31:630–637 (December, 1945).

CHAPTER 20

Criminal Procedure: The Trial

In most states misdemeanants are tried by the judge while the majority of felonious criminal cases are disposed of by some other method than jury trial. A large number of cases are dismissed for lack of satisfactory evidence or because of the apparent innocence of the accused. A notable share of those arrested admit their guilt. Sometimes they admit a lesser offense and through bargaining with the prosecuting attorney are thus in line for a lesser penalty. When a felony case is tried, however, the defendant may receive or waive jury trial, as he sees fit.

TRIAL BY JURY

After the defendant has been duly accused and has had time to secure legal counsel he is given an opportunity to deny or affirm his guilt. If he denies it he is tried for the offense. The county attorney or state's attorney then tries to present evidence to prove the defendant guilty, and the defendant tries to establish his innocence through conflicting evidence and testimony, as we shall discuss in detail. Or the accused may plead that he is not guilty because of insanity. All trials, even where the guilt seems obvious, tend to some uncertainty as to outcome because of human factors which influence the judge and jury's decisions.

Origins of Trial by Jury

Trial by jury is apparently a French contribution to criminal justice. No provision was made for a jury in Roman legal procedure and its origin is said to be derived from the Frankish custom of having royal representatives known as *jurata* to meet with private citizens in the settlement of dispute over land and with reference to offenses against the king. These *jurata* met with private citizens, made an official inquiry (*inquisito*), and gave their report (*veredictum*).[1]

When the Normans invaded England in 1066 they carried this custom with them. During the thirteenth century trial of criminals by jury seems to have been well established in England. However, the defendant could still choose trial by ordeal or torture if he so wished. Early jurors were usually well acquainted with the facts and were often witnesses as well as determiners of guilt.[2]

Basically, jury trials were instituted to provide some measure of justice in the trial of the accused. Men had so frequently been subjected to the capricious and vengeful decisions of the king and royal judges that a trial by men of his own group and rank seemed to provide highly desirable protection to the defendant. Then as now, jurymen must have been carried away by their emotions and have rendered verdicts on the basis of their feelings. At that time there were no psychologists probing into the explanation of verdicts. Fortunately none was excused from jury service because of his occupation, hence the ablest men were not exempt as they so frequently are today. And certainly 12 men sitting in solemn body were a more likely source of a reasonable verdict than a self-righteous judge sitting in his legal aloofness from the accused party. Today trial by jury is no guarantee of justice, as we shall see.

The Jury Panel

Jurors are usually selected from a list of representative citizens in the community drawn up for the purpose. In some states this list is limited to men. In any event, names from the list are placed in a box or wheel and those whose names are drawn from it are asked to serve. Often it is difficult to get a satisfactory jury because so many persons are exempt on the basis of the importance attached to their particular occupations. In virtually all jurisdictions a long list of persons are excused, chiefly because jury duty would presumably prevent them from rendering a necessary service. Thus clergymen, physicians, dentists, undertakers, embalmers, teachers, editors, pilots of vessels, telegraph

---

[1] Cf. Nathaniel Cantor, *Crime, Criminals and Criminal Justice*, Holt, New York, 1932, chap. 13.
[2] *Ibid.*

operators, firemen, policemen, etc., may be excused from jury service. Some states exempt all women categorically although an increasing number are providing for women on the jury. Missouri, for example, in its new constitution makes the following provision for female jurors: "Sec. 22(b). Female Jurors—Optional Exemption.—No citizen shall be disqualified from jury service because of sex, but the court shall excuse any woman who requests exemption therefrom before being sworn as a juror."[3] Because of the extensive exemptions many an impassioned plea has been made to abolish the jury on account of its alleged incompetence.

The Impaneling of the Jury

As the names of jurors are drawn the first person accepted becomes "number 1" and is ordinarily chosen chairman of the jury. This person frequently has undue influence, therefore, through pure chance. The name, sex, and occupation of the jurors drawn are carefully noted and lawyers on both sides may reject any juror. Many persons are rejected quite obviously because of fears that they will be unlikely, because of certain considerations, to give a verdict in favor of the side represented. Thus a labor leader might be challenged in case a union member were the defendant. Women are sometimes rejected because of their alleged intolerance for the frailties of their own sex. A man known to be a member of the Ku Klux Klan would unquestionably be rejected in a trial in which a Jew or Negro was the defendant. The process of rejecting jurors is known as "challenging."

Justice may be delayed in some cases by the challenging of jurors, which goes on for days. In fact challenging is often a device to delay the trial in order to facilitate the appearance of witnesses who are out of town, ill, or otherwise unable to be present. For whatever reason, a delay is usually advantageous to the defendant.

If too many challenges occur the jury panel may be exhausted. Consequently in the larger cities "hangers-on" in the courthouse hallways are frequently called in for jury service. The extent to which these hangers-on are planted in the hallways for the ulterior purpose of packing the jury has never been subjected to any satisfactory ventilation. Any conclusions would necessarily depend on surmise rather than tangible data. Nevertheless, that such packing happens occasionally seems quite likely and any jurors thus sworn into service must inevitably constitute a serious threat to an impartial decision.

[3] Section 22(b), Article I, *Missouri Constitution of 1945.*

At least it is far safer to have all the jurors drawn from a special list of respected citizens. Here there are ordinarily no dangers outside that of the rather general fallibility which characterizes the judgment of all human beings.

The qualifications for jury service usually entail nothing concerning either intelligence or education. Most states are content to insist on "good moral character." A few stipulate that jurors may not have been convicted of a criminal offense.[4] Of course, many competent persons serve as jurors and in some places, New York City for example, jurors seem to be above the average in education and intelligence.[5]

The average juror tends to feel he is wasting his time and that most cases could be equally well settled without a jury trial if lawyers did not profit from drawn-out litigation.[6]

As alterations developed in criminal procedure familiarity with the case before trial became a basis for rejection as a juror, since it was held that such a juror judged the case, as it were, before trial. Since modern dissemination of news makes it almost impossible for any but the most ignorant persons to be unacquainted with certain facts of a crime widely publicized in the press or on the radio, such a basis for rejection of jurors actually limits the possibility of effective jury service severely. Most intelligent people read the newspapers and listen to news reports on the radio.

Raymond Moley does not believe we should take too seriously the protests against the competence of jurors, although he recognizes that jurors are usually less well off financially and less well educated than the exempted groups. Professor Moley holds these facts do not prove *ipso facto* that the deliberation of the jury is a travesty on justice. The juror is not supposed to interpret either the law or the causes of criminal conduct. His function is solely to determine whether the defendant is guilty of breaking a criminal law.

Despite Moley's contention that juries are not supposed to judge the law, his argument can be easily refuted. Actually juries often take the law into their own hands. As a matter of fact, Jefferson maintained that it would be better to omit the people from the legislative than the judiciary department of government since the execution of laws is more important than the making of them.[7] Certainly much of our

---

[4] *Ibid.*

[5] Anonymous ("By a Juryman"), "Just How Stupid Are Juries?" *Harper's Magazine*, 178:84–87 (December, 1938).

[6] R. W. Riis, "The Jury Nuisance," *Reader's Digest*, 32:65–66 (February, 1938).

[7] Letter of Jefferson to L'Abbé Arnond, July 19, 1789 in Vol. III, *Works of Thomas Jefferson*, Washington ed., 1854, pp. 81–82, cited by Mark de Wolfe Howe in "Juries as Judges of Criminal Law," *Harvard Law Review*, 52:582–616 (February, 1939).

pioneer justice indicated an exercise of this theory of democracy, which allowed the jury to determine the law.[8]

The Judge, the Lawyer, and the Jury

The average juror has many prejudices, but prejudice is a common human propensity and applies among highly educated persons and those of the upper income groups. It is not likely, therefore, that juries would be less emotional if there were fewer exemptions from jury service. Emotions are not eradicated by academic education. Class prejudice instead often fires emotions. Nor is hypersuggestibility eliminated by education, although we have reason to believe that it is diminished. Certainly many jurors are "worn down" by the insistence of articulate members irrespective of education.

The major faults of jurors may be reduced to (1) their intellectual incompetence in general and (2) actual corruption in specific instances. Since the average juror has no acquaintance with legal terminology he is often woefully ignorant of what is going on in the courtroom. Upton Close tells of an instance in which the jurors did not know who the defendant was.[9]

The corruption of juries is especially hard to control. The Ruth Commission of Pennsylvania found that in certain counties in the state it was common practice for the defendant to make a call upon every member of the jury panel for the obvious purpose of influencing their verdict, and with apparently effective results. Another variety of corruption was also disclosed: Persons drawn on the jury actually were guilty of sending other persons in their place.[10]

Another serious criticism of jurors is the unpredictable character of their verdicts. Juries tend to render verdicts in accordance with their sympathies. They may free the accused where the evidence would seem to point to indisputable guilt. Occasionally such decisions may be traced to the jurors' misinterpretation of the judge's instructions, as we shall discuss. Further, juries often are asked to render verdicts on cases which exceed any capacity they have for judgment. The necessity for a unanimous verdict presents additional difficulties. The practice of requiring complete accord in the verdict arose as a means of protecting the innocent at a time when the death penalty was exacted for the major share of offenses, but it has endured to obstruct

[8] Mark de Wolfe Howe, *op. cit.*

[9] Upton Close, "Twelve Good Men—Untrue," *Reader's Digest*, 33:12–16 (August, 1938).

[10] *Ibid.*

justice. When a jury is "hung" because of inability to agree a new trial is required, with inevitable expense and loss of time.[11] Except in case of capital offenses there seems to be little valid reason for not accepting a three-fourths vote. Most criminologists believe that jury trials are an unsatisfactory basis either for establishing certainty of guilt or for rendering a verdict involving sentence.

In the trial the lawyers for the defense and the prosecuting attorney are seldom interested in presenting the facts of the case so that the jury may decide intelligently. Instead they engage in a pitched battle, each concerned only with influencing the jury for a favorable verdict. Everything possible is done to disparage the witnesses in the eyes of the jury, to create a favorable emotional attitude toward one or the other side of the case.

When the judge makes the charge to the jury, he is supposed to instruct the members of the jury as to the nature of the law governing the particular case. He likewise reminds the jurors that it is their task to ascertain whether it is established "beyond reasonable doubt" that the defendant has committed the offense of which he is accused. Suitable instructions might alleviate the jurors' confusion about common legal terms employed. Several states have prepared instructions which are given to the jury members.

The judge sometimes instructs the jury in such a way as to influence the verdict. Occasionally judges are corrupt and there have been instances in which they had a financial interest in the outcome of the case. What the jurors seldom realize is that the lawyers for both sides prepare the instructions for the jury which the judge is asked to read. Usually judges look these over and eliminate anything which might be regarded as "reversible error." But even so, an ambiguity of meaning or an erroneous impression may be conveyed to the jury because of the peculiar wording of the instructions and this may occur primarily because one of the lawyers intended to confuse the minds of the jurymen. Ordinarily the lawyers for both sides are supposed to concur in the instructions, but at times the jury has been befuddled through such purposeful shenanigans on the part of the attorneys.

The public, in turn, is often outraged when the jury renders a verdict of "not guilty." The jury, on the other hand, was instructed that unless certain conditions were present the accused must be acquitted; that to be convicted his guilt must be established beyond reasonable doubt. Despite the occasional risk involved in instructing the jury, more authority, rather than less, should ordinarily be given the judge

[11] *Ibid.*

to make clear the law to the jury. And on no count should the judge feel any necessity for accepting his instructions from the lawyers!

The Authority of the Judge

The judge as the presiding officer of the court should have some authority to guide the jury to an intelligent verdict, since practically all jurors are unschooled in law. This information should be offered if only as a means of offsetting the emotionalized appeals which the lawyers make to the jury. In final analysis the function of the jury should be to make a decision on the basis of facts, not on the basis of the distorted facts in the attorneys' impassioned speeches.

The Responsibility of the Judge

The authority vested in the judge for passing sentence on the convicted criminal carries with it a tremendous responsibility. Unfortunately judges are men and not gods, and their decisions, however thoughtfully considered, often carry a heavy weight of personal prejudice and emotionalized attitude. One has only to examine the sentences for the same offense in any state prison. Some judges believe a short sentence is more effective than a long one. Others "crack down" on the offender and give him the limit of the law, with little concern for any personal mitigating factors.

For example, a few years ago a judge in Ohio imposed a severe sentence of 20 years for kidnaping in the case of a young woman employed in a foundling hospital in Cincinnati. The girl took the child to her home, which was across the river in Kentucky. She was low grade in intelligence as well as ignorant of the law, but loved the child and thought she could give it suitable care. She produced no witnesses as to her character at the trial because she thought she could not ask a nun to testify for her, and the judge sentenced her to the federal women's reformatory for 20 years. Here there was no evidence of intent to commit a crime, and the emotionalism of the judge was scarcely a suitable reason for imposing so long a sentence.

Waiver of Jury Trial

During the 20 years preceding World War II there was a definite movement to permit accused persons to waive the right of trial by jury and many laws permitting such waiver were enacted.

A strong impetus to the movement was the fact that very few persons were actually convicted by juries. Instead it has been long recognized that the average guilty person is willing to admit his guilt—in fact he seems to find a certain psychological release in admitting it. The court's chief concern therefore has been with the sentence involved. This was indicated in a study made of felony cases in 24 cities in the United States during the period 1923–1927. A far greater number pleaded guilty than were convicted in 22 cities (in all cities studied except San Francisco and Atlanta, where only 33 and 47 per cent pleaded guilty respectively). For the other cities the number who pleaded guilty ranged from 59 per cent in Cincinnati to 95 per cent in Syracuse.[12]

In a study of cases in Cook County, Illinois, in 1926, of 13,117 felony indictments only 492 were tried by jury. Of these 283 were acquitted, 25 were convicted of lesser offenses, and only 184 were convicted of the offenses charged.[13]

Unhappily the high percentage of confessions is no unmixed blessing. For confessions are frequently an index to the high-pressure third-degree methods of police in dealing with persons under suspicion. We have already discussed this matter in the chapter on police.

The idea of waiving jury trial is not recent. As early as 1810 the Maryland General Assembly made a statutory provision for discretionary choice on the part of the accused as to whether he would submit his case to the court or have a jury trial.[14] In 1874 Connecticut adopted a similar law, which was repealed 2 years later and then reenacted 51 years later, in 1927.[15]

Great Britain likewise adopted a law in 1925 providing that indictable offenses might be dealt with in courts of summary jurisdiction. By 1926 the cases of 69,695 persons were thus disposed of, whereas only 7924 were handed over to trial juries in higher courts.[16]

Present Status of Waiver of Jury Trial

Today nearly half of the states in our country permit waiver of jury trial for felony cases, except those punishable by death. Even so, a sharp conflict exists between two schools of thought on the subject. One group, sometimes designated as the "public interest school,"

[12] Raymond Moley, *Politics and Criminal Prosecution*, Minton, Balch, New York, 1929, chap. 7, "The Vanishing Jury."

[13] *Ibid.*

[14] *Maryland Laws* (November Session, 1809), chap. 144.

[15] *Law Notes*, 31:122 (October, 1927). Cf. also Mabel A. Elliott, *Conflicting Penal Theories in Statutory Criminal Law*, University of Chicago Press, Chicago, 1931, p. 249.

[16] Pendleton Howard, *Century*, 95:683–690 (April, 1929).

maintains that the right of trial by jury shall remain forever inviolate, not as a privilege but as a mandatory aspect of the relation between the individual and the state. In the frequently cited case of *Cancemi* vs. *The People* in New York State it was held that "no one has the right by his own voluntary act to be deprived of his liberty. . . ."[17]

The Supreme Court of the United States has been more liberal in its construction of the Constitution of the United States. In an important decision, *Patton* vs. *United States,* in 1930 the Supreme Court held that, though originally the jury system was developed as a safeguard against cruel and tyrannical monarchs, there is no valid reason today for the accused not to waive jury trial if he so desires.[18]

In the meantime the Ohio legislature in 1929 enacted a law permitting the defendant to waive jury trial. A study made covering the felony cases tried following the adoption of this law during 1930–1931 showed that only 17.8 per cent were tried by the court. In general, trial by the court was most frequently used for sex offenses, offenses against the family, and liquor cases. In Maryland, on the other hand, 85.7 per cent of the trials during this period were conducted by the court alone.[19] Naturally we may assume that long-established practice of waiving jury trial in Maryland accounts for the differential rate in the percentage of waivers.

Waiver of jury trial obviously transfers a major responsibility for determining the guilt or innocence of the defendant to the judge, and there seems to be no question but that considerable time and expense is thus saved.[20]

Despite all the arguments favoring waiver of jury trials, jury trials will undoubtedly figure significantly in criminal procedure for many years to come. The annual conference of the Cincinnati Bar Association in 1937 devoted itself to this topic and a number of distinguished members of the bar from other states participated in the panels and discussion. Eighty-seven per cent of those attending held that jury trial should not be abolished. Sixty per cent held that instead changes should be made in selecting the panel so that jurors would meet certain intellectual, educational, and age qualifications. Approximately 75 per cent held that the present basis of selecting jurors allows a desirable class of persons to evade jury duty. A large majority held the

[17] 18 New York 128 (1858).
[18] Cf. *Patton* vs. *United States,* 281 U.S. 275, 50 Sup. Ct. 253 (1930). Cf. also John Conners, "Current Legislation," *St. John's Law Review,* 12:369–373 (April, 1938).
[19] Pendleton Howard, *op. cit.*
[20] Cf. "Waiver of Jury in Criminal Trials," *Journal of the American Judicature Society,* 18:48–51 (August, 1934).

judge should not comment on the evidence. More than three-fourths of the conference approved a course of instruction for jurors before beginning their service. The conference also recognized the undue influence of the counsel's arguments upon the jury's decision.[21]

EVIDENCE

Since English and American juries are judges of the facts, as brought out in the trial, the law of evidence has tremendous theoretical importance. Actually whatever is said in court whether or not it is "stricken from the record" or ruled out by the judge upon the demand of the opposing attorney cannot be erased from the minds of the jurors. Trial lawyers seize upon this fact for they realize that the major factor in the decision of the jurors is what they, the jurors, believe with reference to the prisoner's guilt. Lawyers tend therefore to pay little attention to the law of evidence in instructing their witnesses with reference to testimony. From a nonlegal point of view evidence is what determines the guilt or innocence of the accused.

Law of Evidence

The law of evidence is essentially the same for civil and criminal trials, save that certain matters pertain ordinarily only to the trial of the criminal.[22] However, the law of evidence has come to be very exacting, for the simple reason that jurors are so easily swayed by irrelevant facts and inadmissible items of information. It is part of the function of the judge to instruct the jury with reference to what facts should be taken into consideration in their verdict, as we have already mentioned. But since judges often give hasty or ambiguous instructions many reversals of conviction are made on the basis of faulty instructions to the jury.[23] For example, an appellate court has ruled that there was a reversible error in the state's presentation of evidence in the case of a man accused of stealing a Dodge car because other evidence was introduced which indicated that he had stolen another car. This evidence was held to have been inadmissible since it was a factor in influencing the jurors, who believed he committed the offense in question because he had committed similar offenses.[24]

[21] "Trial by Jury" (Report on the Cincinnati Conference, 1937), *University of Cincinnati Law Review*, 11:119–259 (March, 1937).

[22] J. H. Wigmore, *A Treatise on the Anglo-American System of Evidence in Trials of Common Law*, Little, Brown, Boston, 3rd ed., 1940, Vol. III, p. 649.

[23] *The Missouri Crime Survey*, Macmillan, New York, 1926, pp. 226–227.

[24] Cf. *Dennison vs. State*, 17 Ala. App. 674, 88 So. 211. Cited in Wigmore, *op. cit.*

Scheming lawyers often make it a point to get some type of reversible error into the record. They then can usually secure a reversal from a higher court and thus indirectly win the case unless it is remanded for new trial. Even when a new trial is stipulated there is every reason to expect the verdict to be less severe, if there is not an acquittal.

However, Roscoe Pound holds that "getting error into the record" is no longer as effective a defense for the accused as it once was. Courts of review are more careful about ascertaining whether the error operates to the prejudice of the accused or not.[25]

Rules of Evidence

Theoretically the rules of evidence are based upon a fundamental belief in the reason, logic, and rationality of the mental processes, although most modern psychologists would have difficulty in ascribing as much rationality to human thinking, even the thinking of those trained in law, as the jurists themselves have ascribed. Instead modern psychology has pretty well demonstrated that most people are guided by emotions rather than reason per se. Nevertheless trial by evidence marks a great advance over the irrationality of trial by ordeal.

Admissibility

Two general rules or "axioms" govern the admissibility of evidence: (1) None but facts having probation value (that is, capable of proving the issue) are admissible; (2) all facts having probation value are admissible unless some specific rule forbids.[26] A legal distinction is also made between admissibility and relevance in that admissibility subsumes relevance and the court is willing to accept it as such. Thus far at least legal rules have not been established with reference to relevance.[27] What is relevant would seem to depend more on the presiding judge than on law itself and we have, therefore, much "case law" on relevance. That is, decisions in previous cases are accepted as establishing precedents.

Admissibility is not proof of guilt but rather an indication that the evidence will contribute toward the proof or disproof of guilt.[28]

---

[25] Roscoe Pound, Criminal Justice in America, Harvard University Press, Cambridge, 1945, Preface to Second Printing.
[26] J. H. Wigmore, op. cit., pp. 291–295.
[27] Ibid., p. 298.
[28] Ibid., p. 299.

Direct Evidence

Evidence may be classified as to whether it offers direct proof of the alleged act. There are two varieties of direct evidence: (1) real or material evidence, which includes such items as a bloody knife, fingerprints, or any object or document which helps to establish the facts of the case; (2) direct testimony of eyewitnesses of the act, or of persons possessing personal knowledge of objects or facts contributing to the establishment of the case or its denial.[29]

Circumstantial or Indirect Evidence

Circumstantial evidence offers indirect or inferential proof of the alleged facts. Ordinarily circumstantial evidence cannot be considered as significant as are eyewitness accounts. Inferential evidence is allowed only when adequate direct evidence is lacking and there is strong presumptive reason for believing the accused has committed the offense. Unfortunately clever lawyers can sometimes build up so convincing a case on circumstantial evidence that occasionally an innocent man is adjudged guilty.

Primary and Secondary Evidence

Evidence may also be classified as "primary" and "secondary." A document which is admissible evidence and proves a fact which indictates indisputably the individual's guilt is primary evidence. A photostatic copy or the testimony of some person that he has seen such a document is secondary evidence. Obviously the original document bears much greater weight as evidence than do copies, which might be faked.

Written or Oral Evidence

Evidence may be further classified as "oral" and "written." Written evidence is admissible when the contents of a document establish a fact. All testimony of witnesses is obviously oral and is admissable under oath.[30]

Testimony of the Accused

Originally the accused could not testify, but English procedure has allowed the accused to testify in his own behalf since 1898.[31] The right

[29] Ibid., p. 396.
[30] Maurice Parmalee, Criminology, Macmillan, New York, 1918, p. 288.
[31] Ibid., pp. 288–289.

to testify in one's own behalf is now generally accepted in American criminal procedure. However, if one offers testimony he must submit to cross-examination by the prosecuting attorney. No accused person can be required to testify against himself and many defense lawyers advise their clients to refuse to take the stand. Since guilty persons often admit their guilt under pressure of questioning some penologists believe it would be a distinct asset to the state to compel the defendant to testify. On the other hand the prosecuting attorney, through leading questions, might incriminate an innocent party, hence most authorities think it better to let the prisoner-at-the-bar decide whether or not he cares to take the witness stand.

DISPOSITION OF CRIMINAL CASES

The average layman assumes that a person who commits a crime is either convicted or acquitted and that if he is guilty he inevitably discovers that the way of the transgressor is hard. Such, however, is not always the case. Many who are guilty do not plead guilty, nor are the guilty always convicted even when there is substantial evidence against them. Even if convicted, a sizable share are never punished for divers reasons. Occasionally a man with no previous record is put on probation, as we discuss in Chapter 21.

If an offender has sufficient means to hire competent legal defense he can nearly always secure a delay or stay of trial for technical reasons which any clever lawyer can present. Since laws are framed so as to protect the innocent as well as to punish the guilty, delays are allowed on a number of grounds, actual and alleged. Such delays make it possible for the defense to work out a scheme either for securing an acquittal or for mitigating the penalties. It is a fact well established that every delay decreases the chance of punishment and increases the possibility that the case will be dismissed or the offender acquitted.[32]

A study of cases brought before the Georgia courts, for example, showed that for 100 cases taken at random in the Fulton Supreme Court, and disposed of within 90 days of filing, 37 pleaded guilty and 41 were convicted. Only 5 were nolle prosequi cases. The rest were acquitted or otherwise disposed of. For 100 cases disposed of in from 91 to 270 days, 25 pleaded guilty, 18 were convicted, and 43 were nol-prossed. Eight were acquitted and 9 otherwise disposed of. For 100 cases not disposed of until after a lapse of 270 days, 17 pleaded guilty,

---

[32] "Crime and the Georgia Law Courts," *Journal of Criminal Law and Criminology*, 16:169–218 (August, 1925).

17 were convicted, and 45 were nol-prossed. Thirteen were acquitted and 8 disposed of otherwise. Expressed differently, only 22 were not punished in the group tried in 90 days; 57 were unpunished in the group tried in from 91 to 270 days. For those who were not tried for over 270 days, 66 went unpunished.[33]

In Missouri in three urban counties 47.85 per cent of the cases were eliminated in the preliminary hearing, 2.81 per cent had information refused or no bill of indictment returned, and an additional 20 per cent were eliminated in the circuit court. In 36 rural counties in the same state only 9.90 per cent of the cases were eliminated in the preliminary hearing and 3.31 per cent had information refused or no bill of indictment returned. In the circuit court of the rural counties, however, 44.72 per cent were dismissed for insufficient charges or other reasons. On the other hand, 42.07 per cent were actually sentenced in rural Missouri circuit courts.[34]

Appeals for retrial are another favorite and effective means of obfuscating justice. In some states as long as a year is allowed for perfecting an appeal. Sometimes the various delays entailed result in postponement of the second hearing for several years. In the meantime important witnesses may have died or moved away and the prosecuting attorney who initiated the case may no longer be in office. Men unfamiliar with what has taken place are forced to try the case and the offender gains a patent advantage in the decline of sentiment against him which the passage of time affords.[35] Sometimes, too, the man released on bail gets lost in what has been called the "double shuffle." Local officials think his case is transferred to the appellate court whereas the attorney for the defense often fails to carry the appeal through, hoping meanwhile that officials will forget all about the case. Upon investigation several hundred cases were found to have been lost thus in Missouri.[36]

A man whose case is lost in such a shuffle has a fair chance of never standing trial. For the most part, however, the wheels of justice grind on and convictions stand. When the judge has pronounced the sentence the prison doors swing open and the offender serves his time behind the bars. Today the sentence tends to be indeterminate as defined by minimum and maximum limits. There are additional reductions in time for good behavior, but this is beyond the jurisdiction of the courts.

[33] *Ibid.* Cases *nolle prosequi* or nol-prossed are those in which the court abandons prosecution because of lack of witnesses, lack of likelihood of conviction, etc.

[34] Cf. *The Missouri Crime Survey*, Table 14, p. 319.

[35] *Ibid.*, p. 356.   [36] *Ibid.*, p. 358.

COURT PROCEDURE IN CASE OF INSANITY

In case of insanity on the part of the accused a different procedure usually takes place. That is, the courts in all states provide for an alteration in the form of trial whenever insanity is alleged. If the court merely suspects insanity some states also make provision for proper examination.

The problem of dealing with the mentally ill who have committed what otherwise constitutes a crime is a very complicated one in most jurisdictions, not only because of the generally retarded standards of public institutions, but because of the whole legal philosophy as to what constitutes both crime and insanity. On the one hand the offender is *de facto* guilty of criminal behavior, of having committed an offense or a series of offenses which are specifically forbidden by law. He is therefore liable to conviction and sentence according to the law.

The law, on the other hand, has long since incorporated the principle of man's "responsibility" for his conduct, whether it be acceptable or condemned, in accordance with the classical and ecclesiastical philosophy out of which this theory grew. Such ecclesiastical theory has held on a *priori* grounds that man is a free, moral agent, one who makes a free choice in his decision to do right or wrong. Men of unsound mind (*non compos mentis*), however, have long been recognized as incompetent to make such decisions. In fact, the new classical school introduced a modification of the free-will theory;[37] hence, by strictest application of legal philosophy, the mentally deranged who have committed crimes have been adjudged "irresponsible because insane." On such grounds many persons suffering from violent mental disturbances have been allowed to go scot free after the commission of what would otherwise have been considered serious offenses. Earlier such persons were acquitted as "not guilty," with no adequate provision for the protection of society against the further damages which similar outbreaks of violence would entail.

That persons may become so mentally or emotionally disturbed as to be incapable of normal reasoning is thus generally recognized. The criteria employed to establish the irresponsible character of an individual's behavior vary, however, from the most scientific techniques of those skilled in psychology and psychiatry to the simple testi-

[37] The author wishes to acknowledge the courtesy of the *Journal of Criminal Law and Criminology* in allowing her to reproduce here certain sections from an article by Mary Goshorn Williams and Mabel A. Elliott, "Court Procedure and Subsequent Treatment in Case of the Criminal Insane," *Journal of Criminal Law and Criminology*, 35:233–241 (November–December, 1944).

mony of untutored laymen. Because of the comparative recency of the scientific development of psychiatry and psychology and the more or less esoteric jargon employed in these subjects, only that part of the public which has received specialized training is capable of understanding psychiatric or psychological testimony offered in defense of the emotionally disturbed or mentally ill. In consequence, the legal profession has been prone to reject psychiatric testimony as illogical or unreasonable. Furthermore, law has its roots in age-old customs, *not* in the acceptance of modern theories as to the dynamic character of human behavior. Moreover, legal decisions have been built upon the complicated system of precedent. Prior verdicts are accepted as true and proper methods for disposing of contemporary problems. So the legal profession today tends to define responsible conduct in terms of the McNaghten-Drummond Case of 1843, in which the basis for deciding upon a man's sanity was established by the famous "right-or-wrong test." According to the decision in this case a man was sane if he knew the difference between right and wrong, insane if he did not.

Previous to this case the best judicial opinion had held that all criminals should be subject to the full penalty of the law unless they were not conscious of the nature of their act or possessed no more reasoning capacity than "a wild beast or an infant." The McNaghten-Drummond Case produced a modification of this practice.[38] Here the defendant's guilt was clear but he was quite obviously insane and was for this reason acquitted by the jury. The House of Lords so disapproved of the decision, however, that they requested a group of judges to define and clarify the right-and-wrong test. The judges in turn formulated a series of questions to be put to the defendant pleading insanity to determine whether, in committing the crime, he knew he was doing wrong.

In general outline this so-called right-and-wrong test has persisted and forms an important part of the proceedings in the case of alleged insanity of the defendant in most criminal trials in the United States. In the course of time the test has been expanded to include a knowledge of consequences in certain jurisdictions, but just as often it stands as defined above. More recently judges have broadened their interpretation of the test and have held the accused is not responsible if his act is the "offspring or product of mental disease."[39]

The conclusions of modern psychiatry and psychology are so widely

[38] See Sheldon Glueck, *Mental Disorder and the Criminal Law*, Little, Brown, Boston, 1925, pp. 161–186 and 368, for a discussion of this famous British case.
[39] *Ibid.*, pp. 187–229,

accepted by recently trained college students that the validity of the right-and-wrong test for measuring normal mental functioning no longer can be accepted by educated men and women. Compulsive behavior is, perhaps, the best example of such inadequacy. For example, a man may be intellectually aware of the nature of his behavior, may know that his conduct is "wrong," so to speak; yet he has a compulsion to behave in a particular manner. Thus, a man may know it is wrong to kill another man but be unable to resist the impulse to kill. He may be convinced that, irrespective of the immoral nature of murder, he *must* kill. Or he may be so emotionally wrought up that he virtually explodes, despite any otherwise rational attitudes he may have on the sanctity of human life.

Both popular opinion and the law attach far less stigma to being adjudged "irresponsible" because of insanity than they do to serving a sentence because of conviction for the offense. It is not surprising therefore that there has been a strong motivation to abuse the plea of "not guilty because of insanity." Such pleas have been particularly frequent among defendants indicted for murder. The extent to which such a plea has been abused cannot be accurately determined, but in any event the public mind has come to regard the plea as a means of escaping the rightful consequences of criminal behavior—in other words, as a legal subterfuge. Part of this public reaction is derived from the customary practice of having the defendant produce alienists to testify on his mental condition. Since the defendant or someone interested in him must pay the fee of such a specialist, the practice tends to be discredited on the grounds that the alienist is paid *to help the defendant and not to give an honest opinion.* To a degree this belief is substantiated by the disparity in opinion existing between the alienists who testify for the state and those testifying for the defendant.

In order to minimize any tendency to give false testimony for a fee it would seem to be a far better procedure for the state to create a psychiatric board consisting of three or so members. These men should receive a stipulated sum for their services so as to preclude any basis for assuming that their testimony might be colored by financial considerations.

Under existing practices there undoubtedly have been many cases in which the plea of insanity was made in an effort to avert conviction. However, outraged legislators have enacted new laws providing for the incarceration of such persons under the special classification of "criminally insane." In place of the old policy that such persons were not guilty because insane, legal provision for another verdict arose, *viz., not guilty, but insane.* Practices in the various states have depended quite naturally upon the legislation enacted in such instances, as well as upon the folkways of local prisons and courts, all these developing with little or no actual statutory provisions. Those of us familiar with treatment of the criminally insane in our own communities ordinarily can express only chagrin for the local practices.

Since there have been no studies indicating exactly what procedures are employed in dealing with those defendants alleging insanity and those adjudged criminally insane in the United States, the author and one of her graduate students undertook the problem of ascertaining procedures for dealing with these situations in the various states some years ago. Letters requesting information were sent out to all the state prison wardens and to all state attorney generals. Approximately one-half answered the first request, one-fourth (one-half of the remaining group) the second request, and information was obtained from practically all through the third letter. All told, 47 attorney generals or state's attorneys and 48 wardens[40] reported the practices in their particular states.[41]

The need for clarification of our criminal procedure in case of alleged insanity of persons under trial has long been obvious to the criminologist and the psychiatrist. Our research made this fact doubly patent, since the prevailing practices were obviously confusing and inconsistent. Upon analysis the returns from the various state's attorneys indicated that the bases for determining sanity of the defendant in criminal cases fell into five distinct classifications.[42] (1) In certain states an ordinary jury trial was held for determining the sanity of the defendant, according to the classical test of whether the defendant knows right from wrong. Further inquiry with reference to the practices in these states, however, disclosed that the testimony of laymen and experts was given as a means of determining the defendant's mental condition. In effect, the procedure in such states did not vary markedly from (2) the procedure in those states which employed a jury trial and made the decision as to the sanity of the defendant on the basis of general evidence of competent laymen, or "expert testimony" from

[40] Two letters received were scarcely literate, embodying in themselves a commentary on penal administration and practice.

[41] These data were classified to the best of our ability. In case of any apparent inconsistency of the state's attorneys the information has been checked and rechecked. The authors accepted the statements of the attorney generals except where there seemed to be important reasons for checking with bibliographical and other sources. These data were published in the article by Mary Goshorn Williams and Mabel A. Elliott referred to in footnote 37.

[42] The data received from the state's attorneys of the several states appear to be authentic with reference to the practices of the particular states.

practicing physicians. Expert testimony was permitted but not required in this group of states. (3) In the third group of states a jury decided the mental condition of the defendant upon the evidence presented by expert testimony alone. (4) A fourth group had abolished the jury trial, and the testimony of physicians alone determined whether or not the defendant was declared insane. (5) Certain states (including some which required a jury trial and others which did not) stipulated that the expert testimony must be given by a physician who is a specialist in mental disease. (6) In two states no general procedure was required.

If we examine each of these classifications in detail we find that in group 1 the right-and-wrong test was the theoretical basis for the jury's decision in case of alleged insanity of the defendant in 14 states, viz., Arizona, Delaware, Illinois, Iowa, Maryland, Mississippi, Missouri, Nevada, New Mexico, South Dakota, Texas, West Virginia, Wisconsin, and Wyoming. This test was, however, offset by the general practice of requiring competent laymen and/or physicians to testify in these states. In no case, however, was the expert necessarily a specialist in mental disease although he occasionally was such.

Texas and several other states required expert testimony but it did not need to be that of psychiatrists. In Illinois the classical right-and-wrong test still prevailed despite the recently enacted (1943) Mental Health Act. If so desired either the state or the defendant might introduce expert testimony, but generally speaking testimony was given by persons who knew the defendant on or about the day the crime was committed.[43]

In Iowa the trial for determining the sanity of a defendant proceeded on the same basis as for any other trial, but the burden of the proof was upon the defendant. If it was determined that the defendant was insane he could not be indicted "until his reason was restored," in which event he might be returned to the custody of the court for trial. If a misdemeanant incarcerated in an Iowa jail became insane, he might be tried before a commission of insanity rather than a regular jury. In this case the medical opinion of a reputable practicing physician was required. The commission of insanity in each county was composed of three members—the clerk of the district court, a reputable physician, and a reputable attorney. It seems obvious that persons guilty of minor offenses in Iowa were thus more likely to receive intelligent disposition than those indicted for felonious offenses.

[43] Jerome Finkle, Executive Secretary of the Legislative Reference Bureau, Springfield, Illinois, correspondence dated April 20, 1944.

However, the prevailing practice in all states in group 1 failed to recognize the incompetence of many general practitioners when testifying with reference to mental disease. Most older medical men engaged in general practice have had little if any training in abnormal psychology or mental disorders. In only a few medical schools is specialization in mental disease possible, hence medical schools must bear part of the blame for the general lack of suitable standards. There actually are not enough psychiatrists to give competent testimony in the courts with reference to what constitutes insanity. In groups 2 and 3 the final decision as to the insanity of the defendant also depended upon a jury of laymen. Group 2 (which included Alabama, Idaho, Kansas, Kentucky, Montana, Nebraska, New Hampshire, Oklahoma, and Pennsylvania) comprised roughly those states which allow either general evidence upon the part of laymen or expert testimony or both. Of this group Alabama also employed the right-and-wrong test. As a matter of fact, notions of right and wrong undoubtedly color the layman's conception of the nature of insanity. If in popular parlance a man is "out of his head" the public is willing to concede that his conduct is unaccountable. Of the states in this group Pennsylvania allowed a most interesting procedure: Whenever in the course of the trial the judge believed a defendant was a mental case he might stay the trial and have the defendant examined.

The 10 states which provided for jury trial and admitted expert evidence only constituted group 4. These were Indiana, Florida, Utah, Minnesota, California, Maine, Tennessee, Virginia, Michigan, and Colorado. Two of these states, Virginia and Colorado, also authorized waiving of jury trial, unless such a trial was demanded. Kansas, which may have a jury trial with both general and expert evidence, also permitted a decision without a jury in case of expert evidence. So also did Maryland, which might also employ the right-and-wrong test with a jury trial. In addition to these 2 states which employed a nonjury trial permissively, 12 other states—Arkansas, Connecticut, Louisiana, Massachusetts, New Jersey, New York, Rhode Island, North Carolina, North Dakota, South Carolina, Vermont, and Washington—authorized a nonjury trial with only expert evidence in all such cases. Patently this was an improvement over the jury decision, but not all physicians are competent to decide such questions, as we have said.

In only 6 states—New York, South Carolina, California, Massachusetts, Arkansas, and Rhode Island (group 5)—was the physician required to be a specialist in mental disease. In Oregon and Nebraska (group 6) there was apparently no fixed rule of procedure but in practice Nebraska fell into group 2, with a jury trial determining the sanity on the basis of testimony from either laymen or reputable physicians.

A few states may have altered their legislation since this study was made, but it seems safe to assume that there have been no significant advances in the methods of determining insanity and responsibility for criminal conduct. Legal practice is largely governed by the opinions of lawyers and relatively few lawyers are interested in the area of criminal law and procedure. Many in fact pride themselves on not taking criminal cases. Thus the average lawyer is not particularly concerned with improving criminal procedure and may be considered partially to blame for the antiquated structure of criminal law.[44]

Trial by jury was itself a social invention of the first-order so far as protecting the individual was concerned. The retention of old and outmoded methods of court procedure today is unfortunate but provides the sociologist with an excellent example of cultural lag in the failure of courts to keep abreast of scientific developments.

[44] Cf. Walter Bromberg and Hervey M. Cleckley, "The Medico-Legal Dilemma," *Journal of Criminology, Criminal Law and Police Science*, 42:739–745 (March–April, 1952), for a recent criticism of existing practices.

SELECTED BIBLIOGRAPHY

Callender, Clarence N., *American Courts, Their Organization and Procedure*, McGraw-Hill, New York, 1927. This is a competent technical analysis of criminal procedure in the United States.

Cantor, Nathaniel, *Crime, Criminals and Criminal Justice*, Holt, New York, 1932, chaps. 11, 12, and 13. Excellent material on criminal procedure is provided in these chapters.

Heinberg, John A., and Breckenridge, A. C., *Law Enforcement in Missouri*, University of Missouri Studies, Columbia, Vol. XVII, No. 1. This study holds that part of the failure of the attorney general to prosecute cases more effectively stems from his numerous other duties.

Howe, Mark de Wolfe, "Juries as Judges of Criminal Law," *Harvard Law Review*, 52:582–616 (February, 1939). The difficulties entailed in having juries act as interpreters of the law are ably presented.

Moley, Raymond, "Bail Bonds," Part V of *The Missouri Crime Survey*, Macmillan, New York, 1926. This section of the survey discloses all of the devices used to defeat the effective administration of criminal justice.

Moley, Raymond, *Our Criminal Courts*, Minton, Balch, New York, 1930. This book presents a rather popular account of the operation of our courts, with all of the defects which characterize the administration of justice in America. Some of the data from the *Missouri Crime Survey* are presented.

Moley, Raymond, *Politics and Criminal Prosecution*, Minton, Balch, New York, 1929. This is an excellent presentation of the interrelationship between corrupt politics and acquittals, cases that never come up for trial, etc.

National Commission on Law Observance and Enforcement, *Report on Prosecution*, No. 4, Washington, 1931. This report gives startling evidence of ineffective prosecution practices in the United States.

Parmalee, Maurice, *Criminology*, Macmillan, New York, 1918. Chapters 17, 18, and 19 give an excellent historical background for understanding modern criminal procedure.

Pound, Roscoe, *Criminal Justice in America*, Harvard University Press, Cambridge, 1945. The former dean (now retired) of Harvard Law School writes on criminal justice with penetrating insight.

Wigmore, John H., *A Treatise on the Anglo-American System of Evidence in Trials of Common Law*, Little, Brown, Boston, 3rd ed., 1940, Vols. I–III. These volumes are considered the most scholarly treatise on the subject of evidence in Anglo-American law.

Williams, Mary Goshorn, and Elliott, Mabel A., "Court Procedure and Subsequent Treatment in Case of the Criminal Insane," *Journal of Criminal Law and Criminology*, 35:233–241 (November–December, 1944). This article summarizes a survey made of existing practices in the several states with reference to the trial of persons who are allegedly insane.

CHAPTER 21

Probation and the Suspended Sentence[1]

What Is Probation?

Some offenders are not considered to be in need of prison treatment. In fact it is a question whether any profit much from such treatment. At least it has been conclusively demonstrated that many young and first offenders will work co-operatively to prove they can be trusted never to repeat their offense, if they are only given a chance. Thus the practice has developed of giving the judge discretionary power to grant probation and suspend the sentence of certain offenders. If the person granted probation makes good, the sentence is never invoked. The threat of such a sentence hangs over the probationer's head, however, until the probation is discharged by the court. If he breaks the terms of his probation at any time during the probationary period he may be imprisoned. Probation is thus the conditional release from commitment to a penal institution, contingent upon good behavior. The sentence is said to be "suspended" and during this period the probationer is ordinarily under the supervision of a probation officer.

Unfortunately there is widespread popular confusion between the terms "probation" and "parole." Parole always refers to conditional release of the offender from prison during the unexpired term of his sentence. When a person is placed on probation he *never* serves the sentence unless his probation is revoked for failure to comply with its terms. Probation is thus a function of the court[2] whereas parole is a function of the parole board and the prison officials who recommend

[1] Mabel A. Elliott, *Conflicting Penal Theories in Statutory Criminal Law*, University of Chicago Press, Chicago, 1931, chap. 7, "Adult Probation and the Suspended Sentence."

[2] *Ibid.*, p. 132.

the parole. It may or may not be affected by the governor as the highest state official.[3] The probationer in turn is generally supervised by probation officers assigned to the court, or by some responsible lay person appointed by the court. Occasionally the probationer is merely required to report regularly to the judge so that some check can be made on his behavior, employment, and anything else which may help in his adjustment. Parole, on the other hand, is generally supervised by officers attached to the prison or by a special board created for that purpose. Parole is never a function of the court.

Antecedents of Probation

Long before there was any statutory provision for probation various methods were developed for permitting offenders to be released without suffering the full penalty of the law. Three forms of such release form the background of present-day probation:

BENEFIT OF CLERGY

The privilege accorded members of the clergy, monks, and nuns was known as "benefit of clergy" in English common law during the early Middle Ages. We mention this right later in connection with another topic. This "benefit" conferred upon members of the clergy and ecclesiastical orders the right to transfer any felonious charge made against them to the jurisdiction of the church courts. Often the church was harsh in its treatment of offenders, but since it opposed the death penalty there were many instances in which the sentence was at least less severe than death, although permanent incarceration might occur.

By the fourteenth and fifteenth centuries the benefit of clergy was extended to all secular clerks, although royal courts instead of church courts assumed jurisdiction in the case of all who were not clergy or members of ecclesiastical orders. Some have doubted whether this device had much influence on practices in the United States except that it gave a precedent for the practice of releasing prisoners without their serving sentence. Benefit of clergy is known to have been an accepted practice in colonial New England, however. It was abolished in Massachusetts because of its excessive abuse in 1784. It was not abolished in England until 1827.[4]

[3] Cf. chap. 27 for a discussion of parole.
[4] Frank W. Grinnell, "Probation as an Orthodox Common Law Practice in Massachusetts Prior to the Statutory System," *Massachusetts Law Quarterly*, 2:595 (August, 1917).

Judicial Reprieve

A reprieve is a stay of sentence and this, too, developed under English common law whenever the judge believed the verdict was unsatisfactory, the evidence questionable, etc. In such cases the convicted person might apply for either conditional or absolute freedom. Reprieves obviously were not granted on the basis of the character of the offender, but on doubt as to the validity of the conviction.

Common-Law Suspension of Sentence

Antecedent to statutory provision for probation many courts in the United States began to suspend sentences in case of young first offenders, partly, we may presume, on the basis of the reprieve practices and the benefit of clergy. Even during colonial times something like probation was permitted. Dalton's *Country Justice*, edition of 1746, mentions "granting good behavior," as it was called, as a discretionary judgment at common law in Massachusetts.[5] Previous to this, and even coexistent with the practice, penalties were often mitigated by plea of benefit of clergy as we have just mentioned.

John Augustus, First Probation Officer

It is to John Augustus, a conscientious and well-to-do Boston shoemaker, however, that we are indebted for the idea of supervision during the suspended sentence. John Augustus became interested in the plight of drunken men and wayward girls (mostly prostitutes) who were brought before the Boston Municipal Court, and in August, 1841, while an onlooker at the court he offered to bail out a man charged with being a common drunkard. The man was apparently still suffering from the effects of intoxication but in conversation with Augustus declared that if he could be saved from the House of Correction he would never taste liquor again. The old man was so earnest that he touched Augustus' sympathy and the latter asked permission to give his bond for the release of the man. This was granted with the stipulation that the man return in 3 weeks. Augustus insisted that the man sign the pledge to forgo all further consumption of liquor. The man straightened up so much within the next 3 weeks that he was scarcely recognizable. The court was pleased and fined him 1 cent and costs, an amount totaling $3.76. What is important of course is that the man continued to live an industrious, sober life.[6]

[5] P. 288, quoted by Frank W. Grinnell, op. cit.
[6] Cf. *John Augustus, First Probation Officer* (reprint of the Original Report of John

Encouraged by this man's improvement, Augustus bailed out 17 other sentenced persons before January 1, 1842. He became convinced that the only way to "save" such persons was to keep them out of houses of correction. He began to hound the courts for he was convinced that the poor and ignorant had little hope of securing justice unless an honest man stood by to see what happened. (All of this sounds very familiar—as a criticism of present-day courts.) He at first met considerable opposition since the police officers lost their fees. Sometimes the judges misinterpreted the offender's testimony and on one occasion Augustus interrupted the court to take a stand in behalf of a woman prisoner. He was rebuffed and the woman sentenced, but the matter weighed on Augustus' conscience and he resolved to help women prisoners as well as men. Soon thereafter he bailed out a drunken woman who became a valiant worker in the cause of temperance. Later he aided many other women convicted of stealing and many who were prostitutes. He was singularly successful in working with young people. He also found good homes for young girls who were in court or otherwise in difficulty. One year, in fact, he obtained temporary homes for 101 women and girls and very few of his charges were ever sent later to the House of Correction. He made thousands of calls and received many persons at his house.

Overwhelmed by the demands made upon him, he found it necessary to establish a "Temporary Home" where girls were given shelter. For others he secured hospital or other needed care. Sometimes he cared for as many as 15 in his own home. Up to 1858 Augustus had bailed out 1152 men and 794 women, most of whom he started on the road to readjustment.[7] During this time Augustus worked hard at his trade so as to make enough money to carry on his work. For 4 years he literally spent all he made at his philanthropic enterprises. Later, so many friends contributed voluntarily to his expenses that he gave up his shop to devote his whole time to work with offenders.[8]

John Augustus died in 1859 and in 1860 Rufus R. Cook, of the Boston Children's Aid Society, became the representative of the friendless at the court. He, like his predecessor, stood bail for many persons ranging in age from older adults to small children. A Boston philanthropist, Benjamin C. Clark, is said to have aided in this work.

Augustus published in Boston in 1852), National Probation Association, New York, 1939, Introduction (by Sheldon Glueck).

[7] Ibid., chap. 1, especially pp. 32–46.

[8] Anonymous, "Letter Concerning the Labors of Mr. John Augustus, The Well Known Philanthropist From One Who Knew Him," privately published, Boston, 1858, quoted in Foreword by Charles L. Clinton to John Augustus, First Probation Officer.

Finally, in 1869 visiting state agents were appointed to assist in the common-law practice of probation in Massachusetts.

The First Probation Law

It was thus more or less inevitable that statutory legislation providing for probation service should develop out of the common-law practice of suspending sentence when someone stood by to sponsor the offender. And it was altogether natural that this should be in Boston where Augustus and his successor had demonstrated that the offender may become a well-adjusted person if given suitable chance and encouragement. Hence the first statute authorizing probation was adopted in Massachusetts in 1878, but this applied only to Boston. The law gave entire discretion to the courts in using probation for both adults and minors and provided for a paid probation officer to investigate and supervise cases and make reports to the court. This was followed in 1880 by a permissory state-wide law authorizing probation for all courts in the state and imposing upon probation officers the supervision of persons released from jail as well. Part of the later confusion between probation and parole seems to be derived from this law. In 1882 Massachusetts changed the permissory law to a mandatory one and required all lower courts to appoint probation officers. These lower court officers were also employed by the higher courts until 1898, when the higher courts were empowered to appoint their own probation officers.[9]

The probation movement spread to other states, at first chiefly as a method of dealing with juveniles, however. Rhode Island, Pennsylvania, Illinois, Indiana, Minnesota, Michigan, Vermont, and Maryland adopted juvenile probation by 1900, and in 2 cities, San Francisco and Washington, D.C., it was permitted by local ordinances. Of these states only Rhode Island had adopted adult probation, by an act passed in 1899,[10] although the Vermont law, wrongly called parole, provided for adult probation.[11] Missouri also instituted a practice known as "bench parole" during this period. It was actually probation, but because of the misleading terminology Missouri was often not credited with having a probation law. This statute (1897) provided that the

[9] Nicholas S. Timasheff, *One Hundred Years of Probation, 1841–1941*, Fordham University Press, New York, 1941, pp. 18–19. Cf. also Mabel A. Elliott, *op. cit.*, pp. 133–134.

[10] Mabel A. Elliott, *op. cit.* Juvenile probation spread with the development of the juvenile court since probation was basic to the juvenile court idea.

[11] Nicholas S. Timasheff, *op. cit.*, p. 19.

courts might allow any offender under 25 years of age to go at large (except in case of murder or robbery). Such a person was required to appear at court and furnish evidence of having complied with the conditions of his "parole" (*which was probation*).[12]

Most of the statutory legislation providing for adult probation has thus been enacted since the turn of the century. In fact much of it was enacted after 1916. Earlier many judges employed the probationary idea in suspending sentences and putting offenders on good behavior without any statutory provision for doing so. The initial Massachusetts law differed from the laws which developed in other states in providing for the suspension of imposition of sentence. This was later made optional in 1900. The judge either could impose a sentence and "suspend" it or could forbear imposing any sentence during good behavior. In this provision the courts were of course assuming some of the governor's executive prerogatives of reprieve. Considerable confusion arose and many legal authorities held that the judge was assuming an unwarranted executive authority in granting reprieves. The United States Supreme Court thus ruled in the Killits case in 1916 that federal judges might use judicial discretion in temporary reprieves but that they had no authority to suspend a sentence permanently. In fact such discretion was characterized as tantamount to refusing to enforce the law.[13]

This decision immediately precipitated the enactment of federal and additional state legislation which specifically granted judges the power to put prisoners on probation and suspend their sentences.[14] Actually the legislation in many states merely gave legal status to existing practices (a fact which is sociologically significant in characterizing much social legislation, we might point out).

In consequence of the legal reasoning in the Killits case it might be equally well alleged that legislatures, rather than judges, were assuming executive authority in passing the law. This legal logic actually prevented the development of suspended-sentence laws in a number of states.[15] In 1925, after considerable effort, a bill was passed by Congress authorizing a federal probation system. Initially this was under the Bureau of Prisons, but in 1941 it was attached to the Administrative Office of the United States Courts.[16]

[12] *Ibid.*, p. 21.

[13] *Ex Parte*, United States, 242 U.S. 27 (1916), cited in *The Attorney General's Survey of Release Procedures*, Vol. II, *Probation*, U.S. Department of Justice, Washington, 1939, pp. 9 and 10.

[14] *Ibid.*, p. 10.   [15] *Ibid.*, pp. 11–15.

[16] Helen D. Pigeon, *Probation and Parole*, National Probation Association, New York, 1942, p. 88.

Extent of Present Probation Provisions

Today adult probation legislation is in effect in all states except Mississippi, Nevada, New Mexico, Oklahoma (in the 2 largest counties, those in which Tulsa and Oklahoma City are located, there are probation laws, however), and South Dakota.[17] In 25 states in which there was information great variation existed in the extent to which probationary treatment was given to prisoners, as Table 21.1 shows. In Rhode Island, 64.6 per cent of prisoners were put on probation in 1945, whereas only 13 per cent were granted probation in Iowa. New Hampshire placed 49.8 per cent on probation and the majority of states employed probation in from 25 to 40 per cent of the cases.

Probation Is Not Parole

Probation and parole have much in common but they are not the same as we have already mentioned. Probation is conditional release by the court from carrying out the sentence. The probationer is under supervision with the sentence suspended during his good behavior. Parole is conditional release from prison after part of the sentence has been served. The parolee is likewise presumably supervised until his sentence expires, depending on his good behavior.

Probation and parole are alike in that the offender is presumably a person who can be trusted to make good if supervised. Probation, as it is in force in the several states and under the Federal Probation System, is usually extended to first or young offenders. The probationer usually lives with his family and often returns to his customary work. All of the pre-sentence investigation, if any, in case of the probationer is made by the probation officer, who works out his plan with the probationer on his interpretation of the total picture as he sees it. He, in fact, often makes the recommendation for placing the offender on probation. On the other hand many judges are erratic and impulsive in placing offenders on probation and thus make the probation officer's job more difficult.

The parole officer has all the accumulated information of the record which was placed before the parole authority before parole was granted. The parolee is often hardened by his prison experience, and skeptical and cynical about the motivations of parole officers. Nevertheless he is accustomed to discipline and on the surface, at least, is willing to accept it.

[17] Information obtained from Sol Rubin, Legal Consultant to the National Probation and Parole Association, correspondence dated July 31, 1950.

TABLE 21.1. Type of Sentence Imposed on Defendants Convicted of Major Offenses, by States, 1945

State	Defendants Convicted and Sentenced	Prison or Reformatory		Probation or Suspended Sentence		Local Jail or Workhouse		Other Sentence	
		Number	Per Cent	Number	Per Cent	Number	Per Cent	Number	Per Cent
Total, 25 states	43,290	16,913[a]	39.1	13,697	31.6	9,034	20.9	3,646	8.4
California	7,088	2,026	28.6	2,326	32.8	2,144	30.2	592	8.4
Colorado	740	57	61.8	220	29.7	36	4.9	27	3.6
Connecticut[b]	921	324	35.2	256	27.8	310	33.7	31	3.4
District of Columbia	956	471	49.3	303	31.7	168	17.6	14	1.5
Idaho	234	123	52.6	67	28.6	29	12.4	15	6.4
Iowa	1,110	484	43.6	144	13.0	286	25.8	196	17.7
Kansas	730	473	64.8	166	22.7	82	11.2	9	1.2
Massachusetts	2,147	1,171[c]	54.5	580	27.0	—	—	396	18.4
Minnesota	821	386	47.0	316	38.5	91	11.1	28	3.4
Montana	207	146	70.5	47	22.7	7	3.4	7	3.4
New Hampshire	235	80	34.0	117	49.8	29	12.3	9	3.8
New Jersey	3,269	1,390	42.5	1,101	33.7	437	13.4	341	10.4
New Mexico	444	272	61.3	114	25.7	24	5.4	34	7.7
New York	5,395	2,120	39.3	1,867	34.6	1,347	25.0	61	1.1
North Dakota	217	103	47.5	34	15.7	53	24.4	27	12.4
Ohio	2,920	1,368	46.8	1,248	42.7	236	8.1	68	2.3
Oregon	533	271	50.8	197	37.0	45	8.4	20	3.8
Pennsylvania	7,725	1,384	17.9	2,083	27.0	3,192	41.3	1,066	13.8
Rhode Island	457	69	15.1	295	64.6	84	18.4	9	2.0
South Dakota	206	120	58.3	40	19.4	33	16.0	13	6.3
Texas	3,546	2,273	64.1	908	25.6	78	2.2	287	8.1
Utah	224	139	62.1	66	29.5	17	7.6	2	0.9
Washington	1,121	536	47.8	442	39.4	101	9.0	42	3.7
Wisconsin	1,847	603	32.6	705	38.2	197	10.7	342	18.5
Wyoming	197	124	62.9	55	27.9	8	4.1	10	5.1

[a] Includes 42 death sentences.
[b] Statistics are for the year July 1, 1945, through June 30, 1946.
[c] Includes defendants sentenced to local jail or workhouse, or to an institution for juvenile delinquents only.

Source: Table 4, Judicial Criminal Statistics, 1945, Summary, Series G-14, No. 76, Bureau of the Census, U.S. Department of Commerce, Washington, p. 5.

Probationers are usually easier to handle, if only for the reason that most of them are very anxious to avoid having to go to jail or prison. They are less likely to be seasoned criminals, less likely to have engaged in criminal careers before coming to trial. At the same time both parole and probation involve helping men who have broken the law to become adjusted to law-abiding community living. Probation usually involves fewer restrictions. Charles H. Z. Meyer says parole is delayed action in releasing the offender, whereas the probationer is not ordinarily removed from the community.[18] In any case the work of supervising such men has so much in common that the National Probation Association extended its membership and became the National Probation and Parole Association in 1947.[19]

Probation Is a Privilege and Not a Right

No person before the bar is automatically entitled to probation, even though certain factors such as youth, good previous record, good family, and others may indicate a favorable prognosis. Whether or not probation is extended rests with the judge to decide. Juries sometimes recommend probation or in nonjury cases the judge may simply decide to give the person a chance on his own.

Factors Determining Probation

Age, type of offense, and standing of the convicted person's family usually have much to do with whether or not probation is granted. That is, young persons who come from highly respected families are very likely to be granted probation if tried and convicted of misdemeanors. Such young persons may also be dismissed without trial. When a respectable person intercedes for the offender and offers to become his sponsor in the community, the chances that probation will be granted are also increased. When a father has children and a wife to support the judge may release him because he knows his dependents will suffer if he is committed to prison. Judges unquestionably try to act wisely but often have little background or training to enable them to predict the probationer's success or failure. There seems to be no doubt that position and status in the community are factors in increasing the offender's chances for probation.

[18] Cf. Charles H. Z. Meyer, "How Do Probationers and Parolees Differ?" *National Probation Association Yearbook*, 1946, New York, 1947, pp. 163–178.

[19] Cf. Foreword, *National Probation and Parole Association Yearbook*, 1947, New York, 1948.

Probation is often regarded as leniency because it is alleged that the probationer does not suffer much for his offense. This is not exactly the case. The probationer is required to prove himself by conformity to the stipulations which are entailed in granting probation; and he is ordinarily placed under the supervision and guidance of a probation officer. It is true, however, that when the offender is placed on probation he does not suffer the same stigma as when he is committed to prison. There is no denying that public attitudes toward the probationer are far more favorable than those toward the convict. Thus the probationer keeps his self-respect because he believes himself to have been regarded as worthy of probation. This attitude in itself is very significant and undoubtedly is to a major degree responsible for the high percentage of successful adjustments among probationers. It is probably the clue to all successful adjustment. The individual has to believe that he is going to be successful before he is able to make the effort to go straight. A man who is convinced he is a derelict, an enemy of society, is likely to prove it in his own conduct.

The Protective Aspect of Probation

It is obvious enough that society should protect itself by putting the dangerous offender where he can be kept from harming members of the community, but the vast majority of offenders are in no sense great social hazards. Furthermore it would be completely impossible to incarcerate every offender. Yet the judge must do something with the guilty person. Quite aside from its rehabilitative aspects probation is the best answer thus far devised for dealing with first offenders who are no great danger to society.[20]

Placing such offenders under the disciplinary supervision of a probation officer is thus a practical social device. It is far better than turning them loose on their own. It is much less expensive than imprisonment. What is more important, probation is a great deal more satisfactory than any other treatment so far as the percentage of success is concerned.

The Public and Probation

There is little public understanding of probation work. The public is interested chiefly in apprehending and convicting offenders. Whatever follows is probably too good for the criminal, in the public's esti-

[20] Sanford Bates, *Protection as a Penal Policy*, U.S. Department of Justice, Washington, 1936, pp. 1–2.

mate, and probation is usually regarded as so much softhearted leniency. It is therefore incumbent on the probation officer to interpret his job to the public. There may be few thrills in probation work but there is drama, pathos, and human interest. The probation officer arouses the co-operation of the probationer through appealing to a child's trust, a woman's interest or religious faith, etc. Of course, effective probation entails much more than this, and making the public realize something of the fine achievements of probation workers would do much to stem the criticism of probation work.[21]

Should Parole and Probation Supervision Be Combined?

Because both probation and parole are concerned with the adjustment of offenders, many people have urged that these services be combined. As a matter of fact, the Federal Probation Service has combined them, as have several of the states. There are, however, good arguments for separating them. In the first place the attitudes and behavior patterns of the probationer (because of the basis of determining probationers) are less distorted than are those of the average parolee. The National Commission on Law Observance and Enforcement has pointed out the essential differences involved in the two services. A parolee has built up a system of habits in prison which make for difficulties in readjustment when he is released. Everything the prisoner does is regulated by rigid rules, as we discuss in Chapter 24. The prisoner has come to regard himself as a convict or common criminal. All of his associates are criminals, and all his loyalties during his prison term are directed toward the group which is undergoing punishment.

The probationer, on the other hand, has not oriented his loyalties to an antisocial group. He is still habituated toward family and institutional controls, which exert a wholesome effect on his everyday existence. If his boss will give him a chance he may even be allowed to keep his old job. Indeed, "Every contact, interest, emotion and habit which can be utilized to keep the individual's relations with his community within the expected norm come automatically into play and become powerful factors, straightening the individual's habit patterns back to normal."[22]

Because of existing social attitudes, parolees inevitably bear much

[21] Cf. Patrick T. Stone, "The Public Is Very Much in the Dark About Probation Work," *Federal Probation*, 12:7–9 (December, 1948).

[22] Cf. National Commission on Law Observance and Enforcement, Report No. 9, *Penal Institutions and Parole*, Washington, 1931, pp. 147–149. Cf. also Joseph P. Murphy, "Shall Probation and Parole Be Combined?" *National Probation Association Yearbook, 1940*, New York, 1940, pp. 239–253.

greater public stigma and public resentment than do probationers. As students of criminology we may and do deplore this stigma, but as realists we must recognize it. Eventually the services may be suitably combined, but since so many parolees exhibit habit patterns of confirmed criminals it is doubtful if identical techniques can ever be employed for both services.[23] The type of offenders will continue to be different. Most probationers are either minor offenders or juveniles.[24] Parolees are usually major offenders or persons with a previous record. Of course the offense in itself is no index to the offender's personality, but public reaction toward the offense complicates the parolee's personality and makes his social adjustment more difficult.

There is, however, one excellent argument for combining probation and parole. The decision to place the offender under probation is a judicial prerogative and the probationer is ordinarily supervised in the local community. Parole, on the other hand, is a prerogative of a parole board, which is an agency of the state with a state-wide service so far as prisoners are concerned. Since parole is a wider service than probation, parole officers are more likely to be professionally trained for their work than is the average probation officer. Consequently, there is often no adult probation officer attached to a court and frequently the probation service amounts to little more than reporting to the sheriff, clerk of courts, or some similar person. Occasionally the judge places the probationer under the sponsorship of some trusted business or professional man who stands ready to vouch for him. Such a sponsor may be well intentioned, but often he possesses little of the insight and understanding necessary to secure effective co-operation from the probationer. Because parole officers usually serve a larger territory and work full time at their profession, higher standards of personnel are easier to maintain.

It is certain that both probation and parole officers need all the skills possible in order to succeed at their task. There are times, moreover, when a combination of services has definite advantages as in the case of probationers who violate their probation, then are committed to prison and later are on parole. Since relatively few probationers fail, as we have already made clear, this is not a very significant argument, but it does lend weight to the proposal for combining services. Walter C. Reckless, well-known American criminologist has developed this argument favoring such a combination.[25]

[23] Joseph P. Murphy, op. cit.   [24] Ibid.
[25] Cf. Walter C. Reckless, "The Democracy of Probation and Parole," National Probation Association Yearbook, 1945, New York, 1946, pp. 99–111.

Techniques in probation work have developed through trial and error, hunches, precepts, and common sense. Research has been slow, partly because of the lack of well-trained sociologists and psychologists working in the probation field. The probation officers themselves have been confronted with the necessity of working out some plan for the probationer. When, through the grace of God, his own increased maturity and insight, or the help and skill of the probation officer, the probationer conforms to the rules of the probationary period his probation is adjudged successful. Needless to say the probation officer is not entitled to take all of the credit. That the probationer is required to conform or have his sentence imposed may be the compelling cause of his good behavior. There is still much room for scientific study in the field of probation. Most probation work has been carried on in the dark.

For effective research in probation, good case records are imperative; so are suitable mechanical devices for conducting statistical research. We need, then, persons adequately trained for gathering, analyzing, and interpreting statistical data. Often persons who are skilled in probation (or parole) work are not trained in research. Nevertheless the probation officer must be available for consultation and interpretation of the data in case records. Sometimes follow-up surveys must be made and probation officers will give many leads as to where ex-probationers can be located. A variety of checks on probationers' present whereabouts may be necessary in order to secure the necessary information.

Qualifications for Probation Officers

Successful probation workers require qualities which are hard to measure. As the committee appointed by the Chief Justice of the United States points out, the two most important qualities of a probation officer are intelligent understanding and devotion to his work.[26] The probation officer requires special abilities in interviewing and eliciting facts, in weighing statements, and in sizing up both individuals and situations. He must be able to formulate his investigation of the case in a clear, concise report. His perception and insight will come partly from experience and partly from his understanding of the mainsprings of human behavior. The probation officer must be kindly in his attitude but know also that it is well-nigh fatal to be naïve. His de-

[26] Cf. "Report of the Committee on Standards of Qualifications of Probation Officers," *Federal Probation*, 6:3–7 (October–December, 1942).

votion to his work must enable him to work beyond the line of duty and after hours, for delinquency problems do not conform to an 8-hour day.

In addition to these special attributes of personality, the probation officer should meet certain educational and other standards. The Committee on Standards of Qualification for Probation Officers recommends that he have a college degree, preferably with training in the social sciences and at least 2 years' experience in welfare work or 2 years' training in a school of social service or in professional social work. He should also be of exemplary character, in good health, and between the ages of 24 and 45 at the time of appointment. Appointments for fledgling probation officers should be made on a trial basis for 6 months, the appointments to become permanent if the trial period is satisfactory.[27]

These, obviously, should be the minimum standards of probation officers and are so regarded by professional workers. Unfortunately most probation officers in rural counties cannot meet them.

The Probation Function in Relation to the Court

In many jurisdictions the court has some supervisory authority over probation. There has been a general tendency, however, for the states to set up boards which control probation, or to place probation under state welfare departments. Probation officers are not concerned so much with interpretation of the law as with the adjustment of the individual, and the trend has been more and more toward regarding probation as social work. Not all judges are in accord with this trend; in fact many of them bitterly oppose the encroaching authority of social workers who seem to the judges to be pre-empting their judicial function.

Eventually, perhaps, judges, along with social workers and criminologists, will come to think of the criminals as maladjusted persons needing all the help that specialists in case work and psychology can give. Judges, as we have noted elsewhere, often assume an omniscience for which their training has not prepared them. They also resent, as an attack on the dignity of their office, having their prerogatives taken from them. At the National Conference on Probation and Parole in Pittsburgh in May, 1950, for example, many judges expressed their growing displeasure at having social workers tell them how to dispose of cases.

[27] Ibid.

The Administration of Probation

Part of the administration of probation is contingent upon the rules affecting eligibility which we have discussed in a preceding section. The *Attorney General's Survey of Release Procedures* indicates that there is no significant relationship between type of offense and behavior on probation[28]—hence most of the eligibility rules based on offense may be said to hamper effective use of the probationary idea.

Three general types of organization have developed to take care of probation. The first is the local administration under the jurisdiction of the courts. The second is some form of state-wide authority for supervising probation. In general a state-wide probation department is a part of the state welfare department—or a state department of correction. A third trend has been to combine the probation and parole departments under a single head. The federal probation and parole systems have been combined since 1930, as we have mentioned.

Pennsylvania's probation service is organized on a district court basis, although there is a state-wide system of parole. There are 58 judicial districts in the state, all but 6 of which coincide with county boundaries. Five districts are composed of 2 counties, and 1 district encompasses 3 counties. As might be expected the widest use of probation is in the 2 metropolitan judicial districts, Philadelphia County and Allegheny County (Pittsburgh). Of 421 paid probation officers in the state, 272 are attached to the courts in these 2 counties. In 45 upstate counties there are only 149 full-time probation officers and in 20 counties there are either no probation officers or only part-time officers. These rural counties rely heavily on volunteer service for particular cases.

The inadequacy of the part-time probation service may be indicated in the salary contrasts, although salary scales for probation officers in large Pennsylvania cities are lower than in large cities in other states. In 1947, for example, a total of $1,156,491 was paid to full-time probation officers, whereas only $11,394 was spent in salaries for part-time officers. Case loads are far too high in Pennsylvania (the average case load is 98.5 persons, compared to a standard load for case workers of 50). On the other hand, federal probation service loads are slightly higher (99) than the Pennsylvania case load. It is suggested that when the number of cases in one county is too low to warrant hiring a well-

[28] *Attorney General's Survey of Release Procedures*, p. 123.

trained probation officer, several counties might suitably co-operate in a joint service.[29]

In general the supervision of children and young persons on probation is better than that of adults in upstate counties in Pennsylvania. However, frequently no home visits at all are made in the case of boys.[30] State supervision of probation services would undoubtedly improve the probation work in the rural counties of Pennsylvania or any other state.

Personnel Standards for Probation Officers

Most early probation officers, like John Augustus, volunteered their services. When probation was authorized by statutory provision, volunteers were replaced by paid officers in the larger cities. In smaller communities volunteers still serve in many courts, or the pay of the probation officer is so low as to constitute "a token payment." Some states, including Michigan, New Jersey, New York, Rhode Island, and Wisconsin, as well as the District of Columbia, have state civil service requirements for probation officers. Several other states, Pennsylvania and Illinois, for example, have civil service requirements for probation officers in the larger cities. But the majority of courts in these states are required merely to appoint discreet persons of good character. Since probation work is now regarded as highly skilled case work, it is to be hoped that standards for probation officers can soon be raised for all courts.[31]

What the Probation Officer's Job Entails

It is self-evident that a probation officer needs professional training in social work, which has emphasized rehabilitative work with offenders. On the job he must recognize the importance of studying the community or territory under his jurisdiction. This in turn involves some knowledge of the economic base of the community, the opportunities for job placement, the status of organized labor, and similar matters. The probation officer must establish effective working relationships with local social agencies. The recreational facilities must be explored. Obviously what the probationer does in his leisure time is

[29] Leon T. Stern, *Probation Service in Pennsylvania* (pamphlet), Pennsylvania Committee on Penal Affairs of the Public Charities Association for the Pennsylvania Association on Probation and Parole, Philadelphia, 1948.

[30] *Ibid.*

[31] Helen D. Pigeon, *op. cit.*, pp. 93–94, and Leon T. Stern, *op. cit.*

often the key to his subsequent adjustment and frequently few wholesome recreational opportunities are open to him. If the probationer has a health problem it must be referred to the proper authorities.

The probation officer must take an objective attitude toward delinquency and recognize that delinquency or criminal behavior is often symptomatic of some deep-seated psychological or social need of the client. Effective training of the probationer must give him the techniques for meeting life situations. Probation work is thus as broad as the range of human personalities and as deep as the mysteries of human conduct.[32]

In-Service Training

Since so many probation officers are untrained and even the trained social worker may be uninformed about certain aspects of his job, in-service training is an important adjunct to successful probation work. In fact nearly all beginners in probation work need some further orientation in their tasks during the first weeks of their appointment. The novitiate should have some experienced officer for a mentor who can point out helpful methods of meeting the clients' needs. New probation officers should be instructed in methods of conducting interviews with relatives, employers, and the probationer. Group meetings in which probation officers discuss techniques and methods of dealing with specific situations are desirable. Three months of such intern type of training will give the newly inducted probation officer much insight into suitable methods to be employed.[33]

Later the intern probation officer will attend staff meetings which may be turned to educational account. One of the staff may present a case, for example, after which there is a general discussion directed by a staff member. Occasionally an outside speaker may give a lecture or a special research topic may be presented. In any event the staff meetings should aim always to be stimulating and helpful.

For advanced workers a university-sponsored training program for a period of a week or two will probably prove most helpful. Here workers may share their experiences, and outstanding authorities may be secured as lecturers and discussion leaders. Short conferences and institutes in connection with either educational institutions or state conferences of social work should be helpful. When workers return to

[32] Cf. "Report on the Committee on Standards of Qualifications of Probation Officers," *op. cit.*

[33] Charles H. Z. Meyer, "Inservice Training Programs," *National Probation Association Yearbook, 1945,* New York, 1946, pp. 263–276.

their own groups they should be asked to present any ideas gleaned from their study to the local group.[34]

Special Types of Probationers

Probationers, like all offenders, are a widely varied group of persons. They may include alcoholics, deserting husbands, sex offenders, embezzlers, and hit-and-run drivers. As such, these offenders need the special kind of help which their particular case requires. We shall present a few well-known types.

THE ALCOHOLIC

The alcoholic who is placed on probation presents certain special problems of re-education. The true alcoholic must learn to give up alcohol completely and the probation officer must help him do so. For medical reasons which are not completely understood the alcoholic cannot drink moderately. He cannot drink without drinking to excess. He must be educated to accept the fact of this disability and to forgo alcohol altogether.

If other members of the family are alcoholic the alcoholic probationer should be removed from his home environment. If he is married, the full support of his wife in enforcing complete abstinence must be secured. The group help of Alcoholics Anonymous may be enlisted. The members of Alcoholics Anonymous have gone through similar difficulties and stand ready to help one in need of assistance. Many distinguished and able people have become interested in the A.A. through their own need for help in fighting alcoholism. This group also extends a sympathetic social acceptance toward others who are fighting the habit and this in itself may be of psychological value to the offender.[35] They approach the problem from the point of view of persons who know the difficulty but have conquered it. They are in a sense a primary group who are able to induce a person like themselves to become socially well adjusted. They understand and "stand by" instead of condemning when the alcoholic "slips" or is on the verge of "slipping."[36]

Alcoholism, like so many behavior deviations, is symptomatic of some other deeper-lying problem. The alcoholic is trying to escape

[34] *Ibid.* Cf. also Louis J. Sharp, "In-Service Training in Probation and Parole, "*Federal Probation,* 15:25–30 (December, 1951).

[35] Cf. Selden Bacon, "Special Problems of the Adult Offender," *National Probation Association Yearbook, 1944,* New York, 1945, pp. 209–234.

[36] *Ibid.*

from a sense of inadequacy. This may be inadequacy on the job, inadequacy in his social role, inadequacy as a father, sexual inadequacy as a husband. If the probation officer is to help the probationer he must get at the source of the difficulty.[37]

THE NARCOTIC ADDICT

The narcotic addict on probation has peculiar difficulties. The mere use of narcotics obtained without a physician's prescription makes the addict a criminal in the eyes of the law. There are criminals with a long record of serious offenses who are addicts, and there are the big-time "dope peddlers." These persons are usually committed to prison. The addict who is merely an addict may be considered a safe person to be treated by probation. Ordinarily the addict should be hospitalized as a part of his probationary treatment. Since his particular difficulty is his addiction the hospital must co-operate in any plan for the probationer's release. A drug addict frequently relapses after release from a narcotic hospital but should not therefore be sent to prison or jail. He should be returned to the hospital for further treatment.

The personality of the narcotic addict must be built up until he is strong enough to resist temptation. The narcotic faces social opprobrium and the probation officer has to extend the probationer support—if he does not fall into the habit again. The drug addict is a sick person; so far as possible he should be treated as one in need of medical and psychological help.[38]

THE PSYCHOPATHIC OFFENDER

Many offenders have queer personalities or "psychopathic egos," to use Dr. Banay's expression. These persons tend to regard themselves as beyond the rule of law. Often they need institutionalization, but many can be helped to face reality better outside of prisons than inside. Frequently well-to-do women are kleptomaniacs; they steal clothes for which they have no need. Psychiatric help is paramount if they are to be retained within the community. Sometimes such persons are epileptic, even though their physical difficulties are of the petit mal variety and therefore not discernible to the layman. Suitable treatment may enable some of these to take their places in society.[39]

[37] Cf. Robert V. Seliger, "Alcohol and the Probationer," *National Probation Association Yearbook*, 1945, New York, 1946, pp. 148–156.

[38] J. D. Richard, "The Role of the Probation Officer in the Treatment of Drug Addiction," *Federal Probation*, 6:15–20 (October–December, 1942).

[39] Cf. Ralph S. Banay, "Therapeutic Experiences with Adult Offenders," *National Probation Association Yearbook*, 1944, New York, 1945, pp. 235–244.

THE MENTALLY DEFICIENT PROBATIONER

The probation (or parole) of the mentally deficient person involves serious difficulties. The feeble-minded person is more suggestible and gullible and is likely to become the tool of clever lawbreakers. Supervision of the mentally low-grade person must obviously be geared to the mental level of the probationer, as well as to the situation in which he is placed. He must therefore be handled very directly; he must also be made to understand the importance of consulting with persons of integrity when confronted with important decisions.

Mentally deficient male probationers are usually placed at physical labor. Women must be placed where there is no great sex temptation since feeble-minded women and girls have little resistance to propositions of an illicit nature. Careful drilling of the feeble-minded both in the nature of the work required of them in job placements and in meeting specific temptations will be the most helpful type of training.[40]

THE CONSCIENTIOUS OBJECTOR

The conscientious objector, as we have discussed in an earlier chapter, poses many questions not involved in ordinary criminal behavior.[41] During World War II a sizable number of conscientious objectors were arrested for refusing to register for the draft for military service. Some courts refused to place such persons on probation in any case; in other instances the conscientious objectors were unwilling to accept probation.

Where the courts refused to place the "C.O.'s" on probation the judges often alleged that probation assumes both that reformation of the offender is possible and that he will make a conscious attempt to conform, whereas this group refused to consider reformation. Nevertheless the 1925 Federal Probation Act in force during World War II held merely that the important considerations were "that the ends of justice and the best interests of the public as well as the defendant will be subserved" by extending probation. The National Service Board for Religious Objectors contended therefore that conscientious objectors were entitled to probation because of the discretionary nature of probation.[42]

[40] Lloyd N. Yepsen, "The Mentally Deficient Probationer and Parolee," *Federal Probation*, 6:30–33 (October–December, 1942).

[41] Cf. "The Conscientious Objector," in chap. 7.

[42] William E. Rostron, Jr., "Conscientious Objectors and Probation" (Letter to the Editor), *Federal Probation*, 13:51 (June, 1949).

Actually conscientious objectors are employing freedom of conscience to disavow their willingness to enter military service and constitutionally they are guaranteed that right. But the facts of social opinion, the nature of modern war compared to war in the eighteenth century, the increase of conscientious objections based on philosophical rather than religious convictions have led to a variety of legal interpretations dependent chiefly upon the philosophical attitudes of the judges trying the cases.

OTHER TYPES

In addition to those just listed we may recognize several other varieties of probationers. These are:

1. The accidental offender who is so humiliated by the fact of his arrest that no further supervision is needed. This person will make every effort to be law abiding by himself.
2. The sharp businessman who seized an illegal opportunity to make big money quickly. This man will more than likely be bitter and think he merely got caught at a widespread practice in the economic world.
3. The unadjusted immigrant or newcomer who is in difficulty chiefly because he fails to understand local attitudes and customs. His problem is primarily one of education in the local mores.
4. The underprivileged youth whose whole story may be written in the word "deprivation" and who needs education in the importance of our property laws. He may also need a job or more training which will enable him to earn for himself the object or objects of his desire.
5. The overly privileged, pampered person who needs to prove himself through the acceptance of responsibility. Placing this type of probationer at a job where he must assume orderly work habits may accomplish wonders in reorienting him toward his own responsibilities as a citizen.

Probation Work Must Utilize Other Agencies

Part of the demand for a state-wide probation and parole authority has arisen out of the need for co-ordinating work with various institutions, various social agencies, and the courts. Often the exchange of records is necessary. This is facilitated if all probation records are filed with one state agency and are readily available to workers who need to consult them throughout the state. Often probationers come from families who are known to social agencies. Sometimes they have moved from one county to another. The development of a well-organized administration of probation (and parole) is never an end in itself, however. It is merely a means toward more effective treatment of the offender.[43]

Probation as Social Work

Although some judges and some probation officers are unwilling to regard probation as social work, this fact may be regarded as an indication that they are ignorant of the nature of social work or have been conditioned against it for some reason. Certainly they are lagging behind the current conceptions of the best probation work. Apparently they fail to understand what social work is, namely, helping the individual adjust to his environment, and instead believe social workers are a combination of "do-gooders" and "professional snoopers."

The intake procedure for probationers is involuntary. Thus there are certain distinctions between the relation of the probation officer to the client and the relationship between the social case worker and the client. That is, the probationer does not ask for help, as do most social welfare clients. The probationer has help thrust upon him. This unquestionably contributes to the difficulties of probation work. But probation is social work nevertheless and the competent probation officer must utilize all the skills of case work in helping the probationer help himself to become a well-adjusted person.

Psychiatry and the Probationer

Some probationers are also in need of psychiatric assistance. Whenever the basic problem of the probationer is essentially a matter of his personality maladjustment and of emotional conflict, psychiatry or the techniques and insights of psychiatry are helpful and should be employed. This statement does not mean, as the majority of psychiatrists apparently believe, that psychiatry is essential to the adjustment of all who indulge in antisocial conduct or have emotional disturbances. Many probationers make an effective adjustment without long and skillful prodding into the recesses of their unconscious or the forgotten

[43] Cf. Marietta Stevenson, "Probation and Parole in Relation to the State Public Welfare System," *National Probation Association Yearbook,* 1941, New York, 1942, pp. 55–74.

experiences of their childhood. Many personality difficulties may be adjusted through the sympathetic understanding of the probation officer and the probationer's own good sense.

The Painful Aspects of Probation

Being on probation is a painful experience to the average probationer because it is tangible evidence of his having offended the criminal law. The probation officer must recognize this and make a special effort to put himself in the position of his charge. He must take a kindly attitude toward the probationer's shortcomings. In many economic crimes the probationer is required to make restitution to the person who suffered the loss. Some probation officers err in attempting to enforce a rigid time limit in such restitution. They must always take into consideration the capacity of the offender to meet the goals laid down. Otherwise the probationer may become bitter and non-cooperative. A plan which makes allowances for the limitations of the probationer, on the other hand, will usually prove satisfactory.[44]

Success on Probation

There has been much controversy over the question of the success of probation in recent years. Many studies have seemed to show that probation was nearly 75 per cent effective insofar as records indicated no serious infractions of probationary regulations. Frederick A. Moran, for example, in a survey of probation in New York State in 1923 maintained that of 139,948 adult men and women on probation during the 14 years 1907–1921, 107,695 or 77 per cent were discharged with improvement, 9076 or 6.5 per cent were discharged without improvement, 13,449 or 9.7 per cent were committed to institutions, and 9698 or 6.8 per cent absconded. Among children the percentage of those who were discharged with improvement was even higher. Of 66,350 children on probation during these years 54,244 or 81.7 per cent were discharged with improvement, 2627 or 4 per cent were discharged without improvement, 9081 or 13.7 per cent were committed to institutions, and 398 or 0.6 per cent absconded.[45]

The *Attorney General's Survey of Release Procedures* studied 19,256 cases in 25 probation districts in 16 states and the District of Colum-

---

[44] Irving E. Cohen, "Probation as Social Case Work Process," *National Probation Association Yearbook*, 1945, New York, 1946, pp. 207–216.

[45] Frederick A. Moran, *Probation in New York State*, New York State Probation Commission, Albany, 1923, pp. 17–18.

bia. This study revealed 61 per cent to have no recorded violations, whereas 7544 or 39 per cent had violated the terms of their probations. Of these, 3497 or 18 per cent committed new crimes and 4047 or 21 per cent violated the probation regulations. In 12 per cent of the cases the violations by new offenses resulted in revocation of probation and in 7 per cent of the cases the violations of rules of probation resulted in such revocation.[46]

Offsetting these figures the research of the Gluecks presents some disturbing conclusions. They studied 1000 delinquent boys over 3 successive 5-year periods. During these 15 years all boys were on probation at some time. In 56.9 per cent of the cases the boys always failed on probation when all their violations were made known; 20.3 per cent were completely successful; and 22.8 per cent were partially successful but had some violations.[47] A study by the same authors of 500 criminal men carried over 15 years found nearly all, 92.4 per cent, were failures on probation.[48] These men may have been failures on probation, but they were also persons who had served reformatory and prison sentences. One cannot very well argue from the failures that the failures will fail! Those never committed to prison are a better sample.

Nevertheless the Gluecks' study of adult criminals indicates that probation is often extended to persons who are bad risks. The whole problem of probation obviously demands further study. At the same time probation seems to offer the best hope of putting an offender in a position where he will exert his best efforts to prove his capacity to become a law-abiding citizen.

Elio D. Monachesi in his study of factors in probation success concluded that those who come from favorable social backgrounds and have had no previous criminal record are the most successful on probation. Where factors of previous criminality, low economic status, poor work record, low occupational level, bad neighborhood, bad family history, continual mobility, and irregular contact with school and church apply, the violation rates are high.[49] The best probationers thus seem to be the accidental criminals—the persons who shouldn't have committed crimes in the first place. Or, if the research of Porterfield and others is correct, persons from this type of background fre-

---

[46] Attorney General's Survey of Release Procedures, Vol. II, Probation, pp. 335–337.
[47] Sheldon and Eleanor T. Glueck, Juvenile Delinquents Grown Up, Commonwealth Fund, New York, 1940, pp. 201–203.
[48] Sheldon and Eleanor T. Glueck, Criminal Careers in Retrospect, Commonwealth Fund, New York, 1943, p. 151.
[49] Elio D. Monachesi, Prediction Factors in Probation, Sociological Press, Hanover, New Hampshire, 1932, pp. 50–64.

quently are not brought before the court. They represent the opinion-making members of society and it is probably much easier to get them to conform to definitions of conduct which they themselves accept, even though they have broken the rules.

The Cost of Probation

Criminologists believe probation is the most satisfactory treatment for those offenders who may be regarded as good risks. They are spared stigma, turn out better, support their families, and do not become public charges. Financially, probation is also a great saving. It costs from 10 to 20 times as much to keep a man in prison as it does to keep him under probation. For example, in 1949 it cost $3.12 a day to keep a man in a federal prison and only slightly more than 18 cents a day to pay for his probation supervision.[50]

SELECTED BIBLIOGRAPHY

Attorney General's Survey of Release Procedures, Vol. II, Probation, U.S. Department of Justice, Washington, 1939. A survey of the development of probation in the United States shows the widely varying practices and standards of probation in the different states.

Beard, Belle Boone, Juvenile Probation: An Analysis of the Case Records of 500 Children Studied at the Judge Baker Foundation Guidance Clinic and Placed on Probation in the Juvenile Court of Boston, American Book, New York, 1934. This is one of the first studies of probation outcome. Some of the author's methods have been widely criticized.

Elliott, Mabel A., Conflicting Penal Theories in Statutory Criminal Law, University of Chicago Press, Chicago, 1931, chap. 7, "Adult Probation and the Suspended Sentence." The conflicting penal theories evidenced in the trends in adult probation and suspended-sentence laws in 13 selected states are analyzed, with a short history of the movement.

Federal Probation. This journal presents current views and conclusions of many outstanding criminologists, penologists, and probation and parole officers and should be consulted by every serious student in the field.

John Augustus, First Probation Officer (reprint of the Original Report of John Augustus, published in 1852, with an Introduction by Sheldon Glueck), National Probation Association, New York, 1939. This gives a fascinating account of the remarkable work of John Augustus, a Boston shoemaker, who befriended thousands of drunken men, sex delinquents, and thieves who appeared before the Boston Municipal Court. Out of his work grew the first probation legislation.

[50] Richard A. Chappell, "The Federal Probation System Today," Federal Probation, 14:30–40 (June, 1950).

Monachesi, Elio D., *Prediction Factors in Probation*, Sociological Press, Hanover, New Hampshire, 1932. The author finds success on probation associated with good family background. All the factors that contribute to delinquency seem to contribute to failure on probation.

National Probation and Parole Association Yearbooks (until 1947 *National Probation Association Yearbooks*). Files of these important yearbooks should be consulted for trends, opinions of leaders in the field, etc.

Pigeon, Helen D., *Probation and Parole in Theory and Practice*, National Probation Association, New York, 1942. This is an excellent survey of both probation and parole with special emphasis upon the probation officer's and parole officer's problems of case work and treatment, and helpful methods of meeting them.

Stern, Leon T., *Probation Service in Pennsylvania*, Pennsylvania Committee on Penal Affairs of the Public Charities Association, Philadelphia, 1948. A telling survey is made of the disparity in standards of probation in one important state.

Timasheff, Nicholas S., *One Hundred Years of Probation, 1841–1941*, Fordham University Press, New York, 1941. This is a survey of probation legislation in the United States and the British Commonwealth, with data on a few other countries.

CHAPTER 22

The American Prison System: State and Federal

The American prison system today consists in (1) the 266 various prisons, reformatories, prison farms, and correctional institutions which are under the jurisdiction of the 48 states (as well as those in the territories) and (2) the federal prison system, made up of the 30-odd prisons and reformatories under the direction of the Federal Bureau of Prisons. Table 22.1 shows the variety of prisons and juvenile institutions in the United States.

Strictly speaking, the prison system in the United States subsumes city and county jails as well as all state and federal prisons and reformatories. Because jails serve as places of detention for those unable to give bail and those guilty of the most serious felonies, they are treated in an earlier chapter. Jails also serve as places of punishment for convicted persons, sometimes for serious offenses where the jury is inclined to be lenient. On April 10, 1950, for example, a Pittsburgh jury sentenced a woman who admitted she shot her husband's mistress to 8 months in jail for voluntary manslaughter. Since she had been confined 5 months awaiting trial this time was deducted from her sentence. The jury was obviously affected by the flippant attitude of her husband while testifying or the penalty might not have been so light.[1] Jails thus occasionally receive offenders who have committed very serious, even though lightly punished, offenses.

Women sex offenders in New York City are frequently sent to the state prison but are just as likely to be sent to the local women's jail, the House of Detention. In general, however, it is the misdemeanant with less than a year's sentence who is committed to jail, whereas the

[1] Pittsburgh *Post-Gazette*, April 11, 1950, p. 1, cols. 6 and 7.

TABLE 22.1. Types of Penal and Correctional Institutions in the Various States

State	Prisons for Men	Prisons for Women	Reformatories for Young Men	Prison Farm or Similar Institution	Institution for Juvenile Boys	Institution for Juvenile Girls
Alabama	3	1	—	2	2	—
Arizona	1	—	—	—	1	—
Arkansas	1	1	—	—	2	—
California	3	1	1	5[a]	4[b]	2
Colorado	1	1	—	—	1	1
Connecticut	1	1	—	—	1	1
Delaware	1	—	—	—	1	—
District of Columbia	—	1	3[c]	—	—	1
Florida	1	—	1	—	1	1
Georgia	3	—	1	2	1	2
Idaho	1	—	—	—	1	—
Illinois	3	1	—	1	1	1
Indiana	1	1	1	1	1	1
Iowa	1	1	1	—	2[d]	1
Kansas	1	1	1	—	1	1
Kentucky	1	1	1	—	1	1
Louisiana	1[e]	—	—	—	2	1
Maine	1	1	1	—	1	1
Maryland	1	1	1	1	—	—
Massachusetts	1	1	1	2	2	1
Michigan	1	—	2	1[f]	1	1
Minnesota	1	1	1	—	1	1
Mississippi	1[e]	—	—	—	1[e]	—
Missouri	1	1	1	—	1	2
Montana	1	—	—	—	1	1
Nebraska	1	1	1	—	1	1
Nevada	1[g]	—	—	—	1[g]	—
New Hampshire	1[g]	—	—	—	1[g]	—
New Jersey	1	1	2	2	1	1
New Mexico	1[g]	—	—	—	1	1
New York	6	2	1	3[h]	5[i]	1
North Carolina	1[j]	—	—	—	3	2
North Dakota	1[g]	—	—	1	1[g]	—
Ohio	1	1	1	1	1	1
Oklahoma	1[g]	—	1	—	2	2
Oregon	1[g]	—	—	—	1	1
Pennsylvania[k]	4	1	—	—	3[h]	—
Rhode Island	1	1	1	1	1	1
South Carolina	1[g]	—	—	—	2	1
South Dakota	1[g]	—	—	—	1[g]	—
Tennessee	2[g]	—	—	1	2	2
Texas	1	1	—	1	—	—
Utah	2[g]	—	—	—	1[g]	—
Vermont	1	1	—	—	1[g]	—
Virginia	1	1	—	4	2	2
Washington	1[g]	—	1	—	1	1
West Virginia	2	1	—	—	2	2
Wisconsin	1	1	1	—	1	1
Wyoming	1	—	—	—	1	—

[a] Under Youth Authority.
[b] Includes diagnostic clinic for both sexes.
[c] Includes D.C. jail and workhouse.
[d] Including juvenile home which takes misdemeanants of both sexes under 18 in certain instances.
[e] Includes women or females.
[f] House of Correction in Detroit includes women and branch prison.
[g] A few females are included among inmates.
[h] Includes hospital for criminal defectives.
[i] Includes 2 for older boys.
[j] Includes women.
[k] There are also several private institutions for delinquents in Pennsylvania.

SOURCE: *State and National Correctional Institutions of the United States of America, Canada, England and Scotland, Official 1949*, American Prison Association, New York, 1949, pp. 1–37.

felons, who are committed for sentences over a year (which in some jurisdictions include those sentenced a year and a day) go to the state prisons. Sometimes prison sentences are for a shorter term.

THE STATE PRISON SYSTEM

The Origin and Evolution of American Prisons

The American prison system in the various states is an outgrowth of British and Continental ideas and practices developed within the peculiar political framework and ideology our Constitution entails. Initially imprisonment was chiefly for detention while awaiting trial, as we discussed in Chapter 18. The British jail, with all of its attendant defects and problems, was transplanted to the American colonies, as soon as local government was set up, as a place to hold offenders pending trial. Pennsylvania seems to have been the only colony for which there is a record of employing imprisonment as a means of punishment.

When William Penn received the grant of land which was to become Pennsylvania he vowed to set up the Quaker idea of the Christian state. Penn arrived in the colony with a band of 100 fellow members of the Society of Friends in 1682. These earnest men of God met in solemn assembly shortly after they arrived and adopted the "Great Law of 1682." This sought specifically (1) to prevent crime through vocational training and work habits, (2) to abolish the death penalty for all offenses except murder, and (3) to provide a jail built upon lines of the workhouses and houses of correction where persons were to be committed for all offenses save murder.

Penn himself had served several prison sentences because of his revolt against the practices of the Established Church and as a result had become much interested in prisons. Following his imprisonment he had toured the Continent and visited the workhouses in Holland. Here he was much impressed with the desirability of providing work for vagrants and debtors rather than either punishing them corporally or locking them up to an idle prison existence.[2] Labor, therefore, Penn believed should be an important aspect of punishment, and crime was to be prevented through vocational training. The "Great Law" stipulated that a jail be erected "for the restraint, correction, and punishment of all persons as shall be hereunto committed by law."[3]

[2] Orlando F. Lewis, The Development of Prisons and Prison Customs, 1776–1845, Prison Association of New York, New York, 1922, p. 12.

[3] Cf. Mabel A. Elliott, Coercion in Penal Treatment: Past and Present, Pacifist Research Bureau, Ithaca, New York, 1947, p. 16.

The same year (1682) a jail of the cage variety 7 by 5 feet was built, next a house was hired for a jail, and by 1695 a brick jail was completed. This was 25 feet long, 14 feet wide, and 2 stories high. It proved unsatisfactory, however, and was declared a public nuisance as early as 1702.[4]

Penn's provisions for treatment of crime were repealed by Queen Anne when she succeeded Charles II, but these laws were soon re-enacted by the Province of Pennsylvania and continued in force until the time of Penn's death in 1718.[5] The Great Law was repealed one day before Penn died because of the quarrel between the Quakers and the Parliamentary Code requiring the person under trial to take an oath. In consequence the royal governor, Gookin, advised the Pennsylvania Assembly that they must accept the British Criminal Code if the Quakers were to be allowed the right of affirmation.[6]

In this criminal code as adopted in 1718 capital punishment was restored for the following offenses:

high treason	rape	manslaughter by stabbing
petty treason	sodomy	witchcraft by conjuration
murder	buggery	malicious maiming
burglary	arson	every other felony or second offense except larceny

Later counterfeiting was added to this list. Larceny was treated by fine, reparation, or imprisonment.[7]

In the meantime, despite the ideals which had imbued its Quaker sponsors, the first jail erected in Philadelphia was condemned as a nuisance and in 1718 a new stone prison was authorized, which was completed in 1723. This early Philadelphia jail was the first politically created institution to be employed for incarcerating convicted felons, although monasteries had given asylum to many serious offenders in early times. However, conditions were apparently none too good in the Philadelphia jail and many complaints were made concerning it. Later when the Walnut Street prison was erected, in 1776, similar protests were heard. Decent people were shocked by the way men, women, and children were herded into one room. Food depended on what the prisoners could afford to buy from the jailer, or on what relatives or friends sent in, and there was no attempt whatsoever to

---

[4] Negley K. Teeters, *They Were in Prison*, Winston, Philadelphia, 1937, pp. 10–11.
[5] Mabel A. Elliott, *op. cit.*, p. 17.
[6] Cf. Harry E. Barnes and Negley K. Teeters, *New Horizons in Criminology*, Prentice-Hall, New York, rev. ed., 1951, pp. 377–379.
[7] Orlando F. Lewis, *op. cit.*, p. 12.

keep the place clean or sanitary. Nevertheless this prison was one step in the direction of humanitarian treatment.

RICHARD WISTAR

Conditions were so bad that Quaker Richard Wistar was prompted to provide soup for the prisoners at his own expense, and shortly before the Revolution he and other humanitarians formed the Philadelphia Society for Alleviating Distressed Prisoners. The next year Philadelphia was in the hands of the British and the Walnut Street Jail became the Provost Prison. Even after the British were driven out the Walnut Street Jail continued to be a military prison.[8] Following the Revolution, Philadelphia citizens reorganized their prison society under the title, The Philadelphia Society for Alleviating the Miseries of Public Prisons. Approximately one-half of its members were Quakers.[9] The Society besieged the state legislature with reform measures, calling attention to the corrupt management of the institution, the drunkenness, filth, and lack of sanitation. They demanded also the abolition of the sale of liquor within the prison, the segregation of the sexes, and solitary confinement at hard labor.[10]

In 1790 the legislature enacted provisions incorporating their recommendations, provided for the erection of a cell block at the back of Walnut Street Jail for hardened offenders, and by the same act made the Walnut Street Jail a state prison. The cell block was called the "penitentiary" and this became the first block prison in the modern sense of the word in America. The Pennsylvania Prison Society, as the Philadelphia Society for Alleviating the Miseries of Public Prisons came to be known, devoted itself manfully to the improvement of the prison and later urged the erection of an entirely separate penitentiary. This latter was to become the famous Eastern Penitentiary, which we shall discuss later on.

BRITISH INFLUENCES IN AMERICA

In the meantime the Britishers John Howard and Jeremy Bentham had been exploring European prisons and carrying back their findings and recommendations to England. Howard published several books at his own expense describing his prison studies and his recommendations for prison reforms. He had become especially interested in the

[8] Cf. Harry E. Barnes and Negley K. Teeters, op. cit.
[9] Edwin H. Sutherland, *Principles of Criminology*, Lippincott, Philadelphia, 4th ed., 1947, pp. 412–413.
[10] Negley K. Teeters, *They Were in Prison*, pp. 448–451.

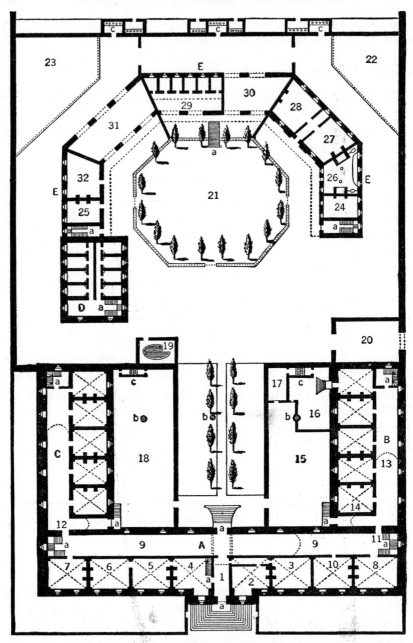

Ground Plan of Walnut Street Jail, Philadelphia, Pennsylvania, 1790. Block
D in this plan shows the cell unit of 16 cells erected in 1790. This introduced cellular confinement in American prisons and laid the basis for the
Pennsylvania system of solitary confinement. (From *Handbook of Correctional Institution Design and Construction*, Bureau of Prisons, U.S. Department of Justice, Washington, 1949, p. 23.)

health conditions in prisons and devoted himself with evangelistic zeal to their improvement. As a matter of fact, Howard was equally interested in hospitals and prisons, and acquired considerable understanding of medicine and public health.[11] Bentham, who is best known as an English scholar and philosopher, was also active in demanding penal reforms and changes in prison architecture.[12]

Of all prisons visited in his travels Howard was most impressed by the famous circular Belgian prison at Ghent. This prison also attracted Bentham's attention, and the latter influenced his brother, who was an architect, to draw plans for a projected prison in Russia. The resulting plan, known as the "Panopticon," became famous for its special features. Briefly, it called for a circular building with outside cells, and for lighting from a glass roof, with the inspector's quarters in the center. Thus each inmate was to be visible at all times to the inspector. Bentham urged the British Parliament to adopt the plans for such a prison. They did so, but the plans were never carried out. Because of a war with Turkey, the Russian prison was not built. Bentham's plans in fact have never been adopted in toto in any prison, although the Richmond, Virginia, prison completed in 1800 did embody some of its major features.[13] The Stateville (Illinois) Prison, erected during 1916–1925, attempted to revive the panopticon features and has four panopticon cell houses.

Prisons in the United States

Following the American Revolution the separate states set up their own penal systems. Initially the state prisons constituted most of our penal system, with the exception of the jails. As the country expanded and as social, economic, and international conditions required more and more federal legislation, a federal penal system more or less inevitably developed.

Imprisonment as a means of punishment for criminal offenses, as established by the Quakers in Philadelphia, became the pattern for penal treatment for all save capital offenses in America. And capital punishment was initially generally restricted to the offenses of murder

[11] Cf. Leona Baumgartner, John Howard (1726–1790) Hospital and Prison Reformer. Reprint from The History of Medicine, 7:5, 6 (May–June, 1939). Cf. also pp. 497–498.
[12] Cf. Jeremy Bentham, An Introduction to the Principles of Morals and Legislation, London, 1823, Vol. II. Cf. also John Bowring, The Works of Jeremy Bentham, Edinburgh, 1843, Vol. IV, for a description of Bentham's plan for the "Panopticon."
[13] Fred E. Haynes, The American Prison System, McGraw-Hill, New York, 1939, p. 24, and Blake McKelvey, American Prisons, University of Chicago Press, Chicago, 1936, p. 7.

and treason. More recently kidnaping, rape, armed robbery, train wrecking, and burglary have been added to the capital offenses in various states. Actually, capital punishment is seldom inflicted for any offense except murder and in only a small percentage of those cases, as we have mentioned.

The history of prisons in the United States, as the *Attorney General's Survey of Release Procedures* indicates, may be divided into 4 periods: (1) the early American prison, 1790–1830, (2) the Pennsylvania and Auburn systems, 1830–1870, (3) the reformatory system, 1870–1900, (4) the industrial prison, 1900–1935. To these we may add (5) the new prison, 1935 on (although the war years 1941–1945 added an interim and temporary shift in prison policies, as we shall discuss later).[14]

Early American Prisons

During the period 1790 to 1830 11 prisons were established, as follows:[15]

Pennsylvania	Walnut Street Jail, Philadelphia	1790
New York	Newgate Prison, New York	1797
New Jersey	State Penitentiary, Lamberton	1798
Kentucky	State Penitentiary, Frankfort	1800
Virginia	State Penitentiary, Richmond	1800
Massachusetts	State Prison, Charlestown	1805
Vermont	State Prison, Windsor	1809
Maryland	State Penitentiary, Baltimore	1812
New Hampshire	State Prison, Concord	1812
Ohio	State Penitentiary, Columbus	1816
Georgia	State Penitentiary, Milledgeville	1817

Of these only the Walnut Street Prison had been erected before the Revolution, and it became the Pennsylvania State Prison in 1790, as we have mentioned. For a few years conditions in the Walnut Street Jail were fairly satisfactory. Sale of liquor was forbidden, men and women were confined in separate compartments, and vocational training in weaving, carving, shoemaking, tailoring, etc., was given. Prisoners were convicted for slight offenses, however, and many had to serve sentences for inability to pay their debts.

[14] *Attorney General's Survey of Release Procedures*, Vol. V, *Prisons*, U.S. Department of Justice, Washington, 1939, p. 2.
[15] Data taken from *ibid.*, p. 4.

With the advent of the yellow fever epidemic in 1798 conditions became increasingly worse. There was serious overcrowding and the sexes were no longer separately quartered. The idea of another prison was vigorously promoted during the years 1803 to 1806 and its construction begun sometime around 1810. Work on this prison, which was erected at the corner of Mulberry (now Arch) and Broad streets, was interrupted and it lay uncompleted for several years. Finally it was finished in 1817. During the early thirties a cholera epidemic swept the Arch Street Prison and it was apparently abandoned in 1836.[16] In the meantime the conditions in the Walnut Street Prison were appalling; and agitation over them had resulted in the development of both the Eastern Penitentiary in 1823 and the House of Refuge for Juvenile Offenders in 1826.

Contract and leased prison labor were common in the period from 1790 to 1830. In Charlestown men were leased out at various trades. In New York both contract and state use labor was employed within the prison. As early as 1801 New York had a real conflict between employed prisoners and "free labor" when the legislature passed a law requiring boots and shoes made by convicts to be stamped with the words "Prison Labor."[17]

In Massachusetts there was an attempt to classify the prisoners into three grades according to behavior and general deportment. In Massachusetts and in New York elementary education was established. In these early prisons there was very little attempt at religious instruction. Pennsylvania, New Jersey, Maryland, Virginia, Kentucky, and Ohio made no provision at all for religious services. In New England various amounts ranging from $25 in New Hampshire to $100 in Vermont and $200 in Massachusetts were appropriated for religious instruction. In New York a clergyman in his seventies was employed to serve several penal institutions.

During the early period overcrowding was general, but the worst conditions applied in Connecticut, where from 15 to 32 were lodged in one room, and in Philadelphia, where from 29 to 31 were so lodged. Then, as now, earnest men recognized the penitentiaries to be schools of crime.[18] Theoretically, however, the separate-cell prison emerged as the ideal of prison construction during this federal period of American history, representing an important transition in the conception

[16] The exact dates are not available. Cf. Negley K. Teeters, *op. cit.*, pp. 70–75.
[17] *Attorney General's Survey of Release Procedures*, Vol. V, *Prisons*, pp. 8–9.
[18] *Ibid.*, pp. 10–14.

of prison architecture. By 1825 the controversy over cellular and congregate prisons had virtually ceased, as the controversy over the Pennsylvania and Auburn systems arose.[19]

The Development of the Pennsylvania and Auburn Systems

When the Walnut Street and Arch Street jails failed so miserably in achieving their purposes, the members of the Pennsylvania Prison Society made a serious study of ways and means of improving prison life. Minutes from their meetings indicate grave concern over conditions in the prisons and the failure of imprisonment as a method of reclaiming offenders.[20]

Undoubtedly the members were influenced by the study of Howard and Bentham's ideas and they began an agitation for the erection of a new prison which would insure solitary and separate confinement. Through the Society's efforts the Pennsylvania legislature in 1818 passed a bill providing for the erection of the Western Penitentiary at Pittsburgh. This bill stipulated that the prison be built specifically so as to permit solitary confinement. In 1821 another bill authorized the erection of the Eastern Penitentiary at Cherry Hill, a suburb of Philadelphia. In the meantime Bentham had been carrying on extended negotiations for the erection of his projected Panopticon in England, but the plan was finally abandoned. Many of his ideas were put into effect, however, in the Cherry Hill Penitentiary through John Haviland, a distant cousin of John Howard's who came to America in 1816. Haviland was engaged to draw the plans for the famous Eastern Penitentiary and later made extensive revisions of the Western Penitentiary. He became the most noted prison architect of his day and subsequently planned the prisons of New Jersey, Rhode Island, and Missouri, as well as the Tombs, the prison of the city of New York.[21]

Both the Eastern and Western Pennsylvania penitentiaries incorporated principles of prison construction as developed by Howard and Bentham. The Western Penitentiary, completed in 1824, was built in an octagon shape, resembling somewhat Bentham's ideal prison plans. The Eastern Penitentiary copied to a marked degree the Wymondham Jail in England, which had been constructed according

[19] Cf. *Handbook of Correctional Institution Design and Construction*, Bureau of Prisons, U.S. Department of Justice, Washington, 1949, pp. 26–27.

[20] Negley K. Teeters, *op. cit.*, chap. 2.

[21] *Handbook of Correctional Institution Design and Construction*, p. 28.

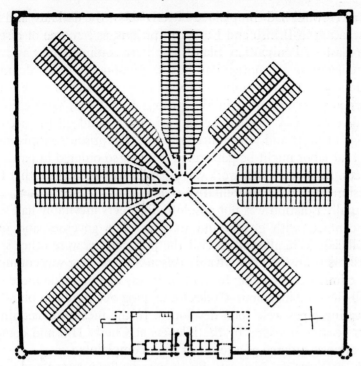

Ground Plan of Eastern Penitentiary at Cherry Hill in Philadelphia, Pennsylvania, 1829. The parent institution of the
Pennsylvania system of prison design and administration. Imitated in a limited way in the United States, but very extensively
in Europe. (From *Handbook of Correctional Institution Design and Construction*, Bureau of Prisons, U.S. Department of
Justice, Washington, 1949, p. 28.)

to the suggestions and recommendations of Howard.[22] The Eastern
Penitentiary was in some respects similar to the Western Penitentiary
with seven tiers of cell blocks radiating from a common center. Each
spokelike tier had cells along the outside walls so that there was outside light for every cell. Each cell had two doors, one leading outside to
an exercise yard and one leading to an inside corridor. Each cell
thus had its own exercise yard—a walled enclosure. To make certain
that the men did not communicate while taking their exercise, those
in adjoining cells were not allowed to exercise at the same time.

The provision for considerable air and yard space with ample light
was unquestionably a result of Howard's demands for healthful prison

[22] Harry Elmer Barnes, "The Historical Origin of the Prison System in America," *Journal of Criminal Law and Criminology*, 12:42–43 (1921); see also his *The Evolution of
Penology in Pennsylvania*, Bobbs-Merrill, Indianapolis, 1927.

quarters. Howard had complained bitterly about the darkness and lack of ventilation in British and European prisons, as a source of disease.

The Eastern Penitentiary plan for solitary confinement was essentially religious in its motivation, but its proponents broke definitely with the earlier Quaker notions of requiring prisoners to work. Many earnest persons interested in the prisons feared that occupation at some diverting task might take the prisoner's mind off his need for a change of heart and repentance. Even so, the prison commissioners noted that labor might be performed if it was so ordered in particular instances. In general such work was regarded as a privilege rather than a punishment and its rehabilitative character was stressed.

Naturally isolation was not absolute. Prisoners inevitably had some social contacts with guards and wardens. The governor and other state officials were allowed to visit the prisoners, as were other specified visitors from the Pennsylvania Prison Society. Nor was communication eliminated by being forbidden. It was merely made more difficult, albeit more ingenious. Codes for tapping out words on plumbing and heating pipes were soon developed. In the meantime certain lay visitors became horrified by the idleness at Cherry Hill and compulsory work was ordered as a result of their complaints.

In New York the Newgate Prison was badly crowded and a new penitentiary was needed. Hence the legislature passed a law in 1816 authorizing the construction of one at Auburn. This was completed in 1824. While drawing up plans, the authorities in New York compared the completely solitary "Pennsylvania" system with the silent system as set up at San Michele, Ghent, and elsewhere, and decided that a system of solitary confinement by night and silent association at common work in the daytime incorporated more desirable features than any plan for complete isolation of the prisoners.

Almost immediately a highly emotional conflict arose between the advocates of the Pennsylvania and Auburn systems. Theoretically the Pennsylvania system had much to commend it, but its plan for meditation and repentance did not work out as predicted. Obviously enough, many prisoners were not reformed and a few convicts became serious mental cases. Dickens, Lafayette, and other visiting Europeans condemned the Eastern Penitentiary roundly and held the solitary confinement to be the cause of mental illness. This conclusion may be questioned, but in any event the Eastern Penitentiary was eventually modified so as to include some form of useful work. And because the inmate population increased rapidly, two men were soon assigned to each cell. Thus the Philadelphia prison became neither silent nor solitary.

Although the Auburn prison system with modifications became the pattern for most American prisons subsequently erected, it was the Pennsylvania type that became widely advocated and adopted in Europe. Or perhaps we should say the European prisons had provided the pattern for the Pennsylvania system in the first place. For although many statements have been made to the effect that the American penitentiary is America's contribution to penology, they are not quite true. The modern prison is essentially the contribution of the Roman Catholic Church to penology. While Pope Clement XI is often given credit for founding the modern prison, his institution was but one step removed from the Penitentials.[23] He too was influenced by other developments. The Amsterdam House of Correction, established in 1589, incorporated the idea of silence by day and separation by night in 1603. This later was copied by Fra Filippo Franci in 1677 and still later by the Ghent prison and by Pope Clement XI.[24] William Penn similarly is said to have been influenced by the Dutch Prison.[25] The Ghent prison gave Jeremy Bentham his inspiration for the Panopticon and influenced John Howard and in turn the Philadelphia Quakers. Modern institutions thrust deeply into the roots of our culture, a fact that is as true of prisons as it is of other organized methods for meeting common social problems.

The architecture of the American penitentiary was, however, a distinctive feature, and in this sense, for good or ill, American penologists have affected the prison structures of the Western world. The Pentonville prison erected in England in 1842 imitated the Pennsylvania design and was widely copied in Europe. The Auburn prison, on the other hand, which was a virtual fortress of stone and steel, became the general pattern for prisons in America. The essential character of the Auburn prison lay in the large congregate rooms where the prisoner worked during the day and in the inside cell block where he slept. The inside cell block, built solely for custodial purposes, consisted in 5 tiers of cells one upon the other, placed back to back down the center of the building with corridors next to the outside walls.

[23] Harry Elmer Barnes, *op. cit.*; cf. also article on "Prisons," *Catholic Encyclopedia*, Vol. XII, pp. 431–432.

[24] Cf. Thorsten Sellin, *Pioneering in Penology. The Amsterdam House of Correction in the Sixteenth and Seventeenth Centuries*, University of Pennsylvania Press, Philadelphia, 1944.

[25] Orlando F. Lewis, *op. cit.*, p. 11.

Sing Sing prison, erected later, affords a typical example of the inside cell block.

This fortress type of prison, commonly called a maximum security prison, is exceedingly expensive to build. Some state prisons constructed according to this pattern during the years 1938 to 1940 cost from $5000 to $7500 per inmate to build. The locking and unlocking of the men in their long rows of cagelike cells puts an unfortunate emphasis upon counting and locking and the purely custodial aspects of prison life. When a man goes to the only space which is truly "his" he must always be locked in or unlocked out. The Auburn type found its extreme construction in the present Western Penitentiary, erected in Pittsburgh in 1892.[26] In more recent years penologists have come to recognize the futility of treating the average prisoner as though he were a dangerous and furious beast, but the majority of state prisons are built as though this were the case.

The philosophy of some of the early wardens was definitely sadistic and had little reference to that of the prison reformers. In a popular article in *Collier's* Freeling Foster gives a thumbnail sketch of Elam Lynds, onetime warden of both Sing Sing and Auburn prisons, as follows:

Of all the prison officials in United States history, the crudest and most intensely hated, even by the public was Elam Lynds who built Sing Sing and alternately managed it and New York's Auburn penitentiary between 1817 and 1845. Lynds introduced the complete silence rule, the shaved head, striped suit, lock step, ball and chain and a dozen forms of torture including the Spanish crib which permanently crippled every person "treated" in it. Being a sadistic savage, he also made his guards, like himself, carry a rawhide whip and use it ruthlessly. One convict was given 6000 lashes in a single week. Such floggings resulted in a number of suicides among the prisoners. Many also went insane or died from their injuries. The first of his victims was a woman who was beaten to death at Auburn. When these deaths forced Lynds to resign from one prison, his political influence would have him returned to the other. After twenty-eight years he was fired and barred from prison work because the public would no longer stand for his inhuman brutality.[27]

There have been many developments in cell block refinement. The modern cell block is chiefly steel instead of stone, and there have been improvements in plumbing, heating, and ventilation. Patented elec-

[26] *Handbook on Correctional Institution Design and Construction,* pp. 32–35.
[27] From Freeling Foster's column, "Keeping up with the World," *Collier's,* 124:8 (September 17, 1949. Quoted by permission of *Collier's.*

trical controls now make it possible to open one cell, a series, or all the cells in a particular tier, at the will of the officer at the controls.

During the period in which the Auburn system developed and spread, little thought was given to making the prisons places where training in trades and crafts might enable the ex-prisoner to earn an honest living. The major emphasis on the work program was concentrated on industrial profits, while the interior cell block type of prison construction was lauded for its security features. Both of these features, so widely heralded at first, have come to be regarded as serious liabilities.[28] During this period the evils of contract labor and the lease system became well established and were not eliminated for more than 50 years. The "animal cage" type of confinement provided by the interior cell block has virtually no justification for any save a very few dangerous or emotionally disturbed offenders who might try to escape. Certainly relatively few prisoners need such maximum security.[29] No one can presume that the psychological effect of locking men in barred cages is desirable. Probably a major reason for such barbaric practices is that relatively few people know anything about prisons. If a penitentiary aims at improving its charges it is safe to say that it never will do so by such shameless methods.[30]

Although considerable emphasis was placed upon the fact that the silent system eliminated communication, actually this was never the case. Prisoners merely learned new devices for communication, such as we have already mentioned. They also learned to talk without using their lips. Consequently in recent years all attempts to maintain arbitrary silence in prisons have been abandoned. In certain complicated production processes carried on by the prisoner talking is more or less automatically ruled out during work periods, particularly if noisy machinery is operated. Quiet talking is generally permitted wherever it does not interfere with the men's work.

The Reformatory Movement, 1870–1900

Thus the American prison system has been a virtual extension of the Auburn prison although markedly affected by the Pennsylvania system. Soon, however, the ideas underlying these early prisons were modified by the growth of the "reformatory" idea, for despite the enthusiastic protagonists for both systems it was soon apparent that

[28] Attorney General's Survey of Release Procedures, Vol. V, Prisons, p. 21.
[29] Ibid.
[30] Cf. Harry Elmer Barnes, in Handbook of Correctional Institution Design and Construction, pp. 110–112.

neither system reformed the prisoner or made him penitent. Many people believed this was because of the harsh penal methods employed, especially in the Auburn system, and a demand arose for a different type of institution aimed at reforming its inmates. This "reformatory movement" crystallized in the organization of the National Prison Association in Cincinnati in 1870. (Later the name of this organization was changed to American Prison Association and in 1941 to the Annual Congress of Correction.) This 1870 congress called for the development of a penal program which would include rewards for good conduct, industrial training and education, and numerous other improvements. In particular it stressed the need for specialized training for prison officials.

In the meantime the New York State legislature had authorized the erection of the Elmira Reformatory for young adult offenders in 1869. This was initially built as a maximum security institution. When it was opened, however, in 1876 Zebulon R. Brockway, its first superintendent, who had been a warden in Michigan, accepted the position on the condition that it be an educational reformatory and that all inmates be given an indeterminate sentence and be eligible for parole. The parole idea as developed at Elmira combined Captain Alexander Maconochie's mark system with Sir Walter Crofton's ticket of leave system, which he had borrowed from Sir Joshua Jebb.[31] The mark system was a plan devised by Maconochie around 1840 to induce good behavior among his charges at the penal colony on Norfolk Island. Instead of receiving a sentence a prisoner received a certain number of marks—the number varying with the seriousness of his crime. These marks were redeemed by good conduct and when a man had redeemed them all he was released.[32] This system is discussed in detail in Chapter 27, "Parole and the Indeterminate Sentence."

This and other experiments in helping the prisoner to adjust after he was released from prison were developed both in Great Britain and on the Continent. Two of the more important of these were the stage system of imprisonment in England and the intermediate-stage method which Crofton developed in Ireland. Both of these systems provided for transitional stages in passing from imprisonment to freedom. If the men passed through several months of co-operative be-

[31] Cf. Sir Hugh Evelyn Ruggles-Brise, *The English Prison System*, Macmillan, London, 1921, pp. 29–30. This is discussed later in chap. 27.
[32] Cf. Sidney and Beatrice Webb, *English Prisons Under Local Government*, Longmans, Green, London, 1922, pp. 165–167.

havior they were given a ticket of leave (or parole) incorporating a conditional pardon. During this period they were aided in securing employment and were required to conduct themselves according to particular rules and regulations until their sentence expired. Otherwise they might be returned to the prison. During the 1850's and 1860's this system attracted wide attention and was actively promoted by Gaylord Hubbell, warden of Sing Sing, Franklin B. Sanborn of the State Board of Charities of Massachusetts, Enoch Wines, and Zebulon R. Brockway. It was to be expected that Brockway would attempt to put the idea of the indeterminate sentence and parole into practice when he developed the first important institution for young adult offenders. These two ideas are now so much a part of our whole penal system that we treat them separately in Chapter 27. Along with these provisions the Elmira Reformatory initiated a program of industrial or vocational training.

After the Elmira institution opened, the reformatory movement spread rapidly, and by 1901, 11 states had established reformatories, viz., New York, Michigan, Pennsylvania, Minnesota, Colorado, Illinois, Kansas, Ohio, Indiana, Wisconsin, and New Jersey. Since that time 10 other reformatories have been built, in Iowa, Washington, Oklahoma, Wyoming, Connecticut, District of Columbia (at Loring, Virginia), Maine, Nebraska, Missouri, and Rhode Island. Very soon, however, prisons took over the special features of the reformatories, and today reformatories are but little different from prisons. In fact it is often said that prisons have become senior reformatories and that reformatories are only junior prisons. Unfortunately, recent surveys of reformatories have given us little reason to be very enthusiastic about any reformation achieved by such institutions. We may assume that the reformatories fail as prisons have failed because of their emphasis upon coercion and repression rather than rehabilitation.

The Industrial Prison, 1900–1935

The industrial feature of the reformatory was its most satisfactory characteristic and this too has been widely copied by prisons. After 1900 practically all prisons established an industrial program; the period from 1900 to 1935 has been designated "the era of industrial programs."[33] Eleven new state prisons were added to the list. One was a development of Jeremy Bentham's Panopticon at Stateville,

[33] *Attorney General's Survey of Release Procedures*, Vol. V, *Prisons*, p. 313.

Illinois; the others were essentially of the Auburn type. In general they were maximum security in type with toolproof steel inside cells, as forbidding in appearance and as secure against escape as it was possible to make them.[34]

Philosophically the penal theory widely held in the United States has been that men are sent to prison at hard labor as punishment, not for punishment. This distinction was offset, however, by the detailed petty rules generally drawn up for prisoners, and every violation of which tended to be scrupulously punished. During this period penal philosophy as developed during the nineteenth century made little advance. Men were required to work at whatever industry was set up. Other programs were all more or less subservient to the aim of producing goods, which might be sold at a profit. The whole program of the prisons was shockingly lacking so far as any reference to the rehabilitation of the offender was concerned. In short, it was "custodial, primitive and industrial." The whole problem of prison labor is so important that we shall discuss it in a separate chapter. Suffice it to say here that this period, 1900 to 1935, was marked by the peak and subsequent decline of the industrial prison, although industrialization had developed earlier with the spread of the Auburn system.[35] A series of laws passed in 1929, 1935, and 1940 have eliminated all interstate commerce in prison-made goods except for a few types of exempt prison products. These are discussed in Chapter 25.

The Interim Period of 1935–1940

The first of these curbs on prison labor became effective in 1935. As soon as the restrictive legislation became operative, prisons were more or less forced to devise ways and means for taking up some of the slack time which the decline in prison employment imposed. Idleness in prison created many problems. Men became easily disgruntled with food, and the monotony of having nothing to do often seemed unbearable. The number of prison riots and escapes increased. In consequence some prisons developed extensive recreational programs to keep the prisoners continually occupied. Others developed more constructive vocational and educational projects. On the whole, however, most prisons were not able to keep the men busy and few wardens had either facilities or foresight enough to make any great change in the prison program. Then World War II came.

[34] *Ibid.*, p. 28.   [35] *Ibid.*, pp. 29–31.

Prisons During World War II

When World War II broke out the problem of prison idleness was temporarily solved by the prisons' participation in war production. Before the attack on Pearl Harbor only 20 per cent of the prisoners (about 27,500 men) were engaged in any sort of industry and only 11,000 of these (about 8 per cent of the total number of prisoners) were regarded as doing any useful industrial production. Production officials believed that this unemployed prison group was an important potential source of war production. The restrictive legislation posed a barrier to using prison labor, but the attorney general ruled that prison production of war materials could not be construed as unfair competition and the prohibition against prison-made goods was temporarily lifted.

In December, 1941, the War Production Board set up a division known later as the Prison War Production Branch. It was given the task of devising ways and means for the prison inmates to contribute to the war effort. On July 9, 1942, President Roosevelt, in keeping with the attorney general's ruling, issued an executive order permitting the federal government to accept prison-made goods and prison agricultural produce. An administrative staff was set up to let contracts to industries which could use prison labor. Soon the prisoners began to produce uniforms and other clothing for the army and navy. Cloth for navy sheets was woven in Alabama prisons. Various prisons made boats, shell crates, ambulance bodies, oilcans, etc. Others produced flags and insignia, ropes, blankets, furniture, brooms, and brushes. North Carolina prisoners built a much-needed 15-mile spur to a railroad.[36]

Certain prisons concentrated on food and dairy products. Many prison farms' major contribution was in furnishing food for their own men and thus releasing commercially prepared foodstuffs for civilians and soldiers. Women prisoners did a great deal of sewing, making flags, shirts, underwear, and uniforms, among other things.[37]

In addition, vocational courses were given in prisons and the men trained as machinists, in metalwork, etc., had great demand for their services.

One of the most important contributions of the prisoners' war effort was its impact on prison morale. Men in prison were stimulated

[36] Arthur G. Eaton and William H. Burke, *Prisons in Wartime*, War Production Board, Washington, 1944, pp. 14–26.

[37] *Ibid.*, pp. 27–40.

to do high-grade work and many prisoners received special National Service Certificates for exceeding their quotas of production. Others were cited for the excellence of their work. Prisoners actually felt their work was important and that they were contributing to the survival of our democratic way of life. Such motivation is harder to achieve in peacetime, but it is important if we would keep either production or morale at a high level.[38]

The problem of co-ordinating prison industries with the rehabilitative program is discussed in greater detail in Chapter 25. The educational program in a prison presumably should emphasize education in ethics and decent attitudes toward the rights of others. Vocational education is directly related to prison industries and should be concerned both with techniques required for the specific job and with the importance of the individual's doing his work well.[39]

The New Prison, 1945 On

At the end of World War II there was no longer any legal basis for permitting the production of prison-made goods. Consequently present-day prison industries must be restricted to items produced and consumed within the several states, or in federal prisons to goods consumed by their own institutions or other federal agencies or institutions.

The restriction on prison labor has created many internal problems. Prisons have seldom wrestled effectively with the need for keeping men active and contented at some suitable task or pursuit. The situation has its negative and positive aspects. Most prison officials or prison boards have made little attempt to work out ways and means for keeping men constructively at work at producing goods which can be consumed within the prison or by other state institutions. In general most prisoners now work at maintenance jobs. A few are employed in making clothes for inmates and discharged prisoners. Others are engaged in making highway signs or automobile license plates. Some make stoves, aluminum ware, mattresses, and other items widely consumed by state institutions. There has been, however, no concerted effort to assay exactly what items are widely consumed by the state and to establish facilities for their manufacture within the

[38] *Ibid.,* pp. 41–44.
[39] John C. Burke, "How Can Proper Correlation Between Prison Industries and Prison Education Be Allowed?" *Proceedings of the American Prison Association,* Boston, 1948, pp. 174–177.

prisons. Every state, for example, needs nurses' uniforms, inmate clothing for persons in insane hospitals, sheets, pillowcases, table-cloths, soap, chairs, tables, lamps, beds, carpets, curtains, dishes. Schools use a countless number of items, as do state and county offices. If a truly intelligent attempt were made to turn out high-grade items by prison labor much of the slack in employment could be eliminated.

On the other hand, the enforced idleness in prisons has made prison wardens re-examine other aspects of their programs. More and more emphasis has been placed upon training the prisoner to do a form of useful labor for which he can find a market when he leaves the prison. If he can be suitably trained and effectively placed at a good job on release from the prison much of the danger of his becoming a recidi-vist may be averted. Perhaps even more important has been the recog-nition that the custodial, punitive, industrial prison is itself but one survival of barbarism in our unfortunately cruel and barbarous age.

An effective program of prison industries can contribute much to preparing prisoners for release, if the capacities and aptitudes of the prisoners are correlated with existing market conditions. The director of prison industries should regard his job as one of vocational coun-seling. Industries must be selected with reference to such practical considerations as available space, funds for purchasing equipment, the need for producing a wide variety of training, and the market for the goods which are produced. In developing any program the personnel is of major importance. Supervisors obviously need to be skilled in the processes they supervise.[40]

Vocational aptitudes of prisoners should determine their assign-ment to particular jobs. The program itself should be motivated by incentives to work well. These may include reduction of sentence, pro-motion, and educational advantage. Wages should be a much more important incentive than they now are; if more adequate wages were paid much of the prejudice against prison-made goods might be elimi-nated.[41]

During World War II prisoners made a notable contribution to the war effort because they felt a new incentive for working to produce food, machinery, and war materials which helped to promote the war effort. Certain prisoners were permitted to enlist in the army and navy and prison populations decreased markedly all over the country.

[40] Charles V. Jenkinson, "How Can Prison Industries Contribute to the Preparation of Inmates for Release?" *Proceedings of the American Prison Association*, Boston, 1948, pp. 159–164.
[41] *Ibid.*

The new prison is an experimental prison. It includes prison farms where young offenders and first offenders are kept from contacts with older, "hardened" offenders. All the modern tools of psychiatry, sociology, and psychology are gradually being introduced to help the prisoner reorient himself and gain self-respect. The prisoner likewise needs to be oriented to the positive values which he can derive from the modern prison program. These and other aspects of prison services today are discussed in the next chapter.

There has been an increasing emphasis upon suitable educational programs, moral education, effective religious services, better medical facilities, a valid classification system—all of which have pointed up the need for treating the whole person of the inmate. These have been instituted for the prisoner's welfare and with the accompanying hope that he will develop a co-operative acceptance of law and order. We know now that no amount of attention to the seriousness or viciousness of the prisoner's offense will ever secure this, nor will any program directed primarily toward profitable industrial production. For the first time in our history an important group of penal administrators are concerned with the methods for accomplishing a re-education in social values. To this end the warden, and all the officials under him, must have some insight into the possibilities of the new approach.

FEDERAL PRISONS, 1895——

Because most criminal law comes within the jurisdiction of the police powers of the several states, federal prisons were not provided for civilian offenders until 1895. Initially the only federal prisons were military prisons and these were under the jurisdiction of the army and navy. As our country developed, many federal laws were enacted both to cover the nebulous boundaries of "interstate" crimes and to enforce restrictions which seemed pertinent to the promotion of the safety of citizens where such restrictions either were not enforced or could not be enforced within the several states.

When distances were greater and communication both less frequent and more difficult, the criminal codes of the several states were fairly adequate devices for defining the prohibited areas of human conduct and for providing means for dealing with offenders. In the few instances in which persons were convicted of crimes designated "federal" in nature such persons were committed to state or territorial institutions. The federal government had jurisdiction, however, over territorial jails or prisons, and the territorial prison built on McNeil

Island in Washington in 1870 later became a federal penitentiary.

The first federal prison was established at Fort Leavenworth, Kansas, in 1895, in a military prison transferred to the Department of Justice from the War Department. The War Department disapproved of its being used for civilian offenders, however, and offered to transfer certain of the land at the Fort for the construction of a civilian prison. This offer was accepted and the prisoners at Fort Leavenworth constructed the Leavenworth Federal Penitentiary. It was a long time in the building and was not opened until 1905. The Atlanta Penitentiary was begun in 1889 and opened in 1902 and the McNeil Island Territorial Penitentiary became a federal prison a few years later. In 1925 a federal reformatory for women was established at Alderson, West Virginia, and a men's reformatory at Chillicothe, Ohio. A small jail for detention purposes was also established in New York City. This brought the number of federal penal institutions to 6 by 1930.

By this time Congress recognized the need for a special agency for supervising federal prisons and created the United States Bureau of Prisons in 1929, defining the Bureau's policies so as to provide for an individualized system of "discipline, care and treatment." The Bureau was organized in 1930. To Sanford R. Bates, who set up the Bureau, and James V. Bennett, who succeeded him as Director, great credit must be given. For these men have built up a prison system organized to help the offender become a socially minded law-abiding citizen.

As a result of the splendid work of the Bureau, personnel standards have been greatly improved and today few state prisons can compare with the standards of penal treatment in the federal institutions. The Bureau of Prisons has also given great impetus to the improvement of standards of prison service in the various states.[42] The Bureau has made important surveys of jails, prisons, and release procedures, under the direction of highly trained criminologists and penologists. Although it has no authoritative supervisory function over state institutions, it has assumed constructive leadership in the promotion of in-training courses, through the Federal Probation Service has sponsored *Federal Probation*, an educational journal on penal matters, and has developed numerous auxiliary services. To carry out the recommendations, Congress passed a number of additional acts in 1930 which (1) created several new institutions to serve special needs, (2) authorized the United States Public Health Service to provide the medical and

[42] *Attorney General's Survey on Release Procedures*, Vol. V, *Prisons*, p. 313. Cf. also Paul W. Tappan, *Contemporary Correction*, McGraw-Hill, New York, 1951, chap. 5.

psychiatric services in federal penal institutions, (3) provided for the development of a system of prison labor, (4) made extensive improvements in the Federal Probation Service, and (5) established a full-time parole board for federal offenders.[43]

Since that time the federal government has greatly extended both its functions and its supervisory regulations. In consquence the number of federal offenders has inevitably increased. The Dyer Act, for example, made the transportation of a stolen automobile across a state line a federal crime. Federal prohibition multiplied the federal offenders during its enforcement. The Social Security Act with its extension of benefits and the accompanying tax program resulted in many evasions and illegal activities which came under the category of crimes.

As the number of convictions increased, further institutional facilities were provided until now there are 30 federal correctional institutions as well as provisions for the criminally insane at St. Elizabeth's Hospital in Washington. Because federal offenders subsume so many different types of persons, the need for classifying them became obvious. A variety of institutions were developed to meet different types of problems presented by the different groups. Thus there are federal institutions for first offenders, young offenders, habitual criminals, sick prisoners, women offenders, conscientious objectors, etc., situated in various parts of the United States. In 1949, as Table 22.2 indicates, there were 20,227 federal prisoners, 17,317 of whom were in federal institutions and the rest in territorial jails or state, county, city, or private institutions. In 1950 the number increased slightly but there were fewer in both these years than in the 2 years preceding.[44] There has been a considerable decrease in commitments during the last 10 years, but most of this may be attributed to a wider use of other facilities rather than to a decrease in crime. Alcoholics, for example, may be referred to clinics instead of being sentenced to prison. Many first offenders are placed on probation. Juvenile offenders in particular are often helped to readjust without the stigma of institutional commitment.[45]

As shown in Table 22.2, the different federal prisons are organized to deal with different types of offenders. From a social viewpoint society must be protected against the intractable, dangerous, or untrustworthy offenders. Gangsters who shoot for a price and without remorse cannot be dealt with in the same fashion as the country boy

[43] *Prison Work as a Career*, Bureau of Prisons, U.S. Department of Justice, Washington, 1944, pp. 10–11.

[44] *Federal Prisons, 1950*, U.S. Department of Justice, Washington, 1951, p. 6.

[45] *Ibid.*, p. 11.

who steals a Ford "to leave home and see the world." Thus on Alcatraz Island, California, a veritable fortress has been erected where those classified as intractable are committed. Because of the isolation from the mainland stern discipline is easier and escape is well-nigh impossible. Serious habitual male offenders who are considered more tractable are nevertheless committed to a maximum security institution either at Leavenworth or at Atlanta. Here armed guards and high walls militate against possible escape. If inmates of these institutions prove refractory, they are often transferred to Alcatraz.

Male offenders who are considered improvable and co-operative are committed to institutions less formidable in their structure and appearance, but with a fairly high degree of security at Lewisburg, McNeil Island, and Terre Haute. Males better suited to an agricultural reformatory life are sent to Petersburg, Virginia. Three reformatories for younger offenders are of the dormitory type.

The institution at Seagoville, Texas, provides an informal type of prison life which has proved highly successful in the short time it has been in effect. Women were originally committed to this reformatory, but during the war period it was turned over to the Immigration and Naturalization Service. Following the war the number of women serving under federal sentences had so declined that it was decided to use the Seagoville plant as a men's reformatory. Built upon a dormitory-like plan with no security facilities, some die-hards thought it would not be a safe place for male offenders but experience has proved otherwise. Of 472 prisoners confined there in 1948, 4 were "lifers," 117 had been committed for 10 years, and 187 for 5 or over. They had committed nearly every federal offense. Here a pleasant attractive atmosphere is maintained, with almost no semblance of traditional prison life. The lock-step type of prison discipline is unknown. In the dining room the men eat at small tables with tablecloths, an unheard-of nicety in men's prisons![46] In 1950 the Bureau of Prisons reported that this institution has exceeded its greatest expectations.[47]

The prison camps, originally developed chiefly to deal with selective service violators, have been retained as minimum custody institutions for male offenders.

The Federal Reformatory for women at Alderson, West Virginia, in the Blue Ridge Mountain area, is of a minimum security type with handsome buildings and grounds laid out in surroundings more beautiful than those of the average college campus. All types of women

[46] *Federal Prisons*, 1948, U.S. Department of Justice, Washington, 1949, pp. 20–21.
[47] *Federal Prisons*, 1950, p. 3.

TABLE 22.2. Average Number of Federal Prisoners, Fiscal Years Ended June 30, 1949 and 1950

	1949	1950	Increase or Decrease
All federal prisoners	20,227	20,652	425
Federal institutions, total	17,317	17,632	315
Bureau of Prisons institutions, total	16,678	16,947	269
Penitentiaries, for:			
Intractable male offenders			
Alcatraz, Calif.	232	216	−16
Habitual tractable male offenders			
Atlanta, Ga.	2,121	2,093	−28
Leavenworth, Kans.	2,184	2,027	−157
Older improvable male offenders			
Lewisburg, Pa.	1,208	1,126	−82
McNeil Island, Wash.	1,050	1,047	−3
Terre Haute, Ind.	1,039	1,034	−5
Reformatories, for:			
Agricultural-type improvable male offenders			
Petersburg, Va.	525	639	114
Younger improvable male offenders			
Chillicothe, Ohio	1,218	1,170	−48
El Reno, Okla.	967	987	20
Englewood, Colo.	311	313	2
Female offenders			
Alderson, W. Va.	428	429	1
Institutions for:			
Male juvenile offenders			
National Training School for Boys, D.C.			
Federal cases	246	245	−1
District of Columbia cases	108	115	7
Natural Bridge Camp, Greenlee, Va.	56	57	1
Correctional institutions, for:			
Short-term male offenders			
Ashland, Ky.	466	592	126
Danbury, Conn.	416	444	28
La Tuna, Texas	586	600	14
Milan, Mich.	544	641	97
Sandstone, Minn.	95[a]	—	−95
Seagoville, Texas	415	406	−9
Tallahassee, Fla.	389	469	80
Texarkana, Texas	374	429	55
Prison camps, for:			
Minimum-custody-type improvable male offenders			
McNeil Island, Wash.	302	290	−12
Mill Point, W. Va.	118	166	48
Montgomery, Ala.	147	154	7
Tucson, Ariz.	213	250	37
Detention headquarters, for:			
Males awaiting trial or with short sentences			
New York, N.Y.	150	180	30
Medical Center, Springfield, Mo., for:			
Physically and mentally maladjusted male offenders			
Hospital	627	663	36
Maintenance unit	143	165	22
Public Health Service Hospitals, total	639	685	46
Fort Worth, Texas (for male narcotic addicts)	145	150	5
Lexington, Ky. (for narcotic addicts)	487	530	43
St. Elizabeths, D.C. (for mental patients)	7	5	−2
Nonfederal institutions, total	2,910	3,020	110
Territorial jails	391	386	−5
State, county, city, and private institutions	2,519	2,634	115

[a] Closed June 14, 1949. Average based on full year.

SOURCE: Table I, *Federal Prisons, 1950*, U.S. Department of Justice, Washington, 1951, p. 6.

from the most vicious and hardened offender to the simple and un-suspecting girl who takes a profferred ride with an interstate auto thief are sent here. Quite naturally there are some escapes, but most of these are soon apprehended. Nearly all of the women are tractable and make no effort to get away. The pleasant surroundings and relative lack of rigid restraint contribute to the program of rehabilitation.

A special institution for maladjusted, physically sick, and mentally ill patients has been developed to which offenders are either com-mitted initially or transferred from other institutions. Because of the character of the inmates received, this institution faces special prob-lems. The men are frequently psychopathic or non-co-operative types who object to every sort of prison rule. During World War II a group of conscientious objectors created a very serious problem here by complaining about the mistreatment of offenders by the staff. Part of these complaints may have been justified. On the other hand con-scientious objectors, being nonconformists by definition, often failed to see the importance of and necessity for rules and regulations within a penal institution, even where they were able men with high scholastic records and other notable achievements. From the prison administra-tor's point of view the men were poorly adjusted when they refused to co-operate with prison rules, irrespective of how ridiculous or un-fair the prisoner thought the rules to be.[48] We have discussed the con-scientious objector at length in an earlier chapter.

The number of children's cases has been reduced in line with the philosophy of the Department of Justice. This department adheres consistently to the belief that wherever possible children should be dealt with in their home communities and through local agencies. Sometimes they cannot be so handled because of either the total lack of local facilities or the lack of suitable facilities. Some children are mental and/or medical cases and no federal institutions exist for meet-ing their peculiar difficulties. In consequence the Bureau of Prisons and the Administrative Office of the United States Courts have to work out arrangements with local authorities. As the Bureau of Prisons is well aware, many unfortunate circumstances still exist.

The detention of juveniles committing federal offenses constitutes one of the most distressing aspects of dealing with the federal juvenile delinquent. A large number of the federal juvenile offenders are ar-rested for transporting automobiles across state lines. These children thus are often far from home. In most instances there are no special

[48] Cf. *Federal Prisons*, 1943, U.S. Department of Justice, Washington, 1944, pp. 11–13.

or suitable places to detain them during investigation. Many therefore are held in county jails. In 1950, 1136 such young offenders spent the period during which they were awaiting trial in jail. This is a notorious fact and the Bureau of Prisons recognizes that the lack of suitable detention facilities or boarding homes for juvenile offenders is a grave problem. Basically it is a community problem since the federal government can scarcely erect detention homes in every county or in every state.[49] The separation of state from federal administration of justice creates many difficulties, but this is an especially serious one when juvenile offenders are so confined and subjected to all the unsavory influences which exist in local jails.

The Offenses for Which Federal Prisoners Are Committed

There are two special types of offenses for which prisoners are received in federal institutions: (1) the "war-related offenses," i.e., those violating our military code and national defense, and (2) offenses against other types of conduct forbidden by federal law ranging from counterfeiting, illegal immigration, and violating liquor laws to offenses committed against government reservation restrictions, the District of Columbia, or territorial jurisdictions. The numbers in each category alter with shifts in both legislation and social circumstances. Liquor law violations decreased about 80 per cent with the repeal of prohibition. Automobile thefts increased considerably with the postwar scarcity of automobiles. War-related offenses increased markedly during the period of the wartime draft but have declined since, as Table 22.3 shows.

Prisons Classified as to Types

MAXIMUM SECURITY INSTITUTIONS

As our discussion has indicated, the various prisons in the several states, as well as the other types of penal and correctional institutions, are usually classified with reference to the degree of custodial security offered. Since custody is one of the functions of the penal institution many persons apparently have believed that a prison should be a fortress against which the prisoner might exert every effort to escape with no success. Most of the older prisons therefore are grim walled structures of stone and steel whose basic purpose is to restrain the prisoner

[49] *Federal Prisons*, 1950, pp. 11 and 84.

TABLE 22.3. All Sentenced Federal Prisoners Received from the Courts, by Offense, Fiscal Years Ended June 30, 1938 to 1950

Offense	1938	1939	1940	1941	1942	1943	1944	1945	1946	1947	1948	1949	1950
Total	23,597	24,750	23,003	21,706	20,027	16,630	19,216	21,200	20,112	19,626	16,787	16,733	18,663
Counterfeiting and forgery	1,710	1,965	1,589	1,289	824	522	536	673	891	1,083	1,018	1,204	1,534
Embezzlement and fraud	704	809	750	796	733	473	452	340	350	396	531	582	609
Immigration	2,844	2,541	2,270	1,695	1,428	1,466	2,674	3,996	3,629	3,989	3,200	3,526	3,463
Juvenile Delinquency Act	—	—	216	428	478	488	834	911	1,211	870	677	607	658
Kidnaping	41	32	37	31	25	42	31	20	21	32	36	23	41
Liquor laws	10,520	11,362	10,735	10,123	8,155	3,502	2,635	2,988	2,425	1,996	1,838	2,035	2,304
National Bank and Federal Reserve Act	155	167	157	161	110	74	67	51	69	50	141	90	165
Narcotic-drug laws	2,332	2,610	2,250	1,596	1,522	1,241	1,306	1,134	1,261	1,447	1,443	1,503	2,029
National Motor Vehicle Theft Act	1,563	1,588	1,512	1,498	1,623	1,150	1,079	1,072	1,997	2,740	2,612	2,471	2,486
Theft from interstate commerce	358	354	313	342	178	216	362	475	448	524	430	378	270
White Slave Traffic Act	447	396	378	357	359	376	255	209	157	183	221	160	185
Government reservation, D.C., high seas territorial cases	994	999	1,021	1,139	1,112	933	991	986	873	974	1,069	1,054	1,145
Other	1,859	1,895	1,719	1,772	1,419	1,370	1,392	1,757	1,965	1,867	1,898	2,012	2,195
National security offenses													
Selective Service Act of 1940	70	32	56	479	2,061	4,777	6,602	6,588	4,805	3,475	1,673	1,088	979
Selective Service Act of 1948	—	—	—	228	1,049	3,145	3,930	2,613	1,446	833	236	152	97
Other national-defense and security laws[a]	—	—	11	151	751	1,121	1,710	2,150	1,143	578	319	182	130
Military court-martial cases:													
Army	70	32	45	100	261	511	954	1,793	2,176	2,014	851	592	666
Navy	—	32	—	—	—	—	8	32	40	50	267	88	107

[a] Commitments under national-defense and security laws in effect prior to 1940 not classified separately.
SOURCE: Table II, in *Federal Prisons, 1950*, U.S. Department of Justice, Washington, 1951, p. 8.

against whatever impulses he might have to break away through bars, stones, gates, and armed guards. But most of the recently constructed prisons for males and the majority of men's reformatories have also been built for maximum security. This group includes such institutions as Sing Sing in New York, Eastern and Western penitentiaries in Pennsylvania, Statesville Penitentiary in Illinois, the federal penitentiaries at Atlanta and Leavenworth, and the majority of other state prisons. The federal penitentiary at Alcatraz Island, California, where dangerous federal convicts are confined offers even greater defense against escape and has been called a super-security institution.[50]

Medium Security Institutions

Many of the federal penal institutions are built on medium security lines, as are a number of the newer state prisons and prison farms. In general, medium security institutions are built without walls and have only a few barred cells for behavior problems within the institution. In the medium security institutions many of the men live in honor-room units where their rooms are not locked, there are central dayrooms or assembly rooms attractively furnished, and the atmosphere generally is pleasant and homelike.

Minimum Security Institutions

Nearly all juvenile institutions are of the minimum security type. Here the semblance of informality prevails, the buildings take on the character of college or school dormitories, and usually there are no fences around the well-kept lawns. The federal government has gone further than the various states in developing this type of prison for adults, although the Walkill Prison in New York possesses some of these characteristics. Likewise the various prison farms which have been developed for younger offenders and first offenders have tried to provide less forbidding surroundings with the hope of securing voluntary co-operation and good behavior. This of course is in the direction of the newer concepts in penology.

The federal prison at Seagoville, Texas, which has already been described, is an outstanding example of a minimum security institution. In fact, it has demonstrated conclusively that most prisoners are not dangerous risks and that a high morale is more effective against prison breaks than stone walls and bars.[51] The problem of custody as such we shall discuss more fully in a later chapter.

[50] *Handbook of Correctional Institutional Design and Construction*, chaps. 4 and 5.
[51] *Ibid.*, p. 103.

THE DECLINE IN THE RATE OF IMPRISONMENT

The discussion of probation in Chapter 21 showed that the philosophy of rehabilitation has been an important factor both in keeping the convict out of prison and in helping him prove himself by suspending his sentence. The wider use of probation and earlier parole have reduced the overcrowding which was such a serious problem during the 1930's. In fact the number of inmates in many prisons is still far below pre-World War II figures despite the much publicized increase in crime rates. In a few states overcrowding still hampers the problem of housing and caring for prisoners effectively. These include Arizona, California, Louisiana, Michigan, New Jersey, New York, North Carolina, Ohio, and West Virginia.

In 1948 San Quentin prison in California, for example, with a normal capacity for 2759 prisoners had 4696 inmates. Folsom Prison with a capacity for 1745 had 2389 inmates, and Soledad Prison with a capacity for 376 had a population of 549. The same year Ohio Prison at Columbus had a similarly serious problem with a normal capacity of 2312 and an average population of 4054. Prisons in the other states mentioned above were also overcrowded. In West Virginia the prisons, including road camps, had a normal capacity for 900 with an average population of 1858. In the North Carolina road camp prisons the 88 units had a capacity of 6500 and an average population of 8000. In most of the states, however, the prison population is far below the normal capacity, which situation seems to be a significant indication of the decline of the prison as a method of treating the offender. To the extent that this is true there is evidence of an important change in penal methods.

Prisons today stand as one of the most disillusioning of social experiments. For initially they were experiments, developed with the idea of substituting imprisonment for brutal physical treatment and the death penalty. Their promoters believed that thus they might make men penitent and reform them. When the prisons appeared to be obviously failing, the reformatory movement was initiated to provide educational and vocational training for young offenders. Less emphasis was placed upon discipline and more upon giving the prisoner a chance to make something of himself.

Unfortunately the reformatory idea spread rapidly without any truly effective means for implementing it. Most prisons theoretically at least adopted the principles and practices of reformatories, but neither the reformatories nor the prisons developed personnel and programs for truly reforming their charges. Various follow-up studies and surveys made during the period from 1926 to 1943 showed clearly that prisons and reformatories were turning out their charges to begin crimes anew. These surveys were mentioned in Chapter 3 in the section on recidivism and will be discussed in another connection in Chapter 27.

The impact of these indictments came at a time when the industrial program of prisons was sharply reduced by restrictive legislation. The enforced idleness in prisons resulting from these laws (described in Chapter 25) has made the necessity for replanning the prison program imperative. Prisoners with time on their hands create so many internal institutional problems that they virtually force prison officials to act as intelligently as possible in working out a constructive program. For that reason the prisons since 1935 have been called "the new prisons," and penal developments have been labeled "the new penology."[52] The introduction of prison psychiatrists to help prisoners reorient their thinking, the better religious and vocational counseling now demanded, the effort to find suitable employment for paroled prisoners, the development of sounder educational programs are all steps in the right direction and should be extensively developed in the future. The federal prisons have been experimenting with an orientation program for several years. This appears to offer the best hope for helping the prisoner reshape his attitudes and conduct and will be discussed further in Chapter 23. Making a man sorry for his mistakes, we have learned after long experience, is not enough. He must also be made glad for the new opportunity to prove himself. Otherwise the ex-convict is overcome by the bitterness and futility of his past and goes out into the world to conform to his own conception of his antisocial role.

SELECTED BIBLIOGRAPHY

Attorney General's Survey of Release Procedures, Vol. V, *Prisons*, U.S. Department of Justice, Washington, 1939. An excellent evaluative survey of state and federal prisons is made by a group of expert penologists commissioned for the purpose.

Barnes, Harry E., "The Historical Origin of the Prison System in America," *Journal of Criminal Law and Criminology*, 12:42–43 (1921). This gives a valuable history of the cultural origins of the American prison system.

Barnes, Harry E., and Teeters, Negley K., *New Horizons in Criminology*,

[52] Cf. Harry E. Barnes and Negley K. Teeters, *op. cit.*, chap. 26, "The New Penology —Elmira Principles and Adult Treatment."

Prentice-Hall, New York, rev. ed., 1951, chaps. 19–26. These chapters from an important textbook give extensive information on prisons.

Elliot, Mabel A., *Coercion in Penal Treatment: Past and Present*, Pacifist Research Bureau, Ithaca, New York, 1947. A short history of American penal institutions is given in this pamphlet.

Handbook of Correctional Institution Design and Construction, Bureau of Prisons, U.S. Department of Justice, Washington, 1949. Prison architecture and its functional relation to penal philosophy are splendidly analyzed.

Haynes, Fred E., *The American Prison System*, McGraw-Hill, New York. This is a concise and valuable history of American prisons.

Lewis, Orlando F., *The Development of Prisons and Prison Customs, 1776–1845*, Prison Association of New York, New York, 1922. This gives an excellent history of early American prisons.

Sellin, Thorsten, *Pioneering in Penology: The Amsterdam House of Correction in the Sixteenth and Seventeenth Centuries*, University of Pennsylvania Press, Philadelphia, 1944. Here is an account of the plan for separation by night and silence by day in the Amsterdam institution during the seventeenth century.

Tappan, Paul W., *Contemporary Correction*, McGraw-Hill, New York, 1951, chaps. 6, 18, and 21. This book gives a number of chapters on prisons by persons active in prison administration.

Teeters, Negley K., *They Were in Prison*, Winston, Philadelphia, 1937. This gives an especially good history of the part played by the Pennsylvania Prison Society in the development of American penal institutions.

CHAPTER 23

Prison Administration and Services

The administration of prisons has been a dark chapter in American penology because few of the persons responsible for it have possessed suitable qualifications for their task. If any institutions should be divorced from partisan politics obviously those which propose to rehabilitate delinquents and criminals should be. Unfortunately it has been the practice in many states for the governor to award the post of warden of the state prison to a fellow politician who has given him major support during his political campaign. In consequence many wardens have been appointed who have known virtually nothing in the field of criminology or penology; in fact they often have never read one book relating to prison work. Totally lacking in suitable training or insight for his job, such a politician tries to proceed on the basis of common sense but often applies only his layman's prejudice to problems of internal discipline and personnel. Or he may turn over most of the administration to a deputy warden and spend his time in practical "politicking." He may even have obtained his job as part of a political deal. In a penitentiary in a western state, for example, the governor appointed a hardware dealer as a warden. This warden had agreed to buy a large amount of agricultural equipment from an agent for a well-known farm machinery firm if he was awarded the post. The hardware agent was the state chairman for the successful political party. He sold a large order of tractors to the state prison, which the warden was able to use only by clearing 1000 acres of river land belonging to the state. At great expense this land was divested of timber, drained, and planted to vegetables which were canned for the prisoners' consumption. The warden then launched a publicity campaign about his remarkable program for first offenders, whom he was keeping from vicious associations with hardened criminals. Only a few people knew that the warden made a tidy sum in connection with the deal. This same warden later introduced ironclad rules for maintaining maximum security in the prison. The rules created extreme tensions within the prison which eventuated in three inmates' kidnaping the warden and escaping. They simply marched him out the front door of the prison and into his own car at the point of the revolver they had wrested from him. The warden was not killed but his hair-raising experience led to his subsequent resignation.

PERSONNEL STANDARDS

Three important standards in determining the administrative personnel in a prison should be (1) professional training, (2) the salary scale, and (3) the matter of tenure. Some people will always be attracted to prison work for humanitarian reasons and a few of these will be so devoted to their work that income is a secondary matter. Most people are forced to consider salary, however, and married persons in particular have to think of suitable standards of living for their families, and the educational expenses of their children as well. It should be obvious that salaries for prison work should be high enough to attract high-caliber men and women who are professionally trained for their jobs.

Professional Training of Personnel

In general all policy-making positions in a prison should be filled by persons who have training in sociology and psychology and some specialized training in criminology. Case workers and probation officers should be graduates of accredited schools of social work. Psychologists and sociologists should have graduate training in their fields. Psychiatrists should be graduates of medical schools and should have specialized in psychiatry.

Persons holding executive positions should have had several years' experience in penal institutions and should be thoroughly familiar with the routine problems of an institution. Furthermore they should have demonstrated the administrative ability which they will need to administer a penal institution. It goes without saying that they should be interested in rehabilitative work and be educators in the sense of being concerned with helping the men reorient their scales of values.

Louis N. Robinson says that no man "is fit to be a warden who lacks deep down in his heart the conviction that a man can be born again as the saying goes, and who does not have a thorough grounding in all the various sciences can contribute to an understanding of human behavior. . . . This calls for a trained educational expert who will be even more dedicated to the re-education of prisoners than is the college president to the education of the boys and girls who are under his tutelage."[1] Certainly unless an educator in this sense of the word is head of the prison we can never expect to make imprisonment a process of re-education. Unfortunately ex-police officers, former army officers, or men who have risen from the ranks of guards too frequently fill the post of warden, if it is not filled by an outright political appointee.[2]

The Salary Scale

Salaries should not only be adequate to maintain desirable living standards; they should make possible the necessary expenditures for professional growth. The scale of salaries should be related both to the value of the service expected and to the incomes of persons in other professions. Such items as the nature of training required, the cost of living in the particular area, whether or not housing and meals are provided, the standing of the particular person in his field, and the responsible duties entailed in the position should all be taken into consideration. Often penal institutions do not differentiate greatly between the qualifications for the various civilian jobs since it is held that all prison jobs involve certain basic principles of dealing with prisoners, even though the individual employee may be concerned chiefly with supervising the men in charge of cleaning out a dairy or be in charge of those detailed to the bakery. Certainly all prison staff members should have some orientation in the policies and rehabilitative program of the institution. The major responsibilities must rest with policy-making staff and members of the classification committee, however, and it is these persons who should be given sufficient salary inducements to make them consider prison work as a lifetime career.[3]

Part of the problem of securing suitable salaries for prison staffs is a matter of the competition of such jobs with those in the so-called free community. Many persons rationalize the low pay of prison offi-

[1] Louis N. Robinson, "Contradictory Purposes in Prisons," *Journal of Criminal Law and Criminology*, 37:449–457 (March–April, 1947).

[2] *Ibid.*

[3] D. Ross Pugmire, *The Administration of Personnel in Correctional Institutions in New York State*, Bureau of Publications, Teachers College, Columbia University, New York, 1937, pp. 123–125.

cials by saying that there is only a certain amount of money available for tax-supported personnel. If prison employees are paid well public health nurses, fire inspectors, schoolteachers, etc., will suffer—so the argument goes. A better administration of prisons, however, might very well reduce recidivism and the total upkeep cost of prisons.

Maintenance of Employees

In some institutions employees are paid a gross salary and not allowed maintenance unless they are required to remain at the institution, when meals, etc., are furnished without charge. A few states, including Florida, give maintenance in addition to a cash salary to all prison employees. In Illinois and Montana employees are discouraged from living within the institution, and this discouragement might suitably be extended by all institutions. It is well known that employees maintain a better perspective on their jobs and are psychologically better adjusted if they can get away from their work. This problem is discussed more fully in another chapter.[4] In Iowa, Mississippi, Nebraska, Nevada, New Jersey, and Virginia, on the other hand, employees are actually encouraged to live on the prison grounds. In Kansas the penal institutions provide living quarters and full maintenance for wardens and superintendents in the men's prisons and reformatories. At the Women's Industrial Farm, however, employees receive full maintenance, which is deducted from the salaries of all except the superintendent of the institution. Massachusetts has no general policy; each institution has its own arrangements. In New York, where it is deemed essential to the functions of institutions for the staff to be on the ground, they are required to live there. In other cases the administrative officers believe that the employees' efficiency is enhanced by "getting away from it all."[5]

The value attached to maintenance varies widely in the different states. Virginia values annual maintenance, consisting of board, room with common bath, medical attention, and laundry, at $300.[6] Wisconsin charges all its employees except superintendents or wardens for maintenance at the rate of $25 for houses and apartments and $15 per month for meals. The superintendents or wardens are given complete maintenance.[7]

[4] Chap. 26, "Women's Prisons and Reformatories."
[5] Cf. Morton Friedman, *State Institutional Employee Maintenance Policies*, Council of State Governments, Chicago, 1945, for a detailed statement of the maintenance policies in each state.
[6] *Ibid.*   [7] *Ibid.*

Personnel Tenure

To secure career-minded persons in prison work, tenure must be assured. So long as the political party in power appoints prison officials, the jobs obviously will be temporary. They may represent mileposts in a political career, but they can never be a matter of permanent concern, since the spoils system will inevitably operate. With a political defeat the appointive officials must go. On the other hand, if jobs are to be filled permanently by trained personnel, sound principles of selection of personnel should be followed. To make certain that selections are satisfactory it is usually wise to have a probationary period and to make permanent appointment contingent upon satisfactory service. Sometimes it is advisable to have some system for transferring personnel within state institutions if this is agreeable to all parties concerned.[8] Transferring personnel without consulting them usually creates unrest and dissatisfaction on the job.

Ex-Inmate Employees

In some prisons ex-inmates have occasionally been hired following the expiration of their sentences. This is probably not a general practice, since many states refuse even to allow a former prison inmate to return for a visit under any circumstances. Nevertheless in occasional instances a prisoner who was employed in a confidential capacity has been retained later at the same or a similar job. In at least one prison in the United States an ex-convict served as the warden's secretary for a succession of wardens. He literally knew more about how the prison was run than the wardens. He met many visitors and determined many policies, since the wardens were for years political appointees with no professional training or experience. It was not strange that much confidential information leaked from the warden's office and spread through the prison grapevine.

PRISON MANAGEMENT

Prison management involves the supervision of a variety of prison functions which may usually be divided into six classifications. First, since the prison is a custodial institution its inmates must be kept in safe custody; this is a major reason for its existence. The

[8] D. Ross Pugmire, op. cit., chap. 7, especially pp. 139–140.

warden is entrusted with custodial duty. This function of prison management is, of course, quite aside from any value to be derived from such custody. Second, the prison must have some plan of organization for assigning the work required in the daily routine of prison housekeeping. This means ordering and preparing the food, keeping the prison and prisoners clean and the clothing washed and repaired, and all the other numerous duties which household management on such a large scale and under such peculiar circumstances entails.

Third is the matter of supervising any or all industrial processes or work programs which provide a means of keeping the prisoners employed. Such work may also be a source of revenue to the prison as well as a means of training the prisoner in a trade at which he will make a living. Fourth, since no prison has a full employment program at present some provision for the slack time of the prisoner must be made. This usually involves planning for the recreation and self-improvement of the prisoners during their long stretches of free time.

Fifth, the best prisons make some provision for educational classes, which are organized for (a) the illiterate and (b) prisoners wishing to pursue specialized courses on technical or cultural subjects. Sixth, and not least, is the religious program of the prison. It must necessarily provide for the different religious faiths (or at least for the religious backgrounds) of the prisoners.

These functions of the prison all come under the direction of the warden, and the problem of weighting and equating the emphasis to be placed upon each must always depend in final analysis upon the attitude and insight of the warden and his immediate assistants. At the same time the best-trained and most competent wardens are public servants and therefore must implement the program of their prisons in the light of public opinion. In particular they must defer to the state boards, which supervise the penal and correctional institutions and more or less determine their broad policies of operation. Most of these special functions of the prison are entrusted to the supervisory staff. Together the functions and activities which are related to them constitute both the workaday life of the prison and its working philosophy and we may profitably explore them in greater detail.

Obviously a major aspect of prison management is suitable personnel. Effective prison management involves several other important considerations. (1) The prison must assure safe custodial supervision of all prisoners, and for the incorrigible, habitual, and non-reformable (if there be those) this custody must be segregated. (2) For the prisoner whose prognosis is favorable every available resource must be utilized to secure rehabilitation and to make certain his satisfactory adjustment on release.[9]

The Custodial Function of the Prison

The custodial functions of the prison are determined by (1) the prison architecture itself, (2) the training and philosophy of the personnel, and (3) the basic program of the prison.

PRISON ARCHITECTURE

Today, as a result of a variety of experiments in classification of prisoners, penologists now recognize that a large share of prisoners are not desperadoes who must be confined in steel cages, behind high walls, encircled by electric fences. Nevertheless the vast majority of adult male prisons and reformatories are built for maximum security. In 1940, 67 state and federal prisons and reformatories had high surrounding stone or brick walls. Of these, 15 were 30 feet or more high; 37 were from 20 to 30 feet high; and 15 were under 20 feet high.[10] Nine had wire fences at the top; 3 of these were electrified. These fences, in case of riot, may be as dangerous to prison guards as to prisoners, hence have never been widely employed. Three other institutions had wire fences without walls, and a fourth had interior cell blocks but neither walls nor fences.[11]

WALL TOWERS. All of the prisons with walls have towers manned by day guards and all but 12 maintain guards at night as well. These towers possess certain hazards since prisoners may seize the guard, take his pistols, overpower him, and make their escape over the walls.

WALL EQUIPMENT. All prisons constructed with walls employ some lighting device such as floodlights or searchlights to guard against escapes at night.[12]

CELL BLOCKS. The Auburn prison, built in 1823, established the pattern for American prison architecture with the interior cell block. Elam Lynds, who planned the prison, developed this idea. It provides for tiers of cells, one above the other, often running as high as five stories. These are set well back from the outside walls and the windows of the outside walls are heavily barred. It is thus virtually impossible

[9] Harry E. Barnes, A Concise Plan for the Organization of a State Department of Correction, Institute of Local Government, Pennsylvania State College, State College, 1945, p. 3.
[10] Attorney General's Survey of Release Procedures, Vol. V, Prisons, U.S. Department of Justice, Washington, 1939, pp. 86–87.
[11] Ibid., p. 87. [12] Ibid., p. 88.

for the prisoner to work his way out of the cell, or to conceal any attempts to filing the bars of his cell windows, as might be possible in case of exterior cells with windows. Sixty-one prisons employ the interior cell as the major type of cell house. Nine of these have both interior and exterior cells, however.[13]

The interior cell admittedly makes escape difficult but it is very expensive to construct and most prison authorities regard its precautionary features as unnecessary for at least two-thirds of the prisoners. Most prisoners are not wholly depraved men and are not likely to break forth to murder and plunder the community. Since many prison administrators are not sure which men are likely to attempt escape they regard the interior cell as a necessary evil. With improved methods of classifying prisoners, most of the prisoners likely to try to escape can be determined. When adequate classification techniques are generally employed we can expect the interior cell to be a small part of the prison's housing equipment.[14]

MODIFICATIONS IN SECURITY PROVISIONS

As our analysis of federal prisons indicated, the federal government has taken the lead in classifying prisoners and developing prisons with reference to the presumed "risks" involved in the different classes of adult prisoners. The federal reformatory in the District of Columbia, built in 1916, was the first dormitory type of reformatory in the United States. Maine built a reformatory with dormitory-type buildings in 1912, but it was not taken over as a state institution until 1919. This institution originally planned to confine all its prisoners in 50-bed dormitory buildings but eventually found it necessary to build an interior cell-house unit for its poor risks. New Jersey and Missouri both constructed dormitory-type reformatories in 1929 without any wall or fence enclosing them. Massachusetts in 1927 constructed a dormitory-type institution within a concrete wall topped with an electric fence. Inside the wall, however, the atmosphere is much like that on a college campus.[15]

Wallkill Prison in New York, built in 1932, follows a different plan of construction. All of the buildings are joined together on a rectangular court, with the buildings themselves forming walls, again much like certain college quadrangles. Only 2 exits are provided, at front and rear.[16] The Rhode Island reformatory at Howard, constructed the same year, is all under one roof—one building within a wall houses dormitories, offices, kitchen, dining room, schoolroom, library, chapel, as

[13] *Ibid.*   [14] *Ibid.*   [15] *Ibid.*, p. 90.   [16] *Ibid.*

well as punishment cells and receiving cells for those newly committed.[17]

In a few other prisons dormitories have been built for selected prisoners within their walls. These are at Stateville, Illinois; Ionia, Michigan; London, Ohio; and Rahway, New Jersey. Illinois also has outside-the-prison-wall dormitories for the prison farm trustees at Menard, Pontiac, and Stateville, as do Kansas and Massachusetts.[18] Kansas has also converted an old cell block into an honor cell house by knocking out the front bars of the cells and constructing washrooms and toilets at the end of wide corridors. The men are permitted to converse and spend their leisure in company during the periods when they are not required to be at work, in the dining room, or elsewhere. The cavelike appearance of these open-front cells is not pleasing, but the plan of rewarding prisoners with good records by allowing them to live in the honor cell house is highly regarded by the prisoners, for here they at least have a degree of freedom within the walls.

Other Security Considerations

THE LAYOUT

There are many other custodial considerations. One is the layout of buildings. Most of our older prisons resemble medieval castles and monasteries chiefly because these very buildings earlier served as prisons, or quasi prisons. The first prisons thus were under one roof or were a series of connected buildings with easy access. Today it is generally recognized that there are a great many advantages to breaking up the prison into several units. Riots are less likely to occur if all men are not under one roof. Fire hazards are less. Custody is easier to insure when unauthorized prisoners are kept out of buildings where they have no reason to be.

THE PROBLEM OF LOCKS

Locking the prisoners in at night—or during punishment, or for minor ailments where the prisoner is not admitted to the hospital—creates many problems. An ingenious electrically controlled panel board has been invented which may unlock all, one, or any given number of cells. Such a board sometimes gets out of order and may present serious hazards in case of fire. The problem of separate keys involves a cumbersome procedure and many prisons use a single-bar arrangement which unlocks or locks all cells, reserving the single key for use when

[17] *Ibid.*   [18] *Ibid.*, p. 91.

only one person is let in or out.[19] Keys entail the risk of copying and prisoners often are skilled in such matters. Stray metal is always to be picked up in a large institution because so many varieties of metal are employed in maintenance and institutional repairs.

As a matter of fact, keeping effective watch over all metal scraps is essential to the safe custody of any prison. For in addition to contriving keys from such scraps some prisoners are actually skillful enough to make knives, guns, and other dangerous instruments. Sharpened pieces of metal can be used to saw through metal bars.

Underground Escapes

Wardens are frequently confounded by the unknown, underground activities of prisoners, such as digging of passageways under the prison walls so as to walk or crawl to escape. The matter of supervising basements used for storage or other purposes, or the supervision of the men who repair plumbing and sewers involves more than merely overseeing the assigned tasks. Always within a prison the administrative staff and the guards must be on the alert to see that nothing untoward is going on behind their backs, or for that matter in front of their eyes.

Departments or Divisions of Correction

The most effective basis for organizing the correctional and penal institutions of the state is to have all of them under a single central direction. In some states the central authority subsumes all the charitable and correctional institutions under the general designation of a department of public welfare. In such cases one of the divisions may be designated as the division of correction.

Experience has proved, however, that the special problems involved in controlling and directing penal and correctional institutions make it desirable for them to operate as an independent unit.[20] Obviously prisons are and should be considered welfare institutions. But the duties involved in the direction of prisons are patently quite different from those entailed in welfare institutions in which poverty, neglect, mental illness, or defect and physical handicaps are the major reasons for providing the institutional care. Certain responsibilities, like feeding, housing, and providing medical care, they share in common. But the basic duty of prisons should be conceived as that of reorienting behavior patterns.

Because so many adult offenders were once young persons who were

[19] *Ibid.*, p. 93.   [20] Harry Elmer Barnes, *op. cit.*, p. 6.

committed to juvenile reformatories or industrial schools it seems obvious that correctional work should start with the juvenile delinquent.[21] For despite the frequently expressed idea that the juvenile delinquent is not a criminal in the eyes of the law, he frequently passes into the stage of the adult offender with no perceptible change in his habit patterns. We should quit talking nonsense. If juvenile delinquents are not to be treated as criminals neither should young adult offenders. We should not stigmatize any offenders who show promise of rehabilitation.

The central correctional authority should therefore supervise all correctional agencies, implement policies, work out a classification system, authorize all transfers, develop work programs and institutional activities and services, and supervise the probation and parole policies.

The director of the correctional authority (or commissioner of correction, as he is often called) should be a highly trained and competent executive and should be assisted by several persons, depending upon the number of penal institutions and the variety of details to be supervised. All of these persons should possess special qualifications in training and experience and should be appointed from civil service lists, or at least on a merit basis. Political affiliation should have no part in the appointment of the commissioner and the assistant commissioners. Salaries should be commensurate with their professional background and training and should compare with those of university presidents, cabinet members, and the like.

Preferably a correctional commission or board of five members should also be appointed, with not over three members from one political party. These persons should be competent, intelligent laymen who are interested in penal matters, who can help determine penal policies and interpret the commission both to the governor and to the political factions in the state. Where possible, persons with some previous professional experience or training should serve as members of such a commission.[22]

In some states, such as Pennsylvania, many of the institutions have separate boards. This practice arose because a group of interested persons initially sponsored the institutions and was instrumental in obtaining charters from the state legislature. Some of the juvenile institutions have always been, in fact, private institutions, although they operate under a state charter, receive children committed by the state courts, and are supported to a major degree by state subsidies. At one time these local boards served an important function and there has

[21] *Ibid.*, p. 7.   [22] *Ibid.*, p. 8.

been an earnest effort to retain them because, it is held, they keep the institutions out of politics. Today such duality of control produces much confusion. Effective central administration will necessitate complete authority. To abolish a long-established pattern is not easy, and states which have muddled along under such an arrangement will be reluctant to yield to a new and obviously better-co-ordinated plan. Since the majority of lay board members are busy people who give little time to the consideration of what is going on in the institutions, graft and poor administrative practices often go unseen and uncorrected.[23]

MEDICAL SERVICES IN PRISON

Once the prisoner has checked in to prison and has been fingerprinted, he is generally sent to quarantine, where he receives a physical examination. Some prisons give such an examination at any hour of the day or night in order to keep down the spread of contagious or infectious disease. Virtually all prisons give serological tests for venereal disease and Xrays for tuberculosis, as well as a general physical examination. Dental services are also maintained. In general medical standards have gone up in prison, and many prisons maintain excellent hospital and diagnostic facilities and take care of all medical problems within the walls. Other prisons arrange to send prisoners to outside hospitals for serious surgical operations.

The problem of maintaining health in prison is complicated by several factors: (1) the prisoners' psychological attitude, (2) their morale, (3) the problem of contagion, (4) the food, (5) the medical staff and the quality of medical services, (6) the mental health services.

Psychological Aspects of Prisoners' Health

Prisoners are often in the depths of despondency, and more or less inevitably feel bitter and frustrated either because they have been imprisoned or because they have made a mess of their lives. Consequently they tend to suffer many physiological manifestations of their emotional tensions, such as indigestion, headaches, etc. Since the anxieties and perplexities of prisoners must be much greater than those of the rank and file of civilians, there is probably a tendency among prisoners to exaggerate minor illnesses and to answer "sick call" without great

[23] *Ibid.*, pp. 9–10.

provocation. At least some wardens say this is true. Hence the daily opportunity to report to prison hospital "sick call" for minor ailments may be a means for the prisoner to gain attention, particularly where the work sessions are short and time seems to drag.

Morale

Morale is often low in prisons, both for individual reasons and because of the lack of sufficient productive work to keep the prisoners busy. Answering sick call may thus provide some interest in an otherwise dull and monotonous day.

Contagion

Because prisons are often overcrowded, the problem of controlling epidemics is continuous. For this reason prisoners are kept in quarantine for a while after entering prison. The time in quarantine varies with the different prisons, running from a few days to two weeks. Isolation of cases with incipient colds or influenza does much to prevent the spread of epidemics among the inmate population.

Food in Prisons

Since nutrition is so closely related to health the problem of adequate food and menu planning should receive more scientific attention than it does. Standards of feeding have gone up in all prisons. Diets usually supply food in generous quantities. They tend to be out of balance in many prisons, however, and to lack essential vitamins. Few prisons give inmates any citrus fruit and many supply very little milk. Meals are usually over-starchy with bread and molasses forming a staple part of each meal. In prisons having their own gardens fresh vegetables may form a higher percentage of the food provided. As it is, unquestionably many problems of indigestion and low resistance are due to the lack of sufficient vitamins and minerals in the diet. Faulty diet coupled with lack of adequate sunshine in the cell houses must affect the health of some of the prisoners adversely.

The Sanitary Aspects of Prisons

The matter of sanitation is always a serious one where large numbers of people live in close quarters. The "public health" problem of a prison includes sewage and garbage disposal, the preparation of food, the regulation of the milk and water supply, proper cleaning of cell houses, dining room, and kitchen, as well as the personal hygiene of each inmate. Many prisons have a "prison smell" which is largely due to the lack of adequate bathing facilities and regulations, although it may be augmented by unpleasant disinfectants. A prison thoroughly scrubbed with soap and water each day does not need strong and ill-smelling purifying agents.

The Medical Service

From any viewpoint it is difficult and humiliating to be a prisoner; to be a prisoner and ill must be a profoundly miserable experience. For this reason, as well as for other sound reasons, prisoners should be supplied with adequate medical service. According to the *Attorney General's Survey of Release Procedures*, there were 77 full-time physicians and 50 part-time physicians in 45 prisons, and in 37 prisons only part-time physicians were employed.[24] In these latter prisons other physicians are consulted when necessary.

Mental Health Services

Mental health services are still relatively undeveloped in prisons although the impetus given to psychiatric treatment of behavior problems in the army during World War II has unquestionably demonstrated its importance. Until recently psychotic prisoners were left to decay like vegetables in secluded sections of the prison. Today many larger prisons employ psychiatrists to supervise psychiatric screening tests for all incoming prisoners and to help men in need of psychiatric assistance as much as possible.

Part of the psychiatric problem of prisons is, as Dr. Lindner holds, a matter of minimizing "the petty tyranny of minor rules and regulations which so interferes with the treatment of criminals."[25] We have already mentioned the rigidity and even absurdity of many of the prison rules to which the inmate must conform or be punished. These rules in themselves so often increase the hostility, discouragement, and suspicion of the prisoner that he may leave the prison far more hostile

[24] *Attorney General's Survey of Release Procedures*, Vol. 5, *Prisons*, chap. 7, "Medical Care."

[25] Robert M. Lindner, "Practical Mental Hygiene for the Prisoner," *Proceedings of the Seventy-Fifth Annual Congress of the American Prison Association*, New York, 1945, pp. 187–194.

toward society than when he entered it. In consequence much of the prison psychiatrist's task is to serve as a buffer between the inmate and rules and prison personnel.[26]

CLASSIFICATION IN PRISONS

The classification system in prisons covers the whole procedure for studying the prisoner and arranging his workaday schedule for living within the prison. The classification involves finding out everything possible about the prisoner's background, family, education, work history, religious affiliation, criminal record, health, mental ability, intellectual habits, emotional maladjustments, special aptitudes, recreational habits, etc., in order to work out a suitable job and institutional placement, and to plan for helping him with reference to his peculiar personal needs.

Classification Procedure

Classification procedure as developed in penal institutions is one of the major advances in modern prison management. As a technique classification has grown out of social case-work techniques. When a difficult problem in case work arises it is customary for social workers to pool their experience and information with reference to the particular client or family concerned. From a discussion of the various aspects of the individual's personality, his assets and liabilities, a plan for helping him is developed. Unfortunately many prisons have no real classification system.

The Classification Committee

The classification committee (where it exists) is in a very real sense the prison's policy-making body. The personnel who suitably determine the principles and policies to be invoked in dealing with the individual offender include the following:

1. The warden.
2. Associate warden for custody.
3. Person in charge of care and treatment of inmates.
4. The supervisor of classification.
5. The social worker or sociologist.
6. The director of academic education.

[26] *Ibid.*

7. The vocational counselor or supervisor.
8. The chief medical officer.
9. The psychiatrist.
10. The psychologist.
11. The chaplain.
12. The institutional parole officer.
13. The officer in charge of reception or quarantine unit of new prisoner.
14. The officer in charge of living quarters of prisoner, in case of a hearing of the inmate who has been "classified."
15. The officer in charge of the work placement in case of reassignment of work placement.[27]

In institutions where some of these appointments do not exist, the classification committee will naturally be less extensive. The important thing is to have all persons possessing special knowledge about the inmate present. All they know should be brought together in order to get a picture of him as a whole to assist in working out a suitable program for him.

Recommendations for the Orientation Period

The pooled experience of many prisons with classification committees has produced a number of further recommendations which we may summarize briefly. Religious counseling during the orientation program may be beneficial. An early interview with the chaplain often contributes to the prisoner's morale. Merely to know someone is interested in his problems may help to reduce the sting and stigma of imprisonment.[28]

The prisoner also should be encouraged to write home as soon as possible, thus keeping in contact with his family. The correspondence will also reveal attitudes of the prisoner and his family which will be helpful to the committee. Correspondence is always closely watched in all prisons.

The Admission

The process of classifying the prisoner begins at the moment he is received behind the forbidding steel doors of the prison. Once the door

---

[27] All but the last two of these recommendations are made in the *Handbook on Classification in Correctional Institutions*, prepared by the Committee on Classification and Case Work of the American Prison Association, New York, 1947, p. 54.
[28] *Ibid.*, p. 29.

is closed the convict has begun to react to the routine of the prison. As we stated, the average prison keeps new inmates in quarantine as a precautionary measure against the spread of contagious disease. Within the first few hours the prisoner is fingerprinted, given a housing (or cell) assignment, issued prison clothing, required to bathe and to present himself for a physical examination. Male prisoners are also given a haircut and a shave. In general the whole admissions process has been a dreary, lonely experience.

Because of the isolation imposed during the quarantine the first few weeks of prison are often worse from an emotional point of view than the trial itself. The prisoner is usually overcome with gloom at the thought of the time he must spend there. Any contact with fellow inmates may serve merely to augment his preoccupation with himself.

The Orientation Program

As a method of dealing more effectively with the newly arrived prisoner the United States Prison Bureau has recently developed one of the most constructive projects in the annals of penology. This is the orientation program which a few prisons have now launched. It has been conceived with the idea of helping the prisoner make the best use of the facilities provided and profit from the mental therapy to be derived from group activity. What was formerly the isolation period is now devoted to giving the prisoner a picture of the vocational, recreational, educational, religious, health, case-work, and counseling services which the prison maintains for his benefit.

Older prison regimes made much of solitary confinement and of the prisoner's reflecting on his past in order to resolve to live the good life. Experience has taught that few prisoners benefit from any concentrated thought about their misconduct. They tend instead to become more emotional and discouraged or rebellious.

One of the new devices employed during the orientation program is group discussions of their problems. Sharing a problem is dividing a problem, according to many psychologists, and prisoners appear to profit from recognizing that other prisoners have just as serious problems as they have. Some authorities have feared that prisoners might contaminate each other by group discussions, but since prisoners always find ways to communicate it is far better to have them discuss their problems under professional guidance if this can be arranged.

New inmates are now introduced to the institution by a conducted tour in a number of prisons. They can see the schools, workshops, recreational activities in action. The use of a series of films made within the institution may also be helpful in explaining programs.

The routine of prison life is explained—that is, what is expected of the inmates in the way of procedures and regulations; the rules of conduct, the methods of discipline; the purpose of the classification committee and its relation to the inmate; the hours for visiting; the health service; the privileges which the prisoner has; the matter of "good time" and of how parole is secured; the need for preserving institutional property; how to use a library; the relationships between inmates and the staff. All these and other items are explained. Especially to be emphasized is the importance of morale and observing rules of mental hygiene.

Obviously some of the topics will come up in group discussions and in the question and answer period. Some can be best explained in the tour. Discussions themselves should be led by those best qualified. As the federal prison officials have found, the staff must work out the orientation program with the personnel and facilities available. The librarian may discuss the library facilities, or a film may provide a good basis for discussion. Films are particularly valuable in arousing interest in education and vocational training. Films are in fact much better mediums for getting across the importance of securing psychiatric counsel for emotional upsets, for overcoming hostility, for presenting health lectures, for creating favorable attitudes toward the law, etc., than any amount of moralizing. A wide variety of films is available on these topics. In the field of vocational guidance there are also many films which give detailed information on the various trades and skilled occupations.[29]

General Recommendations for the Classification Committee

1. The person in charge of the reception center generally writes a letter to the family giving them information about the prisoner's commitment, his probable stay, the rules for visiting, the regulations with reference to correspondence, sending packages, etc.[30] In writing to relatives staff members must be careful to create an atmosphere of sincerity in the letter. After a letter is received from the wife, parents, or other relatives, the officer should try to adapt his style and vocabulary to the educational level of his correspondent. Without sentimentality, the relatives must be told the exact nature of the case. If ex-

[29] This information was derived chiefly from an article, "New Developments in the Admission-Orientation Program," in *Progress Report*, 3:4–16 (January, 1949), published by the Bureau of Prisons, U.S. Department of Justice, Washington.

[30] *Handbook on Classification in Correctional Institutions*, p. 29.

planations are asked with reference to rulings, these should be given courteously. Sometimes relatives get very indignant in their correspondence with prison officials. If the latter would only try to envisage the bitterness, frustration, and grief of the inmate's family it would do much to reduce the tensions which sometimes arise between prison officials and inmate's relatives. Furthermore, where they are convinced of the integrity and friendliness of prison officials the family can do much to assist the prisoner in co-operating with rules and regulations.[31] On the other hand many prisoners come from a background of lawlessness, crime, and vice and in such cases there is little reason to expect any desirable help from the family.

2. The testing program usually comes during the first or second week of the reception period. Most prison authorities apparently encourage this prompt action in order to get the prisoner into the swing of prison life as early as possible. He is given several mental tests, educational achievement tests, personality tests, and interest tests. The psychiatric test is also administered early in order to arrive at an adequate picture of his personality.[32]

There are often good reasons why these tests should be administered later and a good orientation program will take these into consideration. Since most prisoners, particularly first offenders, are emotionally upset about entering prison, they might very well place differently in the intelligence tests if they were administered when the prisoners had become somewhat adjusted to prison life.

3. The educational status of the prisoner may be determined by securing school records and by discovering his educational interests. Educational opportunities within the institution may be explained and special materials may be secured for him to work on in the cell. Here again prison officials may size up the prisoner's abilities and interests wrong because of his difficulties in adjusting to the prison.[33]

4. Vocational placement of the prisoner depends upon a number of considerations. If he possesses certain skills for which there is real need in the maintenance of the prison he may be placed at a task related to his training. Most prisoners are less productive in prison than outside, as we shall discuss elsewhere. When men are belligerent and unco-operative their real capacities may not be discovered. But their belligerent and emotional frame of mind may give real insight into the particular problems they entail as prisoners.

[31] *The Way to Prison Work*, prepared by the Staff of the Bureau of Prisons, U.S. Department of Justice, Washington, 1946, Vol. I, pp. 70–71.

[32] *Handbook on Classification in Correctional Institutions*, p. 30.

[33] *Ibid.*, p. 31.

5. The recreational program in the prison gives opportunity to evaluate the ability of the individual to participate in group activities.[34] His failure to observe rules and regulations may be as indicative as the psychiatric examination of important aspects of his personality. On the other hand many prisoners have never learned to play with others, and this defect may be as much a lack of training as it is of any fundamental antisocial tendency.

6. Where possible those members of the classification committee reporting their opinions at the classification meetings should have some opportunity to interview the prisoner, at least with reference to the specific aspect of his personality on which they are expected to report.

Out of the variety of analyses of the inmate's personality, as outlined above, the classification committee makes reports at a staff conference. After the material presented has been discussed, recommendations for the prisoner's special treatment are made. Sometimes the committee recommends that the prisoner be transferred to another institution. In states where there are several types of institutions transfer may be possible if the practice is permitted by the state board in charge of prisons. Under the Federal Prison System this usually is possible.

Frequently the time element is a serious factor in making adequate recommendations. The plan imposed upon the particular inmate may affect his whole future life and should not be quickly or perfunctorily determined.[35] Fortunately there is always some opportunity for reclassification; in most institutions the inmate himself can petition for reclassification. For the long-term prisoner this right is especially important, because some measure of satisfaction in his daily routine is essential to maintaining his morale. If the prisoner can take a correspondence course and learn to write for publication that is an important achievement. Or he may take equal satisfaction in cultivating a flower bed, in raising vegetables, in weaving a rug, or, as in the case of a Kansas lifer, in raising canaries. Life must go on—and it is well to have it go on as worthily as possible—even in prison.

The classification of prisoners thus proceeds on a variety of assumptions. If the prisoner is mentally defective he must not be expected to make much educational advancement; he cannot be placed in a job requiring judgment and insight. If he is intelligent, he may or may not be strong. If he is not strong, he must be assigned light or clerical tasks. He may be so emotionally disturbed as to be belligerent and en-

[34] *Ibid.*, pp. 31–32.   [35] *Ibid.*, p. 35.

danger the safety of others. In such case he obviously requires psychiatric treatment or at least some psychological assistance. He may have a venereal disease or tuberculosis and require medical treatment. He may be a narcotic addict and be transferred to a special institution. He may be a recidivist and shrewdly adept at thwarting any plans for his readjustment. There are many problems to confuse and confound the classification committee, but in general prisoners tend to fall into types which those in prison service can recognize. Occasionally they err seriously, as in the case of a "trusty" in a western prison who was assigned to work outside the walls as driver for the warden. This man could have escaped any day he tried. He felt on his honor about not trying to escape, but this attitude did not prevent him from being ringleader in a plan within the prison to blow up the prison. He secured some dynamite through outside contacts and enlisting the head cook's aid obtained a kettle in which nitroglycerin could be extracted from the dynamite. This kettle had been brewing on a prison stove for three weeks before the plot was discovered.

It has been the author's privilege to sit in on classification committee meetings in a variety of prisons. Unfortunately no classification committee can go further than its collective insight into the problems which the individual prisoner presents. Many opinions must remain opinions rather than facts and the petty prejudices of the institutionalized personnel sometimes operate against a fair consideration of facts. Personalities rub the wrong way in prison just as they do in any household. Sometimes the suspicion attached to a prisoner may depend upon factors buried in the background of the warden, the psychologist, the schoolteacher, the reception officer, etc. In every prison there probably has been some official who has taken an active dislike to a prisoner for little or no good reason. A man up for parole consideration in a certain prison was once emotionally denounced by the warden at a reclassification hearing in this writer's presence. Actually the prisoner had done nothing, in the opinion of the other officers, to provoke such a tongue-lashing. But because they were subordinate in rank they did not protest the warden's verdict and the prisoner withdrew in embittered silence.

EDUCATION IN PRISONS

Historically, the development of educational opportunities in state prisons (as a serious part of the inmate's institutional experience) began with the opening of the first reformatory at Elmira, New York, as we have already mentioned. The Elmira pattern of education unfortunately declined with the passage of time. Seven additional maximum security reformatories for young men were conducting educational programs of high professional standard by 1940. These were the state reformatories in Illinois, Kansas, Michigan, Minnesota, Pennsylvania, Washington, and Wisconsin. In four minimum security institutions, those in Massachusetts, Missouri, New Jersey, and New York, excellent standards of educational procedure were in effect.

Certain state prisons also had well-developed educational programs: those at San Quentin, California; Stateville, Illinois; Fort Madison, Iowa; Jackson, Michigan; Lincoln, Nebraska; Attica, Clinton, and Sing Sing, New York; the Eastern, Western, and Rockview prisons in Pennsylvania; and the Waupun Prison in Wisconsin. The San Quentin prison, the Waupun Prison, and the prisons in Pennsylvania, incidentally, have had educational programs over a considerable length of time.[36]

In certain prisons an inmate directs the schools, but this policy cannot be recommended. One inmate teacher known to the author in the course of official duties was a dentist who was a chronic forger. He had served in four different state prisons for forgery. In each case he had set up and organized a school for the illiterates and special courses for those wishing to pursue other study. At the Kansas State Penitentiary he developed courses in painting, typing, French, and accounting for the inmates.

There are numerous disadvantages to relying on inmate teachers. When the inmate director's sentence expires, or he is paroled, the school may fold up for want of a leader. Competent teachers thus are often lacking if outside teachers are not hired. Few professional educators, it might be added, are committed to prison. Hence a well-rounded educational program is seldom possible if no civilian teachers are employed.[37]

Varieties of Educational Programs

In general the formal educational programs in prisons consist in two major types: (1) the academic educational program for illiterates and near illiterates with additional training for those who have completed grammar school and wish to pursue high school studies, and (2) adult

[36] Austin H. MacCormick, *Education of Adult Prisoners*, National Society for Penal Information, New York, 1931, pp. 288–289.
[37] *Ibid.*, chap. 16, "The Supervisory and Teaching Staff."

educational programs. These latter fall into 3 types: (a) those of a general cultural or technical level ranging from French literature and the modern novel to courses in accounting, which are given within the prison, (b) correspondence courses in which prisoners pursue study in their cells according to outlines from universities or from correspondence schools, and (c) vocational training courses in the skilled trades, as, for example, radio repair work, piano tuning, etc.

California State Prison at San Quentin, California, has one of the best educational programs of any state prison. Anyone who wishes to attend classes or take extension courses is allowed to do so if his behavior, classification, and educational achievement tests qualify him to do so. Education is not compulsory, but an effort is made to get all men to complete the fifth grade. Western Penitentiary in Pittsburgh, Pennsylvania, goes further in exacting educational requirements and does not release men ordinarily until they have completed the sixth grade.

In the San Quentin prison approximately 2000 are enrolled in the 58 classes which run from 8:30 A.M. to 10:10 P.M. There are two grammar schools, a commercial school, and a high school, a large counseling program and a vocational program. Students completing grammar school and high school receive diplomas from the California State Department of Education with no indication that they pursued their studies in prison. Many also take extension courses from the University of California or other institutions of higher learning. The teachers at the prison are all college graduates and are properly certified for teaching. The accompanying chart showing the schedule of courses given at San Quentin from April 3, 1950, to June 9, 1950, indicates the variety of offerings. This prison gives the inmates a real opportunity to make up their educational deficiencies.

In addition to academic training many prisons provide a wide variety of opportunities for informal education. Most prisons have libraries where books on a wide range of topics and current magazines are available. The Federal Prison System has an especially well-organized library service under the direction of trained librarians. Here the more intellectual prisoners who are so permitted tend to spend much of their leisure time. But all prisoners will usually find some interest in the books, magazines, and newspapers in the prison library. Many library accessions should be chosen with the idea of stimulating reading on the part of the inmate.

Unfortunately state prison libraries often consist chiefly in the cast-off books collected from attics and basements by women's clubs or the

TABLE 23.1. Class Schedules of the 1950 Educational Program at San Quentin Prison, California

Class	Room	Time
Grades 1 and 2 (V)	1	8:30–11:30
Grades 3 and 4 (V)	2	8:30–11:30
Grade 5 (V)	3	8:30–11:30
Commercial Classes	4–11–12	8:30–11:30
Automotive Mechanics, Apprentice (V)	Quonsets 1, 2, and 3	8:30–11:30
Garment Making, Vocational	New Ind. Bldg.	8:30–11:30
General Shop (V)	18	8:30–11:30
Grade 6 (V)	1	12:45–3:45
Grade 7 (V)	2	12:45–3:45
Grade 8 (V)	3	12:45–3:45
Commercial Classes (V)	4–11–12	12:45–3:45
Automotive Mechanics, Apprentice (V)	Quonsets 1, 2, and 3	12:45–3:45
Garment Making, Vocational	New Ind. Bldg.	12:45–3:45
General Shop (V)	18	12:30–3:30
Printing, Vocational (V)	New Ind. Bldg.	8:30–3:45
Shoe Repair, Vocational (V)	New Ind. Bldg.	8:30–3:45
Machinist, Apprentice (V)	Old Ind. Building	8:30–3:45
Drafting, Vocational (V)	Ed. Building	8:30–3:45
Carpentry, Vocational	Room 15	8:30–3:45
Adjustment Counseling "A" (V)	Quonset 5	9:00–11:00 Saturday
Adjustment Counseling "B" (V)	Record Building	12:00–2:00 Saturday
Adjustment Counseling "C" (V)	Record Building	2:00–3:00 Saturday
Guidance Counseling	Record Building	8:30–3:15
Guidance Counseling	GC Room 1	8:30–3:15
Guidance Counseling	GC Room 2	8:30–3:15
Guidance Counseling	GC Room 3	8:30–3:15
Guidance Counseling	GC Room 4	8:30–3:15
Guidance Counseling	GC Room 5	8:30–3:15
Guidance Counseling	GC Room 6	8:30–3:15
Guidance Counseling	GC Room 7	8:30–3:15

Class	Room	Time
World Geography-B (V)	1	6:00–7:00
Public Speaking-B	2	6:00–7:00
High School English-A	7	6:00–7:00
Biological Science-B (V)	8	6:00–7:00
Shop Mathematics	9	6:00–7:00
United States History-B (V)	6	6:00–7:00
Typing—Beginners and Advanced (V)	4	6:00–7:00
Grade 6 (V)	14	6:00–8:00
Grade 7 (V)	10	6:00–8:00
Grade 8 (V)	3	6:00–8:00
Bookkeeping—Beginners and Advanced (V)	5	6:00–8:00
Commercial Art	11 and 12	6:00–8:00
Drafting—Beginners and Advanced	15	6:00–8:00
Agriculture–General (V)	A Room	6:00–8:00
Academic Education, Intermediate (V)	Old Prison	6:00–8:00
Social Living "A"	Old Record Office	6:00–8:00 Mon.–Thur.
Audio Visual Aids	17	6:00–8:00
General Shop—Beginners and Advanced (V)	18	6:00–9:00
Arts and Crafts	Handicraft Shop	6:00–10:00 M-T-W
Arts and Crafts	Handicraft Shop	6:00–10:00 Thur.–Fri.
Physical Science-B (V)	8	7:00–8:00
Civics-B (V)	2	7:00–8:00
Spanish A and B (V)	1	7:00–8:00
Business English-A	7	7:00–8:00
High School Mathematics	9	7:00–8:00
World History-B (V)	6	7:00–8:00
Typing—Beginners and Advanced (V)	4	7:00–8:00
Grades 1 and 2	1	8:00–10:00
Grade 3 (V)	10	8:00–10:00

Salvation Army. No satisfactory prison library can proceed on the
notion that "a book is a book." Most state prison libraries harbor much
trash which should be thrown out. Well-selected volumes can open
up new intellectual horizons for the prisoners. Well-equipped reading
rooms which are open to inmates during stated periods will do much
to relieve the tediousness and loneliness of prison existence and have a
wholesome effect on the prisoners' thinking and emotional life.

Many state prisons publish some sort of inmate journal. All the federal prisons do. Federal prisons probably have a higher proportion of
educated men and some of their journals possess real intellectual merit.
The New Era published by the Leavenworth Penitentiary and the
Atlantian published in Atlanta, for example, are very creditable publications. The United States Bureau of Prisons maintains that these
journals reflect life in the United States rather more accurately than
life in prison, and this assertion is undoubtedly true. Such journals certainly provide stimulating work and training for the editorial staff and
would appear to exert a genuinely desirable influence on the inmates.
They may be compared to collegiate journals, except that there is obviously less emphasis upon loyalty to the institutional ideals in the case
of prison journals. But pride in institutional achievement and in
literary contributions may be stimulated by prison journalism. Furthermore setting up and printing such journals gives splendid vocational
training to the printers, who are usually able to secure placement in
their trade after release. Prison printing plants, particularly those in
the federal system, probably do about the best on-the-job training that
is conducted within prison walls. A good job of printing is a good job
of printing whether within or without a prison.

Vocational Education

As we have observed, many of the San Quentin courses are vocational in nature. Vocational education is exceedingly valuable because
of the importance we must attach to the prisoners' post-institutional
employment. Adjustment after release from the institution will depend to a large degree on the prisoner's ability to do some sort of work
well enough to secure a job. If he can get a job doing something he
both likes and does well, he has cleared an important hurdle.

Vocational education and the classification system sometimes operate at cross-purposes, as Donald Clemmer has pointed out. If a man
appears to be an excellent risk and is transferred to a minimum security institution where he cannot secure the training he desires which

is available at the maximum security prison, the transfer may be a serious mistake.[38] Any vocational training program must take into consideration the capacities of the individual; the location to which he is to be paroled; and the facilities which the prison has. Because there is no longer any extensive market for prison-made goods vocational training in prisons is definitely limited by the variety of articles which can be consumed by other state institutions or facilities.[39]

Within the prison the routine work offers certain opportunities for training in electrical repair work, bricklaying, painting, baking, cooking, tailoring, laundry work, mechanical repair work, etc., and if these processes are properly analyzed they too may be properly taught as subjects for vocational education. All of these processes require skills and these skills can be analyzed and taught under the direction of suitable instructors.

Part of the problem obviously lies in securing suitable teachers. Vocational instructors must know how to resolve the job into processes and how to help estimate and gauge the effectiveness (or lack of effectiveness) of the inmate student's progress. Since many teachers in prison are inmates, they in turn involve problems of emotional instability, of "subversive" methods, of homosexuality and other personality problems which must be considered by the administration.[40]

Education in Women's Prisons

With the exception of the Federal Reformatory for Women, few prisons for women give any adequate educational program. Most of the education given women in prison is that informally acquired in the household arts, cooking, cleaning, sewing, canning. Some prisons also give training in basic principles of agriculture in connection with their farm programs.[41]

This author cannot share Austin H. MacCormick's enthusiasm for such an educational program. A large number of the women in prison were domestically employed before their arrest, conviction, and sentence. That does not prove, as MacCormick seems to think, that further training in the household arts will solve their problems. As a mat-

[38] Donald Clemmer, "A Beginning in Social Education in Correctional Institutions," *Federal Probation*, 13:32–35 (March, 1949).
[39] The federal legislation which limits prison industries is discussed in detail in chap. 25.
[40] Howard L. Briggs, William E. Grady, and Oakley Furney, "Vocational Education," chap. 10 in *Correctional Education Today, First Yearbook of the Committee on Education*, American Prison Association, New York, 1939, pp. 198–221.
[41] Austin H. MacCormick, *op. cit.*, chap. 19.

ter of fact a study of the post-institutional adjustment of Sleighton Farm girls in Pennsylvania showed that 76.4 per cent had just as serious difficulties in adjusting as they had before they were committed.[42]

These same girls were meticulously trained in the household arts. They learned to be excellent cooks, could keep a house beautifully clean, and had mastered the fundamental principles of household decoration. They learned to sew well. They learned to read for self-improvement and became aware of some of the beauties and mysteries of nature. But one could scarcely say that their education had any important therapeutic effect in making them well-adjusted young women. They were instead trained primarily to become good maids or waitresses and were channeled into the very jobs where temptations seem actually to be greatest for the average working girl. Instruction on how to conform to socially approved rules of sex behavior may not be easily incorporated in the educational curriculum of the average women's prison or girls' reformatory. But few if any prisons have actually tried seriously to give such instruction.

Social Education

Austin H. MacCormick has pointed out the need for educating prisoners in social and moral values.[43] How to fill this need without moralizing and calling upon the men to recognize the evil of their ways is a difficult assignment. Nevertheless preaching at men is about as effective in reforming prisoners as is the scolding wife's nagging in reforming her erring husband.

A recent attempt at social education in the correctional institutions under the direction of the Department of Corrections of the District of Columbia has taken an important step toward orienting the prisoner in important facets of social life. The curriculum includes nine courses:[44]

1. Some Principles of Human Behavior (psychology).
2. The Family and Home.
3. Principles of Child Guidance.
4. The Theory of Leisure Time.
5. Community Life and Organization.
6. Social and Economic Trends.
7. Vocational Guidance and Occupational Status.

[42] Mabel A. Elliott, *Correctional Education and the Delinquent Girl,* Commonwealth of Pennsylvania, Harrisburg, 1929, p. 37.
[43] *Op cit.,* chap. 13, "Social Education."
[44] Donald Clemmer, *op. cit.*

8. Money and Personal Budgeting.
9. Significant American Literature.

These courses patently are concerned with understanding the basis and motivations of behavior, the problems of human relationship and interaction in the family and in the community, the major economic and social changes in modern society, and American literature. The latter course we may presume to have some effect upon the leisure-time habits of inmates. The courses in Vocational Guidance and Money and Personal Budgeting should give practical insight into personal problems in post-institutional job hunting and in the matter of personal expenditures. Inability to compete effectively for a job and to live within his legitimate income have contributed to the criminality of many an offender. Such courses may contribute both directly and indirectly to the prisoner's capacity to make effective social adjustments.

Only prisoners who wished to take such courses were enrolled and only those with an I.Q. of 90 or above were allowed to take them. Usually those participating in other educational or religious programs did not have time to take these courses.

Criminology Training for Inmates

Some of the more thoughtful prisoners always turn to the matter of understanding the nature of their own behavior and what contributed to their own criminality. Those capable of self-analysis may profit from such a study. Once the present author was asked to conduct a criminology seminar for selected inmates at the Kansas State Penitentiary. This seminar was arranged by the chaplain at the prisoners' request. About 100 of the prisoners submitted questions in writing in advance. These questions were classified and many were enough alike to be combined. Under the author's direction advanced students in criminology at the university prepared "answers" and they and the author conducted a presentation of the questions and answers before an open meeting of the prisoners. Prisoners raised many questions from the floor about the general causes of crime, as well as problems of personal and post-institutional adjustment. This was an enlightening and heartening experience to the students and professor alike, for the questions involved concrete applications of scientific insight.

Criminologists must recognize in true humility that there remain numerous unexplored and unfinished tasks ahead before they can say positively they know the true and complete explanation of criminal behavior. Nevertheless enough is known to *help* the prisoner understand himself and through that understanding make some advance toward overcoming his propensity to socially condemned conduct.

RECREATION

Recreation in prison serves several purposes. (1) It gives the men a desirable and interesting outlet during their leisure time. True recreation must be enjoyable and when a man is enjoying himself emotional maladjustments and belligerent attitudes tend to disappear. (2) An important therapeutic function is served merely by improving the emotional state of the prisoners. (3) Custodial problems are reduced by keeping the men absorbed. A man engrossed in a basketball game or a movie will not be plotting to escape. (4) An effective recreational program will literally promote group morale and as a result increase industrial output and improve performance on maintenance jobs. (5) With all the current restrictions on marketing prison-made goods as enforced by the various bills discussed in the chapter on prison labor, a full employment program is difficult to achieve in prisons. Inevitably state-use demand for certain types of products must decline. A state prison may manufacture mattresses and garbage pails for other institutions but the demand for such commodities is always limited. Unless the surplus can be put on the public market there must always be dreary stretches of unemployment in prison. Well-behaved prisoners cannot be locked in their cells for long days at a stretch by any conscientious prison administration. Nor should they be left to converse idly for hours on end in the yard. Some provision must be made for taking up these slack periods and organized group recreational activity provides the simplest and best answer to the problem. Here again recreation may be a safety device as well as a therapeutic agent.

In considering all of these items it is important to provide amply for physical activity. A good gymnasium and suitable outside recreational grounds for football, baseball, and basketball should be developed. All of these physically strenuous games will improve the men's health and morale. Competition with outside teams will increase the men's interest and promote their self-respect—another important consideration in the whole matter of rehabilitation.

Prisoners, like many other persons, usually have never learned how to play. One of the important things a prison recreation program can do is to teach the prisoner to find enjoyment in wholesome, beneficial outlets. Some prisoners have undoubtedly looked upon gambling and their hazardous adventures as big-time holdup men as fun. They need to learn that quiet enjoyment, be it a good book, a movie, or a concert, yields many satisfactions; that the co-operative teamwork in a baseball or football game gives an outlet for pent-up energy without any later bitter recriminations.[45]

Sports

In Western Penitentiary at Pittsburgh, for example, most of the men are not employed more than 2 hours a day. For hours they sit idly in the prison yard, but part of their tedium is relieved by baseball games, intramural sports, intermural organizations, playing in one of the three bands, pursuing hobbies, or other activities. In some prisons boxing bouts are permitted.

Contests between cell houses or dormitories afford a wholesome opportunity for recreation both to spectators and to members of the teams. Baseball and football are favorite sports among prisoners and where there are several teams the outstanding members of each may be selected for the prison team which plays against outside teams.[46]

Prison athletics have developed partly in an effort to make prison life less grim and also to take up part of the slack in the prisoner's day because of the lack of industrial employment. Unfortunately most of the athletics is of the spectator variety. Baseball has been especially popular in prisons and has provided an interesting way for men to spend leisure time even though few gain any physical benefit.

Many prisons have calisthenic drills, setting up exercises, or some form of organized quasi-recreational drills which aim at least to help keep the inmates physically fit.

Small Games

Other less strenuous games, of both outdoor and indoor variety, should be provided for prisoners. Croquet, shuffleboard, and tennis might well afford healthy leisure-time diversion. Tennis rackets may seem like expensive equipment, but the men themselves could keep them in repair. Ping-pong tables might be available for inside play. Games requiring mental concentration such as bridge, checkers, chess,

[45] Lewis E. Lawes, "Rehabilitation Comes from Within," *Prison Administration—An Educational Process, Yearbook of the Committee on Education,* American Prison Association, New York, 1940, pp. 57–69.

[46] Kenyon J. Scudder, "A Warden's View on Physical Education and Recreation in Correctional Treatment," *Proceedings of the Seventy-Sixth Annual Congress of Correction of the American Prison Association,* 1946, pp. 145–151.

pinochle, etc., could be provided. Many wardens frown on card playing because gambling is often a serious problem in prison. Gambling is
a problem, however, only when cards are played in secret. If card playing is in the open and under supervision, Warden Kenyon J. Scudder
believes men will co-operate to maintain the privilege.[47]

Dramatics and Music

Dramatics and music permit unexcelled opportunities for self-ex-
pression and have long been recognized as successful methods for obtaining emotional release. Furthermore they may permit development
of skills which will prove useful on release from the prison. Singing societies, prison glee clubs and community singing all have their place
within the prison. Taking part in dramatics does much to give confidence to previously shy individuals.

RELIGIOUS WORK IN PRISONS

Clergymen and nuns were literally the first "professional" social
workers and the early churches provided the first institutions for meeting problems of the wayfarer, the poor, the illegitimate, the sick, et al.,
as well as those who offended the criminal code.[48] Since the origins of
the modern prison were religiously motivated it was inevitable that
the religious life of the prison community should eventually gravitate
to a special religious leader, the prison chaplain. The prison chaplains
in turn became the first social workers in prisons and, so far as the
majority of prisons are concerned, they still are the prison social
workers.

Except in the federal prisons and a few of the more progressive state
prisons, the chaplain performs several important functions in addition to directing the religious services. He usually acts as an adviser
to men who have family difficulties and often establishes some contact with social workers in the prisoner's home community if his
family is in financial need or has other problems of a welfare nature.
Many inmates have serious worries about their wives and children who
have no visible means of support. Other prisoners may be in serious
conflict about their own criminal records and seek the chaplain's aid
in overcoming belligerent attitudes toward police, informants, or other

[47] Ibid.
[48] William J. Ashley, *English Economic History*, Part 2, p. 315, quoted in Amos G.
Warner, Stuart A. Queen, and Ernest B. Harper, *American Charities and Social Work*,
Crowell, New York, 4th ed., 1930, p. 12.

persons whom they believe to be responsible for their arrest and conviction. In a very real sense the chaplain may be a mental hygienist and psychiatric social worker insofar as he affords an opportunity for the prisoner's emotional release and helps him in the development of desirable mental attitudes.

Prisoners often purport to have a religious background and religious affiliation, but it seems obvious that adherence to religious precepts has been singularly lacking among prison inmates. Few men would go to prison, except as conscientious objectors, if they lived by the Ten Commandments and the Sermon on the Mount. A criminal record is generally *ipso facto* admission that the individual has rejected (temporarily at least) the basic principles of ethical conduct which are inherent in the Judaic-Christian tradition. Moreover prisoners are frequently so unprincipled as to enlist the support of chaplains in securing their release with the basic idea of returning to a life of bigger and better crimes. Many prisoners simulate a religious interest when they have none.

Since much of the process of reformation must come from within, it is part of the chaplain's function to stimulate the prisoner to a decision to embark upon a moral and upright life. Few if any truly rehabilitated men have become such without the incentive of belief in resources outside themselves and a reorientation with reference to the validity of moral principles. At least this in final analysis is the message and inspiration of religion.

Religious leaders have supplied the basic concepts of modern penology. It is they who have insisted upon the dignity of human personality, upon the importance of the redemptive power of love and the futility of brutal and vindictive punishment. And it is to the religious leadership within the prison that we must look to help the prisoners understand the creative and regenerative power of love.

Naturally the best of prison chaplains will not be able to help all the men in the prison. And unfortunately many prison chaplains are broken-down ministers who are either too naïve or incompetent to act as an effective spur toward moral rehabilitation. Prison religious work should enlist the ablest and best-trained clergy, if they would reorient the lives of prisoners. In connection with their work chaplains should sit in the classification committee and assist in working out plans for the prisoners' placement and training within the institutions.

Effective religious leadership must provide for religious services and instruction in the Protestant, Jewish, and Catholic faiths. Today the Federal Council of Churches of Christ in America, the Catholic

University of America, and various Jewish organizations are co-operating in developing training programs for men entering prison religious work.[49]

Western Penitentiary in Pittsburgh, Pennsylvania, and Dannemora Prison in New York were the two first prisons in the United States to have chapels used exclusively for religious purposes. In many prisons the stark auditoriums used for movies and for other entertainments make it difficult to create anything resembling a religious atmosphere, even during the services. Religious organizations and foundations might contribute significantly to the religious life of the prisons if they contributed to funds for erecting suitable religious edifices in the prison yards.

Case Work in Prisons

Outside of our federal institutions very little social work on a professional level exists in prisons. In a few states, however, experimental work has been financed by social service agencies. In such cases staff members are usually referred to the prisoners because their families have become clients of the local welfare organization.

Case work in prisons has many facets. Sometimes the moody, restless behavior of a prisoner grows out of resentment against his living arrangements—a studious and cultivated prisoner may be forced to share a cell with a boisterous, crude person. Occasionally a young person serving a sentence for his first offense is placed with notorious criminals. Often men are assigned to the same cell for no other reason than that they work in the same prison shop. Case work would prevent such problems.

REHABILITATION MUST COME FROM WITHIN

Irrespective of the importance to be attached to other considerations, Warden Lewis E. Lawes held stanchly to the idea that rehabilitation can come only from "within," that is, from the prisoner's own rational introspection.[50] To this end he believed the institution should therefore provide some opportunity for the prisoner to evaluate himself and the criminal way of life and to seek help in overcoming his difficulties. He also held that the prison should similarly work at discovering and eliminating the obstacles which the prisoner must over-

---

[49] Most of these ideas on religious work are developed more fully in James V. Bennett's article, "The Role of the Modern Prison Chaplain," *Proceedings of the American Prison Association*, 1937, pp. 379–388.

[50] Lewis E. Lawes, *op. cit.*

come. Sometimes men can find themselves through developing new skills and outlets.

Warden Lawes tells of a man, called "Fred," who was sentenced for 30 years as a third-time offender. Fred's case history read like that of many another recidivist. At the age of 10 he was sent to a truant school, at 12 to a protectory, and at 14 to a juvenile reformatory. Two years later he was sent to an adult reformatory. After each commitment he was returned to the same unsavory home environment. At 18 he was convicted and sentenced to a federal prison for transporting stolen cars across interstate lines. Two years later he was sentenced for 5 years for burglary in a midwestern state. All this before he was sentenced to Sing Sing.

The average classification committee would unquestionably diagnose Fred as a vicious criminal to be confined under maximum security conditions. What to do with him at Sing Sing became a serious problem. He worked 3 years in the knit shop; he attended a few classes in the prison school. His personality showed no improvement whatsoever.

Then the position of civilian bandmaster was created at Sing Sing. A trained musician, the bandmaster directed the musical activities and also instructed men in playing the various instruments. From where he worked in the knit shop, Fred could hear the band playing. One day he went to Mr. Lawes and asked to be assigned to the band. The bandmaster became interested in Fred and taught him to play the trombone. Fred also learned to play other instruments. He began to study music seriously and spent nearly all his institutional earnings on music and books on harmony, counterpoint, and composition.

An orchestra leader from New York City chanced to visit the prison and heard Fred play. He pronounced him one of the best trombone players in the United States. In fact he offered to employ Fred if his parole could be arranged. Unfortunately the length of his sentence would not permit such an early parole. Nevertheless Fred had found himself and in Mr. Lawes' estimation he was rehabilitated. It is unfortunate that New York and other states should retain such rigid laws as to make it impossible for the prisoner to be released when everything seems to point to his effective readjustment.[51] Fred is undoubtedly an exception in the sense that he has developed hidden talents to an astonishing degree.

Finding a niche in which one can do something well that he wants to do, and that someone wants done seriously enough to pay for the

[51] *Ibid.*

service, sums up the major tasks involved in all vocational placement. Many prisoners obviously have never found such a niche in legitimate employment before their imprisonment. Nevertheless all men have some talents or abilities and it should be part of the person's educational counseling to find those talents. For this reason vocational tests should be administered soon after the prisoner is received so that some sensible plan can be developed for discovering his innate skills. Otherwise, although some men stumble onto their vocational interests in a haphazard fashion, the majority may never realize what special capacities they have, nor will the prison officials realize that the prisoners' individual faculties deserve development and training.

In summary we may say that the orientation program represents one of the most salutary developments in the modern prison. For the process of orientation is concerned with the prisoner's making the most advantageous use of the facilities which the prison provides. There are also other alterations which need to be made if the classification system is to accomplish any true rehabilitation of the men. These Nathan Berman has analyzed as follows: (1) Prisoners should be housed according to age, background, and temperament. (2) More attention should be paid to the quality of the food, for this is often a source of discontent. (3) Some provision for participation in self-government should be made so that the inmates may see the relationship between their participation and benefits to the group. (4) The prison should co-operate in co-ordination of the whole problem of crime prevention and treatment under an over-all state organization. (5) The prison itself should participate in helping to extend probation. (6) It should make recommendations for the development of small institutions for the treatment of the younger, more hopeful prisoners. (7) Initially prisons should secure an extension of case-work services to prisoners, through private agencies, in order to demonstrate the effectiveness of helping the individual and working out family problems which are often a matter of serious distress to the prisoner.[52]

SELECTED BIBLIOGRAPHY

Attorney General's Survey of Release Procedures, Vol. V, *Prisons*, U.S. Department of Justice, Washington, 1939. This volume surveys existing conditions in prisons throughout the United States.

Barnes, Harry E., *A Concise Plan for the Organization of a State Department of Correction*, Institute of Local Government, Pennsylvania State

[52] Nathan Berman, "Case-Work Needs in Our Penal Institutions," *Social Service Review*, 19: 516–524 (December, 1945).

College, State College, 1945. This gives a well-thought-out plan for a state department of correction, as developed by a sociologist with a long-time interest in prisoners.

Bennett, James V., "The Role of the Modern Prison Chaplain," *Proceedings of the American Prison Association*, 1937, pp. 379–388. The director of the United States Bureau of Prisons presents his views on the important place of religious leadership in the prison's program of rehabilitation.

Berman, Nathan, "Case-Work Needs in Our Penal Institutions," *Social Service Review*, 19:516–524 (December, 1945). This reviews important "next steps" in case work in prisons.

Clemmer, Donald, "A Beginning in Social Education in Correctional Institutions," *Federal Probation*, 13:32–35 (March, 1949). This article discusses many of the practical aspects of co-ordinating prison administration and classification with the need of the prisoners for educational training.

Correctional Education Today, First Yearbook of the Committee on Education, American Prison Association, New York, 1939. This yearbook gives a comprehensive analysis of educational problems in prisons.

Lawes, Lewis E., "Rehabilitation Comes from Within," *Prison Administration—An Educational Process, Yearbook of the Committee on Education*, American Prison Association, New York, 1940, pp. 57–69. The famous warden of Sing Sing reviews the problem of reorienting the thinking and motivations of prisoners.

MacCormick, Austin H., *Education of Adult Prisoners*, National Society for Penal Information, New York, 1931. Although published 20 years ago, this book is still one of the most important analyses of the problems (and lacks) in educational work in American prisons.

"New Developments in the Admission-Orientation Program," *Progress Report*, Bureau of Prisons, U.S. Department of Justice, Washington, 3:4–11 (January, 1949). A statement of the new developments in orientation is accompanied by suggestions of ways and means of accomplishing a better admissions program for federal prisoners.

Pugmire, D. Ross, *The Administration of Personnel in Correctional Institutions in New York State*, Bureau of Publications, Teachers College, Columbia University, New York, 1937. This gives a practical analysis of the problems of personnel in correctional institutions in New York.

Scudder, Kenyon J., "A Warden's View on Physical Education and Recreation in Correctional Treatment," *Proceedings of the Seventy-Sixth Annual Congress of Correction of the American Prison Association*, 1946, pp. 145–151. This article gives an excellent statement of the importance of physical education and recreation in maintaining the morale of prisoners.

CHAPTER 24

Prison Discipline[1]

The custodial function of the prison is obviously closely related to the problem of prison discipline, which includes the enforcing of rules and regulations and the discovery and punishment of refractory conduct on the part of prisoners. The fortress character of the Auburn type of prison is in itself a crystallization of discipline in architectural terms. This, of course, is an imposed discipline by which the very nature of the structure makes the retention of its inmates relatively certain. The mere fact that a man is deprived of his liberty and confined for a certain period of his life within prison walls is also evidence of the coercive control which the state exercises over at least some of its antisocial members. Social workers, religionists, and penologists frequently question the validity of such coercion, but public opinion has never been much aroused by any scientific evidence with reference to the failure of prisons. In general the opinion seems to be that criminals knew they were breaking the law and they got what they deserved.

Of course a modicum of coercion or highly implemented social control is common to all experience. Theoretically we fight wars for freedom, pass laws guaranteeing freedom, and even wage civil litigation to secure freedom. But freedom to do as one likes is a chimera, an ideal never achieved. In final analysis there is no real (in the sense of complete) freedom in the world of men; there is only a relative freedom, the freedom to behave oneself according to the dictates of the group. Nor is there any certainty that the social group is always consistent in

[1] Most of this chapter is taken from Mabel A. Elliott, *Coercion in Penal Treatment: Past and Present*, Pacifist Research Bureau, Ithaca, New York, 1947, Sections 8 and 9, "Coercive Treatment Within Prisons" and "A Survey of Prison Disciplinary Practices."

648

defining its approval of freedom. Principles are often altered in times of social stress, particularly in wartime.

What sort of freedom do common citizens possess? Freedom to obey the laws, freedom to get a job if there is one, freedom to starve or be on relief rolls if there is not. Each one of us conforms to countless social, economic, climatic, and physiological controls. We are free to dress insuitably and succumb to pneumonia, free to live beyond our income and suffer the hounding of the collector. The husband is free to desert his wife and be haled into court. The student is free to neglect his studies and receive a flunk mark. The mother is free to neglect her children and face the remorse of having a delinquent child. One might go on *ad infinitum*.

There are many areas of social control, but even the law, the type of social control backed by the compulsive power of the state, is enforced as much by the desire to be respected as by the fear of the consequences of breaking a law. Thus the law, just like other forms of social control, exercises restraint over behavior. For whatever reason a person breaks the law he is subject to the special variety of punitive treatment which the law itself requires. Even here, however, the formal regulations on the statute books are limited by judicial decision, common practice, and public opinion. As in other areas of human conduct, attitudes which are generally accepted and customs which generally prevail affect the jury in rendering a verdict and the judge in passing the sentence. "Trials by newspaper" are too well known in American criminal procedure to require any elaboration here. "Class" justice frequently has much to do with the judicial decision. If the judge feels any identity with the offender the penalty is likely to be less, as we have already noted.

Coercion or force in prison routine and prison treatment thus is not markedly different from coercion in civilian life. There is, however, a marked difference in the degree of coercion entailed. When the gates close behind the newly committed convict he has lost a significant degree of whatever freedom to exercise decisions his life on the outside permitted. The convict is no longer free to visit with his friends or his relatives, to drive a car, to order what he wants for dinner; nor is he free to take part in any of the hundreds of other activities which make up the commonplaces of everyday life. Nor, on the other hand, is he free to ply his illegal trade, or to execute any one of the numerous crimes or illicit desires for which he and his fellow convicts are confined. Most of the crimes which the convict might commit outside the prison are well-nigh impossible within the prison walls.

Even so, he may be a member of a group plotting a crime and sometimes he even commits a felonious offense within the prison, albeit with far greater risk than in the world outside. If caught, he is practically certain to be convicted, whereas a surprising number of crimes committed outside are never detected. Of those guilty and arrested outside, many are "nol-prossed." Outside prison walls few if any states authorize punishment for the crime plotted but not committed, however serious the foiled offense may be. Too many imponderables cast doubt on the presumptive intentions of would-be criminals. Within the prison, on the other hand, there is no hesitancy in believing the worst of the offender in case his plan for a crime is brought to light. Except for the small number of serious offenses which take place within the prison, the convict seldom faces trial at all. In case of murder or attempted murder, trial in the regularly constituted courts of the district in which the prison is located may take place. But most offenses for which prisoners are punished are petty matters. A few of the better-run prisons have prison courts which weigh the evidence turned in by the guards. In the majority of instances, however, the convict is merely charged with an offense and seldom has any satisfactory opportunity for denying guilt or establishing innocence. In general the guard or other official is always taken at his word, and if the prisoner denies the accusation he is almost always considered wrong. He may be punished, in fact, for contradicting the guard.

Whatever penalties are exacted depend largely upon the caprice of the warden or of other officials in whom disciplinary authority is vested. Often the deputy warden is the disciplinary officer. Inevitably there tends to be some abuse of authority, even in those cases where there has been some serious misbehavior on the part of the convicts. This is true chiefly because the punishment is administered by an official of the prison rather than by some impartial judge who has no personal concern in the problem.

The Brutality of Within-the-Prison Punishment

Any survey of methods of punishment within the prison shows all too clearly that brutality and extreme measures are frequently employed as punishment for breaking prison rules, and in the majority of instances for very minor offenses. Strictly speaking, the infliction of such punishment within prisons is unconstitutional since there is conviction without trial.[2] Moreover, the accused person is also assured

[2] See Article VI of the first ten Amendments to the Constitution, adopted December

by the American Constitution that no cruel or unusual punishments shall be inflicted,[3] whereas many prisoners are subjected to barbaric cruelties in punishment. Every "prisoner at the bar" outside a prison knows that he need expect no such thing as several penalties for the same offense. Occasionally a fine and a prison sentence are both required, but ordinarily there is a single penalty.

Within a prison, however, the majority of offenses for which men are punished are trivial and could not even be subject to penalty if committed outside the walls. Insolence, complaining about the food, failure to work diligently, lack of neatness in the appearance of one's clothing or one's cell can scarcely be considered criminal conduct, however distasteful such behavior may be. Yet for just such offenses within the walls prisoners may be locked in the "hot box" with the heat turned on and suffer all manner of torture. Some men have even died in such metal cells. Such punishment is not enough, however. In some prisons men so penalized must also lose their "grade" and their "good time" or chance for early release. It would take a clever lawyer to establish any legal validity for such procedure.

The sad truth is that prison officials have seldom, if ever, thought of the constitutional rights of their charges. Theoretically it is true that prisoners have lost certain civil rights. However, this circumstance can scarcely be construed to mean that prison officials may establish rules which allow them to inflict cruel or unusual suffering. It seems obvious that many punishments measure the loss in dignity which officials suffer through infractions of the rules by the inmates. Any elimination of the barbarities practiced in disciplining prisoners would probably demand an arousal of public opinion. Prisoners themselves, along with the inmates of other correctional and eleemosynary institutions, are the involuntary members of their community and cannot "talk back." They can only accept what is meted out to them in a co-operative fashion, "or else."

The officials, on the other hand, whether they be wardens, deputy wardens, principal keepers, or guards, are often products of the spoils system and have seldom had any professional training for their position save in the small group of prisons where excellent personnel standards prevail. As often as not prison employees have no special interest in criminals, but hold their positions solely as a means of making a living.

15, 1791. ("In all criminal prosecutions the accused shall enjoy the right to a speedy and public trial, by an impartial jury. . . .")

[3] Consult Article VIII of the first ten Amendments to the Constitution—"The Bill of Rights." ("Excessive bail shall not be required, nor excessive fines imposed, nor cruel and unusual punishments inflicted.")

Moreover, with the exception of two or three major positions in a prison, the majority of the employees, especially the guards, are ill paid. Naturally the low wage scale does not attract competent men. The turnover in personnel is often high; during the recent war period it was greatly accelerated. Jobs in defense plants which paid several times as well decimated the prison employees throughout the country.

But even in peacetime, personnel problems in prison staffs are legion. Since the pay is low, men are usually untrained. Untrained, insensitive men are more likely to be brutal to the convicts than are better-educated men. Actually many guards come from low-grade social and economic backgrounds themselves and this fact probably accounts for some of their attitudes and their treatment of the prisoners. Undoubtedly part of the brutality is a defense reaction, a means of maintaining the implied "social distance" which is presumed to exist between the criminal and his superior. Unhappily, the only superiority the guard may have often lies in his civilian status. Certainly many of the rank and file of prisoners have as good an education and family background as many of the guards, yet there is probably no hauteur surpassing that of the guard who asserts his superiority over the lawbreaker by inflicting a penalty on him. Guards, like judges, construe their position as one belonging definitely to the ruling class and, like all rulers, usually set themselves apart from the subjects ruled. This is at least a part of the psychological basis for the cruelties imposed by guards.

Prison Rules and Regulations

We have already indicated that most of the rules for which prisoners are punished for breaking could not be enforced in civilian life. In general they are petty regulations involving care of cell, respect for officers, subdued conduct, prompt obedience, etc. In Iowa, for example, the State Penitentiary has published a detailed rule book referring to all sorts of reprehensible behavior, with 71 separate rules which must be observed. In addition there is a long list of specifically forbidden items of lesser nature as follows:[4]

Altering clothing	Crookedness
Bed not properly made	Defaming anything
Clothing not in proper order	Dilatoriness
Communicating by signs	Dirty cell or furnishing
Creating a disturbance	Disorderly cell

[4] *Rule Book*, Iowa State Penitentiary, January, 1943, pp. 11–12.

Disobedience of orders

Disturbance in cell house

Fighting

Grimacing

Hands in pocket

Hands or face not clean

Hair not combed

Having contraband articles on your person or in your cell

Impertinence to vistors

Insolence to officers

Insolence to foreman

Insolence to fellow-inmates

Insolence at work

Inattentive in line

Inattentive in school

Laughing and fooling

Loud talk in cell

Loud reading in cell

Malicious mischief

Neglect of study

Not out of bed promptly

Not wearing outside shirt

Not promptly out of cell when brake is drawn

Out of place in shop or line

Profanity

Quarreling

Refusal to obey

Shirking

Spitting on floor

Staring at visitors

Stealing

Trading

Talking in chapel

Talking in line

Talking from cell to cell

Talking in corridor

Throwing away food

Vile language

Wasting food

Writing unauthorized letters

For these evidences of ill breeding and nonco-operation the prisoners are often severely punished. In the adult civilian world such extreme control over behavior is seldom possible. If we consider how repressed and frustrated the average prisoner is by the mere fact of his sentence we can understand how the rigidity of these regulations creates an even more rebellious attitude. Inevitably the pent-up emotions of the convicts must explode in resentment at the petty character of some of the rules. When the Pennsylvania and Auburn systems were first initiated the whole of prison life was discipline. That is, the major features of both types of prison were hard labor, the deprivation of all but the minimum essentials of living, isolation for 24 or 12 hours a day, noncommunication, moral and Biblical instruction, and an avenging justice.[5] Today this generalized coercion has given way to the required obedience to set rules, such as those in Iowa State Penitentiary.

The *Attorney General's Survey of Release Procedures* found that 60 prisons issued a printed or typewritten list of such rules. All of these were essentially negative in character—with few if any suggestions as to what to do in order to indicate a co-operative and commendable at-

[5] *Attorney General's Survey of Release Procedures*, Vol. V, Prisons, U.S. Department of Justice, Washington, 1939, chap. 5, "Discipline."

titude.[6] According to this survey practically all the punishments were of 4 general types: (1) loss of "good time," (2) solitary confinement, (3) corporal punishment, and (4) loss of privileges.

1. "Good time" refers to the reduction or commutation of sentence which automatically accompanies good behavior in most prisons. Loss of "good time" is therefore a serious penalty since it extends the time the prisoner must serve. Every state made some legal provision for good time, although in Pennsylvania and Utah such provisions were virtually inoperative at the time of the study.[7]

2. Three forms of solitary confinement applied at that time: (a) confinement in cells set aside for isolation only; (b) confinement in a special section of the prison set aside for long periods of isolation; and (c) confinement in the prisoner's own cell. This survey showed solitary confinement was a punishment exacted in all but 4 state prisons: Arkansas, Mississippi, Maryland, and the Wallkill Prison in New York.[8]

3. Corporal punishment was in practice in at least 26 prisons in 1939. Whipping with a strap was allowed in the following states: Alabama, Arkansas, California, Colorado, Delaware, Indiana, Kentucky, Louisiana, Mississippi, Missouri, Tennessee, Texas, Virginia. The number of strokes permitted varied from 1 to 25. Colorado also permitted ball and chain and cold baths; Missouri, Delaware, Montana, Ohio (London Prison), West Virginia, and Wisconsin punished by cuffing to the bars; and Kentucky allowed both ball and chain and bars. The practice known as "spread eagle" was permitted in Virginia. (This form of punishment originated in the navy. A man is lashed while his arms and legs are drawn out as far as possible.) Florida had a sweatbox. In Michigan and Ohio prisoners were confined in a standing position (known as the "cage door") so closely that they could not move.[9] In the Wisconsin prison certain prisoners were gagged. West Virginia used cold baths. Montana and North Carolina shackled prisoners who attempted to escape.

4. Loss of privilege applied usually to minor offenses, although there was no general rule. This meant a reduction in opportunity to write letters, to receive visitors, or to attend the entertainment. Sometimes extra labor was imposed or the "fractious" inmate was required to wear striped clothing.[10]

[6] Ibid.
[7] Ibid., Vol. IV, Parole, chap. 12, "Good Time Laws."
[8] Ibid., Vol. V, Prisons, chap. 5.
[9] Ibid.
[10] Ibid.

The Grading System

In addition to the above-mentioned methods of discipline, certain states attempted to control behavior by giving a meritorious grade to the well-behaved prisoner. In general the grading system is the plan (carried over from the reformatory system) of placing all men who have a record of good behavior in the top grade, designated as Grade A or Grade I. This status is usually earned during the first 60 days of prison life and the inmate stays in the classification as long as he obeys all rules. He may be demoted to Grade B (or II) or Grade C (or III) for misconduct, and if he is demoted he usually loses his "good time." Grade B imposes certain restrictions of privileges and Grade C imposes loss of all privileges and certain loss of "good time." Ordinarily a prisoner is not eligible for parole unless he has been in Grade A for at least 3 months.[11]

In a number of prisons there was some form of inmate participation in the management of an organization or activity, with formal recognition of such participation. In addition, numerous activities, such as publishing a prison magazine, operating a prison library, participating in a prison band, or teaching in a prison school, were recognized in various ways. Self-government was enthusiastically initiated at Sing Sing during Thomas Mott Osborne's wardenship but was practically nonexistent by 1935. Inmate grievance committees met with the wardens in a number of prisons, however.

A FURTHER SURVEY OF PRISON DISCIPLINARY PRACTICES IN THE VARIOUS STATES

Since many states were humiliated at the unfavorable publicity following the publication of the Attorney General's report, the present author decided to make a survey to ascertain, if possible, what punishments for failing to comply with prison rules were in effect in 1945. Because the federal prisons have been distinguished by a much higher type of personnel and regard for the prisoners' welfare and rehabilitation than have many state institutions, this checkup was limited to conditions in the various state prisons. The author sent out letters to the wardens of all state prisons requesting information as to the types of disciplinary methods employed. Several states have had notorious records for brutal treatment of prisoners, and some of the questions were obviously on a delicate subject. The author recognizes that it was much like asking a man if he still beat his wife!

[11] *Ibid.*

There was no way of verifying the replies by observation and it is highly probable that any gross mistreatment of inmates was covered up. However, some improvement undoubtedly has occurred in the administration of prisons. In any event, the material received was analyzed and, according to the wardens' statements, the practices outlined below prevailed. All told, replies were returned by wardens in 42 states. Where replies were not received at least two follow-up letters were sent. If the warden did not reply to the third letter no further attempt was made to secure information. Some of the wardens wrote unusually thoughtful and detailed replies, while others gave only scanty information, and some failed to reply altogether. Hence it was impossible to make any wholly satisfactory analysis. Nevertheless, the reports give an illuminating picture of what is happening in American prisons. It seems obvious that if wardens wished to hide any distressing aspects they might easily do so. In general, however, wardens throughout the nation reported substantially the same sort of prison discipline in the institutions under their direction.

Loss of Privileges

Thirty-one of the states from which information was received indicated that there was a restriction of privileges for infraction of rules. Actually we may assume that loss of privilege is a nearly universal form of punishment, since 37 reported solitary confinement as a form of punishment and this type of punishment inevitably restricts certain privileges.

The type of privileges restricted varied markedly, however. In some states the prisoner was denied the right to receive visitors. California, on the other hand, never denied the prisoner the right to see his wife or parents or the privilege of receiving mail from them. In a large number of instances the actual privileges lost were not indicated, but in general prisoners were denied recreational opportunities, the privilege of writing letters, the right to use tobacco and to receive visitors. Maine reports that offenses were not punished by loss of privilege but by solitary confinement and a bread and water diet. To the author this would seem to be a certain loss of privilege.

The states varied as to what offenses were punished by loss of privilege. Nebraska, for example, deprived a prisoner of his privileges for major offenses; Nevada punished minor offenders by such restrictions in privileges, as did New York and other states. New Hampshire "varied the punishment to suit the offender." In Wisconsin loss of privileges was the major method of punishment, with cumulative loss of privileges for recurrent offenses.

Loss of "good time" was likewise a frequent punishment. In certain states good time was taken away even for minor offenses, in others only for the more serious ones. In general, loss of good time was considered a serious punishment by prisoners and one to be avoided since it lengthens the time in prison.

Solitary Confinement

Thirty-seven of the 42 states reporting admitted that solitary confinement was employed for punishment. The type of solitary confinement varied widely, however. In Arizona solitary confinement was the only punishment meted out to prisoners and was designated as "snakes"! In California prisoners were confined within their regular prison cells, separated from the other cells by screens only. Inmates were thus confined in clean, light, well-ventilated cells and were "not starved, beaten, or abused." At San Quentin prison such punishment was exacted only after several previous punishments by loss of privileges. In case of extreme recalcitrance the prisoner was transferred to the maximum security institution at Folsom. Here solitary confinement was similarly limited to confinement in regular cells and confinees were given exercise daily in the yard. In Oregon men were confined to their own cells for punishment. In Rhode Island the old type of solitary confinement had been abolished and serious infraction of rules was punished by segregation in cells similar to ordinary cells but located on a gallery. Here special privileges were denied and closer supervision was provided than for the co-operative prisoners. In Virginia, similarly, real solitary confinement was not employed. A section of the regular cell block was set apart for men guilty of infraction of rules. They were not allowed yard privileges or contact with other inmates. In Alabama an inmate could not be placed in solitary confinement without an order approved by the state director of the Department of Correction and Institutions.

There was great variation in the type of treatment within the solitary cell. In many states a bread and water diet was enforced, at least for a few days. In New York State solitary confinement was accompanied by a denial of privileges but the prisoner had regular diet and exercise. In some states there were protracted periods of confinement. In Idaho men had been confined as long as 27 months.

As to the extent to which the practice of placing prisoners in solitary confinement was employed we have no accurate information. The warden of the Eastern Penitentiary in Pennsylvania says it was seldom used. Texas had three types of solitary confinement which might extend from 30 to 60 days. In the worst grade of solitary confinement the prisoner had no bed. This was probably true in many prisons, however. In Tennessee solitary prisoners were locked up on week ends on a bread and water diet. In some other states the author has reason to believe that prisoners sometimes have a long bread and water diet.

Corporal Punishment

Corporal punishment, which includes whipping, casting, crippling, and standing on a barrel for long hours at a time, was, according to the wardens' testimonies, seldom employed for purely punitive reasons. Twenty-nine states admitted that corporal punishment or force was used in self-defense or for the protection of life and property, but in only a few states was there open admission of its use in case no such danger to those in authority existed. However, in Alabama corporal punishment was permitted at Draper Prison on the order of the director of prison discipline. In Colorado such punishment was administered "in a few instances." In Mississippi corporal punishment was employed where the prisoner was wholly unmanageable, but this may allow opportunity for wide interpretation. In Tennessee the law allows such punishment but it was "seldom permitted." And the Virginia warden reported that the law permitted such punishment but it was seldom exercised.

Actually corporal punishment is probably much more widespread than these reports indicated. Thirteen of the states reporting made no mention of corporal punishment though there is reason to believe that it is employed in many of them. Oklahoma, Nevada, and Idaho all claimed to have no corporal punishment. But the reports from these states were not very clear as to how much restraint might be exercised in case of an escaping prisoner. The Kansas warden also claimed to have no corporal punishment, and no "dark hole." However, the author has personally visited the "hot box" at the Kansas State Penitentiary and the underofficers freely admitted that the box was frequently used to induce an acquiescent frame of mind on the part of the prisoner. The hot box is a small, dark, metal-lined room equipped with steam heat which can be increased to very high temperatures. The heat is turned on until the prisoner is willing to admit his desire to conform to rules.

The shameless use of hot boxes as a current form of punishment is undoubtedly much more prevalent than is generally known. Since it is so generally condemned, it is a sort of bootleg practice which wardens generally keep quiet. The scandal in the Philadelphia County Prison of Pennsylvania a few years ago, when several men died from such punishment, is a case in point.[12]

Inmate Government Organizations

Thomas Mott Osborne became famous for his plans for reorganizing Sing Sing Prison when he established a form of inmate government known as the Mutual Welfare League in 1914. His efforts did not succeed in gaining any general approval of the idea, however, and were discontinued the year following. Many wardens believe today that the plan is doomed to failure since so few prisoners are trustworthy men. Yet because the acceptance of responsibility for one's conduct is so important an aspect of good citizenship, many others have believed that some form of inmate representation in the management and discipline of an institution would have a salutary effect on both the prisoners and the disciplinary practices. Our survey shows that the majority of states do not favor inmate participation in government. California, which has better-managed prisons than many other states, considers an inmate council impractical and conducive to favoritism. However, California has many inmate-managed organizations for athletics, chess, journalistic projects, and the like.

Maine reported that the officials tried inmate government and it did not work. Former Warden Amrine of Kansas contended that he opposed inmate government because "too many prisoners are unreliable." He reminds us, whether or not correctly, that prisoners are worse than the average person. He held that the decisions and advice of inmates on any democratic basis would therefore not be conducive to the highest ideals of prison government, but would rather incorporate the ideals of criminals.

Unquestionably any plan for permitting prisoners to participate in the administration of rules involving their own discipline presents many difficulties. Prison officials have some basis for thinking prisoners would not be motivated by the highest of ethical ideals. But prisoners have broken only a few of the laws after all, as Sutherland has pointed out. They have obviously obeyed hundreds of laws and

[12] Cf. Harry E. Barnes and Negley K. Teeters, *New Horizons in Criminology*, Prentice-Hall, New York, 1951, p. 425.

have conformed to a large share of the mores. Yet civilians often forget that prisoners are relatively more law abiding than law breaking. If a large part of the civilian population both wittingly and unwittingly commits offenses which are technically crimes, as our earlier discussion has indicated, then lawbreakers are not wholly depraved. We have no reason to suppose that men, imprisoned or not, are devoid of all social sense because they have broken laws.

It is heartening therefore to know that a number of states have developed opportunities for prisoners to have a small voice in prison matters. Draper Prison in Alabama has an inmate council which presents the men's complaints, suggestions, and recommendations to the warden. Louisiana reports an inmate organization, which will permit a degree of self-government, in the process of being set up. In Nebraska inmates have the right to report an officer for "detrimental or abusive action." In New Jersey the prisoners are allowed to write to the warden with reference to any suggestions they wish to make. In New York inmates are allowed a slight amount of self-rule. Certain men act as monitors in shops and when the prisoners march to meals. In Ohio inmates have no voice in disciplinary matters but there are certain self-government privileges in other matters. In Rhode Island men participate in establishing rules and regulations but have no voice in enforcing them. In Washington the inmates have no right to enforce disciplinary rules but they participate in a recreational council. Wisconsin goes farther than some states in having an inmate advisory council; delegates represent each shop or department. The Wisconsin inmates' council meets every Sunday morning to discuss all problems and once each month the warden meets with the council. The warden reports that this council, in its advisory function, has produced many valuable suggestions for the improvement of the institution. Wyoming has an inmate committee of five which may go to the warden with complaints.

In addition to these opportunities for inmate participation several states have attempted to give fairer hearings to inmates by specially constituted courts or committees of the officers. Oklahoma, for example, has a court consisting of the deputy warden, assistant warden, and chaplain, who hear and pass on all cases. The warden retains the right to accept, reduce, or dismiss their recommendations. Virginia also has a court, in this case consisting of the principal keeper, the captain of the guards, and the assistant superintendent. In Washington a somewhat similar group is called the "three-man disciplinary committee." It studies each case and attempts to adapt the penalties to the individual offender. The warden has the right to accept or reject the committee's decision.

Stool Pigeons

Some prison officials make a practice of relying on stool pigeons to secure confidential information about the activities going on within the prison. This means of securing inside information tends to destroy the whole prison morale and wherever possible should be discouraged. When a prisoner is known to have reported on "subversive" behavior of fellow prisoners his life may be in danger. Prison plots are likely to multiply rather than to decrease when prisoners are employed as detectives.

It has been a general practice in many prisons to free a prisoner who furnishes such confidential data in order to prevent possible physical danger or attacks on his life. Even where this is done the resentment against the prison administration tends to persist. If a warden must rely on confidential information it is better to secure it through other channels. "Planted" spies who are presumably convicted and sentenced to prison and who are assumed to be convicts by the prisoners might be a much better means of securing information.

Everyone informed about penal practices knows that stool pigeons are widely used. No confidential information on the practice was gathered in this survey, since the author realized that few if any wardens would care to admit publicly that they resorted to stool pigeons. In general wardens say they have to get the information some way and this is the only way they can unearth plots against the administration.

So much for the general picture of penal treatment in the several states. Since the situation varies from state to state, students will find it profitable to read the summarized reports on discipline in each state as it applied in 1945.

Alabama

(The only information received was from the Draper Prison, which is admittedly more modern and enlightened in its penal practices than the other prisons in the state. We have ample reason to believe conditions far from ideal exist in other Alabama prisons.)

Loss of privileges was applied for minor offenses. Solitary confinement could be imposed only if recommended by the prison officials and authorized by the director of the state Department of Correction and Institutions. Corporal punishment was similarly authorized under the order of the director of prisons. An inmate council presented complaints, suggestions, and recommendations to the warden.

Arizona

According to information received from the warden, solitary confinement, which is popularly called "snakes," was the only form of punishment. There was no corporal punishment or inmate council.

Arkansas

No information was received from Arkansas. (The author was requested to come down and make a "survey.")

California

Loss of privileges for minor offenses was in effect in both San Quentin and Folsom prisons. This includes the loss of rights to attend movies and baseball games and to write letters. Prisoners were not denied the privilege of visits from wife or parents or of receiving mail from them. Persistent loss of privilege led to solitary confinement in both prisons, but it was used only in extreme cases of violation of rules. The solitary confinement section was modern, light, and well ventilated. There was no starvation diet nor were there other brutalities. The confinees were exercised in a yard each day.

Chronic misbehavior in the San Quentin prison might result in transfer to Folsom, the maximum security prison.

Corporal punishment in Folsom Prison was allowed only in protection of life of other prisoners or employees. There was no form of inmate council, but there were many inmate organizations for special-interest groups, for athletics, recreation, etc.

Colorado

Infractions of rules were usually punished by loss of privileges. No information was received as to solitary confinement, but according to information from other sources this exists.

Corporal punishment was inflicted "in a few instances." There is no inmate council or inmate government.

Connecticut

Prisoners suffered reduction in grade and restriction of privileges for infraction of rules. When reduced to third rank they were placed in solitary confinement. There was no corporal punishment or physical force except for protection of life of inmates or officers. There was no inmate government.

Delaware

The only form of punishment was solitary confinement with loss of privileges. There was no corporal punishment "except in self-defense." There was no inmate government.

Florida

Discipline at the Florida State Prison included (1) suspension of privileges, (2) reduction in grade, (3) longer periods in detention building, (4) solitary confinement, and (5) solitary on bread and water.

There was no form of inmate government. There was a Town Hall in which prisoners maintained a round-table discussion. Corporal punishment had not been inflicted "for a number of years."

Georgia

Prisoners were denied tobacco, camp freedom, and other privileges for minor offenses, along with a reduction in "good time." Solitary confinement was permitted for serious offenses, after medical examination. The warden was required to converse with the solitary prisoner every day during his confinement.

Corporal punishment was allowed only in self-defense. There was no inmate government.

Idaho

Prisoners might lose privileges for 1 week to 6 months for offenses. Solitary confinement of two varieties existed: (1) The prisoner might be locked in his own cell; (2) he might be confined in the "hole" on a bread and water diet, with no tobacco or reading material. Some prisoners had been confined as long as 27 months. After their release "such stubborn fellows were model prisoners." There was no inmate government.

Illinois (Pontiac)

At Pontiac there was demotion in grade and loss of "good time" for minor offenses and confinement in solitary for repeated offenses. Physical force was used only in self-defense. There was no inmate government.

Indiana

For minor offenses the prisoners were reprimanded. Solitary confinement was imposed for serious infraction of rules, with a reduction in privileges for 90 days after the solitary confinement. Corporal punishment was permitted only in self-defense. There was no inmate government.

Iowa

Reduction in grade was the penalty for minor offenders, with solitary confinement for serious offenders. Corporal punishment or physical force was used only in self-defense or in case of an escaping prisoner. There was no inmate government.

Kansas

Inmates were deprived of recreational opportunities, especially the movies, and the right to use tobacco and to receive visitors was withdrawn for minor offenses. Solitary confinement was used for serious offenders and to the author's knowledge a dark hole or hot box has been used, although the warden denied this. Corporal punishment, he maintained, did not exist. Inmate government was not permitted because in the warden's opinion prisoners were worse than the average civilian in their notions of ethics. Physical force was "never permitted."

Kentucky

Minor infractions were punished by confinement in cell for 3 to 5 days on bread and water—in more "aggravated" cases 6 months' confinement in cell with yard privilege abandoned, but with regular food. For definitely antisocial offenders and those who had murdered other prisoners there was permanent confinement in cells with no yard privileges.

Corporal punishment was not allowed except in self-defense. There was no form of inmate government.

Louisiana

The Louisiana prison is a prison farm and all the men live in dormitories except for a small number confined in cells for disciplinary reasons. At the time of the survey twelve were so confined. There were three solitary cells, but none was in use at the time of the survey. For minor offenses, punishments included reduction to lower grade, curtailment of mail or visiting privileges, and loss of good conduct privileges.

Corporal punishment was used only in self-defense. An inmate organization permitting a degree of self-government was in the process of being organized at the time of the survey.

Maine

Offenses were not punished by loss of privileges. Prisoners were punished by solitary confinement and might be put on bread and water for 6 days. Thereafter they received the regular noon meal and bread and molasses for supper. The warden said all cases of violence among prisoners were paranoid cases. There was no corporal punishment except in self-defense. There was no inmate government at the time of the survey. The state had "tried it out, but the plan did not work."

Maryland

No reply was received.

Massachusetts

No information was received with reference to loss of privileges. Out of some 700 prisoners about four were locked in solitary confinement each month for a period of from 3 to 10 days. There was no inmate government.

Michigan

SOUTHERN MICHIGAN PRISON

For minor offenses the prisoner might be locked in his own cell; there was loss of "good time"; the privilege of attending the movies, etc., was denied. There was a special disciplinary committee and a sociologist to check each case.

An offender might also be placed in a special detention block for a number of days, usually 5 to 10, with his privileges taken away from him. He could be placed here also on one meal a day.

Mental cases, mental "suspects," the morally unfit, and "professional skaters"[13] were placed under maximum supervision in a special block and not permitted to leave except for meals. A small yard was attached to this block where the inmates might exercise. They had all privileges except contact with the general group.

There was no corporal punishment. "Good time" was reduced only by action of the parole board.

MARQUETTE PRISON

Loss of privileges was the punishment for minor offenses. Solitary confinement was imposed for serious offenses. There was no corporal punishment except in purely defensive situations. There was no inmate government.

According to the warden, 3.92 per cent of the prisoners were reported for minor offenses, 3.6 per cent for major infractions.

Minnesota

None of the information desired was received from Minnesota. The warden submitted a copy of his annual report, which made no mention of coercive treatment within the prison.

Mississippi

Loss of privileges was the penalty for minor offenses, including loss of mail privilege and right to receive visitors. There was no solitary confinement. (The prison is a penal farm, and there are no cells.) Corporal punishment was employed but infrequently. It was used only when the prisoner was wholly unmanageable. Then fifteen lashes were applied on the buttocks with a leather strap 3½ feet long and 5 inches wide. There was no inmate government.

Missouri

No information was received. The warden wrote to the author, "It is not the policy of the Penal Board to permit disclosing of information to other than law-enforcing agencies." The reader may interpret this between the lines.

[13] This is prison parlance for sexually depraved men.

Montana

Ninety per cent of the disciplinary problems were handled through deprivation of privileges. In extreme cases solitary confinement was employed; in 90 per cent of these cases it was limited to 24 hours.

There was no physical force "under any circumstances." There was no inmate government.

According to the warden, over 50 per cent of the prisoners were employed outside the prison in an agricultural production program.

Nebraska

Minor offenses were met with reprimand. For major offenses prisoners were placed in solitary confinement with loss of privileges except mailing privileges. There was no corporal punishment except in self-defense. There was no inmate government. Inmates had the right to report an officer for detrimental or abusive action which was against established principles of the institution.

Nevada

Minor offenses were punished by curtailment of use of tobacco, regular diet, etc., or confinement to own cell. Incorrigibles were placed in a semi-isolated cell. This was an ordinary cell covered with perforated screens. Communication with other prisoners was forbidden and there was restriction of diet within limits of health during the semi-isolation. Complete isolation was no longer used except for inmates who tried to escape or who made an attempt on another prisoner's life. There was no corporal punishment and no inmate government.

New Hampshire

Punishments varied and the seriousness of each case was considered. Some prisoners were deprived of the privileges of correspondence, receiving visitors, and recreation. Others were placed in solitary confinement on a bread and water diet. There was no report on corporal punishment or inmate government.

New Jersey

Troublesome offenders were segregated. They received reading material and adequate food and were permitted a daily period of yard exercise in a separate yard. The chief punishment was the loss of opportunity to work and earn credits. This involved both loss of and remission of "good time."

There was no corporal punishment except in self-defense, and no inmate government. All prisoners might write to the warden, however, and make suggestions.

New Jersey has a classification system. Each prisoner submits to tests given by a psychiatrist, a psychologist, the Director of Education, the Director of Industries, and a number of other key officials. Out of their findings a program is developed for each individual man, to spur him to his best achievement.

New Jersey also employs release on parole more frequently than most states and this, too, provides great impetus to good behavior.

New Mexico

Loss of privileges, loss of "good time," and solitary confinement with a restricted diet were all employed for infraction of rules. All penalties must be approved by the superintendent. Corporal punishment was abolished 30 years ago, except for self-defense. There was no inmate government.

New York

(The same rules cover all New York prisons.)

Loss of privileges was imposed for minor infractions. For serious infractions solitary confinement was employed, but not in the usual sense, since the prisoner had regular meals and exercise. He was denied all recreation, and his rights to receive visitors and to correspond were curtailed. There was no corporal punishment. Force was used only when necessary for protection.

There was a slight amount of inmate government. Men acted as monitors in shops and when men marched to meals. The inmates did not administer discipline.

North Carolina

No information was received.

North Dakota

Minor infractions were met with loss of privileges of recreation, attending religious services and movies, and visiting the library. There was no set punishment. For extreme infractions solitary confinement was inflicted. There was no corporal punishment; no force was employed except for necessary restraint, but this was usually accomplished without weapons. There was no inmate government.

According to the warden, kind treatment, good food of ample quantity, employment with wages, and "good time" allowances have greater bearing on deportment and attitudes of inmates than corporal punishment can possibly have.

Ohio

The Ohio prison has a unique system of courts with a Summary Court, which hears minor violations, a Superior Court, which hears major violations, and a reviewing authority.

More than half the cases of minor violations were placed on probation or suspended sentence. Slightly more than half of those handled by the Superior Court was sentenced to segregated confinement. A slightly smaller number suffered a loss of "good time." There was no inmate organization for disciplinary purposes. There was, however, an inmate organization with certain self-government features.

Oklahoma

Minor offenders might be segregated in third class. Solitary confinement was permitted in a "dark cell" or "hole" with no bed. There was no corporal punishment except in self-defense, and no inmate government.

Oklahoma has a court, consisting of a deputy warden, assistant warden, and chaplain, who pass on disciplinary cases. The warden may accept, lower, or reject their recommendations completely.

Oregon

Loss of "good time" and loss of privileges were the two major forms of punishment. Usually loss of privileges was accompanied by confinement in inmates' own cells. There was no solitary confinement in isolation. Corporal punishment was not employed except in case of attempted escape, etc. No information was received as to inmate government.

Pennsylvania (Eastern Penitentiary)

Loss of privileges was most frequently employed. Solitary confinement was employed but was seldom necessary. Corporal punishment or physical force was not inflicted except in cases of "resistance." There was no inmate government.

Rhode Island

Minor offenders were punished by loss of privileges. "Privileges are rewards for meritorious living." There was no solitary confinement, but there was segregation within the inmate body in case of serious offenses. There was no corporal punishment except in self-defense. There was an inmate organization which participated in the establishment of rules and regulations but not in their enforcement.

South Carolina

No information was received.

South Dakota

Minor violations of rules were punished by loss of privileges and might involve recreation, writing privileges, visiting privileges, tobacco, etc. Serious offenders were punished by solitary confinement on bread and water. In practice this was limited to 10 days. There was no corporal punishment save in self-defense or to preserve order. There was no inmate self-government.

Texas

Punishments were classified according to five gradations. The first minor offense was punished by a simple reprimand and warning. For the second there was reduction of grade or transfer to an outlying farm. For the third there was deprivation of privileges and possible wearing of striped clothing. The fourth called for a form of corporal punishment—an inmate was placed on a barrel or stool in one position for 2 hours at a time. He was allowed to lie down for 1 hour, then obliged to stand in the same position again. No prisoner was allowed to stand thus between the hours of 9 P.M. and breakfast the next morning.

With all the forms of punishment except the first there was a loss of all or part of "good time."

For the fifth type of punishment, in case of extreme misbehavior, inmates were placed in solitary confinement. Such confinement, which was enforced only in case the prisoner had committed a self-inflicted injury or was spreading trouble or unrest among the other prisoners, was of three grades. Grade 3 solitary confinement had no bed. The inmate so punished received bread and water 3 times a day and 1 regular meal every 36 hours. He received no privileges or tobacco. Grade 2 had open cells with no privileges but the prisoner received three meals a day without tea or coffee and had a regular bed. In grade 1 the inmate received limited privileges such as tobacco, coffee, and tea. Most of the isolation sentences extended from 30 to 60 days.

There was no inmate self-government.

Tennessee

Loss of privileges (presumably for minor offenses) and being locked up over week ends with bread and water diet were forms of discipline. Corporal punishment was permitted but seldom exercised.

There was no inmate self-government.

Utah

No information was received.

Vermont

In Vermont discipline was based on a system of reprimands. Each minor offense was reported and if three reprimands were made in 1 year the prisoner received a reduction in grade. There was no use of force except in self-defense. No report was received as to isolation. There was no inmate self-government.

Virginia

Prisoners were punished by loss of privileges, including loss of earnings and loss of correspondence privileges for minor offenses. Serious offenses were punished by confinement in an isolated cell block, in light and airy cells. There was no "solitary confinement." Solitary confinement was permitted but not used. However, Virginia had two farms and 29 road camps as part of the prison system. Inmates were classified and transferred to other units. Corporal punishment was permitted by law but had not been used for a number of years. No force was used except in self-protection. There was no inmate self-government.

All punishments were controlled by a court consisting of the principal keeper, the captain of the guards, and the assistant superintendent.

Washington

For minor offenses there was loss of privileges and loss of "good time" credits. For serious offenses an inmate might be sentenced to solitary confinement up to 30 days, never longer. Corporal punishment was not forbidden but was not employed. Force was used only in self-defense or to protect property. There was no inmate government, but there was an inmate recreational council.

A three-man disciplinary committee investigated cases and passed judgment subject to the decision of the warden. Each case was studied and an attempt was made to adapt the punishment to the individual offender. A life-termer was not deprived of "good time" credits but of personal comforts. In all cases where "good time" was taken away the offenders were given an opportunity to earn back the lost time.

West Virginia

Minor offenders were punished by reprimands and loss of privileges. Serious offenders were punished by solitary confinement and loss of good time. There was no information received as to corporal punishment or inmate government.

Wisconsin

The main method of discipline was loss of privileges. Reprimand was given for ordinary infractions the first time. For the second offense the inmate was given a mark for misconduct on his record. In case he violated rules continually he was given what was called a "thirty-day lock up," which means merely that he was deprived of recreation on Saturdays and Sundays. If he continued to violate rules, he might be placed on second grade, in which he lost visiting and correspondence privileges. In case of still further violation he lost practically all privileges.

Solitary confinement was the punishment administered for rather serious infractions of rules. All men who escaped and were returned and those who got into fights were placed in solitary, ordinarily for only 3 or 4 days. (The solitary cells were light and equipped with beds, and the men there were seen by a doctor at least once a day.) If in the doctor's judgment a man was likely to suffer from a physical stand-point in solitary confinement he was removed. If he was unstable mentally he was kept out of solitary confinement. The Wisconsin prison had an inmate advisory council made up of delegates elected from each shop or department. Delegates met every Sunday morning and discussed all problems they might have on their minds. The warden met with this council once a month and found that this pro-duced many good ideas for the improvement of the institution. The council's suggestions were advisory only, but they obviously served a salutary function. No corporal punishment was allowed except in self-defense.

Wyoming

Restriction of privileges covered most of the punishment for infrac-tion of rules. There was no information received as to solitary confine-ment. (The prison is small, with a population of less than 225.) There was no corporal punishment or force used except in self-protection. There was no inmate self-government, but there was a committee of five inmates which might go to the warden with any complaints.

Although there is undoubtedly more brutality in prisons than these brief summaries indicate, prison discipline has unquestionably become relatively more kind and humane in recent years. Many wardens have the interests of their charges at heart. They know that the mere ob-servance of rules will never rehabilitate the offender. The prisoner must be motivated by a desire to conform to the social controls and must wish to become a respected member of society. Obviously there are many cynical prisoners who will not be reached by kindliness, but remotivation will certainly not be achieved through brutality. Not through coercion but through willing co-operation will the prisoner gain self-control. The recent changes in penal institutions under the California adult authority as discussed in Chapter 29 are an indication of the new trends which may alter the pattern of prison life.

SEX OFFENSES IN PRISON

Sex perversion is one of the most difficult and universal disciplinary problems facing the prison administrator. The sexually isolated life of the prison is in itself conducive to the development of homosexual practices. This isolation in turn tends to emphasize "sex talk" and stimulate sexual desire. In consequence many heretofore sexually normal persons satisfy their sexual urges through homosexual practices.

Some of the prisoners serving sentence for other offenses are sexual deviates when committed, while some prisoners are committed because they are sexual deviates. These men frequently exploit (or attempt to exploit) the younger prisoners. This is one of the reasons for keeping youthful offenders out of prisons where older men are incarcerated. Many of the internal feuds and virtually all of the murders which occur within prison walls grow out of resistance to sexual advances. Homosexual attraction is often greater between races than between members of the same race. Consequently the practice of racial segregation in prison (which often has been roundly condemned as undemocratic) is often enforced by prison officials as an alleged means of reducing sexual perversion. Unfortunately, racial segregation may increase homosexual attraction.

Sex perversions are not limited to male prisoners. They are also rather common among inmates in women's prisons and reformatories. The public meanwhile has paid little attention to the problem. In fact the whole subject of sex in prison has received little ventilation because of taboos on the subject. But laymen and legislators should recognize that imprisonment (especially long-term imprisonment) is in itself conducive to what is generally regarded as sexual depravity.

Mexican prison administrators try to solve the prison sex problem by permitting "marital visits." In the Russian "Bolshevo" prisons (for higher type offenders) prisoners are permitted to take their wives and families to prison where they live in apartments within the penal community. Unmarried prisoners in these institutions are permitted to marry if they have maintained good behavior during a certain part of their sentence. In certain German prisons inmates are permitted to spend week ends or other periods at home as a means of alleviating this problem.

Prisons in the United States have failed rather signally to develop any satisfactory solution to sex problems and the wardens have believed they were more or less powerless to do anything about such matters.[14]

PRISON RIOTS

One of the fears which constantly haunt many wardens is that the prisoners may stage a revolt. In numerous instances prisoners have

[14] Cf. Joseph F. Fishman, *Sex in Prisons*, National Library Press, New York, 1934. Cf. also Benjamin Karpman, "Sex Life in Prison," *Journal of Criminal Law and Criminology*, 38:475–486 (January–February, 1948).

yielded to mob psychology and expressed all their pent-up rebellious emotions in a surge of violence. Sometimes such outbreaks are planned by the masterminds among the inmates (as in the case of the trusty who was cooking nitroglycerin on a kitchen stove in the Kansas State Prison, mentioned in Chapter 23).

Just as often prison riots start as a flash explosion over some relatively minor event. Frequently they occur in the dining room where the presence of so many prisoners makes it fairly easy for them to engage in mass violence. Often the food is the alleged reason. A particularly bad meal, burned soup or gravy, or the fact that food is spoiled, dirty, or otherwise repulsive may be all that is needed to set off the deep-seated resentments which the inmates have kept sullenly to themselves up to then. Communication is easy in a dining room, despite any imposition of silence, and a revolt can spread like wildfire. Table utensils provide dangerous instruments. Forks and knives can be deadly weapons when brandished by aroused and outraged prisoners. Many prisons make special efforts to provide suitable food and a pleasant atmosphere, not only to promote the health and morale of prisoners, but to minimize the problems of discipline and dangers of rioting.

A recent revolt in the West Virginia State Prison at Moundsville affords an excellent example of a prison riot. Here, on October 16, 1951, 1300 convicts staged a revolt in the exercise yard when they refused to enter the prison mess hall. The cook, the prisoners alleged, was "dirty." The revolt was not a spontaneous one but had been mounting. In fact a grievance committee had already appeared before the warden. At first the convicts were not violent, but as their hunger increased they attempted to enter the commissary where foodstuffs were stored. They charged with broken knives and scissors which they had accumulated from various sources. As the night wore on they became cold—but they complained not of this but of the fact that their normal clothing issue was insufficient. The warden admitted there was some truth to the prisoners' complaints.[15]

In April, 1952, three of the worst prison riots in 20 years took place, the first at the New Jersey Prison at Trenton, which was followed by sympathetic outbreaks at the New Prison Farm at Rahway, New Jersey, and at the great Southern Michigan State Prison at Jackson, Michigan. All of these riots took on the nature of strikes with the prisoners demanding better food and living conditions, and more humane treatment. At both the New Jersey Prison Farm and the Michi-

[15] Pittsburgh *Post-Gazette*, October 17, 1951. p. 1.

gan Prison the guards were overpowered and held as hostages until the wardens agreed to make some adjustment. At the Southern Michigan State Prison a mental case was allegedly the ring leader but he had many followers. Between 1000 and 2000 convicts broke out of their cells, many by means of hoarded weapons (many fashioned from stray pieces of metal).[16] This riot lasted for 5 days.

Prison riots evidence every aspect of mob psychology. Mob behavior on the part of prisoners is easy to unleash, because the men are so full of pent-up grievances, bitterness, and frustration. Not only is resentment against food enough to inflame the men. Long sentences and overcrowding are also factors. Men also revolt against the presence of sexual deviates and because of brutal treatment on part of the guards.

Idleness in prison occasioned by the federal restrictive legislation against prison-made goods is undoubtedly a further source of much uneasiness among inmates. Where there is nothing to keep men busy and where no well-organized vocational training or educational program is in effect group resentment and violent action are much easier to foment. Prison labor as related to the problem of prison discipline is discussed in the next chapter.[17]

[16] Cf. *New York Times*, Section 4, "The News in Review," Sunday, April 27, 1952, p. 2E.
[17] Since this chapter is taken largely from the author's study of punishment in prisons as published in *Coercion in Penal Treatment: Past and Present*, Pacifist Research Bureau, Ithaca, New York, pp. 35–56, no selected bibliography is given here.

CHAPTER 25

Prison Labor

A Significant Problem

We have already touched briefly on the subject of prison labor in connection with prison history and prison administration. The topic deserves further detailed consideration, however. Providing the prisoner with some constructive outlet for his energy constitutes one of the most important tasks of prison administrators. Public opinion on the subject of prison labor has been both vindictive and contradictory and has resulted in legislation which has brought prison labor programs to a virtual impasse. Most people, including legislators, believe that the prisoner should work and work hard. On the other hand, laboring men, as "free laborers," objected strenuously to competing with "forced" or convict labor. Manufacturers likewise have fought with all the strength of their resources against the sale of prison-made goods in the open market. Trade unions have maintained that prison-made goods lower wages of free laborers because prisoners are paid little or nothing for their labor. Manufacturers, meanwhile, insist they cannot compete with goods produced under prison conditions because prison industries operate at such a low cost.[1]

The arguments against prison labor are in a sense absurd since if a prisoner cannot work he must be supported at public expense and by the labor of free men. Self-support of prisoners, while desirable, is only one angle of the prison labor problem, as the present discussion hopes to make clear. Prisoners should be trained at vocational pursuits so they can secure suitable employment when they are released. This ob-

[1] John P. Frey, "The Trade Union Attitude Towards Prison Labor," *Annals of the American Academy of Political and Social Sciences*, 48:8–16 (March, 1913), and Louis N. Robinson, *Should Prisoners Work?* Winston, Philadelphia, 1931, pp. 66–77.

jective, however, is seldom achieved by any of the prison labor programs. In general prisons are interested chiefly in keeping operating expenses low and in keeping the men busy so as to minimize the custodial problem.

A Brief Outline of the Origins of Convict Labor

ORIGINS OF PRISON LABOR

Prison labor as such was not in force in ancient times since relatively few offenders were put in prison, except to await trial, as we have already pointed out. In tracing the origins of penal labor, however, we find that forced labor for persons held guilty of criminal offenses has been employed as far back as the ancient Romans and Egyptians. That is, prisoners of war, paupers, children who were sold into bondage, and persons convicted of certain offenses were made slaves. Tradition has it that large numbers of these slaves built the Egyptian pyramids, ancient palaces, roads, and other public works.[2] In Egypt prisoners also worked in the mines. Slaves themselves also committed thefts, murders, and other crimes, but they were punished by their masters.[3] In Greece condemned criminals were often made galley slaves or worked on fortifications or in the government mines.[4]

In Sicily convicts were sometimes required to become agricultural laborers. In Rome citizens who committed crimes might be condemned to slavery and they too worked in mines or in penal colonies.[5] According to Mohler ancient civilization developed "a worthy prototype of our modern public works system."[6] The earliest known convict labor in western Europe was in Spain, where men were sentenced to work in the silver mines.

The first instance of convict labor in France occurred in 1532, when convicts were employed as galley slaves. The practice was not authorized by French legislative enactment until 1561, however.[7] But several years earlier, in 1547, a statute was enacted permitting vagrants who would not work to be sold as slaves.

The houses of correction developed during Elizabethan times in order that idlers (the current name for the unemployed) might

[2] Cf. *Second Annual Report of the United States Commissioner of Labor*, Washington, 1887, pp. 402–403.

[3] *Ibid.*

[4] *Ibid.*, pp. 403–404.

[5] *Ibid.*

[6] Henry C. Mohler, "Convict Labor Policies," *Journal of Criminal Law and Criminology*, 15:530–597 (January–February, 1925).

[7] Cf. *Encyclopaedia Britannica*, (1937 ed.), Vol. IX, p. 984.

be committed to hard labor. Workhouses were later developed, in 1575–1576, where men who were merely out of work might be sentenced.[8] This policy in England was the antecedent to putting men in jail at hard labor for vagrancy in the United States, a practice common until relatively recently.

PRISON LABOR IN COLONIAL AMERICA

When William Penn established the colony of Pennsylvania he reversed earlier British penal philosophy somewhat in the Great Law of 1682 by stipulating that all prisons should be workhouses, rather than requiring workhouses to be virtual prisons. The long list of offenses for which imprisonment was the required punishment, according to the Great Law, represented a significant new direction in penology. As our previous discussion on this topic in Chapter 22 has made clear, the provisions of the Great Law were never put into any effective operation and were abolished in 1718.[9] The stone prison erected that year and the Walnut Street Jail built in 1776 both aroused shocked protests on the part of decent and high-minded citizens of Philadelphia because of the idleness and debauchery among the prisoners.

THE DEVELOPMENT OF PRISON LABOR IN THE UNITED STATES

Following the American Revolution during the period 1790 to 1800 a fairly successful work program was developed. In Philadelphia in 1790 a work program was instituted by law. A kind of contract system was developed on a piece price basis with the prison supplying the tools and materials to be manufactured into articles for sale. This system reportedly worked very well for 10 years or so. But the prison population grew so rapidly and the prison became so overcrowded that effective employment was presently impossible. The situation became so serious that there was agitation for a new and different type of prison which resulted in the legislation providing for the Eastern Penitentiary.[10]

Robert Turnbull, a visitor to the Walnut Street Jail, reported that the inmates "worked at carpentry, joinery, weaving, shoe-making, tailoring and the making of nails. The unskilled convicts were employed in beating hemp and picking moss, wood or oakum. The female convicts worked at spinning cotton yarn, carding wool, picking

[8] Henry C. Mohler, *op. cit.*
[9] Orlando F. Lewis, *The Development of Prisons and Prison Customs, 1776–1845,* Prison Association of New York, New York, 1922, pp. 12–13.
[10] Harry Elmer Barnes, *The Evolution of Penology in Pennsylvania,* Bobbs-Merrill, Indianapolis, 1927, pp. 166–167.

cotton, preparing flax and hemp and washing and mending."[11] Male convicts were paid at the same wages as those outside, or somewhat lower wages, while women "earned small sums."[12] In other early American prisons during this period, including those in New York, New Jersey, and Massachusetts, each prisoner worked in his own cell. Thomas Jefferson also espoused the idea of solitary employment and tried to foster its development in the Virginia prison but his ideas were not carried out. Actually three or four prisoners were confined in each cell in Virginia.[13] It remained for Pennsylvania to take up the cudgels for solitary imprisonment, as we have discussed, while the congregate work program became the dominant pattern in other American prisons. Eventually Pennsylvania also yielded to the weight of social opinion in favor of the factory system.

From 1800 to 1830 various types of work programs were developed in the other prisons which were established. In New Hampshire stone-cutting was the chief employment, and weaving became a principal prison industry in Vermont and Maryland. In general during this period there was no agreement about the reformative influence of work. In Philadelphia the plans for the Eastern Penitentiary initially called for a solitary non-work program in order to permit meditation, but this was soon modified to permit craft work within the cell. With the advent of the Auburn prison in 1824 the idea of putting prisoners to work in a congregate factory type of production spread rapidly and became the pattern for the American prison system.[14]

With the development of the Auburn prison system after 1830 and its spread throughout the country, American prisons in the northern states and those west of the Mississippi all more or less followed the general pattern of the industrial prison. Many legislators were enthusiastic about the opportunities for industrial development which cheap prison labor made possible. Even before this date Auburn Prison was said to be self-supporting and the idea of profiting from prison labor was regarded as a very satisfactory way of making the prisoner suffer for his crimes.

Since the coerced labor of prisoners seldom amounted to "an honest day's work" much of the profit from prison labor was inherent in the very low pay. It was altogether natural, therefore, that the rising labor

[11] Quoted from *Reports of the Prison Discipline Society*, Boston, 1826–1835, Marvin, Boston, 1855, Vol. I, *First Report*, 1826, p. 22, in *Attorney General's Survey of Release Procedures*, Vol. V, *Prisons*, U.S. Department of Justice, Washington, 1939, p. 5.
[12] *Ibid.*
[13] *Attorney General's Survey of Release Procedures*, Vol. V, *Prisons*, p. 6.
[14] Cf. chap. 22, pp. 587–588.

movement should protest against the "unfair competition" which such prison labor entailed. Workers engaged in making furniture, boots and shoes, and in weaving and other industries which were developed in prisons began to oppose prison labor. During the Civil War the increase in factory workers occasioned by the large-scale demand for war materials and soldiers' uniforms and supplies greatly strengthened organized labor. Prison industries also increased, although the reformatory movement which followed during the period 1870 to 1900 created an important change in prison procedures. This was especially apparent in the emphasis on correctional education for younger prisoners.

The industrial prison thus had its beginnings during the early days of our republic and the pattern became widely established during the period 1830–1870 with the spread of the Auburn system. The industrial aspect of prisons was later modified somewhat by the demand for an educational and religious program during the development and spread of reformatories from 1870 to 1900. And with the rise of industrial capitalism to a new degree of large-scale production the prison factory reached its zenith during the twenties but declined sharply by 1935. For the opposition to prison labor resulted in restrictive legislation curtailing most prison-made goods.

Legislation Restricting Prison Labor[15]

The major modifications in prison labor in recent years have been the result of restricting the sale of prison-made goods. There is some evidence that free labor was opposed to employment of prisoners as soon as prison labor systems were established in this country.[16] It was not until the industrialization era following the Civil War (and particularly from 1885 on), however, that the opposition became serious. From then on organized labor and manufacturers alike continued their attack, which ended in the restrictive legislation.

Nevertheless prison industries increased in importance in the prison program until they reached their peak development in 1923, when the monetary value of products made in state prisons was estimated to be $73,668,879.[17] Actually the number of prisoners employed de-

[15] Cf. chap. 22, "The American Prison System: State and Federal," in which restrictive legislation is briefly mentioned.

[16] Louis N. Robinson, op. cit., p. 61.

[17] Richard F. Jones, "Prison Labor in the United States, 1940," Monthly Labor Review, 43:578–606 (September, 1941). Cf. also John R. Commons and John B. Andrews, Principles of Labor Legislation, Harper, New York, 1920, pp. 78–81.

creased from 75 per cent in 1885 to 67 per cent in 1923, however. By 1932 it had declined to 52 per cent and it was further reduced to 44 per cent in 1940. In that year state prison products were worth $48,-995,818.[18] If estimates are correct, approximately 20 per cent of the prisoners were industrially employed in 1950.

During the industrial period agitation against prison labor increased and powerful lobbies on the part of trade unions and manufacturers alike brought about widespread restrictive legislation in the various states. The major reduction in prison labor came through federal legislation, however. The first federal enactment was the Hawes-Cooper Act, passed by Congress in 1929. This act went into effect in 1934 and provided that the several states might prohibit shipping within their boundaries any goods, wares, or merchandise mined or manufactured by prison labor in other states, and that they might prohibit any such goods from being sold to or exchanged with any institution or political division. By 1940 every state in the Union had adopted some provision for carrying out the Hawes-Cooper Act.

The enforcement of such local legislation was made easier by the adoption of the Ashurst-Sumners Act in 1935, which prohibited any transportation company from carrying prison-made goods into any state which had previously prohibited such transportation. By this law prison-made goods were also required to be so labeled, hence was readily recognized by public carriers.

By 1940 a further act, which went into effect on October 14, 1941, prohibited all interstate commerce in prison-made goods with certain exceptions.[19] Farm machinery and farm commodities were exempt from such provisions, as were goods manufactured for the use of states and political subdivisions and all articles made by federal prisons. Any savings incident to the lower production costs of prison labor were thus available to publicly supported institutions. These restrictive laws inevitably were responsible for the rapid decline in productive employment of prison labor.

Wartime Prison Industries, 1942–1945

When the United States was thrown into World War II by the attack on Pearl Harbor, every available source of productive labor was recruited. Leaders in Washington soon turned to prison labor as a means of augmenting the output. Prisoners as well as civilians had a

[18] Ibid.
[19] Richard F. Jones, op. cit. Cf. also Mabel A. Elliott, Coercion in Penal Treatment: Past and Present, Pacifist Research Bureau, Ithaca, New York, 1947, p. 32.

stake in winning the war and were anxious to make some worth-while contribution. The only way that their labor could be utilized was through some special interpretation of the federal legislation.

At the date of the attack on Pearl Harbor only 20 per cent of the prisoners in state prisons were assigned to industrial production and only 40 per cent of these were actually doing any useful industrial work. As a result of the insight and leadership of James V. Bennett, Director of the Federal Bureau of Prisons, and Maury Maverick, then Director of the Government Division of the War Production Board, it was decided to utilize the potential labor power of both state and federal prisoners by making an urgent request for a legal ruling on the matter.[20] On May 6, 1942, Attorney General Francis Biddle, in harmony with the request, ruled that federal legislation should not be construed as restricting the federal government from entering into war contracts with state prisons.

In May, 1942, a Prison War Program Branch of the War Production Board was set up and in July President Roosevelt authorized the federal government to procure any war material from the various prisons that they were able to produce. In letting contracts with prison administrators various devices were established to protect prisoners from exploitation and safeguard the interests of free labor.[21]

Initially some of the federal procurement agencies for the army and navy were hostile toward employing prisoners in the war effort, but eventually this hostility was broken down and the various state prisons entered into what proved to be most satisfactory war contracts. The response from the prisoners themselves was nothing short of amazing. Probably this was the first time in history that prisoners had had any significant incentive to do their best. For the first time, too, they could see that their efforts were important to the safety and well-being of their country, their families, and themselves.[22]

During the year 1943 prisoners produced $11,495,020 worth of goods. Included in their contributions were (1) garments, shirts, and other sewing goods, (2) cloth and textiles, (3) jute, rope and burlap, boats, bunks and chests, (4) metalwork, (5) blankets, (6) furniture, (7) laundry service for the armed forces, (8) mattresses, (9) salvaging copper wire for the navy, (10) bricks, (11) shoe repair, (12) brushes and brooms, (13) foundry work, and (14) a group of miscellaneous

---

[20] Report on the Progress of the State Prison War Program Under the Government Division of the War Production Board, prepared by Harry E. Barnes, Washington, 1944, p. 4.

[21] Ibid., p. 6.

[22] Ibid., p. 8.

items worth over a million and a half dollars. Michigan prisoners made the greatest contribution, with Oregon second and Alabama and Oklahoma third and fourth.[23]

Later other states made stellar contributions. Meanwhile the federal prisons also played an outstanding role. A large share of the army uniforms were made at the Leavenworth prison, for example. The significant thing about the prison war effort from an administrative point of view was that the prisoners were stimulated to superior performance and many prisoners were actually given awards for their meritorious efforts. This achievement points up an important fact for all prison wardens and penologists to consider: The properly motivated prisoner will make an outstanding contribution and the product of his labor will stand up under the sternest scrutiny. If prisoners in wartime can render such excellent service it is obvious that given suitable peacetime incentive they could be stimulated to co-operative endeavor of the highest order. The problem is to secure that motivation.

Lack of incentive in peacetime has undoubtedly created much of the problem of unproductive prison labor. Under the old industrial program it was always difficult to get convicts to do a reasonable day's work. Many wardens have held that prison labor—because it is forced labor—is only about 50 per cent efficient. Part of this inefficiency probably stems from the fact that many prisons do not pay prisoners anything and in the prisons where wages are paid the scale is so ridiculously low as to be insulting. Prisoners under such conditions undoubtedly feel that there is no advantage in making an honest effort to do as well as they can. As an illustration of how little prisoners are paid consider the wages paid in certain states. In 1940 prisoners received no wages at all in 34 prisons. Where wages were paid they varied from the 4 cents a day paid to all prisoners in Kansas (except those working in the mines, who receive much higher amounts—from 50 cents to 70 cents a ton for all coal mined over a certain amount) to 40 cents a day in Maryland.[24] Certain selected prisoners received from 50 cents a day to 20 dollars a month in the Eastern Pennsylvania Penitentiary. Alabama paid men only for work on Sundays and holidays and they received 75 cents a day then.

In Russia after a certain apprentice period prisoners are paid the same wages as those employed at similar tasks outside receive over and above their living costs. Such a system has much to commend it for it helps in maintaining the prisoner's morale, allows him to ac-

[23] *Ibid.*, p. 20.
[24] *Attorney General's Survey of Release Procedures*, Vol. V, *Prisons*, pp. 214–217.

cumulate a backlog for his future, and permits him to contribute to the support of his dependents. Many prisoners have dependent families who suffer severely from the lack of financial support, and reasonable wages might offset the hardship inflicted on the prisoners' families.

Irksome and Cruel Varieties of Prison Labor

Not all punitive labor has been useful. There have been instances of cruel and irksome drudgery devised primarily for punishment and only secondarily for any utility which might be attached to it. In various parts of the world treadmills and other devices of little or no utility have been employed for the purpose of "taming the criminal," as Dr. John L. Gillin has strikingly recounted in his book by that title.[25]

One old practice, the treadmill was introduced in England in 1818 as a means of providing irksome labor for prisoners and some Philadelphians urged adopting this as means of keeping men active in this country. The treadmill was a cylindrical mill made of hollow wood with steps every 7 or 8 inches. The convict stepped from one to another while holding to a handrail so as to keep the mill turning. Later, in 1846, the crank was invented. This was a handwheel similar to the paddle wheel of a steamer. Both of these devices became widely employed in England as means of securing rotary motion for industrial purposes. They were modifications of the treadmill at which animals were used. However, in prisons they were often uselessly employed for punishment purposes alone. By 1865 every convict was required to spend at least 3 months of his sentence at such labor. Fortunately the use of these instruments of torture declined during the next 30 years and they were abolished shortly after the turn of the twentieth century.[26] This particular engine of misery has apparently never been employed in prisons in the United States.

In the United States the most common irksome type of prison labor has probably been "making little ones out of big ones," i.e., breaking large stones with a hammer until they are small enough to be suitable for building hard-surfaced roads. This type of work was widely in vogue both in jails and in prisons as a means of employing slack time as late as 1930. In some prisons such employment has been used for punishing refractory prisoners. At best the prisoners might take out their bitterness and repressions in pounding stones as hard as they

---

[25] Cf. John L. Gillin, *Taming the Criminal*, Macmillan, New York, 1931.
[26] *Encyclopaedia Britannica*, Vol. XXII, p. 437.

liked. With the advent of powerful machinery for crushing stones this practice has virtually ceased.

PRISON LABOR SYSTEMS

Prison Labor Systems in Colonial Times

During the colonial period two specific types of prison labor were developed: (1) indenture and (2) personal account.

INDENTURE

Indenture of lawbreakers was widely practiced before prisons were established, both in the American colonies and in Europe. In the colonies the provincial courts frequently permitted indenture as a punishment for theft where reparation or restitution was impossible. Because indentured men were often brutally treated the practice was abolished. The transportation system was a system of indenture developed by the British to help solve the colonial labor problem and at the same time dispose of their convicts. Where other punishments were not invoked, convicts were "bound out" for a period, usually of 7 years, after which they were given their freedom. The practice of binding out was of course an early counterpart of the later lease system.[27]

PERSONAL ACCOUNT

During colonial times many so-called houses of correction were established. Often relatives of prisoners furnished materials to inmates and the products of the prisoners' labor were sold. Out of the earnings from these sales the prisoner paid for his living expenses and for any fine which might be assessed against him. He was allowed to keep a part of what remained, although some of it usually went into the general treasury.[28]

Prison Labor Systems During the Industrial Prison Era

Since prisoners are now condemned to idleness, interest in the pros and cons of the various prison labor systems has waned. The systems are at least of historical pertinence to the student, however. We are

[27] This system is described in detail in chap. 27, "Parole and the Indeterminate Sentence."

[28] E. T. Hiller, "Development of the Systems of Control of Convict Labor in the United States," Journal of Criminal Law and Criminology, 5:241–269 (July–August, 1914).

also fairly safe in believing that present conditions will not always apply. The major prison labor systems in effect during the rise and decline of prison industries included (1) the contract system, (2) the piece-price system, (3) the lease system, (4) the public account system, (5) state or states' use, and (6) public ways and works.

THE CONTRACT SYSTEM

The contract system was first introduced in Massachusetts in 1807 and soon came to be the prevailing form of prison labor, remaining so until the turn of the century. By 1900 so strong an objection had been raised both by competing industries and by organized labor that 18 states had abolished the practice. By 1911 it was well on the way out of American prisons.[29]

Under the contract system private employers furnished the machinery and raw materials for production, and the prison at a contract price furnished the labor. In certain prisons under the contract system the manufacturers formerly supplied the guards and disciplinary officers. In others the prison authorities supplied the discipline, but supervision of the technical processes of manufacture was left to the manufacturer. The contract system was widely condemned for exploiting the prisoners where manufacturers assumed responsibility for the discipline, since they might enforce long hours or speed up the industrial output without reference to the fatigue of the workers. Most of the condemnation came from those who objected to the undue opportunity for profit accruing to the manufacturer because he paid so little for the prison labor, however.

THE PIECE-PRICE SYSTEM

The piece-price type of contract system was proposed in 1883 by Zebulon R. Brockway, the noted warden of Elmira Reformatory, as a solution to the evils of the contractor-run prison industries. Under this plan the industries supplied the machinery and the material but the prison officers managed the industrial production and had full control over disciplining the prisoners. Contractors paid for prison labor on the basis of output and not according to hours, hence the problem of exploiting the laborer was presumably eliminated.[30] Labor unions and competing manufacturers were not satisfied by this arrangement, however, and made strenuous efforts to secure legislation

[29] Ibid.
[30] Blake McKelvey, American Prisons, University of Chicago Press, Chicago, 1936, p. 95.

abolishing the contract system—which is discussed in a later section.

Certainly the piece-price system provided opportunity for ruthless exploitation of the prisoners through enforced speeding-up of work, since the prison's main interest was also in profits.

The Lease System

The lease system developed along with the contract system during the period 1830–1870.[31] Under this system contractors assumed complete charge of housing, feeding, and disciplining the men, although they were, to a degree at least, subject to statutory regulations. In return they paid the state a relatively small amount for the services of the prisoners. The lease system did not become widely established until the War Between the States practically wiped out the prison system in the southern states. Leasing prisoners was not an innovation occasioned by the Civil War, however, for Kentucky had leased its prisoners as early as 1825.[32] California is said to have leased convicts during the gold rush. In any event the practice of leasing convicts became a definitely accepted procedure in the South after the Civil War.

For years Georgia, Florida, Mississippi, Louisiana, North and South Carolina, Alabama, and Texas leased all or part of their prisoners. This practice promoted a prison labor system which was probably worse than ante-bellum slavery so far as the convicts were concerned. Most of the prisoners were Negroes and discipline was extremely cruel. Corporal punishment was the rule, and the extent to which men were injured or died as a result we shall never know. Enough concerning such cruelties became known, however, to arouse public opinion, and between 1914 and 1923 the lease system was completely abolished and a dark chapter in southern penal annals came to an end.[33]

The Public Account System

In the public account system—or state account system as it is sometimes called—the state furnishes the materials and sells its products on the open market. This system was fought assiduously by organized labor, and today the operation of recent federal laws has abolished most of the public market. An outstanding example of this type of labor was furnished by the state prison at Stillwater, Minnesota, which supplied the farmers of that state with binding twine at a profit to the

[31] *Ibid.*, chap. 5.   [32] *Ibid.*

[33] Cf. Henry C. Mohler, *op. cit.* Cf. also *Prison Labor in the United States*, 1932, Bulletin of the Bureau of Labor Statistics, no. 595, U.S. Department of Labor, Washington, 1933, p. 5.

prison and a saving to the farmers. Today, however, virtually all surplus commodities manufactured by prison labor are confined to the local state's use or use by other state or federal institutions.

STATE OR STATES' USE

Today virtually all prison-made goods not consumed within the respective prisons may be subsumed under the category of "state (or states') use." Under this prison labor system the distribution of prison-made goods is restricted to the local state institutions and agencies, to other state institutions, and to federal institutions and agencies. Thus the Charleston Prison in Massachusetts manufactures aluminum and galvanized ware and other articles for other state institutions. Kansas state institutions receive a sizable share of their coal from that mined at the state prison. During World War II some state prisons manufactured clothing for the army and navy. Others canned surplus foodstuffs for army use. Even in peacetime federal institutions make numerous items for use by the military services or by the various federal institutions and agencies. Since these goods do not compete on the open market and at the same time provide a saving to the taxpayer, this form of prison labor system has met with much less objection than other types.

PUBLIC WAYS AND WORKS

Previous to the development of prisons, persons convicted of crime who were not punished by death, ordeal, or fine were often subjected to compulsory labor on public works or roads.[34] This, of course, is a special variety of state or states' use. During our own colonial days prisoners were employed in building streets and roads, although the practice was not very successful. The lack of sufficient demand for their services led to a general abandonment of the plan.

Not until the advent of the bicycle and later of the automobile was there sufficient demand for good roads to make such prison labor profitable to the state. Prison road gangs then became common in southern states, where the industrial prison had never developed. When the demand for roads arose able-bodied prisoners were considered a suitable source for the heavy construction work, and the penal road camps came into existence. Men were herded like animals into portable cagelike wagons and transported to road-building sites. Frequently the men were chained together while working, so as to

[34] Edwin H. Sutherland, *Principles of Criminology*, Lippincott, Philadelphia, rev. ed., 1947, pp. 464–465.

prevent escapes. They were also chained to the wagons for disciplinary reasons. The cruel and barbaric treatment of these southern chain gangs attracted so much attention in the press and in the movies that a strong movement for their abolition arose. Robert E. Burns' personal account of his escape from a Georgia chain gang[35] was an especially effective protest against the unbelievably inhumane treatment of such prisoners.

The *Attorney General's Survey of Release Procedures* gave a vivid picture of the extent to which southern penal systems employed the chain gang. In North Carolina, for example, there were 26 such state camps in 1937.[36] As late as 1941 a fugitive from a Virginia penal camp related incredible atrocities when arrested in Pennsylvania.[37] We have no authentic data on the extent to which such practices still exist. It is unlikely that all chain gangs have been abolished, although conditions undoubtedly have improved in certain states in recent years. However, in most of the southern states Negroes comprise the majority of convicts, and the worst aspects of race prejudice foster the brutalities of penal treatment. For the guards are white men, generally with no qualifications save brawn and race and possess a sizable degree of racial intolerance.

Of course, certain types of public construction provide reasonable and suitable working conditions. In construction work at various state institutions it is customary to employ inmate labor. For example, inmates from a men's prison are often employed in the erection of new buildings at a women's prison or a boys' or girls' industrial school. In general there is little use of prison labor on construction work for other public purposes today. Such employment of prison laborers is an ancient practice. The pyramids themselves are a monument to prison labor, as we have mentioned previously.

Nonindustrial Types of Prison Work

Inmate workers are naturally employed in (1) prison housekeeping and the specialized services which the prison itself provides and (2) clerical and management jobs.

PRISON HOUSEKEEPING

In many ways prisons resemble other large institutions. Wherever hundreds or thousands of persons are to be housed, fed, and clothed

[35] Robert E. Burns, *I Am a Fugitive from a Georgia Chain Gang*, Vanguard, New York, 1932.

[36] *Attorney General's Survey of Release Procedures*, Vol. V, *Prisons*, p. 40.

[37] Case cited by Harry Elmer Barnes and Negley K. Teeters, *New Horizons in Criminology*, Prentice-Hall, New York, rev. ed., 1951, p. 449.

there is a tremendous amount of detail involved in ordering, preparing, and serving food, purchasing and distributing clothing, keeping the clothing laundered and mended, and providing places to store it. Beds must be provided with mattresses and pillows, bed linens and blankets, and these likewise must be changed and laundered. Buildings must be kept clean, grass must be mowed, vegetable gardens planted, surpluses canned. Small wonder that the average warden is overwhelmed with the business of housekeeping. In addition certain persons assume responsibility in the educational, recreational, record keeping, and business end of running the prison.

In general about 20 to 25 per cent of the prisoners can be suitably employed in operating the prison. Today, because of slack employment, maintenance jobs are often spread so as to take about 20 per cent of the average inmate's time instead of the full time of a small group.

CLERICAL AND MANAGEMENT JOBS WITHIN PRISON

Practically every prison uses some inmates in the numerous quasi-administrative jobs required to keep the institution running, wherever they prove competent. Prisons which have an industrial program employ inmates as foremen, for example. Other prisoners serve as checkers of materials and machinery and examine the finished product.

In some state prisons inmates have successfully taken charge of commissaries, or stores where prisoners may buy personal supplies, such as food, clothing, stationery, soft drinks, tobacco, etc., in addition to that provided by the institution. In these positions prisoners are often wholly reliable, although careful auditing of accounts is always in order. It would seem obvious that embezzlers, forgers, and petty thieves should not be given commissary jobs. The Federal Prison System employs civilians to take charge of commissaries, and the few prisoners employed in them have minor responsibilities, such as delivering newspapers.[38]

In addition many prisons also place a considerable number of their seemingly reliable and competent prisoners in positions involving authority over other prisoners, in charge of confidential records, or in posts which involve judgment concerning the basic policies of the institutions. Such practices are deplorable and are often fraught with grave hazards. This custom of giving certain prisoners "trusty" jobs causes many of the problems of prison discipline and has created many

[38] *The Way to Prison Work*, prepared by the staff of the Bureau of Prisons, U.S. Department of Justice, Washington, 1946, p. 50.

of the scandals of prison mismanagement. Some of the hazards may be evidenced in the following examples:

1. In certain southern prisons, for example in Arkansas, Louisiana, and Mississippi, armed inmate guards have been used exclusively. This practice obviously creates internal tensions within the prison for it gives such prisoners an unwarranted and often resented power over their fellow prisoners. In other states—for example, Missouri—unarmed white inmate guards have directed the agricultural labor of Negro prisoners on prison farms.[39] Although unarmed inmate guards cannot be as seriously condemned as those who are armed, they nevertheless create resentment and racial conflict in case those they are guarding are Negroes.

2. Forty-four prisons, according to the *Attorney General's Survey of Release Procedures*, were using prison help in accounting work.[40] This practice is particularly hazardous for the inmate accountant usually considers his first loyalty to be to his fellow prisoners. In numerous incidents on record an inmate accountant has altered the "good time" record of another prisoner in order to permit the early parole of the prisoner. In a case known to the author when she was a member of the Kansas Public Welfare Commission, an inmate accountant adjusted the record of a long-term prisoner so as to make him eligible for parole 2 years earlier than was legally permissible. No one on the Board of Parole checked the detailed figures in the prisoner's good time record. The inmate prison accountant was said to have received $5000 for the deal. It is believed that he received many other fees from grateful inmates.

3. The use of prisoners in preparing case records with reference to behavior within the walls is especially to be condemned, not merely because of the opportunities which are occasionally taken to alter or manipulate the records, but also because inmate records clerks often betray confidences to the prisoners, by letting some bit of correspondence escape, or make public some opinion expressed by the authorities of the prison. Sometimes such prisoners are regarded in the same light as "stool pigeons" who relay the confidences of prisoners to authorities.

Farming

Farming is often an important part of the prison work program. In many of the southern states, in fact, the whole prison system is a

[39] *Attorney General's Survey of Release Procedures*, Vol. V, Prisons, p. 76.
[40] *Ibid.*, p. 77.

farm system. Initially the farm system was a variety of lease system, but it is no longer so. In 1940 in the 7 states of Alabama, Arkansas, Louisiana, Mississippi, North and South Carolina, and Texas, there were 63 prison farm camps. In general they were poorly equipped. The housing was often unsanitary and seldom fireproof. Ease of escape promoted brutal treatment and many prisoners were killed attempting escape.[41] Financially the prison farms were a great success. However, there is no reason to think that they had any significant rehabilitative or educational influence.

During the last 10 or 15 years a number of states have developed prison farms in conjunction with their institutional prisons, where young and hopeful first offenders are segregated from older and hardened offenders. This plan has proved very productive from an agricultural point of view and has been "promoted" on the basis of its rehabilitative program. Unfortunately there have never been any follow-up studies to find out how far such programs are succeeding in helping the men. They are obviously improving the quality of the prison diet for all the men, both on the prison farm and within the walls of the prison proper.

WORK ASSIGNMENT

Although ideally the classification committees of the various prisons are supposed to consider the skills and interests of men in making work assignments, actually this occurs all too seldom. In the first place there is no provision for classification committees in most prisons. Further, most work assignments are made with reference to places where an additional worker can be of use. Since there must be sufficient men to perform necessary routine tasks these tasks must be taken care of first. The idea of employing a work program for therapeutic purposes is very rare.[42] In only 13 prisons in 1940 was there any attempt to make a special study of the men's experience, skills, or need for vocational training. Many wardens believe a man should be "tried out" at a disagreeable task and public opinion supports this point of view. If a prisoner's trial and conviction has attracted great attention, wardens are often literally afraid to place a prisoner at anything but heavy labor because of fear of public resentment.

A well-known and well-educated banker involved in a bond scandal in a certain state was assigned to work in the prison library, for example. He was a man of cultivated tastes and held two college degrees. It seemed sensible to place him where his talents might be used

[41] *Ibid.*, pp. 40–44.   [42] *Ibid.*, p. 213.

to the benefit of others as well as himself. A newspaper in the state learned of this "outrageous leniency" and published a headline story on the subject. Hundreds of readers sent personal letters to the warden, and the ex-banker was shifted to work in the prison mines, much to the satisfaction of the press and the protesting citizens. This man had never been employed at hard muscular work and he suffered a serious back injury within a week. News of this did not reach the public, and the man was later reassigned to his old post in the library. But the story illustrates both the passing strength and the temporary interest that the public may take in prison labor. Most people believe that any sort of hard work is too good for the lawbreakers, chiefly because most people forget that the purpose of imprisonment is to restore men to a willingness to participate co-operatively in community life.

Wherever possible work assignments should be made with this idea in mind. Every effort should be made to encourage prisoners to reorganize their lives. To this end the vocational training inherent in work assignments should be carefully weighed. Even if such a plan were to cost the state more than does less suitable placing, it would save the state in the end if men went out competently trained to step into jobs at which they could earn an honest living. Such placement in turn might eliminate much of the convict's failure on parole or expiration of sentence, which we discuss in Chapter 27. Effective work assignment is difficult under existing conditions of prison work.

POSSIBLE SOLUTIONS TO THE PRESENT-DAY PRISON IDLENESS

The enforced idleness in prison is a matter of solemn concern to every prison administrator. What solution can be devised for taking up the long stretches of unfilled time is a many-sided problem which should interest every conscientious citizen as well. There are two possible solutions to current unemployment in prisons. One is to bring about widespread agitation for the repeal of existing restrictive legislation. The other is to develop ways and means of extending prison industries within the framework of existing legislation.

The first attack would require the development of national and state committees who would undertake to educate the public, the labor leaders, the rank-and-file members of labor unions, and the industrial leaders who are so fearful of the competition of prison-made goods. Labor leaders and manufacturers must be made to see the folly of opposition to prison work. The belief that prison products are a threat to wages or prices is nonsense. In the boom year of 1923 when prison industries produced approximately $76,000,000 worth of products, this total constituted only 1/10 of 1 per cent of all the goods produced. Obviously this percentage of the total production cannot offer any serious competition. Nevertheless the majority of people, including the articulate lobbyists of both unions and manufacturing groups, do not know this, nor seemingly do members of Congress. Some incisive educational attack on the problem may result in laying low this giant of ignorance.

If labor leaders and manufacturers would only recognize that they as citizens and taxpayers suffer when embittered and untrained men are returned to society, much of their argument would vanish. In making a plea for more constructive utilization of the prisoners' skills and energies the present author is holding no brief for the penal philosophy which characterized the industrial prison. The public must be made to recognize, however, that the present-day idleness in prisons is far worse than any exploitation of men under the earlier system. It is better to wear out than to rot, even in prison.

Antecedent to the restrictive legislation there was nothing like full employment in prisons because of various restrictions and the problem of civilian unemployment. Today, with the federal restrictions, unemployment in prisons has become the rule. Hence the prisoner who may be committed theoretically to from 2 to 5 years at hard labor is actually committed to idleness and boondoggling in most prisons. At the Jackson prison in Michigan Warden Burke estimated 36 per cent of the population were not employed because of lack of work in 1946.[43] This was higher by far than the number employed in most prisons. In fact Wallack estimated that only 42 per cent of all prisoners were employed full time during the war production program in 1943.[44] The situation was regarded as alarming in 1946. By 1950 it was downright appalling. At Western Penitentiary in Pittsburgh in 1950 only about 20 per cent of the men were employed more than an hour or so a day. Any visitor to a prison today cannot avoid being struck by the futility of locking up a thousand or more men to spend weary hour upon hour in idleness. In most prisons there is nothing to do all day

[43] William H. Burke, "A Travesty of Justice," *Proceedings of the Seventy-Sixth Annual Congress of Correction of the American Prison Association,* New York, 1946, pp. 185–196.

[44] Walter M. Wallack, "Some Suggestions for Basic Reforms in Prison Industries for Improved Production and Vocational Training," *Proceedings of the Seventy-Eighth Annual Congress of Correction of American Prison Association,* New York, 1947, pp. 153–160.

long after an hour or two of routine tasks in prison maintenance. If legislators, members of Congress, and members of labor unions and corporation boards could visit a half-dozen prisons they might see for themselves what a serious problem their restrictive legislation has created. Nothing could be more depressing than to witness 1000 or 2000 men sitting within the prison yards, free to think the long hard thoughts of embittered convicts with nothing to do, nothing to look forward to for hours at a stretch, for weeks and months at a time.

In order to spread the work many institutions have resorted to what newspaper reporters have called "broom leaning." That is, an excessive number of inmates are assigned to construction and maintenance tasks and work. What one man could easily do alone is parceled out to four or five men. A 1-day survey of such "broom leaning" was conducted at the Western State Penitentiary at Pittsburgh on April 30, 1947, and at the Eastern Penitentiary at Cherry Hill, Philadelphia, on May 19, 1947. The thinning out of work was much greater at Pittsburgh than at Cherry Hill, as the figures below show. What the percentages not accounted for were doing is not certain.[45]

Work Assignments	Eastern State Penitentiary	Western State Penitentiary
Maintenance and construction	41.2	74.3
Prison industry	6.4	18.2
Definitely idle	23.5	5.7

However, as we have said before, most of those working were working only an hour or two a day.

Women's prisons do a better job of keeping their inmates busy than do men's prisons, largely because the domestic duties which are related to women's prisons can be expanded more or less indefinitely. Women prisoners live in dormitory-type buildings and ordinarily each woman has her own room. She is usually free to make curtains and bedspreads, to weave rugs, and to make her room attractive in any way she wishes, within limits of materials which are provided or the prisoner is permitted to furnish. Women are also generally allowed to wear attractive wash dresses when they are not engaged in menial work and all of these are made at the prison. In addition women frequently do handwork, embroidery, crocheting, knitting, or spend time making aprons, cloth animals, and other items for sale. They may do this

[45] John McCullough and Ralph Cropper, *Idleness in Prisons Is an Unsolved Problem.* Reprint from the Philadelphia *Inquirer*, July 3, 1947.

whenever there is no other work to do. Although much of this work is not particularly constructive in making a better citizen out of a woman it is certainly infinitely better than allowing her to sit idly for hours at a time.

The development of some sort of program of creative hobbies for male prisoners might do much to ease the long hours of empty frustration now so common in prison. Fewer men than women among the rank-and-file prisoners seem to have creative leisure-time skills which they acquired before commitment and to which they can turn for reducing the monotony of "nothing to do." Developing some sort of inexpensive hobby program may be an important next step in prisons for men. This will require careful planning if it is to gain acceptance among criminal men. Many will undoubtedly reject such a program as fit for children and the "women folks," but wood carving, painting, jewelry making, weaving, and similar pursuits are certainly masculine occupations.

The Expansion of a State Use Program

The expansion of a varied state use prison industry program under existing legislation would be more satisfactory, but this is a large order. Nevertheless there are ways in which it might be accomplished. First of all, the list of commodities which are required to run various state institutions might be studied and classified. Obviously not all commodities could be suitably manufactured by prison labor. But hundreds of items ranging from electrical equipment to brooms, mattresses, kitchenware, crockery, uniforms, canned goods, etc., etc., could be competently produced by prisoners. Certain principles would have to be established to determine those most suitable. Shops or factories might then be set up. It would be best to analyze jobs and to use qualified instructors to train men in the steps in the industrial process. High standards of workmanship would necessarily have to be maintained to insure a steady market for the goods.

The majority of inmates would prefer work to the enforced idleness now so characteristic of prisons. Indeed, in some prisons it is now an honor to be chosen for full-time employment. Charles V. Jenkinson believes as many as 25 general types of industries with over 70 kinds of products might be developed in all states except those with very small prison populations. A variety of industries would provide opportunity for a wide program of vocational training and help insure the prisoner's adjustment after release. The unfortunate aspects of the prison labor laws may in the end be offset by certain favorable tendencies. At least the training which seems to be entailed should contribute to the released inmate's capacity to secure and hold a job.[46] The main market for prison-made goods probably will always be in the field of state use. In any event it is doubtful if such a state use program could supply more than a small percentage of the total products consumed by state institutions. There is thus no important enterprise which would be disastrously affected by a well-developed prison industry program. The arguments against prison labor are selfish, prejudiced, and unfounded. Furthermore restrictive legislation is costly insofar as it militates against the development of satisfactory work habits on the part of the prisoner. In final analysis it is criminals which the state cannot afford, and anything which makes their rehabilitation less likely is far more expensive than any infinitesimal threat to a particular industry.[47]

If the co-operation of unions and manufacturers is to be achieved, the most satisfactory prison labor plan would be to pay men adequately for their work. This would require paying them the prevailing wage of free labor with deductions for the proportionate costs of maintaining the prisoner and the prison, which may be rightfully assessed to each inmate. The rest might be allocated in part to the prisoner's family in case of need, in part to pay for his own incidental expenses, and certainly in part to be accumulated against the day he leaves the prison, unless his family is in sore need of it all.

Canadian Experience with Prison Labor

The Department of Reform Institutions in Canada has developed an extensive state use plan and has no problem of finding work for its prisoners. The program provides for slaughtering and processing of meats; manufacturing of furniture; canning; lumbering, both felling trees and sawing lumber; and making sashes and doors. Materials are processed or manufactured in connection with a definite program of training in trade skills. An academic educational program is also well developed. As Director A. R. Virgin says, "It is good business to attempt to make a good citizen of the prisoner."[48]

[46] Charles V. Jenkinson, "How Can Prison Industries Contribute to the Preparation of Inmates for Release?" *Proceedings of the Annual Crongress of Correction of the American Prison Association,* New York, 1948, pp. 159–168.

[47] *Report on the Progress of the State Prison War Program Under the Government Division of the War Production Board,* pp. 45–48.

[48] A. R. Virgin, Toronto, Canada, correspondence dated June 21, 1950.

Prison Labor and the New Penology

Harry E. Barnes and Negley K. Teeters, among others, have heralded the decline of prison industries as the beginning of a new type of prison and a new penology in which the major concern is with the readjustment of the offender.[49] Would that this were truly so! Unquestionably the reduction in prison work has forced prison administrations and prison boards to reassess the whole problem of what to do with their charges.

Unquestionably enforced leisure has made wardens and prison keepers recognize that some other constructive use must be made of the inmate's idle time. In the best prisons highly organized recreational programs under trained leadership are in operation. More bands, ball teams, glee clubs, and hobby clubs are functioning in prison than ever before. Many prisons now show two movies a week where one formerly sufficed. Educational programs are receiving more and more attention. Religious services are under the direction of more competent leadership. These are all to the good, but in the average prison these activities, singly and combined, still do not take up the slack in the prisoner's time.

When civilian unemployment is widespread it is only fair that prisoners should bear a proportionate share of the economic depression. In fact some manufacturers have held that they really "feel" the competition with prison labor only in times of depression.[50] When times are good, however, prisoners should be employed if only for the rehabilitative impact of suitable work. If prison directors can find ways and means of utilizing the creative skills of their charges in their work program the prisoners' pride in honest achievement will go far toward helping them in their post-prison adjustment.

The present-day restrictions may be salutary if they result in our rethinking prison labor in terms of the vocational rehabilitation of the men so that they can take satisfaction in earning a living honestly at tasks which utilize their aptitudes and skills.

Practical Considerations in a Prison Labor Program

In connection with the question of a prison industrial program certain practical considerations must be taken into account before any specific industrial production and training is attempted. One con-

[49] Harry Elmer Barnes and Negley K. Teeters, op. cit., chap. 26, "The New Penology —Elmira Principles and Adult Treatment."

[50] John R. Commons and John B. Andrews, op. cit., p. 79.

sideration is whether the suitable raw materials can be secured at a reasonable outlay. A second is whether or not enough prisoners have the requisite skills to warrant the establishment of a particular industry. A third is whether or not there is a market for the goods, and this obviously has to be found within the present limits of state use.[51]

Basic Reasons for Maintaining a Work Program

In conclusion we may say with Warden Walter M. Wallack that there are three valid reasons for prisoners working: (1) Prisoners should pay for their keep and some form of productive labor is the only way to do it. (2) Work helps keep the men fit physically and mentally, as well as out of mischief, which is a valid reason in itself. (3) Work helps build both habits of industry and skills which any person needs to earn a living. Since 90 per cent of the prisoners are released within less than 10 years, it is very important that they be turned out as competent wage earners.[52]

SELECTED BIBLIOGRAPHY

Attorney General's Survey of Release Procedures, Vol. V, *Prisons*, U.S. Department of Justice, Washington, 1939, Part I, chap. 9, "Prison Industries," and Part II, chap. 6, "Industries." These two chapters give an excellent summary of prison labor up to 1940 in state and federal prisons respectively.

Barnes, Harry Elmer, and Teeters, Negley K., *New Horizons in Criminology*, Prentice-Hall, New York, rev. ed., 1951, chap. 34, "The History and Significance of Prison Labor." A critical and evaluative treatment of the topic is given.

Commons, John R., and Andrews, John B., *Principles of Labor Legislation*, Harper, New York, 1920, pp. 78–81. A brief but significant analysis is made of the fight waged by free labor and industry against prison-made goods.

Elliott, Mabel A., *Coercion in Penal Treatment: Past and Present*, Pacifist Research Bureau, Ithaca, New York, 1947, Section VI, "Prison Labor." This is a concise survey of the major trends in prison labor, the various labor systems, and the restrictive legislation.

Haynes, Fred E., *The American Prison System*, McGraw-Hill, New York, 1939, chap. 14, "Prison Labor." This chapter emphasizes the trends in prison labor during the depression years of the thirties.

[51] Harry Elmer Barnes, *A Concise Plan for the Organization of a State Department of Correction*, Institute of Local Government, Pennsylvania State College, State College, 1945, p. 28.
[52] Walter M. Wallack, *op. cit.*, pp. 153–160.

Hiller, E. T., "Development of the Systems of Control of Convict Labor in the United States," *Journal of Criminal Law and Criminology*, 5:241–269 (July–August, 1914). This is a historical survey of the prison labor problem in the United States.

McKelvey, Blake, *American Prisons*, University of Chicago Press, Chicago, 1936, chap. 5. The prison labor problem in the United States prior to 1900 is exceptionally well presented.

McKelvey, Blake, "The Prison Labor Problem 1875–1900," *Journal of Criminal Law and Criminology*, 25:254–270 (July–August, 1934). This article describes the rise of the industrial prison and the protests of organized labor.

Robinson, Louis N., *Should Prisoners Work?* Winston, Philadelphia, 1931. This discussion of the reasons why prisoners should work effectively demolishes the arguments for curbing prison labor programs.

CHAPTER 26

Women's Prisons and Reformatories

Women's prisons are a neglected area in most treatises on criminology. Greater information and study about women's penal institutions are nonetheless important, for there are many angles of the subject which have never received any objective analysis.

Women's prisons in the United States are of two distinct types: (1) those which are a division of the state prisons run primarily for men and (2) the separate institutions for women. In 23 states all told, including all the southern states except Alabama, North Carolina, and Virginia, women offenders are confined in special sections of men's prisons. Unfortunately there is little satisfactory or extensive information about them. At best the average report on the women's division usually covers only a page or so of the particular prison's annual or biennial report. It seems quite likely that the reason such reports are so scanty is that the staff is untrained and the program very stricted. If the warden is proud of his prison it is usually because of the activities and program of his men's division.

In Florida it has been alleged that the women's building is "frightfully" overcrowded and that there is less separation of the men's and women's quarters than any other prison where both sexes are confined.[1] Wyoming operates no facility for its women prisoners but sends them to Colorado for incarceration. The remaining 24 states—Alabama, Arkansas, California, Connecticut, Delaware, Illinois, Indiana, Iowa, Kansas, Kentucky, Maine, Maryland, Massachusetts, Minnesota, Nebraska, New Jersey, New York, North Carolina, Ohio, Pennsylvania, Rhode Island, Vermont, Virginia, Wisconsin—and the

[1] Fred E. Haynes, *The American Prison System*, McGraw-Hill, New York, 1939, p. 199.

federal government and the District of Columbia all maintain separate institutions. In addition there are several municipal prisons for women.

The separate state institutions for adult women offenders are as follows:

Women's Prisons or Reformatories	Date of Opening
Alabama, Julia Tutweiler Prison for Women, Wetumka	1942
Arkansas Training School for Girls and Reformatory for Women, Alexander	1919
California Institution for Women, Tehachapi	1933
Connecticut State Prison and Farm for Women, East Lynne	1917
Delaware, Women's Prison (adjoining men's prison), Greenbank	1901
District of Columbia, Women's Division of the District of Columbia Workhouse & Reformatory, Occoquan, Va.	1911
Illinois, State Reformatory for Women, Dwight	1930
Indiana Women's Prison, Indianapolis	1873
Iowa Women's Reformatory, Rockwell City	1918
Kansas State Industrial Farm for Women, Lansing	1916
Kentucky State Reformatory, Women's Division, Pewee Valley	1938
Maine, State Reformatory for Women, Skowhegan	1916
Maryland, State Reformatory for Women, Jessups	1940
Massachusetts, Reformatory for Women, Framingham	1877
Minnesota, State Reformatory for Women, Shakopee	1920
Nebraska, State Reformatory for Women, York	1920
New Jersey, State Reformatory for Women, Clinton	1913
New York, Westfield State Farm, Bedford Hills	1901
North Carolina, State Home and Industrial School for Women, Eagle Springs	1918
State Industrial Farm Colony for Women, Kinston	1929
Ohio, Reformatory for Women, Marysville	1916
Pennsylvania, State Industrial Home for Women, Muncy	1920
Rhode Island, State Reformatory for Women, Howard	1925
Vermont, Women's Reformatory, Rutland	1921
Virginia, State Industrial Farm for Women, Goochland	1932
Wisconsin Industrial Home and Prison for Women, Taycheedah	1921

Women Felons Committed to County Jails

Nobody knows how many women are committed to county jails, many of them illegally. In Kansas, for example, the law strictly prohibits women both from being committed to jail while awaiting trial and from receiving a jail sentence following conviction. Nevertheless women are often so committed. Women are held in many county jails following arrest because the community has not provided any other place for their detention. Frequently women are sentenced to jail because judges hesitate to send short-term offenders to prison.

The author once asked a Kansas sheriff why twelve women were illegally confined in the jail under his supervision. The sheriff merely shrugged his shoulders and said, "Where else could they be committed?" In view of the lack of facilities, that is a fair question. Laws which forbid sending women to jail are moribund unless some other provision is made for female offenders.

Number of Women Prisoners

Women prisoners constitute only a small percentage of the total prisoners in the United States, as we have mentioned earlier.[2] In 1950 there were 6316 women prisoners, according to preliminary census data.[3]

Women Who Are Committed to Prison

The courts are, generally speaking, reluctant to commit women to prison and are inclined to extend probation to those women who, theoretically at least, are considered likely to make a satisfactory adjustment in the community. Others are committed to jail. Probation is virtually never authorized for women convicted of murder, although many women convicted ordinarily would (from a psychological viewpoint) be good risks. (Most women murderers, other than a few women gangsters, are convicted for killing their husbands and are not likely to commit a second murder.) Women prisoners as a group are thus either the less promising female offenders or those whose crime is severely condemned by society. Nevertheless in some women's prisons sex offenders and alcoholics form a large percentage of the cases. In Kansas formerly half of the women were committed for having venereal disease. In some states the group may consist almost entirely of felons. At the Tehachapi, California Institution for Women 27 per cent, for example, were convicted for homicide in 1947.[4] There were apparently fewer women murderers the next year, for on December 31,

---

[2] Chap. 4, p. 84.

[3] Ibid. Cf. also National Prisoner Statistics, No. 3, U.S. Department of Justice, Washington, June 25, 1951, p. 2.

[4] Grace E. Barneberg, "The Board of Trustees; Duties and Responsibility," Proceedings of the Seventy-Seventh Annual Congress of Correction of the American Prison Association, 1947, New York, 1947, pp. 221–224.

1948, the distribution of offenses for which the women were committed to the California institution was as follows:[5]

Offense	Per Cent
Homicide	20.5
Robbery	9.4
Assault	6.5
Burglary	7.5
Theft, except auto	16.2
Auto theft	1.6
Forgery and checks	23.7
Rape	0.3
Other sex	0.6
Narcotics	5.5
Escape	2.3
Habitual criminal	—
All other	5.9

Relatively speaking, women prisoners obviously are not an important part of the prison problem. They may give the wardens who are forced to receive them a few bad moments, but for the most part the responsibility for this group is shifted to the women officers. Only when the women become hysterical, stage a riot, or make an escape does the warden pay much attention to their problems. In general women prisoners are rather docile and unless they are in conspiracy with men inmates seldom create much disturbance.

Separate Institutions: A Reform Movement

Sometimes, however, the administration of a women's prison creates a passing scandal. Good people become aroused. Even novelists may take up the theme as did Sinclair Lewis in *Ann Vickers*, when he revealed with bitter irony the conditions in the woman's division at Copperhead Gap Penitentiary. This was a southern penitentiary where politics, ignorance, filth, vermin, contamination, torture, neglect, graft and brutality reigned. Women prisoners were sexually exploited by the guards. Lewis maintained he based his story on conditions essentially accurate.[6]

Most of the social action against the distressing conditions in the women's divisions of prisons has been instigated by women's groups

---

[5] List taken from *California Institution for Women, Tehachapi*, privately printed, no date, p. 13.
[6] Cf. Sinclair Lewis, *Ann Vickers*, Doubleday, New York, 1933.

outraged at the indecencies in the unseparated prisons. Some of these groups have been clubs, others have represented the church women of the state, but in all instances those taking the initiative have had strong religious motivations. The first separate institution for adult women offenders grew out of the protests of Quakers against the conditions under which women prisoners were maintained in Indiana. In 1866 at the yearly meeting of the Society of Friends a committee was appointed to call public attention to the need for a separate prison for women. This movement gained momentum; in 1869 the Indiana legislature passed a law establishing the prison at Indianapolis and in 1873 it was opened as the "Indiana Reformatory Institution for Women and Girls."

Just four years later (in 1877) the Massachusetts Reformatory Prison for Women was opened. Here, too, the influence of Quaker women was an important factor in the inception of a separate and reformatory institution for Massachusetts female offenders. Miss Hannah B. Chickering and Mrs. Ellen Chaney Johnson supplied the motivating force. Miss Chickering had become imbued with the idea that a separate institution for women was needed through visits with Quaker friends in Philadelphia. Her friend, Mrs. Johnson, was widely acquainted with the treatment of women offenders in Massachusetts through her work with soldiers' widows and children during the Civil War. In fact Mrs. Johnson found so many soldiers' widows in jail that she became distressed at their plight and established a Temporary Asylum for women ex-convicts at Dedham, Massachusetts, and was instrumental in having a state-wide survey of the conditions of women prisoners conducted in 1869. The statistics uncovered revealed that a large number of women, mostly sex offenders and alcoholics (many of them young) were too old to be accepted at the institutions for delinquent girls. As a result of the monumental efforts of these women the state legislature in 1870 adopted a law providing for a separate prison.

This law was denounced by the Massachusetts Commission on Prisons on the ground that women prisoners were needed to perform the domestic duties in the men's prison. Manufacturers who had contracts for the women's labor also protested, but the law was nevertheless put in operation. At first several jails were taken over to house the women. In 1874 the building of a special separate prison was authorized and in 1877 it was opened.

Since the movement for the separation of women offenders occurred during the period in which the reformatory idea came into being it was altogether natural that the most progressive correctional philosophy of the period should be incorporated in the women's institutions. The idea of reformation (or rehabilitation) has thus been uppermost in the movement to organize separate women's prisons. Most women's prisons are called reformatories, as the list of such institutions shows. But they are truly women's prisons. They are virtually the only places to which women are committed to "serve time." (Capital offenders are usually kept in a wing of the men's prisons until their date of execution.)

The Philosophy Underlying Women's Reformatories

There have been two types of philosophies underlying the movement for separate women's prisons. The first was a religious conception of women prisoners as "fallen women" who must be led to "repentance" and "salvation." This religious approach was derived from the similar concept which characterized the program of the houses of refuge, mentioned in Chapter 22. The second conception of a women's prison was that it should be an institution closely akin to a reformatory or a training school such as was provided for younger offenders. This philosophy placed the emphasis upon the need of the inmate for special education and protection.[7] It has been the one which has characterized most of the later development of women's reformatories.

The reformatory philosophy underlying what we may call the newer women's prisons was responsible for the development of the cottage system. These early institutions were considered "asylums for the erring," however, and it was in a prayerful and religious spirit that they were originally conducted. The first annual reports of the Indiana institution, for example, emphasized the sinful character of the women and their need for repentance; it gave statistics on the religious services held twice daily. The two philosophies were intertwined and soon extended into development of educational and vocational programs as well as greater provision for recreational opportunities. All of these developments in turn were copied from the programs of the leading institutions for younger girls.[8]

The Board Which Manages Women's Prisons

Where there is a separate board for women's prisons, the majority if not all of the board members are usually women. The board of

[7] Eugenia C. Lekkerkerker, *Reformatories for Women in the United States*, Uitgevers-Maatschappij, Groningen, The Hague, 1931, pp. 164–165.

[8] *Ibid.*, pp. 166–167.

trustees or governing board (whatever its name) of the women's prison often takes a much more personal interest in the individual inmates than is possible in men's prisons. In California all the new inmates are interviewed by the board each month. The policies of the institution are explained and various aspects of the program are presented. One member discusses religion, another education, vocation, and personal adjustments, another the board's duties, matters of parole, etc., while still another gives legal advice. The lone male member of the board discusses morals and appearance, presumably with more psychological effect than any of the women members might exert.[9]

The California board establishes the length of sentence after an evaluation following the first meeting with the woman inmate but this is not the practice in most women's institutions. After half of her sentence is served the individual inmate is again interviewed in the California institution. In the meantime each woman may request a personal interview if she wishes.[10]

In New Jersey the Women's Reformatory at Clinton is under the direction of a separate Board of Managers (as are all the New Jersey penal institutions). It consists of 5 women and 2 men who are appointed by reason of "educational background, tolerance and vision." The board is responsible for the selection of the superintendent of the reformatory, who is a woman, and members of her staff. The board members determine the policies of the institution and also interpret the institution to the community. This New Jersey board has been unusually successful in obtaining a well-trained staff.[11]

Buildings at Women's Reformatories

In general the buildings at the different women's prisons are very attractive in appearance. In fact they often resemble a well-to-do women's college, with the various dormitories or "cottages" (usually housing 50 or more women), an administration building, an educational building, a heating plant, an industrial building or buildings, and in addition the farm buildings (if the institution is located at a farm, as the majority are).

The average women's prison provides a separate room for each inmate, although a few have dormitories for sleeping purposes. With

[9] Grace E. Barneberg, op. cit.
[10] Ibid.
[11] Katherine K. Neuberger, "The Community and the Institution," Proceedings of the Seventy-Sixth Annual Congress of Correction of the American Prison Association, 1946, New York, 1946, pp. 97–99.

the first such institutions the desire on the part of women prisoners to decorate or add decorative touches to their rooms was encouraged and today there are few women's prisons which try to preserve any true "prison atmosphere." Some women's prisons have pleasant cottage living rooms simply furnished with rag rugs which the women have made themselves, a piano, reading lamps, comfortable chairs, and a fireplace as a focus for activities during the colder months. In some prisons the women are permitted to gather in their living room every evening. In others they use the living room only when the officers "call a meeting." Most prison administrators believe that attractive surroundings have a salutary effect on the women and that patterns of thinking and habits of good taste are instilled which persist when they leave the institution.[12]

The Illinois Reformatory for Women at Dwight, Illinois, which opened in 1930, is one of the newest and best equipped women's correctional institutions. Its buildings are pleasing and its educational and correctional programs are more extensive than those in most women's prisons. This may all be attributed to the superintendent, Miss Helen M. Hazard, who assumed charge of the institution when it opened. All the female adult prisoners in the state are now housed here.[13]

The Size of Women's Prisons a Handicap

So far as buildings are concerned it is fairly easy to secure adequate and comparatively high-standard physical equipment for women's prisons. The educational and correctional program is a different matter. Except for the Federal Reformatory for Women few have anything outstanding in the way of vocational or educational programs. Prisons for women cannot compete at present with educational institutions for staff members partly because of the salary scales and partly because of the isolation, as we discuss later in this chapter. Another handicap, as Walter C. Reckless points out, lies in the insignificant size of so many of our state prisons for women. Whereas it seems to be desirable from a social point of view to give women a different type of housing from that available in men's prisons, the relatively few women prisoners do not, in the eyes of legislators, justify the cost of high-grade educational, psychological, and psychiatric services. Dr. Reckless suggests that co-

---

[12] The follow-up survey made by the author of Sleighton Farm girls showed this statement to be true. We have no occasion to believe that it is not also true of older women prisoners. Cf. Mabel A. Elliott, *Correctional Education and the Delinquent Girl*, Commonwealth of Pennsylvania, Harrisburg, 1929, pp. 80–81.

[13] Fred E. Haynes, *op. cit.*, pp. 100–104.

operative provision for women offenders on the part of a group of states would offer a more satisfactory solution.[14] Eventually, perhaps, we may develop a national system of prisons for offenders in the several states. The Federal Prison System so far outranks the standards of the present state systems (with a few exceptions) that this would seem to be a desirable solution. Any such development can come only after major alterations in our present system of federal and state government, but it seems (to this author at least) to offer many advantages so far as maintaining standards in correctional institutions is concerned.

The Educational Program in Women's Institutions

The educational training in women's institutions varies. Some is at best purely vocational. At the Kansas Industrial Farm for Women, for example, there is little or no academic training, chiefly because there are no qualified teachers. The women and girls there receive a certain amount of vocational training in the various activities—in cooking, baking, sewing, and in maintaining their cottages—but the instruction is purely practical and has no theoretical base. Those who work in the laundry are undoubtedly qualified to secure employment in a commercial laundry. The women also receive considerable practical training in gardening and their labor supplies vegetables for the institution's table. This work obviously has little vocational value, since very few women are employed in commercial gardening. The better-educated inmates are often assigned to typing, bookkeeping, and other jobs within the institution and probably learn on the job. The opportunities for self-improvement, however, are extremely limited.

A well-developed educational program is in full swing at Clinton Farms, the New Jersey Reformatory for Women. Here all of the teachers are college trained. Over 20 have a bachelors degree or above. An additional 16 persons have from 1 to 3 years of college training. There is a special teacher to handle music, one to supervise recreation, another to give nursery school instruction, and another to teach domestic science, both theory and practice.[15] All the inmates attend school at least 1 hour a day. Those who are believed able to profit from further education attend 4 hours a day. Special classes are provided for the illiterate girls. In addition to their own program of instruction, quali-

[14] Walter C. Reckless, The Crime Problem, Appleton-Century-Crofts, New York, 1950, p. 449.
[15] Edna Mahan, Superintendent of Clinton Farms, correspondence dated December 4, 1951.

fied inmates takes courses through the Extension Division of Rutgers University, chiefly in commercial and bookkeeping subjects.

The Delaware Women's Prison is a special building at the Delcastle Farms and is known also as the New Castle County Workhouse. The educational activities at this prison are purely vocational and are incidental to the daily work assignments. For the 2 successive years, 1946 and 1947, the supervisor of the Women's Prison made a short report in the shape of a one-page letter and described the activities as follows: "During the year the women have been engaged in making rings, dresses, bed clothes, towels, night gowns, and slips. They have also prepared vegetables for the cannery at Delcastle."[16] As a matter of fact, these women also must have been engaged in sweeping floors, cleaning bathrooms, cooking, washing dishes, washing and ironing clothes, and numerous other activities.

North Carolina apparently has a much higher type of academic and vocational training than do the majority of southern prisons for women.

At Westfield State Farm in Bedford Hills, New York, one of the better women's prisons, over two-thirds of the women attend some sort of educational class. Twenty-odd inmates of this prison successfully completed high school training and received diplomas in 1950 and a few are enrolled in extension work of college grade. Music education is an important feature of the work at Westfield; one versatile instructor gives training in the piano and five other instruments as well as singing.[17] Organized sports are a means of getting rid of frustrations as well as providing healthful exercise. Some other women's prisons also have excellent programs of sports. Others have no organized program but the women themselves sometimes get up baseball teams or are permitted to engage in simple sports.

Libraries in Women's Institutions

Because most of the women's prisons are small their libraries are likewise small, and hence seldom suitably equipped. Far too often they consist largely in books gathered by members of women's clubs or church organizations, and frequently they are the books that these good women would otherwise relegate to the attic or the Salvation

---

[16] *Reports of the Board of Trustees of the New Castle County Workhouse to Levy Court, for the Fiscal Years Ending June 30, 1947 and June 30, 1948,* Wilmington, Delaware, 1948, pp. 19 and 52.

[17] Henry F. and Katharine Pringle, "Convicts with Skirts," *Saturday Evening Post,* 223:34–35 ff. (November 25, 1950). Cf. also Henrietta Additon, "Women's Institutions," in Paul Tappan (ed.), *Contemporary Correction,* McGraw-Hill, New York, 1951, chap. 19.

Army. A prison library should have carefully selected books among the classics and new books of a contemporary interest. There should also be a well-selected list of current magazines to supply wholesome leisure-time reading as well as information on current events and social problems. Most women inmates of prisons are not well educated, but they have more time on their hands than women outside and will read proportionately far more than women of comparable economic and social class on the outside—if suitable reading materials are available.

Edwin I. Friedman recently reported on the findings of his survey of prison libraries covering 120 state and 28 federal institutions (slightly more than half those which were sent a questionnaire). Few libraries had adequate book collections. The larger the institution the poorer the collection—in proportion to need. Among institutions with more than 500 inmates, 38.5 per cent of the federal institutions and 17.5 per cent of the state met minimum standards. Of those with fewer inmates, 87 per cent of the federal and 63 per cent of the state institutions had adequate book collections. More than half had no reading rooms and very few had trained librarians. Generally speaking, magazines are much more widely circulated than books. In some prisons the average number of books circulated per inmate was three annually. The over-all average was 35, however,[18] and this, it must be admitted, is far higher than among the rank-and-file male civilians outside prison walls.

Treatment Programs

All women's prisons attempt to give suitable medical care, although such care varies in both quality and extent of service. Some prisons have excellent resident physicians. Others have good part-time physicians. Still others permit the nurse to diagnose minor ailments. In at least one institution known to the author the nurse prescribes thyroid tablets to a large share of inmates (on the ground that "most of them need thyroid") without administering any metabolism tests.

Virtually all women's prisons require quarantine on entry to keep down contagious diseases. While in isolation women receive routine Wassermann tests, smears, chest X rays, and vaccination for smallpox and typhoid, etc. Most illnesses are cared for "on campus," but serious surgical work is often performed at near-by hospitals.

---

[18] Edwin I. Friedman, "Survey Shows Poor Libraries in Most Penal Institutions," *Library Journal*, 75:1148–1149 (July, 1950). It seems safe to conclude that most state women's prisons did not rank as well as the majority of smaller men's prisons.

Psychiatric examinations and psychological testing should be a part of all prison treatment and these are provided in the better women's prisons. Because of the number of cases which must be interviewed by the small staff the long and expensive process of psychoanalysis can seldom be provided. Often excellent results can be obtained in group treatment, however, since many women and girls have similar problems. For most cases the individual interview is the best opening procedure even though group treatment may come later.

A good prison provides psychological tests measuring intelligence, personality, skills, and occupational interests. A social worker should obtain a complete social history of each case from personal interview with the inmate, from outside agencies, and from other penal institutions if the prisoner has a record. Relatives and friends should also be interviewed—if the best interests of the prisoner can be maintained while so doing.

Serious group discussion in which the women participate, under the effective professional leadership of the psychiatrist, might do much to reduce the cross-fertilization in criminal techniques that is so characteristic of prison life. Inmates in prison, like college students, professors, lawyers, farmers, or any other group in association, come to know each other as persons and to be interested in what they consider their common problems. If prison inmates can think together concerning their mutual difficulties, especially those relating to how they can make an effective adjustment, it should be helpful. How they can rise above the social stigma most of them feel, how they can profit from their institutional experience and go out into the world with the mental, moral, and vocational equipment to succeed are their truly serious problems. Surely some intelligent sharing of these problems would do much to offset the schooling in crime which has been one of the major handicaps of prison experience up to now. Participation in a constructive program for promoting their own adjustment would seem to be an experiment worthy of trial.

The desirability of providing prisoners with individual attention is not a recent idea. A British novelist, posing as a prison matron, writing in the 1860's, pointed out the need for giving more attention to each woman. Then, as now, need for increases in staff, less routine, and more effective recreational programs was recognized.[19]

[19] Frederick William Robinson, *Female Life in Prison*, Sampson Low, Son and Marston, London, 1864, chaps. 4 and 46. (Originally published anonymously, purportedly written by a prison matron, but apparently with the aid of Frederick W. Robinson.)

Classification

The psychiatrist and psychologist can also contribute much to the successful classification of the prisoner by suggestions for placement and educational opportunities, as well as helping the woman directly through counseling. In the better women's prisons the professional staff (including the social workers, psychologist, psychiatrist, physician, and academic teachers) as well as the work supervisor, the housemother, the warden, and the assistant warden usually attend the classification meetings. Here the women's problems are discussed and policies are decided upon with reference to the inmates' best interests.

In prisons where there are relatively few or no professional staff members the classification is much more informal and may consist of a discussion between the warden and the work supervisor. Sometimes, in poorly staffed prisons, the warden talks to the inmate about her problems and makes the decision as to the woman's job placement alone. This is not what our best prisons mean by classification; good classification involves a serious study of the inmate and all her problems, as we discussed in Chapter 23. Where it is effectively operating a classification system the prison aims at truly individualized treatment. In a few women's prisons, notably the Federal Reformatory for Women, there is an excellent classification system.

Miss Helen Hironimus, who was formerly warden of the Federal Reformatory for Women, has stated three important contributions which she believes the classification service in women's prisons has made to the wider field of penology and she believes the same principles might be equally applicable to men's prisons. These are as follows:

1. The classification program is a continuing process in women's prisons (where it is in effect, it should be added). The individual prisoner's progress or regression, physical disabilities or improvements, emotional problems, mental and moral development are reviewed and later discussed frankly with the inmate. Changes in placement, treatment, etc., are then continued or altered in line with her specific needs.

2. The matron or housemother of the inmate who is brought up at a classification meeting is present as a member of the committee. This is a two-way advantage. First, the matron is able to give important information derived from her daily contact with the inmate. The matron herself benefits from attendance at the meetings, where she shares in the discussion and participates in determining what recommendations

are made. Second, she becomes a more valuable officer because she has greater understanding of her charges and she shares in carrying out the recommendations. If the guards in men's prisons shared similarly in classification meetings they might gain much in understanding their charges.

3. Virtually all women inmates, irrespective of background and history, are confined in what may be considered minimum security institutions. "Daring and desperate" women are included in this group and they have caused little difficulty. Miss Hironimus believes that many so-called desperate male offenders also could be dealt with more effectively in situations which more closely approximate community life.[20]

In final analysis women's prisons with all their handicaps were born of the notion that women prisoners were still women and would profit from living under conditions which would demonstrate the values of kindly treatment in clean and attractive surroundings. It seems to be equally true that most men prisoners might be successfully housed in less forbidding structures than the cages of steel and stone which we have built for criminal men. Our treatment of male criminals has verged on the hysterical.

Professional Standards for Staff Members at Women's Institutions

In the Federal Reformatory for Women at Alderson, West Virginia, staff members are relatively well trained; 19 per cent are college graduates.

In many of the state institutions for women few if any of the employees are well educated, with the possible exception of the superintendent. Many superintendents are political appointees, as we mentioned earlier. Even when there are sufficient funds and high personnel requirements it is often difficult to secure well-trained persons to direct the specialized services of the institutions (such as psychologists or psychiatrists) if there is no opportunity for association with other trained persons. Those who are well educated often find it very uninteresting and even irritating to work with other people who are ill qualified for their jobs. The trend toward improvement in personnel appointments at women's prisons is obvious throughout the United States, but many women in prison work still conform to the stereotype of the jail matron who was put in office because her brother was a

[20] Helen Hironimus, "Classification," *Proceedings of the Seventy-Fifth Annual Congress of Correction of the American Prison Association, 1945*, New York, 1945, pp. 59–62.

policeman, or because some other political henchman was able to "speak a word in her behalf."

On the whole the type of woman employed in our prisons for women is far higher than the politically appointed male employee in men's prisons. Nevertheless the women personnel can often be best described as "institutional types." Even in the better state institutions, such as Westfield State Farm, Bedford Hills, New York, some of the employees have as their chief qualification the fact that they have been housewives and "good mothers."[21]

Work Programs

Because women inmates are permitted greater variety in dress, they have more personal laundry than men. They are permitted to have more extensive furnishings in their rooms which entail more care. They have more public living rooms with furniture to keep clean and dusted. Prison housekeeping thus takes more of the individual inmate's time than is true in men's prisons.

The problem of industrial employment is limited in women's prisons by the same legislation which restricts industries in men's prisons, described in Chapter 25. Hence women must be employed at work which will not enter into interstate commerce. The California Institution for Women has a large sewing industry and makes a variety of shirts and dresses for various public agencies, both state and county. The Rutland, Vermont, State Prison and Reformatory for Women runs a laundry widely patronized by the local townspeople. The Federal Reformatory for Women at Alderson makes shirts and underwear for the navy. It requires intelligence and ingenuity to set up effective work programs in prison. In 1950 a program to train inmates at Alderson as hospital attendants was inaugurated.

Discipline in Women's Prisons

Women prisoners (aside from the few political prisoners and a few women murderers who may be relatively cultivated persons without previous criminal record) are not an especially ladylike group. Sometimes they indulge in wholesale vulgar talk and profanity, pull hair when upset, and engage in virtual free-for-alls. Nevertheless the average woman offender is tractable and it is generally agreed that a

[21] Helene de Corse McArthur, "Summary of Meeting, Committee on Women's Institutions," Proceedings of the Seventy-Fifth Annual Congress of Correction of the American Prison Association, 1945, New York, 1945, pp. 127–130.

women's prison is much easier to operate than a men's prison. Women prisoners may be maladjusted but they are seldom violent. They occasionally escape from a prison reformatory, it is true, but in these cases they usually walk out. Women prisoners do not shoot their way out and ordinarily they present no trouble about receiving contraband weapons. Certainly women prisoners do not spend their leisure time within the walls fitting pieces of iron or lead together to make guns and knives—as men prisoners often do.

In some women's prisons there still are appalling methods of discipline enforced. Women may have their heads shaved for "shame," are put in solitary confinement, or are forced to submit to hosing with a heavy stream of cold water. Virginia Kellogg recently described her experiences as a voluntary inmate in one prison and as an observer in several others in a series of articles in *Collier's*. These articles disclosed some of the brutality that still exists in certain women's prisons.[22]

Political Corruption in Women's Prisons

Miss Kellogg's articles also brought out the vicious nature of the political corruption which governs appointments at so many women's prisons. (Of course we should point out that the corruption in men's prisons is as bad, if not worse.) Miss Kellogg recites numerous instances of matrons who give favors to prisoners for money, real estate, etc.

The most effective discipline, in prison as elsewhere, is self-discipline and this, as has been said before, must come from within. Somehow in the prison administration it must be made plain to the inmates that obedience to rules and regulations is not merely expected but required, and that he or she who rebels must not think she can "get away with it." Persuasion, warnings, counseling should precede serious punishment, but some form of deprivation should be given to persons who fail to abide by important rules.[23]

While there can be no justification for physical cruelty or torture in prison, no prison can be administered under lax discipline. Unimportant and foolish rules should be abolished. Intelligent rules are based upon the need for order, harmony, and security within a prison and in these the prisoners themselves will concur if they are properly presented to them and fairly administered.

[22] Virginia Kellogg, "Inside Women's Prisons," *Collier's*, 125:15, 36, and 40–41 (June 3, 1950). (These articles provided the material for the movie "Caged.")

[23] M. F. Amrine, "Prison Discipline," *Proceedings of the Seventy-First Annual Congress of the American Prison Association*, 1941, New York, 1941, pp. 131–135.

The Sex Problem in Women's Prisons

In the states where women are kept in the men's prisons the women prisoners lead a very restricted existence because of problems which would otherwise arise. It is general practice to keep the women prisoners from all contact with the male prisoners. The women are seldom permitted to work outside the walls or to get a desirable amount of fresh air and outdoor exercise,[24] chiefly because it is believed that each sex is disturbed by the sight of the other when kept in confinement. Occasionally successful communication between male and female prisoners takes place. Even where separate institutions exist (as in the case of the Kansas State Penitentiary and the Kansas Industrial Farm for Women, which are only a mile or so apart) men prisoners often work at the women's "farm," at building repairs, plumbing, or assisting in the heaviest farm work. Although communication is theoretically forbidden, the women who work in the kitchen and prepare food for the men prisoners employed on the farm or in the field squads often receive smuggled notes or are tossed a contraband package of cigarettes. Romance flourishes with the slightest opportunity, even when contact is more difficult. The author recalls the case of a young woman (whom she once interviewed in the Kansas prison) who at least thought that she was deeply in love with a fellow prisoner. Their only contacts were smuggled notes. She and her "suitor" were planning to be married when their terms expired.

Because there is no normal opportunity for social relationships sex attraction in prison takes many twists. In women's prisons as in men's there is always the problem of homosexuality. Often such attraction is stronger between Negro and white women than between members of the same race. This fact is the basic reason for racial segregation in prison, at least in our northern institutions. Actually there is little opportunity for overt homosexual practices in women's prisons because most of the prisoners either have a room to themselves or sleep in a dormitory where their behavior is closely observed. The homosexuality in women's prisons takes the form of "mash" notes, present-giving, or other evidences of extreme devotion.

One of the most distressing aspects of women's prisons is the contamination of the relatively young and inexperienced first offenders who are serving sentences for petty offenses. These young women are open prey for the prostitution rings which flourish in some prisons. When a prostitute or narcotic addict with connections in a notorious

[24] Fred E. Haynes, op. cit., p. 88.

prostitution ring is sentenced to prison she often serves as "an inmate contact woman." That is, she literally recruits young inmates for the "houses" she represents. Since in many states the law requires that a convict have a job and a place to live before release can be granted it is relatively easy to work out an offer for work and a home in such a way as to delude members of the board and the superintendent of the prison. Where the prison is located close to a large city such arrangements can be made under the guise of respectable employment. If there are dishonest and corrupt matrons willing to co-operate with such nefarious prisoners the situation may go on undetected.[25]

Where the prison personnel are appointed through civil service examinations or where professional training is required, there is little opportunity for any such disgraceful procedures to take place. But in many states the prisons for both men and women are still politics ridden. New York, New Jersey, and California are generally regarded as having high standards, and the same is true of Vermont, Connecticut, Illinois, as well as a number of other states.

Maternity and Child Care

One of the special features of women's prisons is the provision for maternity care. Every year a large number of pregnant women, most of them illegitimately so, are admitted to prison. In a few states provisions are made for the babies of inmate mothers to be born in hospitals in near-by towns, so that no child will have the stigma of being born in prison. In the Federal Reformatory for Women the children are born in prison in the excellent hospital. Some other prisons have suitable hospital equipment. At the Connecticut State Farm and Prison, for example, 42 babies were born during the fiscal year 1948–1949.[26] In most states mothers care for their children until they are a year or 18 months old, but they are not allowed to remain longer, in accordance with accepted opinion that a prison is no place to rear a child. Many such children are placed for adoption.

At Clinton Farms, as the New Jersey institution is generally known, an excellent maternity cottage is maintained where the mothers give virtually full time to their babies' care. Authorities differ as to what procedures are best for the child, but there is general agreement to the' effect that it is better for the mother to nurse the child if possible, and that the care of the child often has an excellent sobering effect upon

[25] Virginia Kellogg, op. cit.
[26] Report of the Farm and Prison for Women, 1948–1949, Hartford, 1949, from Digest of Connecticut Administrative Reports to the Governor, 1949, Vol. III, p. 466.

the mother. In Connecticut children are supervised by a special pediatrician and at Clinton Farms there is a pre-nursery school for the prison youngsters.[27]

Personnel Problems in Women's Prisons

As Dr. Lekkerkerker points out, women officers in reformatories or prisons should be "physically and mentally healthy, well-balanced, even tempered, socially mature women with steady moral standards and a cheerful disposition."[28] We might add that their educational background should be sufficient to give them proper insight to the problems they will inevitably meet.

There are many fine, well-adjusted women in prison work, but a large share hold their jobs as the result of political favor. This type may or may not be scrupulous. However, maladjusted persons may often be found among the staff members at women's prisons—for several reasons. One is that prison work is occasionally the last refuge of a woman in critical need of employment. A widow of an important clergyman may decide that she can gather "stars for her crown" by devoting her remaining years to prison work. One such case comes to mind. The dear sainted lady taught classes in fine sewing at a state reformatory. She kept herself haughtily aloof from the young women prisoners and when they later brought up their handiwork for inspection she often said icily, "Do not touch me," if they so much as jostled her elbow.

Another type of woman employee that appears to characterize prison workers may be designated, for want of a better name, "the institutional type." Such women have literally grown up within the walls of an institution and have lived so long apart from the general life in the community that they (like certain life prisoners) would find it difficult to live where they had to solve the problems of marketing, housekeeping, laundering, and all the other items which are solved for them within the routinized existence of an institution. They have for years had one responsibility, that of running a piggery, or directing a cannery, or operating the laundry, or supervising a dormitory. Their days are filled with the same monotonous tasks. Mealtimes are spent in recounting their daily experiences.

Of course there are well-trained women (as mentioned earlier) in the Federal Reformatory for Women and a few of the better state institutions. But even where high personnel requirements exist the civil

[27] Eugenia C. Lekkerkerker, *op. cit.*, pp. 529–531.
[28] *Ibid.*, p. 273.

service lists from which candidates are selected have sometimes been a stumbling block. For the written examination ratings of queer, maladjusted persons have occasionally been the highest on the list with the result that extremely intelligent but unbalanced persons have been appointed. Fortunately in recent years the "unassembled examinations" which stress suitable references and experience at previous jobs as part of the examination have been successful in eliminating most of the "malcontents" and "difficult personalities" from the list.

The Geographic Location of Women's Prisons

Another factor which seriously complicates the problem of women's prisons' personnel is the isolated location of so many of the women's prisons. The Federal Reformatory for Women, for instance, located at Alderson, West Virginia, is undoubtedly in one of the garden spots of America. It is laid out like a college campus, with well-kept stretches of green and attractively landscaped grounds which are surrounded in the distance by the magnificent Blue Ridge Mountains. The architecture is excellent, and the whole place amazingly beautiful. One can scarcely believe it is a prison.

But it *is* a prison, and because it is located so far from a large city the leisure time of the staff is to a great degree confined to "on the campus" activities. The recreational resources of the village of Alderson are limited to the movies, a soda at the corner drugstore, and church services. Relatively few staff members have social contacts with the townspeople. This isolation of women's prisons presents serious problems. The staff members of any institution need to get away from the place occasionally for interesting leisure-time pursuits, for the renewal of mental and physical energy in order to maintain balance in their outlook toward their work, their charges, and themselves.

In men's prisons the same problem exists but to a much smaller degree because the majority of men employees are married and live as relatively normal citizens in the community. Instead of spending 24 hours a day within the walls of a prison they put in their 8 hours and occasional overtime, then leave for home and their families. They "get away from their work."

Women employees in prisons need the same sort of escape, but the majority of women's prisons are organized, partially because of their isolation, so as to provide living quarters for them. The House of Detention in New York City is a notable exception. Here the women work on an 8-hour schedule and everyone except the warden lives outside the institution. Thus there is ample opportunity for suitable recreation, friends, and other interests outside of working hours.

Prison work as a profession can be very morbid if workers dwell too much on the background and offenses of the inmates. If a staff member is slightly neurotic she is likely to become more so. State departments of welfare, prison boards, legislators, and others who are responsible for the location of prisons should be apprised of these personnel problems and recognize that a competent, well-trained staff should have access to suitable and wholesome social contacts. A prison in the woods or in the mountains may seem to have great advantages in providing healthful contacts with nature and in reducing disciplinary problems. The interests of the staff deserve major consideration, however, for it is the members of the staff who determine the caliber of the institution.

Parole Policies

Parole policies vary with the different institutions. In California women are given pre-parole instruction over a period of 6 months preceding their release. They are permitted to choose the general area within the state in which they are paroled but are discouraged from locating in the metropolitan areas of San Francisco and Los Angeles. The parole officer always meets the California woman parolee when she arrives in the community where she is to live under parole unless other arrangements for looking after her have been made. If she does not return to her previous home or is not employed in a private home or institution, a room (or housekeeping quarters) is secured in advance for her—always in a respectable neighborhood where community influences will enhance her morale.[29]

The problems on parole are much the same for women as for men, except that women "ex-convicts" tend to be even more severely condemned by public opinion than men. Women parolees sometimes have far more helpful supervision than men, however. Formerly the woman with a record was released with a "paper suitcase," a simple, prison-made wardrobe, and 10 dollars. She was then expected to be able to lead a law-abiding life. Today most parole departments try to secure a satisfactory job placement before releasing women and seek to help them over the difficult first weeks. Unfortunately some states have only one woman parole officer to supervise all women parolees.[30]

[29] Grace E. Barneberg, op. cit.
[30] Cf. chap. 27, "Parole and the Indeterminate Sentence."

Parole Violations of Women Prisoners

Most studies of the post-institutional careers of delinquent and criminal women show a high percentage of parole violation whether it has been detected by parole authorities or not. Miss Miller, Assistant Superintendent at Westfield Prison and Reformatory, says that young girls who are paroled into domestic work are more frequent violators than those from any other type of placement. She attributes this to the loneliness and isolation in such jobs.[31] If this assertion is true we may have the explanation for the high number of failures of women and girls on parole. In a study of the post-institutional adjustment of Sleighton Farm girls made by the author the majority were placed in domestic service and approximately 76 per cent of these girls had serious difficulties or were failures on parole.[32] In the Gluecks' study of 500 criminal women 46.5 per cent were employed as domestic servants at least part of the time while on parole, 11 per cent worked in restaurants and hotels, and 13.7 per cent worked at general housework or at cleaning by the day. The rest were engaged in other employment or fell among the 30.8 per cent who kept house for their husbands or relatives, either for all or for part of the time. The categories in the Glueck study overlap but they indicate the high percentage who were placed as servants. The Gluecks say that parole agents encouraged these women to seek positions as domestics because of the "protected" environment.[33] The "protection" in household employment is dubious because the restrictions in social contacts are resented. Domestic service has many hazards, for girls and women so employed break parole in order to escape their restricted environment.

Women's Reformatories in Contrast with European Institutions for Women Convicts

On the whole the women's reformatories in the United States have made a distinctive contribution to American penology. They have demonstrated that women prisoners are responsive to attractive, home-like surroundings and adequate educational, psychiatric, and other correctional programs. Where women are still incarcerated in special divisions of men's prisons, on the other hand, they are usually in charge of matrons or superintendents who serve under the warden directing

[31] Henry F. and Katharine Pringle, *op. cit.*
[32] Mabel A. Elliott, *op. cit.*, pp. 36–51.
[33] Sheldon and Eleanor T. Glueck, *Five Hundred Delinquent Women*, Knopf, New York, 1934, pp. 210–211.

the prison as a whole. Extensive data on the women's divisions of men's prisons are not available but in general such institutions make little provision for the special needs of women. It was because of the scandalous nature of the women's divisions that the women's reformatories developed, as we have mentioned. There is no reason to believe that any very desirable standards exist in the remaining women's divisions of state prisons today. Because of problems entailed in permitting women to attend joint movies, entertainments, or religious services their lives are often far more restricted than are the men's. At the same time their quarters are more attractive and they are treated less formally than are the men.

Women's prisons in Europe are far removed from our reformatory type of prison. The author has visited women's prisons in Germany under the Nazis, in Russia, and in Hungary. Even during Hitler's regime women's prisons in Germany were still under a high type of civil service control, but the prisons consisted chiefly in grim, gloomy cell blocks where solitary confinement was the rule. In Russia the Soviet penologists before World War II were striving to surpass "capitalistic penology" and were developing excellent educational programs for those who had the capacity to profit from training. Women with a long record of prostitution were given special educational opportunities. The author met and conversed with a number of such women who were being trained as teachers and librarians!

Maria Nostra, the women's prison located near Szob in northern Hungary is apparently the only state prison in the world run by a religious order. This institution admits women convicted of much the same offenses as those in women's prisons in the United States. It is housed in an old monastery which has been beautifully kept and is exceedingly well administered by a group of Roman Catholic sisters who are not merely devoted religious workers but cultivated, educated women. The prison is run on a nonsectarian basis, with special chapels for Jewish and Protestant inmates. The striking characteristic of this prison is that it combines order, cheerfulness, and a belief in the redeemability of the offender with rural life. It also provides educational opportunities and gives the women unexcelled instruction in fine needlework for which the Hungarian shops and well-to-do homes supply a ready market. Ordinarily one may favor the separation of church and state but this prison is an excellent example of how religious ethics may be a factor in aiding the transgressing woman to mend her ways.

Although American penologists have made certain definite contributions in the development of treatment for the woman offender, thus far we have not been able to overcome the stigma which falls like a mantle on our women ex-convicts. Restoring the self-respect of the offender is an important goal that is yet to be achieved.

SELECTED BIBLIOGRAPHY

Additon, Henrietta, "Women's Institutions," chap. 19 in Paul W. Tappan (ed.), *Contemporary Correction*, McGraw-Hill, New York, 1951. This chapter on women's prisons is by the superintendent of Westfield State Farm.

American Prison Association. The *Proceedings* of the various annual congresses of this organization print occasional papers related to the various aspects of women's prisons which give real insight into current problems.

Elliott, Mabel A., *Correctional Education and the Delinquent Girl*, Commonwealth of Pennsylvania, Harrisburg, 1929. This monograph is a follow-up study of Sleighton Farm girls. It also presents the origin and philosophy of a leading correctional institution for younger women and girls.

Glueck, Sheldon and Eleanor T., *Five Hundred Delinquent Women*, Knopf, New York, 1934. This detailed follow-up survey of what happened to women ex-convicts is one of the best studies in this field.

Haynes, Fred E., *The American Prison System*, McGraw-Hill, New York, 1939. This book gives a brief characterization of each of the separate women's reformatories or prisons.

Kellogg, Virginia, "Inside Women's Prisons," *Collier's*, 125:15, 36, and 40–41 (June 3, 1950). A reporter recounts her experiences as a voluntary prisoner and observer in several women's prisons.

Lekkerkerker, Eugenia C., *Reformatories for Women in the United States*, Uitgevers-Maatschappij, Groningen, The Hague, 1931. This is a scholarly survey of women's reformatories, their origin and programs, with an intelligent evaluation of their achievements by a Dutch woman scholar.

Lewis, Sinclair, *Ann Vickers*, Doubleday, New York, 1933. This book contains what Lewis maintained was authentic material depicting the political corruption, lack of sanitation, cruelty, and torture of a women's division of a southern penitentiary.

Pringle, Henry F. and Katharine, "Convicts with Skirts," *Saturday Evening Post*, 223:34–35 ff. (November 25, 1950). This is a popular article but gives important information about Westfield State Farm and Reformatory at Bedford Hills, New York.

Robinson, Frederick William, *Female Life in Prison*, Sampson Low, Son and Marston, London, 1864. This book, first published anonymously in 1862, is a rather scientific study of a British prison. Although actually written by a novelist, it was purportedly the memoirs of a prison matron and was replete with figures to substantiate "her" criticisms. Most of the criticisms sound contemporary and refer to lack of individual treatment, problems of personnel, etc.

CHAPTER 27

Parole and the Indeterminate Sentence

"Parolee from ———— State Penitentiary commits shocking murder." So runs a headline in the leading morning paper. Such statements occur frequently in the press in every important city and often create the impression that the parole of criminals is a direct factor in major crimes. In fact the public tends rather generally to believe that lenient penal practices are basically responsible for sex offenses and murders as well as for other serious crimes.

The average citizen does not take into consideration that practically all prisoners (except the relatively small number of inmates who die during their prison term) are eventually released from prison. Those committed under the indeterminate sentence are released on parole, as are the federal prisoners (who are given definite sentences). But even the state prisoners who are serving definite sentences seldom serve the full term since most of them reduce their sentences by good behavior under the provisions of the state commutation laws. The general tendency, however, is to release most convicts on parole, where they are presumably under supervision until their term has expired.

Statistics for the movement of all prisoners as a whole for 1946 showed that 38,765 prisoners were conditionally released, 29,933 of them on parole. (See Table 27.1.)[1] The same year 7324 persons were returned to prison for conditional release violation (which included those violating parole, conditional pardon, and other conditional releases). The persons returned for such violations are not necessarily those released during the same year. Nevertheless only 18.8 per cent of the number conditionally released were returned for violations. Ob-

[1] *Prisoners in State and Federal Prisons and Reformatories*, 1946, Bureau of the Census, U.S. Department of Commerce, Washington, 1948, p. 3.

726

TABLE 27.1   Movement of Prison Population, by Type of Institution and Sex, for the United States, 1946

Movement of Population	All Institutions			Federal Institutions			State Institutions[a]		
	Total	Male	Female	Total	Male	Female	Total	Male	Female
Prisoners present January 1	134,852	128,585	6,267	18,638	18,112	526	116,214	110,473	5,741
Admitted during year	78,518	73,262	5,256	18,143	17,566	577	60,375	55,696	4,679
Received from court	64,044	59,876	4,168	14,950	14,430	520	49,094	45,446	3,648
Returned as a conditional release violator	7,324	6,807	517	688	661	27	6,636	6,146	490
Returned from escape	2,494	2,364	130	104	94	10	2,390	2,270	120
Returned by court order	321	318	3	3	3	—	318	315	3
Other admissions	4,335	3,897	438	2,398	2,378	20	1,937	1,519	418
Transferred from other institutions	16,355	16,028	327	3,433	3,389	44	12,922	12,639	283
Discharged during year	71,210	65,941	5,269	18,476	17,843	633	52,734	48,098	4,636
All releases	60,240	55,688	4,552	15,544	14,945	599	44,696	40,743	3,953
Unconditional release	21,475	19,799	1,676	4,991	4,824	167	16,484	14,975	1,509
Expiration of sentence	20,778	19,185	1,593	4,869	4,703	166	15,909	14,482	1,427
Pardon	94	90	4	—	—	—	94	90	4
Commutation	603	524	79	122	121	1	481	403	78
Conditional release	38,765	35,889	2,876	10,553	10,121	432	28,212	25,768	2,444
Parole	29,933	27,626	2,307	5,362	5,117	245	24,571	22,509	2,062
Conditional pardon	671	651	20	—	—	—	671	651	20
Other conditional release	8,161	7,612	549	5,191	5,004	187	2,970	2,608	362
Death, except execution	821	802	19	72	71	1	749	731	18
Execution	71	71	—	—	—	—	71	71	—
All other discharges	10,078	9,380	698	2,860	2,827	33	7,218	6,553	665
Escape	2,874	2,745	129	99	89	10	2,775	2,656	119
Court order	1,929	1,866	63	155	152	3	1,774	1,714	60
Other discharges	5,275	4,769	506	2,606	2,586	20	2,669	2,183	486
Transferred to other institutions	17,111	16,759	352	4,116	4,074	42	12,995	12,685	310
Prisoners present December 31	141,404	135,175	6,229	17,622	17,150	472	123,782	118,025	5,757

[a] Includes adjustments and estimates as follows: Alabama, adjustment for incomplete coverage of road camps; Georgia, figures for year ending March 31, 1947, adjusted to a calendar year basis; Mississippi, estimate based on partially reported information. Statistics for Alabama cover county prisoners, those for Pennsylvania are for year ending May 31, and those for Mississippi, for year ending June 30.

SOURCE: *Prisoners in State and Federal Prisons and Reformatories, 1946*, U.S. Department of Commerce, Bureau of the Census, 1948, p. 3.

viously these figures do not mean that 81.2 per cent did not violate any of the terms of release, but merely that they were not returned for any violations. Even so, the showing is commendable, for many of the men become so adjusted to prison existence that they must find the transition to civilian life difficult.

So far as felony prisoners are concerned, a somewhat smaller percentage are released on parole, but of a total of 50,059 felons released in 1946, 34,490 were released before the expiration of their sentence—or nearly 68 per cent, as Table 27.2 shows. However, those released on parole actually served a longer time in prison than those serving a straight sentence. As a matter of fact the majority of the most serious offenders are now given an indeterminate sentence and parole boards may insist on the prisoner's serving more than the minimum sentence

TABLE 27.2. Felony Prisoners Released, by Type of Institution, Time Served Before Release, Method of Release, and Sex, for the United States, 1946

(Median not shown where base is less than 100)

Time Served and Method of Release	All Institutions			Federal Institutions			State Institutions[a]		
	Total	Male	Female	Total	Male	Female	Total	Male	Female
All releases	50,059	47,312	2,747	13,133	12,668	465	36,926	34,644	2,282
Under 6 months	3,559	3,305	254	2,028	1,967	61	1,531	1,338	193
6 to 11 months	9,485	8,647	838	3,373	3,139	234	6,112	5,508	604
12 to 17 months	8,277	7,701	576	1,903	1,807	96	6,374	5,894	480
18 to 23 months	5,853	5,562	291	1,863	1,826	37	3,990	3,736	254
2 years	8,549	8,203	346	2,563	2,539	24	5,986	5,664	322
3 years	4,785	4,618	167	973	965	8	3,812	3,653	159
4 years	2,349	2,264	85	143	143	—	2,206	2,121	85
5 years	1,800	1,736	64	111	109	2	1,689	1,627	62
6 years	1,535	1,491	44	55	55	—	1,480	1,436	44
7 and 8 years	1,575	1,526	49	54	51	3	1,521	1,475	46
9 and 10 years	1,073	1,057	16	37	37	—	1,036	1,020	16
11 to 14 years	719	708	11	12	12	—	707	696	11
15 to 19 years	359	354	5	14	14	—	345	340	5
20 years and over	141	140	1	4	4	—	137	136	1
Median (months)	21.8	22.3	14.9	15.7	16.1	10.4	24.9	25.8	16.3
Expiration of sentence	15,569	14,658	911	2,987	2,919	68	12,582	11,739	843
Under 6 months	2,127	2,013	114	1,350	1,335	15	777	678	99
6 to 11 months	3,868	3,513	355	936	899	37	2,932	2,614	318
12 to 17 months	1,681	1,524	157	73	69	4	1,608	1,455	153
18 to 23 months	1,477	1,401	76	68	66	2	1,409	1,335	74
2 years	2,082	2,000	82	223	218	5	1,859	1,782	77
3 years	1,481	1,422	59	190	186	4	1,291	1,236	55
4 years	716	703	13	47	47	—	669	656	13
5 years	592	570	22	59	58	1	533	512	21
6 years	474	461	13	10	10	—	464	451	13
7 and 8 years	425	416	9	8	8	—	417	408	9
9 and 10 years	325	320	5	7	7	—	318	313	5
11 to 14 years	197	193	4	4	4	—	193	189	4
15 to 19 years	93	92	1	11	11	—	82	81	1
20 years and over	31	30	1	1	1	—	30	29	1
Median (months)	18.4	19.2	11.8	6.9	6.8	—	22.1	23.0	12.2
Other types of release	34,490	32,654	1,836	10,146	9,749	397	24,344	22,905	1,439
Under 6 months	1,432	1,292	140	678	632	46	754	660	94
6 to 11 months	5,617	5,134	483	2,437	2,240	197	3,180	2,894	286
12 to 17 months	6,596	6,177	419	1,830	1,738	92	4,766	4,439	327
18 to 23 months	4,376	4,161	215	1,795	1,760	35	2,581	2,401	180
2 years	6,467	6,203	264	2,340	2,321	19	4,127	3,882	245
3 years	3,304	3,196	108	783	779	4	2,521	2,417	104
4 years	1,633	1,561	72	96	96	—	1,537	1,465	72
5 years	1,208	1,166	42	52	51	1	1,156	1,115	41
6 years	1,061	1,030	31	45	45	—	1,016	985	31
7 and 8 years	1,150	1,110	40	46	43	3	1,104	1,067	37
9 and 10 years	748	737	11	30	30	—	718	707	11
11 to 14 years	522	515	7	8	8	—	514	507	7
15 to 19 years	266	262	4	3	3	—	263	259	4
20 years and over	110	110	—	3	3	—	107	107	—
Median (months)	22.9	23.4	16.2	18.4	18.9	10.6	26.6	27.3	18.4

[a] Includes statistics covering year ending May 31 for Pennsylvania, and for Georgia, statistics for year ending March 31, 1947, adjusted to a calendar year basis; excludes statistics for Michigan and Mississippi.

SOURCE: Table 51 in *Prisoners in State and Federal Prisons and Reformatories, 1946*, Bureau of the Census, U.S. Department of Commerce, Washington, 1948, p. 71.

before releasing him.[2] Table 27.3 shows that Negroes serve a slightly longer part of their sentence than white persons, but this difference is not great, averaging only two-tenths of a month.[3]

Parole—A Definition

Parole may be defined as the conditional release of the prisoner from a prison or reformatory prior to the expiration of his sentence, on the recommendation of the parole authority. During the time the prisoner is so released he must agree to abide by the rules and regulations of the paroling authority and may be returned to the institution from which he was paroled if he commits another crime or if he violates the conditions under which his parole is granted.

As parole systems now operate the parolee is usually released (nominally at least) under the supervision of a parole officer. Basic to the whole idea of parole is effective supervision under a suitable responsible person. Another idea basic to the initial parole concept is that of the indeterminate sentence. Both of these matters will be discussed at some length later.

The Philosophy of Parole

The whole philosophy of parole (notwithstanding its vitriolic critics) is concerned primarily with helping prisoners make an acceptable adjustment to the society which has condemned them to prison. In order to do this it is generally conceded that the time served in prison should be related to the prisoner's social adjustment and that he should manifest indications that he is ready to lead an honest and law-abiding life. Legally, parole is considered a privilege rather than a right and is granted on the discretionary authority of those officers who are given the responsibility for reviewing the case. The prisoner usually makes a request for parole after serving the legally designated minimum term as prescribed by law for his offense in the state in which he is incarcerated. The parole authority (which may be variously constituted as a special state parole board, a committee attached to the prison or a special committee of the supervising board of the prison, or the governor of the state and his assistants) then decides whether the facts in the prisoner's case warrant his parole at that time. If so, the prisoner is released, usually under the supervision of a parole officer and contingent upon his good behavior as defined by rules and

[2] *Ibid.*, p. 70.   [3] *Ibid.*, p. 72.

TABLE 27.3. Male Felony Prisoners Released, by Type of Institution, Time Served Before Release, Method of Release, and Race, for the United States, 1946

(Median not shown where base is less than 100)

Time served and method of release	All Institutions				Federal Institutions				State Institutions[a]			
	Total	White	Negro	Other Races	Total	White	Negro	Other Races	Total	White	Negro	Other Races
All releases	47,312	33,380	13,298	634	12,668	10,009	2,321	338	34,644	23,371	10,977	296
Under 6 months	3,305	2,193	1,080	32	1,967	1,449	492	26	1,338	744	588	6
6 to 11 months	8,647	6,047	2,470	130	3,139	2,358	708	73	5,508	3,689	1,762	57
12 to 17 months	7,701	5,605	1,992	104	1,807	1,410	338	59	5,894	4,195	1,654	45
18 to 23 months	5,562	4,014	1,472	76	1,826	1,484	304	38	3,736	2,530	1,168	38
2 years	8,203	6,053	1,983	167	2,539	2,126	311	102	5,664	3,927	1,672	65
3 years	4,618	3,196	1,378	44	965	820	129	16	3,653	2,376	1,249	28
4 years	2,264	1,576	668	20	143	124	14	5	2,121	1,452	654	15
5 years	1,736	1,200	523	13	109	91	14	4	1,627	1,109	509	9
6 years	1,491	1,008	472	11	55	46	3	6	1,436	962	469	5
7 and 8 years	1,526	992	524	10	51	45	3	3	1,475	947	521	7
9 and 10 years	1,057	705	342	10	37	32	1	4	1,020	673	341	6
11 to 14 years	708	460	243	5	12	9	2	1	696	451	241	4
15 to 19 years	354	239	109	6	14	13	1	—	340	226	108	6
20 years and over	140	92	42	6	4	2	1	1	136	90	41	5
Median (months)	22.3	22.3	22.5	22.0	16.1	17.1	11.7	19.7	25.8	25.6	26.3	24.4
Expiration of sentence	14,658	8,995	5,480	183	2,919	2,186	662	71	11,739	6,809	4,818	112
Under 6 months	2,013	1,254	733	26	1,335	967	343	25	678	287	390	1
6 to 11 months	3,513	2,130	1,340	43	899	659	216	24	2,614	1,471	1,124	19
12 to 17 months	1,524	915	586	23	69	53	14	2	1,455	862	572	21
18 to 23 months	1,401	848	535	18	66	56	8	2	1,335	792	527	16

	(1)	(2)	(3)	(4)	(5)	(6)	(7)	(8)	(9)	(10)	(11)	(12)
2 years	2,000	1,246	725	29	218	181	32	5	1,782	1,065	693	24
3 years	1,422	867	539	16	186	150	31	5	1,236	717	508	11
4 years	703	425	268	10	47	39	5	3	656	386	263	7
5 years	570	377	186	7	58	44	11	3	512	333	175	4
6 years	461	285	175	1	10	10	—	3	451	275	175	1
7 and 8 years	416	255	158	3	8	7	—	1	408	248	158	2
9 and 10 years	320	200	117	3	7	6	—	1	313	194	117	2
11 to 14 years	193	112	81	—	4	3	1	—	189	109	80	—
15 to 19 years	92	64	26	2	11	10	1	—	81	54	25	2
20 years and over	30	17	11	2	1	1	—	—	29	16	11	2
Median (months)	19.2	19.4	18.9	17.9	6.8	7.1	5.8	—	23.0	23.9	21.7	23.6
Other types of release	32,654	24,385	7,818	451	9,749	7,823	1,659	267	22,905	16,562	6,159	184
Under 6 months	1,292	939	347	6	632	482	149	1	660	457	198	5
6 to 11 months	5,134	3,917	1,130	87	2,240	1,699	492	49	2,894	2,218	638	38
12 to 17 months	6,177	4,690	1,406	81	1,738	1,357	324	57	4,439	3,333	1,082	24
18 to 23 months	4,161	3,166	937	58	1,760	1,428	296	36	2,401	1,738	641	22
2 years	6,203	4,807	1,258	138	2,321	1,945	279	97	3,882	2,862	979	41
3 years	3,196	2,329	839	28	779	670	98	11	2,417	1,659	741	17
4 years	1,561	1,151	400	10	96	85	9	2	1,465	1,066	391	8
5 years	1,166	823	337	6	51	47	3	1	1,115	776	334	5
6 years	1,030	723	297	10	45	36	3	6	985	687	294	4
7 and 8 years	1,110	737	366	7	43	38	3	2	1,067	699	363	5
9 and 10 years	737	505	225	7	30	26	1	3	707	479	224	4
11 to 14 years	515	348	162	5	8	6	1	1	507	342	161	4
15 to 19 years	262	175	83	4	3	3	—	—	259	172	83	4
20 years and over	110	75	31	4	3	1	1	1	107	74	30	3
Median (months)	23.4	23.0	24.8	23.3	18.9	19.6	15.5	22.4	27.3	26.2	30.4	24.9

a Includes statistics covering year ending May 31 for Pennsylvania, and for Georgia, statistics for year ending March 31, 1947, adjusted to a calendar year basis; excludes statistics for Michigan and Mississippi.

SOURCE: Table 52 in *Prisoners in State and Federal Prisons and Reformatories, 1946*, Bureau of the Census, U.S. Department of Commerce, Washington, 1948, p. 72.

regulations laid down by the parole authority. If the parolee makes a good record the parole period during which he is supervised on release from the penitentiary is often reduced and he is given discharge before the expiration of the maximum sentence. The basic idea underlying all acceptable standards of parole, then, is the conditional release from prison under supervision of a parole officer until the full term of the sentence is discharged. The aim and justification for parole is to bridge the period between the closely regulated life of the prison and complete freedom in the world outside.

TABLE 27.4.   Median Time Served (in Months) by Felony Prisoners Before Release, by Method of Release, for the United States, 1938 to 1940, 1942 to 1946

Method of Release	1946[a]	1945[b]	1944[b]	1943[b]	1942[b]	1940[c]	1939[b]	1938[a]
All releases	21.8	23.8	24.6	23.9	21.9	18.5	19.5	19.0
Expiration of sentence	18.4	22.2	23.8	23.4	21.1	16.5	19.8	19.7
Other types of release	22.9	24.6	24.9	24.1	22.3	19.3	19.4	18.7

[a] Time served as reported by individual institutions.
[b] Based on difference between date of discharge and date when sentence began for first discharges and redischarges combined.
[c] Based on difference between date of discharge and date when sentence began for first discharges only.
SOURCE: Table 50 in *Prisoners in State and Federal Prisons and Reformatories, 1946*, Bureau of the Census, U.S. Department of Commerce, Washington, 1948, p. 70.

The term "parole" itself is derived from the French word *parole*, which means "word," but it is used in the sense of *parole d'honneur* "word of honor." That is, the prisoner gives his word (or his word of honor) that he will live up to the terms of his conditional release from prison. Some people hold this use of the term unfortunate since prisoners are so generally unreliable. Be that as it may, the idea of parole is closely associated with the idea of reforming the offender which received so much emphasis during the nineteenth century. The notion of reforming the offender has been found in the literature of the scholars and philosophers of ancient times, however. Prosanto Kumar Sen points out several references to the proposition in ancient Hindu law books. Plato later emphasized the idea in ancient Greece, and the churchmen during the seventeenth and eighteenth centuries emphasized reformation as the primary end of penal treatment.[4]

The Antecedents of the Parole Idea

A major antecedent of parole was the French Revolution, which made a decisive impact upon penal theory with its accompanying Dec-

[4] *Attorney General's Survey of Release Procedures*, Vol. IV, *Parole*, U.S. Department of Justice, Washington, 1939, p. 5.

laration on the Rights of Man. One of the intellectual leaders of the Revolution, Mirabeau, proposed in 1791 that a penal system should be developed on principles of labor, segregation, rewards under a marks system, conditional liberation, and aid on discharge.[5]

The first organized parole systems were established in Spain and Germany, however. In Spain, in 1835, Colonel Montesinos developed a system of releasing prisoners from the Valencia prison after two-thirds of their sentence was completed. Only 35 per cent of the men were recommitted for misbehavior, and it seemed to be a successful project. Nevertheless this scheme of release collapsed within 10 years. In Germany Obermaier, formerly governor of the Kaiserlautern prison in Bavaria, was made head of the prison in Munich in 1842. His system of discharging convicts under supervision called for no fixed term and for supervising the men on release through the assistance of a number of prison aid societies.[6]

These developments on the Continent were preceded, however, by the transportation system in England, which in turn led to the development of the marks system introduced by Alexander Maconochie in the penal colony at Norfolk Island in 1840. The marks system, the ticket-of-leave system as evolved by Crofton in Ireland, and the stage system as developed by Sir Joshua Jebb in England are more frequently given credit for leading to modern parole than the experiments of Montesinos and Obermaier.[7] We shall consider these British developments more extensively since American criminal law and penal treatment have been based more than many persons realize on British penal law and practice. Nevertheless the Continental systems also affected the adoption of parole in America.

TRANSPORTATION

The transportation of British prisoners to the American colonies was unquestionably aimed more at solving the colonial labor problem than at reforming criminals. The British began the transportation of regular criminals during the reign of James I, when the practice of sending prisoners to Virginia as indentured servants was instituted. Cromwell had previously sent "political captives" there, but these were not criminals in the accepted sense of the word, but simply orthodox monarchists whom the Cromwellians hesitated to hang. Nevertheless the majority of transported criminals who were sent to Virginia ordi-

[5] Ibid., p. 6.
[6] Ibid., pp. 8–9.
[7] Cf. Frederick H. Wines, Punishment and Reformation, Crowell, New York, 1895, p. 195. Cf. also Attorney General's Survey of Release Procedures, Vol. IV, Parole, p. 9.

narily would have received the death penalty had there not been the great need for labor in the colonies. The idea of putting the men to useful labor was seized upon, therefore, as an admirable solution. Contractors generally handled the men, selling their services to the highest bidders at a public auction in the colony. All this was antecedent to the development of Negro slavery in the colonies, but transportation had many of the attributes of short-term slavery. A man's services were sold for from 7 to 14 years, often for as little as 20 pounds.[8]

Cruel and inhumane practices attended the whole operation of the transportation system. In the first place the transport ships were usually as filthy as the stationary jails and many prisoners died en route from the diseases they contracted. Once indentured, the prisoners were often brutally treated, especially if they were at all refractory in conduct. After the American Revolution the practice of sending British prisoners here was officially abolished, although they were often shipped in illicitly. A few were sent to Africa but so many of them died there that some other plan was imperative. The discovery of Australia afforded another opportunity for shipping prisoners to develop the new colony and the British almost immediately developed a transportation system. In 1787 Captain Arthur Phillip set out for Australia with his "felon fleet" of "nine transports and two men of war."

The transportation of prisoners to Australian developed into one of the most notorious enterprises in which the British government has ever engaged. The actual transportation of convicts was carried out by contractors who were paid sixpence a day for the prisoner's food in addition to an allowance for tonnage. It is claimed that contractors both prolonged the voyages and gave convicts food of poor quality in order to increase their earnings. If the prisoners died they saved the whole amount, and many of the convicts never survived. In 1802, according to the report of a colonial surgeon, 261 men out of 939 sent out on 3 ships died en route, 50 died after landing, and 450 were ill.[9]

Conditions on the boats in which women and girls were transported were literally unspeakable. Officers were permitted liberties without license with whatever women they chose. Nothing in the slave trade probably has so horrified and outraged decent persons as the conditions on the "floating hells," as they were called. There was little ventilation, convicts were often chained together, sometimes to partners who were dead or dying. Meanwhile the officers were so brutal

[8]Arthur Griffiths, *The World's Famous Prisons*, Grolier Society, London, no date, Vol. V, *Prisons Over Seas*, pp. 14–16.

[9] Anonymous, *The History of the Ancient Australian Convict Ship "Success" and Its Most Notorious Prisoners*, compiled from British records, London, 1929, p. 13.

that flogging of the convicts was often a source of their amusement.[10]

For those prisoners who survived the horrible voyage new terrors awaited when they landed in Australia. The men were usually assigned to chain gangs and became the road makers for the new colony. Often the overseers were themselves former convicts, who reveled in treating others as brutally as they had once been treated. Even when the transported convicts' indentures or sentences had supposedly expired many were still kept at forced labor.

While serving their years at forced labor the slightest refractory act of these convicts was often punished by lashing. Countless men died from their floggings. One physician reported that flesh, blood, and skin flew into his face during flogging of one man who received 300 lashes. The British conscience was apparently salved by the law's requiring a physician to be present at such lashings, even though that gesture had no apparent effect upon the severity of the punishment. Some transported convicts were hanged for slight offenses while indentured. During the first 6 years of the penal colony 95 of these prisoners were hanged at Sydney.[11]

Historical surveys have indicated that the political prisoners of the past may be the prototypes of the leaders of tomorrow. This seems to have been especially true of the men transported to Australia. Many of the transported prisoners were men who spoke out against the cruel social injustices of their day, only to face criminal charges for so doing. Thus it happened that in 1912 a monument was erected in Tolpuddle, Dorsetshire, England, to the "Six Men of Dorset." These men had held a meeting in 1834 to consider what could be done about their miserable existence on the pittance wages they were then paid. They had previously asked for an increase of a shilling a week which had been denied. While holding their meeting these men were arrested on charges of conspiracy and sentenced to transportation for 7 years. The undeserved sentence so aroused local Britishers that a demonstration of 50,000 workingmen was held and a petition bearing 266,000 names was presented to the prime minister requesting their pardon. Finally, on January 30, 1837, these men were pardoned and granted free return to England.[12]

Many other men were transported for such trivial offenses as stealing a potato pie or shooting a hare. Some of course were serious offenders and "deserved" punishment.[13] But because there were so many obvious injustices, the governor of New South Wales, as Aus-

---

[10] Ibid., pp. 14–16.
[12] Ibid., chap. 10, "The Six Men of Dorset."
[11] Ibid., chap. 4.
[13] Ibid., chaps. 11–18.

tralia was called, was given right of conditional pardon and as early as 1834 a ticket-of-leave system was established, with grants of land to aid the convicts. This plan failed, however. Finally the whole transportation system's abominable features created so much public indignation that Parliament condemned the practice in 1839 and it was abolished the year following.

2. MACONOCHIE'S "MARK SYSTEM."

Because the 1834 ticket-of-leave plan was unsuccessful, Alexander Maconochie, who was then in charge of the prisoners at Norfolk Island, devised a new plan in 1840. This provided for a system of four stages through which convicts must pass. First, on admission they were kept in strict imprisonment; second, they were placed on government chain gangs; third, they were given quasi-freedom within restricted areas; and fourth, they were finally granted a "ticket of leave" which was followed by full liberty. During each stage in the penal sentence each man was required to earn enough "marks" to secure promotion to the next stage.[14]

This system of grading prisoners and requiring them to earn their privileges through good conduct and diligent labor was of historic importance to subsequent penal developments for it provided both an incentive to good behavior and a transitional period between imprisonment and expiration of sentence. The earlier ticket of leave had made no provision for such a transitional stage. Unfortunately Maconochie's plan was met by a hostile reaction in the community where the men were released. Nevertheless it was the only commendable development under the transportation system.[15]

3. THE STAGE SYSTEMS OF CROFTON AND JEBB.

Sir Walter Crofton in Ireland believed there was much merit in Maconochie's plan if only the community and the convicts could be educated to accept the idea of conditional release through successive stages. As director of the Irish prisons Crofton worked out a three-stage system. Although the idea of stages of imprisonment is now known to have been introduced in Ireland by Sir Joshua Jebb,[16] Crofton may be credited with its development. First, the convict was confined in prison, where he was kept employed and received training. Second, he was released to employment on public works with as little physical

---

[14] *Attorney General's Survey of Release Procedures*, Vol. IV, Parole, pp. 11–12.

[15] *Ibid.* Cf. also George Ives, *History of Penal Methods*, S. Paul, London, 1914, p. 170.

[16] Sir H. Evelyn Ruggles-Brise, *The English Prison System*, Macmillan, London, 1921, pp. 29–30.

restraint as possible. (There were no chain gangs.) Third, he was given a conditional release "on license" pending his adherence to rules. If he violated the regulations he was returned to prison. There was no real supervision, but the men made monthly reports and were required to avoid contacts with other criminals or ex-convicts. These aspects of the conditional release later became common practice in American parole procedures.[17]

THE DEVELOPMENT OF PAROLE IN THE UNITED STATES

The First Parole Law

The first statutory provision for parole in the United States was adopted in New York in 1817. This law gave prison inspectors power to release any convict sentenced for more than 5 years after he had served three-fourths of his sentence, provided he had a record of good behavior.[18] There is, however, no record of any prison inspector's having released prisoners in accordance with this law. As initially conceived, parole was considered a reward for good behavior and differed but little from the provisions for commutation of sentence which soon developed in other states. Thus in 1836 Tennessee authorized commutation of sentence for not more than 2 days each month as a reward for good conduct. Ohio in 1856 provided that 5 days each month should be deducted from the sentence of any prisoner who worked faithfully and had not violated any rules. Similar provisions were soon adopted by other states. Iowa and Massachusetts followed with commutation laws in 1857, and further laws were enacted in New York and Connecticut in 1860, in Illinois in 1863, in Oregon and California in 1864, in Missouri and Nevada in 1867, in New Jersey and Rhode Island in 1868. In the meantime the idea of paroling men under an indeterminate type of sentence was gaining favor.

The Indeterminate Sentence and Parole

The indeterminate sentence is generally considered an important aspect of parole. That is, in the majority of states the prisoner is ordinarily sentenced on an indeterminate basis. The sentence may be from 2 to 5 years, from 3 to 5 years, etc. If the prisoner's prison record is

[17] *Attorney General's Survey of Release Procedures*, Vol. IV, *Parole*, pp. 13–14.
[18] Mabel A. Elliott, *Conflicting Penal Theories in Statutory Criminal Law*, University of Chicago Press, Chicago, 1931, chap. 6, "The Indeterminate Sentence and Parole." Cf. also Helen Leland Witmer, "The History, Theory and Results of Parole," *Journal of Criminal Law and Criminology*, 18:24–64 (May–June, 1927).

satisfactory he is then eligible for parole at the expiration of the minimum sentence, which in the majority of states is reduced even further
through "good time" or commutation of sentence. If parole is granted,
the prisoner is accordingly placed on conditional release from the
prison until his maximum term is completed, or the parole authority
in the particular state may reduce the parole period and release him
before the completion of the maximum period.[19] In many states the
actual parole period often amounts to but 1 year. In the federal penal
system, however, it lasts until the flat sentence is completed.

Although the indeterminate sentence had had many earlier proponents, the first indeterminate sentence law was not adopted until
after the opening of the Elmira Reformatory in 1876. In that year
Zebulon R. Brockway, who had been made superintendent of the new
institution, drafted an unlimited indeterminate sentence law for New
York State which he hoped to have imposed in case of all commitments to the reformatory. Public sentiment opposed a completely indeterminate sentence, however, and accordingly the law as passed in
1877 limited the maximum sentence under the indeterminate sentence
to the maximum prescribed by law for the specific offense. Between
1877 and 1900 parole and the indeterminate sentence idea spread
rapidly, although parole laws were more extensively adopted. At the
turn of the century New York, Massachusetts, Pennsylvania, Ohio,
Michigan, Minnesota, New Jersey, California, Nebraska, North Dakota, Illinois, Kansas, Indiana, Connecticut, Alabama, Idaho, Utah,
Virginia, Colorado, and Wisconsin had adopted parole laws. Of these
New York, Massachusetts, Pennsylvania, Minnesota, Illinois, New
Jersey, Kansas, Ohio, Indiana, Colorado, and Wisconsin had some
form of indeterminate sentence.[20] All told, 20 states had adopted
parole and 11 of these states had also adopted the indeterminate sentence.

In 1928 the present author made a special study of the development
of the indeterminate sentence in 13 states during the years 1900–1925.
At that time the statutes of these states indicated several conflicting
attitudes toward the indeterminate sentence, and the laws of the different states fell into the following 4 types:

1. Those which limited the indeterminate sentence to the less grave
   offenses. (This included the largest number.)
2. Those which applied indeterminate sentence to all prisoners.

[19] Mabel A. Elliott, op. cit.
[20] Edward Lindsey, "A Historical Sketch of the Indeterminate Sentence and Parole
System," Journal of Criminal Law and Criminology, 16:9–126 (May–June, 1925).

3. Those which applied the indeterminate sentence to the more serious offenses or longer commitments.

4. Those which limited the indeterminate sentence to first offenders who had committed less serious offenses.

Some states, however, made no provision for indeterminate sentence.[21]

Parole and Indeterminate Sentence in the Several States Today

By 1944 all states, Alaska, Puerto Rico, and Hawaii had some form of parole system authorized by law, and 25 states now have some form of indeterminate sentence. The indeterminate sentence as it is in effect has been an imperfect instrument for adjusting the sentence so as to suit the problems presented by the individual prisoner. For the judge is still required to decide in advance what the sentence shall be—at least within the limits of the minimums and maximums prescribed.[22]

Eligibility for Parole

The laws vary markedly with reference to eligibility for parole. Some states which have an indeterminate sentence permit all prisoners so committed to be paroled and others do not. Some states permit parole of prisoners committed under definite sentence, whereas others specifically forbid their parole.

TIME LIMITATIONS

In 1950 indeterminate sentence laws in operation in 25 states required that the minimum sentence be served before the prisoner could be paroled. However, in several of these states the prisoner's minimum sentence was further reduced by "good time" allowances. California permitted release on the expiration of one-third of the minimum sentence. In 16 states the laws imposed no specific part of the sentence before the prisoner was eligible for parole. These states include Alabama, Arkansas, and Georgia, and barring certain prisoners who have committed serious offenses parole may be extended at any time the parole authority sees fit in Idaho, Iowa, Louisiana, Maryland, Minnesota, Missouri, New Jersey, Ohio, Oregon, Pennsylvania, Utah, and Wisconsin. In Nevada the prisoner must serve a minimum sentence of 1 year and in the District of Columbia and Michigan the parole board may re-

[21] Mabel A. Elliott, op. cit.

[22] Cf. Randolph E. Wise, "Parole Progress," National Probation and Parole Association Yearbook, 1950, New York, 1951, pp. 111–120.

quest the sentencing court to reduce the minimum sentence. In all other states a substantial part of the sentence must be served before parole may be granted. In general parole may be granted in these states after the expiration of the minimum. In a number of states one-third of the maximum must be served. New Jersey, for example, requires either expiration of the minimum less good time allowance or one-third of the maximum, whichever comes soonest for first offenses, but increases the time limitation with each sentence.[23]

Offense Limitations

Seven of the states which permit parole without time limitations enforce restrictions in case of certain offenses. In Idaho, for example, life termers must serve 10 years, and those convicted of homicide, treason, rape with violence, robbery, kidnaping, burglary when armed, assault with intent to kill, and murder in the second degree all must serve one-third of their sentence. In Iowa life termers and prisoners who have assaulted a prison employee with a deadly weapon are barred from parole.

Many other states (which have definite time limitations) also bar certain offenders from parole. Kansas, for example, will not parole anyone guilty of treason or murder or a person serving a third prison term. North Dakota will not parole a second offender. Pennsylvania does not parole life termers. Tennessee and New York do not permit parole of persons serving definite sentences. Several states, including Delaware, Kentucky, Washington, will not parole rapists. In nine states a life termer may not be paroled; but in other states life termers may be paroled after serving a specific period, usually ranging from 10 to 15 years. Twenty-four states—Alabama, Arizona, Arkansas, California, Colorado, Connecticut, Florida, Georgia, Idaho, Illinois, Maine, Maryland, Massachusetts, Minnesota, Missouri, North Carolina, Oklahoma, Rhode Island, South Carolina, South Dakota, Texas, Utah, Vermont, and Wisconsin—as well as the District of Columbia, Alaska, Hawaii, and Puerto Rico permit all types of offenders to be paroled, although life termers usually serve a considerably longer time than other offenders in these states. In the other states murderers (or life termers), habitual criminals, rapists, and persons who commit deadly assault in prison comprise most of the prisoners who are denied parole because of their offense.[24]

[23] *Ibid.*
[24] *Ibid.* Cf. also Sol Rubin, "Adult Parole Systems in the United States," mimeographed report, National Probation and Parole Association, 1949, pp. 16–26.

Parole authorities often establish their own rules with reference to eligibility for parole even though these are not prescribed by law. For example, the Iowa parole board does not permit parole before 10 months have been served. The Missouri parole authority will consider the parole application of persons who have served one-fifth of their term or after 5 years in case of persons sentenced for 25 or more years.[25]

The Federal Parole Setup

FEDERAL PAROLE LAWS

The first federal parole law was enacted in 1910. It provided that federal offenders might be paroled who were sentenced for 1 year or more and that prisoners might be eligible for parole after the expiration of one-third of their sentence. In 1913 life termers were made eligible for parole after serving 15 years. In 1930 a federal parole board was created to be composed of three persons appointed by the United States attorney general. In 1932 the parole period was specified to extend until the expiration of the maximum sentence or the term imposed upon sentence. Parole in all federal institutions is thus granted by a single body. Parole preparation is under the supervision of parole officers who are staff members of the institution in which the inmate is confined, and his supervision on parole is under the direction of the federal probation officers. They in turn are attached to the Board of Parole in Washington.[26]

FEDERAL PAROLE PROCEDURES

Any federal offender who has served one-third or more of his sentence or any life termer who has served 15 years is eligible for parole if he has had a good record of observing rules within the institution to which he is committed.[27] Such a person makes an application for a hearing. The federal court and district attorney make recommendations and the classification committee and various institutional officers report on his suitability for parole. Hearings are held by the Board of Parole once every 3 months in all federal penal institutions, and a report on the determination of the case is later made from the board after its return to Washington.[28]

If the prisoner is granted parole he must agree to accept the conditions of parole, which are similar to those in most states. He must file

[25] Sol Rubin, *op. cit.*, p. 27.
[26] *Attorney General's Survey of Release Procedures*, Vol. I, *Digest of State Laws on Release Procedures*, U.S. Department of Justice, Washington, 1939, pp. 15–18.
[27] *Ibid.*, p. 18.   [28] *Ibid.*, p. 19.

a report of his arrival at the place where he is paroled (often his old home) and send in monthly reports unless for some reason he must report more frequently. Each parolee is assigned to an advisor, in some cases a person of his own choosing; in other cases the supervising parole officer selects a proper person.[29]

If the federal prisoner violates his parole the Board of Parole may issue a warrant for his arrest, which may be executed by any prison official or federal officer authorized to serve criminal process. Such a warrant must be issued before the parolee's expiration of term. On return to the prison the parolee is given a hearing at the next meeting of the Board of Parole in the institution.[30]

If recommitted to the prison the time spent on parole is not deducted from the original sentence. The prisoner may be reparoled, however. When the released prisoner's parole period is satisfactorily completed he is notified by letter.[31]

Some federal offenders (usually younger persons) are, for various reasons, committed to state reformatories. These persons are subject to the same parole laws as are offenders of the state laws in the same institution. Their parole, however, must be approved by the Federal Board of Parole.[32]

Any federal offender who is denied parole or waives right to apply for parole may be treated as a parolee if he is released before the expiration of his sentence under "good time" regulations, and is subject to the same supervision and to return to prison in case of violation of parole laws.[33]

In an effort to improve the rehabilitation of youthful offenders a Youth Correction Division of the Federal Board of Parole and an Advisory Corrections Council was authorized by Congress on September 30, 1950. The latter is composed of a United States circuit judge, two United States district judges, one person appointed by the Attorney General, the Chairman of the Board of Parole, the Chairman of the Youth Correction Division, and the Chief of Probation of the Administrative Offices of the United States Courts. This group, along with the Director of the Bureau of Prisons, has been authorized to determine the release of all young persons. The law also provides special treatment for offenders and is discussed in Chapter 29.[34] The major aim of the bill is to facilitate treatment which is best for the offender, but it also aims to protect society.

[29] Ibid., pp. 20–21.　　[30] Ibid.
[31] Ibid., p. 23.　　[32] Ibid., p. 24.
[33] Ibid.　　[34] Public Law 865, 81st Congress.

PRESENT-DAY PAROLE ADMINISTRATION

Preparation for Parole

It is the duty of parole officials and specifically of the members of the prison classification committee—if there is one—to assume the task of preparing the inmate for his conditional release. Where there is a classification committee this group tries to uncover all facts which bear upon both the prisoner's offense and his personality, but an intelligent committee will place more emphasis upon understanding the parolee than on weighting the seriousness of his offense. The psychiatrist, the social worker, the supervisor of the prisoner's work detail, the educational director, the recreational director, the chaplain, the dormitory officer, and anyone else who has had direct contact with the prisoner for any length of time should be able to give insight into the quirks of the prisoner's personality, his degree of emotional stability, discernment, and co-operativeness which may measure the degree of his fitness for parole.

Unfortunately the majority of states still have no effective provisions for determining the prisoner's suitability for parole. Of course if a prisoner is to be released on parole at all he must eventually be selected for such release. But a man should not be paroled because of political pressures, because of the pleas of relatives, or because he has broken no prison rule. Some clever crooks purposively obey all rules merely to secure release and get back into their criminal activities. There should be positive evidence that the prisoner can be placed at honest work and is ready to make a constructive effort to become a law-abiding citizen before he is released.

In 1939 the *Attorney General's Survey of Release Procedures* reported that only 11 states and the federal government made a serious study of the prisoner's fitness for parole before releasing him. These states were California, Illinois, Massachusetts, Michigan, Minnesota, New Jersey, New York, North Carolina, Pennsylvania, Washington, and Wisconsin. Some states, including Illinois and Minnesota, have made prediction studies with reference to the prisoner's probable adjustment on release, which have proved fairly accurate in determining success or failure on parole.

These and other prediction studies discussed later in the chapter should be taken into consideration in determining the prisoner's readiness for parole. When unfavorable prediction factors are known to exist in a prisoner's background, steps should be taken to correct them before parole. For example, poor work habits in the pre-institutional period (also discussed later) are known to be correlated with failure on parole. Likewise a previous history of poor use of leisure time appears to indicate a bad parole risk.[35] An individualized type of classification procedure would take such items into consideration and work toward helping the prisoner overcome his bad habits.

As a means of facilitating his adjustment the prisoner should receive specific training and instruction for meeting the problems he will confront on parole. He should be alerted to the difficulties and frustrations he will encounter as an ex-convict. He must respect the conditions of parole even though they may seem absurd and unreasonable if not downright impossible. The prisoner must learn also to accept help from those who are prepared to give it to him. He should be advised to consult his parole officer when he is faced with a difficulty. He may suitably enlist the assistance of clergymen, of social workers, or in particular of prison aid society officials who stand ready to give the ex-convict a helping hand.

The placement officer, psychiatrist of the prison, psychologist, or someone suitably qualified (if one such is available) should secure the confidence of the parolee and help him to recognize his problems in advance and to evaluate the resources and handicaps which he must reckon with in meeting them. In a few prisons the inmates are given an opportunity to discuss their problems in open forums. This seems like a valuable plan for bringing the prisoner's post-prison problems into focus. But each prisoner faces situations which are unique, has peculiar adjustments to make as a member of a family, be it as erring son or erring father, and must cope with local attitudes in the place where he is to be paroled. The fact that the neighbors know him may help, but it is also often embarrassing and for this reason the ex-convict frequently seeks the anonymity of the larger city where he may pass unnoticed in the crowd.

The Parole Authority

Much of the effectiveness of parole inevitably depends upon the way in which it is administered. That is, the parole authority is vested with great responsibility in determining who is to be paroled—within the limits of the laws under which the prisoners are committed. (Prisoners serving definite sentences are automatically released at the

[35] See pp. 757–766 in this chapter for a discussion of predictive factors in success or failure on parole.

expiration of the sentence, as we shall discuss later.) Much of the parolee's success is also effected by paroling him when he has gained as much benefit as he seems likely to receive from his prison training. The supervision the parolee receives is perhaps even more important in effecting his adjustment, and this is vested either in the parole board or in parole officers appointed for the purpose of supervising the men on conditional release from prison.

In general three distinct types of agencies control the operation of parole in the various states: (1) a central state parole board, (2) the governor, who may or may not be assisted by a special board or a "parole attorney," and (3) parole boards which are attached to the particular prisons or reformatories.

The Parole Hearing

When the prisoner appears before the parole authority he is usually tense and worried. He often literally feels that the board is re-trying him for his offense, because he realizes the factors for and against his parole are being weighed. The would-be parolee thus often makes a bad impression just because he is in an abnormal emotional state. He is "frightened, distrustful and unsure of himself." Moreover he feels humiliated, knowing that all the unpleasant facts that the parole board can gather are before them for consideration, as well as any items in his favor. For these reasons the board should attempt to put themselves in his shoes and recognize the strain, embarrassment, and abnormality of the situation. When, on the other hand, the prisoner wishes to be poised and confident, he may seem too confident and cocksure. These outward evidences are indexes to the emotional stress, and the parole board should take them into consideration.[36]

Who Should Be Released on Parole

Modern penologists maintain almost categorically that all prisoners should be released on parole, if they are ever to be released at all. Thus, since with few exceptions convicts are always released from prison, all types of offenders not permanently incarcerated should be released on parole, and as we have seen from our analysis of limitations on parole this practice is becoming general. Even the majority of life termers are released after serving from 10 to 20 years. Nevertheless any expressed belief in making all prisoners eligible for parole usually evokes a storm of protest. "This means," says the outraged layman,

[36] Cf. Melitta Schmidberg, "The Parolee Reports," *Focus*, 29:12–15 (January, 1950).

"that the rapist, the murderer, the kidnaper, the hoodlum, gangster and recidivist should be treated with consideration and as decent men."

It may be true that certain offenders should be permanently incarcerated, but if the state permits their release this is not the fault of parole boards. Nor would it be sensible for legislatures to pass more stringent rules than now exist with reference to parolees. Release, indeed, should be on a much more elastic basis than it now is. Theoretically, as we have indicated, a prisoner should be released on parole when he is ready to make an adequate adjustment to civilian life. He should be released from parole supervision when he has demonstrated his capacity to live a law-abiding life. The exact time when a criminal has reached this stage cannot be determined with any degree of accuracy because prison life adjustment is no index to behavior outside. Although many prisoners fail on parole, enough parolees with very bad previous records have made surprisingly good adjustments to force us to recognize the need for more detailed research into what led these men to go straight. Such research might develop systematic procedures for dealing with the difficult cases, for helping the discouraged, embittered, and avowedly antisocial men. Criminological research needs to go further than merely discovering what factors in the prisoner's make-up and environment will eventually lead him to go straight. It is necessary to know what to do with and for the man who is slated for failure unless he has effective assistance.

Swedish Parole Provisions

Sweden has some interesting new provisions for parole. Prisoners are under parole supervision for 6 months for sentences under a year and for a year or the unexpired term, whichever is longer, in case of longer terms. Since only a few are sentenced for more than a year, most parole periods are not long. Sweden has further legislation providing that certain mentally abnormal offenders and habitual criminals may be committed without any maximum limit to a so-called security prison. Even here, however, there are minimum limits to the sentence, which for the mentally abnormal may not be less than 5 years or more than 12 and for the habitual offender not less than 5 or more than 15. The parole period cannot be for less than 3 years or more than 5 if the parolee conducts himself acceptably. Parole is today obligatory in Sweden, with much of the supervision under volunteer officers.[37]

[37] Thorsten Sellin, "Probation and Parole in Sweden," National Probation and Parole Association Yearbook, 1948, New York, 1949, pp. 239–251.

Parole Risks

The problem of risk on parole has many facets. Some persons are unquestionably better risks than others. The particular offense is no index to the irreformability of the offender, however. Nor is the fact that a man has served two or three sentences instead of one. Many factors should enter into the determination of whether a given prisoner should be granted parole, but most of these are encompassed in a consideration of his present personality adjustment, the environment in which he proposes to live, the attitudes of relatives and friends, the job at which he is to be placed, and the man's own determination (or lack of determination) to make good. Some prisoners are good risks because they have had time to straighten out their thinking under the guidance of intelligent prison officials. Others are obviously made worse by their own embitterment and their contacts with other hardened men.

The alcoholics and narcotic addicts are the worst risk of all. These prisoners are far more in need of psychiatric attention than of imprisonment. Such persons fail on parole because parole officers have no facilities or skills for helping them meet their problems. Sexually abnormal parolees present an extremely serious problem. These persons, too, need psychiatric treatment and probably should have been routed to medical centers rather than to prison. As not all sex offenders represent the same degree of dangerousness, generalities about them are useless. Under present laws the continued incarceration of most sex offenders is impossible. Release from prison on the basis of a truly indeterminate sentence would entail retention of all persons who were diagnosed as socially dangerous. Thus far, at least, there is no adequate provision for retaining them.

It would be safer to release such persons under supervision than to impose a flat sentence and turn them out to become repeaters. Much of the blame laid on parole when these persons get into difficulty should be ascribed to the laws relating to pathological offenders. Sex offenders are admittedly a difficult problem but our failure to devise suitable methods for detecting and treating them is no reason for condemning parole policies in general.

Permanent Incarceration as an Alternative

Permanent incarceration of a small percentage of offenders would be the best protection society could devise. Thus far no state really provides for the permanent incarceration of dangerous offenders, unless offenders are adjudged incurably insane or hopelessly feeble-minded. To date, there is no completely accurate means of determining who will be permanently dangerous and who will not. Moreover, some persons who have always been law abiding suddenly go berserk, for no well-authenticated reasons.

Parole Placement

The problem of job placement is so important that parole laws in many states now stipulate that parolees cannot leave the prison until some form of suitable job is assured. The best prisons are today making an effort to train men for lucrative employment through well-devised programs of vocational education, as we have discussed in Chapter 23. Parole officers in the best institutions spend a major share of their time making arrangements for the sort of jobs in which men can use their skills and talents. The problem of placing parolees is not easy, however. Many businessmen are afraid to employ ex-convicts. On the other hand some businessmen have exhibited real social consciousness in helping parolees get a start and have co-operated effectively with prison officials. Employers naturally have to be careful about their employees and parole officers also should exercise discretion in placing men where they will not be subject to great temptation.

Many factors contribute to parole violation, but one thing is certain, according to the *Attorney General's Survey of Release Procedures:* The parolee who has a good job and is earning a satisfactory wage tends to make good.[38] Jobs entailing obvious risks should be eliminated at the outset, however. For example, a man with a record of embezzlement should not be placed at a cashier's job or in a fund-raising position. Yet some parolees have been actually so unsuitably placed. A woman with a record of prostitution should not be put in a situation where opportunities for returning to her old life are present. She should not work as a waitress, hat-check girl, or in any other job where she has a great many contacts with a great variety of men. Parolees must learn to meet temptation, it is true. But they should not be subjected to conditions which arouse their old weaknesses. It is far wiser to place them in positions where there is some certainty that

[38] *Attorney General's Survey of Release Procedures*, Vol. IV, *Parole*, pp. 442–455.

they can prove themselves. Nothing so contributes to the morale and good adjustment of a prisoner as the feeling that he has done well at an assigned task.

During World War II many prisoners were trained in industrial processes within the prisons because of the need for war materials. In consequence these men were able to step into good jobs outside when they were paroled. This practice should be continued in peacetime.

Parole Is *Conditional* Release

All paroles are conditional releases and, as stated earlier in this chapter, the prisoner has given his "word of honor" that he will live up to the terms of his release. These terms vary from state to state. In general the prisoner must abstain from intoxicants and narcotics. He must report his address promptly and not change it without permission. He must not change employment or marry or drive an automobile or leave the state without permission. He must make a written report on how he is getting along and he must not associate with other parolees or ex-convicts. In addition, of course, he must not break any laws.[39]

Parole Rules

Many states impose additional conditions, as Hans von Hentig has summarized.[40] These include such regulations as are cited below.

Borrowing money or articles of value, going into debt, purchasing on the installment plan or making unnecessary or expensive purchases are forbidden without consent of the parole agent. (Rule 5, state of Minnesota)

The prisoner must make a written report on the last day of each month. This report must state how much money he had at the beginning of the month; how much he has earned during the month; how much he has expended and for what, and how much he has on hand at the end of the month. (Rule 4, state of Connecticut)

Persons on parole are not permitted . . . to loaf, stay out at night, visit public dance halls, associate with doubtful or objectionable company. (Rule 1, state of Minnesota)

[39] *Ibid.*, pp. 212–213.
[40] Hans von Hentig, "Degrees of Parole Violation and Graded Remedial Measures," *Journal of Criminal Law and Criminology,* 33:363–371 (January–February, 1943).

You are strictly forbidden to drive or operate an airplane while on parole, except with the written permission of the State parole officer. (Rule 2, state of California)

You are forbidden to engage in public speaking of any nature or be actively affiliated with any political party or group. (Rule 5, state of California)

I will not associate (the parolee has to affirm) with persons of questionable character, or with anyone on parole, or with any person having a criminal record. (Rule 4, state of Massachusetts)

Nor will I live with any woman not my lawful wife. (Rule 9, state of Massachusetts)

I will not make application for a license to hunt. (Rule 10, state of Massachusetts)

I will not engage in any illegal or illegitimate business. (Rule 6, District of Columbia)

The parolee shall avoid evil associations and not frequent improper places of amusement, nor loiter upon the streets at night. (Rule 10, state of Oregon)

The prisoner . . . must not be away from home after 9:00 o'clock unless granted permission by the Parole Agent. (Rule 6, state of Illinois)

If I should be arrested in another state during the period of my parole, I will waive extradition. (Rule 12, state of New York)

In Louisiana the parolee promises that he "will work diligently and honestly for himself and his employer." (Cf. Form D, Report of the Louisiana State Board of Parole, 1939–1940)

Some states also require regular church attendance.

Dr. von Hentig has stressed the absurdity of many of these rules and regulations. Sanford Bates, on the other hand, insists that such rules are warranted by the necessity of the parolee's proving himself.[41] We may question this, however. In the first place, many of the rules and regulations for parolees impose standards of conduct not imposed upon ordinary law-abiding citizens. The parolees who violate parole regulations and are returned to prison may be guilty of nothing more

[41] Sanford Bates, "On the Uses of Parole Restrictions," *Journal of Criminal Law and Criminology*, 33:435–452 (March–April, 1943).

serious than visiting a dance hall or taking a glass of beer. Furthermore many parole rules are unrealistic because they do not take into consideration the backgrounds and cultural standards of the working class from which the majority of our prisoners come.

Mr. Bates maintains, however, that the man on parole has given the public cause to believe he bears watching, hence any indication that he "is probably about to lapse" may warrant his return to prison. Nevertheless, such constant and picayunish supervision may be a factor in the parolee's recalcitrant and rebellious behavior. Constant checking up on a person and interpreting what the parolee regards as normal association at a beer parlor as a reason for returning the convict to prison is inconsonant with the accepted leisure-time pursuits of the lower classes. It is useless to expect ex-prisoners to visit the "great museums, the exhibitions and zoological gardens," even though Mr. Bates insists that these great opportunities await parolees.[42]

Few, if any, prisons give the prisoners any training in art, advanced science, and the appreciation of nature. Most parolees are not college graduates. Nor are they intellectually oriented toward the "higher life." Forbidding them to participate in social activities common to the members of their social group does not insure their successful parole adjustment. Instead it makes success less likely. The attempt to impose higher standards of behavior on parolees than are required of ordinary rank-and-file civilians is psychologically unsound. It proceeds on the dubious principle that an ex-prisoner must maintain a better record to keep from being returned to prison than the man who has never been in conflict with the law. Actually it is more difficult for the parolee to conform to rigid rules than it is for his brother who never got into trouble. We should not impose impossible standards on the parolee simply because he has a criminal record.[43] Certainly some degree of discretion should be exercised in determining whether the violation of a rule of minor importance is sufficient reason for returning a man to prison.

If they break a rule most parole violators who are returned to prison have no opportunity for a formal trial unless they commit a serious felony. The arbitrary and summary decision on the part of officials that the parolee has no right of trial may be seriously questioned. Yet in approximately half of the states prisoners may be returned without a hearing. How far the fact of having served a sentence should go in

[42] Ibid.
[43] Cf. Mabel A. Elliott, "The von Hentig-Bates Parole Controversy," Journal of Criminal Law and Criminology, 34:96–99 (July–August, 1943).

depriving a parolee (or for that matter a prisoner) of civil rights has never been authoritatively reviewed by our superior courts.[44]

Supervision of the Parolee

Studies have conclusively demonstrated that the quality of parole supervision (which in turn is dependent upon the intelligence, training, and insight of the parole officer) determines to a large degree the success of the parolee, whether he is a juvenile delinquent, a youthful offender, or an adult parolee.[45] Proper supervision is probably most important to adult parolees.[46] That is, though all parolees must be aided in reorienting their attitudes and in reconstructing their habit patterns, the adult offender obviously has a more difficult problem in revising long-established habits and attitudes than a younger person.

In explaining the failures on parole it is often alleged that parole, like Christianity, is an ideal that has not worked because it has never been tried. As a matter of fact parole is working fairly well in certain states, whereas it is purely nominal in others. Where parole failures are excessive, most of the men have had inadequate supervision or virtually none on release from the institution. Until relatively recently parole officers in many states never supervised a single parolee because the number of persons on parole was so large that it was impossible to give them individual attention. During the early thirties, for example, the parole officer of the Kansas State Penitentiary directed parole from his office while 1800 men on parole were supposed to send in a monthly penny post card stating that they were at work and doing well on parole. This sort of practice obviously makes a travesty of the whole idea. The only actual contact the parole officer had with parolees was when they were arrested and it was necessary for him to go after the parole violators to escort them back to prison.

Despite all the handicaps and inadequacies in parole administration parole standards have improved markedly. But only where suitable standards of supervision apply may we expect a high proportion of satisfactory adjustments of parolees. Even then we must always anticipate failures, since not all rebellious, frustrated, or antisocial men can be expected to make satisfactory adjustments in our highly disorganized society.

[44] Cf. in this connection Carter H. White, "Some Legal Aspects of Parole," *Journal of Criminal Law and Criminology*, 32:600–623 (March–April, 1942).

[45] Cf. Mabel A. Elliott, *Correctional Education and the Delinquent Girl*, Commonwealth of Pennsylvania, Harrisburg, 1929, pp. 39–41.

[46] Leon T. Stern, "Popular or Scientific Evaluation of Parole," *National Probation and Parole Association Yearbook*, 1948, New York, 1949, pp. 55–70.

Standards for Parole Personnel

The standards for the parole officer should be essentially the same as those for the probation officer. That is, he should be well grounded in criminology, in correction technique, and in social psychology. He should have had specific courses in probation and parole. Ordinarily the best training is now to be obtained from good departments of sociology and schools of social work.[47]

There has been some controversy as to whether or not parole and probation work is case work.[48] Certainly parole partakes of the nature of case work since parole, like case work, needs to be individualized. Helping the prisoner help himself is an important goal in parole. Parole always must differ from case work chiefly because it is authoritative and backed by the strong arm of penal law. When the recipient no longer needs to accept relief he cannot be forced to accept case-work supervision. A parolee, however, cannot decide for himself that he no longer needs supervision. He must be released from control by someone who has the authority to release him. Thus the relationship between the parolee and the parole officer is very different from that between the client and the case worker. Nevertheless the qualifications for a good parole officer are essentially those of a good case worker, but the former also needs specialized training in his particular task. Unfortunately many parole officers have little of criminological, correctional, or social work training and depend almost entirely upon their common sense.[49] Good parole (we should be reminded) requires professional insights and skills.

SPECIAL ANGLES TO THE PAROLE PROBLEM

Social Relationship of Parolees

The parolee's social relationships are usually complicated. Although slightly more than 50 per cent of prisoners have not been married, those who are married have special problems. Often the marriage is unhappy; sometimes it has been endangered or dissolved by the fact of the offender's felonious conduct. Many states allow divorce on such grounds. If a man's wife "stands by him" in his time of trouble

[47] Walter C. Reckless, "Training Probation and Parole Personnel," *Focus*, 27:44–48 (March, 1948).
[48] Cf. Ben Meeker, "Probation Is Case Work," and M. A. Blake, "Probation Is Not Case Work," *Federal Probation*, 12:51–57 (June, 1948).
[49] Louis Ziskind, "Social Work and the Correctional Field," *Federal Probation*, 14:46–49 (March, 1950).

this may be the greatest asset he has in going straight on parole and after. Belief in his own capacity to make a good adjustment certainly will be fostered by loyal support from his wife.

The relationship between a parolee and his children is another important factor. It is often difficult and embarrassing to parent and child alike. Many children of prisoners have been the butt of mockery from their schoolmates and in turn resent and despise their fathers. An intelligent wife and mother may be able to maintain the children's love and faith in their father and thus facilitate his adjustment.

Political Corruption and Parole

Despite the fact that the leading penologists believe in the importance and desirability of parole as a device for enabling the prisoner to make a better social adjustment on release from prison, parole as it is now administered is subject to a good many hazards. One of the most serious is the lack of suitable supervision, which we have already discussed. Even more serious in subverting the basic purposes of parole is the manipulation of release procedures by corrupt politicians. This obviously makes a travesty out of parole, but such corruption is no reason for throwing out parole. It is merely evidence of the need for removing parole from corrupt political controls.

Unfortunately the governor and members of the legislature in many states have a direct hand in parole. In some states in fact the governor must recommend the parole of all prisoners who are so released from imprisonment. Consequently extreme pressure is often placed upon him to release convicts who have served but a very short part of their maximum sentence. Most candidates for governor are relatively decent "practical politicians," but in order to become governor they accept any sort of political support which will help swing the vote and insure election. They thus frequently place themselves in compromising situations. As ambitious politicians they make "political deals," offering jobs and favors in return for help at election time. Similarly members of the legislature may use "influence" to help the men who aided them. Because they have accepted their aid, politicians are more or less forced to give political protection to certain unscrupulous persons. In fact a governor may literally owe his election to the corrupt machine which got out the vote. If "mobs" and gangsters vote for a governor they require some *quid pro quo*. If a member of a gang which has operated under the protective wing of a political party is convicted and sentenced for a crime his friends and stooges besiege the governor for a reduction in sentence or a parole. They may even go so far as to threaten to expose the unholy alliances which have backed the governor unless he accedes to them. The governor in fear and trembling acquiesces. Legislators are likewise besieged and acquiesce. In consequence few governors or legislators who have any responsibility for parole administration can afford to have their parole policies ventilated. A governor, for example, may be hounded to release some convict not only by the political cohorts who elected him but also by senators or representatives who owe their election to political machines in their constituencies. There is no doubt that such pressures are frequent. *Corruption of parole is not parole,* however, and this the critics of parole often fail to recognize.

Martin Mooney wrote a sensational book in 1939 in which he condemned the whole basis of parole as a political "fixing" device for releasing notorious prisoners. In this book he insists that parole is a failure and should be thrown out; that parole is rotten, a racket for returning unreformed murderers, rapists, and gangsters to pillage and plunder society![50] Mooney furthermore contends that J. Edgar Hoover is correct in calling criminals "rats and vermin," and that it is these "rats and vermin" who are paroled.

What Mooney and others who share his viewpoint are interested in condemning is the manipulation of parole in order that criminals may return to society to commit further crimes without incurring any serious penalties for their nefarious conduct. The scandalous abuse of parole is obviously criminal behavior on the part of the governmental officials, but it is no reason for abolishing parole. It would be as reasonable to propose the abolition of city government because certain government officials are or have been notoriously corrupt or to abolish income taxes because many people do not report all their income.

The situation obviously demands that corruption in parole practices be eliminated by making it impossible for criminals to secure special privileges by manipulating paroles. This can be accomplished only by divorcing politics from parole administration and by appointing professionally trained persons of highest integrity to the parole boards.

The Community and the Parolee

Very often (and certainly too frequently), the parolee is returned to the same community from which he was sentenced to prison. If he can re-establish himself with the people who know his record he

[50] Martin Mooney, *The Parole Scandal,* Lymanhouse, Los Angeles, 1939.

will have achieved a moral victory and his own self-respect. But public sentiment often militates too strongly against the man in his home community. Frequently a new job in a new community where his record is unknown will do more to help him make a satisfactory adjustment.

If a parolee goes back to his old community he may adjust successfully if the supervising official is able to enlist the support of old neighbors and associates in helping him. All men, if they are honest, realize they have made mistakes, often serious ones, which but for the grace of God or status in the community might have put them in the same position as the parolee. Sometimes there is some such man in the community who has made an exceptionally good adjustment. He knows the value of a friendly word, the offer of a job, or a lending hand. If the community resources can only be recruited to help the ex-convict his battle may be won.

On the other hand members of the community often regard the ex-convict with suspicion. Some parole laws require that the proposed release of a prisoner be published in his home county newspaper. Frequently the condemning social attitudes toward the prisoner contribute to his further and complete disorganization. It is easy "to kick a man when he is down" and the rebuffs the ex-prisoner receives make it difficult for him to make good.

We dare not be oversentimental about parole. Some convicts will scorn the proffered help of parole officials and become recidivists. But many recidivists have never had any suitable or satisfactory parole supervision. This fact alone should provide incentive for better parole methods. Probably many men in prison would have done better if they had never been committed to prison in the first place, but if society sends a man to prison and then releases him he deserves a helping hand on release.

The Police and the Parolee

One of the major difficulties in the parolee's adjustment is the tendency of police to hound the released convict on the slightest suspicion. Such tactics are characteristic of police in metropolitan communities. Yet the majority of convicts tend to seek what they believe to be the anonymity of a large city because they dread the hostility they expect to encounter in returning to their home in a smaller community. Unfortunately larger cities offer more temptations and parolees are more likely to get in trouble than in smaller places. Moreover, whenever a crime occurs, police tend quite naturally to be suspicious of a man with a record. But it is likewise true that police often know more about the dangerous exploits of an ex-convict than do parole officers and can thus link certain crimes with certain criminals. In consequence a parolee not guilty of an offense may be arrested on "suspicion" because of his past record. He often has grave difficulty in establishing his innocence simply because he has a record and seems a likely candidate for committing crimes.

On the other hand, parolees, particularly recidivists, frequently return to their underworld practices. Their social contacts in prison being chiefly with fellow prisoners, it is only natural that new alliances with crime may be established during periods of imprisonment. The suspicion of police is thus often warranted and because "they know their criminals" police can be of great assistance to parole authorities in tracking down the illicit activities of parolees. No one objects to the healthy skepticism police attach to the belief that anyone recommended for parole is a good risk. Many ill-intentioned men in prison actually become model prisoners for the sole purpose of securing an early parole so that they may return to their profitable activities as gamblers, racketeers, or holdup men.[51]

PREDICTION OF BEHAVIOR ON PAROLE

One of the questions most frequently subjected to serious study in connection with parole is the matter of attempting to predict whether a man will make good or not when released on parole. In 1923 Hornell Hart pointed out that scientific statistical analysis of the factors in the background of prisoners might be employed to predict rather accurately the percentage of those who would violate parole and those who would not.[52] Following out his suggestion Ernest W. Burgess and his research assistant Clark Tibbitts made the first truly important attempt to discover what factors seem to be positively associated with success and failure on parole. Burgess studied the various factors in the background of 1000 prisoners as given in their prison case records in each of 3 different Illinois penal institutions: the Illinois State Penitentiary at Joliet, the Southern Illinois Penitentiary at Menard, and the Illinois State Reformatory at Pontiac. These men were studied after they had been out of the penitentiary at least 2½ years.

[51] Cf. Wilbur La Roe, *Parole with Honor*, Princeton University Press, Princeton, 1939, chap. 16, "The Police and Parole."
[52] Hornell Hart, "Predicting Parole Success," *Journal of Criminal Law and Criminology*, 14:405–413 (November–December, 1923).

Most of them had been released 3 to 5 years, and some had been out 6 years. The majority, however, had been under parole only 1 year.

Twenty-two factors were studied with reference to these men.[53] These included:

1. Nature of offense.
2. Number of associates in committing offense.
3. Nationality of father.
4. Parental status including broken home.
5. Marital status.
6. Criminal type, i.e., whether
   a. First offender.
   b. Occasional offender.
   c. Habitual offender.
   d. Professional criminal.
7. Social type (farm boy, gangster, ne'er-do-well, etc.)
8. County from which committed.
9. Size of community.
10. Type of neighborhood.
11. Resident or transient where arrested.
12. Statement of trial judge (whether for or against leniency in parolee's case).
13. Whether commitment was on lesser plea.
14. Nature and length of sentence.
15. Time actually served.
16. Previous criminal record.
17. Previous work record.
18. Number of punishments at the institution.
19. Age at parole.
20. Mental age.
21. Psychiatrist's report on personality type.
22. Psychiatry prognosis.

All of these factors (other than the size of the community, which was significant only in the case of the farm boy) were thought to have some relation to adjustment on release from prison.[54] Hence the remaining 21 factors were used to form the prediction tables although they were recognized as not being of equal weight.[55]

---

[53] Ernest W. Burgess, "Factors Determining Success or Failure on Parole," in Andrew A. Bruce, Ernest W. Burgess, Albert J. Harno, and John Landesco, The Workings of the Indeterminate Sentence Law and the Parole System in Illinois, Parole Board of Illinois, Springfield, 1928, p. 221.

[54] Ibid., chap. 28.

[55] Ibid., chap. 30, p. 247.

The Gluecks' Study on Post-Parole Criminality

Sheldon and Eleanor T. Glueck believed that a much more reliable study than that of Burgess *et al.* could be made if reliable life histories of the prisoners could be obtained rather than depending on data in prison records. They therefore undertook an extensive study of post-parole criminality of 510 offenders from the Massachusetts State Reformatory for which they secured verified information with reference to 50 factors in the prisoners' background and history. From their study they concluded that 6 of the 50 factors were reliably related to post-parole criminality. These were: (1) industrial habits previous to commitment (the better worker the man had been before commitment the greater the likelihood of his satisfactory adjustment); (2) the seriousness and frequency of the pre-reformatory crimes (the minor offender and the first offender made the better adjustment); (3) the number of prior arrests (those without prior arrests made the better adjustment); (4) whether or not the prisoner had prior penal experience—i.e., those without prior penal experience made the best adjustment; (5) the economic responsibility of the offender (those who were economically responsible for the support of dependents prior to reformatory experience made better adjustment); (6) mental abnormality (those with mental abnormality made poor adjustment and those without made better adjustment).[56]

In addition to these prognostic factors, the Gluecks found 7 additional factors with reference to adjustment following release from parole supervision. These included: (1) the frequency of offenses in prison (although this was not an absolute factor); (2) criminal conduct on parole (the total failures on parole were prognostic of later difficulties); (3) good work habits after parole (this was related to a low percentage of failures); (4) family relationships following parole (where there were poor family relationships there were 85 per cent failures); (5) economic responsibility following parole (with high economic responsibility the percentage of failures was low); (6) home conditions following parole (favorable home conditions meant a low percentage of failures); and (7) use of leisure (where leisure was put to constructive use the post-parole failures were few, and where it was harmfully used the failures were many).[57] All 13 factors were used in their prognostic tables.

---

[56] Sheldon and Eleanor T. Glueck, *500 Criminal Careers*, Harvard University Press, Cambridge, 1930, pp. 281–282.
[57] *Ibid.*, pp. 283–284.

Each of these factors was related to each offender and he was classified as "good," "fair," or "poor" or as "favorable," "fair," or "unfavorable" so far as the categories were concerned. The number of persons who failed under each category was noted, and the lowest possible total failure score and the highest possible failure score were computed for persons in each group. Every individual was then scored between the limits of scores for the categories "good," "fair," and "poor." It was found that 75 per cent of the successes were those with the most scores of "good"; the partial failures had a fairly even distribution of good, fair, and poor scores; but the total failures had a high number of failure scores.[58]

The Vold Study

George B. Vold of the University of Minnesota believed that the Burgess and Glueck studies both emphasized past conduct too much and that Burgess should have weighted the factors he employed more than he did. Vold undertook a study of the records of 1192 men (542 from the Minnesota State Prison and 650 from the Minnesota State Reformatory) and entered all the information pertaining to pre-parole history in systematic categories covering 44 factors. The paroled men were then classified as (1) non-violators, (2) major violators, or (3) minor violators. The proportions of non-violators, major violators, and minor violators were then calculated according to each of the factors classified by means of the contingency coefficient which was worked out for each category. These were then placed in rank order according to their contingency coefficient.

From these calculations the 17 highest contingency rates for factors in the pre-parole history and parole outcome were studied—as were the 17 lowest contingency rates and a selected group of 25 pre-parole factors. These factors were then compared and it was found that the 25 selected pre-parole factors gave the sharpest distinctions between the violators and non-violators; the 17 highest contingencies came next and the 17 lowest contingencies next. From his study Dr. Vold then constructed prediction tables which were remarkably reliable when checked against the actual number of parole violators in each score class when these men were scored against pre-parole factors. On the basis of the tests, Dr. Vold predicted that 57 out of 282 cases might be expected to violate parole during 1922–1927, whereas 63 actually failed.

The prediction tables still were not accurate in predicting what

[58] *Ibid.*, p. 285.

would happen in a given case but they seemed to indicate that a certain percentage in a hundred cases might be expected to do well and that a certain percentage might violate parole. Vold came to the conclusion that pre-institutional factors are the important ones related to parole outcome, that the "chances in 100" can be stated fairly accurately, and that it did not make a great difference whether the factors were weighted or not. There was a correlation of +.922 when the two methods were compared on Minnesota prisoners.[59]

The Attorney General's Survey of Parole Outcome

A much more elaborate study than those previously mentioned was conducted under the Attorney General's Survey of Release Procedures.[60] Here the factors of race, marital status, number of dependents, recidivism, number of sentences served, age at first arrest, nature of offense committed, conduct record, home conditions, and home community were studied with reference to approximately 85,000 cases paroled from 45 penal institutions in 32 states. Briefly summarized, the findings of this study showed (1) that parole itself was selective at the time the study was made, i.e., white persons were more likely to be granted parole, (2) that unmarried persons were less likely to be granted parole, (3) that recidivists were less likely to be granted parole, (4) that young offenders were less likely to be granted parole, (5) that persons who had associates in crime were less likely to be paroled, (6) that in some communities a certain type of offender was not paroled, whereas in other communities he was, (7) that length of sentence was a factor in parole, (8) that persons who had a job were more likely to be on parole, (9) that a bad conduct record in prison was considered a poor risk, and (10) that persons from rural areas were more likely to be released at the first parole hearing.[61]

With reference to parole outcome the Attorney General's Survey brought out certain important facts.

1. In a total of more than 90,000 cases, white persons had better parole records than Negroes; 26 per cent of the whites and 35 per cent of the Negroes violated parole. (Most of the Negroes were from southern institutions, however.) In a few institutions, including one prison in Alabama, Negroes made a better record than white persons.

2. Unmarried persons violated parole more frequently than mar-

---

[59] Cf. George B. Vold, *Prediction Methods and Parole*, Sociological Press, Hanover, New Hampshire, 1931, especially chaps. 1, 4, 5, 6, and 7. The student is urged to consult this and other studies since it is difficult to condense the whole findings.

[60] *Attorney General's Survey of Release Procedures*, Vol. IV, *Parole*.

[61] *Ibid.*, pp. 486–487.

ried; i.e., 31 per cent of 51,826 unmarried violated parole, while only 19 per cent of 26,145 married persons violated parole. Married persons with children had better records than those without dependents.

3. First offenders had better records than recidivists; 37 per cent of the recidivists violated parole and 24 per cent committed new crimes while only 18 per cent of the first offenders violated terms of parole and only 10 per cent committed new offenses on parole.

4. Offenders who were under 18 years of age at time of arrest were poorer risks than those who were past 22. (This seems to confirm the Gluecks' notion that an offender has to reach a certain maturity before he straightens up.)

5. There was little relationship between committing an offense in a group and parole outcome. However, some "lone wolf" criminals had a worse parole record than those who had been members of gangs.

6. The seriousness of the offense had no apparent relationship to success on parole. Nevertheless when parolees committed new offenses they tended to commit the same type as those for which they were sent to prison.

7. Short-term offenders violated parole less often than long-term offenders.

8. Employment was found to be very important in success on parole. Only 17 per cent of the employed parolees violated parole, in contrast to 53 per cent of those unemployed.

9. Parolees in metropolitan communities failed more often on parole.

10. Married men who returned to their wives seldom violated parole, whereas unmarried offenders had poor records.

11. Native-born offenders were poorer risks than foreign-born offenders.

12. Persons who behaved well in prison were better parole risks than those who were behavior problems in prison.

13. There was some data indicating that parole supervisors can predict with relative accuracy the outcome of parole.[62]

Education and Parole

In a study made by Alfred C. Schnur the relation between educational program in the Wisconsin prison and the prisoner's conduct on parole was correlated. He found that educational treatment of the prisoners for 6 months or longer was significantly related to successful

[62] *Ibid.,* pp. 488–491.

adjustment. Dr. Schnur contends that shorter training periods produced little or no results and that if educational departments of prisons expect to deal effectively with prisoners they should not enroll
men for less than 6 months.[63]

Community to Which Paroled

As an interesting side light on parole Robert E. Clark found that
Illinois parolees made a better adjustment when they were paroled
to a community comparable in size to the one in which they lived before arrest. Apparently lack of familiarity with the type of life in a
community of different size creates further difficulties to adjustment.[64]

Alabama Parolees

Mary Ruth Graham's study of Alabama prisoners paroled between
1939 and 1944 (after the creation of the Alabama Board of Pardons
and Parolees) verified most of the conclusions of the *Attorney General's Survey of Release Procedures* with reference to factors pointing
to successful outcome of parole. She found that Negro parolees, including Negro women parolees, in Alabama made better records than
white parolees. On the other hand white women in general made
much better parole adjustment than did white men.[65] The Attorney
General's Survey showed that in one Alabama prison Negro parolees
made a better record than white prisoners. We must conclude, therefore, that for some reason conditions are more favorable to Negro
parolees in Alabama.

Perhaps more important was the fact that of the 4524 Alabama
parolees studied 89.1 per cent were classified as "successful" and 10.9
per cent as failures. Some of these successful parolees obviously had
not been paroled long enough, however, to test the success of their
parole since the parole period of many had not yet expired.

In the case of 3840 parolees for whom educational data was available, Miss Graham found high educational level negatively related
to parole success. For 734 white parolees, as Table 27.6 shows,
the rate of failures was much higher (31.9 per cent) among those with
superior mental ability than in any other classification. She also found

[63] Alfred C. Schnur, "The Educational Treatment of Prisoners and Recidivism,"
American Journal of Sociology, 54:142–147 (September, 1948).
[64] Robert E. Clark, "Size of Parole Community, as Related to Parole Outcome,"
American Journal of Sociology, 57:43–47 (July, 1951).
[65] Mary Ruth Graham, *These Came Back*, Bureau of Public Administration, University of Alabama Press, University, 1946, p. 103.

the lowest percentage of failures among those with no education, as Table 27.6 indicates. In the case of mental ability only white parolees were included because most of the Negroes were not given mental tests.

TABLE 27.5. Education of Alabama Parolees

| | All Parolees | | Parolees Who Failed on Parole | |
| | | | | Per Cent of |
Education	Number	Per Cent	Number	No. Paroled
No education	670	17.4	59	8.8
Semi-literate (Grades 1–3)	776	20.2	75	9.7
Attended grammar school	1,983	51.7	248	12.5
Attended high school	368	9.6	45	12.2
Attended college	43	1.1	4	9.3
Total	3,840	100.0	431	11.2

SOURCE: Mary Ruth Graham, *These Came Back*, University of Alabama Press, University, 1946, p. 15. Quoted by permission of the Bureau of Public Administration of the University of Alabama.

TABLE 27.6. Mental Classification of White Alabama Parolees

| | All Parolees | | Parolees Who Failed on Parole | |
| | | | | Per Cent of |
Mental Classification	Number	Per Cent	Number	No. Paroled
Imbecile (I.Q. 20–49)	1	0.1	1	100.0
Moron (I.Q. 50–69)	159	21.7	29	18.2
Borderline (I.Q. 70–79)	172	23.4	34	19.8
Dullard (I.Q. 80–89)	156	21.3	31	19.9
Normal (I.Q. 90–109)	199	27.1	39	19.6
Superior (I.Q. 110–119)	47	6.4	15	31.9
Total	734	100.0	149	20.3

SOURCE: Table 7 in Mary Ruth Graham, *These Came Back*, p. 17. Quoted by permission of the Bureau of Public Administration of the University of Alabama.

The Practicability of Prediction Tables

Illinois is the only state which makes extensive use of prediction tables. A study made by Michael Hakeem in Illinois illustrates the application of the Glueck technique. Hakeem applied the Gluecks' method of parole prediction to 1861 burglars in the Illinois penal system. (This constituted all the burglars except Negro burglars who were paroled between January, 1925, and December, 1935, with their praole outcome determined in 1939.) The parolees were divided into the successful, the minor violators (those who broke parole rules), and the major violators (those who committed a new crime). Hakeem related 22 factors to success on parole, and 6 factors emerged as apparently significant in determining parole outcome. These were: (1) psychiatric prognosis (which represented the combined judgment of sociologists and psychiatrists as to the likelihood of the parolee's getting into criminal activities following his release); (2) social type (which was classified into "farmer," "inadequate," "marginal," "maladjusted," "floater" and "ne'er-do-well," "drug addict," and "drunkard"; (3) previous criminal career (in which all known offenses were taken into consideration whether or not a part of his formal record); (4) work record (which included the parolee's entire pre-institutional work history from every available source to indicate whether he was a regular, irregular, or casual worker); (5) classification as to "type of offender" (which meant he was classified as to whether he was a first offender, an occasional offender—that is, with a police record, but no felonies—a recidivist [if more than one felony was to the parolee's credit] or a habitual offender); (6) the pre-institutional community, which was simply a classification of rural (under 2500 population), town and village (2500 to 10,000), small city (10,000 to 25,000), city over 25,000, and Chicago and Cook County, since this was the only metropolitan community represented.[66]

Inmates' "Hunches" as to Fellow Prisoners' Adjustments on Parole

Ferris F. Laune published a study in 1936 in which he summarized his experiments in securing inmate judgments on the success or failure of 150 fellow inmates at Illinois State Penitentiary. These judgments were made and compared with the ratings on questionnaires devised by the inmates which included 1701 questions. These questions the inmates considered important in determining the 42 factors which they employed in arriving at their hunches as to a prisoner's success. The items ranged from excessive interest in clothes, stupidity, timidity, "learned lesson," family ties, emotional instability, selfishness (considered desirable!), conceit (negative), wanderlust, tendency to be an agitator, etc. The coefficient of reliability varied from .5587 $\pm$ .0518 to .8354 $\pm$ .0173, which appeared to be somewhat more reliable than that in Vold's study.[67]

Recently Lloyd E. Ohlin and Richard A. Lawrence conducted another study on Illinois prisoners in which they asked four selected in-

[66] Michael Hakeem, "The Glueck Method of Parole Prediction Applied to 1,861 Cases of Burglars," *Journal of Criminal Law and Criminology*, 36:87–97 (July–August, 1945).

[67] Cf. Ferris F. Laune, *Predicting Criminality*, Northwestern University Studies in the Social Sciences, Evanston and Chicago, 1936, pp. 19–36.

mates to rate parolees. One of them rated 104, two rated 110, and one rated 66 cases. Ohlin and Lawrence compared the inmates' hunches with parolees' scores on the Burgess prediction tables and found the number of errors was almost identical. In other words they concluded that an intelligent inmate can predict the outcome of the parolee's conduct as well as the best prediction devices. The use of inmates for this purpose entails certain problems in prison administration since many prisoners would resent being thus rated by fellow prisoners. This study gives us basis, however, for believing that common-sense judgments in sizing up parolees may be sound if the persons making the judgment know the prisoners' background and habits well enough.[68]

Recent Improvements in Parole Trends

Many favorable trends have developed in parole outcomes in recent years which are probably the result of better parole techniques and better-trained parole officers. Marked improvement was shown, for example, in the survey made in 1947–1948 by the Pennsylvania Committee on Penal Affairs of 1402 men who were paroled from the Eastern State Penitentiary and from the Philadelphia County Prison during the years 1926–1933. This study covered the criminal activities of the men during both their parole and their post-parole periods. Of the 1402, 786 did not violate their parole, 450 did, and 156 committed crimes following the expiration of their parole. [69]

Translated into percentages these figures mean that 67.8 per cent of the men made a successful adjustment on parole. So far as these men were concerned their parole cost the state $361,645.20. Had they remained in prison the bill for their keep would have been $3,191,685; hence the saving to the state was $2,830,039.80. Obviously the rehabilitation of an offender is not to be measured in dollars and cents, but the parole savings were nevertheless impressive.[70]

These men, according to Leon T. Stern, were paroled during a period in which parole supervision was relatively poor. A later checkup on Pennsylvania parolees by two Philadelphia newspapermen, McCullough and Cropper, indicated that 85 per cent of the parolees were making good under the better standards of parole supervision which have been in operation since 1941.[71]

A study was also made, by the Pennsylvania Committee on Penal

[68] Lloyd E. Ohlin and Richard A. Lawrence, "A Comparison of Alternative Methods of Parole Prediction," paper given at the American Sociological Society meetings in Chicago on September 7, 1951.
[69] Leon T. Stern, *op. cit.*   [70] *Ibid.*   [71] *Ibid.*

Affairs, of 225 men who had been given a prediction prognosis and had been paroled and out of prison 12 to 21 years. This study showed that (1) the first offender was a safer risk than the recidivist; (2) men with poor prognoses violated parole sooner than those with better prognoses; (3) nearly all the recidivism occurred within 3½ years of parole. It was also found that (4) the most important problems, as revealed by the prognoses, indicated a need for guidance, aid, and correction of antisocial attitudes. (5) The study demonstrated the value of prognoses to those recommending parole, to the parole authority in granting parole, and to the officers in supervision of parolees.[72]

Parolees in the Armed Services

During World War II (for the first time in the military history of the United States) many men serving sentences in prisons were released on parole to the armed services. Military officers were frankly reluctant to accept such men, but the need for military personnel resulted in pressure to accept prisoners for combat service. We do not have comprehensive figures on how these men turned out, but a study of 3565 men so released in New York State was made in February, 1946. Of this group 1113 men had been discharged by February 1, 1946, and of these 930 were honorably discharged, 75 received blue discharges, and only 108 or 11 per cent were dishonorably discharged. That is, 91.5 per cent received an honorable discharge. This figure compared rather favorably with the 98.6 per cent of honorable discharges granted to the rank and file of men in the military services.

Of these paroled New York prisoners, 750 also received some form of decoration. On the debit side, 211 of the 3565 had delinquent records in the army, and 35 of these were returned either to New York institutions or the prisons in other states. The rest either had their delinquencies "canceled" or were allowed to remain in the armed services although their delinquent record was not released. On the whole the success of these men was striking, for their percentage of failures is far less than the record for most peacetime parolees returned to civilian life. Many of these men exhibited rare courage in the army. They also had an incentive to prove themselves seldom given the parolee in the civilian community, which is probably the significant factor in their success.[73]

[72] Leon T. Stern, "Popular or Scientific Evaluation of Probation and Parole," National Probation and Parole Association Yearbook, 1948, New York, 1949, pp. 55–70.

[73] "Current Notes," National Probation and Parole Association Yearbook, 1948, New York, 1949, pp. 530–532.

The Prison Life and Parole Violations

So far as violations are concerned we must recognize that frequently men become so well adjusted to prison routine that they find it difficult to adjust to the demands of the life outside. Civilian life becomes a leap over the wall for which the restricted and rule-governed prison existence is no preparation. Moreover the association with prisoners and the cross-fertilization of ideas which goes on in prison are conducive to increasingly suspicious and bitter attitudes on the part of the men. Prisoners take on the prisoner's viewpoint. They become conscious of their status as convicts, as men who are against society and whom society is against. The fact is that up to now the prison has not been an effective school for good citizenship. The new developments in orientation and classification indicate that it can contribute more effectively to the prisoner's self-respect and rehabilitation than prisons have done in the past.

SELECTED BIBLIOGRAPHY

Attorney General's Survey of Release Procedures, Vol. IV, *Parole*, U.S. Department of Justice, Washington, 1939. This is the most extensive survey of parole ever made by competent persons, and a valuable reference volume.

Burgess, Ernest, W., "Factors Determining Parole Success," in Andrew A. Bruce, Ernest W. Burgess, Albert J. Harno, and John Landesco, *The Workings of the Indeterminate Sentence Law and the Parole System in Illinois*, Parole Board of Illinois, Springfield, 1921, pp. 205–249. This is the first important research on factors determining success on parole.

Elliott, Mabel A., *Conflicting Penal Theories in Statutory Criminal Law*, University of Chicago Press, Chicago, 1931, chap. 6, "The Indeterminate Sentence and Parole." The conflicting trends in parole and indeterminate sentence legislation in the United States are surveyed.

Glueck, Sheldon and Eleanor T., *500 Criminal Careers*, Harvard University Press, Cambridge, 1930, chap. 18, "Predictability in the Administration of Criminal Justice." One of the important attempts to isolate factors which indicate success or failure on parole is presented.

Graham, Mary Ruth, *These Came Back*, Bureau of Public Administration, University of Alabama, University, 1946. The material in this survey of 4524 Alabama parolees confirms most of the conclusions in the Attorney General's Survey of parole.

Hakeem, Michael, "The Glueck Method of Parole Prediction Applied to 1,861 Cases of Burglars," *Journal of Criminal Law and Criminology*,

36:87–97 (July–August, 1945). This is a verification of the Glueck predictive factors.

La Roe, Wilbur, *Parole with Honor*, Princeton University Press, Princeton, 1939. An incisive treatment of the major criticisms of parole and a statement of the parole ideal are ably presented.

Lindsey, Edward, "A Historical Sketch of the Indeterminate Sentence and the Parole System," *Journal of Criminal Law and Criminology*, 16:9–126 (May–June, 1925). This is an excellent survey of early parole and indeterminate sentence laws.

Mooney, Martin, *The Parole Scandal*, Lymanhouse, Los Angeles, 1939. A startling accusation of parole practices is made by a newspaperman who contends "big-time" convicts secure release by all sorts of devious practices.

Sellin, Thorsten, "Probation and Parole in Sweden," *National Probation and Parole Association Yearbook, 1948*, New York, 1949, pp. 239–251.

Vold, George B., *Prediction Methods and Parole*, Sociological Press, Hanover, New Hampshire, 1931. Here is a splendid statistical study of factors which are of predictive value in parole.

Wines, Frederick H., *Punishment and Reformation*, Crowell, New York, 1895. This is a classic in the field of punishment and treatment.

Witmer, Helen L., "The History, Theory and Results of Parole," *Journal of Criminal Law and Criminology*, 18:24–64 (May–June, 1927). This gives an excellent brief survey parole and its effectiveness at the time the study was made.

SECTION V

Crime Prevention

CHAPTER 28

Crime Prevention on the Juvenile Level

Our study of crime and the factors which have produced antisocial behavior shows crime to be as complicated as the varieties of human motivations, social relationships, and situations which are involved in such behavior. In general society takes a more kindly and intelligent attitude toward juvenile offenders than adult criminals, because juvenile delinquents are generally regarded as victims of circumstance. So far as adult criminals are concerned, the desire to punish is often more obvious in the attempts to put down crime than is any basic wish to help the criminal become a law-abiding citizen.

Out of a wide variety of fumbling (and halfhearted) attempts to prevent crime certain trends have emerged. One is the division of crime prevention projects on the basis of the age level of the offender. That is, (1) there has been a generally accepted belief that a basic attack on crime can come only through preventing juvenile delinquency and, it is argued, thus forestalling adult crime; (2) the second main attack has been the attempt to reduce adult crime by focusing attention on the prevention of recidivism.

Since human life is a continuous process of growth (and deterioration) it is doubtful if any basic dividing line can be effectively drawn between these two attacks on criminal behavior. Youth and maturity are successive biological phases of the life span which occur too gradually to be set off by rigid or artificial divisions of chronological age. To date, however, the crime prevention projects have not overcome this particular hiatus.

A second major development in crime prevention projects has been the shift from piecemeal attacks on the problem to over-all attempts to deal with crime and delinquency on a community, state, national, and international basis. Because the literature on the subject is extensive this chapter will be devoted to the prevention of crime and delinquency on the juvenile level. The next chapter will be devoted to prevention of adult criminality.

PREVENTION PROJECTS ON A JUVENILE DELINQUENCY LEVEL

There is of course great justification for initating preventive projects on the juvenile level since a large number of convicted adult offenders are known to have had records as juvenile delinquents. Any truly preventive program must therefore aim at eliminating juvenile delinquency, by preventing nondelinquents from becoming delinquents and by overcoming early delinquent tendencies in children who have already presented problems in the "pre-delinquent" (or behavior problem) stage have come before courts for their delinquent behavior.

Social Action in Preventing Delinquency

The methods of attacking the problems of preventing juvenile delinquency are hedged in by many factors which limit their effectiveness, as we shall discuss presently. These methods are operating on a variety of levels: (1) the specialized, or piecemeal, attacks of various interested groups and individuals; (2) the planned co-ordinated programs of the various social agencies which are engaged in child welfare activities, usually carried out by a Community Co-ordinating Council or some similar group; (3) projects undertaken by the community as a whole which place the responsibility for preventing and reducing delinquency upon the citizens of the community themselves, relying on a minimum of professional leadership and guidance; (4) city-wide programs of crime and delinquency prevention; (5) statewide organizations which have been created to deal with the problems of delinquency; (6) the various projects on the federal level which aim at giving aid and direction to state and local groups which are attempting to eliminate both juvenile delinquency at the outset and recidivism among those who have already committed "juvenile delinquencies"; (7) the recently organized committee of the Economic and Social Council of the United Nations which aims to foster both crime prevention and more effective penal treatment. Because this committee expects to cover both juvenile delinquency and adult crime it will be discussed in the next chapter.

What Prevention of Delinquency Entails

Prevention of juvenile delinquency involves several approaches. For nondelinquents, for example, it is not merely a matter of preventing children who have wholesome attitudes from developing antisocial tendencies. Children who are not delinquent are not necessarily free from prospective delinquency. Some are under constant threat of becoming delinquents while others are in no such danger. Lowell J. Carr of the University of Michigan has analyzed the various children who need help if there is to be any attempt to control delinquency. These in order of their declining antisocial expectancy are as follows:

1. The delinquents (who are or have been in actual conflict with the law).
2. Children who are in trouble because of behavior problems.
3. Children who are exposed to all sorts of "deviation pressures" which make them potential risks.
4. The normal children who should be kept that way.[1]

Carr maintains, and rightly, that delinquency control involves (1) techniques for the *discovery* of deviant behavior on the part of children, (2) techniques for the *diagnosis*, (3) techniques for *treatment*, and (4) techniques for the *prevention* by (a) removing or controlling pressures conducive to delinquency, (b) introducing positive factors in the environment, and (c) improving the hereditary quality of the population.[2]

At the same time we must remember that part of the disparity in delinquency rates among children unquestionably exists because children in different social and economic groups are reported for their delinquencies with different frequencies, as Porterfield has discussed in his book, *Youth in Trouble*.[3] Children are obviously in greater danger of being considered delinquents if their parents and the neighbors report their infractions of the law. Such children are also in great danger of becoming confirmed delinquents if society takes action against them and labels them "juvenile delinquents." Once stigmatized, it seems difficult for children to avoid further delinquencies.

Since virtually all earnest citizens want children to have the best sort of training opportunities, it is altogether natural that many special groups and interested individuals should "attempt to do something" about juvenile delinquency, according to their special interpretations

[1] Cf. Lowell J. Carr, *Delinquency Control*, Harper, New York, 1950, chaps. 9–14.
[2] *Ibid.*, p. 197.
[3] Published by Leo Potishman Foundation, Fort Worth, 1946. Chap. 2, especially pp. 45–47.

of the problem. It will be impossible to either enumerate or discuss all the projects which have aimed to put down delinquency, but we can point out the most significant ones.

Groups as widely separated in purpose and function as the American Legion (through its Child Welfare Committee) and the Parent-Teachers Association have committees which aim to prevent, reduce, and treat juvenile delinquency. The General Federation of Women's Clubs has made the prevention of delinquency a significant part of its national program, under the skilled direction of Miss Stella Scurlock. The Kiwanis Club (through the impetus of the professional psychologists who are among its members) has developed a noteworthy program. Clergymen, notably the late Father Flanagan of Omaha, have launched one-man attacks on delinquency by developing institutions such as Boys' Town where the positive characteristics of boys in or out of trouble have been fostered under the combined aegis of the Roman Catholic Church, a well-organized school program, and a genuine interest in helping boys who need help.

George Junior Republics

Two institutions known as George Junior Republics—the first of which was founded at Freeville, New York, in 1890, the second at Grove City, Pennsylvania, in 1909—have developed a splendid program for helping young persons (both court and non-court cases) become effective citizens, as the result of the initial interest and efforts of William R. George. The George Junior Republics have functioned on the principle of requiring youngsters to accept responsibility in the community life of the school in an atmosphere which emphasizes the best values of the American way of life. No one can say how many juvenile liabilities these institutions have turned into social assets for there may have been factors other than the institutions at work, but these "republics" have unquestionably helped many hundreds of young people through difficult periods.[4]

Boys' Clubs

Boys' clubs have received much credit for keeping boys out of trouble. Directly, their purpose is to provide wholesome fun and super-

[4] Cf. William R. George and Lyman Beecher Stowe, *Citizens Made and Remade*, Houghton Mifflin, Boston, 1912, and Earle D. Bruner, *A Laboratory Study in Democracy*, Doubleday, New York, 1927, for a detailed description of these two institutions in operation.

vised play for normal, well-adjusted boys. Indirectly, many persons have conceived of the program of boys clubs as essentially one of preventing delinquency, since a boy at play is not "up to something else." Undoubtedly part of the effect of a well-organized boys' club program is to channel the aggressive, hostile, and reckless activities of boys into socially approved types of leisure-time activities.[5]

Much of the interest behind boys' clubs has been religious and charitable in motivation, while the avowed concern is the advancement of boys' moral, mental, and physical well-being. This is achieved by providing youngsters who have no other place to play suitable space and equipment and trained leadership for recreation in sports and games as well as opportunity for reading through library facilities.

A great many people have believed that boys' clubs are a definite preventive measure, but recent studies are not so convincing. Most specialized agencies which aim to prevent delinquency are the "pet ideas" of persons or groups but there seldom has been any attempt to measure the contribution of such agencies. Boys' clubs are among the few specialized agencies whose effectiveness in dealing with delinquency has been subjected to any intensive research. The leaders of boys' clubs were certain that their programs were an important agent in the control of delinquency in the lower-class neighborhoods where most of these clubs were located. As a distinguished former head of the Boys' Clubs of America once said to the author, "If a boy is playing games in a boys' club he certainly is not involved in any delinquency at the time. If that is not prevention I don't know what it is." Many others were of similar opinion, but today we cannot be so sure. Frederick M. Thrasher's study of the extensive operations of a boys' club in New York City over a 4-year period showed that there was no clear relationship between club work and reduction of delinquency. In fact there were more delinquencies in the groups sponsored by the organization than among other boys of the neighborhood.[6]

The School

Many persons have blamed the school for contributing to juvenile delinquency. Although it seems unfair to assign major responsibility to the school for failing to make every child a good citizen, certainly it should share in that task. But the school cannot make up for all the

---

[5] Cf. *Manual of Boys' Club Operation*, Barnes, New York, 1947, chap. 1.

[6] Frederick M. Thrasher, "The Boys' Club and Juvenile Delinquency," *American Journal of Sociology*, 42:66–80 (July, 1936).

inadequacies in the home and the community which also condition the child.

There are numerous ways in which the school might help in reducing "delinquency":

1. Teachers should be able to recognize the danger symptoms that we have already discussed. They should be trained in psychology and sociology as well as in their particular subject matter.

2. School should be made so interesting and vital to the child that he has no desire to play truant. Many children dislike school because their studies are dull. Others dislike it because they are beyond their depth intellectually. Revision of the curriculum to take into consideration the interests and needs of the child would do much to make school a happy experience.

3. The school should give the child some understanding of his community. Some children are truant merely because they want to see what exists beyond the track, the bridge, or over the hill and take time out from school to find out. Well-organized field trips should be helpful in giving the child a chance to learn about his community.

4. Frequently the school ignores the emotional context within which the child lives. Often a child fails because he is upset and worried about a divorce, a sick mother, or an alcoholic father. Sometimes he is ashamed, literally, because his clothes are so inferior to those of other children. Or again an overdressed child may resent being called a "sissy" because his clothes are different. Or the specially talented child may be rejected because "he thinks he is smart."

5. Effective counseling programs should be inaugurated to help the child in difficulty. That is, more adequately trained and better-paid teachers should be a part of the expansion programs of our school systems. Otherwise we cannot hope to have teachers prepared to do this type of work.

6. Where facilities are lacking within the schools the teachers must take steps to refer problem children to diagnostic clinics and case-work agencies outside the institution.[7]

7. Because the school has jurisdiction over all children it is in a particularly strategic position to do much in a constructive way to prevent delinquency by instilling habits of honesty and decency and by emphasizing the need for responsible citizenship. There are many ways in which the children can work together to improve the appearance

[7] Cf. in this connection Mabel A. Elliott and Francis E. Merrill, *Social Disorganization*, Harper, New York, rev. ed., 1950, pp. 85–86. Cf. also William C. Kvaraceus, *Juvenile Delinquency and the School*, World, Yonkers-on-Hudson, 1947, chap. 12, "Frustrating Factors in the School."

of school grounds and buildings. They can also work co-operatively in helping each person improve his performance through encouragement and consideration. Psychiatrists insist that much delinquency grows out of rebellious feelings due to a sense of inferiority. Yet nearly everyone can do a few things well. A little well-distributed and honest praise may do much to give a child the sense of self-respect and individual worth so essential both to his peace of mind and good behavior.

8. The school may work for consideration of others through courtesy and good manners. The teacher can lead discussions of personal habits that are necessary for good citizenship. Likewise such matters can be discussed as how to improve study habits, what constitutes suitable leisure habits, what "good character" consists in, how to get along with people, and finally the ways in which children and young persons can participate in helping reduce delinquency and make their own community a desirable place in which to live.

9. Parents who are incompetent, either because of their own conduct or moral inadequacies or because they are socially and economically unable to provide their children with suitable training and surroundings, are directly or indirectly responsible for a large share of the juvenile delinquents who come before courts. The adequate family is able to meet its problems. It seems obvious that the school should assume responsibility in training children for the responsibilities of family life since many parents cannot provide such training. Such education should be started early enough in the curriculum to reach all students. If all young persons are aware of the child's need for emotional security and of the responsibilities entailed in parenthood and homemaking, the problems of delinquency should be materially reduced in subsequent generations. Knowledge of how to meet problems of family adjustment and child rearing should make it easier for parents to meet their responsibilities.

Mental Hygiene Clinics

Psychologists have seen children misbehave because they were emotionally disturbed or because they were "misunderstood"; they have seen children made fearful and emotionally insecure by those seeking to curb and control their behavior. But many of the difficulties of such children disappeared when the source of their misconduct was revealed. In consequence there has been an emphasis upon the establishment of small diagnostic psychiatric and psychological clinics to which children's behavior problems could be referred. Apparently the first such clinic for children in this country was established in Chicago under the direction of Dr. William Healy in 1909. A second clinic (with the addition of a psychiatric social worker) was established in Baltimore in 1915 by Dr. Adolf Meyer. During the twenties the development of guidance clinics, as they were called, was promoted by the Commonwealth Fund, which financed several in various parts of the country. Since that time the number of clinics has grown until there are several hundred of them, operating either as separate agencies or in co-operation with a university or some other organization.[8] Most psychiatrists and psychiatric social workers tend to believe that psychiatric techniques are essential to resolving delinquent behavior, while sociologists and others have demonstrated the community factors in delinquency to their satisfaction. Both in a sense are right.

Checkups on what has happened to children who have received treatment in these clinics indicate that psychiatry is often effective in reducing delinquency among children who are already delinquent. A study in Berkeley, California, showed that misbehavior of problem children who were treated was reduced 20.6 per cent, whereas there was no reduction in those not treated.[9]

Healy and Bronner's study, *Treatment and What Happened After-wards*[10] showed that favorable results were obtained in 323 out of 400 cases, or 81 per cent, where psychiatric interviews were employed. This group included "behavior problems" as well as delinquents. When delinquents alone were considered results were favorable in only 70 per cent of the cases. In this delinquent group both court cases and non-court cases of delinquency were studied and the percentages were exactly the same for each group.[11]

It seems likely that other factors may also have affected the rate of successful adjustment; parents co-operated in many instances and where children were older their own maturity may have contributed to their changes in conduct.[12]

The preventive, research, and diagnostic facilities for dealing with juvenile delinquency (outside of the juvenile courts and correctional institutions) exist chiefly in the states with large industrial urban populations, including New York, Massachusetts, Connecticut, New Jer-

[8] Cf. Lowell J. Carr, op. cit., p. 220.
[9] Cf. Elise Martens and Helen Russ, The Adjustment of Behavior Problems of School Children, U.S. Office of Education, Washington, 1932.
[10] Published by the Judge Baker Foundation Center, Boston, 1939. P. 42.
[11] Ibid., p. 25.
[12] Cf. Sheldon and Eleanor T. Glueck, Juvenile Delinquents Grown Up, Commonwealth Fund, New York, 1940, chap. 8, "Age, Maturation and Changes in Conduct." The Gluecks believe maturation is an important factor in improvement in conduct.

sey, Ohio, Illinois, and California. Presumably here the need is great, and there is sufficient available wealth to finance such projects.[13] However, Pennsylvania, Michigan, and a number of other states also have large industrial communities and possess great wealth but thus far have not made large contributions to this field although there have been sporadic attempts to provide treatment.

Recreational Projects

Ever since H. W. Thurston wrote his famous volume on *Delinquency and Spare Time*[14] the sociologists, social workers, and other people who read it have been convinced that if there were more and better recreational projects juvenile delinquency would inevitably decline. The first extensive scientific study of the relation between recreation and delinquency was made some 20 years later by Ethel Shanas in Chicago under the general direction of the Chicago Recreation Commission. This study covered 5 communities within Chicago, 4 of which had higher than average delinquency rates and 1 lower. The attendance at recreational activities in the parks, playgrounds, churches, settlements, and community centers was analyzed. One not unexpected conclusion of the study was that there was inadequate provision for recreation in the areas studied. So far as the relation of delinquency to recreation was concerned several important conclusions were made. Recreation was found to be a better preventive than cure for delinquency. It was found difficult, in fact, to interest juvenile delinquents in supervised recreation. They preferred to roam about on their own. Delinquents and non-delinquents were apparently equally fond of the radio. The recreational needs of boys were better provided for than those of girls. Boys past 14 were less interested and harder to hold in supervised recreation projects than younger boys and often preferred street gang activities.

On the positive side the most significant conclusion of the study was that delinquents who did not participate in supervised recreational activities were 30 per cent more likely to become repeaters than those who did participate. However, some delinquents spent more time in the recreational projects than nondelinquents. Recreation thus appeared to be a remedial factor in delinquent behavior but by no means a cure. What was much more significant was that the nondelinquents

[13] Lowell J. Carr, "Organization for Delinquency Control," *Annals of the American Academy of Political and Social Science*, 261:64–76 (January, 1949).

[14] H. W. Thurston, *Delinquency and Spare Time*, Cleveland Recreational Survey, Cleveland, 1918, pp. 105–118.

who were engaged in supervised recreational activities were far more likely to stay well adjusted than those who were not. The latter (those who did not participate) were found to be 270 per cent more likely to become recidivists during the year than those whose leisure time was spent in supervised activities.[15]

Recreation is thus only a partial answer to the question of how to prevent delinquency. Alone it cannot cope with disruptive and disorganizing influences in the community.

The Community Co-ordinating Councils

Community Co-ordinating Councils have been called community attacks on delinquency through social work. They have organized all the existing social service agencies in the community in a general overall preventive program by (1) recognizing delinquent tendencies "on the child's first signal of distress" (and by educating social workers to know the types of behavior which may be regarded as danger signals) and (2) working out methods by which early referrals of delinquents may be achieved, either in the pre-delinquent stage or before delinquent habits become well established.

THE ST. PAUL EXPERIMENT

One of the best known of the co-ordinated attempts on the part of social work and other welfare agencies to launch a united attack on delinquency is the St. Paul Experiment in Child Welfare. This project was officially sponsored by the Social Service Division of the Children's Bureau of the Federal Security Agency, working in co-operation with St. Paul public and private agencies such as the Y.W.C.A., the Y.M.C.A., the Boy Scouts, and the Girl Reserves, as well as with the University of Minnesota, other St. Paul colleges, the Social Welfare Division of the State Department of Social Security, and numerous private groups. The project was essentially a research project aimed at discovering who the delinquent children were and obtaining treatment for them.[16]

The St. Paul Community Chest, a mental hygiene clinic, the County Welfare Board, and the juvenile court acted as the project's local sponsors. The project itself under the title "Community Serv-

[15] Ethel Shanas, *Recreation and Delinquency*, Chicago Recreation Commission, Chicago, 1942, pp. 238–244.

[16] Sybil A. Stone, Elsa Castendyck, and Harold B. Hanson, *Children in the Community*, Publication 317, Children's Bureau, Federal Security Agency, Washington, 1946, p. iii.

ice" was made a member of the local Council of Social Agencies. Initially the staff of the Community Service studied the functions of the various child welfare agencies and discovered that their services were being provided chiefly for children who were removed from their homes rather than for families and children who needed help in meeting their problems within the home.[17]

The project employed a carefully selected staff, including a psychiatrist who served as chairman, a psychologist, 2 case workers who worked with the police and the courts, a group worker, and a social worker from the schools who was assigned with the project, with salary financed by a local agency. This group carried on the various types of individualized service to the children who were referred for assistance.[18]

All told, 1466 children were registered with the project in the 6½ years from January, 1937, to July 31, 1943, when its offices were closed. Of this number 739 were apparently considered minor problems and were registered merely in group activities. The remaining 727 were either those in whom definite behavior problems had been detected or those who had undesirable personality traits. Both of these groups received special services.[19]

The types of misbehavior or personality problems for which these 727 children were referred were as follows:

Academic difficulties	374
Conflict with authority	210
Undesirable personality traits	203
Stealing	178
Physical difficulties	177
School attendance irregularities	165
Conflict with other children	123
Habit problems	120
Failure to observe routines and regulations	114
Social withdrawal	109
Destruction of property	56
Running away	42
Dishonesties	34
Sex	26
Other	54

As might be assumed from the psychiatric approach to the children's difficulties, these children's misbehavior was interpreted as their protest against and disapproval of the world in which they lived. Various

[17] *Ibid.*, p. 8.   [18] *Ibid.*, p. 9.   [19] *Ibid.*, p. 12.

agencies were alerted to the types of behavior regarded as symptomatic of delinquency and in need of help. The kinds of behavior regarded as symptomatic included the following items:[20]

Bashfulness	Gate-crashing	Smoking
Boastfulness	Hitching rides	Speech disturbances
Boisterousness	Ill-mannered behavior	Stealing
Bossiness	Impudence	Stubbornness
Bullying	Inattentiveness	Sullenness
Cheating	Indolence	Tardiness
Cruelty	Lack of orderliness	Tattling
Crying	Masturbation	Teasing
Daydreaming	Nailbiting	Temper displays
Deceit	Negativism	Thumbsucking
Defiance	Obscenity	Tics
Dependence	Overactivity	Timidity
Destructiveness	Over-masculine be-	Truancy from home
Disobedience	havior (of girls)	Truancy from school
Drinking	Profanity	Uncleanliness
Eating disturbances	Quarreling	Uncouth personality
Effeminate behavior	Roughness	Underactivity
(of boys)	Selfishness	Undesirable companions
Enuresis	Sex perversion	Undesirable recreation
Fabrications	Sex play	Unsportsmanship
Failure to perform as-	Sexual activity	Untidiness
signed tasks	Shifting activities	Violation of street-trade
Fighting	Show-off behavior	regulations
Finicalness	Silliness	Violations of traffic regu-
Gambling	Sleep disturbances	lations

Many of the behavior traits which were regarded as danger signs are unquestionably displayed by a large number of children in the process of growing up and attempting to fend for themselves in homes, schools, and communities full of rules and regulations. Even so, many of these traits may be considered serious evidences of delinquency.

Of all the agencies, schools referred nearly half the children (365), the police referred 152, and parents or family members referred 52. The remaining cases were referred chiefly by group-work agencies, case-work agencies, the juvenile court, and health agencies. Individuals referred 15 cases and the churches referred 3. In only 7 cases were the same children referred by 2 different agencies.[21]

The types of services which were given these 727 children included psychiatric, psychological, case work, group work, and tutoring in

[20] *Ibid.*, pp. 47–48.   [21] *Ibid.*, p. 50.

school subjects. Twenty-five children received all 5 services; 88 children received 4 services; 113 received 3; 207 received 2; and 294 received only 1 service. All told, 209 children received psychiatric service, 360 received psychological service, 654 (all but 63) received case work, 217 received group-work service, and 90 were tutored in order to improve their schoolwork.[22]

The variety of services deemed necessary in ironing out these children's problems in itself indicates the complexity of their behavior difficulties. The project grouped the influences which appeared to be causal factors in each child's behavior, and the conclusions of the project staff with reference to their importance are given below:[23]

	Number	Per Cent
Family influence	368	85
Personality deviations	327	76
Economic influences	157	36
Education and training	129	30
Intelligence	105	24
Health	93	22
Community influences	85	20
Undetermined	28	6

As the percentages indicate, there was much overlapping of the alleged causal factors. In the present author's opinion personality deviation, the rating on intelligence tests, and even the matter of health all may be affected by family influences. It would appear to be difficult to make clear-cut diagnoses of these problems. The conclusions of the project itself were to the effect that family difficulties were basically related to the child's problems in many instances and that even where other case workers from local agencies were attempting to meet the family problem they had not recognized that the child was having a difficult problem.[24]

The significance of emotional deprivations in delinquency was clearly demonstrated by this project. Emotional difficulties were considered to be of major importance in the case of 432 children and their families, all but 3 of which were given some sort of therapy. In 53 cases there was deep therapy. In the latter no psychoanalysis was employed, but a strong emotional relationship was established between worker and either the child's parents or the child or both (as the cases varied) in order to get them to understand their motives in delinquent behavior. In 325 cases there was merely surface treat-

---

[22] *Ibid.*, p. 57.   [23] *Ibid.*, p. 68.   [24] *Ibid.*, pp. 74–75.

ment which aimed to help individuals clarify their thinking. For 51 cases there was an attempt to alter the child's behavior through environmental therapy, that is, alteration in the environment.[25] In 406 of the 432 cases given treatment in the experiment, the staff believed that they had a basis for judging the effectiveness of the treatment. Seventy-one cases (or 18 per cent) made major improvement, 265 (or 65 per cent) made partial improvement, and 70 (or 17 per cent) made no improvement. The extent of favorable response convinced the staff that their services were of definite benefit.[26] It is also pertinent to point out that the emotional needs of children seldom adequately can be met by ordinary community facilities.

The school was found to be an important facility for locating delinquent tendencies, as we mentioned earlier. The project committee found, however, that the social workers often failed to take into consideration the rigid routine of the teacher's classroom duties in planning the treatment. The school's major service is obviously to the students as a whole and time for conferences on problem cases has to be adjusted accordingly. Teachers also need to be educated with reference to the validity of the programs of the various social agencies. On the other hand the school's interest in the child may be taken for granted. In working out a child's problem, the families will often cooperate more effectively with a school case worker or visiting teacher than they will with unknown persons from social agencies.[27]

Group-work agencies such as the Y.M.C.A. and the Y.W.C.A. were found to be particularly effective in helping children to adjust to group pressures and to subordinate their own wishes to those of other members of their group, whether the group was concerned with games, hiking, art-craft projects, or some other type of activity. Adjustment took place both among children who were placed in protected groups and among those who were placed in the so-called normal groups with other children. The protected groups were made up of small numbers of disturbed children who required more individualized services than the other groups. The need for case workers to work with group agencies in developing a community preventive project was regarded as definitely established by the St. Paul project.[28]

THE BACK OF THE YARDS NEIGHBORHOOD COUNCIL

Quite in contrast to the methods of the St. Paul project are those of the Back of the Yards Council in Chicago. This organization is in an

[25] Ibid., pp. 70–71.   [26] Ibid., pp. 71–72.
[27] Ibid., p. 95.   [28] Ibid., pp. 140–141.

industrial area of Chicago close to the Stock Yards—generally known as "Back of the Yards." It represents a successful attempt on the part of the citizens to attack the problem of promoting community welfare (including helping delinquents and criminals) through existing groups and institutions. Because it is an area of workingmen's homes in which more than 90 per cent of the population is Roman Catholic, the Roman Catholic Church and organized labor are the two moving factors. The church with the C.I.O. and A.F. of L. labor unions, the local chamber of commerce, veterans' organizations, fraternal groups, and athletic groups have formed the Back of the Yards Neighborhood Council. The organization began before World War I, hence has had ample time to prove that citizens can be aroused to an interest in their own social problems. The Council is made up of the people who live in the neighborhood and are facing these problems, not of outsiders foisted upon them by social work or other agencies.[29]

The work in preventing delinquency in this Back of the Yards neighborhood has been fostered by one of the council's eight committees, which deals with the problems on a common-sense level. If a delinquent boy's father is out of a job that may be the basic problem. At least some kind of job is obtained for him. A community recreational center has been established, littered vacant lots have been cleared to make small parks and playgrounds in the area, the young people themselves have organized to help solve their own problems. This participation has given much insight to older people in dealing with delinquency.

Because they have come to visualize the community's problems as a whole, and to take a community perspective on their problems, the various church and labor groups have come to see that the welfare of each is interlocked with the welfare of all. Much of the activity of the group has been directed toward improving economic conditions, but there has been a general recognition of the need for considering matters of race, child welfare, etc. In the meantime the members of the community have developed great ability in leadership as well as in understanding the nature of their problems. In the Back of the Yards Council the trained personnel has kept to the side lines but has done an excellent job in training leaders, who have gained great understanding themselves as the result of becoming well informed. The professional leader of the Back of the Yards Neighborhood Council, Saul D. Alinsky, has proved exceptionally competent in developing leader-

[29] Saul D. Alinsky, "Community Analysis and Organization," *American Journal of Sociology*, 46:797–808 (May, 1941).

ship resources in the community. These leaders have acquired essential knowledge and skills. There can be no substitute for training and skill, as Lowell J. Carr points out.[30] But it seems obvious that community members can acquire both.[31]

On the other hand amateurs who seek to handle delinquency cases and who work undirected may do untold harm through their "common sense" procedures. Carr cites a telling example of a dentist turned delinquency preventer who botched a case because he failed to recognize that a deep-seated emotional disturbance was responsible for a boy's conduct. The dentist tried to help the boy without discovering what had made the boy behave as he did. He did not know how to get the boy's confidence or his story. He just expected the boy to conform because he (the dentist) took time to see how he was getting along.[32]

THE CHICAGO AREA PROJECT

The Chicago Area Project, first organized in 1930 and incorporated 4 years later, has utilized many of the same principles as the Back of the Yards Neighborhood Council except that it has been basically concerned with reducing delinquency and with making the various areas safe places in which children can grow up. This achievement is possible only when quasi-criminal groups and attitudes which foster delinquency are eliminated from the community.[33] Case workers, psychiatrists, and psychologists can work on individual children and families, but they cannot change the basic characteristics of the community. These the people themselves must first decide to alter; then they must work continuously to keep down unsavory influences. They must also co-operate in supporting any project which aims at building satisfactory community attitudes, both financially and by providing moral support.[34]

The Chicago Area Project is founded on the idea that the roots of delinquency are to be found in the deteriorated area and that social workers (or psychiatrists and psychologists) cannot prevent delinquency. They can help in lending professional advice, but the motivation and the effort to improve a community must come largely from the people themselves. Those who live in the community set the community standards and these cannot be imposed from without. Hence

[30] Lowell J. Carr, *Delinquency Control*, pp. 475–479.

[31] Cf. Saul D. Alinsky, *Reveille for Radicals*, University of Chicago Press, Chicago, 1946, for additional details about the "People's" Council.

[32] Lowell J. Carr, *Delinquency Control*, pp. 475–479.

[33] Clifford R. Shaw, "Annual Report, The Chicago Area Project, 1949–1950" (mimeographed), pp. 1–2.

[34] *Ibid.*

the Area Project has enlisted the support of local leadership, who are organized into neighborhood committees for an orderly attack on problems. The local leaders include local professional people (usually neighborhood boys who return to practice medicine, dentistry, or law in their old community), clergy, teachers, truck drivers, butchers, grocers, druggists, factory workers, and housewives.

The Area Project provides trained personnel, usually a sociologist who is interested in helping the local residents provide their children with a decent and attractive place in which to live. By and large the committee is composed of citizens whose children are growing up in the community.

Local institutions, the church and the school, parks, and health and welfare agencies are enlisted in the co-operative project, in which the social workers advise but do not direct. They are merely members of the committee. Where practicable, local trained persons are recruited for dealing with delinquents, whether as probation, parole, or truant officers.

Many activities are sponsored by the neighborhood committees of the project. Some are purely recreational, in the shape of community centers, camps, sports tournaments, etc. But the committees have also tried to build up the community in other ways, by promoting housing projects, community forums, adult education classes, etc. A major activity has been the rehabilitation program for delinquents or adults who are returned to the community from courts, correctional institutions, or prison. Here there is an attempt to help the child (or adult) readjust by reintegrating him into the life of the community and helping him help himself. The Chicago Area Project maintains that constructive leadership of the residents can do more to prevent delinquency than any diagnostic skills of psychiatrists or social workers. Just as the community itself must institute controls and promote sanitation and education in hygienic living if it would keep down sickness, similarly it must promote effective patterns of wholesome living and eliminate the breeding places of delinquency if it would control delinquency.[35]

The Chicago Area Project is now organized in 10 different high-delinquency areas with 28 separate projects. One of the most important of these has been the project in a South Side Negro community stretching from 22nd to 63rd streets between Cottage Grove and Wentworth avenues. This area has had the highest delinquency rate

[35] *Ibid.*, pp. 14–32. Cf. also *Change the Street* (pamphlet), Chicago Area Project, Chicago, 1951, pp. 22–26.

among boys of any area in the Chicago district. It has been an essentially disorganized section, with poverty, great overcrowding, much prostitution. The chief recreational facilities have been the pool hall, taverns and beer flats while the neighborhood was in a sense a racial ghetto.[36] It seemed obvious that the neighborhood itself was a major factor in the children's delinquency. Even the children who came from good families were often involved in delinquent activities. To make a long story short, local residents were mobilized, volunteer committees were organized, some 11 neighborhood centers and clubs were established, recreational programs were initiated, funds were recruited from public and private sources. The project itself was an experiment in democracy. No longer were social workers or Lady Bountifuls doing things for the community. Mr. and Mrs. Average Citizen were imbued with the idea of doing things for themselves.[37]

In the prevention of delinquency, which was the sole aim of the organization, mothers of delinquents were brought into the organization with the idea of giving them responsibility in helping their children overcome delinquent habits. Residents helped build some of the centers.

During the time the committee has been in operation an incisive dent has been made in local delinquency rates. A group of young girl shoplifters were taken on an educational tour of stores. Many unsavory hangouts, "joints," and "fences" have been cleaned up. Summer camps have been established through efforts of local citizens. In fact as a result of the Southside Community Committee activity the state parks of Illinois have been opened for camping. In the meantime the residents have increased their budget every year. Within 4 years the amount increased fourfold.[38]

What the Chicago Area Project is doing is converting the values of a delinquency-ridden community to concepts of social responsibility and an acceptance of standards of conduct which are approved by the middle class.

These developments in Chicago—the Back of the Yards Council and the Chicago Area Project—represent distinctive approaches to the problem of delinquency. The effort in both is in the direction of building for acceptable standards of good conduct through motivating the residents of the community. The people must become self-respecting and self-sufficing, just as they are in the middle-class and upper-class

[36] *Bright Shadows in Bronzetown*, Southside Community Committee, University of Chicago Press, Chicago, 1949, pp. 18–33. Cf. also Clifford R. Shaw, *op. cit.*, p. 6.
[37] *Ibid.*, chaps. 2, 3, and 4.   [38] *Ibid.*, chap. 5.

areas where juvenile delinquency rates are low. The area projects are committed to the idea that people must care about what happens to young persons.

Experiments in Counseling Juveniles as Crime Prevention Technique

A 10-year experiment in crime prevention carried on in the Cambridge-Somerville Youth Study indicates that the attempt on the part of social workers to supply counseling, special health services, camping trips, and help in working out educational problems to some 325 boys has given no very definite conclusion as to the worth of it all. Certain boys (71 in number) who were thought to have criminal tendencies turned out much better than expected. Only 23 committed serious delinquencies and 31 were not delinquent at all. On the other hand, of the 325 boys who were not given these alleged benefits 163 were held to be probable delinquents, yet only 23 of these were ever committed to correctional institutions.

There were other conclusions. On first sight it seemed that those who had help were no more successful in their adjustment than those who did not. Nevertheless certain facts emerge. More of the control boys were sent to correctional institutions and committed serious offenses than was true of the boys who were helped and some of the boys assisted were apparently "deflected from criminal careers." In general, building of good citizenship could be measured in the more positively satisfactory social adjustments of the nondelinquents.[39]

City-Wide Organization to Prevent Delinquency

Many communities in recent years have developed committees and city-wide plans to attack juvenile delinquency. One city which has made great strides in this direction is Philadelphia, first through the Philadelphia Crime Prevention Association and lately through the Philadelphia Conference to Prevent and Control Delinquency.

THE PHILADELPHIA CRIME ASSOCIATION

Since 1932 Philadelphia has had a Crime Prevention Association. It was developed through the interest of Charles Edwin Fox and Samuel S. Fels, the latter a well-known Philadelphia philanthropist. This association was formed for the purpose of studying the problem and promoting community programs that would remedy conditions which

[39] Edwin Powers, "An Experiment in Prevention of Delinquency," *Annals of the American Academy of Political and Social Science*, 261:77–88 (January, 1949).

were conducive to delinquency. The association asked for and secured the co-operation of the police, which appointed a lieutenant and two policemen to develop a preventive unit. This unit has now grown to 68 policemen, and almost as many have worked in other areas of the program.

A referral plan was developed for all delinquent boys, whether they were picked up by police or were complaint cases received from individuals, agencies, or schools. The boys are referred to different co-operating agencies, who send staff members to visit their homes and who attempt to utilize community resources in helping work out their adjustment. The police unit investigates all places such as movie houses, dance halls, bus terminals, etc., which might be presumed to foster conditions leading to delinquency, as well as investigating all complaints. The unit also scrutinizes places catering to young people and maintains a close relationship with social agencies.[40]

THE PHILADELPHIA CONFERENCE FOR THE PREVENTION AND CONTROL OF DELINQUENCY

As an outgrowth of the National Conference for the Prevention and Control of Juvenile Delinquency which was called in Washington in November, 1946, many new developments and projects were sponsored by various groups on both a local and a national scale.[41] One of the most important of these has been the Philadelphia Conference for the Prevention and Control of Juvenile Delinquency. Philadelphia representatives at the Washington conference reported on the meeting to the local Health and Welfare Council and as a result set up a general planning committee selected from qualified leaders in nine areas of community life having a vital relation to young people. These groups constituted panels in the following fields:

The Church.
The Home.
The Community and Neighborhood.
The Police.
Recreational Facilities.
The Juvenile Court.
The School.
Treatment Resources.
Community Co-ordinating.

[40] J. Francis Finnegan, "The Work of the Crime Prevention Units of Philadelphia," *Proceedings of the Annual Congress of Correction of the American Prison Association,* 1949, New York, 1949, pp. 263–269.
[41] This conference is discussed later in this same chapter.

These groups, which included the outstanding leaders in Philadelphia, spent 2 years gathering material for their reports with suggestions for ways and means of improving services in the nine areas. Naturally the suggestions covered the work of the already existing Crime Prevention Association (which had also given the conference much of its motivation).

Following the conference a continuing committee was established charged with the tasks of planning, co-ordinating, and improving the services of all the agencies now working for better community life. Churches, P.T.A.'s, and civic organizations were urged to participate in community organization. Expansion in family living courses in the teachers colleges were recommended, as well as education in family living in all grades of the public schools. Improvement in the Prevention Division of the police was requested. Co-ordination of recreational facilities was also recommended with a view to securing the establishment of a Department of Parks and Recreation which would direct all leisure-time activities (including libraries and museums) operating under the municipal government. There were many additional recommendations but these are among the most important. The continuing committee hopes to carry out the achievement of these recommendations, which will "improve every facet of human living."[42] The effectiveness of this and every other program will depend upon the degree to which sustained interest and effort can be maintained.

GOVERNMENTAL OVER-ALL PROJECTS

Local Government Projects: A Proposal

The Back of the Yards Council and the Chicago Area Project both seem to be making important strides in reducing and controlling delinquency. Many other community councils have failed to recruit the services of local agencies because the co-operation has been purely voluntary.

Edwin J. Lukas, Executive Director of the Society for the Prevention of Crime in New York City, maintains that any effective co-ordination must come through an over-all community co-ordinating bureau which has mandatory power to mobilize the resources of the public and private agencies in an all-out attack on the problem of de-

---

[42] Cf. The Conservation of Human and Spiritual Resources, A Program Developed by the Philadelphia Conference for the Prevention and Control of Juvenile Delinquency, Albert A. Owens, ed., Philadelphia Crime Association, Philadelphia, 1950, for the extensive details of this conference.

linquency. Furthermore, he would make it compulsory for the private (as well as public) agencies to gear their program to the assigned tasks. Lukas holds the bureau should recommend the revocation of the accredited status of any private agency failing to do so. Such a bureau could really accomplish something. As Lukas recognizes, many bureaus now stop at the canvassing stage or after "studying the problem." After the initial exploration things remain essentially as they were before.[43]

Undoubtedly thoroughgoing attacks on community problems on anything other than a small neighborhood basis will have to come from an authoritative source. But to date most communities have not created delinquency prevention projects within the framework of local government.

State-Wide Crime Prevention Projects

YOUTH CORRECTION AUTHORITIES

The community projects, as we have seen, depend for their success upon the enlistment of sustained citizen support but they also require trained leadership, adequate financial assistance, and suitable facilities. These can seldom be attained on a small voluntary basis in the communities that need them most. This fact became a matter of great concern to the American Law Institute after much consideration of the ways and means by which adequate facilities might be achieved. This body in 1940 proposed a model law, providing for a Youth Correction Authority which incorporated the accepted principles of rehabilitation, which it urged the various states to adopt.

The model act was particularly designed to provide a new type of administrative justice for adolescent offenders past juvenile court age and under 21 at the time of apprehension. Essentially the act aims at supplying treatment which will correct the criminal tendencies of young offenders. Since so many of our criminal group are in the 16 to 21 age classification, the American Law Institute believed its proposal would protect society as well as help young persons to become law-abiding adults.

The plan of the Youth Authority Act calls for committing all young offenders past juvenile court age and under 21 to the Youth Correction Authority in all cases save those extreme ones in which capital punishment or life imprisonment may be invoked, or those involving

---

[43] Edwin J. Lukas, "Crime Prevention: Who Prevents What?" *Federal Probation,* 12:19–23 (June, 1948).

minor offenses for which a fine or very short sentence is imposed. The Authority is empowered to create new places for detention if needed in order to examine and study each case as well as to make use of the various existing private and public agencies; it may create new types of institutions for those not kept in confinement; it is given extensive controls over all persons committed to its charge and may keep offenders in custody for life if necessary; it may place an individual in a correctional institution, in a supervised boarding home, in a hospital or work camp, or any other place that study of the case warrants. The Authority also is authorized to help those who have been released from its custody in securing employment, etc. The act is too long to quote in detail but these are its major points.

California was the first state to adopt a provision for such an authority in 1941 but made it applicable to all young persons under 23 years of age as well as boys and girls from the juvenile court. The California juvenile court already had jurisdiction over all cases under 21 years of age. Since the modal group of offenders runs from 19 to 24 the extension of the age is obviously justified.

In 1943 the name of the California Youth Correction Authority was changed to California Youth Authority and the existing correctional schools and the probation division of the State Welfare Department were both transferred to the Youth Authority. Since that date the work has become a tremendous experiment; 3 more correctional institutions and 4 forestry camps have been added to the administrative services of the Authority. One of the new institutions is a ranch school and the Youth Authority has also subsidized ranch schools connected with the San Francisco and Los Angeles juvenile courts. A field service has been developed for providing consultive services to the various juvenile courts, county probation departments, police departments, and other agencies. There is effective co-operation with the state Departments of Education, Social Welfare, and Public Health, and with the Federal Security Agency. To promote effective contacts for the Youth Authority with local communities the California Youth Committee, made up of lay members throughout the state, is appointed by the governor for a clearing house of youth problems in various parts of the state.[44]

[44] Cf. John R. Ellingston, *Protecting Our Children from Criminal Careers*, Prentice-Hall, New York, 1948, for a detailed description of the California Youth Authority and its origins, and Vandyce Hamren, "California Youth Authority: Organization of the Youth Authority and Outline of Its Program" (mimeographed), Sacramento, California, 1949. For current information see reports in the *California Youth Authority Quarterly*, published by the California Youth Authority, Sacramento.

Today the Youth Authority of California represents the most significant forward step taken thus far in working out plans for helping young people solve their conflicts with society on a satisfactory basis. As Edwin J. Lukas has said, it "embodies all that we know or ought to know in penology. It capitalizes those assets of the present system which are worthy of survival and abolishes those liabilities of which we should have rid ourselves when their obsolescence first became manifest."[45] We may even expect it to lead to new insights.

Four other states have also adopted the Youth Correction Authority plan, at least in part. These are Minnesota, Wisconsin, Massachusetts, and Texas. The Minnesota law, adopted in 1947, created a Youth Conservation Commission, which consists in the Director of the Division of Public Institutions, the Chairman of the State Parole Board, and 5 additional appointees. All persons under 21 who are convicted by the district courts are committed to the Commission, as well as any juvenile court case which may be referred when there is no local probation officer. The state training schools for delinquent boys and girls are supervised by the Commission. Wisconsin created a Youth Service Commission the same year, which operates under the Wisconsin Department of Public Welfare. In Wisconsin all juvenile court commitments are to the Youth Service Commission. California, Minnesota, and Wisconsin thus have jurisdiction over juvenile court cases as well as post-juvenile court age offenders.

Massachusetts (in 1948) and Texas (in 1949) adopted the idea incorporated in the Youth Correction Authority Act except that in both of these states the provisions apply only to juvenile court age offenders. Undoubtedly the juvenile court has not functioned as acceptably as its founders had hoped and this trend is in the right direction. The need for better facilities for adolescent post-juvenile offenders still remains a serious problem in these and the remaining 44 states.[46]

THE NEW JERSEY PREVENTION PROGRAM

New Jersey has a co-ordinated state-wide and local program for delinquency prevention with its direction centered in the Division of Community Services for Delinquency Prevention in the New Jersey State Department of Institutions and Agencies, with the Governor's Committee on Youth serving as its advisory committee.[47] New Jersey

[45] Edwin J. Lukas, "Peno-Correctional Philosophy in Retrospect," Proceedings of National Conference of Social Work, 1948, New York, 1949, p. 364.

[46] Cf. Negley K. Teeters and John O. Reinemann, The Challenge of Delinquency, Prentice-Hall, New York, 1950, pp. 368–370, for a detailed discussion of this matter.

[47] Douglas H. MacNeil, "Two and One-Half Years of State-Local Collaboration in

has made enviable achievements in the development of its state welfare institutions and it seems likely that its co-ordinated program may rival those of the states which have adopted the Youth Correction Authority provisions. In connection with all of these state-wide projects numerous research projects have been carried on.

Federal Efforts to Prevent Delinquency

Throughout its history the Children's Bureau has made many studies and surveys of juvenile delinquency and has gathered statistics on its extent. The Bureau is now a part of the Federal Security Agency but was organized in 1912 as a part of the Department of Commerce and transferred in 1913 to the Department of Labor. The White House Conferences on Child Welfare which have taken place at more or less regular intervals have also considered every phase of the problems of child welfare with detailed studies and reports on juvenile delinquency. Likewise the National Commission on Law Observance and Enforcement made a comprehensive summary of the causes of juvenile delinquency under the direction of Clifford R. Shaw and Henry D. McKay. In addition there have been other constructive efforts to help children in the Aid to Dependent Children program, National Parks, development of 4-H clubs, etc.

The federal government's interest in child welfare and juvenile delinquency thus has been demonstrated over the years. Following World War II there was much talk about the appalling increase in delinquency (much of this talk was the result of misinterpretation of statistics) and prominent citizens and government leaders became much concerned. At their behest an Advisory Panel of 28 persons met in Washington in February, 1946, to discuss ways and means of preventing and controlling delinquency.

The outcome of this meeting was a large national conference on prevention and control of juvenile delinquency in November, 1946, which was attended by over 800 representatives of federal, state, and local governmental agencies as well as private welfare groups. Eighteen detailed reports were presented at this conference on ways in which various organizations and agencies including the whole community could take action in preventing and controlling the problem. We shall mention each briefly.

1. The Community Co-ordination panel stressed the necessity

Delinquency Prevention," *National Probation and Parole Association Yearbook*, 1948, New York, 1949, pp. 252–262.

for seeing the total picture (getting the facts) for providing public understanding of the problem, developing high-type services, relating delinquency to other social problems, co-ordinating existing agencies dealing with young persons, and doing something to get rid of the conditions which contributed to delinquency.[48]

2. The panel on general recommendations for State and Community Action urged that all 48 states call a state conference so as to co-ordinate the efforts to deal with delinquency with representatives of the legislature and members of state departments of education, welfare, health, and correction; training schools, women's clubs, the press, school boards; farm, labor, teachers, and fraternal organizations; commercial recreation groups, etc., as well as representatives of private welfare agencies, boys' and girls' group workers, and the medical profession. It was likewise urged that community conferences be held. In both state and local conferences the participation of young persons was advocated in order to enlist their support in meeting their own problems. Furthermore a continuing committee to carry on the proposed work was recommended and established.[49]

Recommendations relating to their areas of interest were also made for the panels dealing with improvement of:

3. Juvenile Court Laws.
4. Juvenile Court Administration.
5. Juvenile Detention Homes.
6. Institutional Treatment of Delinquents.
7. The Role of the Police in Delinquency.
8. Housing Community Development and Juvenile Delinquency.
9. Recreation.
10. Mental Health and Child Guidance Clinics.
11. Youth Participation.
12. Citizen Participation.
13. Case Work—Group Work.
14. Church Responsibilities.
15. School and Teacher Responsibilities.
16. Home Responsibilities.
17. Rural Aspects of Juvenile Delinquency.
18. Statistics.

[48] Report on Community Coordination, National Conference on Prevention and Control of Juvenile Delinquency, November 20–23, 1946, Washington, 1947, pp. 3–4.
[49] Report on General Recommendations for State and Community Action, National Conference on Prevention and Control of Juvenile Delinquency, November 20–23, 1946, Washington, 1947, pp. 4–11.

Most of these reports summarized ideas already expressed under related topics earlier in this chapter. Reports 11, 17, and 18 deserve further mention.

Report 11, on Youth Participation, stressed the normal need of young persons to escape adult controls. The importance of allowing young persons to plan their programs with friendly adult counsel, but without adult domination, was particularly stressed. In order that youth programs be constructive substitutes for undesirable activities the report recommended providing activities which offered equal interest and excitement, including new experience and adventure. Such activities must make sense from the young person's point of view. But above all the young persons want to have a voice in deciding what is good for them instead of participating in a program planned and executed by adults.

This recommendation is particularly significant for it undoubtedly recognizes the reason for the failure of many recreational and group-work projects to promote wholesome attitudes among children with a record of delinquency. The children wanted to do something which was fun and seemed important to them instead of what adults thought "good for them," or "safe."

Report 17, on Rural Aspects of Delinquency, covered the most neglected aspect of the whole problem. It was one of the longest reports. Although official juvenile delinquency rates are far lower than urban rates, much delinquency is not reported in rural areas; standards of welfare services are much lower if not altogether lacking; there are very few rural police other than the sheriff or township constable (or marshal); rural housing standards are low in many parts of the country; rural schools seldom compare favorably with urban schools; and provision for community recreation often does not exist.[50] Some of the conclusions of this report are more apparent than real.

Since this report made no differentiation between well-to-do farming areas and marginal areas, the problems presented are not truly characteristic of either. Nevertheless most rural areas could profit from an improvement of their church, recreational, and other facilities. On the other hand in many parts of the country, near-by small towns (rather than the open country) have become the social and civic centers for the surrounding farmland. Any promotion of better social services for rural areas should probably be centered in the small towns. With the automobile urban life has been extended to the country and

[50] Report on Rural Aspects of Delinquency, National Conference on Prevention and Control of Juvenile Delinquency, November 20–23, 1946, Washington, 1947, pp. 1–76.

the country has gone to the town. America is becoming what Dr. Kolb calls "rurbanized."[51]

Report 18, on Statistics, stressed (1) the importance of the collection and tabulation of accurate information on delinquency and (2) the need for scientific objective analysis of such data. (Sophia Robison in her book *Can Delinquency Be Measured?*[52] questioned whether we have any common definition of what we mean by delinquency.) Furthermore the disparities in age levels, offenses covered, differences in arrest, inclusion or failure to include "unofficial" cases, etc., all complicate the problem of data.

It was therefore recommended that: (1) All public and private agencies dealing with delinquents should co-operate so that one community resource would give an *unduplicated* count of all delinquents; (2) data on the character of and circumstances surrounding delinquent acts should be reported—whether individual delinquent was committed alone or with a group, whether it was a first offense, etc.; (3) socioeconomic and psychological factors relating to the delinquent should be reported so that an adequate picture of factors relating to juvenile delinquency may be gathered. Such data will give material for understanding and controlling delinquency as well as a better picture of how much delinquency exists. In order for coverage to be detailed there will have to be some governmental facility for gathering the data in the various states. In 1927 (the first year juvenile court statistics were gathered) only 43 courts reported. In 1945, 400 courts representing approximately 37 per cent of the population reported. At present about 25 states have a state-wide agency gathering data and more are expected to follow.[53] The importance of having complete information as to the extent of delinquency is essential in any program which seeks to prevent it.

THE MID-CENTURY WHITE HOUSE CONFERENCE ON CHILDREN AND YOUTH

The mid-century White House Conference on Children and Youth, held in Washington in December, 1950, represented a significant step in the efforts of national organizations in the fields of health, education, welfare, youth services, religion, and communities, as such, to co-ordinate their services on national, state, and local levels.

[51] John H. Kolb and Edmund de S. Brunner, A *Study of Rural Society*, Houghton Mifflin, Boston, 1946, pp. 383–384.
[52] Published by Columbia University Press, New York, 1936.
[53] Report on *Statistics, National Conference on Prevention and Control of Juvenile Delinquency, November* 20–23, 1946, Washington, 1947, pp. 1–25.

More than half the states have held "little White House Conferences" since December, 1950. There have been large meetings such as the Philadelphia Conference described earlier. Many smaller community meetings have taken place. In Iowa 300 meetings were held during 1 month. West Virginia has had 273 meetings. There have also been a number of interstate meetings. Some states have made plans for permanent organizations through legislation and other states are planning such action. A number of colleges have held campus meetings to which the whole community was extended an invitation.

Perhaps the most important development of all has been the organization of a permanent national committee called the National Mid-Century Committee for Children and Youth, which will carry out the work thus far set in motion to aid the various state and local projects as well as to maintain liaison with federal efforts on the behalf of children. This committee expects to maintain 2 advisory councils, 1 for state and local action and 1 for co-ordinating federal activities. The committee will offer field service and information service to various individuals and organizations. It will also develop research projects. It will seek special ways and means for enlisting the co-operation of young persons in solving their own problems.[54]

THE FEDERAL YOUTH CORRECTIONS ACT

In September, 1950, President Truman signed the Federal Youth Corrections Act, which covers young persons under 22 who commit federal offenses. In addition to permitting probation and sentencing (which are standard provisions under the adult laws) 3 new provisions open the way for an entirely new type of treatment. These permit the federal courts (1) to commit a young offender to the Youth Board for an indefinite period up to 6 years and (2) to commit a young person for more than 6 years for supervision and treatment (as, for example, a sex offender), i.e., for an indefinite period not to exceed the maximum sentence. (3) If uncertain what procedure to take the courts may place the young person in the custody of the attorney general for study, diagnosis, and recommendation prior to any imposition of sentence.[55]

Under these new provisions of the act such young persons are placed in a classification center to be studied intensively by a group of trained

[54] Cf. The Child, Vol. 5 (January, 1951). The entire issue is devoted to reporting highlights of the Mid-Century White House Conference on Children and Youth. Cf. also Mid-Century White House Conference on Children and Youth, Progress Bulletin No. 5, June 20, 1951, pp. 1–4.

[55] "The Federal Youth Corrections Act," Prison Journal, 31:39–40 (April, 1951).

specialists, whose reports will go to the Director of Prisons, who will make recommendations to the Youth Correction Division of the Board of Parole. This board and the director will determine the institutional program for young persons.

The act incorporates many of the features of the California Youth Authority and provides for a variety of institutional developments for young offenders including schools, hospitals, forestry camps, as well as special provisions for "accidental offenders" in other private and public agencies.

One of the special features of the act is the creation of an Advisory Corrections Council to be composed of United States judges and administrative courts. This council will study problems related to the prevention of crime and the treatment and correction of offenders and make recommendations to Congress with reference to appropriate legislation. It is to be hoped that this provision will result in a marked increase in the judges' understanding of the problems of delinquent behavior themselves. Often judges are woefully lacking in the understanding which criminology, psychology, and sociology might give them toward such behavior, as we have mentioned briefly in our treatment of criminal procedure.[56]

SUMMARY

This survey of the types of projects sponsored by individuals, groups, committees, the various states, and the federal government indicates both the current interest and the lack of co-ordination in the attempts to deal with the problem of delinquency as a means of crime prevention. This text has not covered the causes of juvenile delinquency and has barely referred to the treatment of juvenile delinquency in other chapters. This chapter may seem out of the frame of reference of the text to some people. If there were not more material than can be included on the general topic of adult criminality greater emphasis might have been placed on juvenile delinquency.

There are, however, two basic reasons for including this discussion. The major reason is that nearly all experiments in crime prevention have emphasized preventing juvenile delinquency. Most of the social action has taken place on the juvenile level. The other reason for including the material is the author's belief that the time for building socially responsible citizens is in childhood and youth. It is during the formative years that our social attitudes and social values are estab-

[56] Chap. 19.

lished. It is during this period that community action can be truly preventive. Most preventive action for adults must be on a rehabilitative basis. This we shall discuss in the next chapter.

SELECTED BIBLIOGRAPHY

Alinsky, Saul D., "Community Analysis and Organization," *American Journal of Sociology*, 46:797–808 (May, 1941). This is an enthusiastic report on the Chicago Back of the Yards Council and its contributions to more effective living.

Carr, Lowell J., *Delinquency Control*, Harper, New York, 1950. In a penetrating analysis, the various facets of the problems involved in preventing, reducing, and controlling delinquency are given.

The Child vol. 5 (January, 1951). The entire issue of this publication is devoted to a report on the Mid-Century White House Conference on Children and Youth. See subsequent issues for further reports.

Ellingston, John R., *Protecting Our Children from Criminal Careers*, Prentice-Hall, New York, 1948. This is a full-scale report on the California Youth Authority with its background.

Hamren, Vandyce, "California Youth Authority" (mimeographed), Sacramento, 1949. This gives a detailed account of the organization of the Youth Authority and its program. Cf. also current reports of the California Youth Authority, which is the most ambitious project in dealing with court cases in the United States.

Kvaraceus, William C., *Juvenile Delinquency and the School*, World, Yonkers-on-Hudson, 1947. This book gives an excellent discussion of the ways in which the school can deal constructively with the program.

Owens, Albert A. (ed.), *The Conservation of Human and Spiritual Resources—A Program Developed by the Philadelphia Conference for the Prevention and Control of Juvenile Delinquency*, Philadelphia Crime Association, 1950. This gives a detailed co-operative plan for meeting delinquency problems in Philadelphia.

Shanas, Ethel, *Recreation and Delinquency*, Chicago Recreation Commission, Chicago, 1942. This volume presents objective data on both the positive and the negative aspects of recreation as a preventive measure.

Shaw, Clifford R., "Annual Report, The Chicago Area Project, Institute for Juvenile Research, 1949–1950" (mimeographed). A report on the sociologically oriented prevention of delinquency project in Chicago recounts its significant successes in reducing delinquency in the various communities within the city.

Shaw, Clifford R., Kolbein, Solomon, and McClaughry, Richard T., *Bright Shadows in Bronzetown*, Southside Community Committee, University of Chicago Press, Chicago, 1949. This is a report on the improvement of the Negro community in the South Side of Chicago.

Stone, Sybil A., Castendyck, Elsa, and Hanson, Harold B., *Children in the Community, The St. Paul Experiment in Child Welfare*, Publication 317, Children's Bureau, Federal Security Agency, Washington, 1946. A comprehensive report is given of the co-ordinated agency attack on the problems of delinquency in St. Paul, Minnesota.

Teeters, Negley K., and Reinemann, John Otto, *The Challenge of Delinquency*, Prentice-Hall, New York, 1950, chaps. 15 and 16. This excellent text contains some fine material on preventive treatment and community action.

Thrasher, Frederick M., "The Boys' Club and Juvenile Delinquency," *American Journal of Sociology*, 42:66–80 (July, 1936). This article summarizes Thrasher's study of boys' clubs as a preventive of delinquency. Boys' clubs are shown to be a partial solution to the problem at best.

Thurston, H. W., *Delinquency and Spare Time*, Cleveland Recreational Survey, Cleveland, 1918. This is the book that launched recreational projects as a preventive to juvenile delinquency.

CHAPTER 29

Crime Prevention on the Adult Level

Social Planning Oriented Toward Crime Prevention

If we are genuinely interested in prevention of crime on an adult level several developments appear to be imperative: (1) We must initiate wide-scale attacks on the social situations which stimulate and foster crime and we must aid in ironing out the personality distortions which lead to criminal behavior. (2) In the estimation of the author of this text our penal system must be converted into a truly correctional system which aims primarily at rehabilitating offenders. (3) The judicial process must be revised by restricting the activities of the judges and courts to the responsibility for determining guilt, while (4) specialists in behavior problems are entrusted with determining the treatment of offenders. (5) In the meantime a wide variety of research projects should be launched so as to discover the most effective ways in which correction and rehabilitation can be accomplished. We must recognize that crime is a function of rules, and rules which restrict human behavior will always be disobeyed by some individuals. But we can educate human beings to an appreciation of the responsibilities demanded of good citizens and attempt at least to establish laws which will promote willing co-operation. This should be the aim of crime prevention in a democracy.[1]

As the author pointed out a good many years ago,[2] the state's supreme concern with reference to penal laws should be with the devel-

[1] Cf. in this connection Arthur L. Beeley, *Social Planning for Crime Control*, University of Utah, Salt Lake City, 1935, for necessary steps in crime reduction and control.

[2] Mabel A. Elliott, *Conflicting Penal Theories in Statutory Criminal Law*; University of Chicago Press, Chicago, 1931.

opment of preventive and corrective legislation based upon a scientific understanding of the crime problem in all its ramifications.[3] But society up to now has never been able to divest itself of the desire to enforce retributory justice. In general the more serious the offense the more severe the punishment, despite a recognized desire to consider the background and personality of the offender in working out any program for dealing with him.

That retributory justice has not prevented crime we hope to have made plain in earlier chapters. The only way that crime and delinquency can be prevented must come through (1) wholehearted attempts on the part of the community to reduce temptations to delinquency and crime, and (2) the development of suitable motivations for good conduct so that children, young persons, and adults desire to behave in conformity to social rules and regulations. (3) For those who have already become confirmed offenders some effective plans for re-education and remotivation must be developed and tested.

We cannot hope to explore all the reasons why more effective programs for crime prevention are not implemented, but a large part of the explanation rests in the difficulty in erasing the desire for revenge that underlies our penal law in most states. Part of the failure to prevent crimes stems from confused thinking and from failure to recognize that we cannot reform a person while antagonizing him by retributory measures. Some of this confusion may lie in our deep-seated desires to hurt others, as the Freudian psychiatrists insist. But much of it must be attributed to the persistence of established habits of action and thinking, even though their ineffectiveness has been demonstrated. Judges, wardens, boards of administration have vested interests in existing procedures which they are unwilling to release in behalf of the offenders' best interests.

Citizens likewise may have a vested interest in crime, as owners of real estate, as police officers, as stockholders in certain industries, as petty gamblers, or as white-collar criminals. Any alteration of the *status quo* in plans for preventing and treating crime has far-reaching ramifications. The various attempts at crime prevention and reduction through punishment, penal reforms, piecemeal attempts to aid offenders, local state and national crime commissions, the California Adult Authority, and prevention at an international level which are presented below should be reviewed with these considerations in mind.

[3] *Ibid.*, p. 240.

Punishment as Prevention

The rationalized motives for punishment conceive punishment as prevention (1) in restraining the would-be offender through fear of the penalties he might otherwise receive and (2) in restraining the offender from further criminal activity after he learns firsthand of the pain of punishment. That this a priori reasoning approach to crime prevention is futile has already been well demonstrated in earlier material. Nevertheless this idea is widely accepted by the average layman. Moreover the average person believes the modern trend toward reformation in prisons is a miscarriage of justice. Convicts are sent to prison for punishment, which if severe enough will deter them, he alleges. But no one who is familiar with the outcome of penal treatment seriously believes that punishment itself is a means of crime prevention. In general punishment merely antagonizes the offender and makes him desire to get even with a society which treated him thus. It is not a constructive method with which to deal with offenders.

Penal Reforms as Crime Preventives

So far as preventing adult crime is concerned, prevention has been conceived largely as a matter of preventing recidivism. Hence most of what has been called crime prevention has been centered on penal treatment. The reformatory, the penitentiary, and probation, as the terms themselves indicate, are all in theory devoted to restoring the individual to the realm of the law abiding—by "reforming" the lawbreaker, by making him "penitent," or by requiring him to "prove" himself on probation.

PENAL INSTITUTIONS AS PREVENTIVES

Thus the introduction of education in penal institutions in the reformatory system and later within most prisons and more recently the development of classification have aimed at correcting the prisoners' criminal behavior. Thus far, at least, most of the institutional methods of penal treatment have proved unsuccessful, for the majority of prisoners are recidivists and a large number of them have committed several offenses. Any effective treatment of criminals obviously must incorporate methods of adjusting offenders to an acceptance of social values and must be related to its actual influence upon the offender's subsequent conduct.

Most institutional treatment has operated on unverified and un-justified assumptions. It has been assumed that if men are deprived of their liberty and privileges for an offense they will not wish to risk such deprivation a second time. Actually it seems that the prison sentence and the prison routine tend to make the majority of offenders bitter and resolved to commit an offense that will make society suffer further for having treated them so. There is nothing about most prisons to make men respect the society which incarcerated them. Hence the ex-convicts are usually cynical about any value to be derived from social conformity.

THE BORSTAL INSTITUTIONS. The Borstal Institutions in Great Britain have attracted much favorable notice for their individualized attention and supervision for youthful offenders—aged 16 to 23. Since this group includes most of the age group (19 to 24) which constitutes the modal group of adult offenders in America, the success of the institutions has been a stimulus to the Youth Correction Authority (and the California Adult Authority) in this country. Most of the British young offenders who serve more than 12 months are committed to Borstal Institutions. There are now 13 "Borstals" each attractively situated and each providing a special type of vocational training. Four of them are without walls. We cannot discuss all the aspects of their program, but a major emphasis is placed upon the influence of staff members and upon maintaining a close relationship with the young men. If a job is assigned, for example, the staff works with the boys, instead of directing them. The philosophy of the Borstal Institutions is that close association with men of high character (who serve as a sort of "father ideal" for the offender) is important in reorienting the young men. Personal influence (rather than psychiatric counseling) is thus a basic part of their therapy. The relationship of the staff is not "moralistic" but friendly. The main aim is to equip the boy to meet temptation when he returns to the world outside and to live as a well-adjusted citizen.

The daily routine is long, compared with American standards. The young men work 8 hours, have 2 hours for schooling, gymnasium, or hobbies, 2½ hours for meals (including tea in the afternoon), 1½ hours for house duties and physical training, 1 hour free, and 9 hours for sleep. This schedule is varied on Saturday, and Sunday is devoted to church, to hikes, lectures, concerts, etc.

The boy's time is virtually all absorbed and he has little time for sulking or rebelling. Furthermore his vocational training is directed by a person skilled not merely in the vocation he is supervising but also in dealing with the problems of the boy's behavior.

There is very little emphasis upon psychological diagnosis of the offenders but great concern that the young men emerge stripped of all the resentment and hostility with which they enter. A survey of the 13,294 "graduates" of the Borstal Institutions in 1936 showed that only 688 served a subsequent sentence or were held in detention. A later (less detailed) survey in 1942 showed most of the 15,000 ex-Borstal young men were married and owned their own homes. The friendly interest and helpful relationships at Borstal appear to be achieving results.[4]

PROBATION AS A METHOD OF CRIME PREVENTION

Probation has accomplished more in restoring American offenders to a law-abiding status than all the other types of penal treatment combined. The recent study of probation services in Alabama indicated that 77 per cent of the 1862 federal probationers in the Northern District of Alabama completed their probation successfully and 83.6 per cent had no further criminal record.[5] This figure is typical, as our analysis of probation in Chapter 21 shows. According to the Alabama study, factors which were associated with no further record were high occupational skill, full-time employment at adequate income, home ownership, marriage, and children. These from a superficial viewpoint are the earmarks of well-adjusted and successful members of civilian society. It seems obvious that it is easier for a man who has a family, a home of his own, and a good job at which he performs a skillful service to make a good adjustment than it is for a man with an unsatisfactory job, low income, and no family ties.

Such an explanation of successful probation is too simple, from this author's point of view. The question is: Why is a man on probation able to make a good living, find a satisfactory mate, own his own home? It must be that probation makes it easier for an offender to achieve these satisfactions. He is given a chance to prove himself with helpful assistance from his probation officer. He has a stimulus to make good and he suffers very little stigma from probation in contrast to what he would have suffered as an ex-convict. He is not continually

[4] Cf. William Healy and Benedict S. Alper, *Criminal Youth and the Borstal System*, Commonwealth Fund, New York, 1941, and Orie L. Phillips, "The Federal Youth Correction Act," *Federal Probation*, 15:3–11 (March, 1951).

[5] Morris G. Caldwell, "Review of a New Type of Probation Study Made in Alabama," *Federal Probation*, 15:3–11 (June, 1951).

restrained, coerced, and restricted by lock step or the routinization of his day. He is a free man so long as he measures up to social demands and he has great incentives to stay out of the restricted and stigmatized life in prison.

PAROLE AS PREVENTION

While satisfactory parole supervision employs the same case-work techniques as probation it is not as effective in producing non-recidivists as probation.[6] There may be several explanations. In the first place the parolees were persons not considered worthy of probation by the court in which they were tried. Secondly, they have suffered all the untoward reactions which prisoners experience in confinement often emerging from prison with a deep-seated hostility for society. Thirdly, our society has a much more kindly attitude toward the man placed on probation than toward the man released on parole. In the fourth place a much larger percentage of convicted offenders are placed on parole than probation, and the case loads of parole officers tend to be so high as to make careful supervision impossible. Much parole is parole in name only. A man is released and is expected to behave himself but often the parole officer never sees him until or unless he (the parolee) gets into trouble.

Private Piecemeal Efforts at Crime Prevention

Most of the organized efforts on the part of the community and local, state, and federal governments toward crime prevention projects have been on the juvenile level, as we discussed in the preceding chapter. The Chicago Area Project and the Back of the Yards Council have been two of the few attempts to include both juvenile and adult offenders in its community-sponsored rehabilitation program.

VOLUNTEER AGENCIES

There have been a variety of social agencies and organizations which have tried to rehabilitate adult offenders, however, including (1) the various Prisoners Aid Societies (by whatever name they may be designated), (2) the Salvation Army, (3) the Volunteers of America, (4) evangelical missions, and (5) Alcoholics Anonymous, as well as other organizations which are attempting, with varying degrees of success, to help ex-prisoners readjust to the community. Virtually all of these agencies have some religious orientation and aim to direct the prisoner

[6] Cf. chap. 27.

to a socially adjusted personality through the implementation of the religious resources of repentance, of prayer supplemented by practical assistance, and of conscious effort on the part of the prisoner to lead a law-abiding life. Undoubtedly many of these societies have done much to help men who are down and out. The Salvation Army and the Volunteers of America have gone after the ex-convict sinner who is both literally and figuratively in the gutter. We shall consider a few of these agencies here.

THE SALVATION ARMY

In recent years the Salvation Army has added professionally trained case workers to its staff and has attempted to understand the personality of the offender, as well as to supply religious motivation for his rehabilitation. The Army maintains a prison visiting committee and assumes the sponsorship for many parolees. The New York City office of the Army cares for approximately 2500 men and 1500 women. The Army also works with alcoholics, both men and women, provides homes for working girls, supplies work for the unemployed, runs boys' clubs, etc. Most of its work may be described as attempts at rehabilitation and prevention of crime and delinquency.[7]

PRISON AID SOCIETIES

Many of the prison aid societies have failed to recognize the need for more than religious appeals in their program of rehabilitation. Prisoners have sometimes accepted financial and other aid from these organizations pledging their intent to "lead a new and upright life" while secretly plotting the execution of another crime.

The Pennsylvania Prison Society is one of the important volunteer societies which has recognized the need for professional assistance. It is the oldest prison society in the country and was a potent factor in implementing penal reforms during both colonial times and the early federal period. Today the society maintains a variety of services to prisoners in prison and while on parole. This prison society sponsors a certain number of men for their first year of parole and helps men meet their adjustment problems on parole. A counseling service is maintained where men are given assistance or referred to other agencies. The society also works with parents in aiding young men and boys on release from institutions. During the 5 years from 1946 to 1950 inclusive the number of persons receiving service from the Pennsylvania Prison So-

[7] Douglas Bethune, correspondence dated August 22, 1951. Cf. also *Time*, 54:38–41 (December 26, 1949), for a feature article, "I Was a Stranger," on the work of the Salvation Army.

ciety varied from 764 to 935. Three full-time social workers and a part-time student assistant make up the professional staff.[8]

The Pennsylvania Prison Society, with its Quaker background, has had a religious orientation with reference to working with prisoners. It is significant that this organization has held to the belief in the redeemability of the offender. Its members pay dues but the organization receives most of its financing through the Philadelphia Community Chest.[9]

THE HELPING HAND INSTITUTE

No one can say how much hope and rehabilitation have come from evangelical missions where food, bed, and an outstretched hand have awaited the friendless ex-prisoner. One of the most notable of these organizations is the Helping Hand Institute in Kansas City, Missouri. Founded in 1894, this organization does not work exclusively with ex-prisoners. For men of all ages who are in need of a place to sleep, food, and help in getting a job are welcome. Here from 8000 to 9000 men are admitted annually. An estimated 80 to 90 per cent of them are alcoholics, a large number of whom have served sentences for misdemeanors in the county jail.[10] And because Kansas City has the largest ex-convict population (proportionately) of any city in the United States, a sizable proportion of the men who are its clients are ex-convicts seeking a temporary haven after release from prison.[11] (Kansas City is the largest city close to the Federal Penitentiary at Leavenworth, the Kansas State Penitentiary at Lansing, and the Missouri Penitentiary at Jefferson City, which location accounts for its floating ex-convict population.)

For those without funds the Helping Hand provides meals and a bed in a dormitory in return for a few hours' work. For those who can afford it beds are available at 10 cents or 25 cents a night, and simple wholesome food is obtainable for a small price. Much of the food is produced on a farm which the institution owns and operates. Many men who come to the institution find work and health in employment at the farm. For men who find employment in the city, individual rooms are available on a weekly basis. In the public rooms the men play games, converse, read, or just sit. Many of the lonely men merely

[8] "One Hundred Sixty-Fourth Annual Report, Pennsylvania Prison Society," *Prison World*, 31:1–12 (January, 1951).

[9] *Ibid.*, p. 26.

[10] J. D. Robins, Jr., Executive Director of Helping Hand Institute, correspondence dated August 1, 1951.

[11] *Ibid.*

sit. If they wish they may go into the chapel for the nonsectarian services held every evening and on Sunday morning, but there is no compulsion. For the men who desire it there is personal counseling. For those who are ill a free medical clinic is maintained and little services such as free telephone, a stamp and stationery, shaving articles, and carfare are also provided.

The Helping Hand also maintains a separate institution for women in dire need and away from home. This is in another part of the city. Because there are fewer "homeless" women the group served is smaller but is equally in need of help.[12]

Both the men's and women's institutions are representative of numerous organizations which are geared to helping those who have nowhere else to turn. Although there never has been any attempt to find out how effective their assistance program is, the staff of the Helping Hand believe they have aided many former misdemeanants and felons to be useful, law-abiding citizens.

ALCOHOLICS ANONYMOUS

While Alcoholics Anonymous helps many men who have not served sentences for being intoxicated, the latter have been just as drunk as the "bums" who are rounded up by the police and committed to the county jail. They are guilty of the same misdemeanor, but most of the members of Alcoholics Anonymous come from a stratum which suffers few arrests—for they are often educated business and professional men who have become confirmed alcoholics.

Alcoholics Anonymous draws from both psychiatry and religion in developing its program, but emphasizes the help and strength which is derived from religious faith in a power higher than oneself. The A.A.'s also depend upon the understanding and help which can come only from those who know what it is to be a victim of alcohol. Hence the A.A. members give the alcoholic who turns to them additional strength to meet his problem. The members of A.A. are living evidence that it is possible to give up drinking and to give it up permanently.

Older A.A. members act as sponsors for new members who are trying to break the habit. They rush to help the man who has the urge to take another drink, and, as has been said, they not merely sit with the patient, they sometimes sit on him to prevent him from taking the one drink which will lead to a drinking spree. Knowledge that the ex-alcoholic can help a fellow alcoholic is a major source of strength to the sponsor. Certainly no other method has been so successful in keep-

[12] *Ibid.*

ing the alcoholic from his cups. According to collected figures 50 per cent of the A.A.'s never drink again and a further 25 per cent are eventually able to break the habit permanently.[13]

In recent years chapters have been organized in the various prisons. At the California Institution for Women at Tehachapi nearly one-fifth of the inmates were members of A.A. in 1946.[14] When a prison A.A. is released, some presently law-abiding citizen who has participated in prison chapter meetings arranges to meet him at the gate. If the ex-prisoner is going to another city he is met there by another A.A. If he is merely in a city for several hours between trains he is also met by a man who takes him for lunch or a cup of coffee and a pleasant chat. Helping the ex-convict A.A. make his initial adjustment in what he probably regards as a hostile and unfriendly world may be a real step in his success on parole.[15]

MIGHT A "PRISONERS ANONYMOUS" HELP?

The success of the Alcoholics Anonymous raises the question as to whether or not an ex-convict or ex-prisoner organization composed of men who have made good might not provide an equally valuable service to newly paroled prisoners. It seems possible that men who are resolved to make good on release from prison might receive powerful assistance from those who have made a successful adjustment.

There is, however, an essential difference between Alcoholics Anonymous and the majority of ex-convicts. Most of the members of Alcoholics Anonymous are relatively well-educated persons, as we have mentioned. They are usually men of extremely sensitive sort and men who thoroughly disapprove of their own disastrous conduct. It seems likely that a much larger share of the total ex-prisoners do not deplore their own conduct than is true of those who have become members of Alcoholics Anonymous. A more satisfactory type of treatment such as that now attempted by the California Adult Authority may induce a larger group of prisoners toward a desire to lead a law-abiding life.[16]

Women Police

A single but important attempt at crime prevention has developed as a function of local government through the creation of women

[13] "A.A.," Alcoholic Foundation, New York, 1943, p. 1–28. John Alexander, "Alcoholics Anonymous," Saturday Evening Post, 9:12 (March 1, 1941).

[14] John R. Ellingston, Protecting Our Children from Criminal Careers, Prentice-Hall, New York, 1948, Appendix, "The Adult Authority," p. 359.

[15] James Finan, "There Is No Prison Problem," Federal Probation, 15:15–21 (March, 1951).

[16] The California Adult Authority is discussed later on in this chapter.

police for both street patrol and investigative duties. Virtually all of the work of policewomen may be considered as crime prevention since they seek out the situations which are conducive to crime and try to keep women and girls (and children, whether boys or girls) from becoming delinquent or criminal.

In general policewomen are social workers armed with the authority of the law (whether or not they are graduates of duly qualified schools of social work). Portland, Oregon, claims to have had the first woman police. She was authorized to deal with the various women who were in trouble or in difficulty at the World's Fair held there in 1905.[17] The appointment of policewomen increased slowly until World War I, when the need for them was highlighted by the wartime problems of prostitution, as well as by the necessity for protecting women employed in war production plants.

The contribution of policewomen has proved itself during the years and today there are 1000 such police employed in 141 cities over 2,500,000 in population.[18] The majority of policewomen are employed in the larger cities although there are a few policewomen in the smaller places. The policewomen's bailiwick is in patrolling those streets and keeping an eye on questionable places where young girls may be in special danger, e.g., bus stations, amusement places, taverns and other places serving alcoholic drinks. The policewoman ferrets out the places where crimes and delinquencies among women may be expected to occur and "nips them in the bud" where possible. She is thus engaged in "on the spot" prevention as well as in law enforcement.[19] The preventive work of policewomen has provided the background for the development of preventive work for police departments as a whole, as discussed briefly in Chapter 17.

The Role of the Judge in Crime Prevention

The role of the judge in any present-day rehabilitative program is a crucial one, and one which is too often fraught with both confusion and professional jealousy. At the meetings of the National Probation and Parole Association held in Pittsburgh in 1951, for example, juvenile court judges expressed both fear and disdain in apprehension lest the social workers should pre-empt the judges' tasks in deal-

---

[17] Cf. Mabel A. Elliott, *Conflicting Penal Theories in Statutory Criminal Law*, University of Chicago Press, Chicago, 1931, p. 162.

[18] Anonymous, *The American City*, 63:17 (February, 1948).

[19] Cf. National Advisory Police Committee on Social Protection of the Federal Security Agency, *Techniques of Law Enforcement in the Use of Policewomen with Special Reference to Social Protection*, Federal Security Agency, Washington, 1945, pp. 1–14.

ing with offenders. Many judges apparently believe that their traditional authority is sacrosanct, whereas case workers, psychologists, and psychiatrists are convinced that few judges really know how to deal with the cases after the verdict is in and the sentence imposed.

Frequently, in fact, judges pursue little pet formulas. A juvenile court judge known to the author in a large midwestern city dismissed virtually every boy brought into court with a dime and the injunction to learn the Lord's Prayer and to report back in 2 weeks. If the boys could repeat the Lord's Prayer the judge apparently believed that they were on the way to successful readjustment. On the other hand, judges sometimes receive undeserved praise. A Temporary Study Committee on Crime and Delinquency of the New York School of Social Work made a proposal recently that the judicial practice be raised to a new level of performance, stating that "most infractions of the law can be and are dealt with by judges without the need of correctional treatment by institution or probation officer, some four-fifths of all cases are disposed of by the judge through reprimand and fine or order of restitution."[20]

This committee, which numbers among its members nationally known social workers, should know that no judge can expect to have the insight and understanding to deal with an offender as effectively as might a probation officer who has made a detailed investigation of the case. It has been traditional for judges to assume an omniscience they do not have in dealing with criminal and delinquency cases and it is high time they were made aware of their limitations. In fact, in this same report the committee pointed out the enormous power, the diverse decisions, and the lack of information and understanding which characterize the judges' manipulation of cases and maintained that judges should refer offenders to an appropriately constituted statutory authority which should take charge of their treatment and rehabilitation.[21]

SOCIAL ACTION IN CRIME PREVENTION

Community Attempts at Crime Control

As the result of increased understanding there have been many attacks on the crime program by local communities and by state groups both civil and governmental. Most of the community efforts have been through voluntary citizen organizations. In fact co-ordinated commu-

[20] Philip Klein, Next Steps in Dealing with Delinquency, Bulletin of the New York School of Social Work, New York, July, 1945, p. 12.
[21] Ibid., p. 40.

nity action on adult crime control has developed chiefly in the form of local crime commissions.

The following crime commissions are now functioning in their respective local communities:[22]

Baltimore Criminal Justice Commission, Inc., Baltimore, Maryland.

Chicago Crime Commission, Chicago, Illinois.

Cleveland Crime Commission, Cleveland, Ohio.

Dallas Crime Commission, Dallas, Texas.

Gary Crime Commission, Gary, Indiana.

Citizens Crime Commission, Indianapolis, Indiana.

The Crime Commission of Greater Jacksonville, Jacksonville, Florida.

Kansas City Crime Commission, Kansas City, Missouri.

Crime Commission of Greater Miami, Miami, Florida.

The New York City Anti-Crime Committee, Inc., New York, New York.

Commercial Crime Commission, New York, New York.

Crime Prevention Ass'n of Philadelphia, Philadelphia, Pennsylvania.

St. Louis Crime Commission, St. Louis, Missouri.

Hillsborough County Crime Commission, Tampa, Florida.

Washington Criminal Justice Association, Washington, D.C.

Most of the local crime commissions grew out of the general alarm following World War I at the increase in crime and especially in violent crime which characterized the period. Citizens became so aroused that many state and local governments or groups of citizens operating independently set up organizations both to study crime conditions and to develop ways and means for dealing with them. Many of these have persisted as local gadfly organizations. In addition there are various state, interstate, and national commissions which have been organized from time to time to investigate conditions and suggest remedies for the prevention and control of crime. We shall consider a few of the important local and state commissions as well as the recent interstate and national commissions.

THE CHICAGO CRIME COMMISSION

The Chicago Crime Commission is believed to be the earliest organization attempting to deal with the rising crime rate following

[22] Data furnished by Virgil W. Peterson, Operating Director of Chicago Crime Commission, as of June 8, 1951.

World War I. As a matter of fact this commission grew out of the public indignation occasioned by the robbing of the pay-roll money for employees of a plant producing shell casings for munitions in 1917. A committee of 10 appointed to investigate the crime proposed the creation of a local crime commission. Out of this recommendation the Chicago Crime Commission was organized in January, 1919. Comprised "of important business interests and the best citizens," it became the first citizens' gadfly organization in putting down crime. The Chicago Crime Commission since has developed unusual resources in investigating crime and checking on the administration of criminal justice and has stimulated many other cities to form similar organizations.[23]

The Chicago Crime Commission has functioned continuously ever since its organization. It now has a membership of approximately 130, including prominent businessmen, industrialists, and professional men. In addition to the usual list of officers there is a full-time operating staff, the head of which is designated "operating director." The group includes an assistant operating director, an administrative assistant, a docket and statistical department staff, filing department staff, court observers (who go to court hearings and trials to check on the administration of criminal justice), investigational department staff, stenographers, and secretary.

The investigational department makes investigations of cases in which authorities do not live up to their duties and more or less compels them to perform properly. The Commission has been effective, for example, in securing a reform in a notorious bail bond situation and in the waiving of felony counts in Chicago. The Commission sponsored the Uniform Motor Vehicle Theft Act which reduced interstate activities on the part of automobile thieves. Racketeering has been widely curbed by the Commission. In addition to other objectives it is trying (1) to remove police from political control, (2) to put suitable job prerequisites for police into effect, (3) to remove civil service from political controls, (4) to destroy the "unholy" alliance between organized crime and politics, (5) to improve the caliber of men in public office, and (6) to keep the public informed with reference to existing crime conditions.[24]

The work of the court observers, who "put the fear of the Lord" into the hearts of the judges and prosecuting attorneys, and the extensive investigations carried on by the Chicago Crime Commission have fur-

---

[23] Virgil W. Peterson, *Crime Commissions in the United States*, Chicago Crime Commission, Chicago, 1945, pp. 1–3.

[24] *Ibid.*, pp. 28–29.

ther demonstrated that citizens can exercise some coercion over corrupt officials and lawbreakers in their midst. The Commission has come to be a vigilance committee for the citizens as a whole.

The present operating director, Mr. Virgil W. Peterson, a trained lawyer who formerly served with the F.B.I., has become one of the best-informed men in America on the far-reaching network of organized crime in our several states. Mr. Peterson's testimony before the Senate hearings on organized crime formed the groundwork for the hearings held in various metropolitan cities by the Senate Commission on Organized Crime (popularly known as the Kefauver Committee) during 1950–1951. It is fortunate that citizens in Chicago have recognized that crime is a perennial problem and that a continuing organization of public-minded citizens is essential to keeping down crime. A number of excellent organizations (such as the Kansas City Law Enforcement Association of Kansas City, Missouri) have been organized to combat a serious crime situation and have later passed out of existence. The Kansas City group was organized in 1920 and ceased functioning 12 years later. Similarly the Los Angeles Commission, created in 1922, went out of existence in 1928.[25]

State and Interstate Commissions

Most of the state and federal action with reference to adult crime has been on the investigative level. A number of states thus have made "crime surveys" which have varied in purpose and procedure. Two of the more important have been the *Missouri Crime Survey* (published in 1926), which was concerned mainly with the administration of justice, and the *Illinois Crime Survey*, which was concerned primarily with the treatment of the offender. Both of these surveys contained material which should have aroused the public, but the materials were never made the basis of any significant educational campaign. The Missouri Survey we have already discussed, in Chapter 19.

The Illinois Crime Survey

The *Illinois Crime Survey* (published in 1929)[26] was sponsored by the Illinois Association for Criminal Justice, a state-wide organization composed of the representatives of a wide variety of organizations including the Illinois Chamber of Commerce, the Illinois Federation of Labor, the Illinois State Bankers Association, the Industrial Club of Chicago, the Chicago Crime Commission, the Illinois Federation of

[25] *Ibid.*, pp. 3–4.
[26] The *Illinois Crime Survey*, directed by Arthur V. Lashly and edited by John H. Wigmore, Illinois Association for Criminal Justice, Chicago, 1929.

Women's Clubs, the Illinois League of Women Voters, and other interested private and public welfare agencies.[27]

This survey covered 3 general areas:

1. The machinery of justice.
2. Specific types of offenses and offenders.
3. Organized crime in Chicago.

The first section of the survey, on the machinery of justice, embraced the general methods of criminal procedure—grand jury investigations, preliminary hearings, trials, convictions, dispositions, sentences, bail, probation and parole, and numerous other items. In this connection the whole problem of time lapses, the matter of bond forfeiture, "nolle prosses," the integrity of judges, and many other items which enter into determining whether or not the guilty are convicted were covered.

The second part of the survey was concerned with an exploration of juvenile delinquency in Illinois and a special analysis of defective and deranged offenders. The survey on organized crime in Chicago ventilated the extensive ramifications of prostitution and gambling and the interrelated problems of racketeering, bootlegging, and gang warfare. This Illinois survey was in fact one of the first fearless attacks on the gangsters involved in Chicago's underworld. Life histories of certain notorious gangsters were made public, and the intimate connection between corrupt politics and organized crime was exposed. By this survey every criminologist in America was made aware of the fabulous returns accruing from the illicit liquor industry. The study also established the antisocial philosophy of the gangsters who scorned the honest workingman's struggle for an honest pittance when a fortune could be made through racketeering. The *Illinois Crime Survey* proved to be the historical antecedent to the hearings conducted by the United States Senate Special Committee to Investigate Organized Crime in Interstate Commerce during 1950 and 1951 which is discussed later on in this chapter.

OTHER EARLY STATE CRIME COMMISSIONS

There were other state crime commissions of varying importance. In 1926 there was so much lawlessness in the widely separated states of Nebraska and New York that both of these states also created crime commissions. The sheriffs and county attorneys were instrumental in forming the state organization in Nebraska. The Nebraska commission was organized by persons chosen because of their local leadership (chiefly businessmen) in the various counties of the state.

[27] *Ibid.*, p. 11.

The New York State Crime Commission was created by legislative enactment in 1926 and consisted of 11 members, 6 from the state legislature and 5 appointed by the governor. This organization grew out of the earlier work of the New York State Senate's Crime Commission, which enacted the so-called Baumes Law (or habitual offender act) in 1926. There were six subcommissions appointed to serve under the New York Commission to study and report to the legislature on (1) statistics of crime, (2) the causes and effects of crime, (3) the police problems, (4) penal institutions in New York, (5) the adjustment of sentences, and (6) the courts. This commission served for 5 years (from 1926 to 1931).[28]

THE CALIFORNIA ADULT AUTHORITY

California is now engaged in the most notable experiment in penal treatment which has been undertaken by any state, with the idea of rehabilitating the offender. In 1944 California adopted a Prison Reorganization Act which aims to apply the same principles as those incorporated in the Youth Authority to adult criminals. This act provided for a Director of Corrections and three-member Adult Authority. Working together, they have the responsibility for developing (1) diagnostic services, (2) treatment based upon the diagnosis, and (3) replacement of offenders in society. These services intend to replace the old "patchwork" type of facilities and services which previously met the needs of prisoners.[29]

According to the provisions of the act, two Guidance Centers were set up at which all men committed by the courts are received (except those awaiting the death penalty). These Guidance Centers, supervised by the Classification Bureau, are located at San Quentin and at the Vocational Institution at Lancaster, but eventually they will be moved to Vacaville and Chino. Here the men are studied from various angles. Information is obtained from the prisoner's family (and other relatives), the police, the sheriff, the officer who accompanies him to the center, and his former associates. These data are elicited by a questionnaire, which is mailed to the informant in a plain envelope so as to minimize embarrassment to the person addressed.[30]

At the Guidance Center the men themselves are asked to explore their own problems in consultation with staff members in order to make them see their "quarrel with society." Group discussions are held

28 Virgil W. Peterson, op. cit., pp. 6–8.
29 John R. Ellingston, op. cit.
30 Ibid., pp. 353–354.

to help the men understand that theirs are common difficulties. The fact that the California's correctional system is organized with the idea of helping the men is presented and emphasized.[31] After a period of from 4 to 8 weeks at the diagnostic center a report is sent to the Adult Authority which the members of the Authority study (along with any other data they may have secured). The prisoner is then asked to appear before the Authority in an informal hearing. On the basis of this and a consideration of all the facts the man or woman receives a definite sentence to one of the California correction institutions. This sentence can be reduced at any time and parole may be permitted at any time that it is deemed advisable.[32] In short, the whole program is individualized.

The institution to which the prisoner is assigned is presumably the one best suited to his particular needs. In order to make this placement possible the Adult Authority has developed a variety of institutions for different types of offenders. The Authority inherited the maximum security state prison at Folsom for dangerous offenders, the industrial prison at San Quentin for older and hardened offenders, and the minimum security prison at Chino for younger and less hardened offenders. Forestry camps have operated out of both San Quentin and Chino, and at San Quentin road-building camps were developed for working on the state highways. The camp work of these institutions has since been extended; three facilities have been added for adult correction. These include the California Medium Custody prison at Soledad, which has a work program almost entirely agricultural; the California Vocational Institution at Lancaster (which is shared with the Youth Authority), for young persons from both the youth and adult groups who need more supervision and training than either Chino or the institutions for more stable youths supply; and the Medical Facility at Vacaville, which provides medical and psychiatric treatment for the chronically ill, the mentally ill, the defective, the psychopathic, and the sexual deviates (chiefly homosexuals). In addition the Women's Institution at Tehachapi, which it proposes to move near Chino, is now under the Adult Authority.[33]

The Adult Authority has already made many changes in the penal treatment of California convicts. As a result of its recommendations, the habitual offender laws of California have been revised downward, although they still limit the minimum sentence and individual treatment possible for habitual offenders. The classification system of each institution now prepares men for parole, but the parole officers work directly with the Adult Authority.

[31] *Ibid.*, pp. 354–355.   [32] *Ibid.*, p. 355.   [33] *Ibid.*, pp. 356–358.

The Adult Authority has recognized the need for providing more adequate funds to tide the parolees over the period between "gate release" and securing a job, and has been able to persuade the legislature to give each man $40 instead of the customary $10. Paroled prisoners have also had their privileges extended. They now have the right to marry and to transfer property restored. As must be obvious many profound changes in attitudes are necessary for any state correctional institution to enter wholeheartedly into developing a system basically committed to helping the men become socially adjusted. The Authority has likewise been engaged in studying the influences which operate in building constructive and destructive attitudes among the men in all institutions.[34] Although limitations are still imposed by the maximum security institutions and habitual offender laws, California is obviously taking a significant step in the right direction, and one in harmony with the trend in the federal Bureau of Prisons.

THE INTERSTATE COMMISSION ON CRIME AND ITS PROPOSALS

Many crime problems are interstate in nature because criminals are continually crossing state borders. In order to alleviate some of the difficulties involved in arresting fugitive criminals (as well as in cooperating in other ways in the administration of justice) an Interstate Commission on Crime was organized in 1942. It is composed of official representatives of all 48 states and the federal government and aims basically at securing uniform legislation in the several states with reference to certain distinct problems. These legislative proposals include the following:

1. The adoption of a uniform act with reference to "fresh pursuit" of criminals across state lines, in order to permit the sheriff or police officers to cross state lines to apprehend and arrest criminals.[35] By 1951, 37 states and the federal government had adopted such legislation, according to information received from the various state attorney generals.

2. The adoption of a uniform extradition act providing that fugitives of justice be returned by the warrant of the governor in the state in which such fugitives are hiding to the proper agents of the states in which the fugitives are wanted for the crimes.[36] By 1951, 40 states had adopted such provisions.[37]

[34] Ibid., pp. 360–363.
[35] The Handbook on Interstate Crime Control, Interstate Commission on Crime, Newark, New Jersey, 1942, pp. 16–22.
[36] Ibid., pp. 23–31.
[37] Information was received by correspondence with the various attorney generals covering states which had not enacted the legislation at the time the handbook was issued.

These two provisions offer more effective means for apprehending offenders who might otherwise be able to flee from justice. Formerly it was very difficult to secure the return of criminals from distant states. As the discussion on frontier mores in an early chapter indicates, there were many outlaws in the newly settled western states. Governors were expected to facilitate the return of criminals by the provision of the federal Constitution, but often there was no machinery either to facilitate or to compel this. These provisions represent two important ways of bringing offenders to justice and have been regarded as means of making punishment far more certain than before such law existed. The Interstate Commission on Crime has also developed model laws for providing for a uniform arrest act for interstate supervision of probationers and parolees, and additional laws providing for the restriction of the use of firearms and for the gathering of uniform statistics on the part of all the states. The uniform arrest act provides for stopping persons under reasonable suspicion and detaining them for as long as 2 hours. This act also makes it possible to arrest persons reasonably presumed to have committed a misdemeanor. Since common-law usage permits arrests on suspicion only for suspected felonies, such a provision might conceivably result in wider apprehension of offenders. The uniform arrest act has not had wide support, however.

Since so many serious crimes are committed by armed criminals, some method of reducing the carrying of dangerous weapons is patently desirable. During the twenties and thirties numerous laws were enacted to increase the penalties in case criminals employed firearms, but these laws were seldom invoked.[38] The proposed uniform act aims to make it "harder for criminals to secure a pistol and more dangerous for them to keep one."[39]

The need for more effective supervision of probationers and parolees has been discussed in earlier chapters. Anything which the several states can promote through interstate legislation to make it possible to place probationers and parolees to their own advantage is a step in the right direction and one which promises mutual helpfulness in reducing recidivism. More than three-fourths of the states have signed compacts to supervise probationers and parolees. Here, unfortunately, the spirit is willing but the facilities are weak. There are many difficulties inherent in transportation of parolees and probationers. There is possibility of their defying rules, the lack of adequate supervision because

[38] Cf. Mabel A. Elliott, op. cit., chap. 11.
[39] The Handbook on Interstate Crime Control, p. 110.

of too heavy case loads, etc. The problem of returning a parole or probation violator from a distance is also complicated by interstate supervision. Extradition agreements or laws are not binding on parolees or probationers. Many persons believe therefore that reciprocal agreements permitting placements between adjoining states are far more satisfactory in case of probationers and parolees than general agreements involving the United States as a whole.

A fifth proposal of the Interstate Crime Commission is for a uniform criminal statistics act to be enacted by the several states. Present-day statistics on the extent of crime are incomplete and wholly unreliable, as we discussed in Chapter 3, "The Extent and Distribution of Crime." If the model act proposed were enacted by all 48 states and the District of Columbia it would require designated officials to report crimes accurately and to give detailed social data with reference to age, sex, race, nativity, mental and physical characteristics, educational achievement, and vocational history, as well as previous criminal record. This proposal is to be commended, for only with reliable and accurate information on the extent of crime can we evaluate the effectiveness of any rehabilitative or preventive programs.[40]

In 1946 the Bureau of the Census abandoned its practice of gathering statistics on prisoners and turned this duty over to the federal Bureau of Prisons.[41] The latter unfortunately has no power to compel state and local prisons to submit statistical data nor has it had adequate financial appropriations to publish the data it has collected. Criminal statistics of offenses reported to the police, collected by the F.B.I., cover urban areas, and rates in smaller places and the open country are estimations. Police statistics are notoriously inaccurate, depending upon many variables, as we have already mentioned.[42] An accurate picture of the extent of crime is desirable in developing any program of crime prevention.

Federal Commissions

THE NATIONAL COMMISSION ON LAW OBSERVANCE AND ENFORCEMENT

Although most of our crime problem is a matter of state rather than federal jurisdiction, the federal government has conducted surveys on

---

[40] Thorsten Sellin, "The Uniform Criminal Statistics Act," *Journal of Criminal Law and Criminology*, 40:679–700 (March–April, 1950).

[41] *Ibid.* Cf. also chap. 3.

[42] Chap. 3, pp. 49–51.

various aspects of interstate crime problems. One of the most important of these national surveys on crime was that conducted by the National Commission on Law Observance and Enforcement and incorporated in 14 monumental volumes which the commission published in 1931.[43] Scholars of national reputation were recruited for the various studies the Commission undertook. These covered many areas of law-breaking and law enforcement, ranging from the juvenile offender to the adult criminal and from the police to the deportation of foreign-born criminals. The Commission's report on the *Enforcement of the Prohibition Laws in the United States*,[44] however, was its most important survey for its findings led to the repeal of the national prohibition amendment. The repeal occurred chiefly, that is, because of the disclosures as to the lawlessness which the prohibition of liquor manufacture and sale appeared to stimulate. The enormous profits in bootlegging, the tremendous corruption in metropolitan politics, the great expense entailed in maintaining prohibition agents and police in the attempt to prevent the manufacture and sale of liquor were all exposed. In consequence many honest persons, including John D. Rockefeller, Jr.,[45] became convinced that prohibition laws were actually promoting a great reign of lawlessness rather than inducing sobriety. Moreover the lawless purveyors of illicit liquor not only were carrying on warfare among themselves, they were terrorizing law-abiding citizens in many cities and undermining the whole structure of government as well.

The repeal of the Nineteenth Amendment in November, 1932, was thus a direct result of the federal report. How much crime repeal has prevented is hard to say. Alcoholism has not decreased and there is still much illicit activity in the promotion of the liquor trade, as discussed in Chapter 6. Nevertheless the profits of bootlegging and the gunfire between rival gangster groups on city streets have both declined.

Many important recommendations were made by the Commission with reference to the appointment of police, lawlessness of police, the unfortunate lack of training and insecurity of office of chiefs of police. The need for uniformity in our criminal laws and criminal statistics was stressed, as well as the need for men of character and ability in positions of prosecuting attorneys. The Commission also published

---

[43] Published by the United States Printing Office, 1931.

[44] Cf. National Commission on Law Observance and Enforcement, *Enforcement of the Prohibition Laws*, Washington, 1931, Vols. I–V.

[45] John D. Rockefeller, Jr., "The Failure of Prohibition," *Review of Reviews*, 86:42 (July, 1932).

two of the most important compilations on the causes of delinquency and crime.[46]

THE SENATE INVESTIGATION OF ORGANIZED CRIME—1950–1951

The repeal of prohibition did not put an end to crime. Instead crime rates have increased with successive years. In fact following World War II crimes and rumors of crimes began to plague the conscience of the nation. In consequence a Special Committee to Investigate Organized Crime in Interstate Commerce of the United States Senate was set up under Senate Resolution 202 of the Eighty-First Congress. This committee, popularly known as the Kefauver Committee (because Senator Estes Kefauver served as its chairman) conducted widely publicized hearings on organized crime at the request of local officials in many of the larger cities throughout the country. The hearings were given much space in the press and many of them were broadcast. The fabulous hearings in New York City in which Frank Costello and other underworld figures and former Mayor O'Dwyer appeared were televised. Stenographic reports of the hearings were printed in a series of some 19 reports (with separate reports published for hearings in the particular state). Such hearings were held in Florida, Louisiana, California, Missouri, Illinois, Pennsylvania, New York, and elsewhere. The major revelations were the enormous income derived from gambling throughout the country and the close affiliation between gambling and other types of organized crime and local corrupt politics. The extensive network of relationships among gamblers was also revealed. Many of these gamblers who were also gangsters were in the numbers and policy rackets. The testimony indicated that gangsters were getting their information by wire and telephone. This made it obvious that some sort of interstate regulation of gambling might be inaugurated by prohibiting interstate use of communications systems for such a purpose.[47]

As a result of the hearings local clean-up campaigns were stimulated, and a number of gangsters and gamblers were indicted for perjury. Actually Congress has no control over most of the activities in which the gangsters engage, but these hearings have been an entering wedge in the development of interstate crime control. One of the truly salu-

[46] Cf. Reports 1–14 of the National Commission on Law Observance and Enforcement, op. cit.

[47] Cf. Investigation of Organized Crime in Interstate Commerce, Hearings Before the Special Committee to Investigate Organized Crime in Interstate Commerce, U.S. Senate, 81st Congress, 2nd Session, and 82nd Congress, 1st Session. Reports 1 to 19, Washington, 1950, 1951.

tary aspects of the hearings has been the awakened public conscience and the impetus to improving law enforcement on the state and municipal level. Aroused citizens have demanded improvements in policing, and local investigations have been made where the Kefauver Committee did not hold hearings. Awareness of any problem is a first step in solving it, and the Kefauver Committee has apprised every hamlet in the country of the extensive lawlessness on the part of "respectable" citizens who gamble as well as that of the professional gamblers and racketeers. One of the rackets publicized was the extensive gambling on slot machines. As a result Congress passed a law forbidding the sale of slot machines as an article of interstate commerce, as mentioned earlier. The law undoubtedly decreased this form of lawlessness. Virtually all states but Nevada had laws forbidding their operation earlier, but they were widely installed in private clubs, resort hotels, etc.[48]

Certain states have since forbidden the transmission of racing form numbers until after races are run. Others have forbidden the transmission of gambling information by wire or telephone, but control of communication is obviously very difficult. Meanwhile the federal law requiring gamblers to register and pay a tax has dealt a crushing blow to gambling as we have mentioned earlier.

Prevention on an International Level

We are in the process of recognizing that any effective program for crime prevention for the nation as a whole must operate on federal, state, and local level. We are likewise just beginning to recognize that crime, like disease, is not confined by national boundaries, and that many problems in the reduction and prevention of crime are international in character. In fact the greatest criminals of our generation may well be the international gangsters who have plundered and pillaged countries and condemned millions of people to death or torture in their mad pursuit for power in the game of geopolitics. This international aspect of gangster tactics is a question which owing to its nature and complexity we cannot discuss in detail. But we must point out that the horrors and values of modern war are so disruptive to the accepted ethical concepts of civilized society that they provoke aggressive and hostile tendencies which persist when war is over. Meanwhile the destruction of war produces (for those peoples vanquished or

[48] This topic has been discussed in chap. 6, "The Professional Criminal and Organized Crime."

despoiled by war) the very frustrations which lead to criminal conduct.

From a purely ethical point of view war is an outrage against all the concepts of civilized behavior. In modern society war may also be defined as a crime perpetrated on one nation or group of nations by another nation or group of nations. But the crime of aggressive war is met by another, defensive aggression. The brutality, violence, deception, and destruction which carrying on war entails must set back our moral behavior just as surely as a depression sets back our expenditure. War presents many moral dilemmas to the modern state because it authorizes crimes in the name of political security. How far international efforts can go in reducing crime while engaging in warfare is a major question.

In the meantime the United Nations has concluded that crime and its control is both an internal national problem and one of international importance. At its seventh session, in August, 1948, the Economic and Social Council of the United Nations assumed the responsibility for attempting to prevent crime (and to treat offenders) on an international level. This phase of this United Nations committee's work has functioned chiefly through existing organizations specifically devoted to crime and penal affairs. These organizations include:

The International Association of Penal Law.

Nordic Association of Criminologists.

International Bureau for Unification of Penal Law.

International Penal and Penitentiary Commission.

International Criminal Police Commission.

Howard League for Penal Reform.

Several other international organizations which are concerned with economic, health, education, law, child welfare, and statistical research have also participated in the meetings on crime prevention and treatment because it is recognized that all these welfare problems are related to the problem of crime. These other organizations are:

International Labor Organization.

World Health Organization.

United Nations Educational, Scientific and Cultural Organization.

International Institute of Statistics.

International Law Association.

International Union for Child Welfare.

A wide variety of studies on crime prevention and penal treatment international in scope have been proposed and are on the agenda for the

Economic and Social Council. In the meantime the organization is aiming to improve the administration of criminal justice in backward countries and to exchange information on research and experience in advanced countries.[49]

RESEARCH IN CRIME PREVENTION

The discovery of ways and means of preventing crime is obviously part of the picture. All enlightened attempts at the prevention of crime should take into consideration the interrelated nature of the various community welfare problems. This recognition was clearly demonstrated by a second research project in St. Paul. The Community Research Associates, Incorporated, under Bradley Buell's direction, made an intensive study of all the families who presented problems and received service from the city's 108 public and private agencies dealing with dependency, ill health, maladjustment, and lack of recreational opportunity. Maladjustment covered two categories: (1) officially recorded antisocial behavior and (2) diagnosed mental or emotional illness or incapacity to assume proper responsibility. The findings have been summarized by Richard A. Chappell.[50]

From the study it was found that economic need, ill health, and maladjustment were clustered in the same families. Forty-one thousand families were serviced by the various agencies in 1 month. Of these families, the 6600 which had two or more difficulties absorbed 68 per cent of the dependency services, 46 per cent of the health services, and 55 per cent of the adjustment services.

These data indicate clearly that people who come to an agency because of one difficulty usually have several different problems. It would seem that effective co-operation by the agencies might do much to help these families achieve social adjustment when this is the basic problem. Any preventive program on the part of welfare agencies should certainly include joint planning of services, since ill health, economic insecurity, mental illness, family tensions, and antisocial behavior are so closely related.

Richard A. Chappell, Chief of the Federal Probation Service, suggests that a "family mental health center," equipped with an able psychiatrist, psychologist, and case worker, should be able to diagnose

[49] Adolphe Delierneux, "The United Nations in the Field of Prevention of Crime and Treatment of Offenders," *National Probation and Parole Association Yearbook*, 1949, New York, 1950, pp. 248–258.

[50] Richard A. Chappell, "Some Realities in the Prevention of Social Maladjustment," *Federal Probation*, 15:33–36 (June, 1951).

and treat the various disturbances which are so disruptive to family life, since so much delinquency and crime apparently stem from broken homes and all the attendant economic and emotional insecurity broken homes occasion.[51]

Need for Further Research

Whatever preventive programs are launched, at this juncture at least, should be undertaken on the basis of the insights our study of offenders has given up to now. Many programs are by the very nature of the situation experimental because one cannot be certain how far they may succeed. Treatment which overcomes the frustrations of the individual, for example, would, from the psychiatrist's viewpoint, offer some hope of overcoming the delinquencies which grow out of that kind of despair. The only way this viewpoint can be tested is to run a series of tests with enough cases to give some reliable index to the success or failure of such treatment.

Treatment of the offender can probably be improved in many ways. More effective classification procedures could probably be achieved if the outcome of cases were studied after certain procedures had been initiated.[52] It seems likely that the success of any classification program must depend upon the impact of the staff upon the individual prisoner, and this is more difficult to measure than to observe. We have already emphasized the importance of the classification service in producing a well-adjusted prisoner. Classification procedures are still in the experimental stage. It is therefore important to study and analyze the classification process with reference to its effect upon the prisoner's adjustment.

Predictive studies of probable success or failure on parole have been useful in determining parole policies in certain states and have apparently prevented recidivism, at least to a certain extent. We can look forward to predictive studies in relation to classification.[53]

PHILOSOPHICAL CONSIDERATIONS OF THE PROBLEM

To prevent crime in any complete sense would inevitably entail either the removal of all stimulus, temptation, or opportunity to com-

---

[51] *Ibid.*
[52] Pauline V. and Erle F. Young, "The Uses of Statistics in Planning a Rehabilitative Program," *Proceedings of the Seventy-First Annual Congress of the American Prison Association,* 1941, New York, 1941, pp. 477–486.
[53] *Ibid.*

mit crime, or the elimination of envy, greed, hatred, frustration, care-lessness, ignorance, desire for status in the group, and all the other personality characteristics which condition individuals to behave in socially condemned ways. The prevention of all crime and delinquency will probably remain an ideal which can never be approximated. Since we must live in a practical world the question therefore becomes not so much how to prevent crime as how to reduce crime to the lowest minimum possible under existing circumstances.

With this reservation in mind the question then resolves itself into two parts: (1) How can we prevent delinquency and crime from being committed, and (2) how can we prevent criminals from being re-cidivists? And since we know that so many adult criminals are simply juvenile delinquents "older grown" the crime prevention program should aim at preventing delinquency among children. A crime pre-vention program must also rehabilitate the young and first offender and aim at restoring the recidivist to the ranks of good citizenship. Furthermore the community and the institutions which serve the com-munity must utilize every possible device to help the offenders become law-abiding citizens. The achievement of these goals can never be easy because there are so many forces which tend to promote delinquent and criminal conduct.

Motivation of Socially Accepted Conduct

The motivation of socially accepted conduct therefore must be a major phase of any effective attempt to reduce crime. To live accepta-bly as a good citizen in modern society means that the individual must co-operate willingly in abiding by the restrictions placed upon his be-havior as laid down by the law-making, law-interpreting and law-en-forcing bodies. In a society such as ours there are many complicated restrictions upon conduct which in themselves increase the extent of lawbreaking among adults. Some lawbreaking is unwitting because of ignorance. Some is rebellious because laws run counter to previously established habits. Some stems both from honest and unconscientious disapproval of the law. To children all laws are forms of social restric-tion which must be explained and interpreted if they are to see any value or reason for their acceptance. Education in social values is thus a significant part of inducing social conformity.

Frequently a child thinks there is no conformity at all between the conduct which is permitted him within the home and the conduct for

which he is punished outside. Thus Johnny may take an orange from the bowl of fruit in the pantry at home with no serious consequences. But parents seldom properly instruct Johnny so that he understands that the oranges outside the grocer's window are not to be shared without payment. The difference between "taking" and "stealing" is not immediately apparent to the child. If, however, society places such great stress upon the importance of private property it should place equal stress upon educating children to comprehend the meaning and place of private property in our ethical concepts and legal taboos. To the child life is a sort of daily experiment in which he discovers what it is that he is allowed to do, how much he can insist upon, what he is permitted to eat, play with, or appropriate for himself without being punished.

The individual must learn to adjust his aggressive tendencies. No matter how much we may do to improve environmental influences individuals will probably always have to learn to curb their selfish impulses themselves. Irrespective of the social order in which he lives life presents problems of adjustment to the individual. Just as it is not always easy to be a Christian, similarly it is not always easy to abide by secular rules and regulations. But society can hope to work out methods for helping its members accept and abide by social rules through developing educational procedures for instructing young persons in our basic social values.

Moral Education

Likewise increased emphasis upon moral education is essential if we expect to increase the degree of moral conduct. No one seems to know the best way this can be accomplished, but somehow parents must be impressed with the seriousness of their responsibility in bringing up their children. The child must learn to understand that it is not only wrong to steal, it is right to be honest, decent, and kind. Teachers must recognize their strategic importance in stressing honesty and decency and human kindliness in everyday conduct. Labor organizations must be concerned with the caliber of men's work on the job and their reliability if the rank-and-file workers are to develop a concern for earning an honest living as well as a concern for a high standard of living. For despite the many persons who live on a relatively low income we have achieved the highest standard of living in the world. But in our struggle for material well-being we have often forgotten the importance of making it clear to young people that integrity and thoroughgoing honesty are as essential as material success (if not more so).

Concepts of absolute honesty are often difficult to comprehend or to accept, however. In fact, honesty appears to be a wholly relative concept to many persons. Corrupt politicians thus do not steal from their neighbors' houses, nor do white-collar criminals. And these same persons often do not conceive of their illicit business or professional activities as crime. Much stealing on the part of the poor, and especially on the part of servants, is likewise "rationalized" as suitable conduct. If any employer is wealthy and has extensive possessions, servants sometimes insist that "Mrs. Jones will never miss this, and I need it." The disparity in economic circumstances rather than absolute need is a factor both in inducing and in justifying the theft.

Unhappily such rationalizations for dishonesty exist in many circles, and crimes in high places make it difficult to reduce crimes lower down in the social scale. The politician who receives a cut in the graft, the contractor who pads his expense account for a government loan, and the extensive crimes among big businessmen are all stimuli to the organized crimes of the underworld.

Religion and Crime Prevention

As we have seen, many crime prevention programs (as thus far developed) have emphasized improvement in the machinery of justice in order to make certain the quick detection, apprehension, trial, and conviction of the offender. In recent years there has been increasing emphasis upon the improvement of the penal treatments for the convicted offender. To date at least there has been little concern expressed about keeping the adult from committing offenses in the first place. Nevertheless preventing offenses is the only true crime prevention.

We have long recognized this in case of the child. The ancient Jews pointed out that a child trained the way he should go will not depart therefrom. Religious teaching, however, has also maintained that man's earthly struggle against evil is never over. From a religious viewpoint the best men must continually strive to overcome envy, malice, suspicion, selfishness, hate, lust, anger, and pride (if not downright dishonesty) and need the help of the church for achieving an acceptable spiritual life. If the spiritual impact of the church can help men overcome these emotions which are sins from the religious point of view, crime may also be reduced. At least these same emotions provide much of the impetus to criminal conduct. Many of the traditional crimes have long been condemned by Judaic-Christian religious tenets as sins—murder, adultery, stealing, lying, etc. To the religionist such crimes are more than secular legal taboos; they are offenses against "laws of the universe."

What the actual impact of religion is or can be in rehabilitating the offender has never been subjected to any thoroughgoing scientific analysis. Much of the religious leadership in prisons is of a dubious quality and much of the religious orientation of prisons has not been effectively related to helping men overcome their conflict with organized society. Similarly much of the profession of religious interest by prisoners has been insincere.

Thus far the Christian Scientists have been the only religious group which has been thoroughly committed to analyzing religious experience in relation to a social problem. Their major concern has been health. Whatever the objections which some may raise against their teachings, Christian Scientists deserve great credit for turning their attention to the psychogenic aspects of sickness and health. In so doing they have made an important contribution to medicine itself.

Since religion is basically concerned with the problem of evil, and crime in a social sense is evil, a major attempt to consider crime from a religious perspective may be equally fruitful. Thus far there has been no important research with reference to the impact of worship, prayer, and belief upon antisocial conduct, partially because so much of religion is "faith, the substance of things hoped for, the evidence of things not seen." Many research persons are also definitely antireligious in their approach to the crime problem.

One of the complicating factors in criminal conduct is that much that is now called crime was formerly considered acceptable behavior. The constantly shifting perspective from which conduct is judged makes it difficult for some individuals to accept newly defined crimes as truly antisocial. Modern definitions of acceptable conduct tend, however, more and more to be in harmony with widening concepts of democracy and love for one's neighbor. These ideas are rooted in religion. Hence religious leaders may conceivably make a contribution to the prevention of crime in relating religious ideas to legal ethics. Religion would appear also to offer greater motivation to acceptable conduct than many of the so-called rational approaches. Helping the individual reorient his thinking is important, but in the end the individual himself must make a determined effort to adhere to the values of the group if he is to become a law-abiding citizen.[54]

SELECTED BIBLIOGRAPHY

Beeley, Arthur L., *Social Planning for Crime Control*, University of Utah Press, Salt Lake City, 1935. A proposal for improving the treatment of crime so as to prevent crime is presented along with ideas for improving law enforcement, court procedures, and correctional measures.

Delierneux, Adolphe, "The United Nations in the Field of Prevention of Crime and Treatment of Offenders," *National Probation and Parole Association Yearbook, 1949*, New York, 1950, pp. 248–258. This gives a statement of the activities of the Social and Economic Council of the United Nations in this field.

Ellingston, John R., *Protecting Our Children from Criminal Careers*, Prentice-Hall, New York, 1948, Appendix, "The California Adult Authority." The appendix to this book gives a full statement of the law, its provisions, and the plan of operation of the most significant step taken by any state to rehabilitate the offender.

Elliott, Mabel A., *Conflicting Penal Theories in Statutory Criminal Law*, University of Chicago Press, Chicago, 1931. The central thesis of this analysis is that the irreconcilable conflicts in our penal laws must be resolved if any effective program of crime control (or prevention) is to be established.

Glueck, Sheldon and Eleanor T., *Preventing Crime*, McGraw-Hill, New York, 1936. This book presents a number of the various projects on crime prevention.

Handbook in Interstate Crime Control, Interstate Crime Commission, Newark, New Jersey, 1942. This book presents the proposed uniform legislation believed desirable for apprehending prisoners and supervising probationers and parolees and for gathering statistics.

Investigation of Organized Crime in Interstate Commerce, Hearings Before the Special Committee to Investigate Organized Crime in Interstate Commerce, U.S. Senate, 81st Congress, 2nd Session, and 82nd Congress, 1st Session, Reports 1 to 19, Washington, 1950, 1951. These reports are a stenographic record of what happened at the various hearings held by the widely publicized Kefauver Committee. The startling revelations at these hearings led to a number of convictions. They also led to extensive improvements in law enforcement on the local fronts.

National Commission on Law Observance and Enforcement, Reports 1–14, Washington, 1931. These reports have been the basis for social action in various states and communities.

[54] The author is indebted to Victor H. Evjen, Managing Editor of *Federal Probation*, for suggesting the importance of research in this area.

Peterson, Virgil W., *Crime Commissions in the United States*, Chicago Crime Commission, Chicago, 1945. This is a discussion of the social action taken by various communities and states in an effort to control crime.

Wigmore, John H. (ed.), *The Illinois Crime Survey*, Illinois Association for Criminal Justice, Chicago, 1929. One of the most important early disclosures with reference to gangster activities was made in this survey.

Young, Pauline V. and Erle F., "The Uses of Statistics in Planning a Rehabilitative Program," *Proceedings of the Seventy-First Annual Congress of the American Prison Association, 1941*, New York, 1941, pp. 477–486. As the title indicates, this article discusses the importance of statistical research in evaluating the worth of rehabilitative projects.

Indexes

INDEX OF NAMES

Abbott, Edith, 222, 284, 286, 287, 288, 311, 498, 510, 511
Abel, 193
Abrahamsen, David, 335, 336, 345, 401, 402, 405
Adam, Hargrave L., 205, 225, 255
Additon, Henrietta, 711, 725
Adler, Herman M., 27, 80, 328
Adler, Mortimer J., 387, 388, 389, 392, 393, 406
Alexander, Franz, 331, 401, 405
Alexander, John, 814
Alinsky, Saul D., 787, 788, 803
Allen, Carleton Kemp, 30
Allen, Edward J., 491
Alper, Benedict S., 809
Amrine, M. F., 124, 659, 717
Anderson, R. L., 470
Andrews, John B., 681, 699, 700
Anne, Queen, 421, 582
Annenberg, Moses, 169
Aquinas, St. Thomas, 21, 194
Arnold, Thurman, 283
Asbury, Herbert, 162, 255
Aschaffenburg, Gustav, 26
Ashley, William J., 642
Augustine, St., 194
Augustus, John, 456, 555, 556, 557, 568, 577

Bacon, Selden, 570
Banay, Ralph S., 571
Bane, Frank, 510
Bar, Karl L. von, 433
Barneberg, Grace E., 704, 708, 722
Barnes, Harry Elmer, 49, 108, 110, 131, 168, 285, 365, 405, 445, 582, 583, 589, 591, 593, 610, 618, 621, 622, 623, 646, 659, 679, 683, 690, 699, 700
Bass, Sam, 324
Bates, Sanford, 562, 601, 750, 751
Baumgartner, Leona, 585

Beard, Belle Boone, 577
Beavers, Etta, 228
Beccaria, Cesare B., 102, 384, 438, 440, 441, 453
Beeley, Arthur L., 805, 836
Beesley, Thomas Q., 149
Bennett, James V., 187, 188, 195, 601, 644, 647, 683
Bentham, Jeremy, 384, 438, 439, 453, 583, 585, 588, 591, 595
Bentley, Elizabeth, 185
Berman, Louis, 324
Berman, Nathan, 646, 647
Bethune, Douglas, 811
Biddle, Francis, 683
Binaggio, Charles, 149, 152
Biscailuz, Eugene, 510
Bjerre, Andreas, 128, 129, 131
Blake, M. A., 753
Blanche, Ernest, 162, 164
Blodgett, Ralph H., 111
Boies, Henry M., 321
Bolitho, William, 273, 391
Bonger, William A., 26, 297, 311, 375, 381, 385, 405
Borchard, Edwin M., 425, 518
Boring, Edwin G., 316
Bowler, Alida C., 289, 293, 295, 311
Bowles, J. D., 307
Bowring, John, 585
Bradley, F. H., 397, 445, 453
Branham, Vernon C., 183
Brasol, Boris, 114
Brearley, H. C., 126, 127, 131, 132
Breckenridge, A. C., 519, 551
Breckenridge, Sophonisba P., 222
Briggs, Howard L., 637
Brissand, Jean, 440
Brockway, Zebulon R., 509, 594, 595, 687, 738
Broeke, James Ten, 20
Bromberg, Walter, 330, 333, 335, 345

Bronner, Augusta F., 27, 327, 350, 351, 381, 391, 780
Brown, Francis J., 293, 312
Brown, Sam, 324
Browning, Elizabeth, 202
Bruce, Andrew A., 758, 768
Bruner, Earle D., 776
Brunner, Edmund de S., 800
Buell, Bradley, 830
Burgess, Ernest W., 757, 758, 759, 760, 766, 768
Burke, John C., 598
Burke, William H., 597, 598, 695
Burns, Robert E., 690
Burt, Cyril L., 28, 377, 394, 395

Caldwell, Charles, 315
Caldwell, Morris G., 809
Calhoun, Arthur W., 306
Callender, Clarence N., 520, 521, 551
Cannon, Walter B., 325
Cantor, Nathaniel, 358, 522, 525, 532, 551
Capone, Al, 138, 139, 149, 156, 159, 169, 274
Cardozo, Benjamin, 529
Carr, Lowell J., 775, 780, 781, 788, 803
Carter, Sam R., 114, 115, 116, 125
Casey, James, 324
Casey, Roy, 498, 500, 502, 511
Castendyck, Elsa, 782, 783, 784, 785, 786, 804
Cavan, Ruth Shonle, 97, 358, 405
Chambers, Whittaker, 184, 185, 186
Chapin, F. Stuart, 432, 433
Chappell, Richard A., 577, 830
Charles II, 264, 582
Charles V, 417
Chickering, Hannah B., 706
Chopra, G. S., 176
Chopra, R. N., 176
Cicero, 415
Clancy, Frank J., 158
Clark, Benjamin C., 556
Clark, Carroll D., 498, 511
Clark, Charles L., 62
Clark, Robert E., 763
Classen, E., 128, 131
Clement XI, 591
Clemmer, Donald, 636, 637, 638, 647
Clinard, Marshall B., 28, 30, 154
Clinton, Charles L., 556
Close, Upton, 535, 536
Cohen, Irving E., 575
Collins, Ruth E., 211, 228
Collins, Ted, 123
Commons, John R., 681, 699, 700
Conners, John, 539
Conwell, "Chic," 136

Corle, Edwin, 310
Cornell, Julien, 191
Cooke, Alistair, 184
Cooper, Courtney Ryley, 161, 168
Costello, Frank, 148, 149, 150, 155, 156, 372, 827
de Crevecoeur, J. Hector St. John, 286
Crile, George W., 325
Crofton, Sir Walter, 594, 733, 736
Cromwell, Oliver, 285, 733
Cropper, Ralph, 696

Dallin, David J., 181
Darrow, Clarence, 445, 513
Davenport, Charles B., 286
Davis, O. C. M., 397, 398
Dawley, Almena, 224, 225, 255
Deets, Lee E., 433
Delierneux, Adolphe, 830, 836
De Toledano, Ralph, 184
Dewey, Thomas E., 518
Diamond, "Legs," 139
Dick, Everett, 269, 283
Dickens, Charles, 590
Dillinger, John, 139, 226
Dimsdale, Thomas J., 268, 270, 283
Dooling, James H., 504, 505, 506, 507
Downing, George Fletcher, 470
Drahms, August, 318
Drake, Sir Francis, 260
Dugdale, Richard L., 286
Dunn, C. V., 365
Dykstra, Clarence A., 191

Earle, Alice Morse, 419, 420, 433
Eaton, Arthur G., 597, 598
Edwards, Chilperic, 413, 414, 415, 433
Eliot, George Fielding, 187
Ellingston, John R., 795, 803, 814, 821, 822, 823, 836
Elliott, Mabel A., 27, 96, 114, 124, 139, 149, 165, 168, 178, 222, 223, 224, 225, 227, 231, 252, 255, 259, 273, 278, 297, 300, 308, 327, 339, 340, 350, 359, 360, 362, 363, 370, 371, 372, 375, 377, 380, 381, 384, 403, 410, 434, 436, 453, 484, 498, 509, 511, 538, 545, 548, 552, 553, 557, 577, 581, 582, 611, 638, 648, 682, 700, 709, 723, 725, 737, 738, 739, 751, 752, 768, 778, 805, 806, 815, 824, 836
Engels, Friedrich, 374, 385
Eppstein, Foline, 498, 500, 501, 511
Ervin, Spencer, 527
Estabrook, Arthur Howard, 286
Eubank, Earl E., 62
Evjen, Victor H., 836

Faris, Robert E. Lee, 366
Fels, Samuel S., 791

Fernald, Mabel R., 224, 225, 255
Ferrero, Gina Lombroso, 345, 405, 441, 453
Ferri, Enrico, 26, 102, 104, 132, 438, 441, 443, 444, 453
Feuerbach, Paul J. A., 384, 438, 439
Finan, James, 814
Fink, Arthur E., 314, 315, 321, 346, 406
Finkle, Jerome, 549
Finnegan, J. Francis, 792
Fishman, Joseph F., 674
Fiske, John, 264, 265, 266, 267, 283
Flanagan, Father, 776
Floyd, "Pretty Boy," 139
Fosdick, Raymond B., 455, 493, 528
Foster, Freeling, 592
Fox, Charles Edwin, 791
Fox, J. C., 417
Franci, Fra Filippo, 591
Franklin, Benjamin, 284, 286
Frazier, E. Franklin, 304, 305
Freud, Sigmund, 119, 329, 333
Frey, John P., 677
Friedman, Edwin I., 712
Friedman, Morton, 615
Fromm, Eric, 199
Fry, Elizabeth, 384
Fuchs, Klaus E. J., 186
Furney, Oakley, 637

Galen, 392
Gall, Franz Joseph, 315
Gargotta, Charles, 150, 159
Garis, Roy L., 285, 286, 289, 295
Garner, James W., 440
Garofalo, Raffaele, 26, 102, 103, 132, 441, 442, 443, 448
Garraud, R., 417
Gault, Robert H., 12, 25, 26, 30, 386
Gemmill, Paul F., 111
George, William R., 776
Gibbs, Angelica, 123
Gillin, John L., 27, 30, 104, 105, 106, 107, 108, 109, 115, 118, 119, 120, 121, 122, 123, 124, 125, 128, 132, 440, 441, 454, 685
Gilson, Etienne, 21
Glueck, Eleanor T., 27, 28, 38, 92, 97, 116, 213, 221, 222, 223, 224, 225, 255, 340, 341, 342 343, 344, 349, 350, 351, 381, 391, 395, 404, 576, 723, 725, 759, 760, 762, 764, 765, 768, 780, 836
Glueck, Sheldon, 27, 28, 38, 92, 97, 116, 213, 221, 222, 223, 224, 225, 255, 340, 341, 342, 343, 344, 349, 350, 351, 381, 391, 395, 404, 546, 556, 576, 577, 723, 725, 759, 760, 762, 764, 765, 768, 780, 836
Goddard, Henry H., 327, 400

Gold, Harry, 186
Goring, Charles B., 27, 80, 103, 317, 325, 326, 327, 346
Grady, William E., 637
Graham, Mary Ruth, 763, 764, 768
Graper, Elmer D., 456
Gray, M. A., 336
Green, Thomas Hill, 446, 454
Greenglass, David, 183
Greening, J. A., 457, 459
Griffiths, Arthur, 734
Grinnell, Frank W., 554, 555
Gross, Fred, 505, 511
Gross, Hans, 26
Guerry, A. M., 316, 385

Hadley, James, 434
Haines, William H., 123
Hakeem, Michael, 334, 336, 764, 765, 768
Haldane, Lord, 449
Hale, Nathan, 185
Hall, Jerome, 29
Hall, Winfield Scott, 321
Hammurabi, 16, 20, 412, 413, 414, 415
Hamren, Vandyce, 795, 803
Hanson, Harold B., 782, 783, 784, 785, 786, 804
Hardin, Clara A., 293
Harkness, Georgia E., 367
Harno, Albert J., 758, 768
Harper, Charles, 324
Harper, Ernest B., 642
Harris, Mary B., 228, 255
Hart, Hornell, 757
Harum, David, 84
Haviland, John, 588
Hawthorne, Nathaniel, 420
Hayes, Mary H. S., 224, 225, 255
Haynes, Fred E., 585, 611, 700, 702, 709, 718, 725
Hazard, Helen M., 709
Healy, William, 27, 327, 350, 351, 381, 391, 401, 405, 780, 809
Heinberg, John G., 519, 551
Heirens, William, 123, 130, 131
Henderson, Charles R., 26, 317, 385, 386
Henderson, Leon, 154
Henry VIII, 156, 418
von Hentig, Hans, 24, 62, 73, 121, 132, 207, 208, 298, 299, 301, 302, 303, 311, 312, 314, 315, 320, 324, 333, 346, 353, 354, 357, 376, 381, 418, 434, 749, 750, 751
Hershey, General, 191
Herskovits, Melville J., 306
Heyward, Dorothy, 307
Heyward, DuBose, 307
Hickey, M., 410, 411

Hickock, Wild Bill, 324
Hiller, E. T., 686, 701
Hironimus, Helen, 215, 217, 225, 228, 255, 714, 715
Hiss, Alger, 184, 185, 186
Hobhouse, L. T., 17, 18, 31
Hoffmann, Harry R., 123
Hogben, Herbert I., 17
Hohman, Leslie B., 116, 117, 118, 132
Holbrook, Stewart H., 123
Holstrom, J. D., 458
Hooft, Wisser 'T., 367
Hooton, Earnest A., 318, 319, 320, 346
Hoover, J. Edgar, 169, 479, 489, 493, 755
Hopkins, Ernest J., 487, 488, 489, 490, 493
Horduk, Margaret M., 297
Horton, Henry P., 317, 346, 442
Hostetter, Gordon L., 149
Hough, Emerson, 270, 283
Howard, John, 384, 497, 498, 512, 583, 585, 588, 589, 590, 591
Howard, Pendleton, 538, 539
Howe, Mark de Wolfe, 534, 535, 551
Hubbell, Gaylord, 595
Hulton, Thomas A., 299
Hussey, L. M., 45
Hynd, Alan, 139, 169

Insull, Samuel, 39, 164
Ives, George, 736

Jackson, Joseph Henry, 269
James I, 177, 733
James, Jesse, 324
James, T. E., 406
James, William, 433
Jameson, John Franklin, 267
Jansen, William, 176
Jastrow, Rachel S., 437, 454
Jebb, Sir Joshua, 594, 733, 736
Jefferson, Thomas, 23, 514, 534, 680
Jellinek, E. M., 178
Jenkinson, Charles V., 599, 697, 698
Johnson, Allen, 268, 270, 283
Johnson, Charles S., 363
Johnson, Ellen Chaney, 706
Johnson, Guy B., 300, 307, 312
Jones, Richard F., 681, 682

Kaffits, Otto C., 470
Kant, Immanuel, 446
Karpman, Benjamin, 335, 451, 452, 454, 674
Kastel, Phil, 156
Kefauver, Estes, 134, 152, 168, 357, 819, 827, 828, 836
Kelley, Joseph F., 438, 453
Kelley, Kathryne Thorne, 226
Kelley, "Machine Gun" George, 226

Kellogg, Virginia, 717, 719, 725
Kellor, Frances, 318
Kennedy, Foster, 123
Kenny, Courtney S., 447
Key, V. O., Jr., 485, 493
Kinsella, Nina, 216, 499, 512
Kinsey, Alfred C., 35, 61, 116, 117, 169
Kirchheimer, Otto, 416, 417, 418, 434
Kirchwey, George W., 445, 446
Klein, Philip, 816
Kliner, John H., 299
Kolb, John H., 800
Kolb, Lawrence, 173, 174, 175
Kolbein, Solomon, 803
Kolling, Ruth D., 498, 511
Kooken, Don L., 491, 493
Kretschmer, E., 325
Krug, J. A., 310, 312
Kutash, Samuel B., 183
Kvaraceus, William C., 364, 365, 778, 803

Lafayette, General, 590
Landesco, John, 758, 768
Langer, William L., 412
La Roe, Wilbur, 757, 769
Lashly, Arthur V., 819, 820
Laughlin, H. H., 295
Laune, Ferris F., 765
Lawes, Lewis E., 641, 644, 645, 647
Lawrence, Richard A., 765, 766
Lazia, John, 149
Leach, William H., 367
Lekkerkerker, Eugenia C., 707, 720, 725
Levin, Yale, 316
Lewis, Orlando F., 422, 434, 508, 509, 581, 582, 591, 611, 679
Lewis, Sinclair, 705, 725
Leyburn, James G., 262, 268, 283
Lieck, Albert, 46
Lindbergh, Charles A., 67
Lindesmith, Alfred R., 174, 197, 198, 316
Lindner, Robert M., 625, 626
Lindquist, G. E. E., 310
Lindsey, Edward, 738, 769
Lisle, John, 438, 453
Lombroso, Cesare, 26, 80, 102, 103, 127, 316, 317, 318, 325, 345, 346, 384, 405, 441, 442, 453
Lowrey, Lawson G., 333
Lukas, Edwin J., 793, 794, 796
Lynds, Elam, 592, 618

MacCormick, Austin H., 504, 505, 506, 507, 512, 633, 637, 638, 647
MacDonald, John C. R., 143, 169
MacNeil, Douglas H., 796
Macniven, Angus, 332
Maconochie, Alexander, 594, 733, 736
McArthur, Helene de Corse, 716

McClaughry, Richard T., 803
McClellan, William Smith, 267
McConnell, Ray M., 445, 446, 448
McCullough, John, 696
McElroy, Henry, 165
McKay, Henry D., 27, 339, 374, 375, 382, 395, 797
McKelvey, Blake, 585, 687, 688, 701
McVey, R. E., 321
Mahan, Edna, 710
Malinowski, Bronislaw, 17, 412
Malmstrom, Olaf, 129
Maltbie, W. M., 178
Mannheim, Hermann, 220, 452, 453
Martens, Elise, 780
Martin, Clyde, 61, 116, 169
Marx, Karl, 374, 385
Massing, Hede, 185, 198
Maudsley, Henry, 385
Maverick, Maury, 683
Mawrer, David W., 144, 145, 146, 160, 169
Mayer, Edward E., 119
Meeker, Ben, 753
Menninger, Karl A., 331, 338, 445
Merrill, Francis E., 96, 124, 139, 149, 165, 168, 178, 206, 225, 231, 252, 255, 273, 278, 300, 308, 359, 371, 372, 375, 380, 381, 403, 484, 778
Meyer, Adolf, 780
Meyer, Charles H. Z., 561, 569
Michael, Jerome, 387, 388, 389, 392, 393, 406
Michaelis, Karin, 113
Millar, Robert W., 103, 442, 443
Miller, Miss, 723
Miller, Herbert A., 293
Millspaugh, Arthur C., 476, 493
Mirabeau, 733
Mohler, Henry C., 678, 679, 688
Moley, Raymond, 522, 523, 524, 534, 538, 551
Monachesi, Elio D., 337, 338, 339, 576, 578
Monahan, Florence, 228, 255
Montesinos, Colonel, 733
Mooney, Martin, 148, 755, 769
Moore, Merrill, 336
Moran, Frederick A., 575
Morel, Benedict A., 385
Morris, Norval, 115, 132
Morris, Richard B., 264
Munchausen, Baron, 129
Murchison, Carl, 80
Murphy, Fred J., 33, 34, 73
Murphy, Joseph P., 563, 564

Nash, Jolin, 479
Neuberger, Katherine K., 708

Nicolaevsky, Boris J., 181
Nitti, Frank, 139
Nolan, James B., 492

Obermaier, Georg M. von, 733
O'Dwyer, William, 168, 827
Ohlin, Lloyd E., 765, 766
Oldham, J. A., 367
Ormsbee, Hazel Grant, 350
Osborne, Thomas Mott, 655, 659
Owens, Albert A., 793, 803

Parmalee, Maurice, 27, 121, 375, 382, 542, 552
Pasley, Fred D., 149, 274
Paul, Cedar, 374
Paul, Eden, 374
Pendergast, Thomas, 165, 166, 169, 372, 485
Penn, William, 421, 422, 581, 582, 591, 679
Pennypacker, Governor, 471
Perkins, Rollin M., 470, 493
Perloff, William H., 119
Pescor, M. J., 175
Petersen, Hans, 113
Peterson, Virgil W., 148, 150, 151, 156, 157, 404, 817, 818, 819, 821, 837
Pettee, George S., 187, 198
Phillip, Arthur, 734
Phillips, Orie L., 809
Pigeon, Helen D., 558, 568, 578
Pinel, Phillipe, 384
Plato, 732
Ploscowe, Morris, 156, 157
Plummer, Henry, 270
Polcyn, John C., 458
Pollak, Otto, 199, 200, 206
Pomeroy, Wardell B., 61, 116, 169
Porterfield, Austin L., 28, 33, 34, 35, 36, 73, 79, 363, 576, 775
Pound, Roscoe, 29, 527, 528, 541, 552
Powers, Edwin, 73, 791
Pringle, Henry F., 711, 723, 725
Pringle, Katharine, 711, 723, 725
Pugmire, D. Ross, 614, 616, 647

Quantrill, 266, 324
Queen, Stuart A., 510, 512, 642
Quetlet, A., 316, 385
Quinn, John Philip, 156
de Quiros, C. Bernaldo, 26, 31, 317, 384, 406

Radzinowicz, L., 45, 331, 332, 346, 398, 399
Reckless, Walter C., 279, 564, 709, 710, 753
Rees, J. R., 331

Reid, Ira de A., 382
Reinemann, John Otto, 796, 804
Reiwald, Paul, 406
Richard, J. D., 571
Riis, R. W., 534
Robins, J. D., 812, 813
Robinson, Frederick William, 713, 725
Robinson, Louis N., 498, 508, 509, 510, 512, 614, 677, 681, 701
Robinson, William M., Jr., 268
Robison, Sophia, 800
Rockefeller, John D., Jr., 826
Roethlisberger, F. J., 354
Romilly, 384
Roosevelt, Eleanor, 21, 31
Roosevelt, Franklin Delano, 282, 597
Rosenberg, Mrs. Julius, 183
Rosenberg, Julius, 183
Rostron, William E., Jr., 572
Rotnam, David B., 179, 198
Roucek, Joseph S., 293, 312
Rousseau, Jean Jacques, 396, 437, 438
Rubin, Sol, 559, 740, 741
Ruggles-Brise, Sir Hugh Evelyn, 594, 736
Rusche, George, 416, 417, 418, 434
Russ, Helen, 780

Saleilles, Raymond, 26, 437, 454
Salvio, Alfonso de, 406
Sanborn, Franklin B., 595
Sankey, Verne, 139
Sartre, Jean Paul, 49
Schaffner, Bertram, 116, 117, 118, 132
Schlapp, Max G., 127, 325, 346
Schmidberg, Melitta, 745
Schmidt, B., 418
Schnur, Alfred C., 762, 763
Scott, G. M., 398, 399
Scudder, Kenyon J., 641, 642, 647
Scurlock, Stella, 776
Seliger, Robert V., 571
Sellin, Thorsten, 50, 51, 73, 108, 508, 591, 611, 746, 769, 825
Semmes, Raphael, 421
Sen, Prosanto Kumar, 447, 449, 454, 732
Shalloo, Jeremiah P., 481, 482, 483, 493
Shanas, Ethel, 781, 782, 803
Sharp, Louis J., 570
Shaw, Clifford R., 27, 339, 374, 375, 382, 390, 395, 788, 789, 790, 797, 803
Shideler, Ernest H., 350
Shirley, Mary M., 33, 34, 73
Sibley, Mulford Q., 190, 192, 193, 194, 196, 198
Simon, Richard, 468, 469, 493
Slack, Alfred Dean, 186
Smith, Bailey, 130
Smith, Bruce, 458, 459, 460, 462, 471, 472, 473, 474, 484, 492, 493

Smith, Edward H., 127, 325, 346
Smith, Lillian, 308
Smith, Philip M., 365
Smith, S. J., 325
Sobell, Morton, 183
Socrates, 79
Sprigle, Ray, 161, 165, 486, 494
Spurzheim, John Gaspar, 315
Staub, Hugo, 331
Stearns, Myron, 109, 110
Steiner, Franklin, 365
Steinhausen, A., 417
Stern, Leon T., 568, 578, 752, 766, 767
Stevens, W. H. N., 470
Stevenson, Marietta, 574
Stone, Patrick T., 563
Stone, Sybil, 782, 783, 784, 785, 786, 804
Stowe, Lyman Beecher, 776
Sullenger, T. Earl, 221
Sumner, William Graham, 432
Sunderland, Edson R., 525, 526
Sutherland, Edwin H., 27, 28, 33, 38, 39, 40, 41, 42, 43, 44, 45, 47, 58, 74, 136, 141, 147, 165, 201, 274, 279, 280, 283, 295, 296, 326, 347, 360, 362, 365, 377, 401, 402, 406, 423, 432, 496, 583, 659, 689

Talbert, Robert H., 362
Tappan, Paul W., 601, 611, 725
Tarde, Gabriel, 26
Tarkington, Booth, 84
Teeters, Negley K., 49, 108, 110, 131, 168, 285, 365, 405, 582, 583, 587, 588, 610, 611, 659, 690, 699, 700, 796, 804
Thomas, Dorothy Swaine, 375, 376, 382, 395
Thomas, William I., 27, 395, 411, 412
Thompson, Big Bill, 372
Thompson, Charles B., 333
Thrasher, Frederick H., 352, 360, 382, 777, 804
Thurston, H. W., 781, 804
Tibbitts, Clark, 757
Timasheff, Nicholas S., 557, 578
Toby, Jackson, 369, 370
Train, Arthur W., 273
Truman, Harry S., 162, 177, 801
Tuck, William, 502
Tulchin, Simon H., 328, 346
Turnbull, Robert, 679
Turner, Frederick L., 281, 283
Turner, J. W. C., 46, 331, 332, 346, 398, 399

Urschel, Charles, 226
Useem, John, 95

Van Huyten, Peter, 130
van Kleeck, Mary, 349, 355, 356, 382
van Vechten, Courtlandt C., 295, 296
van Waters, Miriam, 366
Virgin, A. R., 698
Villard, Oswald G., 518
Vold, George B., 377, 760, 761, 769
Voltaire, 438

Wadleigh, Henry Julian, 186
Waldner, Mary, 95
Wallack, Walter M., 695, 700
Wallerstein, James S., 33, 36, 37, 74, 79
Ward, Leo R., 21
Wardlaw, Ada, 190, 192, 193, 194, 196, 198
Warmoth, Governor, 157
Warner, Amos G., 642
Webb, Beatrice, 594
Webb, Sidney, 594
Webb, Walter P., 271, 272, 283
West, Rebecca, 198
White, Carter H., 752
White, Stewart Edward, 268
White, William Alanson, 397, 399, 445, 450
Whiteside, Thomas, 389
Whitman, Howard, 119, 170
Whitney, Richard, 39
Whyte, William F., 359, 360
Wigmore, John H., 447, 449, 454, 540, 541, 542, 552, 819, 820, 837
Wile, Ira S., 119

Williams, Frankwood, 370
Williams, Mary Goshorn, 545, 548, 552
Willoughby, W. W., 446
Wilshire, F. A., 397, 398
Wilson, C. W., 212
Wilson, Donald P., 173
Wilson, Margaret, 285
Wilson, Woodrow, 46
Wines, Enoch, 595
Wines, Frederick H., 317, 409, 420, 434, 733, 769
Winslow, Emma A., 382
Wise, Randolph E., 739
Wistar, Richard, 583
Witmer, Helen L., 33, 34, 73, 737, 769
Wolff, Pablo O., 174, 176
Woofter, T. L., 309
Work, Monroe N., 308
Worthington, Myrtle R., 80, 328
Wright, Hamilton, 172
Wycherley, George, 266, 283
Wyle, Clement J., 33, 36, 37, 74, 79

Yepsen, Lloyd N., 572
Young, Erle F., 831, 837
Young, Pauline V., 831, 837

Zane, John M., 451, 454
Zeleny, Leslie D., 328, 346
Zilborg, Gregory, 331
Ziskind, Louis, 753
Znaniecki, Florian, 27

INDEX OF SUBJECTS

Abandonment of children, as a female offense, 253–255; social workers' attitude toward, 253

Abortions, 148

Accusation, in criminal procedure, 520–521

See also Indictment

Acquittals, 543

Administrative personnel of prisons, professional standards for, 612–613

Adolescence and crime, 352–353

Adultery, 229

Advisory Corrections Council of Federal Youth Correction Division, 802

Age of consent, 229

Age groups, and comparative crime rates, 351–352

Aggravated assault, rate of, 52

Alcatraz Federal Penitentiary, 603

Aldermen's courts, 524

Alien status and arrest, 297

Alienists, private vs. public, 547

Allegheny County League of Women Voters, 487

Allegheny County League of Women Voters Police Survey, 463–468

All-Ukrainian Cabinet for Research in Criminality and the Criminal, 127, 128

Alcoholics, 171, 177

Alcoholics Anonymous, 813–814; chapters in prison, 814; membership of, 813; religious character of, 813

Alcoholism, arrests for, lower class aspects of, 178; as defense for other crimes, 179; emotional factors in, 252–253; extent of, 178; as factor in other crimes, 178–179; relation to consumption of hard liquors, 177; and sex offenses, 179; in upper classes, 178

See also Drunkenness

Ambulance chasing, 152–153

American Bankers Association, 483

American crime, cultural aspects of, 361

American criminal procedure, origins of, 514–515

American culture, nature of and crime, 283

American Indian, crime rates, 309–310; cultural factors in, 311; economic factor in, 310; minority status factors in, 309

American Indian crimes, alcoholism, 310; drunkenness, 309

American Institute of Criminal Law and Criminology, 26

American Journal of Ortho-Psychiatry, 9

American standard of living, and crime, 280, 281; stimulus to crime, 273, 274, 275–276

American women's prisons, distinctive features of, 723–724

Americans, lack of respect of law, 277

Amsterdam House of Correction, 508

Anthropometric studies of crime, 318–320, 325–326

Anti-social acts, in contrast to legal crimes, 23

Arch Street prison, 587

Armstrong racing publications, 157

Arraignment, 521

Arrests, criminal procedure in, 519–520; false, 64; as index to crime, 65; in murder cases, 64; number of, 65; and police, 64

Ashurst-Sumners Act of 1935, 682

Associational offenders, number of, 402

Atavism and criminality, see Lombroso's classification of criminals, the born criminal

Atlanta Penitentiary, 601

The Atlantian, 636

Atomic bomb secrets, and espionage, 185

Attorney General's Survey on Release Procedures, 743, 748, 761

Auburn Prison System, 588–593; architecture of, 591; cage type of confinement, 593; conflict with Pennsylvania System, 591; contract labor in, 593; derived from European pattern, 591; forerunner to industrial prison, 591; inside-cell block, feature in, 591, 593; pattern for American prison organization, 591–592

Auburn system of factory labor, development and spread of, 680–681

Augustus, John, first probation officer, 555–556

Auto theft, rate of, 52

Bail, abuses of, 523; advantages of to criminal, 524; as aid to unscrupulous, 523–524; origins of, 522; scandals, 523; temporary defaulting of, 524; unavailable to poor offenders, 523–524

"Bail deals," dishonorable, 523

Bail forfeiture, lack of collection of, 523

Baltimore, drug addiction among teen-agers, 176–177

Bank embezzlement, high rates of, 112

Banking laws, offenses against, 110–113; employees as offenders, 111–112; technicalities in, 112

Baptists, conscientious objectors among, 194; among criminals, 365

Baumes Laws, see Habitual offender laws

Beat men, see Police, foot patrol

Beccaria, classical penal theories of, 438

Bedford Hills Reformatory for Women, 213

Bell boys, relation to hotel thieving, 141

Benefit of clergy, 554, 555

Bentham, Jeremy, penal theories of, 439; Panopticon plan for circular prison, 585

Berkeley, California, 462, 492

Berlin, traffic problems in, 460

Bestiality, 119

Better Business Bureaus, attacks on crime of, 147

Big business methods, gambling characteristic of, 164–165

Bigamy and Indian custom, 311

Bilboes, 419

Bill of Rights, 181

Biological defects and crime, 400

Biological factors in crime, anatomical characteristics and, 316; phrenological characteristics and, 315–316

"Black hand societies," 133

Black Magic, 16

Black market, businessmen and, 154–155; extent of, 154; farmers and, 154; in meat, 154; in sugar and syrup, 155; racketeers and, 155

Blackmail, 62

Blood feud, 417

Blumenfield syndicate, 156

Boards of women prisons, nature of, 707–708

Bolshevo (Russian prisons for high type offenders), 674

Bonger's theory of relation of cost of living to crime, 375

Bookmaking, 158–161; in college athletics, 160–161; definition of, 158–159; extent of, 159; fake varieties, 160

Bootlegging, 133, 138

Born criminal, 284, 317, 338
   See also Lombroso's classification of criminals, the born criminal

Borstal Institutions, methods of, 808–809; success of, 809

Boston, traffic regulation in, 460

Boston Municipal Court, early probation service of, 555

Boston delinquents and nondelinquents compared, 351

Boy gangs, types of, 352–353

Boys' Town, 776

Branding, 418; in Athens, 420; in New England, 420; in Rome, 420

Brank, 420

Breaking stones, as form of prison labor, 685

British county jails, 495–497; forerunner to modern prisons, 495

British penal methods, see Borstal Institutions; Marks system; Ticket-of-leave system; Transportation system

British transportation system, see Transportation of British prisoners

Britishers, influence on American prisons, 583–584

Broken home and crime, 350–351

"Broom-leaning" in prisons, 696

Brutality of punishment, constitutional prohibition of, 650–651; in 16th century, 418; within prisons, 650–652

Bureau of Crime Prevention, 492

Bureau of the Customs, intelligence unit of, 475

Bureau of Internal Revenue, 139; intelligence unit of, 475

Bureau of Narcotics, 476

Burglary, 139; losses from, 140; rate of, 52

Burns, William J., International Detective Association, 483

Business and crime, 279–280

Business cycle, relation to crime, 376–377

California Adult Authority, 808; guidance centers of, 821; rehabilitation work of, 821–823; reorganization of penal treatment involved, 821; services of, 821–823

California Institution for Women, The, 708, 814

California Youth Authority, 795–796; co-operation with other social agencies, 795; forward looking nature of, 796; reorganization of correctional schools and probation system involved, 795

Cambridge-Somerville Youth Study of Youth Counseling, 33; as delinquency preventive, 791; success of, 791; unexpected results of, 791

Camorra, 133, 273

Capital offenses, 426–427

Capital punishment, in 16th century, 418; today, 508

Capitalism and crime, 374, 403

Capone, Al, crime and vice interests, 138–139; the gang, 156
    See also Cicero

Carolinas, piracy in, 267

Case work in prison, experimental nature of, 644; lack of, 644; need for, 644

Caste system and discriminatory criminal law, 265

Caste system in administration of criminal law, for lower-class whites, 280; for Negroes, 280

Catholic Church, contribution of to modern prison, 591; penitentials of, 591

Cattle thieves, 271

Causes of crime, early research in, 384; imponderables in, 25; multiple aspects of, 389

Cell locks, 620–621

Cells, interior, 618–619; open, 620; punishment, 657–658

Chaplain, functions of, in prison work, 643

Chicago, drug addiction among teen-agers, 176; gangsters in, 138–139, 149; underworld, 372

Chicago Area Project, 404; activities of, 789–790; basis of organization, 788; community leadership in, 789; delinquency prevention of, 788–791; elimination of criminal groups and attitudes from community, 788; extent of, institutional participation, 789–790; success of, 790–791

Chicago Back of the Yards Council project in delinquency prevention, 786–788; citizens participation in, 787, 788; community improvement and, 787; labor unions and, 787; leaders and, 787–788; Roman Catholic Church and, 787

Chicago Crime Commission, 150, 817–819; activities of, 818–819

Chicago Police Department, chart of, 461; organization of, 458

Child abandonment, 253–255; comparative

reprehensibility in case of men and women, 253–254

Children, age of responsibility for conduct, 397–398; born in prison, 719–720; federal juvenile offenders, 605–606; in jails, 504–506; responsibility for, 253
    See also Child abandonment

Children of the foreign born, crime rate of, 362

Christian state, Quaker model of, 421

Christian teachings, effect on criminal law, 415; relation to law, 21

Church, failure in meeting social problems, 366; influence of on criminal conduct, 365; methods for preventing crime, 367; work of with criminals, 367

Church of the Brethren, conscientious objectors among, 193

Cicero, Capone's interests in, 139

Cincinnati workhouse, 506

Circumstantial (or indirect) evidence, see Evidence

City-wide projects in delinquency prevention, 791–793

Civil rights, 181

Civil service appointments for prison personnel, 719

Class distinctions in medieval penalties, 417–418

"Class" justice, 649

Class structure, and crime, 359, 361

Classical penal theories, 437–441, 495; conflict with positive penal theories, 436; nature of, 437; origins of, 437; reform character of, 437

Classification committee, limitations of, 632; members of, 626–627; recommendations of, 631; study of prisoner, 631

Classification of prisoners, 600, 626–632; according to personal characteristics, 104; individualization of, 631–632; nature of, 626, 645; procedures, 626, 629–630; women prisoners, 714

Cleft stick, 420

Clergy, corruption of, in Virginia, 264

Climate and crime, 401

Clinton Farms (New Jersey Institution for Women), 719–720

"Clues" to crimes, 63–64

Coal and iron police, 481; abolition of, 482; brutal tactics of, 482

Coast Guard, 475

Code of Hammurabi, 20, 412–415; provisions of, 413–415; relation to Jewish and Roman legal codes, 413

Coercion in prison, 649; compared to civilian life, 649

College athletics, and gambling, 160–161

College graduates, among criminals, 369

College professors, as victims of fraud, 146

College students' delinquency, compared to juvenile court cases, 35–36

Colonial period crimes, in New England, 259–263; piracy, 266–268; in Southern colonies, 263–266

Colorado, mean age of criminals in, 85

Commercialized vice, 148, 207

Common-sense judgments on parole success, 765–766

Common-sense procedures in delinquency prevention, dangers of, 788

Communists, as political offenders, 182

Community, disorganization of, and crime, 374; as factor in crime, 358; as related to parole success, 755–756, 761, 763

Community action in delinquency prevention, need for sustained effort in, 794

Community Co-ordinating Councils for delinquency prevention, 782–786; St. Paul experiment, 782–786

Community planning for delinquency prevention, 793

Comparative crime rates among men and women, 204–205

Competition, as factor in men's crimes, 202

Composition, see Compounding of crime

Compounding of crime, 411, 417

Compulsive behavior, 397; and criminal conduct, 547

"Con" men, see Confidence men

Concepts of crime, social origins of, 29

Confidence men, 140, 141, 144–145; victims of, 144

Conflict in penal theories, see Penal theories, conflicts in

Connecticut State Farm and Prison, 719

Conscientious objectors, and attempts at prison reform, 195–196; charges for which convicted, 196; constitutional rights of, 190; number of, 191; philosophical and religious types, 190–191; psychotics among, 196; religious affiliation of, 192–194; religious basis for exemption, 190–191; serving sentence, 189, 192, 193; types of non-compliance, 196

Conspicuous wealth, as stimulus to crime, 134, 136

Constable, duties of, 474; origin of, 455

Continental Press Service, gambling and racing information, 159, 167

Controlled experiments in delinquency, 404; difficulties in, 405

Convicting the innocent, 518

Convictions, 543

Convicts, 77
   See also Prisoners

Cook County jail, 505

Corporal punishment, in prisons, extent of, 654, 658–659

Corporation lawyers, 46

Corporations, and crime, see White collar crimes; lobby of, 46

Correctional institutions as factors in recidivism, see Prisons, as factors in recidivism

Correspondence of prisoners, importance of, 627

Corrupt politics, and organized crime, 135

Cost of living, and crime, 375

Costello, criminal activities of, 148; gang, 156

Counseling, as delinquency preventive, 791

Counterfeiting, 71, 133

Counterspying, 186

Country lawyers, control over criminal procedure, 527

County attorney, 531
   See also State prosecuting attorney

County courts, 524

County jails, women prisoners in, 703–704

Court procedure, outmoded character of, 551

Courts, conflicting jurisdiction of, 528; institutional aspects of, 433; need for simplification of, 528

"Coveteveness," and crime, 315; and economic crimes, 315; and selfishness, 315

Crank, as a punitive device, 685

Crime, aggressive behavior, 40; as anachronistic behavior, 391; case studies on, 6; Colonial southern, 263; community aspects of, 358; community explanation for, 390; comparative rates in cities, 54; complex factors in, 389–390; complicated nature of, 24; definition of, 13, 387; differential patterning of, 361; as disease, 321; early sociological theories concerning, 385; education and, 181; environmental factors in, 399; feeble-mindedness and, 400; as function of the mores, 403; as legal-social problem, 13; as function of social disorganization, 403–404; as function of social organization, 402–403; and function of variables, 389, 391; gradation in, 438; illiteracy and, 81; intelligence and, 80; internal migration and, 207; law's relation to, 19; learned aspects of, 402; legal control, 278; legal technicalities of, 111–112; modern social organization and, 360; multiple factors in, 394–395; multiple theories of, 394–395; national patterns of, 274; nature of, pseudoscientific opinions on, 11; newer concepts of, 18; normal tendency to, 345; norms of behavior in relation to, 359–360; physical traits and, 80; psychiatric explanations for, 390; psychological motivation of, 336–337; as psychological problem, 12; as psycho-social problem, 13; as rebellious conduct, 336–337; in relation to culture, 358; seasonal factors in, 377–378; sin and, 80; as social problem, 11–12; as symbolic behavior, 334–335, 401; theological views of, 320; traditional concepts of, 15; treatment of, 6; types of, 14–18; unreported, 39, 58–59; variations of conduct involved, 5; variations in definition of, 62, 386, 387; varieties of, 389, 392; vested interests in, 806; youth as factor in, 391

Crime among businessmen, 39
  See also White collar crimes

Crime commissions, see International organizations for crime prevention; Local crime commissions; State and interstate crime commissions

Crime prevention, 7–8; on adult level, 805–836; disruptive factors in families of offenders, 830; good government and, 7; on juvenile level, 773–804; methods, 806; need for further research in testing theories of crime, 831; as police function, 491–493; police's relation to, 491–493; research in, 830–831; through community organization, 816–817

Crime problem, related to its own generation, 7

Crime rate, age groups and, 88; biological factors in, 314–325; increase in, 59; Indian, 309–310; nativity and, 284–299; Negroes and, 297–309; population figures and, 60; regional variations in, 56–58; social factors in, 348–357; syphilis as factor, 304; tuberculosis as factor, 304; upper age groups, 88; western frontier and, 268
  See also Foreign-born

Crime reported, seriousness of offense and, 63

Crime statistics, 48, 51–54, 206; factors affecting, 59; give distorted picture, 279; inaccuracies of, 59

Crimes, classification of, 14–15; against person, 376, 378; against social welfare, 15; primitive, 16; vs. dignity and security of state, 14

Criminal behavior, changing definitions of, 835; learned aspects of, 402

Criminal cases, disposition of, 543

Criminal conduct, among great corporations, 39–43; among "respectable" population, 32–33, 37

Criminal courts, types of, 524–525

Criminal justice, administration of, 432–433; drawn-out proceedings of, 527; long-range planning for, 452–453; rural origins of, 527; system of in relation to crime, 371

Criminal law, antiquated structure of, 551; basic concepts of, 450; comparative rigidity in, 23–24; ethical developments in, 19–20; function of ruling class, 416–417; relation to religion and ethics, 19; social welfare and, 19

Criminal procedure, in case of insanity, 548–551

Criminal theory, 383–406; complicated aspects of, 389–390; prejudice and, 5; variations in, 387

Criminal women, classification of offenses of, 210–211; parents of, 227; poor background of majority, 227; romantic conception of, 226; types of, 226–259
  See also Women offenders

Criminality, a common trait, see White collar crimes; current theories of, 393; emotional insecurity and, 391; frustrating experiences as a factor in, 108; function of other factors, 387; group explanations for, 391; multiple factors in, 395; psychiatric theory of, 451–452; unitary theories of, 394

Criminality among women, comparative rate of, 85
  See also Women, crime rate of

Criminally insane, types of psychoses among, 331

Criminaloid, 317

Criminals, characteristics of, 77–79; classification of by Ferri, 104; classification of by Garofalo, 102–103; classification of by Lombroso, 101–102; classification by offense, 96; deficient in pity and probity, 103; lascivious, 103; marginal men, 133; marital status of, 90; median age of, 83, 85; morphological characteristics of, 319–320; motives of, 443; physical defects of, 103; physical stigmata and, 441; psychological anomalies of, 442; sex of, 83–84; variety of social types among, 83; youth of, 85

Criminals and noncriminals, differences between, 81; similar characteristics, 313
  See also Goring's anthropometric studies of English convicts; Intelligence

Criminological Institute, as proposed by Michael and Adler, 388–389

Criminological research, 25–28; contributions of sociologists, 29; defects in, 387–388, 392; gaps in, 29; limits on social experiments for, 29; Michael and Adler's rejection of, 387–388; need for new directions in, 30

Criminologists, contributions of, 389; European, 26

Criminology, defined, 24; as an educational subject for prisoners, 639–640; historical aspects of, 279; limitations of, 8–9; popular interest in, 4; scientific research in, recency of, 5; reference journals in, 30; sociological frame of reference for, 8; texts in, 27; vocational aspects of, 3–4

Criminology as field of study, 3, 4; for administrators of penal institutions, 3; for sociology students, 4; for lawyers, 3; for psychology students, 3; for social workers, 3

Crofton's ticket-of-leave system, 594–595

Cultural conflict and crime, 238, 272–274, 283, 284, 296–297, 311, 349, 362–363

Cultural differences between prisoners and their wives, 107

Cultural heterogeneity as factor in delinquency, 362

Cultural lag, in the courts, 551; in social-welfare concepts, 19

Cultural norms, and delinquency rates, 363; and methods of punishment, 449

Culture, a factor in low female crime rate, 201–203; factor in crime, 259–284

Custom as factor in enforcing law, 21

"Dead-end justice," 490

Death penalty, 424–428, 444; in Colonial America, 421; crime rate and, 425–426; decline in use of, 425, 426–429; in England during 17th and 18th centuries, 421; federal offenses authorizing, 425; geographical variations in rates, 429–431; in Pennsylvania, 421; in present-day United States, 424–429; racial factor in, 428; regional aspects of, 428; states abolishing, 425

Decisions against industrial corporations, 40–42

Decline in criminality with age, 339–345, 387

Degradation as punishment, 420

Delay in trials, 544

Delinquency areas, 390; Chicago, Philadelphia, Boston, Cincinnati, Cleveland, Richmond, Columbus, Birmingham, Little Rock, Denver, 374

Delinquent boys, normal aspects of, 338

Delinquent girls, emotional disturbances of, 338

Delinquents, multiple factors in background, 394–395

Dementia praecox, 332
See also Schizophrenia

Democracy, dangers and benefits, 283

Democratic government as political expression of Christian ethics, 21

Departments of correction, 621

Destructiveness to property, and crime, 315; and murder, 315

Determinism, and criminal conduct, 399–400

Deterrence motive of punishment, 447

Detroit, gambling in, 156

Detroit House of Correction, 506, 509

"Deviation pressures," 775

Dictionary of Sociology, 9

Differential association, crime and, 274; defects of theory, 402; as factor in crime, 347–348; limitations of theory, 348

Direct evidence, see Evidence

Discipline in women's prisons, 716–717; brutality of, 717

Disease, as a cause of crime, 321

Dismissals, 544

Disorderly conduct, 207

Distribution of police, 458–459

District attorney, see State prosecuting attorney

District courts, 524, 527–528

District judge, popular election of, 528

Division of correction, 621

Domestic employment for women ex-convicts, 637–638; dangers in, 638

"Dope" peddlers, 177

Double shuffle, 544

Draft evaders, 183, 188
See also Selective Service violators

Draper Prison, 660

Dress, Puritans' restrictions on, 262

Drug addiction, 171–175; dangers of, 172–174; extent of, 173; hospitalization vs. penal sentence, 175; physicians and, 175; and the underworld, 174
See also Narcotics

Drug racket, 174

Drunken driving, 178

Drunkenness, as defense for crime, 398–399; among Negroes, 308–309; among Indians, 309–310; as offense, 398; causes of, 179; first English law concerning, 177–178; murder and, 179; personality problems and, 179
See also Alcoholism

Dunking stool, 421

Dyer Act, 70

Eastern European immigrants, break with "foreign" churches, 365

Eastern Europeans, crime rate of, 289

Eastern Penitentiary, 587, 658; architectural features of, 589–590; ground plan of, 589; relation to Bentham's panopticon and Howard's ideas, 588–589; solitary aspect of, 588, 590

Economic class and crime, 109, 373–374

Economic conditions and crime, 375–376

Economic factors in crime, 385, 401, 416–418; in Indian crime rate, 310; in Negro crime, 298, 304, 308

Economic structure and crime, 373–377

Economic success, emphasis on and crime, 109

Education, in crime, 347–348; for family life, as a delinquency preventive, 779; for maturity, 404

Education in prisons, 600, 632–640; informal, 634, 636; need for suitable teachers, 637; variations in, 633–636; women's prisons, 638–639

Educational achievement, increase in among prisoners, 371; related to criminality, 368–369

Educational differentials, as factor in crime rates, 369

Educational status of prisoner compared to his wife, 106

Ego, 329, 331, 336, 400

Eighteenth-century philosophy of responsibility, 445

Electrocution, 432

Elimination motive of punishment, 443

Elliott Survey of Disciplinary Practices, 655–673

Elmira Reformatory, 594–595, 632–633; first institution to use indeterminate sentence, 738

Embezzlement, 348; fraud and, 71; standard of living factor in, 110, 247; temptation easy, 109–110

Embezzlers, 246–248; characteristics of, 109, 113; class status of, 246; women, 246–249

Emotional factors in crime, 279, 328–336; conflicts, 391; dissatisfaction, 108; insecurity, 249–250, 252–253, 391; women's crimes, 227, 255

Emotional instability in general population, 336–337

Emotional training, need for, 370

Employment, as factor in parole success, 748–749; in women's prisons, 696–697

Encyclopedia of Criminology, 9

Endocrine imbalance and crime, 324–325

Enemies as sources of information, 490–491

Engel's theory of capitalism and crime, 374

England, low crime rate in, 275, 361

English convicts, physical characteristics compared to University students, 326–327

Environmental factors in crime, 326
See also Crime, environmental factors in

Episcopalians, conscientious objectors among, 194

Espionage, 184–186, 223; among women, 216, 223; peacetime, 185; penalties for, 185–186; professional nature of, 187; wartime, 185–186

Evidence, admissibility of, 541–542; circumstantial, 542; definition of, 540; direct, 542; types of, 542
See also Law of evidence

Execution, 426–430; methods of, 425–432; racial rates of, 428; rape cases, 428; statistics on, 426–432

Exemption from jury service, 532–533

Experimental work in prisons, 600

Expert testimony for determining insanity, 549

European outlaws, see Camorra; Mafia

European women's prisons, contrasted with American women's prisons, 724

"Eye-for-eye" justice, 435

Failures on parole, 810

False arrest, 64, 232, 485, 488–489, 520
See also Arrests, false

Family and crime, 349–350

Family mental health centers as crime prevention, 831–832

Family training and crime prevention, 832–833

Federal board of Parole, Youth Correction Division, 742

Federal Bureau of Investigation, 186, 476–480; criminal investigation division, 479; functions of, 476–477; personnel standards for, 477–479; training program of, 479

Federal Bureau of Investigation Laboratory, 479

Federal Bureau of Investigation National Academy, 479

Federal Bureau of Prisons, 498, 601

Federal Crime Commissions, 825–827

Federal District Attorney, political patronage and, 515

Federal Jail Survey, 498

Federal judges, credentials of, 528

Federal Juvenile Delinquency Act, 216

Federal juvenile offenders, 70

Federal Kidnapping Act, 216, 477

Federal Military Police, 476

Federal offenders, increase in, 602

Federal offenses, classification of, 607; comparative ratios of specific crimes, 72; conduct forbidden by federal law, 606; on government reservation, in D.C., high seas and territorial offenses, 71; juvenile, 605–606; shifts in, 606; war-related offenses, 606

Federal parole, of youthful offenders, 742

Federal parole laws, 741

Federal parole procedures, 742

Federal parole violation regulations, 742

Federal police, 475–480; special varieties of, 476

Federal prisoners, 89; received from courts, by offenses, 607

Federal prisons, 600–606; children's cases in, 605; development of, 600–601; list of, 604; standards of, 601; types of, 602–604

Federal probation service, 601–602

Federal probation system, 558, 559

Federal projects in delinquency prevention, 797–802

Federal Reformatory for Women, 214, 240, 603, 709, 716, 719, 720, 721; classification system of, 714; professional qualifications for staff members of, 715

Federal Wage and Hour Law, 301

Federal Youth Corrections Act, 801; provisions for rehabilitation of young offenders, 801–802

Fee system criticized, 504

Feeble-mindedness and crime, 13, 327–328

Fees, of justice of the peace, 525; of sheriff, 502

Felonies, 14
See also Crimes, classification of

Felony indictments, 538

Felony prisoners, 80–81; ages of, 80–81; according to age groups, 99–101; according to offense, 99–101; median age of, 80–81; sex of, 80–81

Female crime rates, in relation to women's mode of life, 201, 202

Female criminal, 201
See also Women offenders

Female criminal roles, in relation to marriage, 201, 202

"Fences," 62, 139, 142; varieties of, 142

Ferri, and Lombroso, views contrasted, 444–445; theories of punishment of, 443–444

Feuerbach, penal theories of, 439

Financial aid, in helping parolees adjust, 823

Financial fraud and violation of trust, 39

Financial manipulations, by corporations, 43

Fines, 422–423, 503; fiscal considerations of, 417; inability to pay, 423; installment plan for paying, 423, 503–504; need for revision of, 423; proportion of crimes

punished by, 423; theory of, 422–423; under Roman Republic, 415

Fire, fish, and game wardens, 472

Firearms, illegal use of, 131; relation to murder, 131

First families of Virginia, transportation and, 264

"Fix," the, 139, 141

Flogging, 418, 421

Follow-up surveys, 339–345

Foreign-born, and crime, 96; crime rates of, 289–297; criminality of in comparison to native white population, 289; residence of, 374; rural crimes of, 96

Foreign-born, children of, delinquency rates of, 296–297

Foreign-born young men, high crime rate of, 295

Foreign-born, younger and older male groups, crime rates compared, 295–296

Foreign- and native-born comparative crime rates, 293; according to age and sex groups, 293–295

Foreign churches, decline in identification with among immigrant families, 366

Foreigner, ignorance and crime, 297

Forgers, 248–250

Forgery, emotional factors in, 249, 250–251

Fornication, 229

Fort Riley, 214

Fort Robert, 214

Fort Sumter, 214

Fort Worth study, see Unreported delinquency, college students and

Fraud, 43; misrepresentation in advertising, 42

Fraudulent medical testimony, 59

Freedom, desire for, 282; lawlessness and, 282; political limitations on, 180–182; relative aspect of, 648–649

Free-will theory and criminal law, 545

French Code of 1791, classical provisions of, 440; penalties of, 440

Freudian conception of crime, 329

Food, as factor in prison riots, 675

Ford Committee for Investigating Crime Among Immigrants, 287

Foreign nativity, and crime, 284

Fortune-tellers, 162

Frontier crimes, border lawlessness, 271; cattle rustling, 269; on cattle trails, 269–270; in gold and silver mining country, 270; murder, 269; robbery and holdups, 269, 270; shooting scrapes, 269

Frontier mores, crime and, 265–266, 358; relation to modern crime rate, 361; in western states, 268–272

Frustration, and crime, 308

Gamblers, occupational tax on, 167; respectable activities of, 156

Gambling, activities, 155–156; big business and, 138, 151; dice and cards, 148; difficulties in controlling, 163; forms of, 158–163; hazards of, 164; historical aspects of, 156–157; human factors in, 163; illegality of, 167; press interests, 159–160; in prison, 642; in private resorts and hotels, 163; prohibition of, 156–157; regulation of, 167; tie-up with other illicit activities, 155–156; wire services, 159–160

Gambling information, transmission of, 169

Gambling laws, difficulties in enforcing, 163

Gangsters, 166, 167, 274, 372; activities of, 149; conspiracy of silence of, 150; economic motivation of, 360; investments in hotels and restaurants and in other agencies, 151; investments in liquor interests, 151; real estate racket, 150–151

Garofalo, list of criminal types, 442; theories of punishment, 442–443

Glandular malfunctioning, and crime, see Endocrine imbalance and crime

Gluecks' follow-up studies, 340–345

"Gold Coast," Chicago, 360

"Good time," loss of, as punishment, 654, 657

Goring's anthropometric studies of English convicts, 325–326

Government projects in delinquency prevention, 793–804

Governors and their parole policies, 754–755

Grading systems for convicts, 655

Grand jury, 521

Granting good behavior, see Suspended sentence, relation to probation

Green, Thomas Hill, theories of punishment of, 446

"Grilling," 489

Group relationships and crime, 348–357

Group stimuli, and crime, 401; theories of criminality, 400

Group therapy, in prisons, 629; in women's prisons, 713

Guidance centers, preventive work of, 821

Gunrunning, 148

Habitual offender laws, 114

Habitual offenders, 113; backgrounds of, 116; not necessarily dangerous, 116; variations in types of, 114–115

Hanging, as method of execution, 428

Harrison Anti-Narcotic Act, 171–173

"Hashish" drug, 176
    See also Marihuana

Hawes Cooper Act of 1929, 682

Healy and Bronner study of factors in delinquency, 327

Hearings, court procedure in, 522

Hebrew Code, severe penalties provided, 414–415

Helping Hand Institute (Kansas City), 812–813; rehabilitative work with ex-prisoners, 812–813

Henderson's study of causes and cures of crime, 385

Hennepin County Home School, 338

Henry VIII, harsh penalties under, 418

Heredity, as factor in crime, 316–317, 320–322

Heterogeneity of population and crime, 363

High conviction rates, political aspects of, 523–524

High standard of living, crime and, 360; stimulus to crime, 134

Highway police, 471–472

Hobbs-Wagner bill, 530

Hohman and Schaffner sex study, 116–118

Holmesburg Prison, 506

Home, background as factor in crimes, 241; and delinquency, 351

Homicide rate among Negroes, 298

Homogeneous population, relation to low crime rate, 297

Homosexuality, 117, 118, 119, 120; Freudian theory of, 119; in women's prisons, 718

Homosexuals, characteristics of, 117, 119, 120

"Honest" graft, 48

"Honor among thieves," 140

"Honor cells," 620

"Honor road camps," 510

Hooton's theory of crime, 318–320

Horse thieves, 271

"Hot boxes," 658–659

Hot ice (diamonds), 148

Hotels and restaurants, in gambling racket, 151–152

House of Correction, Chicago, 509

Houses of correction, 507; in England, 678; industrial training in, 507–508; programs of, 509
    See also Jails

House of Detention, New York City, 213, 721–722; statistics for persons sentenced and detained at, 209, 210–211

House of Refuge for Juvenile Offenders, Philadelphia, 587

Household employment, parole hazards of, 723

Household training for women prisoners, 638; dangerous aspects of, 638–639

Housekeeping activities in women's prisons, 696–697

Houses of detention, see Jails

Housing, in relation to crime rate of Negroes, 308

Howard, John, influence on American prisons, 584–585; interest in prison reform, 585; State of the Prisons, 497

Human behavior, a major aspect of criminal behavior, 385–386

Human weakness and crime, 135

"Hung," juries, 536

Hunting rules, breaches of, 16
 See also Crimes, primitive

Hutterites, German, crime rates among, 96

Ideological conflicts, and crime, 182

Idleness in prison, comparative lack of in women's prisons, 696–697; serious aspects of, 694–695; prison riots and, 676; recreation and, 640

Ignorance, factor in crime, 357; factor retarding criminology, 435

Illegal entry, 223; among women, 223

Illegitimacy, Puritans' treatment of, 262

Illicit drug business, adjuncts to, 177

Illinois Crime Survey, 819–820

Illinois Mental Health Act, 1943, 549

Illinois State Penitentiary, 328, 333

Illinois State Reformatory, 328

Illiteracy, as factor in crime, 328

Immaturity and crime, 330

Immigrant parents, conflict with children, 274; criminals and paupers among, 287–288

Immigrants, charged with increasing criminals and paupers, 287–288; crimes and deportation, 287; offenses of, 71; quota restriction of, 288

Immigration Act of 1917, 288

Immigration laws, violations of, 70–71

Immigration restrictions, in attempt to reduce crime, 287–289

Imprisonment, 423–424; decline in rate of, 609; as substitute for capital punishment, 582, 585

Incest, 118, 120, 121; characteristics of incest cases, 120; and other primitive breaches of sexual morality, 16; penalties for, 118; rape charges in cases of, 120
 See also Crimes, primitive

Incidental criminal, 402

Indemnity, 448

Indenture, 686
 See also Transportation of British prisoners

Indeterminate sentence, 443, 737–739; defects of, 739; Elmira Reformatory and, 738; legislation, growth and development of, 738–739; minimum and maximum features of, 738–739; states authorizing today, 739; time limitations on, 739–740; varieties of, 738–739

Indian uprisings, 271

Indiana prisoners, methods of punishment of, 664

Indiana Reformatory, Institution for Women and Girls, first women's prison in U.S., 706

Indictment, procedure in, 520, 521

Individual effort and law-abiding behavior, 836

Individualization of punishment, theories of, 444

Individualized treatment of prisoners, 713

Industrial discontent, and crimes, 417

Industrial espionage, 42

Industrial police, 480–482

Industrial prisons, 595–596, 680–681; rise and decline of, 681

Industrial tensions and violent crimes, 354

Inferiority feelings and crime, 335

Information, procedure in case of, 521

Informer, 490–491

Infringements of patents, trade-marks, and copyrights, 39

Inmate clerks, 691, 692

Inmate councils, 660

Inmate government organizations, 655, 659–661; objections to, 659–660

Inmate guards, 692

Inmate hunches and parole success, 765–766

Inmate teachers in prison schools, 637; personality problems of, 637

Inner weakness, and crime, theory of, 401

Innocent, conviction of, see Convicting the innocent

Insane criminals, punishment of, 442

Insanity, basis for determining in criminal cases, 548–551; court procedure in cases of, 545–551; right and wrong test for, 397, 549, 550; unscientific practices in determining, 547–551

In-service training for police, see Police, in-service training

Inside-cell blocks, custodial aspects of, 591–592

Institutional relationships in relation to crime, 363–373

"Institutional types," women's prison employees, 716

Insurance companies, ambulance chasing of, 152–153; fraudulent activities of, 152–153

Intelligence, of criminals compared to soldiers, 80–81, 328; as factor differentiating non-criminals from criminals, 326; relation to crime, 326–328

Intelligence agencies, in relation to political offenders, 187

Interior cell blocks, 618–619

International aspects of crime, 378

International Opium Convention, 172

International organizations for crime prevention, 828–830; other international organizations, 829–830; United Nations organizations, 829

International tensions and political offenses, 182

Interstate Commission on Crime, legislative proposals of, 823; membership of, 823; organization of, 823

Intimidation by foreign agents, 186

Iowa prisoners, methods of punishment of, 664

Irresponsibility, 545; because of insanity, 547

Isolation of women's prisons, 721–722

Italian crime rate, 300; in relation to educational differential, 370

Italian immigrants, crime patterns, 273; and organized crime, 296; professional criminals among, 134

Italian prisoners, Lombroso's study of, 316

Jail fever, 497

Jail keeper, sheriff's role as, 502

Jail sentences, instead of fine, 503–504

Jails, children in, 504–506; conditions in, 497–503; early functions of, 495; education in, 506–507; fee system and, 501; number of, 496; origins of, 495; outmoded type of institution, 502; present functions, 495–496; as prisons, 579–580; proposed abolition of, 510; public apathy toward, 502; sanitation, 502–503; standards, need for decent, 501–502, 511; teachers for, 507; types of prisoners in, 496, 503

Jealousy, factor in reporting crimes, 63, 251

Jehovah's Witnesses, conscientious objectors among, 193; selective service violators among, 188–190, 192–193

Jewelers Security Alliance, 483

Jewish crime rate, in relation to educational differential, 370

Job mobility and crime, 106

Journal of Criminal Law and Criminology and Police Science, 9

Judges, 528–530; attitudes toward probationers, 816; attitudes toward social workers, 815; authority of, 537; corruption of, 536; as factor in crime prevention, 815–816; importance of personality, 529; importance of training, 529; law interpreting functions of, 528; not legislators, 438; responsibility of, 537; salaries of, 529–530

Judge Baker Foundation Clinic, 340

Judicial reprieve, 555

Judicial statistics, 51

  See also Statistics, judicial

Jurors, challenging of, 533; competence of, 534; corruption of, 535; function of, 534; incompetence of, 535; prejudice of, 535; rejection of, 533; unpredictable nature of verdicts, 535

Jury, chairman of, 533; function of, 537; impaneling of, 533–534; instructions to, 536; panel, 532

Jury service, 532; qualifications for, 534

Jury trial, for determining insanity, 548–549; waiver of, 537–540

Justices, part-time, 525–526

Justices of peace, 525; educational standards for, 526; fees of, 525; solicitation of business of, 525

Juvenile delinquency prevention, as crime prevention, 774–804; among normal children, 775; methods, 774; techniques involved, 775; in wartime, 379

Juvenile delinquency prevention projects, piecemeal, 776; boys clubs, 776–777; Boys Town, 776; George Junior Republics, 776; mental hygiene clinics, 779–781; recreational projects, 781–782; the school and, 777–779

Juvenile Delinquency Act, 71

Juvenile delinquents, federal, special problems, 605–606; institutions for, 605–606

Kaiserlautern prison, 733

"Kangaroo court," 499, 503

Kansas City, corrupt politics and, 165–166, 372; gambling in, 145, 150, 152, 165

Kansas habitual offenders, characteristics of, 114–116

Kansas jails, 498; conditions in, 500–501; illegal incarceration in, 501; inmates of, 500–501; recidivists in, 500; sanitation in, 501; survey, 500–501

Kansas murderers, characteristics of, 125–126

Kansas prisoners, methods of punishing, 664

Kansas State Industrial Farm for Women, 213, 710, 718

Kansas State Penitentiary, 639, 658, 812

Kefauver Committee, 134, 168

  See also Special Committee to Investigate Organized Crime in Interstate Commerce of the U.S. Senate, 81st Congress

Kentucky prisoners, methods of punishment, 664

Kidnaping, 68, 71, 133

Killits case, restriction on suspended sentence, 558

King's peace, 14, 416–417

Kinsey report, 61, 116, 117

Labor, as punishment, 596

Labor spies, 43

Larceny, 52, 139, 140

Law, arbitrary character of, 23–24; arbitrary, advantages of, 24; conflict with psychiatric theory and, 450; enforceability of, 23; formalized character of, 24; lack of respect for, and crime, 277–278; limitations of, in interpretation, 649

Law enforcement, by police, 459–460

Law of evidence, 540–541; exacting nature of, 540

Law-abiding, among criminals, 82

Lawbreaking, among Americans, 79; among general population, 32–33, 79; and bill of rights, 23; not occupation of most criminals, 356; psychiatric theories of, 451–452; and social values, 22–23; unwitting, 45

Lawlessness, American examples of, 277–278

Laws, multiplicity of, 277

Lawyers, vested interest of in existing criminal law, 453

Leavenworth Federal Penitentiary, 601, 812

Left-handedness and crime, 324

Legal controls, too extensive nature of, 278

Legal-philosophical theories of crime, 395

"Legal spies," 186

Leisure-time activities, prisoners' education for, 639

Lethal gas, as method of execution, 432

Letter writing, loss of privilege of, 656

Lex talionis, 435

Libido, 329

Libraries, in prisons, 634, 636, 712; in federal prison system, 634; in jails, 507; low quality of in state prisons, 636; in women's prisons, 711–712

Liquor interests, tie-up with vice, gambling, underworld, 138, 149

Liquor law, offenses, 71; violation of, 250–251

Loan sharks, 148

Local crime commissions, 817

Local government projects in delinquency prevention, 793–794

Lockups, see Jails

Lombroso, list of criminal types, 442; theory of crime, 80, 384; theory of criminality, 316–318; theory of criminality disproved, 317; theory of punishment, 442

Lombroso's classification of criminals, the born criminal, 103; the criminal by passion, 103; the criminaloid, 103; the habitual criminal, 103; the insane criminal, 103; the occasional criminal, 103; the pseudo-criminal, 103

London, traffic problems in, 460

Los Angeles, gambling in, 139

Louisiana, gambling in, 157; legalized lottery in, 157

Louisiana prisoners, methods of punishment of, 665

Love (Christian), as basis of treatment for offenders, 415

Lower courts, 524

Low-grade mentality and crime, see Feeble-mindedness and crime

Loyalty of criminals to their profession, 64

Luxurious living, relation to crime, 376

Lynch law, 271; origins of, 265

Maconochie's mark system, 733, 736

McNaghten Case, 397, 546

McNeil Island Territorial Penitentiary, 601

Mafia, 133, 273

Magistrate's courts, 524, 526; dismissals of, 527; functions of, 526; jurisdiction of, 526

Mail, use to defraud, 144

Maine prisoners, methods of punishment of, 665

"Making the punishment fit the crime," 435

Male prostitutes, see Prostitutes, male

Male sex, aggressiveness of and crime, 353, 354; and crime, 302, 353–354

Man, as free moral agent, 445

Man price, see Wergeld

Manic depressive psychoses, and murder, 332; and suicide, 332

Mann Act, 215; violators of, 236–238

Mannheim's classification of crimes, 452

Manslaughter, rate of, 52

Marihuana, addiction to, 176; laws, 177

Marital disharmony and crime, 106

Marital factor in women's offenses, 217–218

Marital status of criminals, 90

See also Criminals, marital status of

Marital visits, 674

Marks system of Alexander Maconochie, 594, 733, 736

Marriage, as factor in crime, 218; as factor in criminal's adjustment, 340

Marxian doctrine of crime, 374, 385

Maryland prisoners, methods of punishment of, 665

Massachusetts prisoners, methods of punishment of, 665

Massachusetts Reformatory Prison for Women, 222–223, 706

Massachusetts "state constables," 471

Material values, as factors in crime problem, 834

Maternal favoritism and crime, 106

Maternity and child care services in women's prisons, 719–720

Mathematical criminal theory (as proposed by Michael and Adler), 388

Maturity, as factor in prisoner's adjustment, 339–345; and law-abiding behavior, 339–345

Maximum-security prisons, limitations of, 596

May Act, 214, 215

Median age, of federal convicts, men and women, 88–89; of state convicts, men and women, 88

Medical center for federal prisoners, 604–605

Medical opinion and crime, 321, 322

Medical service in prisons, 623–624; in women's prisons, 712

Medieval bishop, power of, 417

Medieval criminal law, 416, 417

Men and women offenders, comparative marital status of, 90, 92, 217–218

Mennonites, conscientious objectors among, 193; German-Russian, crime rates among, 96

Mental ability and crime, see Feeble-mindedness and crime

Mental deficiency and crime, see Feeble-mindedness and crime

Mental disease and crime, see Psychoses, and crime

Mental hygiene, 9

Mental hygiene clinics, as aids in delinquency prevention, 780; extent of, 780; need for greater number, 781

Mental illness, lawyers' ignorance concerning, 550
    See also Psychoses, and crime

Mentally ill, not responsible for crime, 396–397

Methodists, conscientious objectors among, 193

Mexican immigrant, crime rate of, 295

Miami, gambling in, 139, 156

Michael and Adler's rejection of criminal research, 387

Michigan prisoners, methods of punishment of, 665–666

Military executions, number of, 427

Milwaukee, law and order school for citizens, 463; police personnel requirements, 462–463; police training school, 463

Minneapolis Juvenile Court, 338

Minnesota prisoners, methods of punishment of, 666

Minor offenders, punishment of, 496

Misappropriation of private funds, 59

Misdemeanants, 509, 511

Misdemeanor, 14
    See also Crime, classification of

Misrepresentation in advertising, 39, 42
    See also Fraud

Mississippi prisoners, methods of punishment of, 666

Missouri, conditions in Missouri jails, 499–500; methods of punishment of prisoners in, 666; organized crime in, 166

Missouri Crime Survey, 523, 819

Missouri Jail Survey, 498, 499–500

Missouri Penitentiary, 812

Mobility, crime and, 273

Modern Criminal Science Series, 26

Modern technology and crime, 97

Molasses Act, 267

Monachesi study of factors in successful probation, 576

Monachesi study of personality differences of delinquents and non-delinquents, 337–339

Montana prisoners, methods of punishment of, 667

Moral concepts, relation to crime, 278

Moral depravity, 321

Moral education, 600; as crime prevention, 833–834; in schools, 370

"Moral insanity," Maudsley's concept of, 385

Moral law, conscientious objector and, 197; Puritan concept of, 261

Moral responsibility, Christian teachings on, 396; limited, theory of, 396; limiting factors: alcoholism, 398–399; coercion, 399; mental defect, 396–397; nonage, 397–398; theory of, 395

Morals, double standard of, 229, 231; on frontier, 269

Mortality as factor in Negro crime rates, 303–304

Mosaic Code, 20, 447; relation to Code of Hammurabi, 20–21, 414–415

Motivation of socially acceptable conduct, as crime prevention, 832–833

Motivations of punishment, rationalizations of, 449
    See also Punishment, motives of

Multiple factors in crime, 337

Municipal courts, 524, 526–527; rural origins of, 526

Murder, alcoholism's relation to, 125; death penalty permitted, 427; executions for, 427; marital factors in, 130; psychology of, 128; related to economic conditions, 208; seasonal aspects of, 378; under coercion, 399; under influence of liquor, 398; victims of, 357

"Murder, Incorporated," 149

Murder rates, 52, 126; among farmers, 130; comparative rate for Negroes, 126; pistol carrying and, 131; reliability of, 62; sex and age a factor, 301; in urban and rural areas, 53

Murderers, 123–131; biological degeneracy and, 127; Bjerre's theory of, 128, 129; educational background, 126; as first offenders, 130; as frustrated types, 124, 125; Kansas cases of, 125–126; Negroes, 127; occupations of, 126; reactions to their crime, 128; sense of inferiority of, 129; as "shamming" types, 129; theories pertaining to, 127–128; United States, cases of, 126–127; as weaklings in conflict, 127–129; weapons of, 131; Wisconsin cases of, 123–125

Mutilation, as punishment, 418, 420

Mutual Welfare League (Sing Sing), 659

Naïveté, as factor in women's crimes, 201, 227, 236–237, 238, 239

Narcotic addicts, 173–177; alliance with underworld of, 174; among teen-agers, 176–177

Narcotic drug peddlers, 141

Narcotic law, 215; offenses against, 71
    See also Harrison Anti-Narcotic Act

"Narcotic ring," 70

Narcotics, 133, 148; crimes committed under influence of, 174–175

National aspects of crime, 378

National Association of Manufacturers, 43

National Bank Act, 477

National Bank and Federal Reserve Act, offenses against, 71

National Commission on Law Observance and Enforcement, 138, 563, 797, 825–827; recommendations of, 826; repeal of Prohibition and, 826; reports made by, 826

National Conference on Criminal Law and Criminology, 1909, 25, 386

National Conference on Prevention and Control of Juvenile Delinquency, 797–800

National council against conscription, 191

National Crime Commission, proposed, 168

National Crime Syndicate, 486

National danger and restriction of civil rights, 181–182

National Motor Vehicle Theft Act, 71, 477

National patterns of crime, in America, 274–276; in England, 275; in Russia, 274–275

National security offenses, Selective Service Act of 1940, 71; Selective Service Act of 1948, 71; other national defense and security laws, 71; military court-martial cases, 71

National Service Board for Religious Objectors, 191–192

National Stolen Property Act, 216

Nationality groups, comparative delinquency rates, 362

Native-born white crime rate, higher than foreign-born rate, 295–296

Navigation Acts, 267

Nazi Germany, 180

Nebraska prisoners, methods of punishment of, 667

Nebraska State Crime Commission, 820

"Need and Greed" as cause of crime, 108

Negro crime rate, caste system factor, 300, 307–308; as compared to white, 298–299, 303; cultural factor in, 307; drunkenness and, 308–309; economic factors in, 298; emotional factors in, 308; false arrests and, 300; housing factor in, 308; in 1950, 299; poverty and, 300; race prejudice and, 300; recreational factor in, 309; social and economic factors affecting, 300; urban factor in, 300
    See also Crime rate, Negroes and

Negroes, arrests compared to whites, 299–303; comparative delinquency rates, 363; and crime, 297; crimes compared to those of foreign-born, 299; desertion rates as factor in crime, 304; discrimination against and crime, 298; educational limitations of and crimes, 298–299; execution rate, 428; false arrests of, 298; female crime rates compared to white females, 303; mortality as factor in comparative crime rate, 303–304; parole success of, 761, 763; sex offenses of, 304, 306; sex ratio and crime, 302–303

Neo-classists, 440–441

Neuroses, and criminality, 327, 334–335; and types of crime: arson, 335; robbery, 335; swindling, 335; theft, 335

Nevada, gambling in, 157; mean age of criminals in, 85

Nevada prisoners, methods of punishment of, 667

New England (Colonial), penal restrictions in, 261
New Era, 77, 636
New Hampshire prisoners, methods of punishment of, 667
New Jersey Prevention Program, community services of, 796–797
New Jersey prisoners, methods of punishment of, 667–668
New Jersey Women's Reformatory, 708
New immigration, crime rates of, 295
New laws and crime, 403
New Mexico prisoners, methods of punishment of, 668
New Orleans, drug addiction among teenagers, 176–177; gambling in, 139
"New penology," rehabilitative character of, 610
New York, gambling in, 139, 156, 157
New York City, drug addiction among teen-agers, 176
New York City police, false arrests of, 488, 489; plan of organization, chart, 460
New York prisoners, methods of punishment of, 668
New York State Crime Commission, 820–821
Night club racket, 148
Nol-prossed, see Nolle prosequi cases
Nolle prosequi cases, 515, 518, 543, 544
Non-compliance of conscientious objectors, types of, 196
Non compos mentis, 545
Non-conformers, Puritans' treatment of, 262
Non-delinquent boys, emotional disturbances of, 338
Non-residence and crime, 94
North and South Europeans, disparity in lawbreaking, 296–297
North Carolina, lawlessness in during Colonial period, 265
North Carolina prisoners, methods of punishment of, 668
North Dakota prisoners, methods of punishment of, 668–669
Northern Europeans and crime rates, 289, 363
Northwestern University Law School, 25
Numbers game, 161–162; losses from, 162; and low-income groups, 161; and Negroes, 161

Occasional criminal, 402
Occupation and crime, 106, 354–355
Occupational and employment records of prisoners, 356
Occupational maladjustments and crime, 354

Occupations, of Negro and white convicts, 355; of women offenders, 220–221
Offenders, classification of, see Criminals, classification of; sumptuary, 171
Offense limitations, on parole, 740
Offenses, according to marital status, 91; among "respectable" men and women, 36–38; condemned by ruling class, 47; federal, types of, 70; of older persons, 38; variations in, 70
Ohio court for trial of prisoners' offenses, 669
Ohio prisoners, methods of punishment of, 669
Oklahoma prisoners, methods of punishment of, 669
"Old American" crime rate, 318
Old World habits and crime, 96
Opium, addiction to, 174–175; control law, 172
   See also Harrison Anti-Narcotic Act
Oral evidence, 542
Oregon prisoners, methods of punishment of, 669
Organized crime, 47, 133–168, 357; changing aspects of, 137; in Chicago, 820; corrupt politics and, 44–48, 165–168; current types of, 139; during Prohibition, 137; losses from, 47; nature of, 136; and ordinary crimes, compared, 73; prey to human weakness, 135; rate of punishment, 135; and white collar crime, differences in, 47
   See also Professional Criminal; Special Committee to Investigate Organized Crime in Interstate Commerce of U.S. Senate, 81st Congress
Orientals, crime rates of, 311
Orientation program for prisoners, 627; in federal prisons, 628–629
Outlawry, and red hair, 324
Outlaws on western frontier, 268–269

Pacifist Research Bureau, 194
Panopticon, Bentham's plan for circular prison, 585; influenced by Ghent, Belgian circular prison, 585
Paranoia psychoses, and character assassination, 333; and embezzlement, 333; and libel, 333; and obscenity, 333
Pardons, unethical nature of, 424; unsystematic granting of, 432
Paris, traffic regulation in, 460
Park police, see Police, park
Parole, 424; abuse by politicians, 755; adjustment, see Parole success; administration today, 743–746; adopted in all states today, 739; aim of, 732; alcoholics as parole risks, 749; alternative to, 747–

748; as conditional release, 732; control of, 745; corruption by government officials, 754–755; defined, 729; economic advantage of, to state, 766; eligibility, controversies concerning, 745–746; eligibility, as established by parole authorities, 741; eligibility, variations in, 739, 740–741; federal, see Federal parole; first systems of, 733; first, in United States, 737; forerunners of, 732–733; hazards of, 754; as method of crime prevention, 810; narcotics offenders as parole risks, 749; need for research concerning, 746; officers, lack of training of, 753; officers, personnel standards for, 753; outcome, Attorney General's study of factors affecting, 761; outcome, improvement in, 766; outcome, trends in, 766; parole hearing, 745; philosophy underlying, 729; placement, 748–749; in home community, 755–756; job risks in, 748; policies, 745–746; for federal prisoners, 742; of women's prisons, 722; political corruption and, 754; prediction, 757–766; prediction factors employed in Illinois penal system, 764–765; prediction tables and parole policy, 764; preparation, 743–744; a privilege not a right, 729; public misunderstanding of, 726; quality of supervision as factor in parolee's success, 756; relation of to indeterminate sentence, 737–739; restrictions, in case of certain offenses, 740; restrictions, civil rights and, 751; risks, 749; scandals, relation to political corruption, 754–755; sex offenders as parole risks, 749; standards for, 732; statistics, 726–727; suitability, methods of determining, 743–744; training of prisoners for, 744; violators returned to prison, 727; summary punishment of violators, 751

Parole authority, the, 729–730, 745

Parole regulations, 749–751; absurdities in, 750–751; difficulties in enforcing, 750–751; high standards of conduct imposed, 750–751

Parole success, according to race of offender, 761, 763; according to type of community, 762, 763; and age at time of arrest, 762; Burgess' study of factors determining, 757–758; common-sense judgments and, 765–766; and educational training in prison, 762–763; and employment, 762; factors determining, 757–766; and fellow inmates hunches, 765–766; good supervision in relation to, 766–767; and length of term, 758,

762; and marital status of offender, 761–762; and nativity, 762; and parole supervisor's prognosis, 762; of recidivists and first offenders, compared, 762; as related to educational achievement, 763; and relation of individual or group offense, 762; in relation to job placement, 748–749; relation to orientation and classification, 768; in relation to prison behavior, 767; unrelated to seriousness of offense, 762

Parole supervision, 752; inadequacies of, 752; postcard variety of, 752; quality of, 752; relation to parole success, 766–767

Parolees, in armed services, relative success of, 767; contact with former prisoners, 757; family of, 750; recidivism of, 757; social attitudes toward, 563–564; social relationships of, 753–754; suspicion of, 756; time served before release, 728

Patent infringement, 41–42

Patent violations, see Patent infringement

"Pay-off," 145

Peace churches, historic, 193

Penal institutions, number of, 580; for juveniles, 580; prison farms, 580; prisons, 580; prisons for women, 580; reformatories, 580

Penal methods, African, 411; American Indian, 410–411; Babylonian, 412–415; lack of progress in, 409–410

Penal reform, as crime preventive, 807
　　See also Classification of prisoners; Howard, John; Parole; Pennsylvania Prison Society; Quakers, penal reform

"Penal substitutes," 444

Penal systems, irreconcilable character of, 449; vested interests in, 806

Penal theories, conflicts in, 435–453; and philosophical opinion, 383; positive, 441–445; prejudice factor in, 435; as rationalization, 433; and theological opinion, 383
　　See also Ferri; Garofalo; Lombroso; Mannheim; Sutherland

Penance, 417

Pendergast machine, 165–166, 372

Penn, William, Great Law of 1682, 581–582; interest in jails and prisons, 581–583

Pennsylvania, gambling legislation in, 157; Great Law of 1682, 421, 508; methods of punishment of prisoners, 669–670; "state constabulary," 471

Pennsylvania Eastern State Penitentiary, 321

Pennsylvania Prison Society, 583, 811–812

Pennsylvania prison system, conflict with Auburn system, 590; solitary nature of, 588–593

Penology, 435–453; classical school, 435–441; early theories of, 383–384; positive school, 441–453

Permanent incarceration for certain offenders, 747–748

Personal offenses, 14
See also Crimes, classification of

Personal vengeance, 17
See also Vengeance

Personality differences, between delinquents and non-delinquents, 337–339

Personality disturbances, among non-delinquents, 338–339

Personality studies, importance of, 345

Personality theories of criminality, 400

Personnel standards, for prison administrative personnel, 613–614
See also Parole officers, personnel standards for; Probation officer, personnel standards for

Philadelphia, Crime Prevention Bureau, 492; drug addiction among teen-agers, 176–177

Philadelphia Conference for Prevention and Control of Delinquency, 792; continuing committee of, 793; institutions co-operating in, 792–793; plans for improving leisure-time and other activities, 793

Philadelphia County Prison, 659

Philadelphia Crime Prevention Association, 791–792

Philadelphia Society for Alleviating Miseries of Public Prisons, 583
See also Pennsylvania Prison Society

Philoprogenitiveness, and crime, 315; and infanticide, 315

Philosophical objectors to military training, 193, 194, 195; as activists, 195

Phrenology, 315–321; crime theory of, 315, 384

Physical characteristics of criminals, Hooton theory of, 319–320; related to specific crimes (Lombrosian theory), 317–320; similarities of criminals and noncriminals, 317–318

Physical environment and crime, see Climate and crime

Physical stigmata, as factor in crime, 316–317

Physicians, incompetency of most for determining mental illness, 550

Physique and crime, 325–326

Pillory, 263, 419

Pinball games, 148

Pinkerton National Detective Agency, 483

Pioneer News Company, 159

Pioneer systems of justice, 527

Piracy, in Colonial times, 266–267

Pirates, a variety of gangster, 268

Pittsburgh, gambling in, 161, 165; police, exposes of, 486–487

Planning for criminal justice, 452–453

Playgroups and crime, 352

Poisoning and allied offenses, 16

Police, ancient Greek and Roman, 456; arrests, discretionary nature of, 485; attitudes toward parolees, 756; bribery of, 485; Chicago, plan of organization chart, 461; college graduates among, 462; Colonial, 456; common welfare and, 456; corrupt politics and, 458, 467; county police, see Rural police, county; crime prevention and, 491–493; cruel methods of, 489; disarming of, 490; educational standards for, 462; effective distribution of, 459; ethics in methods, 491; foot patrol, 466; fragmentation of services of, 458; functions of, 455–457; gunplay of, 489–490; headquarters control of, 461; highway, 471–472; honest administration of, 486; in-service training, 468–470; law enforcement by, 459; lawlessness of, 487–489; Los Angeles, 469; needs served by, 456; night watchmen, 456; origins of, 455–456; park, 475; personnel standards, 461–462, 467; platoons, 459; politics and appointments, 467; precinct offices, 461; protection, 459; records, 460–461; roll call training of, 468; salary scales, 467–468; science curriculum, 469–470; services, changing nature of, 458–459; services, classified, 456–457; services, common welfare and, 456; social work features of, 492; suburban, see Rural police, suburban; surveys, 463; training, methods of, 463; training, teaching materials for, 470; types of, 457; in totalitarian countries, 456; violent methods of, 488; Wichita, 469–470

Police Athletic League, 492

Police corruption, 141, 166, 484–487; explanations for, 485; false arrests and, 484; gambling and, 484–485; liquor and, 484–485; prostitution and, 484–485
See also Police, corrupt politics and

Police standards, in cities over 250,000, 464–468; Berkeley, 462; Milwaukee, 462; Toledo, 462; Wichita, 462

Policy racket, 148, 161; extent of losses, 162
See also Numbers game

Political appointees in women's prisons, 715–716

Political corruption, as factor in organized crime, 371–372

Political crimes, in totalitarian states, 180

Political freedom, in the United States, 181

Political offenders, 179–197; American, 181; difference from other types of offenders, 180; German, 180; number of, 182; idealistic nature of, 180; in totalitarian state, 180; types of, 183

Political protection of organized crime, 135

Pollak's theory of women's criminality, refutation of, 200

Positive penal theory, 441–445

Positive School of Penology, see Penology, positive school

Post-institutional behavior, 339–345

Post office inspectors, 476

Post-parole behavior, Glueck's study of factors affecting, 759

Poverty, crime and, 359, 377; in relation to other factors, 377
  See also Economic factors in crime

"Poverty of blood," as cause of crime, 321

Preliminary examination, 522

Preliminary hearing, 521

Presbyterians, conscientious objectors among, 194

Present-day penal methods, 422; death penalty, 424–428; fines, 422; imprisonment, 423; parole, 424; pardon, 424; probation, 423; warning, 422

Pre-sentence employment and crime, 355

Presentments, 521

Prevention of juvenile delinquency, see Crime prevention on juvenile level; Juvenile delinquency prevention

Preventive measures in penal institutions, 807–808

Price of cereal and crime rate, 375

Primary evidence, 542

Primitive crimes, 16; types of, 411

Primitive penal methods, see Penal methods

Priority regulations, violations of, 43

Prison, administration, 612–646; administrative staff, need for improvement, 615; architecture, custodial features, 618–619; architecture, modifications in security provisions, 619; architecture, security features, 618–621; chaplains, 643–644; chaplains, need for well-trained religious personnel, 643–644; "college dormitory" type, 619–620; discipline, relation to custodial function, 648; educational programs, types of, 633–634; factory system, modified by reformatory movement, 681; farms, 692–693; journals, 636; layout, 620; libraries, 711–712; prison-made goods, federal legislation prohibiting, 682; prison-made goods, legal restrictions on, 596; prison-made goods, possible markets for, 599; prison-made goods, possible opportunities for, 599; management, 616–618; officials, prejudices of, 632; products, percentage of total industrial production, 695; programs, need for re-examination of, 599; routine, as factor in parole violation, 768; rules and regulations, 652–653; rules and regulations, irritating aspects of, 653; rules and regulations, negative aspects of, 653; rules and regulations, petty nature of, 653–654; statistics, 75; treatment, ineffective methods of, 808
  See also State prison farms; Statistics of prisoners

Prison Aid Societies, rehabilitative work with criminals, 811–812

Prison boards, qualifications for members, 622

Prison labor, absurdity of arguments against, 677; alleged competition with free labor, 695; clerical and supervisory prison jobs, 691–693; in Colonial America, 679; cruel and irksome varieties of, 685–686; development of in United States, 679–681; early forms of in England, 678, 679; early forms of in Western Europe, 678; efficiency of, 684; farming, 692–693; federal legislation restricting, 681–682; low percentage of prisoners employed, 695; low productivity of most, 680–681; markets, 700; and morale, 597–598, 599; non-industrial types, 690–692; opposition of labor unions toward, 677; opposition of manufacturers toward, 677; origins of in Egypt, Rome, Sicily, 678; peacetime, low productivity of, 684; prison housekeeping, 690–691; production, peak value of, 681; program, arguments in behalf of, 700; provisions in Great Law of 1682, 679; public construction work, 690; public opinion, contradictory nature of, 677; as punishment, 693; restrictions on, 598; under Auburn system (factory system), 680; work assignment, 693–694

Prison labor during World War II, 682–684; incentives for, 683; productiveness of, 683–684

Prison labor systems, chain gangs, 690; contract system, 687; during Colonial times, 686; during industrial prison era, 686–689; during present time, 689–690; indenture, 686; lease system, 688; personal account, 686; piece-price system, 687–688; public account system, 688–689; public ways and works, 689–690; state or states use, 689; types of, 685–690

Prison riots, 596; ease with which precipitated, 675; emotional frustrations and, 676; factors related to, 674–676; food as a factor in, 675; mob psychology involved, 676; as sympathetic outbreaks, 675–676

Prison staff, ex-inmate employees undesirable, 611; maintenance of, 615; need for improvement of, 614–615; personnel tenure, 616; residence of, 615; salary scale, 614

Prisoners, admission of, 627–628; attitudes, reorientation of, 610; censuses of, 51; classification, importance of to future adjustment and to morale, 630; comparative lack of religious motivation, 366; as criminals, 72–73; dependents of, 685; and economic insecurity, 107; educational classification of, 369; educational status compared to civilians, 369; favorable assets of, 356; female, in proportion to number arrested, 224; grievances of, as factors in prison riots: 675–676; health, contagion and, 624; food and, 624; medical staff and, 625; mental health services and, 625–626; prisoner's attitudes and, 624; sanitation and, 624–625; isolation period of, 628; low educational achievement, 369; methods of release, 730–731; previous institutional experience of, 622; reading habits of, 712; received from court, 68–69; recidivism, rate of, 92; recidivism according to sex of offenders, 92–94; released on parole, 727–728; released from state and federal institutions, 728; religious counseling of, 610; as representatives of criminal class, 83; residence of, 94–95; siblings and, 105–107; time served before release of, 730–731; truthfulness of, 105, 115; vocational counseling of, 610; vocational placement of, 630; wages, see Wages of prisoners

Prisoners Anonymous, a proposal, 814

Prisons, administration of, 612–618; centralized control, 622; in Colonial America, Holland prisons influence on, 581; custodial function of, 616, 618–620; as factors in recidivism, 372; failures of, 610; failure as a penal method, 410; functions of, 616–617; idleness in, 596; institutional aspects of, 433; maximum-security prisons, 608; medium-security prisons, 608; minimum-security prisons, 608; need for constructive program in, 610; number of, 579, 580; as patterns of behavior, 433; petty rules in, 596; relation of workhouses to, 508; testing program of, 630; types of persons sentenced to, 65–72; unemployment in, 695–696; in United States following American Revolution, 586; in United States, varieties of, 579–580; varieties of centralized control over, 621–622; wall equipment, 618; wall towers, 618

Prisons, state, 581–600; architectural features of, 591, 592–593; Auburn System, 588–593; Bentham's influence on, 591; early prisons, 586–588; Howard's influence on, 589, 591; idleness in, 596; industrial prisons, 595–596; maximum-security type, 592–593; new prison, 598–600; Pennsylvania system, 588–593; Quakers' influence on, 585; reformatory movement in, 594–595; silent system, 593; solitary system, 590; World War II developments, 597–599

Private detectives, 483

Private piece-meal attempts at crime prevention, 810–814

Private police, 480–484; types of, 480

Private prosecutor, 514

Private watchmen, 482–483; powers of, 482–483

Privateers, 268

Probation, 65, 423; administration, types of, 567–568; advantages over parole, 563; arguments for combining probation and parole, 563–564; comparative costs of, 577; conditional nature of, 553; confusion with parole, 553; a court function, 566; crime prevention and, 809–810; difference from parole, 553; extent of present provisions, 559–560; factors determining granting of, 561–562; historical antecedents, 554–555; legislation, Boston first in United States, 557; legislation, growth and spread of, 557–558; leniency not a factor in, 552; nature of effective, 563; painful aspects of, 575; preserves self-respect of probationer, 562; privilege (not a right), 561; probation work in relation to other social agencies, 573–574; protective aspects of, 562; public misunderstanding of, 563; rehabilitative aspect, 562; relative stigma of probation and parole, 563–564; research, 565; service, difference from parole service, 559; social work aspect of, 574; success of, 575–577; techniques of, 565; types of offenders to which granted, 564

Probation officer, educational and other qualifications needed, 565–566, 568–569; in-service training for, 569; personnel standards for, 568; salaries of, 567–568; skills needed for, 565

Probationers, factors in success of, 576, 809–810; Gluecks' study of, 576; Monachesi's study of, 576; psychic factors in adjustment of, 809–810; psychiatric needs of, 575; relative success of, 809–810; special types of, 570–573; the alcoholic, 570–571; the conscientious objector, 572–573; the mentally deficient, 572; the narcotic addict, 571; the psychopathic offender, 571–572; other types, 573; violations of, 576

Professional bondsmen, 523

Professional crime, 47

Professional criminal, 166; defined, 136; goals of, 136; income of, 136; types of, 133

Professional gambler, 164

Professional persons, exemptions from jury service, 532

Professional standards, for women's prison staff members, 715–716

Professional teachers in prison, 633

Professional thief, 276

Prognostic factors in parole adjustment, 757, 766

Prohibition, crime and, 277, 826

Promiscuity, among Negroes, 306–307

Property crimes, in rural and urban areas, 53

Prosecuting attorney, 528
  See also State prosecuting attorney

Prosperity, sex offenses and, 121

Prostitutes, 133, 231–234; case studies of, 232–238; false arrests of, 232; "high grade," 232–234; male, 231

Prostitution, 94, 214, 215, 232–236, 238; among criminal women, 218; corrupt politics and, 166; federal attempts to reduce, 207; Federal Bureau of Investigation and, 214; rates as affected by wartime condition, 214; recidivism and, 94; relation to narcotic addiction, 232; rings in women's prisons, 718–719

Protestant teachings and the law, 21

Psychiatric conception of crime, 390

Psychiatric examinations, in women's prisons, 713

Psychiatric opinion, limitations of, 334, 336–337; naïveté of, 334

Psychiatric theory, of crime, 400; of criminality, 329; disparities in, 451–452

See also Criminality, psychiatric theory of

Psychiatric viewpoint, unscientific nature of, 334

Psychiatrists conflict with legal theory, 397

Psychiatry, conflict with the law and, 450; in prison, 624–625
  See also Psychiatry and the law, disparity between

Psychiatry and the law, disparity between, 450–452

Psychological testing, in women's prisons, 713

Psychopathic factors in delinquency, 327

Psychopathic personality and crime, 335–336

Psychopathy, and murder, 335; and sex offenses, 335

Psychoses, classification of, 331; conflicting viewpoint concerning extent of among prisoners, 333–334; and crime, 384; dementia praecox and crime, 332; involutional melancholia and crime, 332; manic-depressive psychoses and crime, 331–332; paranoia and crime, 332–333; schizophrenia and crime, 332; types of and crime, 331–333
  See also Schizophrenia

Puberty and crime, see Adolescence and crime

Public apathy, crime and, 404

Public health service hospitals for narcotic addicts, 604

Public police, 457

Public prosecutor, origin of, 514

Public utility corporations, 44
  See also White collar crimes

Punishment, basis for, 373; Beccaria's criterion for, 438; Bentham's objects of, 439; as crime prevention, 807; gradations in, 438; institutional aspects of, 433; as logical consequence of law breaking, 439; loss of privileges as, 654, 656–657; methods of, rationalizations on, 449; motives of, 445–450; rationalized motives of, 807; social defense theory of, 443

Punishment in the American Colonies, 418; bilboes, 419; branding, 420; brank, 420; cruel methods of, 418–422; death penalty, 421–422; mutilation, 420; pillory, 419; whipping post, 421

Punishment within prisons, classified by states, 661–673; types of, 654; without trial, 650

Pure Food and Drug Act, violations of, 42

Puritan crime, 259–266

Puritan concept of crime, relative to sin and vice, 262
Puritan tradition in frontier mores, 263

Quakers, belief in solitary confinement of, 447; conscientious objectors among, 190; penal reforms, 384; prison reforms, 581, 583, 585
Quantrill's Raid, Lawrence, Kansas, 266
"Quashing" of indictments, 521

Race, factor in homosexual attraction, 674; infliction of death penalty and, 428
    See also American Indian crimes; Negro crime rate; Negroes, and crime; Orientals, crime rates of
Race tracks, rackets at, 148
Racial segregation in prison, 674
Racing information, 159–160, 168
Racketeering, defined, 147; stimulation of, 147
Racketeers, 372, 486
Rackets, types of, 148
Railroad police, 480–481; functions of, 481
Ramsey County Home School, 338
Randen Foundation, 36
Rape, 118, 230; definitions of, 118; executions for, 427; forcible, 121–123; inaccuracies of charges, 380; inaccuracies of statistics on, 380; punishment of, 120; punishment of by United States Army, 380; rate of, 52; rate of in urban and rural areas, 53; seasonal aspects of, 378; in wartime, 380
Rapid transportation, and crime, 378
Rapists, characteristics of, 121; marital status and, 121
Rationalized conduct, as factor in crime, 834
Real estate booms, gambling character of, 165
Real estate racket, 148, 150–151
Rebelliousness of lower-class members and crime, 361–362
Receivers of stolen goods, 62
Receiving homes, 505
Receiving stolen goods, 139
Recidivism, 92, 339–345; among delinquent children in supervised recreational projects, 781–782; among prisoners, 92–94; related to type of offense, 224
Reclassification of prisoners, 631
Recreation, as delinquency cure, 781; as preventive, 781–782
Recreation in prison, 640–642; card playing, 642; dramatics, 642; functions of, 640; music, 642; programs, 631; sports, value of, 641; therapeutic aspects of, 640

Recreational activities, prisoners lack of training for, 640–641
Red hair and crime, 319, 320, 324
Reformatories, education and, 594; growth of, 595; parole and, 594–595; indeterminate sentence and, 594–595
Reformatory motive of punishment, 447
Reformatory movement, 593–595; antecedents of, 594; incorporation of reformatory idea in prison organization, 594–595; indeterminate sentence and, 594; parole and, 594
Rehabilitation of prisoners, inner aspect of, 644–645; prison's responsibility for assistance, 644–645; stimulated by present restrictions on prison labor, 699; through new skills and interests, 645–646
Relative poverty, a factor in crime, 377
Relatives, prison's contacts with, 629–630
Relief status, of foreign-born, 374; of Negroes, 374
Religion, degree of among criminals, 364, 643; in relation to crime, 261; as source of criminal law, 19
Religious affiliation, of criminals, 364–366; unreliable nature of, 364–366
Religious attitudes, as factors in crime prevention, 835–836; lack of sincerity of in prisoners, 643; need for research in, 835–836
Religious basis for selective service exemption, 195
Religious concepts, as involved in definitions of crime, 835
Religious convictions, of criminals, 366
Religious differences of prisoners and their wives, 107
Religious exemptions for military service, 191
    See also Conscientious objectors, religious basis for exemption
Religious motivation among prisoners, 366
Religious work in prisons, 642–644
Religious training, and crime prevention, 835–836
Remittance men, 285
Reparation, 104; motive of punishment, 443, 444, 447
Research, in crime prevention, 820; in criminology, recency of, 25
    See also Crime prevention, research in
Respect for law, among foreign-born, 296
Respectable people, crimes of, 279
    See also White collar crimes
Responsibility, and crime, 385; in mental cases, 545; right and wrong test for, 397
Restraint of trade, 39
Restraints upon convicts, 649–650

Restrictive laws, 46; and crime, 281; growth of, 281

Retainers, 147

Retaliation, 417; in Code of Hammurabi, 412–414; in Mosaic Code, 414–415

Retrial, appeals for, 544

Retribution, motive for punishment, 448

Retributory justice, failure of, 806

Reversible error, 536, 540, 541

Rhode Island prisoners, methods of punishment of, 670

"Right and wrong test" for insanity, 546, 547, 549, 550; rejection of by psychiatrists and psychologists, 546–547

Rigidity in morals, of Puritans, 262–263

Robbery, 139, 140; rate of, 52

Rochester, New York, crime prevention program, 492

Roman Catholics, among criminals, 365; conscientious objectors among, 194

Roman classification of crimes, 415–416

Roman Code of Laws, 415

Roman justice, state system of, 415

Roman legal procedure, 531

Roman penalties for crimes, 416

"Roper," 145

Rousseau's philosophy of social contract, 437

Rules of evidence, rational character of, 541

Ruling class, and criminal law, 416–417; and law, 22; and morality, 22

Rural aspects of delinquency, neglected nature of, 799–800

Rural courts, 525–526

Rural crime, characteristics of, 95; increase in, 55; lack of professional crime among, 96; nature of compared to urban crimes, 95; predominant types of, 95; rates, 55; in relation to rural habits and lack of police protection, 56; in South Dakota, 95–96; relation of to urbanization, 360

Rural justice, 527

Rural police, 472–475; county, 474–475; suburban, 474–475

Sacrilege, 16

St. Bridget's Well, 507

St. Elizabeth's Hospital, 602

St. Louis, drug addiction among teenagers, 176–177

St. Louis House of Correction, 509

St. Paul experiment in delinquency prevention, 782–786; agencies participating, 782–783; behavior problems covered, 783; children referred to, 783; conclusions from, 786; influences evaluated as significant, 785; services rendered, 784–

785; staff of, 783; symptomatic behavior studied, 784

St. Thomas, teachings of in relation to law, 21

Salvation Army, preventive work, 811; work with criminals, 367

San Francisco, drug addiction among teenagers, 176–177

San Quentin prison, education program of, 634–635; school, class schedules of, 635

School, co-operation with community agencies, 778; counseling and delinquency prevention, 778; curriculum in relation to delinquency, 778; delinquency and crime and, 367–368; ways in which it can reduce delinquency, 778–779

Scriptural sins, 262

Seagoville, Texas prison, attractive features in, 603; dormitory plan of, 603; response of men to, 603

Seasonal factors in crime, 377, 378, 385
See also Crime, seasonal factors in

Secondary evidence, 542

Secret Service, 475

Selective Service Act, 187, 191

Selective service violators, special character of their crime, 187; types of, 188–191
See also Conscientious objectors

Sense of guilt, as motivation for crime, 330–331

Sentences, comparative length of white and Negro, 729; long, damaging characteristics of, 373

Seriousness of offense, decline in, with increase in age, 344

Servants, petty offenses of, 206

Servicemen's allowances, illegally secured, 215–216

Severe penal measures, 418; for women offenders, 205, 253–254

Sex, attraction as factor in crime, 245, 354; attraction, factor in women's crimes, 217, 226, 235; impulses, and arson, 335; impulses, and pyromania, 335; morals, in 17th century, 260; laxity among Negroes, cultural factors in, 306–307; murderers, 122–123; murderers, psychopathic type, 130–131; murderers, recidivism among, 130–131; perversion, 123; perversion in prison, 673–674; perversion, racial factor in, 718; perversion in women prisons, 674, 718; problems in prisons, attempts at solution of, 674; ratio and crime, 302–303; ratios, disparity between and Negro crime rates, 303–304

Sex offenders, 116–122, 208, 228–237;

characteristics of, 104; detection of, 119; in New York City, 121; Puritan attitude toward, 262–263; Puritan treatment of, 262

Sex offenses, 228–237; and age of consent, 229; college students and, 35; cultural definition of, 311; double standard of, 200, 229; in prison, see Sex, perversion in prison; mental disorders a factor in, 335–336; proportion of women's offenses, 211; ratio of women punished, 200; types of, 229–230; under influence of liquor, 398
  See also Prostitution; Rape

Sexual deviates in prison, 674

Sexual passivity, as factor in women's crime, 199–200

Sexes, comparative ratio of, among offenders, 220

Sheep thieves, 271

Sheriff, in Anglo-Saxon times, 472; duties of, 473; fees of, 473; lack of training, 474; major task of, 473; origin of, 455; personnel requirements for, 473; role as jail keeper, 502; in the United States, 472–474

Sheriff's wife, role of, 502–503

"Shills," 145

Sibling rivalry, crime and, 335

Silent system, see Auburn Prison System

Sin and crime, Puritan conceptions of, 262–263

Situational aspect of crime, 347

Slave labor camps in Soviet Russia, 181

Slavery, lynch law and, 265

Sleighton Farm, 223; Sleighton Farm study, 224, 327, 350, 638

Slot machines, 157, 162–163, 167; federal legislation prohibiting, 162–163; in Idaho, 157; in Nevada, 157; in Washington state, 157

Slums and crime, 360

Small jails, special problems of, 500, 511

Social action, in crime prevention, 816–830; in delinquency prevention, 774, 802–803

Social attitudes toward criminals, 409–410

Social change and crime, 97, 403

Social conscience, lack of, and social suffering, 23; lawyers' need for, 530

Social contract, 396, 437

Social controls, need for democratic processes in developing, 24; rejection of, in relation to crime, 282–283

Social disorganization, confusion in social values and, 361; crime and, 135, 260, 273, 276, 378, 379, 527; emotional disturbances factor in, 337; relation to crime rate, 278, 361

Social education, 638–639; curriculum for, 638–639; as factor in reducing delinquency, 779; work of Department of Corrections of District of Columbia, 638–639

Social factors in crime, 348–375

Social immaturity, as a factor in behavior, 339–345

Social institutions, lack of and crime rates, 266, 269

Social legislation and lawbreaking, 282

Social orientation, and adjustment, 345

Social planning for crime prevention, 805

Social relationships, types of and crime, 349

Social utility, motive of punishment, 448

Social welfare, and crime, 97

Society of Friends (Quakers), conscientious objectors among, 193

Sociologists, contribution of to criminology, 29; determinism theory and, 399–400; early theories of crime, 317–318
  See also Criminological research, contribution of sociologists

Sodomy, 117, 118–120

Solitary confinement, as punishment within prison, 654; 657–658; bread and water diets during, 657–658; types of, 657–658

Solitary employment in prisons, 680

Solutions to prison labor program, expansion of educational program, 699; expansion of states use program, 697–698; hobbies; 697; public education, 695; recreation, 699; vocational training, 699; wages on equal basis with free labor, 698

South Carolina prisoners, methods of punishment of, 670

South Dakota, rural crime rate in, 95–96

South Dakota prisoners, methods of punishment of, 670

South Europeans, crime rate of, 289, 294, 363

Southern prison labor, brutal aspects of, 688, 690

Soviet Russia, patterns of crime in, 361

Soviet Union crime, 274–275; cultural aspects of, 361

Soviet Union espionage, 185–187

Spanish prisoner swindle, 146

Spare time and delinquency, 781

Special Committee to Investigate Organized Crime in Interstate Commerce of United States Senate, 81st Congress, 134, 150, 152, 167, 168, 328, 357, 820, 827–828; hearings of, 827–828

Special courts, 524

Spies, 183, 184; types of, 186
  See also Espionage

Stage system of releasing prisoners, 733, 736–737
Stamp Act, 267
Standard of living, and crime, 108, 356, 375
Standards of acceptable conduct, lower class, 84; and their relation to religious values, 835–836; upper class, 84
Standards of prison service, improvements of, 601–602
State and interstate crime commissions, 819–820
State attorney general, duties of, 518
State police, 471–472; limited authority of, 472
State prison farms, 510
State prosecuting attorney, 516–518; authority of, 517; conviction rates of, 517; corruption of, 517; curbs on, 518; functions of, 517; lack of supervision of, 516; political ambitions and, 516, 517, 518
State's attorney, 531
        See also State prosecuting attorney
States Use Prison Labor System, possible expansion of, 697–698; practical consideration of, 699–700
State-wide delinquency prevention projects, 794–797
State witness, turning, 490
Statistics, judicial, 51
Statistics of crime, as collected by states, 51; general characteristics of, 49–50; inaccuracies of, 48; lack of authority to collect complete statistics, 50; limitations of, 50; methods of gathering, 50; reported by police, 51; variation in coverage, 50
Statistics of delinquency, coverage of, 800; unscientific nature of, 800
Statistics of prisoners, 65–67; federal, 67–73; state variations in, 67
Status, achieved by delinquent behavior, 338
Statutory rape, 120–121
Steps in criminal process, 519–530
Stimulus to anti-social activities, 348; economic, 349; emotional, 349
Stocks and bonds racket, 148
"Stool pigeon," 490–491, 661
Street corner society, 359
Subversive activities, see Espionage; Political offenders; Spies; Traitors
Sugar Act of 1764, 267
Sumptuary offenders, see Offenders, sumptuary
Super-ego, 329, 331, 336, 400; distorted, a factor in crime, 336

Supervised recreation, and recidivism among delinquents, 781–782
Suspended sentence, relation to probation, 561
Suspicion, factor in arrest, 284
Swedish parole provisions, 746
Swindlers' victims, as factor in crime, 357
Swindling, 39, 133, 142–143; human frailty and, 142; methods of, 143; varieties of, 146; victims of, 142–143
Symbolic factors in crime, 401

Tammany Hall, 168
Tax evasion, by corporations, 44; excess-profits, 44
Teachers in women's prisons, 710–711
Teen-agers, drug addiction among, 176
        See also Adolescence and crime; Narcotic addicts among teen-agers
Tennessee prisoners, methods of punishment of, 671
Testimony of the accused, 542
Testing of criminal theories, 404
Texas prisoners, methods of punishment of, 670–671
Texas Rangers, 271–272, 471
Theft from interstate commerce, 71
Theologians' theory of crime, 80
Theories of criminality, 383–406; prejudicial thinking and, 383
Thieving, 133, 139; types of, 140
Third degree, 297, 489
Ticket-of-leave system of Crofton, 733, 736
Time served, comparative length of Negro and white offenders, 729, 730–731
Tips to criminals, 141, 143, 144
Toledo, Ohio, police, 462
Toledo Police Academy, 470
"Tooth-for-tooth" justice, 435
Traffic regulation, function of police, 460; problems of, 460
Traffic violations, among college students, 35; punishment of, 496
Traffic police, 459–460
Traitors, 183–184
        See also Espionage; Political offenders
Transportation of British prisoners, abolition of, 736; in America, 286–287; to American Colonies, 285–286, 286–287, 733; as factor in crime to Africa, 734; to Australia, 286, 734–736; rebuffed by colonies, 286
Transylvania University, 35
Treadmill, 685
Treason, 180–184; general characteristics of, 180; among women, 216; primitive, 16
        See also Espionage; Political offenders

Treatment of offenders, major facets of, 432
    See also Discipline in women's prisons; Imprisonment; Pardons; Parole; Probation
Trial, 531–552
Trial-and-error arrest, 488
Trial by jury, 531–540, 551; basic concepts underlying, 532; criminal insane and, 542–551; French origins of, 531–532; present trends, 531; waiver of, 538–539
"Trial by newspaper," 649
Truancy, 367–368; as background of delinquents and criminals, 368
"Trustees," 631, 691
Turning state witness, 490
Twelve tables, Roman, 415
Type of crime, relation to physical characteristics, 319–320
Typical criminals, Garofalo's theory of, 103

Unanimous verdict of juries, criticism of, 536
Unconscious, a factor in crime, 329
Underground escapes of prisoners, 621
Underprivilege, as a factor in crime, 347
Underworld, 47, 274; crimes, enemy reports on, 63
    See also Organized crime
Unemployment, and crime, 355–356; in prison, a factor in riots, 596, 676
    See also Economic factors in crime
Unfair labor practices, 42–43; as defined by the National Labor Relations Act and other laws, 39
Uniform Arrest Act, 824
Uniform compact for supervision of parolees and probationers, 824
Uniform crime reports, 60, 480
Uniform Criminal Statistics Act, 826
Uniform Dangerous Weapons Act, 824
Uniform Extradition Act, 823
Uniform Fresh Pursuit of Criminals Act, 823
Uniform Motor Vehicle Act, 818
Unitarian Church, selective service violators among, 195
Unitary theories of crime, absurdity of, 394
United Nations Economic and Social Council, studies in crime prevention and penal treatment, 829–830
United States District Attorney, 515
United States Pententiary, Leavenworth, 77
Unpunished crimes, 46, 58, 81
    See also Crimes, unreported; White collar crimes

Unreported crime, 80, 135, 146, 147; among domestic servants, 60–61; blackmail and, 62; men and women compared as to extent of, 38; sex offenses, 61; varieties of, 61
Unreported delinquency, in Cambridge and Somerville, 34; college students and, 34
Upper class, in relation to punishment, 36
Upper-middle class, as lawmakers, 49; belief in the law, 49
Urban crime, predominant types, 95
Urban life, anonymity of and crime, 53
Urban police, 457–460; organization of, 458
Urban residents, conviction rate of, 94
Urban women prisoners, compared to rural, 94
Urbanization, and crime, 360
Use of mails to defraud, 139, 144
Utah prisoners, methods of punishment of, 671

Vagrancy, 207, 508; punished by hard labor, 679
Valentine Day murders (Chicago), 149
Varieties of crime, *see* Crime, varieties of
Venereal disease, 215; imprisonment for in Kansas, 209, 212
Vengeance, in Code of Hammurabi, 415; in Mosaic Code, 415; motive for punishment, 446–447, 448
    See also Retaliation; Retribution, motive for punishment
Vermont prisoners, methods of punishment of, 671
Vermont State Prison and Reformatory for Women, 716
Vice, 138
Victim, as factor in crime, 357; as stimulus to crime, 357
Vigilantes, 270–271, 483–484
    See also Frontier mores, crime and; Lynch law
Village magistrate, 525
Violations of war regulations, 40
    See also Black market
Violent crimes, related to alcoholism, 336
Violent criminals, 103
Virginia, crimes in Colonial period, 263
Virginia prisoners, methods of punishment of, 671
Vocational education in prisons, 598, 636–637; classification in relation to, 636–637; opportunities for in routine work, 637
Vocational placement of prisoners, 630
Vocational training of prisoners, 677; of

women prisoners, 716; in work assignments, 694

Volstead Act, 151; crime resulting from, 277

Voluntary police, see Vigilantes

Volunteer agencies in crime prevention, 810–814

Volunteers of America, work with criminals, 367

Wages of Negroes, and crime rate, 301

Wages of prisoners, low rate of, 684; in Russia, 684–685; in United States, 684

Waiver of jury trial, 537; attitudes toward, 539–540; extent of, 538; origins of, 538; present status of, 538–540; state court decisions on, 539; supreme court decisions on, 539–540
   See also Jury trial, waiver of

Wall Street manipulations, relation to gambling, 165

Wallerstein-Wyle study, 33, 36–38

Wallkill prison, 619

Walnut Street jail, conditions in, 582–583, 586–587; labor in, 679; plan of, 584; role as Pennsylvania State Prison, 586–587

War, decline of crime during, 379; effect upon crime rate, 278–279, 379, 829; effect upon drunkenness, 208; effect upon prostitution, 208, 214–215; effect upon women's crime rates, 206–208; effort of prisoners, motivation for, 683, 684; embargoes, violation of, 44; production in prison, quality of, 597–598; regulations, violations of, 43; sex offenses and, 380; values of, and crime, 380

War Resisters' League, 194

Wardens, incompetence of, 612; lack of professional training of, 651; qualifications for, 613; of women's prisons, 228

Warning, 422

Warrant, 520

Wartime offenses, black market, 153–155; selective service violators, 188–197

Wartime Prison Industries 1942–1945, 682–684; types of goods produced, 683–684

Washington, drug addiction among teenagers, 176–177

Washington prisoners, methods of punishment of, 672

Weak government, a factor in crime, 371

Wealth, factor in crime, 273, 376

Wergeld, 416

West Virginia prisoners, methods of punishment of, 672

Western frontier, lawlessness of, 268–270
   See also Frontier mores

Westfield Farm, New York prison for Women, 71, 213, 716

Whipping post, in Colonial times, 421; in Delaware, 421

White collar crimes, 38–45, 280, 362, 377, 402; big business varieties, 39; compared to ordinary crimes, 73; manufacturing corporations, 39–43; mercantile corporations, 39–43; public utility corporations, 44–45; punishment of, 40, 45; types of offenses, 39–45

White House Conference on Child Welfare, 797, 800

White Slave Traffic Act, 71

White slavery, 215
   See also Mann Act, violators of

Wichita, Kansas, police, crime prevention of, 492; standards of, 462

Willoughby, theories of punishment of, 446

Winter, a factor in economic crimes, 377–378

Wire tapping, 144

Wisconsin prisoners, characteristics of, 105–109; in comparison to non-prisoner brothers, 105–108; methods of punishment of, 672–673

Wisconsin survey of prisoners, 104–109; methods of, 104–105

Witchcraft, 16

Women, crime rate, in proportion to men, 203; cultural factors in behavior of, 201; effect of war upon crime rate of, 206–208; exemption from jury service, 533; Eric Fromm's theory of behavior of, 199; gangsters, 239–240; goals and criminal behavior, 201; goals dominated by marriage and family interests, 202; as instigators of men's crimes, 354; Otto Pollak's theory of women's crimes, 199; police, 492; police, as a crime prevention service, 814–815; rate of imprisonment, 84; rate of imprisonment as compared to men, 84; reformatories for, see Women's prisons, reformatory character of; wages, Negro, 301

Women offenders, 199–255; age of, 218; alcoholics, 251–253; backgrounds of, 227–228; case studies of, 232–255; child abandoners, 253–255; early home environment of, 221–223; embezzlers, 246–248; English median age of, 220; federal prisoners, 214; federal offenses of, 214, 216; forgers, 248–250; judges' attitude toward, 206; in Kansas, statistics for, 212–213; leniency toward, 206; marital status of, 217; murderers, 205; nativity of, 222; in New York State, 223; occupations of in Massachusetts, 221; occupations of in Omaha, 220–221; recidivism according to offense, 223–224; sensational literature on, 205; severe penalties for certain types, 205; sex attraction and, 217, 218; sex offenders, 228–237; statistics for, inaccurate, 206; statistics on arrests, 204; tax evaders, 250–251; thieves, 246; types of, 210–211; unfortunate marriages and, 217, 218; unreported cases, 206

Women's court, 525

Women's offenses, convictions for in relation to arrests, 204; inaccurate statistics for, 206; in rural and urban areas, 212–213

Women parolees, 722–723; parole violators among, 723; special difficulties of, 722; supervision of, 722; work placement of, in relation to violations of parole, 703

Women prisoners, 84, 90–92, 210–211, 704–705; age of compared to men, 218, 219; comparative number of, to those arrested in relation to men, 224; in county jails, 703–704; marital status of, 90–92; median age of, 218–219; offenses committed by, 704–705; percentage of total prisoners, 704; in relation to number arrested, 224; recidivism among, 223–224; recidivism related to type of offense, 224; relative proportion to men, 704, 705

Women's prisons, administration of, 717; architecture of, 708–709; board members, 707–708; campus atmosphere of, 708–709; contribution of, to penology, 714–715; division of men's prisons, distressing conditions in, 705–706; divisions of men's prisons, sex problems in, 705;

educational programs in, 709–710; European contrasted with American, 724; geographical isolation of, 721–722; limited services of, 709–710; management of, 707–708; medical care in, 713; personnel problems of, 720–721; philosophy underlying, 707; political corruption in, 717; recreation in, 711; reformatory character of, 707; rehabilitation motive in, 707; religious orientation of, 707; separate institutions, dates of opening, 703; separate institution, a reform movement, 705–706; small population of, 709; staff members, 709–710; 715–716; types of, 702–703; vocational training in, 710–711; wardens of, 228

Work assignment, factors determining, 693–694

Work details, 690–691

Work history, and crime, 106, 355

Work placement, of women parolees, 723

Workhouse, 507–508; concept of, 508; origins of, 508; poor farm's relation to, 508; program of, 508; substitute for corporal and capital punishment, 508; vagrants and, 679

    See also Houses of correction; Jails

Working mothers, effect upon delinquency rates, 379

Written evidence, 542

Wyoming prisoners, methods of punishment of, 673

Youth, and crime, 302, 391

Youth Correction Authorities, 794–796; California Youth Authority, 795–796; Massachusetts provision for, 796; Minnesota provision for, 796; Texas provision for, 796; Wisconsin provision for, 796